A WORLD OF DIFFERENCE

A World of DIFFERENCE

Second Edition

Encountering and Contesting Development

**Eric Sheppard,
Philip W. Porter, David R. Faust,
and Richa Nagar**

THE GUILFORD PRESS
New York London

A Division of Guilford Publications, Inc.
72 Spring Street, New York, NY 10012
www.guilford.com

Printed in the United States of America

This book is printed on acid-free paper.

Last digit is print number: 9 8 7 6 5 4 3 2 1

Library of Congress Cataloging-in-Publication Data

A world of difference : encountering and contesting development / Eric Sheppard ... [et al.]. — 2nd ed.

p. cm.

Includes bibliographical references and index.

ISBN 978-1-60623-262-0 (pbk.) — ISBN 978-1-60623-263-7 (hardcover)

1. Geography. 2. Economic development. 3. Sustainable development.

I. Sheppard, Eric S.

G116.W67 2009

910—dc22

2009014573

"Your idea of the 'Third World' and mine must be so impossibly different."

"Why impossibly different?"

"You write about it—that's your job. I live in it—that's my fate. Don't you see the difference?"

—Shiva Naipaul, *A Hot Country*

Preface and Acknowledgments

In the preface to the first edition of this book a decade ago, its two authors, Eric Sheppard (ES) and Philip W. Porter (PWP), began by noting: "We share a white, masculine, middle-class education as professional geographers in the Anglo-American tradition. This makes us, like anyone, different from most people on the planet, but occupying a privileged situation from which to discuss issues of development." Now we are four, linked together by the common experience of teaching, writing, and working together to convey to a privileged audience (by global standards) of students and colleagues the complexity of the third world—the part of the planet that has labored under colonialism, and been forced to come to terms with development, and now neoliberalism. We are more than white males, and grounded in more parts of that world than before, but we face the same challenges of narrating it from our shared positionality as geographers and feminists trained in the West, to an audience even less familiar with it than we are.

In preparing this second edition, we paid close attention to changes on the ground, to evolving conceptual paradigms for making sense of it, and to the voices of instructors and students who had used the first edition (including those in our own classes). We retain the vision and the bulk of the topics from the first edition, but have also made many changes (detailed in Chapter 1). We have diversified the theoretical voices to integrate feminist and postcolonial sensibilities more fully throughout, without abandoning the insights of political economy. We have moved away from a structure that separated nature from society (and made it easy to teach around nature, for those uncomfortable with its presence), to one where the human and nonhuman aspects of our world cohabit the book. We have made the empirical examples less Afrocentric, and have paid more attention to many contestations of and alternatives to Occidental norms that are being practiced in diverse places throughout the third world. Also, we contest the common narrative structure (in both conservative and progressive accounts) of beginning with global processes, which then seem to enframe local practices. We start instead with the excluded spaces—subjects and scales of global capitalist development—before turning to the dominant ones (whose power cannot be wished away).

Concretely, the second edition differs from the first as follows:

- Chapter 1 was rewritten to explicate the new conceptual framework summarized above, and to explain how the second edition differs from the first. Statistical expressions of poverty have been separated into Chapter 2; materials from Chapters 2–4 of the first edition were largely removed.
- Chapters 5 and 6 from the first edition were expanded into three chapters (3–5),

extending the discussion to draw out parallels among colonialism, development, and globalization, and to integrate questions of gender.

- The second section of the book focuses on pursuing livelihoods in a more-than-human world, rather than on environment. The discussion of population (Chapter 6 of the first edition) was reframed to bring out discourses and contestations centering around population and environment (Chapters 6 and 7); discussions of biophysical processes were shortened and focused more squarely on the implications of biophysical processes for livelihood possibilities, particularly in tropical environments (for a discussion of tropicality, see Chapter 1). Empirical materials repeated from the first edition were updated.
- The third section of the book is much as it was before, with all empirical materials updated and with the discussions reframed to reflect the new conceptual approach. The (updated) chapter on the earth's crust was relocated here, because fuels and minerals have been so central to the dynamics of global capitalism. With Bongman Seo's help, Chapters 22 and 23 were comprehensively rewritten to take into account new research on global finance and the shift in global policymaking from structural adjustment to poverty reduction. The chapter on tourism from the first edition was reduced and integrated into Chapter 21.
- The concluding chapter was completely rewritten to highlight grassroots initiatives toward remaking a more-than-capitalist world of difference.

Neither edition of this book could have been finished without invaluable help from loved ones, friends, colleagues, and students. The two editions cannot be separated from one another, so we simultaneously acknowledge contributions to both. Eight strong and inspiring women, the loves of our lives, have put up (in some cases for 20 years!) with what became a Herculean task with good grace, patience, and tremendous support during many dark moments: Pat, Helga, Vibha, Alice, Janet, Kirstin, Medha, and Sara. It is no longer possible to disentangle from our own knowledge all that we have learned from our colleagues within and beyond our department and discipline, from the undergraduates to whom we have taught this material for 15 years, and from the current and former graduate students with whom we have worked in the Department of Geography; Gender, Women, and Sexuality Studies; and the Interdisciplinary Center for the Study of Global Change, all at the University of Minnesota. We are particularly grateful to Bongman Seo, coauthor of Chapters 22 and 23. We have learned as much over the years from our many friends, acquaintances, collaborators, and companions in Africa, Asia, Europe, and Latin America, especially from the *saathis* of Sangtin Kisaan Mazdoor Sangathan (Sangtin Peasants and Workers Organization) in Sitapur, India. These individuals—both those we remember and those we do not—peopled the networks that have helped create these ideas. Many might rightfully wish to disown any implication of responsibility for what follows, but it would not have happened without them.

In addition to several generations of students whose classroom comments on the manuscript were invariably useful, we are particularly grateful to seven people who read complete drafts of the first edition. Their detailed and very different reactions have helped us rethink what we were trying to do and, we hope, strengthened the final manuscript: Trevor Barnes, Jim Glassman, Helga Leitner, Earl Scott, Peter Wissoker, and two anonymous reviewers. For the second edition, we thank (again) Jim Glassman, as well as two other anonymous reviewers, for their comments on the entire manuscript. We also would like to thank colleagues who read at least one chapter in areas of their expertise at one point or another, helping us correct egregious errors of fact and interpretation: Donald Baker, Todd Benson, Richard

Butler, Bilal Butt, Francis P. Conant, Ton Dietz, William Gartner, Phil Gersmehl, Vinay Gidwani, Kim Holmén, Susan McClary, Roger Miller, Phil O'Neill, John Rice, Suzanne Romaine, David Slater, Connie Weil, and Elvin Wyly. We also acknowledge and thank John Benson, Donna Brogan, Todd Federenko, Kirstin Leitner, Kefa Otiso, and Jun Zhang, who helped prepare material for sections of the book, and Nicki Simms for her editorial assistance. We thank Joni Seager for help in obtaining permission to include two maps from *The Penguin Atlas of Women in the World.* Members of the Cartography Laboratory and the Social Science Research Facilities Center at the University of Minnesota have provided invaluable conceptual and practical help with the many original and adapted illustrations in the book: Mui Le (who tutored PWP in CorelDRAW), Elizabeth Fairley, Mark Lindberg, Liesa Stromberg, Jonathan Schroeder, Philip Voxland, and Allan Willis. We also are grateful to the Center for Advanced Study in the Behavioral Sciences (Stanford, California) for hosting two of us (Richa Nagar [RN] and ES) during the writing of the second edition, and for hosting the four of us for a crucial week of collaborative writing, during 2005–2006.

Finally, various editors at The Guilford Press deserve our undying gratitude (and, we hope, the thanks of our readers) for ensuring that this book came to be: Janet Crane, who in the early 1980s broached with Phil the idea of writing the book (as an update of an earlier Association of American Geographers Resource Paper, "Underdevelopment and Modernization of the Third World," written with Tony de Souza); Seymour Weingarten, whose carrot-and-stick strategy kept us from giving up; Peter Wissoker, without whose patience, encouragement, and gentle but firm hand the first edition would never have seen the light of day; and particularly Kristal Hawkins, who has patiently shepherded us through the second edition. Finally, we acknowledge our debt to each of those employed or engaged by Guilford who have helped turn our manuscript into this book, particularly William Meyer and Marie Sprayberry.

ERIC SHEPPARD
PHILIP W. PORTER
DAVID R. FAUST
RICHA NAGAR

Measurement, Acronyms, and Abbreviations

MEASUREMENT

For the most part, we have used the International System of Units (the Système International d'Unités, or SI) in stating units of measurement.

Length

centimeter	0.3937 inches
kilometer	0.62 miles
meter	3.28 feet
millimeter	0.03937 inches

Area

hectare	2.471 acres
square kilometer	0.386 square miles

Weight

bar	10^5 newtons/square meter
gram	0.035 ounces
kilogram	2.2 pounds
millibar	unit of pressure; 0.001 bar
quintal	100 kilograms

Energy

becquerel	unit of radioactivity
calorie	heat required to raise 1 gram of H_2O by 1°C
Celsius	temperature scale; H_2O freezes at 0°C, boils at 100°C
kilocalorie	1,000 calories
kilolangley	1,000 langleys
kilowatt	1,000 watts
langley	unit of illumination; 1 gram calorie/square centimeter
watt	unit of power; 1 joule/second

ACRONYMS AND ABBREVIATIONS

AAWORD	Association of African Women for Research and Development
ACLL	Anti-Corn Law League
ADC	African District Council
AID	Agency for International Development
AIDS	acquired immune deficiency syndrome
AK47	Kalashnikov automatic rifle model of 1947
ALBA	Alternativa Bolivariana para los Pueblos de Nuestra América [Bolivarian Alternative for the Americas]
APDF	Association for the Progress and Defense of Women's Rights
ARV	antiretroviral (therapy for HIV/AIDS)
ASAL	Arid and Semi-Arid Lands Programme
ASEAN	Association of Southeast Asian Nations
ATTAC	Association pour la Taxation des Transactions pour l'Aide aux Citoyens
AT&T	American Telephone and Telegraph Company
BIS	Bank of International Settlements
Bq/k	becquerels/kilogram
^{o}C	temperature in degrees Celsius
Cd	cadmium
CEC	cation exchange capacity
CFCs	chlorofluorocarbons
CGIAR	Consultative Group on International Agricultural Research
CH_2O	carbohydrates/sugar
CH_4	methane
CIA	Central Intelligence Agency
CIAT	Centro Internacional de Agricultura Tropical
CIFOR	Center for International Forestry Research
CIMMYT	Centro Internacional Mejormiento de Maíz y Trigo
CIP	Centro Internacional de la Papa
CO_2	carbon dioxide
COMECON	Council for Mutual Economic Assistance (eastern European bloc)
CPD	critical population density
DALY	disability-adjusted life year
DAWN	Development Alternatives with Women for a New Era
D.C.O.	Dominions, Colonies, and Overseas
DDT	dichlorodiphenyltrichloroethane
DRF	David R. Faust (author)
DNA	deoxyribonucleic acid
D.O.	district officer
EA	enumeration area (Tanzania)
EAAFRO	East African Agricultural and Forestry Research Organization
EAVRO	East African Veterinary Research Organization
ECLA	Economic Commission for Latin America
EEC	European Economic Community
EFTA	European Free Trade Association
EOI	export-oriented industrialization
EPZ	export-processing zone

ES	Eric Sheppard (author)
ESI	environmental sustainability index
EU	European Union
FAO	Food and Agriculture Organization
FDA	Food and Drug Administration
FDI	foreign direct investment
FGM	female genital mutilation
FTAA	Free Trade Agreement of the Americas
G3	automatic rifle made by German manufacturer Heckler and Koch
G8	Group of Eight (Canada, France, Germany, Italy, Japan, Russia, United Kingdom, United States)
G20+	Group of Twenty [Plus] (a formal bloc of developing countries within the World Trade Organization)
GAD	gender and development
GATT	General Agreement on Tariffs and Trade
GBD	global burden of disease
GDP	gross domestic product
GNH	gross national happiness
GNI	global national income
GNP	gross national product
GRAIN	an international nongovernmental organization (NGO) that promotes the sustainable management and use of agricultural biodiversity, based on people's control over genetic resources and local knowledge
GSP	generalized system of preferences
H_2O	water
HCFCs	hydrochlorofluorocarbons
HDI	human development index
HFCs	hydrofluorocarbons
HIPC	Heavily Indebted Poor Countries (World Bank/International Monetary Fund initiative)
HIV	human immunodeficiency virus
IBEA	Imperial British East Africa Company
IBM	International Business Machines Corporation
IBRD	International Bank for Reconstruction and Development, an affiliate (and the original institution) of the World Bank
ICARDA	International Center for Agricultural Research in the Dry Areas
ICLARM	International Center for Living Aquatic Resources Management
ICRAF	International Center for Research on Agro-Forestry
ICRISAT	International Crop Research Institute for the Semi-Arid Tropics
IDA	International Development Association, an affiliate of the World Bank
IFPRI	International Food Policy Research Institute
IIMI	International Irrigation Management Institute
IITA	International Institute for Tropical Agriculture
ILO	International Labour Organization
ILRI	International Livestock Research Institute
IMF	International Monetary Fund
INEAC	Institut National pour l'Étude Agronomique du Congo Belge

IPCC	Intergovernmental Panel on Climate Change
IPGRI	International Plant Genetic Resources Institute
IPRs	intellectual property rights
IRRI	International Rice Research Institute
ISI	import substitution industrialization
ISNAR	International Service for National Agricultural Research
ITC	information technology and communication
ITCZ	intertropical convergence zone
ITD	intertropical discontinuity
ITDG	Intermediate Technology Development Group
ITT	International Telephone and Telegraph (now ITT Industries Inc.)
KARI	Kenya Agricultural Research Institute
LETS	local exchange trading systems
MERCOSUR	Mercado Común del Sur (Southern Common Market)
MFN	most favored nation
MSF	Médecins sans Frontières (Doctors without Borders)
MVA	manufacturing value added
N_2O	nitrous oxide
NAFTA	North American Free Trade Agreement
NASA	National Aeronautics and Space Administration
NBA	Narmada Bachao Andolan (Movement to Save the Narmada River)
NBTT	net barter terms of trade
NGO	nongovernmental organization
NICs	newly industrializing countries
NIEO	new international economic order
NTB	nontariff barrier
OAU	Organization of African Unity
ODA	official development aid
OECD	Organization for Economic Cooperation and Development
OFCs	offshore financial centers
OPEC	Organization of the Petroleum Exporting Countries
OTA	Office of Technology Assessment
PCBs	polychlorinated biphenyls
pH	potential of hydrogen, a measure of acidity or alkalinity
PL 480	Public Law 480 Food Aid Program (United States)
ppm	parts per million
PPP	purchasing power parity
PQLI	physical quality of life index
PRGF	Poverty Reduction and Growth Facility
PRM	participatory resource management
PRSP	Poverty Reduction Strategy Program
PTA	preferential trading arrangement
PVP	plant variety protection
PWP	Philip W. Porter (author)
R&D	research and development
RAINBOW	Research Action Information Network for Bodily Integrity of Women
RN	Richa Nagar (author)
SARDEP	Sustainable Animal and Range Development Programme

SKMS	Sangtin Kisaan Mazdoor Sangathan (Sangtin Peasants and Workers Organization)
spp.	species (with genus names)
STDs	sexually transmitted diseases
STIT	Sindicato de Trabajadores de la Industria Textil
TB	tuberculosis
TCDD	2,3,7,8-tetrochlorobenzo-para-dioxin
TNC	transnational corporation
TRIPS	Trade-Related Aspects of International Property Rights
UNAIDS	Joint United Nations Programme on HIV/AIDS
UNCTAD	United Nations Conference on Trade and Development
UNCTC	United Nations Centre on Transnational Corporations
UNDP	United Nations Development Programme
UNESCO	United Nations Educational, Scientific, and Cultural Organization
UNFPA	United Nations Fund for Population Activities
UNICEF	United Nations Children's Fund
UNIDO	United Nations Industrial Development Organization
USAID	U.S. Agency for International Development
USDA	U.S. Department of Agriculture
USGS	U.S. Geological Survey
US/LEAP	U.S. Labor Education in the Americas Project
USSR	Union of Soviet Socialist Republics
WAD	women and development
WAEMU	West African Economic and Monetary Union
WARDA	West African Rice Development Association
WCD	World Commission on Dams
WEU	West European Union
WHO	World Health Organization
WID	women in development
WTO	World Trade Organization

Contents

Part II. Differentiated Livelihoods and the Nonhuman World

Part I Differentiated Ways of Knowing

1 Introduction

"THIRD WORLD"—FIRST IMPRESSIONS

Were you to stand in the center of a village in Africa, Asia, or Latin America—in a so-called "less developed" country—you could watch the daily comings and goings of villagers. Let's say that this is an African village, in the country of Kenya. Soon a man in his late 20s asks a young girl in school uniform to fetch a chair for you, and he invites you to sit in the shade. Depending on whether you know the village well (perhaps even were born there) or are a first-time visitor, you can make mental notes on the material conditions of life and, by talking with passers-by, learn about the hopes, joys, and problems of the people living there. You may see much poverty, but you may also be struck by the richness and vibrancy of the social life around you.

Local conditions seem to explain local life. It is not always apparent that virtually any village is part of a global political economy, a world system. Your first impressions may lead you to ask whether the poverty in the village has stemmed from a complex product of checks, impediments, and constraints—partly of an environmental sort (poor soils, inadequate, unreliable rainfall, endemic diseases), and partly related to sociocultural attitudes and practices that either exhibit adjustments to local environmental circumstances, or are often regarded as "barriers" to technical and attitudinal changes that might lead to greater productivity and well-being.

You are curious about the man who has just asked the girl to bring out a chair for you. Who is he, and what does he do? What does he think of his village and the world? What about the girl? Is she his daughter or niece? Where is the rest of her family? Does her mother work on the farm or sell anything at the market? Is her mother involved in the local nongovernmental organization (NGO) that works on human immunodeficiency virus/acquired immune deficiency syndrome (HIV/AIDS) and reproductive health in the village?

But the young man has taken an interest in you and why you are there! He tells you his name, Wambua Muathe, and asks yours. He tells you proudly that he has gone to college. He is not disconnected from the world. Indeed, he appears to be quite knowledgeable about current events, and if you come from the United States he quizzes you about

U.S. foreign policy, much of which puzzles and dismays him. His older sister, Leila, works in the capital city, and he talks with her frequently by cell phone. (You note the Reeboks and Levis that he is wearing.) There is a cybercafé in the nearby market town, and although it is mostly down due to frequent power outages, Wambua has learned how to use the Internet. His uncle, Mwinjuma, has lived for some time in Rochester, Minnesota, and he likes to be in touch with him.

As you visit, you notice that not everyone is dressed like Wambua. Wambua has sent packing a large bunch of curious kids who gathered around you as you sat down. Some young boys in neat school uniforms run by on their way to football (soccer) practice. Some school girls, in uniform as well, run with the boys; others, including Wambua's niece, Ngina, who brought the chair for you, get busy with afternoon chores at home. But you note other youngsters, dressed in worn, torn garments. They appear not to go to school at all; some have herniated, protuberant navels and leg sores, and a few show signs of malnutrition. Some of the girls and boys are taking care of younger siblings. The older women move between outdoor kitchen and the insides of their houses. Some return from a nearby hand pump with buckets and jerri cans filled with water. There is a constant round of activities. In one of the houses, a radio loudly plays "Kwassa Kwassa," a popular number by a Congolese Swahili band named Kanda Bongo Man; farther along from another house you can hear the percussive sound of rap music, something you vaguely recognize as being by 50 Cent. Why are there so few men? Some of them are away working on estates, plantations, or mines; others have jobs in cities, working for one multinational corporation or another. They return home from time to time, and some manage to send money back to help their families. Kavindu, Ngina's mother and Wambua's sister-in-law, calls and asks him to help haul more water, so he excuses himself.

You are forming the impression that there are features of the stereotypical first world that show up in third world settings—popular music, athletic shoes, blue jeans, jobs in multinational corporations, as well as a constant flow of information about happenings elsewhere in the world. You try to compare this poverty with the poverty and limited access to education and health care you have seen in your own country, and you suddenly think of questions you never thought of asking when you were "back home." You realize that all these elements you have been observing are interconnected. The world has been interconnected for a long time—perhaps not so instantaneously as today (with the Internet, transmission of video, audio, and text messages from anywhere to everywhere is possible within nanoseconds), but connected nonetheless.

Most readers of this page, of course, are not standing in a village in Africa (or Asia or Latin America). For many readers (at least those whose immediate experience is limited to western, industrialized societies), their understanding of lives in such places is generally secondhand, vicarious; their knowledge and assumptions about these "other" worlds are anecdotal and unsystematic.

The planes flown into the World Trade Center and the Pentagon, on September 11, 2001, provided a spectacular reminder that alienation and poverty elsewhere cannot be explained as simply local events, and that distant consequences can come home to roost. Many Americans reacted to this particular shocking act of terrorism by asking, "Why do they hate us?" They were puzzled that people in distant lands, drawn to Islamic extremism, could be and were willing to engage in "this kind of attack on us," seemingly out of the blue. Can these acts really be explained as coming from a "hatred of freedom" or of what Americans do at home? Too few Americans understood how such acts can be traced to alienating experiences with colonialism and development, stretching back over centuries, and grievances for which the United States as a nation and

U.S.-based corporations were readily identifiable as both symbols and culpable parties (not least because of the United States' historical associations with violence in strategic parts of the third world)—notwithstanding the fact that many victims were themselves not Americans. These acts reinforced tendencies to equate Islam with violent fundamentalism and the Middle East, overlooking how the powerlessness with which many ordinary people experience globalization has catalyzed a turn to (often xenophobic) extremisms—Christian, Jewish, Hindu, and Muslim—also in North America and South Asia.

In the post-9/11 world, it is especially important that we become more systematically informed about the meanings and processes pertaining to development and underdevelopment in the third world. We hope this book will help. We use geographical and historical methods of analysis to explore the nature and structure of relations in what is becoming more and more each day a "globalized" world. It should already be clear that "first world" and "third world" are not monolithic categories. We must constantly question and problematize these labels, even as we grapple with why and how to understand the complexity of lives and struggles in the third world. To borrow a phrase from a colleague, Yi-Fu Tuan, our goal is to increase the "burden of awareness" of our readers (see sidebar: "Understanding Poverty?").

TRANSCENDING ENLIGHTENMENT IN A WORLD OF DIFFERENCE

> A cultural theory which stresses the hybridities and impurities that are the legacy of colonialism and global capitalism and which recognizes the continuously transforming impact of global inequalities on the lives of the marginal people in the Third World can better account both for the conditions in which claims to indigenousness are politically effective and for those situations which do not allow for such claims to be mustered . . . "indigenous knowledge" is not a static or closed system but is itself heterogeneous, hierarchical, and infused by relations of power and inequality; . . . the effectiveness of "indigenous" identity depends on its *recognition* by hegemonic discourses of imperialist nostalgia, where poor and marginal people are romanticized at the same time that their way of life is destroyed . . .
>
> —AKHIL GUPTA (1998:18)

So far, you have been reading references to "poverty" in conjunction with a world that we are painting as being different from the "first world"—a world that we call the "third world." But how do we know poverty when we see it? Is it something we can touch, measure, evaluate, and fix? Lest we assume that definitions of "poor" and "poverty" are universally shared or as old as language itself, it is critical to remind ourselves that poverty is sociopolitically constructed (see sidebar: "The TV Set in the Mud Hut") in much the same way that the idea of the third world is (see Chapter 2). However, the constructed nature of these ideas does not minimize the magnitude of their lived meanings, or the effects of the dichotomies that they implicitly or explicitly invoke (e.g., "underdeveloped" vs. "(over)developed," "backward" vs. "modern," "have-nots" vs. "haves"). All of these have become a critical part of our everyday lives and cultures—who we are, what we are becoming, what we want to become, and how.

We have often learned to see development as diffusing the benefits of modernity to those who have not yet received them. However, this view is complicated by the rise of postmodernist thinking, which arose to contest modernist pretensions. Therefore, some might see our inquiry into poverty and development as indicative of a titanic struggle between two contrasting visions of the world. One is generally regarded as linear and progressive, originating in the European Enlightenment; the other, a "Counter-Enlightenment" vision (to use Isaiah Berlin's term), tends to be circular, ecological, and decentralizing, standing in reaction to the

Understanding Poverty?

One of our most remarkable capacities as humans is our ability to live with contradictions. Those of us living in comfortable circumstances know that a world of poverty and inequality exists, and we know that the values in which we are instructed from childhood in our homes, schools, and places of worship argue for greater equity and for the worth and dignity of human life. Yet thoughts about inequality do not dominate our waking moments, and certainly not our actions. There is much else to life. For most U.S. residents, as for many wealthy people across the globe, the world's poverty and its problems are remote. The Czech novelist Franz Kafka (1948: 418) wrote in his diary for August 1914: "Germany has declared war against Russia. Afternoon, swimming pool." The world's problems are felt to be too large and complex to be assumed as an individual burden. Yet Robert Heilbroner, in *The Great Ascent* (1963), attempted to present a vivid tableau of underdevelopment by describing his view of what it would take to transform a typical U.S. family into an equally typical family of the underdeveloped world. He argued that the transformation could be described in terms of a string of subtractions, removing material and nonmaterial things from the family. First, almost all of the furniture, clothing, and food would be taken away, and then the house itself (a nearby shed would have to suffice). This would be followed by communications—gone would be TV, telephone, newspapers, and books, as well as the family's literacy itself. One radio would remain for the neighborhood. This would be followed by the removal of services—schools, health clinics, doctors, police, and fire services. Thus, saying an individual lives on less than $2 per day shows what it would take to convert a typical U.S. family into one living in third world poverty. This view, despite its gendered and racialized oversimplifications, vividly illustrates the material dimensions of privilege and deprivation that characterize the global politics of development.

excesses and destructive tendencies of the first vision (Berlin, 1979). The Enlightenment project is viewed by its proponents as a positive, progressive movement, whose ultimate goal is the liberation of humankind from poverty and oppression. Its keywords are "progress," "simplicity," "universalism," and "rationality." The Enlightenment began with such philosophers as John Locke and Gottfried Wilhelm Leibnitz in the 17th century, so it has had over 300 years to work toward its objectives. It cannot be said that it has made much headway in a large part of the world, and indeed Counter-Enlightenment scholars question whether it can or should.

The goals of the Counter-Enlightenment are similar to those of the Enlightenment—the liberation of humankind from poverty and oppression—but its strategy is different. First, it is critical of the excessively reductionist ways of knowing and essentialist thinking that the Enlightenment brought. Stemming from that, it exhibits a deep suspicion of western instrumentalities: capitalism and market-driven economics; advanced technologies and the sciences; the central power of the state. It is also critical of the way capitalism, technology, and the state have combined to use up the earth's natural resources and degrade the environment, all the while (through a global reach of advertising, marketing, trade, and communications) seeking to transform the wants and desires of third world peoples by projecting first world products and ideals onto them. The Counter-Enlightenment's proponents point to the grotesque, wasteful, irrational consumption of resources in the first world, while millions in the third world live in misery and poverty. Instead, for first and third world people alike, the Counter-Enlightenment celebrates diversity; localism and community; egalitarianism; ecological sustainability, a small scale, and self-sufficiency; and pride in local culture, ethnicity, and traditions. It seeks to do away with structures that support and protect the powerful—for example, classism, patriarchy, sexism, homophobia, and racism—and to achieve a world in which

The TV Set in the Mud Hut

How do we know "poverty" when we see it? Majid Rahnema (1992: 158–159) argues that poverty is historically, politically, and geographically constructed:

> For long and in many cultures of the world, poor was not always the opposite of rich. Other considerations such as falling from one's station in life, being deprived of one's instruments of labor, the loss of one's status or the marks of one's profession (for a cleric, the loss of his books; for a noble, the loss of his horse or arms), lack of protection, exclusion from one's community, abandonment, infirmity, or public humiliation defined the poor. The Tswana people of South Africa recognized their poor by their reactions to the appearance of locusts. Whereas the rich people were appalled lest the locusts ate the grass needed by their cattle, the poor who had no cattle rejoiced because they could themselves eat the locusts.
>
> In Europe, for ages, the pauper was opposed to the *potens* (the powerful), rather than the rich. In the 9th century, the pauper was considered a free man whose freedom was imperiled only by the *potentes*. In the . . . 11th century, . . . the word, poor, could be applied to the owner of a little alleu (a tax-free property), a wandering merchant, and even to any non-fighter, including the unescorted wives of knights. On the whole, the poor were quite respectable persons who had only lost, or stood in the danger of losing, their "berth."
>
> In that same period in Europe, a whole new category of poor appeared on the social stage—the voluntary poor who chose to share the life of the destitute and the berthless. For these, living poorly was a sign of elevation rather than degradation. Respect and admiration for the voluntary poor had, of course, always existed in Eastern traditions.
>
> It was only after the expansion of the mercantile economy, the processes of urbanization leading to massive pauperization and, indeed, the monetization of society that the poor were defined as lacking what the rich could have in terms of money and possessions.
>
> A common denominator for most perceptions of poverty remains the notion of "lack" or "deficiency." The notion reflects only the basic relativity of the concept, for a utopian "complete" man would not be lacking anything. Besides, when poor is defined as lacking a number of things necessary to life, the questions could be asked: What is necessary and for whom? And who is qualified to define all that? In smaller communities, where people are less strangers to one another and things are easier to compare, such questions are already difficult to answer. In a world of the mass media, the old familiar horizons and communally defined bases of comparison are all destroyed. Everyone may think of themselves as poor when it is the TV set in the mud hut which defines the necessities of life, often in terms of the wildest and fanciest consumers appearing on the screen.

people enjoy freedom, equality, community, and material well-being.

If we accept the idea of a great dialectical contest between the forces of modernity and the forces arrayed in opposition to it, one way to make sense of these contrasting logics is in terms of what Tuan (1996) views as a struggle between cosmos and hearth. "Cosmos" refers to the high-modern Enlightenment project based on what are presumed to be universal forms of reason, science, the application of technology, and democracy. "Hearth" represents a postmodern radical reaction to Enlightenment modernization. The Counter-Enlightenment, which seeks to recover the time-honored virtues and blessings of the hearth, features deconstruction of modernity's hegemonic megastructures—philosophical, sociopolitical, historical, literary, and scientific (Giddens, 1991: 27 ff.). In Tuan's provocative image, the playing field among cultures is leveled by deconstructing the megastructures of "high culture," so that they are reduced in size to those of the "miniworks of preliterate peoples, folks, peasant immigrants, ethnics"; "we are then left with differences between one opinion, one work, and another, all spread out as it were on a flat plane, a colorful mosaic of sharply bounded, incommensurate units, rather than ranked judgments of ideas and works, a topography of peaks, plains and troughs" (Tuan, 1996: 128).

Another way to work through this tension is by confronting the myth of development which, despite repeated failures, continues to be justified on the grounds that the failures are caused by local, regional, or national problems, not by the logic of development itself. For Latouche (1993), development and underdevelopment are part of an asymmetrical world system, but culture exists as prior to and alongside economic domination. The idea of development is fundamentally a western cultural invention that has been poorly grafted in the third world, while the perception of what is underdeveloped is a result of the collision of different cultural universes—western and nonwestern. This perspective recognizes that the desire for development exists in the third world, but it questions whether development and opulence will have long-term viability for the west (or anywhere else), given the extensive environmental destruction and the level of human alienation that it has caused. To transcend the development narrative, Latouche and others conceive of a postwestern world arising out of the nebula of informal economy and alternative social relations: "While modern society is seen as detaching the economic from the social, the informal society is regarded as embedding the economic with the social by reactivating networks of solidarity and reciprocity" (Saunders, 2002a: 22).

The notion of contestations over the diffusion of modernity may not be the most useful way to think about development. The distinction between what is or is not modern is murky. Latour argues in the title of his 1993 book that *We Have Never Been Modern*, and Gidwani (2002) argues for the notion of multiple and context-specific modernities. To frame the problem in terms of Enlightenment and Counter-Enlightenment, cosmos and hearth, or modern and informal runs the grave risk of reifying the artificial dichotomy between the west and the rest, while overlooking the unexpected intersections among the globe-spanning legacies of the modernist projects of colonialism, nationalism, and development—intersections that are regarded as the defining features of the "postcolonial condition." Engaging with these intersections, as Gupta (1998: 20) points out, requires us to grapple with hybrid discourses and practices, to delineate the intertwining of "local" practices with global and national projects of development, and to unsettle the binaries of colonial and nationalist thought by pointing to the imbrication of the indigenous in modernist discourse. Rather than determining whether something is authentic, original, or uncontaminated, we must accept cultural hybridity as a starting point in political projects that seek to empower subaltern, poor, and marginal groups. At the same time, Gupta (1998: 24) is careful to remind us that "the postcolonial" cannot be a synonym for "the third world." Since postcolonial theory is profoundly shaped by the failure to constitute a modern nation that mimics the development trajectory of the "west," it has much less influence in locations or with groups that have had a longer period of formal independence (e.g., parts of Latin America); among people who are still colonized (e.g., native and aboriginal peoples of North America and Australia); and in places where the optimism of nationhood has not yet yielded to the disillusion of postcoloniality (e.g., South Africa).

The diverse trajectories of decolonization make it important that any attempt to understand the postcolonial dilemma attends analytically to these similarities and differences:

> On the one hand, it is important to see modernity, colonialism, capitalism, development discourse, and international science as *global* phenomena that have far reaching and systematic consequences for the regions that they

> affect. On the other hand, it is crucial not to overlook the differences in the forms taken by these global phenomena in multiple locations, differences that arise from contestation, reworking, and rearticulation. The opposition between "the global" and "the local" itself depends on a spatialized dichotomy that needs to be questioned. (Gupta, 1998: 24)

CULTURES AND REPRESENTATIONAL ASYMMETRIES

> "Culture is who we are and who we are becoming." It is the food we put on the table; the way we cook it; the utensils with which we eat it; the relations between the people who sit at the table and the people who cook and serve; what is done with the leftovers; what is discussed during the meal; what music, dancing, poetry, or theater accompany it; and the social and spiritual values of those present—for, when we say culture, we include the visions, dreams, and aspirations of humanity.
>
> How is it possible to talk of social and economic development without talking about culture? . . . How can we address the question of literacy if we ignore the question of what there is to read? Do we want women to learn to read and write merely so that they can follow the instructions in packages of birth control pills? Or do we want them to be able to read their own lives, write their own destinies, and claim their share?
>
> —MEREDITH Tax with MARJORIE AGOSIN, AMA ATA AIDOO, RITU MENON, NINOTCHKA ROSCA, and MARIELLA SALA (1999: 113)

The processes and politics of development are inextricably intertwined with the manner in which "cultures" are invoked, defined, and evaluated—often in terms of "backward" or "progressive," "traditional" or "modern," "dynamic" or "static." Our aim in this book is not to define, explain, or assess cultures. Indeed, we agree with Appadurai (1996) that culture should be approached not as a noun, but as an adjective, "cultural"—culture not as substance, but as the dimensionality of difference. He sees things cultural as "situated difference, that is, difference in relation to something local, embodied, and significant" (Appadurai, 1996: 12). But a commitment to approach the cultural as situated difference brings with itself enormous responsibilities and challenges: How and from which locations can we speak about, write, and represent that which is different and thereby becomes our "other," and for what purposes? These challenges are strikingly similar to the ones that Ella Shohat (1998: 8–9) describes in her elaboration of feminist alliance work that shuttles "back and forth between concentric circles of affiliation riven by power asymmetries." For Shohat,

> The critique of white feminists who speak for all women might be extrapolated to cases in which upper-middle class "Third World" women come to unilaterally represent "other" working class sisters, or to [cases in which] diasporic feminists [operate] within First World representational practices. Metropolitan feminists of color have to be aware of these hierarchies, just as "Third World" feminists cannot ignore class or religious privileges when "speaking for our sisters." The possibility of speaking for Third World sisters (even if of the same color) is rooted in global structural inequalities that generate such representational asymmetries, whereby some voices and some modes of speaking are amplified more than others. . . . Even with the very best intentions, a fetishized focus on African female genital mutilation or on Asian foot-binding ends up as complicit with a Eurocentric victimology that reduces African or Asian cultures and women to such practices, while muting or marginalizing African or Asian agency and organizing. A multicultural feminist critique disrupts the narrative of center/periphery when talking "about" the "Third World," showing feminist resistant practices within a conflictual community, where opposition to such practices does not perpetuate the false dichotomy of savagery versus civilization or tradition versus modernity. . . . [It is] less concerned with identities as something one has than in identification as something one does. While rejecting fixed, essentialist and reductionist formulations of identity, it

> fosters a mutually enriching politics of intercommunity representation.

To internalize Shohat's concerns and apply them—even minimally—to our own project, we must struggle with the challenge of rejecting fixed, essentialized, and reductionist formulations of the third world, while highlighting the processes by which the dynamic specificities of communities and lives in the third world are erased, are homogenized, are retained, or become points of contestation in development thought and practice. This task, of course, is more easily summarized than enacted, and must become part of a lifelong journey dedicated to learning how to become responsible teachers and students of difference.

As a starting point, we can think of two ways to embark on this journey in U.S. academic spaces. First, we can make a conscious attempt to disrupt any borders or boundaries that seek to make a stark separation between the "there" of a backward, oppressed, traditional third world on the one hand, and the "here" of a progressive, emancipated, modern first world on the other (see sidebar: "Shoes, Veils, and Murders"). Second, we must mark moments of tension and contradictions in our own generalizations about the third world, and be critically reflexive of the possibilities and limitations that such generalizations enable.

Tropicality: The More-than-Human World

One such generalization, popular again, is that nature (not culture) is what makes the third world different from the first. In particular, the generalization is made that the third world is tropical, and that tropical environments stand in the way of development (e.g., Diamond, 1997; Sachs, Mellinger, and Gallup, 2001). Many parts of the global south are not tropical (Chapter 2), but the persistence of poverty and malnutrition in sub-Saharan Africa continues to invite this environmental explanation. The danger, again, is slippage into a mode of thinking that separates a tropical "there" from a temperate "here." We seek to take the more-than-human world seriously, while contesting such thinking.

We examine particularities of tropical environments in Chapters 8–12. Locations close to the equator do indeed experience particular temperature and rainfall regimes and soil conditions, and particular disease clusters. Yet the claim that tropicality prevents development is based on the presumption that the nonhuman world can be thought of as separate from and determinant of human livelihood possibilities. In fact, society and environment are mutually constitutive (Chapter 7). Thus the continued presence of distinct, hazardous disease clusters in tropical environments is not simply caused by the tropics. To take the perspective of western medicine, their persistence is due to the lack of effort devoted to finding preventative measures or cures for diseases in these impoverished parts of the world. For example, the persistence of malaria in tropical Africa and its absence from the southern United States is not because of climatic differences, but because of historical efforts in the United States to eliminate the environmental conditions favoring anophelene mosquitoes, as well as the mosquitoes themselves. (When analysts attribute the prevalence of HIV/AIDS to tropicality, simply because of its presence across sub-Saharan Africa, it is a prime example of such muddle-headed thinking. HIV is spread through human-to-human contact, not through biophysical processes.)

Another important shaper of livelihood possibilities is agriculture. Tropical environments do pose particular challenges, but it does not follow that climate is the principal cause of the livelihood challenges faced by tropical agriculturalists. Under colonialism, some indigenous farmers were displaced from those environments best suited to rapid crop growth, which were given to European farmers; others were required to grow export crops to sell to uncertain markets,

Shoes, Veils, and Murders

The work of shuttling back and forth, of disrupting stereotypes, of pushing ourselves to be critical of the ways in which "we" ourselves are oppressed (even as we are eager to identify the "other" as victim, and to help emancipate that victim) is hard intellectual, political, and emotional labor. However, there are many examples in feminist work where such labor has been creatively undertaken. Uma Narayan (1997), a U.S.-based feminist scholar, contrasts popular representations of murders by "dowry deaths" in India with those by domestic violence in the United States. Nawal El Saadawi (1994), an Egyptian feminist writer and activist, has similarly compared the oppressions inflicted by two kinds of veils: that covering a woman's head and body (*hijaab, burqa*) and that covering her face (makeup). She argues that these are two sides of the same patriarchal coin that objectifies women's bodies to suit its ends, and it should be added that both are equally complex in how, why, and when they are embraced by women in specific locations and contexts. A third example of such comparisons, which pushes the "self" to insert itself in its reading of the "other," comes from an exhibit at the University of British Columbia's Museum of Anthropology. The exhibit displayed two cultural artifacts commonly described as "shoes." A silk shoe from late-19th-century China, invoked in the west as symbolic of Chinese women's bound feet, was imaginatively paired with a high-heeled shoe from 1990s North America. Presented with a commentary by Anna Nobile (1999; provided courtesy of James F. Glassman, January 4, 2000), the display sought to mark specific continuities across times and cultures:

. . . thought to be erotic . . .
Shoes, China, late 19th century
Artist unknown
Silk

> The practice of foot binding began in China during the Song Dynasty (960–1270 AD). Girls, beginning at seven or eight years old, had their feet tightly wrapped and bent until the arch broke and the toes were permanently bent under. The practice was extremely painful and limited the mobility and agility of bound-foot women for centuries. Initially, the practice was limited to the upper classes, but because bound feet were associated with wealth and status, they soon became an essential prerequisite to any advantageous marriage. Small feet in women were thought to be erotic and became euphemistically known as "golden lotuses." The practice lasted into the early twentieth century.

Shoes, North America, 1998
Leather

> Today, we still have the high-heeled shoe. In many societies, the female foot is still considered erotic and the high-heeled shoe has become a fetish object. High heels force the buttocks and breasts out while decreasing a woman's mobility and agility. They also compress the toes (leading to calluses and corns), put double the weight on the ball of the foot (leading to bunions and neuromas), strain the tendons around the knees and prolong the pressure across the knee joints and on the back. The practice of wearing high-heeled shoes is prevalent among all social classes throughout the world.
>
> . . . Despite our cultural and racial differences, we are often very much the same.

and/or were encouraged to use technologies that proved inappropriate to their particular social and environmental conditions. From the point of view of western agricultural know-how, after colonialism less effort has been devoted to improving the yields of tropical food crops than to increasing those at home in temperate climates. Beyond this, the global agribusiness economy, along with subsidies to farmers in the United States, Europe, and Japan, have done more to undermine the profitability of agriculture in the global south than any environmental constraints have.

Nevertheless, environmental conditions make a difference. Although local residents have developed effective means of managing these (Chapter 12), plants grow more slowly in the warm, humid lowland tropics than in the middle latitudes, and soils are often more fragile (Chapters 10 and 11). Such environments favor agricultural and societal practices that are oriented toward subsistence, rather than toward maximizing agricultural surplus as a basis for economic and population growth. If we think in terms of western, growth-oriented cultural and economic systems as being the only way to the good life, such conditions and livelihoods seem disadvantageous. But this, again, is to equate such systems with "modern" and tropical subsistence livelihoods with "backward." In fact, as we begin to realize how much our growth-oriented culture is transforming the nonhuman world through global warming and resource exhaustion, we would be well advised to jettison such hierarchical thinking. What we can learn from such tropical subsistence-oriented livelihoods that can help us learn how to live better?

AFFECT HUNGER AND THE ORIGINS OF CULTURE

For some time now, you have been reading what we have written. What enables you to do this? Your ability is the result of a long learning process that began at birth. Elsewhere in this book, you will encounter discussions of "Orientalism" and the "other." We have a lot to say about the problems of prejudice and stereotyping that western observers frequently exhibit regarding nonwestern cultures—sweeping overgeneralizations that pit "them" against "us."

At the same time, it might be important to consider the perspective that emphasizes the fundamental importance of the "other" in human development and the creation and transmission of culture. Our first "other" had an "m" in front of it! Everything we know and think stems in some way from an interaction with an "other." Thus is the individual body (the self) brought into the community. Thus does the individual come to know and understand the society and culture of which she or he is a part. These interactive processes and relationships through which we as humans are constantly living and becoming with our "others" are referred to by anthropologist Walter Goldschmidt (2006) as "affect hunger" (see sidebars: "Goldschmidt on Affect Hunger" and "Calculating Kinship").

Our human evolution is now guided by social and cultural factors as well as biological factors. Although affect hunger is expressed in myriad ways in different cultures, it is a fundamental underlying impulse in individual growth and, by extension, in societal and cultural change. As we consider the distortions, deprivations, inequalities, violence, and injustices that individuals, particularly children, experience as they grow up (not only in the third world, but in much of the rest of the world), we can wonder at the long-term effects of losses—the decreases in family cohesion; the diminished sense of place and neighborhood; the disappearance of lodges and clubs; the impoverishment of social and religious networks; the deskilling of labor; impersonal, alienating market and bureaucratic transactions; and loneliness and isolation among the elderly. Affect hunger will find ways to satisfy its cravings, and some of those ways can jeopardize the very cultures in which they emerge—for example, urban gangs in Los Angeles neighborhoods where family structure has broken down and children are left to their own devices. A gang provides a young person with support, identity, security, and a sense of belonging, however antisocial the gang's actions may be deemed by the "other."

The concept of affect hunger serves to remind us that all human beings of every culture seek recognition and expressions of affection from others. Every society has institutions and practices that provide for and validate an individual's efforts to belong and be valued. We are inherently social beings with social needs. Modern capitalist society, in which impersonal market relations and bureaucratic transactions crowd out genuinely human interactions, can limit the scope for healthy social interchange and can lead to alienation and antisocial behavior. As neoliberal globalization increases its penetration of lives among third world people, compromising or destroying aspects of society that provide value and recognition to individuals, we should keep in mind that affect hunger does not cease; an individual's needs for support and validation will still be met, one way or another.

REWRITING *A WORLD OF DIFFERENCE*

A Microsoft Thesaurus search on the word "collaboration" yields the following results: "teamwork," "partnership," "group effort," "alliance," "relationship," "cooperation." The objectives of teamwork are by definition "shared," but the complex process by which each partnership or alliance arrives at its shared goals makes every collaboration unique. This uniqueness emanates from the manner in which the collaborators negotiate their positionalities (their geographical, sociopolitical, and institutional locations), investments, individual goals (personal, political, intellectual, etc.), and processes for creating a set of common strategies and an agenda that they wish to pursue. Such complex processes of negotiation in an academic collaboration, when specified and analyzed (however partially), can provide useful insights into how we become learners, users, evaluators, and producers of knowledges. Here we want to touch briefly on some of these aspects in the making of the second edition of *A World of Difference*. Our aim is not to achieve perfect transparency before our readers in terms of who we are, how we met, or why we jointly undertook this project. Rather, we want to reflect on some of the ways in which the present collaboration among four authors (Sheppard, Porter, Faust, and Nagar) makes this book significantly different in nature and scope from the first edition (Porter and Sheppard, 1998).

To begin with, this new edition makes a conscious effort to move away from the dualism of Enlightenment and Counter-Enlightenment by engaging more systematically with development theory that has deployed a range of poststructuralist and feminist perspectives. The initial five chapters of the book, in particular, attempt to provide a historically specific account of how the third world gets constructed as a "knowable" entity and evolves as such, through colonial encounters, state-led development, and neoliberal globalization.

Relatedly, whereas the book's engagement with feminisms was primarily confined to a chapter section on gender and development (GAD) in the first edition, the second edition actively incorporates insights from feminist approaches to development and difference. Rather than averaging out "feminist approaches" in a broader philosophical discussion about development, we consider feminisms as internally varied and diverse in terms of intellectual stances and political goals. We also note the ways in which the language of feminism itself has been mainstreamed in development rhetoric and practice, with mixed results.

Third, we are more attentive to the theme of contestation at a number of levels. For example, we explore how narratives of empowerment or violence (as in "female literacy," "reduced fertility," and "genital mutilation") are multilayered, and how "emancipation" might carry very different meanings for different groups. We also examine the ways in which contestations around nature, resources, development, and globalization are articulated at multiple scales, sometimes in dissonance and at other times in harmony with one another.

But the process of interrogating a preexisting narrative, revising it by inserting contestation and disharmony into it,

Goldschmidt on Affect Hunger

The cover of Goldschmidt's *The Bridge to Humanity: How Affect Hunger Trumps the Selfish Gene* (2006) has a hauntingly evocative portrait by Pablo Picasso (an early, representational work) of a mother nursing her baby. This image intrudes constantly as one reads the book, whose essential argument is that with the invention of culture, the *social* (affect hunger) assumed priority over the *biological* (genetics) in human evolution. "Affect hunger is the urge to get expressions of affection from others" (Goldschmidt, 2006: 47). This sidebar summarizes Goldschmidt's argument by tracing the steps whereby hominids reached the point of having culture. (All page numbers in what follows are from Goldschmidt, 2006.)

For evolution to occur, two things are necessary. Put most succinctly, they are death and the taking of life. "Change comes only as new generations acquire new traits that render the old obsolete" (ix). "Understanding that others must have died for us to live and the inevitability that we must, in turn, die that others may live reinforces the sense of our continuity with eternity" (ix). Furthermore, "we must all eat to live, must take life to have life. In no other way could the earth support a continuing population—an integral part of the evolutionary process" (ix). Another central fact concerns "mutuality"—the facts that mammalians of all sorts cooperate, and that nurturance is deeply embedded in mammalian behavior (ix).

"The basic lifestyle of each species is always inherited, but the degree and nature of this adaptability vary widely among living things, and this *variability is itself a genetic heritage*" (1; emphasis in original). "Homo sapiens is by far the most adaptable of all species" (1).

Fundamental human behavioral characteristics that enable people to live nearly everywhere on earth are (1) the ability to control internal body temperature; (2) the complex of features involved in viviparous birth (uterine feeding, mammary feeding, and the long dependency period of the infant that requires bonding between infant and parents); and (3) sociability—that is, mutuality and cooperation, which, along with competition, characterize human social life (13–14). Learning is key to all three. "Culture is, by definition, learned behavior, making learning crucial to the human condition" (16–17). A syllogism summarizes the point of the foregoing: "Many genetic instructions that make us human are indeterminate, requiring fine adjustments. These adjustments are responses to situational conditions. The actions of other humans create some situational conditions. Therefore, social and biological cannot be separate realms" (19).

Goldschmidt advances the argument that language and tool making exhibit similarities in logic and structure, and thus must have evolved at the same time. This puts language development much earlier in the development of *Homo sapiens*. Trading quadrupedal for bipedal locomotion and a large head (containing a large brain) for fighting effectiveness (prothaganous jaw, large canines, and an acute sense of smell) made possible "the two things that distinguish Homo sapiens from other forms of life: talking and making things" (21). "The mental processes involved in speaking and in making things are essentially alike" (21). Speech involves (1) the articulation of delicately nuanced sounds (sounds); (2) the formulation of conceptual categories (words and categories); and (3) structuring the relations among the elements brought together in utterances (grammar). In this, humans are truly unique. Summarizing Noam Chomsky, Goldschmidt writes that "humans are endowed with some special mental capacity for learning [the rules of syntax] through experiencing their use by those around them" (24). A human who does not hear human speech by puberty is forever incapable of learning grammar.

A mother cat vigorously licks and grooms her kittens. In so doing, she promotes the "normal growth of dentrites and a full complement of synapses on [the kitten's] nerve cells" (47); that is, the stimulation helps the brain develop. Infants deprived of such "tactile stimulation" do not develop normally. One is reminded of Victor, the "the wild boy of Aveyron." He was found in a wooded part of the southern Massif Central in France, in 1799. He had somehow lived much of his first 12 years separate from human society. Although his mentor, Jean Marc Gaspard Itard, worked unceasingly to educate the young man, Victor never developed human capabilities. He died aged about 40 (Itard, 1801/1962).

"Affect hunger can only be gratified by others; it is therefore immediately implicated in the existence and nature of social relations. It is ratified in many different specific ways, but there are two general ways to meet this need: belonging, and performance. Belonging involves a sense of oneness with others in the environment.

. . . Performance means ability and proficiency in doing things that the individual feels is worthwhile" (58). "The result [of teaching] is to transform the neonate into a responsible and competent member of his or her society. In the long, intimate affective 'conversations' that take place between infant and caretaker, the child gradually acquires the subtle qualities of character and behavior of that culture by learning what evokes the affective responses it is seeking and what wards off painful rejections" (61–62).

Kinship terms are not about persons per se, but about relationships. "Every infant in tribal societies grows up in immediate contact with his mother, father, siblings, and kinship systems expand the dyadic relationships of this domestic ménage outward into the community to engulf everyone, extrapolating the experiences of infancy to the ever-widening relationships in the community" (110). (See sidebar: "Calculating Kinship.") "Kinship systems extend the feelings laid down in the bosom of the family, building on the experiences each member of the family had at the outset of his life" (111). "We apparently have an inherent capacity for bonding, creating an emotional tonus between the neonate and his immediate social environment that gets attached to the words as well as the human referent, extending the expected sentiments to all belonging to that category" (111). "The evolutionary advantage of affect hunger lay in its ability to induce the individual to be committed to the community—to be a socially responsible person. But it did this by giving humans an internal *physiological need*" (119; emphasis in original).

"It is the nurturant love, and the affect hunger that energizes it, that induces us to live in concert with others, to collaborate in creating and maintaining social order, and to inspire us to a creativity that has constantly raised our sights to build ever more elaborate edifices—social and physical" (138).

and negotiating these changes among four people—two of whom authored the first edition—was bound to be marked by tensions reflecting the varying positionalities of individual authors. Philip W. Porter (PWP) and Eric Sheppard (ES) entered the academy during the development decades (Chapter 4), albeit 15 years apart. PWP's views were shaped by decades of fieldwork among farmers and pastoralists in East Africa, whereas ES brought a much more macro-level political economy and regional comparative perspective. Richa Nagar (RN) and David R. Faust (DRF) studied with PWP and ES, cutting their teeth on feminism and post-development theory (Chapter 5), informed by fieldwork and a range of other complex long-term relationships in India and Tanzania. Bringing these perspectives and commitments to the collaboration strengthened the book—not as a new synthetic statement integrating all views, but by broadening, complicating, and sometimes maintaining the tensions among ourselves, even as we created a narrative to represent different views in the volume.

Among the tensions that became sources of productive dialogue among us, four have been central. One was the question of the specific languages that each of us was used to (words, theories, figures, maps, graphs), due to our subdisciplinary and interdisciplinary trainings, locations, and intellectual investments. A second had to do with our different approaches to questions of literacy and empowerment. Yet another challenge had to do with working through the tension between what can and ought to be generalized, and what must be specified as contingent and as historically and geographically located. Finally, there was the challenge of how to speak or write about the making and unmaking of "other worlds" without thereby "othering" the people, places, and cultures of that world.

Not all of these tensions could be resolved. In fact, rather than pretending that we could arrive at resolution through careful rewriting or editorial work, we want to recognize some characteristics that make our collaboration (and hence this book) different from several other critical texts on the politics of development and global political economy. To begin with, we strive to main-

Calculating Kinship

The concept of "family" in Africa may be so broad that it encompasses an entire community and involves unrelated individuals. The notion of "family" or "household" is relaxed, flexible, hospitable, and open. Every adult woman is a mother or aunt. A child in trouble is the responsibility of anyone, man or woman. Westerners are frequently surprised at the degree to which kinship is claimed and traced over great "distances." Once I (PWP) showed a poem by Rebeka Njau, a Kenyan poet, to Njeri Wang'ati, a Kenyan student who lived with my family for several years in the late 1980s in Minneapolis while attending the University of Minnesota. "Oh! That's my auntie," she exclaimed. I asked her to explain the relationship. "She's my grandmother's stepsister's son-in-law's sister," she said, without a pause to think. Stated another way, her dad's grandfather had a second wife whose granddaughter married Rebeka Njau's brother. It requires seven steps and four generations to link Njeri to Rebeka Njau (see the accompanying figure). I had to ask her to diagram it for me on an envelope, and you probably would too. For her, the links were already "wired" in her mind—established, instantaneously known, and readily explained.

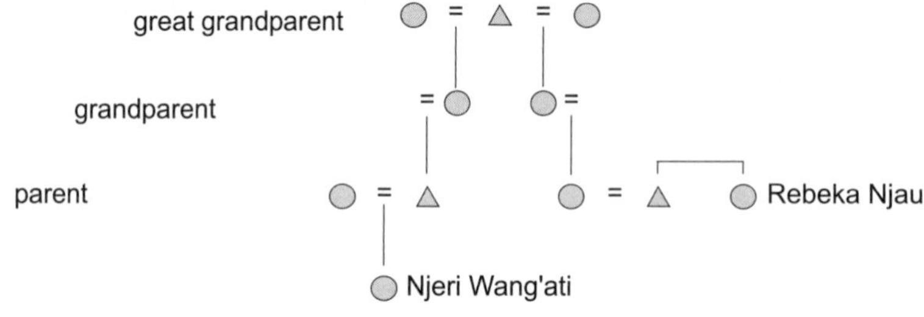

tain substantial depth in areas ranging from development theory to human–environment interactions and industrialization in the global south. In so doing, we engage with a broad set of interconnected processes, but we do not always impose a sense of flow, interconnection, or sequential development in coverage of all topics. Our desire to resist such imposition of sequence or flow emanates, in part, from the presence of theoretical/political dissonances and disjunctures that reflect our own difficult dialogues on the issues we cover in this book.

Thus, even as our framing of this new edition of *A World of Difference* is critical of north–south dualisms, colonial spatial imaginaries, and the colonial gaze, we sometimes use empirical data or sidebars that can be seen as reinforcing such dualisms and imaginaries. At other times, two different chapters, two sections of the same chapter, or two sidebars may highlight competing arguments or approaches in the text. Far from regarding this as a flaw or limitation of our collaboration, we find this an exciting opportunity for you, our readers, in two specific ways. First, we invite you to juxtapose and read the empirical material in the latter half of the book with and against the theoretical debates raised in the introductory chapters. Second, we invite you to identify how the various disjunctures in this book allow for complicating the concept of difference by interweaving the focus on difference with a focus on knowledge. The two concepts are interrelated: Material differentiation is realized through different knowledges, which in turn both reproduce and justify material differences. We hope that, in its entirety, this book will allow you to gain not only a comprehensive understanding of the world in which you live, but also a scholarly appreciation of the ways in which our world of difference is reproduced through different knowledges and relations to power that undergird those knowledges.

BODY, COMMUNITY, GLOBE: FRAMING A WORLD OF DIFFERENCE

The idea that "the local is global" or that "we all live in a global village" has become a commonly shared wisdom, thanks to Levis and Reeboks as well as to the NGOs, the UN conferences, and the U.S. Agency for International Development (USAID) projects that have done their share to popularize these truths. We know that the lives of Wambua Muathe and his neighbors are shaped by the negotiations in the World Trade Organization (WTO); the policies of the International Monetary Fund (IMF) and the World Bank; the rural development programs adopted by the state; and the activities of Dole, Coca-Cola, ExxonMobil, the International Business Machines Corporation (IBM), and Google. But other truths—that the global is also local; or that, for those largely excluded from the "global village," the global might still be defined by two villages and a nearby town (Sangtin Writers, 2006)—seem to find little space in popular understandings about the global and the local. Indeed, much of the talk about globalization that has pervaded the academic literature and the mass media has persistently focused on some spaces, scales, and subjects, while excluding others. Typically,

> discourses of global capitalism continue to position women, minorities, the poor, and southern places in ways that constitute globalization as dominant. Images of passive women and places (frequently southern, but also deindustrialized places in the north) are constructed and simultaneously serve to construct discourses of globalization as capitalist, as Western-centric, and as the only possible future for the "global economy." The result is "capitalist myopia," by which researchers assume that global capitalism is all encompassing and they cannot see, or consider salient, other non-capitalist, nonpublic spheres and actors. (Nagar, Lawson, McDowell, and Hanson, 2002: 262–263)

This second edition of *A World of Difference* seeks to respond to these erasures by starting with the excluded spaces, subjects, and scales of global capitalist development, before turning its attention to the dominant ones. At the same time, our analysis resists a compartmentalization between the local and the global on the one hand, and the dominant and subordinated places and actors on the other; we recognize these as always deeply intertwined and mutually constitutive. In our effort to do justice to both of these tasks, we have organized the chapters of this book into three sections. Part I provides a framework of multiple differences and how they become a part of the theories and practices of development; Part II considers social relations of difference and how they articulate with biophysical processes; and Part III addresses social relations of difference and how they articulate with large-scale global processes. Although the major themes of the first edition—society, nature, and development—are still at the core of our concerns, the present tripartite structure allows us to examine the relationships among culture, nature, development, and neoliberal globalization as contingent and constructed discursive practices and materialities, without privileging that which is already dominant.

2 Measuring, Describing, and Mapping Difference and Development

Measuring development is often an exercise in sorting, classifying, and ranking countries as if they were homogeneous entities. However, the opening lines of an editorial by the Indian journalist P. Sainath (2006) may give you a sense of the vast gulfs that separate the many worlds within the borders of a single nation state (in this case, India):

> Farm suicides in Vidharbha crossed 400 this week. The Sensex share index crossed the 11,000 mark. And Lakme Fashion Week issued over 500 media passes to journalists. All three are firsts. All happened the same week. And each captures in a brilliant if bizarre way a sense of where India's Brave New World is headed. A powerful measure of a massive disconnect. Of the gap between the haves and the have-mores on the one hand, and the dispossessed and desperate, on the other.

The purpose of this chapter is to provide basic data on how the people of the world confront difference. This is an almost insurmountable and necessarily problematic task because of the various structures that trap us at every turn. First, there is language itself. A collection of words has emerged over time to form a vocabulary for discussing difference and development. The ways we use these words in framing arguments about, descriptions of, and conclusions concerning difference and development constitute a discourse (see Chapter 3). Consider this long list of words:

development	race
property	class
poverty	resource
literacy	scarcity
autonomy	the population problem
freedom	nature
trade	biodiversity
income	oppression
wealth	truth
sustainability	honor
environmental degradation	shame
pollution	progress
rank	universalism
life expectancy	rationality
health	diversity
gender	

Each and every one of these words and phrases is theory-laden. Each can carry a vastly different meaning for a peasant woman in Cambodia, for a development official working for the Thai government, for a stockbroker in New York City, or even for two students in the same classroom.

Second, there are the collection and organization of data. For the most part, data are collected by political units—states (from which the very term "statistics" derives). International organizations collect data, but in many respects they depend on nation states for much of the information. This leads analysts, for lack of an alternative, to discuss difference and development in terms of nations. A statistic that the per capita global national income (GNI) of Brazil was $3,090 in 2004 may hide as much as it reveals.[1] The average "income" is silent about the range of incomes among the people of Brazil, and about how income is distributed among that population. (In fact, the average person in the top 10% income group in Brazil has 93 times as much income as the average person in the lowest 10% income group.) A further pernicious feature of using national data is the tendency we have to rank and group states, suggesting, in so doing, that Luxembourg, which ranks 1st, is better than Denmark, which ranks 5th, and way better than Burundi, which ranks dead last, at 208th.

A third problem stems from the first two—the conventions we use to characterize difference and development. There are the familiar ones: gross national product (GNP), gross domestic product (GDP, which does not include money remitted from abroad or sent abroad), the physical quality of life index (PQLI), and the United Nations' human development index (HDI). None of these indices measures how happy individuals are, or whether they feel life provides opportunities for self-realization and fulfillment, although some get closer than others. Scholars are constantly trying to improve measures of difference and development. One recent effort that originated in the Kingdom of Bhutan tries to calculate not GDP, but gross national happiness (GNH). It has encouraged others to try to devise measures of development that consider not just income, but "also access to health care, free time with family, conservation of natural resources and other non-economic factors" (Revkin, 2005b: D1).

THE THIRD WORLD! WHERE DID THE TERM COME FROM?

Words have lives of their own. The term "third world" started life with a meaning far different from that which it commonly has today—that is, of poor, less developed countries somewhere to the "south."[2] The term "third world" (we use lower case for it throughout the book unless we quote others) was invented in 1955 as a way of identifying the "nonaligned movement." It is thus political, not economic, in origin, and is a product of the Cold War. In 1955, representatives of 29 nations met in Indonesia for what became known as the Bandung Conference. Among leading participants were Sukarno (Indonesia), Chou En-Lai (People's Republic of China), Nasser (Egypt), and Nehru (India). The term "third world" was intended as a political statement—to distinguish newly independent, decolonized countries, intending to pursue a neutral, unaligned foreign policy vis-à-vis the "first world," the capitalist economies of western Europe and North America, and the "second world," the state or centrally planned economies of eastern Europe and the Soviet Union. The Latin American countries were not present at the Bandung Conference. Apparently they were not invited, on the grounds that their economies were too closely tied to that of the United States for them to follow an unaligned foreign policy. In July 2003, Asian and African nations met again in Bandung, reasserting the principles of the 1955 conference (Co-Chairs' Statement, 2003).

The nonaligned movement reconvened in 1961 in Belgrade, Yugoslavia, with Marshal Tito as host. This time many Latin American countries participated. The countries identifying themselves as "third world" gradually expanded in number and broadened their agenda to include economic concerns. These developments took place within the United Nations; among them was the creation of the United Nations Conference on Trade and Development (UNCTAD) in 1962, with its first meeting held in 1964. UNCTAD provided an institutional framework within which third world countries could negotiate (1) the prices of commodities they produced, (2) the reduction of trade barriers, and (3) the provision of more capital investment in third world countries. From UNCTAD came all the international trading agreements, covering such products as cocoa, coffee, copper, and so forth. The work of UNCTAD also influenced trading negotiations in the General Agreement on Tariffs and Trade (GATT). The GATT was first signed in 1947 and renegotiated periodically (the last "Uruguay round" was concluded in 1994), providing a venue for all trading nations to negotiate trade and tariff matters. Since its establishment in 1995, the World Trade Organization (WTO) has taken on responsibility for trade discussions, with the current round of negotiations, the "Doha [Qatar] round," starting in November 2001. These discussions were resumed in Hong Kong in December 2005.

In 1974, third world nations were instrumental in calling for a "new international economic order" (NIEO)—not that first world countries were ready to listen. The NIEO proposed meeting "basic needs" as a goal of development in less developed countries. The Group of 77 emerged as a subset of the third world, comprising 77 of the poorest nations with the greatest unmet "basic needs." The Group of 77 eventually grew to include over 130 nations.

There have been other initiatives from third world countries, often through UN channels, to reduce asymmetries in power, such as the proposed new international information order developed within the United Nations Educational, Scientific, and Cultural Organization (UNESCO), which seeks to change power relations of the press and communications industries vis-à-vis third world governments and countries. This initiative met with stiff resistance from the United States, and was in part the cause for the United States to withdraw its membership in and financial support of UNESCO for a number of years.

EMPIRICAL EXPRESSIONS OF POVERTY

> [While women] represent 50 per cent of the world adult population and one third of the official labour force, they perform nearly two thirds of all working hours, receive only one tenth of the world income and own less than one per cent of world property.
>
> —UNITED NATIONS (1980: para. 16)

The oft-repeated quotation above points to important gulfs in a world where gender differences translate into significant material inequalities. Yet the quote is silent on how girlhood or womanhood can be experienced in vastly different ways by two females living in very close quarters even in a single village: in terms of their differential access to income, education, health care, or property; their aspirations for themselves and their families; their ability to pursue their dreams in life. Consider the following quotation from a book where seven rural activists from one district of north India came together to reflect on the different meanings of deprivation they experienced as little girls in the same villages:

> when we connected the stories of our seven lives we repeatedly found ourselves tied with the thick rope of casteism, sometimes at opposite ends . . . each one of us had suffered deprivation, but the ways in which caste-based violence shapes, deepens and poisons that deprivation became the theme of our discussions. . . . It was difficult for some of us to accept that even in the midst of our poverty, the very accident of birth in an upper caste had made our survival far easier than others. The pain of hunger is the same for all children, but the circumstances and means by which that hunger is satisfied make one child's hunger different than another's. How can we not distinguish between a circumstance where there

is nothing to eat or cook in one home and the mother has to lay her newborn baby on the edge of someone's farm to pick up the remains from a harvested field, and another situation in which, despite many problems, a mother is able to save a few lentils, peanuts, and rice to feed her hungry children? . . . And then again, we find that a starved Brahman girl has an opportunity to kill her family's hunger by stealing food at a neighbor's death ceremony, whereas a Dalit girl in her place could have only hoped to find some leftovers after the caste Hindus had thrown away their plates on the street. (Sangtin Writers and Nagar, 2006: 26–27)

Socioeconomic and political differences along the axes of class, race, gender, caste, religion, ethnicity, and geographical location interlock in complex ways that make each of us simultaneously unique, yet socially marked in somewhat predictable ways. This tension between what is unique and what is predictable is a hard but necessary tension to understand and negotiate as we learn to grapple with a world of difference. To go back to the quotation above, for example, we can predict the ways in which hunger and deprivation in a caste-ridden context can never be the same for a Brahman girl as they would be for a Dalit or "untouchable" girl. At the same time, it would be irresponsible (even dangerous) to generalize that every Brahman girl and Dalit girl who inhabit the same village in India experience hunger in ways similar to the two girls compared above.

This is a point to remember in examining statistics that describe average characteristics of groups, such as populations of a country. In this section we explore our worlds of difference in relation to the economy of the nation state, and to three frequently used, though seriously flawed, measures of development: global national income (GNI); physical quality of life index (PQLI); and human development index (HDI). Color Plate 2.1 (facing page 44) shows a classification of the global economy. It is the first in a series of maps used in this text to display aspects of our world of difference. Table 2.1 and Color Plate 2.1 present the countries of the world cross-classified according to several ideas: center versus periphery relationships, market versus transitional economies, presence of a special attribute (e.g., some are

TABLE 2.1. Basic Data on the Global Economy

Country	Area (sq. miles)	Population (2004, in millions)	GNI (2004, U.S. $)	PQLI (2001)	HDI (2001)	Gini index	% pop. <$2/day
		Group A. Industrial market/core					
Australia	2,966,155	20.1	26,900	97	0.939	35.2	—
Austria	32,377	7.5	32,300	97	0.929	23.1	—
Bahamas	5,382	0.3	14,920	86	0.812	—	—
Belgium	11,783	10.4	31,030	97	0.937	25.0	—
Canada	3,849,674	31.9	28,390	98	0.937	31.5	—
Cyprus	2,276	0.8	17,580	96	0.891	—	—
Denmark	16,638	5.4	40,650	96	0.930	24.7	—
Finland	130,559	5.2	32,790	97	0.930	25.6	—
France	211,208	60.0	30,090	97	0.925	32.7	—
Germany	96,027	82.6	30,120	97	0.921	30.0	—
Greece	50,944	11.1	16,610	96	0.892	32.7	—
Iceland	39,769	0.4	38,620	98	0.924	—	—
Ireland	27,136	4.0	34,280	95	0.930	35.9	—
Israel	8,019	6.8	17,380	96	0.905	35.5	—
Italy	116,320	57.6	26,120	97	0.916	27.3	—

(cont.)

TABLE 2.1. *(cont.)*

Country	Area (sq. miles)	Population (2004, in millions)	GNI (2004, U.S. $)	PQLI (2001)	HDI (2001)	Gini index	% pop. <$2/day
Japan	144,870	127.8	31,700	100	0.932	24.9	—
Luxembourg	998	0.5	56,230	96	0.930	26.9	—
Malta	122	0.4	12,250	94	0.856	—	—
Netherlands	16,133	16.3	24,300	97	0.938	32.6	—
New Zealand	103,519	4.1	20,310	97	0.917	—	—
Norway	149,412	4.6	52,030	97	0.944	25.8	—
Portugal	35,516	10.4	14,350	93	0.896	35.6	—
Spain	194,885	41.3	21,210	97	0.918	32.5	—
Sweden	173,732	9.0	35,770	98	0.941	25.0	—
Switzerland	15,943	7.4	48,320	97	0.932	33.1	—
United Kingdom	93,629	59.4	33,940	96	0.930	36.1	—
United States	3,679,245	293.5	41,400	95	0.937	40.8	—
Group B. Industrial transition/core							
Belarus	80,155	9.8	2,120	89	0.804	21.7	0.7
Cuba	42,804	11.4	2,800	94	0.806	—	—
Czech Republic	30,450	10.2	9,150	94	0.861	25.4	0.2
Estonia	7,413	1.4	7,010	91	0.833	37.6	—
Hungary	35,920	10.1	8,270	91	0.837	24.4	1.5
Poland	120,728	38.2	6,090	93	0.841	31.6	1.2
Russian Federation	6,592,849	142.8	3,410	87	0.779	48.7	23.8
Slovenia	7,820	2.0	14,810	95	0.881	28.4	0.1
Ukraine	233,090	48.0	1,260	88	0.766	29.0	31.4
Group C. Middle-income NICs/semipheriphery							
Argentina	1,073,400	38.2	3,720	91	0.849	52.2	14.3
Brazil	3,286,488	178.7	3,090	82	0.777	59.1	22.4
Hong Kong	412	6.9	26,810	—	0.889	—	—
Korea, Rep.	38,025	48.1	13,980	94	0.879	31.6	—
Malaysia	127,502	25.2	4,650	88	0.790	49.2	9.3
Puerto Rico	3,515	3.9	10,950	62	—	—	—
Singapore	239	4.3	24,220	95	0.884	—	—
South Africa	433,680	45.6	3,630	69	0.684	59.3	34.1
Taiwan	13,900	22.9	23,400	86	—	—	—
Turkey	300,948	71.7	3,750	82	0.734	41.5	10.3
Group D. Middle-income oil-exporting/semiperiphery							
Bahrain	256	0.7	17,100	89	0.839	—	—
Kuwait	6,880	2.5	17,970	89	0.820	—	
Mexico	761,605	103.8	6,770	88	0.800	51.9	26.3
Oman	82,030	2.7	*7,890*	83	0.755	—	—
Qatar	4,416	0.6	*21,500*	86	0.826	—	—
Saudi Arabia	864,869	23.2	10,430	83	0.769	—	—
United Arab Emirates	32,278	4.3	*23,200*	86	0.816	—	—
Venezuela	352,145	26.1	4,020	89	0.775	48.8	30.6
Group E. Middle-income oil-exporting/periphery							
Algeria	919,595	32.4	2,280	75	0.704	35.3	15.1
Angola	481,354	14.0	1,030	27	0.377	—	—
Brunei	2,226	0.4	*18,600*	93	0.872	—	—
Ecuador	109,484	13.2	2,180	86	0.731	43.7	36.1

(cont.)

TABLE 2.1. *(cont.)*

Country	Area (sq. miles)	Population (2004, in millions)	GNI (2004, U.S. $)	PQLI (2001)	HDI (2001)	Gini index	% pop. <$2/day
Egypt	386,662	68.7	1,310	71	0.648	28.9	44.0
Gabon	103,347	1.4	3,940	63	0.653	—	—
Indonesia	741,101	217.6	1,140	80	0.682	51.7	34.3
Iran	636,296	66.9	2,300	79	0.719	—	—
Iraq	169,235	25.3	*1,600*	62	0.599	—	—
Libya	679,362	5.7	4,450	85	0.783	—	—
Nigeria	356,669	139.8	390	51	0.463	50.6	90.8
Syria	71,498	17.8	1,190	81	0.685	—	—
Tunisia	63,170	10.0	2,630	81	0.740	41.7	6.6
Group F. Middle-income transitional/semiperiphery							
Bosnia and Herzegovina	19,741	3.5	2,040	90	0.777	—	—
Bulgaria	42,823	7.8	2,740	90	0.795	26.4	—
Croatia	21,829	4.5	6,590	94	0.818	29.0	0.5
Kazahkstan	1,049,156	15.0	2,260	80	0.765	35.4	8.5
Latvia	24,595	2.3	5,460	90	0.811	32.4	11.5
Lithuania	25,212	3.4	5,740	92	0.824	32.4	6.9
Macedonia	9,928	2.1	2,350	89	0.784	—	—
Moldova	13,012	4.2	710	86	0.700	40.6	64.1
Romania	91,699	21.6	2,920	89	0.773	28.2	20.5
Serbia Montenegro	39,449	10.8	2,620	88	—	—	—
Slovakia	18,933	5.4	6,480	93	0.836	19.5	—
Turkmenistan	188,456	4.9	1,340	78	0.748	40.8	44.0
Uzbekistan	172,742	25.9	460	84	0.729	33.3	71.7
Group G. Middle-income/periphery							
Antigua and Barbuda	171	0.1	10,000	89	0.798	—	—
Barbados	166	0.3	9,270	95	0.888	—	—
Belize	8,866	0.3	3,940	86	0.776	—	—
Bolivia	424,165	0.0	960	74	0.672	58.9	34.3
Botswana	224,711	1.7	4,340	53	0.614	—	55.7
Cameroon	183,569	16.4	800	52	0.499	—	50.6
Cape Verde	1,557	0.5	1,770	79	0.727	—	—
Chile	292,135	16.0	4,910	94	0.831	57.5	9.6
Colombia	440,831	45.3	2,000	88	0.779	57.1	22.6
Congo	132,047	3.9	770	57	0.502	—	—
Costa Rica	19,730	4.1	4,670	95	0.832	45.9	9.5
Dominica	290	0.1	3,650	91	0.776	—	—
Dominican Republic	18,704	8.9	2,080	78	0.737	47.4	0.8
El Salvador	8,124	6.7	2,350	81	0.719	50.8	58.0
Fiji	7,078	0.9	2,690	87	0.754	—	—
Grenada	133	0.1	3,760	84	0.738	—	—
Guadeloupe	687	0.4	*7,900*	76	—	—	—
Guatemala	42,042	12.6	2,130	72	0.652	—	37.4
Honduras	43,277	7.1	1,030	78	0.667	59.0	44.0
Jamaica	4,244	2.7	2,900	89	0.757	36.4	13.3
Jordan	37,737	5.4	2,140	86	0.743	36.4	7.4
Kyrgyzstan	76,641	5.1	400	82	0.727	40.5	—
Lebanon	4,015	4..6	4,980	86	0.752	—	—
Macao (part of China)	7	0.4	*19,400*	—	—	—	—

(cont.)

TABLE 2.1. *(cont.)*

Country	Area (sq. miles)	Population (2004, in millions)	GNI (2004, U.S. $)	PQLI (2001)	HDI (2001)	Gini index	% pop. <$2/day
Maldives	115	0.3	2,510	81	0.751	—	—
Martinique	425	0.4	*14,400*	—	—	—	—
Mauritius	788	1.2	4,640	86	0.779	—	—
Morocco	172,414	30.6	1,520	68	0.606	39.5	14.3
Namibia	317,818	2.0	2,370	61	0.627	—	55.8
Panama	29,762	3.0	4,450	90	0.788	48.5	17.6
Papua New Guinea	178,704	5.6	580	60	0.548	50.9	—
Paraguay	157,048	5.8	1,170	86	0.751	57.7	30.3
Peru	496,225	27.6	2,360	84	0.752	46.2	37.7
Philippines	115,831	83.0	1,170	86	0.751	46.2	47.5
Réunion	967	0.8	*6,000*	—	—	—	—
Senegal	75,951	10.5	670	46	0.430	41.3	—
Seychelles	175	0.1	*2,300*	89	0.840	—	—
St. Kitts–Nevis	104	0.4	7,600	88	0.808	—	—
St. Lucia	238	0.2	4,310	87	0.775	42.6	—
St. Vincent and Grenadines	150	0.1	3,650	88	0.755	—	—
Suriname	63,251	4.0	2,250	87	0.762	—	—
Swaziland	6,704	1.1	1,660	45	0.547	60.9	22.6
Thailand	198,115	62.4	2,540	87	0.768	41.4	32.5
Trinidad and Tobago	1,980	1.3	8,850	90	0.802	40.3	20.0
Uruguay	67,574	3.4	3,950	93	0.834	42.3	3.9
Vanuatu	4,706	0.2	1,340	64	0.568	—	—
Western Samoa	1,097	0.2	*5,600*	88	0.775	—	—
Group H. Low-income/semiperiphery							
Albania	11,100	3.2	2,080	86	0.735	—	11.8
Armenia	11,506	3.0	1,120	88	0.729	44.4	49.0
Azerbaijan	33,436	8.3	950	82	0.744	36.0	33.4
China	3,718,782	1,296.5	1,290	83	0.721	40.3	71.0
Georgia	26,911	4.5	1,040	94	0.746	37.1	15.7
India	1,237,062	1,079.7	620	64	0.590	37.8	32.5
Korea, Dem. Peop. Rep.	46,540	22.8	*1,000*	56	—	—	—
Tajikistan	55,251	6.4	280	83	0.677	—	58.7
Group I. Low-income/semiperiphery							
Africa							
Benin	43,484	6.9	530	43	0.411	—	—
Burkina Faso	105,869	12.4	360	33	0.330	48.2	81.0
Burundi	10,745	7.34	90	35	0.337	33.3	87.6
Central African Rep.	245,535	4.0	310	34	0.363	61.3	84.0
Chad	495,755	8.8	260	36	0.376	—	—
Comoros	838	0.6	530	62	0.528	—	—
Congo, Dem. Rep. (Zaire)	905,568	54.8	120	37	0.363	—	
Côte d'Ivoire	123,847	17.1	770	38	0.396	36.7	—
Djibouti	8,958	0.7	1,030	47	0.462	—	—
Equatorial Guinea	10,831	0.5	*2,700*	56	0.664	—	—
Eritrea	36,170	4.5	180	53	0.446	—	—

(cont.)

TABLE 2.1. *(cont.)*

Country	Area (sq. miles)	Population (2004, in millions)	GNI (2004, U.S. $)	PQLI (2001)	HDI (2001)	Gini index	% pop. <$2/day
Ethiopia	446,953	70.0	110	36	0.359	40.0	77.8
Gambia	4,361	1.5	290	46	0.463	47.8	54.3
Ghana	92,098	21.1	380	65	0.567	39.6	79.8
Guinea	94,926	8.1	460	40	0.425	40.3	—
Guinea–Bissau	13,948	1.5	160	33	0.373	56.2	—
Kenya	224,961	32.5	460	57	0.489	44.5	58.3
Lesotho	11,720	1.8	740	49	0.510	56.0	56.1
Liberia	38,250	3.5	110	33	*0.311*	—	—
Madagascar	226,658	17.3	300	56	0.468	46.0	85.1
Malawi	45,747	11.2	170	37	0.387	—	76.1
Mali	478,767	12.0	360	30	0.337	50.5	90.6
Mauritania	397,956	2.9	420	41	0.454	37.3	63.1
Mozambique	308,642	19.1	250	31	0.356	39.6	78.4
Niger	489,191	12.1	230	22	0.292	50.5	85.8
Rwanda	10,169	8.4	220	42	0.422	28.9	—
São Tomé and Principe	372	0.2	1,200	78	0.639	—	—
Sierra Leone	27,925	5.4	200	15	0.275	62.9	—
Somalia	246,201	9.9	500	24	*0.221*	—	—
Sudan	967,500	34.4	530	58	0.503	—	—
Tanzania	364,900	36.6	330	49	0.400	38.2	72.5
Togo	21,925	5.0	380	51	0.501	—	—
Uganda	93,104	25.9	270	50	0.484	37.4	96.6
Western Sahara	102,703	0.2	—	—	—	—	—
Zambia	290,586	10.6	450	39	0.386	52.6	87.4
Zimbabwe	150,873	13.2	480	50	0.496	56.8	83.0
Asia							
Afghanistan	251,826	27.2	700	*13*	*0.229*	—	—
Bangladesh	55,598	140.5	440	58	0.502	33.6	82.8
Bhutan	17,954	0.9	760	58	0.511	—	—
Cambodia (Kampuchea)	69,898	13.6	320	58	0.556	40.4	77.7
Laos	91,429	5.8	390	56	0.525	37.0	—
Mongolia	604,250	2.5	590	78	0.661	33.2	74.9
Myanmar (Burma)	261,228	49.9	*700*	66	0.549	—	—
Nepal	56,827	25.2	260	55	0.499	36.7	8.9
Occupied Palestinian territories	2,401	3.5	1,120	87	0.731	—	—
Pakistan	339,732	152.1	600	54	0.499	31.2	65.6
Sri Lanka	24,962	19.4	1,010	89	0.730	34.4	45.4
Vietnam	127,242	82.2	550	84	0.688	36.1	—
Yemen	75,290	19.8	570	55	0.470	33.4	45.2
Latin America/ Caribbean							
French Guiana	35,135	0.1	—	—	—	—	—
Guyana	83,000	0.8	990	79	0.740	40.2	11.2
Haiti	10,714	8.6	390	48	0.467	—	—
Netherlands Antilles	309	0.2	—	*82*	—	—	—
Nicaragua	50,193	5.6	790	75	0.643	60.3	78.7

(cont.)

TABLE 2.1. *(cont.)*

Country	Area (sq. miles)	Population (2004, in millions)	GNI (2004, U.S. $)	PQLI (2001)	HDI (2001)	Gini index	% pop. <$2/day
Oceania							
East Timor	5,347	0.7	—	—	—	—	—
French Polynesia	1,544	0.3	—	—	—	—	—
New Caledonia	7,366	0.2	—	—	—	—	—
Pacific Islands	721	0.2	1,990	—	—	—	—
Solomon Islands	10,954	0.4	*1,990*	80	0.632	—	—

Note. Data in italics indicate use of earlier data, or in case of GNI, use of purchasing power parity (PPP).

Sources: Data on area are from *Goode's World Atlas* (1995). Data on population, GNI, PQLI, and HDI are from World Bank (2005b). Data on income inequality and percent of people living on less than $2/day from World Bank (2004g) and United Nations Development Programme (UNDP) (2004).

newly industrializing countries [NICs] or petroleum-producing nations), and income levels. A much more complex division of the world results when such intersecting categories are used.[3] Because of the attempts in the former Soviet Union and eastern Europe since 1989 to make a transition to a market economy like that of the first world, we have classified the countries of the former Soviet Union, eastern Europe, and the former Yugoslavia, depending on their stage of industrialization, as "industrial transitional/core" countries or "middle-income transitional/semiperiphery" countries.

Gross National Product or Global National Income

GNP has been described as a "grotesque" measure of development, since when expressed on a per capita basis, it does not consider the distribution of wealth within a population. Moreover, expenditures for armaments, hospital surgery, environmental cleanup, and car repair resulting from automobile accidents contribute positively to GNP, whereas anything that is not monetized or not countable is ignored—including the underground economy, the value of goods that are bartered, the value of goods and services provided by the environment, and the value of goods and services provided within the household (such as self-provisioning of food, clothing, and shelter, or unpaid household work).[4] GNP or (more recently) GNI is nonetheless widely used as a way of measuring the economic productivity of countries, and because data have been so widely collected for so long, GNP or GNI provides one of the few statistical bases for international comparisons. So, even as we subject it to critical scrutiny, we must occasionally use it. (As indicated in note 1, we use GNI in our discussion from here on.)

Although economic (i.e., GNI) growth is commonly touted as the cure for poverty, the 2005 *Human Development Report* (United Nations Development Programme [UNDP], 2005) found that economic growth has failed for a great part of the world's people. Much of the growth of recent decades has not enhanced the incomes of the poor; rather, it has flowed to the already wealthier. It is projected that by 2015, 827 million people will live in extreme poverty (Martens, 2005: 3). Inequality between "haves" and "have-nots" is increasing. "The world's richest 500 individuals have a combined income greater than that of the poorest 416 million. Beyond these extremes, the 2.5 billion people living on less than $2 a day—40% of the world's population—account for 5% of global income" (UNDP, 2005: 4).

In 70 developing countries, 1996 levels of income per capita were lower than they were in the 1960s and 1970s. The chasm between rich and poor countries has long been great and is increasing. In 1970, 88.1% of the world's wealth was accounted for by the wealthiest 20%, while the world's poorest 20% accounted for 2.0% of global GNI. In 1993, the world's wealthiest 20% of the population (47 countries) accounted for 86% of GNI, while the world's poorest 20% (24 countries, including India and Bangladesh) received 1.1% of global GNI. At the high end, average per capita GNI ranged from $37,400 (Luxembourg) to $3,350 (Hungary). At the low end, it ranged between $300 (India) and $90 (Mozambique). In 2005, the world's wealthiest 20% of the population (68 countries) accounted for 85% of the global GNI, while the world's poorest 20% (44 countries, including Bangladesh and Pakistan) received 1.1% of the global GNI. At the high end, average per capita GNI ranged between $56,230 (Luxembourg) and $3,750 (Turkey). At the low end, it ranged between $600 (Pakistan) and $90 (Burundi). In summary, as of 2005, income inequalities between the wealthiest and the poorest 20% had not been significantly reduced (UNDP, 2005: 4).

Let us look at these figures again, contrasting the first world with all other countries. In 1970, the total GNI of the first world was about twice that of the rest of the world, $8.4 trillion vs. $4.2 trillion (in constant 1995 U.S. dollars). The first world constituted 21.3% of the world's population at the time. By 1993, the first world's total GNI had grown to $20 trillion, and that of the rest of the world had reached $5.6 trillion, giving a ratio of 3.6:1. By 2004, the first world constituted less than 14% of the world's population; the first world's GNI had grown to $29.6 trillion, and that of the rest of the world had reached $9.7 trillion (in constant 2004 U.S. dollars), giving a ratio of 3.1:1. Inequalities within countries are also increasing. The Gini coefficient (see below) measures inequality in distribution within populations of a country. In 53 countries (among 73 for which data were available), inequality in income distribution increased. These 53 countries accounted for 80% of the world's population (UNDP, 2005: 4).

By 2004, among groups of countries outside the first world (Color Plate 2.1), only the middle-income NICs/semiperiphery group showed consistent gains; all other groups experienced ups and downs, or just downs. For example, the low-income/periphery countries had a total GNI in 2004 of $463 billion, whereas in 1970 their total GNI was $363 billion. During this time, their population grew from 439 million to 1,041 million. The 59 low-income/periphery countries (and their 1.04 billion people) thus stand in relation to the 879 million people of the first world as 1 does to 76—$444 versus $33,656 per capita GNI. To make the contrast more dramatic, the ratio in per capita GNI of Mozambique's 19.1 million people to Australia's 20.1 million people is 1:108, and even more striking comparisons could be made. These figures give some first, imperfect inklings of the gap between rich and poor.

In 1967, Herman Kahn and Norbert Wiener published a book called *The Year 2000*, subtitled *A Framework for Speculation in the Next Thirty-Three Years*. Using stages or levels of development associated with the writings of W. W. Rostow (1960; see Chapter 4 of the present volume), they projected, among other things, population growth and economic growth (as measured by GNI) to the end of the century (Figure 2.1). They predicted the paths of development for groups of countries, such as what was then the European Economic Community (EEC), the Middle East and north Africa, Latin America, and so forth. For example, they predicted that eastern Europe would have passed from an industrial phase through the phase of mass consumption, and would be entering the postindustrial era in the year 2000. Latin America, with a flatter trajectory, would be just entering the industrial stage. Black Africa, although still in the preindustrial stage, would be about to enter the transitional stage by the year 2000. It is instructive to see how, in fact, some of

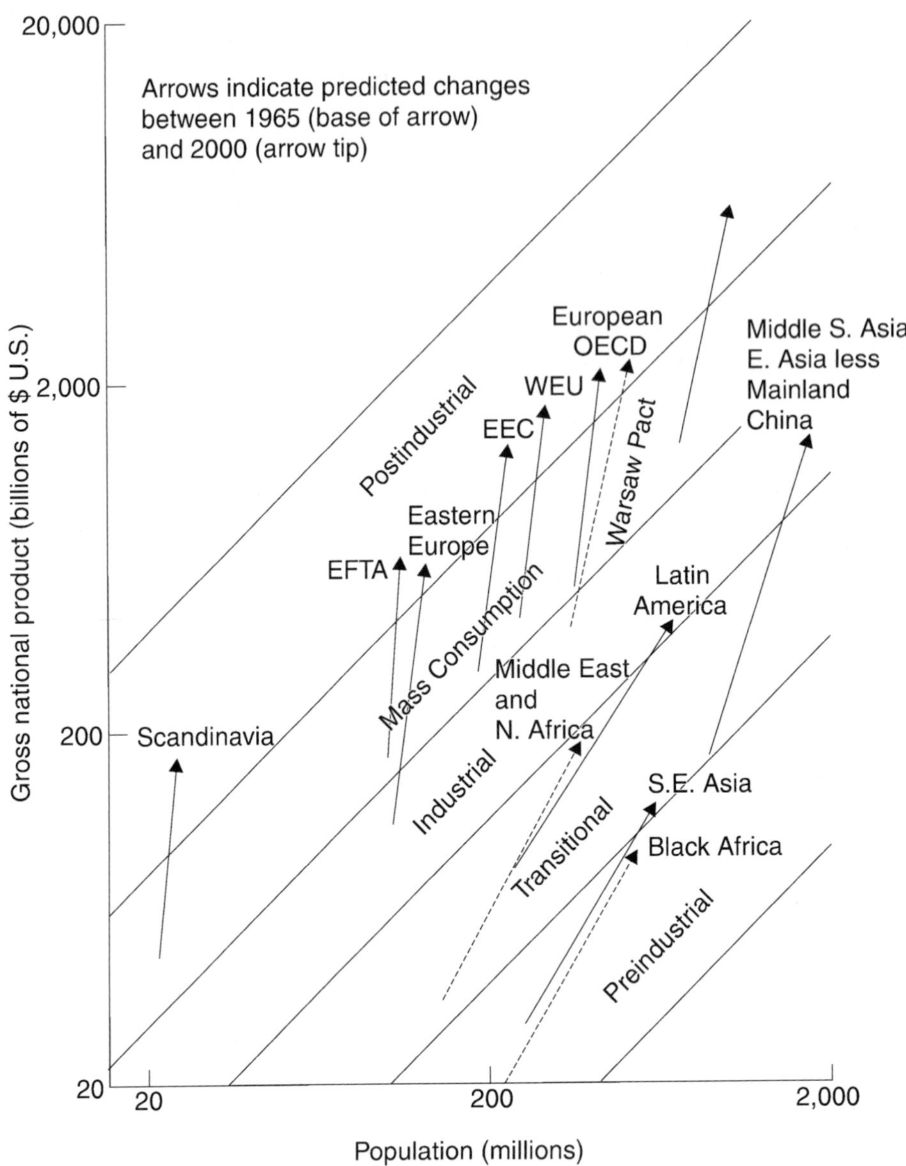

FIGURE 2.1. Projected changes in economic development by major world regions, 1965-2000. EEC, European Economic Community; EFTA, European Free Trade Association; OECD, Organization for Economic Cooperation and Development; WEU, West European Union. *Source:* Adapted from Kahn and Wiener (1967). Copyright 1967 by the Hudson Institute, Inc. Adapted by permission of Simon and Schuster, Inc.

the regional groupings have fared. We must remember that Kahn and Wiener wrote during the middle of the Cold War—before the Organization of the Petroleum Exporting Countries (OPEC) was formed and decades before the breakup of the Soviet Union. In an effort to compare the paths predicted with the paths that various groups of nations have followed, we have prepared Figures 2.2 and 2.3.

Accepting for the sake of illustration the economic categories used by Kahn and Wiener, we show these, together with the per capita income separating them, in Table 2.2. Figure 2.2 compares total GNI and total population at five dates (1970, 1980, 1990, 1993, and 2004) for the nine groups in the classification of the global economy described earlier. On the graph, 2004 figures are shown by large circles, whereas figures for earlier dates are shown with smaller circles. The long diagonal lines show per capita income values that represent approximately the point at which countries move from one stage of economic development to the next—say, industrial to mass consumption, the per capita income value being $7,000. (All the GNI values in Figures 2.2 and 2.3 are shown in 1995 U.S. dollar equivalents, in order to eliminate the effects of inflation and to show real trends. As a consequence, the positions of the 2004 circles on the graph differ from the numbers given in the text.) If the trajectory of a group of countries parallels the diagonal lines, this means that it is "running in place"—that is, adding people at the same rate as it is adding GNI. With that fixed reference in mind, let us examine what has happened to various groups between 1970 and 2004.

The first world (industrial market/core) stands apart from all other groups in two respects: (1) in trajectory (adding much GNI, yet comparatively few people from 1970 to 2004), and (2) in absolute levels of GNI. Total GNI (in real dollars) for the first world increased over threefold, from about $8.4 trillion to $29.6 trillion. This is as predicted by Kahn and Wiener (1967). Over the same period, the low-income/periphery countries went from $363 billion (in 1970) to $498 billion (in 1980), but retreated to $337 billion by 1993, and was only 463 billion in 2004. Essentially, these economies stagnated or lost ground during two and a half decades. The numbers of people in each group in 2004 are roughly comparable—879 million in the first world, 1,041 million in all low-

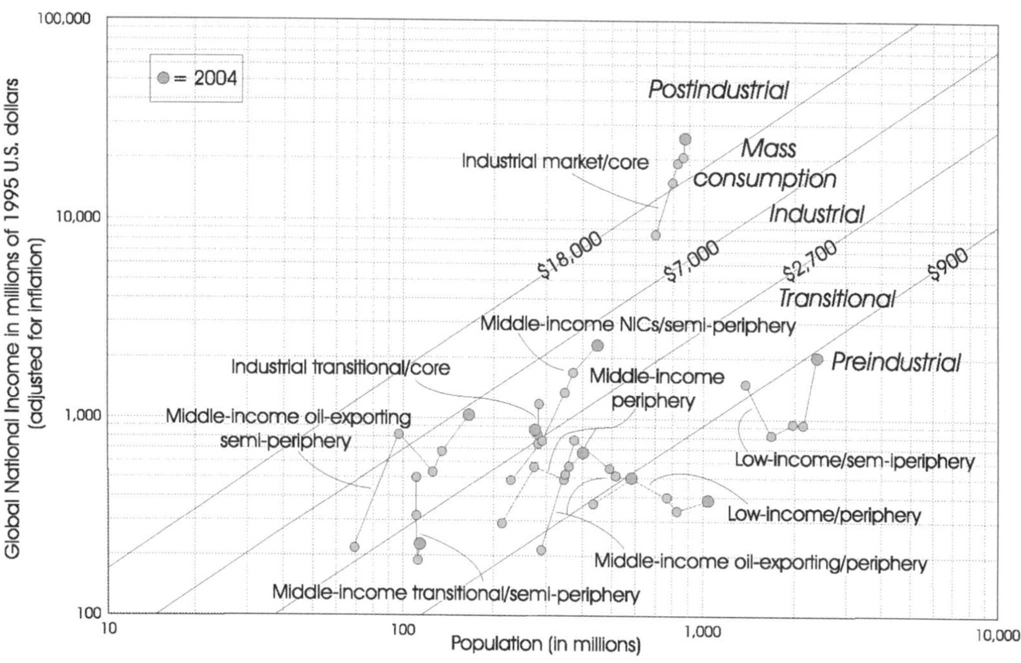

FIGURE 2.2. Population and GNI compared for 1970, 1980, 1990, 1993, and 2004 (logarithmic scales). *Source*: Data are from World Bank (2005b).

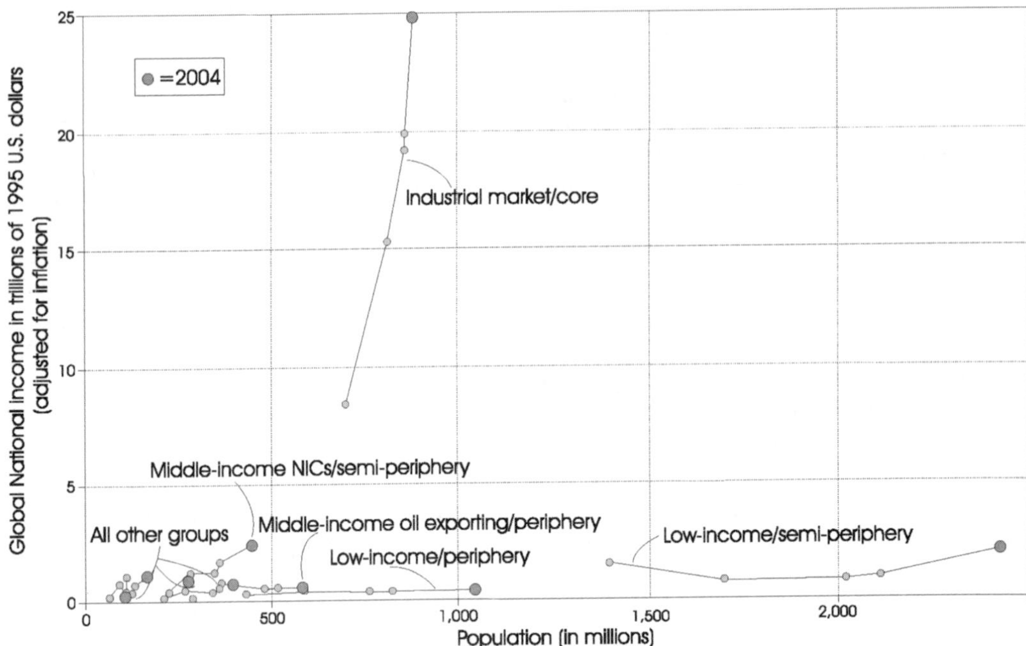

FIGURE 2.3. Population and GNI compared for 1970, 1980, 1990, 1993, and 2004 (arithmetic scales). *Source*: Data are from World Bank (2005b).

income/periphery countries (see Table 2.3, below). The low-income/periphery countries did even less well than the modest growth projections of Kahn and Wiener predicted (for black Africa, the Middle East and north Africa, and southeast Asia).

It is clear from the graph that the period 1970–1980 was a lot better from the standpoint of economic growth than the period succeeding it was. Many of the sets of symbols rise during the earlier decade and plunge in the later ones. The pattern is especially marked among the middle-income oil-exporting groupings. In the 1970s, many groups experienced dramatic economic growth, but they gave up some of it in the 1980s and early 1990s. Nonetheless, three groups more than doubled their per capita GNI: the middle-income NICs/semiperiphery group (increasing by a factor of 3.4), the middle-income oil-exporting/semiperiphery group (3.0), and the middle-income oil-exporting/periphery group (2.3). In the middle-income/periphery group (essentially, China and India), per capita GNI decreased by about 40% between 1970 and 1993.

TABLE 2.2. Projected Levels of Income and Industrial Development in the Year 2000

Range in per capita income in U.S. dollars	1965	1995 (adj.)
1. Preindustrial	50–200	225–900
2. Partially industrialized or transitional	200–600	900–2,700
3. Industrial	600–1,500	2,700–7,000
4. Mass consumption or advanced industrial	1,500–4,000	7,000–18,000
5. Postindustrial	4,000–20,000	18,000–90,000

Sources: Data are from U.S. Department of Commerce (1976: 41 and 1992: 24) and *Standard and Poor's Current Statistics* (1996: 12).

TABLE 2.3. Summary of the Global Economy

Group	Area (sq. miles)	Population (mid-2004, in millions)	Av. GNI (2004, U.S. $)	GNI range	Av. PQLI (2001)	PQLI range	Av. HDI (2001)	HDI range
A. Industrial market/core	12,172,121	879.3	34,325	56,230–12,550	96.7	100–86	0.930	0.944–0.812
B. Industrial transitional/core	7,161,229	273.8	3,829	14,810–1,260	88.9	95–87	0.794	0.881–0.766
C. Middle-income NICs/semiperiphery	5,278,109	445.6	6,254	26,810–3,090	87.2	95–62	0.782	0.889–0.734
D. Middle-income oil-exporting/semiperiphery	2,104,479	163.9	7,569	23,200–4,020	87.4	98–83	0.792	0.839–0.755
E. Middle-income oil-exporting/periphery	4,719,999	613.1	3,310	18,600–390	70.2	93–51	0.626	0.872–0.377
F. Middle-income transitional/semiperiphery	1,717,575	111.4	2,486	6,480–460	85.2	93–78	0.751	0.836–0.700
G. Middle-income periphery	3,861,069	396.5	2,049	19,400–400	80.8	95–45	0.717	0.888–0.430
H. Low-income semiperiphery	5,140,588	2,424.4	985	2,080–280	87.1	95–56	0.662	0.746–0.590
I. Low-income periphery								
Africa	7,133,036	481.7	312	2,700–90	42.8	78–15	0.413	0.664–0.221
Asia	1,976,382	542.6	557	1,120–260	60.4	89–13	0.531	0.731–0.229
Latin America/Caribbean	179,531	15.2	575	990–390	60.0	82–48	0.547	0.740–0.467
Oceania	20,585	1.8	1,990	1,900	80.0	80	0.632	0.632
All low-income/periphery	9,309,534	1,041.3	445	2,700–90	54.4	89–13	0.484	0.740–0.221
World	51,464,703	6,349.3	6,179	56,230–90	80.3	100–13	0.688	0.944–0.221

Sources: See Table 2.1.

Since then there has been a dramatic turnaround, particularly in China, which has experienced unprecedented rates of economic growth. The per capita GNI in China more than doubled in real terms between 1993 and 2004. Thus, to use Kahn and Wiener's terminology, during the three decades the NICs went from the transitional to the industrial stage; the middle-income oil-exporting/periphery group went from the preindustrial to the transitional stage, but then lost most of the gains between 1980 and 2004. Although the middle-income oil-exporting/periphery's total GNI has more than doubled since 1970, its population has grown just as fast, so it still finds itself in the preindustrial zone.

The industrial transitional/core economies of eastern Europe experienced a retrograde movement, having declined from a position close to the border of mass consumption in 1970 (their data for that year are not shown in Figure 2.2) to the edge of the transitional stage by 2004. The per capita GNI declined over 50%. For the middle-income transitional/semiperiphery countries, the decline was even more marked. In summary, the gap between first world economies and virtually all groups of third and (former) second world economies increased massively between 1970 and 2004. For the most part, Kahn and Wiener's predictions on where regional economic groups would be by the year 2000 have not been borne out.

Figure 2.2 uses logarithmic coordinates for both GNI and population, allowing us to show large and small values on the same graph; however, differences shown on log scales are difficult to grasp fully. In Figure 2.3, which uses arithmetic scales, the magnitudes of the gap and their intensification over a 34-year period become dramatically clear. We are reminded of the atmosphere on Mars: It becomes so cold on Mars at night that the atmosphere falls down and lies on the ground. Whereas GNI in the industrialized market economies increased greatly over the 34-year period, with moderate growth in population, other groups added population at a high rate, but their GNI increased at a comparatively slow pace or even declined. This was particularly true for the low-income/periphery group and the low-income/semiperiphery group (although China and India showed marked gains in per capita GNI). Aside from the industrial market/core countries, the only group that can be said to have added GNI faster than it added people is the middle-income NICs/semiperiphery group. The contrasting trajectories shown on Figure 2.3 (first world vs. all other groups) follow almost orthogonal directions. In terms of GNI and population, the first world is adding most of the income; the rest of the world is adding most of the people.

The Kahn and Wiener (1967) projections of the economic paths that the various country groupings would take between 1963 and 2000 for the most part have not been confirmed by events (Figs. 2.1, 2.2, and 2.3).[5] To deal first with the groupings with continued positive change to 2004, the Industrial market/core moved into the postindustrial zone by 1980, and between 1993 and 2004, though it added GNI faster than people, its gains were modest. The middle-income NICs/semiperiphery approached closer to the mass consumption line. The middle-income oil-exporting/semiperiphery saw a positive growth between 1990 and 2004. The same is true for the low-income/semiperiphery (which includes China and India), although it still sat in the preindustrial zone. [Possibly one could find a better term than "preindustrial" as this classification is merely due to the fact that the per capita GNI for this grouping was only $985 in 2004. Nonetheless, the rate of GNI growth greatly exceeded the rate of growth in population.] The middle-income/periphery experienced a small increase between 1990 and 2004.

Three groupings of countries showed significant losses. The middle-income transitional/semiperiphery (mainly former states of the Union of Soviet Socialist Republics [USSR], including several of the "-stans"), went from industrial to transitional, losing GNI while population barely grew. The industrial transitional/core (the Russian Federation and several eastern European states) not only lost GNI, but also actually declined in population between 1993 and 2004. The greatest losers were countries in the low-income periphery (mostly African and Asian countries), which after 1980 experienced two decades of decline in GNI values while adding greatly to population.

Physical Quality of Life Index

> "I would like to be like those young women who are well-educated, who have learned French and Arabic, who know how to read well. That's what I would like. Of course, there are women who are educated and those who aren't, but we are all women just the same. Women are just as capable as men, and I hope that women—through their education—will come to be more equal to men. . . . I want my daughters to go very far in their education. I want them to work and to have a good future. I have learned to read a bit here,

but I want to learn so much more. I want to know about *everything*."

When we left the center a few hours later, the interpreter told me that several days before, the young trainee had been found peeling labels off the canned goods stores in the kitchen. Having no access to books—or to money with which to buy them—she collected the labels in order to practice her reading. It mattered little to her that the words on the labels listed only the ingredients of a soup.

—PERDITA HUSTON (1979: 90), quoting and describing an unnamed Tunisian woman

There is no doubt that [the women's empowerment and literacy program] transformed many of us from overworked domestic creatures into fiery feminists. . . . It lit a fire in our hearts by showing us how we were oppressed as women. . . . But when we started searching and addressing the most profound and hidden causes of our oppressions, it removed the support from under us. . . . What was the use of lighting the fire in our hearts, then? Just to cause more burnout and bitterness? . . . What do we do with a Band-Aid feminism that is happy when we label our feudal men as our enemies, but terribly unhappy when we critique the government, take issues with water privatization policies, or challenge the community forestry schemes of the World Bank?

—SHIVANI, a woman interviewed by RN in Tehri Garhwal, May 1999

Knowing the alphabet, argue critical literacy activists, does not constitute education. Yet the statements by the unnamed Tunisian woman and Shivani quoted above suggest that an opportunity to gain knowledge of the alphabet may become a necessary precondition to becoming educated in ways that allow us to develop a critical understanding of our world, and to participate in changing the structures and institutions that oppress or liberate us (see sidebar: "Multiple Literacies"). These critical aspects of development and human well-being are not directly described by GNI. The PQLI is an effort to find surrogate measures of human well-being. The PQLI is a composite index based on three measures that, to an extent, are the properties of each of us, and thus good measures of individual well-being: our life expectancy at age 1, our literacy, and our society's rate of infant mortality (see sidebar: "Fairness"). The sidebar "Physical Quality of Life Index" works through an example showing how M. D. Morris (1979) arrived at the PQLI numbers for Nigeria, India, and the United States. There are striking anomalies in the GNI and PQLI columns in Table 2.1—for example, a relatively low PQLI (63) in oil-rich Gabon, where per capita GNI was $3,940 in 2004, and a relatively high PQLI (89) in Sri Lanka, where per capita GNI was only $1,010. Although there is a general relationship between GNI and PQLI, we can conclude that wealth is no guarantee of human well-being, and that a low per capita income does not inevitably mean a low level of human well-being.

Table 2.3 presents a summary, according to the ninefold classification used in Table 2.1, of the average GNI and the average PQLI for each part of the world economy. Values are weighted by populations, and instances where data were lacking are omitted. In order to help readers make some sense of the data contained in Tables 2.1 and 2.3, we have prepared seven graphs (Figures 2.4 through 2.10) to illustrate differences between the first world and the third world.

Figure 2.4 shows the relationship between per capita GNI (2004) and PQLI (2001). As in Figure 2.2, we use a logarithmic scaling for GNI. The industrial market/core scores high. The graph shows, however, that there is no necessary relationship between the two measures. Some countries (e.g., Puerto Rico, which is a self-governing U.S. commonwealth and is often treated statistically as a separate entity) have a high per capita GNI value but a low PQLI value. Conversely, some countries with very low per capita GNI values score well on the items measured in the PQLI. Moldova, Vietnam, and Kyrgyzstan are notable outliers on the graph, with per capita GNIs of $750 or less,

Multiple Literacies

In order to understand how power works in the context of diverse cultures and communities, it is important to recognize transactional functional literacy, and to distinguish (1) among different kinds of social literacies (e.g., prose literacy, document literacy, quantitative literacy); and (2) between cultural literacies (vernacular, local, or community literacies) on the one hand, and formal literacies (associated with formal education, law, medicine, and government, etc.) on the other (Rassool, 1999). For Rassool, this attention to multiple and differentiated political and social landscapes of literacy must be rooted in an understanding that literacy constitutes simultaneously a social practice, an ideological practice, a cultural practice, and an educational practice. Thus, when literacy is defined in terms of "individual empowerment," "social transformation," or "fundamental human right," we have to bear in mind that literacy policy and provision arise within the organization of particular social systems and forms of governance, as well as economic, social, and political priorities identified within the context of the state. These priorities include such issues as routes of access to participation in the democratic process; fiscal policies pertaining to educational and/or language provision; social controls; inclusions and exclusions related to technological developments; the linguistic and cultural rights of minority groups, asylum seekers, and refugees; and the role and influence of external funding bodies (Rassool, 1999: 47).

Rassool provides useful examples from Tanzania (development of Swahili as a national language at the expense of other languages), Ethiopia (one-language policy and multiple-language policy used as strategic tools by different parties to gain and consolidate political power), Iran (peasants targeted *for* specific literacies and women excluded *from* specific literacies after revolution), Nicaragua (multiple literacies as key tools for building a people's movement).

yet PQLI values ranging from 82 to 86. The low-income/periphery group occupies the lower left zone of the diagram. The middle-income/periphery group covers a wide range of values: The PQLI is as low as 46 in Senegal (per capita GNI = $670) and as high as 95 in Barbados (per capita GNI = $9,270).

When the same data are shown with arithmetic scaling (Figure 2.5), we see that most third world countries have both low GNI and low PQLI values. Table 2.3 summarizes these measures according to the nine global economic groups (with added regional detail for the low-income/periphery group). At the high end sits the industrial market/core group, with an average PQLI of 96.7, and an average per capita GNI of $34,325. The industrial transitional/core group has an average PQLI of 88.9 with a per capita GNI of $3,829. At the other end of the scale lie 482 million people in 36 sub-Saharan African countries, with an average PQLI of 42.8 and an average per capita GNI of $312 in 2004.

Human Development Index

A third means of assessing human well-being, the HDI, has been devised more recently by the UNDP. Data for 2001 are shown in Figure 2.6, wherein the HDI is plotted against average annual population growth for countries over the period 1975–2003. The HDI combines three measures of well-being: (1) life expectancy; (2) education (in which the adult literacy rate counts two-thirds and average years of schooling count one-third); and (3) "purchasing power," a weighted measure of real GDP per capita, reflecting the returns to human well-being (at first increasing, but ultimately diminishing) made possible by increases in purchasing power (Thomas, 1994: 74–75; UNDP, 1996). One drawback to the HDI is that inclusion of purchasing power biases the assessment of development in favor of countries with the greatest commodification or monetization of goods and services. In many societies, considerable wealth is produced but never monetized. Thus the values of crops grown

Fairness

It is not fair that a child born in the third world has a 20% chance of dying within the first 5 years of life. The 84-year-old mother of one of us (PWP), beginning her hospice round-the-clock care at home, observed how lucky she was and how lucky she had been. The age–sex pyramid of a less developed country does not have the shape of that in a just society, no matter how caring and enlightened its institutions (see Chapter 6, Figure 6.6). The just society not only needs to include all the attributes one normally associates with equity and nondiscriminatory behavior; it should also ensure that everyone born has the maximum opportunity to live a full, normal life span.

Recall the notable "I've Been to the Mountaintop" address that Dr. Martin Luther King, Jr., gave at Bishop Charles Mason Temple in Memphis on April 3, 1968, the evening before he was assassinated:

> Well, I don't know what will happen now. We've got some difficult days ahead. But it really doesn't matter with me now, because I've been to the mountaintop. And I don't mind. Like anybody, I would like to live a long life. Longevity has its place. But I'm not concerned about that now. I just want to do God's will. And He's allowed me to go up to the mountain, and I've looked over, and I've seen the promised land. I may not get there with you. But I want you to know tonight, that we, as a people, will get to the promised land. And so I'm happy tonight. I'm not worried about anything. I'm not fearing any man. Mine eyes have seen the glory of the coming of the Lord. (Quoted in Garrow, 1986: 621)

Leaving aside the uncanny parallels with the Last Supper, we want to focus on these phrases: "Like anybody, I would like to live a long life. Longevity has its place." Any definition of development should include the prospect that each child born has a carefully designed and equal chance to live out a full life span. In our view, a nation that does not provide this "basic right" cannot be considered developed.

and consumed at home, of houses built for personal use, and so forth are not counted at all in largely self-provisioning societies.

From Figure 2.6, we can see that first world industrialized market economies cluster in one corner of the diagram, with HDI values over 0.90, and population growth rates generally under 1% per year. The former socialist countries have HDIs between 0.70 and 0.90, and low or even negative population growth rates (Bulgaria, Georgia, Hungary). At the other extreme is sub-Saharan Africa, with most countries showing HDI values under 0.50 and growth rates between 2.0% and 3.5% per year. Other regional groupings lie between the two extremes of HDI, and even these groups have their outliers or anomalies (most of which are annotated on the diagram). In south Asia, the HDI ranges between 0.50 and 0.73. Three countries with growth rates in excess of 4.0% per year are Middle Eastern oil-producing states (United Arab Emirates, Qatar, and Saudi Arabia). Other Middle Eastern or oil-exporting countries have had annual rates of population growth greater than 3%. These growth rates include net migration as well as natural increase, and thus reflect the large migration streams of guest workers from other nations, particularly Asians and Palestinians. Migrants have contributed about 30% of the population growth in these countries. The HDI diagram (Figure 2.6) tells much the same story as the PQLI diagrams (Figures 2.4 and 2.5): The countries with high individual well-being have generally high per capita income and low population growth rates; other countries, especially those in sub-Saharan Africa and south Asia, combine moderate to low HDI values with comparatively high rates of population increase.

Figure 2.7 shows the HDI for 169 countries for two dates, 1993 and 2001. In that 8-year span, 117 countries showed an increase in their index number, and 50 countries showed a decline (two exhibited no change). On the graph, any country above the diagonal line had a higher HDI value in 2001 than it had in 1993. One can see that many countries with quite low HDI values (0.2–0.6) improved during the period. The exceptions are noted on the graph. China and India, the two most populous nations on earth, made notable improvements in HDI values. Two former eastern European states (the Czech Republic and Lithuania) improved their HDI. Countries in the 0.7–0.9 HDI range that experienced a decline of over 5% are mostly from the Caribbean and Latin America (see shaded area on Figure 2.7): Antigua and Barbuda, Bahamas, Chile, Colombia, Costa Rica, Mexico, Panama, St. Kitts–Nevis, Trinidad, Uruguay, and Venezuela (Argentina and Ecuador were just under 5%). Other countries with declines greater than 5%, in order of magnitude, are Albania (21.2), Botswana (17.1), Fiji (11.6), Thailand (7.7), Zimbabwe (7.1), Swaziland (6.7), Zambia (6.1), and Mauritius (5.6). The AIDS pandemic is partly responsible for the declines in some of these countries.

One might think, intuitively, that poverty and inequality go hand in hand, but that may not be the case. If we compare the Gini index regarding the distribution of income with the percentage of the population living on less than two U.S. dollars a day (measured in purchasing power parity [PPP] terms), we find that there is almost no statistical relationship (Figure 2.8).[6] With a Gini coefficient of 1.0, one person has all the income. With a coefficient of 0.0, all income is equally distributed among the population. The Gini index expresses the values as percentages, and thus ranges between 0 and 100. Namibia, with a Gini index value of 70.7, had the greatest income inequality,

Physical Quality of Life Index

The PQLI is derived from three measures: life expectancy at age 1, percentage of people over age 15 who are literate, and rate of infant mortality. Each item contributes equally to the index. The range in values of each of the measures is indexed from 0 to 100, from the lowest to the highest of generally expectable values of life expectancy, infant mortality, and literacy.

The life expectancy at age one index ranges from 38 to 77 years; the infant mortality index ranges from 229 to 7 per thousand live births; the literacy index ranges from 0 literacy to 100 percent literacy. [The attached table] shows for three countries how the indicators were changed to index numbers and then averaged (equally weighted) to form the PQLI. (Morris, 1979: 45)

Thus each 0.39 years of life expectancy equals 1 unit on the PQLI scale; it takes a change of 2.22 live births per 1,000 to change the infant mortality index by 1 point. The PQLI is determined by averaging its three component indices, which are calculated as follows:

Life expectancy at age 1: (Life expectancy at age 1 – 38)/0.39
Infant mortality: (229 – infant mortality rate per 1,000)/2.22
Literacy index numbers correspond to the actual data

Life Expectancy at Age 1, Infant Mortality, and Literacy: Actual Data and Index Numbers, Early 1970s

	Life expectancy		Infant mortality		Literacy		
	Years	Index number	Per 1,000 live births	Index number	%	Index number	PQLI number
Nigeria	49	28	180	22	25	25	25
India	56	46	122	48	34	34	42
United States	72	88	16	96	99	99	94

Source: Adapted from Morris (1979). Copyright by Overseas Development Council. Adapted by permission of the author.

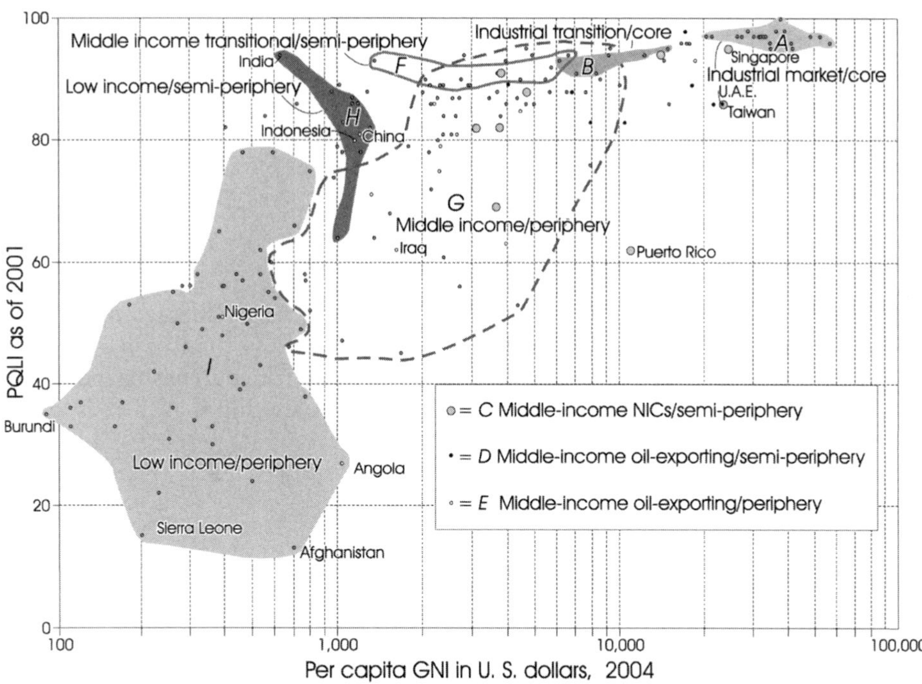

FIGURE 2.4. Relationship between per capita GNI (semilogarithmic scales) and PQLI. *Source*: Data are from World Bank (2005b).

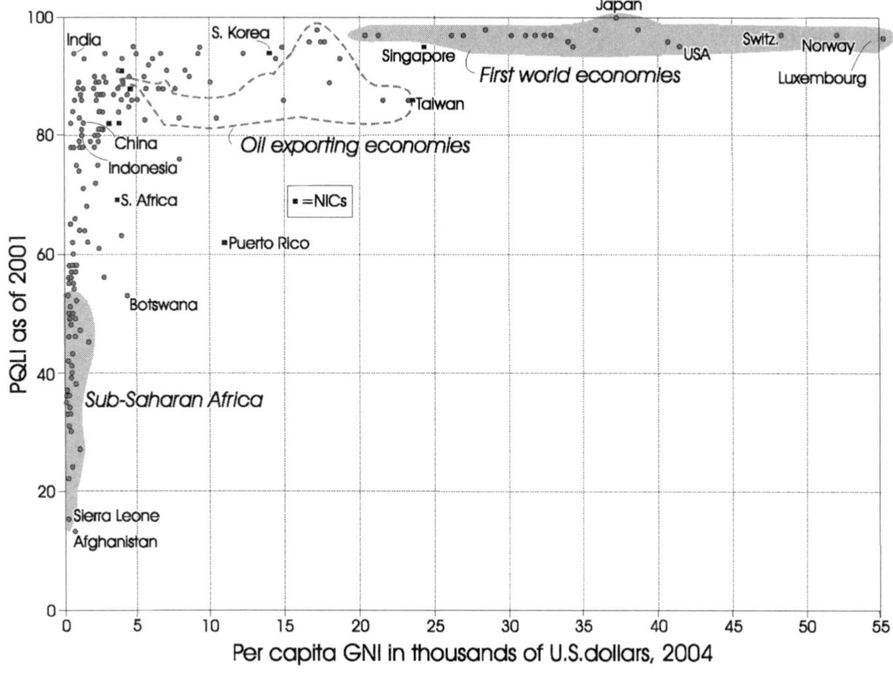

FIGURE 2.5. Relationship between per capita GNI (arithmetic scales) and PQLI. *Source*: Data are from World Bank (2005b).

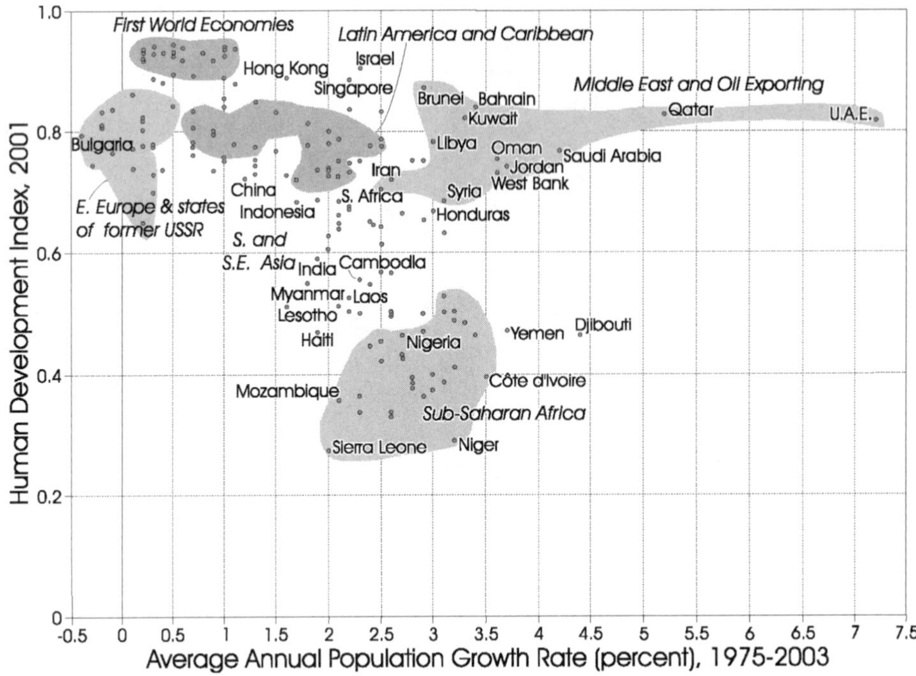

FIGURE 2.6. Population growth and HDI. *Sources*: Data are from World Bank (2005b) and UNDP (2005).

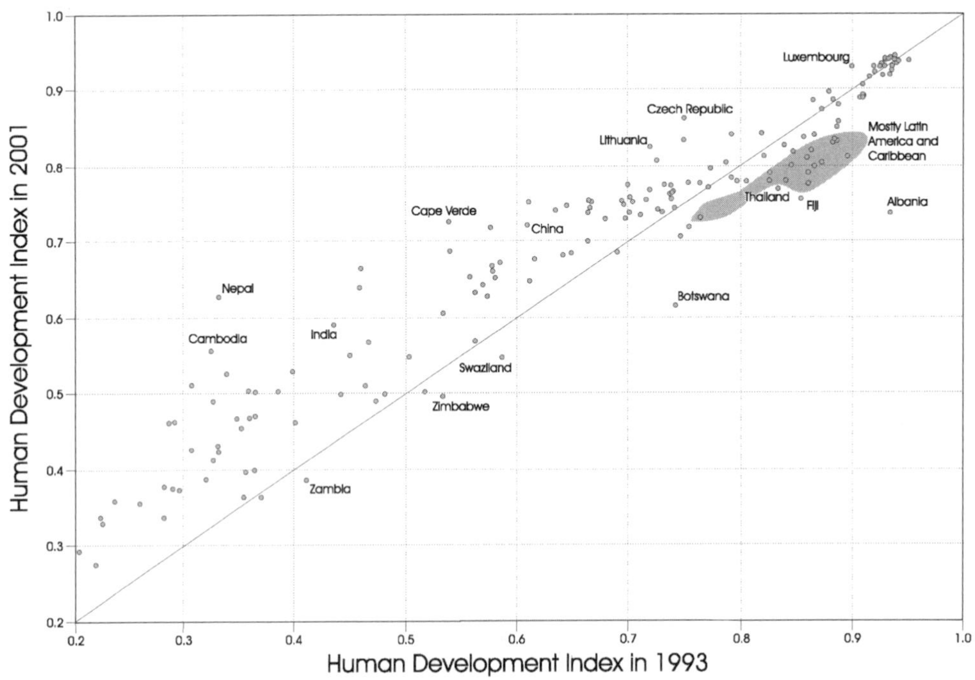

FIGURE 2.7. HDI, 1993 and 2001. *Sources*: Data are from World Resources Institute (1996b) and World Bank (2005b).

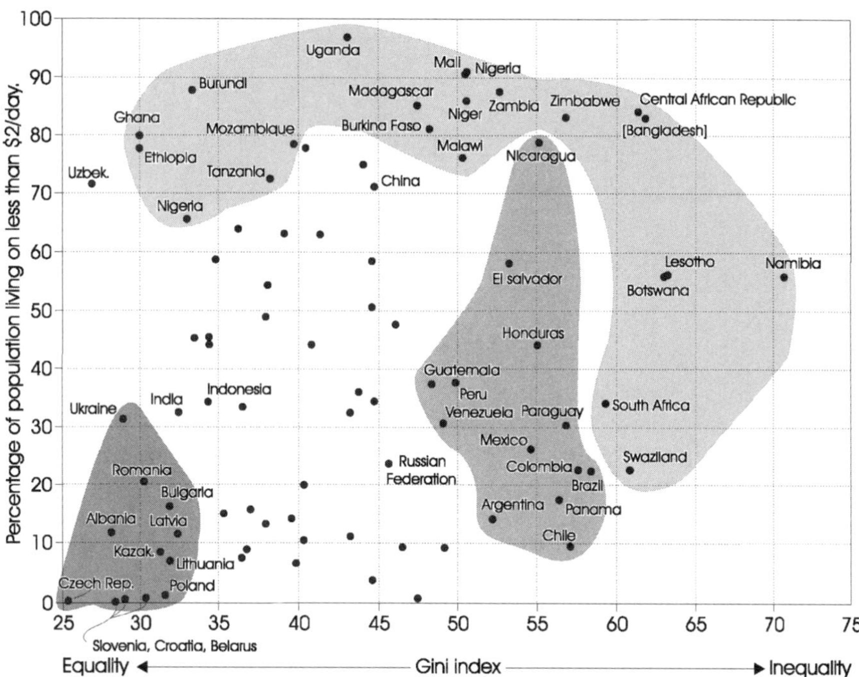

FIGURE 2.8. Gini index and percentage of people living on less than $2/day, with annotations. *Source*: Data are from World Bank (2008).

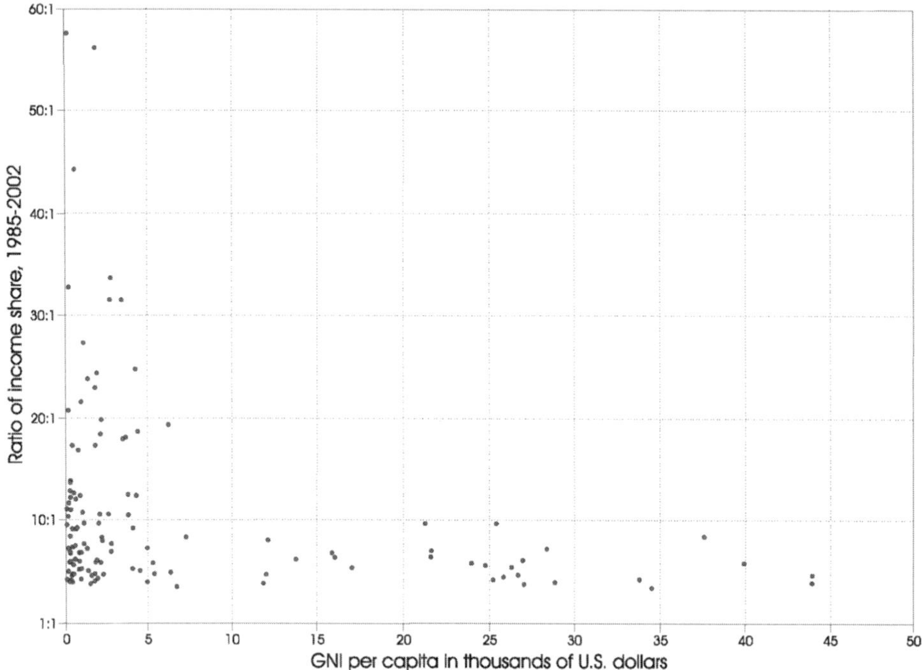

FIGURE 2.9. Income disparities: Ratio of highest 20% to lowest 20% (arithmetic scale). *Sources*: Data are from World Bank (2009) and UNDP (2004).

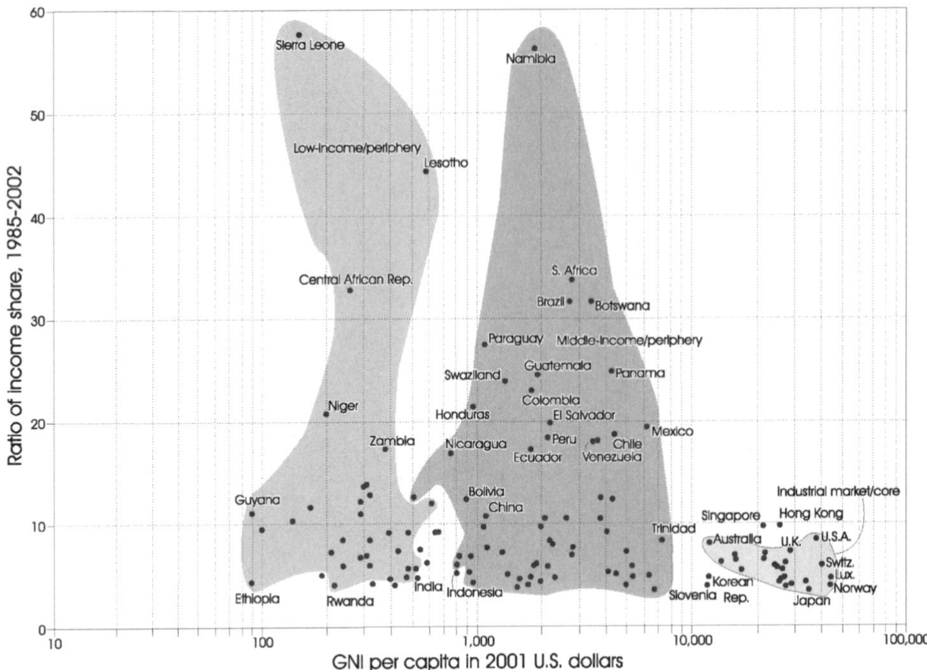

FIGURE 2.10. Income disparities: Ratio of highest 20% to lowest 20% (semilogarithmic scale). *Sources*: Data are from World Bank (2009) and UNDP (2004).

and 55.8% of its people lived on less than \$2/day. Less than 8% of the variation of percentage of people living on less than \$2/day is explained by the distribution of income as measured by the Gini index ($r^2 = 0.075$).

At first glance, the graph appears almost random, but closer study of the countries involved reveals certain patterns. Those countries on the outer margins of the graph—that is, with high percentages living on less than \$2/day, yet varying Gini index values—are almost entirely African (Figure 2.8.). A second set, consisting entirely of Latin American countries, has Gini values ranging between 37 and 60. With the exceptions of Nicaragua, El Salvador, and Honduras, they have between 10% and 40% of their populations living on less than \$2/day. A third set of countries has low Gini numbers and low percentages living on less than \$2/day. Here there is greater equality in income distribution. These countries are eastern European countries or parts of the former Soviet Union. The positions of other countries of interest are noted in Figure 2.7 (China, India, Indonesia, and the Russian Federation).

Empirical expressions of income disparities in different countries are shown in Figures 2.9 and 2.10. Figure 2.9 shows income disparities using an arithmetic scale. On the *X* (horizontal) axis is per capita GNI, and on the *Y* axis is the ratio of income of the richest 20% to the poorest 20% of the population. The immediate message is that the disparities are greatest in countries where overall GNI is low, less than \$4,000 per capita. Use of a semilogarithmic scale for per capita GNI (as in Figure 2.10) reveals details among countries. Some observers say that when the ratio of the top 20% of the people in a country to the bottom 20% begins to exceed 8:1, the economic disparities lead to social unrest, social disorder, authoritarian reactions on the part of the state, and an undermining of the "solidarity" and acceptance of the social contract necessary for civil society. Figure 2.10 shows that nearly all first world countries have income inequality ratios under 8:1. Some countries have notably low ratios—for example, Japan (3.4:1), Norway (3.9:1), Sweden (4.0:1), Denmark (4.3:1), Germany (4.3:1), and Belgium (4.5:1). Slovenia (3.9:1), Slovakia (4.0:1), and Hungary (4.9:1), all part of the former second world, also have low ratios, though midrange GNI/capita. The United States (8.4:1 in 2000) has long exceeded the 8:1 ratio. Middle-income countries exhibit a wide range of disparities, with the highest being Namibia (56.2:1), followed by South Africa (33.3:1), Brazil (32.2:1), and Botswana (32.0:1). The top 20% of Brazilians have on average nearly 32 cruzeiros to spend for every cruzeiro paid to the bottom 20% of Brazilians. Low-income/periphery countries also have a wide range of ratios, some of them rather spectacular. In Sierra Leone, with an average GNI of only $200, the ratio is 57.6:1, and in Lesotho it is 44.2:1. If we compare the top 10% with the bottom 10%, the disparities are even more striking. For Namibia, the ratio is 128.8:1; for Lesotho, 105:1; and for Brazil, 93:1.

These generalized measures (GNI, PQLI, HDI, Gini index, and quintile and decile income inequalities), even as they try to suggest the circumstances of individuals, deal in averages and aggregate data. The figures and tables in this chapter provide a first look at a world of difference. They will reward further study. To appreciate the nature and causes of poverty, however, one needs to meet particular people in the places where they live.

Maps and Locations

Remapping Patterns and Assumptions

Maps constitute a language. They have their own vocabulary, syntax, and conventions. They are subject to the same features of written and spoken languages, in that each map is selective. It shows some things and not others. At the same time, maps are not entirely independent of other "languages"; they often rely on other representations that support similar discourses. In choosing what and how to show information, the cartographer may rely on some labels and categories that highlight some facts, while erasing or marginalizing others. The making of a map is thus an exercise in power. Moreover, even when a map seeks to destabilize some dominant categories or representations, it can inadvertently reproduce others. Figures 2.11 and 2.12, from an atlas by Joni Seager (2003), allow us to consider some of these necessarily complex (and perhaps not entirely resolvable) aspects of the language of maps by portraying distributions not found in conventional atlases.

Gay and lesbian people throughout the world have increasingly asserted their human right to be treated equally under the law, often in the face of severe repression and outlawing of homosexuality in many countries (see Figure 2.11). They have sought to decriminalize homosexual behavior and to promote a broader acceptance of "nontraditional" families or households. Seager (2003: 24) notes also that when "women step outside of heterosexual norms, they are seen as being doubly subversive—both as members of a sexual minority, and also as women who are rejecting male authority." At the same time, it would be wrong to assume on the basis of this map that first world countries are necessarily more "advanced" than African, Middle Eastern, and south Asian countries when it comes to visibility, freedom, or persecution of lesbian and gay peoples. Here it is important to ask who is protected by the law and which categories the law privileges. The global discourse of homosexuality often ignores the poor and rural women in much of the third world who develop and nurture their same-sex relationships and practices in the absence of any formal lesbian organizations, and sometimes in the absence of even an identifiable community of women in same-sex relationships. The world's most economically and politically marginalized women frequently exercise their sexual agency and publicly cultivate their sexual and emotional intima-

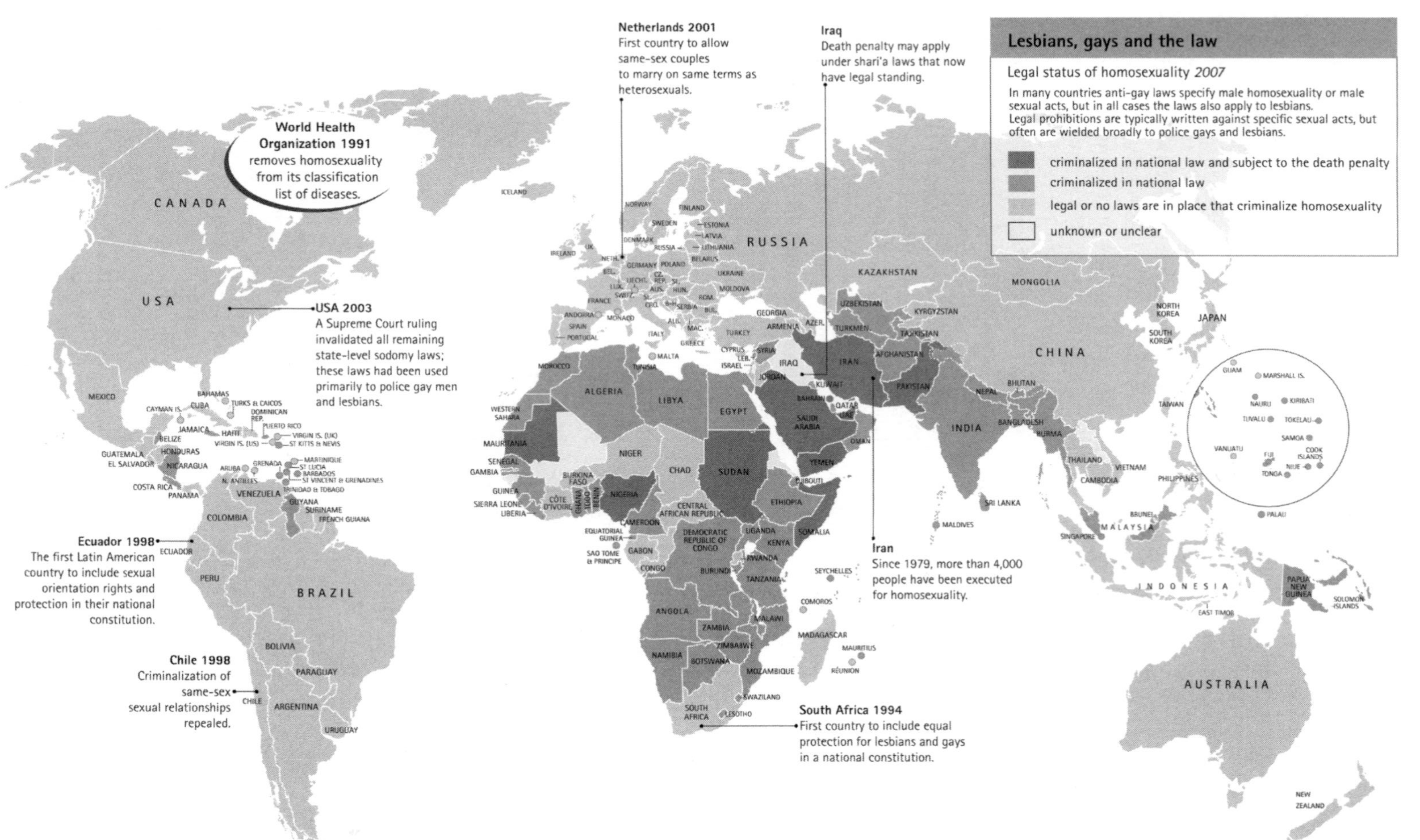

FIGURE 2.11. Challenging the heterosexual norm: Female homosexuality. *Source:* Seager (2009): plate 6, 24–25. Reprinted by permission of Myriad Editions.

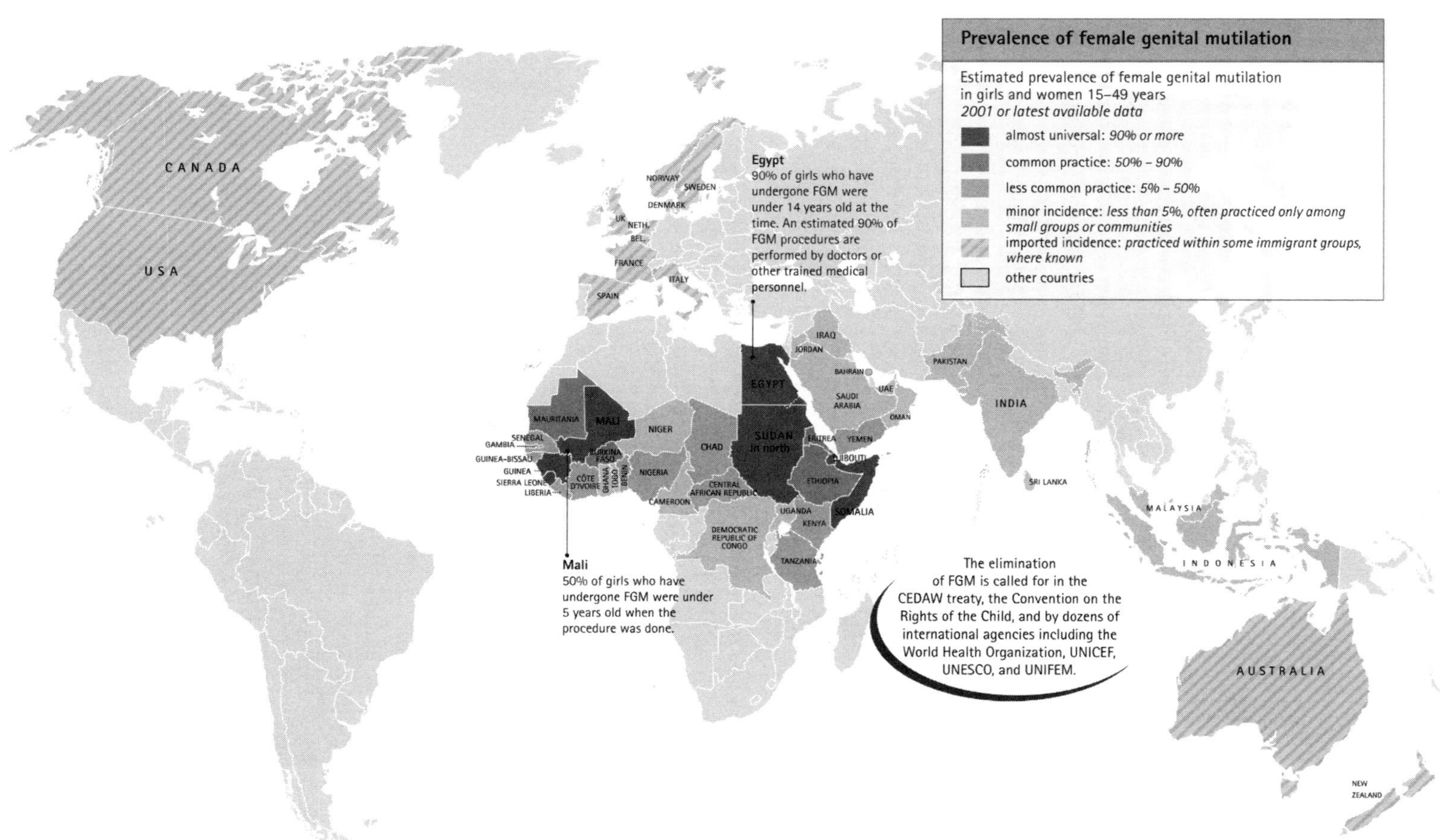

FIGURE 2.12. The contentious practice of genital cutting. *Source*: Seager (2009): plate 18, 54–55. Reprinted by permission of Myriad Editions.

cies with women in relation to their other battles for everyday survival (such as those over access to clean water, land, electricity, and minimum wages) and in highly contextualized, place- and class-specific ways. Terms such as "lesbian" can be incomplete, inapplicable, or even offensive, depending on contexts and histories, even though scholarship, organizations and conferences often rely on such terms, concepts, and identities with little or no interrogation (Swarr and Nagar, 2004).

Let us now consider another sensitive cultural terrain—the practice of what has been popularly termed "female genital mutilation" (FGM), also referred to (wrongly, some point out) as "female circumcision" (Figure 2.12), and understood to be typically performed on girls as a preparation for marriage. According to Seager (2003: 54), an "estimated 130 million girls and women in the world have undergone genital cutting; each year another 2 million join their ranks." The practice is deeply embedded culturally, regardless of the strong presence of Christianity or Islam. Figure 2.12 indicates that this practice is widespread in sub-Saharan Africa, with occurrences also in the Middle East and south Asia. Through migration, it is now found among migrant groups in parts of Europe, North America, and Australia and New Zealand. Things we cannot afford to forget here, however, are that (1) the practices of genital cutting are as varied in their nature, degrees, styles, and social meanings as are the communities in which they are performed; and (2) naming this practice indiscriminately as a "violent" act practiced by the "other" may itself translate into a violent form of representation. Alice Walker and Pratibha Parmar's failure to attend to such nuances in their film *Warrior Marks* (Parmar and Walker, 1993) on the subject of FGM led a group of feminist critics from Africa to make some instructive points that are quite relevant to our discussion of difference, representation, power, and inequality (see sidebar: "Responding to *Warrior Marks*").

Locating the Third World

If we accept conventional definitions of which countries belong to the third world, such as that adopted by the United Nations, some 140 countries are classed as third world. The third world, so defined, is almost entirely confined to the tropics and subtropics (from the equator to about 35°N and 35°S latitudes). These are lands dominated by the intertropical convergence zone (ITCZ) and areas of subtropical high pressure, the main exceptions being northern China, Mongolia, Korea, and the southern parts of Argentina and Chile (see Chapter 9).

Figure 2.13 illustrates the preponderance of third world land in tropical and subtropical areas.[7] In Figure 2.13, the lands in the southern hemisphere have been "folded over" so that all land appears on a graph, plotted against distance from the equator. From this figure we can derive some statistics. The third world occupies nearly 60% of the earth's land (our analysis excludes Antarctica). If we make 35° of latitude our division point between the tropics/subtropics and the middle and high latitudes, we find that about 86% of the third world lies in the tropics and subtropics, whereas less than 18% of the land classed as the first and second worlds lies within the tropical/subtropical zone, most of which is Australian desert and the southern part of the United States.

Of course, there is immense variety within the categories of third world, second world, and first world. Whereas some of the third world countries are seen as getting ready to graduate to first world status (such as some so-called NICs—Hong Kong,[8] Taiwan, Singapore, and South Korea), economic and social conditions have worsened in others, and the suffering of the poor has increased. The notion of a "second world" has become less and less salient since the end of the Cold War and the turning of most former second world countries away from command economies toward free market economies.

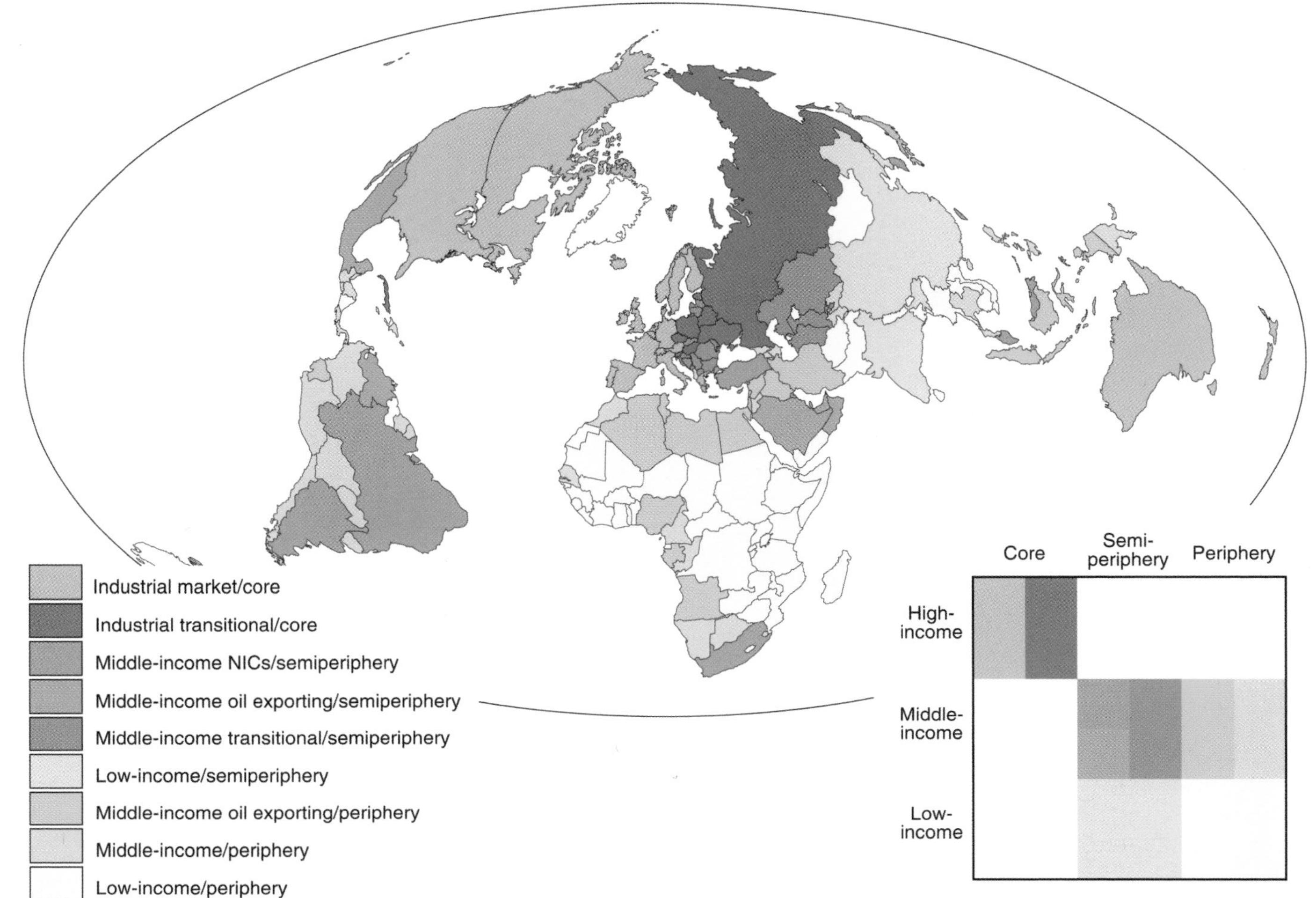

COLOR PLATE 2.1. A classification of the global economy.

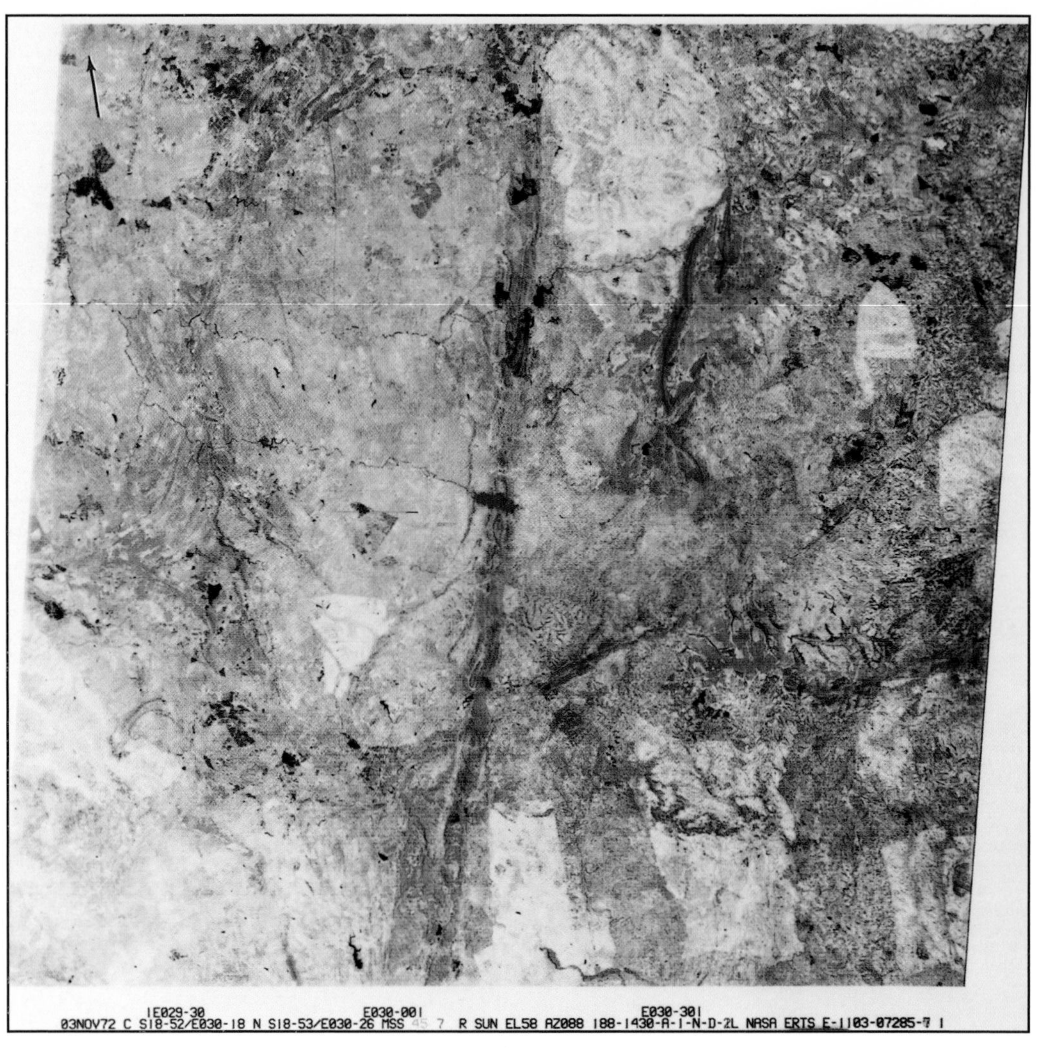

COLOR PLATE 14.1. LANDSAT scene of central Zimbabwe, southwest of Harare, taken on November 3, 1972. The scene measures about 185 kilometers (115 miles) on a side and covers an area of about 34,000 square kilometers (13,000 square miles). Elevation is 1,200 meters (4,000 feet). Crossing north to south through the photo is the Great Dike, a narrow line of hills about 100 meters (300 feet) above the general terrain, formed of ancient intruded Pre-Cambrian rocks that are highly mineralized. The Great Dike and surrounding areas of older Pre-Cambrian rocks (3 billion years old) are mined for chromium, manganese, iron ore, and gold. There is much gold mining around Kwekwe, lower left on the photo (see Figure 14.6). The very light patches, many of which have straight edges, are African land units from which much vegetation has been removed by grazing, wood cutting, and farming. Population densities are high, whereas they are low in other areas where vegetation (red and pink tones) is more abundant (see Chapter 14). In 1972 these areas were in the hands of white Rhodesian farmers. Landsat photo courtesy of National Aeronautics and Space Administration (NASA), Image I.D. 1103-07285. See Short, Lowman, Freden, and Finch (1976).

Responding to *Warrior Marks*

In response to the film *Warrior Marks* (Parmar and Walker, 1993), Salem Mekuria, an assistant professor of art at Wellesley College and an independent film maker from Ethiopia, brought together in one article the arguments made by Rashidah Ismaili AbuBakr from Niger, associate director of the Higher Education Opportunity Program at Pratt Institute in New York; Asma Abdel Haleem, a lawyer from the Sudan and a board member of the Center for Women, Law and Development in Washington, D.C.; Seble Dawit, a lawyer, an Ethiopian, working as an independent consultant in human rights; and Nahid Toubia, a physician from the Sudan and executive director of the Research Action Information Network for Bodily Integrity of Women (RAINBOW) in New York. The authors place serious question marks on such condemnations of FGM that "focus our attention on Africa as a continent of physically mutilated, psychologically deficient, and mentally deranged women" and have no time for explanations and/or discussions with the very people whom these condemnations are seeking to save. In turning a blind eye to the wider context within which possible methods of eradicating FGM can be effected, the educational moment is lost. Mekuria (1995) and colleagues argue:

> The diverse and diffuse situations in which FGM is considered acceptable becomes significant only in seeing the true complexity and depth with which the tradition is entrenched in a wide variety of cultures. . . . Commonly cited reasons for the preservation of the practice include: cleanliness, aesthetics, prevention of stillbirths, promotion of social and political cohesion, prevention of promiscuity, improvement of male sexual pleasure, increased matrimonial opportunities, good health, fertility and . . . preservation of virginity. . . . Some societies believe that undergoing this practice has a healthy calming effect on women as well as [helps] them to regulate fertility. It is also important to note that in most African societies, fertility is a tool of negotiation for women to earn power within the family and the society at large. . . . Furthermore, women are socially expected to show that they have no sexual desires. This is not uniquely an African condition. It exists in every society where unequal gender relations dictate the conditions under which women have to live.
>
> The persistence of female genital mutilation in Africa cannot, therefore, be separated from the power imbalance in gender relations, from the low levels of education, economic and social status of most women. The latest United Nations figure shows that 75% of African women over the age of twenty-five are illiterate. . . . At fifty years, African women have the lowest life expectancy in the world . . . , with maternal mortality rate of 675 per 100,000 live births. . . . Europe has less than 75 per 100,000. Furthermore, it belongs squarely within a *continuum of gender oppression* [emphasis in original] that includes the murder of female children, less health care for girls, less nutritious foods, less schooling, harder work, child marriage and early pregnancy, breast implants/reductions, anorexia nervosa, and the millions of dollars we spend on cosmetics and harmful diet programs. All of these stem from an ideology of women as producers and reproducers, objects, imperfect as we are, to be shaped and molded, cut and tucked, into a more appealing commodity for man's pleasure. Neglecting to make the connection between the physical pain suffered in female genital mutilation and other, less obvious yet equally powerful ways in which women suffer, results in a shallow—if not irresponsible—analysis of the issue.
>
> The current furor in the West about female genital mutilation . . . strips the practice from the social and political reality of gender relations. How effective can this ultimately be in helping African women? Raising the social status and economic independence of the African woman are factors as important in and integral to determining her overall health and happiness as will be stopping her genitals from being excised.
>
> The work of several women's groups in Africa is instructive in supporting our argument. Maendeleo Ya Wanawake Organization in Kenya, after successfully doing qualitative and quantitative studies among four national groups, is now implementing strategies for eradication developed by women from and for their regions. The Uganda chapter of the Inter Africa Committee trains traditional circumcisers for other profitable vocations and has seen exciting results. The Association for the Progress and Defense of Women's Rights (APDF) in Mali works closely with the government to develop policy level intervention

on female genital mutilation within the framework of violence against women. There are several other groups working to eradicate this practice in every country where it exists. Our task should be to find out how all these groups are faring, ask them what they need to advance their struggle and how best they can use our special talents.

Those both inside and outside of the "village" can help to socially and economically empower the women who are our elders, to come together and find a rite that will achieve the desired ritualistic need. As the "village" consists of men and women, children and elders, they too must be included in the process. If outside agencies would like to help, let them sponsor a Council of Women to come together from the four corners of Africa and other areas of the globe, to develop a non-invasive, non hazardous means of ritualizing passage and status. Encourage positive usage of various holy books—the Torah, the Bible, and the Koran—to point the way. Support the work of locally based African women who live daily the realities and can propose sensible interventions. But, for any of this to have meaning, we must first locate and challenge our own position as rigorously as we challenge that of others.

Source: Mekuria (1995). Reprinted by permission of the Association of Concerned Africa Scholars.

Still another way to think of "worlds" would be to move to a subnational scale and study how much third world underdevelopment is found in first and second world countries, and, conversely, the extent of first world consumption patterns and living levels among some classes in third world countries.[9] How many people live the equivalent of third world lives in the United States, lacking access to schools, adequate diets, health facilities, housing, and employment? The UNDP (2005) *Human Development Report* observed that 45 million (of 290.8 million) people in the United States did not have basic health insurance in 2003—a situation found disproportionately among Hispanics and African-Americans (Martens, 2005: 4). How many people lead essentially first world lives in Caracas or Jakarta? South Africa might be taken as a country where from 1948 to the present time (despite recent major changes), a white minority has pursued or benefited disproportionately from policies that have divided its population into an affluent first world and an impoverished, disenfranchised third world.

Before we explore and locate the third world in greater detail, we need to decide on a frame for so doing. We need to choose our maps. Maps can be symbols of our world; maps can be tools for analyzing it. If we must have a symbol, let it be Frank Borman's famous photograph taken during the Apollo VIII mission, showing the earth with the moon's light-brown cratered surface across the foreground, and let Archibald MacLeish write the caption:

> To see the earth as we now see it, small and blue and beautiful on that eternal silence where it floats, is to see ourselves as riders on the earth together, brothers on that bright loveliness in the unending light—brothers who see now they are truly brothers. (MacLeish, 1978: xiv)

Let us immediately help MacLeish out by adding "sisters," "all humanity," and indeed "all life," while also recognizing that exclusionary masculinist constructions cannot always be fixed through addenda. So much for symbols.

But for analysis, let us find a map that represents the countries of the world in a useful and relatively nonchauvinist manner. This task cannot be done without slighting some places and offending their inhabitants. The penguins of Antarctica may never be satisfied, since their land is almost always marginalized or omitted on world maps. The earth's land constitutes only about 30% of the total surface. Much more land lies north of the equator than lies south of it, as we

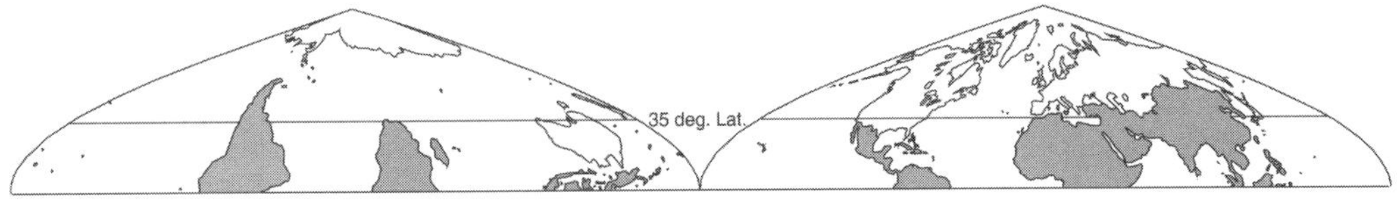

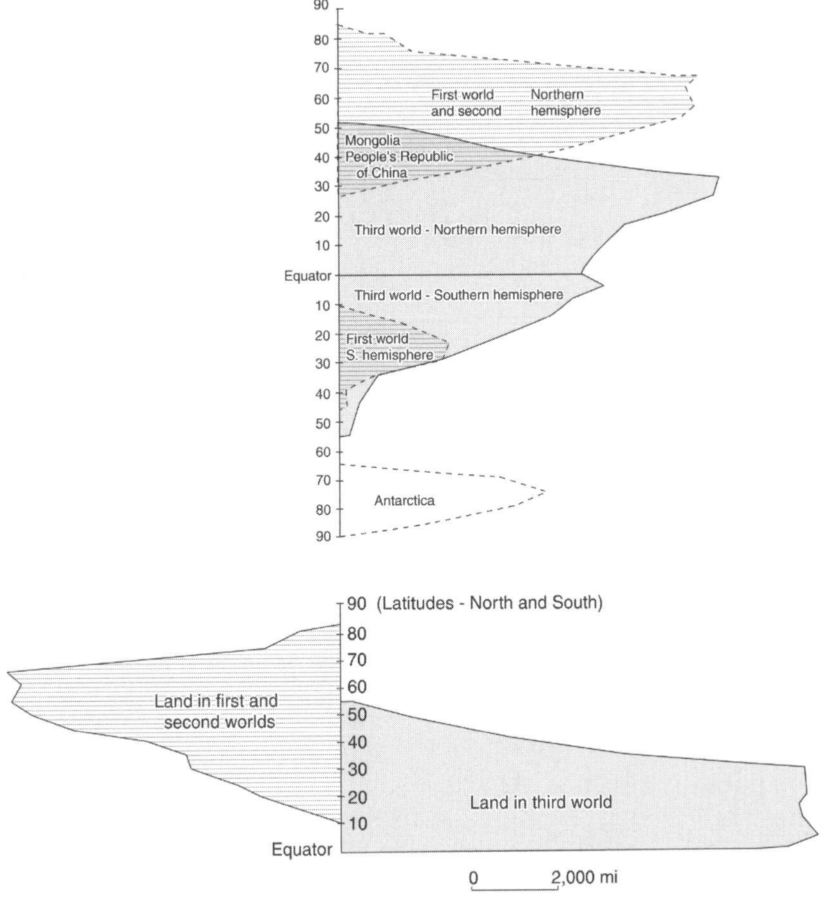

FIGURE 2.13. The tropics, subtropics, and land in the third world.

have seen in Figure 2.13. Much more land lies 90° of longitude east and west of Greenwich meridian than in the "back" 180°. In fact, the center of gravity of the land hemisphere is located at about 1°W longitude and 47°N latitude, near Nantes, France.

Equivalence—that is to say, equal area—is a valuable property in maps used for comparative purposes. We have chosen a Briesemeister projection, named for William A. Briesemeister, who developed the projection at the American Geographical Society in 1953 (Figure 2.14). This is an equal-area projection similar but not identical to the more familiar Mollweide projection (Figure 2.15). The Briesemeister provides an oblique view of the earth. The projection has been rotated so that the point closest to the viewer is at 45°N latitude and 10°E longitude.[10] This map has the following advantages: (1)

FIGURE 2.14. Briesemeister projection, centered on 45°N, 10°E.

FIGURE 2.15. Mollweide projection, centered on 0° latitude and longitude.

It is an equal-area projection; (2) it shows the world centered on the land surface; (3) it has a global or spherical "feel" to it; (4) it does not distort the shapes of third world countries too badly; and (5) it shows the main arenas of movement and conflict in the colonial and postcolonial periods, on both the land and the sea. Its weakness, of course, lies in not representing spatial relationships well for the Pacific Ocean and Pacific rim countries.

Each "oval" on these maps is a circle on the earth that covers one million square miles (2.59 million square kilometers). The degree to which each diagnostic oval departs from being a true circle is an indication of shape distortion in that part of the map. On the Mollweide and Briesemeister projections, areas are always true, always the same; however, shapes are true only at the point of tangency of these projections (0° latitude and 0° longitude in Mollweide, and 45°N latitude and 10°E longitude in Briesemeister). Even though directions and distances cannot be read from this projection, many geographic relationships can be discerned by using the curved graticule to guide the eye. We can see, for example, that traveling due south from Chicago will take us through the Yucatan and into the Pacific Ocean, or that northern Mexico's latitude is similar to those of northern Egypt and northern India. Admittedly, the Briesemeister projection is "Eurocentric," but then so too is the "land hemisphere." Much of the history of the world since 1500 can be traced to diffusions, for good or for ill, from the "hearth" of western Europe, and the projection we have chosen reinforces many aspects of our discussion about core and periphery. We could have chosen a non-Eurocentric projection. For example, we could have been "population-centric" and brought the bulk of the world's people front and center, placing China and India at the point of tangency (Figure 2.16). The change to this new projection center would be a matter of indifference to the always marginalized Antarctic penguins, but it would make it difficult to track patterns in the Americas. Look to see where the Chicago–Yucatan path now lies.

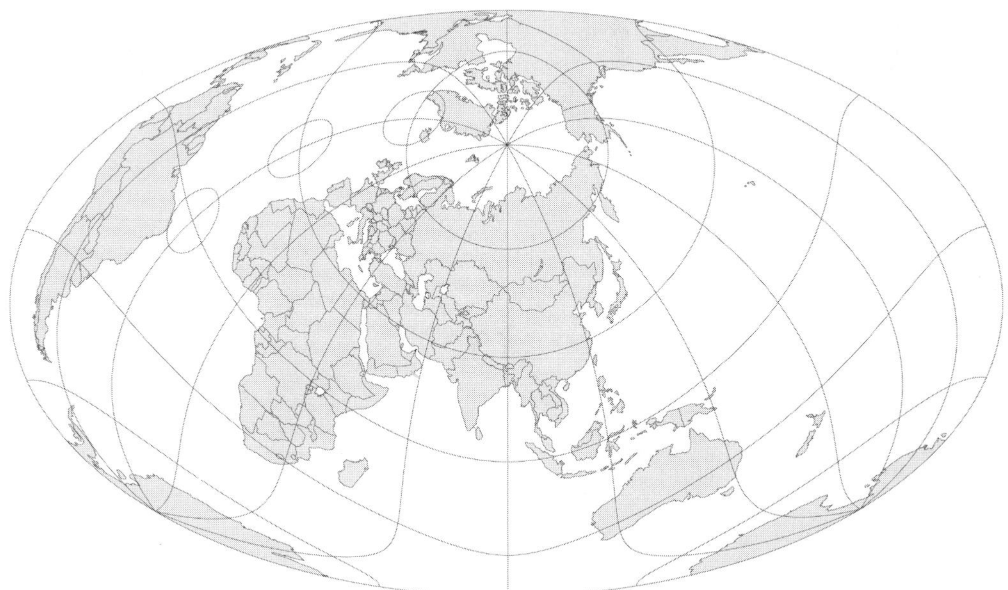

FIGURE 2.16. Briesemeister projection, centered on 45°N, 90°E.

CONCLUSIONS

In this chapter, we have made a first attempt to explore our worlds of difference, concentrating on some of the conventional measures used to describe differences in development, wealth and poverty, human well-being, and life chances. These measures are clearly imperfect; they deal in aggregates (usually countries); and they say nothing about causes of differences. We have noticed a greater spread in the values within the categories we established for the first edition (industrial market/core, industrial transition/core, etc.) A number of countries have moved in different directions. Some countries that were in one grouping in the first edition of this book (Porter and Sheppard, 1998) probably could have been placed in another for this edition (2009), but that would have destroyed the comparative analysis over 34 years. Papua New Guinea, for example, classed as middle-income/periphery in 1993 (GNI of $1,130), really now belongs in the low-income/periphery group, since its GNI in 2004 was $580, not adjusted for inflation. At least 13 countries in the low-income/periphery group had GNIs that were higher.

We have traced the origins of the idea of "first world," "second world," and "third world"—terms that are problematic in a number of ways, not least of which is the assumption that "first" is superior to "third." We have also chosen the map projection that we use throughout the book, explaining its properties and why we have chosen it. Our next task is to consider concepts of development from several different standpoints, and to begin the task of revealing and understanding the causes for the immense differences we find in wealth, poverty, and ideas—practices and realities associated with human well-being throughout the world.

NOTES

1. Global national income (GNI) is the same thing as gross national product (GNP). Both consist of gross domestic income (GDP) plus net receipts of primary income from external sources. The calculation of GNI is based on the Atlas method of the 1993 United Nations System of National Accounts. It uses a 3-year average of exchange rates in order to moderate the transitory effects of fluctuating exchange rates. We use GNI in place of GNP throughout this chapter.

2. The idea of "South" is frequently used as an alternative to the term "third world" for distinguishing former colonies and less industrialized nations from countries of the more affluent and industrialized north. "South" is preferred by those who see the "third world" as connoting third-ranked rather than its original meaning of a nonaligned or third path, independent of the capitalist "first world" and the socialist "second world." However, the term "south" is also problematic in at least two ways. First, the countries of the south are defined through their location with respect to the United States and western Europe; second, they are concentrated in the tropics and subtropics of both northern and southern hemispheres. To avoid such problems, some scholars use the terms "the one-third world" in conjunction with the "first world/north" and "the two-thirds world" in conjunction with "third world/south" to represent the relative fractions of global population based on quality of life led by peoples and communities (Mohanty, 2003). The popularization of the terms "south" and "north" is sometimes attributed to the publication of two reports by the Brandt Commission (Brandt, 1980, 1983). Convened by Willy Brandt of West Germany to study critical issues arising from the economic and social disparities of the global community, this self-appointed commission highlighted a codependent relationship between the northern nations (which relied on the poor countries for their wealth) and the southern nations (which depended on the wealthier north for their development). With food, agriculture, aid, energy, trade, financial reform, and global negotiations as their focus, the Brandt Commission reports sought to promote "adequate solutions to the problems involved in development and in attacking absolute poverty" (Brandt, 1980: 8), while also addressing issues concerning the environment, the arms race, population growth, and the uncertain prospects of the global economy that the commission viewed as common to both north and south.

3. This classification is derived by combining

six sets of measures or ideas about the world system: (1) core versus semiperiphery versus periphery; (2) income; (3) oil-exporting status (including OPEC membership); (4) NIC membership; (5) industrial versus nonindustrial; and (6) market versus nonmarket orientation. We have divided the global economy into nine classes, which differentiate the first, second, and third worlds along several significant axes. (The exercise actually resulted in 11 classes, but some had so few instances and people that they were combined with larger classes.)

4. The documentary *Who's Counting?: Marilyn Waring on Sex, Lies and Global Economics* (Bullfrog Films, 1995) focuses on the inclusions and exclusions created by GNP. Produced by the National Film Board of Canada, this film is based on critical contributions made by Marilyn Waring, an internationally recognized political economist, former member of the New Zealand Parliament, and author of *If Women Counted* (Waring, 1988). Waring critically analyzes how economic value, economic growth, and economic development are measured; who and what they privilege; and who and what they erase. Her argument unpacks, for instance, the ways in which war and environmental disasters contribute to making a country more powerful in terms of GNP. In contrast, the contributions of those who labor for subsistence, raise children, protect the environment, or work for peace, go unregistered (or even registers as negative) in the GNP calculations. Unfortunately, however, most critical decisions about resource allocations in the global political economic system are made on the basis of GNP or GNI rankings.

5. Note on Figures 2.1 and 2.2: Some of the data points among the various national groupings are virtually identical, and this results in a circle for one series covering the circle of another series. In a few places in Figures 2.1 and 2.2, solid or dashed lines connecting data points have been used to aid the reader. The dollar values were adjusted to 1995 rather than 2004, because it was simpler to adjust one set of 2004 values to the other four sets. The resulting data can be compared, and there is no need to recalculate the per capita GNP/GNI boundaries between categories (preindustrial, transitional, industrial, etc.). Between 1995 and 2004, the amount of inflation was modest: One U.S. dollar in 1995 was worth $0.836 in 2004.

6. Values are expressed in purchasing power parity (PPP). This is a system in which a bundle of goods is identified, and then, for each country, the cost to purchase that bundle is calculated using the local currency. This permits us to make comparisons among countries and to calculate exchange rates.

7. The areal diagrams in Figure 2.13 were prepared by laying lines of latitude spaced at 5° intervals on a map wherein lines of latitude are straight, parallel to each other, and in true scale. Sanson's sinusoidal map projection meets these requirements. The length of longitude interrupted by third world and by first/second world land was determined for each latitude, summed, and multiplied by the length of 5° of latitude.

8. Strictly speaking, Hong Kong was not and is not now a country, but it has commonly been grouped with other NICs. Hong Kong was transferred from the United Kingdom to China on July 1, 1997, under an agreement enabling it to retain a distinctive economic and political system for 50 years.

9. With the breakup of the former USSR in 1989, 15 new states came into being. We have included the Russian Federation and the developed portions of the former USSR in a category called "industrial transitional/core." A few of the new countries, such as Armenia, Azerbaijan, the Republic of Georgia, and Tajikistan, have been assigned to the low-income/semiperiphery group.

10. The major difference between the Mollweide and the Briesemeister projections is that in the Mollweide the lines of latitude are parallel, whereas those of the Briesemeister are slightly curved. It is, in fact, an oblique Hammer projection. The north–south "amplitude" of the Briesemeister is also a bit greater, giving better shapes to land masses.

3 Knowing the Third World

Colonial Encounters

The terms "third world" and "development" seem, to us, self-evident and closely intertwined.

"Developed society" conjures up in the minds of most readers of this book, no doubt, images of life in these regions: north America (north, that is, of the Rio Grande); western Europe (west of a line that used to divide the first and second worlds, but now is moving east to embrace some new, formerly communist members of the European Union [EU]); and Australia, New Zealand, and Japan. Furthermore, in those countries the image would also be positive, invoking a comfortable middle-class lifestyle. By contrast, other places and livelihood possibilities, such as those we associate with the third world, seem incomplete or inadequate—less than fully developed (third world = third best). Of course, a moment's thought reminds us that some people in those countries associated in our mind with the third world live as well as or better than middle-class persons in "developed societies." It also reminds us of people in "developed societies" whose livelihood chances are inadequate by anyone's standards. In addition, as discussed in Chapter 2, the term "third world" was coined to mean a third way (neither capitalist nor communist), not third best. Nevertheless, the representations of development and third world caricatured above are incredibly resilient and persistent; indeed, in European thought, they can be traced back several hundred years. The purpose of this and the following two chapters is to critically dissect where these representations come from, in order to call them into question—an exercise that Jacques Derrida (1976) terms "deconstruction."

In critically interrogating how we think about development and the third world, we need to pay attention to discourse. Words, and the representations they unconsciously and automatically invoke in our minds, are far from innocent. "Discourse" refers to the set of social and cultural practices and norms that limit and shape what can be said (i.e., what seems normal, legitimate, and truthful, and what does not), in ways that we are quite unaware of unless we challenge ourselves. In short, discourse sorts out what is taken to be knowledge from what is taken to be belief. At times, these discursive meanings are formally articulated and given verbal precision through theories (of, say, development). However, what seems normal and truthful in one context may seem bizarre in another. In short, knowledge is situated: Ideas and representations of development and the third world held by a female trader in northern Niger will be quite different from those held by a New York City stockbroker. Thus "knowledge" is not singular but multiple: "knowledges."

Very often, the very different knowledges that emerge out of distinct social, historical, and geographical contexts cannot coexist: Like oil and water, they repel one another. But this polyvalence evaporates as one form of knowledge not only overpowers others, but also delegitimizes them—successfully representing them as inadequate beliefs about the world. In short, as Michel Foucault (1980) argues, there is an intimate relationship between knowledge and power: What we take to be knowledge is shaped by the power of a particular discourse, and of those who hold it, to shape how we think. In order to get a critical perspective on current norms about development and the third world, it is necessary to try to reconstruct struggles between differently situated knowledges out of which our consensus has emerged. Foucault refers to this as "genealogy"—reconstruction of the origins and development of discourses by revealing their rootedness in a field of forces.

This is not simply a historical task, but also a geographical one—of situating different discourses in their geographical context, sorting out how some contexts come to dominate our thinking and what we accept as knowledge, and tracing the consequences of this. Given that imperialism and colonialism still haunt both livelihood possibilities and knowledge production (how many universities or great thinkers can you name from the third world?), we need to pay attention to this imprint—on the ongoing centrality of the colonial/imperial encounter for how we think and act, even in this era of globalization. David Slater (2004) defines this as focusing on how colonizer and colonized, or globalizer and globalized, have shaped one another; on recovering and giving priority to "nonwestern" knowledges that have been whitewashed by "western" knowledge; on using these as a foundation to question the "western" knowledge now taken for granted; and on reasserting autonomy and popular resistance to "western" penetration. The use of the term "western" alerts us immediately to a problem: "Western" and "nonwestern" are at best arbitrary divisions of the world. Indeed, this division is actually a product of the very discourses that we seek to deconstruct, making it a problematic starting point! We could use "north–south" instead, but that also is a vast geographical oversimplification (see Chapters 1 and 2). Thus we resort in this and the following chapters to the terms "core" and "periphery," referring respectively to those social and geographical locations that, at any given point in time, respectively are geopolitically dominant or dominated.

Such an analysis reminds us that the process of knowledge production is geographical: People located in different places have experienced and come to know colonialism, development, and globalization very differently. In these chapters, we sketch the historical geography of struggles over knowledge and representations of development and the third world, examining how and why certain ideas (like those summarized above) have become dominant, and we begin to recover other possible forms of knowledge. As a result, instead of assuming that there is one way of thinking about development, we can begin to identify alternatives. Of course, tracing such debates across the world and over several centuries is an impossible task. Thus we offer only a crude sketch, delineating three historical phases (colonialism and empire, nation-state-led development, and globalization), and two broad and vaguely defined geopolitical regions (core and periphery).

As we will see, views from the core typically adopt a "diffusionist" view of social change and development (Blaut, 1993). Spatial diffusion describes a process whereby initial differences between places disappear as the entity concerned (be it an idea, virus, or commodity) spreads from places where it is already present to places where it is absent. Applied to development, this is the view that nations should copy the practices of wealthier societies in order to "catch up" with their development achievements. It envisions a single path to development for all places, and looks forward to a progressive elimination of geographical differences in development. This perspective, with modulations, can be traced from colonialism to the present day. It is not exclusively a procapitalist position, however; a number of Marxist scholars and second world policymakers have seen the European experience with socialism or communism also as a model for social change, also to be propagated worldwide. The situated perspective of the periphery offers a very different experience, from which development is *encountered* rather than propagated (Escobar, 1995). For its residents, development is typically associated with the violence of colonialism, gunboat diplomacy, and wars between superpowers; impoverishment; external control over domestic affairs; the dissolution of indigenous institutions and cultures; and environmental deterioration. As is so often the case with human ideas, a peripheral position has facilitated a questioning—or even deconstruction—of thinking that is taken for granted in the core, resulting in a revolution in development thinking.

VIEWS FROM THE CORE

European Ideas of Progress and the Discovery of Development

In the history of European thought about social change, a transition from cyclical to progress-oriented thinking can be discerned. Aristotle, for example, described the development of organisms as following a cycle of birth, maturity, death, and decay—and applied the same idea to the state. Cyclical ways of thinking about social change remained important into the 18th century. This thinking was central to Edward Gibbon's (1776–1787/1993) *Decline and Fall of the Roman Empire*, one of the most influential books of the late 18th century, and many others drew analogies from cycles of nature to describe human societies in similar terms. This suggested that social change is bounded by limits, that things eventually fall apart, and that not much can be done to prevent this. Such ideas still persist today in discussions of the limits posed by spaceship Earth, or in analyses suggesting that American dominance, like that of Rome, will decline.

In Christian thought, however, the idea of progress became influential. In articulating a view of the natural and social world as shaped by God's plan, St. Augustine of Hippo described a universal history, applicable to all humankind, embedding into this the particular developmental histories of nonhuman processes and society (Rist, 1997). This still had a cyclical component (from Adam to Christ and the final judgment), but its trajectory could be influenced by human intervention. A Christian society, brought to all corners of the earth through adherence to religious doctrine and evangelism, would maximize the number of souls to be saved when the final judgment came. Space was thus created for a project of development. Under the trusteeship of experts—those with the knowledge and accorded the responsibility and power to realize God's plan—corruption and deviance from the plan could be minimized in order to realize the best possible outcome (Cowen and Shenton, 1996).

The emergence of Enlightenment thought in Europe in the 18th century adopted this idea of progress, but replaced God with man as its principal architect. Scottish philosophy was particularly influential. John Locke argued that man's labor, exerted over an inert nature, created value that gave individuals the right to possess the nature they had thereby improved (Mehta, 1999). Locke went on to argue that private property was necessary to realize individual freedom—a core idea of contemporary neoliberalism. At issue, however, was whether this individual right was also good for society. Without a persuasive argument to this effect, it would be impossible to challenge the prevailing discourse that society should conform to God's plan. Scottish and English political economy of the 18th and 19th centuries provided such an argument, thereby reframing conceptions of progress and development. Scottish moral philosophy articulated a theory of subjectivity, theorizing desire, self-interest, and virtue. Bernard Mandeville (1714/1970), in *The Fable of the Bees*, argued that the actions of self-interested free individuals are also good for society. Instead of natural laws based in religious morality, to which human behavior should conform, he thus proposed a law of human behavior, the pursuit of self-interest, which also results in a moral society. Despite occasional trenchant criticisms of liberalism and untrammeled self-interest, Adam Smith (1776, Book I, Chapter 2) developed this into the economic theory of the "invisible hand" in *The Wealth of Nations*: "It is not from the benevolence of the brewer, or the baker that we expect our dinner, but from their regard for their own self-interest."

By the mid-19th century, the idea of development began to emerge among British thinkers. It came to be recognized that progress was not necessarily orderly, particularly in the face of the gales of creative destruction accompanying Britain's transition from an agricultural land-owning society to industrial capitalism. Development was seen as intervention, by those entrusted to do so (typically the state), to address and mitigate the negative aspects that seemed to accompany social change and get progress back on track (Cowen and Shenton, 1996). Initially conceived of as a domestic challenge, soon it was taken abroad to India and other British colonies.

From British Ideas to Global Knowledge

Today, the idea that unobstructed capitalism is best for society is hegemonic (i.e., broadly taken for granted as self-evident). It is worth reflecting, however, on how philosophical reflections emanating from the northern tip of a small island nation in the Atlantic took the world by storm; and how ideas of individual liberty were related to contemporaneous practices of colonialism that took away the liberty, and lives, of so many. The influence of Locke's private property liberalism and Smith's hidden hand cannot simply be traced to the intelligence of these men. There is no doubt about their exceptional intellect, but exceptional intellects can be found in many places. The ability of their arguments to gain traction and travel the world is in part rooted in the global geographical distribution of power and influence. Prior to 1492, pockets of prosperity, wealth, and sophisticated knowledge production could be found scattered throughout Europe, Asia, and Africa. Indeed, European political systems, knowledge, and technical prowess were not particularly high by comparison with those elsewhere. The wealth of China and India were legendary in Europe, whose merchants found it hard to persuade Asians and Africans to buy their products.

Europe rose to global prominence after the discovery of the Americas, and by the 18th century Britain was Europe's hegemonic global military and economic power, with by far the most extensive colonies. It was widely said that the sun never set on the British Empire. Recalling that power and knowledge are intimately related, we can see how Britain's Enlightenment philosophers were particularly well positioned. Their local ideas became global knowledge once they gained acceptance in Britain, where they legitimized a nascent urban industrial capitalism (e.g., Adam Smith's optimism about the invisible hand contributed to his popularity, according to Perelman, 2000). Their instantiation in British economic policy after the 1830s gave them global scope.

Application to the Colonies

Philosophical principles about the rights of individuals were applied unevenly, however. Within Britain, for a long time they were restricted to men with property, were only gradually extended to enfranchise all men during the 19th century, and were finally extended to women in 1918. The United States abrogated these rights to itself in its 1776 Declaration of Independence ("We hold these truths to be self-evident, that all men are created equal, that they are endowed by their Creator with certain unalienable Rights, that among these are Life, Liberty and the pursuit of Happiness"), but did not extend them to Native Americans or slaves. It was recognized that such rights should apply to settlers in the European settler colonies (Australia, Canada, New Zealand, South Africa), but not to the indigenous populations of these colonies, or to other colonies. Thus James Mill wrote a "conceptual" history of India while working for the East India Company in London (never bothering to visit India), in which he defined India as less than civilized—inscrutable, superstitious, and childlike. Contravening liberalism's focus on individual rights, he dubbed all Indians immature simply because they lived in such a place (Mehta, 1999). His son John Stuart Mill, founding father of liberal thought, drew on Locke's idea that children could not be accorded individual rights until tutored by their fathers and teachers, to conclude that severe colonial rule was the only way to bring liberalism to the immature nonwhite colonies: "There are . . . conditions of society in which a vigorous despotism is in itself the best mode of government" (Mill, 1862/1966: 408).

Stephen Jay Gould (1981) has noted that Herbert Spencer drew on biology to legitimate a similar view, popular in 19th-century Britain. Darwin's 1859 *The Origin of Species* was the most influential scientific argument of the day. Spencer, interpreting it erroneously to say that evolution means that the fittest organisms (humans) always rises to the top, argued that the same applies to human races: The fittest are the most successful, and are justified in thriving at the expense of the weak, as in colonialism. This "social Darwinism" later led to eugenic movements seeking to breed the best (white) individuals.

Climate, Race, and Representation

The notion that the indigenous civilizations of Asia, Africa, and Latin America were inadequate by European standards was commonplace in European discourse during the 18th and 19th centuries, expressed in different ways. Some of this was explicitly geographical: the idea that the environment you live in determines who you are and what you can do. The American geographer Ellen Churchill Semple (1911: 620), drawing on ideas that go back to Montesquieu (1689–1755), gave many examples of how environment influenced human culture and behavior, often describing this in racial terms:

> In general a close correspondence obtains between climate and temperament. The northern peoples of Europe are energetic, provident, serious, thoughtful rather than emotional, cautious rather than impulsive. The southerners of the sub-tropical Mediterranean basin are easy-going, gay, emotional, imaginative, all qualities which among the negroes of the equatorial belt degenerate into grave racial faults.

Others framed this through more explicit racism. Joseph Arthur, Comte de Gobineau (1816–1882), a French novelist, aristocrat, and diplomat, rejected the ideals of the French Revolution—*liberté, egalité, fraternité*. He, perhaps more than any other, helped graft ideas of racism onto those of nationalism. In Europe in the 19th century, much research was being done in philology, anthropology, and paleolinguistics—research establishing, for example, the linguistic links between Sanskrit and other Indo-European (including Teutonic) languages. Gobineau believed that language and race are related, that the languages of certain racial groups are superior to those of others, and that the resulting civilizations reflect this superiority (Seillière, 1903). In his four-volume *Essai sur l'Inégalité des Races Humaines* (1853–1855), Gobineau speculated on a mystery that engaged the minds of many 19th-century scholars: the decline and fall of civilizations. He argued that the failure of civilizations is not to be found in war; rather, civilizations thrive so long as they remain racially pure. They fall when "miscegenation with lower races" leads to the dilution of the purity of the population (quoted in Spring, 1932). According to Gobineau, the Aryan (or Nordic) race is the most superior. "Aryan"—a Sanskrit word meaning "ruler," "aristocrat," "noble," or "pure," according to Snyder (1939: 80)—came eventually during Nazi Germany's Third Reich to mean "master race" or *Herrenvolk*, supposedly destined to rule the "inferior" races.

Gobineau's ideas found favor in Bismarck's Germany, in a period of national unification, a time of *Blut und Eisen* ("blood and iron"). Gobineau's ideas were popularized in the writings and music of Richard Wagner, and in turn influenced Wagner's protégé, Friedrich Nietzsche, in his romantic idealism and philosophy of will. Gobineau's science of racial superiority was really pseudoscience—a confused, eclectic muddle of a priori reasoning (Snyder, 1939: 37). It was taken to ridiculous extremes by some German scholars:

> Generally speaking, the Nordic race alone can emit sounds of untroubled clearness, whereas among non-Nordic men and races, the pronunciation is impurer, the individual sounds more confused and more like the noises made by animals, such as barking, snoring, sniffling and squeaking. That birds can learn to talk better than other animals is explained by the fact that their mouths are Nordic in structure—that is to say, high, narrow, and short-tongued. The shape of the Nordic gum allows a superior movement of the tongue, which is the reason why Nordic talking and singing are fuller. (H. Gauch, quoted in Snyder, 1939: 121)

The concept of racial superiority has had a long and pernicious history, infecting all the social sciences in one way or another, and continues to have influence today (Littlefield, Lieberman, and Reynolds, 1982). In the title of a 1964 book, Ashley Montagu called this concept *Man's Most Dangerous Myth*, but it has had great appeal. Gobineau's ideas were taken over in their entirety by Houston Stewart Chamberlain, a "renegade Englishman" who married one of Wagner's daughters, Eva. Chamberlain added an anti-Jewish component that had not been present in Gobineau's work. His *Die Grundlagen des neunzehnten Jahrhunderts* (1899/1904) had an enormous popularity in Germany, and was a favorite book of Kaiser Wilhelm II (Montagu, 1964: 58). Hitler drew heavily on Gobineau and Chamberlain in writing *Mein Kampf*, and in creating the Third Reich and justifying its policies (Hitler, 1925/1943).

Racism and anti-Semitic sentiments occurred throughout Europe from Portugal to Scotland, from France to Russia, in the 16th century as well as in the 19th and 20th centuries. They were invoked to support slavery in one period, and the acquisition of colonies and social, economic, and political discrimination in another.

In the early decades of the 20th century, a development related to racism gained strength: eugenics. Founded by Francis Galton in 1883 as the science of improving stock, eugenics was particularly popular in Great Britain and the United States (Gould, 1981: 201). Although the movement started with laudable aims—to create a more humane, healthy humanity—it soon was pressed into the service of class interests (Montagu, 1964: 226). Geographers played a part in its history in America. Ellsworth Huntington, in particular, was a key figure over a span of nearly 30 years (1918–1945), serving as the president of the American Eugenics Society in 1934, and holding posts at other times in the Eugenics Research Association, the National Society for the Legalization of Euthanasia, and *Birth Control Review* (Martin, 1973: 176–191, 301). Although Huntington and many other American scholars interested in heredity and eugenics repudiated any racial basis for their work, the movement found it so difficult to avoid an aura of racism that the term "eugenics" itself fell into disfavor (Kevles, 1985). In 1969, *The Eugenics Quarterly* became *The Journal of Social Biology*; in 1954, the British journal *Annals of Eugenics* was renamed *Annals of Human Genetics* (Paul, 1986: 27).

Such ideas were to be found throughout European society, drilled into schoolchildren from an early age. In the 1850s, young Americans learned the fundamental facts about how the world was divided from *Smith's First Book in Geography*. The chapter on Africa states: "The people are generally idolaters or pagans, and show little signs of intelligence. Their complexion is mostly black" (Smith, 1854: 139). The catechismal question at the base of the page asks: "What is the religion and complexion of the inhabitants?" As a further illustration, here is Lesson XIII in its entirety:

Seasons, Productions, Animals

Q. What are the seasons of the Torrid Zone?
A. Two; the wet and the dry.
Q. What are its most valuable vegetable productions?
A. Coffee, tea, sugar-cane, bread-fruit, oranges, spices, &c.
Q. What are the most noted animals?
A. The elephant, camel, rhinoceros, lion, crocodile, &c.
Q. Will you describe the inhabitants?
A. They are dark-colored, passionate, and indolent.
Q. What are the seasons of the Frigid Zones?
A. A short and warm summer, and a long, cold winter.
Q. What animals live in the Frigid Zone?
A. The white bear, dog, reindeer, sable, ermine, &c.
Q. Will you describe the inhabitants?
A. They are dark-colored, low in stature, ignorant and indolent.
Q. What are the seasons of the Temperate Zones?
A. Four; Spring, Summer, Autumn or Fall, and Winter.
Q. What are the chief productions?
A. Wheat, rice, maize, cotton, tobacco, grass, fruit.
Q. What are the most noted wild animals?
A. Buffaloes, elks, wolves, bears, panthers, foxes, deer.
Q. What are some of the domestic and useful animals?
A. The horse, ox, sheep, swine.
Q. Will you describe the inhabitants?
A. Generally fair, robust, intelligent, and industrious. (Smith, 1854: 170–171)

Figure 3.1 is from *Johnson's New Illustrated Family Atlas of the World* (Johnson, 1877), one of the most popular and widely owned atlases in North America in the late 19th century. The atlas contains one of the earliest thematic maps portraying the worldwide distribution of the races, prepared by a well-known Swiss geographer, Arnold Guyot of Princeton College. The portion of the legend shown speaks for itself.

Albert Schweitzer—philosopher, theologian, musician, and medical missionary—was in his time perhaps the most famous person on earth. From 1913 until his death in 1965, his views on world events were constantly sought out by reporters who traveled by launch up the Ogooué River (with Conrad's *Heart of Darkness* tucked into their luggage) to Lambaréné, Gabon, to ask his reaction to the atomic blast at Hiroshima, or the construction of the Berlin Wall. He expressed a paternalism common in colonial administrative circles:

> A word about the relations between the whites and the blacks. What must be the general character of the intercourse between them? Am I to treat the black man as my equal or as my inferior? I must show him that I can respect the dignity of human personality in everyone, and . . . the essential thing is that there shall be a real feeling of brotherliness. . . . The Negro is a child, and with children nothing can be done without the use of authority. We must, therefore, so arrange the circumstances of daily life that my natural authority can find expression. With regard to the Negroes, then, I have coined the formula: "I am your brother, it is true, but your elder brother." (Schweitzer, in Joy, 1947: 157)

Whereas Schweitzer's approach was emblematic of paternalistic Europeans' views toward those colonized societies that they saw as always backward, the situation was more complicated for societies of the

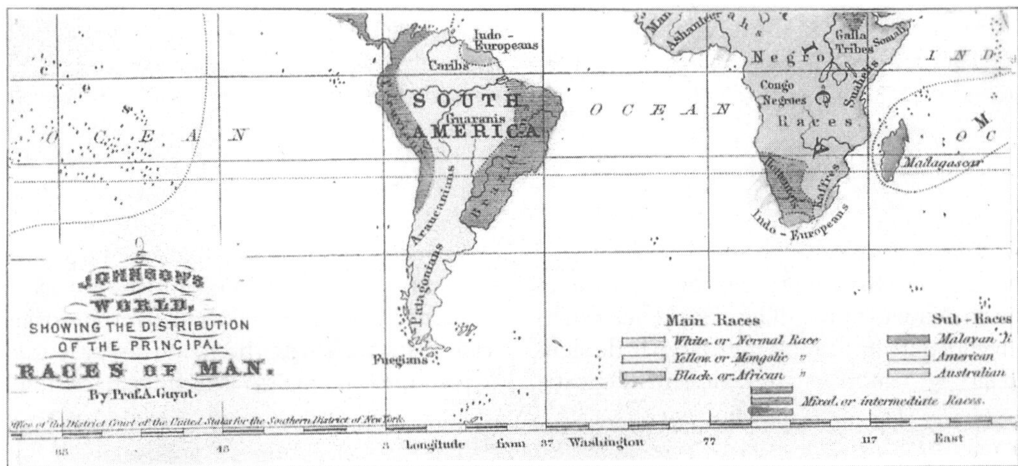

Legend and map reproduced at scale. Hand-applied aquatint affects appearance of legend boxes.

FIGURE 3.1. A portion of *Johnson's New Illustrated Family Atlas of the World* (Johnson, 1877), showing the distribution of the "Principal Races of Man."

Middle East and south and east Asia, where Europeans recognized the historical presence of what they acknowledged as great civilizations. Whereas the civilizing white men and women wanted to become elder brothers (and fathers, mothers, and saviors) of those who were seen as savage or uncivilized, the "great civilizations" of Asia were seen as having fallen from grace. The Palestinian American literary theorist Edward Said (1978) coined the term "Orientalism" to refer to discourses marginalizing these societies by comparison to Europe—discourses already prevalent in the 18th century, but persisting to the present day (think, for example, about how Arabs are portrayed in Hollywood movies or in U.S. television series).

Said argued that European (particularly 19th-century British and French) scholars, artists, and writers created, as a result of contact with cultures to the east, a deliberate "other" as a counterfoil to what is "western." Although racism is a fundamental underlying presupposition of Orientalism, Orientalism has even deeper effects because it appears to be benign or neutral. While acknowledging the richness, complexity, and beauty of Oriental cultures, these creators of Orientalism also invested it with traits and values that set it apart from, put it in opposition to, and characterized it as less worthy than western civilization. The contrast in cultural motifs can best be represented in a succession of paired opposites, and the assignment will be obvious:

rational–superstitious
cultured–close to nature
just–despotic
mature–childish
civilized–barbaric
plain–seductively pretty
straightforward–devious
open–mysterious
honest–corrupt
prudish–licentious
orderly–chaotic
peace-loving–violent
manly–effeminate
judicious–fanatical

It is worth noting that such hierarchies were also used to differentiate Europeans: Irish and Italian immigrants to the United States a hundred years ago were categorized as nonwhites by the British, German, and French immigrants who had preceded them.

Paternalism and Orientalism reinforced one another. For example, the same colonizers who were curbing the women's suffrage movement in Europe articulated their responsibility in terms of white men saving brown women (and brown civilizations) from brown men. Leila Ahmed (1992) has termed this particular articulation of orientalism "colonial feminism," as it deployed (and still deploys, we would argue) the language of feminism to legitimize colonial occupation:

> Even as the Victorian male establishment devised theories to contest the claims of feminism, and derided and rejected . . . the notion of men's oppressing women with respect to itself, it captured the language of feminism and redirected it, in the service of colonialism, toward Other men and the cultures of Other men. . . . The idea that . . . men in colonized societies . . . oppressed women was to be used, in the rhetoric of colonialism, to render morally justifiable its project of undermining or eradicating the cultures of colonized peoples. (Ahmed, 1992: 151)

Economic Theories

By the mid-19th century, discussions of social change in Europe had become dominated by economic questions, reflecting the influence of British political economy over social discourse. It was simply assumed that economic explanations of social change in Europe would apply everywhere—that Europe was the mirror in which colonies could see their own future. Prior to 1800, there were two prominent views on how to accelerate economic growth in European countries. In the period of the 16th, 17th, and early 18th centuries, the dominant view was "mercantilism." This viewpoint emphasized that the state should be made strong, and that the basis for this strength lay in monetary wealth, particularly in the form of precious metals. The principal mechanism for bringing this about was seen as the export of more goods than were imported, leading to what we would call today a positive monetary trade balance. This emphasis on trade is unsurprising in a historical period when western Europe was exploiting the benefits of an inequitable exchange of commodities with its colonies and eastern Europe (see Chapter 13). This viewpoint was surpassed in the latter half of the 18th century by that of the "physiocrats," who argued, in a period when new farming methods in Europe were revolutionizing the economic surplus that could be drawn from the land, that the sole source of economic growth for a nation lay in exploiting the land—a natural resource provided freely by nature (Quesnay, 1753–1758).

The industrial revolution brought about an explosion of thinking about the economic base of society. The British political economists all recognized that human labor is a necessary input to producing an economic surplus; yet they held divergent views on the implications of this for the development of society. Adam Smith (1776: 1) saw the difference between the developed and the less developed worlds as lying in the "skill, dexterity, and judgment with which labor is applied." Thomas Malthus (1798/1992) argued that population growth would outstrip the environmental constraints on food production, creating famine unless humans changed their morals and practiced sex less often (see Chapter 6 for a fuller discussion of Malthus). Instead of focusing on scarcity, David Ricardo (1817/1951: 12) stressed how societies produce industrial goods that "may be multiplied, not in one country alone, but in many, almost without any assignable limit, if we are disposed to bestow the labor necessary to obtain them." He held, however, the Malthusian position that because such products require inputs from an exhaustible supply of land and natural resources, a capitalist economy would eventually stagnate as more and more economic surplus must be devoted to exploiting increasingly inefficient locations. Smith believed that such limits on economic development could be overcome by technological improvements.[1]

Ricardo also popularized a model of free trade that claimed to demonstrate which goods each country should produce in an international economy. He showed that under certain assumptions, if two countries were together producing two goods, then a greater total quantity of both goods could be produced if each country completely specialized in producing the good that could be produced with relatively less labor domestically than by any other strategy. Each country could then obtain the good it did not produce by trading with the other country. Ricardo argued that this made possible increased economic growth for both countries if they followed such a strategy of specialization and trade. The fact that the example he used (England producing "corn"—i.e., wheat—and Portugal producing wine) led to the ruin of the Portuguese wine industry when it was pursued in practice (Chapter 15) has not prevented this free trade doctrine from continuing to dominate thinking about development strategies for less developed nations to this day.

Smith, Malthus, and Ricardo saw themselves as extending and elucidating the economic implication of Scottish enlightenment liberalism in the spirit of Locke. As with the free trade doctrine, economic mechanisms accelerating progress in Europe were seen as directly applicable to the colonies. The other great classical economist, Karl Marx, was a very different thinker, however. Unlike his predecessors, Marx did not unquestioningly accept as a natural and permanent state of affairs—for Europe and everywhere else—the capitalist society in which he lived. Rather, he saw capitalism as a step forward, but riven with contradictions that would sooner or later pull it apart (Marx, 1867) (see sidebar: "Marx on Capitalism and Global Development").

Marx saw capitalism as just one of several possible forms that economic production has taken and could take in society—a form that (like such earlier systems as feudalism) would eventually be superseded by something better. He argued that production might take a limited number of distinct forms, termed "modes of production." Each of these includes a distinctive set of "production relations" (the technology used in production, and the division of labor) and of "social relations" (describing who owns the means of production, the mechanisms governing the provision of labor for production, and how and to whom the benefits of economic production accrue). He concentrated on five modes of production, ordered into a sequence based on his interpretation of the European experience: slavery, feudalism, capitalism, socialism, and communism. He saw each mode of production as having a historical role to play in increasing both humankind's control over/exploitation of the material natural environment, and human emancipation. At the same time, however, limits faced by each mode due to its own set of internal contradictions would eventually lead to its replacement by another mode. These transformations, resisted by those who benefited from the previous system, were seen as governed by the material needs of society—Marx's method of historical materialism.

Like Smith and Ricardo, Marx maintained that the capitalist mode of production is both feasible and necessary in all countries at some point if they are to develop. "The country which is more developed industrially only shows, to the less developed, the image of its own future" (Marx, 1867, Preface). But he was aware that his European outlook might lead him to be mistaken on this point. In a letter written late in life, he emphasized that the situation in other countries might not parallel his analysis of the European case as closely as he had claimed, warning that one should not "metamorphose [his] historical sketch of the genesis of capital in Western Europe into an historical–philosophical theory of the general path every people is fated to tread, whatever the historical circumstances in which it finds itself" (Marx, 1877/1989: 200). He argued in favor of a distinctive "Asiatic" mode of production that had not occurred in Europe, and

Marx on Capitalism and Global Development

Marx argued as follows:

1. The source of profit in a capitalist economy is labor. Marx reached this fundamental conclusion as follows. If commodities are valued by the number of hours of labor that directly or indirectly have gone into their production (the "labor value" of a commodity), then labor itself is a unique commodity, because it is both the source of value and must also have an economic value. By definition, the labor value of an hour of work equals one (the "value of labor power"). However, unless the labor value of the goods consumed by that worker, and his or her family, in a working day is less than the number of hours worked, it will be impossible for the purchasers of that labor ("capitalists") to make a monetary profit. This inequality in labor value terms always exists when labor is supplied in a freely operating labor market.
2. The dynamism of capitalist production, which requires continued growth and reinvestment of these profits in order to survive in a competitive market, means that this system will inevitably seek to expand the geographical area under its influence.
3. Capitalism by its very nature is an unstable and wasteful system of production, oriented toward maximizing the monetary value rather than social utility of production, but it is also a far more dynamic mode of production than anything preceding it. It has brought not only great technological advances in productivity, but also social advancement. The principles of individual freedom and democracy—a necessary ideological basis of the private ownership and free labor market that characterize capitalist social relations—are as much a result of capitalism as are its technologies.
4. The impact of capitalist expansion on noncapitalist countries may be catastrophic in the short run. An example of this is the destruction of a healthy domestic textile industry in India by the British in order to create a new market for British industrialists. However, the long-run effect of this has been "the laying of the material foundations of Western society in Asia" (Chilcote, 1984: 14). Only in situations dominated by mercantile rather than industrial capitalists would this kind of full capitalist development have been prevented (Brewer, 1980).
5. Capitalism, like every mode of production, is fraught with internal contradictions and can only bring about development up to a point. Sooner or later these contradictions, the wastefulness of the system, and the highly concentrated ownership of the means of production and the fruits thereof should create the conditions for its replacement by a socialist mode of production with collective ownership of the means of production. Human development, then, will be fulfilled through a transition to socialism and then communism.

also foresaw some possibility that socialism could evolve in Russia without a period of capitalism (Palma, 1981). Thus the sequence feudalism → capitalism → socialism should perhaps be seen as a model of what might happen in western Europe, rather than, as some have claimed, a false universal prediction of his historical materialist theory of social change. A historical materialist approach is simply the claim that the development of society stems from the material needs of humankind to subsist and develop its potential through interaction with the biophysical environment and other people; it need not imply some universal sequence of development stages.

Marx differed from the other classical economists in five important ways. First, he sought to place capitalism within a broader geographical and historical context. Second, he discussed not only economic aspects, but also social and political aspects, of social change. Third, his analysis was openly critical of the capitalist society in which he lived, whereas the others took capitalism's persistence for granted and were simply interested in analyzing this status quo. Fourth, he argued that capitalism would spell economic ruin as it diffused, inevitably, to the colonies. Fifth, he "came to the idea that the true or full development of humanity hinged on the intent of the human subject to develop . . . through the expanded freedom of activity in general" (Cowen and Shenton, 1996: 119). Rather than leaving development to the state, or even a socialist elite, people must take control of society to realize their own freedom. By the end of the 19th century Marx's ideas were to be swept aside in economics in favor of the Lockean liberalism of Ricardo and Smith, although they did affect social policy where a progressive liberalism emerged justifying state intervention to address the poverty associated with industrial capitalism. This developmental strategy was not extended, however, to the nonsettler colonies.

A fundamental split in western social science thought persists to this day along these lines, between those believing that the free market system (with perhaps some modification) can underwrite development and human well-being, and those believing that it is fundamentally flawed and must be replaced.

Justifying Colonialism

It should be evident from the discussion above that perspectives from the core divided the world in two. The European colonizing powers and their settler colonies (colonies whose indigenous populations had been largely wiped out and replaced by settlers from Europe) had desirable qualities missing in other societies. This provided a convenient discourse justifying, in Europeans' eyes, the violence that was colonialism: European "civilization" was good for everyone, and it was up to Europeans to "civilize the natives" so that they too could live like Europeans. In the case of those societies that were acknowledged to have once been civilized, it was up to Europeans to set them back on the right path. With an appropriate mix of tutelage and discipline, they could be advanced toward civilization. This moral justification for colonialism as a development strategy permeated everyday life. English author Rudyard Kipling, author of the *Jungle Book* fables about India, penned a poem in 1899 urging the United States to assume the task of developing the Philippines, which it had just colonized. This became an anthem for the age:

> Take up the White Man's burden—
> Send forth the best ye breed—
> Go bind your sons to exile
> To serve your captives' need. . . .(Kipling, 1917: 215)

France's most famous author, Victor Hugo, author of *Les Miserables* and supporter of John Brown and Abraham Lincoln, opined at a banquet commemorating the abolition of slavery in Paris (quoted in Rist, 1997: 51):

> To fashion a new Africa, to make the old Africa amenable to civilization—that is the problem. And Europe will solve it.
>
> Go forward, the nations! Grasp this land! Take it! From whom? From no one. Take this land from God! . . . God offers Africa to Europe. . . . Change your proletarians into property owners! . . . Grow, cultivate, colonize, multiply! . . . may the divine spirit assert itself through peace and the human spirit through liberty!

In 1885, France's Chamber of Deputies gave this view quasi-official status, passing three principles on the basis of which the colonies were to be turned to account (*mise en valeur*) (Rist, 1997: 52):

1. "Colonial policy is the daughter of industrial policy." Growth of production requires new outlets in new places, especially as international competition is intense.
2. The "higher races" have rights and duties toward the "lower races," and must share with them the benefits of science and progress.
3. Colonization is necessary for France to avoid "the high road to decay." If France

does not colonize, other nations will, but in the name of less noble values and with less talent.

The view that emerged in 19th-century Europe—that each nation was differently positioned on the same development path, and thus could be ranked from less to more developed and civilized—had profound consequences. It meant that non-European societies (i.e., those not predominantly peopled by Europeans and residents of European extraction) were represented as not only different but also inferior; thus an inferiority was associated with non-Christians, nonwhites, and nontemperate environments. It meant that there was only one path to development (that already trodden by the industrial capitalist European nations of northwestern Europe). And it meant that Europeans, experienced with this path, should colonize the world to accelerate everyone toward civilization—no matter what the short-term cost. It justified European views on what constituted a proper nation state, on which places could be occupied because they did not qualify for this status, and where boundaries should be drawn to create national territories where none previously existed. It also justified European actions to remake nature in order to serve colonial expansion. These actions range from the Columbian exchange—bringing European disease complexes, crops, animals, and production methods to the New World—to the occupation of environments best suited to European agriculture, enclosure of common lands, exploitation and extraction of resources, and global relocation of cash crops. (Nature, feared and revered in feudal Europe, had by now come to be seen by Europeans as something to be dominated, controlled, and exploited—just like the nonsettler colonies.) Tea, coffee, sugar, bananas, and other crops—efficient sources of energy and stimulus for the European workers—were moved from one world region to another, to keep their production under colonial control and to ensure cheap production, often based on slavery. The very idea of factory production was invented in these plantations.

As a diffusionist narrative, justifying action on the basis of universal principles, and in the name of development, these views created a particular spatial imaginary: a common destiny for all, to be achieved by "draining the swamp" of ignorance, tradition, and difference.

VIEWS FROM THE COLONIAL PERIPHERY

Contesting Colonial Ideology and Practice

We know little about views from the periphery until colonialism had nearly run its course. These views often were not written down; even when they were written down, they did not make it into the European literatures dominating global knowledge production. One exception is India, where Prithwish Chandra Roy, Subramania Iyer, Romesh Dutt, and particularly Dadabhai Naoroji articulated a theory of underdevelopment. In his book *Poverty and Un-British Rule in India*, Naoroji (1871/1962) articulated what he called "drain theory," describing how India suffered from unequal relationships with Britain that drained India, violating British claims that India was benefiting from colonial development strategies. Although these ideas had limited influence, they provided the groundwork for a peripheral theory of underdevelopment, emanating from Latin America, that had significant influence after the end of colonialism. Cowen and Shenton (1996) trace the idea of underdevelopment to Cardinal Newman, writing about the corrupting influence of Protestantism in 1845. It is reasonable to suppose, however, that Naoroji and his compatriots independently came up with their formulation, which was rooted in their experiences of the violence and disruption associated with British rule in India.

In Latin America, José Martí (1891/1961) wrote about the need for Latin American autonomy in the face of the "colossus of the north" (the United States) emerging to replace Spain, warning against a trade agreement between Mexico and the United States. In 1896, Argentinean diplomat Carlos Calvo challenged attempts by European states and the United States to assert the right to protect their nationals and their nationals' property anywhere in the world, culminating in the Drago Doctrine of 1902. The Drago Doctrine, stating that public international law was based on the presumption that all nation states were equal under the law, was rejected by the United States at the 1906 Pan-American Conference (Slater, 2004).

Evidence that controverted the rationale for the white man's burden was not welcome. Until 1957, for example, Ethiopia and Liberia, which had been independent since 1847, were the only independent black countries in Africa. The rest of Africa consisted of colonies, protectorates, League of Nations mandates/UN trusteeship territories, High Commission Territories, and so forth. Liberia and Ethiopia constituted counterexamples of widespread European opinion on the "ability of the Negro to govern"—a view that Africans were not capable of governing themselves and needed a long period of benevolent tutelage at the hands of "strong high-minded white men" (Anderson, 1952: 115, 97).

One of us once spent several months in the library of the Royal Empire Society, London, reading everything available on Liberia. An inordinate amount, perhaps a majority of what was written, was polemical and concerned the fitness of Americo-Liberians (freed ex-slaves from the United States and the Caribbean who had resettled on the west African coast) to govern themselves and the indigenous people. Figure 3.2 shows trends (using a 3-year moving average) in the number of books and articles about Liberia published in Great Britain, Liberia, the United States, France, Germany, and other countries. Note that the largest number of publications appeared in Britain. The peaks in writing about Liberia occurred mainly in times of some diplomatic or financial crisis in Liberia, reflecting the ambivalence of European colonial powers over the existence of a country governed by Africans themselves. A large proportion of the published works concerned either commercial activities and possibilities in Liberia, or the debate about slavery sparked by a controversial book by Lady Simon, the wife of the British Foreign Secretary.

This book, *Slavery*, published in 1929, created a sensation in Britain, Europe, and the United States. It accused the government of Liberia of engaging in labor practices "which are barely distinguishable from slavery" (Simon, 1929: 82). It claimed that the government used *corvée* (forced) labor in the country, compelling young men from the Cape Palmas area to work on cocoa plantations in Fernando Po (Vice President Yancy, it was claimed, was the chief organizer and beneficiary of the contracting). Moreover, the government was said to tolerate "pawning," a system wherein a person (often a child) was given in servitude to another in exchange for money or some other consideration. The resulting public outcry led to an official investigation by the League of Nations and a concerted effort by major European colonial powers (the Christy Commission, the Brunot Commission) to put Liberia into receivership.

The "plan of assistance" devised by the League would have placed white men in all positions of power: "a 'Chief Advisor,' whose function it would be to tell the President of Liberia what he might and might not do," and white provincial and deputy commissioners (Anderson, 1952: 115). Although President King and Vice President Yancy resigned, Liberian leaders staved off the attack; in the process, they became more closely tied to the United States, and fiscally subordinate to the Firestone Plantations Company.

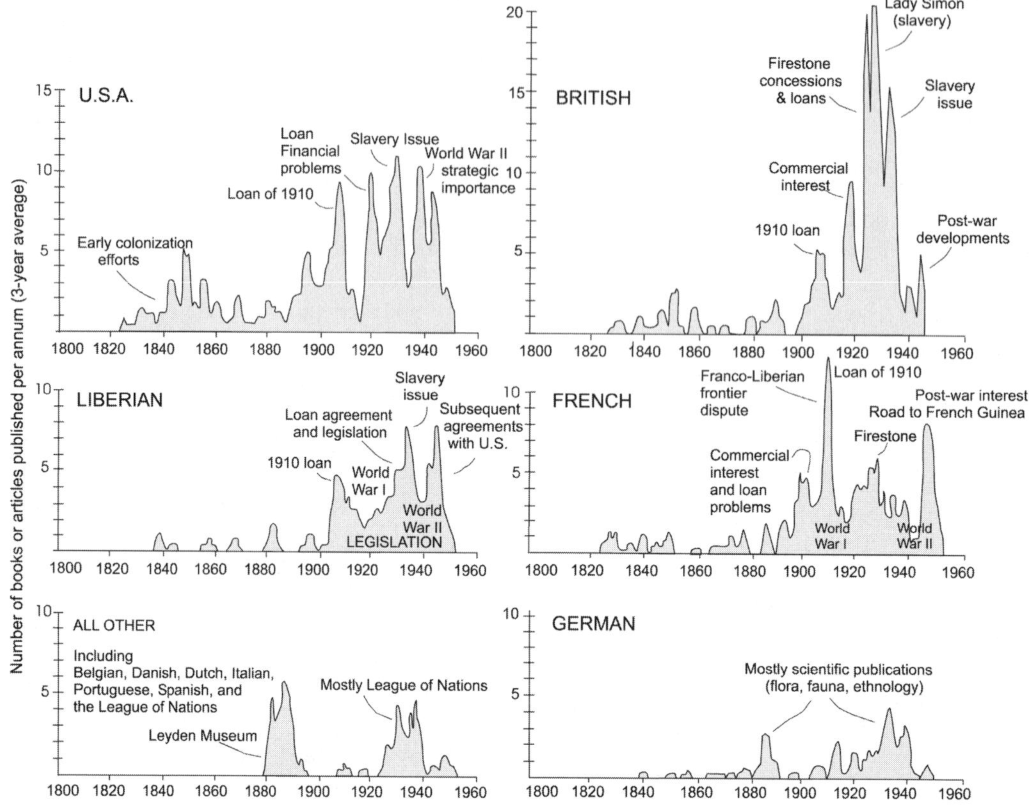

FIGURE 3.2. Number of books and articles about Liberia published in different countries, 1825–1960s.

Querying the Origins of European Capitalism

Much more recently, the U.S. geographer James Blaut has provided a critical reexamination of how colonialism was essential to Europe's rise as the core of the global economy; his presentation resonates with the arguments of Naoroji, Martí, and Calvo (Blaut, 1976, 1993). He argues that the success of European capitalism is not a result of the cultural, political, or economic superiority of European society, as argued by most other European and North American scholars (whether their affinities are with neoclassical economics or Marxism). Instead, he argues (Blaut, 1992: 2–3):

1. "Medieval Europe was no more advanced or progressive than medieval Africa and medieval Asia, and had . . . no unique gift of 'rationality' or 'venturesomeness.' "

2. Europe became the center of global capitalism after the 15th century because of its geographic situation (i.e., its access to the New World). Discovery of the New World stimulated a rapid shift from feudal to capitalist society in Europe, and gave Europe a decisive locational advantage over competing foci of incipient capitalism in Africa and Asia.

3. Colonial exploitation of the New World produced a major transformation of European society. The influx of capital from the New World broke down European class systems, enabling the bourgeois revolutions of the 17th century; in addition, economic power combined with new markets enabled

a decisive concentration of capitalist production within Europe to occur.

In this view, European merchants and capitalists (and, by extension, other Europeans) were fortunate by comparison to African and Asians, rather than gifted (cf. Abu Lughod, 1989; Amin, 1988; Frank, 1978b). Their advantage was geographical rather than cultural. Furthermore, Europe did not exert a one-way influence over other parts of the world, however pervasive that influence might have been. Without the opportunities of the New World, the European and American prosperity that is taken for granted almost as a birthright in western societies might have happened much later, if at all.

A logical consequence of this analysis is to further question the assumption that Europe and America constitute the development model for everyone else. If European capitalism prospered by luck rather than superiority, the possible existence of other equally effective development models that were not as lucky cannot be ignored. In short, Blaut departs from the diffusionist position, which he argues is Eurocentric: It entails the dual assumptions that European capitalism is superior by comparison with its predecessors in Europe and contemporaneous systems elsewhere, and that others must copy the European experience if they wish to experience first world prosperity. By showing that a nation's situation within the world economy can shape its development paths, he seeks to undermine the notion that third world nations have only one development path to choose from, and have only themselves to blame for not pursuing it.

CONCLUSIONS

Societies throughout Asia, Africa, and Latin America were clearly at least as capable of large-scale social organization and developmental strategies of their own prior to the era of colonialism as were those emanating from Europe. It is telling that these achievements generally are not described as development projects, even by critics of colonialism. This shows how deeply academic and policy thinking has been pervaded by discourses that equate development with European (and, more recently, American) thinking (Gidwani, 2002). This discourse has been so pervasive that successful struggles against colonialism, fought on the basis of views from the periphery of the kind summarized here, resulted in independent governments that then took it upon themselves to implement the European development project domestically. Mexico in the 1860s, Chile, Argentina, and Brazil (which still has "progress and order" in its flag) pursued European ideas of development, seeking to "civilize" their own non-European populations; Nehru pursued this in India; and, more recently, the African National Congress has done this in postapartheid South Africa (Cowen and Shenton, 1996). It is to this development project, as it emerged after 1945 in the first world and newly independent third world countries, that we now turn.

NOTE

1. Writing at a time when British population growth was exploding while incomes were falling, Malthus was interested in the interaction between population and economic surplus. He argued that population would grow at a geometric rate, but that the productivity of land could not increase as quickly. He neglected the possibility that specialization in industry can increase productivity, and did not discuss how a nation's social inequality affects the likelihood of malnutrition at any given level of food production. Today, the viewpoint that environmental constraints are (or will be) a constraint on economic growth is still known as the "Malthusian" view (Chapter 6).

4 Knowing the Third World

The Development Decades

To acquire a horizon means that one learns to look beyond what is close at hand—not in order to look away from it, but to see it better within a larger whole and in truer proportion.

—HANS-GEORG GADAMER (1993: 305)

By 1950, colonialism was on its last legs, as a result of forces from both above and below. From above, the United States used its emergent global influence, and particularly the dependence of western European wartime allies on U.S. finance and materiel for victory and postwar reconstruction, to rewrite the global geopolitical order. As part of the Bretton Woods agreement negotiated during the war (Chapter 15), these European powers agreed to end colonialism, which would allow the United States to trade with and invest in the large parts of Asia and Africa where colonial preferences had ruled. This signaled a move from a world of colonial empires, in which the United States was a marginal player, to a world of nation states in which the United States was a major power. Defeat of Germany, Italy, and Japan also resulted in the breakup of their colonies and spheres of influence. From below, anticolonial independence movements throughout Asia and then Africa further catalyzed this process, often at a faster pace than European overlords and their U.S. allies were comfortable with—including the creation of political regimes in these newly independent countries that were ideologically opposed to capitalism (China, India, Cuba, Tanzania, Vietnam, etc.). The presence of a cluster of socialist nation states in eastern Europe under the heavy-handed tutelage of the Soviet Union, now secure within its own borders, created a second world of nominally communist regimes to which such oppositional postcolonial regimes could appeal for support.

As a result of these contestations of a colonial geopolitical world order, a new geopolitics emerged. As a result of geographical rescaling, nation states became the principal form of political regulation, overlain by a first world–second world superpower rivalry embracing much of the world by the early 1970s. This world of independent nation states, each (at least in principle) accorded sovereign powers over domestic political, social, and economic affairs, was accompanied by new ways of thinking about the third world. U.S. President Harry Truman framed a new way of thinking from the core in his inaugural address in January 1949. He organized U.S. policy for the postwar Bretton Woods world, in opposition to the communism then spreading through eastern Europe, around four points: "unfaltering support to the United Nations and related agencies"; "world economic recovery," organized around economic reconstruction in Europe and Japan and free trade; international alliances to oppose communism; and "a bold new program for making the benefits of our scientific advances and industrial progress available for the improvement and growth of underdeveloped areas." The fourth point is worth quoting in detail:

> More than half the people of the world are living in conditions approaching misery. Their food is inadequate. They are victims of disease. Their economic life is primitive and stagnant. Their poverty is a handicap and a threat both to them and to more prosperous areas.
>
> For the first time in history, humanity possesses the knowledge and the skill to relieve the suffering of these people. The United States is pre-eminent among nations in the development of industrial and scientific techniques. The material resources which we can afford to use for the assistance of other peoples are limited. But our imponderable resources in technical knowledge are constantly growing and are inexhaustible.
>
> I believe that we should make available *to peace-loving peoples* the benefits of our store of technical knowledge in order to help them realize their aspirations for a better life. And, in cooperation with other nations, we should foster capital investment in areas needing development. Our aim should be to help *the free peoples of the world*, through their own efforts, to produce more food, more clothing, more materials for housing, and more mechanical power to lighten their burdens.
>
> We invite other countries to pool their technological resources in this undertaking. Their contributions will be warmly welcomed. This should be a cooperative enterprise in which all nations work together through the United Nations and its specialized agencies wherever practicable. It must be a worldwide effort for the achievement of peace, plenty, and freedom.
>
> With the cooperation of business, private capital, agriculture, and labor in this country, this program can greatly increase the industrial activity in other nations and can raise substantially their standards of living.
>
> Such new economic developments must be devised and controlled to benefit the peoples of the areas in which they are established. Guarantees to the investor must be balanced by guarantees in the interest of the people whose resources and whose labor go into these developments.
>
> The old imperialism—exploitation for foreign profit—has no place in our plans. What we envisage is a program of development based on the concepts of *democratic fair-dealing*. (Truman, 1949; emphasis added)

Truman's speech essentially inaugurated an era of thinking that framed social change in terms of national economic development. Indeed, some argue that this constituted the invention of development (Escobar, 1995; Rist, 1997), although the circulation of the idea in 19th-century Britain suggests that it is more accurate to refer to this as a period in which the idea became global in its scope and influence (Cowen and Shenton, 1996). Several aspects of this focus are worth noting. To begin with, it put economic processes at the core of development—as the essential element around which other societal processes would coalesce. In so doing, it attempted to construct a "new" discourse that replaced "the old imperialism" with developmentalism, while carefully adhering to the colonial logic of the white man's burden: A primitive and stagnant third world, steeped in poverty, disease, and misery, now needed to be saved by a "humanity" that "for the first time in history . . . possesses the knowledge and the skill to relieve the suffering of these people." The picture painted here is strikingly reminiscent of the Malthusian discourse on population (Chapter 6). Although Truman's address was framed in terms of "humanity" rather than "mankind," his conceptualization of peace, plenty, and freedom was guided by a technocratic logic that rendered it implicitly masculinist. Business, privatization, labor, and industrial activity were called upon to cooperate in ways that left little room for reciprocity between nature and humanity, or for alternative definitions of progress where peace, plenty, and freedom might exist outside of state-led capitalist economic development.

Three other features of Truman's speech helped flesh out this discursive framework.

First, it placed nation states at the center of thinking, as the scale where development would happen (replacing the scale of colonial empires, with which the United States, with its own history of anticolonial struggle followed by colonial possessions, had long had an uncomfortable relationship). Second, Truman excluded any nation states that in his view were not "peace-loving," "free," or "democratic" (by which he meant nation-states that did not organize themselves around the U.S.–European norm of capitalism and representative democracy). Finally, as under colonialism, societal change was conceptualized as a common set of stages—now described in terms of moving from less to more developed, or from traditional to modern, rather than from uncivilized or primitive to civilized. From the core, this was seen as a transition that any and every country could and should follow, catalyzing a series of theories of modernization and development. The peripheral perspective and experience were very different, however, catalyzing theories of underdevelopment and dependency.

VIEWS FROM THE CORE

Modernization Theories

The central tenet of modernization theories is the proposition that all nations occupy positions on a spectrum running from "traditional" societies at one extreme to "modern" societies at the other, and that nations may move from the former to the latter group by adopting the characteristics of "modern" societies. As we have described in Chapter 3, the roots of this approach lie back in the 19th century, in the social Darwinism of Herbert Spencer and others. Similar ideas underlay the social theories of Tönnies (1887/1957) and Durkheim (1893), and also accounted for the popularity of environmental determinism in geography at the turn of the century (Peet, 1985). However, the most influential recent research stemmed from the Americans Walt Rostow (1960) and Talcott Parsons (1961), who wrote major works during the optimism of the post-World War II economic boom.

Walt Rostow was an economic historian and an advisor to President John F. Kennedy. The subtitle of his 1960 book (*A Non-Communist Manifesto*) indicates his purpose: to refute Marx's theory of economic development. His ideas are worthy of scrutiny because they typify American optimism of the time that third world poverty could be eradicated through a diffusion of free market capitalism throughout the world; they also have renewed relevance today as precursors for structural adjustment policies. He envisioned five stages through which a society passes from traditional characteristics to maturity (see Table 4.1).

Rostow proposed a "dynamic theory of production" to explain the evolution from stage 2 to stage 5:

> . . . it is possible to define theoretical equilibrium positions not only for output, investment, and consumption as a whole, but for each sector of the economy. Within the framework set by forces determining the total level of output, sectoral optimum positions are determined on the side of demand, by the levels of income and of population, and by the character of tastes; on the side of supply, by the state of technology and the quality of entrepreneurship. . . . One must introduce an extremely significant empirical hypothesis: namely that deceleration is the normal optimum path of a sector, due to . . . supply and demand. . . . The equilibria which emerge from the application of these criteria are a set of sectoral paths, from which flows . . . a sequence of optimum patterns of investment. . . . The economic history of growing societies takes a part of its rude shape from the effort of societies to approximate the optimum sectoral paths. (1960: 13–14)

This passage reads impressively, but does not stand up well to theoretical analysis. Essentially, Rostow was asserting that consumer demand, entrepreneurship, and technical knowledge push the economy toward optimal paths of growth for each sector; and he implied that national economic growth

TABLE 4.1. Rostow's Stages of Economic Growth

Stage	Characteristics
1. Traditional society	Production and productivity are limited. Scientific knowledge is "pre-Newtonian." Society is heavily agricultural. The social and political structure is hierarchical. The value system is geared to fatalism.
2. Preconditions for takeoff	Productivity is still limited. The nation state is a necessary political development. Economic progress comes to be seen as necessary for public good. These preconditions generally come from some "external intrusion."
3. The takeoff	A rise in savings, and in investment in economic expansion, occurs. Agriculture becomes mechanized and commercialized. New production methods are developed. An expanding class of capitalists arises. "Compound interest gets built into" [the nation's] habits and institutional structure (Rostow, 1960: 36).
4. The drive to maturity	Output increases faster than population. The nation engages in specialization and international trade. A nation can produce what it chooses. "Dependence is a matter of economic choice rather than a technological or institutional necessity" (Rostow, 160: 10).
5. Age of high mass consumption	Production shifts to consumer goods and services. Real income can purchase much more than food and shelter. Quality of life becomes important, no longer being dominated by the wish to expand technology.
6. Beyond mass consumption	Increased value is given to nonmonetary aspects of life.

Source: Based on a discussion in Rostow (1960: 4–12.)

is governed by a dynamic tendency toward these optimal paths, interrupted by external shocks. He envisioned, then, a smoothly operating, relatively harmonious progression that approximates the best society can do, and that is governed by individual desires and initiative. However, he made no attempt to explain what processes bring this about; thus in the end the theory amounts to an assertion. Rostow's vision has been enduringly popular—partly because his assertions coincided with the theoretical conclusions reached by the dominant western economic theory of economic development, the neoclassical theory (see the next section); and partly because of its similarity to popular contemporary optimism that the rapid postwar growth being experienced by Europe and America would diffuse to the third world as former colonies gained their independence.

It is also unclear how, in Rostow's explanation, the preconditions for takeoff were developed endogenously in Europe, but only arrived in other countries by "external intrusion." There was certainly a Eurocentric sense here of some innate superiority in Britain or western Europe that brought about an early transition there, despite historical evidence suggesting otherwise (Blaut, 1993). Although Rostow saw his theory as a refutation of Marx's conception of economic development, he expounded a crude and inaccurate impression of Marx's own views. Rostow (1960: 149–156) argued that his theory was different from Marxism in the following ways:

1. Marx assumed that behavior is entirely governed by rational calculation of economic costs and benefits, whereas Rostow saw his own approach as allowing for the fact that people seek "also power, leisure, adventure, continuity of experience and security" (149). He argued that this was what made Marx's theory excessively dependent on economic determinism.
2. Marx adopted an excessively Malthusian view of population change, by comparison to Rostow.
3. Marx thought that the ownership of capital would become increasingly concentrated, and that economic crises would become increasingly severe as a result of long-run declines in profits, whereas Rostow argued that this was not true.

The first two points are clearly misdirected. It is widely accepted, by critics and supporters alike, that Marx had a very broad view of humankind; indeed, it was the neoclassical economists, whose theory supported Rostow's assumptions, who were known for their use of the assumption of "rational economic man" (Hollis and Nell, 1975). Furthermore, Marx's theory of population explicitly and fundamentally opposed that of Malthus.

Although Rostow laid an economic foundation for a theory of modernization, this theory has been most widely propagated as a sociological concept. Its modern roots are in American sociologist Talcott Parsons's influential "structural–functional" theory of society (Parsons, 1948), which he later applied to the question of social change (Parsons, 1961, 1966). Other prominent writers on modernization included Hoselitz (1955), Lerner (1957), McClelland (1961), and Eisenstadt (1965). Briefly, to summarize a very ingenious and complex argument, Parsons's theory was an attempt to use systems theory to account for the relationship between actions taken by individuals, and the broader structure of society. On the one hand, he asserted individual actions to be the result of conscious decisions made by actors. The structure of society was seen as important, however, in determining the "pattern variables," which form the context in which such decisions are taken. Parsons took the functionalist view that since societies seem by and large stable and able to reproduce themselves from one year to the next, then the structure of society must influence the pattern variables to take a form ensuring that the conscious decisions made by individuals will be consistent with what is required for that society to continue to exist. In this way, he conceptualized individuals as having freedom to act as they wish, without those actions threatening the stability of the society of which they are a part. As a result, Parsons saw a society as analogous to a natural organism, containing a set of necessary roles and functions that have to be, and will be, performed by members of that society (see sidebar: "Parsons on Social Change").

Parsons's theory implies that all societies are on a path toward greater and greater complexity, implying increased differentiation and specialization of roles. This common path became termed "modernization." Thus it was suggested that more modern societies are those with a more sophisticated division of labor, a stronger individualistic motivation to achieve success, a competitive capitalist system of production and exchange, a more integrated society with well-developed and flexible systems of transportation and communication, better education, and greater individual participation in political processes (Hoselitz, 1955; McClelland, 1961; Riddell, 1970; Soja and Tobin, 1977; Taaffe, Morrill, and Gould, 1963).

This conclusion was strengthened by combining Parsons's conclusions with the proposition of Max Weber that a characteristic of modernization is an increase in

Parsons on Social Change

Parsons argued:

1. A society is thought to be in a state of equilibrium with its environment. Social change should be analyzed with respect to the way in which changes in this environment introduce stress into a social system, upsetting this equilibrium.
2. The society must then move from its old equilibrium to a new equilibrium. This can only be done by creating new roles within society, which can carry out the new tasks necessitated by incorporating the external change.
3. Consequently, the system must become more and more complex over time, with an increasingly sophisticated differentiation in the roles it performs. All transitions from one equilibrium to another require increased differentiation, since a more complex system is better able to adapt to its environment.
4. Reintegratory mechanisms must therefore be created during the transition period from one equilibrium to the next, in order to handle conflicts that arise during the transition. Either new institutions must be formed for this purpose, or old ones must be adapted.

activities involving calculated rational action directed toward certain well-defined goals. The degree to which societies have achieved these goals then became taken as an empirical measure of their degree of integration (Taylor, 1979). It also led to proposals for facilitating development by inculcating the entrepreneurial ethic into populations of third world countries, as McClelland (1961) proposed for India. Modernization theorists saw the mechanisms that should ensure the dominance of the pattern variables representing a "modern" society over other variables as including the creation of innovative modernizing elites (Eisenstadt, 1965) to promote capitalist production/exchange, pluralist political systems, urbanization, education, and a more nationalistic military (Taylor, 1979).

A critical evaluation of the theory of modernization must start with an examination of Parsons's structural–functional theory (Taylor, 1979). Recall the functional argument that since societies are relatively stable, then there must exist pattern variables that are ensuring a consistency between individual action and social reproduction. In making this argument, Parsons did not provide any theory to deduce, from the requirements of the social system, exactly which phenomena must be present to ensure societal reproduction. Essentially, he was asserting that in each society the appropriate institutions will develop to satisfy its functional needs, without telling us how this happens (cf. Chapter 1 sidebar, "Goldschmidt on Affect Hunger"). The theory then depends on an inductive conclusion from the observation that societies are fairly stable, rather than providing a deductive explanation of how stability comes about. This logical problem, a feature of all functionalist explanations, means that Parsons was unable to tell us exactly which phenomena must be present in a society. Consequently, he fell back on an empirical generalization: Those phenomena that we do observe in a society must be playing this role. However, his theory is thus distinctly oriented toward the status quo: The phenomena that are deduced as necessary for a society to survive are restricted to those we observe around us. Consequently, Parsons and other modernization theorists were forced to conclude that the characteristics of "modern" societies are necessary for development, and should be adopted by others seeking to modernize.

The modernization theories propounded by Rostow and Parsons have two principal weaknesses. First, there is no attempt to explain why the external changes occur to which the social system then responds. Implicitly these are seen as diffusing in from other, "more advanced" societies. But how, then, did change originate in *these* societies? This is not discussed. Second, the set of phenomena supposed to ensure societal reproduction is established by observing "modern" societies, rather than deduced from analysis of other possibilities. The only information available to explain how, say, Chad can modernize today are observations on how other societies have modernized in the past. It is thus small wonder that the blueprint for modernization has a Eurocentric flavor to it; the theories provide no mechanism that allows one to go beyond generalizations based in historical observations. Indeed, the key assertion suggesting a path of development—that increased societal differentiation and specialization will always occur (points 2 and 3 in the Parsons sidebar)—is also not deduced in any way, but is at best an analogy from our knowledge of the development of natural organisms, and of "modern" societies.

Marginalist Theories of Economic Growth

Shortly after the publication of Marx's devastating critique of classical economic thought in 1867, an alternative viewpoint emerged in European economics. This view attempted to turn the classical political economic thinking of Smith and Ricardo (see Chapter 3) on its head: Instead of analyzing the conditions by which societies can increase their production of goods and a surplus, as Ricardo and Marx had, it focused on the allocation of scarce resources among competing ends, emphasizing the importance of demand in determining the market price of these goods. This school then naturally concentrated on exchange in the market rather than on production, leading to a completely different set of questions from those that Marx had been able to exploit successfully. These ideas had circulated since the 1830s (cf. Cournot, 1838), but they were unpopular until the 1870s, when several people reinvented them simultaneously, in Britain, Austria and France (Jevons, 1871; Menger, 1871; Walras, 1874; for an elaboration, see Pasinetti, 1981).

This paradigm became known as the "marginalist" revolution, because it was based on the principle that the worth of a good is equal to its marginal utility (which in turn depends on its scarcity; the more of a good that a person has, the less use an extra unit of it is to her or him). This approach became central to economic thinking about development once it was extended to consider not only the price of goods bought by consumers, but also the price of capital and labor bought by producers. This extension was supposed to integrate the classical economists' concerns about production into the marginalist approach, producing what has become known as the "neoclassical synthesis."

This approach produces a simplified model by means of which the dynamics of economic growth in a country are deduced. The simplest version of this approach starts with the following assumptions:

a. Economic production can be represented in a simplified form by a relationship called a "production function." This states that the quantity of goods produced in a country depends on the quantity of labor, capital, and technical knowledge available in that country. These three inputs are themselves known as "factors of production."

b. Typically, the production function is assumed to have the following properties: (1) If the amount of all factors of production is increased by an equal proportion, then the quantity of goods produced also increases by this proportion ("constant returns to scale"); and (2) if the amount of any one factor is increased by a certain proportion, while the supply available of the other factors remains the same, then the quantity of goods produced will increase by less than this proportion ("diminishing returns to a factor of production" or "diminishing marginal productivity"). Taken together, these characteristics imply that the quantity of goods produced in a nation, and thus its rate of economic growth, depend on the *relative* availability of production factors.

c. Labor and capital are fully employed; there is no unemployment, and no money, land, or equipment is underutilized.

d. If economic markets are allowed to operate freely, the wage paid to labor, and the rate of profit made on capital, are each equal to the technical contribution that the labor and capital present in a country will make to economic production. Thus, for example, if it can be shown that the present levels of technical knowledge, capital, and labor available imply that one extra laborer will increase the hourly output of goods in a country by a value of $3.75, then the wage paid to that worker in a free market will be $3.75. In other words, the economic price of a factor of production is equal to its marginal productivity.

e. The greater the relative availability of a production factor in a country, the lower its marginal productivity, and consequently the lower its price.

Starting with these assumptions, and mathematically analyzing their consequences, the American and British neoclassical theorists and Nobel laureates Robert Solow and George Meade reached the following conclusions about national economic growth (Meade, 1961; Solow, 1956):

1. The best long-run rate of economic growth is a rate balancing the rate of growth of the labor force and of technical knowledge.

2. Under conditions of free competition (see assumption d above), the national economy will adjust itself, automatically converging on this optimal growth rate over time.

The central proposition of the neoclassical theory, then, is that an optimal rate of economic growth can be achieved if free capitalist competition prevails in a nation. Having reached this conclusion, neoclassical writers were then faced with explaining why the rate of growth has historically been less in third world countries that have attempted to follow the capitalist path to development. Both internal and external conditions have been seen as explaining this. Internally, the barriers to a higher rate of growth in the third world have been argued to include such things as excessive population growth, creating too much labor for the nation to absorb (which violates the full employment assumption); lack of education and technical knowledge; lack of domestic saving; and restrictions on economic competition, which result in an inefficient allocation of productive resources among economic sectors. Note that each of these explains the difference in terms of a claimed deficiency in third world nations by comparison to a first world model. Externally, it is argued that the world market does not operate freely. Restrictions on the international movement of factors of production, and on international commodity trade, must be removed if all countries are to achieve equal rates of economic growth.

To understand the rationale for this last argument, it is necessary to understand how removal of these restrictions will, in the neoclassical view, lead to a reduction in growth rate differentials between developed and underdeveloped nations. Let us consider each in turn. Consider first the flow of production factors. We use a simple example to lay open the basis of the neoclassical argument. Suppose there are two countries: one with a skilled labor force, relatively low unemployment rates, and a generally capital-intensive economy; and the other with unskilled labor, high unemployment, and generally little in the way of capital investment. Let us call the former a core country and the latter a country of the periphery. In the core, we would expect to observe a high growth rate, a relative shortage of labor, and a relative surplus of capital, whereas the opposite conditions hold in the periphery. Under these conditions (using the assumptions defining a production function, the payment of labor and capital according to their productivity, and marginal productivity as falling with the availability of capital or labor), neoclassical theory would suggest that wages will be higher in the core where labor is short, and similarly that profit rates will be higher in the periphery. If we further assume that unrestricted international movement of production factors will lead to a flow of labor from the periphery to the core (seeking higher wages), and a reverse flow of capital (seeking higher profits), then the following theoretical conclusion can be added:

3. An unrestricted international market for labor and capital will lead to a reduction in growth rate differences between the core and the periphery. This occurs because the imbalances in the relative quantity of labor and capital between core and periphery will largely disappear, as a result of the international movement of production factors in response to geographical differences in the economic rewards (wages and profits) that these factors can earn.

Conclusion 3 follows from the earlier propositions. If the growth rate depends on the relative availability of production factors (assumption b), and if these factors migrate in such a way as to reduce international inequalities in their relative availability, then the growth rates must become more and more equal as time goes on. The role of differences in technology has been ignored in this argument, but it can be easily introduced without changing the results. Indeed, technical knowledge is treated as a production factor like labor and capital—a factor that, in an unfettered global market, will flow from places of surplus (the core) to places of shortage.

At the international scale, it is often thought that a free international movement of capital and labor mobility is unlikely. However, this is not a major problem in the neoclassical view, because there exists another mechanism that will equalize the chances for economic development even in the absence of such mobility. This mechanism is free trade. Neoclassical theory has taken the free trade argument of Torrens and Ricardo and generalized it to apply under the neoclassical assumptions described above. This doctrine is captured in the following theoretical proposition (based on the arguments of Hecksher, 1919; Ohlin, 1933; Samuelson, 1953–1954):

4. Countries stand to gain economically if they specialize in producing certain commodities, and if they trade the excess they produce to other countries in exchange for other imports. In order to benefit from this, a country should examine the relative quantity of the various production factors available locally, and the inputs required to produce various commodities. It should then specialize in those economic activities requiring more of the production factor or factors that are locally most abundant. If many countries do this, then together they will produce more of all commodities than they would by a strategy of self-sufficiency.

This result also stems from the basic assumptions outlined above, particularly assumptions d and e, which state that the most abundant factor will be the cheapest one. If countries use a lot of their cheapest factors, then specialization and trade provide for a greater surplus than self-sufficiency does. This is intuitively appealing, since instead of saying that local conditions in a country can act as a barrier to growth, it argues that countries stand to gain by exploiting these differences. However, it fails to answer the crucial question of how this surplus is divided up between the trading countries. For example, if underdeveloped countries gain by 10% from specialization and trade, but developed countries gain by 15%, then, although both may gain, the differences in growth rates between core and periphery will only widen. Thus free trade, even under the assumptions of the neoclassical theory, provides no guarantee of any international convergence of growth rates. We return to this issue in Chapters 15 and 16.

In summary, the neoclassical viewpoint clearly promotes the position that equality in development can be promoted by allowing for as free an operation as possible of market forces in the world economy, supporting the global propagation of a capitalist economic system. However, the argument is based on acceptance of the five key assumptions (a–e). It was thought for some time that the assumptions that wages and profits will equal the marginal productivity of labor and capital, respectively (assumption d), and that marginal productivity will fall with the availability of capital or labor (assumption e), were not assumptions at all, but could be logically deduced from the assumptions of a production function, diminishing returns, and full employment of labor and capital. This has now been shown to be untrue, however. Indeed, such a deduction is only valid under the same limiting conditions that allowed Marx to claim that labor values equal prices (i.e., every economic sector uses the identical technology); this is ironic, given that neoclassical researchers gained much mileage from criticizing Marx's theory for the narrowness of these conditions (Harcourt, 1972). Furthermore, it has been shown that if assumptions d and e are invalid, then none of the theoretical propositions 1–3 is necessarily true. Thus we may conclude that although the neoclassical theory provides one viewpoint, there is no basis for accepting it as a superior explanation.

The neoclassical theory was popular in the 1950s and early 1960s—a period when the postwar economic boom seemed to provide the potential of prosperity for all (at least from the perspective of the developed countries). During the global economic crises of the late 1960s and 1970s, it fell out of favor, to be replaced by the theories of dualism and core–periphery (discussed below). Now, however, with the apparently corroborative evidence of rapid development in at least some third world countries, and with new mathematical pyrotechnics, it is receiving a new lease on life; under the new moniker of "neoliberal globalization," it is once again becoming the development theory of choice in the international policy arena (Chapter 5).

Dualism and Core–Periphery Approaches

West Indian/British economist W. Arthur Lewis (1954), recognizing that development within third world countries was creating a polarization between a "modern" and a "traditional" sector that did not seem to be diminishing, developed a Nobel Prize-winning dualist theory of economic development. The traditional sector is characterized by subsistence wages and a surplus of labor. This surplus is characterized as "inefficient"; the same agricultural production could be obtained from a much smaller labor force. The modern sector is characterized by capitalist production using more productive and capital-intensive technologies. In Lewis's theory, these two sectors essentially exist in parallel with one another, the former being left over from traditional society. The traditional sector is seen as a sphere into which modernization is having trouble diffusing, but this barrier to complete modernization can be broken down by fostering capitalist initiative. If capitalists hire workers from the traditional sector at a wage just a bit above subsistence levels, they can attract workers from the traditional sector and also make significant profits because of these low wages. The size of these profits should induce capitalists to reinvest them in expanded production, gradually attracting more and more of the surplus labor from the traditional sector until labor is efficiently allocated between the two sectors. Some labor will remain in "traditional" activities because, as more people take up work in the modern sector, there will eventually develop a shortage of food production due to a shortage of labor. As a result, food prices increase, making participation in the traditional sector more attractive.

It is clear from this description that Lewis's theory brings together explicitly the theories of modernization and of neoclassical economics. The modern–traditional dualism is characteristic of the former, whereas the relation between optimal production and the reallocation of labor is a neoclassical idea. Lewis's theory shows how closely intertwined the two approaches are. Concomitantly, several criticisms of these two approaches can also be applied to his theory.

Swedish economist and Nobel laureate Gunnar Myrdal (1957), together with American economist Albert Hirschman (1958) and Austrian/American planner John Friedmann (1966), developed a dualistic perspective similar to that of Lewis, but focusing more on geographical differences within both first world and third world nations, and with varying degrees of pessimism about whether such spatial dualisms can be overcome. These authors were concerned with the geographical equivalent of Lewis's dualism—particularly the way in which third world societies were polarizing into a growing "modern" core region linked to the international economy, and a stagnating "traditional" periphery. They saw this split occurring both at an international scale (between rich and poor lands) and also within countries. The core of their analyses is a critique of the assumption in neoclassical and modernization theories that the dynamics of capitalist development are characterized by a progressive elimination of geographical differences in economic welfare. They pointed out that the multiplier effects of an investment tend to be localized and will not diffuse readily to other locations. Myrdal captured this idea in the concept of "circular and cumulative causation." He argued that instead of development spreading out in space, there is instead a "backwash" effect: The flows of migration, capital, and international trade can exacerbate rather than reduce inequalities. Hirschman and Friedmann developed similar arguments that spatially unbalanced growth is the rule rather than the exception. Whereas Hirschman and Friedmann were somewhat optimistic that ways can be found to overcome these imbalances, and even to exploit them by concentrating investment in peripheral regions in the hope that the local multiplier effect will help stimulate these places, Myrdal was quite pessimistic and foresaw no significant reduction in inequalities. These authors offered no well-crafted theory of the processes causing spatial polarization, since they concentrated on revealing limitations of neoclassical theory. The challenge of constructing such a theory was to be taken up by Latin American writers (see "Views from the Periphery," below).

State-Led Development

As noted above, policies of economic development were conceived within a particular geopolitical framework—that of nation states. During the 1940s, the idea of *the* national economy became commonplace for the first time (Mitchell, 2002). National sovereignty was viewed as including the power to control the national border (regulating trade, capital, technology, and labor crossings), and to regulate and manage economic activities within that border, in the name of maximizing economic growth. Although markets were seen as vital to economic prosperity, it was also generally agreed across the political spectrum that continual state intervention is necessary, because markets often fail to deliver on the theoretical promise. From the perspective of the core, this came to mean a Keynesian or Fordist approach to managing the national economy. In brief, the idea was that the state can intervene in times of economic crisis by spending money to stimulate consumer demand, which should then catalyze new economic production. Henry Ford pursued this principle in his Model T plant, where he paid his workers enough to buy the cars they were making. Franklin D. Roosevelt applied the same idea at the national scale to pull the U.S. out of the Great Depression, through public works programs and (particularly after 1941) war-related expenditures. British economist John Maynard Keynes provided the economic theory justifying such policies.

Throughout the 1950s and 1960s, first world nation states fostered a particular regulatory arrangement between capitalists and organized labor: a policy of big business, big labor, and big government. Indeed, in a number of "corporatist" political regimes in western Europe (e.g., Germany, Austria, Sweden), the national economy was managed through a formal cooperation among large corporations, labor unions, and the nation state. A symbiotic policy was conceived, whereby unionized workers were paid good wages, and would purchase the durable consumer goods that large corporations specialized in producing (automobiles, homes, appliances). The state helped manage labor relations along these lines; provided subsidies and other state spending to further catalyze such demand (e.g., the U.S. tax break on mortgage interest, and highway construction stimulating suburbanization); and underwrote all of this with welfare state policies providing a safety net for the least well off (Aglietta, 1979; Dunford, 1990; Walker, 1981). A social contract thus emerged between nation states and their citizens (it was unequally extended to noncitizens), guaranteeing certain individual rights and protections in return for the expectation that citizens would act responsibly by paying taxes, voting, and contributing to national welfare. Those unable or unwilling to contribute became caught in the safety net, placed under the tutelage and supervision of state agencies charged with getting them back on track. Through such processes, which Foucault (1991) has termed "governmentality," individuals internalized and reproduced expected behavior (see also Rose, 1999). At the subnational scale, Fordism also often involved policies aimed at equalizing opportunity across space (seeking to reduce geographical differences in prosperity, access to employment, etc.).

In short, markets were regulated at the national scale, to mitigate social conflict in order to underwrite national growth combined with broad socioeconomic prosperity. Following the stageist nature of core thinking about development (i.e., the concept that development means passing through a predetermined sequence of stages), it was expected that Fordist principles should also be followed by third world states. Thus attempts by certain more "advanced" third world nations to foster their own durable manufacturing behind tariff walls (import-substituting industrialization) were looked on favorably by first world nation states and the supranational Bretton Woods institutions (the International Monetary Fund [IMF] and the World Bank; see Chapter 23) that they dominated. Yet this was much easier to manage in first world nations, which were able to maintain favorable trade relations with third world nations that allowed first world countries to keep production costs low while exporting surplus manufacturing production. Even in the first world, however, this regulatory system soon showed signs of strain (Chapter 5). Internally, many were left out of the symbiosis between organized labor and the private sector, and high wages eventually became a burden for industries where profits were stagnating. Externally, third world nations (as well as low-wage regions within first world nations) offered low-wage production locations that, together with new technologies, pushed first world firms to outsource jobs abroad.

Women in Development

As struggles for emancipation of "women" progressed in the first world, core thinking about development expanded to embrace questions of gender.[1] Such core thinking was encapsulated in the idea of "women in development" (WID). Prior to WID, welfarism existed as an extension of liberal western ideologies of relief aid and addressed itself to the needs of vulnerable groups, poor women being its major clients. In the male-dominated realm of development agencies, a bourgeois definition of "woman" and her essential identity as a wife and mother had framed welfare strategies that were defined as appropriate for impoverished third world women. Accordingly, such approaches centered on programs that addressed nutritional education, home economics, reproductive role of women, mother–child health, and family planning. The issues of population and its management, rather than being seen as structural or power-laden, were regarded in this approach as functions of the dissemination of birth control information and contraceptives (Crehan, 1983; Saunders, 2002b; Urdang, 1983).

Three works that are regarded as among the best illustrations of WID arguments are Boserup's (1970) seminal *Women's Role in Economic Development*, along with Tinker's (1976) and Rogers's (1980) critiques of mainstream development and its adverse impact on women. Although these authors accepted the modernist classification of societies into subsistence and modern sectors and sometimes drew rather heavily on the neoclassical notion of universal economic rationality, they questioned the assumptions that (1) the benefits of development will automatically trickle down to the poor, and that (2) women everywhere are confined to the private or "nonproductive" sphere of economic activities. For example, Boserup (1970: 50) contrasted the "male farming systems" of south and west Asia with what she labeled as the "female farming systems" of sub-Saharan Africa and parts of southeast Asia, and pointed out how women in the latter regions enjoyed "considerable freedom of movement and some economic independence." She further identified how the prevailing norms of male privilege in training and access to credit led to men's dominance in the formal, paid employment in the "modern" sector, while the women remained confined primarily to the subsistence and informal sectors. WID theorists criticized development planners for rendering women invisible in the planning process (Tinker, 1976) and for treating them as secondary earners who were only deemed fit to be trained as more efficient housewives (Boserup, 1970). In making policy recommendations, then, these critics advocated better-designed opportunities that could help women to enhance their competitiveness and productivity in a male-dominated economy without superimposing western values regarding appropriate work for women (Rogers, 1980).

In this way, WID attacked the dominant welfarist image of women as mere nurturers and sought to establish them as capable of fully participating in rational, aggressive, and competitive market-driven capitalist development. It articulated an efficiency-based argument for the integration of women into development through access to training and resources. Influenced simultaneously by the institutionalized field of modernization and development and the feminist movement in the west in the 1970s, WID initially emerged as a women's caucus within the Society for International Development to promote professional employment opportunities for women in development agencies, and to compile data exploring the proposition that development was adversely affecting impoverished women in the third world. WID became hegemonic in the field of feminist development practices, experiencing increasing legitimacy and integration with major bilateral and multilateral development agencies, as well as in international advocacy and organizations such as the United Nations. Ironically, however, the advocates of WID "continued to perpetuate images of impoverished Third World women as helpless victims of patriarchy, since such representation authorized their right to organize a planned liberation of this client population, construed as lacking the sovereign power to liberate itself" (Saunders, 2002a: 5; see also Spivak, 2000).

Imperialism as Pioneer of Capitalism

Planning the liberation of a client population, or creating stagist theories of social change based in economic mechanisms, is far from the exclusive province of mainstream and neoclassical economists. We have suggested earlier that Marx's vision of development can also be interpreted as a universal schema for all nations. In such an interpretation (and not necessarily Marx's), all societies need to pass through the disruptive but highly technologically and politically liberating stage of capitalism before true emancipation of all people can be achieved, by the abandonment of capitalism for socialist and communist social systems. Capitalism is seen as a necessary evil, creating the democratic institutions and technological skills necessary to uncover the inequities and contradictions of capitalism and to progress beyond it. A particularly diffusionist application of Marxist thinking can be found in the work of British Marxist Bill Warren (1980). He has argued that all third world nations must experience capitalist development as part of the path to development, and that any processes accelerating the diffusion of first world style capitalism throughout the third world are politically progressive because they accelerate third world development. In this view, the failure of communism in the Soviet Union can be explained by the fact that this region did not experience capitalist development, because through the Bolshevik Revolution Russia leapfrogged from feudalism directly into communism.

Warren's view differs radically from most other diffusionist views of the 20th century, which see capitalism not as a necessary evil on the path to development, but as the desirable endpoint of that path. Nonetheless, all diffusionist views assume that there is a single best path to development; that this path approximates the historical experience of the first world; and that imperialism and the global reach of large corporations are good for the third world in the long run, no matter what short-term adjustment problems they cause. Indeed, a reading of Warren's empirical analysis shows a remarkable similarity to neoliberal development theory in its interpretation of how the spread of markets relates to improvements in economic welfare, and how shared visions of development can transcend political ideologies. In fact, there was much debate among Marxists in the early years of the 20th century about the role of imperialism in third world nations and about whether capitalism is necessary to development. As we see in the following section, Lenin's negative answer to the latter question provided an intellectual foundation for the Bolshevik intervention, and also opened the door for alternative paths to development.

VIEWS FROM THE PERIPHERY

> When we consider what is happening both in our country and in other parts of the world, we are forced to take another look at the idea of development at top speed at any cost. Let us forget for a moment the crimes and stupidities that have been committed in the name of development from Communist Russia to India, from [the] Argentina of Perón to the Egypt of Nasser, and let us look at what is happening in the United States and Western Europe: the destruction of the ecological balance, the contamination of lungs and of spirits, the psychic damage to the young, the abandoning of the elderly, the erosion of the sensibilities, the corruption of the imagination, the debasement of sex, the accumulation of wastes, the explosions of hatred. Faced as we are by all this, how can we not turn away and seek another mode of development? It is an urgent task that requires both science and imagination,

> both honesty and sensitivity; a task without precedence, because all of the modes of development that we know, whether they come from the West or the East, lead to disaster. Under the present circumstances the race toward development is mere haste to reach ruin. . . .
>
> Can we devise more humane models that correspond to what we are? As people on the fringes, inhabitants of the suburbs of history, we Latin Americans are uninvited guests who have sneaked in through the West's back door, intruders who have arrived at the feast of modernity as the lights were about to be put out. We arrive late everywhere, we were born when it was already late in history, we have no past or, if we have one, we spit on its remains. . . . Will we now, at last, be capable of thinking for ourselves?
>
> —OCTAVIO PAZ (1972: 46–47; ix–x)[2]

Mexican writer Octavio Paz is no political radical, yet he perceives well that third world experiences of development are quite different from first world experiences. Different experiences engender different ways of thinking about the world. Diffusionist thinking is rooted in a positive experience, and in the belief that others also should and can benefit from this success. Thus development is seen as a common goal, to be reached by paths that have already proven successful and that can universalize this experience of development if they are propagated from more to less developed places. There is an Enlightenment optimism about development, holding out the prospect of prosperity without limits or regrets, and a confidence that the first world knows how to achieve it.

Third world experiences (whether in third world nations or within third world enclaves of first world nations) are different. The interrogations emanating from these experiences has brought about a revolution in development thinking—challenging the tenets of modernization theory and seeking to rewrite what "development" means (Slater, 2004).

The experience of national political independence from colonial masters was followed by greater differences in economic prosperity between most first and third world nations, rather than the promised convergence. Because of this, writers taking a peripheral perspective have argued that the very mechanisms hypothesized by Rostow and his successors as prerequisites for development have the opposite effect. Dependency theorists and their successors share a similar vision of development (as economic prosperity) with diffusionist thinkers, but have assembled evidence and arguments to show how the integration of third world nations into a world system of nation states and global capitalism has created underdevelopment in the periphery of this system. In the hands of these theorists, "underdevelopment" has been reconceptualized from an original condition that must be overcome to an active process that German sociologist André Gunder Frank dubbed "the development of underdevelopment." The notion that different parts of the world might experience different trajectories of development dates back to Bolshevik debates in Russia (then on the European periphery) in the 1920s, particularly the ideas of Vladimir Lenin. Argentinian economist Raúl Prebisch, other *dependentistas* from Latin America, and Egyptian economist Samir Amin have made central contributions in this area. Frank has popularized dependency theory in the Anglophone literature, and American sociologist Immanuel Wallerstein and Italian American sociologist Giovanni Arrighi have also made signal Anglophone contributions.

The Development of Underdevelopment

The term "underdevelopment" was originally used by core thinkers such as Rostow to refer to the conditions found in a country before development begins (i.e., the barriers and limits to be overcome by development and modernization). This view itself entails a pejorative view of societies that have not joined the development bandwagon; it implies that life begins with development, and that other "traditional" or "primitive" social systems are not to be taken seriously and must be abandoned to achieve progress. However, the persistent political and social problems of development faced by countries outside western Europe and North America after 1945 led academics and policymakers in these countries to question the thesis that it was only a matter of time before the benefits of development would diffuse to these locations. Rather than seeing underdevelopment as a problem that the diffusion of development can overcome, they began to argue that underdevelopment itself is intricately linked to the worldwide spread of capitalist production and market exchange. These views bear some similarity to those of Lewis, Myrdal, and Hirschman, but their early exponents predate these authors (Bagú, 1949; Lenin, 1917/1933).

Development in the European Periphery and the Theory of Imperialism

Debates in Russia between the 1890s and 1920s about the direction that development should take catalyzed the first influential European challenge to the assumption that all countries follow the same path to development. After the social revolution of 1905, Tsar Nicholas II's minister Peter Stolypin attempted to stave off further social unrest by introducing capitalist reforms into Russia in order to create economic prosperity, much as Russian politicians attempted to do in the 1990s. This brought to a head a furious debate among the radical opponents of Tsarist Russia, both before and after the Bolshevik Revolution of 1917 that finally overthrew the Tsar, about whether Russia should proceed to capitalism as a necessary precursor to socialism (Palma, 1981). Notwithstanding their serious differences, most proponents in this debate agreed that economic relations between the European capitalist nations and Russia had already created conditions in Russia that were sufficiently different to suggest that the European path of capitalism was not necessarily appropriate for Russia.

The view that became most influential, both within Russia and for development theory more generally, was that of Vladimir Lenin. Lenin's analysis of the Russian situation concentrated on the situation of Russia with respect to the European capitalist nations, in the context of the existing political, social, and economic institutions of Tsarist Russia. On the one hand, the late start of industrial production meant a much slower process of industrialization in Russia—partly because it had to compete with surviving traditional structures, and partly because of international competition with the more efficient producers of Europe. On the other hand, there was already extensive investment of foreign capital from Europe in Russia, which, though accelerating the process of industrialization, tended to limit the possibility of indigenous Russian capitalism. At the same time, Lenin argued that the considerable concentration of the ownership of financial and productive capital in a few hands made it easier to transfer these assets to state ownership. Thus, he argued, the situation of Russia in the world economy suggested the need for an alternative path to economic development—a direct transition to socialism.

This analysis was generalized into a theory of imperialism (Lenin, 1916/1970). Lenin's theory contains the following propositions:

1. Capitalism has reached the phase where a considerable portion of capital is concentrated in the hands of relatively few monopolies.
2. Because of their monopoly position, these companies retain an excess of profits, and an overaccumulation of capital results. This money is under the control of a financial oligarchy, finance capital, formed from a merger of banks and industrial producers.
3. This excess of capital is exported to underdeveloped countries, where a higher

rate of profit on production is possible because of available raw materials and cheap labor.
4. The result is an international diffusion of commodity production under the control of companies of the industrialized world.

Lenin's approach represented a turning point, because for the first time it was being argued that the penetration of capitalism into a noncapitalist society could lead to effects other than those already observed in other capitalist societies. In short, it allowed for the possibility of alternative paths to development, or to underdevelopment (Palma, 1981). This contrasted with the views of previous writers on imperialism such as Marx who contended that although imperialism hinders industrial development, the disappearance of colonial bonds and monopolies should eventually lead to industrialization. Yet, while Lenin wrote that capitalism brings about greater underdevelopment, he did not incorporate this fully into his theory of imperialism, and never spelled out under what conditions it occurs (Howe, 1981). This conclusion was nevertheless used to justify Soviet support for socialist revolution in the third world.

Whereas Lenin saw the theory of imperialism as a logical consequence of applying Marx's theory to a situation that Marx had never analyzed (i.e., monopoly capitalism), others have taken this theory in different directions. Barratt-Brown (1974) points out that imperialism, as an expression of how global economic and political relations have created inequalities of power and asymmetrical relations of dependence between nations, has been discussed by neoclassical, Keynesian, and Marxist economists. Within Marxist research, there have been differences in opinion about whether imperialism requires the superprofits associated with monopoly capitalism (Emmanuel, 1972; Luxemburg, 1915/1951), and about whether it is a permanent feature of global capitalism (Emmanuel, 1972) or a temporary holdover from the colonial era (Warren, 1980). There is nonetheless a common logic to these theories of imperialism (see sidebar: "Galtung's Structural Theory of Imperialism").

Trade and Underdevelopment

The United Nations Economic Commission for Latin America (ECLA) was organized in 1948 as a regional commission headquartered in Santiago, Chile. In the 1950s, it forged a considerable name for itself with a distinctive explanation of development under the aegis of its director, economist Raúl Prebisch. Prebisch (1959) argued that the lack of development in Latin America could be attributed to the unequal effects of international trade. The argument was as follows:

1. Historically, the rate of growth of productivity in industrial production has been faster than that for primary goods.
2. Increased productivity in manufacturing leads to a lowering of their costs, and this should theoretically be translated into a lowering of their price compared to primary products. This has not happened, however, because the struggle between organized labor and capitalists in the developed countries has kept wages high there. They have been able to pass the costs of this on to less developed countries in the form of higher prices because of their political and economic power in the international market. By contrast, the prices of primary products have fallen; however, since these are primarily exported, the main beneficiaries of this have been consumers in the industrial countries rather than consumers in the underdeveloped countries.
3. Therefore, the developed countries have been able to gain a disproportionate share of the gains accruing from technological progress and from trade, in the form of capital that could be used to fuel a faster rate of growth in those countries.
4. The result is that international trade exacerbates rather than reduces interna-

Galtung's Structural Theory of Imperialism

Swedish sociologist Johann Galtung (1971) concisely summarized the overall logic of imperialism. He began by noting that the world economy can be divided into "center" and "periphery" nations, and that within each such nation there is also an "elite," defined as the influential social and political groups, and a "non-elite," defined as the remaining members of society. He then argued that imperialism is a relation between a center and a periphery nation, whereby (1) there is a harmony of interest between the elites in the center nation and the elites in the periphery nation; (2) there is conflict of interest between elites and non-elites in both the center and periphery nations, but this conflict is greater within the periphery nation; and (3) there is disharmony of interest between the non-elites in the center nation and the non-elites in the periphery nation.

In this view, imperialism is a consequence of economic, political, and cultural relations between center and periphery nations, propagated by the elites of the center nations and accepted by the elites of the periphery because they stand to gain from these relations. For this reason, imperialism is not restricted to periods of colonialism, but can occur whenever the interests of center elites coincide with those of peripheral elites. Yet, since these relations serve peripheral elites, they are against the development interests of non-elites in the periphery. Finally, although there is a conflict of interest between elites and non-elites in the center, imperialist relations hurting peripheral elites are actually beneficial to center non-elites. This secures the support of all social groups in the center, together with elites in the periphery, for imperialist relations that hurt non-elites in the periphery—numerically by far the largest of these four social groups in the world economy.

tional inequalities in levels of economic development.

This argument, in which manufacturing prices are influenced more by production costs and political power than by demand, is essentially rooted in Keynesian economics. Not surprisingly, this compromise between neoclassical and Marxist explanations has been criticized from both the left and the right. Neoclassical economists argue that it ignores the role of demand; if prices for industrial goods stay high, it is because people value these goods, and thus high (and low) prices cannot be construed as unfair. In response to this, later ECLA analyses included a discussion of demand, invoking "Engel's law": As people become richer, their demand for food falls relative to that for other goods, leading to a decline in the price of food exports (Hirschman, 1961; see also Chapter 16). Marxists have pointed out that the ECLA analysis is primarily an attempt to modify a flawed theory of international trade, and fails to clarify which social classes in the developed and Latin American countries benefit.

Both neoclassical and radical analysts have also objected to the political conclusions that ECLA drew. ECLA argued that the key to development in Latin America is the promotion of industrialization (ECLA, 1951; Prebisch, 1959). This can only be achieved by state intervention in the short run in order to establish industrial enterprises, in addition to primary production for export, and to protect them from international competition. The state should place tariffs on key imported industrial goods, and financially subsidize domestic production of these goods until indigenous industry is ready to compete internationally. This protection of nascent industry should be combined with policies providing scarce foreign currency to the most productive sectors, giving industrial workers reasonable wages, organizing underdeveloped countries into trading blocs, encouraging domestic consumption, and allowing selective investment by European and American firms. Such actions were seen as necessary because the situation of these countries within the world economy means that the free operation of market forces is inefficient. It was thought that with this kind of temporary state intervention, the barriers to development can be broken down, and development in the third world should follow to a point where the free market can take over again.

The Organization of American States proposed the adoption of many of these policies in 1961 (Cardoso, 1977), resulting in an era of what has become known as "import substitution industrialization" (ISI), and ECLA was also a driving force behind the creation of a Latin American common market. Such actions were taken without any effective attempt to deal with the external conditions that formed the backcloth of the ECLA analysis, however, and this policy ran into trouble in the 1970s (Chapter 17). Thus the guarded optimism of ECLA's earlier work gave way to pessimism about the possibility of third world development within a capitalist world economy. This pessimism increased the popularity, both within and outside ECLA, of a more radical Latin American interpretation: "dependency theory."

Dependency Theory

Dependency theory originated with the writings of Bagú (1949), and took up an implicit theme of Prebisch's theory—that links between the developed and less developed nations are causing economic conditions in the third world to worsen. Consequently, underdevelopment came to be seen not as an original condition, to be overcome by closer integration of the world economy, but as a process brought about by that integration. Dependency theory represents a common conceptualization of the nature and causes of underdevelopment, put forward from varying theoretical positions by a prolific school of writers. For the purpose of this overview, we identify three Latin American groups: the "classical" dependency theorists, the ECLA group, and the "contextual" dependency theorists. It is important to note, however, that a similar approach, no doubt emanating from similarly frustrating experiences with development in the third world, can be found in the writings of African and South Asian development theorists.

André Gunder Frank popularized dependency theory among English readers, although it should be stressed that he was a relative latecomer to the circles within which dependency theory evolved (Frank, 1967, 1978a). Frank argued not only that development in Latin America is hindered by the expansion of capitalist production there, but that this expansion is the cause of underdevelopment: "the development of underdevelopment." His theory drew on a detailed historical study of development in Chile and Brazil, which showed that even the most remote parts of these countries had been profoundly influenced by their exchanges with Europe since the 16th century. As a result, he was convinced that capitalism cannot be viewed as a progressive economic force that has only recently come to stimulate development in Latin America. Rather, it has been there for a long time, and thus must have contributed to continued underdevelopment (see sidebar: "Frank's Dependency Theory").

Frank combined his empirical research (points 1, 5, and 6 in the sidebar) with elements of Prebisch's theory (sidebar point 2) and Marxist analyses of imperialism (sidebar point 4) into an ingenious synthesis forming a relentless critique of the modernization and dualism theories. He also contributed to political debate about the development of Latin America, taking issue with the prevailing view among Latin American communist parties of capitalism as a positive step toward socialism—a view that had led these parties to form alliances with national bourgeoisies as well as with ECLA (Cardoso, 1977; Henfrey, 1981). The *dependentistas* argued for an immediate transition to socialism, because of the fundamentally detrimental nature of capitalism in a periph-

Frank's Dependency Theory

Frank has argued:

1. Since its "discovery" by Europeans, Latin America has had a capitalist market economy, because it has always been involved in the exchange of commodities with the capitalist countries of Europe and North America.
2. This exchange has been unequal, because Latin America has historically been dependent on the capitalist countries both militarily and economically.
3. Its current state of underdevelopment must then largely be a result of these historical relations.
4. Since these exchange relations have been and continue to be a necessary part of continued capital accumulation in the capitalist countries, and thus are part of the system of capitalism itself, the underdevelopment of Latin America must be a consequence of capitalism.
5. The nature of class relations in the less developed countries is also a result of the external linkages. The elites of these countries act as the agents propagating the interests of external capitalism, and their domestic relations with the other social classes facilitate the participation of the latter in the international capitalist economy.
6. Empirically, these countries experience their greatest degree of development in those places where, and those time periods when, links with the advanced capitalist countries are weakest.
7. Underdevelopment in Latin America is therefore qualitatively different from that observed before the industrial revolution in Europe, because Europe was not linked in this way to an external capitalist economy.
8. The thesis that there exists a unique set of stages of growth or modernization, and the thesis that Latin American societies have a dual structure, must then both be rejected.

eral context. During the economic crises of the late 1960s and early 1970s in Latin America, dependency theory and its political program gained considerable popularity.

Frank called his theory a Marxist theory of development, but there are clear contradictions between it and a Marxist approach (Laclau, 1971). These stem from Frank's geographical definition of "capitalism." By arguing that all parts of the globe participating in exchange with the advanced capitalist countries are themselves capitalist, he used a definition of capitalism that is inconsistent with Marx's theory. In that theory, as we have shown in Chapter 3, a country is capitalist if it possesses the social relationships necessary for *production* to occur in a capitalist way, not because it engages in *exchange* with capitalists. This need not imply that the theory itself is inappropriate; it only questions Frank's claim that it is an updating of Marxist theories. Whatever its actual intellectual heritage, dependency theory had an enormous impact on thinking about global development.

Frank's argument has been subjected to three further major criticisms by many different authors (e.g., Henfrey, 1981; Howe, 1981). First, its focus on the national scale, and on the expropriation of economic surplus by the developed countries, neglects the allocation of this surplus among individuals and social classes within these nations. This can be seen if the status of point 5 in Frank's theoretical scheme (see the sidebar) is analyzed. Essentially, this point could be dropped without affecting the rest of the argument. The second sentence in point 5 does not follow from points 1–4, nor do points 6–8 depend on 5. A second, and closely related, criticism is that this focus on just one aspect provides as simplistic a view of the process of development as that of the modernists or ECLA. Although the argument is inverted, and the conclusions are diametrically opposed, underdevelopment is as inevitable for Frank as modernization is for Parsons. Henfrey (1981) has suggested that this may be because Frank's purpose was more political than academic: He wished to provide a counterthesis to the arguments of ECLA and the Latin American communist parties favoring capitalism. The outcome of these two criticisms is the characterization of dependency theory as focusing too much on external and economic relations and too little on internal and social class relations. Third, a number of authors have objected to the form of Frank's argument. He concentrated on showing how capitalism has not developed in Latin America in the way that it did in Europe; as a result, he wrote what Henfrey calls a "nonhistory"—a history of what might have occurred (but did not). By taking this approach, Frank could avoid directly confronting the reality of many differences between countries that cannot be accounted for by simply labeling them all as members of the global periphery.

It is important, however, not to equate dependency theory with Frank's viewpoint. Within Latin America, it circulated as a far richer and more nuanced body of ideas than can be found in Frank's formulation. Two other contributors emphasizing economic aspects of dependency theory are worth noting: Brazilian economists Theotônio dos Santos and Ruy Marini. Dos Santos (1970) was concerned with the differences between nations in the nature of dependency. He identified essentially three different forms of dependency: "colonial," being the earlier phase of mercantile colonialism; "industrial–financial," representing the investment of capital from the core countries into producing primary goods in the periphery; and "technological–industrial," representing the direct investment by transnational corporations (TNCs) in production for local consumption in the third world. He saw this third type as the result of the ECLA-induced development policies of the 1960s. This classification at least made it possible to ask how different internal situations may interact differently with the external relations of dependence.

Marini (1973) contributed an analysis of "dependent capitalism," explaining how a peripheral positionality in the world economy entails a different set of laws of development than those appropriate in North America and western Europe. He argued that since third world producers sell their products abroad, there is no incentive to stimulate domestic consumption. Since it is not necessary to keep wages high, profits are increased by lengthening the working day rather than by increasing productivity, while the lack of domestic markets makes third world nations unattractive for industrial production. This represents a self-sustaining cycle of dependency.

An "ECLA school" of dependency theory developed, as some ECLA members became pessimistic about the possibility of development in Latin America. Recognizing the limited and even deleterious effects of earlier ECLA-inspired policies, they placed more stress on the role of domestic factors than Frank or Prebisch did. Argentinean economist Carlos Furtado (1966) argued that Brazilian industrialization at that time was concentrated in capital-intensive luxury goods benefiting only the elite, with little employment potential for other social classes or investment potential for foreign capital; he saw the result as a "stagnationist" cycle of dependency. Subsequent improvements in trade relationships for some Latin American countries led later writers in this dependency school to be optimistic, arguing that domestic consumption in some Latin American countries had reached the level that made production for the national market attractive enough to allow at least for the possibility of growth. Because this growth was in consumer goods, the capital goods required to produce these still had to be imported from the first world. Furthermore, third world production was dominated by foreign corporations, supported by indigenous elites who consumed the goods these firms produced. However, Chilean economist Osvaldo Sunkel (1973) argued that nationalist action reorienting production toward the basic needs of the majority was in some cases resulting in a successful form of peripheral capitalism.

It is important to recognize that Latin American dependency theory was far less economistic, and pessimistic, than Frank's analysis would suggest. Brazilian sociologists Fernando Cardoso and Enzo Faletto took issue with the tradition–modernization dichotomy—a key theme among the *dependentistas*. Observing that some "dependent development" was occurring in a few countries, they argued (Cardoso and Faletto, 1979) that no deterministic general theory of dependency is possible. They did not impose a single conception of dependency on all countries; they laid more stress on the intervening role played by national social and class relations (the alliances and conflicts between different social groups, and the legal and de facto powers that they have to realize their own goals). They argued that these vary from country to country. The best that can be done is to define the various contradictions and conflicts that are endemic to third world countries, given their position in the world economy. Such a necessarily partial and incomplete outline must be filled out in each case with the historical developments specific to that place. They argued that dependency theory is only useful for empirical analysis if it is employed as the basis for historical analysis of concrete situations of dependency.

They then set out to examine the "concrete situations" of actual social and political developments in individual Latin American countries—identifying key social factors varying between them, and focusing on the historical role of different political classes with particular concern for national elites and the state. They argued that particular conjunctures of internal conditions do allow for dependent development, and that in cases where development does not occur, there is room for national populist movements to correct such deficiencies as long as they can command the nationalist agenda. This approach has been criticized, however, for failing to identify which factors are crucial for dependent development, thus providing no clear guidelines for development policy. (Cardoso became president of Brazil from 1995 to 2003, overseeing its neoliberalization; see Chapter 5.)

Other *dependentistas* stressed still different aspects (Slater, 2004). An important political theme was the importance of sovereignty and autonomous development. Brazilian political scientist Octavio Ianni (1971) suggested that the militarization of Latin American society and the accompanying culture of violence are essential to the reproduction of dependency. Mexican philosopher Leopoldo Zea (1963) stressed cultural questions of identity and difference, examining the impact of dependency on modes of thinking, and seeking to resurrect a right to recognition and independent identity. The contributions of intellectuals such as Cardoso, Faletto, Ianni, and Zea go some way toward redressing the critiques, addressed to Frank, that dependency theory is overly economistic and pessimistic. The failure of influential Anglophone representations of dependency theory to take full account of its diversity (including this account) reflect the asymmetrical nature of contemporary knowledge production, whereby Anglophone ideas move very easily and pervasively from north to south, whereas southern intellectuals' lack of access to northern circuits of knowledge production, and northern intellectuals' inadequate language skills, undermine the reciprocal movement of peripheral formulations from south to north—even when they are written down. Of course, this reinforces the marginalization of peripheral forms of knowledge. The trajectory of world system theory is a case in point.

World System Theory

The term "world system theory" was originated by the American Immanuel Wallerstein, but Samir Amin simultaneously and independently developed this approach. Although it has close affinities to imperialism and dependency theory, its claim to distinctiveness lies in its explicit attempt to analyze the entire extent of the global economic system that is linked economically to capitalism. Wallerstein (1979) defined a "world economy" as being such a globally extensive interdependent economic system, and noted that capitalism is the only sustained example of such a system that history has yet provided. There were other world systems, such as the Chinese empire, but these were different since they were political rather than economic systems. Amin and Wallerstein both placed the world system at the center of their analysis; for both, events occurring within this system are to be explained in terms of the demands of the system as a whole. Both were also concerned with the fact that within this system capitalist and noncapitalist production coexist. They wished to understand why noncapitalist production persists, and what the implications of this are for understanding global inequalities in development. Finally, both authors grounded their theories in impressive historical analyses of the evolution of this system. Amin (1974) first developed this approach (see sidebar: "Amin's Theory of World Capitalism").

Wallerstein's analysis differs from that of Amin in several respects. Instead of simply classifying countries into core and periphery, he divided economic processes into "core" processes and "peripheral" processes. He then argued that core activities will tend to be located together, defining a place where this occurs as a core country; similarly, peripheral processes will tend to gravitate together, defining countries of the periphery. Second, he introduced the category of a "semiperipheral" country as being one where a mixture of core and periphery processes coexists. Third, Wallerstein emphasized that the world economy evolves in a cyclical manner. The crisis of overproduction identified by Amin is not dealt with gradually, but erupts as periods when production drops off drastically, since the oversupply means that adequate profits can no longer be realized. These cyclical downturns are a time of great upheaval among capitalists, during which inefficient producers are eliminated and the whole process of production and labor is modified to increase productivity. At the same time, a redistribution of income in favor of workers in core countries, and the elite in the periphery, occurs. Together, these increase demand; increased productivity reduces prices while incomes rise.

Such actions cannot solve the inherent contradictions of a capitalist mode of production, however, and so at less frequent intervals full-scale world crises occur, which the system must be able to overcome in order not to collapse. During these full-scale crises, the membership of the core and periphery may change. Wallerstein saw the states of the semiperiphery as playing a crucial role at this point, as they are the ones best equipped to move up into the core. He did, however, emphasize that while the membership may change, "the distribution of the roles (how many in each role: i.e., core, semi-periphery, periphery) has remained remarkably constant, proportionally, over the history of the world-economy" (Wallerstein, 1984: 7). He implied that this distribution is required by the system.

There are clearly strong affinities between world system theorists and the classical dependency theory of Frank. Both use the nation state as the unit of analysis, and emphasize the circulation of economic surplus and its disproportionate appropriation by countries of the core. These similarities have led to explicit cooperation between researchers from these two schools (Amin, Arrighi, Frank, and Wallerstein, 1982). Thus Amin and Wallerstein have been subject to criticisms similar to those leveled at Frank; that is, they have been accused of ignoring internal conditions and paying too much attention to external exchange relations (Brenner, 1977; Petras, 1981). World system theorists also do not provide an explanation of how wage differentials and underdevel-

Amin's Theory of World Capitalism

Amin (1974) developed his account of the global capitalist system as follows:

1. The expansion of capitalist production in Europe and North America required raw materials from the third world. The precapitalist modes of production existing in the third world made it possible to obtain these while paying workers there wages at levels well below what was regarded as a subsistence wage in the capitalist countries. In this manner, selected countries of the third world were drawn into the trading sphere of the industrial capitalist countries without themselves becoming industrial producers. Amin distinguished between the two groups of countries by calling the former the "periphery" and the latter the "core" of the global capitalist system.
2. This set up a fundamental difference between countries of the core and those of the periphery in real terms and in money wages. As a result, unequal exchange has led to the persistent transfer of economic surplus from the periphery to the core.
3. This transfer has meant that a disproportionate share of the economic surplus produced in the world has accumulated in the core countries. This surplus has also been historically invested in the core countries for the kinds of reasons already suggested by Marini (1973) and Sunkel (1973). Workers in the periphery can continue to be paid much lower wages, as long as they continue to be subject to precapitalist social relations. This means that the market for consumer goods in the periphery remains small. As a result, investment in production in peripheral locations to satisfy this demand has remained relatively limited. It is only recently that increased production has occurred in these locations, because the wage differential is so high that it is now possible for corporations to perform labor-intensive production for markets in the countries of the core more cheaply by locating that production in the periphery (Fröbel, Heinrichs, and Kreye, 1980).
4. Political power plays a vital role in reinforcing this process of unequal exchange and in maintaining the geographical patterns of specialization and trade that this process requires.
5. As a result, unequal development between the core and the periphery is, and will continue to be, the rule.
6. The superprofits being made in the third world pose a threat to continued capital accumulation, because the low wages and low demand there mean that in the system as a whole, workers do not earn enough to purchase all the commodities that are produced when those profits are invested in increased production. This threat is contained by acceding to demands for higher wages in the core countries—an action that can also have the effect of securing support for the global system from workers in the core, because they benefit from it (Emmanuel, 1972).
7. The form that development takes in countries of the periphery depends both on the nature of precapitalist social formations there and on when, and the manner by which, they were integrated into the world economy. However, development in all countries of the periphery is distorted by comparison with core countries in three ways: much greater export orientation to provide for the demands of core countries; a withering of manufacturing and abnormal expansion of service activities; and a tendency to use less productive technologies.

opment have resulted from the structural features of capitalist production. Rather, they (particularly Wallerstein) have tended to assume that observed developments have occurred because they are required by the (capitalist) world system—a functionalist explanation similar to that of Parsons.

One important difference, however, is that dependency theory is unable to explain the success of any third world nation, making its applicability questionable in the light of the prosperity of South Korea and some other "newly industrializing countries" (NICs; see Chapter 2, Table 2.1). By contrast, world system theory, at least as formulated by Wallerstein, allows countries to progress from the periphery to the core or vice versa, but does not allow all (or even a majority of) countries to belong simultaneously to the core of a global capitalist system, and thus to experience prosperity. Yet, though world systems theory provides structural circumstances that create a space for countries to move into the semiperiphery and even the core of the world economy, this does not account for which countries have been successful.

Developmental States

In the periphery, nation states also sought to exert influence over economic growth and national prosperity, with great success in some cases. On the one hand, anticolonial movements brought to power new elites with politically progressive programs, such as African socialism in Tanzania. In a world where nation states were overlain by superpower rivalry between the first and second worlds, it was singularly possible for newly independent states (e.g., Egypt, India) to carve out a third way for the third world, by playing the Soviets and Chinese off against the Americans and Europeans. On the other hand, general support for state-led programs on national economic development encouraged third world nation states also to intervene massively in domestic society (and, in too many cases, to abrogate democratic powers). Their peripheral position led to distinctive kinds of policies, such as import-substituting industrialization (e.g., Brazil, Bolivia) and rules about domestic ownership of firms (e.g., Indonesia); to state-owned industries (some, as in India, locally developed; others created by nationalizing foreign branch plants, as in India, the Philippines, and Cuba); to state suppression of unionization movements (e.g., Taiwan, South Korea); to reengineering of first world know-how (e.g., South Korea); and to welfare, health, population management, and education programs built from the ground up (e.g., Taiwan, South Korea).

In short, state intervention in third world countries could not simply follow the Fordist model, but required a distinctive set of strategies adapted to their peripheral positionality—the "developmental state" (Amsden, 1989; Evans, 1995; Glassman and Samatar, 1997; Wade, 1990). A developmentalist state takes a proactive role in the development process, using a combination of regulatory and deregulatory trade and investment policies and selective incentives to promote the success of certain firms and industries, often under the kind of close collaboration with state agencies and financial institutions that is frowned on by the World Bank (Chapter 17). Within the intellectual tradition of world system theory, it is argued that the situation of third world nations within the global economy has made this distinctive kind of state intervention necessary to achieving economic prosperity (Glassman and Samatar, 1997).

Women, Gender, and Development

WID's privileging of sex inequality as the fundamental problem facing all women; its simplistic assumptions about a universal sisterhood; and its peripheralization of class and national hierarchies came under serious attack in the 1980s. On the one hand, these problems with WID helped to trigger a new era of feminist theorizing marked, in particular, by the emergence of critical third world feminist voices located in U.S. academia. In her now canonical essay "Under Western Eyes," for example, Mohanty (1984) dismantled the very category of "third world women" as created by the hegemonic development discourse, while also highlighting the necessity of reclaiming and recasting that category. Several of these authors (Lazreg, 1988; Mohanty, 1984; Trinh, 1989) highlighted the contradictions and dangers inherent in a feminist project where "difference" is only allowed to unfold according to external standards and within an external frame of reference. The Algerian feminist Marnia Lazreg (1988: 81) wrote:

> Under these circumstances, the consciousness

> of one's womanhood coincides with the realization that it has already been appropriated in one form or another by outsiders, women as well as men, experts in things Middle Eastern. In this sense, the feminist project is warped and rarely brings with it the potential for personal liberation that it does in this country [the United States] or in Europe.

On the other hand, WID sparked structuralist critiques and alternative articulations on the question of "women and development" (WAD) by networks of third world activists, policymakers, and researchers, such as the Association of African Women for Research and Development (AAWORD) and Development Alternatives with Women for a New Era (DAWN). Whereas WID was concerned with inserting women *in* development by maximizing their access to the modern sector, the structuralist and dependency perspectives on WAD sought to problematize third world women's relationship to development and modernization. For WAD theorists, women's inclusion in or exclusion from development processes is related to the hierarchical spatialization of the global capitalist economy that shapes the differentiated spaces of center, semiperiphery, and periphery; of urban and rural areas; and of market and subsistence sectors. Rather than problematically treating third world men as direct oppressors of the third world's poorest women, then, this framework regarded the growth of highly capital-intensive relations of production as a major cause of third world poverty, from which women suffer very disproportionately (Kabeer, 1994). For instance, Nash and Safa (1980: xi) argued that "It is not men who keep women at home . . . but the structure of the capitalist system, which benefits from the unpaid labor of housewives, or, in wartime, draws upon this reserve labor supply." Furthermore, they contended that working-class men's frustration with the class system is what gives rise to masculinist violence and aggression against women. In short, they argued that the accumulation processes of global capitalism produce gender and class hierarchies that can be understood in terms of an Althusserian base–superstructure metaphor, in which the economic is foundational, whereas ideology, including gender ideology, is relegated (along with politics) to a superstructure of secondary causal importance (Saunders, 2002b).

But not all structuralist feminists viewed gender as subordinate to class. A group of feminists working in Germany in the development field, for instance, rejected the prioritizing of class as the primary contradiction and argued that women's relegation to the unpaid subsistence serves the system of capitalist *and* patriarchal domination, in which men profit from the system *as men*, rather than as members of the ruling class. Most prominent among these thinkers was Maria Mies (1980), who argued that both men's and women's essence of being has emerged from their laboring activities since the days of hunting and gathering. Whereas women's laboring activities in biosocial reproduction are sensuous, self-fulfilling, nonalienating, and ultimately revolutionary because of these traits, men's activities are mediated by tools of destruction. Founded on the interrelated processes of colonialism and housewifization, then, capitalist patriarchy has propelled the pervasive exploitation of weak by strong and has led less powerful men to imitate the "big white men." By focusing on the sexually differentiated body as an important site for the enactment of power relations in this way, Mies opened up the analysis of women's oppression to a whole range of issues centering around body politics that had been downplayed in traditional Marxist approaches. At the same time, however, her approach was criticized for its failure to question the assumed internal coherence of monolithic categories such as "the global patriarchy," "women," and "the colonies," and for conceptualizing "big white men" as the centrifugal force through which all other forms of power are articulated (Kabeer, 1994; Saunders, 2002b).

The economic determinism of WAD approaches as a whole has been critiqued by the gender and development (GAD) theorists, who have attempted to rethink development as a complex field comprising processes of social transformation involving diverse actors at multiple geographical scales. Focusing on the interwoven nature of power and knowledge on the one hand, and of theory and practice on the other, feminists working in the GAD paradigm have attended to the interlocking relationships among rules, resources, and institutional practices through which social inequalities of gender, caste, class, and so forth are constituted and played out in specific contexts (Kabeer and Subrahmanian, 1999: viii). Rather than making a radical break from WAD perspectives, furthermore, some GAD authors drew on third world networks such as AAWORD and DAWN to argue that development theories and practices should start from the vantage point of the poor third world woman. This, argues Kabeer (1994: 81), is not because this figure is inherently more knowledgeable than all others, but because (1) she offers a viewpoint from below that can help to realign development paradigms more closely to the "real" order of things; and (2) a structural transformation of the lives of the poorest and most oppressed sections of all societies is a prerequisite for development and equity. GAD thinkers, moreover, have challenged the opposition posited by WID between welfare and efficiency and argued for the redistributive role of state welfare, and the significance of state subsidies in education, health and child care, housing, and pensions, the reduction of which increases the reproductive burdens of women.

GAD has been subjected to criticism by postcolonial feminist critics (see Saunders, 2002b), however, for exhibiting "gynocentrism"—that is, a narrow focus on women that tends to essentialize womanhood and femininity, and to align GAD with WID at the level of practice. In particular, the mainstreaming of gender and the institutionalization of sustainability and empowerment through global platforms (e.g., the United Nations) and donor-led nongovernmental organizations (NGOs) can be seen as contributing to an unintentional merging of WID and GAD to promote the professionalization of grassroots activism and a deradicalization of transformative politics (Armstrong, 2004; Kamat, 2002; Roy, 2004).

CONCLUSIONS

Through the three "decades of development" after World War II, diffusionist views from the core, seeking to propagate development around the third world, were counterposed by third world perspectives, encountering development, that stressed its negative effects outside the first world. Although economics was very much the language of development, similar oppositions could be found among those examining the role of the (generally national) state and of women. Notwithstanding considerable advances in the theoretical sophistication of these theories and associated discourses, the tenor of debate often paralleled that of the colonial era. Yet there was one crucial difference: Third world perspectives gained much more attention and influence in the wake of the 1955 Bandung conference, circulating through Latin America before being taken up after 1968 in the first world. Economic crises in the mid-1970s ushered in a new phase of thinking, however—one in which "development" gave way to "globalization," and first world perspectives began to reassert themselves.

NOTES

1. "Woman" has always been a contested category in (and outside) the first world, due to the inclusions and exclusions it has involved along the lines of social hierarchies such as race and class, which articulate in complex historically and geographically specific ways with gender.

2. The passage from Paz (1972) is reprinted by permission of the Grove Press.

5 The Third World and Neoliberal Globalization

INVENTING GLOBALIZATION

The dynamic of "globalization"—the increased range, speed, and intensity of human-induced connections between different parts of the world (Held, McGrew, Goldblatt, and Perraton, 1999)—is almost as old as humankind. We still debate exactly when and where *Homo sapiens* emerged (almost certainly in Africa), and probably will never resolve this exactly; however, we know that men and women spread rapidly around the world, and that they have had at least intermittent contact even across the largest oceans for the last 2,000 years. Although no one can question that globalization has increased in recent years, it would be erroneous to treat it as a recent phenomenon. Hirst and Thompson (1996) assemble plenty of evidence to suggest that the nations of the world were at least as interdependent, and the world at least as "globalized," 100 years ago as they and it are today. Ruddiman (2003) finds evidence that humans were noticeably warming the earth 8,000 years ago. Why, then, is globalization commonly presented as a recent phenomenon? Whereas the practice dates back millennia, the rise of globalization as a dominant discursive metaphor only goes back a decade. An online search revealed that "globalization" was mentioned less than 200 times in 1996, but that this increased more than eight times in 3 years, to some 1,700 mentions by 1999 (Taylor, Watts, and Johnston, 2002).

A clue to understanding this increase is to pay attention to how the processes driving globalization are conceptualized. Obviously, there are many ways to imagine the world becoming more interdependent: Over 160 years ago, Marx and Engels proclaimed: "Workers of the world, unite!" This is not, however, the imaginary that is invoked by globalization these days. Rather, globalization is taken to be synonymous with market-led or neoliberal globalization. The term "neoliberalism" was borrowed by Austro-British economist Friedrich Hayek to envision a society in which unfettered markets allocate society's wealth according to individuals' desires (preferences) and productivity. In this view, the state and other institutions of civil society should leave as much as possible to a deregulated private sector, in order to maximize personal liberty.

Into the 1970s, this vision was unpopular (Chapter 4). In the first world, prosperity was seen as being best ensured by a Fordist cooperation among the state, corporations, and unions in demand-led growth; in effect, this was a national application of Henry Ford's idea that if he paid his workers more, they would buy more of his Model T's. The state dominated the economy in the second world, and in large parts of the third world a strong developmentalist state was seen as the key to economic growth. In this view, personal liberty was maximized through state intervention to help the least well off—those people and places impoverished by capitalism. Yet a confluence of forces, from the mid-1970s to the late 1980s, combined to deconstruct this consensus. First world economies stagnated as increased wages ate into capitalists' profits, and cheaper and better manufactures from abroad undermined their heavy industries, the core of Fordism. Third world countries had trouble realizing state-led development behind national barriers. The second world imploded, vitiating the industrialized world's principal alternative to capitalism. This led to a shift in thinking about the economics of social change. Whereas state intervention and regulation, and ideas from dependency theory, possessed a lot of global currency in nations and multilateral development institutions in the 1970s, they were quickly displaced by neoliberal ideas. Hayek, laughed out of British economics in the 1930s, was a surprise winner of the Nobel Prize in economics in 1974, along with the ideologically progressive Swedish economist Gunnar Myrdal. Since then, more than 25% of the awardees have taught at or held a doctorate from the University of Chicago, the home institution of neoliberal economic thinking.

After the mid-1970s, this shift began profoundly affecting thinking about the third world. The Central Intelligence Agency (CIA)-backed coup in Chile in September 1973 provided an opportunity to experiment with authoritarian market reform, and for some time the term "neoliberalism" circulated primarily in Latin America to describe such processes of market "shock therapy." New York City's fiscal crisis in 1976 provided an opportunity to experiment with neoliberalism within the first world (Harvey, 2005), and by the end of the 1980s neoliberal policies had replaced Fordism under President Ronald Reagan in the United States and Prime Minister Margaret Thatcher in the United Kingdom. International institutions such as the World Bank and the International Monetary Fund (IMF) shifted their thinking and policy recommendations from Keynesianism to neoliberalism, as formulated in their structural adjustment programs (Chapter 23). By the 1990s, even nations from the second world, pressured by the World Bank and advised by U.S. economists, were pursuing a trajectory toward market-led growth—a transition from state socialism to capitalism.

Initially, neoliberalism focused on changing domestic and local conditions in order to "liberalize" markets. Increasingly, however, it came to be associated with globalization. From the core, globalization has replaced development as the framework within which to think about trajectories of change in the third world; it is the diffusionist paradigm in new clothes. Societal progress is still equated with capitalist economic growth, but development is equated with both deregulating the domestic market economy and opening a country to international markets instead of state-led development. Third world elites, with a few prominent exceptions (Cuba, Venezuela, North Korea), have come to embrace neoliberal ideas as the key to progress. From the periphery, marginalized communities, confronted with the negative consequences of market-led globalization plus development, put forth alternative analyses of this process. These are often designated by core commentators as "antiglobalization" (i.e., as opposed to any kind of globalization), even if, as is often the case, it is only *neoliberal* globalization that they object to (cf. Kitching, 2001).

VIEWS FROM THE CORE: ONE WORLD

The Evolving Principles of Neoliberal Globalization

By the mid-1980s, development theory from the core was beginning to change course. The year 1985 saw the publication of two articles of enduring influence: Booth's, describing the "impasse" in development sociology (Booth, 1985); and Lal's, discussing the "misconceptions" of development economics. In neoclassical economic thought, government involvement in the economy is warranted when markets fail to perform their task of efficiently allocating resources. Among economists, a shift had been occurring from the view that pervasive market failures must be addressed by state action to a view that, because of politics and rent-seeking behavior, states are not capable of remedying market failure, and in fact state intervention actually makes things worse. Lal (1985: 13) encapsulated well this shift in thinking: "Most of the serious distortions are due not to the inherent imperfections of the market mechanism but to irrational government intervention." At the heart of the neoliberal revolution is the principle that prosperity is best assured by "liberalizing" market mechanisms—both domestically, by reducing state regulation of and participation in the economy; and internationally, by eliminating border controls over the trade of commodities and the movements of labor and capital, while also strengthening protection for investors and traders. Yet neoliberal ideas are also important at the micro scale, shaping how we think and act. Individual freedom becomes redefined as the capacity for self-realization and freedom from bureaucracy, rather than freedom from want; and all aspects of human behavior are reconceptualized along economic lines. Individuals are empowered to become active in making choices that further their interest, and are made responsible for acting in this way to advance both their own well-being and that of society.

Neoliberal policies were initially tried out in vulnerable locations in the 1970s, as noted above. Fertile conditions were necessary, however, for this shift in thinking to diffuse around the world, and globalization was particularly important. The internationalization of global manufacturing systems (Chapter 20) was already posing major difficulties for nation states seeking to maintain control over affairs within their own borders. In the early 1970s, such trends were seen as a threat to national social and economic policy. There was substantial national support for border controls (restricting trade, investment, and labor flows between countries), domestic content rules (restricting the degree to which a firm could be controlled by foreigners or a product could be built with foreign parts), and even the nationalization of foreign firms. In the 1980s, by contrast, neoliberal thinking constructed globalization as the key to creating free markets and free trade globally, not just domestically. Globalization thus came to be seen as the key to a free and prosperous global society, creating a level playing field on which a girl in a Bangkok slum has the same opportunities to prosper as a boy in Beverly Hills.

This approach has come to dominate academic thinking about the third world, as well as being central to the books of globalization pundits, whose popularity has helped shape public opinion in the core (Ash, 2005; Friedman, 2005). It propounds a new kind of theory of development via globalization. Advocating a return to "market fundamentals" and Adam Smith, proponents of globalization argue that nations will develop if they pursue an open-border, export-oriented approach. Nation states should thus abrogate their powers of sovereignty over national boundaries, in order to enable, and indeed encourage, free trade in commodities and services, the unrestricted international movement of capital and labor, and the activities of foreign investors. Although many residents will object to the disruptions resulting from encouraging globalization in this way, it is argued that resistance is futile and counterproductive—that globalization not only is inevitable, but offers the best chance for national development. The perspective from the core parallels that taken during the eras of colonialism and development (Chapters 3 and 4): There is one approach to prosperity, which worked in the core and should be applied to the periphery (now defined to include both the newly independent states emerging from state socialism, and the formerly colonized third world).

The neoliberal approach has changed over the years. The early emphasis in neoliberal structural adjustment and other policy prescriptions, as promoted by the U.S. and U.K. governments and by the World Bank and IMF, was to reduce state ownership, spending, and regulation of the economy. In response to such prescriptions, national governments substantially harmonized their systems of economic governance—a form of political governance. If they deviated too much from "sound" financial and economic governance, they would be penalized—both by international financial markets, through refusals to lend money or through speculation driving down their currency; and by the surveillance, lending, and support practices of supranational institutions. However, by the mid-1980s it was already becoming clear that reducing the economic role of the state did not, by itself, set nations on the road to prosperity. Developing countries also needed a broader environment in which markets could thrive. To help create and support a market-friendly environment, it was necessary to bring the state back into development thinking, but under the limited banner of good governance. Indeed, countries' performance is increasingly measured by the degree to which they conform to the global desiderata of best practice and good governance. "Best practice" means adopting what experts, typically from the core, deem to be the best response to a particular problem. "Good governance" is commonly seen as entailing such things as rule of law, participation, transparency, and accountability. Recent World Bank studies argue that high scores on the following six key dimensions of governance will bring higher economic growth (Kaufmann, Kray, and Mastruzzi, 2005):

1. *Voice and accountability*—measuring political, civil, and human rights.
2. *Political instability and violence*—measuring the likelihood of violent threats to, or changes in, government (including terrorism).
3. *Government effectiveness*—measuring the competence of the bureaucracy and the quality of public service delivery.
4. *Regulatory burden*—measuring the incidence of market-unfriendly policies.
5. *Rule of law*—measuring the quality of contract enforcement, the police, and the courts, as well as the likelihood of crime and violence.
6. *Control of corruption*—measuring the exercise of public power for private gain, including both petty and grand corruption and state capture.

In the early 1990s, as it was becoming clear that even adding good governance to markets did not guarantee development, the neoliberal approach was expanded again, to address people's ability to participate in development activities. People, too, were brought back into development theory, through the concepts of participation, civil society, and social capital. Differences in the ability of various individuals and groups to participate and make their voices heard were accounted for by differing quantities of "social capital"—the civil associations allowing people to establish trusting relationships that make collective action possible. Citizen participation can be facilitated by nongovernmental organizations (NGOs),[1] which are assumed to be expressions of civil society's collective action. Several critics have observed, however, that good governance, participation, and social capital, as conceived by the World Bank and other proponents of neoliberalism, are analytically fuzzy enough to mean whatever a user wants them to mean, on the one hand. On the other hand, these concepts are profoundly depoliticizing, because they focus on notions of civil society while ignoring both organized political society and structures of social difference and their associated power relations (see the following section).

Concerns with good governance and civil society have stimulated nation states to decentralize and devolve governance structures, on the grounds that this can increase political responsiveness and participation at the local level. However, we must note that this is happening at a time of increasing centralization of corporate power. In such a condition, local governments, rather than responding to local needs, may be put in the position where they are forced to inform their citizens that there is no choice but to accept the choices presented by corporate interests.[2] Thus formal measures of democracy increase, while the space for democratic decision making shrinks. This risk is magnified at a time when attacks on unions have eroded the bargaining power of labor as well.

Increasingly, it has been recognized within the neoliberal camp that even this expanded agenda is overly simplistic. Jeffrey Sachs, formerly a leading advocate of shock therapy as the way to transform state socialism into capitalism, now argues that countries can become prisoners of their immutable geography. In arguments redolent of the logic of environmental determinist thinking under colonialism, closeness to the equator and distance from navigable waterways are seen as causing poverty (Sachs et al., 2001). Like Rostow, Sachs (2004) argues that economic growth proceeds in stages (in his case, precommercial, commercial, industrial, and knowledge—with even less emphasis on noneconomic aspects than in Rostow's theory). But progress is impeded because geography creates an uneven playing field, preventing neoliberal globalization from equally benefiting all. This in turn requires extra efforts by the first world to level the playing field and help such places eliminate poverty (Sachs, 2005).

Joseph Stiglitz (2002), a Nobel-winning economist with extensive insider experience in the Clinton administration and the World Bank, argues that the institutions managing globalization (the IMF, the World Bank, the World Trade Organization [WTO], and the U.S. administration) have systematically favored the interests of global financial and mercantile capital, and the United States and other key first world countries, at the expense of the poor and the third world. Stiglitz locates this problem in a promarket and pro-U.S. approach that pushes ideology at the expense of economic science, by failing to recognize the necessity for state intervention to address the ineradicable imperfections of markets that penalize the least well off. Noting that globalization is inevitable, and that it will be difficult to prevent the rich countries from tilting the playing field in their favor, he argues for more democratic, participatory, and transparent governance for the institutions managing globalization, giving them a taste of the good governance agenda. He also contends that third world countries should

> assume responsibility for their well-being themselves . . . live within their means . . . eliminate protectionist barriers which force consumers to pay higher prices . . . put in place strong regulations to protect themselves from speculators from the outside or corporate misbehavior from the inside. Most important, [they] need effective governments, with strong and independent judiciaries, democratic accountability, openness, and transparency . . . (Stiglitz, 2002: 251)

Such qualifications about globalization remain focused on markets as the least bad mechanism to ensure social prosperity and free choice for all. They are dismissive of Marxist critiques of capitalism, and seek to resuscitate Keynesian philosophies about the need for state regulation to rein in markets' negative consequences. Nevertheless, these economists' departure from the neoliberal position (sometimes known as the Washington consensus; see Chapter 23) has made them into controversial public figures. The same is true for third world elites who attempt to moderate market mechanisms, as when Malaysia's Prime Minister Mahathir imposed controls on international capital flows. Neoliberals are willing to countenance strong state action, but only in the name of eradicating the state as a market player.

Geographically, globalization is widely argued to herald a smaller world—a global village in which distance is increasingly irrelevant. Places are seen as increasingly penetrated by global processes and thus as losing their distinctive local identities. Distance no longer matters, as transportation costs fall and global telecommunications networks connect the most distant parts of the globe almost instantaneously, easing the movement of information, knowledge, and capital (Cairncross, 1997; O'Brien, 1992). Kenishi Ohmae (1995) has famously argued that nation states are no longer the relevant spatial units for organizing the global economy. It is also argued that globalization is creating an ever faster, 24/7 world, in which financial markets are always open and trading somewhere; stores are open all day; and the working day increasingly encroaches on the times and places that used to be thought of as dedicated to family and social activities and recreation. In a grander sense, writing on the eve of the disappearance of the second world, Francis Fukuyama (1989: 4) argued that globalization means the end of history—"the end point of mankind's ideological evolution and the universalization of Western liberal democracy as the final form of human government." David Harvey (1989), a passionate critic of neoliberal globalization, recalls Marx's aphorism that we are experiencing the annihilation of space by time.

Certainly the world is becoming smaller and faster, but it does not follow that either its geography or its history is becoming irrelevant. Its geography is changing, of course, as it always has. In part, we can identify a shift in the geographical scales that matter. The nation state scale is becoming less dominant, or "hollowed out" (Jessop, 1999), as both supranational scales (think how such acronyms as UN, IMF, WTO, EU [the European Union], and NAFTA [the North American Free Trade Agreement] have become commonplace) and subnational scales (cities, industrial districts, and export-processing zones [EPZs]) have become more important in shaping the global economy (Swyngedouw, 1997). New supranational scales are being created, such as the EU or the Organization of African Unity (OAU). Whether nation states have been pushed into abrogating sovereign powers (powers that in principle they still can exercise) or whether they have jumped, it is certainly the case that borders are increasingly open—except when poor people try to enter rich countries.

The argument that distance no longer matters leads to the conclusion that promotion of good governance under globalization creates the necessary conditions for a country to succeed by competing with other countries (geoeconomics rather than geopolitics). Implicitly, it also implies that every country is equally situated with respect to other countries—that there need be no cores or peripheries under globalization. The one departure from this argument is Sachs et al.' (2001) claim that places are disadvantaged by proximity to the tropics and distance from navigable waterways. Just as individuals are made responsible for behaving appropriately (being entrepreneurial, self-interested) to make the most of their opportunities under neoliberalism, so countries on this leveled playing field are now made responsible for their own success or failure (cf. Stiglitz, 2002). This clearly rejects the presuppositions of dependency and world system theory (Chapter 4). Geographers argue, however, that distance—in the sense of relative position within the global system—does still matter (Massey, 2005; Sheppard, 2002). Distance is subject to manipulation through the development of new transportation and communications technologies (accessibility cannot be measured as simply distance to a navigable water body). But in a smaller and faster world, small time periods and small differences in relative position matter more. Expectations about what constitutes an adequate time for financial information to be transmitted from New York to London have fallen dramatically over the last 200 years, from weeks to milliseconds. The Barings Bank of the UK, an imperial institution founded in 1763, went bankrupt in 1995 after one of its traders, Nick Leeson, lost one billion U.S. dollars speculating on tenths-of-a-second differences in futures prices in Osaka and Singapore. If the speed of communication linking two other places has only fallen from weeks to minutes during this time frame, then, by comparison to New York and London, those two places now would be relatively farther away from one another than before. Even in cyberspace, where the crucial factor affecting accessibility to the World Wide Web is "the last mile" (the quality of your home connection and computer), historical global inequalities in accessibility are remarkably persistent (Graham and Marvin, 2001). Information travels as quickly over the Internet between Frankfurt and Los Angeles as it does between Nairobi and Johannesburg. The global cable systems on which high-bandwidth information exchange relies heavily are very dense within and among North America, Europe, and Japan, but still bypass much of Africa (where the cables are laid in international waters, with individual connections extended into particular countries) and low-income neighborhoods in cities like New York. To give a more specific example, the much-celebrated arrival of the Internet in the remotest rural districts in India does not mean much for people living in the many villages of the state of Uttar Pradesh, which receive less than 7 hours of electricity daily. Inequities in physical travel also still exist: Although it might take only 2 hours for an Indian of means to cover the 1,300 kilometers separating Mumbai and Lucknow (the capital of Uttar Pradesh), a 110-kilometer-long trip from Lucknow to a village in Sitapur district can easily take 4 hours for an ordinary woman living in one of those villages.

Thus differences in relative position may be increasing between different places and people in different social locations, even as time and space shrink in an absolute sense, raising the question of whether dependency theory and world system theory can be dismissed as easily as globalization pundits would like. If space- and place-based differences are disappearing, then a stages-of-growth or linear historical view of socioeconomic change becomes the only logical possibility. The argument that every country can pursue the same path to development presumes that positionality does not matter. If differences in relative position persist, however, and places retain their distinctiveness despite their openness to global influences, then this implies a very different spatiotemporal conception of socioeconomic change: Even if all places adopt the same approach, not all gain from it. It then follows that there must be room for different visions of development and the good life, and distinct ways of going about achieving these. This alternative conception can be found not only in dependency and world system theories, but also in postcolonial theory, which has emerged in the last 20 years to challenge the relevance of a linear model of history to account for what has been happening in countries affected by colonialism (Dirlik, 1997; Massey, 1999).

Since the mid-1970s, three issues have become central to thinking about societal change: the biophysical environment; social differences, such as gender; and religion. These issues seem at first glance to challenge a market-based, neoliberal logic, each catalyzing significant resistance to neoliberalism. In each case, however, perspectives from the core have sought to incorporate them into the neoliberal model. With respect to the biophysical environment, for example, early concerns about natural limits to economic growth (i.e., that sustainability and growth are mutually contradictory) have been countered by the argument that markets can anticipate and develop innovations to address emergent environmental problems (e.g., an oil shortage or pollution). In principle, such market "externalities" can be "internalized" as long as mechanisms exist to account for the full social and environmental costs and benefits of a particular commodity, and include this "full-cost" accounting in market pricing. The result, it is argued, will be sustainable development, with the two proceeding hand in hand rather than in opposition to one another. There are two problems with this argument, however. In a world of difference, it is not clear that it is possible, even in principle, to satisfactorily calculate the full social and environmental costs of a commodity. Second, this argument inadequately addresses the fact that measures to internalize externalities are profoundly political—and that capitalist enterprises often have the incentive and power to block them (see also Chapter 7). We turn now to how neoliberalism has incorporated the social issues.

Neoliberalism, Social Capital, and the Mainstreaming of Difference, Participation, and Empowerment

In 1987, Margaret Thatcher famously stated that "there is no such thing as society. There are individual men and women, and there are families"—who, we might add, are supposed to interact as rational individuals in self-regulating markets. But a decade later, this high neoliberalist position was under challenge by the viewpoint that society, in the guise of social capital, is the "missing link" in development studies (Grootaert, 1998). (Note the language here; "missing link" usually refers to a gap in the evolutionary record between apes and humans.) The neoliberal discovery and embrace of social capital have not, however, translated into an engagement with social difference and the associated structures of power. Academics and activists have long critiqued exclusions and inclusions along the lines of such social differences as gender, race, class, and caste in the processes of liberalization, development, and sustainable development. They have also highlighted how dominant masculinist perspectives from the core fail to attend to the construction or reification of most of these differences, and how they shape people's selective inclusions in processes of "liberalization." This lack of attention emanates from the premise that some of these differences (e.g., race, caste, "tribe") are irrelevant, and that class differences can be explained by individual merit while other forms of difference (e.g., religion) can be completely separated from secular society. Religious values, for example, are regarded as simply one of many factors determining individuals' preferences—preferences that are then best met through market exchange (including competition between religions).

With respect to gender, the picture becomes more complicated. Recall that with the emergence of women in development (WID), gender mainstreaming became a key component of international development institutions (Chapter 4). The Office of the Special Adviser on Gender Issues and Advancement of Women (2005) at the United Nations defines "gender mainstreaming" as "promotion of gender equality at all levels—in research, legislation, policy development and in activities on the ground, and to ensure that women as well as men can influence, participate in and benefit from development efforts." In short, as long as women are fully empowered, and their issues and preferences receive equal attention in the economy, they should be able to participate as fully in, and gain as much from, market-led development initiatives as men do. According to this view, success or failure in a neoliberal world cannot be explained by people's gender, but is their individual responsibility.

At the same time, the question of whether and how gender should be mainstreamed in the context of market liberalization, and the pros and cons of such mainstreaming, have been vigorously debated in feminist circles. The 1980s saw the growth of a rich body of literature on gendered labor and free trade zones, as third world women workers became a critical part of global commodity chains, producing manufactures exclusively for export to the rich countries (Nisonoff, 1997: 179). A recurring issue in these writings has been the question of whether EPZs and free trade zones, such as the *maquiladoras* (export assembly plants in Mexico along the U.S. border), have liberated women wage workers from patriarchal domination, or whether the exploitative and poor working conditions in factories and the changes pushing women out of homes to support their natal or marital families symbolize a deepening or redefinition of patriarchal relations.

For example, Linda Lim (1983/1997) argues that multinational corporations generally offer better employment alternatives to women than local enterprises in modern and traditional sectors of the economy, and also provide a limited escape from the domestic roles imposed by traditional patriarchy. According to Diane Elson and Ruth Pearson (1981), women are hired in such factories because of a discourse of "natural" womanly qualities, such as nimble fingers and docility, which are results of specific socialization processes. Thus women's participation in the new labor regimes has tended to (1) *intensify* existing forms of gender subordination, through active preservation and deployment of traditional forms of patriarchal power; (2) *decompose* existing gender relations, through such practices as commodification of women's bodies and marriages; and (3) *recompose* new forms of gender relations, by subjecting women to subordination by their male factory bosses instead of their male relatives in the household. Similarly, Baneria (1989) views feminization of global capital as a function of three factors (labor control and malleability, productivity, and flexible labor), and sees the predominance of women workers in temporary contracts and in part-time work as facilitating all these aspects. More recently, Wright (2001, 2006) has extended this conversation by arguing that plans to redevelop third world cities, such as Ciudad Juarez on the U.S.–Mexico border, into new industrial districts are dependent on reproducing the currently existing cities—marked by poverty, inadequate infrastructure, and unskilled low-wage laborers willing to work in labor-intensive industries. She shows how disposability of temporary workers, collusion between tradition and femininity, the linking of progress to masculinity, and the construction of femmes fatales and masculine heroes all become key elements in the new proposals that seek to transform an "unskilled, low-tech, high-crime ghetto into a high-tech value adding city, one teeming with middle-class services, skilled professionals, and safe neighborhoods" (Wright, 2001: 93).

Other key concerns in feminist writing have included the new forms of consciousness enabled by free trade processes. Even though *maquiladoras* have taken advantage of women's vulnerability in the job market, and although the organization of labor in specific plants has not automatically resulted in feelings of solidarity, the nature and conditions of *maquila* work have allowed women workers to confront new challenges and develop new forms of consciousness in the realms of household relations, morality, virtue, and femininity (Fernandez-Kelly, 1984; Wright, 2006). Ong's (1987) work on Malay peasant women in Japanese-owned factories in Malaysia has complicated analyses of factory labor by challenging the dichotomy between "traditional" patriarchy on the one hand, and liberation through "modern capitalism" on the other. Although young women's working conditions are frequently negotiated for them by their male family members, they have innovatively resisted the imposition of new tasks and schedules through claims of spirit possession, which require ceremonies to "free" them or the machines. In this framework, patriarchy, cultural practices, and everyday play of power and resistance have become thoroughly interwoven in the workplace, community, and family.

By the mid-1990s, however, critics of liberalization became concerned with how processes of mainstreaming are no longer confined to the woman issue, but are also spreading in the areas of participation and empowerment. NGOs, community-based "participatory" schemes, and new social movements are proliferating hand in hand with neoliberal globalization—a phenomenon that has sometimes been labeled "NGO-ization." Geoff Wood (1997) argues that the term "franchise state" best characterizes this new relationship between NGOs and a neoliberal state, because NGOs subcontract the management and administration of essential social services from the state. Writing in the very different contexts of Latin America and Germany, respectively, Sonia Alvarez (1998: 306) and Sabine Lang (2002) observe the ways in which "NGO-ization of feminisms" has transformed radical/grassroots feminist movements into professional managers of women's issues, in pretty much the same ways as state institutions are managed.

For Sangeeta Kamat (2002: 166–167), this "NGO-ization of grassroots struggles"—feminist or otherwise—represents continuities within the sphere of the "new politics" of state and civil society. Unlike many scholars of new social movements, who see autonomous civil society organizations as symbolizing the devolution of power from the state to the public, Kamat illustrates how the structure and praxis of grassroots organizations may contribute to reproducing the status quo state, particularly in the era of capitalist globalization. She notes that the seemingly different discourses of empowerment and corporatization share a philosophy of change. Both suggest that in order to ensure the progress of the whole nation, the state and civil society need to work together to direct the productive forces of society (including people). The actualization of the productive forces of the nation, furthermore, is only deemed possible through structural and moral disciplining so that all classes can produce to the best of their capacity, and the poor can get the special assistance they need to realize that capacity. Downsizing the welfare state may then be acceptable to many NGOs, argues Kamat, as long as the state institutions and international community remain committed to the development of productive forces.

VIEWS FROM THE PERIPHERY: ENCOUNTERING DEVELOPMENT AND GLOBALIZATION

Notwithstanding renewed debates over development, thinkers in the core largely agree that development consists first and foremost of economic growth, and that both the knowledge about how to achieve growth and the growth itself should diffuse from the core to the periphery. Yet the experiences of many people of the periphery continue to raise questions about what development has proven itself to be about, and whether it really is a good thing. The experiential basis for this thinking lies in third world encounters with innumerable development failures or "unintended consequences," resulting in a variety of social, cultural, economic, political, and environmental crises. These experiences include alienation; the persistence of poverty and even impoverishment amid increasing affluence; growing gaps between rich and poor; environmental destruction; and processes of cultural hegemony. Such experiences in turn cause or exacerbate increasing levels of tension and contestation along lines of gender, race, ethnicity, religion, and region, and provoke increasing levels of oppression by militarized states. It is important to emphasize that domination, malnutrition, and environmental damage did not originate with development. However, while development has increased material production and the wealth of some, it has tended to reduce the power of the poorest and most vulnerable social groups to control their own lives. Such people have often found development destructive—undermining their social and cultural livelihood systems and degrading their environment, without providing them with suitable alternatives.

There is a long history of a grassroots resistance to development interventions, particularly among the rural poor, who have often been on the losing end of development (see Scott, 1985). The crises mentioned above have caused such popular resistance to blossom since the 1970s, with an expanding number of social movements and local experiments becoming increasingly important throughout much of the third world. These movements have emerged from contestations of people for whom the experience of development has been one of deepening oppression, impoverishment, exploitation, and displacement. Locally rooted social movements may increasingly "scale up" or jump scales from the local to the national or global, in order to gain leverage in their struggles against destructive development or neoliberal globalization, while still remaining rooted in the different social realities of highly differing contexts of development (Glassman, 2001). Some argue that these movements and experiments—including environmental movements, women's movements, farmers' movements, and movements to defend local communities—not only demonstrate the bankruptcy of development, but also hold the key to rethinking development and producing an alternative globalization from below (Brecher, Costello, and Smith, 2000; Escobar, 1995; Slater, 2004; Wignaraja, Hussain, Sethi, and Wignaraja, 1991).

People working from within some of the traditions of development thought discussed earlier in this chapter and in the preceding two chapters recognize many of these same problems and patterns. For example, conventional development proponents often argue that the negative experiences mentioned above, though painful, are in some cases the result of tactical errors or failures of execution, and that in others they represent necessary but short-term pains of adjustment ("to make an omelet, you must break eggs") or gaps that will be filled in over time. Therefore, although these phenomena must be minimized and smoothed out, they are not seen as evidence of fundamental flaws in the development project.

On the other hand, a number of thinkers hold that the evolution of these problems throughout the world cannot be explained satisfactorily by available theories even after refinement. Instead, they argue that the kinds of polarization created by development are ubiquitous and insoluble within the model of the mainstream development project and its associated notions of state, market, and civil society (Banuri, 1990; Escobar, 1992; Sachs, 1992; Yapa, 1996a). Many such thinkers, drawing on the work of the French philosopher Michel Foucault, emphasize that knowledge is power, because it shapes what we see and what we believe to be possible. Their work centrally addresses the politics of representation and the ways in which a reality "colonized" by a western masculinist politics of representation has worked to the disadvantage of particular social groups. We briefly touch on two such approaches: postcolonialism and postdevelopment.

Postcolonialism

Ironically, perhaps, postcolonialism is an approach that refuses to relegate colonialism to the past. Although formal colonialism has ended for all but a handful of territories, the material and discursive legacies of colonialism are very much in force, meaning that an intellectual and institutional continuity remains—a colonial present (Gregory, 2004). Postcolonial scholarship seeks to disrupt the legacies of colonialism; it argues that nationalism cannot adequately claim to represent the colonized (and subsequently decolonized) subjects under the name of, or any community called, a "nation" (Bhabha, 1994; Ismail, 1999; cf. Said, 1978; Spivak, 1988).

Thinkers embracing postcolonial frameworks are particularly sensitive to the ways in which systems of knowledge affect thought and action, and therefore represent power.

Works such as Said's (1978) *Orientalism* have demonstrated how colonial discourses laden with ethnocentric assumptions constituted the lens through which the world was viewed; through which norms were set; and through which governing policies and institutions were imagined, operated, and justified (Chapter 3). Postcolonial critiques argue that theorizing about the world is still produced primarily in western institutions and continues to systematically generate concepts and theories that set the west apart from and above others. They argue that western thought cannot explain the rest; rather, it homogenizes the rest of the world and locates it as an inferior other. They focus on problems of difference, agency, subjectivity, and resistance in ways that seek to challenge or destabilize such western and nationalist discourses of civilization, modernization, development, and globalization. This is done by (1) foregrounding the importance of colonial and imperial politics; (2) explaining the manner in which the categories of colonizer and colonized, center and periphery, globalizer and globalized necessarily constitute one another; and (3) questioning who the agents of knowledge are, where they are located, for whom they speak, and what their priorities are.

Postcolonial approaches further argue that mainstream discourses of knowledge have silenced the voices of sociopolitically marginalized peoples (sometimes referred to as "subalterns"), and that this silencing implies three things. First, a subaltern subject can only appear as inadequate, even to her- or himself. Second, although it is important to "recover" the voices, agency, and resistance of marginalized people that have been erased by the dominant discourses of knowledge and power, it is also important to recognize that such attempts at recovery will always remained buried in contradictions. Third, the voices, thoughts, and actions of subalterns cannot be accessed in completely transparent ways (Spivak, 1988).[3] Finally, postcolonial thinkers emphasize the need to revalidate autonomy, resistance to subversion, and alternative ways of knowing and doing. In so doing, they often draw out cases from the peripheries or the south as a way of making more visible the global realities of geopolitical power and representation (McEwan, 2002; Slater, 2004).

Several strands of this critique have come alive in feminist engagements with development, especially as the mainstreaming of gender in such institutions as the United Nations and the World Bank has produced the monolithic third world woman as victim who must be saved, liberated, and empowered through development. The political and intellectual mediation and representation of the third world woman in western feminist discursive practices and in development institutions have constituted a central theme in this writing. For example, Marnia Lazreg (1988) has addressed how the tendency to see gender relations as determined by Islam displaces the actual existence of Algerian women by ahistorical signifiers of tradition such as the veil, seclusion, or clitoridectomy. Chandra Talpade Mohanty (1984) has described the creation of a monolithic category of third world woman as discursive colonization, where third world women are defined as victims of male violence while western women are positioned as true feminist subjects. For Aihwa Ong (1987), such tendencies in hegemonic feminism construct third world women and men in essentialist terms, while Cheryl Johnson-Odim (1991) points out how an exclusive focus on third world women's cultural practices, coupled with a disengagement from questions of political and economic domination of the third world by the west, effectively places first world feminists in the service of western imperialism. Taken together, these insights give us tools to complicate two ideas. First, "woman" cannot be seen as a predefined category based on some shared essence. Rather, "woman"—particularly the subaltern woman on whom hinge the projects of modernization, empowerment, and emancipation—is a *political* subject. Second, both the development discourse and the broader feminist discourse that it interacts with are loaded with political stakes.

Critics argue that postcolonial theorists write in a jargon that is accessible only to academic specialists, thereby perpetuating the exclusion of the colonized and oppressed from the conversation. A second criticism is that postcolonial approaches have developed a theoretical sophistication at the expense of material concerns, and that by focusing on discourse they neglect material power relationships and economic relationships, while also undermining a focus on the political and intellectual possibilities of alliance work. A final criticism points out that these approaches have been preoccupied with the past and have had little to say about ways to address immediate problems or about postcolonial futures. Nevertheless, postcolonial writings have acted as correctives to the Eurocentrism and masculinism of elite knowledges, and have promoted a recognition of diversity and of the possibility of alternatives (McEwan, 2002: 130).

Postdevelopment

Postdevelopment (sometimes also called "antidevelopment") thinking draws from and parallels postcolonial thinking. Postdevelopment sees development as

> a particular vision and one that is neither benign nor innocent. It is a set of knowledges, interventions, and world-views (in short a "discourse") that are also powers—to intervene, to transform, and to rule. It embodies a geopolitics, in that its origins are bound up with Western power and strategy for the third world, enacted and implemented through local third world elites. (Sidaway, 2002: 16)

Two important critiques are that development disempowers and impoverishes its supposed beneficiaries.

Development as Disempowerment

Postdevelopmentalists argue that development disempowers its supposed beneficiaries in two ways: first, by giving them no voice in defining the ends of development; and, second, by excluding them from discussions of the means by which those ends are to be reached. The development discourse ignores the fact that different societies have different histories, geographies, cultures, institutions, and conceptions of the good life: "societies of the third world are not seen as diverse and incomparable possibilities of human living arrangements, but are placed on a single 'progressive' track, more or less advanced according to the criteria and direction of the hegemonic nations" (Sachs, 1990: 9). Consideration of alternative futures is foreclosed; consequently, for two-thirds of the world's population, notes Gustavo Esteva (1992), thinking of development of any kind requires thinking of themselves as underdeveloped. Such a self-perception, far from being the simple acceptance of objective reality, entails a voluntary intellectual surrender: It impedes thinking of one's own objectives; it undermines confidence in oneself and one's own culture; it leads one to demand management from the top down; and it converts participation into a manipulative trick that engages people in struggles for getting what the powerful want to impose on them (Esteva, 1992: 7–8).

This construction of development as learning the lessons of the developed countries in order to catch up with them allows developmentalists to position development as a narrowly technical endeavor that must be directed by a set of specialized professionals and institutions who alone can develop, validate, and put to use the knowledge required to carry out such a complex task (Escobar, 1988: 430). The knowledge produced and employed by these professionals is seen to be scientific, objective, universally applicable, and the only valid knowledge. All other forms of knowledge are considered to be subjective, contaminated by particular values and agendas, and therefore inferior. Consequently, people who are not trained specialists, or who are outside development institutions, the state, or big business, are considered to possess little knowledge relevant to their own development and to have no valid standpoint from which to critique the knowledges produced and deployed by development institutions. Their only role is to be passive subjects of development who participate by going along with the plans of the developers. This intellectual positioning of the development discourse removes any need for substantive consultation with, or accountability to, those in whose name development is carried out. On the contrary, it serves to sanctify any intervention by the "more developed" in the lives of those declared to be "underdeveloped" in the name of a higher evolutionary goal (Sachs, 1990: 11–12).

Postdevelopmentalists argue that the knowledge system underlying development is actually a central reason why development interventions do not help their putative beneficiaries. This is because even specialist scientific knowledge, far from being universal and objective, is just one *culture* of situated knowledge, shaped by the social positions of specialists and their institutions. Such knowledge thus reflects interests, priorities, and ways of thinking that are Eurocentric, middle-class, masculine, and weighted in favor of powerful political and economic interests. The biases in scientific knowledge are both hidden and also compounded by the reductionist nature of science (Shiva, 1991). Reductionism is based on the assumption that all systems are made up of the same basic discrete and atomistic constituents, and that all basic processes are mechanical. A reductionist approach allows researchers to construct simplified models that allow them to focus very precisely on one particular aspect of a complex reality. At the same time, a reductionist approach throws other aspects of that same reality out of focus, rendering them distorted or invisible. Scientific managers using such models often attempt to simplify and homogenize reality to make it into a replica of their models (Alvares, 1992; Scott, 1994). When they do so, the result is that the aspects of reality that were ignored usually manifest themselves in the form of unanticipated negative consequences.

Scott (1994) and Shiva (1991, 1993) cite scientific forestry as a striking example of this reductionist process of simplification, homogenization, and the consequent disruptions. The first simplification is to assume that the key consideration is to maximize annual income from timber sales. That assumption leads scientific forestry to reduce a forest to an assemblage of commercial trees. These are then reduced to abstract trees representing a volume of lumber, pulp, or firewood. Finally, over time the forests and land are manipulated to increase production of the most highly valued commercial trees—a process that often culminates in the conversion of complex and diverse forests to a monoculture of even-aged tree farms. This calculus of scientific forestry misses almost everything, including the existence value and ecological value of all noncommercial flora and fauna; the important role of the forest in sustaining the environmental systems upon which all life depends; and the "vast and complex, negotiated social uses of the forest for hunting and gathering, pasturage, digging valuable minerals, fishing, charcoal-making, trapping, and food collection as well as its significance for magic, worship, refuge, etc." (Scott, 1994: 3).

The particular simplifications employed in scientific forestry have allowed it to serve the state's revenue needs, overlooking both environmental destruction and the violence done to people who can no longer use forests to provide for their survival. Such biases, which are the taken-for-granted simplifications of scientific management, are one way in which scientific knowledge and practices are used (also innocently and by well-meaning people) to promote and justify projects and policies whose consequences include the devaluation, exclusion, and use of violence against marginal social groups—particularly people of lower classes and those whose ways of knowing are nonreductionist, non-European, and/or nonmasculinist.

The scientific metaphor of nature as a

machine characterized by divisibility and manipulability is to be contrasted, says Shiva (1993), with organic metaphors in which concepts of order and power are based on interdependence and reciprocity. The organic metaphor requires contextualized and holistic ways of acquiring and validating knowledge. Indigenous or traditional knowledges generally rely on the organic metaphor, and their knowledge is directly coded in cultural practice. For example, nutritional knowledge is embodied in dietary customs, and agricultural knowledge is embodied in such farming practices as seed selection and cropping patterns (Chapter 12). Indigenous knowledges are not static, contrary to often-held assumptions; they evolve with experience, innovation, and adaptation of other knowledges to which they are exposed, and shape local culture and institutions. Such knowledges are devalued by development thinking, despite the fact that traditional knowledge and systems of land use and production have proved far more environmentally appropriate, resilient, and complex than initially supposed by outside experts (Colchester, 1994: 69).

Development as Impoverishment

Antidevelopment thinkers make another point that relates to the ways in which scientific forestry provides certain values while impoverishing forests ecologically and impoverishing peoples who rely on forests. According to this argument, development thinking produces and justifies policies, programs, and projects that, though often providing increasing flows of commodities to the upper middle and upper classes, simultaneously create scarcity in other spheres, degrade the environment, and undercut the physical and cultural support systems of the many people who are impoverished and vulnerable. This can happen in part because the knowledge system of development is not even equipped with the intellectual tools to recognize the destruction it produces (Yapa, 1996a).

The practice of development, a form of social engineering, relies on two other questionable yet unquestioned beliefs: (1) that rapid global national income (GNI) growth is the key to development, because all human benefits derive from economic growth; and (2) that rapid GNI growth will result from technology transfer and industrialization achieved through market and/or state institutions. "In the economists' world of capitalist development the agents of change are the multinational corporation, technology transfer, the state, the planning bureaucracy and the project manager. . . . In the Marxists' world of socialist development the agents of change are the vanguard intellectual, the socialist party, the state, the planning bureaucracy and the project manager" (Yapa, 1993b: 11). This implies a progressive expansion of the influence of states and/or markets to areas of life previously governed by relationships between people based on local knowledge and ties of mutual obligation and reciprocity. Such relationships traditionally provided some social rights for the poor, who have little power in interactions with market or state. Thus development results in an institutionalized weakening of the less well off, complementing their intellectual disempowerment.

GNI growth has not generally "trickled down" to benefit the poor. Furthermore, in focusing on GNI growth, reductionist conceptions of development highlight commodity production and thereby tend to render invisible other kinds of production, as well as any values that are not represented in prices (Chapter 2). One invisible category is "self-provisioning"—production by people (often women) of goods and services primarily for consumption by their own households. When people eat home-grown food, live in self-built houses of natural materials, or wear homemade clothes of natural fiber, their production and consumption are generally overlooked, and they are defined as poor in prevailing development discourse. More importantly, the resources that they use are held to be underutilized because they have not been turned into commodities. The power dynamics of development arbitrarily reallocate such resources to commodity production through such devices as state imposition of new property rights regimes and/or expropriation of land by the state or by powerful people, without compensating the holders of traditional or customary rights.

> Development for some means underdevelopment and dispossession of many. Development interventions aimed at commercialization of natural resources involve a major shift in the manner in which rights to resources are perceived and exercised. It transforms commons into commodities, and deprives the politically weak communities of access to resources, and robs resources from nature, to generate growth on the market for the more privileged groups in society. (Shiva, 1991: 10)

One prominent example of this commercialization—the hybrid seeds of the Green Revolution developed by first world scientists to improve third world food production—is a case in point (see sidebar: "What Are Improved Seeds?").

A second invisible category is natural production by the ecological processes providing the environment that makes human life possible (Shiva, 1991; 1993: 75). Economists are only beginning to develop ways to assign values to ecological services (e.g., maintenance of hydrologic regimes) and to search for ways to take account of how the naturally produced wealth that has accumulated historically (e.g., soils, forests, biodiversity) is now being destroyed in the process of creating commodity wealth. Furthermore, the economic valuation of some of the hitherto invisible forms of value, such as nonmarket consumption, ecological services, and the intrinsic value of biological species, ranges from problematic to impossible (Blaikie, 1995: 212). Indeed, a substantial proportion of what appears in GNI statistics as net economic growth may actually represent the consumption of ecological wealth (e.g., clear-cutting forests), which is destroying unmeasured or unquantifiable values. This suggests a very different view of human–environment relations from that presumed in discussions of sustainable development (Chapter 7). If economic exploitation of the biophysical environment carries with it ecological degradation, then no amount of management can create ecologically sustainable development, let alone socially sustainable development (Escobar, 1995; Mies and Shiva, 1993).

The development discourse of mainstream and Marxist economic development theorists disempowers and impoverishes the poor by closing off opportunities for them to participate in decisions shaping the conditions under which they will live their lives. Therefore, postdevelopmentalists are interested in alternatives to development. Such alternatives will emerge from an emphasis on local cultures and knowledges; a critical stance toward (or outright rejection of) established scientific discourses; and a defense and promotion of localized, pluralistic grassroots movements (Escobar, 1995: 215; see also Rahnema and Bawtree, 1997).

There are several critiques of postdevelopment. The first is that it offers very little that is new, not moving much beyond the earlier work of critics such as Mahatma Gandhi, E. F. Schumacher, Ivan Illich, and Franz Fanon (Corbridge, 1998). A second criticism is that whereas postdevelopment theorists, like postcolonialists, seek to challenge or destabilize western discourses of civilization, modernization, development, and globalization, they often begin their analysis with Truman's 1949 inaugural address (Chapter 4) and thereby overlook the colonial and imperial processes that their postcolonial colleagues highlight as central to understanding the colonial present. A related criticism is that postdevelopment theorists do not adequately explore the ways in which development involves complex and mutually constitutive relationships among the multiple parties that constitute the development encounter. Postdevelopment theorists seem to critique modernity and reason, while failing to engage adequately with the possibil-

What Are Improved Seeds?

Lakshman Yapa (1993a: 259) argues that poverty is not about a lack of development; rather it is, "a routine, everyday, normal manifestation of the very process of economic development." This fact is not commonly recognized in academia, he maintains, because developmentalist thinking directs our attention elsewhere and distorts understanding of the problem. He uses the example of Green Revolution seeds to demonstrate how new seeds are a means for the domination of people and destruction of nature that create scarcity at the same time as they provide high yields. He argues that the fragmented nature of conventional development paradigms conceives new seeds as purely technical improvements, despite the fact that these seeds also embody a web of social, ecological, cultural, political, and academic interrelationships leading not only to technical achievements, but also to social, ecological, cultural, political, and academic changes. What happens when new seed technologies are evaluated according to all these attributes?

- *Technical attributes*: They produce higher grain yields when used as intended.
- *Social attributes*: The technical attributes of new seeds mean that they cannot be used in all places or be adopted by all farmers, so their use confers benefits of higher production unequally on different social classes and regions.
- *Ecological attributes*: The new seeds are genetically uniform and require irrigation, chemical fertilizers, and pesticides—encouraging loss of biodiversity, increased soil erosion, contamination of groundwater, eutrophication of water bodies, and depletion of water tables. This degrades the long-term capacity of the land to provide subsistence. Alternative indigenous technologies, such as multicropping and crop rotation, biological fixation of nitrogen, and biological pest controls, are ignored or suppressed.
- *Cultural attributes*: The diffusion of improved seeds is also the diffusion of a new culture—one that devalues the production of subsistence and erodes the principle of local reproduction using the alternative technologies above, by creating a need for external inputs (to control soil erosion, groundwater contamination, etc.). The new seeds thus effectively become bearers of a hegemonic culture of science, capital, and authority that subjugates tradition and the keepers of that knowledge.
- *Political attributes*: The state, encouraged by the fertilizer and pesticide lobbies, becomes the chief architect of agricultural modernization through high-input seeds, while failing to promote alternative means of increasing food production, such as land reform.
- *Academic attributes*: Seed technologies are arrived at through academic processes of research carried out in the context of social scientific theory that sees grain shortfalls as the problem and high-yielding seeds as the solution. In addition to hiding this academic blind spot itself, these processes conceal the social causes of hunger, the alternative solutions to grain shortfalls; and the social, ecological, and cultural attributes of new seeds.

Such an alternative approach to thinking about the Green Revolution illuminates the nexus of technological, social, ecological, cultural, and academic relations that new seeds embody, making it clear how new seeds create scarcity along with higher yields.

ity that there can be multiple modernities and rationalities existing in varied times and places. Furthermore, they fail to deal adequately with other forms of heterogeneity on a number of levels, by romanticizing the local and neglecting to explore (1) how local customs and social movements can be oppressive as well as liberating; (2) how development itself is heterogeneous and contested, and produces outcomes that can be both good and bad; and (3) how local communities are characterized by hierarchical structures of difference (Gidwani, 2002).

These criticisms must be taken seriously. They point to ways in which post-development thinking could become more rigorous and nuanced through a more serious engagement with both political economy and postcolonial theory. At the same time, it is worth noting that the aim of postdevelopment theory is more political than academic. It seeks to disrupt a development discourse that has proven remarkably stable, sturdy, and resilient. For example, Escobar (1995) goes to great lengths to show how the development complex absorbs and transforms criticisms in ways that rob the criticisms of their critical power. And it is not clear that postdevelopmentalists are opposed to rationality and reason in general. More often, they critique forms of reason based on narrowly instrumentalist rationality and reductionist systems of knowledge.

Critics also hold that postdevelopment overstates the case against development. If "development" is a concept that stands for a better life (whatever that means in a particular context), then it is something that everyone wants. Therefore, we should not be looking to postdevelopment or antidevelopment, but rather to improved development—development that is better specified and executed. Human efforts are always imperfect, but the mainstream development discourse already recognizes (to some degree) the incomplete, uneven, and contradictory nature of development, and it is always being revised to improve development processes. Therefore, to throw out development because of its imperfections might be seen as throwing the baby out with the bathwater.

Postdevelopment theorists do not criticize the idea that people may want development in the sense of a better life. Rather, they observe that a second sense of the word "development" refers to the *particular* discourse discussed above, and that the first sense of the word has become inextricably bound up with the second sense. As a result, development has, as Escobar (1995: 39) observes, "created a space in which only certain things could be said or even imagined." Therefore, for the majority of people in the third world, improved lives can only come when the mainstream development discourse and its associated complex of power, knowledge, and institutions are transcended. Transcending this discourse and this complex requires critical analytical tools, political courage, and collective energies that internalize a commitment to heterogeneity and pluralism, as well as to the necessity of continuous self-reflexive interrogation.

We might think of postcolonial and postdevelopment thought as complementary to each other. Whereas postcolonial thought is subtle and theoretically sophisticated, yet often distanced from material realities, postdevelopment thought is marked by an outraged demand for change that comes from engaging with the raw wounds of the human and environmental tragedies inflicted, and overlooked or glibly explained away, by the system of power and knowledge that constitutes development. Both postcolonialism and postdevelopmentalism look for hope, not in developing the next superior doctrine, but in the kind of open-ended, pluralistic, radically democratic processes of change exemplified in the Zapatista uprising in Mexico and related forms of globalization from below, such as the World Social Forum (Slater, 2004; see sidebar: "Notes from Nowhere").

NOTES

1. The term "nongovernmental" is somewhat self-contradictory, because in many parts of the third world, NGOs have virtually become an arm of the state and have stepped in (with governmental support) to provide the basic services that were once seen as the responsibility of the state.

2. For example, on the one hand, corporations demand uniformly strong international protection of intellectual property through the WTO agreement on Trade Related Aspects of Intellectual Property Rights (TRIPS). On the other hand, workers are told that they must compete for corporate investment and jobs by limiting demands for wages, benefits, worker health and safety, or trade unionization. In addition, localities must compete by providing concessions such as low cost financing, infrastructure subsidies, tax breaks and/or weakened regulatory oversight

Notes from Nowhere

The editorial collective Notes from Nowhere (2003) imagines struggles against corporate globalization as revolutionary movements that must genuinely listen and reflect as they grow. This approach commits itself to a global political project that represents diverse, people-centered alternatives and is "defined by notions of diversity, autonomy, ecology, democracy, self-organization, and direct action" (29). Such a political journey can only advance as a listening rebellion, in which getting lost may be an important part of the process.

> The idea of listening rebellion turns preconceived notions of struggle on their head. Zapatismo [the approach of the Zapatistas in Chiapas, Mexico] throws political certainty to the wind, and out of the shape shifting, flowing mist, it grasps change; change not as banal revolutionary slogan, but as actual process. Change as the ability of revolutionaries to admit wrong, to stop and question everything. Change as the desire to dissolve the vertical structures of power and replace them with radical horizontality: real political participation. Change as the willingness to listen, the wisdom to grow, the commitment to transform. . . . Learning true democracy is not something you arrive at, and then sit still, clutching it tightly. It falters, starts up again, and requires constant rejuvenation and experimentation. It is a series of skills that require practice, self-knowledge, self-confidence, self-awareness. Walking and asking questions.
>
> A movement that stops asking questions will become more ruthless, possibly more "effective" in the short term, but ultimately, repressive, doctrinaire, unable to respond to new threats or opportunities. We begin, in short to resemble what we oppose. We ossify, and are toppled by those who innovate while we stagnate and pontificate. We refuse this fate that has befallen so many radical movements. We commit ourselves to move on and reconstitute rather than let that happen. (Notes from Nowhere, 2003: 507)

The authors use fences, real and metaphorical, as a way to bring together divergent struggles. Their aim is to provide mutual support and encouragement in the project of tearing down all of the fences of exclusion or imprisonment. Through this open-ended process, both alternative forms of development and alternatives to development may emerge:

> The fence surrounding the military base in Chiapas is the same fence that surrounds the G8 [Group of Eight] meeting in Genoa. It's the fence that divides the powerful from the powerless; those whose voices decree from those whose voices are silenced. And it is replicated everywhere.
>
> For the fence surrounds gated communities of rich neighborhoods from Washington to Johannesburg—islands of prosperity that float in seas of poverty. It surrounds vast estates of lands in Brazil, keeping millions who live in poverty from growing food. It's patrolled by armed guards who keep the downtrodden and the disaffected out of shopping malls. It's hung with signs warning you to "Keep out" of places where your mother and grandmother played freely. This fence stretches across borders between rich and poor worlds. For the unlucky poor who are caught trying to cross into the rich world, the fence encloses the detention centres where refugees live behind razor wire.
>
> Built to keep all the ordinary people of the world out of the way, out of sight, far from the decision makers and at the mercy of their policies, this fence also separates us from those things which are our birthright as human beings—land, shelter, culture, good health, nourishment, clean air, water. For a world entranced by profit, public space is privatized, land fenced off, seeds, medicines and genes patented, water metered, and democracy turned into purchasing power. The fences are also inside us. Interior borders run through our atomized minds and hearts, telling us we should look out only for ourselves, that we are alone.
>
> But borders, enclosures, fences, walls, silences are being torn down, punctured, invaded by human hands, warm bodies, strong voices which call out the most revolutionary of messages: "You are not alone!"
>
> For we are everywhere.
>
> We are in Seattle, Prague, Genoa and Washington. We are in Buenos Aires, Bangalore, Manila,

Durban and Quito. Many of these place names have been made iconic by protest, symbols of resistance and hope in a world which increasingly offers little room for either.

The Zapatistas have joined with thousands around the world who believe that fences are made to be broken. Refugees detained in the Australian desert tear down prison fences, and are secreted to safety by supporters outside. The poor, rural landless of Brazil cut the wire that keeps them out of vast uncultivated plantations and swarm onto the properties of rich, absentee landlords, claim the land, create settlements, and begin to farm. Protestors in Quebec city tear down the fence known as the "wall of shame" surrounding the summit meeting of the Free Trade Area of the Americas, and raise their voices in a joyful yell as it buckles under the weight of those dancing on its bent back, engulfed in euphoria even while the toxic blooms of tear gas hit. The radical guerrilla electricians in South Africa break the fence of privatization that keeps the poor from having electricity by installing illegal connections themselves. Peasant women across Asia gather to freely swap seed, defying the fences of market logic that would have them go into debt to buy commercial seed. "Keep the seeds in your hands, sister!" they declare. (Notes from Nowhere, 2003: 21).

and weakened environmental laws. Sometimes these concessions are all provided as a package in the form of Special Economic Zones or Export Processing Zones.

3. Spivak's essay "Can the Subaltern Speak?" (1988a) perhaps best demonstrates her concern for the processes whereby postcolonial studies ironically reinscribe and coopt neocolonial imperatives of political domination, economic exploitation, and cultural erasure. In a helpful summary of Spivak's complex essay, Benjamin Graves (1998) summarizes her central question thus: Is the postcolonial critic unknowingly complicit in the task of imperialism? Is "postcolonialism" a specifically first world, male, privileged, academic, institutionalized discourse that classifies and surveys the east in the same measure as the actual modes of colonial dominance it seeks to dismantle? According to Spivak, postcolonial studies must encourage postcolonial intellectuals to learn that their privilege is their loss. In "Can the Subaltern Speak?," Spivak encourages but also criticizes the efforts of the subaltern studies group, a project led by Ranajit Guha that has reappropriated Gramsci's term "subaltern" (the economically dispossesed) in order to locate and reestablish a "voice" or collective locus of agency in postcolonial India. Although Spivak acknowledges the "epistemic violence" done to Indian subalterns, she suggests that any attempt from the outside to ameliorate subalterns' condition by granting them collective speech will invariably encounter the following problems: (a) a logocentric assumption of cultural solidarity among a heterogeneous people, and (b) a dependence on western intellectuals to "speak for" the subaltern condition rather than allowing subalterns to speak for themselves. As Spivak argues, by speaking out and reclaiming a collective cultural identity, subalterns will in fact reinforce their subordinate position in society. The academic assumption of a subaltern collectivity becomes akin to an ethnocentric extension of western logos—a totalizing, essentialist "mythology," as Derrida might describe it—that doesn't account for the heterogeneity of the colonized body politic.

Part II Differentiated Livelihoods and the Nonhuman World

6 Geographies of Population

Discourse and Politics

> In general, underdeveloped countries . . . are not industrialized. They tend to have inefficient, usually subsistence agricultural systems, extremely low gross national products and per capita incomes, high illiteracy rates, and incredibly high rates of population growth . . . Most of these countries . . . could quite accurately be called "never-to-be-developed countries" [and they] . . . will be unable to escape from poverty and misery unless their populations are controlled. . . . The "have-nots" of the world are in an unprecedented position today. . . . Magazines, movies, transistor radios, and even television have brought them news and pictures of our way of life—our fine homes, highly varied diet, . . . our automobiles, airplanes, tractors, refrigerators. . . . Naturally they want to share our affluence. . . . It takes no political genius to guess the results of not just a continual frustration of these expectations, but an actual deterioration of living standards as well. Population pressure has been described as numbers of people pressing against values. For many people in the [underdeveloped countries] there are relatively few values left to press against, and even these are doomed if mankind continues on its present course.
>
> —PAUL R. EHRLICH AND ANNE H. EHRLICH (1970: 2–3)

> Could it be—possibly, shockingly—that the United States itself has a population problem? That not just the poorest nation in the world, but also the richest is suffering from too many children being born too fast taxing too many resources which are being consumed too fast? That it is time for this country to stop preaching to others and to do something about its own population growth? Not long ago, these questions would have seemed ridiculous, even bizarre. That is no longer the case.
>
> —DANIEL CALLAHAN (1971: xi–xii)

> Until the 1980s . . . population studies was not only virtually non-existent in most parts of the less developed world, the general public also had a very hazy idea about [population issues]. . . . Today . . . anyone . . . immediately spouts his or her pet theory about high fertility. . . . This public concern with population issues and, even more, this public opinion about the determinants of population growth

> is only partly a result of the great publicity that the population problem has received in recent years thanks to concerted efforts by official national and international agencies. The fact that there exist so many popular views about the causes of high fertility testifies also to (a) the high visibility of different influential groups with definite views about the determinants of fertility and (b) the ease with which fertility can be politicized by lobbies of any persuasion; no theory of fertility decline sounds terribly outlandish because every theory can drum up at least some empirical evidence in its favour.
>
> —ALAKA MALWADE BASU (1997: 14)

The quotations above offer a glimpse of the passionate arguments that the subject of population has been stirring in relation to development politics for the last four decades. Even more remarkable—if not necessarily evident from these quotes—is the widespread existence of a political and public consensus: on the assumed "overpopulation" of the global south and the curbing of fertility rates as its "solution." This can be found in the views expressed in third world countries about themselves and in the perceptions in the first world countries with regard to the so-called "population crisis" in the third world (Basu, 1997; Hartmann, 1995; Johnson, 1995). This consensus (however contested, and notwithstanding caution among today's academics about positing causal relationships between population growth and "development" processes) views human population numbers and fertility rates as key causes of poverty, environmental degradation, and social conflict, and as impediments to economic development. Although much of this book highlights the centrality of geographical location in shaping sociocultural, political–economic, and biophysical *processes*, here we deploy a geographical sensibility to approach some of these competing *discourses*. We argue that narratives focusing on population, fertility, and the natural increase of human beings are inextricably bound up with geographically and historically specific social agendas. How, and by whom, is control over reproduction and fertility exercised and contested over different geographical scales? And what are the consequences? To answer these questions, we consider some key theoretical frameworks that have helped to produce the above-mentioned consensus, as well as those that complicate the basic premises of that consensus and recast the terms and issues at stake in the "population debates."

The historical and projected growth of population, summarized in a graph (Figure 6.1), shows that human population levels were low and stable for centuries, but began to grow significantly from about 1500 A.D.—which marked the beginnings of European exploration and trade expansion, and of course the European discovery of the New World. It is estimated that in 1650 there were about 500 million people on earth; 190 years later (1840), the number had reached one billion. The world passed the two billion mark about 1920 (after 80 years), the three billion mark in 1965 (after 45 years), the four billion mark in 1979 (after 14 years), and the five billion mark in 1986 (taking 7 years; Coale, 1974; 16, Population Reference Bureau, 1986). By January, 2009, the world population had reached an estimated 6,751,602,449 (U.S. Census Bureau, 2009).

These aggregate population growth figures cannot show the effects of colonial histories of plunder, enslavement, and acquisition of wealth, or the processes of production, consumption, and redistribution that have continued to create haves and have-nots after the formerly colonized nations won their independence. Nor can they show the effects of policies and conditionalities of governments and international organizations. Such socioeconomic processes can create differing population dynamics in different places.

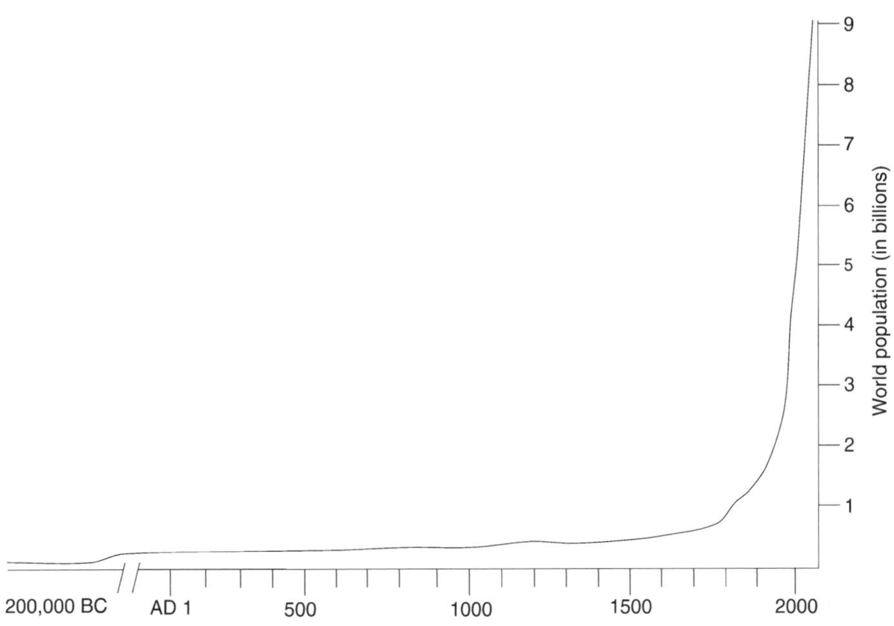

FIGURE 6.1. World population growth. *Source:* Adapted from Gore (1992). Copyright 1992 by Senator Al Gore. Adapted by permission of Houghton Mifflin Harcourt Publishing Company. For Gore's sources, see Gore (1992: 408).

Thus Blaut (1993) connects the post-1500 growth of European population, industry, and commerce to a locational advantage that made it easier for Europe to pursue sea travel to the Americas—allowing the conquest, plunder, and development of the resources of the New World, which Blaut terms the "first fruits of colonialism" (179). The other side of the same process was the rapid, severe, and widespread depopulation of the Americas due to war and epidemics of exotic diseases introduced by Europeans (Blaut, 1993: 184; see also Chapter 14, Figure 14.1).

Numerous debates on population since the 1960s have attempted to address these societal questions. For example, the role of the United States in controlling the populations of poor nations, and the ecological destabilization caused by the size and consumption rates of the U.S. population, have been vigorously debated (Bouvier and Grant, 1994; Callahan, 1971; Johnson, 1995)—as has the specter of China arriving at the global dinner table (Brown, 1995). Yet, at the level of policies (and the taken-for-granted "truths" that provide their rationale), a preoccupation with population numbers and fertility reduction has guided the agendas of governments and development/aid organizations, and this preoccupation has translated into interventions in the lives and bodies of the third world's poor.

In the following sections, we begin by contrasting two overarching frameworks with very different sets of assumptions, logics, and prescriptions on the question of population. The first focuses on population as a pressure on resources, with debates centering on a race between human population growth and the ability of human ingenuity to find ways to provide for the growing numbers of people. The second underscores the centrality of social organization in (re) shaping human needs, and the relationships of production, reproduction, consumption, and distribution that determine human impact on the environment. After discussing these broad approaches, we consider how the "demographic transition" model has been used to understand patterns of demographic change. Next we move to a critical scale that is frequently ignored in earlier framings of the population issue—the scale of the body. Here human reproduction and sexuality become key sites of conflict and struggle between different interest groups over the "means, ends and meanings of childbearing" (Greenhalgh and Li quoted in Kaler, 2000: 878). Finally, we reflect on selectivities in the population debates by examining the human immunodeficiency virus/acquired immune deficiency syndrome (HIV/AIDS) pandemic in Africa and the issue of literacy, which is often considered as having an important causal relationship with fertility.

FRAMEWORKS FOR UNDERSTANDING WORLD POPULATION GROWTH AND ITS RELATIONSHIP TO SOCIAL AND ENVIRONMENTAL PROBLEMS

Population versus Resources Approaches

The adjective "Malthusian" has been with us for many generations—an ominous pedalpoint to the world's song of life; a constant reminder that the genetic capability of people to increase their numbers requires of human beings an equivalent capability for ingenuity and innovation to keep the means of sustaining them in balance with the numbers of people. A major axis for debates on the question of population is the Malthusian perspective, which has inspired both pessimists and optimists who disagree on whether population increases faster than carrying capacity of land, or vice versa. Both sides see social and technological innovation as the key to solving the "imbalance" between population and resources, but disagree on the speed and limits of such innovation. We briefly consider the views of Malthus, the original pessimist, as well as those working within the same framework who have taken more optimistic views, such as economists Ester Boserup and Julian Simon.

The Malthusian Argument

The Reverend Thomas Robert Malthus published his celebrated study *An Essay on the Principle of Population* in 1798, at the age of 33. He wrote from the standpoint of an Anglican clergyman, a member of and servant to the propertied class. The gist of his population argument reads thus (this and the following quotations are from Malthus, 1798/1992):

> Taking the population of the world at any number, a thousand million, for instance, the human species would increase in the ratio of—1, 2, 4, 8, 16, 32, 64, 128, 256, 512 &c. and subsistence as—1, 2, 3, 4, 5, 6, 7, 8, 9, 10 &c. In two centuries and a quarter, the population would be to the means of subsistence as 512 is to 10: in three centuries as 4096 to 13, and in two thousand years the difference would be almost incalculable, though the produce in that time would have increased to an immense extent. (9)

In this scenario, population quickly outstrips subsistence. Malthus held that people might exercise what he called "preventive" checks on population growth—for example, by eschewing or delaying marriage. But when these checks on population growth were not effective, "positive" checks (e.g., war, famine, disease, revolution, and high infant mortality among families living in misery) would inevitably occur as a result of overpopulation. He argued that the preventive check of delayed marriage operated across all sections of society in Britain as men calculated the costs of taking on a dependent wife and children; yet he also suggested that the poor in Britain and elsewhere would continue to increase their population until nature, through positive checks, reestablished a balance between resources and population numbers.

> The vices of mankind are active and able ministers of depopulation. . . . But should they fail in this war of extermination, sickly seasons, epidemics, pestilence, and plague, advance in terrific array, and sweep off their thousands and ten thousands. Should success be still

> incomplete, gigantic inevitable famine stalks in the rear, and with one mighty blow, levels the population with the food of the world (49).

Malthus devised this argument on population as a way to counter the French Revolution's ideals of *liberté*, *egalité*, and *fraternité*, which were diffusing across the English Channel and threatening the English upper classes. He used his theory of population to defend privilege and social inequality, and to justify the immiseration of the lower classes as the product of natural forces and therefore humanly impossible to remedy through social change. First, he saw class differences as inevitable and moral. "When these two fundamental laws of society, the security of property and the institution of marriage, were once established, inequality of conditions must necessarily follow" (71). Second, he argued that even in the most benevolent and egalitarian society, as population outstripped sustenance, all the evils of the existing British society would inevitably emerge: "violence, oppression, falsehood, misery, every hateful vice, and every form of distress, which degrade and sadden the present state of society, seem to have been generated by the most imperious circumstances, by laws inherent in the nature of man, and absolutely independent of all human regulations" (67).

Malthus argued that the English Poor Laws, which provided public assistance to the poor, should be eliminated because they would depress the general condition of the poor, while creating more of them. In any case, "dependent poverty ought to be held disgraceful" (29). In addition to seeing women primarily as men's possessions, Malthus had a low opinion of the "lower classes," in regard to both their moral and sexual behavior and their intellectual promise. He frequently expressed disdain and opprobrium toward the poor, their supposed sexual licentiousness, and their tendency to proliferate:

> The cravings of hunger, the love of liquor, the desire of possessing a beautiful woman, will urge men to actions, of the fatal consequences of which, to the general interests of society, they are perfectly well convinced, even at the very time they commit them. (89)

> [The] principal argument of this essay tends to place in a strong point of view, the improbability, that the lower classes of people in any country, should ever be sufficiently free from want and labour, to obtain any high degree of intellectual improvement. (76)

In short, Malthus used the inadequate data available to him, along with his personal beliefs about the possibilities for change, to propose two independent "natural" trajectories of increase—one for sustenance and the other for population. Based on these "natural" laws of population, he argued that any attempt to make society more egalitarian, or even to ameliorate the condition of the poor, was idealistic, not possible in the real world, and doomed to failure. In fact, providing resources to the lower classes would be counterproductive, because it would reduce the well-being of all and result in greater numbers of immiserated poor. On the one hand, it was natural and inevitable that the misery of positive checks would fall first and most heavily on the lower classes. On the other hand, this immiseration—as well as war, famine, disease, revolution, and high infant mortality—can be seen as both a symptom of and a check upon overpopulation.

Neo-Malthusians

After World War II, problems of development and later environmental sustainability gave rise to a renewed and updated Malthusianism. Population growth was taken to explain such problems as poverty, hunger, malnutrition, and environmental degradation, making population control—in the guise of family planning—a central part of development strategies, first in India and later worldwide.

In 1968, Stanford University biologist Paul Ehrlich published *The Population Bomb*, warning that there would soon be more people than the earth could support and that hundreds of millions of people could die in the 1970s because it would be impossible to feed so many mouths. The next year, Garrett Hardin, a professor of biological sciences and environmental studies at the University of California at Santa Barbara, scaled up Malthusian ethics to the globe. Hardin (1969, 1974) advocated the notion of "lifeboat ethics" (an oxymoron of stupendous callousness). In his schema, nations are thought of as lifeboats, and their immigration policies govern what one does about nearby drowning swimmers, imploring to be pulled aboard. His argument appropriates still another image, this time from the World War I battlefields of France—the concept of *triage* ("to sort"). In triage, overwhelmed medics divided the wounded into three classes: those who would probably recover without immediate medical attention; those who were going to die anyway; and those who might survive if attended to there on the battlefield. Hardin argued that the 170 or so lifeboats comprising the world's nations could be similarly subjected to triage, and that the attention of the "medical" personnel should be directed toward those countries with some evident potential of surviving and achieving a balance in their populations and resources.

For Hardin and many others, a country like Bangladesh is already an international "basket case," and should be allowed to experience the ravages invoked by Malthus: famine, war, pestilence, sickly seasons, and the convulsions of nature. (And indeed Bangladesh, receiving the runoff from the denuded landscapes of highland Nepal, India, and Bhutan, did experience the last of these in the terrible flooding of 1988 that made millions homeless.)

In thinking of nations as a set of lifeboats, one has to ignore a number of inconvenient facts. First, it raises this question: How did all these lifeboats get built in the first place? For U.S. readers, how did the U.S. lifeboat come to be built? Second, there is an implicit assumption that the present distribution of access to resources is fair. The construction and maintenance of the lifeboat called the United States has depended on a continuing flow of commodities, ideas, and capital from other lifeboats. A population that constitutes under 5% of the world's population generates and consumes 31% of the global gross national income (GNI), and a considerable portion of that product has been hauled in over its gunwales from other lifeboats.

If one were to choose as "basket cases" those nations in which the per capita GNI was less than $500 in 2004, the resultant list would consist of 28 sub-Saharan African countries (including Ethiopia's 70 million people and Nigeria's 140 million people), and 7 countries in Asia, including the 141 million people of Bangladesh (Table 6.1). Overall, some 560 million Africans (over half the people of Africa) and 223 million Asians would be chosen for triage, for a grand total of 782 million people. This of course says nothing about the one billion or more people in other countries who individually live on less than $500/year. This simple calculation, determining the locations of supposedly disposable populations by neo-Malthusian logic, is reminiscent of a statement by Levi-Strauss (quoted in Harvey, 1974: 275–276): "Once men begin to feel cramped in their geographical, social and mental habitat, they are in danger of being tempted by the simple solution of denying one section of the species the right to be considered human."

Imagine that people themselves are weightless, but that they walk about with the average GNI of their country of citizenship stacked on their heads—$41,400 for the "mean" American in 2004, $90 for the average citizen of Burundi. (We leave aside the differences *within* countries—say, the head of Occidental Petroleum [quite a balancing act], and a bag lady in Washington, D.C. [with her $50 tucked under a scarf].) We could calculate a "GNIPopulation density" for different countries. In some degree, it represents the demand (if not the "insult") each of us makes on the environment to

TABLE 6.1. Triage: Countries to Abandon? (Annual Per Capita GNI $500 or Less, in U.S. Dollars)

Country	Population (2004, in millions)
Africa	
Burkina Faso	12.4
Burundi	7.4
Central African Republic	4.0
Chad	8.8
Congo	54.8
Eritrea	4.5
Ethiopia	70.0
Gambia	1.5
Ghana	21.2
Guinea	8.1
Guinea–Bissau	1.5
Kenya	32.5
Liberia	3.5
Madagascar	17.3
Malawi	11.2
Mali	12.0
Mauritania	2.9
Mozambique	19.1
Niger	12.1
Nigeria	139.8
Rwanda	8.4
Sierra Leone	5.4
Somalia	9.9
Tanzania	36.6
Togo	5.0
Uganda	25.9
Zambia	10.6
Zimbabwe	13.2
Total	559.6
Asia	
Bangladesh	140.5
Cambodia	13.6
Kyrgyzstan	5.1
Laos	5.8
Nepal	25.2
Tajikistan	6.4
Uzbekistan	25.9
Total	222.5
Combined total	782.1

Source: Data are from World Bank (2005b)

sustain us. The normative expectation for (and of) a child born in America is to be well clothed, fed, and educated (probably through college); protected from disease and violence; and in due course to own an iPod, a car, a house, and so forth—the conventional American dream. Of course, most people on earth do not come even close to achieving this dream.

If one indexes the world GNIPopulation density at 1.0, it shows that a U.S. citizen uses resources at a rate of 4.33 per square mile, whereas the average person in Niger uses resources at a rate of 0.008 per square mile—a ratio of 541:1 (Table 6.2). An advanced country with little land, such as Japan, has a very high GNIPopulation density, whereas countries like Canada and the Russian Federation have low density values. The Japanese "intensity of land use" as a combination of people and income has an impact per square mile in Japan that is 37 times the world average, and 4,585 times that of the land use intensity (similarly defined) in Niger. The notion of GNIPopulation density is kindred, but inverse, to the idea of the "ecological footprint" proposed by Wackernagel and Rees (1996). The ecological footprint is how many resources (productive marine waters are included) it takes to support a nation's population in relation to the sustainable resources produced each year in that nation. It is expressed as an area, in relation to the area of the country. The footprint for industrial first world economies resembles that of Godzilla, stomping over an area much larger than the country itself.

The issues of social difference highlighted above are important, and we return to them shortly. But first let us note that some scholars have a much more optimistic "take" on the population versus resources question, disputing Malthusian and neo-Malthusian contentions about both popu-

TABLE 6.2. Population Pressure Redefined: Comparative 2004 GNIPopulations and GNIPopulation Densities for Selected Countries

Country	Population (in millions)	Per capita GNI (U.S. $)	GNIPopulation (U.S. $) (in millions)	Area (sq. mi.)	GNIPopulation (millions)[a]	Index[b]
Japan	127.8	31,700	4,051,260	144,870	27.965	36.68
United States	293.5	41,400	12,150,900	3,679,245	3.303	4.33
Sweden	9.0	55,770	501,930	173,732	2.889	3.79
Poland	38.2	6,090	232,638	120,728	1.927	2.53
Bangladesh	140.5	440	61,820	55,598	1.112	1.46
Canada	31.9	28,390	905,641	3,849,674	0.235	0.31
China	1,296.5	1,290	1,672485	3,718,782	0.450	0.59
Russian Fed.	142.8	3,410	486,948	6,592,849	0.074	0.09
Niger	12.1	230	2,783	489,191	0.006	0.008
World	6,349.3	6,179	39,232,325	51,464,703	0.762	1.00

Source: Data are from World Bank (2005b).

[a]GNIPopulation density = total income/area in square miles.

[b]Index calculated by dividing GNIPopulation density by the world average (0.762).

lation and sustenance. Malthus began his argument with two baseless assertions: that population grows geometrically, and that subsistence grows only arithmetically. Both have been proven spectacularly wrong. Malthus could not understand the innovativeness of humans at controlling their fertility even in his own time, much less the development of new birth control technologies. Equally, he had a narrow and unrealistic view about the possibilities of innovation and adoption of agrarian innovations. We explore the optimistic side of the argument through the work of Ester Boserup and Julian Simon.

Ester Boserup Inverts Malthus

In 1965, Ester Boserup, a Danish economist, turned Malthus's argument upside down: She showed how even in preindustrial agrarian societies, population pressure has often led to enhanced agricultural productivity, not immiseration and Malthusian checks. On the basis of her field observations in India (1957–1960) and extensive reading about agricultural history in other areas (Europe, Latin America, Africa, and Asia), Boserup (1965) argued that the potential for increase in agricultural production is in fact complex and not limited to Malthus's asserted arithmetic increase. She found that agricultural production has been highly responsive to human innovation. Indeed, in her view, population pressure has been the engine driving agricultural improvement.

Boserup described examples of societies in which people, subjected to slow sustained pressure of population on resources, figured out ways to make their agriculture more productive per unit of land (i.e., to increase crop yields). Her first insight was to place all agricultural land on a continuum and to consider the requisites in tools, labor, infrastructure, and social and economic institutions appropriate to (and even necessary for) the *kinds* of landscapes that emerge at the end of characteristic fallow periods, when the land is again ready for use. Her types of vegetated landscapes form a sequence, each representing a more intensive use of the land (forest fallow -> bush fallow -> short fallow -> annual cropping -> multicropping). Although there are certain problems in applying Boserup's scheme universally (to grasslands where there is no forest and where grass-mounding agricultural techniques are found, or to areas that because of poor resource endowment cannot be intensified to reach the annual cropping and multicropping stages of her continuum), she forced many people to rethink the connections among biophysical elements, agricultural technology, and social institutions and practices.

Boserup gave great attention to the mobilization of labor, and showed how as agriculture intensifies, societies invent ways to spread out labor over longer periods (irrigating, using environments with different growing seasons, etc.), and to make people work harder. Such institutions or practices as domestic slavery, polygyny, "groom service" (the groom's working for his wife's family), work parties, and endogamous castes (castes whose members are not allowed to marry outside their group) are shown to aid in the mobilization of labor. She also showed that permanent investments in land—terraces, irrigation furrows, fruit trees, regular use of fertilizers—help increase yields even as the fallow period is reduced. She argued that predictable changes in attitudes and practices attend changes in the form of agriculture as it becomes intensified.

Boserup carefully examined agricultural growth in stages and posited a fascinating suite of expectations about what happens as intensification occurs—expectations relating to tools, techniques, the place of livestock and grazing land, settlement forms and circulation patterns, labor inputs, capital inputs, marginal returns, land tenure, and social and political characteristics that are appropriate to each stage of agricultural growth (Table 6.3). Although her analysis has been criticized for failing to take adequately into account the role of state systems, the distortions in social and economic relations caused by market relations and capitalist penetration, and the misappropriation of surplus, many of her insights are well accepted by scholars of third world agrarian change (Blaikie, 1985; Datoo, 1978; Turner and Ali, 1996).

People, the Ultimate Resource

Julian Simon, Chicago-trained American economist and senior fellow of the Heritage Foundation and the Cato Institute (conservative think tanks), went even further in turning the Malthusian argument upside down, proposing in two book titles (Simon, 1981, 1996) that humans are *The Ultimate Resource*. Simon (1996: 12) argued that "In the short run, all resources are limited. . . . The longer run, however, is a different story. The standard of living has risen along with the size of the world's population since the beginning of recorded time. There is no convincing economic reason why these trends toward a better life should not continue indefinitely." In this view, there is virtually no limit to the human population that capitalist societies can sustain.

Human ingenuity, guided by market incentives, is the resource that drives these trends. For Simon, "a larger population influences the production of knowledge, by creating more minds to generate new ideas (the supply side) and more consumers to drive up prices and create the financial incentives for the creation of new knowledge (the demand side). This creation of knowledge ultimately makes us wealthier and solves the problems that population growth and rising income may cause" (Ahlburg, 1998: 322). Simon supported his argument with over 100 graphs of data on key aspects of the population–environment debate, many of them going back over 100 years. These data showed that as population and affluence have increased, human well-being and life spans have increased, and prices for primary goods (a measure of economic scarcity) have trended down. Putting his money where his mouth was, Simon made a famous bet in 1980 with neo-Malthusian ecologist Paul Ehrlich that any five metals of Ehrlich's choice would be cheaper in 1990 than in 1980 (a falling price implying less scarcity). Simon won; in 1990, all five were cheaper.

Simon's insights and arguments, supported by substantial statistical evidence, constitute a powerful counterweight to Malthusian pessimism. However, his argument that people are the ultimate resource depends on market price signals to provide direction and on the ability of societies to efficiently develop new knowledge and practices to address problems. These conditions may not always hold. For example, Kelley

TABLE 6.3. Summary of Ester Boserup's Observations and Expectations with Respect to Agricultural Growth and Intensification

Boserup's agricultural stages	Boserup L.U.[a]	William Allan's land classification terms	Allan L.U.[a]	Tools	Role of livestock[b]	Settlement form	Population density
Multi-cropping	0.3 - 0.5	Permanent cultivation	< 1	Irrigation, tractors, improved seed insecticides, etc.	Stock may be eliminated as being uncompetitive.	As in item below, but more intensively and rapidly.	High, very high (1,000/sq. mi., 400/sq. km)
Annual cropping	1		1	These need not be associated with multi- or annual cropping, but commonly are.	Severe conflicts over grazing/ cultivation rights. Increasing provision of fodder.	Urbanized to some extent. Investment in infrastructure occurs.	High (500/sq. mi., 200/sq. km)
Short fallow	2 - 3	Semipermanent cultivation Discontinuity	2.5 - 3	Hoe, plow, fire, draft animals.	Stock used in plowing and as manure source. Conflicts over cultivation/ grazing rights.	Permanent settlements, wells, roads.	Moderate (100-250/sq. mi., 40-100/sq. km)
	/\/\/\/\/\/\/\/\/\		/\/\/\/\/\/\/\/\/\	↑ Better *makes* of tools			
Bush fallow	7 - 13	Recurrent cultivation	4 - 8 (10)	Fire, ax, hoe.	Beginnings of stock use for manuring some fields.	Stable settlements. some larger settlements.	Low (20-150/sq. mi., 8-60/sq. km)
Forest fallow	10 - 26	Shifting cultivation	>10	Digging stick, ax, fire.	Stock not integrated with agriculture.	Unstable, dispersed.	Very low (2-50/sq. mi., 1-20/sq. km)

Boserup's agricultural stages	Transport network	Social and political organization	Wage economy money transactions	Social infrastructure	Land tenure	Division of labor	Marginal productivity
Multi-cropping	More feeder roads, trucks.	Shifts of power to (remote) urban centers. Cooperatives, marketing organizations.	Increasing percentage of labor force is wage-earning in nonagri-cultural as well as agricultural pursuits.	↑	Permanent ownership, investment (consolidation?) Emergence of landless group.	Out-migration.	
Annual cropping	↑ Increasing efficiency in having a road net.		Land owners/ tenants (rent) ↖ Peasant land ownership, smaller farms (freehold) ↗ "modern tenure"	should be increasing and should be reaching a greater percentage of the population.	Fragmentation.	Long hours of work, greater subdivision of labor; landless/ wage laborer group. (Servile labor)	(Input) Labor (more even distribution of labor time); (Output) Production/work hour (not including industrial agriculture sector)
Short fallow	Roads and trails.	Differentiated forms of social organization.	Increasing use of money in transactions; emergence (of concept) of private property. Redistribution of land becomes less frequent.		Individual usufructary tenure.	Some nonagri-cultural full-time professional artisans.	(Output) Production/work hour
Bush fallow		A little more central power.		Health services Water supply Social services Education	Specific right to cultivate a given plot of land; individual occupies arable land subject to "feudal" authority.	Some division of labor; village markets. Part-time artisans.	(Output) Production/unit area
Forest fallow	Trails.	No central power.			General right to cultivate land. Individual does not permanently occupy particular plots.	Little division of labor.	

Sources: Data are from Boserup (1985) and Allan (1965).

[a]Approximate land use factor, in years.

[b]In production system only.

and Schmidt (1996) found a negative association between population growth and per capita income growth in the 1980s. Simon's reasoning also relies on the assumption that environmental change is gradual, continuous, and reversible; however, scientists are increasingly finding that environmental change can be nonlinear, with discontinuities, and that such change is sometimes irreversible. In such cases the market triggers a response only after irreversible damage has been done, so a precautionary principle rather than a market principle is needed. Finally, Simon's belief that societies will always create and apply the knowledge that is required to provide for continuously growing population and consumption is simply an act of faith based on his understanding of the historical trends he examined (Ahlberg, 1998: 320–323).

A Critical Look at Population versus Resources Approaches

We have sketched some key arguments in a long-running and intense debate over which "naturally" increases faster—the population of humans, or their ability to provide for their sustenance. This debate has often addressed the speed of, and limits to, social and technological innovation. It is difficult to come to a definitive resolution of this debate, because it is too confined. In a nutshell, the debate centers on how many people are "too many," without considering that different people and different systems of production and consumption put different types and degrees of stress on social and natural systems. Those issues are labeled "black boxes" and set aside, allowing this approach to focus on the notion of what we now call "carrying capacity." Ecologists developed the concept of carrying capacity to indicate the number of animals that can be sustained in a given area of land without causing degradation. So, for example, let us assume that a particular area of pasture land could support up to 100 wild horses for many years. If the population of horses increased to, say, 120, the horses would overgraze and trample the pasture and actually damage its capacity to support them. The horse population would then have to decrease, either through migration or die-off.

The concept of carrying capacity has been criticized even when used for animals, but it is especially problematic in talking about humans. Other animals tend to have a small and stable range of consumption per individual compared to humans, and they cannot rapidly or dramatically alter their technologies of production or consumption. By contrast, the consumption per human is infinitely variable from a biological minimum upward toward infinity. And social and technical systems of production are equally variable. Carrying capacity arguments for animals can focus on population numbers, because there is relative stability and equality among the consumption and damage caused by all individuals. This equality is emphatically not the case for humans, with some individuals subsisting at close to biological minimum consumption, others being mass-consuming members of the middle class, and record numbers of hyperconsuming ultra-rich. It is clear that the carrying capacity for socially differentiated human societies depends on the character of that differentiation—and that the issues of what the various sections of those societies produce and consume, and of the social and technological systems by which they produce and consume, are obscured by the framing of the population versus resources debate (see sidebar: "Carrying Capacity?").

Each of the approaches discussed above legitimizes the status quo in different ways. Malthus employed the population versus resources framework to protect the privileged few by arguing that such a social order is created and maintained by laws of nature, not human institutions. At the other extreme, Simon argued that we need not worry about either privilege or resources, because free markets and innovation will bring us all increasing well-being. The neo-Malthusian argument might allow for widespread dif-

Carrying Capacity?

Timothy Mitchell (2002) provides a powerful empirical critique of arguments based on the idea of carrying capacity. He does so by systematically undoing the claims of reports presented by development organizations such as the U.S. Agency for International Development (USAID) and the World Bank for the case of Egypt.

Not Enough Land? For Whom?

In 1976, a USAID study cited by Mitchell concluded that there was just not enough land to go around in Egypt: The average size of a land holding was less than 2 acres; 94% of these holdings were smaller than 5 acres; and only 0.2% of the land owners had at least 50 acres each. The study painted a picture of too many farmers crowded into the available space and glossed over the following critical points:

- Five acres is enough! With Egypt's fertile soils, year-round sunshine, and irrigation waters, a landholding of 5 acres allows a family of five to cultivate on its own, working full time, without hired labor. The minimum farm size required for such a family to feed itself was only 0.625 acres by 1988.
- Where did the land go? A USAID study found that in 1976, 6% of landholders controlled 33% of Egypt's agricultural area. In 1982, 10% of landholders controlled 47.5% of the country's cultivated areas. In the 1980s, agribusiness corporations managed large estates, such as a 10,000-acre estate managed by Bechtel International Agribusiness division, and a 40,000-acre estate that was a joint venture with Delta Sugar.
- If land reforms were to place the ceiling on landholdings at 3 acres, at least 2.6 million acres of land would be available for redistribution to the landless or near-landless, and every household in Egypt would have at least 0.625 acres to feed itself.

However, official studies enumerating hurdles to development in Egypt never broached the question of land reform. On the contrary, USAID helped to introduce a "free market" program for rural Egypt that began to undo earlier reforms and consolidate land into larger farms.

Not Enough Food? For Whom?

Mitchell (2002) notes that between 1965 and 1980, the World Bank tables reported Egypt's annual rate of population growth as 2.1% and that of its agricultural production as 2.7%. During the 1980s, population grew at the rate of 2.4%, while food production per capita grew faster—by 17%. Yet the country had to import ever increasing amounts of food, and the prevalence of undernutrition is estimated to have more than doubled. This was not due to lack of food, but to important shifts in what was being eaten and by whom. Consider the following:

- During the oil boom from the late 1970s to mid-1980s, the income share of the wealthiest 5% in Egypt grew to 25% in rural households and to 29% in urban households. This inequality became worse when the USAID and the IMF imposed restructuring policies that removed price subsidies, increased unemployment, and brought economic recession.
- The 1980s witnessed a rapid rise in demand for meat and other animal products, consumed primarily by resident foreigners, tourists, and middle- and upper-class urban residents. In 1981–82, the chicken and beef consumption of the richest 25% was about three times higher than that of the poorest 25%. In the oil boom years, a combination of income growth and extensive U.S. and Egyptian government subsidies resulted in a broader switch from diets based on legumes and corn to less healthy diets of wheat and meat products.
- Between 1980 and 1987, crop production grew by 10% but livestock production grew by almost 50%. It takes 10 kilograms of cereals to produce 1 kilogram of red meat. Think of the implications of this

correlation for the diversion of staple food supplies from direct human consumption to animal fodder (which eventually feeds far fewer, but wealthier, people).
- Following Mitchell's (2002) line of argument, can you articulate three questions that you might ask in response to the following statement: "The population explosion in Bangladesh needs to be the urgent priority of its government, because there are simply too many people crammed into the Ganges delta"?

fusion of development, but the cost of this development has to be paid for through population control. Because the population versus resources framework fails to address differences, it continues to naturalize most aspects of existing social hierarchies and social definition of wants and needs, along with systems of production and their consequences, thereby taking them "off the table" and promoting acceptance of the status quo. In so doing, the neo-Malthusian pessimists in this debate (who have generally guided population programs and policy in the post-World War II years) have made population control both the means and the end, while overlooking social difference and foreclosing spaces for naming or locating human actors and social structures whose practices result in poverty and environmental degradation on the one hand, or restoration and equitable, sustainable use on the other. Furthermore, the impacts of population control programs themselves are not distributed evenly across societies. The rich or the men are not the ones targeted by family planning programs; rather, low-income and marginalized women are more typically the targets of family planning programs. There remains little room to hold state or non-state actors accountable when the poor have to bear the burden of state- (and international aid-) sponsored birth control programs, displacement in the name of "national" development schemes, or reduced access to resources.

Social Organization Approaches

The critiques provided in the "Carrying Capacity?" sidebar constitute a good example of a social organization approach to the so-called "population problem." Unlike the Malthusians, thinkers focusing on social organization do not see rapid population growth relative to resources as the root cause of poverty, hunger, malnutrition, environmental degradation, and conflict. Although social organization perspectives on population are by no means monolithic—ranging from different shades of Marxists to varied degrees of identification with the label "feminist"—they tend to converge in one critical respect: They see these problems as emerging from the ways in which societies define their needs and organize their systems of production and distribution.

Capitalism, Surplus Population, and Degradation

Karl Marx, writing in mid-19th-century Europe, sought to debunk Malthus's claim that population dynamics and poverty are the inevitable products of universal natural laws; he argued instead that they are the products of social factors. In Marx's scheme, the notion of "overpopulation" is replaced by the class-specific concept of "surplus laboring population." In a capitalist mode of production based on individual capitalists' surviving by maximizing profit, a surplus laboring population becomes a condition of existence for capital accumulation. All available means (technological and social innovation, as well as political and economic power) are deployed to minimize costs and maximize revenues in a structure that seeks continued economic growth. As the economy approaches full employment, wages are forced upward and less efficient producers go bankrupt, increasing unemployment, decreasing pressure on wages, and producing an unemployed "surplus" population, regardless of population size or density. Thus, contrary to Malthus, Marx specifically argued that the poverty of the laboring classes could not be explained away by appeal to some natural law; it was "an endemic condition internal to the capitalist mode of production" (Harvey, 1974: 269).

Not only does a capitalist mode of production systematically generate an unemployed surplus population, but ecological Marxists such as O'Connor (1998) argue that capitalism also systematically tends to degrade the conditions necessary for production, including both worker health and safety and the environment. This is because worker health and safety, as well as environmental stewardship, represent investments on which there is often comparatively little direct return. The results are systematic underinvestment in these areas, and a resultant degradation of the very conditions upon which the system depends. This degradation, caused by the incentives built into the capitalist system itself, often provokes a social response in the form of struggles for occupational health and safety, public health, environmental protection, and similar measures.

Subsistence, Resources, and Scarcities Redefined

The insights of David Harvey, a British/U.S. geographer, are helpful in unpacking the relationship among population, consumption, and the environment. Harvey (1974: 272) highlights the social factors that are obscured in the Malthusian and other population versus resources approaches by highlighting the ways in which the forms and meanings of "subsistence," "resources," and "scarcity" in any society are shaped by social organization. If needs are perceived as socioculturally created rather than "natural," then the definition of subsistence becomes endogenous to a mode of production and subject to change over space and time. Similarly, materials available "in nature" can only be defined as "resources" with respect to a particular interplay of technical, cultural, political, and economic factors at specific times and places. By this logic, "scarcity" of resources refers to the lack of means to accomplish specific sociopolitical ends with the existing technology and production system. Such scarcity is often created by human activity and managed by social organization. This argument dismantles the very idea that overpopulation can be defined by scarcity of available resources. Instead, it emphasizes the way that needs and ends—and the means of achieving them—are all *constructed* through dynamic relationships within a hierarchical social organization that is in place to pursue those needs and ends. Thus, states Harvey (1974), when someone says that resources are scarce, it really means that "the particular ends we have in view (together with the social organization we have) and the materials available in nature, that we have the way and the will to use, are not sufficient to provide us with those things to which we are accustomed" (272).

When reframed in this way, the so-called "population problem" gives rise to an expanded set of questions that go beyond the population versus resources focus propelled by a (neo)-Malthusian logic. As we discuss in more detail later, a focus on social organization helps us understand demographic change itself. Why should enforcing population control upon selected groups of people (frequently from the most marginalized classes, communities, and nations, which qualify as "basket cases" in Hardin's logic) be the chief way of addressing environment and development problems? Should not the targets of change be shifted to question dominant definitions of (1) social ends; (2) technical and cultural appraisals of nature; and (3) things, needs, and lifestyles to which the more privileged populations of the world are accustomed (Harvey, 1974)?

A social organization view is reinforced by Indian/British economist and Nobel laureate Amartya Sen's research on famine. His detailed research on four 20th-century famines demonstrates that famines, hunger, and starvation do not happen because of a lack of food, but because people lose their command over the means that help them secure their entitlement to food (Sen, 1981, 1987; Drèze and Sen, 1990–1991). Famine deaths result from a loss of income or other claims on food entitlements, not from the unavailability of food in famine areas.

Environmental Security: A Social Organization Approach?

In 1994, the *Atlantic Monthly* published a polemical essay by journalist Robert Kaplan, entitled "The Coming Anarchy: How Scarcity, Crime, Overpopulation, and Disease Are Rapidly Destroying the Social Fabric of Our Planet." It painted a dire picture of surging population and environmental degradation leading to mass migrations and group conflicts. The Clinton administration embraced Kaplan's argument, and environmental degradation caused by resource scarcity and population growth became key concerns of the U.S. national security establishment (Peluso and Watts, 2001: 3–4).

Thomas Homer-Dixon, a Canadian political scientist, has been one of the most influential academic theorists in the field of environmental security—the field popularized by Kaplan's essay. In Homer-Dixon's (1999) model, environmental "scarcity" is a key cause of violent conflict. The logic of the model is as follows: Scarcity can occur because supply of a resource shrinks (e.g., through environmental degradation) while demand increases (population grows), or as a result of structural inequalities (inequitable distribution of resources). When scarcity increases, the problem may be exacerbated by elites' attempting to capture a larger proportion of the resource, thus increasing structural scarcity. Structural scarcity, combined with population growth, can force poor people to migrate onto marginal lands, which then become degraded—a process called "ecological marginalization." In all the jockeying for control of scarce resources, social groups become increasingly polarized and antagonistic, while the state is likely to be weakened and lose its ability to mediate social conflicts. This process can culminate in ethnic conflicts, insurgencies, and coups d'état whose effects can spill across international borders (e.g., through human-made disasters, refugee flows, or financial crises). Therefore, dealing with environmental scarcity is a matter of international security concern. Political strife in such places as Haiti, Rwanda, and the Mexican state of Chiapas is attributed to environmental stress produced by excess numbers of people; this attribution is used to justify the (continued) enforcement of population control policies on the poorest communities of the third world, this time in the name of a new global security agenda.

Although the Homer-Dixon model bears some surface similarities to a social organization model, it has a Malthusian heart. First, environmental scarcity is treated as the central explanatory variable, but it is an underspecified combination of other variables, the most visible of which is population growth. Population control, therefore, stands out as the clearest preventative measure against scarcity. While all of the variables that make up scarcity are socially defined and produced, social factors enter the model only in tightly constrained and mechanistic ways that are incapable of addressing how scarcity is constructed. Second, resource capture often results from greed, power, and the desire to control sources of wealth, not from increased "scarcity"—as, for example, Watts's (2001) work on "petro-violence" shows. Finally, ecological marginalization can be better seen as a symptom of the social marginalization, displacement, and disempowerment of certain social groups, rather than as a product of environmental scarcity.

From the perspective of those officials, experts, and formally educated members of upper and middle classes who choose to look at issues of poverty, hunger, and malnutrition; environmental degradation; loss of "wilderness," habitats, and biodiversity; and related conflicts through Malthusian lenses, such an approach is attractive for many reasons. It is simple and intuitive to grasp (the problem is overpopulation), and it provides a clear solution (the solution is fertility reduction). It echoes a "common sense" that is already universally well established through the development apparatus, and it is entirely nonthreatening to the privileged sections of global society. Indeed, a fertility reduction agenda can be a powerful tool for entrenching the power, status, and employment prospects of the more privileged social groups globally, while also allowing them to feel good about such interventions at the same time. This happens because Malthusian lenses obscure the social causes of all the problems noted above.

Social organization approaches highlight how the causes of the problems listed in the preceding paragraph flow from the ways in which societies define their needs and organize their systems of production and distribution, not primarily from overpopulation and scarcity. As Harvey (1974) argues, there are several ways to address these social problems: We can (1) change the needs we have in mind (e.g., compare a Gandhian or Buddhist definition of need with a capitalist/consumerist one) and alter the social organization of scarcity (needs are socially constructed and can be redefined); (2) change our technical and cultural appraisals of nature (different lifestyles and technologies lead to different pressures on the biophysical world); (3) make our systems of access to resources and consumption patterns more egalitarian; and/or (4) reduce the number of people. There is evidence as suggested by the demographic transition theory (discussed below) that pursuing approaches 1–3 would create the social conditions that would lead to approach 4 as well. Similarly, women's empowerment perspectives on population argue that 3 is a precondition to 4. However, a unidimensional focus on the fourth strategy does nothing to advance the first three.

Social organization approaches usefully complicate our understanding of social definition of needs and the centrality of processes of production, accumulation, and redistribution in shaping the politics of population, environment, and development. In the remainder of this chapter, we focus on sociopolitical processes of demographic change.

DEMOGRAPHIC CHANGE: PATTERNS, MEANINGS, AND POLITICS

Tracking the Demographic Transition

The "demographic transition," as a theoretical tool, was constructed on the basis of the historical experience of birth rates and death rates in European countries as they industrialized. European countries experienced an initial phase in which both birth rates and death rates were relatively high and roughly equal. Then death rates declined, followed by a decline in birth rates, until the rates were again roughly equal, but at a lower level. The demographic transition model generalizes this experience, arguing that modernization and development will produce a similar set of historical changes in the birth rates and the death rates of other countries. Over a period of several generations, a country will proceed from an initial equilibrium stage, through a period of dynamic change and population growth, to a final equilibrium stage. In the first stage, both birth rates and death rates are high (say, 40 and 30 per 1,000 per year, respectively), and population growth is slow (only 1.0% per year). The middle stage commences when public health measures, cleaner water supplies, and medical advances help to reduce the death rate (to, say, 15 per 1,000), while the birth rate continues to be high. During this period, there is rapid population growth. The final stage is entered as people choose to have fewer children, birth rates decline (say, to fewer than 20 per 1,000), and population growth rates become low once again. A special graph is used to track the transition. It shows several interrelated phenomena: birth rates, death rates, and rates of natural increase (Figure 6.2). In principle, we can watch the unfolding of demographic changes by plotting birth and death rates for a country year by year on this diagram, with its axes showing death rates and birth rates.

Figure 6.2 shows Japan, frequently cited as an example of a country that has completed the demographic transition. Since the Meiji period (1867–1912), Japan had a population that was growing only slowly, because a moderately high birth rate (30–35 per 1,000) was counterbalanced by a similarly high death rate (20–25 per 1,000). The diagram shows, overall, a steady decline in birth and death rates since 1905, but with several striking aberrations in both birth rates and death rates. Jumps in death rates occurred in 1919, during the worldwide influenza pandemic, and again in 1945—the last year of World War II, with high military casualties and, more significantly, the megadeaths that occurred when atomic bombs exploded over

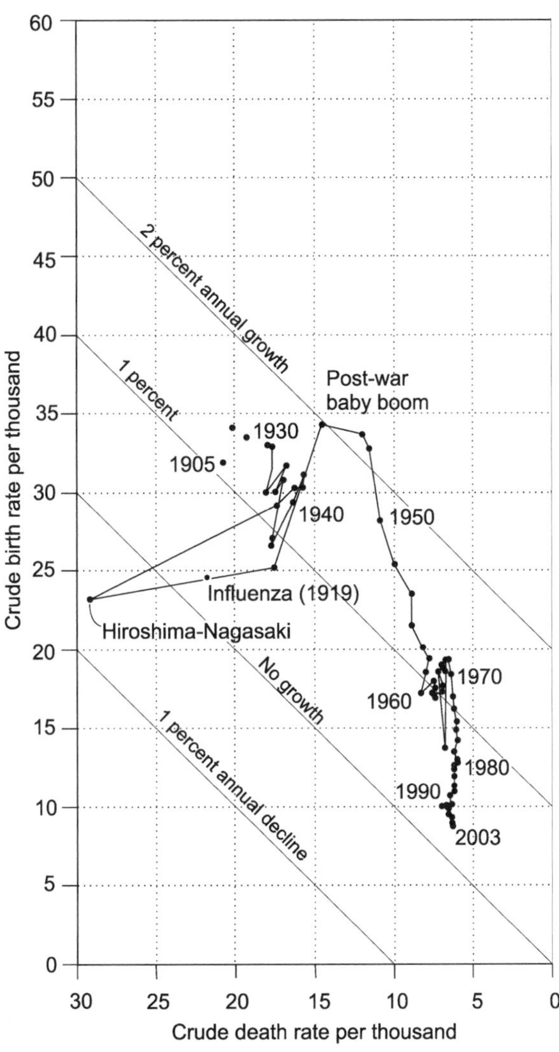

FIGURE 6.2. The demographic transition in Japan, 1905–2003. *Source:* Data are from United Nations (1948–2004).

Hiroshima and Nagasaki, adding to those in the earlier firebombings of Tokyo and other cities. The period 1947–1949 saw a postwar baby boom in Japan, but birth rates declined rapidly after 1950, so that by 1955 Japan had essentially "completed" its demographic transition. The birth rate in 2006 was 9 per 1,000, the death rate was 8 per 1,000, and the annual rate of increase was under 0.1% in a nation of 127.8 million people.

Let us now turn to the continent of Africa for another set of patterns. Figure 6.3 shows the nations of Africa at two dates: 1966 and 2002. The year 1966 is a useful early date at which to anchor our analysis of demographic change, because it marks a major turning point—the time by which most African colonies had gained political independence. If one regards the black dots on the diagrams as a swarm or a cloud, one sees that in 1966 the main swarm (consisting of at least 38 countries) was located in the portion of the diagram that represents stage 1 in the demographic transition—high to very high birth rates (40–60 per 1,000) and high to very high death rates (20–35 per 1,000). A few countries were entering stage 2, with lowered death rates but continued high birth rates. No country had completed the demographic transition.

The impression the cloud of little dots provides in 2002 is quite different. Almost all countries have moved out of the very high death rate category, and most have moved out of the very high birth rate category. Overall population growth for the main swarm is higher (exceeding 3.0% per year), compared to 1966, when the general rate was 2.5% per year. These countries have entered the second phase of the transition.

Three African countries seem to be on the way to completing a transition. These are on the northern margins of continental Africa: Morocco, Algeria, and Egypt.

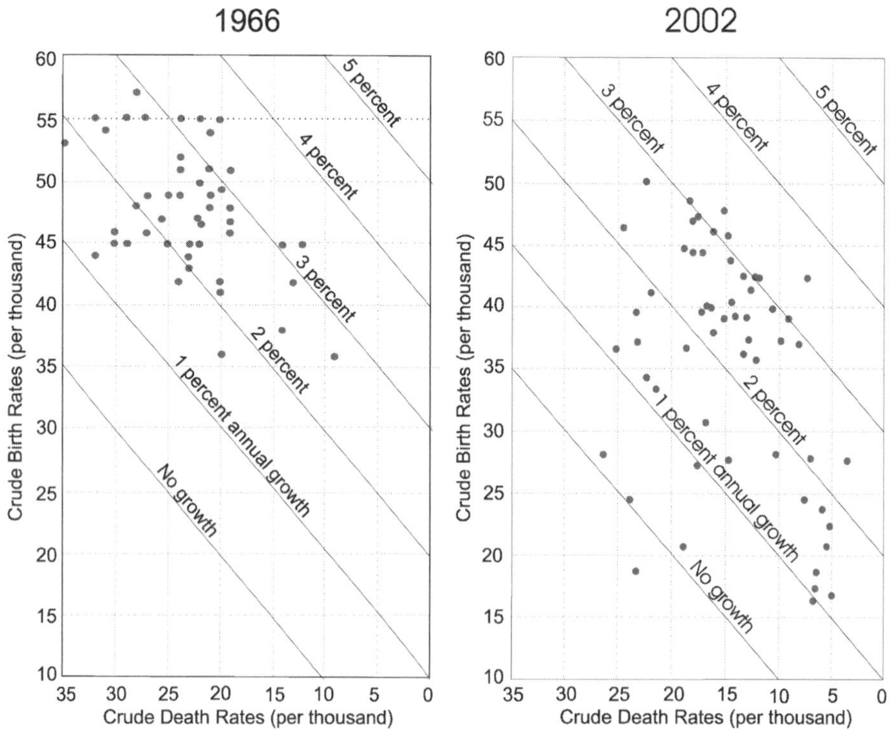

FIGURE 6.3. Crude birth and death rates, Africa, 1966 and 2002. *Sources:* Data are from World Resources Institute (1996b) and Population Reference Bureau (2002).

Only four African countries (Mauritius, Seychelles, Réunion, and Tunisia), three of which are island nations, have essentially completed the demographic transition. They have achieved slow growth (<1.5% per year). In 2002, the annual rate of increase in sub-Saharan Africa was 2.5%, and average life expectancy was 49 years.

Key comparative differences between crude birth and death rates in Africa, for the rest of the third world, and for the world as a whole are shown in Figures 6.4 and 6.5. Whereas most other third world countries have reduced their annual death rates below 15 per 1,000 (the exceptions being Afghanistan, East Timor, and Haiti), about half of African countries have death rates ranging from 15 to 27 per 1,000.

Similarly, whereas almost all of these other countries have reduced their annual birth rate to under 40 per 1,000, nearly three-quarters of African countries have annual rates above 40, ranging up to 55 per 1,000. This means that numbers characteristic of the third stage of the demographic transition (low birth rates and low death rates) are occurring in many parts of the third world, but not in Africa. Most African countries seem to be either in the early stages of a transition, or are in the second stage (lowered death rates, continuing high birth rates), during which there is a rapid growth in population.

Some groups within the mass of "other" third world countries show very distinct signs of completing the demographic transition. Several NICs (Hong Kong, Singapore, South Korea, and Taiwan) have done so (Table 6.4).

Premises, Policies, and Politics

Several premises and definitions underlie the "theory" of the demographic transition. At the most basic level, it assumes—as some of the social organization thinkers do—that if families are assured of the long-term survival of children, they will have fewer children. Second, it is based on the idea that national averages of birth and death rates are good indicators of the transitions happening throughout a country. In other words, it does not take into account the stark inequalities in access to resources that lead to wide-ranging differences in patterns of demographic transition from one community, one locality, or one subregion to another *within* a country.

Third, the demographic transition model oversimplifies the meanings associated with death rates (Figure 6.5). A country midway in the demographic transition may have death rates considerably lower than those of advanced industrialized countries: 3–5 versus 10–15 per 1,000 (see sidebar: "Demographic Definitions"). In a country where fertility is high, people are "arriving" at a high rate all the time, swelling the numbers of "thousands" against which the death rate is calculated. There is also an element of "borrowed time" in the occurrence of a low death rate in some third world countries. People in different age cohorts, of course, do not have equal risks of dying. Eventually, the larger numbers living longer, because of environmental sanitation, public health measures, and the like, will begin to contribute to the statistics on mortality. As a population matures, its age–sex pyramid is expected to assume the shape of the Washington Monument, rather than that of the pyramids at Giza (Egypt), with death rates reaching a steady state of 10–15 per 1,000 per year (Figure 6.6).

Gender, Poverty, and Fertility Decline in the Realms of Theory and Practice

On a superficial level, the idea of demographic transition does not carry any value judgments or prescriptions about desirable versus undesirable forms of "development." The conventional wisdom is that by improving technology and rationalizing the organization of production and labor, countries will be able to improve their people's standard of living, which in turn will carry the society through the demographic transition.

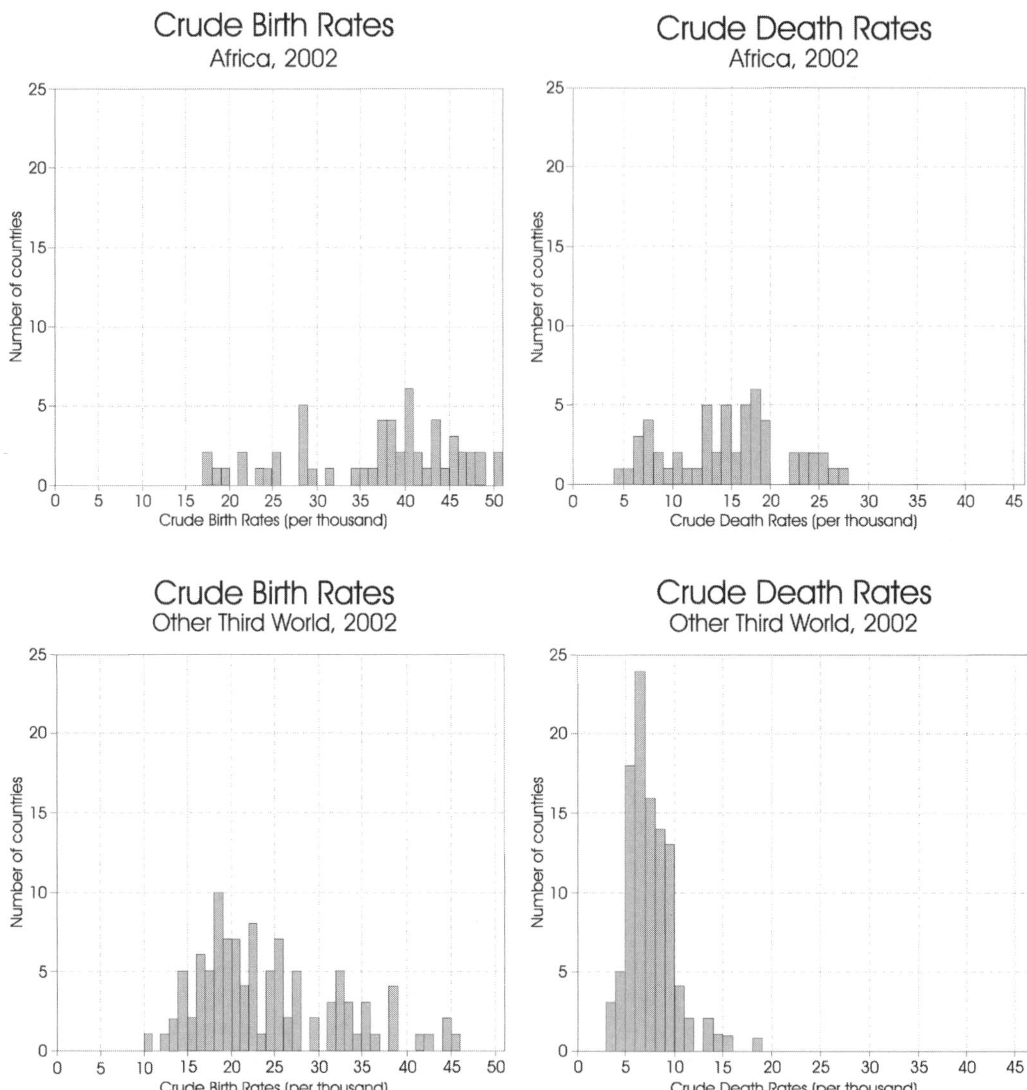

FIGURE 6.4. Crude birth and death rates 1966 and 2002, comparing Africa and the rest of the third world. *Sources:* Data are from World Resources Institute (1996b) and Population Reference Bureau (2002).

However, Barry Commoner (1975) inverted the argument. He pointed out from a social organization perspective that if one first made people sufficiently well off through a redistribution of wealth, the demographic transition would then happen automatically as people limited the sizes of their families while simultaneously developing productive forces and improving their standard of living. He argued that the threshold at which the transition would have a chance to take place was somewhere between \$500 and \$900 in per capita GNI. Commoner linked the failure of the demographic transition to take place in the colonized world to the fact that the colonial powers appropriated the surplus created in the colonies and prevented the local populace from industrializing and thereby passing through the demographic transition.

In reality, however, much of neo-Malthusian policy making is directed toward fitting third world countries into the model of demographic transition experienced by Europe. Strikingly reminiscent of Rostow's (1960) model of economic growth, the demographic transition model has been widely deployed to predict when a third world country would catch up with the first world levels on the basis of the relationship between industrialization and rates of natural increase. Such deployments overlook the ways in which demographic transition at various levels of fertility and mortality is intricately interwoven with changes in social structures, state welfare policies, and struggles for social justice—all of which shape the landscape of women's empowerment and rights/entitlements in a given country. Indeed, demographers have con-

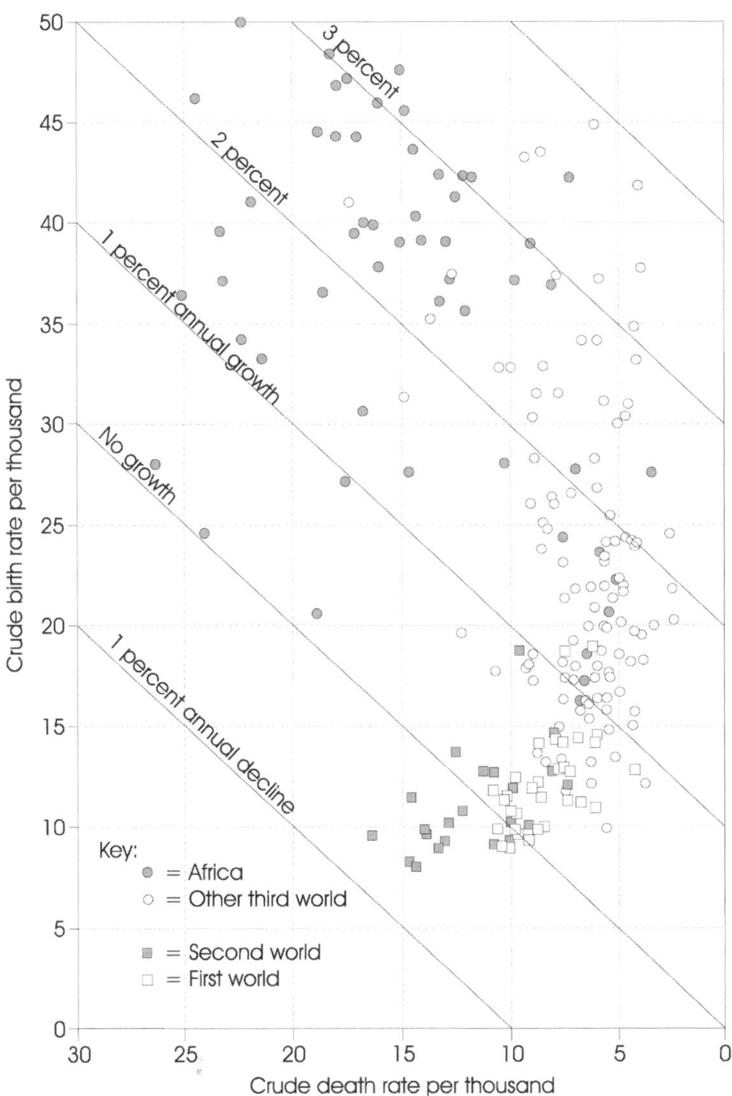

FIGURE 6.5. Crude birth and death rates, world, 2003. *Source:* Data are from Population Reference Bureau (2003).

TABLE 6.4. NICs and the Demographic Transition

Country	Birth rate (2002, per 1,000)	Death rate (2002, per 1,000)	Annual growth rate (%)	Per capita GNI (2000, U.S. $)
Hong Kong	7	5	0.2	16,419
Singapore	12	4	0.8	17,746
South Korea	13	5	0.8	38,324
Taiwan	11	6	0.6	13,969

Source: Data are from Population Reference Bureau (2002).

cluded that up to 60% of the variation in fertility changes in less developed countries is accounted for by social and economic changes, and that only 15% can be attributed to the effects of family planning. It is estimated that if on average each woman were to have two children (the approximate replacement rate) between now and the year 2030, and if the demographic transition were to apply everywhere, the world's population would stabilize at 10 billion by the year 2050; if not, the estimates have the world reaching a "stabilized" population in 2050 of 17 billion instead.

It is important to emphasize, moreover, that social organization of class *and gender* is a key determinant of population processes themselves—a point variously made by feminist critics and organizations. Simply stated, rather than being poor because they have many children, people may choose to have many children because they are poor. One reason cited for high fertility is the greater socioeconomic value of children in contexts

Demographic Definitions

"Crude birth rate" is the number of births per 1,000 population in a year.

"Crude death rate" is the number of deaths per 1,000 population in a year.

"Fertility" refers to the actual reproduction performance of an individual, a couple, a group, or a population.

"Fertility rate" is the number of live births per 1,000 women ages 15–44 years in a given year.

"Total fertility rate" is a measure of the reproductive performance of the female sector of a population ages 15–44, or a woman's childbearing years. It is the average number of children born to a woman during her lifetime. Total fertility rate exceeds 6.0 in many third world countries (mostly African), a number far greater than fertility rates in the first and second world (e.g., western Europe, 1.5; eastern Europe, 1.2; North America, 2.1). Sub-Saharan Africa averages 5.6, with the highest value in 2002 given as 7.2 for Somalia; a high rate was also cited for Yemen, 7.0 (Population Reference Bureau, 2002). To replace a population without relying on migration, a rate of at least 2.1 is needed. Since infertility among women of childbearing age is common in the third world (as well as in the first and second worlds—an estimated 17% in the United States), a total fertility rate that averages 6 means that many women are having many more than 6 children during their lifetimes—10, 12, and even more.

"Infant mortality rate" is the number of deaths of infants under age 1 per 1,000 live births in a given year.

"Population growth rate" refers to the rate at which population is increasing or decreasing in a given year due to natural increase and net migration. This rate is expressed as a percentage of the base population.

"Replacement level" is the level of fertility at which a group of women on average are having only enough daughters to replace themselves in the population.

Sources: Based on Newman and Matzke (1984) and Hewitt and Smyth (1992), except as noted above.

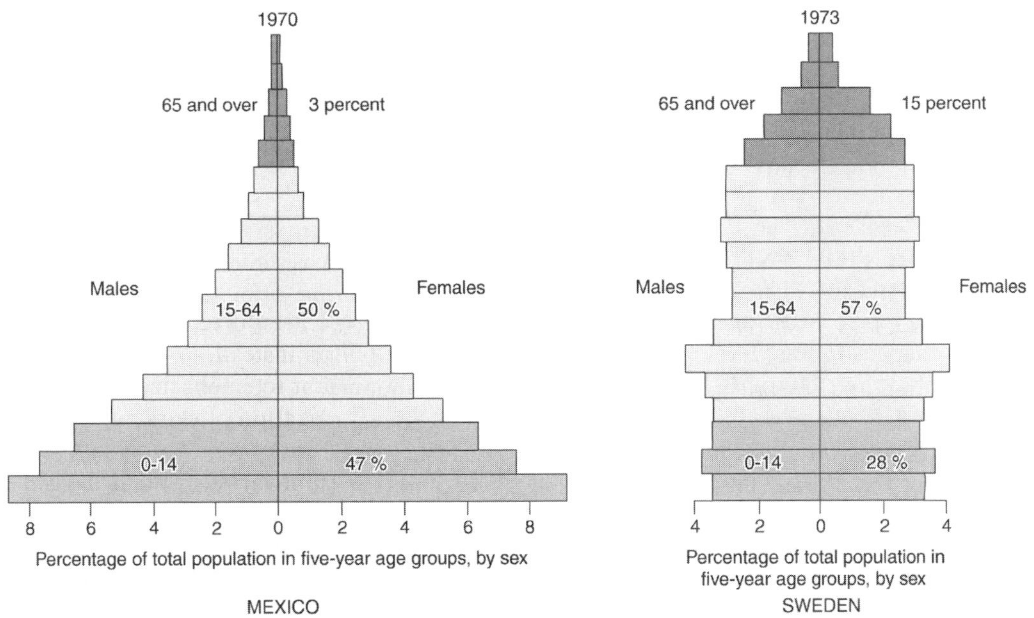

FIGURE 6.6. Age-sex pyramids for Mexico and Sweden. *Source:* Adapted from Broek and Webb (1978). Copyright 1978 by McGraw-Hill.

where social security (e.g., in the form of pensions or savings) for the elderly is low and where children provide their parents with security in old age. In addition, children's labor is valuable, both as a source of household income and as labor within the household that can supplement their parents' labor or release their parents to seek outside income. Another reason, despite the often-cited mortality decline in the third world, is that health and sanitary conditions are far from adequate for many, and fatal diseases among children continue. The higher the number of children under age 5 dying from causes related to poverty, malnutrition, or inadequate health care, the greater the likelihood of families' having more children to compensate for possible losses.

Sri Lanka, Thailand, Cuba, and the state of Kerala in south India have recorded remarkable declines in fertility rates because they have provided more widespread access to social resources such as health care, education, and employment, particularly for women. It is argued that access to such resources encourages more egalitarian gender relations within and outside the household, and in turn reshapes other crucial sociopolitical determinants of fertility—for example, social pressures to marry and bear children, relocation of women and their labor after marriage, preference for sons, expenses and expectations involved in raising boys and girls, and dominant norms concerning men's and women's desires and familial status (Hewitt and Smith, 1992: 88–89). Women with access to improved education and employment opportunities are expected (1) to be less dependent on their children for economic security and social recognition; (2) to better safeguard the health of their children, thus contributing to the reduction of infant mortality; and (3) to gain better access to contraceptive information and mechanisms. What we begin to see here, then, is that rather than being external to the gendered body, social structures are intimately connected to the forms of contestations and negotiations that socially marked bodies actively participate in constituting. We take a more systematic look at this mutually constitutive relationship between human bodies and sociopolitical hierarchies in the next section.

REPRODUCTION AND SEXUALITY AS SITES OF CONFLICT AND STRUGGLE

Reproduction and sexuality have long been sites of conflict and struggle at multiple geographical scales. At the scale of the state, the bodies of marginalized subjects are frequently also marked by politics of gender, ethnicity, race, caste, and/or religion. At the scale of the household, fertility control is imposed, regulated, negotiated, and resisted by gendered and sexualized subjects in myriad ways. Yet other complex politics of scale come into play when specific political groups and lobbies tap into global- and national-scale discourses of population to politicize fertility for their own gains at regional and local scales.

At the scale of the state, U.S. feminist scholars Loretta Ross (1994) and Dorothy Roberts (1997) present a historical analysis of the intersections of race, class, and gender in population control programs in the United States. Ross (1994) considers the emergence of the eugenics movement in the 1870s United States. Proponents of Malthusian theories joined white nativist Protestants to make eugenics laws into state policy between 1907 and 1945, sterilizing 45,000 Americans who were seen as "poor and unfit." Dhanraj's (1991) film *Something like a War* vividly captures how the most dispossessed and least powerful populations in terms of caste, gender, and access to resources inadvertently became the victims of the government of India's compulsory sterilization schemes (see sidebar: "*Something like a War*"). In a strikingly similar vein, the 1907 compulsory sterilization law of Indiana—the first state to enact such policy—applied to the "mentally deficient, those with certain types of mental illness, epileptics, sexual perverts and criminals" (quoted in Ross, 1994: 20). Thirty other states followed Indiana's example.

Roberts (1997) complicates the dominant narrative of U.S. women's increasing control over their reproductive decisions, centered on the right to an abortion. She highlights the long, often silenced, and dehumanizing history of "the systematic, institutionalized denial of reproductive freedom" that has uniquely marked the lives of African American women. She paints a picture of the powerful link between race and reproductive freedom in the United States by "considering this history—from slave masters' economic stake in bonded women's fertility to the racist stains of early birth control policy to sterilization abuse of Black women during the 1960s and 1970s to the current campaign to implant Norplant or inject Depo-Provera in the arms of Black teenagers and welfare mothers" in order to provide reliable long-term contraception (Roberts, 1997: 4).

The ways in which interwoven processes at the scales of the body, household, community, and state work to shape reproductive politics are approached by U.S. feminist sociologist Amy Kaler, whose study of contraceptive diffusion in colonial Zimbabwe (Southern Rhodesia) highlights how "power and conflicts over power, whether overt, covert, or evaded altogether, are at the hearts of interpersonal relations surrounding fertility" (Kaler, 2000: 679). Since fertility is both the means of producing human beings and a symbol of cultural continuity, control over women's fertility constitutes a transhistorical and transcultural basis of power. As a power that is biologically the property of the young and the female, but also a necessity for the social power of men and elders, human fertility is inevitably implicated in symbolic and material struggles between the genders and across generations. Kaler (2000: 677–678) situates her work as part of the intellectual movement that views broad

Something like a War

Something like a War (1991), a film directed by Deepa Dhanraj, examines India's massive centrally enforced family-planning program from the point of view of the women who are its primary targets. To do so, it traces the history of this program, characterized by bureaucratic cynicism, corruption, and brutality, while also creating a space for a group of women (as part of the film-making process) to critically analyze their own locations with respect to such issues as sexuality, fertility control, health, and socioeconomic values. The film juxtaposes a neo-Malthusian approach with a social organization approach that critically addresses sexuality, women's bodies, the state, and the politics of fertility. The neo-Malthusian approach is exemplified by a surgeon (and the government medical apparatus in general) who is invested in sterilizing as many women as possible, and for whom population control has become a sacred necessity for the nation's welfare. For him, the ends justify the means, even as he upholds the idea of shame and provides it as one of the justifications for why (forced) sterilization is a superior method. The second approach is exemplified by a women's group, meeting in a small town to critically analyze the politics of sexuality and fertility control in the context of patriarchal and class-based relationships in which its members are inserted—both in their homes and with respect to the state. Through a critical analysis of sexualities, patriarchies, economic values, preference for sons, state pressures, and so on, the women's group tries to imagine and enact empowerment and community building on its own terms—possibilities that are entirely precluded by the surgeon's approach.

Both sides view population control as a kind of war, but as a result of very different logics. In the first view, it is a war to prevent destructive population growth, where the ends justify the means; in the second view, it is a war against the poor and their self-empowerment and rights. The women's group resists giving a single "feminist" interpretation to the politics of childbearing and birth control, and highlights multiple interpretations, desires, contradictions, and tensions. The film also draws our attention to how the idea of population control is translated through social structures and institutions into processes and events that affect people of different social groups differently, and that change over time.

demographic changes "from the ground on which they occur"—that is, the daily lives of women and men—in order to challenge existing demographic descriptions of fertility change that ignore conflict, resistance, and subversion in regulation of fertility. She argues that the contraceptive pill and the Depo-Provera injection allowed women to meet their desires for autonomy and control of their fertility, and thereby enabled them to subvert the will of men and elders. At the same time, these contraceptive technologies were inscribed within racist power relations as instruments of the white Southern Rhodesian elite. Rather than being invested in empowerment or in enhancing the lives of the women among whom the technology was diffused, "the state was largely motivated by the desire to neutralize the demographic and political threat allegedly posed by the growing African population" (Kaler, 2000: 682). Thus women inadvertently participated in one of the Southern Rhodesian government's project of racial domination, even as they appropriated the contraception for their own ends.

The complex contestations and alliances in the story of contraception in Zimbabwe did not end with the colonial period. Kaler (1998) documents how women's bodies became the foremost sites where the politics of masculinity, nationalism, and morality intertwined in the postcolonial period. A central population control strategy of the white minority government in the 1960s and 1970s, Depo-Provera had come to symbolize medical colonization of the African body in the masculinist national imagination. Despite the contraceptive's immense popularity among women in the 1970s, the nation's fear of "disorderly" women—combined with genuine health risks posed by the synthetic hormones in Depo-Provera—led to its being banned by Zimbabwe's Ministry of Health in 1981.

Attention to the politics of fertility at narrower and more interpersonal geographical scales is not necessarily feminist or progressive, as U.S.-based demographer Alaka Malwade Basu's argument about the politicization of fertility suggests. Basu (1997) has observed increasing use of demographic arguments to achieve nondemographic objectives, ranging from women's empowerment to political polarization. This kind of politicization of fertility is enabled, first, through a wide consensus that third world countries benefit from reduced fertility. Second, there is no grand theory for fertility decline, yet it is possible to find a relationship between almost any variable and fertility. Third, the pressure on demographic research to be policy-relevant provides an incentive to draw linkages between fertility and other phenomena. In this environment,

> any sufficiently strident pressure group [can] base its demands on a presumed fertility-reducing effect of these demands . . . Such a strategy, whether conscious or not, carries more weight than a claim bolstered only by the support that [fertility decline] is just or right, or wanted for itself. What impact these . . . demands have on social change and social stability if they are fulfilled in turn depends on the nature of these demands. (Basu, 1997: 7)

Fertility can be politicized in the service of either progressive or regressive goals at all scales (community, neighborhood, household, body) where everyday lives are lived. Basu discusses two examples from India. In one case, the pressure group consists of women's organizations whose collective strategy of deploying fertility-related arguments to improve the overall status of women turns out to be a progressive force, resulting in a number of gains for women in the sphere of state policy. And the prominence of World Bank programs for women's health, literacy, and empowerment derives from their presumed effectiveness at lowering fertility. This is a risky strategy, however, because if another variable is found to be more effective at reducing fertility, programs for gender justice could be undermined.

In a contrasting case, the pressure group consists of right-wing Hindu communal organizations, which use fertility-based arguments in a fear-mongering strategy to bolster their own political base and to threaten the social identity of Muslim minority groups; this approach culminates in an exacerbation of communal tensions on the one hand, and a further marginalization of Muslim women's collective status on the other. Basu elaborates on several invalid assertions made by the Hindu right about Muslims in India: (1) that the Muslim population will soon outnumber the Hindu majority in terms of absolute numbers; and (2) that Muslim fertility is higher than Hindu fertility because (a) Muslim men tend to have multiple wives, and (b) Islam is opposed to family planning. Basu (1997: 10) underscores these lessons from this case:

> First, there is just enough plausibility in such fertility-based communal assertions to make it possible for vested interests to politicize the issue. Secondly, there is enough counter evidence for [the above] assertions which a committed opposition could just as easily muster to politicize the issue in a more desirable direction. By the same token, demographic arguments to be used by a Muslim majority to antagonize a Hindu minority can be formulated.

Basu's broader point is that "the ease with which fertility can be politicized means that it can have an impact on societal welfare in ways which are not necessarily dependent on actual growth rates or pressures on resources" (1997: 14). The politicized arguments about fertility can lead to the same forms and degrees of political and social instability that demographic change is presumed to cause.

SELECTIVITIES IN POPULATION RHETORIC AND PRACTICE

Let us further reflect on the selectivities embedded in the idea of demographic transition, and in the rhetoric and practice of population policies more generally, by briefly considering two issues that are intimately linked with the politics of fertility and mortality: the AIDS pandemic in sub-Saharan Africa, and the focus on literacy as a catalyst for fertility decline.

AIDS and Fertility

Lynn Brown (2004: 291) reports as follows about the HIV/AIDS epidemic:

> Since . . . the early 1980s, more than 60 million people have been infected, five million people in 2001 alone, with 3.4 million of these in sub-Saharan Africa. In 2001, 14,000 people per day were infected with the HIV virus, 95 percent of these in the developing world. In the past two decades some 14 million adults have died of AIDS, 82 percent in sub-Saharan Africa. In 2001, three million people, adults and children, died of AIDS, 2.3 million of them in sub-Saharan Africa. . . . Today, more than 95 percent of all HIV-infected live in the developing world, where in 1998, more than 23 percent of the population lived on less than U.S. $1 a day and 800 million people were food insecure. In sub-Saharan Africa more than 48 percent of the population lives on less than U.S. $1 a day. . . . Recognition that the HIV/AIDS pandemic was more than a severe health issue and would drive overburdened development budgets near bankruptcy was slow in coming. But, in the past decade, the perceived impact of HIV/AIDS has shifted from one of a disease affecting individuals to a disease which potentially affects the development of nations.

Mainstream development discourse may have just begun to acknowledge the human costs of AIDS in sub-Saharan Africa, but for those living in countries such as Zimbabwe with high AIDS prevalence rates, it is impossible to talk about family planning or reproductive decision making in isolation from the devastating effects and implications of the AIDS epidemic (Grieser, Gittelsohn, Shankar, Koppenhaver, Legrand, Marindo, Mahvu, and Hill, 2001). The life expectancies for many African countries, including South Africa and Botswana were expected to increase to over age 65 by the year 2000 without AIDS. With AIDS, these rates have plummeted to less than age 40 in several countries, including Botswana, Malawi, Mozambique, and Swaziland (Craddock, 2004: 2–3).

Despite the effects of the deadly virus, however, the necessity of reducing fertility and the need for unabated structural adjustment remain deeply entrenched faiths for international development agencies. It is disturbing if not surprising that the push for population control over famine relief and AIDS prevention has intensified in Africa, and although a Global Fund was created to fight AIDS under the auspices of the Joint United Nations Programme on HIV/AIDS (UNAIDS), less than 8% of an annual targeted budget of $10 billion had been met by 2004 (Bandarage, 1997; Craddock, 2004: 10). There is widespread evidence that AIDS has been exacerbated by deepening poverty "in the aftermath of war, civil unrest and refugee movements; that migration patterns necessitated by underemployment in chronically underfinanced economies ensure both an increase in rates of transmission and a spread from rural to urban areas; and that governments shackled by poor terms of trade and crippling debts have neither the finances nor the personnel to address the problem adequately" (Craddock, 2004: 5). In such a scenario, critics argue, the international apathy toward AIDS amounts to a genocide that is legitimated (at least in part) by a Malthusian logic according to which AIDS's negative impact on population size will reduce pressure on available resources, improving the world's ability to sustain and feed itself (Brown, 2004: 295).

Literacy as a Vehicle for Population Control

The example of child labor can serve as an entry point into some observations about literacy. In the early 1990s, the boycotting of products made by child labor in the third world became a point of passionate debate in the United States and in many countries of the third world. Iowa Senator Tom Harkin became a hero in the mass media for drawing attention to the plight of poor children who worked in dark and dangerous factories of countries such as Pakistan and India, making footballs, rugs, and glassware. These children, he argued, were being robbed of their childhoods, deprived of education, and forced to work under extremely exploitative conditions that amounted to slavery. Although there was a general agreement that every child should have a right to a decent childhood and education, some critics pointed out a series of contradictions—that the call to boycott child labor should come at exactly the same time when the structural adjustment programs were making the family members of the same children unemployed; when hospitals and schools were becoming inaccessible to these very same children; and when elimination of food subsidies were increasing malnourishment and starvation among those child laborers and their family members. It was ironic that the plight of enslaved children was being articulated in isolation from the policies that made these children the breadwinners for their households. Also, those calling for the boycott of the products made by children had little to say about what these children would do, where they would study, or how

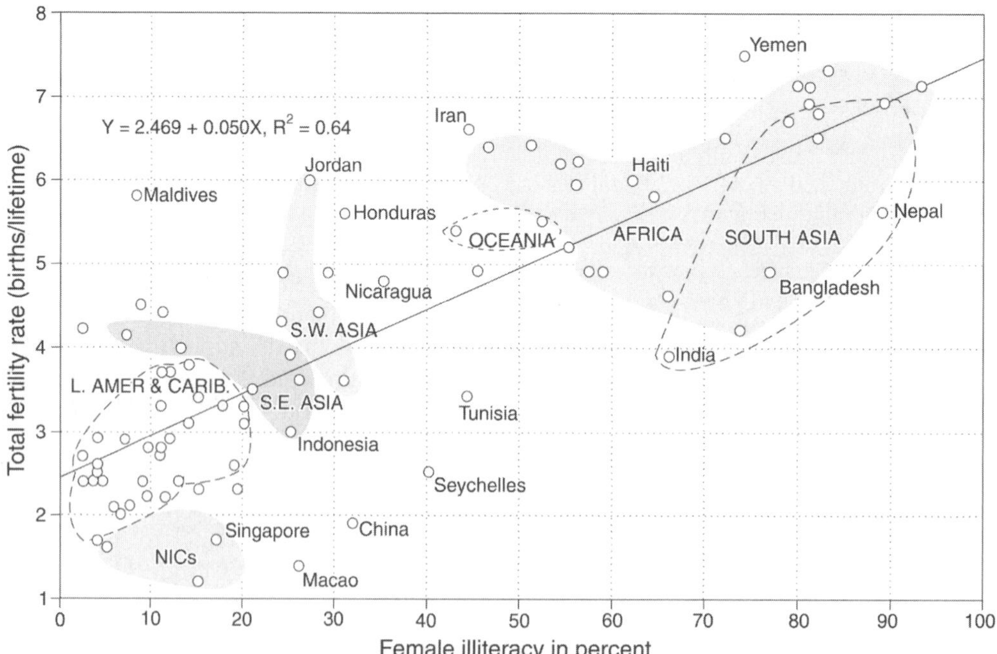

FIGURE 6.7. Total fertility (1993) and female illiteracy (1990). *Source:* Fertility data are from World Resources Institute (1996b), which used data from the United Nations Population Division, and illiteracy data are from World Resources Institute (1996b).

they would feed themselves once they were released from their jobs (Forum of Indian Leftists; FOIL, 1996).

Literacy, often perceived as a key to empowerment and in turn to demographic transition, is surrounded by a similar irony. It is argued that if the poorest women in the rural areas of the third world could become literate, the population problem would automatically sort itself out. Indeed, our final graph for this chapter (Figure 6.7) shows that there is a statistically significant relationship between total fertility of women and female illiteracy. In general, in countries where most women are literate (under 20% illiteracy), total fertility (births per lifetime) is low to moderate (2–4). In tropical Africa, where total fertility rates are high (6–7), female illiteracy rates generally range between 70% and 95%.

But we may want to pause and ask this question: What kind of literacy are we talking about when efforts to make the poorest women literate often operate in conjunction with policies that impoverish and displace them? For example, the Education for All scheme sponsored by the World Bank through central governments of countries such as India target the same women for their literacy programs whose access to water, forests, and lands is steadily diminishing in the face of privatization of these resources. The basic education infrastructure, furthermore, is in a constantly declining state in many rural areas of Asia and Africa, and if the learning of the alphabet is meant to help incorporate these women and their children into the system, chances are that they are only going to get incorporated at the very bottom. This raises these questions: What kind of literacy, for whom, and for what purpose? Is literacy merely an instrument to decrease poor women's fertility and help them to buy the new brands of soaps, toothpastes, and contraceptives in increasingly globalized markets? Or is it to create the conditions by which the formerly "illiterate" can draw critical connections among the processes that serve to place them on the margins of socioeconomic and political systems, and figure out the ways in which they might transform the meanings of those margins?

BRAIDING THEORY WITH POLICY

> A feminist analysis of reproduction must necessarily distinguish itself from both anti-natalist Malthusian population control as well as right wing pro-natalism, especially religious fundamentalism.
>
> —ASOKA BANDERAGE (1997: 8)

The wide-ranging conversations on demographic change covered in the previous sections paint a complex picture of the patterns, processes, conflicts, and selectivities involved in attempts to understand demographic change. We have seen that demographic transitions are more multifaceted and complicated than they have been presumed to be, and that they are not simply universal or automatic responses to industrialization or development. Fertility is related to access to social services, as well as to the politics of such social differences as gender, ethnicity, race, caste, and religion. Approaches that underscore bodies and sexuality as sites of contestation and strategic intervention combine sensitivity to societal structures and power hierarchies with an attentiveness to the complexities of agency. The earlier discussion of such contestations in Southern Rhodesia/Zimbabwe and India exemplifies how the construction of the population problem as a discourse at global, national, and communal levels goes hand in hand with the manner in which (1) governments and experts perceive and manage bodies that are sociopolitically marked (by gender, race, class, religion, caste, location, etc.); and (2) those marked bodies resist or negotiate the management of their own bodies.

We can discern here ever more clearly the workings of a complex politics of scale. Malthusian doctrine gains legitimacy, at least in part, by establishing itself as indispensable for addressing the "big picture" of a world that is in grave danger of overpopulation, which must be addressed through expeditious population control. Questions of empowerment through land and income redistribution at the national or regional scales, or of the ways in which the "targets" or "victims" of population control policies maneuver their own relationships with reproductive rights and wrongs at the levels of their households and bodies (Hartmann, 1999), are deemed too narrow to be significant in the "big picture." Yet neither antinatalist Malthusian nor pronatalist fundamentalist positions that claim legitimacy on the basis of the "big picture" argument can maintain their dominance if they do not actively rework their rhetoric and practice at all geographical scales.

Some scholars who view women's empowerment as a necessary precondition to fertility decline make an important distinction between population control and birth control. "Birth control" refers to the right of women and couples to control childbearing (timing, spacing, and the total number of children) on the basis of individual choice and circumstances. "Population control," in contrast, is a top-down policy aimed at controlling childbearing for the population as a whole, and it is based on demographic imperatives such as a perceived need to cut the population growth rate. According to this view, family planning should be available, but it is doomed to fail unless women's socioeconomic and political empowerment becomes a primary goal of development agencies. Fertility reduction has to be a secondary goal, to be adopted by women themselves according to their needs and desires (Hewitt and Smyth, 1992: 90).

Developed and publicized by feminist lobbyists and alliances since the 1970s and 1980s, arguments centering on women's socioeconomic and reproductive rights led to major shifts in the rhetoric of key development organizations in the 1990s. Recognizing the centrality of women's role in affecting population growth, the United Nations Fund for Population Activities (UNFPA) placed women at the center of the "population–environment–development triangle" in 1992 (cited in Hartmann, 1995: 135). Similarly, the World Resources Institute (1994) pointed out how population pressures in many regions of the global south cause deforestation and reduce access to fuel, water, and other natural resources, exponentially increasing the burdens of women who have to spend more time walking to collect water, fuelwood, and fodder. However, the inclusion of gender rhetoric in such reports did little to undermine the Malthusian emphasis on "overpopulation."

Like the discourse of feminism and women's rights that was deployed in the service of colonialism in Egypt and India (Chapter 3), a supposedly progressive rhetoric of gender, environment, and sustainability was now being deployed to serve an old Malthusian agenda. "Overpopulation" was claimed to be the root cause behind third world women's oppression and a key determinant in the chain of environmental destruction, poverty, high fertility, and food insecurity. Thus the agenda for "women's reproductive rights" remained consistently synonymous with the emphasis on fertility control (Bandarage, 1997: 52–53). The findings of the World Bank's own studies that fertility decrease is frequently correlated with increases in incomes of the poor rather than the rich, furthermore, did very little either to reduce the World Bank's vigorous opposition to income redistribution or to change its conviction that "it is possible for fertility to decline and contraceptive use to increase without much change in those social, economic and health variables generally believed to be crucial preconditions for demographic change" (quoted in Bandarage, 1997: 43).

To use the language of population control versus birth control, then, international and national agencies have been more concerned with population control than with birth control. Although the positive value of women's choice in childbearing is sometimes acknowledged on paper by such organizations as the UNFPA, there has been relatively little effort to incorporate this crucial understanding into family-planning programs—to determine what methods of contraception should be developed or the type of information that should be available to enable women to make a free and informed choice, to decide how and when to use a specific contraception method, and to decide where and from whom contraceptives should be available.

Finally, our discussion suggests that "problems" concerning society, poverty, environment, and development cannot productively be addressed through approaches that frame the question at hand in terms of the pressure of population on resources. Instead, we must consider who consumes what, why, and how; which alternative modes of production, consumption, and distribution acquire legitimacy; and which ones are silenced, overlooked, or deemed "impractical."

7 Contested Environments

The Entanglements of Nature, Development, and Globalization

SUSTAINABLE DEVELOPMENT, SUSTAINABILITY, AND ENVIRONMENTAL JUSTICE

Chapter 6 has considered the interrelationships between people and resources, examining how the policies and programs that conceptualize and control those interrelationships have resided at the core of development politics across the borders of first and third worlds, donors and recipients, and policymakers and "target populations." In this chapter, we extend the discussion to focus on society–environment relations more broadly. It is important to note at the outset that the environment (biophysical processes surrounding social life) and society coevolve, each shaping the other. We have described in Chapter 6 how society and resources are mutually related, and this is true of societal relationships with all kinds of biological, meteorological, and geological processes. These are complex relations, often with unexpected consequences: Humans seek to tame nature, only to find that nature's own agency escapes these confines to affect society in unexpected and often unpleasant ways—just as humans often profoundly reshape the environment in their efforts to escape its confines. These constantly changing relationships between environments and societies are produced through social and environmental processes (often contested) that reshape the life chances and livelihood possibilities of all people in different ways, depending on where they are located socially, economically, and physically. Thus our focus here is on the interrelated themes of social and environmental justice and sustainability. We begin with the idea of sustainable development in a world of difference.

Ever since a satellite image of the earth catalyzed concern in the first world about the limits of "spaceship earth" in the early 1970s, various efforts have been made to conceptualize how humans can take advantage of their environment without destroying it. "Sustainable development" has become the new maxim. Beginning with publications such as the World Commission on Environment and Development's (1987) report entitled *Our Common Future* (also known as the "Brundtland Report"), and with meetings such as the 1992 World Conference on Environment and Development or "Earth Summit" at Rio de Janeiro (and its various spinoffs and follow-ups), sustainable development has become a sprawling umbrella concept and a major industry. Mainstream thinking on sustainable development has focused on finding forms of capitalist economic growth and development that also maintain or enhance desired flows of environmental services. A common catchphrase is "development which meets the needs of the present without compromising the ability of future generations to meet their own needs" (World Commission on Environment and Development, 1987: 43). With the emergent popularity of neoliberal globalization, the belief that such market mechanisms as full-cost pricing and pollution trading can guarantee sustainable development has become increasingly influential.

Initial thinking presumed that sustainable development would also cure poverty; more recently, it is being recognized that this is not necessarily true. Nevertheless, concerns about poverty often take second place to those about the environment in such discussions. Indeed, the poor are often presumed to be major contributors to environmental degradation, because of the miserable environments in which they are often found. This presumption is ironic, since poor people and peripheral locations generally bear a disproportionately large share of the environmental costs of development—an imbalance that is exacerbated as systems of production and consumption become increasingly globalized, and as hazardous production and waste-processing work moves to the third world.

Critics note that mainstream sustainable development discourses often display other blind spots and biases. Such discourses privilege "global" environmental problems and institutions over "local" ones; conceptualize poverty, rather than consumption and poverty-producing conditions, as the root cause of environmental degradation; reproduce economistic and developmentalist biases (cf. Chapter 4); and advance a highly reductive interpretation of the environment as a static "resource" (Escobar, 1995: 48–54; Sneddon, 2000: 525). First world countries tell tropical countries such as Brazil and Indonesia to conserve their rainforests as sources of biodiversity, sequesterers of carbon, and producers of oxygen for the global good, despite the fact that forest clearances were once central to industrialization and wealth creation in Europe and North America. Those targeted in such discourses reasonably complain about double standards—new rules for today's poor and peripheral locations that reinforce *developmental discourses* while erecting barriers to achieving *development*. At the same time, concerns about recycling waste rather than reducing consumption, and policies creating protected areas (e.g., national parks) and species (e.g., tigers or whales), often take precedence over allowing poor people access to environmental resources vital to their livelihoods. Moreover "not in my backyard" movements in many guises relocate dirty wastes, polluting industries, and other environmental risks from richer to poorer places.

We are often taught to see the environment as an assemblage of biological and physical things (ranging from subatomic particles, to plants and animals, to the continents, oceans, and atmosphere) that work according to a set of biophysical laws and processes (e.g., laws of physics and chemistry, the hydrologic cycle, the nutrient cycle, atmospheric cycles) operating at temporal scales ranging from nanoseconds to millennia and spatial scales ranging from the infinitesimal to the global. Mainstream sustainable development often treats these as stable, predictable resources subject to human management. However, disciplines such as the "new ecology" suggest that the biophysical environment is heterogeneous, complex, and dynamic—and less linear, predictable, and manageable than had been frequently presumed (Sneddon, 2000). Thus the biophysical world is more an agent with which societies negotiate than a machine that they control. Consequently, we can never have more than an imperfect understanding of the ways in which social and biophysical processes and things interact to change environments on multiple geographical scales (e.g., complexities of ecosystem change), or of the spatial ramifications of an event or change (e.g., global climate change or the 2004 Indian Ocean tsunami).

Innovative work in such areas as political ecology, environmental history, the new institutional economics, ecological economics, the new ecology, science studies, and sustainable livelihoods have addressed environment–society relationships at multiple geographical scales and across time. This multidisciplinary work highlights the importance of addressing difference, context, scale, and the social and environmental systems that connect places to each other. Such approaches help us think about environment–society relations not as involving discrete, manageable natural and social units, but instead as a set of complex interactions through which biophysical environments and human societies are continuously coproducing each other through their mutual interactions at multiple scales. In any given place, the environment provides a dynamic set of conditions and processes that both facilitate and limit human activities. Through interaction with the environment, human societies create meanings; produce, reproduce, and change their forms of social organization; appropriate valued goods and services; and also affect processes of environment change. These elements are intimately interwoven in myriad dynamic environment–society complexes, all interacting with other such complexes.

A consideration of the many third world people's movements that focus on the environment can also help us understand the complexities of environment–society relations. Such movements differ from mainstream environmentalism or sustainable development: They are generally couched in terms of defending not only particular environments, but also the lives and livelihoods that those environments sustain. For people in the third world who derive their livelihoods from the forests, fields, and waters around them, sustainability is intimately related to rights of communal ownership, collectively shared ways of knowing, cultural autonomy, religious rituals, and freedom from externally imposed programs that seek to promote someone else's vision of how to conserve or develop the environments they depend upon. We might describe such movements as "environmental livelihoods" movements, and they are frequently cast as "environmental justice" movements. Yet we must also be cautious about taking for granted the sustainability and equity of local livelihood systems. They are interlinked with other dynamic social and biophysical systems and can involve hierarchies along multiple dimensions—for example, gender, class, and caste. We must examine the particulars of each case. This link among the environment, sustainability, and sociopolitical justice is a key theme of the present chapter.

DIFFERENCE AND A CONTESTED BIOPHYSICAL ENVIRONMENT

In a world of difference, people with differing class locations, livelihoods, ways of knowing, values, and social institutions are all interacting with their environments to meet their varied needs. As a consequence, we should expect that they have different wants, needs, and dreams, and therefore that they will seek varied paths toward differing visions or goals as they look to the future. Consider the variety of values that humans derive from the environment in a particular place. Below is a list that, though not comprehensive, provides examples of several different types of values.

1. *Intrinsic existence value* of the biophysical world and all of its inhabitants.
2. *Recreational or scenic value* of places, or the ways that they give meaning to life.
3. *Life support value*: the "natural economy" of the biophysical world reproducing the conditions necessary to sustain life.
4. *Commodity value*: environment as a source of resources that are appropri-

ated to be sold, including both renewable resources (e.g., water, land, forests) and nonrenewable resources (e.g., oil, minerals).

5. *Use value*: resources (renewable and nonrenewable) appropriated from the local ecosystem for direct consumption.
6. *Sink value*: the environment as a "free" disposal site for wastes.

Now think of the contrasting needs, values, and livelihood systems of several different social groups. For example, in the Amazon rainforest, international and local environmentalists may emphasize various aspects of values 1 through 3 to justify protecting the forests as both a local and a global asset, while capitalists and consumers interested in timber and/or livestock production for the global market are necessarily concerned with values 4 and 6. Marginalized migrants from the city may be interested in the combination of 4 and 5 as they attempt to make a living off the land as small farmers. Indigenous forest dwellers would have their own combinations of 1–6, based on unique combinations of their physical and sociopolitical locations and the values they might articulate to urge their own uses of the forest. Already, the issue of the Amazon rainforest looks complex and ripe for conflict, even with this simplified list of contending actors and often mutually exclusive uses.

Faced with this tangle of interests, we might simply ask who has the *right* to use the land. This, as we shall see, is an area of profound contestation, as changing power configurations in society also change the systems of rights and responsibilities. This question is made even more vexed by the fact that the broad and deep interconnectedness of social and biophysical systems creates a situation in which human uses of the environment produce social and environmental consequences that reach far beyond the users themselves—through the effects, for example, of pollution, ecosystem change, or global climate change. Economists refer to these consequences as "externalities," because they are external to market transactions and therefore ignored in market calculations. We might more aptly refer to the costs of environmental degradation as "socialized" costs or "transferred" costs, because they are costs imposed upon one part of society, without its consent, by the behavior of another part. Externalized, socialized costs are not spread evenly over all people, but are often transferred to those who are not responsible for these costs and who cannot afford them.

The issue of socialized or transferred environmental costs is increasingly important. First, economic globalization makes it easier to distance the place of consumption decisions (both physically and psychologically) from the place of their effects. For example, when we fill our cars with gasoline in the United States, the price we pay at the pump does not go toward compensating for the social and environmental destruction caused by oil production in the Niger River Delta. These costs of providing us with gasoline are borne by the people and environments there. Second, the increasing scale of human activities and power of human technologies makes possible increasingly widespread and pronounced environmental change. For example, the Intergovernmental Panel on Climate Change (IPCC, 2007a) has found that although first world countries are primarily responsible for climate change, poor third world people will suffer the most severe consequences. In both cases, some people are being made to pay for social and environmental ramifications of decisions made by others. The issue of some groups' capturing flows of benefits (through systems of production and consumption), while socializing or transferring the costs and risks of their actions, is at the center of contestations over development and globalization.

As in Chapter 6, we are interested in the contested social institutions and processes that structure the rights to access, use, and make decisions over the biophysical environment. These range from conquest and armed struggle, to regulatory systems, to systems of property rights and customary practices. One obvious means of controlling uses of the environment is evident in the armed struggle for strategic control of a geographical site that yields a valuable resource, such as gold, timber, oil, or fresh water. The Spanish and Portuguese conquest of many parts of the Americas after 1492 was motivated largely by the desire to capture their gold and silver supplies. Subsequent colonial expansion by the British, French, and other European powers was similarly motivated by a desire to control key resources. Today, access to oil remains a central motivating factor in American policies in the Arab world, notably the 1980–1988, 1990–1991, and 2003–present Persian Gulf wars (Chapter 18).

Beyond blatantly violent processes of war and conquest, we can find a more pervasive set of lower-key but vital contestations over who gets to use which aspects of the environment, for what purpose, under what conditions, for whose benefit, and at whose cost. These struggles are played out through contestations over the social institutions that structure environmental access and decision making. By using social, economic, and political power to change the shape of institutions (such as systems of property rights, environmental regulations, customary practices, and economic systems), some groups capture flows of benefits from the environment, while other groups are left to deal disproportionately with the more dire consequences of such decisions.

Understanding such struggles involves engaging with (1) differences between parties articulating differing values, systems of knowledge, and/or institutions for resource access, control, and use (e.g., third world vs. first world, urban vs. rural); and (2) social heterogeneity within each country, region, locality, and even household involved in such struggles (e.g., with regard to class, gender, inherited or acquired skills, livelihood systems, and ways of appropriating value from nature). Such differences also involve stratification in terms of political and economic power. Thus some voices are amplified and others are stifled.

In the following sections, we examine three contested processes of changing social institutions around the environment, and discuss how some sets of actors change the rules of the game in ways that create flows of benefits to themselves, while often shifting costs to others. These processes are commodification of the environment, development projects, and conservation projects. The first of these three is the broadest, and has been ongoing for centuries.

MARKET EXPANSION, COMMODIFICATION, AND ENVIRONMENTAL CONTESTATION

For most of human history, people have relied upon directly appropriating what they need from their local ecosystems through such activities as hunting and gathering, herding, and/or agriculture. These are often referred to as "subsistence livelihoods," because households directly produce most of what they need for their own subsistence. Subsistence-based societies continually develop experience-based knowledges that are embodied in practices for using the environment and that evolve as their local environments evolve (Chapters 9–12). The Social institutions that have developed around such livelihoods often involve forms of barter exchange, institutions for sharing of labor and other resources, and communal ownership of common-pool resources (such as forests, pastures, and fisheries). Historically, participation in markets has been a marginal part of such livelihood systems. One of the tasks of colonialism was to find ways to compel colonized peoples to participate in colonial markets (Chapters 13–14).

Although colonialism, development, and globalization have expanded market penetration to virtually all corners of the world, many people in the third world continue to meet most of their needs primarily through what they can produce or appropriate directly from their local ecosystems for local consumption, and there are continual struggles between commercial and noncommercial values. These struggles are conditioned by structures of difference along such lines as gender, class, and caste, which shape people's needs, aspirations, and ability to appropriate resources for themselves; they are also conditioned by the environments in which people live (see sidebar: "Development and Access to Water in Bangladesh").

The spread and deepening of capitalist relations entails a continual reworking of relations between society and the biophysical world. One of the key requirements for a capitalist economy is that raw materials, means of production, and products can all be freely bought and sold through markets. This in turn requires the institution of transferable private property; the development of a set of laws to define, and mechanisms to enforce, property rights; and the extension of such institutions to cover elements of the biophysical world, such as land. When the market is not the primary mechanism for organizing social and economic life, as in precapitalist or noncapitalist societies, there is no need for this type of property system, and social relations with the biophysical world are typically governed by locally specific and often complex and multilayered systems of use rights, customs, and obligations, where different people have varied sets of rights and obligations with respect to the land and to each other. These sets of rights and obligations represent different varieties of "common-property" systems (see sidebar: "Property Regimes")—or, as with the genetic information represented in seeds or animal breeds, it may be considered the common heritage of all humanity.

In order for part of the biophysical world to be made into a commodity for exchange in the market, it must be removed from the realm of things commonly owned, by legally delimiting (or enclosing) and privatizing it. This process takes the rights to nature away from most of the erstwhile users and assigns them to a single owner. In essence, this is theft by legal fiat. Termed "primitive" accumulation or "original" accumulation by Marx, processes of enclosure and privatization are still ongoing. Harvey (2003)

Development and Access to Water in Bangladesh: Entanglements of Gender, Class, and Nature

In the first world, access to safe water—central to human life—is nearly universal and relatively inexpensive. This is not the case in much of the third world. Examples from Bangladesh illustrate how access to water is mediated by environmental processes and social relations of class and gender, and how development activities can create multidimensional conflicts involving both social and environmental change.

Generally speaking, people of the third world secure access to water in four ways: (1) They own land from which they can access water with a pump; (2) they buy water, perhaps from a neighbor with a pump; (3) they have communal rights of access to a river, pond, or public tank; or (4) the state provides water, such as municipal tapwater or irrigation. It is common for people to access water in more than one of these ways. Wealthier households generally have a more reliable and more easily accessible supply of water than poorer households do. The water to which poor households have access is often both inadequate and unsafe.

Within poorer households, the gender division of labor interacts with these material inequalities in accessing water. Women are primarily responsible for domestic work, which includes provision of water for household needs, and may also involve growing a kitchen garden or raising animals for household consumption. Men often dominate decision making regarding all four modes of social access to water. Men are also primarily responsible for irrigated commercial agriculture, and they are therefore more immediately concerned with "economic" uses of water for irrigation than with "domestic" uses of water, such as for drinking, cooking, sanitation, and kitchen gardens. Poor women's access to water may thus be disadvantaged by both difficulties in physical access to water and the low priority assigned to responsibilities undertaken by women. These difficulties increase the likelihood of adverse health affects for poor families. With this broad picture in mind, let us consider three specific changes in Bangladesh, as discussion points on how development activities interact with class, gender, and the environment to produce inequitable results and conflicts.

- *First change: Drinking water supply undermined by irrigation wells.* In Bangladesh, development brought two contradictory kinds of changes in systems of groundwater access. Since groundwater is usually safer than surface water, development programs diffused hand pumps across the country, bringing safe drinking water within reach of some 97% of the population. These hand pumps draw water from no deeper than 25–30 feet. Subsequently, powered deep wells with motorized pumps were sunk for irrigation. These wells pumped so much water that they lowered groundwater tables, threatening access to clean drinking water by leaving between one-third and one-half of the drinking water hand pumps dry for part of the year. Male-dominated economic uses of water for economic growth thus clashed with and subverted female-oriented priorities of domestic water supply and health. In this case, the sectoral divisions in planning and priorities (health vs. economy), the gender division of labor, the hydrology of the region, and the technologies of water extraction combined in particular ways that led to inequitable access to water and promoted conflict while diminishing health.
- *Second change: Unanticipated biophysical consequences of water programs.* Much of the groundwater in Bangladesh has become contaminated with arsenic, so groundwater provision has ironically turned out to entail mass poisoning. The sediments in much of the country contain natural deposits of arsenic. The process by which this arsenic is released into the water is still under debate, but it is clear that irrigation and drinking water programs have provided arsenic-contaminated water to tens of millions of people. Some 20 million people have been exposed to contaminated water, and 70 million more are at risk. The issue is made more complex by the spatial variation in contamination levels. Different wells in the same village can have different degrees of contamination, meaning that all wells must be tested. Identifying contaminated wells and purifying water are costly, and people may simply have to choose between the long-term risk of arsenic poisoning and the short-term risk of illnesses borne by surface water. The effects of the arsenic problem are structured by class and gender. It seems that deep wells that richer people can afford are less contaminated than shallow wells. Intrahousehold gender dynamics mean that females generally eat last and least. People in poor households, females in particular, are less well nourished and therefore are more susceptible to the effects of arsenicosis. As water providers, women and girls may be involved in conflicts over access to cleaner water supplies and may have to spend more time getting clean water. As the symptoms of arsenicosis (such as skin ulcers and lesions) emerge, women and girls get less access to health care; they may also be socially ostracized and considered unmarriageable, or abandoned by husbands. At the same time, it is estimated that fewer people will die from arsenicosis than have been saved by access to groundwater, which brought about a steep decline in deaths due to diarrheal disease, cutting infant mortality rates in half.
- *Third change: Export shrimp aquaculture.* In the 1980s, the production of saltwater shrimp for export began to flourish in coastal areas of Bangladesh. Farmers flood tracts of land with seawater for shrimp culture, threatening the Sundarban mangrove forests and reducing opportunities for gathering livelihood resources. More prosperous farmers often take land from poorer people for shrimp farms, forcing the poor to become laborers. However, the labor on shrimp farms is hazardous to health, and shrimp culture provides fewer income-earning opportunities than did the rice farming the poor were forced to abandon. The rise of shrimp culture has also caused salinization of groundwater, increasing the burden on women who must supply household water, while also reducing the possibilities for supplementing diets through kitchen gardens and domestic livestock. Nutrition is adversely affected, especially in the poorest homes, where gender once again becomes an important variable in determining access to food.

Source: Based on Crow and Sultana (2002).

Property Regimes

> It is essential to understand that *property* is not an object such as land, but rather is a *right to a benefit stream that is only as secure as the duty of all others to respect the conditions that protect that stream*. When one has a *right* one has the expectation in both the law and in practice that their claims will be respected by those with duty.
>
> —BROMLEY (1991: 22; emphasis in original)

A "property regime" is a set of institutional arrangements that structures the rights and duties of individuals with respect to a particular object or resource. For our purposes, we can consider four different property regimes as ideal types:

- *Private property*: An individual (or legal individual, such as a corporation) has the right to exclude others from the resource and has a wide range of discretion over resource use.
- *State property*: Rights to control resource access and use are vested in the state, although the state may grant individuals and groups the privilege to use the resources.
- *Common property*: Control and use of a designated resource with known boundaries is in the hands of a well-defined social group, within which management rules are developed, incentives exist for member-users to follow mutually accepted institutional arrangements, and sanctions work to ensure compliance.
- *Open access*: Access and usage are available to anyone, and there are no enforceable obligations.

Historically, humans have treated the biophysical world principally as either common property or open access. States have played an important role in facilitating commodification by forcing the conversion of common property into either state property or private property, often on the grounds that common-property regimes lead to resource degradation (the "tragedy of the commons") and/or to economically "inefficient" resource use. Both the degradation and the inefficiency arguments are fallacious. The well-known and tragically (but not innocently) misnamed "tragedy of the commons" parable (Hardin, 1969) indicates that individuals have the incentive to overuse the commons, leading to its degradation. This parable is flawed on its own terms; more importantly, it applies to a situation of open access, not to a common-property regime, which by definition involves a set of use rules and obligations to limit overuse and degradation. On the ground, common property has proven no more prone to resource degradation than either private or state property. Furthermore, institutional economists have demonstrated that private property is inherently no more economically efficient than common property (Bromley, 1991; Vatn, 2001). The upshot, in the words of Vatn (2001: 677), is that

> choosing property regimes is about choosing between which interests are to be defended, which costs will be invoked, and even which interests will develop and be sustained. There is a tendency to believe that regimes are chosen on the basis of efficiency considerations; that is, over time, modernisation brings society from less efficient to more efficient systems. The main step is often understood as the move from common to private property—so often endorsed in contemporary development programmes around the world. The argument is, however, inconsistent. As long as what is efficient depends on which interests are to be defended, no objective or independent source of facts on which to base that judgment exists.

describes this as "accumulation by dispossession," because a few people accumulate wealth through the dispossession of others, rather than by creating new wealth.

Accumulation by dispossession—institutional change in who has rights of access, use, and control over parts of the biophysical environment—is intertwined with two further changes. Commodifying the environment brings qualitative and quantitative changes in the ways people use the environment, as capitalists produce different goods and services (commodities) to sell to those with purchasing power. These changes lead in turn to changes in the biophysical environment and its ability to supply various values. O'Connor (1998: 23; emphasis in original) characterizes the process thus:

> Original accumulation was the separation of human and nonhuman nature, and the separation of the elements of both, *in fact*—the breakup or enclosure of common lands and common property, the seizure of the commons by the well-to-do, and New World slavery, hence the *real* separation of nature or land and human beings. This forcible change violently divided human from nonhuman nature, helping to transform land into a commodity. By making many of the direct producers propertyless, original accumulation helped to break up their communities and forced them (and more importantly historically, their offspring) to sell their laborpower to survive. . . . The commodification and capitalization of nature resulting from "primitive accumulation," and later competitive accumulation, removed traditional socioeconomic and cultural constraints on land use, hence created the potential for ecologically destructive production methods.

Neither the capitalist market economy nor the process of accumulation by dispossession emerged "naturally," as the working out of some abstract natural law; both were produced through a series of contested social and institutional changes. Even Europe, much of which witnessed the expansion of the market economy in the absence of colonizers, could not avoid wrenching transitions in the making of a predominantly capitalist society. Physical enclosures of common land by local elites and legal changes combined to gradually extinguish the system of the commons, and to propagate a more standardized private property system. Many of those who lost their rights to the commons resisted these enclosures. In England, for instance, underground protests and local uprisings against these changes occurred from the mid-16th through the mid-19th centuries.

European colonial powers diffused their property systems and the related enclosures to their colonies. In order to find a reliable way to get colonial subjects to produce crops for the export market and to efficiently collect tax revenues to pay for the colonial administration, agricultural land was widely surveyed and assigned to the ownership of individual men who would be responsible for production and taxes. Colonial governments pursued not only privatization strategies, but also nationalization, transferring common land and resources to state control. They nationalized forest and other nonagricultural land in order to manage land use and extract revenue. For example, in colonial India the government nationalized forest lands under the control of the forest department, and "waste" lands (land not suitable for agricultural production) under the control of the revenue department. The respective departments then set policies for who could use such land and at what cost. The forest areas with the most valuable timber were contracted out to logging companies, enclosing the forests and extinguishing the rights of the erstwhile user-managers to the extent possible.

As in Europe, colonial processes of accumulation by dispossession undermined common-property systems and severely curtailed customary rights to natural resources, leading to protest and resistance, and giving impetus to independence movements. Nevertheless, postindependence states did little to redress past grievances, and generally continued processes of enclosing and commodifying the biophysical world in the name of national development, leading to renewed environmental livelihoods movements across the third world. Under neoliberal globalization, "free" trade agreements and pressure from the World Bank and IMF (as well as U.S. administrations) have provided leverage for transnational corporations (TNCs) seeking to advance their accumulation strategies by extending enclosure and commodification to such things as genetic material, seeds, fresh water/water services, and the Internet.

These strategies are being contested by place-based and transnational social mobilizations around the globe.

Mexico provides an example of the contestation over privatization and commodification of land. At the beginning of the 20th century, land in Mexico was concentrated in relatively few hands. Thus agrarian reform was a key issue in the Mexican revolution of 1910. The postrevolution constitution of 1917 and related agrarian regulations restored *ejido* land tenure—a form of common property in which families may control their own plots, but land is owned by the community and cannot be sold. As a result of government land redistributions, *ejidos* came to control some 40% of the country's agricultural land, providing secure access to resources for their members. However, in the process of negotiating and implementing the North American Free Trade Agreement (NAFTA), the United States insisted upon many changes to Mexican domestic law. These included a 1992 amendment to the Mexican constitution that allowed the privatization and sale of *ejido* land. This was merely the latest in a number of measures chipping away at the rights of indigenous peoples. Overt resistance to Mexican state policy crystallized on the 500th anniversary in 1992 of Columbus's arrival in the New World, and on January 1, 1994 (the day that NAFTA took effect), thousands of armed Zapatistas took over major population centers and perhaps 500 ranches in the state of Chiapas in southern Mexico. The Mexican army moved in but was not able to crush the Zapatistas, and eventually a cease-fire was signed. Despite the low-intensity conflict that has prevailed since then, the Zapatistas have worked to build a locally grounded alternative social and economic order that is autonomous, democratic, and equitable (Slater, 2004; Mexican Solidarity Network, 2006).

Struggles over enclosures are ongoing not only at the national scale, but globally as well, with the World Trade Organization (WTO) setting rules protecting Trade-Related Aspects of Intellectual Property Rights (TRIPS) and their embodiment in seeds, and discussions about the patenting of life forms (see Chapter 16 sidebar, "The WTO, Intellectual Property, and Patenting Plants"). Social movements, including so-called "antiglobalization movements," contest this form of accumulation by dispossession. For example, struggles have blossomed around the world over the issue of patenting of life forms and over the "biopiracy" that such patents enable. In addition, local movements such as the *Beej Bachao Andolan* ("Save the Seeds Movement") in India preserve diverse traditional seeds and associated farming systems. Various movements contest water commodification and water service privatization in international fora and on the ground. For example, in the April 2000 "water war" in Cochabamba, Bolivia, a broad community uprising reversed the World Bank-promoted privatization of water services into the hands of a subsidiary of Bechtel Corporation.

It is important to note that when processes of commodification extinguish previously existing rights of access use and control of a resource, erstwhile users are dispossessed and thereby lose their livelihoods, either entirely or in part. The poorest communities (and particularly women of those communities) rely most heavily on common resources, so their survival is threatened as their ability to support themselves outside the market is reduced. Such people must increase their reliance on wage labor, usually by entering at the very bottom of the labor market, doing low-paid and part-time or seasonal work, and often migrating to urban slums.

At the same time, as a resource is commodified, competitive pressures and the need to maximize profits in a capitalist economy drive capitalist enterprises to capture and internalize flows of benefits while externalizing or socializing costs and risks. Therefore, commodification brings changes in the understandings and social uses of the biophysical world, along with new technologies, production systems, labor processes, and sets of outputs—all geared to maximize the net revenue from commodity sales. In addition, commodification often entails a rescaling and relocation of the control and use of the biophysical environments (see sidebar: "Commodification and Technological 'Progress' "). As commodified outputs from an environment are traded over longer distances, the decision makers (e.g., corporate managers, consumers) who affect how that environment is used also become distanced from the local context, and rarely experience any of the social and environmental consequences of their own decisions. Thus the violence and environmental disruptions stemming from pollution of air, water, and land in the vicinity of mines or factories, or from the damage wrought by the expanding shrimp aquaculture of Bangladesh, may be devastating locally, but generally do not enter in a sustained way into the calculations of either consumers or corporate managers. In this way, environmental and social costs become "external" to the retail commodity transaction, even though these costs are central to its provision. Such "externalities" represent an involuntary subsidy, often provided by those least able to afford it. We should thus not be surprised when the human and environmental subsidizers of others' consumption contest their position.

DEVELOPMENT PROJECTS

The Distribution of Costs, Risks, and Benefits

Development often proceeds through projects that aim to extract primary resources through mining, forestry, or fisheries; to build infrastructure, such as roads, railways, and electrical power systems; to set up industrial facilities, such as steel mills or manufacturing plants; or to transform agricultural production. All such projects entail sets of costs and benefits that flow unevenly to different social groups, as well as environmental impacts that also have ramifications at various scales. Decisions about whether and how to proceed with such projects are usually informed by cost–benefit analyses that estimate whether the financial returns from a proposed project will exceed the financial costs. For example, when state planners or capitalists, working together or separately, formulate a development project such as an electronics factory, steel mill, or large dam,

Commodification and Technological "Progress"

Technological changes over time and space are often viewed as based in a "scientific progress" that is value-neutral or meeting the universal good of humanity as a whole. However, technology is also sociopolitically constructed and mediated. On the one hand, technological change has distinct sociopolitical consequences for nature and society; on the other, societal structures and hierarchies—and their relationships with nature—shape the forms of new technological development, as well as the diffusion, accessibility, uses, and effects of new technologies. A central strand running through many cases of technological transformation is the privatization of benefits that flow from that change (e.g., as a result of patent laws) even as the risks of those changes are increasingly socialized (through, e.g., state subsidization of research and development [R&D] and attempts to limit the liability of producers). When examined through this lens, the narrative of the march of benevolent scientific progress and modernization via technological change becomes a narrative of shifting relationships among privatization and socialization of risks and benefits; commodification of nature, society, and the reciprocity between them; and ideological, sociopolitical, and "scientific" forms of domination and control. Deborah Barndt's 2002 study of the "tomato trail," and a 2004 report by Focus on the Global South and GRAIN (an international nongovernmental organization [NGO] promoting the sustainable management and use of agricultural biodiversity) on new seed laws in Iraq, vividly highlight these shifting relationships

Industrialization of global agriculture and loss of biodiversity in seeds are social, cultural, and political processes. Focusing on the story of the tomato, Deborah Barndt (2002: 31–48) explores these processes as "tangled routes of contemporary agriculture" through five key historical "moments" since the 16th century. The term "moment" describes convergences of various economic, political, and ideological forces that make possible the emergence of specific kinds of practices.

1. *The scientific moment and colonialism* (beginning circa 16th and 17th centuries). Whereas many indigenous communities and *campesinos* have long celebrated the self-regenerative capacity of nature, regarding plants and animals as imbued with spirit, the emergence of western science during the colonial period meant that plants and animals—along with "savages"—were declared soulless. In asserting the superiority of "civilized" humans, this science has denied humans a sense of reciprocity with other living things, which in their own life cycles sustain the humans. Our difficulty in seeing the tomato as a living entity, then, is rooted in the emergence of a reductionist and fragmented science that has denied the self-generating qualities of nature.
2. *The industrial moment and capitalism* (beginning circa 18th and 19th centuries). The roots of the word "resource" mean "to rise again." With the onset of the industrial revolution in Europe, however, the predominant meaning of "resource" was transformed from a self-generating living system to a mere raw material to be extracted from the colonies and nature, and converted into an input for industrial commodity production and colonial trade. The key components of agricultural industrialization—mechanization, chemicalization, and new crop-breeding priorities—addressed problems such as labor inefficiency and yield, but they also created new problems: erosion, energy dependency, capital expenses, interest payments, larger farms, fewer farmers, and loss of livelihood. The tomato became subjected to a range of industrial processes and products, including the greenhouses that produce the seedlings; fertilizers, pesticides, and irrigation systems; the plastic sheets that keep the moisture in the ground while keeping the pests out; and the pails, boxes, netting, skids, and forklifts that help carry the tomato all the way from the field to the refrigerated rooms.
3. *The chemical moment and development* (beginning circa mid-20th century). Marked by the diffusion and imposition of the Green Revolution and "technological packages," this moment saw a shift from ecological processes of production, through self-generation, to technological processes of nonregenerative production. In the case of Mexico, for instance, technological packages for crops including the tomato comprise hybrid seeds, which make self-generation impossible; a diverse range of fertilizers, pesticides, insecticides, and fungicides; applicators (from backpack sprays to tractor-drawn spray rigs and airplanes); and more water and the irrigation systems and pumps to deliver it. Such chemical treadmills became a very expensive venture for third world peasants, leading to acute dispossession. The shift from self-generative to nonregenerative processes also caused drastic reduction of biodiversity, due to loss of soil fertility; emergence of new pests, weeds, and fungi; and disruption of ecological systems by the diversion of rivers and construction of dams.
4. *The genetic moment and neoliberalism* (beginning circa late 20th century). Transgenic organisms that cross species (as opposed to hybridization within species) are "canaries in the gold [*sic*] mines of the New World Order, Inc.," where profit, power, and bodily rearrangements define biotechnology as a global practice (Haraway, quoted in Barndt, 2002: 39). Genetic engineering involves taking genes and segments of deoxyribonucleic acid (DNA) that are coded for certain characteristics from one species and inserting them into another species. Multinational corporations have received protection through U.S. patent laws as well as from recent multilateral agreements (e.g., the Biodiversity Convention and Trade-Related Intellectual Property Measures [TRIPs] that came out of the Uruguay round of the General Agreement on Tariffs and Trade [GATT]). Companies that finance biogenetic research and development often use the resources of biodiversity-rich third world countries. By changing one element in the genetic makeup of a resource, they can claim a patent on the new material or on the innovative processes used to engineer the new product. TRIPs recognizes intellectual property rights (IPRs) only as private rights, thus excluding the collective nature of ideas shared in an "intellectual commons"

among *campesinos* or indigenous communities. Furthermore, only innovations that are capable of industrial application are considered as IPRs, undermining other uses aimed at the social good rather than at maximizing profits.

Barndt provides the example of the Flavr Savr tomato to illustrate how technoscientific, political, economic, ecological, and epistemological aspects of bioengineering interact. Developed in the late 1980s by Calegne (a company based in Davis, California) with the help of researchers from the University of California, the Flavr Savr tomato promised to provide "the summer taste" all year round. Technically, this involved the development of a process called "antisense," which effectively silences the promoter gene that contributes to the ripening and rotting of tomatoes. Between 1992 and 1994, Calegne had obtained a U.S. patent on its improved tomato and on the antisense technology; permission from the U.S. Department of Agriculture (USDA) to grow genetically engineered tomatoes commercially without USDA permits; and a notice from the Food and Drug Administration (FDA) that the new tomato satisfied its food safety requirements. By 1995, however, another company called Enzo Biochem launched a lawsuit against Calegne, alleging infringement of its antisense technology patents. To make matters worse for Calgene, Campbell's Soup Company, which along with Zeneca A.V.P. had exclusive rights to products based on Flavr Savrs, backed out of the deal in 1995 because of customers' nervousness about genetically modified foods. The ensuing financial losses ultimately caused Calegne's demise; it was subsequently bought out by Monsanto. Although the Flavr Savr tomato has disappeared, Monsanto is applying the same research on biogenetics to other foods.

5. *The computer moment and globalization* (beginning circa late 20th century). Computerization has replaced certain tasks, has precipitated a shift from full-time to contingent employment, and has facilitated increased monitoring of workers such as cashiers. Scanning data are used to check productivity levels, with high-scoring employees given more work hours and below-average scanners subjected to disciplinary action. Similarly, the bar code serves functions ranging from advertising, recording a sale, and inventory to documenting personal and group history, organizational surveillance, rational decision making, and self-monitoring. "Just as the corporate tomato is monitored by agribusinesses, brokers, wholesalers, and retailers who control inventory for just-in-time production, so, too, is every movement of the workers who pack tomatoes in Mexico and scan tomatoes in Canada computer monitored. Fruit/ commodity, worker and technology are totally intertwined and controlled within the silicon chip" (Barndt, 2002: 46–47).

Through these five moments, then, both crops and workers become commodified, through a fragmentation within the food system and through a uniformity that allows ever-increasing control by corporate decision makers. Although Barndt separates these moments analytically, they can be found simultaneously at work in the present time. Iraq is a case in point. According to a report issued by Focus on the Global South and GRAIN (2004), new legislation put in place by the United States prevents farmers in U.S.-occupied Iraq from reusing seeds of "new" plant varieties registered under the law. This means that they cannot save those seeds for reuse; in effect, it hands over the seed market to transnational corporations such as Monsanto. To quote from the report:

> In 2002, FAO [the Food and Agriculture Organization, United Nations] estimated that 97 percent of Iraqi farmers used saved seeds from their own stocks from [previous] year's harvest or purchased from local markets. When the new law—on plant variety protection (PVP)—is put into effect, seed saving will be illegal and the market will only offer proprietary "PVP-protected" planting material "invented" by transnational agribusiness corporations. . . . Its consequences are the loss of farmers' freedoms and a grave threat to food sovereignty in Iraq. In this way, the U.S. has declared a new war against the Iraqi farmer. (Focus on the Global South and GRAIN, 2004)

they envisage a set of monetary costs (e.g., financing, land acquisition and construction costs). The flow of income that the project is projected to generate is balanced against these costs. This kind of financial exercise is a standard way of evaluating projects, but in the enthusiasm to move ahead benefits are often overestimated and costs underestimated. Furthermore, parties that expect to profit from the construction of the project itself are particularly vociferous about touting the benefits of the project and about minimizing its costs.

Government agencies are important arenas for the play of power politics in development projects. Through acts of both commission and omission, such agencies often play a central role in shaping a project's costs and benefits and their social distribution. State agencies use powers of eminent domain to take control of land (without adequately compensating those displaced) and turn it over to mining or industrial concerns, or flood it behind dams. Such projects are usually built on land that people are using, and affect the environmental services that resident (and sometimes distant) communities rely on. These social and environmental costs are complex, are difficult to quantify, and have generally been downplayed when they can be socialized. By disregarding most of the negative social and environmental effects of a project, officials tacitly approve the socialization or transfer of these costs onto those who can be ignored or rendered voiceless. These burdens are passed on to people marginalized by specific intersections of gender, class, location, and ethnicity (many of whom become destitute migrants to urban slums), or they manifest themselves as environmental degradation. The case of large dams illustrates some of these processes.

The Promises and Perils of Large Dams

The global debate about large dams is at once overwhelmingly complex and fundamentally simple. It is complex because the issues are not confined to the design, construction, and operation of dams themselves, but embrace the range of social, environmental, and political choices on which the human aspirations to development and improved well-being depend. Dams fundamentally alter rivers and the use of a natural resource, frequently entailing a reallocation of benefits from local riparian users to new groups of beneficiaries at a regional or national level. At the heart of the debate about dams are issues of equity, governance, justice, and power—issues that underlie the many intractable problems faced by humanity (World Commission on Dams [WCD], 2000: xxvii–xxviii).

A large dam is the quintessential development project. Intended to provide hydroelectric power, flood control, and/or irrigation, large dams involve wide-ranging planning and monumental construction works to create enormous social and environmental transformations. They are also powerful technological symbols of modernist development. Although societies have been constructing dams since ancient times, a rapid growth in the construction of large dams (defined as 15 meters or more from foundation to crest) after World War II coincided with waves of decolonization and the growth of the development industry. There were 5,268 large dams in 1950; their number increased to more than 36,000 by 1986 and to more than 40,000 by 2005. China alone built nearly 19,000 large dams, while India built nearly 1,600. Large dams were constructed in Latin America, and several newly independent African countries built dams in the 1960s (McCully, 1986: 2–5).

With this dam-building boom, concerns arose about their environmental effects. Concerns about the social costs of dams, however, were pushed aside. Although planners have always recognized that dams displace people, rarely have they done more than pay lip service to the need to relocate and rehabilitate those whose homes and lands are flooded, and people displaced by dam-related construction and infrastructure are often completely overlooked. In practice, the people to be displaced by dam construction and submergence were rarely even counted, let alone compensated. The resulting toll of immiseration has been enormous. The World Bank (1994) has estimated that some four million people are displaced annually by dams, and that many of these are left impoverished. McCully (1996) estimated that between 30 and 60 million people, few of whom are ever able to recover either economically or psychologically, have been displaced by large dams.

Despite growing concerns about the social and environmental costs of dams, and the emergence of large-scale social movements contesting dams, alliances among government development agencies, international funders such as the World Bank, construction companies, and prospective beneficiaries have ensured the continuation of new dam projects. Facing such powerful international interests, social movements struggling against large dams throughout the world have themselves found it necessary to form domestic and international networks in order to have an impact.

In western India in the 1990s, the *Narmada Bachao Andolan* (NBA, or Movement to Save the Narmada) formed alliances across scales ranging from the village to the state and to the national and international. Initially, the NBA was struggling to ensure that those displaced by the Sardar Sarovar dam and related projects in the Narmada River valley would receive a just resettlement and rehabilitation package. Later the NBA broadened its critique to oppose the model of development based on large dams, because its members believe that backers for such projects underestimate costs and overestimate benefits to make such projects appear viable—and, most importantly, because large dams have such enormous social and environmental costs. The NBA made international alliances that pressured international funders of the Sardar Sarovar project to reexamine the project on the grounds that their own standards were not being followed, particularly regarding environmental impact and the resettlement and rehabilitation of displaced people. A World Bank inspection team largely verified the NBA's claims. The work of the NBA and its allies was instrumental in ending both Japanese government and World Bank funding of the Sardar Sarovar dam on the Narmada River, and in stalling the dam's construction in court. The project proceeds slowly, with continuing rounds of resistance and repression in the Narmada River valley, public appeals, protest rallies, and court cases. The NBA is still demanding that those involuntarily displaced be equitably resettled and rehabilitated.

The debates generated by this struggle and the growing international uproar over the social and ecological costs of large dams led to the establishment of the WCD, a multistakeholder fact-finding commission charged with developing a broad, deep, and unbiased understanding of the full range of costs and benefits of large dams, as well as the distribution of those costs and benefits, and to develop a framework for decision making. The WCD's 2000 report runs to nearly 400 pages, but a summary of key findings on the performance of large dams is instructive (see sidebar: "The Performance of Large Dams"). The report emphasizes that the social and environmental costs and risks of large dams flow overwhelmingly to the poor, the otherwise vulnerable, and future generations, while the social and economic benefits flow primarily to the comparatively well off of today; it finds this outcome unacceptable, given existing commitments to human rights and sustainable development (WCD, 2000: xxxi).

If a similar commission examined mining operations, oil wells, or industrial facilities, the conclusions would be similar. For example, Gadgil and Guha (1995) estimate that the principal beneficiaries of development constitute only about one-sixth of India's population, while nearly a third of the population has been forced to become

The Performance of Large Dams

The knowledge base indicates that shortfalls in the technical, financial, and economic performance of large dams have occurred and are compounded by significant social and environmental impacts, the costs of which are often disproportionately borne by poor people, indigenous peoples, and other vulnerable groups. Given the large capital investment in large dams, the World Commission on Dams (WCD) was disturbed to find that substantive evaluations of completed projects are few in number, narrow in scope, poorly integrated across impact categories and scales, and inadequately linked to decisions on operations. In assessing the large dams it reviewed, the WCD (2000) found the following:

- Large dams display a high degree of variability in delivering predicted water and electricity services (and related social benefits), with a considerable portion falling short of physical and economic targets, while others continue generating benefits after 30–40 years.
- Large dams have demonstrated a marked tendency toward schedule delays and significant cost overruns.
- Large dams designed to deliver irrigation services have typically fallen short of physical targets, did not recover their costs, and have been less profitable in economic terms than expected.
- Large hydropower dams tend to perform closer to (but still below) targets for power generation; they generally meet their financial targets but demonstrate variable economic performance relative to targets, with a number of notable under- and overperformers.
- Large dams generally have a range of extensive impacts on rivers, watersheds, and aquatic ecosystems. These impacts are more negative than positive, and in many cases have led to irreversible loss of species and ecosystems.
- Efforts to date to counter the ecosystem impacts of large dams have met with limited success, owing to the lack of attention to anticipating and avoiding impacts, the poor quality and uncertainty of predictions, the difficulty of coping with all impacts, and the only partial implementation and success of mitigation measures.
- Pervasive and systematic failures to assess the range of potential negative impacts and to implement adequate mitigation, resettlement, and development programmes for the displaced, as well as failures to account for the consequences of large dams for downstream livelihoods have led to the impoverishment and suffering of millions, giving rise to growing opposition to dams by affected communities worldwide.
- Since the environmental and social costs of large dams have been poorly accounted for in economic terms, the true profitability of these schemes remains elusive.

Perhaps of most significance is the fact that social groups bearing the social and environmental costs and risks of large dams, especially the poor, vulnerable, and future generations, are often not the same groups that receive the water and electricity services, or the social and economic benefits from these. Applying a "balance sheet" approach to assess the costs and benefits of large dams, where large inequities exist in the distribution of these costs and benefits, is seen as unacceptable given existing commitments to human rights and sustainable development.

Source: Adapted from WCD (2000: xxxi).

ecological refugees. The people who are marginalized or excluded from decision-making processes find themselves subject to one or more of the following "five D's," giving them a reason to engage in contestation centering around social uses of the environment:

- *Disease/injury*: People suffer illness or injury because their jobs or their environments become less safe. For example, factories and power plants often entail increased chronic exposure to hazardous pollutants that poison the surrounding air, water, and/or land. Agricultural fertilizers and pesticides can themselves be hazardous to the people and environments where they are used, as well as to the places they are transported by the movement of air and water (not to mention the risks to consumers of foods treated with agrochemicals). Dams and irrigation systems facilitate the territorial expansion of disease vectors, such as malarial mosquitoes or the snails that carry schistosomiasis.

• *Disaster risk*: People's risk of suffering from a "natural" or human-induced disastrous event is increased. Union Carbide produced pesticides in a crowded area of the Indian city of Bhopal until a leak of poisonous gas shortly after midnight on December 3, 1984, became the world's most deadly industrial accident. Safety systems were not working, and there was no alarm. Some 500,000 people were exposed to the gas, mostly as they slept. Twenty thousand have died as a result of their exposure, and over 120,000 people, many of whom are disabled, suffer from ailments caused by the accident and the pollution at the plant site (which has yet to be cleaned up). After 5 years of wrangling, Union Carbide paid $470 million in compensation to the Indian government, but many victims still await compensation. Dams can increase risk of earthquakes, and dam failures create flash floods. Denudation of hillsides can contribute to landslides on the hills and floods on the plains below.

• *Degradation*: External actors directly and indirectly cause degradation of environments that people depend on for lives and livelihoods, and that give meaning to their lives. Thus excessive extraction of groundwater by those who can afford pumps draws down the water table, leaving those who must depend on shallow wells without access to adequate water supplies. Pollution, logging, or mining operations may degrade resources that the rural poor rely on for food, cooking fuel, or income. Degraded land and water may also impair crop and livestock production. Taken together, these degradations reduce nutrition and impair health.

• *Displacement*: People are physically removed from the environments that they depend on for livelihoods and sustenance. A World Bank study estimated that development projects in the third world cause involuntary displacement of at least 10 million people per year, most of whom are poor at the outset and find themselves further impoverished and their social support networks disintegrate as a result of displacement (World Bank, 1994).

• *Dispossession*: People are dispossessed of rights to access, control, and/or use of environments that they depend on for sustenance and livelihoods. For example, forests are made state property and then leased to timber contractors, while local people are excluded.

In fact, we can see all of the five D's above as examples of accumulation by dispossession related to the environment. It is therefore not surprising that such projects frequently spawn protests, which are often met by repression. Such protests are sometimes characterized as antidevelopment, but it is clear that they are actually protests against the power politics embodied in a form of development in which benefits flow predominantly to some social groups, while costs are socialized and transferred to others. We might ask what it would take to move toward societies that design and execute initiatives or projects that are socially and environmentally equitable and sustainable in a world of difference.

CONSERVATION AND CONFLICT

Commodification and development are not the only processes that arbitrarily redistribute the benefits of the environment away from subsistence users, producing contestation. The same is true even for programs for environmental conservation or regeneration.

A common way to promote conservation is to mark off a protected area, such as a national park, to which human access is limited and customary uses of the area by local people are either banned or severely restricted. Because this limits the use of hitherto common resources—an uncompensated loss for the erstwhile users—spaces of conservation become arenas of conflict that result in distinctive patterns of resource management (Zimmerer and Bassett, 2003: 5). Ironically, the so-called "global" or "abstract" decontextualized visions of ecology can produce frameworks that are at odds with place-specific ecologies. This happens, for example, when environmental planning seeks to protect nature as environment around marketable activities, while local conservation efforts of rural women, peasants, and indigenous peoples seek to protect nature as the environment around their homes and hearths.

When protection is connected to commercial activity, as is often the case with forest management, the opportunities for conflict are even stronger: Timber and pulp companies, environmentalists, and local forest users all seek to advance their interests. The famous *Chipko* ("hug a tree") movement in northern India provides an example. The British had nationalized forests in India in the name of sound forest management. Their concern was principally with ensuring a continuous supply of timber, so they restricted the access of local users and instead allowed commercial contractors to harvest timber. This practice continued after independence. *Chipko* sought to protect local forests from the axes of commercial forest contractors so that local households could receive environmental benefits from the forests, as well as forest produce, firewood, and small timber for household needs. As a result of pressure generated by movements such as *Chipko* and their domestic and international allies, the Indian government changed forest regulations and enforcement to strengthen conservation. But the state apparatus failed to apprehend how its new regulations to conserve forests also ended up harming those, such as the members of *Chipko*, who had fought to protect local lives and livelihoods by limiting commercial timber operations. This short-sightedness provoked renewed contestation, including protest movements to cut down trees in retaliation (Guha, 2000; Rangan, 2000).

Although *Chipko* itself was quite heterogeneous, this vignette suggests that its struggle was not simply about the environment, but also about the manner in which livelihoods and justice are inextricably linked with the uses of the environment. In this case, the colonial and postcolonial state and commercial interests used discourses of conservation and sustainable forest management as pretexts for accumulation by dispossession. Ecotourism, often seen as a happy blending of commerce and conservation, can create the same troubled dynamics if ecotourism ventures exclude local users from particular areas in order to sell exotic environments to wealthy vacationers.

An increasingly popular approach, often referred to as "participatory resource management" (PRM), seeks to address questions of development, equity, and sustainability by bringing local stakeholders back to the table as the future of local resource use is decided. In PRM—for example, participatory forest management or participatory watershed management—members of a community come together with relevant government officials and experts to jointly chart the priorities and management of their local resources, balancing the varied needs and interests of the stakeholders. PRM comes, at least in part, from a belated recognition of the fact that interventions made in the name of modernization, progress, or development have frequently disrupted preexisting systems of management that were often more sustainable and socially equitable. In so doing, PRM attempts to revive many of the kinds of practices that existed under earlier common-property systems.

Although PRM approaches promise to promote both environmental and social justice values, they must negotiate a complex terrain. On the one hand, it is crucial to recognize that " 'communities' are characterized as much by their heterogeneity as by their (uneasy) alliance around certain issues" (Zimmerer and Bassett, 2003: 6). Communities have their own power dynamics and exclusions, based on gender, caste, class, religion, or other dimensions and hierarchies of difference. On the other hand, these internally diverse PRM groups are embedded in social and biophysical processes at multiple scales. Therefore, the effectiveness and sustainability of local participatory institutions are mediated by the ways in which their members interact (both individually and collectively) with such nonlocal actors and institutions as social networks, commercial enterprises, government functionaries, and nongovernmental organization (NGO) intermediaries—each of which may have its own values, priorities, and knowledge systems, as well as a different relationship to individual members. These "conservation encounters" can shape landscapes and livelihoods in contradictory ways. For example, NGOs are "important yet ambivalent intermediaries in linking local and global concerns over conservation and development" (Zimmerer and Bassett, 2003: 6).

In addition, biophysical dynamics (such as seasonality, precipitation patterns, erosion and deposition, and the life cycles of plants and animals) and related ecosystem changes can play a significant role in shaping the evolution of resource use institutions and conflict. Furthermore, these processes rarely operate at scales that correspond with social jurisdictions, meaning that what a PRM group does also affects those outside its borders, raising the possibility of conflict.

PRM at its best must be a democratic, accountable process for provisionally resolving the multidimensional conflicts that are continuously produced by the context-specific interactions of the social actors and biophysical processes. As such, it is not an institutional model to be diffused, but a long-term process of change that seeks to foster inclusion and negotiation of difference on an equitable basis. With all of its risks and complexities, PRM also holds out the possibility of social justice and environmental sustainability for local environments. But is it possible to "scale up" participatory management to the whole world? How can localized participatory systems be sustained in the face of external pressures?

CONCLUSIONS

Throughout this chapter, we have examined the ways in which contestation over the environment is produced—not principally as a result of a declining resource base, but through struggles over the distribution of costs and benefits in dynamic processes that mediate and regulate the social uses of the environment. As a way to conclude this discussion of environment and social conflict, it is useful to touch on three sources of contestations to which we have directly or indirectly alluded in our themes and examples.

First, we need to reflect on the ways in which the shifting power configurations of third world states since the end of the Cold War have compromised, enhanced, or shaped the nature of their participation in projects of sustainable development. Third world states, with the assistance of international development agencies, have often been the dominant postindependence actors in developing and managing such resources as water and forests. Since the 1970s, this state-centered approach has come under fire from three directions: (1) Various social movements around the world have challenged state management as inequitable and environmentally unsustainable, and have sought broader popular participation in resource management; (2) the neoliberal revolution of the 1980s launched attacks on the state, asserting the importance of private ownership and markets as a means to assure efficient resource allocation and rapid economic growth; and (3) advocates of pragmatic concerns within state and international agencies have grappled with the burgeoning financial costs of, say, forest and water management. Together, these changes have opened the door to more possibilities for local participation in managing local uses of the environment, at least where such uses do not conflict with commercial interests. On the other hand, neoliberal policies may mean that states promulgate and enforce fewer regulations on business as they sign international agreements and pass laws to allow enclosures in more and more realms.

A second dimension relates to how gender equality, and the notion of women's participation more generally, have been highlighted, politicized, or reductively deployed in popular conceptualizations of sustainable development. In the years immediately following the 1992 Earth Summit, the World Resources Institute and the World Bank inserted women into their conceptualization of sustainable development. The World Resources Institute (1994: 43), for instance, defined the concept of "sustainable development" as

> based on the recognition that a nation cannot reach its economic goals without also achieving social and environmental goals—that is, universal education and employment opportunity, universal health and reproductive care, equitable access to and distribution of resources, stable populations, and a sustained natural resource base. While often difficult to quantify because of the lack of or local nature of data, there is also increasing recognition that, if women do indeed have a significant—and in some cases disproportionate—influence on many cross-cutting components of sustainable development, then the achievement of sustainable development is inextricably bound up with the establishment of women's equality; one cannot be accomplished without the other.

However, this definition of sustainable development continued to imply that the environmental problem is primarily a problem of the poor (and predominantly rural) women of the global south who need to be educated about how to become better managers of the rural environment. It also failed to make any mention of various kinds of interventions made in the name of modern progress that had disrupted many preexisting environmental management practices, which were often relatively more sustainable and socially equitable.

The institutionalization of gender, participation, empowerment, and sustainability in donor-driven development programs has generated possibilities to create new agendas, but the politically limiting and status-quo-reinforcing nature of many of these programs has also caused frustrations. For example, donor-sponsored women's empowerment programs in some third would countries allow women to agitate to save their seeds, while effectively prohibiting them from participating in agitations against state policies privatizing water and forests. This subject is a delicate one. On the one hand, rural women's widespread sociopolitically constructed role as the primary managers of natural resources in their communities ties their social interests closely to their environment; in fact, many grassroots movements pertaining to access or dispossession of natural resources have been initiated, led, or sustained by women. At the same time, appropriation of the sustainable development discourses by donor agencies and mainstream development programs has often focused exclusively on women as decontextualized objects who simply need to be targeted as agents of development so that they can become better natural resource managers—a classic Malthusian practice. Furthermore, participation itself has often been used as a decontextualized idea that can be uniformly applied in every local community, rather than a practice whose contours are to be collectively configured, negotiated, and implemented (sometimes in starkly different ways) in each community where it is embraced.

Third, we must consider how the roles, responsibilities, and interests of the first world and third world have been politicized or erased in popularization of the sustainable development discourse. As Paul Ekins (1993: 99) has argued, sustainable development is possible only if the following three principles are met: (1) The northern establishment must recognize its countries' primary responsibility for the present environmental crisis and determine to take radical action against it. (2) The north must further recognize that current hierarchical structures of interdependence (of trade, aid, and debt) make sustainable development in the south impossible; institutions such as the General Agreement on Tariffs and Trade (GATT), the World Bank, and the IMF need to be totally reformed if true sustainability is to be achieved. (3) Southern elites must recognize that the principal concern of sustainable development should be with the poorest people in their countries. Continuing campaigns for democracy, accountability, and sustainability that mature through contestations among specific local actors and social movements in many parts of the third world have brought these realizations to powerful state and international actors.

We might also consider the dangers of always pairing the concept of "sustainability" with that of "development." Context-specific considerations of "sustainability" can be used in more nuanced, flexible, and antihierarchical ways than can "sustainable development," because "sustainability" has not yet been coopted into a narrow mainstream interpretation. Context specificity is important, because it forces the crucial questions: What exactly is being sustained, at what scale, by and for whom, and using what institutional mechanisms (Sneddon, 2000: 525)?

> Rather than listening to politicians and state officials intone the sustainable development mantra and reacting, diverse actors might instead use as starting point the fact that sustainability is simultaneously an ideological stance, a point of convergence for political struggles, and a measure of performance for development activities. The first aspect can be converted to vision and political action based on affinity, the second to an organizing tool and the third to a means of holding public–private development projects accountable. (Sneddon, 2000: 525)

In the end, multidimensionality, contextuality, dynamism, and accountability must be critical in determining whether sustainable development can serve as a useful tool because of its wide acceptance in discourses across institutions and social contexts—or whether it wiser to reject sustainable development on the grounds that it is coopted and oversimplified, and to replace it with new articulations of sociopolitical and environmental justice that are attentive to the nuances of each struggle.

8 Disease and Health[1]

As we write this book, there is an ongoing national debate in the United States about how to provide universal health care. The cost of health services has been said to constitute 16% of the U.S. gross domestic product (GDP) (Centers for Medicare & Medicaid Services, 2008). It is a huge topic, yet it interests us that geography books about the United States rarely devote much space to the geography of disease and disease control. Disease is an ever-present matter in the third world. It shortens life expectancy significantly, and it affects the work and well-being of all.

With few exceptions, there have not been major improvements in patterns and prevalence of diseases since the first edition of *A World of Difference* was published. Three notable success stories come from Africa. First, there has been a considerable reduction in the prevalence of onchoceriasis (river blindness), which has been virtually eliminated from 11 west African countries. The World Health Organization (WHO, 1999b) reported that 1.5 million people in west Africa who had been infected no longer were, and that 300,000 cases of river blindness had been prevented. A second success story concerns Guinea worm disease. The Carter Center, based in Atlanta, Georgia, has had a worldwide program to eliminate Guinea worm disease (dracunculaisis). In 1986, there were 3.5 million people with this disease; in 2004, there were only 16,026 cases (mostly in Ghana and Sudan)—a reduction of 99.5% (Carter Center, 2005). The third success story concerns the human immunodeficiency virus (HIV) and acquired immune deficiency syndrome (AIDS) in Uganda, where between 1991 and 2001 HIV-positive rates declined from 21.1% to 6.4% (Low-Beer, 2005: 480). On the other hand, in the past decade HIV and AIDS have spread throughout the world; the incidence of associated diseases, such as tuberculosis (TB), has increased as well. In this chapter we limit revisions to an analysis of the HIV/AIDS pandemic during the past decade, projecting its future course worldwide, as well as the demographic, social, and economic impacts that are likely to ensue.

FIRST AND SECOND WORLDS VERSUS THIRD WORLD: COMPARISONS

Figure 8.1 suggests in a disturbing way the contrast in the timing of death between first world and third world countries (Madeley,

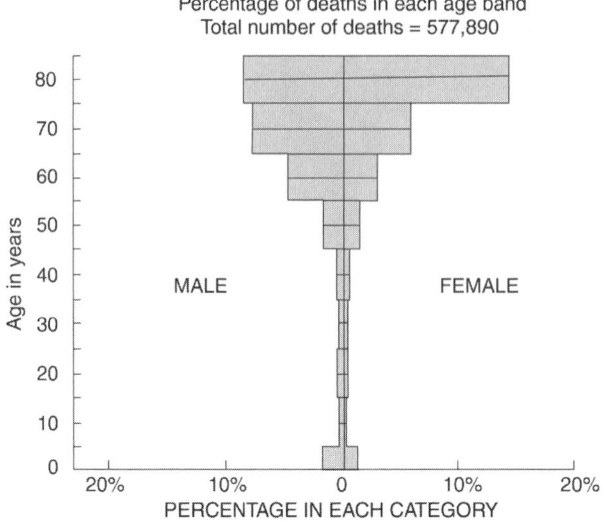

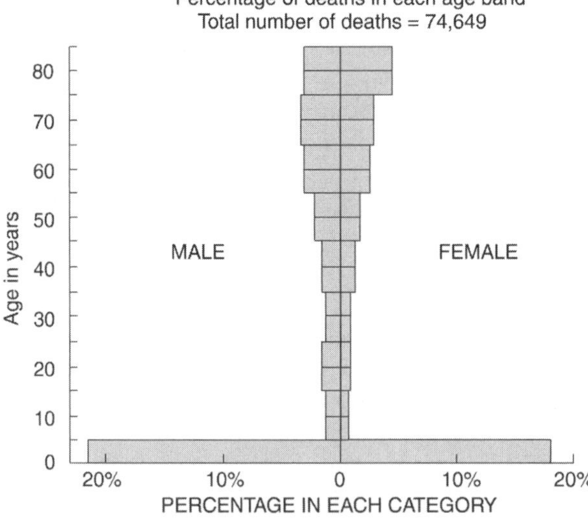

FIGURE 8.1. The timing of death: England and Wales, 1981, and Venezuela, 1979. *Source:* Adapted from Madeley, Jelley, Epstein, and O'Keefe (1984). Copyright 1984 by the Royal Swedish Academy of Sciences. Adapted by permission.

Jelley, Epstein, and O'Keefe, 1984). It shows that in Venezuela, 40% of deaths each year are in the age cohort 0–4 years, and that death comes at an earlier age in every cohort (compared with England and Wales) until age 55. Health problems can be grouped into three broad types: communicable diseases, noncommunicable diseases, and injuries. Diseases are major contributors to third world mortality and morbidity (illness). As we will see, among third world people the disease burden attributable to communicable (infectious and parasitic) diseases and to insanitary conditions is very great, and these diseases frequently have direct links to environmental conditions. We cannot cover all the diseases, but by providing some examples, we hope to give a sense of the scope of the challenge in improving the health of third world peoples.

How should one measure the seriousness of disease and injuries? Days lost from work and numbers of deaths constitute common ways to assess disease effects. Demographers at WHO, however, have begun to use a measure called the "disability-adjusted life year" (DALY) as a means of describing the burden of disease. The DALY is a measure of the years of healthy life "not lived"—that is, lost because of premature death or disability. The measure is based on a projected life expectancy of 82.5 years for women and 80 years for men; a complicated system of discounted "age weights" (the value of a year of life at age X, with age 25 having the highest value); and a six-class measure of the severity of disability (World Bank, 1993: 26, 213). The part of the DALY contributed by disability assessments has been criticized as being flawed and unreflective of the sorts of productive and fulfilling lives that are possible for severely disabled people (Metts, 2001). Nonetheless, we can gain useful comparative information from the DALY. The total loss of DALYs is called the "global burden of disease" (GBD). Although the data presented here are based on the most authoritative, official government statistics available, they are subject to great variability in accuracy and completeness. "Comparability is limited because of variation in data collection, statistical methods, and definitions" (World Bank, 1993: 195). We can make only general comparisons from the information used.

More than 853,000 children ages 0–4 died from malaria in 2003 (Centers for Disease Control and Prevention, 2005). A statement like that has immediacy and is readily understood. The ideas of DALY and GBD are more abstract, but they provide a systematic way of comparing particular regions, as well as of comparing the first and second worlds with the third world. Careful study of Figures 8.2–8.5 in conjunction with Tables 8.1–8.3 will help the reader understand much about disease patterns and consequences. (Note that in these figures, the light-shaded bars refer to the less developed world and the dark-shaded bars to the developed world.)

If the burden of disease were equally distributed among the peoples of the world, we would expect the first and second worlds, with 22% of the world's population, to carry about 22% of it. In fact, their burden is 11%, the other 89% being shouldered by third world people. Since the numbers of people are different between developed and less developed economies (1,114 million compared with 4,123 million), in much of this presentation we use DALYs/1,000 population—a ratio that standardizes data and permits comparison.

Obviously, since third world people do not live as long, they have their illnesses earlier in life than first/second world people do. The kinds of illnesses and injuries are thereby different from those encountered by older folk. For communicable diseases, 62.8% of the DALYs lost occur during the first 5 years of life in the third world (696.7 DALYs/1,000 population). By contrast, in the first and second worlds, communicable diseases account for 36.6% of DALYs lost for the same age group, 0–4 years (and result in only 66.1 DALYs/1,000 population, less than 10% of the third world rate). For noncommunicable diseases, the largest contributors to DALYs lost are cardiovascular diseases, malignant neoplasms (cancers), and neuropsychiatric illnesses. As for injuries, nearly all DALYs (91%) are associated with ages 0–44 in the third world, whereas in the developed world 89% of DALYs are associated with ages 15–60+.

Figure 8.2 shows the sources of the global disease burden among males, and partitions it between third world economies

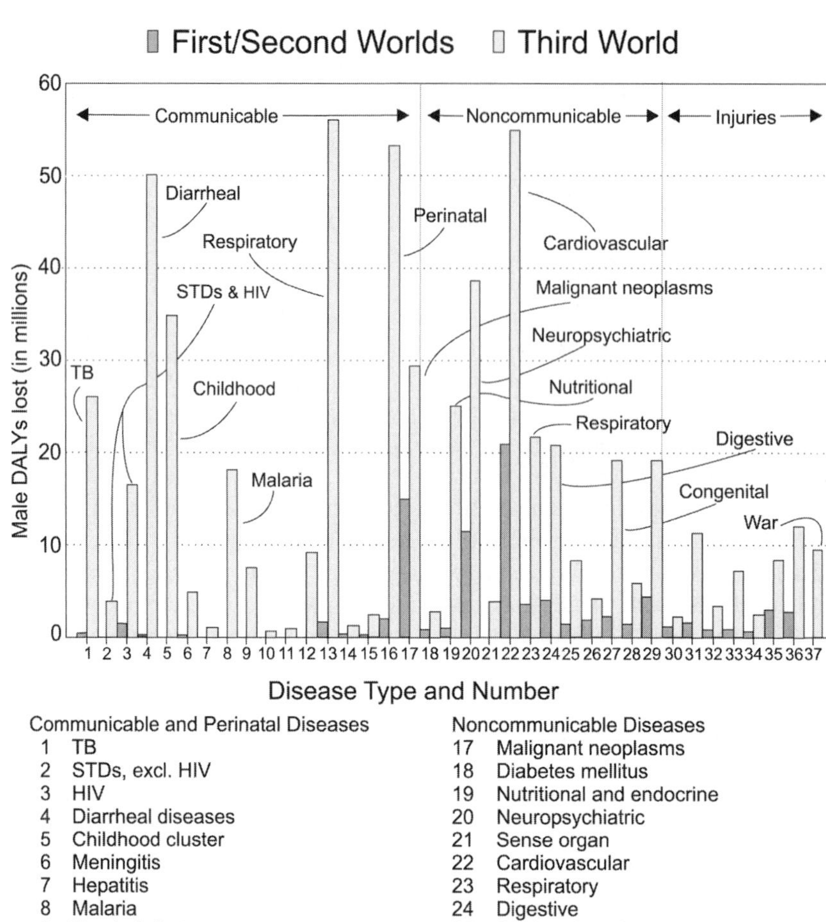

FIGURE 8.2. Total male disease burden (in millions of disability-adjusted life years, or DALYs). *Source:* Data are from World Bank (1993).

(light-shaded bars) and first/second world economies (dark-shaded bars) (World Bank, 1993). The figure should be read with Table 8.1. The left part of the figure deals with communicable diseases, most of which are infectious and/or parasitic. The first of these is TB, which is probably increasing in incidence and resistance to antibiotics worldwide. Among sexually transmitted diseases (STDs), HIV is also diffusing in a pandemic

TABLE 8.1. Total Male Disease Burden, 1990 (in Millions of Disability-Adjusted Life Years, or DALYs)

No.	Disease type	First and second worlds	Third world	Total	Third world's percentage of DALYs
Communicable and perinatal					
1	TB	4.1	260.5	264.6	98.5
2	STDs, excl. HIV	0.3	38.3	38.6	99.2
3	HIV	13.7	165.5	179.2	92.4
4	Diarrheal diseases	2.3	499.4	501.7	99.5
5	Childhood cluster	0.7	347.7	348.4	99.8
6	Meningitis	1.4	48.4	49.8	97.2
7	Hepatitis	0.6	9.8	10.4	94.2
8	Malaria	0.0	182.3	182.3	100.0
9	Tropical cluster	0.0	75.0	75.0	100.0
10	Leprosy	0.0	5.1	5.1	100.0
11	Trachoma	0.0	9.3	9.3	100.0
12	Intestinal helminths	0.0	91.8	91.8	100.0
13	Lower respiratory infections	5.4	560.9	576.3	97.3
14	Upper respiratory infections	2.9	11.9	14.8	80.4
15	Otitis media	2.3	23.6	25.9	91.1
16	Perinatal	19.8	532.0	551.8	96.4
Noncommunicable					
17	Malignant neoplasms	149.4	294.6	444.0	66.4
18	Diabetes mellitus	7.9	26.8	34.7	77.2
19	Nutritional and endocrine	9.8	250.6	260.4	96.2
20	Neuropsychiatric	113.4	386.4	499.8	77.3
21	Sense organ	0.5	38.6	39.1	98.7
22	Cardiovascular	210.7	548.6	759.3	72.3
23	Respiratory	34.2	217.1	251.3	86.4
24	Digestive	37.9	207.8	245.7	84.6
25	Genitourinary	13.8	81.9	95.6	85.6
26	Musculoskeletal	17.3	40.9	58.2	70.3
27	Congenital abnormalities	20.7	190.7	211.4	90.2
28	Oral health	12.5	56.5	69.0	81.9
Injuries					
29	Motor vehicle	41.2	190.1	231.3	82.2
30	Poisoning	8.7	20.7	29.4	70.4
31	Falls	13.6	110.6	124.4	89.0
32	Fires	5.8	32.7	38.5	84.9
33	Drowning	7.0	70.2	77.2	90.0
34	Occupational	4.4	22.3	26.7	83.5
35	Self-inflicted	26.3	79.7	106.0	75.2
36	Homicide and violence	23.7	118.3	142.0	83.3
37	War	0.0	92.5	92.5	100.0
	Total	822.3	5,939.0	6,761.3	87.8

Source: Data are from World Bank (1993).

(3). Two groups of infectious diseases have major impacts on young children: diarrheal diseases (4) and the "childhood cluster" (5), the latter of which includes pertussis (whooping cough), polio, diphtheria, measles, and tetanus. Diarrheal diseases killed 2,866,000 people in the third world in 1990, and 86% (2,465,000) were ages 0–4 years. Some 86% of the 1,860,000 deaths from childhood diseases occurred among children ages 0–4. Meningitis (6) and hepatitis (7) are comparatively less important. Malaria (8) also has its major impact on infants and children to age 5, and over 68% of the 926,000 deaths caused by malaria in 1990 were among children ages 0–4.

Another group of infectious diseases is called the "tropical cluster" (9) and includes trypanosomiasis, Chagas's disease (American trypanosomiasis), schistosomiasis, leishmaniasis, lymphatic filariasis (elephantiasis), and onchocerciasis (river blindness). Leprosy (10) occurs at low levels and trachoma (12) at moderate levels in the third world, and they are essentially absent elsewhere. Intestinal helminths (11), such as ascaris (roundworm), trichuris (whipworm), and hookworm, are common in the third world; they are particularly serious in southeast Asia and the Pacific islands, China, and Latin America and the Caribbean. The next-to-last tall spike in this survey of communicable diseases (Figure 8.2) is for lower respiratory infections (13). The reader will have noted that across the span of communicable diseases, the first and second worlds show up only with respect to HIV and perinatal diseases (16). By and large, communicable diseases have been brought under control in the developed world.

Residents of developed countries are afflicted at higher levels when we consider noncommunicable diseases and injuries. Three groups of noncommunicable diseases—cardiovascular diseases (22), malignant neoplasms or cancers (17), and neuropsychiatric illnesses (20)—have the only substantial spikes representing people in first/second world economies. Still, well over two-thirds of the DALYs generated by these diseases are borne by people in the third world. Nutritional and endocrine diseases (19) are overwhelmingly third world problems. (Endocrine diseases affect the thyroid, pituitary, adrenal, and other glands, whose secretions govern human growth and vascular and skeletal development.) Among nutritional diseases are kwashiorkor (protein–energy malnutrition), particularly serious in India; goiter (iodine deficiency), a condition that can be easily and inexpensively remedied by iodizing salt; vitamin A deficiency; and anemia. Other diseases of malnutrition are pellagra (a vitamin B [niacin] deficiency), scurvy (a vitamin C deficiency), and rickets (a vitamin D deficiency that results in deficient bone growth).

Injuries can be divided into unintentional injuries (i.e., accidents) and intentional ones: self-inflicted injuries (including suicide), those caused by homicide and violence (36), and those caused by war (37). It is notable that the 92.5 million DALYs attributed to war in 1990 all occurred in the third world; none occurred in the developed world. Among unintentional injuries, the most notable are those caused by motor vehicle accidents (29). The types of injuries immediately to the right of motor vehicle injuries in the diagram are those resulting from poisoning (30), falls (31), fires (32), drowning (33), and occupational accidents (34). They are all much more prevalent in the third world than they are in the first and second worlds.

Figure 8.3 shows disease patterns for women (and should be read with Table 8.2). The patterns are by and large the same as those for men, so we highlight here the major differences; before doing so, however, we must stress that diseases in third world women (as well as first world women) are less well documented than those in men, because of gaps, absences, inattention, and "silences" in medical research on women (Holloway, 1994). Some argue that women's diseases are less well documented simply because they have not been recognized as dis-

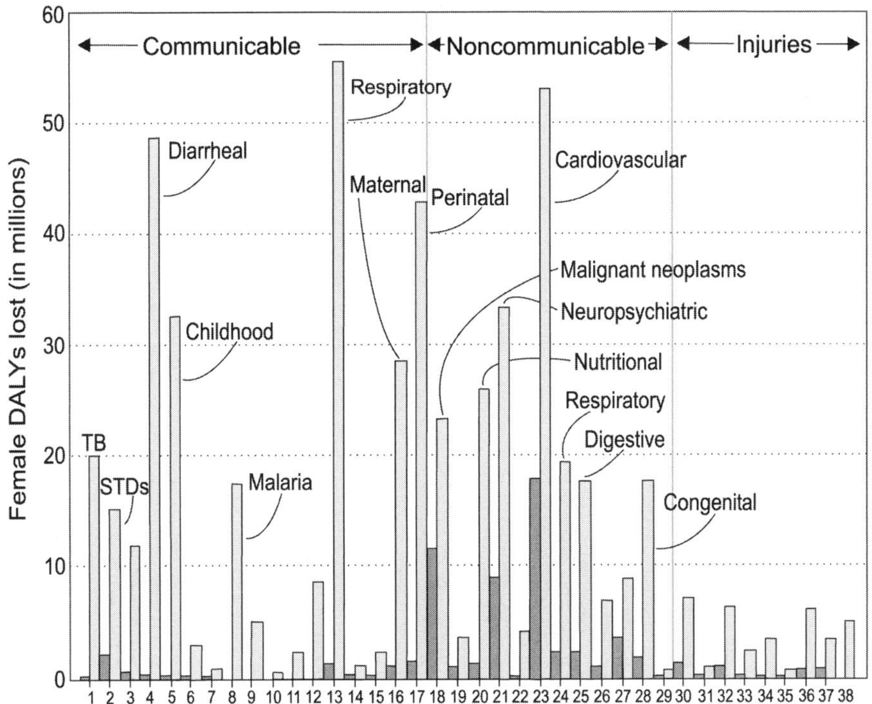

FIGURE 8.3. Total female disease burden (in millions of DALYs). *Source:* Data are from World Bank (1993).

TABLE 8.2. Total Female Disease Burden, 1990 (Millions of DALYs)

No.	Disease type	First and second worlds	Third world	Total	Third world's percentage of DALYs
Communicable, maternal, and perinatal					
1	TB	1.0	198.8	199.8	99.5
2	STDs, excl. HIV	20.5	151.7	172.2	88.1
3	HIV	3.6	119.1	122.7	97.1
4	Diarrheal diseases	2.2	487.2	498.4	99.6
5	Childhood cluster	0.6	327.1	327.7	99.8
6	Meningitis	1.0	30.1	31.1	96.8
7	Hepatitis	0.4	8.4	8.8	95.5
8	Malaria	0.0	175.0	175.0	100.0
9	Tropical cluster	0.0	51.0	51.0	100.0
10	Leprosy	0.0	5.1	5.1	100.0
11	Trachoma	0.0	23.7	23.7	100.0
12	Intestinal helminths	0.0	87.9	87.9	100.0
13	Lower respiratory infections	12.8	558.3	571.1	97.8
14	Upper respiratory infections	3.3	11.1	14.4	77.1
15	Otitis media	2.2	23.1	25.3	91.3
16	Maternal	10.4	286.8	297.2	96.5
17	Perinatal	14.5	430.3	444.8	96.7
Noncommunicable					
18	Malignant neoplasms	115.5	234.7	350.2	67.0
19	Diabetes mellitus	9.5	35.5	45.0	78.9
20	Nutritional and endocrine	13.7	262.1	275.8	95.0
21	Neuropsychiatric	91.3	335.3	426.6	78.6
22	Sense organ	0.9	42.2	43.1	97.9
23	Cardiovascular	180.3	532.9	713.2	74.7
24	Respiratory	22.6	196.3	218.9	89.7
25	Digestive	23.2	177.8	201.0	88.5
26	Genitourinary	10.0	69.5	79.5	87.4
27	Musculoskeletal	35.8	90.2	126.0	71.6
28	Congenital abnormalities	18.6	178.4	197.0	90.6
29	Oral health	1.2	8.5	9.7	87.6
Injuries					
30	Motor vehicle	13.7	72.6	86.3	84.1
31	Poisoning	2.5	11.4	13.9	82.0
32	Falls	10.2	64.4	74.6	86.3
33	Fires	3.1	25.7	28.8	89.2
34	Drowning	1.4	36.7	37.1	96.2
35	Occupational	0.7	7.0	7.7	90.9
36	Self-inflicted	7.4	61.9	69.3	89.9
37	Homicide and violence	7.5	34.0	41.5	81.9
38	War	0.0	49.8	49.8	100.0
	Total	641.6	5,500.6	6,142.2	89.6

Source: Data are from World Bank (1993).

eases by male-oriented physicians; this may lead to a degree of undercounting in the incidence of some diseases in women. Women are also less commonly included in clinical trials. Girls have higher rates of malnutrition (the rate of stunting [low height for age] in girls in India is about five times what it is for boys); moreover, female fetuses are often "selected" for abortion when sonograms inform parents of a fetus's gender. Amatyar Sen has estimated that there are 100 million women missing from the world's population because of social practices relating to abortion and to differential feeding and child care (cited in Holloway, 1994: 80). Girls are subjected in some societies to genital mutilation (infibulation and clitoridectomy or so-called "female circumcision"), sometimes with fatal complications from sepsis and infection. Some two million women in 26 African countries are clitoridectomized or infibulated each year, and the total may reach 114 million women living who have undergone the operation (Holloway, 1994: 83; see also Chapters 2 and 12). "Social customs, health policies and a largely male medical community have tended to treat women as wives and wombs and little else" (Holloway, 1994: 77).

DALYs associated with STDs are noticeably higher in women, largely because of pelvic inflammatory disease and chlamydia disease, to which men are not vulnerable. The next major disease group, one unique to women, is maternal; it includes hemorrhage, sepsis, eclampsia (coma and convulsions during pregnancy), hypertension, obstructed labor, and abortion. Of these, hemorrhage, sepsis, and obstructed labor account for 78% of the DALYs lost. Third world women, because of their work patterns, sustain injuries and exposures to disease that result in maternal and other illnesses. For example, the tumpline used by many Kenyan women to carry heavy loads of wood and water affects the spinal column and pelvic area, leading to complications in childbirth. Cooking in smoke-filled kitchens or sheds contributes to the prevalence of respiratory diseases among women. The DALY values for musculoskeletal diseases (27 in Figure 8.3), which include rheumatoid arthritis and osteoarthritis, are considerably higher for women than for men. However, rates for all categories of injuries are lower among women than among men (see Table 8.3).

The total female and male disease burdens are shown in a second way in Figures 8.4 and 8.5. Whereas the earlier set of figures contrasts the overall disease burden between the first and second worlds and the third world, this set shows the DALYs/1,000 population. It can be said that we all will die of something, and relatively few of us will have "old age" or "worn out" written on our death certificates. Most people die of some disease or other. Thus the dark-shaded bars for the developed world are much taller in Figures 8.4 and 8.5 than in Figures 8.2 and 8.3, and the noncommunicable diseases, especially those whose prevalence increases with age, are featured prominently (for women, cardiovascular diseases [23], malignant neoplasms [18], and neuropsychiatric illnesses [21]; for men, the corresponding numbers in Figure 8.5 are 22, 17, and 20). Lower but significant DALYs/1,000 among women are recorded for respiratory (24), digestive (25), musculoskeletal (27), and congenital (28) diseases, as well as HIV (3) and other STDs (2). For men, many of the same diseases, but with slightly higher rates, are notable: respiratory (23), digestive (24), and congenital (27) diseases. Also important are injuries: motor vehicle (29), self-inflicted (35), and homicide and violence (36). In sum (and by comparison), third world people "escape" the three big killers in the developed world (heart disease, cancer, and neuropsychiatric disorders), but only because so many people die young as a consequence of communicable diseases, complications from malnutrition, and accidents. Since we are making the broadest of comparisons (first/second worlds vs. third world), we miss much variation within each category. For example, many of the differences within

TABLE 8.3. Male and Female Disease Ratios, First/Second Worlds and Third World, Expressed in DALYs/1,000 Population

No. and name	Male first/ second worlds (1 + 2)	Male third world (3)	Ratio: 3/(1 + 2)
Communicable and perinatal			
1 TB	0.74	12.41	16.8
2 STDS	0.05	1.82	33.7
3 HIV	2.47	7.88	3.2
4 Diarrheal	0.42	23.79	57.3
5 Childhood cluster	0.13	16.56	131.0
6 Meningitis	0.25	2.31	9.1
7 Hepatitis	0.11	0.47	4.3
8 Malaria	0.00	8.68	Inf.
9 Tropical cluster	0.00	3.57	Inf.
10 Leprosy	0.00	0.24	Inf.
11 Trachoma	0.00	0.44	Inf.
12 Intestinal helminths	0.00	4.37	Inf.
13 Lower respiratory infections	2.78	26.72	9.6
14 Upper respiratory infections	0.52	0.57	1.1
15 Otitis media	0.42	1.12	2.7
16 Perinatal	3.58	25.34	7.1
Noncommunicable			
17 Malignant neoplasms	26.98	14.03	0.5
18 Diabetes mellitus	1.43	1.28	0.9
19 Nutritional and endocrine	1.77	11.94	6.7
20 Neuropsychiatric	20.48	18.41	0.9
21 Sense organ	0.09	1.84	20.4
22 Cardiovascular	38.05	26.13	0.7
23 Respiratory	6.18	10.34	1.7
24 Digestive	6.84	9.90	1.4
25 Genitourinary	2.49	3.90	1.6
26 Musculoskeletal	3.12	1.95	0.6
27 Congenital abnormalities	3.74	9.08	2.4
28 Oral health	2.26	2.69	1.2
Injuries			
29 Motor vehicle	7.44	9.06	1.2
30 Poisoning	1.57	0.99	0.6
31 Falls	2.46	5.27	2.1
32 Fires	1.05	1.56	1.5
33 Drowning	1.26	3.34	2.6
34 Occupational	0.79	1.06	1.3
35 Self-inflicted	4.75	3.80	0.8
36 Homicide and violence	4.28	5.64	1.3
37 War	0.00	4.41	Inf.
Total	148.51	282.91	1.9

No. and name	Female first/ second worlds (1 + 2)	Female third world (3)	Ratio: 3/(1 + 2)
Communicable, perinatal, and maternal			
1 TB	0.17	9.82	58.0
2 STDS	3.47	7.49	2.2
3 HIV	0.61	5.88	9.6
4 Diarrheal	0.37	24.07	64.6
5 Childhood cluster	0.10	16.16	159.0
6 Meningitis	0.17	1.49	8.8
7 Hepatitis	0.07	0.42	6.1
8 Malaria	0.00	8.65	Inf.
9 Tropical cluster	0.00	2.52	Inf.
10 Leprosy	0.00	0.25	Inf.
11 Trachoma	0.00	1.17	Inf.
12 Intestinal helminths	0.00	4.34	Inf.
13 Lower respiratory infections	2.17	27.58	12.7
14 Upper respiratory infections	0.56	0.55	1.0
15 Otitis media	0.37	1.14	3.1
16 Maternal	1.76	14.17	8.0
17 Perinatal	2.46	21.26	8.7
Noncommunicable			
18 Malignant neoplasms	19.57	11.60	0.6
19 Diabetes mellitus	1.61	1.75	1.1
20 Nutritional and endocrine	2.32	12.95	5.6
21 Neuropsychiatric	15.47	16.57	1.1
22 Sense organ	0.15	2.08	13.7
23 Cardiovascular	30.54	26.33	0.9
24 Respiratory	3.83	9.70	2.5
25 Digestive	3.93	8.78	2.2
26 Genitourinary	1.69	3.43	2.0
27 Musculoskeletal	6.06	4.46	0.7
28 Congenital abnormalities	3.15	8.81	2.8
29 Oral health	0.20	0.42	2.1
Injuries			
30 Motor vehicle	2.32	3.59	1.5
31 Poisoning	0.42	0.56	1.3
32 Falls	1.73	3.18	1.8
33 Fires	0.53	1.27	2.4
34 Drowning	0.24	1.76	7.4
35 Occupational	0.12	0.35	2.9
36 Self-inflicted	1.25	3.06	2.4
37 Homicide and violence	1.27	1.68	1.3
38 War	0.00	2.46	Inf.
Total	108.69	271.75	2.5

Note. Inf., infinity.
Source: Data are from World Bank (1993).

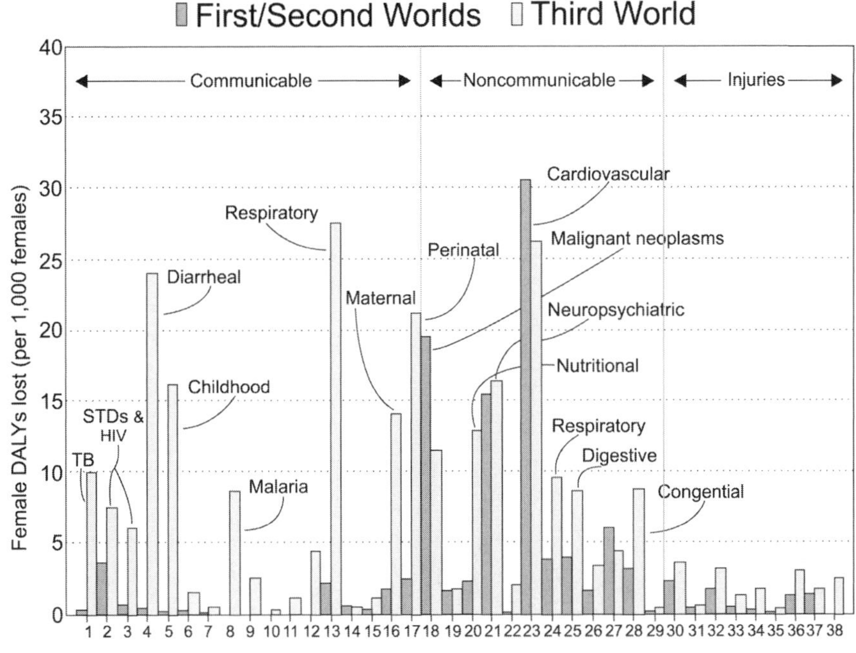

Disease Type and Number

Communicable, Maternal, and Perinatal Diseases
1 TB
2 STDs, excl. HIV
3 HIV
4 Diarrheal cluster
5 Childhood cluster
6 Meningitis
7 Hepatitis
8 Malaria
9 Tropical cluster
10 Leprosy
11 Trachoma
12 Intestinal helminths
13 Lower respiratory infections
14 Upper respiratory infections
15 Otitis media
16 Maternal
17 Perinatal

Noncommunicable Diseases
18 Malignant neoplasms
19 Diabetes mellitus
20 Nutritional and endocrine
21 Neuropsychiatric
22 Sense organ
23 Cardiovascular
24 Respiratory
25 Digestive
26 Genitourinary
27 Musculoskeletal
28 Congenital abnormalities
29 Oral health

Injuries
30 Motor vehicle
31 Poisoning
32 Falls
33 Fire
34 Drowning
35 Occupational
36 Self-inflicted
37 Homicide and violence
38 War

FIGURE 8.4. Female disease burden rates (in DALYs/1,000 females). *Source:* Data are from World Bank (1993).

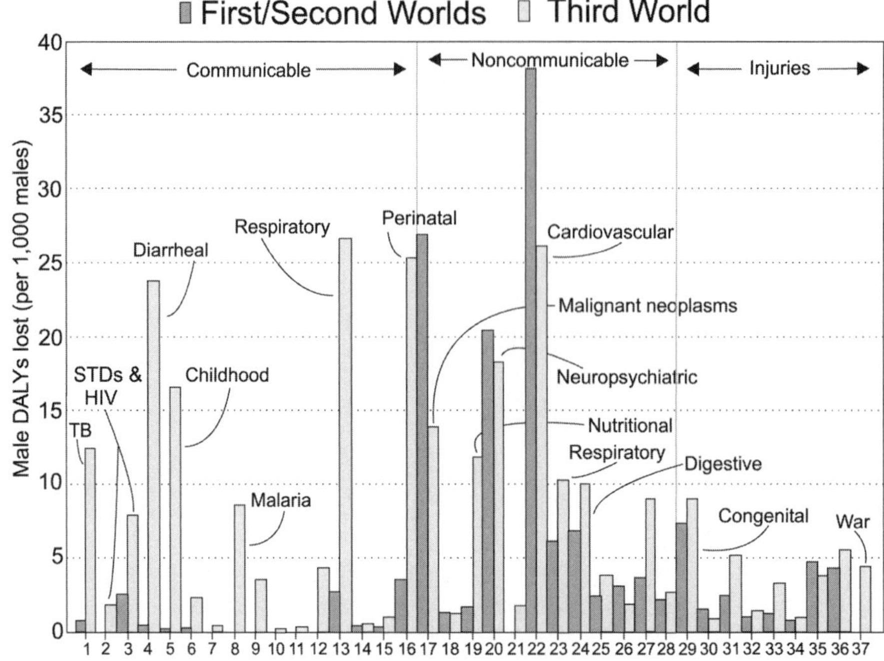

Disease Type and Number

Communicable and Perinatal Diseases
1 TB
2 STDs, excl. HIV
3 HIV
4 Diarrheal diseases
5 Childhood cluster
6 Meningitis
7 Hepatitis
8 Malaria
9 Tropical cluster
10 Leprosy
11 Intestinal helminths
12 Trachoma
13 Lower respiratory infections
14 Upper respiratory infections
15 Otitis media
16 Perinatal

Noncommunicable Diseases
17 Malignant neoplasms
18 Diabetes mellitus
19 Nutritional and endocrine
20 Neuropsychiatric
21 Sense organ
22 Cardiovascular
23 Respiratory
24 Digestive
25 Genitourinary
26 Musculoskeletal
27 Congenital abnormalities
28 Oral health

Injuries
29 Motor vehicle
30 Poisoning
31 Falls
32 Fire
33 Drowning
34 Occupational
35 Self-inflicted
36 Homicide and violence
37 War

FIGURE 8.5. Male disease burden rates (in DALYs/1,000 males). *Source:* Data are from World Bank (1993).

Latin America—both among countries and among sectors of society within countries—are explored in Weil and Scarpaci (1992). In the face of public health crises, such as the 1991 cholera epidemic and the HIV/AIDS pandemic, Latin American countries exhibit different ways of coping.

Certain diseases are many times more common in the third world than in the first and second worlds. Table 8.3 gives the ratios of some diseases. Of course, if a disease occurs in the third world but is absent from the first and second worlds, the ratio is infinite. Infinite ratios among both men and women are recorded for malaria, the tropical disease cluster (trypanosomiasis, schistosomiasis, leishmaniasis, lymphatic filariasis, and onchocerciasis), leprosy, trachoma, intestinal helminths, and war. Some of the most striking ratios among men are found for childhood diseases (5) at 131:1, diarrheal diseases (4) at 57:1, STDs other than HIV (2) at 34:1, and sense organ diseases (especially blindness) (21) at 20:1. Among women, there are striking differences as follows: childhood diseases (5) at 159:1, diarrheal diseases (4) at 65:1, TB (1) at 58:1, sense organ diseases (22) at 14:1, HIV (3) at 10:1; lower respiratory diseases (13) at 13:1, and maternal diseases (16) at 8:1. Any value in Table 8.3 that is less than 1.0 shows a ratio where more people in the developed world per 1,000 suffer death or disability from the disease. The most extreme of these ratios is only 0.52, or 1.92:1, among men; that is, about twice as many men per 1,000 in the first and second worlds as in the third world develop cancer.

Another way to look at the GBD is to study DALYs in relation to expenditures for health care. There is a huge difference in the amounts spent between the first world and the third world, but large expenditure is not synonymous with a low burden of DALYs. Note in Figure 8.6 that China, despite an annual expenditure of only $11 per capita on health services, has a remarkably low health burden as measured by DALYs. The same may be said of the former socialist economies (the second world). Their burden is only marginally greater than that of the established market economies (the first world), which spent an average $1,860 per person in 1990. The region with the greatest per capita burden as measured by DALYs is sub-Saharan Africa, where only $24 was spent per capita for health care. Some of the differences between China and sub-Saharan Africa may lie in their respective sanitation, water supplies, and public health programs, all of which are of higher quality in China. Another factor is that China is largely spared (or has successfully prevented) the diarrheal diseases, malaria, and diseases of the childhood and tropical clusters. Also, it has only half the DALY figure for respiratory infections and one-third the figure for maternal diseases.

Third world countries and first/second world countries share some problems in health care: (1) the misallocation of already scarce resources—for example, spending money for very costly teaching hospitals, but not carrying out highly cost-effective programs, such as immunization for childhood diseases or treating TB; (2) inequity—for example, spending money disproportionately for wealthy urban users, while ignoring rural clinic-level services; and (3) inefficiency—for example, wasting money on brand-name pharmaceuticals when generic drugs do as well. However, the impact of all three of these problems is more dramatic in the third world, where overall expenditures are much lower and where basic nutritional and health needs are unmet (World Bank, 1993: 3–4).

SIGNIFICANT DISEASE GROUPS IN THE THIRD WORLD

Having laid out a general picture of disease patterns, we turn to particular groups of diseases of importance in the third world, most of which have strong environmental components. Our objective is to show that environmental conditions, poverty, diet, settlement patterns, gender roles, and livelihood prac-

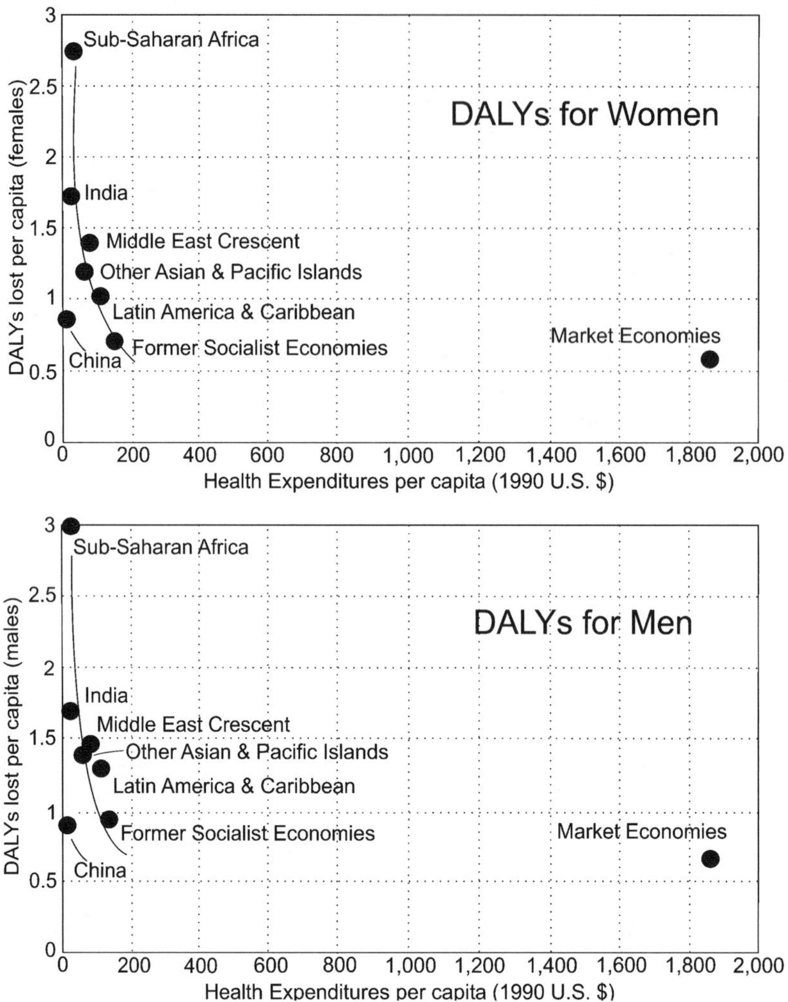

FIGURE 8.6. Health expenditures per capita, and disease burden (in DALYs) per capita, for women and men. *Source:* Data are from World Bank (1993).

tices interact, often leading to conditions that promote the occurrence and spread of disease.

Malnutrition and Diarrheal Diseases

The consequences for health of nutritional diseases in 1990 are displayed in Table 8.4, taken from the World Bank (1993: 76) report. In third world economies, some 14.4 million DALYs were attributed to malnutrition or its indirect effects, or 3.5 DALYs/1,000 population. Malnutrition alone accounted for 18.3 DALYs/1,000 population in India, and the figure for sub-Saharan Africa was 13.8. Not surprisingly, 55% of DALYs attributed to malnutrition occurred among children ages 0–4. Wisner (1989: 155–156) gave estimates of the percentage of children who were malnourished in Africa in 1984. At the low end was Mauritius with about 2%, and at the high end was Burkina Faso with 40%. About 23% of Nigeria's population ages 6–60 months, more than 15 million children, were malnourished.

Diarrhea is not only a serious factor in

several diseases; it also functions as a form of malnutrition. As we have noted above, diarrhea is a major killer of children ages 0–4, particularly because of the effects of dehydration. Diarrhea, which is caused by insanitary conditions in food and water, plays a significant role in malnutrition, because the food ingested is not metabolized by the body, but lost through the bowels. It occurs frequently at the onset of weaning. In addition to its role in disease, diarrhea can be viewed as a form of starvation.

Other sources of malnutrition lie in the extent to which healthful food is available and in the way it is shared in the household. It is common for children to be served last, or just before adult women in the household. The men frequently consume more of the food and get the choice parts (e.g., when meat is eaten). When children go to school, there is less time for roaming in the countryside collecting wild fruits, nuts, seeds, and other bush foods. Furthermore, as women turn more and more to the market for their food, they have less time for foraging for bush foods, and their knowledge (and their children's knowledge) of bush foods and famine foods declines (Tallantire, 1975: 244). When farmers become involved in growing labor-demanding cash crops, such as cotton, tea, or tobacco, they may plant food crops that require less attention. One example is cassava, planted in lieu of small grains such as finger millet, sorghum, or

TABLE 8.4. Direct and Indirect Contributions of Malnutrition to the Global Burden of Disease (GBD), 1990 (in Millions of DALYs, except as Specified)

Types of malnutrition	Sub-Saharan Africa	India	China	Other Asia and PI	Latin Amer. and Cbn.	Middle East cres.	Former soc. econ.	Estab. mkt. econ.	World
Direct effects									
Protein–energy malnutrition	2.2	5.6	1.7	0.9	1.0	1.0	0.2	0.2	12.7
Vitamin A deficiency	2.2	4.1	1.0	2.5	1.4	0.5	0.0	0.0	11.8
Iodine deficiency	1.7	1.4	1.0	1.3	0.5	1.4	0.0	0.0	7.2
Anemia	1.0	4.5	2.7	2.3	1.0	1.5	0.4	0.6	14.0
Total direct	7.0	15.5	6.3	7.0	3.9	4.5	0.6	0.9	45.7
Total DALYs per 1,000 population	13.8	18.3	5.6	10.3	8.9	8.9	1.7	1.1	8.7
Indirect effects (minimum estimate)									
Mortality from other diseases attributed to mild or moderate underweight[a]	23.6	14.9	3.3	8.0	2.4	8.0	0.0	0.0	60.4
Mortality from other diseases attributed to vitamin A deficiency[b]	13.4	14.0	1.0	7.0	1.8	2.0	0.0	0.0	39.1

Note. PI, Pacific islands; Cbn., Caribbean; cres., crescent; soc. econ., socialist economies; mkt. econ., market economies.

Source: World Bank (1993: 76). Copyright 1993 by The International Bank for Reconstruction and Development (IBRD). Reprinted by permission of Oxford University Press.

[a]Based on the GBD attributable to deaths from tuberculosis, measles, pertussis, malaria, and diarrheal and respiratory diseases in children under age 5; in developing countries, 25% of those deaths are attributed to mild or moderate underweight.

[b]Based on estimated deaths attributable to vitamin A deficiency in the age groups 6–11 months and 1–4 years. These account for, respectively, 10% and 30% of all such deaths in high-risk countries and for 3% and 10% of all such deaths in other countries. Thirty lost DALYs are attributed to each child death; losses are redistributed to the regional classification in this report.

bulrush millet. It can be planted and left to grow pretty much by itself, and can be harvested over a long period once the roots have matured. Unfortunately, although cassava is high in carbohydrate value, it is low in protein and many other nutrients, and its successful use in the diet requires that it be supplemented by other foods to ensure a balanced diet. There are many examples from the colonial era of developments that led to an impoverishment of the diet (Porter, 1979: 69–76).

Sharman (1970: 77, citing two 1966 articles by Scrimshaw) summarized the many human costs of malnutrition:

> The cost of malnutrition in less developed areas is exceedingly high; it includes the waste of resources in rearing infants who die before they can become useful citizens and the reduced working capacity of malnourished adults. From a quarter to a third or more of the children die before they reach school age, largely from infections that would not be fatal to a well-nourished child or from clinical malnourishment precipitated by a prior episode of acute infectious disease. . . . Nearly all children among the less privileged populations of underdeveloped countries show retarded growth and development at the time they reach school age; and although they are rarely seriously malnourished during school years, they do not make up for the deficit acquired during preschool years.
>
> Recent evidence suggests that retardation in physical development in infancy is paralleled by impaired mental development that is probably permanent. This means that the future development of a country is compromised by serious malnutrition in young children. Moreover, attempts to provide adequate medical care are complicated and made more costly by both the greater amount and longer duration of illness of both malnourished children and adults.

Respiratory Diseases

Respiratory diseases take many forms and are caused by a large number of bacteria (especially *Streptococcus pneumoniae*), as well as by rhinoviruses, influenza viruses, adenoviruses, and other viral forms (Benenson, 1990: 367 ff.). The most common forms, however, are pneumonia and childhood pneumonia, and they constitute the greatest killers in the third world. The World Bank (1993) estimated that 4,314,000 people died of these and other respiratory infections in 1990. The DALY from respiratory diseases for the developing world was 119 million in 1990, which translates into 28.8 DALYs/1,000 population.

Air pollution in third world cities and homes contributes to respiratory diseases, as does the smoking of tobacco. A major source of insult to lungs is the carbon monoxide issuing from cars and trucks as they inch along in the traffic congestion of third world cities. It hangs like a pall over many third world urban neighborhoods. Smoke from fires and cookstoves in homes is particularly harmful to women and children; it is said that by reducing indoor pollution, the incidence of childhood pneumonias could be cut in half. Crowding is another cause of respiratory illnesses, because airborne droplet transmission is facilitated. Exposure to dust in mines and factories, as well as to the fine dust that accompanies the dry season in many third world areas, is yet another cause of respiratory problems.

Air pollution is much more serious in some places than in others. For example, Mexico City, in its enclosed basin, has serious air pollution levels compared with Dakar, which is swept by oceanic onshore breezes much of the time. Mexico City is attempting to reduce motor vehicle emissions to improve air quality (World Bank, 1993: 97).

Malaria

We have earlier noted the seriousness of malaria, citing the fact that over 68% of the 926,000 deaths caused by malaria in 1990 were among children ages 0–4. The vector is the female anopheline mosquito. In Africa, the *Anopheles gambiae* is the most important vector. It is dominant in the coasts and in low, wet areas; in highlands, the vector is largely absent. There is no practical way of wiping out the vector or environments favorable for it. Mosquitoes breed in stagnant water in ditches, ponds, latrines, depressions, tin cans, and abandoned automobile tires. (The tire, to make a point of interest to the topologist, has a most distressing dimensionality: No matter which way you turn it or leave it lying, it will catch and retain rainwater, providing an ideal breeding environment for mosquitoes.)

Malaria is reported to have almost 100% prevalence in infested areas. Everyone has it, and most who survive develop an immunity to it. Sickle cell disease, a form of anemia, is related to a resistance to malaria and emerged through a selection process. It derives its name from the shape of red blood cells, which, when normal, are round. The condition is prevalent among west Africans and is also found in many African Americans.

There are four types of malaria, some of them quite horrible. Although people develop a tolerance to it, it leaves them in a generally weakened state and makes them less able to work. People periodically get attacks of malaria that will keep them away from work for a few days.

Can malaria be conquered? It is doubtful that the wily mosquito can be eliminated in wet and wet–dry tropical environments, but local supremacy in areas of human settlement can be achieved. Recent success in mosquito control has been achieved by inexpensive means: bed nets soaked in a nontoxic pyrethrum-based solution. Mosquitoes, attracted by the carbon dioxide (CO_2) and body odors of sleeping humans, land on the net and subsequently die. Since they do not survive to breed, the mosquito population is reduced. Another technique tried in Zanzibar and northeastern Tanzania has been to cover stagnant water (in ponds, pools, ditches, and particularly latrines) with inexpensive polystyrene beads, which cover the surface and prevent mosquito larvae from breathing. One test population showed a decline in infection by filariasis, which is also mosquito-borne, from 50% to 3% over a 5-year period (World Bank, 1993: 94).

Recently, clinical trials of a malaria vaccine (developed by Colombian researchers) have been undertaken. It would be good to have a vaccine, because the plasmodium (the malaria parasite) develops resistance to drugs over time. In Thailand, there is now no drug that can be used for malaria protection, since the local mosquitoes have become resistant to all of those available. In 1992, the U.S. Department of State began to require all members of diplomatic and international aid missions to take mefloquine (or sign a waiver relating thereto), after 24 people in the diplomatic mission in Kampala, Uganda, simultaneously contracted malaria, even though they were taking chloroquine. The sustained taking of these antimalarial medicines is probably not desirable, since they can affect eyesight, among other things. For the people of the third world, who cannot fly away to a midlatitude home, long-term solutions raise tricky questions. If people are vaccinated, are they protected for a lifetime? What are the dangers of protecting a large proportion of the population, only later to expose them to a new strain to which they have not developed immunity? These and other considerations must enter into the development of policy on disease eradication and control in the third world.

Acquired Immune Deficiency Syndrome

First, we characterize AIDS and HIV with a quotation:

> AIDS is a severe, life-threatening clinical condition. . . . [It] represents the late clinical stage of infection with the human immunodeficiency virus (HIV), which most often results in progressive damage to the immune and other organ systems, especially the CNS [central nervous system]. . . . The severity of HIV-related illnesses is, in general, directly correlated with the degree of immune system dysfunction. Onset of clinical illness is usually insidious with non-specific symptoms such as lymphadenopathy [swollen lymph nodes],

anorexia, chronic diarrhea, weight loss, fever and fatigue. (Benenson, 1990: 1)

The Global Pattern

In 2004, over 40 million people worldwide were infected with HIV (Table 8.5). Estimates range widely; and cumulatively for the world there is a high estimate of 49.7 million for the number of HIV/AIDS cases and a low estimate of 34.2 million (Joint United Nations Programme on HIV/AIDS [UNAIDS], 2005). Yet there is much uncertainty: In November 2007, the United Nations (Bernard, 2007) reduced its own estimate of the number of HIV-infected individuals from 40 million to 33 million. New cases of HIV in 2003 were estimated at between 4.2 and 6.3 million. Only a small percentage of people in low- and middle-income countries who needed antiretroviral (ARV) medicines were receiving them.

Given the presence in east, south, and southeast Asia of 3.7 billion people (about 57% of the world's total), what happens in controlling (or failing to control) the spread of HIV/AIDS there will determine the world's demographic future. "If prevalence rates in China, Indonesia, and India were to increase to rates now seen in Thailand and Cambodia," the number of people who are HIV/AIDS infected would double (World Bank, 2004b: 1). There are currently estimated to be 1.1 million HIV-infected people in east Asia and the Pacific. The east Asian figure is projected to rise to 11.9 million by 2010. Of the 6.4 million HIV-infected individuals in south and southeast Asia, over 5.1 million live in India. The World Bank lists

> significant structural and socioeconomic factors which put South Asia at risk for a full-blown AIDS epidemic: More than 35 percent of the population lives below the poverty line; Low levels of literacy; Porous borders; Rural to urban and intrastate migration of male populations; Trafficking in women and girls into prostitution; High stigma related to sex and sexuality; Structured commercial sex and casual sex with non-regular partners; Male resistance to condom use; High prevalence of sexually transmitted diseases (STDs); [and] Low status of women, leading to an inability to negotiate safe sex. (World Bank, 2004c: 1–2)

This list of factors is generally applicable in other regions where HIV/AIDS is prevalent, although it should be noted that there are vastly different attitudes, behaviors,

TABLE 8.5. Estimated Number of People with HIV/AIDS, 2003

Region	Estimated number of HIV-infected people
Australia and New Zealand/Oceania	35,000
Caribbean	440,000
East Asia and Pacific[a]	2,300,000
Europe and central Asia	1,400,000
Latin America	2,000,000
Middle East and north Africa	540,000
North America	1,000,000
South and southeast Asia[a]	7,100,000
Sub-Saharan Africa[a]	25,400,000
Western Europe	570,000
Total	41,085,000

Data are from Joint United Nations Programme on HIV/AIDS (UNAIDS, 2005); World Bank (2004a: 1, 2004b: 1).
[a]Different figures from other sources are used in the text.

and practices relating to sex and sexuality in different cultures—stigmatized in some, viewed as natural in others.

In Latin America and the Caribbean, two million people are infected with HIV. Rates vary considerably country by country, and within countries by particular groups at risk—drug users in Argentina and Uruguay; homosexual partners in Peru and Mexico; and heterosexual transmissions in Bahamas, Haiti, and Guyana (Stanecki, 2004: 12). In the Caribbean, HIV infections are highest in Haiti (6.1% among adults) (Stanecki, 2004: A-5). In some places, ARV therapies are having promising results: The HIV/AIDS mortality rate in Barbados fell by 43% after ARV drugs became universally available in January 2002 (World Bank, 2004d: 2), and Brazil has also made great progress in the use of ARV drugs (Stanecki, 2004: 13).

In the Middle East and north Africa, HIV prevalence is still low, which provides a significant opportunity to "stem the tide" of the pandemic (World Bank, 2004e: 1). It has been estimated that 0.3% of the adult population in those areas is HIV-seropositive. In Europe and central Asia, the adult HIV prevalence rate is over 1%, and the AIDS epidemic is growing rapidly: "AIDS claimed an estimated 60,000 lives and some 210,000 people were newly infected" (World Bank, 2004f: 1). The most serious epidemics were in Ukraine and the Russian Federation. Elsewhere, particular groups are at high risk (young people and injecting drug users). Of particular concern is the spread of TB among peoples of the former Soviet Union, because those with weakened immune systems are vulnerable, and TB is latent in many individuals.

With the production of generic versions of ARV drugs, therapies for an individual can cost as little as $150 a year (Over, 2004: 311). This encouraging news must be tempered by the realization that millions of HIV-positive people live on less than $1/day and cannot remotely afford to pay for ARV therapy.

HIV/AIDS in Sub-Saharan Africa

Some years ago, a delightful film fantasy titled *Back to the Future* appeared. A film about sub-Saharan Africa, given the current HIV/AIDS crisis, would have to be titled *Forward to the Past*, and it is no fantasy. The projected future for the people of sub-Saharan Africa is most dire, particularly for those in southern Africa. According to one estimate, about 70% of the world's 40 million HIV-positive people are in sub-Saharan Africa—some 28.5 million (Stanecki, 2004: 11). African women account for 58% of the HIV-positive infections. Seven countries at the southern end of Africa have HIV prevalence rates above 20% among adults ages 15–49: Botswana, Lesotho, Namibia, South Africa, Swaziland, Zambia, and Zimbabwe. The high rates in these nations may be attributable in part to the high level of labor migration to mines, factories, and farms, which separates men from their families (Jayne, Villareal, Pingali, and Hemich, 2004: 5); men often live in crowded dormitories and housing complexes for long periods, with increased possibilities for risky sexual behavior (Campbell, 2004). Botswana had the highest estimated seropositive rate, 38.8% of adults ages 15–49. Lower rates of HIV are found in west Africa. This may be related to the presence of HIV-2 as well as HIV-1; this second type of HIV, discovered in 1986, appears to be less infectious and for a shorter period. The immunodeficiency "seems to develop more slowly and be milder" (Centers for Disease Control and Prevention, 2006). In sub-Saharan Africa, a person who becomes HIV-positive generally dies within 10 years. The ominous prospects for population, economy, and society could return sub-Saharan Africa to conditions akin in some ways to those of the late 19th century (Figures 8.7 and 8.8).

The net effect of AIDS on future population in 37 sub-Saharan countries is to move all but one country (Senegal) out of the 0–10 range in crude death rate (Figure 8.8).

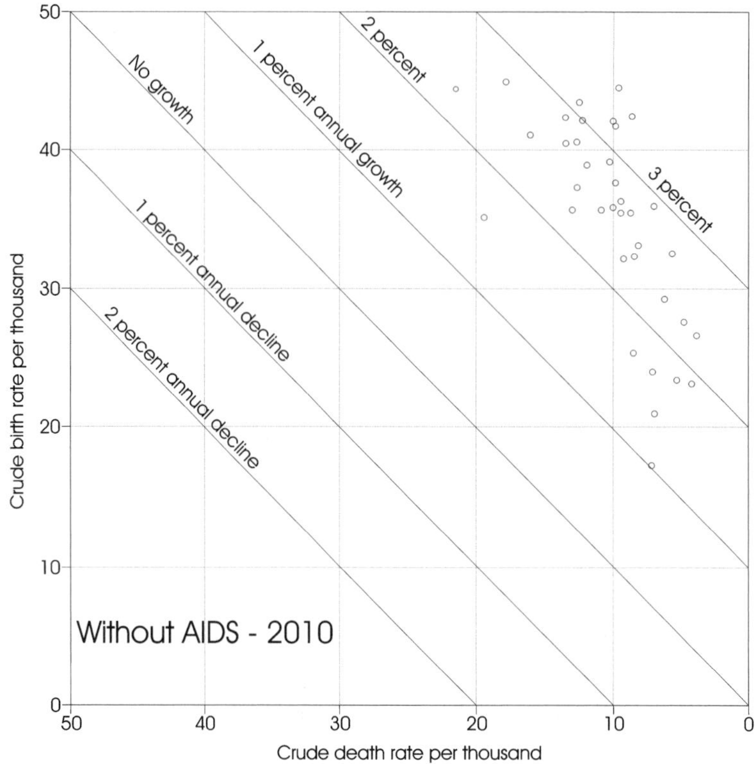

FIGURE 8.7. Sub-Saharan Africa: Projected crude birth rates and crude death rates for 2010 without AIDS. *Source*: Data are from Stanecki (2004: 17)

Another effect is to lower the rate of annual increase by about 1%; most countries would go from a 2–3+% to 1.5–2.5% rate. Several countries would experience actual population declines. These are Mozambique, Swaziland, Lesotho, South Africa, and (most notably) Botswana, where the decline would exceed 2% per year.

As deaths occur within a population, they become reflected in the proportion of people in different age cohorts, as shown in age–sex pyramids. Botswana is an interesting case to consider for two reasons. First, it has experienced impressive economic growth and social betterment in recent decades (Samatar, 1999). Second, it has the world's highest HIV-positive rate. Botswana's future, given the AIDS picture there—and what it might have been, had it avoided the AIDS pandemic—place in bold relief demographic and other outcomes that are likely to occur there, and to a lesser (but still significant) degree in other countries experiencing AIDS. Figure 8.9 illustrates what the population structure of Botswana would probably be in 2020 if it were not afflicted with AIDS, and what it is projected to be, given the AIDS situation there now (du Guerny, 2002). Demographers have never seen population pyramids like this before (Stanecki, 2000). Life expectancy in Botswana in 2010 is projected to be 26.7 years; without AIDS, it would have been about 74.7 years (Stanecki, 2004: 17). Eleven countries in sub-Saharan Africa are projected to have life expectancies of less than 40 years by 2010. These are rates that have not been seen since the end of the 19th century.

When AIDS becomes a serious presence in a population, it sets in train long, interlocking effects in every sector of society. Let us examine them in sequence. The first to be greatly affected are men and women ages 15–39, who are in their most productive years. These are people who have been educated and who form the productive core of a society. They are the parents of children and caregivers to the elderly. With them gone, there are ramifications for the younger cohorts of the population. The death of parents makes orphans of their children. Responsibility for the well-being of children must be shifted laterally to brothers or sisters (or other kin), or cross-generationally to grandparents. Moreover, HIV/AIDS reduces female fertility rates and reduces the numbers of children born. Figure 8.9 shows that approximately 300,000 children ages 0–14, who would have been born were it not for AIDS, are predicted to be absent from the population. The age–sex pattern of those older than 40 becomes a narrow "chimney" rather than a pyramid. Those who have survived to old age may be more likely to contract TB from family members who have contracted it because of AIDS (du Guerny, 2002: 3). Most strikingly, the cohort of men and women between the ages of 30 and 39 has many fewer women than men. In 2000, the age category 35–39 had 90 men for every 100 women. In 2020, the ratio is projected to be 138 men for every 100 women, and the total numbers of both will be greatly reduced. This will have profound implications not only for the availability and quality of labor, but also for the division of labor. In rural areas, there is likely to be a severe shortage in agricultural labor; a decline in food productivity; an increase in food insecurity, with shifts to less valuable and nutritious foods; and out-migration to urban areas. Rural people in urban areas are at

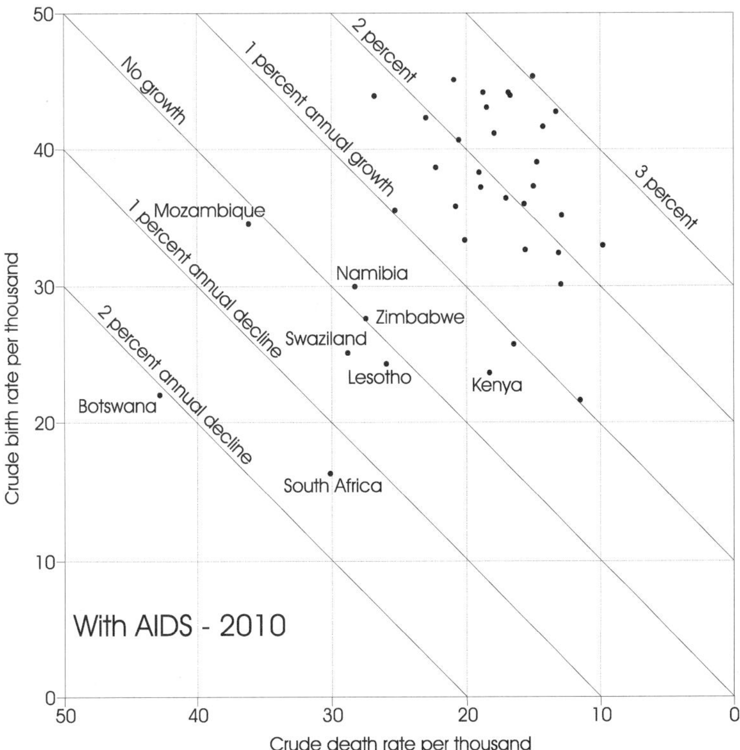

FIGURE 8.8. Sub-Saharan Africa: Projected crude birth rates and crude death rates for 2010 with AIDS. *Source:* Data are from Stanecki (2004: 17)

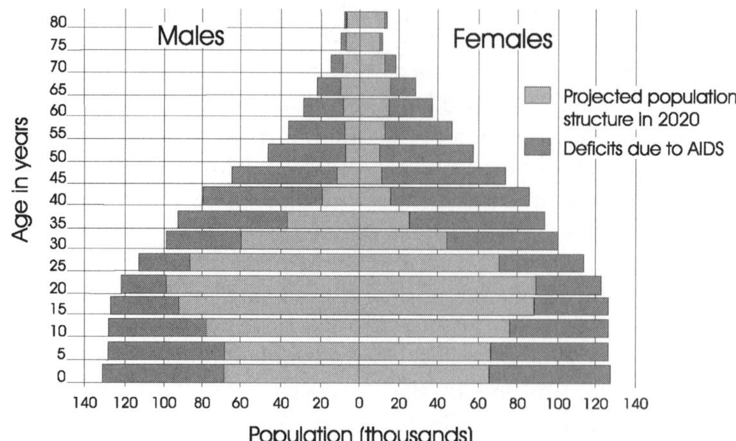

FIGURE 8.9. Projected population structure with and without the AIDS epidemic, Botswana, 2020. *Source*: du Guerny (2002: 8).

much greater risk of becoming infected with HIV. By 2020, it is projected that Botswana will have lost 23.2% of its agricultural labor force (du Guerny, 2002: 4). Women in an AIDS pandemic are particularly vulnerable. Louise Thomas-Mapleh has stated:

> The HIV/AIDS problem is a gender issue because the female gender is generally more vulnerable due to biological, epidemiological and social reasons. Deeply rooted gender imbalances, economic marginalisation, cultural practices such as wife inheritance and the increasing need for alternative sources of survival by women in African expose them to the risk of HIV infection. (Inter Press Service, Women and Law in Southern Africa Research Trust, Southern Africa AIDS Information Dissemination Service [IPS/WLSA/SAfAIDS], 2001: 1)

The labor force is affected by much more than deaths from AIDS. People with HIV/AIDS are in poorer health and can do less work; they need care from others (and such care costs money that is thereby unavailable for other uses); and their deaths can involve those still living in lengthy periods of mourning (Jayne et al., 2004: 4). Another potentially serious loss brought about by AIDS deaths is the transmission of local knowledge and skills from parent to child (Jayne et al., 2004: 4). In particular, women's knowledge of plants for medicinal, famine-preventing, and other purposes can be lost. This may be another instance in which grandparents have to take on a task that parents are not there to do (du Guerny, 2002: 6).

Overall, the HIV/AIDS pandemic is the most serious developmental issue facing the world. All governments and many international organizations (the United Nations, the World Bank, the International Monetary Fund [IMF], the Food and Agriculture Organization [FAO], the United Nations Educational, Scientific, and Cultural Organization [UNESCO], the U.S. Agency for International Development [USAID], etc.) are working to try to limit the effects of the pandemic, reduce infection rates, prevent maternal transmission of HIV during pregnancy, and use ARV therapies to improve health and life expectancies of those living with HIV. With active, committed intervention, much can be done to lessen the effects of HIV/AIDS, as is illustrated by a graph for Botswana (Figure 8.10) (Masha, 2004: 302). Low-Beer (2005: 480) notes that in "successful African responses to AIDS, the universal building blocks of HIV prevention are apparent: primary sexual behavior change, open communications about AIDS and people with AIDS, and community-level structures of support, contact and care." The HIV/AIDS pandemic, this "slow plague" of the 21st century, has many chapters yet to be written (Gould, 1993; Barnett and Blaikie, 1992).

The "Tropical Cluster"

The "tropical cluster" is a term used by the World Bank (1993) in its *Investing in Health* report. All but one of the diseases of the tropical cluster are parasitic diseases, and most are transmitted by a biting insect—a mosquito, tsetse fly, black fly, sandfly, or cone-nosed bug. The exception is schistosomiasis, whose transmission occurs in water when the trematode, in a free-swimming larval form, enters the body through the skin. Most of these diseases have an "alternate host" form, with the reservoirs being animals other than people. These diseases raise specific environmental concerns related to sanitation, garbage disposal, and denying the vectors breeding grounds near homes (Hunter, Rey, Chu, Adekolu-John, and Mott, 1993).

Malaria, which can occur in midlatitude areas, is not included in this group. These diseases are found mainly in the tropics, but they could spread to higher latitudes if there is significant global warming. If a 5°C warming were to occur, it is highly likely that malaria would spread northward into Europe, Russia, northern China, and the United States east of the Rockies (Stone, 1995: 957). The diseases of the tropical cluster (schistosomiasis, filariasis, onchocerciasis, trypanosomiasis, dengue, and yellow fever) would also expand their range.

Trypanosomiasis (and Chagas's Disease)

Trypanosomiasis is called "sleeping sickness" in humans and *nagana* in cattle. It is caused by a single-celled parasite living in the bloodstream and is transmitted by the bite of the tsetse fly (*Glossina*); it is thus an "alternate host" disease. Animals may carry the parasite that affects humans, but the animals themselves are affected by other species that do not harm people. Brush and bush, which provide shade, are necessary for the tsetse fly. It likes to bite people, particularly on the back on the neck. It looks like a deerfly; the wings characteristically fold one on top of the other.

Tsetse flies spread from woodland into savanna in the wet season. The flies must have a blood meal. People are not the favored hosts; animals are. If tsetse flies can be deprived of shade, they die. Temperatures above 40°C (104°F) are fatal to tsetse. Different kinds of *Glossina* have different life habits; some live along streams, others in bush.

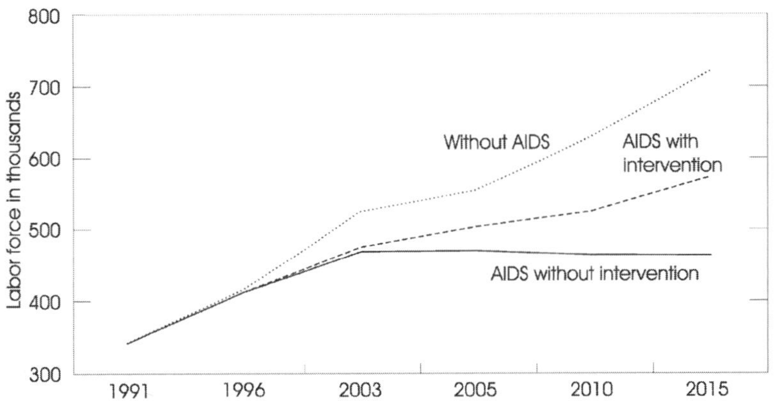

FIGURE 8.10. Botswana's labor force size in thousands. *Source*: Data are from Masha (2004: 302).

There are two types of the disease: *Trypanosoma rhodiense*, which is rapid and fatal, and *Trypanosoma gambiense*, which is milder but eventually terminal. In most of Africa one finds the *T. gambiense* form. The person affected with *T. gambiense* exhibits general lassitude and characteristics resembling *petit mal* epilepsy. Although death is the final result, it can be a long time in coming. A person can live many years, yet not be a productive member of society.

There have been tremendous outbreaks at times. For example, there was an epidemic in 1910 in what is now Rwanda and Burundi, when the area was under German colonial rule. The reports from veterinary departments of that era read like war bulletins, with fronts, salients, attacks, advances, retreats, and strategies for defeating the enemy.

Mixed farming, with crops and livestock, has many advantages for African development. It has dietary advantages, land use advantages (crop production can be concentrated on good land and grazing on marginal land), and advantages relating to the use of stock as draft animals and suppliers of farmyard manure. However, as long as tsetse flies are transmitting *nagana*, it keeps mixed farming from developing well. "The tsetse fly is the real ruler of Africa" is an old saying.

Many attempts at control have been tried. Clearly, these can be successful if the human population density is high enough and the land is under control. Thus vegetation control, or bush clearance, is the most commonly used method. People have also tried game destruction (since game animals are important reservoirs of infection, even though animals tolerate the parasite). They have sprayed with insecticides (dichlorodiphenyltrichloroethane [DDT] and dieldrin) from ground and from the air. They have resorted to dipping and spraying cattle when the cattle are about to be sent through tsetse areas. They have sent cattle into cleared areas to catch the last few flies. Formerly, they used traps, but mainly to count frequencies. Other techniques tried include release of sterile males, use of ethidium bromide, and inoculations, although they have found that resistant strains of tsetse fly soon develop. People have also tried fencing of land (to control movement of animals) and drug therapy. James Newman, who worked among the Sandawe in Tanzania, has described travels in a Land Rover through fly-infested bush when the flies were so thick that they piled up on the hood and windshield as if they were snowdrifts (personal communication, July 1966).

A novel approach to tsetse fly control has been developed in recent years in central and eastern Africa—a tsetse fly trap known as the Challier trap. The tsetse fly is attracted by the breath of cattle (as well as by the movement of cattle), and it homes in on it. The trap is devised to resemble, at least to tsetse flies, a cow (see Plate 8.1). Apparently the colors used and the height at which the "cow's" back is placed were determined by careful experiments. The trap is sewn out of inexpensive cloth in three colors: black, blue, and white. (Since the trap sits unattended out in the bush, the cloth has to be made useless for other purposes, such as clothing for people; thus the cloth is "prepared" by making dozens of small snips all over the cloth.) The blue cloth forms the body, the black forms the forelimbs and chest, and the white suggests the head. When the trap was first developed, the cloth was dipped in cow's urine, but it has been found that the cow's breath can be simulated by using octenol and acetone. The "surrogate" cow is strung up with sticks and sisal twine. Atop the head is a plastic bag. The fly lands and then seeks the light, moving upward. It enters the bag and becomes trapped. In a few days, one cloth cow can clear a highly infested tsetse fly area the size of 1 square kilometer, reducing fly levels by over 95%. This inexpensive way to clear fly-infested woodland, leaving vegetation and wildlife undisturbed, could have major beneficial consequences for African land use and settlement.

PLATE 8.1. A Challier trap, intended to catch tsetse flies in southeastern Rwanda. The tsetse fly is attracted by a cow's breath (as well as its movement). This inexpensive yet effective trap is devised to resemble, at least to tsetse flies, a cow's shape and breath odor (the latter is simulated by using octenol and acetone). The trap is sewn out of inexpensive cloth in three colors: black, blue, and white. The fly lands, seeks the light, moves upward, enters a plastic bag, and becomes trapped.

The number of deaths attributed to trypanosomiasis in 1990 was 55,000; an additional 23,000 were attributed to Chagas's disease, the Latin American form of trypanosomiasis. The DALYs lost among third world peoples because of these two diseases were estimated in 1990 as being 2.4 million for men and 2.1 million for women (World Bank, 1993).

Schistosomiasis

Schistosomiasis (or bilharzia), as noted earlier, is a blood fluke (trematode) infection that enters people when they are standing or swimming in water. The free-swimming larval forms (cercariae) enter the body through soft tissue. There are two main forms: (1) *Schistosoma mansoni* and *S. japoni*, which generally lead to intestinal pain and hepatic (liver) problems; and (2) *Schistosoma haematobium*, which affects the urinary tract. The snail is the intermediate host (Weil and Kvale, 1985: 197). *S. mansoni* is found in Africa, the Arabian peninsula, and portions of Latin America (Suriname, Venezuela, Brazil, and some Caribbean islands). *S. haematobium* also occurs across Africa and includes the Middle East. Other forms are found in peninsular southeast Asia (Laos, Cambodia, and Thailand), as well as Indonesia and the Philippines. The number of deaths caused by schistosomiasis in 1990 was estimated at 38,000. The bulk of the DALYs occur in Africa, predominantly among men, and amount to 6.8/1,000 population.

Since the schistosomiasis cycle involves an intermediate host, there is the possibility of interrupting it, but a lot of things have to fall into place: (1) sanitation that prevents human feces and urine containing the eggs of the parasite from contaminating water; (2) avoidance of exposure to the free-swimming larvae; (3) reduction of the intermediate host population through use of molluscicides; and (4) treatment of infected individuals to prevent them from spreading eggs. A fifth control measure may involve monitoring the in- and out-migration of an area. Other key variables in transmission are the frequency, extent, and duration of exposure to water containing cercariae. In areas where irrigation is important, the residents frequently have very high rates of infection—for example, cotton growers of the Gezira in the Sudan, and irrigation farmers in Mali in the area developed by the Office du Niger. In the Gezira, a huge area irrigated with waters from the Blue Nile, women have brief contact with water when collecting it, "while men and children were more likely to immerse themselves for long periods during activities such as working in the fields or swimming" (Weil and Kvale, 1985: 209).

Leishmaniasis

Leishmaniasis is a skin disease caused by an intracellular protozoan. It is manifested as skin lesions and ulcers, and is transmitted by the bite of female sandflies. The host population includes humans, wild rodents, sloths, marsupials, carnivores (including domestic dogs), and horses (in urban areas). It occurs widely, especially in Pakistan, the Middle East, Afghanistan, the west African savanna states (including Sudan), the Ethiopian highlands, and from east Africa southward to Namibia. It is also found in all of Central America and most of South America. A variant is *kala-azar*, or visceral leishmaniasis, which affects the liver, spleen, and intestines. If untreated, leishmaniasis is fatal. Found essentially in the third world, leishmaniasis constitutes a burden of 1.7 million DALYs, or 0.4 DALYs/1,000 population; the World Bank estimate for deaths from leishmaniasis was 54,000 in 1990 (World Bank, 1993).

Lymphatic Filariasis and Intestinal Worms

The parasite that causes lymphatic filariasis is a long threadlike worm, transmitted via mosquito bites. The reservoir includes humans, cats, and nonhuman primates. The female worms produce microfilariae, which, in one form that is common in Africa, circulate in the peripheral blood at night (10 P.M. to 2 A.M.). Although those affected may experience fever and nocturnal asthma, the most common expression is elephantiasis of the legs below the knees (see Plate 8.2). Chronic effects of the disease are expressed as hydrocele (serum-like fluids in the testes); chyluria; and elephantiasis of the limbs, breasts, and genitalia. Filariasis is endemic across the wet humid tropics, with special variants occurring in Indonesia and the island of Timor. The affliction is more common among men than women. Overall, only 0.2 DALYs/1,000 population were recorded for filariasis in 1990, but for those affected it is a serious affliction.

Although intestinal worm infestations are not part of the tropical cluster as defined by the World Bank (1993), we mention them here along with filariasis because of their widespread occurrence in the third world. Like filarial worms, the intestinal worms or helminths, such as ascaris (roundworm), trichuris (whipworm), and hookworm, can be controlled by improving sanitation, water supplies, and personal hygiene. The third world disease burden from all helminths combined amounts to 4.3 DALYs/1,000 population. Ascaris is particularly severe in southeast Asia and the Pacific islands, China, and Latin America, averaging 3.7 DALYs/1,000 population. The other two types are much less prevalent, except that trichuris causes 3.5 DALYs/1,000 population in southeast Asia and the Pacific islands. It has been estimated that 29,000 people died in 1990 from helminth infestations.

PLATE 8.2. A man with elephantiasis, in Bagamoyo, Tanzania, takes on all comers at the game of *bao*. He supports himself through wagers on the outcome of the game. His left leg is swollen with the disease, and his right leg, having been amputated, is wooden.

Onchocerciasis (River Blindness)

Onchocerciasis is a usually nonfatal disease caused by nematodes; it leads to the buildup of irritating fibrous nodules under the skin, and frequently also to blindness. It is transmitted during the blood meal of a black fly (*Simulium* species [spp.]) and is found all across wet and wet–dry Africa, especially west Africa. It is also found in the western parts of Latin America from southern Mexico (the states of Chiapas and Oaxaca) to Ecuador and western Brazil. The fly lives in aerated running water. Control is achieved by avoiding fly bites and spraying biodegradable insecticides. Aerial spraying has been used to cover breeding areas in west Africa, where a particularly successful control program on the Volta River system has been undertaken. The GBD of onchocerciasis is felt almost entirely in Africa and amounts to 640,000 DALYs, or 1.25 DALYs/1,000 population. Deaths from river blindness in 1990 were estimated to be 30,000.

Other Diseases

Benenson (1990) listed 101 arthropod-borne viruses—that is, viruses spread by mosquitoes, ticks, and sandflies; occasionally by midges or gnats; or as aerosols. The better-known arthropod virus diseases are dengue (or breakbone fever), tick-borne encephalitis, yellow fever, Rift Valley fever, and hemorrhagic fever. There are many other diseases we could have, and perhaps should have, considered more fully—TB (whose occurrence has increased explosively in recent years), meningitis, yaws (tropical syphilis), and the tick-borne diseases that affect livestock (east coast fever, anaplasmosis, piroplasmosis, redwater fever, heartwater fever)—but space does not permit us to do so. There could also have been a long section on chronic alcoholism and its economic and social effects. Alcoholism is a particularly serious problem among men.

DISEASE PREVENTION AND TREATMENT: THIRD WORLD PROBLEMS AND SOLUTIONS

Problems associated with the prevention and treatment of diseases in the third world are huge and sobering. Environmental conditions (heat, shade, dust, stagnant water, and insanitary conditions) play a central role in the origin and control of many diseases, and the resources available in terms of both funding and trained personnel are limited.

The Role of Traditional Health Care Providers

Development aid to Africa for health amounted to $1,251 million in 1990, or $2.45 per person, and this constituted 10.4% of Africa's health expenditures (World Bank, 1993). The figure scales up to $23.55 total per capita expenditures on health. Omitted from the World Bank's calculations, no doubt, are expenditures (both cash and in kind) for health care provided by traditional practitioners (Good, 1987). These health care providers are granted professional recognition in varying degrees, depending on the country. In China, there is a well-established system of "barefoot doctors" and traditional health care providers. Even the training of "western" doctors in China includes a considerable exposure to traditional medicines and treatments. In Tanzania, the government certifies traditional doctors (see sidebar: "Osman Waziri, Traditional Doctor"; another such practitioner from Tanzania is described at greater length below). These practitioners often have an extensive pharmacological knowledge, as well as understanding of human nature. At times when "the doctor is in," one may find long queues lined up along a road or path leading to the doctor's "surgery" (clinic). Such doctors make important contributions to the health of third world peoples.

A continuing problem in research on disease and testing by drug companies in industrialized nations concerns diseases that affect large numbers of people who would not be able to pay for drugs or treatment should they be discovered. Most research and development (R&D) efforts are directed toward diseases of the first world. Pharmaceutical companies are reluctant to spend great sums of money to develop drugs needed in third world settings, since they will probably be unaffordable for those affected by the diseases. Notwithstanding a reluctance to give consideration to the health needs of third world peoples, western drug companies search for new medicines in the floral, fauna, and fungal diversity to be found in the tropics. Third world practitioners of homeopathic medicine, who are otherwise denigrated by western scientists, are useful in helping western medical researchers identify materials with active ingredients that may form the basis for new drugs.

An Example from Tanzania: The Apothecary of Dr. Mtemi

A large sign displayed at the Sunday market in Magoma, northeastern Tanzania, lists diseases and afflictions that can be cured by Dr. Mtemi Alahu Maswumale, a seller of medicines and other services (see Plate 8.3). (Although the photo was taken on February 28, 1993, we use the "ethnographic present tense" in this section to describe Dr. Mtemi and his sign.)

The Market

Magoma market is spread out on both sides of a north–south highway that runs through the Lwengera Valley north from Korogwe.

Osman Waziri, Traditional Doctor

The following is an entry from the journal kept by one of us (PWP) and a family member during fieldwork in Tanzania:

> By 9 A.M. [February 15, 1993] we were interviewing Osman (Athumani) Waziri, 66, who thanked God that he is still here to talk with us. From time to time during the interview he would absent himself to go to his office, a thatch-roofed building next to his house—to bring out a notebook (to check birth dates of his children), a certificate, a sheaf of papers. He had a large family: a second wife (his first wife died), four sons, and eight daughters. Osman liked to keep records, and he had a very neat hand [we saw an example of his handwriting]. We learned during the interview that he is a local *mganga* [doctor]. Indeed, he has a certificate from Muhimbili Hospital [in Dar es Salaam] dated in 1992 certifying him to be a local traditional doctor for the Mgera area. His "surgery" had a table with many bottles on it, and the rafters were festooned with plant materials. Outside the "surgery" were clumps of artemisia and a kind of mint that he used in his medical work. (Porter and Porter, 1993: 71–72)

PLATE 8.3. A large sign displayed at the Sunday market in Magoma, northeastern Tanzania, lists the diseases and afflictions that Dr. Mtemi Alahu Maswumale offers to cure. The medicines are sold in small glass and plastic containers that once contained medicines manufactured by pharmaceutical companies. Further details on the diseases and problems listed on the sign are given in the text.

Users of the market come from nearby sisal estates and from the hills to the east and the west. Because market day is Sunday, the people working on the sisal estates have free time to attend. It is a big, lively, noisy market: People call out their wares, trying to attract customers, and chickens (carried about with legs bound by sisal twine) squawk in alarm while tethered goats bleat apprehensively. There is the smell of fish, sun-baked earth, dust, and rotted fruit and vegetables. Periodically a lorry approaches from the distance, raising a huge cloud of dust and forcing people to scramble to the side of the road to avoid being hit. Buses arrive with new customers.

The market has many products for sale. In addition to medicines, fruit, vegetables, and fish, one finds cooked foods of all sorts, meat, jewelry, cosmetics, kitchenware, underwear, bras, T-shirts, belts, straps, shoes and sandals, knives, Arab caps (*kofia*), and other clothing of all kinds. There are large printed cotton *kitenges* and *khangas*, and vast quantities of secondhand clothing spread out on plastic sheets. The used clothes are jokingly referred to as *kafa Ulaya*—that is, "from a person who died in Europe."

Dr. Mtemi's Stall and Its Contents

Dr. Mtemi's stall is centrally situated along the axis of the market on the eastern edge, with room for people to walk behind and in front of his display. The sign faces the main crowd, and he and his associate sit next to it. He offers medicines for a wide range of illnesses, including some that may originate more in the mind than in the body. We do not know much about the specificity of action. In some cases, the medicines are made from herbs and roots that have very active ingredients; in other cases, there may be no active ingredients. For example, some treatments involve writing a verse from the Qu'ran on a slip of paper and placing it in water. After the ink has dissolved, the patient drinks the water and recites the quotation.

Medicines are administered in various ways. Many are ingested; some are applied topically; still others may be heated in a *chetezo* (clay bowl), vaporized, and inhaled, with the patient bent over the bowl, completely covered with a cloth or blanket. Some medicines are poured into bathwater or worked into incisions, and others (particularly those protecting against hostile threats) may be placed above the entrances to houses, poured out on the earth around a house, or sprinkled "along the way." Much practice has to do with belief, because if everyone around a person believes in the efficacy of amulets, charms, or medicines, that person may also conform.

The medicines are sold in small glass or plastic containers that once contained medicines manufactured by pharmaceutical companies. The spent containers are obtained from hospitals and health clinics. Some people may be reluctant to ask for medicines for problems of a personal nature (impotence, missed menstrual period, etc.), and we do not know how privacy or confidentiality is provided for such people. Some traditional doctors have permanent surgeries, and at markets may have booths or enclosures that provide privacy.

It should be noted that Dr. Mtemi does not advertise medicines specifically for ulcers. This may be because ulcers are not a problem, or it may be because ulcers are diagnosed differently—as gastric pains, in the pit of the stomach (*chembe cha moyo*, in Kiswahili).

As for AIDS, Dr. Mtemi does not claim to have a cure for it, although less scrupulous peddlers of medicines may make such claims. AIDS itself is very difficult to diagnose, since blood tests are not reliable and since the symptoms may be similar to those associated with chronic malaria, anemia, TB, parasitic illnesses, diarrheal disorders, and other diseases. Traditional doctors generally do not claim to cure AIDS, but they have been able, through nutrition and medicines, to prolong patients' lives.

Dr. Mtemi's Sign

Dr. Mtemi's sign (see Plate 8.3 and sidebar: "Dr. Mtemi's Sign") begins with a general invitation, and then lists the problems he cures.

Traditional Medicine in Tanzania

In Tanzania, there is about 1 western-trained doctor for every 20,800 people, whereas there are about 60,000 bona fide, registered traditional doctors in the country (a ratio of 1:463). Certificates are granted to the traditional doctors (*waganga*) by Muhimbili Hospital, Dar es Salaam, after careful evaluation. There is a difference in accessibility to medical services: Western hospitals and clinics may be many miles away and may be costly, whereas local doctors are usually much closer and cheaper. Distrust and rivalry exist between the two sorts of doctors, with western-trained doctors looking down on the traditional doctors and dismissing the medicines and treatments they offer. Actually, a *mganga* is not a witch doctor, but a doctor who (among other things) treats *against* witchcraft, as many of the medicines listed in the sidebar attest. There is a place for Dr. Mtemi and his 60,000 colleagues in providing health services to Tanzania's people.

CONCLUSIONS

In this discussion, we have concentrated our attention on the deaths and disabilities resulting from diseases (and injuries) in the third world, and noted the high proportion of the burden borne by infants and children. It should not be forgotten that many diseases, though not fatal or even disabling, nonetheless have ongoing effects on millions of people. They constitute a persistent drain on energy, capacity to do work, feelings of well-being, and household finances. Although many aspects of development may be argued, including how diseases should be controlled and the ill should be treated, we can agree on the goal of improving health and ensuring that more of those millions of DALYs—the years of healthy life "not lived"—get to be lived, and lived productively. An encouraging development is that the Bill and Melinda Gates Foundation has made a long-term commitment to fund research and delivery programs in efforts to eliminate many third world diseases, some of which have long been neglected by western medical scientists and pharmaceutical companies (Paulson, 2001).

NOTE

1. Two excellent and indispensable works have been used in writing this chapter on disease and health. The first is Abram Benenson's (1990) *Control of Communicable Diseases in Man*. The second is one of the World Bank's annual *World Bank Development Reports* (the 16th such report), which in 1993 was devoted to health and is subtitled *Investing in Health* (World Bank, 1993). Also recommended are Gesler (1991), Good (1987), Learmonth (1988), Meade, Florin, and Gesler (1988), and Wisner (1989). Wisner proposes a strong "basic needs approach," wherein local groups take control of organizations, local political power, and initiative in providing for their own health, food, and other needs.

Dr. Mtemi's Sign

Kiswahili	English
Tangazo	Attention.
Tiba Za Jadi Kutana na Mimi	Authentic/Traditional Cures. Meet with Me
Dk. Mtemi Wengi Wamepona	Dr. Mtemi. Many Have Been Cured.
Wengine Wananafuu	Others Are Getting Better.
Mungu Mkubwa Tetea	God Is Great. Protect
Afya Yako Usikonde Bule	Your Health. Don't Waste Away for Nothing.
1 *Ngili*	Hernia
2 *Kiuno*	Loin
3 *Mshipa*	Swollen scrotum (from filariasis/elephantiasis)*
4 *Kambaku*	Painkiller for aching tooth
5 *Tambazi*	Varicose veins
6 *Dulazi*	Recurring cold, low-grade fever, and fatigue*
7 *Kichwa*	Headache*
8 *Koo*	Throat
9 *Macho*	Eyes
10 *Meno*	Teeth
11 *Wengu*	Spleen
12 *Ini*	Liver
13 *Mgoro*	Rectal hernia*
14 *Kizuka*	Apparition, ghost (nocturnal)
15 *Kichocho*	Bilharzia
16 *Kisonono*	Gonorrhea
17 *Kaswende*	Syphilis
18 *Kiguma*	Stammering, stuttering
19 *Muku*	Burnout or fatigue from overwork*
20 *Kiume*	Impotence (literally, "maleness")
21 *Kiteza*	Goiter
22 *Nkomo moyo*	Heart disease
23 *Masikio*	Earache (may also help deafness)
24 *Figo*	Kidney
25 *Chashi*	?
26 *Mba*	Tinea or candida, fungal infection, yeast infection, or ringworm*
27 *Maleiia*	Malaria
28 *Ndele*	Love potion*
29 *Kusafisha nyota*	Improve (literally, "cleanse") one's luck
30 *Kutoa mkosi*	To expunge a bad omen
31 *Kutumia sana*	To control excessive menstrual flow*
32 *Kichefuchefu*	Nausea
33 *Kifafa*	Fits, convulsions, epilepsy
34 *Mke kukosa hamu ya mume*	Literally, "woman fails the yearnings of a man"
35 *Mume kukosa hamu ya mke*	Literally, "man fails the yearnings of a woman"
36 *Opresheni ya sili*	Confidential operation*
37 *Kuumwa tumbo*	Stomachache
38 *Kukosa choo*	Constipation
39 *Kwikwi kutoshika mimba*	Hiccups, inability to conceive*
40 *Kinga ya mwili*	To protect the body
41 *Kukopea mbegu*	To invigorate semen*
42 *Kinga ya boma*	To protect the homestead
43 *Kukosa siku bila sababu*	Inconsistent menstruation
44 *Upere*	Scabies
45 *Pumu*	Asthma, chest complaint
46 *Tegu kibuga*	Big tapeworm
47 *Miguu kuwanga*	Aching leg (pain within the bone)*
48 *Jinanamizi*	Nightmares
49 *Kigwasho*	Itching or sting (from insects)
50 *Henia kichomi*	Hernia (undescended) with stabbing pain
51 *Wavi na uhanisi mchango*	Impotence, caused by hernia*
52 *Pete ya bahati njema*	Good luck ring
53 *Tiibii changa*	Incipient or "young" TB (may also refer to other chest problems)
54 *Kukosa siku*	Missed menstrual period*
54† *Ndoa yenye matatizo*	Marriage having complications

55 *Moyo kusokota*	Pounding heart, possibly angina*
56 *Kibishi kujikunna*	"Phantom" itches (no visible inflammation)
Jitibu na Dawa za Mtemi	Treat yourself with the medicines of Mtemi
Alahu Maswumale	Alahu Maswumale

†As in the original sign, there are two 54's; see Plate 8.3.

Note on Orthography

Spellings in vernacular language frequently do not agree with those of standard Kiswahili. The L and R sounds get mixed up; thus *Usikonde Bule* should be *Usikonde Bure, Ngili* should be *Ngiri*, and *Opresheni ya sili* should be *Opresheni ya siri.* Other words get misspelled: *Jinanamizi* should be *Jinamizi, Kigwasho* should be *Kiwasho*, and so forth.

*** Notes Giving Added Information and Context**

3 *Mshipa*/swollen scrotum: A degree of respect is accorded to someone who has *mshipa.* The person with *mshipa* is supposed to prepare a bag in which to protect and carry the enlarged scrotum. The term *mwinyi* is associated with *mshipa. Mwinyi* is a term of respect and is linked with power and prestige. One is supposed to do things for such a person. *Mwinyi mkuu* refers to a chief; *mwinyi mwenyekitu* refers to one who has valuable things, such as a man with a large coconut grove or many wives, but it can also refer to one who carries a "thing."

6 *Dulazi*/recurring cold, low-grade fever, and fatigue: If diagnosed in a hospital, *dulazi* may be found to be caused by worms, tuberculosis, clinical malaria, or malnutrition. It is an unidentified ailment.

7 *Kichwa*/headache: There are many kinds of headache, specified by location (forehead, side, etc.).

13 *Mgoro*/rectal hernia: This is associated with constipation; part of the intestine emerges.

19 *Muku*/burnout or fatigue from overwork: Women in particular may experience burnout because they work so hard and have so little to eat.

26 *Mba*/ . . . ringworm: Ringworm is quite common along the coast and is called *shilinge shilinge*, since the worm coils up under the skin and occupies a space about the size of the old shilling coin.

28 *Ndele*/love potion: This can be used by men and women, young or old, but is frequently used by older women to regain or attract affection. The potion may be poured on meat, which is then held in the vagina. Later the meat is cooked with other meat for the man to consume, making him fall in love with the woman.

31 *Kutumia sana*/to control excessive menstrual flow: This item, the inverse of items 43 or 54, is thought to be caused by witchcraft practiced by a jealous co-wife or rival woman—someone who is trying to "hold" another woman's fertility. Care is taken that menstrual blood does not fall into improper hands. Sanitary napkins are washed clean of blood and then buried as a safeguard.

36 *Opresheni ya sili*/confidential operation: One can only speculate on the sort of operation Dr. Mtemi may perform. (He will refer a hernia operation to a hospital.) It may involve incisions with cupping, or possibly penile rectification to prevent excessive penetration during intercourse; otherwise women may refuse a man's advances.

39 *Kwikwi kutoshika mimba*/hiccups, inability to conceive: Our informants believe that this illness refers to hiccups developing in the man during intercourse, leading to coitus interruptus and consequently the couple's inability to conceive. The problem is attributed to someone's wish to harm the couple.

41 *Kukopea mbegu*/to invigorate semen: The medicine is made of high-protein ground seeds, such as pumpkin seeds or peanuts.

47 *Miguu kuwanga*/aching leg (pain within the bone): This problem occurs particularly in women at the time of menopause.

51 *Wavi na uhanisi mchango*/impotence, caused by hernia: *Mchango* means "wormlike or snakelike shape," and refers to the way a hernia feels through the skin.

54 *Kukosa siku*/missed menstrual period: This does not refer to abortion. It is traced, as in item 31, to witchcraft.

55 *Moyo kusokota*/pounding heart, possibly angina: *Kusohota* means "twisted," as in the motions of making a rope.

We wish to thank Theodora Bali, Simeon Mesaki, Kefa Otiso, and Charles Pike, all of the University of Minnesota, and Pitio M. B. Ndyeshumba, Mlingano Agricultural Research Institute, Tanzania, for assistance in translating and interpreting the words on Dr. Mtemi's sign.

9 Uncertain Rains

The Atmospheric Energy Cycle and the Hydrologic Cycle

MEET KITEMU WA NGULI AND HIS FAMILY

Kitemu wa Nguli is a maternal grandparent of Wambua Muathe, whom we have met in Chapter 1. He and his extended family live in Kilungu, not far from Kibwezi, in Ukambani in southeastern Kenya. Culturally, Kitemu is Akamba. He is 77 years old and has two wives, Mbeke and Mbula. Mbeke has three sons and two daughters. One son, named Kioko, lives on Kitemu's farm. Daughters Sukali and Nzilani are married and live elsewhere. Mbula had two sons and two daughters (one of whom died when she was about 1 year old). Both sons, Mutisya and John, are married, and they and their families live with Kitemu. Daughter Katura is married and lives nearby. It is a large family, numbering over 20 people when all are gathered together (some of them are depicted in Plate 9.1). We will look in on Kitemu and his family from time to time in this and later chapters, in order to understand environment and resources from the standpoint of local people.

Consider the following sentence:

> Agriculture began between five and ten thousand years ago when there were approximately five million people in the world. Population doubled eight times, increasing to about 1.6 billion people by the middle of the nineteenth century. (Norgaard, 1994: 40)

All this was accomplished by people interacting with their local environment in adaptive and mostly sustainable ways. The result was a mosaic of thousands of livelihood systems throughout the world. Each tile in the mosaic was managed by people with local knowledge of themselves and their place.

Agriculture is a complex system. Richard Norgaard (1994: 81) has argued that all complex systems emerge through interactions over long periods among many elements. They result from a coevolutionary process between a *social* system and its *environmental* system. Agriculture illustrates humankind's intelligence and ingenuity in matching the management of crops in fields with the nature of the environment being used. We will examine ways in which Kitemu and his family adapt their farming practices to the changing possibilities and challenges presented by nature, noting that such adaptations are also conditioned by the changing economic and social context in which people on the land are embedded.

Farming is central to the livelihoods

PLATE 9.1. Kitemu wa Nguli and part of his family. Kitemu is on the left. Mbeke is seated in the center. John is at extreme right.

of most third world people, although stock keeping, fishing, hunting, forestry, collection of wild products, and various crafts and home manufactures can be important. Historically, and in varying ways today, one's kinship position in these societies shapes one's role in the social division of labor, and thus one's life chances and expectations. Since agriculture is the central and pervasive economic activity, we arbitrarily call this "lineage agriculture," though it should be understood that societies focused purely on fishing or livestock keeping, and even the few hundred thousand people who rely on hunting and gathering, share many of the same characteristics. It could be called "(precolonial) family agriculture," and some would wish us to call it a precapitalist mode of production. We borrow an earlier exposition (Porter, 1979: 31–32):

> First let us characterize lineage agriculture, paying particular attention to the manner in which it is made to be reliable as well as productive. Those who participate are interested primarily in using what they produce rather than in exchanging or selling it to buy things they need. Of course, exchange of surpluses may take place and even be commonplace, but the farm family produces most of what it consumes. Polanyi (1971) called this *use value* rather than *exchange value*. . . . The pre-colonial farm family's enterprise has to be judged in terms of what Chayanov called the labor–consumer balance "between the satisfaction of family needs and the drudgery (or irksomeness) of labor" (Chayanov, 1966: xv). The net product (what remained after the farm had been restored "to the same level of production it possessed at the beginning of the agricultural year, i.e., seed, fodder, repairs, replacement of expired livestock and worn out equipment, etc.") could then be divided between consumption, capital investment to

> raise the farm's potential for production, and savings (Chayanov, 1966: xv).

For Kitemu's family living in the semi-arid part of east Africa, Figure 9.1 shows a set of connections and relationships that were generally operative during the period of colonial occupation, although many elements predate the colonial period. Although Figure 9.1 pertains to a particular place, time, and type of environment (central Kenya, early 1960s, semi-arid), it represents general circumstances found throughout the third world. The first thing to note is that the producer and consumer are one and the same—the family living on the farm. The second thing to note is the diversity of connections. There is much more going on here than cultivation of crops: stock keeping, hunting, fishing, collecting, and many other enterprises that create products useful in the community (crafts and manufactures) and valuable for trade. Most "self-provisioning" societies (the U.S. Agency for International Development's [USAID's] preferred term) engage in some trade, often over long distances. Few societies are totally self-sufficient.

The third thing to notice is the purpose of all these different activities. The idea is to buffer the family against food shortages and other hardships. The strategies for this are many and change over time as the social, economic, and environmental context changes. However, these livelihood strategies may be grouped into three sorts: (1) those that exploit the site, (2) those that exploit the biophysical situation, and (3) those that use the social situation.

Strategies in the first group, those involving exploitation of site, are based on what a group knows about its environment. Those western-trained scientists who have inquired into the matter always find an indigenous understanding of the environment. It is usually practically adequate (i.e., practical and useful), and in many instances it is complex, sophisticated, subtle, and highly effective (Conklin, 1957; Frake, 1962; Richards, 1985; Porter, 2006). It represents an accumulated knowledge based on experience,

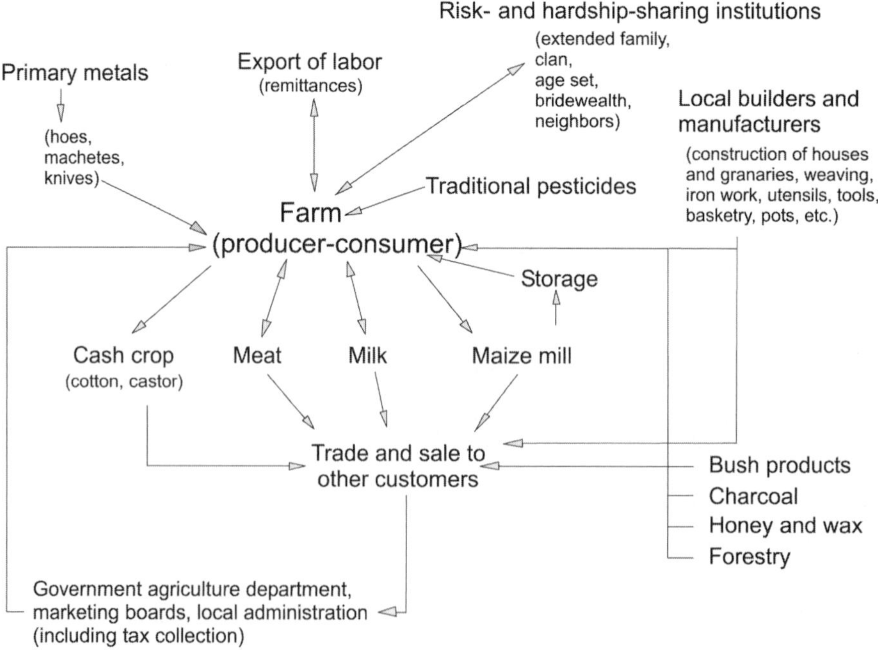

FIGURE 9.1. Kin-based rural economy: An example from a semi-arid part of Kenya.

observation, and trial and error, even though it may not be a result of the experimental design and hypothesis-testing methods of standard western science. A central strategy in self-provisioning societies in east Africa is to plant large enough areas so that even if rains are poor, the resulting low yields will provide at least a minimal subsistence. This means that in most years, farm families will produce somewhat more than their minimal needs. William Allan (1965) termed the result of this practice the "normal surplus" (see Chapter 10 of the present volume).

Farmers exploit their biophysical situation (the second group of strategies) through varied strategies of diversifying their livelihoods, by locally specific combinations of farming practices, hunting, fishing, and/or gathering needs from common lands. In east Africa, for example, farmers commonly place fields far from one another. Rainstorms in large parts of the tropics are commonly small and intense. A good harvest may be ensured by a single good rain (Jackson, 1969). Field dispersal is a form of insurance: If the rains fail in one area, perhaps they will be adequate in another. In areas of great local topographic relief, very different ecological zones may be within walking distance, and people may arrange their residence, land use, and political territory to enable each family to use several differing environments (Porter, 1976a; see Chapter 12). Ways in which people exploit their social situation (the third group of strategies) are considered in Chapter 12, and Chapter 7 has shown some of the ways in which social changes at broader scales, through processes of colonialism, development, and globalization, affect the livelihood possibilities of such people (see also Chapters 13–14).

Figure 9.2 shows rainfall distribution where Kitemu and his family live. The pattern is bimodal; that is, there are two rainy seasons, one peaking in April and the other in November (locally called the "grass rains"). The November rains are heavier. There is great variability in the amount of any given month during the rainy season. For example, in November 1960 the amount was 13 millimeters, whereas November 1962 brought 626 millimeters. The rains of one month don't tell how the rains will be in a subsequent month. Figure 9.3 shows a scatter diagram in which November's rains are used to predict December's rains. The rains of each month can be regarded as statistically independent, since November rains explain only 1% of December's rains. Stated another way, we can assure Kitemu and his family that if November's rain was 160 millimeters, we predict that December's rain will be 140 ± 167 millimeters. In other words, we are 95% confident that precipitation will be at least 0 and less than 307 millimeters! It is to the unknowability and variability of the rainfall that Kitemu's farming must adapt.

In the past year, Kitemu's family had the following crops under cultivation: maize, cowpeas, sorghum, bulrush and another kind of millet, pigeon peas, calabashes, marrow, pawpaw, and tobacco. Table 9.1 lists some 20 crops, 8 of them grains. Growing crops in Kilungu involves many strategies, one of which is to plant many different seeds all together in each field. Crops need to be planted on time, so that the growing season of the crop matches the time when rains are plentiful. One can see that the onset of the November rains is quite abrupt. Why are the rains in Kilungu bimodal? Why are they so variable and unreliable? To answer these questions, we have to go back to basic principles concerning the energy and hydrologic cycles.

A SHIFT IN SCALE

Part of the excitement in studying the biophysical world, including the tropics and subtropics, is that our ability to understand it has progressed from a descriptive, natural history level to a processual, analytical level. The different elements and flows that make up the biosphere can be measured and interlinked. Thus any place in the third world can

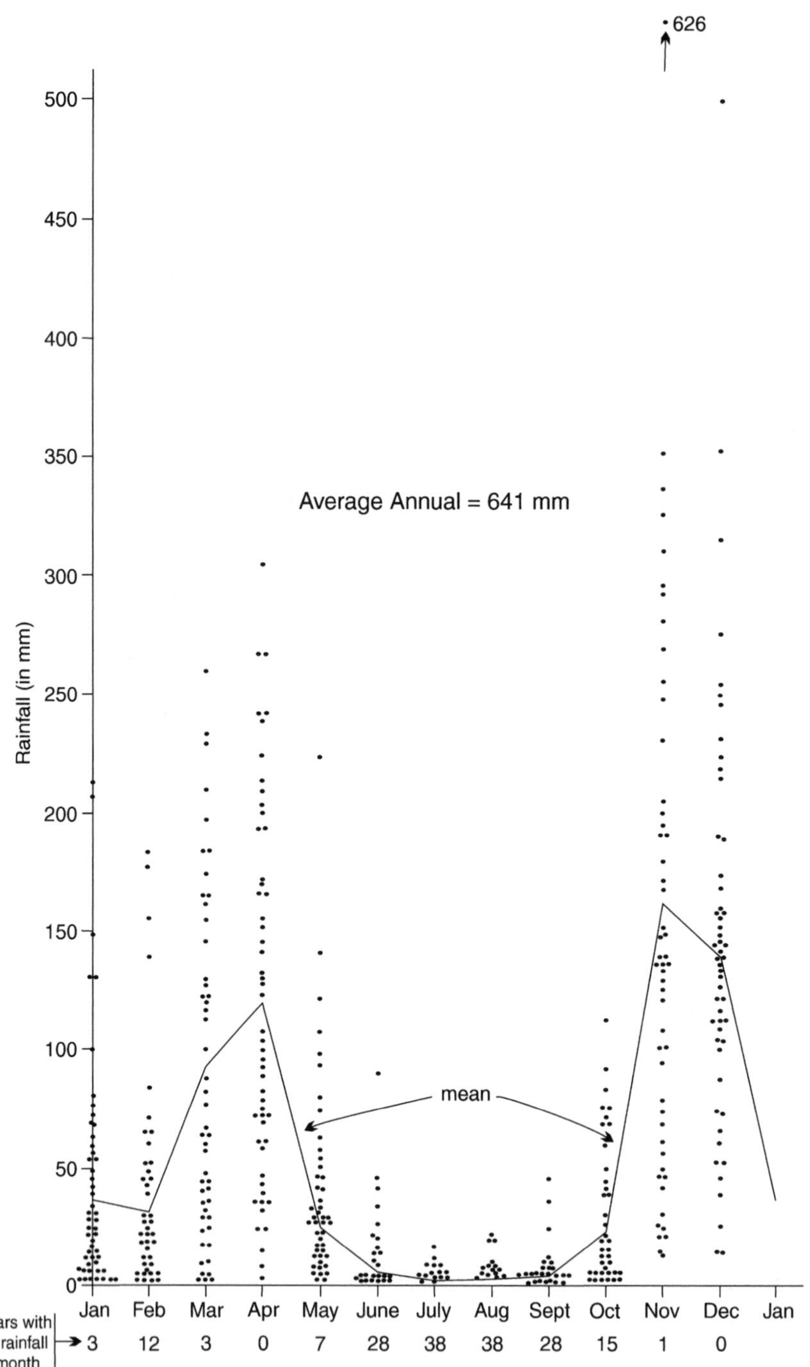

FIGURE 9.2. Rainfall diagram for Kibwezi, Kenya (covering 53 years). *Source*: Adapted from Porter (1979), who used data from the East African Meteorological Department. Copyright 1979 by the Maxwell School of Citizenship and Public Affairs, Syracuse University. Adapted by permission.

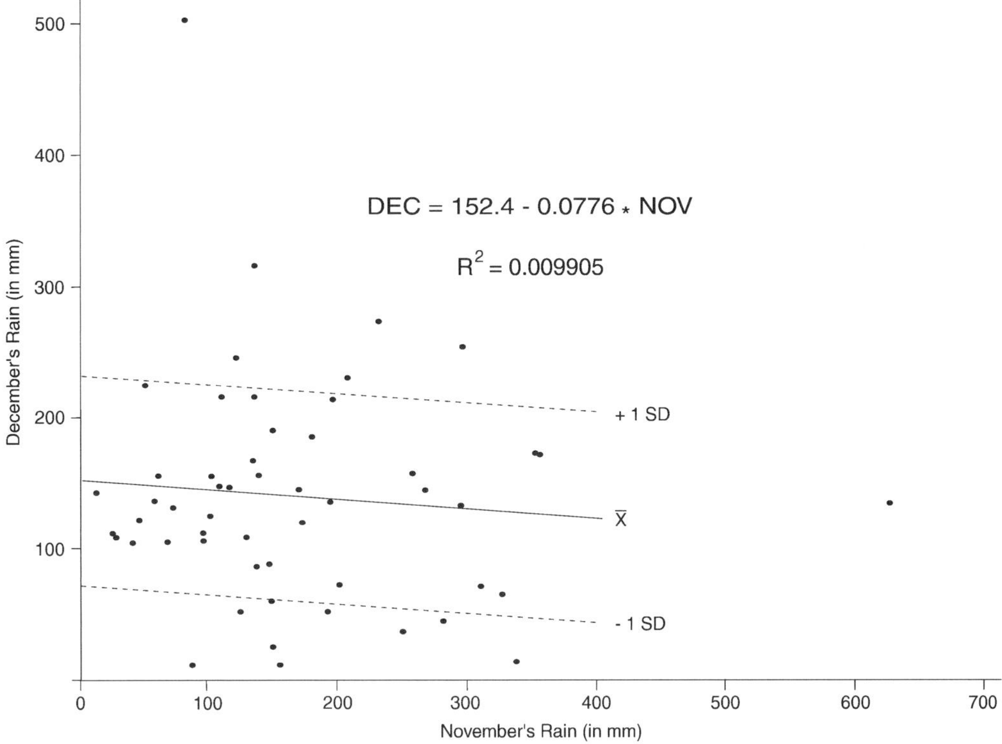

FIGURE 9.3. November as predictor of December's rainfall, Kibwezi, Kenya, 1918–1970. *Source*: Adapted from Porter (1979), who used data from the East African Meteorological Department. Copyright 1979 by the Maxwell School of Citizenship and Public Affairs, Syracuse University. Adapted by permission.

be studied as to its biophysical nature and its potentialities for human use.

It is useful to understand the differences in environmental possibilities set in train, in the first instance by the flow of the sun's energy in the biosphere, and in the second instance by the interaction of energy and moisture at particular places—a concept known as the "energy–water balance" or "energy–water budget." Patterns of energy and moisture provide a fundamental setting within which human activities occur. They affect chemical, physical, and biological reactions in soils and vegetation; they affect hydrology, agriculture, livestock keeping, forestry, transportation, architecture, urban planning, and commodity markets, as well as daily and seasonal rhythms of life. Thus, although some of the material presented in this chapter (and in Chapters 10 and 11) may be unfamiliar and challenging, the reader will, we hope, gain from them a better understanding of the second of the three megastructures of difference around which this book is built (social/cultural difference, environmental/resource difference, and political/economic difference).

The rainfall and sunshine at a place constitute part of that place's resources. Kitemu and his family have to understand it if they are to create a viable livelihood. They may not understand what causes the rain to come when it does, or why it is so variable; nevertheless, they have to cope with the environment they use. The reader of this book does not *need* to understand the causes either, but it is important to know the patterns in resources that result from the

TABLE 9.1. The Agricultural Year at Kilungu, Machakos District, Kenya

Crop	Aug.	Sept.	Oct.	Nov.	Dec.	Jan.	Feb.	Mar.	Apr.	May	June	July	Aug.
Maize			Plant —	weed 1 2				Harvest					
Maize (2nd planting)								Plant — weed - weed	(if the rains are good)		Harvest		
Millet													
muvovi								Plant			Harvest	Birds a problem	
muthio								Plant			Harvest		
mwembe (common)				Plant							Harvest		
muveta				Plant			Harvest		Plant		Harvest		
Sorghum			Plant				Harvest						
Finger millet			Plant							Harvest			
Beans			Plant —	weed 1 2			Harvest						
Cowpeas			Plant —	weed 1 2			Harvest — (of the dry beans) (Start eating them green; others allowed to dry.)						Harvest
Pigeon peas				Plant								Harvest	
Pumpkins				Plant				Start producing		Three main times of harvest 1	2	3	
Calabashes				Plant						1	2	3	
Sweet potatoes				Plant				No proper harvest time, goes on for two years, not stored					
Cassava				Plant						Ready now, but not harvested, can be left in ground 12 months			

N. B. Most of the above crops grow through the entire agricultural year, i.e., through both rains, to maturity. Exceptions are maize, beans, sorghum and three varieties of millet. Other crops grown: tomatoes, groundnuts, *kyondomelo* (a red millet), castor, and bulrush millet.

circulation of the atmosphere and flows in the hydrologic cycle. Probably the best way to know the patterns is to understand how they come into being. A discussion of the earth's energy budget and atmospheric circulation was included in the first edition of this book with that purpose in mind. Since many students felt that this discussion was too technical and far from their interest in development, we have removed it. A reader wishing to understand the causes of climatic patterns is referred to the first edition. Here we concentrate mainly on the resulting patterns, which, as we have noted, constitute a set of resources farmers and herders must take into account as they devise strategies for making a living.

Atmospheric Circulation

Solar radiation strikes the earth and drives a vast engine: the atmosphere. The atmosphere is a thin film of gases (90% of the mass of the troposphere is within 10 kilometers of the earth's surface) held near the earth by gravity. Air density is greatest at ground level and lower aloft. (Recall the standard temperature and pressure assumptions of your high school physics class: 1013.25 millibars, 20°C at mean sea level.) This skin of air is really thin—a vaporous envelope that would not be detectable by your hand if reduced at scale to a 16-inch globe, since its height above sea level (like that of Mount Everest) is less than 0.002% of the radius of the earth, or 0.0003 inches on such a globe.

This shallow layer of atmosphere is in constant, complex motion, largely because radiant energy from the sun heats the air and the underlying surfaces differentially—strongly in the tropics and subtropics, but only seasonally in higher latitudes. The atmosphere (and the ocean beneath it) acts as a sort of machine for redistributing heat, but it is only partly successful. The working of the machine, and sometimes its failure to work perfectly, give the tropics and subtropics their characteristic regimes of rainy and dry seasons; from these, in interaction with bedrock geology, elevation, and life forms, have come tropical and subtropical soils, vegetation, and biota. There is a lot more to global atmospheric circulation than the movement on energy and moisture from one place to another (see sidebar: "Global Warming, Arctic and Elsewhere"). Furthermore, the atmosphere is full of all kinds of stuff that moves about and gets deposited

Global Warming, Arctic and Elsewhere

The Arctic region is showing evidence of global warming in dramatic ways. Glaciers are retreating, ice sheets are thinning, permafrost is thawing, and coastlines are collapsing. The consequences are serious, and are immediate as well as long-term. The result is disruption in the lifeways of the four million people who live in Arctic areas, as well as in those of its wildlife (Myers, Revkin, Romero, and Krauss, 2005). As warming occurs, thousand of ice-covered Arctic lakes, which because of their high albedo normally reflect solar radiation back into outer space, are melting. Open water has a much lower albedo than ice. Furthermore, as the soil thaws, some lakes drain away, leaving a darker land surface that absorbs more energy and warms still further. This endangers plant and animal life, as well as fishing and other human activity (Biever, 2005).

The melting of permafrost removes the very foundations for structures built by people—houses, roads, pipelines, airstrips. As houses sink into the ground, much remedial work has to be done to save them.

Some 14% of the world's surficial carbon is found in Arctic soils (see Chapter 10, Figure 10.2). As Arctic lands thaw, this carbon becomes available for release into the atmosphere through bacterial action, further increasing the rate of global warming (Solcomhouse, 2005: 4). The atmosphere at the start of the industrial revolution contained 280 parts per million (ppm) of carbon dioxide (CO_2), a value it had had for thousands of years. By 2000, the CO_2 level had risen to ~370, and it rises about 1.5 ppm each year (World Climate Report, 2004).

In the event that the polar seas of the Arctic become ice-free throughout the winter, the fabled northwest passage (via Hudson Strait and Beaufort Sea) may become a reality, as well as ocean traffic from Europe to east Asia via the Barents Sea. Work is already in hand for the time when Churchill, Manitoba, on Hudson Bay, will receive tanker traffic coming from northern Siberia. This would quickly become a standard route for oil tankers to take, with attendant risk to the fishing industry as well as wildlife stemming from oil spills. Traffic is also likely to develop from northern Siberia to east Asian destinations (Japan, China, and Korea).

The consequences of global warming are felt not only in the Arctic. Scientists predict increasing frequency of drought for southern Africa, as a result of warming of the Indian Ocean, which lacks the natural variability of the Atlantic and Pacific. At the same time, the Sahelian states, which were wracked with drought and famine in the 1970s (although they may enjoy higher rainfalls overall for the next 50 years), are likely to experience more extremely dry years, with serious effects on their vulnerable populations (Revkin, 2005a: D3). Among the most serious potential consequences of global warming, which scientists are currently studying carefully, are (1) evapotranspiration shifts and their consequences for agriculture; (2) loss of biodiversity; (3) bleaching of the world's coral reefs, with attendant changes in world fisheries; (4) a rise in sea level, which will take 10,000 years to reverse; and (5) a possible shutdown within 200 years of ocean currents that moderate the climate of northern Europe. These are examples of what we have referred to in Chapter 7 as environmental "externalities," or the socialization of the environmental costs of the choices made by particular individuals.

on land and in the ocean (see sidebar: "No Place Is Remote").

Rainfall Distribution

Figures 9.4 and 9.5 are two maps showing our world of difference—average January precipitation and average July precipitation. We suggest that you take a few minutes to study these two maps and notice ways in which they are different. They characterize in a rough way the rainfall situation in the summer of the southern hemisphere (January) and the summer of the northern hemisphere (July). How do these patterns come to be? Can you explain them?

If we could trace the history of each parcel of air in the atmosphere over the 3–4 weeks prior to January (or July), we would be able to see where these air streams were coming from and where they were going, much as we see moving weather patterns shown on our local TV. Although we do not go into the causes of the atmosphere's movement here, we do consider the resulting patterns, using a "genetic" air mass climatology—"genetic" because it results from study of the processes that generate the persistent patterns of air movement in January and July.

January represents the height of summer in southern hemisphere subtropical and midlatitude locations, just as July does for northern hemisphere places (and for most of the readers of this book). Figure 9.4 shows that in January the highest levels of precipitation are centered on areas south of the equator—the Amazon basin, southern Africa, northern Australia, and the island archipelago of southeast Asia. The highest monthly amounts are on the order of 300–400 millimeters (12–16 inches).

Since there is much more land in the northern hemisphere, heating the atmosphere during its summer, the pattern in July (Figure 9.5) shows greater extremes. These are most notable on the Indian subcontinent (where monsoon rains bring monthly amounts exceeding 400 millimeters of precipitation to a large zone stretching from the Gulf of Siam to Delhi), but are also striking in two other southwest monsoon locations: coastal west Africa (Sierra Leone, Liberia, and Côte d'Ivoire) and peninsular Central America (Guatemala, Honduras, and Nicaragua). The best time for farming in the subtropics is the summer period, which brings both warmth and rainfall. Because the cooler temperatures of the "low-sun period" coincide in the subtropics with the low rainfall of those periods, these are not good times for plant growth. As we will see, the areas close to the equator (where winter never comes) commonly have a bimodal distribution of rainfall; depending on the amounts that come, this makes possible continuous cultivation, two crop seasons, or only a single crop season.

AN AIR MASS CLIMATOLOGY OF THE THIRD WORLD

Air close to the earth's surface within the tropics moves from areas of high pressure to areas of low pressure. As an equilibrium-seeking redistribution system, it is clearly imperfect and in a constant state of flux. In studying the trajectories of air streams from highs to lows (taking note of how the streams interact with the oceanic and land surfaces they traverse), we can develop a dynamic and synoptic view of air masses and a rudimentary air mass climatology. By so doing, we create a map of global climates that will help us understand thermal and moisture differences from place to place in the less developed world. This map in turn is useful in understanding the biological, chemical, and physical processes that affect soils and vegetation.

John Borchert (1953) generated a useful genetic classification of the climates of the earth by examining regions having persistent air mass characteristics (areas of gradual climatic gradients—i.e., exhibiting similarity in air pressure, humidity, etc.) and the boundaries between them (zones of rapid

No Place Is Remote

The circulation of the atmosphere involves much more than the redistribution of energy and heat. The "effluents" of human activity also circulate globally, and end up far from their points of origin. They get deposited on land and in oceans, and some of them get taken up through the food chain and concentrate in the fatty tissues and other parts of animals, both terrestrial and marine. Thus animals, including humans, become sinks for all sorts of dangerous, health-threatening substances. The list of such substances is long. In addition to all the "greenhouse" gases—carbon dioxide (CO_2), nitrous oxide (N_2O), and methane (CH_4)—that are responsible for global warming, the list includes polychlorinated biphenyls (PCBs); mercury; dioxins, the best known being 2,3,7,8-tetrachlorobenzo-para-dioxin (TCDD); hydrofluorocarbons (HFCs); chlorofluorocarbons (CFCs); hydrochlorofluorocarbons (HCFCs); and DDT. No wonder we resort to abbreviations. We can add to the list radioactive elements that concentrate in plants and subsequently move into animals and humans when the plants are eaten.

In 1986, the nuclear meltdown at Chernobyl sent vast quantities of radioactive material across the Soviet Union, eastern Europe, and the Scandinavian countries. Large quantities of cesium 137 and strontium 90 were deposited in Sweden and Norway in bands where it happened to rain that day, and were taken up by lichens, a major food for reindeer. The Sami people have historically depended on the reindeer for their subsistence. Reindeer make up an important part of their diet. All at once, the reindeer in parts of Norway were exhibiting high levels of radioactivity (70,000 becquerels/kilogram of body weight or more). The "safe" level for human consumption of reindeer meat was set at 300 becquerels/kilogram in Sweden and 6,000 in Norway (Stevens, 1987: 2). The fallout also contaminated the water, milk, and fish (Strand, Selnaes, Boe, Harbitz, and Andersson-Sorlie, 1992: 385).

The Sami, faced with a serious disruption in their food supply as well as their livelihood, differentiated among the population as to the levels of contamination in meat acceptable for people to consume—either safe, already stored meat or meat with low levels of radioactivity for children and pregnant women, or meat showing higher levels for older people. Contaminated meat was marked with blue, to prevent sale to humans. Some of it was fed to mink and fox in fur-breeding farms, and much was buried in uninhabited areas—"essentially nuclear waste disposal sites" (Stevens, 1987: 4). Without these actions, Sami intake of radiocesium would have been 400–700% higher than it actually was (Strand et al., 1992: 1).

The most profound consequences were psychological. The Sami felt "profound dislocation, a sense that "thing have split part" in the aftermath of Chernobyl." Ivan Toven, a South Sami herder in Norway, expressed his feelings thus:

> One of the worst things is the pretending. We know that the work of our hands just ends in animals being thrown into the ground. But the only ways we know how to handle the deer are the careful ways our fathers taught us and that we hope to teach to our children. So we pretend and we hope. What else can we do? This is the life I know. (Toven, quoted in Stevens, 1987: 4)

This quotation can only suggest the deep trauma the Sami people experienced as their culture and all that gave meaning to their way of life was suddenly destroyed.

Now let's consider *mercury*. Methyl mercury poisoning can have severe consequences and lead to death, as happened in Minimata Bay, Japan, in the 1950s (where fish were contaminated from the discharge of a factory making plastics, drugs, and perfumes). Nearly every system of the body seems to be compromised by mercury—neurological, gastrointestinal, cardiovascular, kidney, and immune. Mercury is emitted into the atmosphere by coal-burning plants for generating electrical power, as well as in many manufacturing processes (remember the Mad Hatter in *Alice in Wonderland*?). Cremation, burning of fossil fuels, and incineration of refuse put 11,500 tons of mercury into the atmosphere each year. Its pathway to humans is as follows: from air into water (and land), where it sinks to the lake or sea floor; bacterial action there turns mercury into methyl mercury, mercury's most deadly form (U.S. Geological Survey, 2000: 2). It then enters and moves up the food chain: phytoplankton → zooplankton → small fish → larger fish → mammals and birds that prey on fish. "Mammals and birds that prey on fish—such as seals, whales, loons, and osprey—also have large amounts of mercury in their tissues" (Gardner, 2005: 3).

The diet of the Inuit people of Alaska and northern Canada consists mostly of fish and seal blubber. "Because of their diet the Inuit people . . . are among the most mercury-exposed people on earth" (Gardner, 2005: 2). But again, as with the Sami people, the Inuit view fishing and seal hunting as central to their way life and their economy. Issuing "fish advisories" suggesting that they change their diet to avoid mercury ignores important cultural and religious features of Inuit livelihood. Governments should solve the problem. It should change the behaviors of mercury producers, not at-risk mercury consumers. If fabric filters were fitted to smokestacks, 99% of mercury emissions from coal-fired generators could be eliminated (Gardner, 2005: 5).

A story similar to that for mercury and the Inuit could be told regarding lead, derived from gasoline additive processes and waste treatment, and cadmium, which is emitted mainly from fossil fuel burning in the United States and industrial processes in Canada. These metals circulate in the atmosphere and food chains in the same way. Lead was found in Inuit communities in the Belcher Islands, in southeast Hudson Bay, at levels far above permissible daily intake levels (Hermanson and Brosowski, 2005: 1308).

Let's also consider dioxins and PCBs. These are persistent organic pollutants that "bioaccumulate" in the food chain. They are found throughout the world, in "air, soil, water, sediment, and food, especially dairy products, meat, fish and shellfish" (World Health Organization [WHO], 1999a: 1). Sources for dioxins are "a wide range of manufacturing processes, including smelting, bleaching of paper pulp and the manufacturing of some herbicides and pesticides" (WHO, 1999a: 1). Health consequences of dioxins in humans are many. They include cancer, effects on reproductive processes, effects on the hormonal system, delay in development of the nervous system, diabetes, liver and heart diseases, skin problems (chloracne), conjunctivitis, and fatigue. Problems associated with PCBs are similar. The Inuit show high levels of dioxins and PCBs in their bodies. PCBs evaporate in the midlatitudes and become condensates in high latitudes.

Well, that's enough. We have shown how actions taken in one part of the world have ramifications for others thousands of miles away, and how when one group of people takes particular actions for their own benefit, they shift environmental and social costs to others in different places (Chapter 7). Suppose, instead of everyone having the implicit right to harm others in pursuit of their own good, everyone had the right not to be harmed by the affects of other peoples' production and consumption. How might societies change production systems and consumption decisions in such a world?

but locationally persistent weather "gradients"). In examining the general circulation of the atmosphere, he found four boundary-generating factors: "1) boundaries between contrasting surfaces [land and sea], 2) steep orographic gradients, 3) boundaries between air streams from unlike source regions, and 4) belts of rapidly increasing divergence of the lower air" (Borchert, 1953: 15).

Before we proceed, it is useful to fix two terms in our minds: "divergence" and "convergence." In a high-pressure cell, air at sea level (commonly overlying an ocean surface) diverges, or moves outward toward areas of lower pressure, rather like a scatter-brained knight on horseback who rides off in all directions. As air moves out of a high-pressure zone, it is replaced from aloft by subsident air. Such areas of subsidence are characterized by clear blue skies, no rain, and air containing very little moisture.

Whether over land or sea, these zones are deserts. Air streams fed by subsidence from aloft stay relatively dry and stable, but if air flows long enough across a surface, it interacts with it. For example, air moving across a warmer ocean will itself become warmer and will increase its moisture content. At some point in the movement of air from high- to low-pressure areas, air streams begin to parallel each other and eventually, as they approach the low-pressure zone, begin to converge. In converging, they "jostle" adjacent streams to occupy the same

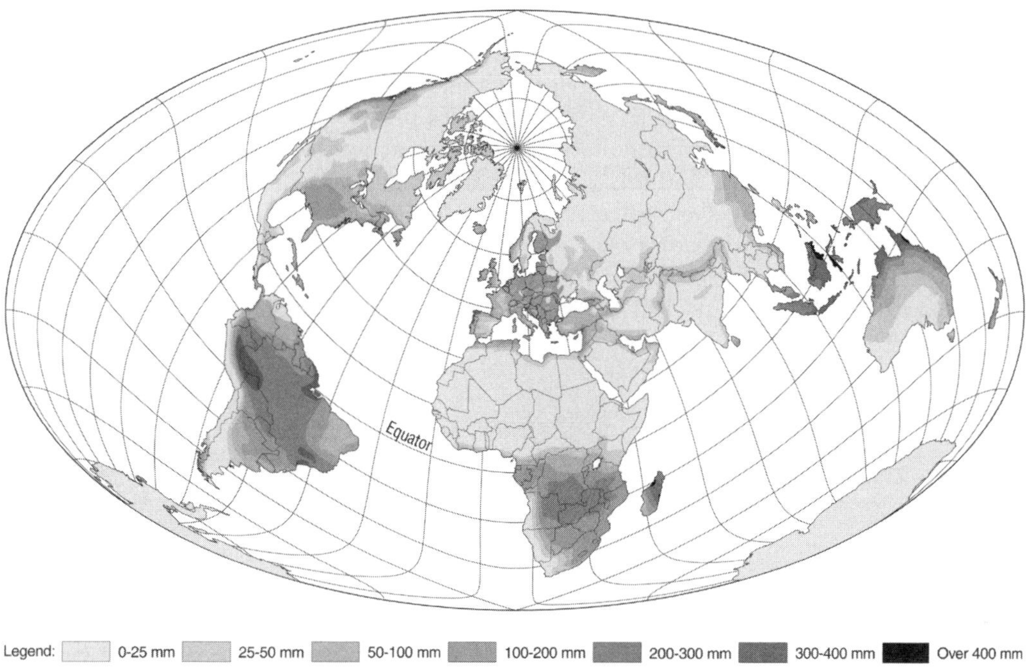

FIGURE 9.4. Average January precipitation. *Source*: Adapted from Bartholomew (1950). Copyright 1950 by John Bartholomew and Son, Ltd.

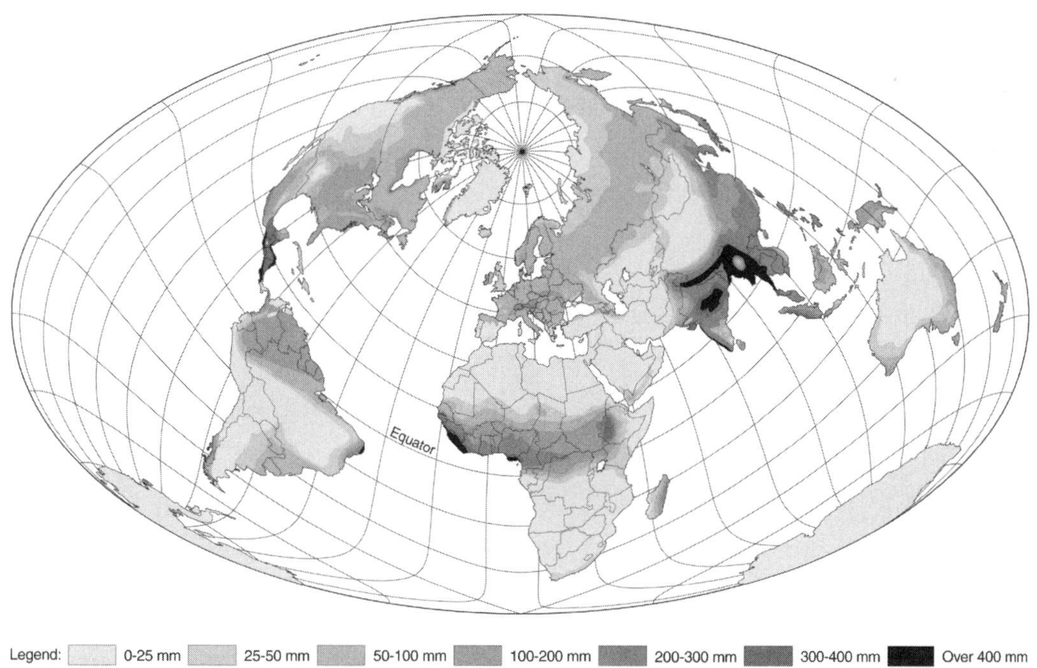

FIGURE 9.5. Average July precipitation. *Source:* Adapted from Bartholomew (1950). Copyright 1950 by John Bartholomew and Son, Ltd.

space, and some air masses are forced aloft or become unstable; this gives rise to large-scale general convectional rains, a feature of the low-latitude, rainy tropics.

Figure 9.6 shows the zonal circulation of the atmosphere in January and July. Polar easterlies lie poleward of the midlatitude westerlies, which in turn border on low-latitude easterlies. The westerlies bring cyclonic winter storms to portions of the third world, to northern hemisphere subtropics in January (the Caribbean, north Africa, central China), and to southern hemisphere subtropics in July (Uruguay and southern Brazil, coastal South Africa, and southern Australia). Figures 9.7 and 9.8 show the regional differences in the prevailing winds for January and July, respectively. The maps use the following conventions as the source regions for air streams: *P*, polar ice cap; *C*, dry conti-

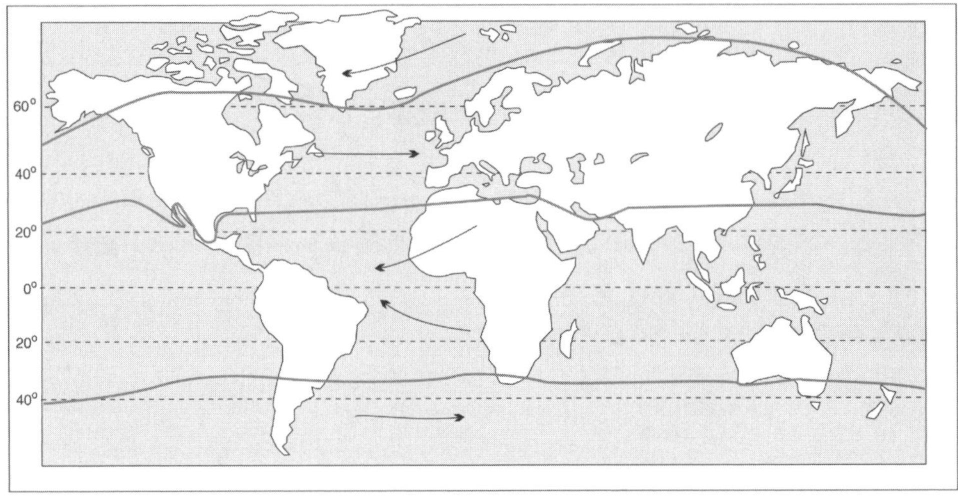

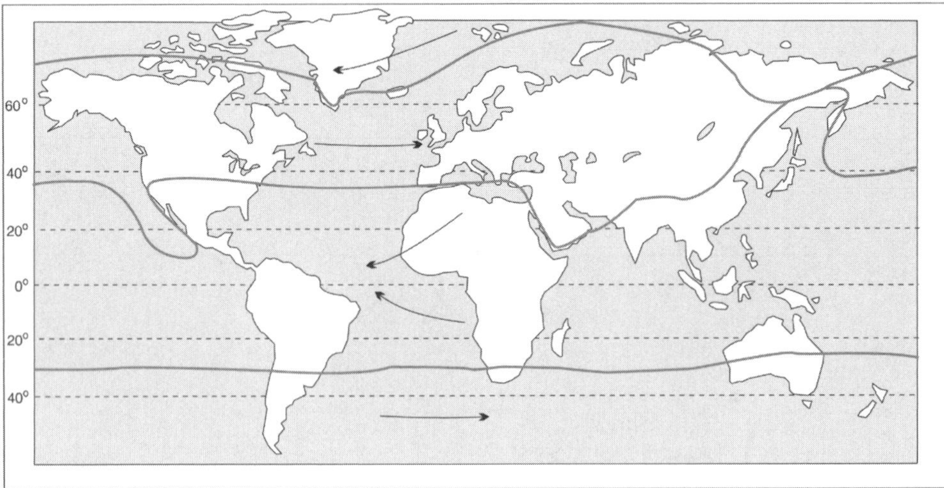

FIGURE 9.6. Zonal boundaries between the high-latitude easterlies, middle-latitude westerlies, and low-latitude easterlies for January (top) and July (bottom). *Source*: Adapted from Borchert (1953). Copyright 1953 by Association of American Geographers. Adapted by permission of Blackwell Publishers, Ltd.

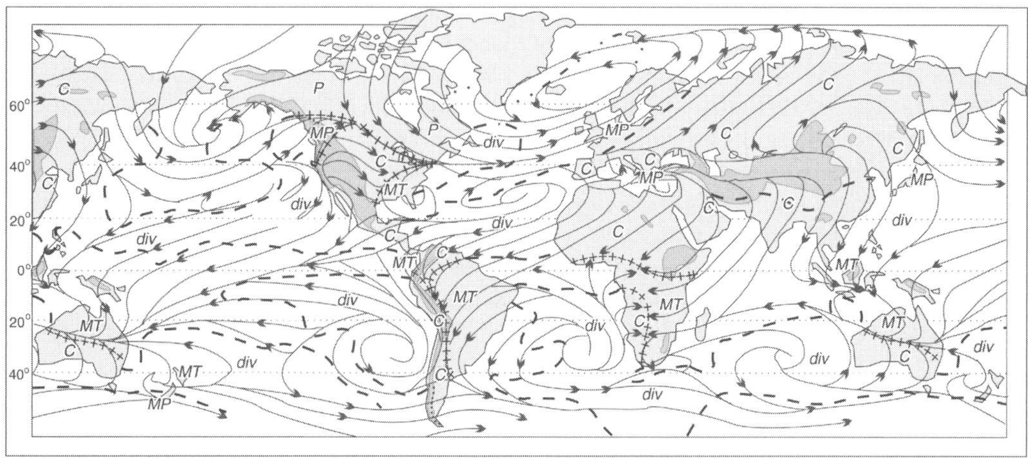

FIGURE 9.7. Major regional differences in the prevailing winds for January. The following symbols are used to designate air streams according to their sources: *P*, polar ice cap; *C*, dry continental; *MP*, relatively warm middle-latitude oceans; and *MT*, tropical oceans. Symbols used to designate regional boundaries according to the way in which they are generated are as follows: crosses, streams from unlike sources; dashed lines, divergence; dotted lines, orographic barriers in a maritime stream; solid lines, coast lines; dotted/dashed lines, ice cap boundaries. Mountain areas and their enclosed plateaus with a general elevation greater than 5,000 feet above sea level are shaded. Areas of mean divergence over the oceans are labeled "*div*." *Source*: Adapted from Borchert (1953). Copyright 1953 by Association of American Geographers. Adapted by permission of Blackwell Publishers, Ltd.

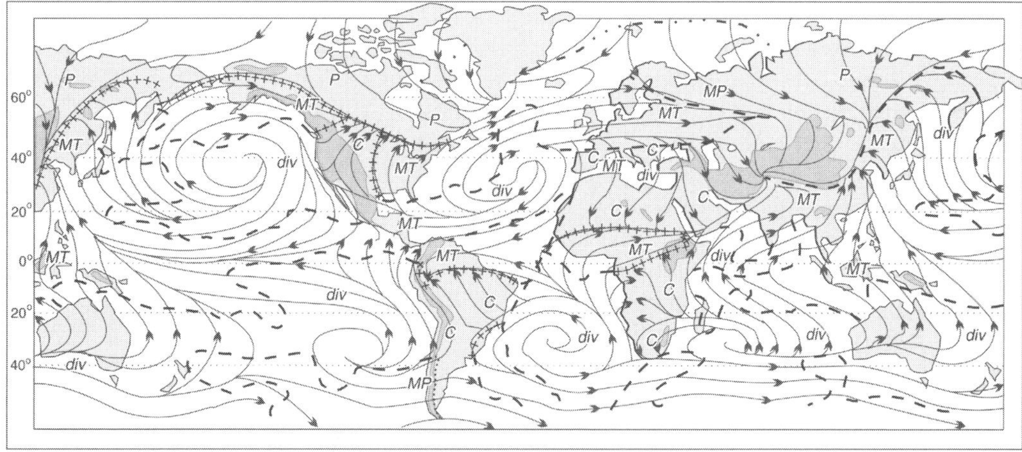

FIGURE 9.8. Major regional differences in the prevailing winds for July. Symbols are the same as for Figure 9.7. *Source*: Adapted from Borchert (1953). Copyright 1953 by Association of American Geographers. Adapted by permission of Blackwell Publishers, Ltd.

nental; *MP*, maritime polar (relatively warm middle-latitude) oceans; and *MT*, maritime tropical oceans. Areas of mean divergence over oceans are marked *div* on the map. Boundaries between regional air masses are marked by different lines according to the boundary-generating cause (the different boundaries are listed in the caption to Figure 9.7). Areas above 1,624 meters (5,000 feet) have a dark shading. A key transitional boundary (shown by a dashed line in Figures 9.7 and 9.8) marks the place where air streams over oceans change from being divergent to being convergent, since this signals a shift in weather possibilities from one in which precipitation is unlikely to occur (unless orographically induced) to one in which large-scale precipitation becomes highly probable.

The January pattern shows that areas receiving rain at that time of year (the southern hemisphere continental land masses) are dominated by maritime air. (The zones can be picked out in Figure 9.7 by finding the symbol *MT* and converging arrows.) Third world nations mainly in the southern hemisphere receive the bulk of their rain during this season, although the western coasts of southern continents, bathed by divergent air streams with trajectories over cool, poleward margins of oceans, get little rainfall and experience frequent temperature inversions (when a layer of warm air overlies a colder layer) and coastal fogs (Chile, Peru, Namibia, Angola).

In the northern hemisphere in January, third world nations are generally overrun by dry continental air. This is their cool, winter dry season. Exceptions are west coast midlatitude areas, such as Morocco, Algeria, and Tunisia, where cyclonic storms at the equatorial margins of the westerlies bring winter precipitation and occasional frosts—the so-called "Mediterranean climates."

In July, the summer of the northern hemisphere, patterns are reversed and indeed heightened because of the development of an intense low-pressure zone over the subcontinent of Asia, with an extension into northern Africa. There is a northward shift in the position of the subtropical high-pressure anticyclones, while in both southern and northern oceans these high-pressure zones shift westward, bringing clear skies and dry conditions to the southern parts of South America and Africa. This time of year brings rain to tropical areas north of the equator (the monsoonal rains of the Indian subcontinent and southeast Asia), while areas lying within zones of the subtropical highs, such as north Africa, remain rainless.

By superimposing the January and July maps of air mass boundary positions (Figure 9.9), we obtain a simple but informative process-related map of world climates. The pattern is process-related because it has been generated by examination of the temporal positions (January and July) of flowing air in the light of surface differences, relief, latitude, and boundary interactions. For the third world, the main "climates" resulting from this superimposition are *MT-MT* (the rainy tropics), *MT-C* and *C-MT* (the wet–dry tropics), and *C-C* (deserts). Areas lying on the margins of these "climates" are transitional types—for example, semi-arid savannas and steppes. Study of the pattern of air mass "climates" with reference to third world state boundaries will reward the reader with a valuable introduction to the geography of the climatically conditioned resource base of the less developed world (compare Figure 9.9 with Figures 9.4 and 9.5). After all, the vast majority of third world people live by some form of agriculture; the amounts of water available for farming, and whether these come seasonally, all the time, or hardly ever, thus have great consequences for people in their efforts to devise successful livelihoods.

It may be useful to sketch the main environmental characteristics associated with the air mass climates we have described (Figure 9.9). We can expect most of the rainy tropics (*MT-MT*) to exhibit leached soils, to support tropical forest (if undisturbed), and to have forms of agriculture based on a lengthy fallow period and usually root crops or irrigated rice as the main staple. In the third

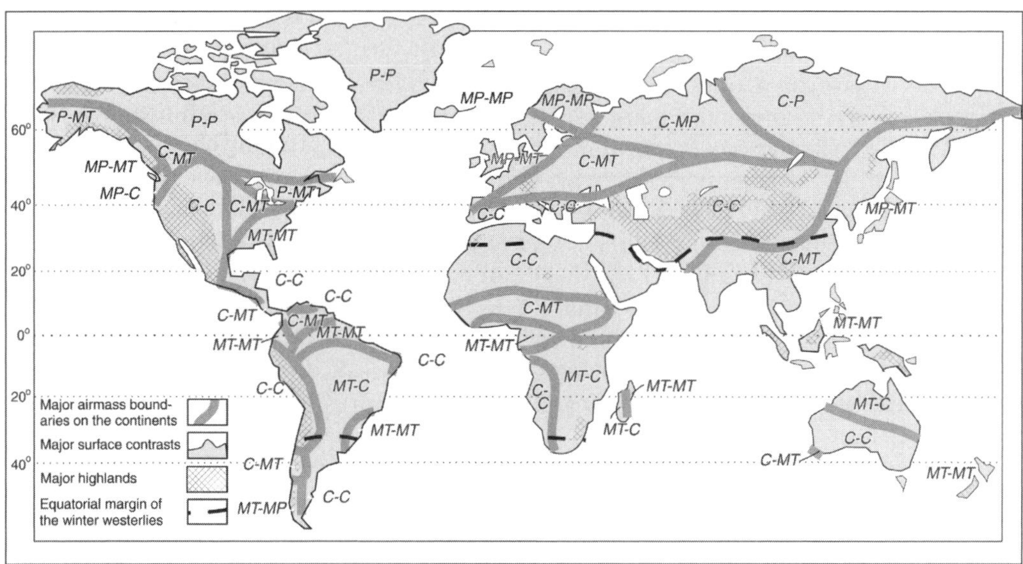

FIGURE 9.9. Major static climatic regions derived from prevailing air mass maps. The first letter symbol in each position describes the prevailing air mass in January; the second, in July. *Source*: Adapted from Borchert (1953). Copyright 1953 by Association of American Geographers. Adapted by permission of Blackwell Publishers, Ltd.

world, there are not many areas of *MT-MT* (portions of Ecuador and Colombia; the Guianas; the northern part of the Amazon basin of Brazil; coastal west Africa; parts of Cameroon, the Central African Republic, Gabon, and the Republic of the Congo; the northern Democratic Republic of Congo [formerly Zaire]; and eastern Madagascar). In Asia, we find *MT-MT* climates over the various island archipelagoes—of Indonesia, the Philippines, and Papua New Guinea.

The wet–dry tropics (*MT-C* or *C-MT*) are many times larger, perhaps by a factor of 10, than the rainy tropics. By definition, they experience one wet season and one dry season; of course, the lengths of both vary greatly from place to place, and from year to year at a given place (discussed more fully below). The wet–dry tropics also feature leached soils, more open forms of woodlands and savannas, and agriculture based on annual crops (particularly cereal grains, such as pearl millet, sorghum, and maize). Livestock keeping also is more important. The seasonal rhythm of agricultural life is adjusted to a single period of sustained labor, during which crops are planted, weeded, and harvested.

The wet–dry tropics are found over much of Brazil, in coastal Colombia and Venezuela, and in parts of Central America. In Africa, this climatic type covers the Sahelian states of west Africa (a band of states from Senegal to Chad); southern Sudan and Ethiopia north of the equator; and, south of the equator, highland Africa from Kenya to South Africa, including highland Angola and Mozambique. On the Indian subcontinent, strongly monsoonal, wet–dry climates are found over much of India, Bangladesh, peninsular southeast Asia, and southern China.

The arid climates (*C-C*) are marked by very marginal cultivation or no cultivation at all, except in specially favored areas with an "exotic" water source (a river such as the Nile, or an underground spring or aquifer). In such places one may find an oasis community. These areas tend to be very hot and dusty. Architecture and clothing may show special adaptations to hot, dry conditions.

Buildings tend to have massive walls, special ventilation chimneys, and inner courtyards filled with orchard trees and gardens. Livestock keeping is often the main livelihood. The C-C climates cover portions of the Caribbean, the northeast coast of Brazil (Fortaleza), and the Peruvian and north Chilean coast. In Africa it covers the vast Sahara, as well as the Namib and Kalahari Deserts in the southwest. In Asia, virtually all of the Middle Eastern states are classified as semi-arid or arid, and these environments extend to Pakistan, northwest India, and central Asia.

The reader should note that air mass boundaries between different climates are transition zones and are not necessarily marked clearly in the landscape, although occasionally vegetative boundaries can be very sharp. The windward and leeward sides of hills are often spectacularly different in vegetative cover.

Much of the interest and excitement in studying livelihood systems in the tropical lands stems from discovering the ingenuity and intelligence that people have shown in adapting to both the regularities and the vagaries of the atmospheric distribution system, which affects so profoundly the spatial and seasonal distribution of moisture and thermal energy.

THE HYDROLOGIC CYCLE

If you try to write a topic sentence conveying the centrality of water in life, you will find that there do not seem to be superlatives powerful enough to convey water's importance. It constitutes 97% of our bodies. Without water to drink, we die in a matter of days. For example, if you found yourself in a desert where maximum daily temperatures reach 120°F (49°C) in the shade, you had 2 quarts of water, and you walked only at night until exhausted, resting thereafter, you would survive for 2 days (*Approach*, 1964: 26).

Water covers 70% of the earth (the salinity of our blood, by the way, closely matches the salinity of the seas). Yet when we partition water into the various domains where it is found, we discover that the water that is so important to us represents just a tiny portion of the total. Table 9.2 gives such a partitioning, listing the total amounts, the depth equivalent if spread over the earth's surface, and the "dwell time" or "residence time"—that is, how long the water stays in a particular domain before moving elsewhere in a closed, balanced system we call the "hydrologic cycle" (see below). The water so important to human life is biological; atmospheric; surficial (freshwater lakes

TABLE 9.2. World Water Balance

Parameter	Volume (km^3)	Equivalent depth[a]	Average residence time
Atmospheric water	13,000	25 mm	8–10 days
Oceans and seas	1,370 × 106	2.5 km	4,000+ years
Freshwater lakes and reservoirs	125,000	250 mm	
River channels	1,700	3 mm	2 weeks
Swamps	3,600	7 mm	On the order of years
Biological water	700	1 mm	1 week
Moisture in soil and the unsaturated zone	65,000	130 mm	2 weeks to 1 year
Groundwater	4 × 106 to 60 × 106	8–20 m	From days to tens of thousands of years
Frozen water	30 × 106	60 m	Tens to thousands of years

Source: Data are from UNESCO (1971: 17).

[a]Computed as though the storage were uniformly distributed over the entire surface of the earth.

and reservoirs, river channels, and in soils and swamps); and, in specialized circumstances and varying degrees, groundwater (tapped by artesian and pump wells). The percentages of the earth's water residing in these domains (leaving aside groundwater) is virtually a trace, in comparison with the amount in the oceans. Even terrestrial ice and groundwater taken together constitute only 7.6% of the earth's water. The easiest way to visualize the relationships is to see water distributed uniformly over the surface of the earth. The resulting depth of atmospheric water (water in clouds and as vapor in the air) is 25 millimeters, an inch high. Biological water (contained in all vegetation, microorganisms, and animals, including humans) stands tall, 1 millimeter high! At the other ends of the scale are melted ice, 60 meters high (197 feet), and the oceans themselves, 2.5 kilometers high (8,200 feet).

The system that moves water from the oceans to the atmosphere (evaporation), then to land and the terrestrial biosphere (precipitation), and finally back to the oceans (runoff and drainage) is known as the "hydrologic cycle." It is only through the workings of the hydrologic cycle that the "trace" of water on which terrestrial life depends is available. In this section we consider the importance of water in the hydrologic cycle in three ways: (1) its geographical distribution, (2) its seasonal distribution and temporal variability, and (3) its relation to the kinds of livelihoods possible in different places. Some of the broad patterns in the distribution of moisture have been established earlier in the discussion of the atmospheric energy cycle. Here we give closer scrutiny to the links among water, plant growth, and livelihood.

Figure 9.10 shows the moisture flows between the main domains in the hydrologic cycle (Postel, Daily, and Ehrlich, 1996). On balance there is a net transfer of 40,000 cubic kilometers of water from ocean to land in the course of a year, through evaporation from the ocean and precipitation onto land, and a corresponding return of 40,000 cubic kilometers to the oceans through runoff and drainage. Among facts not intuitively obvious regarding moisture sources is that the source of 70,000 cubic kilometers (i.e., about 64%) of terrestrial precipitation is moisture that has evaporated from land,

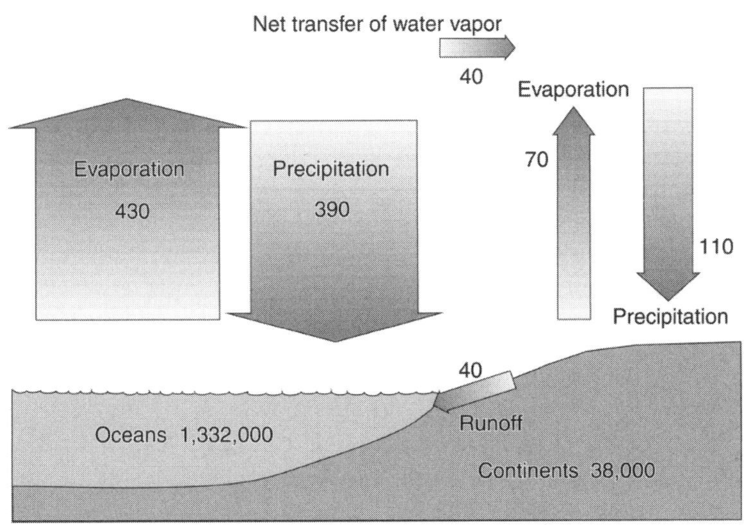

FIGURE 9.10. World water balance: Moisture flows in the hydrologic cycle. *Source*: Data are from Postel et al. (1996).

not the ocean surface. Most of the rain that falls in Uganda and the Lake Victoria basin, for example, consists of water that fell earlier in the dense forests of the former Zaire and was then returned to the atmosphere by transpiration and evaporation. Another surprising fact is that approximately 20% of global runoff is accounted for by the Amazon, whose plume of sweet water penetrates up to 300 kilometers into the Atlantic Ocean (United Nations Educational, Scientific, and Cultural Organization [UNESCO], 1971). Indeed, Vincente Yanez Pinzon, the first European to explore the Amazon shores and delta, was led to suspect the nearby presence of land because the crew observed land vegetation floating in the water and because the water was not salty.

The Energy–Water Balance

It is one thing to get 1,000 millimeters (about 40 inches) of rainfall on average each year at a place, and another thing for that rainfall to be suitable for agriculture. It all depends! It depends on such aspects as when precipitation comes in relation to radiant energy, how much net radiation there is (heating the atmosphere and driving evaporation and plant transpiration), how the rainfall is distributed through the year, and how reliably rainfall comes year by year. In a place where rainfall varies considerably from year to year, farmers may face considerable risk of getting too much or not enough for their crops.

To get some idea of the distribution of these varying characteristics of precipitation (for our purposes, rainfall), we need to understand the energy–water balance, which is an approach to a place's hydrology. It helps greatly to use the energy–water balance as a way of understanding the potentialities of a place. Figure 9.11 shows an energy–water balance diagram based on the data given in Table 9.3; it tracks month-by-month flows of energy and water at Bissau, the main city of Guinea–Bissau and a port on the Atlantic coast of west Africa (see Figure 9.13, below).

Before studying Figures 9.11 and 9.12 in detail, we need to define some terms. The energy–water balance, developed by C. Warren Thornthwaite (1948), consists of studying the interrelations of three curves: (1) actual evapotranspiration (AE), (2) potential evapotranspiration (PE), and (3) precipitation (P). AE refers to the moisture that is actually evaporated or transpired by plants during any particular month, although values of AE are inferred, not measured directly. The moisture making up AE can come from two sources: (1) rain that falls during the month, and (2) moisture drawn from the soil (ST, or storage—a supply already present in the soil at the beginning of the month). Stated another way, $AE = P + \Delta ST$, where ΔST is the change in storage between the previous month and the month in question.

PE is the amount of moisture that can be evaporated or transpired by a vegetated land surface freely and continuously supplied with moisture. If PE exceeds AE during a month, there is a water deficit (WD). AE cannot exceed PE. P is rainfall (and in places this includes ice, sleet, and snow).

The interplay of the three curves (above, coincident with, or below one another) helps define agronomically significant periods and characterize the degree to which water and energy are balanced, in surplus, or in deficit. In dry seasons when $PE > AE$, there is a WD (November through May in Bissau; see Figure 9.11). At the beginnings of drier periods, if sufficient moisture is drawn from moisture stored in the soil (termed "soil moisture use" or SMU), AE may equal PE. AE comes close in November, but it doesn't equal PE (118 vs. 136 millimeters); and during the dry season, the soil, through SMU, contributes 283 millimeters of moisture to AE.

During rainy seasons, P may exceed PE (June through October in Bissau). At such times, the moisture that is not used for PE goes first to recharge the soil. If soils reach a point of moisture content called "field capacity," runoff and drainage (loss of water through subsoil) occur. The first of these two phases is called soil moisture recharge

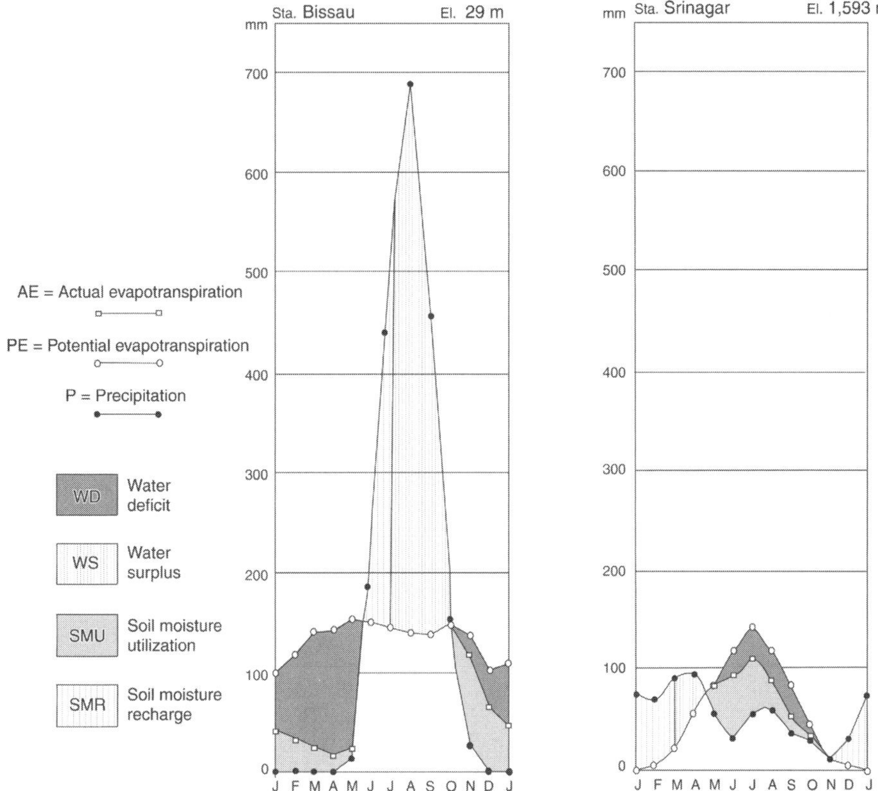

FIGURE 9.11. Energy–water balance diagrams—Bissau and Srinagar. *Source*: Data are taken from Table 9.3.

(SMR) (June and part of July in Bissau), and the second is called water surplus (WS), or runoff (July through October in Bissau).

For global comparisons, Thornthwaite (1948) adopted a convention of assuming an average soil with a storage capacity of 300 millimeters. Note that in Bissau (Table 9.3 and Figure 9.11), ST shows a figure of 300 in July. During July SMR reaches 300 millimeters, and a WS of 52 occurs (WS = P – PE – ΔST, or 52 = 444 – 145 – [300 – 53]). A WS continues for several more months. The balance between PE and P is characterized in a measure called the moisture index (I_m), which varies from perhumid to arid (Table 9.4; the formula for calculating I_m is provided in a footnote to the table). If on an annual basis at a place, P and PE are exactly equal (say, both are 932 millimeters), then I_m = 0 and the place is said to be on the zero water balance line (neither humid nor arid). If we calculate I_m for Bissau, we get a value of 23, which means that the place is on the humid side of the water balance line. Figure 9.13 shows the average zero water balance line for the land areas of the earth. Darker-shaded areas on the map receive on average more P than PE on an annual basis, and lighter-shaded areas receive less.

Bissau (Figure 9.11) lies about 140 kilometers south of that line in west Africa. Farmers live in the real world, not an abstract world of annual averages. What does the statement "I_m = 23" mean to a farmer? Farmers in the humid zone of west Africa grow crops such as rice, maize, and groundnuts during their high sun period (roughly April–September). Farther north,

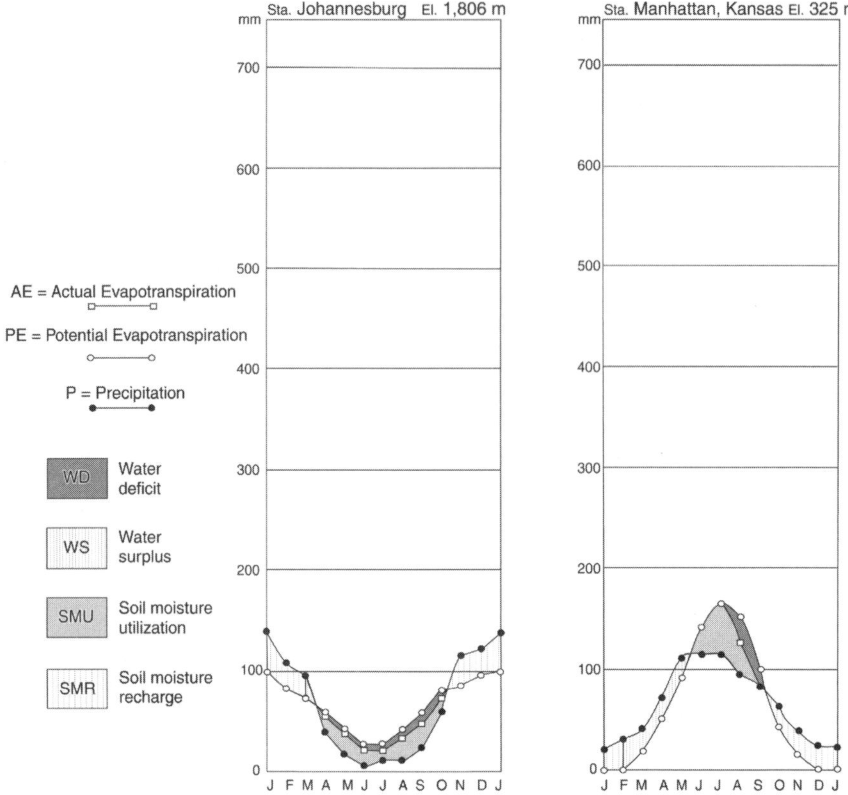

FIGURE 9.12. Energy–water balance diagrams—Johannesburg and Manhattan, Kansas. *Source*: Data are taken from Table 9.3.

in semi-arid areas where rain is concentrated in a 3- or 4-month period, crops such as pearl millet and sorghum are chosen to fit that "window of opportunity," the shorter agricultural season. It is clear from the diagram of Bissau (Figure 9.11) that there is one rainy season (June–October) and a dry season (November–May). If we calculate I_m for these two contrasting seasons, we get a striking result: From June through October, Bissau is a hot, wet, "perhumid" area (I_m = 177); from November through May, Bissau is a dry, dusty desert, an "arid" area, I_m = –96). Thus we need to look "behind" annual averages (such as the annual I_m figure) to understand what really goes on at a place.

Contrast Bissau with Manhattan, Kansas (Figures 9.11 and 9.12). Manhattan has an I_m value of 2, which places it in the moist subhumid class, almost atop the zero water balance line. Month by month, on average, there is an almost perfect match between PE and AE. In other words, whatever the energy demand for moisture, it is nearly always supplied in full either by P or by a combination of P and SMU. The implication for farmers is that reliable rainfed agriculture may be possible, since there is generally a good match between water need (as expressed by PE) and water supply (as expressed by AE). Of course, the diagram shows average conditions, and year-to-year variations need to be taken into account. Some of the most dramatic images of drought come from photographs taken in Kansas during the "dust bowl" period of the 1930s. Consider now Johannesburg, South Africa, with an I_m value of –2; this classifies it as dry subhumid, again almost atop

TABLE 9.3. Water Balance Data (in Millimeters) for Four Cities

	J	F	M	A	M	J	J	A	S	O	N	D	Year
Bissau, Guinea–Bissau, el. 29 meters, I_m = 23, humid													
PE	102	117	141	143	152	149	145	138	135	145	136	101	1,604
P	0	1	0	0	13	185	444	682	462	157	22	1	1,967
ST	102	69	43	26	17	53	300	300	300	300	204	143	—
AE	41	34	26	17	22	149	145	138	135	145	118	62	1,032
WD	61	83	115	126	130	0	0	0	0	0	18	45	578
WS	0	0	0	0	0	0	52	544	327	12	0	0	935
Srinagar, India, el. 1,593 meters, I_m = –7, dry subhumid													
PE	0	3	21	50	89	118	142	131	87	45	17	4	707
P	74	71	91	94	61	36	58	61	38	30	10	33	657
ST	200	268	300	300	273	214	156	123	104	99	97	126	—
AE	0	3	21	50	88	95	116	94	57	35	12	4	575
WD	0	0	0	0	1	23	26	37	3	10	5	0	132
WS	0	0	38	44	0	0	0	0	0	0	0	0	82
Johannesburg, South Africa, el. 1,806 meters, I_m = –2, dry subhumid													
PE	99	82	76	58	40	27	27	40	58	80	83	96	766
P	139	108	97	38	18	5	11	11	22	61	119	120	749
ST	271	297	300	280	260	241	228	207	183	171	207	231	—
AE	99	82	76	58	38	24	24	32	46	73	83	96	731
WD	0	0	0	0	2	3	3	8	12	7	0	0	35
WS	0	0	18	0	0	0	0	0	0	0	0	0	18
Manhattan, Kansas, el. 325 meters, I_m = 2, moist subhumid													
PE	0	0	19	51	93	139	164	150	101	52	14	0	783
P	20	30	38	71	111	117	115	95	86	58	38	22	801
ST[a]	72	100	100	100	100	78	29	0	0	6	30		52
AE	0	0	19	51	93	139	164	124	86	52	14	0	742
WD	0	0	0	0	0	0	0	26	15	0	0	0	41
WS	0	2	19	20	17	0	0	0	0	0	0	0	58

Note. I_m is the moisture index (see Table 9.5).
Source: Data are from Laboratory of Climatology (1962–1965).
[a]Assumed storage capacity = 100 millimeters.

TABLE 9.4. Moisture Index

Designator	Name	I_m boundary
A	Perhumid	
		100
B	Humid	
		20
C2	Moist subhumid	
		0 (zero water balance line)
C1	Dry subhumid	
		–33
D	Semi-arid	
		–67
E	Arid	

Note. Formula for calculating the moisture index: $I_m = 100\ (P/PE - 1)$.

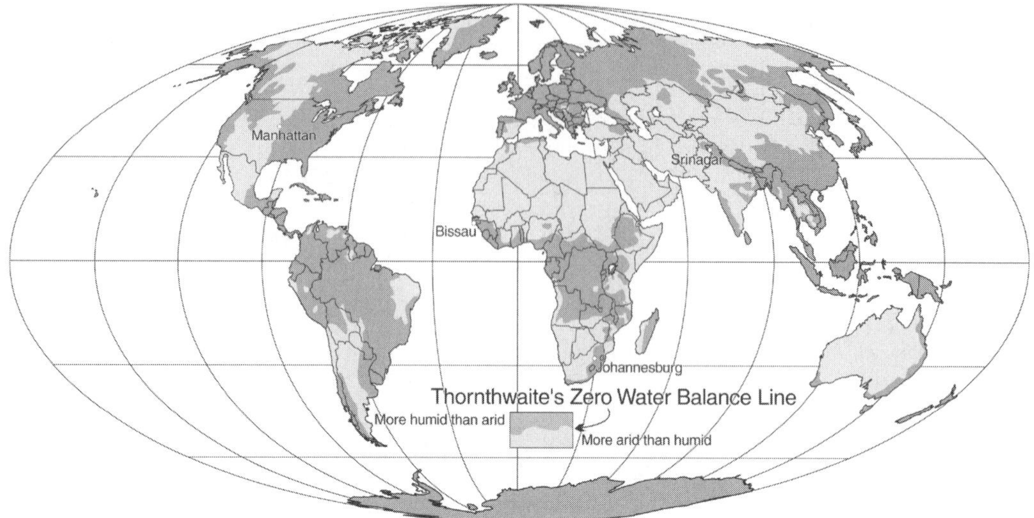

FIGURE 9.13. The zero water balance line. *Source*: Adapted from Willmott and Feddema (1992). Copyright 1992 by Association of American Geographers. Adapted by permission of Taylor & Francis.

the zero water balance line (Figure 9.12). As was the case with Manhattan, Kansas, the average match between what can be termed water need and water supply is very close, only the tiniest of deficits occurs, and that during the winter period.

In Srinagar (Figure 9.11 and Table 9.3) in highland Jammu and Kashmir, India, by contrast, there are rains through the year, and they are not well matched with evaporative need. During most of the low-sun period (November through March), there is lots of rain; however, during the summer period (May through September), PE is much higher than rainfall. Consequently, a serious WD develops during Srinagar's main agricultural season. The implications in this case are that crops need to be chosen in terms of drought tolerance or drought escape (quick-maturing varieties), or that supplemental irrigation is needed.

Rainfall Variability

The Bissau water balance diagram (Figure 9.11) masks another kind of variation. We can see that the average January is very different from the average July in Bissau, but are all Julys alike? Variability within a given month is illustrated in Figure 9.14, which shows 36 years of rainfall records for Dodoma, on the central plateau of Tanzania. Each dot on Figure 9.14 represents 1 month's rain in Dodoma, and each month has 36 dots (actually dots plus the months with no rain at all, shown as a number beneath the month). Rainfall in December in Dodoma averages about 100 millimeters, but can vary wildly from year to year. There was one year with no rain at all, and another with 220 millimeters. One year in four brings less than 50 millimeters of rain in December. Like Bissau, Dodoma has a 5-month rainy season and a 7-month dry season; however, Dodoma's average annual rainfall is less than Bissau's (536 vs. 1,967 millimeters), while the January peak reflects its southern hemisphere location.

How confident can farmers be about getting the needed amount of rainfall each year for their crops? Study of rainfall variability provides an answer, and for much of the wet–dry tropics (see Figure 9.9, above), the answer is not reassuring. On the face of it, one would expect rainfall variability to be greatest in arid and semi-arid areas; perhaps

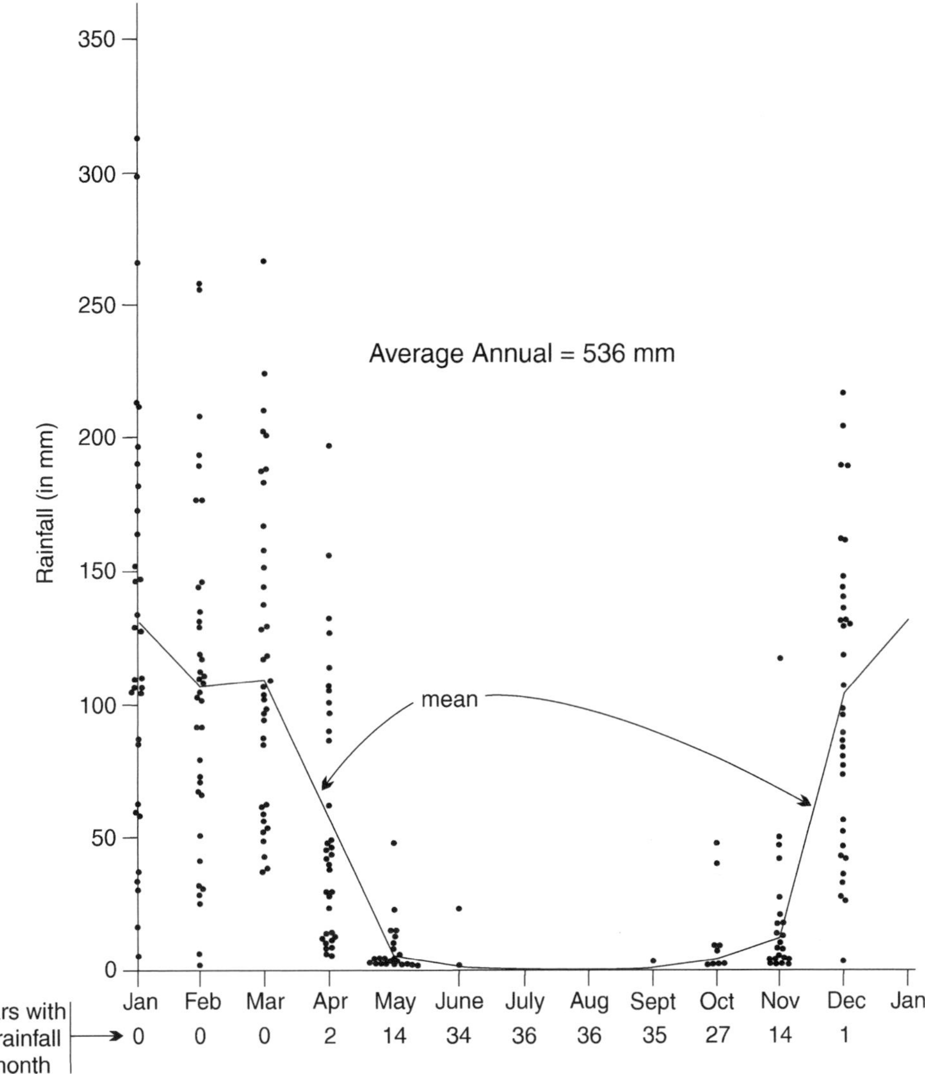

FIGURE 9.14. Rainfall diagram for Dodoma, Tanzania (covering 36 years). *Source*: Adapted from Porter (1979), who used data from the East African Meteorological Department. Copyright 1979 by the Maxwell School of Citizenship and Public Affairs, Syracuse University. Adapted by permission.

in a statistical sense it is, since it is common for occasional storms to bring unusually large amounts of precipitation, which skew the average. In fact, rainfall may vary only somewhat more in arid and semi-arid areas than in the wetter tropics and in midlatitude wet areas (Jackson, 1977: 46 ff.), but the consequences for agriculture and stock keeping of low amounts of precipitation are so great that people no doubt have a heightened sense of rainfall variability in semi-arid lands. Rainfall variability is best studied not as a departure from an annual mean (rainfall data are generally not normally distributed, and thus not appropriately described by such statistical measures as standard deviation from the mean), but in relation to crucial moments in the annual livelihood cycle, such as variability in the onset of the rains, variability in the amounts received during the crop season, and probability of rain failures during the flowering period.

In a zone circling the earth near the equator, one finds still another distributional pattern of consequence: two distinct rainy seasons, each associated with the overhead passage of the sun and, a few weeks later, the arrival and onward journey of the intertropical discontinuity (ITD) or ITCZ. The generally bimodal pattern is found over a latitudinal belt that ranges between 200 and 1,000 kilometers in width. Earlier in this chapter, Figure 9.2 has shown the two seasons at Kibwezi, Kenya (2°20' south of the equator)—one peaking in April, and a somewhat wetter season peaking in November. Again, as with Dodoma, variability within any given rainy month can be great.

Learning about systematic patterns helps us to understand the nature of the climatic benefits and challenges that farmers in particular places face. When we shift scales back to the local, we observe that it would be good if Kitemu wa Nguli and other farmers could tell at the beginning of a season whether it is going to be a dry one or a wet one. They could at least plan (and plant) accordingly. At first glance, this seems impossible (Figures 9.2 and 9.3). How can a farmer plan for such vagaries in a basic agricultural element? In fact, research by Ian Stewart has shown that planning is possible; some 50 days into the crop season, a farmer can at least hedge bets as to whether the rains will be average/above average, or average/below average (Stewart and Hash, 1982; Stewart, 1988). This turns out to be quite useful information. Systems of indigenous knowledge in the third world provide many examples of successful adaptation to uncertainty and agricultural risks, in response to the capricious behavior of water as it moves in the atmospheric energy and hydrologic cycles. Such knowledge systems are intertwined with particular social systems and livelihood strategies that have themselves been changing through processes of colonialism, development, and globalization; thus they can be fragile. Useful knowledge for one generation may be lost, or irrelevant to the conditions of the next. We return to these themes in Chapters 10 and 12.

10 Other Challenges to Rural Livelihood

Soils, Vegetation, and Pests

Kitemu wa Nguli copes not only with a variable and unreliable rainfall, but with a host of other threats and conditions surrounding his livelihood. His farming might better be called "agropastoral," because the family manages many cattle, sheep, and goats. He recognizes four soil types: *muthanga mwiu* (black soil), *muthanga mutune* (red soil), *nthangathi* (sandy soil), and *ilivi* (black cotton soil). The first two are oxisols, the third is an entisol, and the fourth a vertisol. He plants crops only in *muthanga mwiu* and *muthanga mutune*. Land for crops is plentiful in Kilungu, and the interesting thing about Kitemu's practice is that he preserves strategic areas of grazing near his home (and livestock *kraals*), so that the animals can graze and browse as they go to and from the place where they get water. Pests and vermin exact a varying, sometimes very serious toll on Kitemu's crops, both as they grow in the field and after harvest. Other concerns—especially for Kitemu's wives, Mbeke and Mbula, and for some of their children—include water for domestic uses, as well as water for livestock. We now consider each of these topics more broadly.

TROPICAL SOILS

We sometimes wonder whether soils are even more complex and individual than people. Our colleague Phil Gersmehl says that about 50% of the variation in soils usually occurs as a person takes 100 steps away from any place (and often within just a meter or two). Any topic of inquiry so variegated and spatially complicated makes geographic generalizations at regional and global scales extremely problematic.[1] There are, however, ways around our difficulty with soils. We can characterize and typify the sorts of ensembles of soils found in the third world with respect to the parent materials, the way they weather, the chemical and biological processes going on in them, and the resulting characteristics as repositories of nutrients and water. We can also describe what happens to typical soils when people use them in various ways. Thus, although we cannot present to readers the exact character of a soil at any place, we can convey a general idea of the sorts of soils encountered and the implications these have for crop production, soil erosion, roadway engineering, and so forth. Since agriculture and transport are two of the major conditioners in the production and circulation of goods, the soils of the third world have direct consequences for livelihood.

Carbon

We begin with carbon, using two maps that present a vivid contrast. Figure 10.1 shows the global distribution of carbon produced annually, as biomass; Figure 10.2 shows the global distribution of carbon preserved in soils (Box and Meentemeyer, 1991). It is clear that carbon stands mainly above ground in the tropics and is not preserved in the soil, whereas in the midlatitudes less biomass is produced annually, but higher percentages of carbon are retained in the soil.

These two maps can be regarded as metaphors or emblems for the processes at work in the environment and the strategies of plants and plant manipulators. On the one hand, midlatitude soils are repositories for carbon and mineral nutrients; they are like cellars, where things that are useful but not currently needed are stored. In the tropical soils, there is not much of a below-ground cellar or basement, hardly even a crawl space. Carbon and plant minerals are stored mainly in the plants themselves. To switch metaphors, if vegetation is a biomass factory, it uses a "just-in-time" system of production in the tropics, but it has an inventory/warehouse system in the soils of drier and cooler environments. On the tropical forest floor there is scant litter, and the soils themselves are generally low in carbon and in available nitrogen, potassium, and phosphorus. Nutrients are either quickly incorporated in plant tissue, or they are leached (i.e., dissolved and washed away) from the soil.

The Antiquity and Nature of Most Third World Soils

Most tropical and subtropical land is part of ancient Gondwana (one of the "supercontinents" that, with Laurasia, figures centrally in the study of plate tectonics). Gondwana has broken apart to become South America, Africa, south Asia (India, Pakistan, and Bangladesh), Australia, and Antarctica; its surfaces have been exposed to subaerial pro-

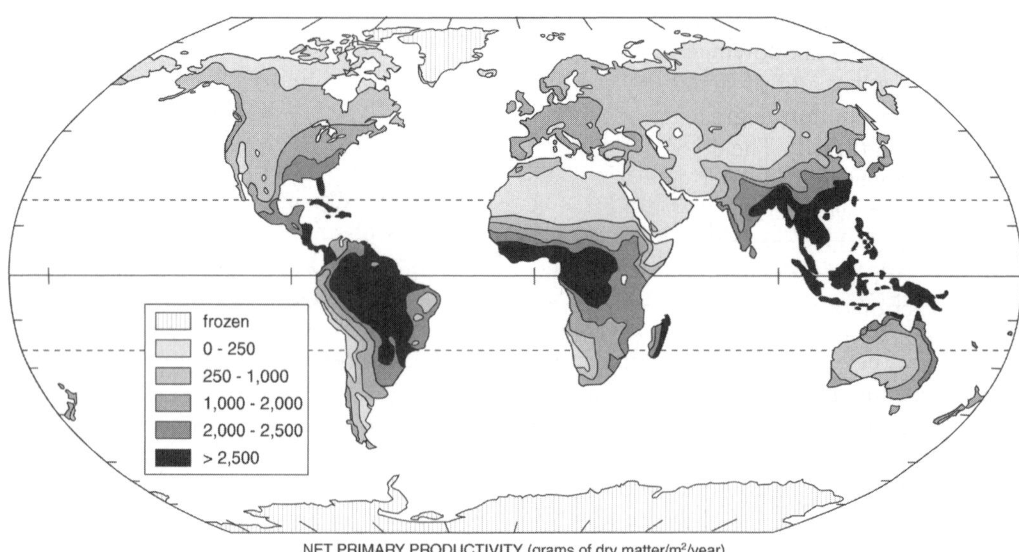

FIGURE 10.1. Global distribution of carbon produced annually. *Source:* Adapted from Box and Meentemeyer (1991). Copyright 1991 by Elsevier Science, Inc. Adapted by permission.

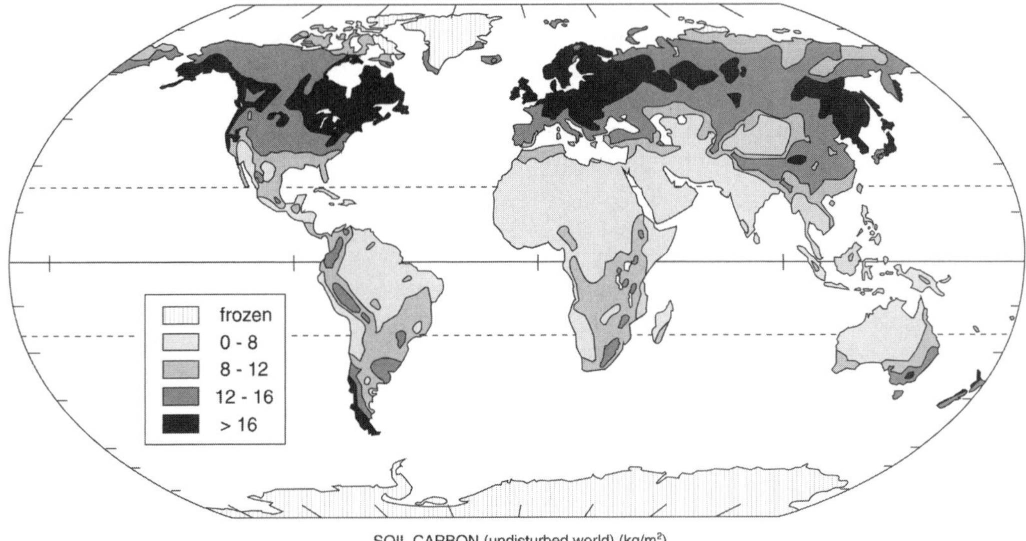

FIGURE 10.2. Global distribution of carbon preserved in soils. *Source:* Adapted from Box and Meentemeyer (1991). Copyright 1991 by Elsevier Science, Inc. Adapted by permission.

cesses of sun, wind, water, and microbial activity for long periods, typically 65 million years or more. Considerably smaller areas of soil have formed from more recent volcanic outflows, or are alluvial or depositional in origin. The parent material varies greatly, of course, but large portions of it are composed of ancient Archean quartzites, gneisses, and granites (which break down into sharp granular, sandy soils), and of shales, slates, and marls (which contain a greater fraction of clay when weathered). The dominant weathering in the wet and the wet–dry tropics is chemical—the weathering and leaching of minerals, and the formation of oxides of iron and aluminum through hydrolysis (the chemical action of acidic water) or oxidation. These processes can be accelerated when the protective cover of forest is removed, although the hydrologic front, where these processes are occurring, is deep in the soil column. Nonetheless, an undisturbed forest at higher elevations can develop a carbon-rich, nutrient-rich deep soil.

When vegetation is cut down, as in shifting cultivation, major changes take place: in temperature of the soil (it rises), in aerobic activity (it increases), and in the local hydrology (runoff and evaporation increase, and they more than offset decreased transpiration). If an area is not permitted to recover, nutrient loss, soil acidification and toxification, and soil erosion and gullying may ensue; the water table may drop; and changes in grass, shrub, and tree species may occur, tending toward less desirable types. Frequently, difficult weedy grasses (such as *Imperata cylindrica* or *Chloris pycnothrix*) invade, and thickets may form.

In semi-arid and arid areas, where rainfall is less, oxidation and actual physical processes (rock heating and cooling, wind abrasion) become dominant. Here undisturbed soils tend to be covered by grasses and small shrubs and trees, rather than forest or woodland. The heat load is much greater, and soil temperatures are higher. Aerobic activity of microorganisms is greatly accelerated, breaking down organic matter and oxidizing nutrients. (Organic matter decomposes much more rapidly in the tropics than it does in the midlatitudes. One study gives the ratio of decomposition rate in tropical Africa to that in Rothamsted,

England, as 4:1, and ratios even higher have been cited by Meentemeyer, 1984.) Moisture is vaporized quickly, and there is a tendency for moisture to move, at least seasonally, by capillary action toward the surface. Soil horizons (profile differences with depth) are shallower, and rain penetrates less deeply into the ground.

Ninety-two percent of soils in the humid tropics can be accounted for by four orders: oxisols (35%), ultisols (28%), inceptisols (15%), and entisols (14%) (Table 10.1). Oxisols have excellent physical properties (they are easily worked and well aerated), but are very low in nutrients and have low water-holding capacities. They have low clay content. Ultisols, though similar to oxisols physically, have greater amounts of clay at depth. These soils are slightly better endowed with minerals, although they too are acidic and have low fertility. (Note that ultisols are particularly abundant in the Asian humid tropics.) They are often found on steeper slopes and are easily eroded. The oxisols and ultisols—the red, highly leached "latosols," to use an alternate, old-fashioned term—can be considered together. Iron oxides are what give tropical soils their characteristically vivid red colors. "Their main limitations are chemical: high soil acidity; aluminum toxicity; deficiency of phosphorus, potassium, calcium, magnesium, sulfur, and other micro-nutrients, and low effective cation-exchange capacity, which last indicates a high leaching potential" (National Research Council, 1982: 44).

Inceptisols and entisols are young soils. Inceptisols are commonly of fluvial origin and of moderate to high fertility. The andept inceptisols (now placed in a new order of andosols) are volcanic in origin and are particularly prominent in parts of southeast Asia, where they are used for permanent irrigated cultivation and support high population densities. Entisols are not soils in a classic sense, since they are so young that they do not yet exhibit a vertical profile. They include alluvial soils of high fertility, infertile acid psammants (deep sand soils—beach terraces and the like), and infertile lithosols (rocky and shallow).

Three other soil orders may be noted: alfisols, vertisols, and mollisols. These are well-drained soils having high fertility. Alfisols resemble oxisols and ultisols physically and in color, but have "high base content"; that is, they have minerals that can be taken up by plants.[2] Some alfisols have poorer physical properties, usually exhibiting a coarse-textured surface horizon and clayey

TABLE 10.1. Geographical Distribution (in Millions of Hectares) of Soils of the Humid Tropics

Soil order	Humid tropics, total	Humid tropical America	Humid tropical Africa	Humid tropical Asia
Oxisols	525	332	179	14
Ultisols	413	213	69	131
Inceptisols	226	61	75	90
Entisols	212	31	91	90
Alfisols	53	18	20	15
Histosols	27	—	4	23
Spodosols	19	10	3	6
Mollisols	7	—	—	7
Vertisols	5	1	2	2
Aridosols	2	—	1	1
Total	1,489	666	444	379

Source: National Research Council (1982: 41). Copyright 1982 by the National Academy of Sciences. Reprinted by permission of the National Academy Press.

subsurface layer. Given their weak structure, they are susceptible to crusting, compaction, and erosion. They constitute only 3.6% of the soils of the humid tropics, but they are very important agriculturally. Vertisols—the infamous "black cotton soils," as they are called in Africa, where they have mired so many Land Rovers—are found in low places. These areas are usually treeless, grass-covered, seasonally flooded zones, and in eastern and southern Africa are commonly termed *mbuga*, *dambo*, or *vlei*. In the rainy season they are impassable, and in the dry seasons these "cracking clays" develop deep polygonal fissures. These heavy clays are fertile, although they lack nitrogen and phosphorus. Vertisols have poor physical properties and are difficult to work.

Mollisols, which in midlatitudes are among the best agricultural soils (imagine western Iowa), are in the tropics associated with limestone and with slopes. Mollisols are uncommon in Latin America and Africa, and constitute less than 2% of soils in humid tropical Asia. Overall, Asia has larger proportions of good agricultural soils than do Latin America and Africa.

Nitrogen

Nitrogen poses special problems. Nitrogen is very low in tropical soils, but it is needed if high amounts of dry matter and protein are to be obtained from crops. One possible source is leguminous plants, which are found at all latitudes. The herbaceous legumes are characteristic of higher latitudes: alfalfa, vetch, peas, and clover (the Faboideae). There are also a few larger pod-bearing species, such as the locust and catalpa (the Caesalpinioideae). Nitrogen-fixing, leguminous plants become more woody as one moves closer to the equator. Cowpeas, pigeon peas, greengrams, and groundnuts all fix nitrogen, but pigeon peas, if left to grow as a perennial, become large woody bushes. *Acacia* and *Albizzia* (the Mimosoideae) are also pod-bearing, nitrogen-fixing plants, but their nitrogen is not in a form that is easily available to improve the soil.

Tropical research stations have conducted experiments with indigenous and imported nitrogen-fixing plants, using cuttings from the plants when they are still shrubs as mulch and as green manure. The most successful has been *Leucaena leucocephala*. The plant is associated with the term "alley cropping," wherein it is planted in hedgerows with cultivated areas between the rows. Cuttings from the plant are mixed into the soil, to which they add significant amounts of nitrogen, potassium, phosphorus, calcium, and magnesium (International Institute for Tropical Agriculture ([IITA], 1986: 29).

The Soil Catena

Although soils exhibit tremendous local variability, in the tropics certain regularities in the variation are associated with slope, drainage, and elevation. Milne (1935) developed the notion of the "soil catena" (Latin for chain)—a set of regular soil differences exhibited along hill slopes, wherein each part of the slope (hilltop, valley side, valley bottom) exhibits its own special character in soil texture, drainage, presence or absence of concretionary bands, and so forth.

In Chapter 12, we discuss the way the Pokot of west central Kenya think about their soils. Figure 10.3 names the soils of "their" catena, or soil–topography association, and gives the closest possible approximations to comparable terms used in western soil science.[3] The complexity in this single example of soil changes along a single slope may be extended in the mind of the reader to every hill and valley in the third world. Truly, the assessment of agricultural possibilities in the tropics and subtropics is a local, place-specific matter. There are answers, but they are not general.

Although soil science has developed generalizations and principles of management that transcend location, each place presents

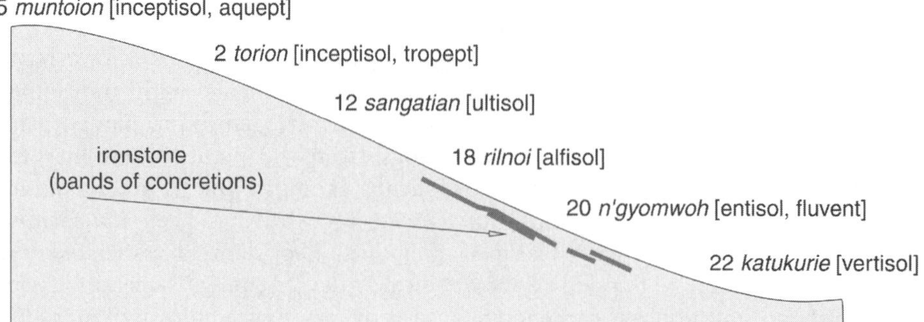

FIGURE 10.3. Pokot soil catena.

its own set of soils and attendant management requirements. The fact that indigenous knowledge of soils is complex reflects the fact that soils themselves are complex. Local knowledge of soils developed in order to enable people to adapt agricultural and pastoral practices to nature's possibilities.

VEGETATION

Kitemu and his family can read the vegetation very skillfully. They can tell by what is growing on it which land is good for farming and for grazing, which land has been disturbed, which land is poor or worn out, and which land is ready to be used again. For example, the following grasses and trees are indicative of good land: *mbwea* (*Panicum maximum*), *kikii* (*Themeda triandra*), *ikoka* (*Cynodon* spp.), *nthata kivumbu* (*Cenchrus pennisetiformis*), *mbeethua* (*Eragrostis superba*), *kisemei* (*Acacia nilotica*), and *kithii* (*Acacia mellifera*). The weed *muvongolo* (*Datura strimonium*) indicates that a field has been manured, for this plant, itself poisonous to humans, is associated with seeds eaten by stock and passed through the animal. It is a plant one finds growing around cattle bomas. Plants reveal soil characteristics and moisture conditions. There is also a rich knowledge among the Akamba of which plants to use for food, medicines, poisons, crafts, and building construction, firewood, and charcoal.

The Strategies of Plants

Tropical forests are well known for their floral diversity, and for the strategies various plant forms use to thrive, seeking both water and light. The higher the rainfall, the greater the tendency for vegetation to be multistoried. A closed-canopy tropical lowland forest will have three or four stories. The floor of the forest may be quite open, though gloomy. The larger trees commonly have flared and buttress-like root systems. One will find climbing plants (lianes) and, in upper branches, epiphytes (plants that depend on others for support, but not nutrition) such as orchids. There may be as many as 100 different tree species per hectare. Another common feature is "cauliflory," in which bloom and fruit grow on short stalks directly from branches or the main trunk. (A truly startling sight is the huge, bizarre, ungainly jack fruit, *Artocarpus heterophyllus*, growing directly out of tree branches in a tropical village.)

As one moves to cooler and to drier locations, the vegetation will adjust, growing to lower heights, becoming more open in canopy, with greater presence of shrubs and grasses. Figure 10.4 shows the general types of vegetation found in Africa as one goes from wet to dry and from hot to cool areas. Similar patterns are found in South America and Asia, although the particular grass and tree species will be different.

In some cases distinctive vegetational

assemblages arise because of special adaptations—to a severe dry season, annual fires, or special soil or groundwater conditions. For example, the *Brachystegia* woodland is adapted to a single rainy season (summer) with a long, severe dry season. This type of woodland exists in warm areas that have insufficient water to produce rain forest, but too much rain to produce thorn forest. It is physiologically adapted to a long dry season, and the trees flower and put out leaves in the period just before the dry season ends. In Figure 10.4, along the left margin, vegetation that exists in areas of low rainfall ranges from hot desert conditions through *Acacia–Commiphora* bushland, to thorn forest and thicket, to cooler grasslands, and finally to Afro-alpine heath and moorland. Alpine vegetation on equatorial mountains sometimes has to adapt to "crazy" conditions—an annual cycle every day, since it freezes every night (winter) and warms up every day (summer)! *Acacia* savannas occur in moderate temperature and moisture conditions, and the characteristic flat-topped, small-leaved trees are familiar to anyone who watches nature documentaries on television. *Combretum* savannas feature *Combretum* trees and shrubs, which are large-leaved and more numerous on the landscape. They tend to occur in somewhat cooler, wetter areas than *Acacia* savannas.

Along the right side of the diagram, hot lowlands can have tropical forest as described above. With increases in elevation, temperatures decline; species diversity also declines somewhat (down to maxima of 40 species per hectare); there may be only two stories; and climbing vines are fewer. Epiphytes are common.

Managing Soils and Vegetation

Third-world farmers, through trial and error, have learned to adapt to the unique sets of benefits and constraints of tropical and subtropical environments. For example, Kitemu and his family practice a form of shifting cultivation. The interplanting of crops and the complex schedule of planting, harvesting, and planting for a second season give the field an appearance of chaos, but

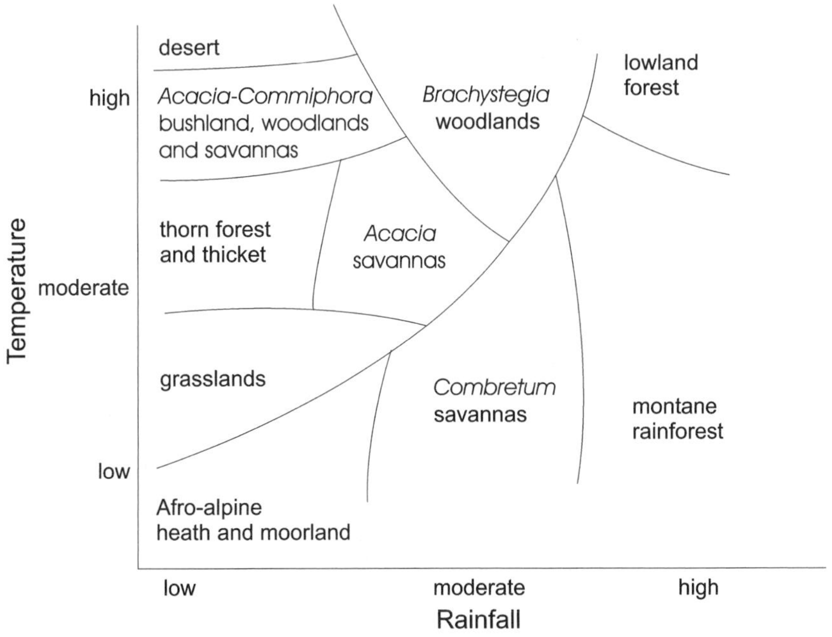

FIGURE 10.4. African vegetation.

there are many ingenious and adaptive elements designed to ensure a moisture supply and a protective environment for the crops. Most of the points listed below were made by informants in Kilungu, though some of the observations come from plant physiologists and agroclimatologists.

First, visualize the sequence.[4] A Kilungu farmer plants maize, beans, cowpeas, sorghum, groundnuts, bulrush millet, red millet, cassava, pumpkins, calabashes, and pigeon peas, all mixed together in one large field (Plate 10.1). The crops come up together in a riotous profusion of vines, leaves, and stems. Weeds have little chance. The phosphorus flush in the soil that comes with the first rains is taken advantage of by these crops. Crops (e.g., maize) that might be indolent about putting down roots and strong tillers in a soil well supplied with moisture have to compete with the other plants, and thus they put down roots to a depth of more than 1 meter. These deeper roots come into play later in the season. Although the rate of moisture use of all these crops planted together is high, it occurs at the one time of the season when enough moisture is likely to be available. Furthermore, the interplanting provides a good continuous canopy within which photosynthesis can proceed. Since tropical areas have a relatively uniform radiation income all year around, a continuous leaf canopy is the most efficient user of radiant energy for photosynthesis (Chang, 1968). Both the farmer's interplanted field and the full-canopied, sometimes multistoried, natural vegetation of many tropical ecosystems show adaptation to the uniformities of radiation in the tropics (Geertz, 1963).

After about 7–8 weeks, some of the crops are harvested. Beans may be harvested as green vegetables. As the season

PLATE 10.1. Part of the main field of Kitemu wa Nguli. *Acacia* and *Commiphora* bushes with scattered *Euphorbia* form the background.

progresses, the millet is harvested; beans for seed are also taken, and the vines are pulled up. The number of plants per square meter of soil begins to decline, and only crops requiring a longer time to mature are left. The bare weedless soil between the plants is dry, which forms a vapor barrier to the movement of moisture to the surface. Evapotranspiration is thus reduced. The sparse plant population remaining is able to tap moisture from a larger volume of soil without competition from adjacent plants. This moisture, combined with the lesser amounts of rain that come at the end of the "grass rains," is often sufficient to bring the maize and the longer growing millets to harvest. The plants also provide some shade for crops set out to get a start on the main rains. The thick mat of plant cover in the first weeks of the "grass rains" and the second rains also serves to hold the soil. There is also the adaptive fact that if the rains do give out, some crops will have been harvested, and the agricultural effort will not have been a total loss. Furthermore, interplanting reduces the amount of work considerably by reducing the time farmers spend weeding. Labor for weeding is often the most serious impediment to agriculture and the management of larger hectarages.

In the Kilungu area, farmers characteristically place fields far from one another. This dispersal of fields has the effect of ensuring that if the rains fail in one area, the farming effort for that season will not necessarily be a total loss. Storms are often very small; one good rain or its absence can make or break the crops in a particular field. Field dispersal is a form of insurance.

Managing Soils and Vegetation, Considered More Generally

Soils and vegetation can be managed so that they do not degrade and so that there is little or no species loss, but doing so requires a thorough understanding of each particular tropical ecosystem. Most soils in Latin America and Africa are marginal upland types. There is little land suitable for irrigation, and that which is suitable may be in areas with serious health risks—from schistosomiasis, onchocerciasis (river blindness), and malaria (Lal, 1987).

The two tricks in soil management for agricultural purposes are (1) to prevent it from eroding, and (2) to preserve and enhance its capacity to hold minerals and water. One should concentrate on surface and slope. The surface should never be so exposed that rain can wash the soil away. By its nature, shifting cultivation leaves much litter in the field, thereby protecting the soil from rain and sun, reducing erosion, and conserving soil moisture. Contemporary techniques such as zero tillage and mulching also do much to preserve soil and moisture (Blaut, 1963, 1993: 74). As to slope, if the land can be made level, it will reduce the potential for erosion and increase the ability of soil to capture all rainfall, thereby reducing or delaying runoff.

In shifting cultivation, the soil, after being used, is brought back to an earlier level of fertility by a long fallow period for vegetative regrowth. (The growing plants immobilize carbon and other mineral nutrients above ground.) In shifting cultivation, farmers also depend on plant roots to improve the soil structure; leaf litter and mulching to control erosion; burning, which contributes nutrients and ash (thus improving pH); deep-rooted perennials, which bring nutrients above ground where they can again be incorporated into the soil; and the intermixture in fields of a wide range of crop species, in order to control pests.

A comparison of the figures presented in Table 10.2 shows that when soil is well covered, as with thicket or grass, there is virtually no soil loss or runoff. When soils are cleared and exposed, however, the increases can be dramatic. Several methods, many of which have been devised by local farmers, may be used in preventing or reducing runoff and soil loss. These include plowing and ridging on the contour after harvest; mulching and incorporating manure and crop residues

TABLE 10.2. Accelerated Erosion and Runoff, Depending on Surface Cover

Treatment	Soil lost by erosion (metric tons/hectare)	Water lost by runoff (percent of rainfall)
Ungrazed thicket	0.0	0.4
Grass	0.0	1.9
Millet	78.0	26.0
Bare fallow	146.2	50.4

Source: Data from Sundborg and Rapp (1986: 216).

into the soil; using crop rotations, including grass leys (i.e., treating a field for a time as a meadow or pasture); strip cropping; and terracing. There are many kinds of terracing, the most common being narrow-based (ridge-type) terrace, narrow-based (channel-type) terrace, *fanya juu* (explained below), forward-sloping bench terrace, level bench terrace, backward-sloping bench terrace, and modified bench terrace (also known as step terrace or orchard terrace) (Thomas, 1978: 33). The narrow-based (ridge-type) terrace and narrow-based (channel-type) terrace are for slopes up to 10°, and the other types are for slopes up to 27°. The modified bench terrace is for still steeper slopes.

Terracing techniques may also involve use of barriers, diversion ditches, strip cropping, and grassed drainageways (Ngugi, Karau, and Ngoyo, 1978: 49). One widely used technique in Kenya is called *fanya juu* (roughly, "make it upward"), wherein a ditch is dug along the contour of a sloping field, and the earth from the ditch is thrown immediately upslope. In its turn, erosion brings sediment downslope, and they meet. Over time this creates a barrier to the flow of water, improves infiltration during rains, and reduces or stops soil loss. Terraces can be very complex, even underlain by tiles that direct water flow toward the back of the seedbed and then along it (below ground) to grassed drainageways at the ends of terraces.

Although terracing, where slopes require it, is the best way to prevent erosion and to enhance soil fertility and moisture availability, it is also a most backbreaking and time-consuming enterprise. Collins (1987: 32) stated that it took 752 person-days to build a hectare of absorption terracing in Peru—terraces that would last for 20 years with little maintenance. Terracing accomplished by forced labor in Tanzania and Kenya was so unpopular that it became an issue around which the independence movement mobilized in the late 1950s (Young and Fosbrooke, 1960). Of course, the work of building terraces also has to be incorporated into the schedule of all the other regular work of the agricultural year.

With mechanical land clearing, where heavy equipment (such as tractors and bulldozers) is used, "soils are often more compacted, leaching and erosion rates increase, soil fertility is rapidly depleted, productive capacity on a given site soon tends to decline, and recovery is much slower than under conditions created by hand clearing" (National Research Council, 1982: 164). Examination of Table 10.3 shows this clearly. When heavy machinery was used, followed by conventional western tillage, the loss of water through runoff increased greatly (from 0.6% to 56%) and soil loss went from nil (0.01 tons/hectare) to 19.57 tons/hectare. Although yields were somewhat greater (0.5–1.8 tons/hectare), clearly farming cannot long be sustained by using such practices. In addition, compacted soils are more difficult to work.

With regard to forestry, the very diversity in species in tropical forest presents special problems. One cannot harvest pure stands of mature trees (as in some midlatitude forests), and for the sake of economics, one must be willing to take several kinds of hardwoods, which may have to be handled differently. Clear-cutting of a tropical forest frequently leads to such species loss that the vegetation will never regain its former state; indeed, it may lead to the emergence of new landscapes—derived savannas or grasslands. It also leads to soil compaction and acidification of groundwater.

Vegeculture and Horticulture

Many African humid tropical systems are forms of horticulture or vegeculture, wherein cuttings of a plant are set out, rather than germinated from seed. These systems depend heavily on root crops such as cassava, yams, potatoes, sweet potato, taro, arrowroot, and ensete, and tree (or tree-like) crops such as coconuts, citrus, and bananas. (Bananas are not actually trees, since they are propagated through planting of root stock, and essentially cannot be propagated from seed.)

There is a link between these systems and the natural systems they displace. Many (perhaps most) parts of tropical and subtropical Africa that are well peopled would, in the absence of human settlement and depending on the soils and climatic conditions, form some kind of forest or woodland. The same could be said of Asia and Latin America. There would be large areas of closed-canopy forest, and still larger areas of open-canopy deciduous woodland and bushland. In other words, the landscape would be dominated by trees. Removal of trees, as we have noted earlier, sets in train a series of changes in soil conditions (soil moisture, soil tempera-

TABLE 10.3. Effects of Alternative Land Clearing and Preparation Systems on Soil Properties and Maize Yields in an Alfisol, Ibadan, Nigeria

Land-clearing method	Land preparation method	Labor used for clearing (person-days/ha)	Tractor time (h/ha)	Erosion loss (tons/ha)	Runoff loss (% of rainfall)	Maize grain yields (tons/ha)	Topsoil pH	Available P (Bray) (ppm)
Traditional slash and planting burn	Hand	57	—	0.01	0.6	0.5	6.6	14
Slash and burn complete	Zero tillage	117	—	0.37	3.5	1.6	6.8	13
Slash and burn complete	Conventional tillage	117	—	4.64	12.1	1.6	6.8	19
Bulldozer with shear blade	Zero tillage	—	1.9	3.82	19.1	2.0	6.2	10
Bulldozer with tree pusher and root rake	Zero tillage	—	2.7	15.36	34.2	1.4	6.3	4
Bulldozer with tree pusher and root rake	Conventional tillage	—	2.7	19.57	56.0	1.8	6.5	10

Note. Abbreviations in column heads: ha, hectare; h, hours; pH, acidity–alkalinity; P, phosphorus; ppm, parts per million. "Bray" refers to R. H. Bray, who developed a widely used flame photometric method for phosphorus determination.

Source: National Research Council (1982: 164), which used 1980 data from the International Institute for Tropical Agriculture (IITA). Copyright 1982 by the National Academy of Sciences. Reprinted by permission of the National Academy Press.

ture, soil chemistry, soil movement/erosion, and hydrologic conditions) that alter the landscape and its capability to support its characteristic vegetative cover. To some degree, indigenous agricultural systems in tropical areas mimic the vegetative forms and environmental outcomes of forests, as Geertz (1963) noted long ago for Indonesian agriculture—multistoried, marked by intercropping, intensive cultivation, and a host of other features. These systems are examples of Norgaard's (1994: 81) "coevolutionary process"—that is, the joint evolution of environmental and social systems in a context-specific (i.e., place- and time-specific) manner, not according to some presumed universal process.

AGRICULTURAL PESTS AND VERMIN

Kitemu has a great deal of trouble with agricultural vermin, particularly porcupines which eat maize and marrows. There is an insect pest, *ivivi*, that damages the pigeon peas and the cowpeas; but fortunately there is no maize stalkborer. Birds attack millet and sorghum. The type of bird that does the most damage is called *ngwei* (*Quelea quelea aethiopica*). "Agricultural pests and vermin" is the term applied to the animals, birds, and insects that consume crops at every stage of the agricultural cycle—as newly planted seeds, as growing crops, and as stored harvest.

We establish the environmental context of the problem of agricultural vermin by quoting Solomon (1949) and Owen (1973):

> In a broad way, there is a geographical zonation of degrees of ecological complexity. The fact that terrestrial life tends to be less abundant and varied as one moves from tropical forest to temperate regions and thence to polar and other barren regions is widely recognized. . . . We should expect a corresponding trend from smaller to greater variability in the densities of populations. There is evidence to support this conclusion. . . . Periodic outbreaks of forest insects are more common and marked toward the arctic regions; they are perhaps the least evident in tropical forests.
>
> . . . There is a general tendency for population densities of most species in the tropical forests to be relatively low, perhaps as a result of a more intense struggle against enemies and competitors. . . . In a very heterogeneous physical environment, there is more likely to be a continual supply of favourable microhabitats, however changeable the general conditions may be; on the other hand, only a certain fraction of such an environment is likely to be favourable at any one time; these circumstances would be likely to operate against any tendency to extreme variation in the density of population. (Solomon, 1949: 30)

> Any tendency towards monoculture is likely to generate an increase in the population size of insects that feed on the crop or on related wild species. The diversity of species of crops grown by rural cultivators reduces the impact of insects on the crops, but any attempt to grow a crop on a large scale over a wide area encourages the build-up of pest populations. It would therefore seem that plans to develop agriculture by converting large areas of land to a single crop are doomed to failure unless precautions are taken to control the buildup of pest populations. (Owen, 1973: 85)

It may seem surprising that we would include a section on agricultural pests and vermin in a chapter on the management of tropical and subtropical ecosystems, but they constitute a very serious problem, whether approached from the standpoint of indigenous practice or from that of western science. Farmers in third world countries face staggering losses, both before harvest time in their fields, and in after harvest in granaries and other storage spaces. Here is a vivid description of vermin damage in Tanzania:

> In an assessment in the Tanga district in 1944 it was estimated that in the south, 10–15 percent, and in the north 25–35 percent of the crop was ruined by wild pigs. . . . In 1952 birds threatened to create near-famine conditions in the West Kilimanjaro area when they began to attack grain crops in areas where the food supply had already been depleted because of drought. In several parts of the Eastern

Province it was estimated in 1958 that rats, baboons, monkeys, and pigs had consumed as much as one-third of the food crops produced. (Mascarenhas, 1971: 259)

According to Howe (1965: 285), "Losses caused by insect infestations in stored foods in the tropics can vary from 10 per cent to 50 per cent." Importing food from first world countries is no solution, as one journal points out:

> Very roughly [food losses] amount, according to the various cases, to between 30 and 50 percent of what has been grown (whether still growing or already stored). But the cost of replacement is two to three times greater because the food that must be imported to replace the lost crops is more elaborate and needs conditioning, and transport costs must be added. (*Ceres*, 1976: 8)

Vermin in Context: Research from Tanzania

As an illustration of how serious third world people consider pests and vermin to be, consider Tables 10.4 and 10.5, which are based on data developed from a University of Dar es Salaam study associated with the first Agricultural Census of Tanzania and the Agro-climatological Survey of Tanzania (Porter, 1976b).[5]

The seriousness of problems with birds, insects, and other vermin came as something of a surprise to the university researchers. As "first-ranked difficulty" (see Table 10.4), bush pigs and other vermin were at the top of the list; they were cited as a serious problem by 9 of every 10 households. Amounts and timing of rain came second and third as "first-ranked difficulty," followed by birds and insects; however, birds were cited at twice the rate of rainfall problems (67% vs. 34.9% for rainfall timing and 36.2% for amounts). Many other constraints to agricultural development, all of which are central concerns for first world farmers—crop prices, quality of transport, lack of capital, poor soils, land shortages—figured much less prominently in Tanzanian farmers' minds. In terms of times problems were cited, vermin–birds–insects scored 1,663; water-related problems (including floods) scored 811; land-related items scored 293;

TABLE 10.4. Tanzanian Farmers' Rankings of the Problems They Face

Problem	First-ranked	Second-ranked	Third-ranked	Cited but not ranked in top three	Total citations	Total % of all EAs[a]
Bush pigs and other vermin	366	245	112	105	828	90.4
Too little rain	89	47	54	142	332	36.2
Rain coming at wrong time	87	45	51	137	320	34.9
Birds	80	165	94	275	614	67.0
Insects	56	70	68	27	221	24.1
Shortage of land	46	21	32	60	159	17.4
Changing prices	38	90	82	138	348	38.0
Isolation and poor communications	29	60	50	121	260	28.4
Too much rain	22	21	17	81	141	15.4
Thieves	18	29	46	106	199	21.7
Poor soil	10	7	16	11	44	4.8
Shortage of capital	7	3	6	41	57	6.2
Floods	3	4	1	10	18	2.0

Source: Porter (1976b, using responses to question 1 of block 3, Agro-climatological Survey of Tanzania, November 1972).

[a]All enumeration areas (EAs; $N = 916$).

TABLE 10.5. Vermin Ranked by Tanzanian Farmers on the Basis of the Damage They Do to Crops

Vermin type	Number of EAs first-ranked	Number of EAs second-ranked	Sum of all four ranks	Citations as a percentage of all EAs (N = 916)[a]
Bush pigs	430	102	554	60.5
Birds	144	208	517	56.4
Monkeys	88	127	292	31.9
Insects	56	70	222	24.2
Rats and mice	36	34	112	12.2
Baboons	28	38	85	9.3
Porcupines	18	24	57	6.2
Elephants	10	13	42	4.6
Hippopotami	9	15	37	4.0
Other[b]	31	31	94	10.3

Source: Porter (1976b, using responses to question 2 of block 3, Agro-climatological Survey of Tanzania, November 1972).

[a]Total citations: 219.6 (or 2.2 vermin per EA).

[b]Included in "Other" are antelopes, buffalo, bush squirrels, cattle, goats, hedgehogs, hyenas, jackals, leopards, lions, moles, mongooses, rabbits, rhinoceri, sheep, snails, and wart hogs.

and all other problems (all of them socioeconomic) scored 864. Vermin–birds–insects constituted nearly 60% of farmers' first-ranked problems.

Table 10.5 shows how farmers ranked vermin according to the seriousness of the damage they caused. Again, bush pigs topped the list, with birds not far behind. There are significant regional variations in Tanzania as to where particular vermin are a serious problem. For example, porcupines have become a significant problem in the cotton-growing area of Sukumaland, in Mwanza Province, south of Lake Victoria. Elephants are more frequently a problem in settlements near game reserves; destruction by hippos is generally associated with areas near rivers and lakes. Damage can be seasonal, and since some vermin (e.g., bush pigs, porcupines, wart hogs, rodents, and hippos) are nocturnal and others (e.g., monkeys, baboons, and birds) do their damage during the day, guarding crops becomes a 24-hour job at times. The sidebar "Destructive Animals and Insects in Tanzania" provides capsule summaries of the main vermin in Tanzania, the sorts of damage they cause, and the timing and locations of this damage.

It is clear from the sidebar that different vermin have to be controlled in different ways. Furthermore, the vegetation of Tanzania is a mosaic of cultivated fields, interspersed with fallow land, grazing land, forest, and bush; this reduces vulnerability to insects, but also makes it impossible to deprive vermin of all potential habitats. Large game reserves also provide reservoirs for pests. Game parks in Tanzania date from 1896. More and more people are living at the margins of national and local game parks, game reserves, conservation areas, and controlled areas as the general population increases; this brings farmers and their crops and livestock into direct competition with the country's wildlife.

The problems of human competition with other life forms for ecological dominance, or at least parity (so that livelihood can be sustained), carry over into many other domains. For example, the tsetse fly, the alternate host for trypanosomiasis, is widespread in tropical Africa and prevents the keeping of cattle over large areas of the

Destructive Animals and Insects in Tanzania

Bush Pigs

Bush pigs (see figure below) forage at night; travel in "sounders" of 5–20; and are terribly destructive, especially to maize and cassava. They live in thickets, long tall grass, reed beds, and dense bush. A large male may weigh 77 kilograms and have a shoulder height of 80 centimeters. They root up crops with their tusks, and do great damage to standing crops, as much from their trampling as from what they eat. Along the coast of Tanzania, the killing of a bush pig has no associated food benefit, because Islamic people do not eat pork.

The African Bush Pig. Drawing by Sara Porter.

Birds

Birds of many varieties are agricultural pests. One of the most important is the *Quelea quelea aethiopica*, also known as the Sudan dioch and the weaver bird, after its neatly woven nests. These birds travel in great swarms, swooping down on fields to eat the seed. One million birds can consume 55,000 kilograms of grain per day. Much time can be spent guarding against bird swarms when grain is ripening.

A favorite nesting site is *Acacia mellifera*, and the birds are generally associated with areas getting about 750 millimeters of precipitation a year (Disney and Haylock, 1956). Nesting areas can be destroyed through aerial and ground spraying, flame throwers, and hand labor (which involves large work parties). Where birds nest in large numbers, eradication teams may place numerous pans of gasoline or kerosene under the trees at night and ignite them simultaneously, so that a huge fireball erupts, killing all the birds at once. Mascarenhas (1971: 262) presented estimates on the numbers of *Quelea quelea* killed over a 13-year period (see figure, overleaf).

Monkeys

Monkeys travel in groups of 20–30. The common vervet monkey is very gregarious, active, cunning, and inquisitive, and is fearfully destructive to all agricultural produce, particularly fruit and maize. One study cited losses from monkey depredations as follows: bananas, 28% (of total crop); cotton, 21%; maize, 20%; groundnuts, 18%; and cassava, 19% (Mascarenhas, 1967).

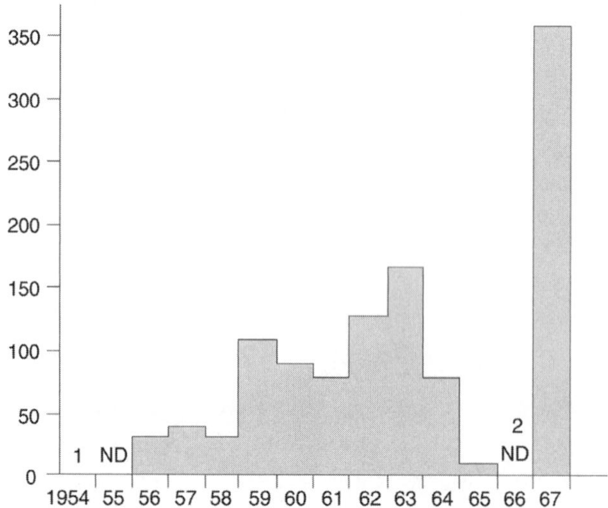

Millions of *Quela quela* birds killed: Estimates from 1954 through 1967.
Source: Data are from Mascarenhas (1971).

Insects

There are, of course, hundreds of kinds of insects that affect crops, both while growing and when stored. For example, 45 of the 800 important pests of coffee are found in Tanzania (Price Jones, 1974: 184). Crop losses to insects are probably greater than those to animals, but farmers may not be aware of the magnitude of the former. Losses to bush pigs are spectacular, whereas losses to insects are less so. The losses caused by insects may be general, accounted for by many pests and shared among many crops. The sort of vegetation mosaic found in Tanzania, as in tropical forests, tends to be biotically complex and varied. There are fewer outbreaks and rapid changes in insect populations, as we have noted in the text.

The interplanting of crops (a ubiquitous practice in Tanzania) helps reduce insect pests and disease levels, partly because a large, single food supply, advantageous to one pest, is not produced. The farmer probably tolerates a relatively constant loss to insects, except when particular circumstances (such as periodic cycles or heavy rains) lead to insect outbreaks. In short, insects levy a tolerable, somewhat fluctuating tax on farmers. When farmers begin monocropping, they may face much larger damage. Losses are very high in cotton, for example.

Special problems are presented by locusts (e.g., the red locust, the desert locust), which commonly breed in remote areas. If they reach the gregarious stage, they begin to swarm, staying together and allowing themselves to be carried by convergent air streams to areas where there is likely to be more abundant rain and green vegetation, ready to be consumed (Rowley, 1993). Over the years, the Desert Locust Survey has monitored areas where the desert locust breeds. If these insects are caught while the locusts are still in the solitary stage, potential plagues can be prevented. Many other swarming insects could be described, such as the army worm (*Spodoptera exempta*), which can cover the ground so deeply that the wheels of train engines spin uselessly. Depending on when an insect outbreak occurs, it may force farmers to replant their crops, or it may result in loss of the harvest.

Rats and Mice

Nearly all members of the Rodentia order are found throughout Tanzania. Rats and mice, including the giant rat and cane rat, are nocturnal and are serious pests to crops (especially grains), both in field and in storage. They usually burrow underground in areas of dense bush or thicket. It is essentially impossible to deprive them of suitable habitats, and Tanzanian farmers are generally indifferent to rats and mice except when they reach plague proportions.

Baboons

Baboons are found everywhere in Tanzania, but especially in rocky or mountainous forested and wooded areas. They do serious damage to coffee, bananas, cashews, cassava, beans, groundnuts, maize, and sweet potatoes.

Porcupines and Hedgehogs

Porcupines and east African hedgehogs live in underground burrows and are nocturnal. Adults weigh from 9 to 13 kilograms and travel up to 16 kilometers at night in search of food. They are particularly destructive of root crops, such as sweet potatoes, groundnuts, and cassava. Poisons are often used to eradicate porcupines. Placing the poison in burrows puts it out of harm's way for humans.

Elephants

Bush elephants are widely distributed, especially in national parks, game reserves, and controlled areas. They are fearfully destructive, trampling everything under foot. They have touristic value, so there is a government policy to protect them. Yet they endanger life, property, and livelihood, and thus have also been treated as vermin. Usually if the leader of the herd (always a female) is killed, the rest can be made to move into unsettled areas. Between 1955 and 1967, the Tanzanian Game Department killed 34,174 elephants; this was only a fraction of the animals causing the damage.

Hippopotami

Hippopotami are river and lake dwellers. They are nocturnal feeders, grazing on vegetation in areas adjacent to water. They are protected game in most areas, and can cause an immense amount of damage where settlement occurs near rivers on large floodplains.

Other Vermin

Respondents to the survey described in the text mentioned many other creatures as being destructive of their crops: hyraxes, jumping hares, ratels or honey badgers, bush squirrels, hyenas, wild dogs, lions as predators, buffalo, and pythons (see also Table 10.5).

continent. Where land is cleared of its vegetative cover, the fly can be brought under control and the disease eliminated. Another disease vector affecting livestock is the tick (*Amblyomma* spp.). Tick-borne diseases affect livestock and wildlife throughout the tropical and subtropical world, causing heartwater fever, redwater fever, east coast fever, and anaplasmosis.

Postharvest Losses

Postharvest losses are a problem worthy of separate consideration; in addition to animals and insects, we should consider various moulds and fungi that destroy the sale and use value of crops. The numerous techniques third world farmers have devised to save crops in storage are well summarized by Goldman (1991), who draws examples from Kenya. Among traditional techniques to manage postharvest losses are selection of the best crop or variety to grow in the first place; sun drying; storage of maize in husk (often outdoors on hanging racks or frames); sealing seed hermetically in pots or gourds (especially next year's seed); smoking or fumigating grain in storage; sorting out infested grain before placing the harvest in storage, since insect infestation begins in the field; mixing grain with ashes or powdered chilies; cleaning the storage crib completely before placing a new harvest in it; and planting insect repellent plants (e.g., marigolds) around the granary. Increasingly, people dust their stored crop with commercial pesticides, including malathion. Another "technique" is to sell the crop rather than store it, letting someone else deal with possible infestations.

WATER

Fetching water is just one of a multitude of tasks that Mbeke and Mbula do. A description of women's roles, taken from a Kikamba reading book (*Kitabu tja Kusoma*), is given by Lindblom (1920: 543–544):

> The woman's work is to powder maize, grind flour, chop wood, fetch water, look for vegetables and cook them, cook food for her husband and to eat it herself (!). Her other duties are: to milk the cows and churn butter, to dig (the field), sow and plant, gather in the maize, thrash the millet and Penicillaria and the [cowpeas]; to cut and carry home grass for thatching, sweep the hut, shut the entrance to the craal and clean it after the cattle (this is seldom done, however); to plait bags and mend calabashes; feed children (a very important duty), suckle them, look after them and bring them up (there is, however, no education in our sense of the word).

The list above omits weeding, an endless task during the agricultural months.

According to men (and perhaps women too), an Akamba wife is supposed to be doing something useful at all times. That is the hallmark of a good Akamba woman. I (PWP) have heard Akamba men comment approvingly about several women, seen walking along a road, whose hands were busy weaving craft objects—sisal baskets or bags.

Domestic Water Supplies

In rural areas, water used at the house for cooking, washing dishes and utensils, and cleaning must usually be brought from a distance (Adams, 1992; Gischler, 1979; White, Bradley, and White, 1972; Thompson, Porras, Tumwine, Mujwahuzi, Katui-Katua, Johnstone, and Wood, 2004). This may require great amounts of time, particularly on the part of women and children. One study of nine villages (167 households) showed that in 92% of the households, the women and children usually carried the water (Warner, 1969). This can mean as many as four trips per day to the water source, with a child generally able to carry about a third as much as an adult woman. Women in eastern Africa carry plastic pails or jerri cans, usually balanced on their heads, containing about 18 liters (weighing about 18 kilograms or 40 pounds). There are, naturally, systematic relationships between the time it takes to get water and the distance traveled (Figure 10.5) (Warner, 1969; Tschannerl, 1971). The relationships between the amount of water consumed in a household and the distance it has to be carried are less strong (Figure 10.6). In any event, adult women in a household may devote several hours each day (usually in the morning) to carrying water. When water is taken from a nearby outdoor tap, water use may be only marginally greater than when water is carried in from some distance. However, it is said that when the water supply enters the house itself, with

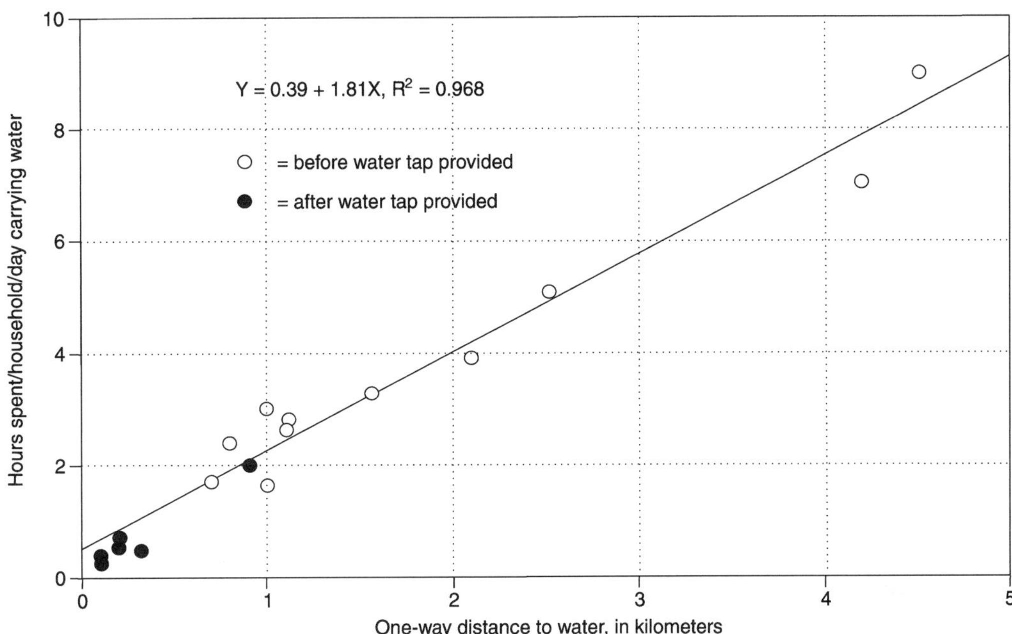

FIGURE 10.5. Water: Time–distance relation for 11 Tanzanian villages. *Sources:* Data are from Warner (1969) and Tschannerl (1971).

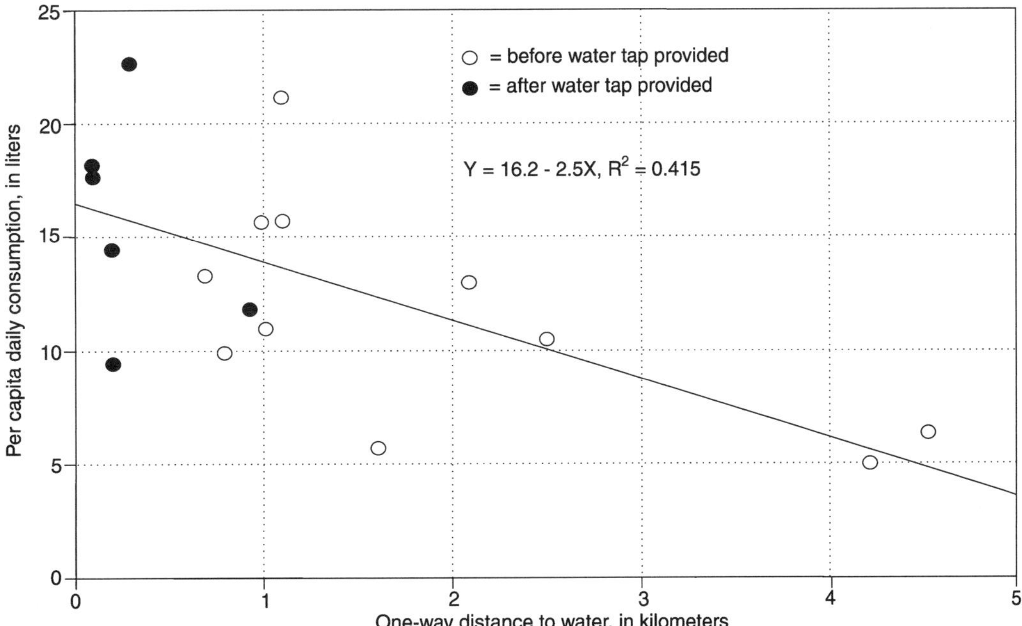

FIGURE 10.6. Water: Consumption–distance relation for 11 Tanzanian villages. *Sources:* Data are from Warner (1969) and Tschannerl (1971).

indoor plumbing (which includes toilets and showers, along with water taps), consumption increases 20-fold (Wang'ati, personal communication, 1989). Water tends to be regarded as a free good in African societies, equally available to all (Carruthers, 1969: 12). This attitude may be carried over to water supplied through a project sponsored by a government or a nongovernmental organization (NGO). Thus, in any water development project, one needs to anticipate how costs are to be met.

Improvements in water supply need to be considered not only from the standpoint of labor time, distance, and amounts; issues of water quality and health must also be taken into account. Heijnen and Conyers (1971: 55–62) developed 14 hypotheses about the effects of water development, which are worth reviewing here:

1. The distance walked to obtain water decreases.
2. The quality of water used improves.
3. The time and energy expended decrease.
4. The quantity of water used increases.
5. Improved supplies are more reliable.
6. All people who do not live too far from the improved supply will make use of it.
7. The additional time made available through improved supply may be put to productive use.
8. Improved supply means better health.
9. By providing more and better water for livestock, an improved water supply increases the returns for animal husbandry.
10. The economic benefits of water supply projects may be increased by using excess water for small-scale irrigation.
11. The economic benefits of surface water resources may be increased by using them for fishing.
12. An improved water supply provides a stimulus for the development of secondary economic activity.
13. A new water supply will encourage the clustering of settlement around the water point.
14. The input of improved water acts as an incentive to overall rural development.

Although undoubted benefits come from improvements in water supply, not all developments are positive. The time taken to reach the water point may be less, but one may encounter a long queue, and the savings in time may be less than expected. The quality of water may or may not be better. Taste, smell, and clarity–turbidity are very important aspects of water quality, and sometimes users may prefer the old to the new source. An improved supply may not be as reliable, particularly with bore holes or pump systems that may break down or encounter maintenance problems. The robustness and simplicity of water supply systems are key considerations for long-term development. Communal waterpoints, particularly if there is standing water (basins, troughs, ponds, hafirs), may pose serious health risks: They may transmit coliform bacteria; contagious diseases (e.g., cholera, typhoid); and hookworm, bilharzia, and malaria. If a water point also serves livestock, one may find the area soon trampled and churned, the graze in the immediate surroundings entirely gone, and increased gullying and soil erosion.

Environmental Sanitation

Water also needs to be examined from the standpoint of its quality after it is used. It is very easy to pollute water supplies with industrial wastes, sewage, garbage, and household waste, as well as with pesticides and chemical fertilizer runoff from fields. The larger the urban place, the more important it becomes to manage return water and pollution sources. Few third world towns and cities have water supplies, storm drains/sewers, and sewage treatment systems that meet the needs of the population. Trash removal in many cities is not provided. Instead, outside each house one finds a pit into which trash is tossed and periodically burned, sending a pall of acrid stench across the neighborhood. During the rains, many neighborhoods become flooded, and the effluent of pit latrines mixes with garbage and excess rainwater; the resulting conditions are hazardous to health, as well as unpleasant to live with.

The cost of building and maintaining water and sewage systems may be beyond a city government's means. In the early 1970s, the water supply for Dar es Salaam—piped from an intake on the Ruvu River, some 63 kilometers away—was so safe and clean that anyone could drink it straight from the tap. Pressure was good, and the supply was assured. By the early 1990s, in a city whose population had in the meantime more than doubled, the supply was irregular; water pressure was variable and inadequate to serve buildings at higher elevations; and water had to be boiled and filtered. Water left to settle overnight produced a layer of sediment at the bottom of the pan. These sorts of problems sometimes concatenate. Thus the fuel (electricity, wood, charcoal) needed to boil water to make it safe represents a waste of time, money, and resources.

AGRICULTURE AND LIVELIHOOD IN THE RURAL THIRD WORLD

We have been looking in on Kitemu wa Nguli and his family from time to time. In what follows, we describe kin-based livelihoods more generally, and consider ways they may be improved.

The Economy of Affection[6]

A kin-based society provides each of its members a life of wholeness: One produces what one consumes, makes what one uses, builds the house one lives in, helps and is helped in coping with hardship and risk by an extended network of kinfolk and neighbors, and lives a life comparatively clear in its values and expectations. One is within nature, not an entity seeking to subdue it. Ways of interpreting experience focus on and reinforce the whole—poetry, song, story, and dance; plastic representation and domestic art; and religious practice. One belongs; one is part of the community by virtue of birth—the *Gemeinschaft* of Tönnies (1887/1957). Opportunities to do things with others are not assessed by typical western cost accounting ("What's in it for me? What will it cost? How much time will it take?"). Göran Hydén (1983), a Swedish student of African development, has called this an "economy of affection," in contrast to the market economy or the centrally planned economy of modern industrialized states. Nearly everywhere, the economy of affection has been penetrated and affected by the global market economy. On the other hand, elements of kin-based society persist in varying degrees in modern societies—in barter, mutual aid, and other informal arrangements. Kin-based elements are most strongly developed and preserved among the poor and among minority groups, in part because these people are kept from participating in a significant portion of the market economy. Carol Stack (1974, 1996) has found patterns similar to those described here among African Americans: extensive, intricate patterns of kinship links and mutual aid, connecting urban dwellers in northern U.S. cities with their rural roots in the South.

The bonds among sisters are especially strong and enduring. Young men of a given age group also form strong lifelong friendships. Authority is commonly vested in a patriarchal gerontocracy. Young men and women experience age-graded rites of passage. In a kin-based society, one belongs by right of birth, and one has a clear view of life's course. The answers to various questions—"Who am I? What will I do? What will become of me?"—are all clearly known. Each person is part of a kinship that forms an unending river of the living, those not yet born, and those who have gone before.

We should not confuse the economy of affection with such emotions as fondness. According to Hydén (1983: 8), the economy of affection "denotes a network of support, connections and interaction among structurally defined groups connected by blood, kin, community or other affinities, for example, religion." Kin-based, rural, settled life provides ample scope for ill feeling and interpersonal conflict. Along with cooperation and mutual obligations of reciprocity (exchanges and sharing) come less congenial features: covert hostility, fear, aggression (generally expressed indirectly), tensions and inequalities between generations and between sexes, envy, discontent, gossip, and witchcraft (Edgerton, 1971; Lee, 1984: 87 ff.). In many instances, the powerful exploit the weak and control scarce resources unequally.

We should take special note of ways in which families use the economy of affection to distribute risks and share hardship. All human groups have a repertoire of institutions and ways of doing things that can be called upon to solve problems. A vast anthropological literature treats every phase of this theme—ways in which mutual aid is obligated and provided through kinship, through membership in the same age grade or clan, or through marriage or other contracts. We present one example in some detail, to give the reader a feel for the richness and social ramifications of ways of ensuring well-being for the members of a lineage-based society.

Pastoralism, which shares many commonalities with lineage agriculture, is a lifeway that requires unremitting attention to the needs and well-being of livestock. The members of a herding family must provide their stock with grazing, water, salt, and protection, day in and day out. It is a livelihood fraught with many and different risks. Some of the social institutions pastoralists have invented help disperse risks, and in doing this they accomplish other important social purposes.

At the base of Mount Elgon (in eastern Uganda), along the mountain's northwestern side, lives a group of Sebei-speaking people who devote much effort to herding (Goldschmidt, 1969, 1976). In managing a herd to distribute risk, a man has at least five ways of transferring cattle to another person. One of these is called the *namanya*, and it may be regarded as a "cattle futures" contract. Labu and Mwanga (not their real names) agree to an exchange of cattle. Labu needs a bullock for a feast and receives one in exchange for a heifer. Mwanga keeps the heifer until she has produced a heifer that in turn has matured sufficiently to show that she too is fertile, at which point the original heifer is returned to Labu along with any bull calves she has produced. This cycle takes a minimum of 5 years, and the average is closer to 10. Think of all that can happen in 10 years. Sebei herders may have scores of *namanya* arrangements with other people (kin and friends, living nearby and living far away). They have a saying: "Sweet is the cow of debt." These distributions of stock reduce the risk of having all of one's stock wiped out by disease, killed by lightning, or stolen. If stock are stolen and those in the *kraal* belong to many people, it is easier to mobilize help in pursuit of the thieves. If one's stock are dispersed, they are more difficult to count and tax.

Goldschmidt found that the Sebei herd is structured as a man's household is, in relation to the man himself, his wives, and his children. The cattle line is a lineage, with an indefinite continuity expressed in the pattern of inheritance, which itself reinforces the continuity of the family line. If a man chooses, he may allocate cattle to a wife in a ceremony called *teita nye kityeilwo* ("cattle that have been smeared"). The wife smears these cattle with cow dung; she holds them thereafter in trust for her sons. No one, including the husband, can sell them, trade them, or make any other arrangement regarding them without her permission. In Sebei society, it is an act that gives status to a wife and pleases her greatly.

When a wealthy herdsman—one with many *namanya* and other contractual arrangements—dies, he leaves behind a complicated estate. Goldschmidt observed the "probate" of Kambuya's estate:

> No experience so impressed me with the individuation of cattle as the recounting by Salima

> [Kambuya's eldest son] of the animals in his father's herd, in which he gave data on some 700 animals, their source, the exchanges made with them, the amounts received in cash, the person with whom trades were made, and occasionally idiosyncratic characteristics of the animals, covering a period of time extending back to before his own birth. (Goldschmidt, personal communication, 1968)

Salima could keep track because each animal belonged to a lineage. All cattle "belong." Through the *namanya* and other forms of exchange, the fortunes of Sebei pastoralists are inextricably linked. Contracts take so long to run their course that Sebei herders inevitably find themselves sharing interests over many years. (Another Sebei saying is "A debt never rots.") They develop deep friendships through their stock arrangements. Thus an institution that reduces economic risk also generates social obligations, responsibilities, common interests, and friendships. Lineage-based societies are characterized by their extended nature. Within a network of rights and obligations, they provide mutual aid and share out risk and hardship. Chapter 12 of this book presents a case study of social and spatial institutions among the Pokot of western Kenya (near neighbors to the Sebei); it describes how different rights and obligations, integral to Pokot management of their ecosystem for farming and for keeping livestock, make their livelihood and lives secure and resilient when under stress.

Third World Agricultural Productivity

There is no doubt that the yields per unit of area achieved by many local systems of agriculture in the third world are low in comparison with those achieved by using improved seeds and other technological inputs, such as fertilizers, pesticides, and herbicides (see Chapter 11, Table 11.1). However, these local systems, in comparison with industrial agriculture, often give high yields per unit of labor and sometimes (as with kitchen gardens or intensive horticultural forms) give high yields per unit area. They also characteristically do not require much financial outlay. The problem with these systems is their vulnerability when pressed to serve larger numbers of people using a fixed resource. When farming systems expand into areas unsuited to them, or when farmers use the same system more heavily without meliorating actions to preserve soil fertility, the system becomes stressed and environmental deterioration results. Full recovery of former soil fertility at the end of fallow before the next planting is crucial.

In 1965, a book containing many of Ester Boserup's ideas appeared: *The African Husbandman*, by William Allan (see Chapter 6, Table 6.3). It summarized research Allan had done much earlier in what is now Zambia. In the 1930s, working with the ecologist Colin Trapnell and the anthropologist Max Gluckman, Allan devised a method of determining how much land African groups need for their livelihoods. This method involves assessing soils and vegetation in any area, calculating the land's "carrying capacity," and using the livelihood system of the group in question. He asked local people four key questions: (1) "Which soils do you name and use in your farming?" (2) "How long do you rest each of these named soils after you have used it?" (3) "How many times do you cultivate this soil before letting it rest?" (4) "How many fields in fallow are needed, in addition to each garden in use in the current year?" He then measured fields to determine how much land a family needed. With this information in hand about any agricultural system, he could survey unused land, identify the amounts of different soils available, and calculate a critical population density (CPD) beyond which the environment would be stressed, fail to recover fertility, and begin to degrade.

According to Allan, if an area exceeds the CPD, permanent environmental degradation should in due course ensue, as people become caught in a downward spiral of declining yields. Lower yields should force farmers to return to fields before the customary fallow period has ended—that is, before fertility has been restored. When cropped, those fields should give lower yields than formerly, forcing the farmer to plant a larger area, which in turn should encroach further on the fallow land. There is thus a multiplier effect, and land deterioration is inevitable unless the system is changed, the population–resource relationship is rebalanced by out-migration, or measures are taken to restore soil fertility. To be sustainable, the means used must not degrade the soil in the long term, either through actual loss (erosion) or through change in chemical and physical structure. Allan arrived independently at Boserup's insight of viewing land as a continuum and agriculture as a management of different vegetation–soil complexes, depending on fallow length. Some of his terms are incorporated in Table 6.3.

The four questions Allan asked are incorporated in the formula for calculating the CPD:

$$\text{CPD} = 640/(100 \cdot \text{LU} \cdot \text{C/P})$$

where CPD is the critical population density, an ecological threshold; LU is the land use factor = (fl/cl + 1), fallow length in number of years (fl) divided by cultivation length in number of years (cl) plus 1 (this answers Allan's question 4, above); C is the cultivation factor, the average acreage planted per capita per year; and P is the cultivable percentage of the land. A worked example of calculating CPD is shown in Table 10.6.

Allan's is simultaneously the best approach and the worst approach. It is best because it seriously links the physical resource (soil–vegetation nexus) with actual human use of it, with a view to sustaining an equilibrium in fertility (offtake of nutrients, return of nutrients). It is worst because its equilibrium is maintained within a closed system, a status quo in which change is not envisaged. Agricultural systems are usually dynamic and change over time. Allan, working as a British colonial officer, applied a "game park" or "range management" model to peasant agriculture. On ranches and game parks, if an imbalance develops between graze/browse and stock, stock may be killed, sold, or moved to restore balance. In ensuring that the CPD is not exceeded, Allan's system would require the human equivalent—restricting entry into an area or removing people when the CPD is exceeded. Static, simplistic formulation is one of the serious inadequacies of models of agricultural carrying capacity.

Answers to the agricultural productivity conundrum do not lie in taking sides

TABLE 10.6. William Allan's CPD: A Worked Example

Suppose an area of 1 square mile (640 acres, 259 hectares) is cultivable as follows:

	LU factor	Percentage time[a]	Acres in crop	Acres in fallow	Acres not used
10% can be used every year	LU = 1	100	64.0	—	—
20% can be used every other year	LU = 2	50	64.0	64.0	—
60% can be used every 10 years	LU = 11	9	34.9	349.1	—
10% cannot be used	—	—	—	—	64.0
Totals			162.9	413.1	64.0

Note. The cultivable percentage (P) is 90.

The average LU factor is 3.54—that is, the total fallow land divided by the total cropped land (413.1/162.9 = 2.54) + 1.

Suppose that the cultivation factor (C) is 1.0.

Substituting in Allan's formula,

$$\text{CPD} = 640/(100 \cdot 3.54 \cdot 1.0/90) = 640/(354 \cdot 0.0111) = 640/3.9294 = 162.9.$$

Thus the CPD is 162.9 people per square mile, or 62.9 people per square kilometer.

[a]Percentage of time a given piece of land can be cropped.

Sustainable Agriculture in Cuba

An interesting "natural experiment" in sustainable agriculture was forced upon Cuba by the breakup of the Soviet Union in 1989 and the cessation of oil and other subsidies the USSR had provided Cuba until then (Rosset and Benjamin, 1994a). Virtually overnight, the supply of oil dropped 53%, and the price of gasoline rose to prohibitive levels. The availability of fertilizers, pesticides, and other chemicals dropped over 80% (Rosset and Benjamin, 1994b: 83). By 1992, Cuba's highly mechanized state farms found it necessary to idle about 20,000 tractors.

The government was not unprepared for the exigency of having external inputs cut off, since such possibilities had long been part of military preparedness (Levins, 1990: 134). Civil defense manuals covered agricultural production; municipal gardens have been a feature of Cuban agriculture for years; and Cubans have long had an interest in organic farming and sustainable agriculture.

In responding to events, a government-led "back to the land" program has reconfigured state farms as cooperative farms in which organic farming, use of animal traction for plowing and transport, locally made fertilizers (from compost, farmyard manure, etc.), integrated pest management, and increased human labor have been substituted for the previous agroindustrial methods. Science has not been rejected by Cuba in this transformation. Instead, it has been refashioned to use biological and organic approaches to soil, crop, and pest management, rather than the high-energy and high-chemical-input approach formerly used. Sophisticated use is made of pheromone traps, ant colonies (*Tetramorium*), parasitic wasps (*Trichogramma*), and bacillary and fungal sprays to control insect pests. Interplanting of "companion crops" (e.g., sweet potatoes with corn, cassava with beans) is used to enhance soil quality and use soil nutrients effectively.

Cuba's largely urban population has participated in this agricultural transformation. Some families have joined cooperative farms in return for housing and other perks. Some state farms have been reconstituted as cooperative farms by groups of urban families. On a rotating schedule, school children, government employees, factory workers, and other urban dwellers spend 2 weeks on rural cooperative farms during the agricultural season, providing labor. In the cities, many people cultivate "allotments" (small community gardens), thereby adding to food production. Classes in food canning and preservation have brought back methods reminiscent of U.S. family farms in the 19th and early 20th centuries.

This forced experiment in sustainable agriculture has succeeded in the sense that the Cuban people have been able to feed themselves. It has required considerable reordering of labor priorities, food rationing, and some degree of hardship; however, it provides interesting lessons related to sustainable farming—farming that is no longer dependent on high energy and high chemical inputs.

for or against organic farming or industrial agriculture (see sidebar: "Sustainable Agriculture in Cuba"). Either one by itself—careful husbandry or use of technical inputs—will increase yields, but when both are used in combination, yields are still further enhanced. The "maize diamonds" of A. Y. Allan (1969) illustrate this point nicely (Figure 10.7). The diamonds, based on actual field trials, illustrate the relative value of good husbandry versus use of technical inputs, and the gains to be made by using them together. Allan found that it availed nothing to pay for technical inputs but to use poor husbandry; the costs negated the benefits (358 vs. 327 Kenya shillings). Good husbandry, with no technical inputs, more than doubled yields (49.0 vs. 19.8 quintals/hectare). Good husbandry combined with the use of hybrid seed and fertilizers *quadrupled* yields (80.4 vs. 19.8 quintals/hectare).

Adoption of modern inputs has a serious disadvantage, however. As farmers give up using their own local seed in favor of hybrid seed, they enter a world with new and ramifying relations (Yapa, 1993a, 1996b; see Chapter 5 sidebar, "What Are Improved Seeds?"). First, they must purchase hybrid

Good Husbandry (GH) = planting early, at start of rains and correct population. 35,880 plants/hectare and clean weeding until tasselling.
Bad Husbandry (BH) = late planting, 4 weeks after start of rains and low population. 18,830 plants/hectare and one late weeding only.
Local Maize (LM) = unimproved seed from good local farmers.
Hybrid Maize (HM) = Hybrid 613 from Kitale, Kenya.
Fertilizers (F) = 280 kg/ha of single supers at planting plus 306 kg/ha of A.S.N. top-dressed at knee-height.

Diamond 1 showing specific combinations of treatments:

BH + LM, without F
BH + HM + F
GH + LM, without F
GH + HM + F

Diamond 2 showing yields: quintals/hectare (increases in parentheses)

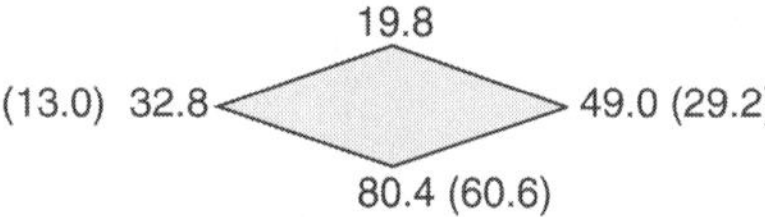

Diamond 3 showing extra costs/hectare: data in Kenya shillings (1969)

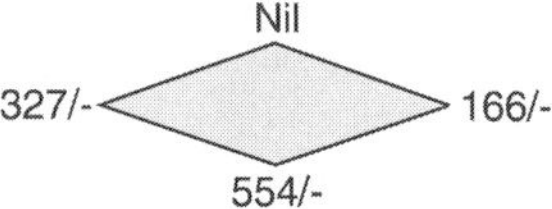

Diamond 4 showing extra gross income/hectare compared with income from 19.8 quintals/hectare:

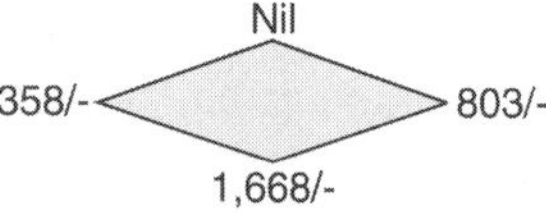

Diamond 5 showing differences between extra gross income and extra cost of obtaining that gross income:

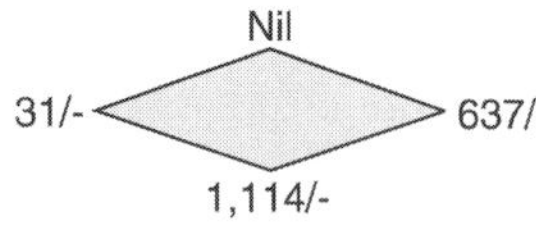

FIGURE 10.7. Maize diamonds, illustrating the value of good husbandry versus technical inputs. *Source:* Adapted from A. Y. Allan (1969). "Single supers" refers to a phosphate fertilizer; "A.S.N." refers to ammonium sulfate nitrogen.

seed. Second, farmers cannot use seed saved from the harvest of a crop grown with hybrid seed for the next season's crop; fresh seed must be bought for each subsequent planting. Third, farmers become dependent on an external organization for the timely delivery of hybrid seed and associated inputs. Fourth, the value in using hybrid seed is only realized by using the other components of the Green Revolution package of which the seeds are a part, as well as the associated labor discipline. Farmers are expected to purchase herbicides, pesticides, fungicides, and fertilizers to gain the yield increase from hybrids (see Figure 10.7). Provision of irrigation water may also be required and entail further costs. Fifth, there is a psychological dimension to switching to hybrid seed—an abrupt break in a feeling of continuity in farming. No longer is the planted seed something a farmer grew and saved for next year, and thus emblematic of a kind of genealogical connection with past crops. The seed is not in safe keeping in the house during the nonagricultural season. Rather, it becomes a commodity purchased elsewhere, symbolic of a new set of dependent relations with the supplier of seed and other inputs.

Agricultural Commodity Trade

The course of agricultural development in the third world cannot be understood without giving attention to the world food system, the international division of labor, and industrialization in the third world in recent decades. In 1950 third world countries accounted for 53% of agricultural exports, but by 1992 the figure had slipped to 24%. During this time, Japan and a group of middle-income third world countries increased their share of world manufacturing output from 19% to 37%. This was accomplished in part by food policies as well as industrial policies. When the General Agreement on Tariffs and Trade (GATT) was established in 1947, agricultural products, at the insistence of the United States, were specifically excluded from this effort to liberalize trade and remove tariff barriers. Thus the United States protected American farmers through import quotas and import tariffs, as well as crop price subsidies. The price supports went mainly to five crops: wheat, corn (maize), rice, sugar, and cotton. Thus protected, U.S. farmers generated surplus food.

The Public Law 480 Food Aid Program (known as PL 480), passed by the U.S. Congress in 1954, aided U.S. farmers in finding overseas markets for the surplus food. There were three parts to the PL 480 program: Title I, commercial sales at discounted prices, using local currencies; Title II, famine relief and food aid; and Title III, barter for strategic materials, usually minerals. Food aid early became the main component of the PL 480 program, much of it used to relieve third world food shortages. Since crop prices were subsidized, the food produced could be sold in foreign markets at low prices, competing heavily with local farmers. This became one of a number of assaults on rural livelihoods. As rural livelihoods became more difficult, many people left rural areas and migrated to cities, where they joined the ranks of low-paid and/or marginally employed workers. In some cases, such as South Korea, migrants became part of the low-paid industrial workforce and thereby helped to facilitate the country's ambitious industrialization goals. By contrast, much of Colombian agriculture collapsed under the impact of food aid, but there were few industrial jobs for those forced to migrate to the cities. Thus PL 480, and the international food regime that it helped to create, undermined third world agriculture and contributed to the development of burgeoning urban slums housing the underemployed people forced off the land, although in a few cases it aided third world industrialization (McMichael, 1996: 59–73).

By 1966, 80% of U.S. wheat exports were for food aid, and the United States accounted for 90% of all food aid (McMichael, 1996: 62). The local currencies generated by PL 480 were used as part of U.S. international development planning to foster U.S. business penetration and to change local food tastes, particularly those of urban populations. For example, in South Korea, breads and pastries made from imported wheat made tremendous gains at the expense of rice. McMichael (1996: 61) cites U.S.-subsidized programs in which bread was provided free of charge to school lunch programs and South Korean women were taught how to make sandwiches. Efforts to change third world diets also included promotion of consumption of beef, pork, and poultry. In agribusiness feedlot terms, cattle, pigs, and chickens are dependent on some combination of feed grains (maize, sorghum, oats, barley), alfalfa, and soybeans. The world's maize trade increased spectacularly, and in the late 1980s it was six times greater than that of wheat—a direct consequence of the growth in the third world's livestock industry (McMichael, 1996: 67).

In global terms, food production has kept ahead of population growth since 1960. World per capita food production grew by about 25% from 1961 to 2003 (Figure 10.8). Asia, in particular, increased its production by 43%. Food production in Africa, south of the Sahara, has been relatively stagnant, and by 2003 stood only 8% above the index value 42 years earlier. Grain imports have met some of this worsening food deficit, although food imports consumed valuable hard currency that could have been used in other ways (Figure 10.9) (Watts and Bassett, 1985: 23). Grain imports to Africa since 1961 have increased 10-fold and reflect some of the impacts of the PL 480 program.

Toxic Chemicals and Their Movement in the Biosphere

The use of pesticides is increasing in third world countries, whereas it is stabilizing or even declining in midlatitude areas because of burgeoning interest in integrated pest management.[7] Pesticides, herbicides, and fungicides may control pests and weeds, but they also create a serious pollution problem. The various compounds used (organochlorine and organophosphorus compounds, benzene hexachloride, and copper fungicides) are persistent in the soil, groundwater, and life forms (Adams, 1990: 117–122). They retain toxicity for a long time. When they enter the food chain, they can concentrate at higher trophic levels—for example, in fish, game animals, and livestock—and ultimately in the humans who consume these creatures (see Chapter 9 sidebar, "No Place Is Remote"). People also consume pesticides because of residues found on the surfaces and in the interior of fruits, vegetables, and grains.

A related problem is that as more pesticides are used, target pests develop greater resistance to them (National Research Council, 1986). For example, one report stated that by 1984, "638 pest species worldwide (428 arthropods, 50 weeds, 150 plant pathogens, and 10 small mammal pests and plant-attacking nematodes) were known to possess strains resistant to one or more pre-

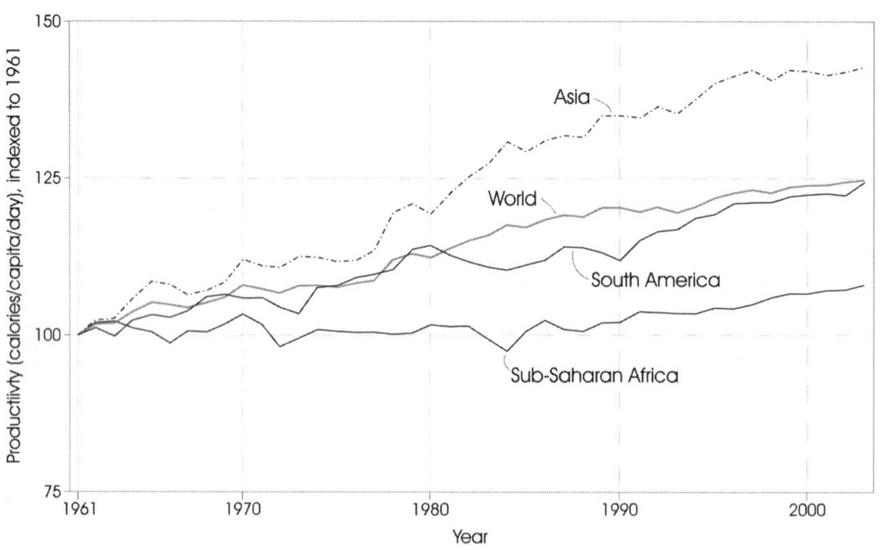

FIGURE 10.8. World per capita production of food, 1961 through 2003. *Source:* Data are from Food and Agriculture Organization (2006).

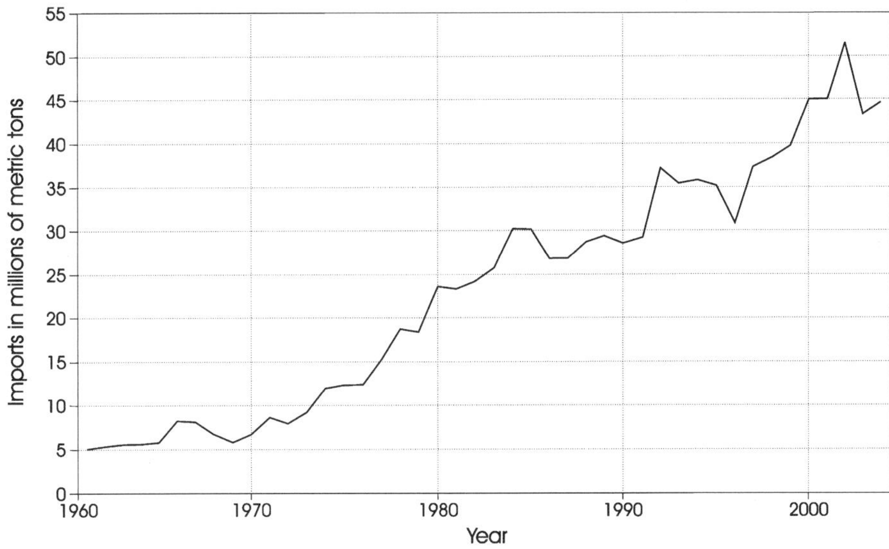

FIGURE 10.9. Cereal imports to Africa, 1961 through 2004. *Source:* Data are from Food and Agriculture Organization (2006).

viously effective pesticides" (Office of Technology Assessment [OTA], 1988: 261). The development of resistance to pesticides can lead to overuse (Norman, 1978).

The flow of toxic chemicals into third world countries is not well documented, but it is increasing greatly. In India, consumption of pesticides (a key component of the Green Revolution) rose 40-fold in two decades, from 2,000 tons annually in the 1950s to more than 80,000 tons in the mid-1980s (still a small amount on a per capita basis). Postel (1988: 121) stated: "Between 400,000 and 2 million pesticide poisonings occur worldwide each year, most of them among farmers in developing countries." An estimated 10,000–40,000 deaths occur each year from pesticide poisonings, and there are also health effects from chronic, low-level exposure. The Bhopal disaster—an industrial explosion at a Union Carbide pesticide plant in Bhopal, India, in 1984, which sent toxic fumes over the city, killing nearly 7,000 people and damaging the long-term health of hundreds of thousands of other residents—was only a spectacular example of the harmful effects of exposure to pesticides, whether such exposure is accidental or not.

The control of pesticides in third world countries is very lax (Bull, 1982). One can go into nearly any third world market and find small plastic packets of dangerous pesticides for sale—bags with no identification of the pesticides' names and no instructions on their use. Under such circumstances, a pesticide is likely to be handled in a dangerous manner, and frequently too much of it will be used on crops. Instances of mothers, uninformed as to the dangers, rubbing pesticides onto the heads of youngsters to kill head lice are common. According to the OTA (1988: 261), "about 25 percent of U.S. pesticide exports were chemicals that have been heavily restricted, suspended, or prohibited in domestic markets." The organochlorides (e.g., dichlorodiphenyltrichloroethane, or DDT) used in the 1950s have largely, but not entirely, been phased out of use in the third world. Many third world countries currently do not have in place the necessary laws or the institutional capacity (inspections, record keeping, quarantine facilities, etc.) to control the flow of poten-

Sustainability Science

As Ruttan (1994: 211) observed, "It is not uncommon for a social movement to achieve the status of an ideology while still in search of a methodology or a technology." Another feature is that new terms proposed by a progressive but marginalized group may be coopted or undergo "establishment appropriation" by mainstream organizations (Ruttan, 1994: 211). This has happened to sustainability. In some definitions, sustainability may be valued for the fact that it obscures equity issues tied to class and social relations, and focuses instead on an abstraction—the protection of nature.

Ideas about sustainability and sustainability science have developed considerably in scope and sophistication since the first edition of *A World of Difference* was published. In 2005, at the World Economic Forum in Davos, Switzerland, the environmental sustainability index (ESI) was unveiled (Yale Center for Environmental Law and Policy, 2005a). The ESI is based on 76 *variables* (data sets about the environment), which are collapsed into 21 *indicators* of environmental sustainability, and five fundamental *components* of sustainability. "The ESI ranks countries on 21 elements of environmental sustainability, covering natural resource endowments, past and present pollution levels, environmental management efforts, contributions to protection of the global commons, and a society's capacity to improve its environmental performance over time" (Yale Center for Environmental Law and Policy, 2005b: 1). For example, nitrogen dioxide, sulfur dioxide, and particulate concentrations in the atmosphere, plus indoor air quality, constitute the variables for air quality (one of the 21 indicators). Air quality, biodiversity, land, water quality, and water quantity together constitute environmental systems. The other four components are reducing environmental stresses, reducing human vulnerability, social and institutional capacity, and global stewardship. One of the central goals of the ESI research and publication program is to provide benchmarks for individual countries so that they can see how they compare with other countries—where they are strong and where they could improve their performance. The benchmarks provide quantitative data that are supposed to enable governments to make "data-driven" policy. The variables that correlate most closely with the ESI are civil and political—civil and political liberties, government effectiveness, political institutions, and participation in international environmental agreements.

No country is fully environmentally sustainable at this point, but some do much better than others. Finland, with a score of 75.1, ranks first, while North Korea, with 29.2, ranks 146th. The United States ranks 45th, between Armenia and Myanmar. On certain scores, such as water quality and environmental protection capacity, the United States ranks high, but when greenhouse emissions and waste generation are added, its overall score is much lower. There are many online sources of information about ESI (see *www.yale.edu/esi*).

tially disease-bearing plants and dangerous pesticides.

Pesticides are increasingly popular with third world farmers, and they are particularly effective in protecting foods in storage. There are undoubted benefits in using pesticides for crop protection as they are growing. Sometimes the yield benefits are an order of magnitude (10 times) greater than the yield for an unprotected crop. The trick will be to walk the fine line between precise, targeted use in the right amounts and at the right times, and overuse and misuse, resulting in health problems, needless expense, and the emergence of pesticide resistance in pest species.

Agricultural Research

For third world people to meet their food needs, they will have to increase their agricultural research and extension services, and to incorporate certain technological advances. How is this to be done? Answers may lie in building the institutional capacity to do basic research for each important crop in every agroclimatic region of the world (Ruttan, 1986: 307). Small third world countries have an especially difficult task in building such capacity, and regional consortia have not proved effective.

Global institutions designed to increase agricultural production began with the colonial agricultural services—for example, Great Britain's Empire Cotton Growing Corporation, founded in 1917 (Masefield, 1950: 87). The United Nations established the Food and Agriculture Organization (FAO) in the early 1950s. Efforts by the Ford Foundation and the Rockefeller Foundation in international agricultural research, begun in the late 1950s, evolved into the 15+ institutions that made up the Consultative Group on International Agricultural Research (CGIAR) in 2005. Figure 10.10 gives the full names of the member institutions of the CGIAR. The first four CGIAR institutions were started with Ford and Rockefeller support: the International Rice Research Institute (IRRI) in 1960; the Centro Internacional de Mejoramiento de Maíz y Trigo (CIMMYT) in 1966; IITA in 1967; and the Centro Internacional de Agricultura Tropical (CIAT) in 1968. These centers concentrated respectively on rice, maize/wheat, and tropical food crops (cassava, yams, sweet potatoes, and tropical pulses). Between 1968 and 1980, nine more institutions were added, and in recent years several more have been created (Figure 10.10). All but three of the CGIAR institu-

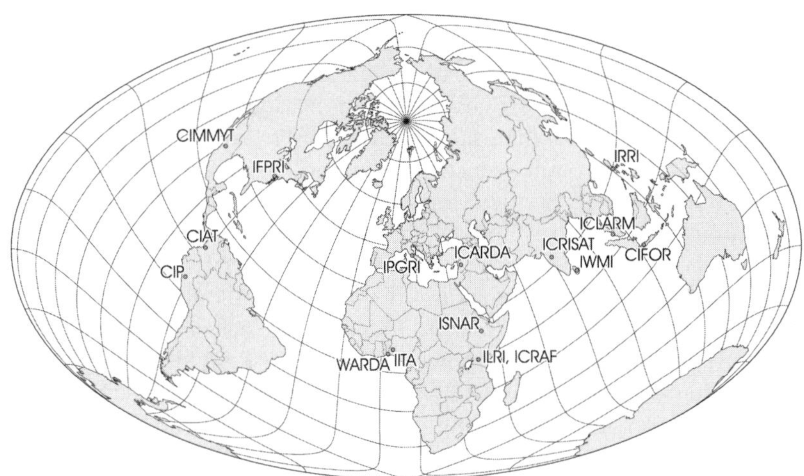

CGIAR - The Consultative Group on International Agricultural Research

Africa Rice Center (formerly WARDA), Cotonou, Benin
CIAT - Centro Internacional de Agricultura Tropical, Cali, Colombia
CIFOR - Center for International Forestry Research, Bogor, Indonesia
CIMMYT - Centro Internacional Mejoramiento de Maiz y Trigo, Mexico City, Mexico (maize and wheat)
CIP - Centro Internacional de la Papa, Lima, Peru (potatoes)
ICARDA - International Center for Agricultural Research in Dry Areas, Aleppo, Syrian Arab Republic
ICRISAT - International Crops Research Institute for the Semi-Arid Tropics, Patancheru, India
IFPRI - International Food Policy Research Institute, Washington, D.C., U.S.A.
IITA - International Institute of Tropical Agriculture, Ibadan, Nigeria
ILRI - International Livestock Research Institute, Nairobi, Kenya
IPGRI - International Plant Genetic Resources Institute, Rome, Italy
IRRI - International Rice Research Institute, Los Baños, Philippines
ISNAR - International Service for Agricultural Research, Addis Ababa, Ethiopia
IWMI - International Water Management Institute, Colombo, Sri Lanka
World AgroForestry Centre (formerly ICRAF), Nairobi, Kenya
WorldFish Center (formerly ICLARM), Penang, Malaysia

FIGURE 10.10. The Consultative Group on International Agricultural Research (CGIAR) and its member groups.

tions are in tropical or subtropical locations. They have expanded the research focus to include potatoes (the Centro Internacional de la Papa [CIP], Lima, Peru); semi-arid crops, such as chickpeas, pigeon peas, pearl millet, sorghum, and groundnuts (the International Crop Research Institute for the Semi-Arid Tropics [ICRISAT], Patancheru, India, and the International Center for Agricultural Research in the Dry Areas [ICARDA], Aleppo, Syria); rice (the Africa Rice Center, formerly the West African Rice Development Association [WARDA], Cotonou, Benin); and livestock and livestock disease control (the International Livestock Research Institute [ILRI], Nairobi, Kenya). The two centers presently outside tropical and subtropical locations are in Washington, D.C. (the International Food Policy Research Institute [IFPRI], which deals with food policy worldwide), and Rome, Italy (the International Plant Genetic Resources Institute [IPGRI], which collects, inventories, and maintains a worldwide collection of plant genetic resources). The International Service for National Agricultural Research (ISNAR), which deals with agricultural research and institution building, closed its operations in The Hague, The Netherlands, in 2003, and moved to Addis Ababa, Ethiopia; it is now under IFPRI governance. Among CGIAR's strengths have been its oversight and its long-term planning. Research institutions are autonomous, but are reviewed and periodically evaluated by CGIAR and a Technical Advisory Committee.

In the early 1990s, four other international agricultural centers joined the CGIAR system: the International Water Management Institute (IWMI); the Center for International Forestry Research (CIFOR); the International Center for Research on Agro-Forestry (ICRAF), since renamed the World Agroforestry Centre; and the International Center for Living Aquatic Research Management (ICLARM), renamed the World-Fish Center, which deals with aquaculture and fisheries. As the system has expanded, however, funding for both the established and the new centers has declined. In part, they are victims of the end of the Cold War. Furthermore, some of the older centers have experienced a decline in the élan, dynamism, and productivity of their early years. This reflects the "natural history of research institutes"—cycles of creativity and stagnation that occur in all institutions (Ruttan, 1986: 312–313).

Meanwhile, what of national centers in third world countries? East Africa provides an example that may be replicated in many other third world countries. When independence came to Kenya, Uganda, and Tanganyika (1961–1963), a superb agricultural and forestry research organization existed at Muguga, 31 kilometers west of Nairobi, Kenya. It was known as the East African Agricultural and Forestry Research Organization (EAAFRO). A companion organization, the East African Veterinary Research Organization (EAVRO), flourished nearby. EAAFRO's extensive research library had been built around a German research library formerly located at Amani, Tanganyika, which was confiscated by the British during World War I. With the breakup of the East African Community in late 1976, the cooperative science institutions were dismembered. EAAFRO became the Kenya Agricultural Research Institute (KARI), and the Ugandan and Tanzanian staff members returned home. External sources of funding declined. Expatriate scientists left and Kenyan scientists gradually replaced them, although often these staff members were overseas (Australia, The Netherlands, United Kingdom, etc.) taking courses or pursuing advanced degrees. KARI's institutional capacity to run a research program was weakened. Indeed, the CGIAR institutions attracted some of the better scientists away from national agricultural research institutions, offering higher pay and better opportunities to conduct research (Wang'ati, personal communication, 1989).

In 1993, one of us (PWP) and a family member spent some months at Mlingano Agricultural Research Institute, in Tanga

Region, northeastern Tanzania. It is the premier soils research institution in Tanzania, responsible for formulating research policy respecting soils and agriculture and for mapping Tanzania's soils. While we were there, lack of electricity was a constant problem. A couple of quotes from our journal explain:

> 22 February 1993—We picked up Pitio, prior to going to Mzundu, and he relayed the bad news that the lease on the generator at Mlingano has ended and the company that owns the generator has come and taken it away, leaving Mlingano Agricultural Research Institute and the associated Agricultural Training Institute without electricity. No work is being done, no laboratory work, no computers can be run, cartography, printing, and lots of analytical procedures. Tanesco [the national electricity company] doubled the late bill (two months late) and there continues to be a big argument. Meanwhile the Dutch team [helping develop Tanzanian soils research capacity] had a big discussion to decide what they might do. (When I talked with them Tuesday they said they might simply withdraw and return to the Netherlands, since the idea is to build capacity among Tanzanians, and that would not be accomplished if the Dutch team withdrew to Tanga and continued its work there by themselves. That would not help with institution building, which was the topic of a big conference in early November.) (Porter and Porter, 1993: 77)

> 10 March 1993—Went to Mlingano in the morning. Everyone was at a meeting and there was still no electricity. We went to the library, but not even the librarian was there, just a few people reading newspapers. It seemed to me that most of the journals in the library stopped at about 1973. (Porter and Porter, 1993: 88)

The difficulty of creating and sustaining effective national agricultural research systems is summarized by Ruttan (1986: 318–319):

> 1) Excessive investment in research facility relative to development of scientific staff . . . , 2) Excessive administrative burden that stifles both routine investigations and research entrepreneurship . . . , 3) Location decisions for major research facilities, often made with the advice of assistance agency consultants, have frequently failed to give adequate weight to the actors that contribute to a productive research location [well-chosen agroclimate location, appropriate professional infrastructure, resources (soils, water), and infrastructure (electricity, transport, and amenities)] . . . , 4) Lack of congruence between research budgets and the economic importance of major commodities or commodity groupings . . . , 5) The apparent presumption in some national systems that it is possible to do research in agricultural science without scientists . . . , 6) The cycles of development and erosion of capacity that have characterized a number of national agricultural research systems . . . , and 7) Lack of information and analysis that goes into establishment of research priorities . . .

AGRICULTURE AND SUSTAINABILITY

As human populations grow in the third world, the task of increasing agricultural productivity on a sustainable basis becomes more urgent. In the past, increases in agricultural production were gained mainly by adding land; in the current century, increased production over much of the world must come from intensification of agriculture on land already in use (Ruttan, 1994: 212). In the first world, there has been a decrease in yield response to use of fertilizer; "maintenance research" (keeping current yields from declining) has increased as a proportion of the research effort (Plucknett and Smith, 1986).

As concern for the environment has increased, there is greater interest in finding ways to use the environment that can be sustained indefinitely. The current litany of environmental concerns includes the threat of chlorofluorocarbons (CFCs) to the ozone layer; global warming, with attendant risks of rise in sea level; the poleward spread of tropical diseases; stresses on vegetation and agriculture that are related to climate change; floral and faunal decline and species extinctions; land degradation, soil erosion, impoverishment, waterlogging, and salinization; deforestation; industrial and urban pollution of air, soil, subsoil, and marine environments; and, finally, the questions about generational equity and ethics that these changes raise.[8] Thus, over a short period, "sustainability" has become a new watchword, although it is a term variously (and vaguely) defined and appropriated by groups with different goals and objectives (see sidebar: "Sustainability Science"). Williams and Millington (2004: 99) cited a study that gave "80 different, often competing and sometimes contradictory definitions" of sustainability. Agricultural production will have to increase while the above-listed global changes are occurring, and it needs ultimately to be done in a sustainable way.

Because there is an immense plasticity in plant materials, there is great scope for improving the yields and productivity of tropical crops. Many of these have not yet been well studied by western agronomy, but their characteristics and virtues are part of indigenous knowledge. We note in Chapter 11 the claim by the Board on Science and Technology for International Development (1996) that there are 2,000 native grains and fruits ready for "rediscovery" and exploitation. As western science directs greater attention to crops it has not yet studied extensively, such as amaranth (*Amaranthus* spp.), bonavist beans (*Lablab niger*), quinoa (*Chenopodium quinoa*), mung beans (*Phaseolus aureus*), and many others, the local knowledge of third world farming men and women—their science and their technology—can help materially in the quest for sustainable agriculture and food security.

CONCLUSIONS

We hope this chapter has conveyed the idea that biophysical environments in the third world are complex, are easy to injure, and offer different sets of opportunities and challenges than higher-latitude environments do. This does not mean that third world places are poor or marginalized because of their biophysical environments. Rather, it means that people must take care to adjust to the particular opportunities and challenges of the tropics and subtropics. Management of tropical and subtropical systems (soils, vegetation, insect and animal pests, and water) requires great knowledge if they are not to be harmed. Techniques both from local knowledge and from western agronomy and engineering play key roles in determining what can be done sustainably from place to place in agriculture in the third world. A significant body of environmental wisdom is bound up in the hard-earned knowledge of indigenous groups, learned by experiment and by trial and error over long periods. Western agronomic knowledge also evolved over a long period of time, particularly in northern Europe in another geographical context. It should not surprise anyone that the application of western agronomic practices in tropical environments does not always work as planned.

It would be folly to argue that local practice is always wise and environmentally sound, or that western techniques are always harmful. We can be hopeful for the sustained human use of the tropical world. There is much scope for a fruitful sharing of knowledge and experience about tropical and subtropical ecosystems, and it should be clear that genuine, beneficial exchanges can occur in both directions (Breemer, Drijver, and Venema, 1995; Goldman, 1995).

Many urgent tasks lie ahead for agricultural research in the tropics and subtropics. There is a special need to design viable short-rotation systems to replace the more extensive slash-and-burn or other long-rotation systems now in use, and to find ways to increase nitrogen fixation, such as alley cropping, discussed earlier (Ruttan, 1986: 315). "If the less-developed countries are to establish a viable base for self-sustained scientific effort leading to productivity growth, it is important that they establish a capacity to work on the fundamental problems that are of particular significance in tropical environments" (Ruttan, 1986: 310). And we must never lose sight of the fact that sustainable productivity growth is not merely (or perhaps even principally) a technical concern, but one tied up in diverse values, knowledges, institutions, livelihoods, and economies. Cooperation and collaboration, rather than competition, are called for between international and national research systems and those who live by agriculture. Local knowledge, like that exhibited by Kitemu wa Nguli and his family, also needs to contribute to the tasks of framing priorities, designing and carrying out research, and evaluating its usefulness.

NOTES

1. Although there is fearful complexity in the study of soils in tropical and subtropical areas, there are some very useful references. For further reading, we recommend Coleman (1996), Gersmehl, Kammrath, and Gross (1980), Greenland and Lal (1977), Moran (1987), National Research Council (1982), Sanchez and Cochrane (1980), and Silva (1985).

2. Cation exchange capacity (CEC) is a measure of the ability of soil particles to retain positively charged ions of such minerals as calcium, magnesium, and phosphorus. In other words, CEC is the size of the storage box. Base saturation (the percentage of positively charged ions other than aluminum and hydrogen—e.g., magnesium, potassium, calcium) is the percentage of CEC occupied by usable bases, a measure of minerals available for plant uptake. These tend to be low in highly leached soils, such as oxisols and the upper layers of entisols, and higher in soils with greater clay fractions. (No generalization is without exception: Leached soils can be high in CEC, and nonleached soils, with high base saturation, can be low in CEC.) The pH, which expresses a soil's degree of acidity–alkalinity, is a measure of the balance between free ions of hydrogen and other elements. When they are in balance, the number is 7. The scale runs from 1 to 14, and each integer represents a change by an order of magnitude. Thus a soil with a pH of 6 is 10 times more acid than one at 7, and one with a pH of 5 is 100 times more acidic (values higher than 7 indicate alkalinity). In our experience, tropical soils range between a pH of 7.2 for montane forest soils and a pH of 4.5 for highly leached oxisols. Not only is the latter soil poor in plant nutrients, but it has two other drawbacks: (a) It probably has a low CEC, as well as low base saturation (and thus is not able to retain minerals when they are supplied by the farmer); and (b) the soil probably has a low water-holding capacity, which makes crops vulnerable to moisture stress when rains are poor. Most soils in third world locations are somewhat acidic (say, a pH of 6.5), although soils with low CEC do not even store hydrogen or aluminum ions, and can therefore test neutral.

3. An extended footnote describing these soils according to Scott's (1969) soils map can be found in the first edition of this book.

4. This section draws from Porter (1976a: 134–135).

5. The Agro-climatological Survey of Tanzania was a research project of the Bureau of Resource Assessment and Land Use Planning, University of Dar es Salaam, Tanzania. In the period September 1971 to October 1972, the first Agricultural Census of Tanzania was undertaken. The census was actually a sample survey of approximately 16,000 farm households, carried out by 380 field investigators. The survey was based on a sample of 1,083 enumeration areas (EAs) stratified by region, district, and division, and sampled in proportion to the number of people in the division. Census schedules of the Agro-climatological Survey of Tanzania, administered in October and November 1972, were completed for 1,040 EAs. Of these, 916 (88%) were deemed worthy of further analysis. The analysis, then, was based implicitly on a sample survey of about 16,000 farm households.

6. The first part of this section is adapted from Porter (1987: 3–4). Copyright 1987 by *Geografiska Annaler.* Adapted by permission.

7. One of the best sources for current research on pesticides, toxic substances in the biosphere, and many other environmental concerns is the Swedish journal of the human environment, *Ambio*. In covering topics ranging from acidification to zinc, it gives considerable attention to atmospheric pollution, cadmium, DDT, energy, forests, fresh waters, health, heavy metals, marine waters, mercury, nitrogen, nuclear power, nuclear war, organochlorines, ozone, PCBs, pesticides, pollution, and waste (*Ambio*, 1986).

8. Under the general rubric of sustainable development (Wilbanks, 1994), there has been

much discussion in recent years about biological diversity and species extinction (Wolf, 1988); desertification and land degradation, a concern of long standing (Dalby and Church, 1973; Eckholm and Brown, 1977; Brown and Wolf, 1985; Adams, 1990; Little and Horowitz with Nyerges, 1987; African Academy of Sciences, 1989; Blaikie, 1985; Bot, Nachtergale, and Young, 2000; Food and Agriculture Organization, 2000); habitat loss in the cutting of tropical forests; the cultivation and overgrazing of woodlands and savannas; sustainable management of ecosystems (Merchant, 1992; Brown et al., 1984–2007; Gore, 1992; Turner, 1990); and environmental ethics and generational equity (Naess, 1990; Norgaard, 1994; Kalof and Satterfield, 2005; Curtin, 2005; Paavola and Lowe, 2005).

11 Nature as Latitudinal Trickster

The Carbon Cycle and Plant Growth

Kitemu has estimated that from his large field (see Plate 10.1) in a good season, he would get 40 bags of maize, four bags of cowpeas, two bags of sorghum, and six bags of millet (90.9-kilogram bags). Of this yield, he would only consider about eight bags as surplus that he might sell. He never sells cowpeas. Pigeon peas do not do well here, but they do much better at the Mukokoni farm. In the past few years, Kitemu's total harvest from all fields in Kilungu has averaged six bags of food—crops of all types—and he has been forced to buy maize. At the Mukokoni farm, Kitemu should in a good year obtain 80 bags of maize, six bags of cowpeas, nine bags of millet, seven bags of sorghum, and eight bags of pigeon peas. For the past few years, the harvest has been about two or three bags of maize, two bags of millet, one bag of sorghum, and one bag of cowpeas; the pigeon peas have failed almost completely. As one can see, yields fluctuate tremendously from good years to bad years, so an "average yield" has a rather artificial meaning. In Kitemu's fields, then, yields in a good year work out to be about 6.1 quintals/hectare, and in a poor year they work out to be about 1.1 quintals/hectare or less. (A quintal is 100 kilograms or 220 pounds; a hectare is 2.471 acres.)

This is a very low yield, and it is no wonder that Kitemu plants such a large area, given that the yield per unit area is so low. He knows that yields in high-potential areas elsewhere in Ukambani are much higher, but he does not know the whole story. He is unaware of the "dirty trick" nature has played on those who live in the tropics and who grow grains. Perhaps some readers as well are not fully informed about nature as "latitudinal trickster."

PHOTOSYNTHESIS AND THE CARBON CYCLE

"Where winter never comes!" This is a pleasant idea, evoking images of warmth, vegetative luxuriance, and relaxed living in the minds of many readers. Indeed, the phrase provided the title for a book by Marston Bates (1952), subtitled *A Study of Man and Nature in the Tropics*. A view widely held by the general public is that although the tropics may have some environmental drawbacks (poor soils, unreliable rains, endemic diseases), there is no thermal problem; one can grow almost anything. This view ignores a fact of fundamental importance, however. There are major differences in the worldwide distribution of potential photosynthesis—differences that give midlatitude lands a considerable agricultural advantage over tropical lands. This advantage has been "built in" by nature; no amount of biotechnological tinkering is likely to eliminate it. This chapter explores this important difference.

Photosynthesis in plants is a chemical process in which chlorophyll uses visible light to produce the carbohydrates needed for plant growth out of water and carbon dioxide (CO_2). Carbon participates in a continuous, complex flow of creation and decomposition, which we call the "carbon cycle." In its simplest form, the carbon cycle can be expressed in the equation shown below.

There is a "fearful symmetry" to this equation. Carbon is organized for a time, bound with hydrogen and oxygen atoms in the form of carbohydrates, while simultaneously oxygen is released to the atmosphere. Ultimately, however, with decomposition, the carbohydrates revert to their earlier state (H_2O and CO_2), but with a twist in the story line—*heat* rather than *light* as the end product. (One could find *heaven* and *hell* in this progression.)

Perhaps the symmetry is better regarded as reassuring, because the global distribution of carbon exhibits equilibrium in the long term—with carbon, hydrogen, and oxygen flowing among different parts of the biosphere, maintaining an oxygenated atmosphere so vital to communities of living organisms (see sidebar: "The Biological Carbon Cycle"). Indeed, even at geological time scales, the picture is generally reassuring: Even though there have been immense fluctuations in CO_2 in the atmosphere (in Cretaceous times, 100 million years ago, there was probably 18 times as much CO_2 in the atmosphere as we have today), life has flourished and evolved (Berner and Lasaga, 1989: 19).

Agriculture may be defined as the exploitation of solar energy, conditioned by the genetic constitution of plants, in the presence of an adequate supply of water and soil nutrients. When temperature is not limiting, and CO_2 concentration in the air is constant, the photosynthetic rate increases with solar radiation to a point known as "saturation light intensity." The relationship between light and photosynthesis (Figure 11.1) as given by Monteith (1965: 18) is described by this equation:

$$P = (a + b/I)^{-1}$$

where P is the rate of photosynthesis, *a* is a constant proportional to the resistance of the diffusion of CO_2, *b* is a constant proportional to photochemical resistance, and I is light intensity in gram calories/square centimeter/minute.

When P is expressed in grams of carbohydrate/square meter of leaf/hour, and I is expressed in langleys/minute, the value of *b* is almost constant at 3×10^4 calories/gram, but the value of *a* varies with the plant species—ranging, for example, from 0.25 per square meter/hour/gram for sugar cane to 1.30 per square meter/hour/gram for tomatoes. (A langley is a measure of energy; 1 langley = 1 gram calorie/square centimeter, and 590 gram calories/square centimeter is sufficient to evaporate or vaporize 1 cubic centimeter of water. This last value is useful to know when one is considering evaporation and crop water requirements.) Figure 11.1 shows that the rate of photosynthesis increases rapidly as solar radiation increases, but then

$$\text{light} + H_2O + CO_2 \rightarrow O_2 + \underset{\text{[carbohydrates]}}{[CH_2O]_n} \rightarrow \underset{\text{[decomposition]}}{CO_2 + H_2O + \text{heat}}$$

The Biological Carbon Cycle

The flow of carbon in the biosphere is shown schematically in the adjacent figure. There are two distinct but related cycles—one between the atmosphere and land, the other between the atmosphere and the ocean (and ocean floor). Before the industrial revolution and widespread human use of fossil hydrocarbons (coal and oil), the system was in balance. The combustion of coal and oil, which releases CO_2 into the atmosphere, has set the biosphere on a course wherein over the past 150 years there has been a gradual increase in the amount of CO_2 in the atmosphere. CO_2 levels were generally about 280 parts per million (ppm) before humankind began burning coal in great quantities. By the year 2000, the levels had reached ~370 ppm.

Concerns about the "greenhouse effect" and global warming are very much in the news these days, and meteorologists and oceanographers have reached a consensus that recent warming represents an ongoing, long-term change in global climates (Intergovernmental Panel on Climate Change [IPCC], 2007a, 2007b).

There is no agreement as to what actions government, industry, and individuals should take (see National Geographic Society, 1993). Although in theory an increase in CO_2 in the atmosphere increases the amount of carbon fixation in living plants, the warming of the atmosphere has even greater impacts—reflected in increased evaporation and water requirements of plants; heat and moisture stress on plant communities adapted to cooler environments; and so forth (see Chapter 9 sidebar, "Global Warming, Arctic and Elsewhere").

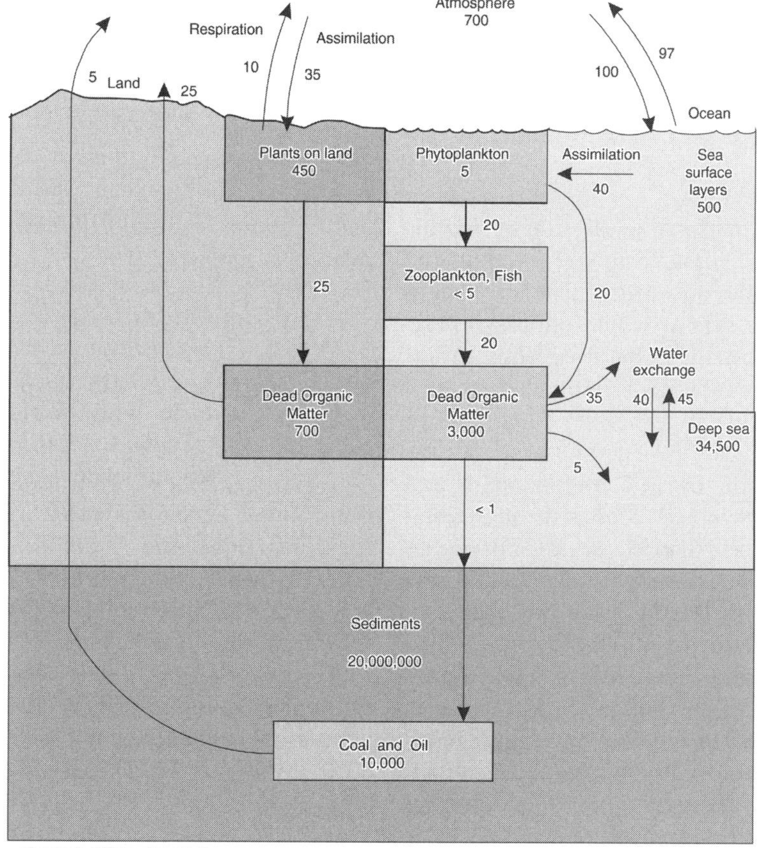

The Biological Carbon Cycle. Carbon circulation in the biosphere. *Source*: Adapted from Bolin (1970). Copyright 1970 by *Scientific American*, Inc. Adapted by permission.

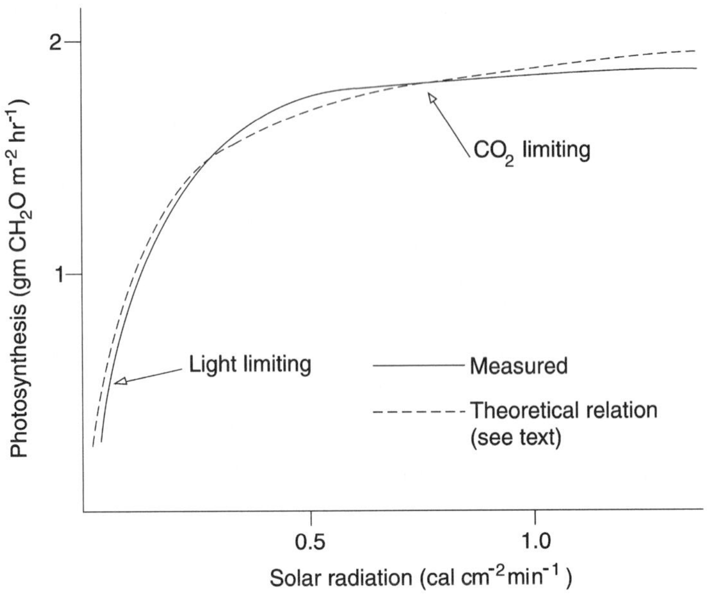

FIGURE 11.1. Assimilation rate of sugar beet leaf. Photosynthesis is given in grams of carbohydrate/square meter of leaf/hour; solar radiation is given in gram calories/square centimeter/minute (i.e., langleys/minute). *Source:* Adapted from Monteith (1966). Copyright 1966 by Cambridge University Press. Adapted by permission.

levels off. The reason it levels off (at 0.5 calories/centimeter square/minute) is that the stomata (cellular structure of the leaf) begin to control the rate at which photosynthesis takes place. Visualize a bathtub: You can add more water, but it will drain only so fast.

The chemical processes involved in plant growth also use energy, which means that some of the organic compounds stored through photosynthesis are lost through respiration—a process that releases CO_2 back into the atmosphere. Photosynthesis occurs only during daylight (leaving aside the complexities of crassulacean acid metabolism, which do not concern us here), whereas respiration occurs all the time. At night, dark respiration is continuous. During the day, photo respiration and photosynthesis proceed together, with a net balance in favor of fixing more CO_2 than is respired. Indeed, there is a daily cycle in the content of CO_2 in the air at treetop level (Figure 11.2), decreasing to about 305 ppm at noon and rising to about 340 ppm during the night (Bolin, 1970).

Respiration increases linearly with temperature. For example, alfalfa shows this relationship (Chang, 1968):

$$R = 0.533 + 0.078T$$

where R is grams of CO_2 respired/64 minutes and T is temperature in degrees Celsius (°C).

The net effect of respiration is to reduce the amount of photosynthate permanently fixed in plant tissue. It could be viewed as a "tax" (gross photosynthesis – respiration loss = net or potential photosynthesis). In temperate climates, most plants have a respiration loss of 20–30% of gross photosynthesis. In the tropics, respiration losses are more commonly in the range of 50–60% (Chang, 1968; Monteith, 1972: 756).

PHOTOSYNTHESIS AND LATITUDINAL CONTRASTS

A striking geography of potential photosynthesis emerges when we examine the geographic and temporal distribution of light and temperature. In the tropics, where winter never comes, every day is almost exactly 12 hours long. Moments after the sun sets (and depending on moon and weather), the sky is lit with a million stars. There is never a long twilight. At middle and high latitudes, however, the summer season brings long days and short nights. Photosynthesis can occur for many hours each day, and dark respiration is reduced because of the shortened night. Warm days and cool nights are ideal for plant growth, because dark (nighttime) respiration is lower than it is in areas that have warm nights. Length of daylight and rates of dark respiration vary systematically with latitude and season. Although on an annual basis the tropics have a higher potential photosynthesis, for periods of 4–5 months (the "window" within which most major grains are grown) during the summer of the hemisphere, the rates of potential photosynthesis are far greater in midlatitude locations than those possible in the tropics. After all, any one month is pretty much like every other month at the equator as far as daylength is concerned.

When we combine longer periods of daylight with reduced dark respiration, we find a significantly enhanced potential for photosynthesis in middle and higher latitudes during the 4-month summer season. Figure 11.3 shows the pattern of potential photosynthesis based on the best 4 months of the year (May–August in the northern hemisphere, November–February in the southern hemisphere). Rates of potential photosynthesis in the third world tropics are generally less than 25 grams/square meter/day, rising to 30 at the margins of the subtropics. Note that the world's "breadbaskets"—the plains areas where wheat and maize are grown (the Great Plains and Corn Belt of the United States, and the plains areas of

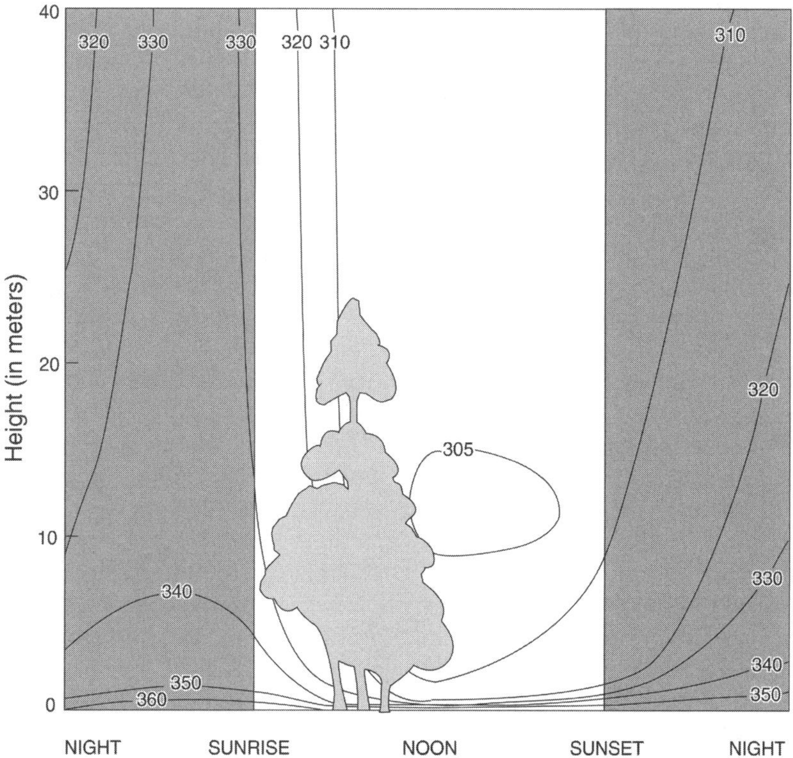

FIGURE 11.2. Vertical and diurnal distribution of CO_2 (in parts per million). *Source:* Adapted from Bolin (1970). Copyright 1970 by *Scientific American*, Inc. Adapted by permission.

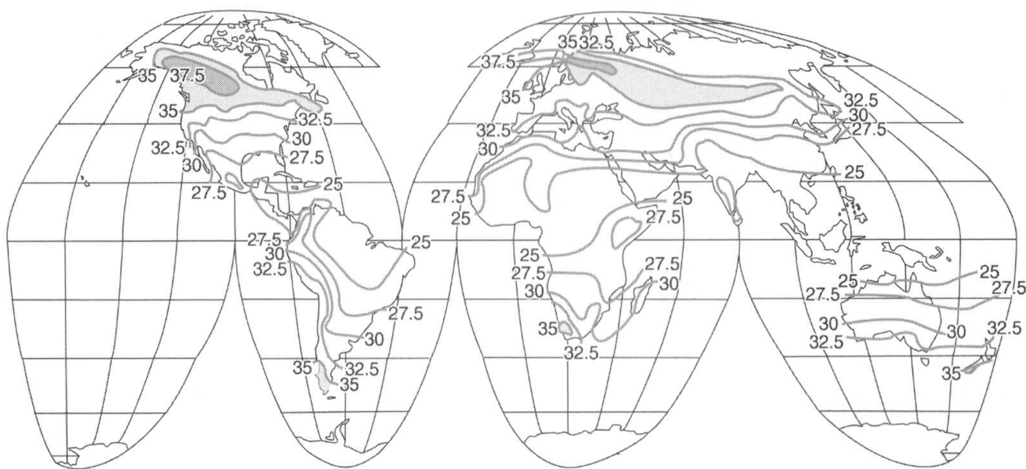

FIGURE 11.3. Potential photosynthesis (in grams/square meter/day) for 4-month season (May–August in northern hemisphere, November–February in southern hemisphere). *Source:* Adapted from Chang (1970). Copyright 1970 by Association of American Geographers. Adapted by permission of Blackwell Publishers, Ltd.

Canada, Europe, the former Soviet Union, Argentina, southern Australia, and northern China)—are all areas with potential photosynthetic rates exceeding 30 grams/square meter/day, rising in Canada and the former Soviet Union to vast areas over 35 grams/square meter/day (Chang, 1970).

The difference in crop potential reappears strikingly when one looks at graphs showing potential photosynthesis and the yield performance of different countries. Figures 11.4 and 11.5 show the relationship between estimated potential photosynthesis and rice and cotton yields for selected countries, measured over the growing season. Countries with low yields tend to be in low-latitude parts of the third world. Could this difference be explained simply by differences in technology and in the quality of husbandry? Chang (1968) reported on experiments in which agronomists at research stations were asked to grow rice using the best techniques. Two midlatitude locales (Japan and Australia) averaged 14.3 metric tons/hectare, while two tropical countries (the Philippines and Malaysia) averaged 12.3—a difference of 16%. Thus the difference in agricultural potential between the tropics and the midlatitudes is real. No matter what the farmers of Tanzania and Uganda do, cotton yields in Egypt and Israel are likely to exceed theirs by 30–40% (Isaacman and Roberts, 1995: 47). In the longer term, some of the difference in crop yields may be reduced by applying the agronomic and plant-breeding technologies of the Green Revolution to cereals, legumes, and root crops that are indigenous to Africa, such as ensete (*Ensete edulis*), teff (*Eragrostic tef*), finger millet (*Eleusine coracana*), pearl or bulrush millet (*Pennesitum typhoideum*), fonio or "hungry rice" (*Digitaria exilis*), caudatum and other local sorghums (*Sorghum vulgare*), cowpeas (*Vigna unguiculata*), pigeon peas (*Cajanus cajan*), bambara nuts (*Voandzeia subterranea*), Guinea yam (*Dioscorea* spp.), and so forth. A report by the Board on Science and Technology for International Development (1996) states that there are 2,000 native grains and fruits ready for "rediscovery" and exploitation.

Grain produced in the midlatitudes will continue to constitute a large part of world grain production and trade. The most pro-

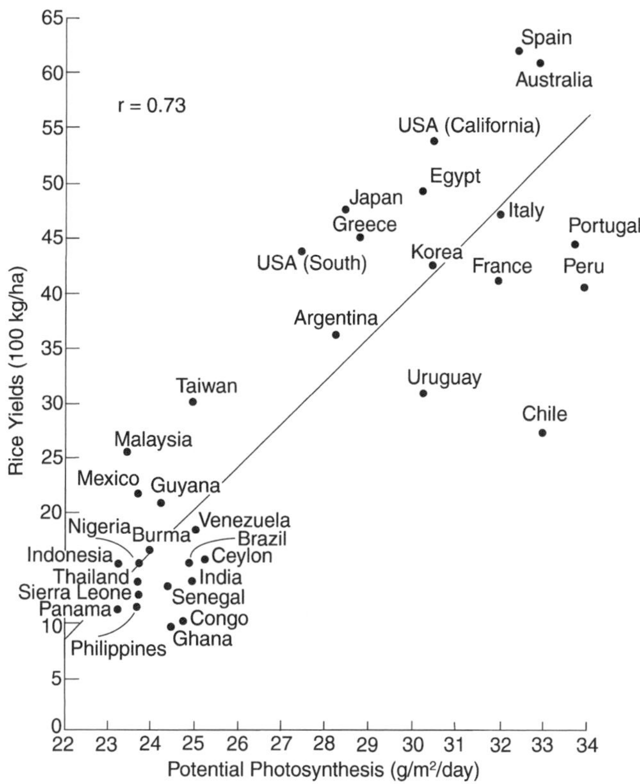

FIGURE 11.4. Relationship between rice yields and potential photosynthesis for 4-month period. Yields are given in units of 100 kilograms/hectare; potential photosynthesis is given in grams/square meter/day. *Source:* Adapted from Chang (1970). Copyright 1970 by Association of American Geographers. Adapted by permission of Blackwell Publishers, Ltd.

found consequence of the yield advantage enjoyed by growers in the midlatitudes is that they can control the world market prices of the major grains (wheat, maize, rice, oats, sorghum, barley), and western grain merchants will continue to dominate world grain trade.

Do the winterless tropics have any advantages? After all, there is a year-round growing season, and two or even three crops can be harvested per year. In the production of certain perennial crops, the humid tropics have an undeniable advantage. Crops that develop a large, permanent canopy of branches and leaves are more nearly like the characteristic vegetation of the humid and subhumid tropics; like evergreen and deciduous tropical forests, they interrupt much of the incident light and are as efficient photosynthetic users of it as is possible under such warm conditions. In part this is because their large "infrastructure" of branches and leaves can engage in photosynthesis for about 12 hours daily, and in part it is because they develop an extensive rooting system, which may be able to adapt to an annual dry season. Rubber is harvested every day, and tea leaves are picked nearly every day. Crops that grow throughout the year or tolerate only a brief dry season—rubber, cacao, coffee, tea, bananas, oranges and other citrus fruits, cashew nuts, coconuts, and oil palm—all do well in tropical areas.

Annual crops (such as maize, sorghum, rice, beans, and peas) can of course be grown a second time, but this doubles the amount of labor and technical inputs (such as fertilizer, seed, and perhaps irrigation water) needed. In economic terms, the longer growing season provides little advantage over that enjoyed by the midlatitude farmer.

Still another feature of potential photosynthesis mitigates, to some extent, the "dirty trick" nature has played on the people of the tropics. Tropical highlands have a considerably better potential for photosynthesis of annual crops than lowlands do. The advantage can be traced to two elements. One is that average temperatures are lower and diurnal temperatures (i.e., the range in daily high and low temperatures) are greater in highland locations, resulting in much lower dark respiration rates; the other is that an annual crop spends more time assimilating photosynthetic material in the seed or fruit than does the same crop at lower elevations. Table 11.1 shows that the advantage is on the order of 2:1 between highland areas in eastern Africa and the adjacent Indian Ocean coast.

The makers of food policy in third world countries need to work through the complexities of several contradictory goals: national food self-sufficiency; economy and efficiency in food provision; support for indigenous farmers; development of markets for the agricultural sector; and effective use of hard currency for imports. On the one hand, it might be cheaper to import the major food grains (wheat, rice, maize) for local consumption, but to do so would have drawbacks: (1) undermining local producers and impeding the development of local agriculture, (2) using precious hard currency, and (3) making the nation dependent on external sources of supply. On the other hand, reliance on local production might result in higher prices (or costly counterbalancing governmental subsidies, since governments are keenly watchful for signs of urban unrest) and irregular or unreliable supplies (caused by drought, pest infestation, and inadequate systems of transport). Many third world countries pursue a mixed strat-

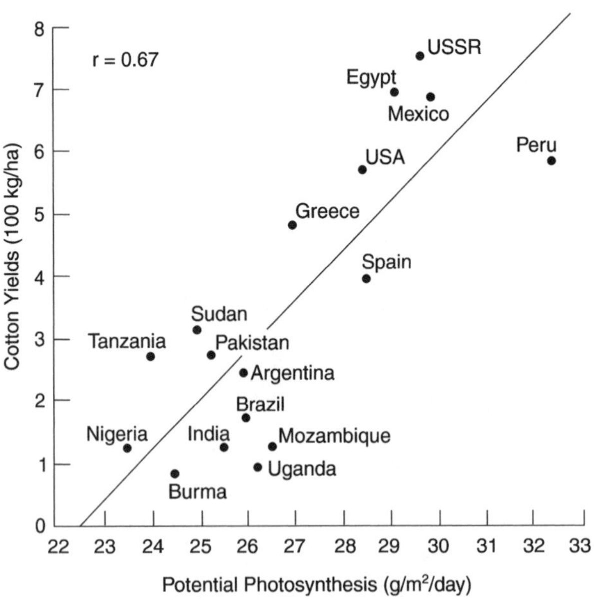

FIGURE 11.5. Relationship between cotton yields and potential photosynthesis for 8-month period. Yields are given in units of 100 kilograms/hectare; potential photosynthesis is given in grams/square meter/day. *Source:* Adapted from Chang (1970). Copyright 1970 by Association of American Geographers. Adapted by permission of Blackwell Publishers, Ltd.

TABLE 11.1. Observed Maize Yields for Three Altitudinal Zones in East Africa

	Yields[a]			Yield advantage (%) of highlands over intermediate and lowland zones	
Maize type	0–850 meters (lowlands)	900–1,600 meters (intermediate)	Over 1,650 meters (highlands)	Intermediate (base 100)	Lowland (base 100)
Local farmers'	25.7	32.6	49.9	153	194
H611C[b]	33.8	45.3	71.1	157	210
H613B[b]	29.3	40.4	69.6	172	238

Source: Adapted from Porter (1979: 23). Copyright 1979 by the Maxwell School of Citizenship and Public Affairs, Syracuse University. Adapted by permission.
[a]Yields are in quintals/hectare. A quintal is 100 kilograms or 220 pounds; a hectare is 2.471 acres.
[b]These are the names of hybrid varieties especially developed for farms at elevations above 6,000 feet (1,829 meters).

egy in their agricultural policy. The larger the internal market in a country, the larger the potential for local farmers to satisfy its food requirements.

The implications of latitudinal and altitudinal differences in potential photosynthesis for the nations of the third world are serious, but manageable. Those third world countries with tropical highlands have a resource of which they should take special advantage. In colonial times, these were the high-potential areas appropriated by European settlers (see Chapters 13 and 14). Third world countries, at a disadvantage with respect to grain yields, should nonetheless avoid dependence on midlatitude suppliers as much as possible, since grain prices respond to other pressures (midlatitude drought, crop diseases, aflatoxin outbreaks, etc.). It is much more sustainable to promote indigenous food production for urban markets, including the various tuberous crops that yield well in the tropics. Some countries have made notable gains toward achieving food security. Indonesia, for example, is self-sufficient in rice production.

The environmentally generated "locational advantage" enjoyed by the tropics means that farmers should, if possible, become regional specialists, growing those crops that do best there. As noted above, these are mostly forest-like, perennial crops (rubber, coffee, cacao, bananas, citrus fruit, etc.). Unfortunately, these crops are not basic foods, and incomes depend on export markets in the midlatitudes. Companies that import these tropical products will always seek to minimize costs, and thus will try to ensure a plentiful supply and alternative sources, including synthetic or midlatitude-grown substitutes. Attempts to form cartels in tropical products, similar to the Organization of the Petroleum Exporting Countries (OPEC) for oil, have not worked. Whether international agreements controlling production of tropical products can ensure reasonable and stable prices remains an open question (see Chapter 16).

12 The Management of Tropical and Subtropical Ecosystems

The Pokot of West Central Kenya—An Indigenous Knowledge System[1]

This chapter presents part of the world of ecological knowledge and practice of the Pokot, a Kalenjin-speaking people who are linguistically part of the Highland Nilotic group, and closely related to the Marakwet and Karasuk peoples (Ehret, 1969). There are many details and many totally unfamiliar terms in the text that follows. We suggest that the reader approach it not to master the details and terms, but rather to gain a general appreciation of the complexity of the Pokot world view and the intelligence and originality demonstrated in their local knowledge—the ways they have read nature (and political economy) and fashioned their economic and social institutions to use their environment.

The Pokot, numbering some 308,000 in 1999, live in West Pokot District, largely west of the great Rift Valley in west central Kenya, at elevations ranging from 1,000 meters (3,500 feet) to 3,350 meters (11,000 feet). We examine three systems: pastoral livelihood on the semi-arid plains of Masol; agricultural livelihood in Tamkal Valley; and irrigation among the Kurut, a group of several hundred Pokot families who live on the floor of the Rift Valley along its western edge and who depend almost entirely on irrigation for their crops. The purpose of this case study is to give the reader a feel for life in a third world setting in which an indigenous system of knowledge and practice prevails. Although British colonial administration had great impacts upon the Pokot, largely through confining them to a much smaller area than that to which they had had access in the 19th century, we frame this discussion almost entirely in terms of indigenous knowledge and practice. In comparison to many groups in colonial Kenya, the Pokot were much less affected.

THE POLITICAL ECONOMY OF POKOT COUNTRY, 1880–1962

We begin with a sketch of major events affecting the Pokot. A regionally integrated specialization in economy—farming in the hills, pastoralism on the plains—was distinct and probably of long standing by 1880. The agricultural Pokot used irrigation and were restricted in their farming to areas where irrigation was present and needed. Agricultural settlement was thus found in Cheptulel, Lomut, Mwina, Weiwei, and Sekerr, as well as in the interior basin centering on the drainage of the Murun and Iun Rivers (Figure 12.1). Here, near present-day Sebit and Ortum, population was sparse, but the irrigation system appears to have been well established.

No evidence of agricultural communities that were wholly independent of irrigation has been encountered in an extensive search of the literature on the Pokot. The names Chepkondol and Mbaara, for example (both agricultural communities that don't require irrigation), do not appear in the writings about the Pokot up to 1933. These settlements may not be new, but their fame as granaries has come only recently.

The Kiplegit agriculturalists formed the stable nucleus of Pokot culture in Cheptulel, Lomut, Mwina, and Weiwei. The Kacheripkwo agriculturalists were found strung out along the highlands of the Rift Valley, between Marich Pass and the Turkwell River gorge. A large number of the Kacheripkwo

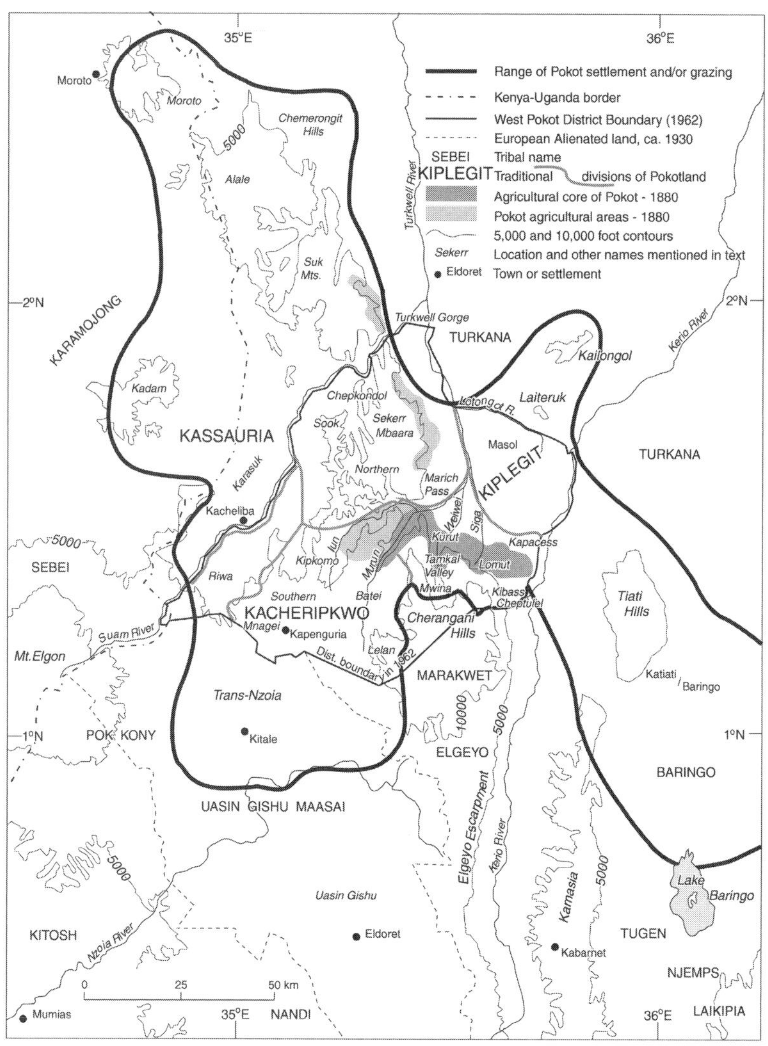

FIGURE 12.1. Pokot core and extent: 1880–1930.

were pastoralists who apparently took to farming when forced to by lack of adequate grazing land for their cattle (Kenya Land Commission, 1934, Vol. 2: 1744).

The decade of the 1890s was one of spectacular stock loss in east Africa generally, and Pokot country was no exception (Ford, 1971). From 1894 to 1896, rinderpest (*lopit* or *molmolei*) swept through Pokot and Karamoja, killing 90% of the cattle and causing widespread famine (Dietz, 1987: 88). There was a near-collapse of pastoralism. People migrated and were forced to place greater reliance on small stock and crops. Given the Pokot's ever-present interest in cattle, they began to rebuild their herds. Increasing numbers, which to the Pokot represented regaining the status quo, were interpreted by district veterinary officers as an alarming, uncontrolled, and ecologically unsustainable growth.

The coming of British administration to Uganda and northern Kenya, and the alienation of the Trans-Nzoia for European settlement, began to constrain Pokot movement and livelihood in about 1908. Prior to this time the Pokot had been buffeted on occasion from all sides, but if forced to retreat on one front, they were able to expand on another. The general component of movement in the late years of the 19th century was from east to west and north to south—out of Turkana country on the north and east, and into Karamoja on the west and the Trans-Nzoia and Baringo on the south. (The Turkana are pastoralists who border on the Pokot to the north.) From the late 1920s onward, the Pokot were bounded on all sides, and their livelihood henceforth evolved within a circumscribed territory. Population increased greatly in the hill country of Mnagei and Lelan.

The effect of the boundary constraints introduced by the British was fundamental. Hemmed in on the south by Europeans, deprived of historic grazing areas west and north of the Suam River in Karamoja, moved out of Laiteruk back to the Lotongot River (to the advantage of the Turkana), and continually harassed by the government and competing groups in their attempt to expand in Baringo, the Pokot obviously had only one place to go—up. The consequent devastation when a plains technology of grazing and firing was applied to the steep slopes of the hill lands in Mwina, Batei, Kipkomo, and Mnagei is a kind of epic theme in the veterinary officers' files. Limitations of space prevented the Pokot from observing their usual practice of letting bush rest for a year so that the grass would recover (Kenya Land Commission, 1934, Vol. 2: 1734).

The colonial administration's efforts to introduce and enforce grazing schemes did not take into account the overall livelihood requirements of the Pokot. As established by 1960, the grazing schemes accommodated only 20% of Pokot livestock, leaving some 100,000 cattle and 120,000 sheep and goats outside the schemes to bring even more devastation to the land.

The governmental grazing schemes were born in distrust and outright defiance (DYM, or *dini ya msambwa*, a millenarian protest movement, held up the grazing scheme in Kipkomo); they matured amidst hostility, trespass, and noncompliance; and in the postindependence period they were abandoned as Pokot herders decided they had had their fill of governmental control over their affairs.

The fixing of boundaries in West Pokot, which constrained the Pokot and their cattle after 1926, ignored a fundamental element in the geography of Pokot life—the imperative of mobility to seek out graze for livestock. Loduk, son of Atuchalei, summed it up perfectly from the Pokot point of view in 1932 when he said: "All is well in our land except the boundary" (quoted in Kenya Land Commission, 1934, Vol. 2: 1733).

POKOT LOCAL KNOWLEDGE AND LIVELIHOOD

The Pokot have created a workable livelihood within several differing ecological zones to satisfy their economic needs; they have also established economic specialization and regional trade, particularly in grain and livestock between farming and herding sectors. The risks that inhere in farming and herding are distributed both spatially and socially by specific social institutions.

We want to allow the Pokot's view of their environment to be heard. Imagine that Merkol is explaining the following material (see Plate 12.1); indeed, Merkol himself explained many of the things described in this chapter. It is, after all, on the Pokot's understanding of nature that their decisions and actions are based. Pokot ideas about seasons, climates, soil, and terrain types prove to be closely related to the body of custom and practice that guides agricultural and pastoral activities. Presented herein is what the Pokot say about their terrain and their soils. Although the "ethnographic present tense" is used in most of this chapter, the time is 1962, just prior to Kenya's independence. We end the chapter with comments on events since independence (1963) and the current situation.

POKOT CLIMATIC/TERRAIN TYPES

We introduce the three areas of Pokot country through a block diagram (Figure 12.2). The Pokot use a clear, consistent set of terms to describe the kinds of country in which they live: *keo'gh*, *tourku*, *masob*, *kamass*, *touh*, *sos*, and *kide*. Because of the dramatic and abrupt changes in relief in the eastern part of the district, where the plains give

PLATE 12.1. Merkol points across Tamkal Valley, explaining the Pokot climatic types that change with altitude and give the *korok* its zonal character (see Figure 12.2).

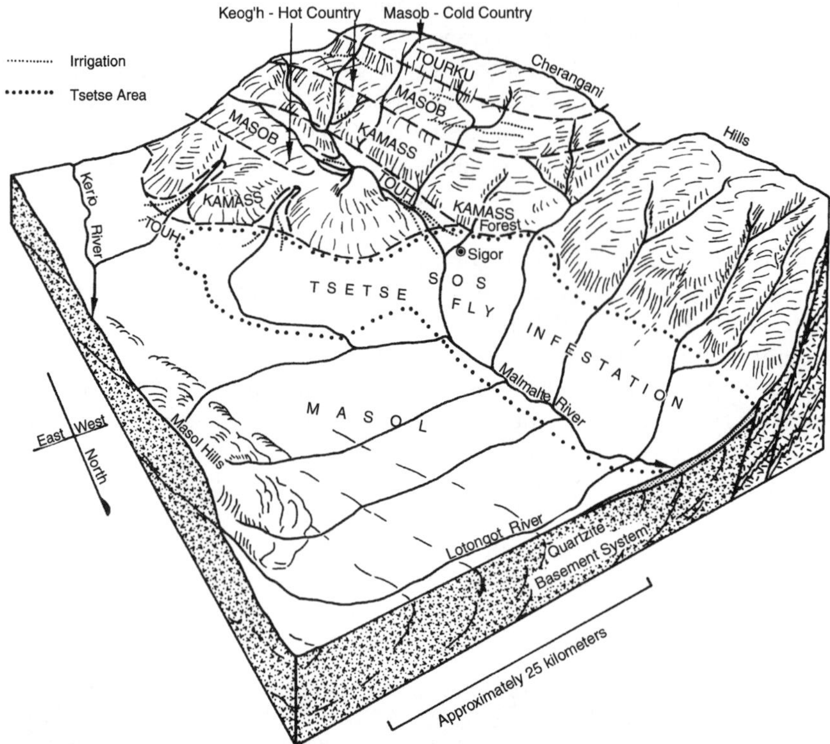

FIGURE 12.2. Block diagram of Pokot environment: Western edge of the Rift Valley, northwestern Kenya. *Source:* Knight and Newman (1976). Copyright 1976 by Prentice-Hall. Adapted by permission.

way on the west to the escarpment of the Rift Valley, the boundaries between terrain types are in most places sharply marked. There is no question where *touh* becomes *kamass* and so forth.

There are two main kinds of "climate" in West Pokot District. The Pokot do not separate the climate from the land where it is found; thus the climate called *masob* means "cold country," not "cold climate." The other type, on the lower hills and valleys and out onto the plains, is called *keo'gh*, "hot country." These two kinds of country can be subdivided still further. The cold, high, forested country is called *tourku*. *Tourku* is an area of moist montane forests, bamboo groves, and small patches of bracken and heath. The forests are on the sloping lands in the high valleys. The grassland/heath, which was formerly less extensive, occupies the hilltops. There aren't many people there. Thus, by default, when the Pokot say *masob*, they usually mean the better-populated area that lies below the forests on a bench of land (at 2,100 meters) that runs along the mountainside high above the valley. This high country is cloud-covered much of the time; there is more rain and less sun than at lower elevations in *keo'gh*.

Keo'gh, the hot country, is divided in the hill area into two parts: *kamass* and *touh*. *Kamass* is the area of lower hill slopes. Houses, *kraals* (thornbush enclosures for livestock), and some of the fields are up on the *kamass*. The houses are built there partly to avoid malaria, which is in the valley, and partly historically for reasons of defense. People also build their houses in *kamass* for the view (Conant, 1966, Chapter 5: 15c). In addition, the valleys get cold at night—colder than *kamass*—and they are bad places to keep cattle. The valley floor is *touh*. Here fields are served by irrigation furrows, which take off from streams farther up the valley. As the crop season advances, these furrows are opened to supplement diminishing rains.

Two other terrain regions are on the plains, not in the hills. One, an area called *sos*, is near the edge of the mountain, and consists of dense bush—an *Acacia–Sansevieria* thicket about 5 meters high. The low alluvial plains on either side of the perennial rivers that flow through these thickets onto the plains are subject to flooding in the rainy season. Farther out on the plains, where it is very dry and hot, is a terrain called *kide*. (The term we use a good deal is *masol*, after a kind of grass that is good for cattle.) *Kide*, which is associated with "east," has been described as having almost no soil, and for much of the year there is no water; however, it is a good place for cattle, since there is little disease.

Life in Pokot country requires use of more than one zone, regardless of where one lives. The pastoralists occupy the Masol plains (Figure 12.2), with seasonal movements into the Masol Hills and the fly-infested zone west of the Malmalte River; the Tamkal Valley farmers occupy the valley that runs south of Sigor; and the Kurut occupy the plains and hillside (*kamass*) immediately south of Sigor, where the irrigation channels are shown.

THE MASOL PASTORALISTS

The family of Lopetakwang, plainsman and herder, lives in the heat and dryness of Masol. He is of the Kakolmong *korok* (a territorial unit explained below). Here he was born and raised; he has never traveled far. A man of about 45, he has two wives (one quite young) and seven children ranging in age from 2 to 15. His first wife, Cemkaya, has borne him seven children, four of whom have survived. Life on Masol is not easy. Ceparason, his second wife, has had three children and is expecting a fourth.

The actions of Lopetakwang and his family are shaped by his membership in a particular "color section" of a *sapana* or age set. The age set provides a structure for organizing labor, planning strategies for stock management or military actions, and determining precedence at ceremonies. There are two *sapana* sets, based on the Turkana model (*athapan*, Turkana for "to initiate"), which alternate in a cycle about every 25 years. The color sections are established by a ceremony called *munian*, which assigns an age cohort to one of two groups within the *sapana: camarmar* ("zebra") or *nyimur* ("stones"). The color sections change about every 12 years. One can read a Pokot man's color section from his *atoro*, the front half of the *syoliup* or mud/hair skullcap, which is painted either in reddish brown stripes on a white background (zebra) or in reddish brown dots on a white background (stones). Lopetakwang did his *sapana* in the 1930s, and is a member of the *camarmar* color group.

The *sapana* marks a young man's entry into adult life; it occurs individually, usually after circumcision and prior to marriage. It is thus not a competitive, arduous rite of passage, but rather the initiation of a junior member into a group of age mates. Indeed, the *sapana* forms part of a young man's strategy to begin to build a herd so that he can eventually marry. Ages of young men undergoing *sapana* range generally between 12 and the mid-20s. Typically, a young man's father enters into a *tilia* (see below) agreement with a friend, obtaining an ox, which his son then spears for his age mates and others (women and older men) who attend the ceremony. The ceremony should be well attended, and much meat (including goat) and many calabashes of sour milk should be eaten and drunk during the dancing and feasting. This wonderful 3-day party (a bit reminiscent of a potlatch) is intended to place a large number of age mates and others in the young man's debt, so that he can, through time and with stock exchanges, build his herd (Peristiany, 1951). There is no formal ceremony for women comparable to *sapana* to mark their transition from childhood to adult life. Their identity, in this society that contains strong elements of patriarchy, is defined by their fathers before marriage and by their husbands after marriage.

Many stock-keeping terms in Masol are Turkana words, although there is usually a Pokot equivalent "for use in considered speech, as before a council of household heads" (Conant, 1966, Chapter 4: 23). It may be a fanciful idea, but use of Turkana terms perhaps adds a cachet, just as English borrows from French and vice versa. (On the ferry across the English Channel, we once heard the voice on the public address system telling passengers in English about the opening of the buffet, and in French about the opening of "*le snack bar.*")

Neither Lopetawkang nor anyone in his family has ever attended school, and the prospects that his children will go to school are remote. The life of the family centers on its livestock (see Plates 12.2, 12.3, 12.4a, and 12.4b). Lopetawkang has in his *kraal* 13 cattle and somewhat more than 20 goats. He actually owns other stock but keeps them in a neighbor's *kraal*, thus spreading his risks outside the one herd. In general wealth and status among his peers out on these plains, he is neither conspicuously high or low, though a little below average. At times he has earned money as a grazing guard for the Masol Grazing Scheme. This pays 30 East African shillings a month, the equivalent of $36 in 1996 U.S. dollars.

In the absence of government interference, Pokot use of the Masol plains and adjacent hills and streams to the east and west for their livestock is a carefully crafted yet flexible seasonal "dance" that is sensitive to time, place, distance, stock-grazing habits, stock endurance, and the happenstance of rain. There are competing pushes

PLATE 12.2. Masol Pokot bringing cattle home to the *kraal* for evening milking.

PLATE 12.3. A pastoralist's *manyatta* on the plains, Masol. Inside the large thorn *kraal* that surrounds Lopetakwang's *manyatta* are several smaller enclosures for calves and goats. The houses, with roofs freshly covered with mud and dung, are of recent construction. Vegetation here is *Acacia reficiens* with *Aristida* spp. grasses dominant.

and pulls: the need to provide water at least every third day, preferably more frequently; the need to provide grass and seed pods for grazers, and leaves, bark, twigs, and seed pods for browsers; the need to ensure that necessary forage is saved for a later time; the need to go where rains have made pasturage abundant; the need to provide salt; and the need to trade for food with Pokot in the hills to the west in areas where grain has been harvested. Francis Conant (1966, Chapter 4:14) likened the way a household reaches a decision about where to run its stock to a vector analysis of forces. Essentially, during the wet season there is a concentration of households and stock in the center of Masol, and during the dry season there is a dispersal of stock in temporary camps to areas far to the east and west.

The annual and shorter cycles of movement of stock take place within six types of vegetative zones (Table 12.1). Each zone has its season, its suitability for browsers and grazers, and its proximity to other resources. The resultant "dance" has a strong east–west component. Stock are concentrated in the *Acacia* thorn scrub in central Masol during the rainy season (April–August), and are dispersed during the dry months (September or October–March). *Turtur*, the word for February, means "to separate, to disperse." In the dry season, mature stock travel farthest to graze the Rift Valley foothills and the Masol Hills (where the grazings are called *keitakat*, "the grass that has been saved for later"). Immature stock and sheep are moved into the galerie forest (taller trees found along river courses) along the Malmalte River, now safe from tsetse-borne disease, and onto the *Acacia* thorn scrub lowland plains and foothills to the west. The thicket areas may be used in passing, but generally are avoided. The browsers—goats, donkeys, and camels—move east into semidesert thorn scrub. The arrangements take into account the disappearance of surface water and the digging of step wells. Favorite places for digging step wells are the Lotongot, Malmalte, and Kerio

(a)

(b)

PLATES 12.4a and 12.4b. Milking time in Masol. Cemkaya, Lopetakwang's first wife, milks while Ceparason comforts the animal, which is somewhat fierce, with the hide of its recently deceased calf. The hair style, beads, rings, armlets, numerous necklaces, and leather apron are standard style for women in Masol. Note also the wooden milk pail.

TABLE 12.1. Seasonal Aspects of Stock Management among the Masol Pokot; Vegetation Zones Are Arranged along a West–East Transect

Vegetation type	Area		Season when used	Livestock type[a]	Elevation/terrain
	Sq. km	Percentage			
West					
Commiphora scrub	70	5.0	Dry	Mature	Rift Valley hills and foothills and adjacent plains
Acacia–Themeda	57	4.0	Dry	Mature	
Acacia thorn scrub	60	4.3	Dry	Immature and sheep	
Sansevieria thicket	134	9.5	Dry (generally avoided)	—	Western Rift Valley plains
Dense thicket	87	6.2			
Riverine forest	107	7.6	Dry	Immature	Malmalte River
Acacia thorn scrub with and without scattered thicket	308	21.9	Wet	All stock	West–central Masol
Grassland on black cotton soils	34	2.4	Wet	All stock	West–central Masol
Semidesert thorn scrub	405	28.7	All year, esp. dry	Goats, donkeys, camels (browsers)	East–central Masol and Kerio Valley
Commiphora scrub	147	10.4	Dry	Mature	Masol hills
East					

[a]Cattle, unless otherwise specified.

Rivers (Figure 12.2). The lesser north–south component of stock movements reflects the capriciousness of rainstorms and quality of pastures, as well as the availability of food grains in the adjacent hills—at times plentiful in Sekerr, far to the northwest; at other times found in Tamkal Valley or Lomut, along the Rift Valley to the southwest.

Young boys and girls do many household chores, such as "drawing water, gathering brush for fences and firewood, collecting dung, care of stock in the household yard (especially de-ticking), help with milking chores and in the preparation of foodstuffs, including the trapping or collection of locusts, termites, honey, gum arabic, and the digging for edible roots" (Conant, 1966, Chapter 4: 32). Young men in their late teens and early 20s may form trading bands and spend several months together on trading expeditions. Sometimes a farming family will send a son as herdboy to the plains in exchange for stock. The herdboy may in due course return with the nucleus of his own herd (Conant, 1966, Chapter 4: 43).

As the dry season wears on, stream flow dwindles until finally the broad, flat sand floors of these intermittent streams are revealed. These wide stream channels, choked with alluvium, are unhappily characteristic of areas that have been devastated by overgrazing. In such areas, stripped of vegetation, runoff is immediate and complete. Much sediment is thereby moved into the stream channels, and it comes to rest as stream levels and velocity become reduced. The water table drops below the surface and is progressively reached by digging step wells (*kakhpipigh*) into the sand. As the dry season wears on, the water table continues to drop; on the beds of larger river courses, such as the Lotongot River, wells are dug down and down until depths in excess of 20 meters are reached. Women generally, but not always, operate these wells in bucket-brigade fashion: Hollowed wooden bowls are passed up from one woman to the next, continually replenishing a larger wooden trough to which the men bring the stock for drink.

During the dry season, the Pokot must

move their stock great distances for both grass and water. Land is not owned; it is simply used. Just as no one can designate which water from a stream one's livestock will drink, no one can set aside specific grazing land for one's cattle alone. During the rainy season, all is well: Streams have water; the *hafirs* (simple seasonal dams along water courses), if they haven't been destroyed by crocodiles, are full; and grazing is plentiful on the plains in the vicinity of the *manyattas* (thornbush-enclosed *kraals* with houses). As the dry season intensifies, greater motion is introduced into stock management. During the most trying part of the dry season, the stock must go 3 days after each watering. It takes a sturdy beast to survive the vicissitudes of Masol during the dry season. Stock that can go for 3 days without water are hardy indeed.

According to Schneider (1959: 151), the Pokot castrate all male cattle, keeping only a few bulls for breeding purposes. The veterinary officer in 1952–1953 noted a similar phenomenon: ". . . the Masol people, like the Turkana, remove one testicle from their bulls believing that it enables them to withstand the severe droughts better" (Department of Veterinary Services, 1953).

Some families normally live up in the Masol Hills. During the dry season, they spend 2 days in these hills with their stock and then go to the river for 1 day to let their stock drink. People who normally live on the plains alternate, spending 1 day in the hills and the next at the Malmalte. People living on the west slope of the Masol Hills, from Nan'gaita to Lotongot, go to the Malmalte River when other sources have failed.

Those living on the eastern slopes take their stock to the Kerio River. In August, the Lotongot people begin to get water from wells dug in the river. Sometimes they can last through the dry season without going to the Malmalte, but this is rare. Although there is a belt of bad tsetse infestation along the Malmalte, it is safe enough in the dry season to take the stock to the river; furthermore, valuable graze and browse can be found along the way. This dry season hill–plains circuit is so traditional that there are terms for the arrangement: *kabatich rongo*, literally "cattle went to graze on the mountain," and *kabatich keoh*, literally "cattle went to graze on the plains." As noted earlier, there is also *keitakat*, for "the grass that has been saved for later"; this is always in the mountains.

The grasses common in this area are *Panicum*, *Eragrostis*, *Chloris transiens*, *Aristida*, and others; the browse plants are *Acacia mellifera*, *A. misera*, and other *Acacia*. There is one salty grass, worthy of mention, that Masol cattle can eat. It is called *n'geeleet* (*Sporobolus marginatus* or *S. melimis*, molasses grass); it is ubiquitous and available in all seasons. Salt is also obtained in Turkana country: "The Masol people use the Kula salt lick which is just inside Turkana. This is a warm spring of saline content which flows out through the rock" (Department of Veterinary Services, 1953).

This pattern of movement between hill graze and lowland river drinking point is completely characteristic of pastoralists throughout the district. Movement into the hill country is not without its perils, however. The east coast fever belt, which "acts as a grazing control in itself during the rains," is of necessity invaded by stock during the dry season (Department of Veterinary Services, 1953). Sometimes the losses are light, but sometimes they are heavy. In addition, outbreaks of bovine pleuropneumonia (*sok*), hoof-and-mouth disease (*norien*), mange, and tick-borne heartwater fever sometimes occur in the higher areas.

Opportunities for agriculture in Masol are almost nil, although informants speak of sporadic attempts to grow finger millet and sorghum. A little tobacco is reportedly grown in the Masol Hills, and there is evidence in aerial photographs of attempts to cultivate a few small fields in the southernmost part of the hill country. The carrying capacity is extremely low in Masol. The Jarrett (1957) tsetse fly survey recommended a 1:40 ratio (i.e., 1 beast for 40 acres, or 1:16 hectares, of grazing land) for the Masol Hills; a 1:30–40 ratio (1:12–16 hectares) along the Malmalte River; and a 1:30 ratio (1:12 hectares) on the black cotton soils to the south (outside the grazing scheme proper). However, noting that about a third of the area is bare ground, the survey suggested increasing the ratios accordingly (Jarrett, 1957). Masol is simply not suited to support a population density much above 1 person per square kilometer. The mean family size in Masol is 7.03 people.

The Pokot have a special term for permanent settlements: *kamasino*, the "*manyattas* of a long time," in contrast to *kaleipin*, the temporary cattle camps set up during the dry season diaspora. Air photographs taken for the Kenya government in February 1956 have preserved an earlier pattern of settlement. The *manyattas* are, by and large, concentrated on the higher shelving plain not far from the base of the hills in semidesert thorn scrub. They lie within easy access of the Masol Hills and on a direct line to the Malmalte River. Houses and *kraals* are scattered on a north–south axis all along this higher plains country. There are several reasons for not settling closer to the Malmalte River. In addition to tsetse fly and malaria, there is an abundance of elephant and buffalo in this *Acacia* thorn scrub and thicket country.

The Pokot diet in Masol consists mainly of milk and milk products; food prepared from grain obtained through trade with people living in the hills to the west; and blood taken from cattle by means of a blocked arrow (see Plate 12.5). Blood and milk are commonly mixed when consumed (see Plate 12.6).

PLATE 12.5. Pokot herders catch a heifer preparatory to taking blood. A blocked arrow is used, shot from close range into the jugular vein. About a liter of blood is removed, and then the wound is sealed with earth. The young man who is kneeling does not yet wear a *syoliup* (mud/hair skullcap on head), because he has not performed the *sapana* ceremony and been circumcised.

Important though cattle are for subsistence, they affect several other dimensions of Pokot life (Conant, 1965; Herskovits, 1926). The attachment of herdsmen to their stock is expressed in a variety of ways: by taking a favorite ox's name for oneself; by affection for and identification with cattle; by insistence on certain sex taboos over the management of stock; and by the involvement of stock in the ceremonies that attend life's rites of passage—birth, circumcision, marriage, and death. Pokot simply enjoy cattle; they like to look at them, smell them, touch them. A most important institution is "bridewealth" (*kandin*). Harold K. Schneider, though insisting on the primacy of the subsistence role of cattle, agreed with Herskovits that "the 'cattle complex' [with] some slight revisions and qualifications from one culture to another, . . . still holds good for East African pastoral people" (Schneider, 1957: 278). According to Schneider, the Pokot divide aesthetic beauty into two parts: (1) that which is pleasant to contemplate and novel (*pachigh*); and (2) that which is functional, utilitarian, and good (*karam*). Cattle in all cases are *karam*, although the colors and patterns of their hides may be *pachigh* (Schneider, 1956). There are dozens of terms to describe the colors, patterns, scarifications, horn shapes, personalities, and other details of cattle. The most highly prized ox—one that has had his horns artificially bent from youth, one pointing forward, the other pointing backward—is called *kamar* (Peristiany, 1951: 201). Oh, the songs one can sing about such a noble beast; the elephants he has slain!

Although stock are slaughtered and eaten during the *sapana* ceremony and on many other ritual occasions, a herdsman keeps the cattle he owns dispersed through a series of stock deals—a kind of formal partnership called *tilia*, *tilya*, or *tilyatain*, literally "cattle-kin" (Peristiany, 1951; Schneider, 1957; Conant, 1966). In essence, this

PLATE 12.6. Mealtime for Lopetakwang's children in Masol. Komolingole, a friend of Lopetakwang, gives mixed milk and cow's blood to Lopetakwang's young children, each in turn. The stance of the Pokot bystander is eloquently characteristic.

is the exchange of a bull for a heifer. The recipient of the bull slaughters it for food (perhaps in a ceremony), or pays off a debt, or pays for a divination. The recipient of the heifer keeps her until she has produced a heifer of her own that has proved that she too can bear offspring, at which point the donor of the original heifer can claim offspring of the heifer and even offspring of descendants of the original heifer. The cycle takes a minimum of 6 years (the average is 10 years), and some *tilia* arrangements can be inherited by sons. The possible variations under the *tilia* arrangement are many. Francis Conant described five variations on the *tilyatain*: two incomplete exchanges in which (1) a heifer is given but no ox is taken, or (2) an ox is given, but nothing is taken in return; (3) an exchange that does not involve cattle (e.g., a goat is exchanged for several beehives); (4) a return of bridewealth; and (5) a trading relationship between plains people and hill farmers (the latter supplying grain). The latter two variants are the most frequent sources of "complicated and litiginous case histories" (Conant, 1966, Chapter 4: 41). Stock simply herded on behalf of another are called *kemanakan*.

The economic arrangements embodied in *tilia* and other exchanges among the Pokot in Masol and between Masol and hill people are long-lived, as well as "intricate, burdensome, and rewarding" (Conant, 1966, Chapter 4: 44). "The tilyatain relationship, which may well have started with a youngster and several goats setting off on a trading expedition, may span more than half a century and create a network of dependency relationships which indirectly crosscuts ties of blood, marriage, and peer group affiliations" (Conant, 1966, Chapter 4: 40).

Because of stock exchanges, the size of a family's herd is not revealed by the number of stock in the *kraal*. Lopetakwang as a number of *tilia* arrangements, and so his fortunes are inextricably enmeshed with those of his neighbors. The network of *tilia* partnerships not only insures Lopetakwang against complete loss and ruin through disease or theft; it gives him a resource in friendship that he can call upon when he is in trouble (e.g., over an accidental killing).

The *tilia* deals take on a heightened significance when one examines the *korok* (a political territory, discussed in the next section), which is modified when applied to the plains. The *korok* in Masol does not help in the maintenance of strength in clan or lineage. There is a striking difference in the personnel who make up a *korok* on the plains and in the hills. Whereas the *korok* in the hills tends to consist of people of just a few clans or lineages, on the plains a great number of lineages is represented in a *korok* (Conant, 1965: 431). Peristiany (1954: 24) stated: "Constant individual movements have prevented the localization of lineages and there are fewer kinship bonds linking together the members of a [pastoral Pokot] village than among the irrigation people."

Prestige comes of owning cattle, and with them the good things of life—notably suitable marriage partners and grain from the hill settlements in the west, and as far afield as Kadam and the Tiati Hills, farther south. Cattle are coin of the realm (Schneider, 1964). They are subsistence insurance. In the worst of times, they are killed and the meat consumed; in normal times, they provide milk and blood for all—and meat on special occasions. Indeed, how could one properly entertain one's friends at a feast if there were no meat?

TAMKAL VALLEY

Tamkal Valley is a narrow valley that lies nestled between the Rift Valley wall on the west, and a limb of high country on the east (see Figure 12.2). Its entrance from the north is commanded by a peak called Koh; this means "cow's hump," which it resembles (see Plates 12.7 and [below] 12.11). Annual precipitation in Tamkal Valley exceeds 1,000 millimeters. A second crop season,

PLATE 12.7. Tamkal Valley, West Pokot District, viewed from Kokwatandwa. Panorama of Tamkal Valley, viewed southeast. The photo shows the Marin and Kale Rivers, whose confluence forms the Weiwei River. The land between the Marin and Kale is the *korok* of Asar. To the left (east of the Marin River) lie, from north to south, the *korok* named Kitonyo, Wator, Kamicich, Tirtoi, Ptalam, Sungwut, and Marin (see Figure 12.3). The prominent peak, *Koh*, lies down the valley to the left. The valley bottoms (*touh*) are irrigated and used mostly to grow maize and some sorghum. The lower slopes of the valley (*kamass*) are planted on a bush fallow basis to finger millet. Some of these fields can be irrigated. Settlement is clustered in the *kamass*. On a bench of land higher up on the valley side (*masob*), more fields and settlements are found. The higher forested country (*tourku*) is here, typically, enshrouded in cloud.

based largely on sorghum, is possible along lower valley floors in Tamkal. The vegetation of the area of dense settlement in Tamkal Valley is *Combretum–Hyparrhenia*, grading into *Acacia–Themeda* on the valley floor and on the drier east-facing slope. In Tamkal Valley, population densities exceed 40 people/square kilometer (100/square mile). The mean family size in Tamkal Valley is 4.75. After explaining the *korok* and other terms important in Pokot society, and sketching Pokot ideas about soils, we turn to agricultural and stock-rearing practices in Tamkal Valley.

The Korok

The *kokwa* and the *korok* are Pokot institutions specifically designed to organize the use of the different climatic/terrain types described earlier. The *kokwa* is a kind of council, a meeting at which decisions regarding the life of the group are reached. The membership of the *kokwa* consists of heads of households in a particular area. The meeting is presided over by male elders or respected individuals (the *kirwokin*, "good talkers"). The *kokwa* is not determined by clan or other kinship affiliation, although there is a tendency for members of one or two clans to be numerically dominant in the *kokwa*. Rather, the *kokwa* is defined as the people who live within particular geographic boundaries. This geopolitical space is called the *korok*. It is the smallest political territorial unit in Pokot country. It normally consists of land bounded at the lowest elevation by a main trunk stream; the sides are defined by streams that come down off the hillside approximately at right angles to the trunk stream, and the hill crest forms the upper boundary (Figure 12.3).

Stated another way, the *korok* is a unit of geographic space designed to include some each of *touh* (valley flats), *kamass* (lower hill slopes), *masob* (higher hill land), and in Tamkal Valley the bench at 2,100 meters, within its boundaries. There are many exceptions—for example, *korok* that include no part of *masob*, *korok* that begin in *masob* and run upslope into *tourku*, and the like. Generally, however, the objective of including land with differing environmental potentials in a single political space is achieved. In some *korok*, hill spurs rather than streams mark off the sloping side boundaries. Still more interesting things happen to the *korok* as it is applied to plains areas in Masol, where the people lead a wholly pastoral kind of life. The *korok* in Masol, though more nearly two-dimensional, is still demarcated

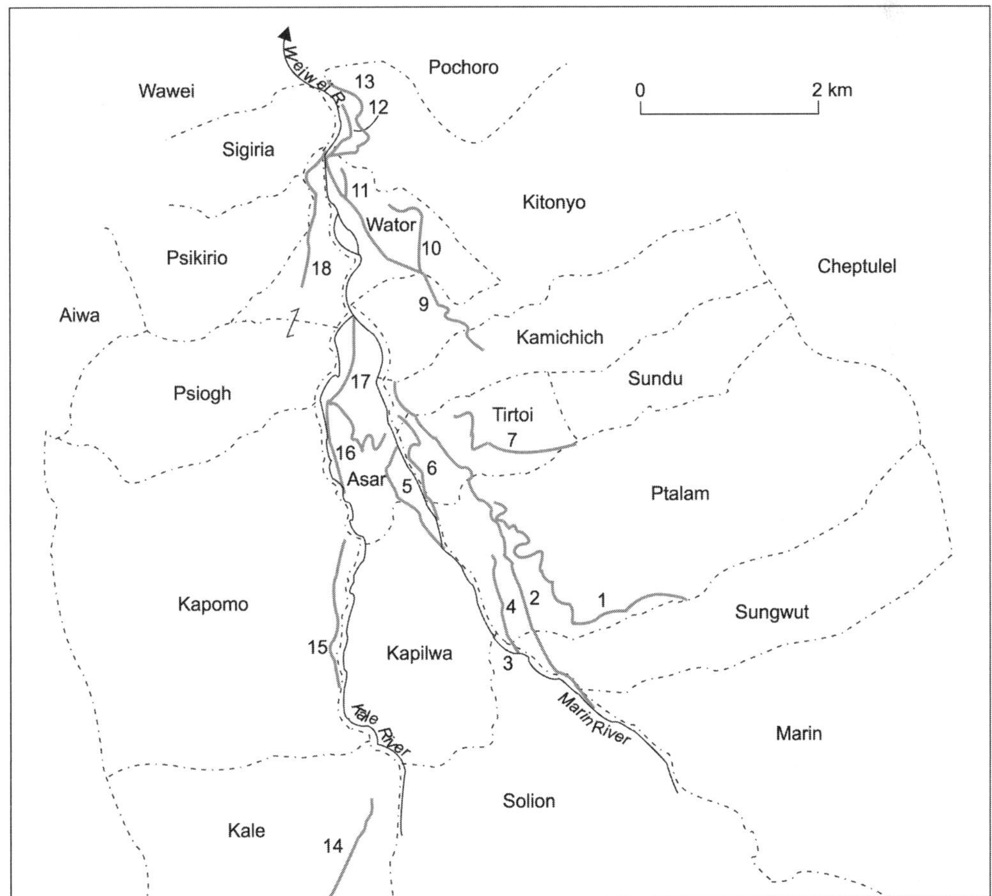

FIGURE 12.3. *Korok* and furrows in Tamkal Valley, Mwina Location, West Pokot District. Numbers refer to furrows' names as given in Table 12.5.

by a stream bounding the base and two sides of this political and social entity (Conant, 1965).

The *korok* is thus a Pokot invention, a geopolitical instrument whose purpose is to give its members control of several ecological zones. The Pokot see clearly that livelihoods are safer and more productive for *korok* members when these are gained not from one, but from a range of environments. The way in which this works out in actual agricultural practice is considered in a later section of this chapter.

Pokot Ideas Concerning Soils

Pokot farmers know the facts about soils that are important to their agricultural use.[2] The main fact to emerge from a study of Pokot soil types is that the notion of "catenary association," as first advanced by Milne (1935: 183) and subsequently widely adopted by other soil scientists in tropical Africa (Scott, 1962: 67–76; Chenery, 1960), is present in Pokot thinking. A "catena" is "any regular repetition of soil sequence down a slope which may have been caused by changes in the parent material as well as those brought about by topography" (Scott, 1962: 71). Each Pokot soil type is described below in terms of Pokot understanding of it, and its pertinent attributes are given. (See also Chapter 10 of the present volume, Figure 10.3.)

Pokot soils may be ordered by geographical site along a mountain–valley cross-section. The only additional complexity is caused by variations in terminology from Tamkal to Kurut–Sigor to Masol. First come *torion* and *muntoion* forest and grassland soils of the highest elevations; then come *nun'gutian nyoh to* once-forested black soils of the *masob* bench; these are followed by *sangatian* or *ngoriow*, which are poor soils to be found on the steep slopes of the *kamass*. Immediately below them in the *kamass* one finds *pirirwok*, a red, somewhat leached soil that supports crops of finger millet. *Rilnoi*, a white or gray soil, occurs in limited areas in the same transitional zone of the *kamass*. On the flat narrow valley floor in *touh*, one encounters two colluvial–alluvial soils: *munoh*, a clay loam, and *n'gyomwoh*, a sandy alluvium, both much prized for agricultural purposes. Near the riverbanks in touh is found *ramian*, a sandy soil that may be related to *n'gyomwoh*. In the Kurut–Sigor area, this sand soil is called *tokoyon*; in Masol, it is called *ngayam*. The sticky clay *munoh* of the narrow Tamkal Valley is called *munion* in the Kurut–Sigor area, and *katukurie* or *arai'yon* in Masol.

• *Torion*: The meaning attached to this word includes both "blackness" and "charcoal." One informant said that it denotes "the *shamba* [field] that was just started and burned." The soil is black, the *torion* being a mixture of charcoal with the earth. *Torion* occurs in the thick *Podocarpus* and cedar forest in the higher parts of *masob*. If you walk on it, your feet will sink because of all the decayed trees and leaves. The soil is black, but not completely black; it can be brownish or bluish black. There is water underneath, but not on top. If you dig down, you encounter water. Crops that can be grown in it are finger millet, English potatoes, and maize; maize thrives only at the lower elevations where *torion* occurs.

• *Muntoion*: This is a companion soil to *torion*. It is a grassland soil of high elevations. In some areas, it is black and sticky; in other areas, it is greatly mixed with stones. On lower elevations of this grassland soil, one can grow maize and finger millet. At higher elevations, only potatoes, beans, and perhaps peas can be grown.

• *Nun'gutian nyoh to*: Literally, this means "soil that is black." *Nun'gutian* is the Pokot word for "soil," and *to* means "black." This soil occurs mainly in the *masob* and at lower elevations in bush. It is a good soil that is best suited for maize; indeed, one can plant a crop of maize 4 or 5 years in a row in this soil. It is not sticky. The soil is sometimes used for mudding the walls of houses. One informant said: "We know that wherever we find the soil, the area was once forested." This observation might provide a way to map areas from which forest has been removed in historic times.

• *Sangatian* or *n'goriow*: This is a mixture of soil and stones, with more stones than soil. The stones can be found mixed with red and/or black soils. Finger millet alone can be grown on this soil, and then only for 1 year. This soil is found in *kamass* on slopes, commonly above *pirirwok* (see below).

• *Pirirwok* or *pirirnoh*: *Pirir* means "red." It is found in the valley where the slope begins, not near the river. There is no sand in this soil; there is much clay, and with it small stones. Finger millet is the best crop for this soil. Maize can only last for 1 year on such soil; finger millet can only be grown for 1 year also, but that is because weeds compete too strongly in the second year. Cassava and sorghum do well on this soil. It is usual to irrigate crops on *pirirwok* unless the rains are heavy. *Pirirwok* can be mixed with plain salt (bought in a shop) to give to goats; it is also used for mudding the walls of houses.

• *Rilnoi*: This is a kind of white or gray soil; *ril* (or *rel*) means "white" or perhaps "whiteness." The soil is clay-like, absorbs water very easily, and when soft is easily eroded and carried away by runoff. Maize can be grown on this soil, but not for many years. Finger millet can be grown for 1 year. *Rilnoi* occurs in limited parts of the *kamass*. Goats, but not cattle, lick it for salt. It is also used for mudding walls and is used by girls at circumcision time to spread on their bodies.

• *Munoh*: This word means "sticky." The adjective evidently is restricted to the description of soil, and is not applied to other substances. Something covered with honey is not *munoh*, for example. *Munoh* is used in making pots and clay pipes; the word is used to describe the material from which pots are made. *Munoh* is a prized agricultural soil.

• *Munion*: The word denotes black soil, mud, and black cotton soil. It is good for growing sorghum, finger millet, and maize. It is also used for mudding the walls of houses. It is definitely a lowland soil. It may also be used in making pots and clay pipes, although the name applied to material used in making pots and pipes is *munoh*, as noted above.

• *Arai'yon* or *katukurie*: Both are terms applied by the people of Masol to the well-known, endlessly cursed black cotton soil. It has no agricultural uses, but young Masol men who have not undergone the *sapana* ceremony use it in making their *lotokon*, or bun at the back of the head. *Arai'yon* and *katukurie* probably have characteristics resembling those of two other Pokot lowland soils, *munion* and *munoh*.

• *N'gyomwoh*: This is sandy alluvium. Both *n'gyomwoh* and *munoh–pirirwok* produce equally well. The sand soil is "warmer," and maize planted in both soils at the same time grows quicker and matures sooner on the *n'gyomwoh*. *N'gyomwoh*, although an agricultural soil in the hills, is taken to mean in Masol the sand and small stones that choke the dry river channels.

• *Ramian* or *ngayam*: *Ramian* is the term used in the hills; *ngayam* is used on the plains by Masol people. This soil is found along the banks of rivers. Soil that has come from the *kamass* has been deposited beside the river; sometimes the river itself overflows and adds some more. *Ramian* is a mixture of all kinds of soils. It is mostly soil, but there are small stones as well. It is good for almost any crop, but is usually planted to maize and sorghum; it can be used for maize as long as 10 years. The trouble with this kind of soil is that it can be swept away by the river in flood, taking the crops too. The soil is very deep.

There remain a number of distinguishable "soils" in Pokot country that are wholly nonagricultural. The Pokot make this important difference clear in separating soil, *nun'gutian*, from clay, *munyan kapagh'yat*.[3] At least eight kinds of clay used in the making of head packs have been collected in Masol. One of these, *pikos*, is a widely used red clay that is found only in one place in Mwina, at Psoi. Circumcised boys smear it on their bodies for decoration. Circumcised girls spread the soil on their precircumcision beads, and before dances they spread oil and then *pikos* on their bodies to make themselves pretty.

N'yen'g is a subsurface "soil"; it is salty and fed to livestock. It is found along the banks of the big rivers in flat country. Its colors differentiate it. Thus one can speak of *n'yen'g nyoh ril* (white) and *n'yen'g nyoh pirir* (red). It can be found along the Weiwei, Samakitok, and Marich Rivers.

Tolot (also *talan*) is a soil moisture condition. It has been said to mean "with water inside," and used to describe a soil when it is wet or saturated. An informant said: "If you find the land flat, and water spreading through inside, and green things like grass always growing there, then it is *tolot*." The *masob* people call such areas *sos*.

Table 12.2 gives a western soil science description of the Pokot catena. The terminology in English is derived from the map of soils in *The Natural Resources of East Africa* (Scott, 1962: Map 6). This map offers a remarkable cartographic solution to the problem of showing catenary detail. Thirty-six soil types are recognized. These are combined and recombined according to terrain, slope, and elevation to form 48 soil–topography associations. This permits one to read from the map a great amount of detailed information about the soils of particular places.

The Pokot soil catena jumps, in Scott's classification, from a humid region (2) to a semiarid region (12) type, which highlights the strong contrast between moist *masob* areas and the excessively drained *kamass* (see Figure 12.2). The Pokot acknowledge this sharp gradient by using several altitudinal zones, and by maintaining an elaborate network of irrigation channels, which are opened as needed during the crop-ripening season.

The Pokot make many real distinctions among soil types; they have a well-developed functional knowledge of soils. Despite the variation in terminology among Tamkal Valley (Mwina), Kurut–Sigor, and Masol, the Pokot are consistent in selecting significant criteria to divide soils from one another. Laboratory analyses have shown that even soils that are grouped together in

TABLE 12.2. The Pokot Soil Catena

English description	Pokot soil name
Well-drained soils	
Humid region	
2[a] Dark brown loams (ando-like soils)	*Torion*
	Nun'gutian nyoh to
Semi-arid region	
12 Dark red sandy clay loams	*Sangatian*
	Pirirwok
12/18	*Munoh*
Soils with slight seasonally impeded drainage	
18 Red to dark red friable clays with laterite horizon	*Rilnoi*
	Munion
20 Strong brown to pale yellow loamy sands with a laterite horizon	*N'gyomwoh*
	Ramian
	Tokoyon
	Ngayam
Soils with impeded drainage	
22 Black to dark gray clays soils (grumosolic soils)	*Kutukurie*
	Arai'yon
Poorly drained soils	
25 Dark grayish brown to very dark brown loams (alpine meadow soils)	*Muntoion*

[a]The numbers are Scott's Soil Topography Associations. *Source:* Scott (1962: Map 6).

TABLE 12.3. Characteristics Distinguishing among Pokot Soils

Soil pairs	Main difference between pairs attributable to:
Torion *Mungutian*	Texture, phosphorus
Sangatian *Pirirwok*	Texture, pH
Sangatian *Munoh*	pH, percentage organic matter, phosphorus
Pirirwok *Munoh*	Texture, pH, percentage organic matter, phosphorus
N'gyomwoh *Ngayam*	Color, pH, percentage organic matter, phosphorus, and potassium

Scott's classification are physically different from one another. Many of the soil differences noted by the Pokot are not based on color, but on texture, percentage of organic matter, or other attributes. Table 12.3 shows what distinguishes the Pokot soils that are grouped *together* in Table 12.2. Pokot farmers, of course, do not separate soils from one another according to all of the criteria listed in Table 12.3; again, color, texture, presence of organic matter, taste, and moisture are their guides.

On a second count, the Pokot also perform well—that of knowing the agricultural potential of their soils. This potential is as much a matter of sunshine and rainfall as it is of soil, but the Pokot know how long a field may be used, what to plant where, when to irrigate, and when to cut bush for a new field. They speak of quick soils and warm soils, have a term for moisture saturation, and distinguish soil from unaltered earth (clay, "the stones that are not hard"). Pokot knowledge of soil may not fit certain rigorous classification schemes, but it is internally consistent and results in categories of soil that are meaningful in Pokot life.

Farming in Tamkal Valley

The life of the Lorongelosi family is described in this section. Pkite Lorongelosi, a resident of Tirtoi *korok*, is in his mid-30s. He is separated from his first wife, who bore him no children. By Cheptonjyo, his second wife, he has had a son and three daughters, all of whom are living (see Plate 12.8). Two of the children are preadolescents, and the others are under 4 years old. Pkite's older brother, Kisitut, who lives in a house close by, completes the family group. Pkite has traveled a good deal and has had more schooling (5 years) than most Pokot of his age. Like his father, he was born and brought up in Tirtoi; his religious adherence is to traditional Pokot beliefs. He is well off by Pokot standards and high in the social esteem of his peers. He estimated his 1962 income at 30 East African shillings from the sale of tobacco, but it must have been more, very likely as a result of the sale of surplus maize and bananas. In any event, Pkite's cash income is minimal, and his involvement in the "world" economy is small even by Pokot standards.

Pkite is powerfully built and extremely hard-working. He seems to have an almost Calvinist attitude toward the job of farming, which cannot be said to be generally characteristic of the Pokot. He is also somewhat experimental in his farming, which is unusual. In most ways, however, Pkite is representative of farmers of Tamkal Valley.

In his ownership of livestock, Pkite is representative of people living in the valley. He has two cows, five sheep, and five goats. Nearly all heads of households own stock, and the average figures (from data collected by Francis Conant) are five cattle, four sheep,

PLATE 12.8. Pkite, a resident of Tamkal Valley, prepares a gourd by drilling several small holes in a circle and knocking out the center piece, later used as a stopper. The gourd will be dry-cured by keeping it close to the embers of a fire. A common use for such a gourd is for storing beer that has been brewed at home. Pkite himself does not drink beer, but his kin and neighbors certainly do. Photo courtesy of Francis P. Conant.

and three goats. Pkite's livestock are herded with the stock of another brother, Chirotwa, who is not willing to divulge any details concerning the stock he owns.

Ownership of and Control over Land

Pkite has abundant land, most of which he inherited from his father. There are at least 14 separate parcels, fewer than half of which are in crop at any one time. It cannot be said that Pkite is land-rich, for just as there is enough air for all to breathe, there is enough land in the valley for all to farm. Land is owned and inherited in Tamkal Valley, in contrast to the communal control of land among the Masol pastoralists. It is surveyed after a fashion, the boundaries being marked by especially fashioned stones (*kaeghae*) driven vertically into the ground. These boundary stones are spaced along property lines at intervals of about 8–10 meters. Land is not bought and sold in the sense that westerners normally use these terms. The usual transaction involves the payment of a goat by the person obtaining the land. A goat, valued in 1962 at 20–22 East African shillings (the U.S. equivalent was about $3 at the time, or $15.40 in 1996) is a token, something that makes the exchange tangible. Indeed, land that has been so acquired goes by the name *paragh*, "the *shamba* of the goat(s)." Such land is held in perpetuity by the owner, who wills it to his sons. Part of one of Pkite's fields is *paragh*—one that he purchased from Chepchoy, a clan brother who moved away and wanted to sell his land. Each field that Pkite has inherited is called *parenjya*, literally "the field that is ours," or if fallow, *wutenjya*, "the bush that is ours."

Both *paragh* and *parenjya* should be considered freehold. A second type of tenure, which could be termed quit-rent or just temporary loan of land, is called *kimanaken*. It is not actually rented; according to Pkite, "that cannot happen" in Pokot country. But if, for example, a man wants to use one of Pkite's fields only for a short time (say, for 1 or 2 years), he will brew beer for Pkite. This is a token even more modest and transient than giving a goat. Pkite can ask the man to quit his land any time after harvest. It is a form of land holding in Pokot that exists, but does not seem to be widely practiced. The term *kimanaken* can apply to cattle as well as to land. The borrower gets only the milk. Any calves produced during the loan period go back to the lender when he collects the cow. The lender brings a pot of beer when he comes to collect his stock.

Just as there is no rented land, there is no common land. Farms are made in which the fences are built and maintained in common. Furrows that supply water to fields are held and administered in common. After the harvest, the stubble is grazed at will by any and all livestock, and no one will keep them out. The large fields in which several people have land in crop are called *paraghomucho*. Land that is used by everyone for pasture is called *gomucho*. Francis Conant (1966, Chapter 5: 19) collected two other terms for large, communally managed fields: *kanasian* and *psigirio*.

A point that becomes clear as we examine Pkite's fields is that the *paraghomucho* is a functional agricultural entity of the greatest importance in Pokot life. It is an organizational unit that involves a farmer with kin and neighbors. It has social implications, inasmuch as people must agree on which *paraghomucho* to open next, who is to be included, and when the work of preparation will be done. The work of cutting the bush, burning it, and building the fence and trash terraces is done by the men as a group. The planting and the seemingly interminable stooping labor of weeding give the women long hours under the hot sun together. Yet through it all, each ripening head of finger millet has one ultimate owner—a woman (generally a wife) who places it in her private granary. She controls its subsequent use. The fields, in narrow strips running up the hill slope, may not be evident, but beneath the vivid green of the finger millet may be found the lines of stones that set each parcel off from the others. It is part of being a Pokot farmer to be involved with many others through the *paraghomoucho*, as well as by sharing in turn water from the furrows. As we explore the details of Pkite's land holdings, it becomes apparent how intricate and many-skeined is the web of involvement in a Pokot farming community.

Gender and the Division of Labor

Pokot women, by virtue of their agricultural labor, have considerable control over resources and decisions regarding those resources. The harvest from a woman's fields goes into her granary. She decides what, when, and how much of the stored food to use. If part of the crop she has raised is to be sold, she must agree. Thus, whereas men make decisions regarding the high-prestige aspect of Pokot economy (the keeping of livestock), women perform most of the labor and make decisions on the more fundamentally important part of the economy (the production of grain and other food crops). Planting seed is exclusively a woman's domain, and, sometimes with the help of children, women do the continuous tasks—digging, weeding, and guarding the fields (Conant, 1966, Chapter 5: 10; see also Conant, 1973, 1982b). Among plains households, women may manage goats and sheep, but men always manage the cattle.

Wives have power and autonomy in still other ways. One way is the remote, but ever-present, possibility of poisoning the food served to a husband. There is sometimes a fear in men of witchcraft practices among women (Edgerton, 1971: 288 ff.); however, these are hidden, covert, seldom-used sanctions. There is a more public sanction to which Pokot women may resort—the *kilapat*, or shaming party. If a man abuses a wife, she may enlist the aid of co-wives, sisters, and other women in the community, who gang up on the man, tie him to a stake or tree, and subject him to verbal ridicule as well as physical actions of extreme insult, such as placing a foot on his shoulder, thereby exposing their private parts to him (Edgerton and Conant, 1964). As in other third world societies, Pokot women are not without means of empowerment and control of resources.

The Fields

Pkite has six fields in crop, and at least eight parcels of bush, perhaps more (Table 12.4 and Figure 12.4).[4] Although exact areas have been calculated for the fields in cultivation, we can only guess at the size of the parcels of bush. Even these could be mapped if necessary, for in the bush still lie the boundary stones from the last time the area was used. Rediscovery of the stones is part of the normal process of preparing a field from bush. We can assume that the fallow fields have a range in size comparable to the fields Pkite currently has in crop. His first field (No. 1), planted in maize (*alpa*), is near his house, which sits up in *kamass* on the east side of the valley, overlooking the ravine of a short tributary of the Mbaya River. At its edge is a house where the goats and sheep are kept, and just downhill from this house has been built up a pile of droppings, which are used in the adjacent field. As a consequence, this field is called *paraskon*—roughly, "the field of dung."

Across the ravine is a field of finger millet (*maiwa*) and maize (No. 2), which can be irrigated by the furrow that is called Mbokor. Close by is a field, shared with Chirotwa, of maize, cassava, bananas, and a miscellany of vegetables (No. 3). It is a small field (0.3 hectares) that has a special name, *paran'gion*. This is a little garden that Pokot men have, but not women; yet it resembles the sort of kitchen garden that women in other African cultures commonly have near their houses.

Across the Marin on the west side, Pkite has two small maize–beans fields (Nos. 4 and 5) in a large *paraghomucho* in which there are 29 other parcels, the concern of 25 of Pkite's neighbors. This field is served by an excellent furrow called Chemwanya, which takes off upstream along the Marin River.

The remaining cultivated parcel (No. 6) owned by Pkite lies about 2.5 kilometers to the south in more remote wooded country in the narrow valley of the Runu River, a tributary of the Marin. Field No. 6 is in finger millet. It is a large farm on a steep slope (54%) in the *kamass* to the south, remote from the other fields. Fourteen people are involved in this field, nine of them related to Pkite, and all of them resident in *korok* lying east of the Marin River. Pkite's parcel in the field is unusual because he and Chirotwa own it jointly. Their father died before saying whose field it would become. The field is too narrow to be divided, so Pkite and Chirotwa share its produce equally, and Cheptonjyo and Chirotwa's wife share the work of weeding and so forth. The location of a large finger millet field so far removed from Pkite's other currently used fields is purposeful. As he puts it, "If you have separate *shambas*, you can fail in one and not fail in all of them. For example, the stalk borer ruined the maize *shamba* near my house this year, but I have good crops in *shambas* elsewhere, and thus there will be food." It appears that location of fields far from one another, but in the same valley environment, is a measure against disease pests rather than against the vagaries of rainfall.

In addition to the currently unused bush, Pkite has control over some low-lying open pasture land that is near his field No. 3. All told, Pkite has about 1.13 hectares in maize, 0.61 hectares in finger millet, and 0.28 hectares in areas devoted to bananas, cassava, and vegetables, for a total of about 2 hectares under crop.

We have explored some of the static elements of Pkite's life. We have seen how Pkite's fields enmesh his fortunes deeply with those of 34 other people. We turn next to management of farming and herding in Tamkal Valley.

Opening Fields and Raising Crops

If a new field is to be opened, the work should be started in February. In order to see the process at its simplest, let us make it a small field that Pkite and his wife, Cheptonjyo, can clear. She cuts bush with a small billhook called a *mor*. Pkite uses the ubiquitous

TABLE 12.4. Farms in Which Pkite Lorongelosi Is Involved

Field no.	Description	Names of participants	Kin of Pkite	*Korok* in which owner resides	Residence E or W side of Marin River
1	Maize field near Pkite's house	Pkite		Tirtoi	E
2	Finger millet opposite Pkite's house	Pkite		Tirtoi	E
		**Kanakwang	k	Tirtoi	E
		**Chepokoweri	k	Tirtoi	E
		**Cheptonjyo (f)	k	Tirtoi	E
3	Maize, beans, banana field	Pkite		Tirtoi	E
		***Chirotwa	k	Tirtoi	E
4 and 5	Large communal maize farm across Marin River	Pkite (2)		Tirtoi	E
		***Chirotwa	k	Tirtoi	E
		**Lotilem	k	Tirtoi	E
		**Kanakwang	k	Tirtoi	E
		**Psintag	k	Tirtoi	E
		**Chepokoweri	k	Tirtoi	E
		**Cheptonjyo (f)	k	Tirtoi	E
		**Yaranyang	k	Tirtoi	E
		Lokor		Asar	W
		Kapkai (2)		Asar	W
		Kapasir (2)		Asar	W
		Lomonyong		Kapilwa	W
		Kisitut		Tirtoi	E
		Perechu		Tirtoi	E
		Sangwate		Tirtoi	E
		Kortchome		Tirtoi	E
		Chepenut (2)		Asar	W
		Kinjeltum		Tirtoi	E
		Lokwameru		Kokwatandwa	W
		Psirkoi		Kapkomo	W
		Koitum		Asar	W
		Lokalis		Asar	W
		Lorongolima		Asar	W
		Murun		Psiogh	W
		Longurasia (2)		Asar	W
		Siwareign		Asar	
6	Finger millet farm far to the south	Pkite and ***Chirotwa		Tirtoi	E
		**Psintag		Tirtoi	E
		Kisiautum		Tirtoi	E
		Mokono		Tirtoi	E
		Karuno		?	?
		**Lotilem		Tirtoi	E
		Tambach		Tirtoi	E
		**Yaranyang		Tirtoi	E
		Loitareigm		Tirtoi	E
		Chepinyin		Tirtoi	E
		Chepenyorio (f)		Kitonyo	E
		Kapchok		Ptalam	E
		Kapundos		Ptalam	E

Key: ** = name appears twice; *** = name appears thrice; k = member of same subclan as Pkite; (f) = female; (2) = has two fields in this farm. Total number of people involved is 35.

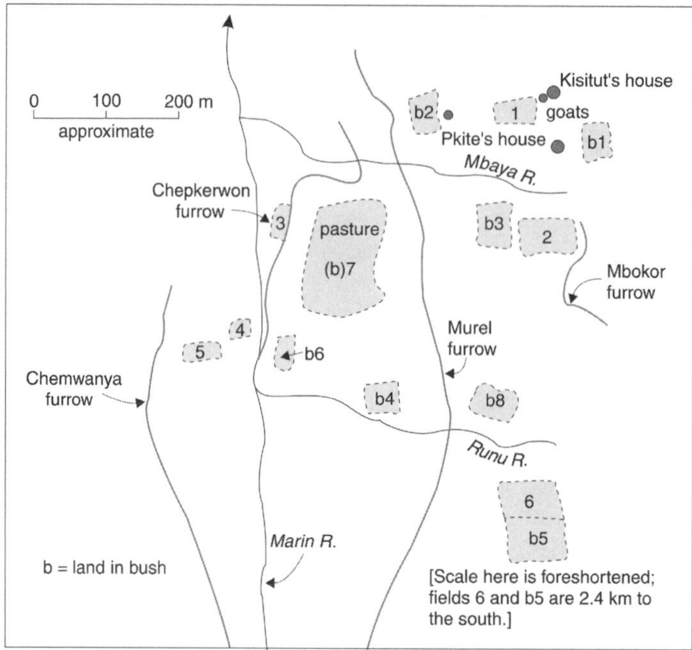

FIGURE 12.4. Sketch map of the land holdings of Pkite Lorongelosi's family.

panga, a flat, broad-bladed cutlass. They cut all the bush except the big trees. The lower branches of the big trees are lopped off as well. Other tools used in cutting the bush are the *oiwa*, a Pokot-made axe, and the *chouk*, a large sheath knife smaller than a *panga*, which is sharpened on both sides.[5] It is really a sort of short sword.

The bush is left to dry for a month, until the middle of March. Fires are set to it at the bottom of the field and allowed to burn uphill. Sometimes these fires get out of hand and have to be put out by hitting the flames with green-leaved branches. After the bush has burned, the field is left for a week. Pkite then collects all the unburned litter, some of which he burns and some of which he uses to build the fence, which is nearly 2 meters high and very dense at the base. The next day Cheptonjyo accompanies him to the field, and while Pkite continues work on the fence, she begins to sow finger millet seed and to cultivate the field. She does this with a small hoe called a *kapemba*. Pkite constructs trash terraces at the same time he makes the fence.[6] Commonly, of course, this work is done with others, in larger fields.

When the finger millet is 25–30 centimeters high, it is weeded. If Cheptonjyo isn't getting the weeding done quickly enough, Pkite comes to help. The weeding is done in June and takes a full 4 weeks. Now the field is left until August, when it will be ready for harvest. A few weeks before harvest, troubles with birds begin during the day; the task of guarding the crops now occupies the time of small children, who sit on platforms and sling stones and pellets at the birds. White quartz rocks are placed on stumps and rocks to glisten in the sun and frighten away any birds. The birds are called *sawatch*; they are small finches with brown backs and white breasts. They flit to and fro, moving in groups. The birds are troublesome only at harvest time. During this period, moreover, it is necessary to patrol the fields day and night against animals—birds, baboons, monkeys, and goats by day, and bush pigs, porcupines, and jackals by night. For this purpose, temporary huts are commonly built right in the field.

The harvesting of finger millet is done in Pkite's land only by Cheptonjyo, using a small knife. She puts the finger millet seed clusters in a big sack called a *sambur*, and takes them to her granary. Each day more finger millet is added to the store. This continues until all the finger millet has been harvested. If Pkite's first wife were still living with him, she too would have a field of finger millet and her own granary. Pkite has his own granary for maize. Maize and millet are not mixed in the same granary, although both can be stored in the same granary at different levels.

The finger millet is cleaned little by little as it is used. The heads are beaten with a sharp stone to break the hulls and stems away from the grain. The millet is hand-winnowed, and the grain and shells are hand-rubbed. The grain is then placed in an animal's skin, in a cloth sack called a *rupka*, or in shallow bamboo baskets called *kusa*. A rudimentary milling process is used to make flour of maize, finger millet, and sorghum.

The management details concerning a maize field on flat land are slightly different from those concerning a finger millet field on the slopes of the *kamass*. The field is prepared in about the same way and time as a hill farm, except that the fence is made after the land has been cultivated, and the maize seeds are planted in rows. As soon as the plant has about five leaves, the field is weeded, after which it is left until the weeds come up again. This first weeding is in June; a second weeding is done at the end of the month. A hoe is used in both planting and weeding maize. The harvest, in August, Pkite and Cheptonjyo can handle by themselves. The disposition of the harvest is Pkite's affair. It goes to his granary, and he may sell some or all of it as he pleases. If he decides to sell, he can perhaps get 6 shillings ($0.84 in 1962 or $4.30 in 1996 U.S. dollars) for a *debe* (5-gallon tin, U.S. gallons; 19.9 liters) of shelled maize at the shops or from the police station in Sigor.[7] Or again, if there is enough surplus, he can exchange it for a goat. People from Masol, Roruk, and Kapacess come to the mountain valleys to buy maize and finger millet in exchange for milk and livestock.

If it becomes apparent that some agricultural task is going to be more than Pkite and Cheptonjyo can accomplish, they may resort to giving a *kiyuch*, or work party. This will definitely be the case if Cheptonjyo becomes ill or gives birth to a child just at harvest time. But the usual use of the *kiyuch* is for weeding finger millet. Pkite brews three or four calabashes of beer—either *kumbachai* made from store-bought sugar; *kumbamageen*, a mead beer made from fermented honey; or a millet beer (*maiwa*), made from maize and sprouted finger millet. News of the beer preparation and the work party will circulate, or Pkite may actually visit neighbors to recruit participants. Some 10 or more neighbors—men, women, and girls; mostly clan relatives—will come. They will weed in one or two finger millet fields during the day, until enough work has been done. Then they will sit down, relax, and talk while Pkite brings out and distributes the beer.

Irrigation

Figure 12.3 shows the distribution of irrigation furrows (*orapagh*, "path of water"), which originate in the *kamass* and *touh* portions of Tamkal Valley. There are at least 22, beginning with a furrow named Mbrunuh whose takeoff point is high up on the Runu River. At the lower end of the valley are two large furrow systems that supply water for all of the Kurut people, a group that farms the plains near Sigor (discussed below). Excluding these very long Kurut furrows, the average length of the irrigation channels is 1.4 kilometers. The Murel, 3.7 kilometers long, is the longest furrow in the valley itself. The aggregate length of the 17 furrows in an 8-kilometer segment of Tamkal Valley is 24.6 kilometers. This is the equivalent to three furrows running the full length of this segment of the valley. Furrows are commonly short and contained within a single *korok*. A few start in another *korok*, but do not involve much irrigable land in the upstream *korok* and are therefore not subject to dispute. Two of the furrows are long, and disputes over water from these furrows do develop between *korok*. The Murel furrow passes through the Sungwut, Ptalam, Tirtoi, and Kamicich *korok*. The Ataril, farther downstream and 2.4 kilometers in length, flows through Wator and Kitonyo *korok*. Table 12.5 gives particulars about these furrows.

The origins of these furrows are not known. The Pokot claim that some of the furrows were there when they came to this country. It is certain that the technique is old and is known to most people in east Africa. Much more impressive feats of irrigation engineering can be found among the Elgeyo and Marakwet, who occupy the Elgeyo Escarpment, stretching south of Pokot country to Tambach. There, high flumes carry water across ravines, and the water is made to flow great distances to the fields.

The furrows in Tamkal Valley proper (excluding the Kurut farmers, whose system is described later) should be considered as antidrought measures. So long as the rains continue to be adequate, the furrows remain unused. But if the rains seem insufficient and the crops are beginning to show signs of drought, the people will take the necessary steps to repair and open the furrows.

FURROW MAINTENANCE AND CONSTRUCTION. When it becomes apparent that resorting to supplemental irrigation water will be necessary, the men call a *kokwa*. If the furrow involved runs through several *korok*, a *kokwa* in each *korok* will be called. Necessary repairs of the furrow will be done, the people of each *korok* taking care of their segment of furrow. If one

TABLE 12.5. Furrow Lengths in Tamkal Valley and Kurut

Number	Name	Length (meters)	Number of *korok* through which furrow flows
Tamkal Valley furrows			
1	Mbrunuh	2,960	1
2	Murel	3,705	4
3	Sangat	425	1
4	Tapar	840	1
5	Chemwanya	1,340	2
6	Songoch	995	1
7	Mbokor	1,595	1
8	Cheperkwon	275	1
9	Narah	1,145	2
10	Sirimun	925	1
11	Chepkirnoi	1,460	1
12	Ataril	2,400	2
13	Chepkontol	?	?
14	?, in Kale *korok*	945	1
15	?, in Nurpotwa *korok*	1,450	1
16	Psintag	2,140	1
17	Turkowo	1,040	1
18	?, in Psiogh *korok*	890	1
Kurut furrows			
19	Ara Pupuh Kan'gora	8,015	1
20	Ara Pupuh Mochowun	6,920	1
21	Ara Pupuh Kapirich	?	1
22	Right bank Weiwei furrow	4,510	1

group finishes its repairs early, its members will go help the others. This work usually takes place in late August and in September, just before the water is needed.

The men involved will be those who have fields and plan to use some of the water. The repairs are accomplished by work parties. A family that does not plan to use the water need not participate in the work parties. However, if later the members of this family decide to use water after all, then they must kill a male goat and give the meat to the people who did the work. There is no individual responsibility for the work of furrow renewal (it is not based, for example, on the length of furrow fronting on an individual's field). This is community work, and all help until it is done.

Pokot furrows are simple structures. The takeoff point consists of a ponded area, made by piling rocks up in the stream bed, at one edge of which is a sluice that regulates the flow of water into the furrow. The furrows in *kamass* hug the sides of hills, describing the path of slightly inclined contours. In *touh*, they strike out from the takeoff point to follow along the sharp change in slope between *touh* and *kamass*, thereby making it possible to irrigate any land between the furrow and the main stream. Construction and repairs are carried out during the rainy season, when water can be run into the furrow to gauge the slope. A shallow trench is dug, and the excavated material is placed downslope to form a continuous embankment. After a section has been dug, water dammed in an upstream segment is allowed to trickle into the new section. If it ponds or fails to run to the far end, the trench is dug deeper and the slope is increased. When the slope of a typical furrow in *touh* was surveyed, the average loss in elevation per 100 meters was about 50 centimeters; this is high for an irrigation channel built to western standards, but perfectly adequate for Pokot needs. The rate of elevation loss of *kamass* furrows is different. Long sections may run at a rate of about 50 centimeters lost per 100 meters, when suddenly the channel will drop abruptly and then take up its nearly level course once again. The reasons for this have to do with the kinds of land to be irrigated. Some land is so steep that it is not irrigated. Thus a sudden loss of altitude serves merely to keep the furrow on the high side of land that will be irrigated. Often water from a furrow will plunge into a ravine, join a stream, and travel along the stream course for a way. Then, a little farther on, the entire flow (furrow and stream) will be diverted into a continuation of the furrow.

The channel along which water flows from the main furrow into the field is called *sochyot*. The small channels that distribute water within the field are called *morut*. A field of sorghum or maize is irrigated from the top down. Commonly the water runs along the boundary a farmer's field makes with an adjacent field. A series of chevron-like incisions is made to divert water into a portion of the field. When that portion is sufficiently wetted, the little ditches are removed, and a new set of incisions is made lower down in the field. The process for ridged crops, such as sweet potatoes and cassava, is different. The ridges run approximately on the contour or are level, and each depression between rows is watered in turn.

FURROW USE AND OWNERSHIP. The opening of a furrow is performed by the oldest male member of the *korok*. This individual, who offers an invocation, is known as the *itcyotyon*, or "leader"; depending on the context in which it is used, the term can mean "judge," "opener of irrigation furrows," or "maker of feasts" (Conant, 1966, Chapter 5: 25). Once the furrow has been set in operation, decisions regarding the use of water are made by the *kokwa*. While irrigation continues, there is a *kokwa* as often as every afternoon to decide whose farm is driest and most in need of water. These decisions are made day by day. If two *korok*—say, Ptalam and Tirtoi—are concerned, a span of 5 days will be set aside for Ptalam; then it will be Tirtoi's turn to receive water for 5 days. If the people of one *kokwa* finish irrigating before the 5 days are up, they inform the other *kokwa* that it is all right to begin irrigating again.

There are quarrels when someone takes water before another has finished. Bad feeling sometimes develops between the people of adjacent *korok* over the use of a shared furrow. No one owns a furrow, however. If, for example, a person builds a furrow to irrigate a field, the builder will have to allow others to extend the furrow. Generally there is enough water to go around, and there is little occasion for friction to develop because of water scarcity.

In summary, the furrows, like the *paraghomucho*, are features of daily life in which the people share a common concern. Where furrows cross *korok* boundaries, the sharing of water is sometimes a matter of dispute between people of adjacent *kokwatin*. Agriculture in Tamkal Valley is based mostly on precipitation. In wet years, furrows will not be used at all. Thus, in Tamkal Valley at least, irrigation can be considered an agricultural device whereby the Pokot are enabled to prolong the rainy season and to counteract the inherent variability of rainfall from year to year.

The Daily Round

The rhythm of the daily round in Tamkal Valley is measured by an enormous clock—the valley itself, with sun and shadow silently ticking off the progress of time. Tamkal Valley is high-walled, and its axis has an almost perfect north–south orientation. There is therefore a succession of kinds of lighting in the valley from morning (*tpokwogho*) through afternoon (*munon*):

1. At the time of sunrise (*kaposoasis*), about 6 A.M., the sky overhead is light, but no land is in sunlight.
2. At about 7 A.M. occurs *kawatasis*, "the mark of the sun," when the sun begins to illumine areas high up on the west wall of the valley.
3. Eventually the sun itself can be seen in the valley bottom, and within minutes the entire valley is bathed in sunlight. This is *kechoachasis*, roughly, "the sun is going high." This is between 9 and 10 A.M.
4. Midday, when the sun reaches its zenith, is called *keghioasis* (*keghio*, "to stand").
5. The period when the sun is beginning definitely to incline to the west, between 1 and 2 P.M., is called *kamalassis*.
6. When the sun "sets"—which is fairly early, since it is still high in the sky when obscured by the Cherangani Hills—the term is *karaetoasis*.
7. Soon the edge of shadow has climbed the east wall of the valley, and now comes the period of *kapirtoi rurwonya*, which means that the whole valley is sunless. This persists until about 6:30 P.M.

Taking Pkite's livestock as an example, let us fit them into the round of daily activities. Pkite doesn't herd his cattle. His cattle are kept in Chirotwa's *kraal*, and Chirotwa, Pkite's older brother, herds them along with his own. At about *kawatasis* (7 A.M.), the cows are milked; the calves are allowed to feed, and then the calves are closed up in the house while the cows go off to graze. Chirotwa accompanies them and stays with them most of the morning. About midday, he goes off to his own work. The cattle remain unattended, but he checks on them a few times during the afternoon. Just before sunset, he goes to the cattle and takes them back to the *kraal*. They reach the *kraal* just before dark. The women now milk the cows and let the calves feed, after which the calves are locked in the house and the cattle are closed in the *kraal*.

The calves are separated from the cows when still young, until they have been weaned. After that they are allowed to go with the cows. The calves spend the first part of the morning locked in the house. At about 9 A.M., Chirotwa takes the calves off a little way from the house in a direction different from that in which he took the cows. The calves are then allowed to graze. Sometimes the calves go off and find their mothers.

Pkite keeps the goats near his own house and cares for them himself. Actually, the goats are not herded at all, but are left to fend for themselves. Sometimes Pkite takes them down onto the flat land near the Marin River and lets them find their own way back to the *kraal*.

The daily round of Cheptonjyo and other women is governed by milking, which, in a sense, marks the beginning and end of the day. Weeding and other agricultural tasks are usually done in the morning when it is cool. Household tasks, milling of maize and finger millet, making beer, and so forth are more commonly reserved for the afternoon.

The Seasonal Pattern of Agriculture

There are seasonal as well as daily rhythms in agriculture and in livestock management. It is worthwhile describing these seasonal rhythms in detail, for through them we gain many insights into the Pokot's understanding of ecological differences and the implications of these differences for their livelihood.

The seasonal round for farmers is complicated in Tamkal Valley by the fact that they are using simultaneously land in *touh*, *kamass*, *masob*, and even *tourku*, each with its own seasonal characteristics. We have already examined the land-holding and agricultural round of Pkite and his family, who live in *kamass*, with fields in cultivation in *touh* and *kamass* (see Plate 12.9). We give one more example to show in a more formal way the seasonal rhythm to the distribution of labor, shared among several zones.

A family living in *masob* (Figure 12.5) will own some land also in *kamass* and *touh*. In any one year they will be likely to have a maize field in *touh*, one finger millet field in *kamass*, and one maize and one finger millet field in *masob* (see Plate 12.10). The diagram shows the succession of work for the husband, and more importantly for the wife or wives. In using three altitudinal zones, the family schedules the planting over a 3-month period, the weeding over a 2-month period, and the harvest over a 3- or 4-month period. In *kamass* and *touh*, they plant finger millet and maize in March; in *masob*, the planting of maize is in April, and that of finger millet in late April and May. Maize and finger millet take only 6 months to mature in *touh* and *kamass*, whereas in *masob* they take 7 or 8 months. It would take even longer there, but they delay the *masob* plantings so that the grain ripens in the dry months of October and November, when there is sunshine in all the valley and it is warm in *masob*. The Pokot explain this use of several environments as serving two purposes: (1) to distribute work more evenly through the agricultural year, and (2) to spread the risk of loss of crops because of disease or lack of water.

The diet of a Pokot family reflects the dominant economy of the place where it lives. Pastoralists consume more stock products, farmers more grains and vegetables. All Pokot, however, consume *ugali*, a porridge usually made from ground finger millet, sorghum, or maize. Porridge prepared from sorghum or finger millet is preferred. Also included in the diet are cassava, both roots and leaves (which make a nutritious spinach), and items from small kitchen gardens, such as tomatoes, onions, sweet potatoes, cabbages, and bananas (both sweet and in plantain form). At higher elevations, English potatoes are eaten. People also collect or eat in passing bush products, berries, fruits, and seeds encountered as part of the daily round of walking from one place to another or herding livestock. Beehives are maintained to collect honey, which is eaten raw or made into a fermented mead. Another kind of beer is made from finger millet. Hunting brings in meat, such as small antelope, dik-dik, or colobus monkey. Eggs are eaten. The Pokot do not fish. The pastoral people rely more heavily on milk—fresh as well as soured or curdled, or made into a kind of soft cheese. They eat more meat, especially goat meat,

PLATE 12.9. A hill settlement with *kraal* for stock, Lomut. The houses and granaries are situated on the *kamass*, away from the malarial and tsetse-ridden plains below. In the lowland on the left can be seen irrigated sorghum fields through which runs an irrigation furrow, marked by paths on both sides. The size of the opening to the *kraal* shows that only goats and sheep are kept by this family.

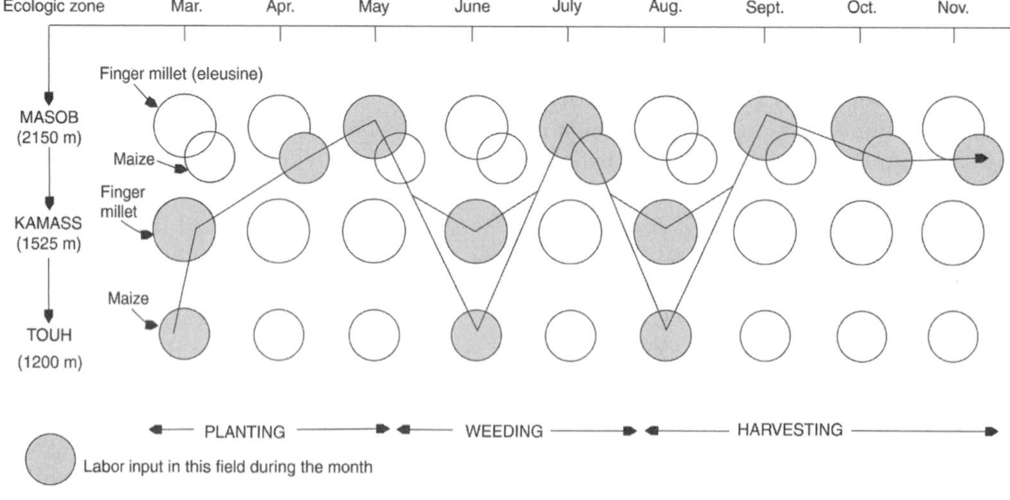

FIGURE 12.5. Planting, weeding, and harvesting cycle in Tamkal Valley, West Pokot District: Idealized example of work patterns of one family living in *masob*. *Source:* Knight and Newman (1976). Copyright 1976 by Prentice-Hall. Adapted by permission.

Plate 12.10. Finger millet in the *masob* country, Kokwatandwa. This field, managed by the families of Samuel Ptiso Chumakemer and his brother, is planted to finger millet (*Eleusine coracana*), which can be grown here for only 1 year. In the second year, competition from weeds becomes too intense. Standing tree stumps, whose branches have been lopped, are characteristic sights. Sunshine is reduced in Kokwatandwa, and the crops need all the sun they can get. A high bush fence is seen on the left, climbing the steep incline. Trash terraces to reduce soil creep and soil wash are built at the insistence of agricultural aides.

and consume blood from cattle when it is fresh or after it has coagulated. Although maize, finger millet, and livestock products predominate, the Pokot diet overall is varied and balanced.

Because the Pokot use land at several altitudes, they are able to schedule planting, weeding, and harvesting *en echelon*. Thus there is never any month in which they cannot cope with the agricultural tasks. Their management of livestock also reflects a keen awareness of seasonal ecological differences. When work demands in the fields close to home are at their highest, the local graze is at its best; during much of the dry season, when agricultural activities have been suspended, there is time to take the cattle farther afield in search of graze. There is little doubt that in the Pokot's view, a livelihood based solely on one altitudinal zone is not possible. The shape and geographic layout of the *korok* are consistent with their view that control and use of several altitudinal zones are necessary.

THE KURUT

The Kurut are a group of several hundred households, whose members live on the *kamass* to the west and southeast of the Weiwei River, where it flows onto the plains past

Sigor. By comparison with other Pokot, the Kurut people have enormous irrigated fields on the flat alluvium (*sos*) on either side of the Weiwei River (see Plate 12.11). Agriculture cannot be based on rainfall alone in this area. In fact, only April in Sigor can be considered a nondrought month. The people are therefore almost wholly dependent on the Weiwei River for water with which to irrigate their crops, mainly sorghum (*masong*).

The first matter to observe is the layout of furrows and fields on this alluvial area (Figure 12.6). There are three furrows on the west side of the Weiwei, two of which share a common takeoff point. There is another furrow on the right bank. The furrows on the left bank are named Ara Pupuh Kan'gora, Ara Pupuh Mochowun, and Ara Pupuh Kapirich (a small one). Downslope from the main takeoff point on the left, the land for several hundred meters is not farmed because of gravelly soils. A bifurcation occurs after about 1,800 meters; Ara Pupuh Kan'gora flows across higher ground close to Sigor, whereas Ara Pupuh Mochowun traverses lower ground nearer the Weiwei River.

The latter furrow flows for part of its course along the edge of a forest named Oluwa. This forest in former times was a place to which the people could flee for refuge and common defense if an attack occurred while they were in their fields. Although the need for flight is less today, the forest still stands. These two furrows effectively divide the Kurut people west of the Weiwei into two independent groups: the N'gora people, served by Ara Pupuh Kan'gora, and the Ptakough people, served by the Ara Pupuh Mochowun. Very few people have land in both furrow zones, although people from the two groups intermarry.

The farm is a large communal enterprise involving as many as 100 heads of households. There is a common fence around the entire planted area, "which it would take you an hour to walk around," according to

PLATE 12.11. Kurut irrigated sorghum. The Kurut people have enormous, irrigated, communal fields on the flat alluvium (*sos*) on either side of the Weiwei River. The landmark known as Koh, meaning "cow's hump," is on the left (see Figure 12.2).

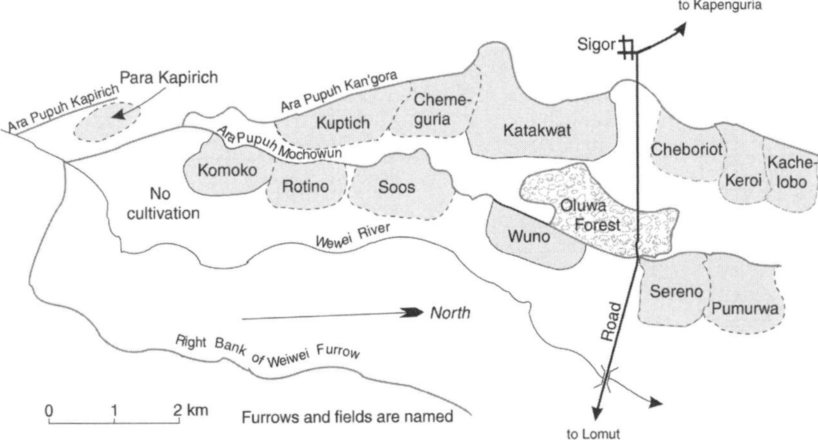

FIGURE 12.6. Kurut irrigation furrows and farms (schematic).

an informant. The fields of six large farms are served by a single furrow. The six farms have names and appear to be used one after another in an orderly sequence (Table 12.6).

There are two crop seasons a year. The major crop season is during the main rains (March–September); work on the second crop season begins with the decrease of the rains and runs through to the end of the dry season. Sometimes the Weiwei by January has been reduced to a mere trickle of water, and irrigation is no longer possible. In such instances the yields of crops will be reduced. The dry season crop is to some extent a famine measure; that is, if the yield from the first crop is adequate, the people may decide not to plant during the second season. In most years, however, a second planting is done. If a field is planted, it is wholly planted, for it is not good to have enclaves of bush.

A representative Kurut family is that of Aranyatom Likeno. Aranyatom is old now, probably well into his 60s. He was born in Weiwei Location, as were his father and his father's father. He was a member of the African District Council (ADC) criminal court for 2 years, but otherwise has not been involved in the administration of the district. The farthest he has been away from home is Karasuk, scarcely 80 kilometers away. He has had no schooling; there were no schools when Aranyatom was a boy.

Aranyatom has two fields in cultivation in August, and more than a dozen other fields in fallow. All of these are irrigable by the same furrow, Ara Pupuh Kan'gora. During the main rains, the large farm named Kuptich is under cultivation; the farm in line to be cultivated that September is Katakwat. Aranyatom has two plots of ground in Kuptich cultivated and another left in fallow. One of the fields is that of Sikohwa, the wife he inherited. The other fields he inherited from his father. The field attached to Sikohwa will be passed on to her sons. The distribution of fields at Aranyatom's disposal is shown in Table 12.7.

Aranyatom, with himself and two wives to feed, has nearly a hectare in crops. His sons have some fields of their own. The area in sorghum is 0.6 hectares; the area in finger millet is 0.16 hectares. He estimates his yield from the small sorghum field (area: 0.15 hectares) at 4 *somburh*. This works out to a yield of 1,125 kilograms/hectare. His estimates for the large field are 10 *somburh* of sorghum and 3–4 *somburh* of finger millet, which translates into yields of 980 kilograms/hectare for the sorghum, and 900–1,125 kilograms/hectare for the finger millet. The food produced in a year, assum-

TABLE 12.6. Sequential Use of the Farms Served by Ara Pupuh Kan'gora

Month	Year	Name of field
September	1962	Katakwat
January	1962	Kuptich
September	1961	Cheboriot
January	1961	Keroi
September	1960	Katakwat
January	1960	Cheboriot and Kachelobo
September	1959	Keroi
January	1959	Katakwat
September	1958	Chemeguria
January	1958	Kuptich
September	1957	Chemeguria

South - - - - -Kup - - - - -Chem - - - - -Kat - - - - - - -Cheb - - - - - -Ker - - - - - - - -Kac - - - - - -North

Time:	Kup	Chem	Kat	Cheb	Ker	Kac
S/62			*			
J/62	*					
S/61				*		
J/61					*	
S/60			*			
J/60				* - - - - -	- - - - - - -	- - -*
S/59					*	
J/59			*			
S/58		*				
J/58	*					
S/57		*				

ing a second planting of about 0.8 hectare, will be on the order of 1,640 kilograms of small grains, which seems sufficient for the needs of his family.

The annual agricultural cycle is shown in Table 12.6. There are really two cycles running concurrently. In August, the harvest of sorghum and finger millet is underway in Kuptich. During the daily *kokwatin*, however, plans are being laid to clear the farm named Katakwat, and work parties to put the necessary additional segment of furrow in readiness are being organized. Finger millet is planted after sorghum in May and harvested in August, just before the sorghum matures. The tools are the same as those in Tamkal Valley. Other crops grown by the Kurut people are cassava and a little maize. Tobacco is grown in the *kamass* around the houses. Tobacco and maize are grown partly as cash crops for local trade, particularly with the people of Masol. The money is

TABLE 12.7. Aranyatom's Fields

Farm name	Number of fields inherited from Aranyatom's father (worked by Chesalawich)	Number of fields on which Aranyatom has interim claim (worked by Sikohwa)
Kuptich	2	1
Katakwat	4	2
Cheboriot	2	1
Keroi	1 (very large)	1
Kachelobo	1	1

Note. Fields are listed in the order cited by Aranyatom. He made no mention of any fields in Chemeguria.

used to buy aluminum pots and pans, beads, wire, clothing, and other trade goods at small shops in Sigor.

The *kokwa* decides which farm is to be planted, and arranges for the repair of furrows and the distribution of water. A reconstruction of the movement from farm to farm follows a rough sequence in which fields are used serially one after another up and down the length of the furrow (see Figure 12.6 and Table 12.6). The pattern of 12 seasons suggests that the farm at the southern end of the furrow near the takeoff point has been left in fallow longer than the farms in the center (Katakwat, Cheboriot, and Keroi). This may stem from the fact that the sandy soils in Kuptich (they are *pirirwok* and *n'gyomwoh*) cannot support repeated croppings. The invocation with which the *itcyotyon*, or leader, opens the furrow is longer among the Kurut, where much more depends on irrigation water for success (Conant, 1966, Chapter 5: 30).

With over 100 families involved in a single common farm, there are obvious problems connected with the distribution of the irrigation water. During the irrigation season, the *kokwa* meets daily. The order in which people receive water is a function of nearness to the start of the furrow, but everyone has a turn (see Plate 12.12). Users at higher elevations receive water before those at lower elevations. A person gets water rights overnight and all the next day, and gets to use the furrow again about a week later. The users are divided into groups of six or eight people who use a common small channel called a *sochyot*. The people decide among themselves who is to use the water on a certain day. Aranyatom and his son estimate that there are perhaps 20 such groups in the one communal farm, which indicates something in excess of 100 households.

The fields are in strips, as they are in Tamkal Valley, and the strips usually run half the width of the farm; that is, there are two plots running from the furrow downslope to the low edge of the farm. The boundaries are marked by stones and have been fixed for many years. They are not a source of dispute. Disputes over water do arise, especially among the young men. These disputes are settled in the *kokwa*.

Work parties are strong regular features of the Kurut management of agriculture. Aranyatom always arranges work parties for larger tasks, and participates in those that others hold. In the first season of this particular year (1962), he has had two work parties in his large field, one for bush clearance and one for cultivating. For a third work party, he provided no beer (this consisted of children who did weeding). Children are given the important task of guarding against birds. Spaced at intervals of perhaps 25–30 meters are platforms on which children sit and keep the swarms of weaver birds away. They use long flexible sticks (*sitoprum*) onto which moist mud balls are pressed and then hurled at the birds. Aranyatom notes the following crop pests and diseases in the Kurut area: wild pigs, birds, black-faced monkeys, porcupines, baboons, and a worm called *machon* that attacks the sorghum and sometimes the finger millet. As the season advances and mature sorghum stalks reach heights of 2–3 meters, the stalks are tied in bundles as they stand to protect against wind damage, giving the field something of the appearance of a giant mangrove forest at low tide.

The Kurut area is surrounded by dense *Acacia–Sansevieria* thicket, which is infested with tsetse flies. The area is also malarial. As a consequence, both people and livestock live on the *kamass* and descend to the plains by day. Few cattle are kept by the Kurut people, but they do have many sheep and goats. Aranyatom will not say how many head of stock he has, but he does say that the average flock includes 15 sheep and goats, and that average cattle numbers are 1 or 2, although some people have a lot of cattle. Most of the cattle are herded elsewhere by clan brothers or friends. He claims that few people have many sheep.

Aranyatom has one of his grandsons look after the sheep and goats. His livestock

PLATE 12.12. Aranyatom, a Kurut farmer, closes off an irrigation channel after diverting his share of irrigation water into his field of sorghum. He cooperates with four other farmers in using the water on a rota basis. His is one of several hundred farm families that use the waters of the Weiwei River to irrigate lowlands near Sigor (see Figure 12.6).

can graze between the furrow and *kamass* when there are crops growing. They can move to Katakwat, which is currently in fallow. In the rainy season, the goats and sheep are grazed in the *kamass*. Many Kurut people keep cattle elsewhere, in Batei and Kipkomo, above Ortum (to the west); and some cattle are kept in Masol, but not many, because they commonly die during the dry season for lack of grass.

The goats give a small, uncertain amount of milk, and also supply blood, meat, and hide. In a sense, goats replace cattle in both subsistence and ritual. Like the cattle in Masol, the goats are bled, and the blood is mixed with milk. Instead of the short blocked arrow used in Masol, a thin hollow reed is jabbed into the goat at a place below the eyelid, and the blood is collected.

The Kurut don't hunt much, but some of the people fish in the Weiwei River, using hooks and lines. They also use baskets and weirs. Aranyatom has about 10 beehives and obtains honey four times a year. The Kurut are distinctive among the Pokot in the size and labor intensity of their agricultural operations. Almost all activities are concentrated in the one zone called *sos*. The *kamass* west of Sigor is so dry that the land cannot be farmed. Nonetheless, these two environments are necessary to life, for neither people nor livestock can live in *sos*.

INDIGENOUS KNOWLEDGE AND ADAPTIVENESS AMONG THE POKOT

The Pokot have a lively and informed understanding of their environment and the possibilities it provides for living. Furthermore, they take advantage of their informed understanding of their lands in their organization of space, use of resources, organization of internal social relations, and actions and reactions to external social and economic phenomena. It would be good if it were possible to discuss these elements under these headings, but in practice they become so intertwined that we ask the reader to look for them in the following summary. For example, the *korok* concerns organization of space and appraisal of natural resources; it also has implications for social relations in the distribution of individual and community risks, in settlement pattern, and in the mobilization of labor.

First, there are areal specializations and interregional trade. This gives a basic division of labor, with some communities specializing in livestock and others engaged in growing crops. The integration of farming and herding takes many forms. For example, farmers may own stock cattle and small stock that are managed by *tilia* kin or affines on the plains. Younger sons of farmers serve periods as herdboys in families of Masol, returning later to the farms. Farm daughters are married into plains households, and the bridewealth livestock stay where they always were.

There are gradations and admixtures of farming and stock keeping everywhere in Pokot country—an emphasis on goats here, a greater reliance on sorghum and bulrush millet there, an absence of irrigation in some highland communities. Each variation reflects the Pokot's reasoned appraisal of environmental suitability. The Kurut community provides an instance of cooperation on a grand scale, permitting several hundred people to use a large potential resource (arable land irrigated by one large furrow taken from the Weiwei River) in an area that is otherwise very marginal. Cooperation is organized hierarchically (households; groups of about five families sharing irrigation water; and the *kokwa*, encompassing 100 families using a single large field at a time).

The *korok*, the bounded territory of a Pokot community, is specifically designed where possible to encompass different ecological zones. This gives individual Pokot households, as well as entire communities, opportunities to grow different crops, to disperse in space and thereby reduce the risk of crop failure, and to lengthen and even out labor inputs. The *korok* works best in hill country, where different ecological zones are close together. It is less important in pastoral areas, where mobility and social bonds based on cattle deals (*tilia*, *kamanakan*) become more important.

Many collaborative practices associated with the management of the *paraghomucho* and individual fields reflect Pokot knowledge. By managing a field as a group, the people mobilize labor; provide for sociability (e.g., in communal weeding by women); reduce labor costs (e.g., in guarding ripe sorghum or finger millet against birds, or in fencing one large field rather than many smaller ones); and yet provide for individual ownership by women of the harvest from their individually marked fields. The Pokot lop and pollard tree branches to ensure that crops are not shaded from the sun. They put manure and household ashes in their kitchen gardens to enrich the soil. The choice of crops, timing of planting, use of supplemental irrigation, and intercropping are all examples of Pokot field management that work. Other practices may be borrowed or introduced; for example, trash terraces were constructed at the insistence of the district agricultural officer (although the Pokot said they did it before the agricultural officers came—Conant, 1966, Chapter 5: 12), and the growing of white potatoes was introduced by Europeans in the 1930s. However, most borrowed practices are old, and their origins are lost in the mists of time. For example the Pokot may have learned to irrigate from now-vanished Sirikwa people. Indigenous knowledges are therefore not static, but are continually evolving as they incorporate useful practices from others and adapt to changing conditions.

Irrigation is used as a buffer or insurance system in many farming communities. Labor is expended to bring irrigation channels into operation when it becomes necessary. This minimizes risk without using labor unnecessarily.

Livestock movements both in Masol and in Tamkal Valley are carefully scheduled. In Masol, the schedule is built around the seasonal availability of water and the location of pastures. The distribution of good pasture itself can change as small storms occur during the rains, benefiting one catchment and missing another. Moves can take place over considerable distances and involve establishing new camps. In Tamkal Valley, the scheduling of stock movement is a less vital matter and does not involve moves by the entire community. Scheduling takes into account the labor demands associated with farming. There are times when stock can be taken quite far away for grazing, and others when there is too much work to do in the fields.

The pastoralists of Masol show striking differences from the farmers of Tamkal Valley in individual and community behavior and in emphasis on social institutions, despite the fact that they share many values and social practices. The major difference stems from the settledness of life and the steady annual round of activities in the farming hills, as compared with the mobility, uncertainty, and instability of livestock keeping on the plains. The former encourages codified practice and regular behavior; the latter encourages, and even demands, flexibility and decisiveness. The *korok*, *kokwa*, *paraghomucho*, *kiyuch* (work party), and clan are central and stable elements in the hills. The *tilia*, *kamanakan*, trading bands, and allocation of tasks by age sets (*sapana* groups) disperse the locations of effort and risk in the plains. Although clans and the *kokwa* are elements of social life among the plains pastoralists, their importance is obscured in the flux of cattle exchanges; in the seasonal fragmentations and reunions of families and herds in the ongoing succession of rainy, dry, and drought periods; and in the changing fortunes of families linked by bridewealth or disrupted by stock disease or theft.

Depending on the potential of the land, the Pokot bring into play one strategy or another, often several simultaneously. Pokot match management practices with the potentialities of their land. Their strategy may call on a management practice that is spatial/geopolitical (*korok*), environmental/resource-specific (irrigation in Kurut), socioeconomic (*tilia*), or linked to a larger political economy (seeking work in the Trans-Nzoia, or sending a child to boarding school to have one fewer mouth to feed). In every case, however, the strategy represents an appraisal of what is possible, what is desirable, and what the likely outcome may be (in reduced risk, assured production, or increased wealth). The Pokot have many ways of reaching a realistic understanding of their material and social world. Each circumstance and setting brings into play different techniques and institutional arrangements. For most Pokot, notwithstanding all that has happened to them between 1963 and 2008 (described in the following section), the dream of a good life is embodied in autonomy, good grazing lands, some fields in crop, a large herd, and a prosperous family.

THE POKOT AND KENYA'S POLITICAL ECONOMY

The foregoing presentation has purposely concentrated on the Pokot indigenous knowledge system and practice; however, life for the Pokot has always been affected by people and events elsewhere. We end this chapter with a sketch of what has happened to the Pokot since Kenya became independent in 1963. Year by year, they have become drawn more deeply into political and economic relationships with the rest of Kenya and the global economy (Dietz, 1987 and personal communication, June 8, 2005; Andiema, Dietz, and Kotomei, 2003). Recent events in

Pokot country prefigure themes that are the subjects of Part III of this book ("Differentiated Social Relations Encountering Global Strategies"). A consciousness among people in Europe and North America that there are people in Kenya who call themselves Pokot was greatly aided by the athletic accomplishments of Tegla Loroupe, a Pokot runner who has won many marathon races, beginning with the New York marathon in 1994 at the age of 21.[8]

In general, West Pokot District has remained a peripheral part of Kenya since independence. The rule of law weakened during the 1960s and 1970s as cattle raiding and the emergence of *ngoroko* gangs brought economic and social disruption to eastern, northern, and northwestern parts of the district. Some of these bands originated in Uganda out of the turmoil created during Idi Amin's period of misrule; certainly many of the high-powered arms of the *ngorokos* were obtained from Uganda. Disruption has continued through the 1980s, the 1990s, and the first years of the new century. There is some evidence that arms have been coming via southern Sudan, as well as from Kenyan and Somali arms merchants (Dietz, personal communication, June 8, 2005).

The district was the focus in the early 1970s of a major development effort of the government—the Special Rural Development Programme, which concentrated on livestock marketing and associated veterinary services, maize demonstrations, and community development and self-help projects (Widstrand, 1973: 36). Purebred Corriedale sheep were successfully introduced into Lelan, and commercial growing of hybrid maize, pyrethrum, beans, other vegetables (e.g., cabbage, kale), and fruit was expanded in Mnagei, the southern high country, far from Tamkal Valley and Masol. Elsewhere, however, there was a dramatic loss of cattle and small stock, and in some areas a decline in attention to farming, with attendant neglect of irrigation furrows.

This decline and neglect were offset by a gold rush, participated in by thousands of Pokot. Since 1979 alluvial gold has been panned in many localities in Mwina, as well as in Sekerr and Sook Locations (in central Pokot, and elsewhere in the district).[9] Pokot have panned for gold in large part as an "off-season" activity, and income from it has supplemented their incomes in a significant way, even though the main beneficiaries have been gold traders and those who have supplied goods and services in the mining communities. Gold mining is a part-time activity for many, mainly during the dry season between November and April (Dietz, van Haastrecht, and Schomaker, 1983c: 15). Panning for gold continues to be a small-scale activity, especially in bad years, involving thousands of men, women, and children. The gold traders are partly Somali, but many are Pokot as well. Active areas for gold panning include the lower Murun River between Ortum and Sigor.

In Mnagei and Lelan there has been encroachment on forested lands, as both Pokot and non-Pokot clear areas to make new farms. The Kapkanyar Forest was "degazetted" (i.e., removed from governmental protection) in 1982 by presidential decree (Dietz, van Haastrecht, and Schomaker, 1983a: 6). There continues to be illegal felling of trees in the Kapkanyar forest in Lelan (*Daily Nation*, February 28, 2005). Some improvement in transport has occurred, in part because of the development of the Turkwell Gorge Multipurpose Hydroelectric Project, the building of a tarmac road through the Marich Pass connecting Kitale with Lodwar, and road improvements attendant on the gold mining.[10]

In Tamkal Valley, compared with the 1960s, people are more inclined to use hired labor, to buy food, to be involved in the cash economy, and to send their children to school (Dietz, van Haastrecht, and Schomaker, 1983b: 19). The road into Tamkal from Sigor was greatly improved in the mid-1980s.

There has been a decline in the use of irrigation furrows in Tamkal Valley (Dietz et al., 1983b: 22). This decline can be attributed in part to the fact that many farmers have stopped growing a second crop of sorghum. Sorghum grown as a second crop invariably used irrigation and required that the furrows be functioning. Significant numbers of people were caught up in the gold fever, or moved to Mnagei and Lelan or sought wage work (Dietz et al., 1983b: 24).

On the Masol Plains, strife between the Pokot and Turkana resumed in 1967, and it was especially bad in the period 1974–1977. The eastern plains were emptied of Pokot (Dietz et al., 1983b: 19). This led to terrible economic hardship, with the Pokot clustered in refugee camps along the base of the escarpment, west of the Malmalte River (Conant, 1982a). It also led to vegetational changes in the areas occupied by the refugees, but also in the Masol Plains they had abandoned, where thicket formation, featuring *Acacia* spp., encroached on grassed areas (Conant, 1981).

Population data showed increased numbers of non-Pokot living in the district by 1979. A large share of these non-Pokot lived in Mnagei Location (in the south central highlands, adjacent to Trans-Nzoia District), many of them government officers. The enterprise of these people, and of some wealthy Pokot, has increased social stratification and intensified economic disparities in Mnagei Location (Reynolds, 1982). The 1999 census of Kenya placed the population of Pokot District at 308,086 (Central Bureau of Statistics, 1999, Vol. 1: Table 3). This compares with a figure of 170,000 in 1979. For a partly pastoral society, it was growing rapidly, 2.4% annually (Lang and Bollig, n.d.: 1). The younger Pokot generation shows both disaffection from and interest in the old way of life, and there are generational tensions. Dietz (personal communication, June 8, 2005) has noticed a "revival of 'pastoral identity' among youth, and it manifests itself for instance in a very strong 'repokotization' of identity markers among the young men in places like Kacheliba. The long black robes are very much back on market days. Many young men have again chosen to be warriors, even those with education."

No simple conclusions about the growth of disparities can be drawn with respect to the Pokot. As is true of most other groups in east Africa, there have always been "big men" and poor people among the Pokot. Age is a factor, since young married couples are generally poorer than older, established families. A class of landless, dispossessed in-migrants (both Pokot and non-Pokot) has emerged, who work for others. In West Pokot District, they commonly live in Mnagei and Lelan (the southern high country adjacent to Trans-Nzoia District), clearing land, making charcoal, and farming for a few years until the owner takes over farming and livestock raising. These landless people must then go elsewhere, hoping to repeat the sequence with another landowner.

The Pokot's fears that, with the arrival of independence, others would come in and take over land in Mnagei have proved to be true. Despite considerable efforts on the part of Pokot to control land registration, non-Pokot were able to gain title to land. Two local organizations (the Pokot Welfare Association and the Cherangany Union) proved to be ineffective in controlling land registration to accord with the wishes of Pokot and Sengwer residents.

Political changes in the district have also affected Pokot autonomy. The official policy of the Kenyan government in the 1960s and 1970s was to centralize power in the executive branch. In 1969, the government transferred responsibility for health services, education, and roads to its own ministries—thus effectively removing power and purpose from local and district councils, such as the Pokot Area Council (Reynolds, 1982: 124). In addition, ethnic associations were urged to cease operations or to keep their efforts entirely nonpolitical (Reynolds, 1982: 218). Furthermore, according to Reynolds (1982: 5; emphasis in original), the *harambee*—a fund-raising technique combining self-help with governmental matching of funds—was coopted by government officials and turned into "an agency for community *under*development," often supporting nonproductive services or projects that benefited few people.

Other events in more recent times affecting the Pokot include serious droughts in 1984, 1986, 1992–1993, and 2002, and a decline in the government's ability to fund the Arid and Semi-Arid Lands Programme (ASAL, the successor to the Special Rural Development Programme). The ASAL lasted from 1981 to 2000, and was funded by the Dutch Development Agency. The Kenyan government, itself short of funds to support development, asked donor countries to "adopt" districts in the arid and semi-arid parts of Kenya. The Netherlands "adopted" West Pokot and Elgeyo–Marakwet, immediately to its south, and later on Kajiado and Laikipia. The program evolved into a multisectoral development effort (health, education, agriculture, livestock/veterinary, afforestation, water supply, and social services—especially for women and children). The ASAL strategy was one of low donor profile, and its ultimate aim was to help local councils and civil servants from various ministries take responsibility for running the program (Dietz and de Leeuw, 1999: 43).

Dietz and his Pokot coworkers, Rachel Andiema and Albino Kotomei, did an evaluation of the ASAL experience, to gauge Pokot views on the successes and failures of ASAL and other organizations that operated in the district in the 1980s and 1990s. By and large, Pokot viewed any project connected with the government as "bad," and those connected with a church or a nongovernmental organization (NGO) as "good," although NGOs tended to be perceived as engaging in many unsustainable projects (Andiema et al., 2003: 11–12). Churches of many denominations, as well as church-related NGOs, are active in Pokot District. Higher cash incomes occurred among small farmers and pastoralists in ASAL areas as compared to areas where ASAL did not work (Dietz and de Leeuw, 1999: 51). This may not have been because of ASAL itself: "Cash income generation was also largely beyond the domain of ASAL programmes, as trade in livestock, gold, precious stones, minerals, miraa (i.e., qat [a narcotic plant]) and arms was largely outside the government's orbit" (Dietz and de Leeuw, 1999: 51).

After multiparty democratization began in Kenya in 1991, tensions between Pokot and non-Pokot residents emerged. The impetus for this was the promulgation in October 1991 of *majimboism* (regionalism) in Kenya's Kalenjin-dominated ruling party (Kenya African National Union) led by President Daniel Arap Moi. The idea, a return to pre-1964 policies, was that Kenya's government should be strongly decentralized and that regional government should be based largely on ethnicity. In the aftermath of an armed conflict in North Narok in October 1993, in which 17 people were killed and many more wounded, 30,000 mostly Kikuyu-speaking people fled Narok District. Subsequently, in December 1994, many of the refugees were forcibly repatriated to their "ancestral habitation" in Central Province (Dietz, 1996: 7). The Pokot, who are linguistically and culturally of Kalenjin ethnicity, shared in the general Maasai and Kalenjin view of the Kikuyu people as "expatriates," with at best only temporary rights in the ancestral lands of the Kalenjin and Maasai. Thus, in 1993, there began a kind of "ethnic cleansing" of Pokot District—particularly in Mnagei and Lelan, where many Kikuyu had taken up land. In this less publicized but active struggle, the Kikuyu and other "ethnic outsiders" were forced to abandon their homes and farms (Dietz and van Woersem, 1996: 18). "The ethnic hatred, politically instigated, [led] to the most dramatic results, so far, in West Pokot, where a large part of the non-Pokot population was chased away (or fled in panic and did not dare to return)" (Dietz and van Woersem, 1996: 21). Migration continues as a major factor in Pokot life, both as labor movements to employment opportunities around Kapenguria, Lelan, and Trans-Nzoia District, but also as permanent settlement on new lands in Trans-

Nzoia District (Dietz, personal communication, Jun 8, 2005). Pokot leaders now claim part or all of Trans-Nzoia as "traditional Pokot territory," a claim validated by reference to the testimony Pokot gave before the Carter Commission in 1934 (Kenya Land Commission, 1934, Vol. 2: 1763). There are ongoing disputes over idle, absentee-owned former ADC lands in Trans-Nzoia. David Pkosing, of the Kitale Peace and Justice Commission, said that 60,000 acres of ADC lands lay idle in Trans-Nzoia District (*Daily Nation*, October 17, 2004). There is also considerable pastoral movement that takes Pokot livestock into Uganda; into Trans-Nzoia District; and from Masol, Sekerr, and Sigor eastward into northern Baringo District. Trans-Nzoia District also experienced disruption in the first months of 2008, when the presidential election was being disputed between Mwai Kibaki and Ralia Odinga, though the turmoil was nothing to match what occurred in Eldoret District.

Since the late 1990s, the people of Pokot District have endured continuous disruptions in their lives and livelihoods because of banditry and cattle rustling. There are reports that cattle rustlers are now using mobile phones to coordinate their activities and monitor police movement (Obare, 2008). The economic costs in loss of cattle and crops were large. For all of Kenya, losses of $400 million were attributed to cattle rustling from 1990 to 1999 (Intermediate Technology Development Group [ITDG], 2003: 1). Banditry claimed 1,200 lives between 1995 and 2000. In addition, an ever-growing population has put pressure on land and grazing resources.

The cattle raiding, thievery, and banditry have been carried out by armed groups of Pokot, within the district, and by other groups from adjacent areas (especially Turkana, Karamojong, and Sabiny [Sebei]), but to a lesser extent by the Marakwet. Interethnic raiding has a long history (Bollig, 1990). The gangs, called *ngoroko*, are armed with AK47s and Heckler–Koch G3 assault rifles, as well as the usual spears. The Catholic Church Peace and Justice Commission reported that there were 60,000 illegal guns in the hands of West Pokot herdsmen (Obare and Maero, 2005).

The disruption these gangs cause goes far beyond loss of livestock and other possessions. People are killed during raids; women are raped and widowed; homesteads are burned; people flee, abandoning their homes and fields; schools are closed; health clinics are abandoned; and social institutions stop functioning. Someone benefits from these cattle raids, and it is possible that influential cattle and arms merchants are organizing and profiting from the raids. One report noted "that within two or three days of cattle rustling incidents, lorry loads of cattle are seen being transported out of the area yet no action is taken to ascertain their connection with the raids" (Ramani, 2001). One study estimated that 40% (nearly 16,000) of the people in Kasei and Alale Divisions had been directly affected by conflict, and that another 24% had been indirectly affected (Pkalya, Adan, and Masinde, 2003: 44). Pastoralism has not collapsed, but it has diminished greatly as a form of livelihood (Dietz, 2005: 2). Considerable numbers of the displaced people have moved to higher elevations, increasing land pressure there.

Certain other projects have been funded. The Italian government gave 1 billion Kenyan shillings ($12.6 million in 1994 U.S. dollars) for the Weiwei irrigation project, and the scheme has been deemed a great success (*Daily Nation*, December 18, 2004). In 2004, the Kerio Valley Development Authority (KVDA) was negotiating with the Spanish government for the development of a sugar irrigation project, which was projected to cost 24 billion Kenyan shillings (*Daily Nation*, December 18, 2004).

There are even efforts to promote tourism in Pokot District. One effort, funded by Swiss donors, is the Pokot Lomut Cultural Village (*The East African Standard*, March 5, 2005). Yet it is hard to see how tourism can flourish when visitors to the district are advised as a first step to stop at a police station to arrange for an armed escort (Butt, personal communication, March 26, 2005).

Overall, it is fair to say that life has not improved for most Pokot in the past decade. An extremely disturbing recent development is the fact that the HIV/AIDS pandemic is claiming an increasing number of Pokot victims (Dietz, personal communication, June 8, 2005). The Pokot continue to try to maintain their distinctive dual regional economy of pastoralists and farmers, with regular trade and marriage between the two sectors; however, with the constant threat from armed gangs (and now from HIV/AIDS), no one's livelihood is safe and secure (Bollig, 1998, 2000; Bollig and Schulte, 1999; Wagongo, 2003). There are calls for mediation between warring groups, disarmament, and conflict resolution from the government, church leaders, NGOs, donor countries, and the Pokot themselves, but they have not as yet brought lasting peace to the land and the people (*The East African Standard*, February 5, 2005; ITDG, 2003; Pkalya et al., 2003; Musambyai, 2003; Bollig, 1993).

NOTES

1. This chapter is a condensed version of a much longer study of the Pokot that forms part of *Adaptation in Ecological Context: Studies of Four East African Societies* (Porter, n.d.).

2. Soil names and characteristics are based on information provided by Lokweliapit (an agricultural instructor in Tamkal Valley, previously from Lomut); Pkite Lorongelosi of Mwina; Samuel Ptiso Chumakemer of Kokwatandwa; Lotinyang Alen'ga of Lelan; and an elder named Kitumo. Verification of terms and uses occurred constantly as we mapped farms and took soil samples. Francis Conant provided useful criticism of this section. Also consulted for this section were works by Alexander and Cady (1962), Buckman and Brady (1962), Gelens, Kinyanjui, and van de Weg (1976), and Siderius and Njeru (1976). The English renderings of Pokot soil terms given here are broad glosses rather than strict literal translations. Although there seem to be local terms for the same soil types in different parts of Pokot country, this should not be construed as evidence of dialect differences. A person from Masol will understand the Tamkal term *munoh* and the Kurut term *munion* for a clay soil, even though the term used in Masol is *arai'yon*. We omit discussion of the laboratory analyses of the soils we had done.

3. The distinction is between altered earth material that has agricultural uses and relatively unaltered earth material that is unsuitable for agriculture. It is the distinction that soil scientists make between weathered soils that exhibit vertical profiles (evidence of the interaction of plants, heat, organisms, minerals, and water) and desert mantle that shows no vertical zonation and accordingly is not classed as a true soil.

4. Again, to give the tour of the fields greater presence, the present tense is retained. The description refers to conditions as of August 1962. (The same is true for the discussion of Kurut agriculture, later in the chapter.)

5. The Pokot are sometimes called Suk by other groups in Kenya. Suk appears to be a term the Maasai gave to the Pokot, and it has been conjectured, not altogether convincingly, that the word can be traced to the characteristic sheath knife (*chouk*) that the Pokot sometimes wear.

6. These trash terraces were a requirement of the *bwana shamba* (district agricultural officer), and each community was subject to periodic inspection by the agricultural instructor.

7. Local maize prices in Sigor in 1962 were 44 East African shillings ($6.16) for a 200-pound bag (90.9 kilograms) of shelled maize.

8. Tegla Loroupe has won many marathons. She won again in New York in 1995; in Rotterdam three times between 1997 and 1999; in London and Rome in 2000; and in Lausanne, Switzerland, in 2002.

9. The boom in panning for gold is one of the more spectacular developments in the district. A European named Van Wijk, with Turkana laborers, panned gold in the Turkwell Gorge from the 1940s until 1963, when he left the district (Dietz et al., 1983b: 19). The gold mining grew enormously beginning in about 1980. An estimated 5,000 people were panning gold in April 1983 in Sekerr Location, and during 1982 they produced about 40 kilograms of gold, earning about 4 million Kenyan shillings (Dietz et al., 1983b: 23–24). A spectacular find at Kriich in Sook Location in 1981 brought in up to 2,000 people at times. In Korpu, a big center in Alale Location, gold pro-

duction in 1982 exceeded 10 kilograms (Dietz et al., 1983b: 23).

10. The controversial Turkwell Gorge Hydro-Electric Power project cost $450 million, three times its original estimate, and has produced only about half the power it was supposed to—85 versus 160 megawatts (Hawley, 2003: 29). The Suam River, which becomes the Turkwell at Kongelai, flows from Mount Elgon and is the major source for the dam. The hydrologic analyses done at Kongelai and in the Turkwell Gorge itself were inadequate and severely misestimated flow volumes, overestimating annual discharge and badly underestimating flash flooding from intense afternoon storms (Radwan, ca. 1995). It has been estimated that 160 million cubic meters of silt per year are transported by the Suam River and its tributaries (Dietz et al., 1983c: 26–27). There has been extensive sedimentation in the lake; the reservoir level was 50 meters below full capacity as of 2000; environmental deterioration has occurred below the dam; and the irrigation that was supposed to develop below the dam has not benefited the Turkana and Pokot. Irrigation waters have gone to serve export-oriented large-scale farms (Hawley, 2003: 28 ff.). There was great corruption in the way the contract was awarded to Spie Batignolles and Sogreah, both French companies. A Japanese development group is now trying to develop an irrigation project on the Turkwell River, but finds it difficult to staff the project because social conditions are so unstable (Butt, personal communication, March 26, 2005).

Part III Differentiated Social Relations Encountering Global Strategies

13 The Historical Geography of Colonialism and the Slave Trade

To understand our world of difference today, it is important to understand that 500 years of colonialism remade the world and our views of it in ways that are still important, not least for the millions of living people for whom colonialism is part of their life histories. We take the colonial era to be the 500 years beginning about 1492, when the European imagination was forever changed by the "discovery" of the Americas. The colonial era witnessed the production and evolution of a global economy and associated structures of power and knowledge, in which the exploitation and reworking of difference was both a driving force and a product. In this chapter, we briefly sketch some of the changing patterns of colonialism over time and space, with a particular emphasis on the slave trade.

Although the colonial era lasted five centuries, the beginning, end, and duration of colonization of any particular place varied greatly, as did the experience of colonialism. We can begin to chart the historical geography of colonialism by plotting over time the waves of colonialism, the major colonial powers, and the places colonized. The first wave of colonialism began at the end of the 15th century, crested in the late 18th century, and fell off as the countries of the Americas gained their independence, reaching a low point in 1825. In the second wave, there was a renewed increase in colonialism from 1825 to 1925, followed by a decline until 1990, when independence came to Namibia (Figures 13.1 and 13.2). (We leave in limbo a number of overseas territories and dependencies, as well as the continued disputed status of phosphate-rich Western Sahara, the object of three decades of war between Morocco and the Polisario Front of Mauritania.) We can also see that Spanish and Portuguese colonization of the Americas dominated the earliest phase, followed by the rise of British, French, and Dutch colonization, and then the decline of Spain, Portugal, and The Netherlands as colonial powers. The second wave of colonization was dominated by British and French colonial expansion in Asia and Africa, followed by independence struggles and formal independence worldwide. What these graphs cannot show is that the first wave of colonization saw a rise in the importance of merchant capitalism and then the beginnings of industrial capitalism. This wave also brought with it the rise and

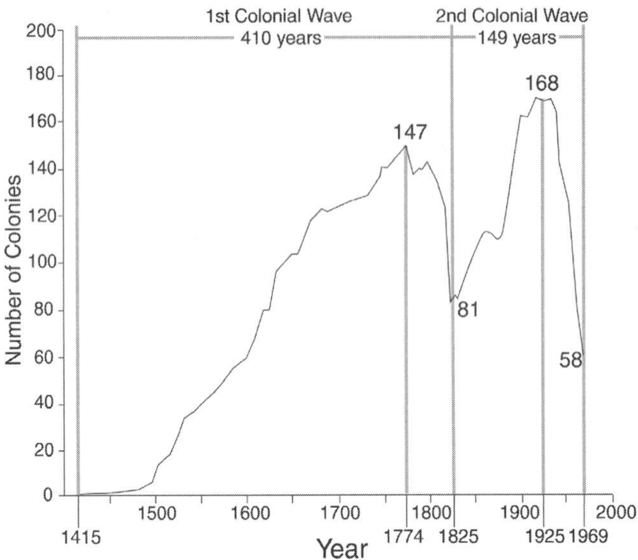

FIGURE 13.1. Waves of colonialism. *Source*: Adapted from De Souza (1986). Copyright 1986 by the American Geographical Society. Adapted by permission.

fall of the slave trade. The second wave witnessed the growth and evolution of industrial capitalism.

It interests us that most of the countries currently defined as belonging to the third world were once colonies. The exceptions are higher-latitude countries, such as Canada, New Zealand, Australia, and the United States, whose indigenous populations were decimated and marginalized as people of Anglo-European culture largely remade those places in their own image. Of further interest are the large movements of people within the third world that occurred during each of these colonial eras. In addition to the forced migration of millions of people from Africa, discussed below, are the migrations that occurred to and from west, south, and east Asian lands—Syrian and Lebanese to west Africa; Indians, frequently as indentured laborers, to east Africa, south Africa, Mauritius, Malaysia, Fiji, and the British Caribbean; Malays to Cape Province in South Africa; Chinese to southeast Asia, to the Americas, and even to South Africa; and Europeans themselves to third world destinations. Plants, animals, and diseases also diffused to new locations, both in the service of colonial empires and as unintended consequences of the sea trade. The same is true of intangibles, such as knowledge, ideologies, and institutions.

COLONIALISM: THE FIRST PHASE

In 1492, the world was made up of a great variety of societies, large and small, with varying degrees of urbanization, diverse artisanal industries and agricultural systems, and different degrees and types of social hierarchies. Most people supported their households through agriculture. Merchants and traders supplied luxury goods to elites, sometimes over great distances. Europe was not exceptional in its social or technological development or its engagement in merchant trade. In fact, it was on the western periphery of the Eurasian–African trade economy. The two major European powers of the 15th century, Spain and Portugal, vied with each other to be the first to secure a feasible sea route to the Orient, since overland travel had become dangerous, costly,

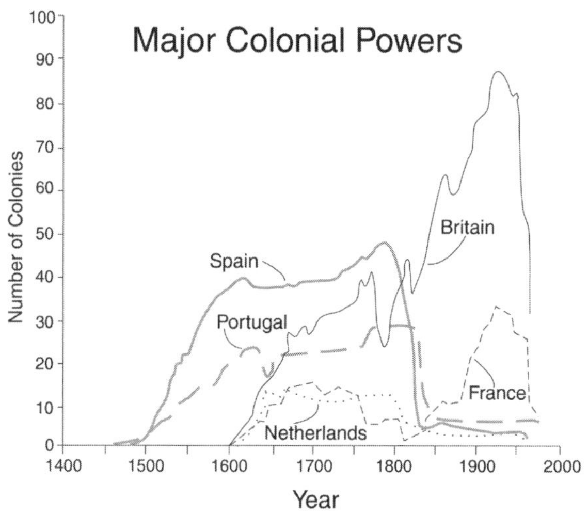

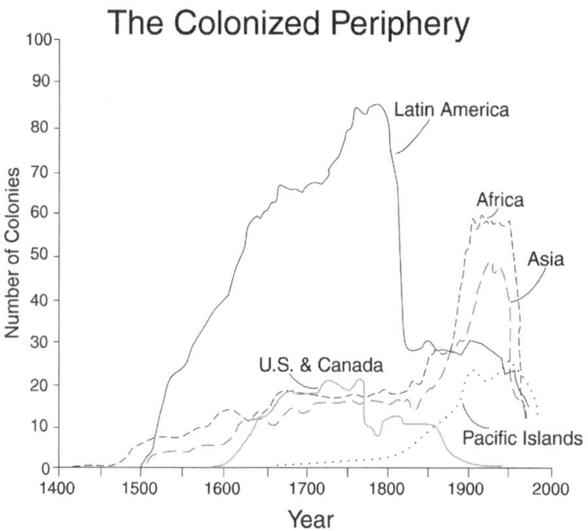

FIGURE 13.2. Major colonial powers and the colonized periphery. *Source:* Adapted from De Souza (1986). Copyright 1986 by the American Geographical Society. Adapted by permission.

and uncertain (Porter, 1958; Martin, 1981). The land route was controlled on the west by the Ottoman Empire and, east of that, by the strife-torn remnants of the Mongol Empire. The Portuguese, having the better estimate of the circumference of the earth, decided that the shortest route would be around Africa. Prince Henry the Navigator had pressed along the African coast during the 15th century. At his death in 1460, Henry's sailors had explored the Atlantic coast as far as Sierra Leone. His successor, King John II, continued the work, letting it out on contract to explorers/entrepreneurs such as Fernão Gomes, who in 1469 undertook to discover "one hundred leagues of coast" (644 kilometers) beyond Sierra Leone over a 5-year period (de Barros, 1552). Columbus convinced the Spanish queen that the shortest route to the Orient was to the west, and she gave her support for the 1492 voyage in which he stumbled onto the Americas. By the time Columbus headed west on his epochal journey across the Atlantic, the Portuguese had rounded the Cape of Good Hope and stood poised to cross the Indian Ocean. Vasco da Gama did so in 1498, reaching the west coast of India.

In 1494, in the Treaty of Tordesillas, the Pope agreed to a division of the world into two hemispheres of interest—one for the Portuguese, including Africa and India; and one for the Spanish, including the Americas and much of the Pacific (Figure 13.3). The meridian, which was set at the present-day longitude of 53° west of Greenwich (whose prime or zero meridian did not become the international standard until 1884), cut on the other side of the sphere through the Spice Islands of the Moluccas. As a consequence, the discovery for Europeans of the lands of the rest of the Old World was accomplished largely by the Portuguese, who explored along Africa and onward to the Indian subcontinent, Sumatra, Java, the Moluccas, and the southeast coast of Japan (all by 1513), while Spanish fleets explored the Americas.

Nevertheless, some exceptions to this general tendency did occur. In 1500, a Portuguese expedition led by Pedro Alvares Cabral was blown off course on a voyage to the Orient, and Cabral found himself cruising the coast of Brazil. Although he probably did not know his precise longitude, he knew he had encountered land well east of the line established by the Treaty of Tordesillas (the eastern tip of Brazil lies at about 35°W longitude). Thus the coast Cabral saw fell within the Portuguese sphere; he claimed it for the crown of Portugal, sending one of his ships back with the news while he continued on to India. Among Spanish explorers, only Magellan in his circumnavigation of 1521 gave Spain a claim to territories in Asia, since his expedition reached the Philippines before any recorded visit by the Portuguese. The Philippines, in fact, lie west of the Tordesillas treaty line, but nonetheless Spain was eventually able to claim them as a colony. It is from such happenstance events—a papal bull drawing a line on a map of a not-yet-known world, a navigational mishap, a "first arrival" claim—that we get centuries later a Portuguese Timor

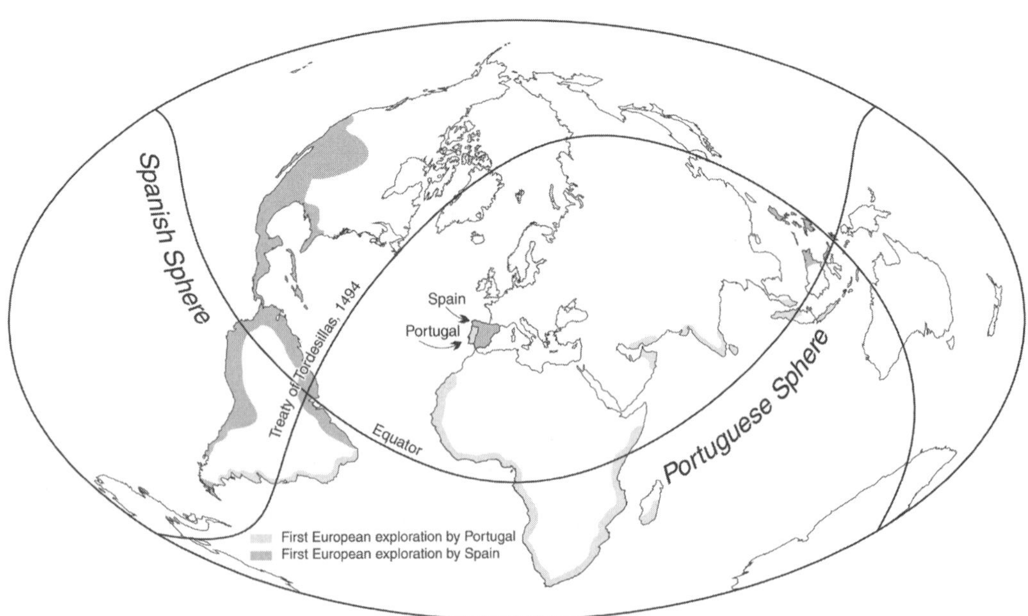

FIGURE 13.3. Spanish and Portuguese spheres of influence, 1494.

(invaded by government forces from Indonesia), Spanish influence in the Philippines, Portuguese influence in Macao, Portuguese spoken in Brazil, and so forth.

Figure 13.2 shows that most of the colonies formed in the period from 1500 to 1774 were established in the Americas. Spanish *conquistadors* conquered the Aztec and Inca empires. After looting the wealth of these empires, they focused on mining precious metals, using forced labor in both the mines and the agricultural estates that supplied them with food. From 1503 to 1660, Spanish shipments from Latin America tripled the amount of silver in Europe. Between 1600 and 1810, 22,000 tons of silver and 185 tons of gold were transferred from Latin America (Peru) to Spain. From 1750 to 1810, Portuguese mines in Brazil produced 800 tons of gold (Thomas, 1994: 28). Meanwhile, between 1500 and 1600, the Portuguese developed an empire consisting of strategically located trading and provisioning ports with which they sought to monopolize the lucrative spice and textile trade between Europe and Asia, as well as to profit from trade within Asia.

Maritime northern European countries were exploring the Americas contemporaneously with Spain and Portugal (the Cabots did so for England in 1497 and 1508, and Cartier for France in 1534), but they did not begin to pose a real threat to their Iberian rivals until the 17th century (Palmer, 1957: 141). The Dutch, English, and French all established claims and counterclaims to lands in the New World. Figure 13.4 shows where the Dutch contested other European powers; although they lost out almost everywhere in the end, their presence is still to be found in place names in New York State along the Hudson River, and in architecture and in other ways in the Netherlands Antilles—Curaçao, Aruba, Bonaire, and Dutch Guiana (Suriname). The Dutch had a more lasting influence through the East India Company (founded in 1602) in Sumatra, Java, and South Africa, where a revictualing way station on the Cape of Good Hope eventually became a retirement center and a destination for Dutch settlement, as well as the progenitor of Afrikaans and Afrikaner nationalism.

In 1776, as we all know, 13 colonies along the Atlantic coast declared independence from Great Britain. There followed the world-shaking French revolution in 1789, which set the stage for wars of independence throughout Latin America and the Caribbean. The precipitous decline in numbers of colonies from 1800 to 1825 is traced to decolonization all across Central and South America, almost all of them losses for Spain and Portugal (De Souza, 1986). It started with Toussaint L'Ouverture, who succeeded in liberating Haiti from the French in 1801, and ended with the military triumphs of José de San Martín and Simón Bolívar over the Spanish, which brought independence to Bolivia in 1825. The main states of South America emerged during this period: La Plata (Argentina) in 1816, Chile in 1818, Colombia in 1819, Peru in 1821, and Brazil in 1822.

As European merchant capitalism strengthened from the 16th century onward, European traders began to consolidate the first international division of labor. The Americas and eastern Europe produced raw materials; Africa provided labor; Asia produced luxury commodities; and western Europe directed these operations and focused increasingly on industry (Stavrianos, 1988: 449). The tropical and subtropical environments of the Caribbean and the southern United States provided conditions in which plantation agriculture could be organized on an industrial basis to produce crops for export to Europe, if only a large, disciplined labor force could be provided. Slaves could provide such a labor force, but from where? Because Native Americans died in epidemic proportions from smallpox and other introduced diseases to which they were not resistant, they could not provide sufficient numbers. Moreover, the European settlers believed that the indigenous people in the New World were unenslavable—that

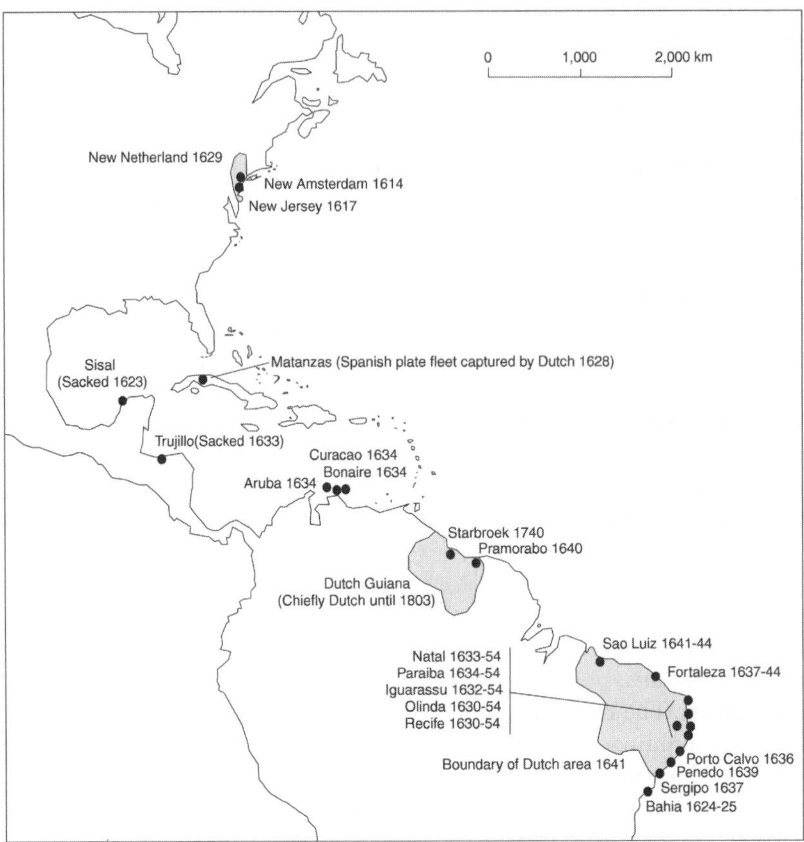

FIGURE 13.4. Dutch activities in the New World, 17th and 18th centuries.

they would just escape to the hills. Therefore, the cheapest way to provide labor was by importing slave labor from Africa.

THE SLAVE TRADE

Iino ya mmiini maiini mo.
—From a Kiswahili slave poem (see BENNETT, 1974: 70)

Although slavery is an institution of great antiquity, its apogee in the modern era was reached in the 18th century, developing out of an African trade that began taking enslaved people to Portugal and Bahia (the northeast coast of Brazil) as early as 1570 (Inikori, 1992). In this section, we consider the actors in the slave trade, the way the trade worked, the middle passage, the impact of enslavement on those captured, the eventual suppression of the trade, and some of its consequences for Africa and the world.

The Actors

European slave traders dealt with viable states on the African coast, entering into collaborative arrangements with them to obtain slaves in return for arms, gunpowder, and trade goods. The sailors also operated their own separate settlements, frequently forts (Oliver and Fage, 1962: 112 ff.). They relied on Africans to capture others to sell them into slavery. Occasionally, European slavers dealt with African states in a subservient status. Wydah, for example, was a center for the trade in Dahomey (now Benin). Dahomey had been located in the interior, away from the Atlantic Ocean, but it broke through to the coast in order to control the whole trade; it did not want an intermediary. The slave trade shifted the balance of power to the coast. Wydah had a French Quarter, a Dutch Quarter, and an English Quarter. The European residents were restricted in their movements. Because they were "guests," food was brought to them. They were told when to come to the market to inspect and purchase slaves. The terms of the trade were also set by local people.

European–African trade had started a long time before with the "ounce trade" in gold, wherein so many bundles of iron, bolts of cloth, guns, and other manufactured goods were specified for an ounce of gold (Polanyi, 1964). Liquor was an important item of trade, as were pans, pots, shoes, mirrors, and salted meats. The European traders dealt with the more organized states—Akan (Ashanti), Fon (Dahomey), Yoruba, Benin (Niger River delta), Calabar, and Congo—along the coast to Angola. Most of the raiding was in the zone from Elmina to Calabar, although all of coastal Africa south of the Sahara was affected. North American colonists developed a significant trade even on the east coast of Africa.

The Dutch and the British systematized the "triangular trade," a lucrative production and trading complex that transformed Africa, Europe, and the Americas. The "triangular trade," involved traffic among three destinations—the New World, Europe, and Africa. Sugar and tobacco went from the New World to Europe. These were the most valuable commodities in the triangular trade, but labor was needed to produce these goods. The second leg of the triangular trade was from Europe to Africa, and it consisted of manufactured goods, rum, guns/gunpowder, and other items as mentioned earlier. From Africa, slaves were conveyed to the New World, thus completing the triangle. The Spanish shaped the geography of slave trading via its *asiento de negros*, which granted monopoly rights after 1543 to other European countries (Portugal, France, Britain), in return for a fee, over the delivery of slaves to its New World colonies.

The Dutch have the dubious distinction of bringing the first slave shipment to the British colonies, possibly to Jamestown, Virginia, in 1619. Thus some descendants of slaves can claim to have come to North America before the landing of the *Mayflower.* The English began to take an active interest in supplying slaves in about 1660, when the Company of Royal Adventurers was formed in Liverpool. The wealth of Liverpool was created through the slave and triangular trade, evidence of which is still to be seen in very old warehouses, buildings, and street names in the city's port area. Penny Lane was named for James Penny, an 18th-century slave ship owner.

The maximum activity in the slave trade took place between 1660 and 1780. Toward its end, 100,000 slaves were taken by European ships from the west African coast each year. Some 45 million people may have been captured; however, it is believed that fewer than 15 million made it to the New World. One estimate (Kuczynski, cited in Curtin, 1969: 5) of numbers of slaves landed in the Americas by century is as follows:

16th century	900,000
17th century	2,750,000
18th century	7,000,000
19th century	4,000,000
Total	14,650,000

The captives moved mainly through European maritime agency, and to a lesser extent through Arab agency, for sale to European and New World slavers or to traders in the Middle East. One-third died en route to the coast; another third died in the middle passage (see below). Bagamoyo, which in Kiswahili means "crush (or break) your heart," was the eastern terminus of caravan routes from the upper Congo. In a museum in Bagamoyo, one can read that only one in five of those captured actually made it to the coast. In the mid-1800s, some 60,000 to 70,000 slaves were being exported annually. There is a large margin for error in all these estimates, of course (Curtin, 1969: 5).

The geographical structure of the trade on land in Africa was divided. Along the coast in west Africa and southward to Angola, as described above, strong local African states controlled the trade and dealt with European ship owners (Figure 13.5). On the drier margins of populated Africa—that is, across the Sahel and Sudan, in northern Africa, and along the east African coast as far as Mozambique—Arab slavers with their caravans were generally in control. In some instances, middlemen interposed some control (e.g., Muslim kingdoms in west Africa—Mandingo, Songhay, Fulani/Hausa).

How the Trade Worked

The slavers worked mainly through powerful states, but constantly cruised up and down the coast to lesser places, to see what opportunities might arise. Also, they tried to intercept free-lancers and interlopers. The strong states were the Benin states, Dahomey, and Ashanti. These states had factories and forts with living quarters, defenses, dungeons, and open pens (stockades). People were branded and placed in stockades or temporary shelters (called *barracoons*).

In eastern Africa, several routes were used to penetrate to the interior Congo

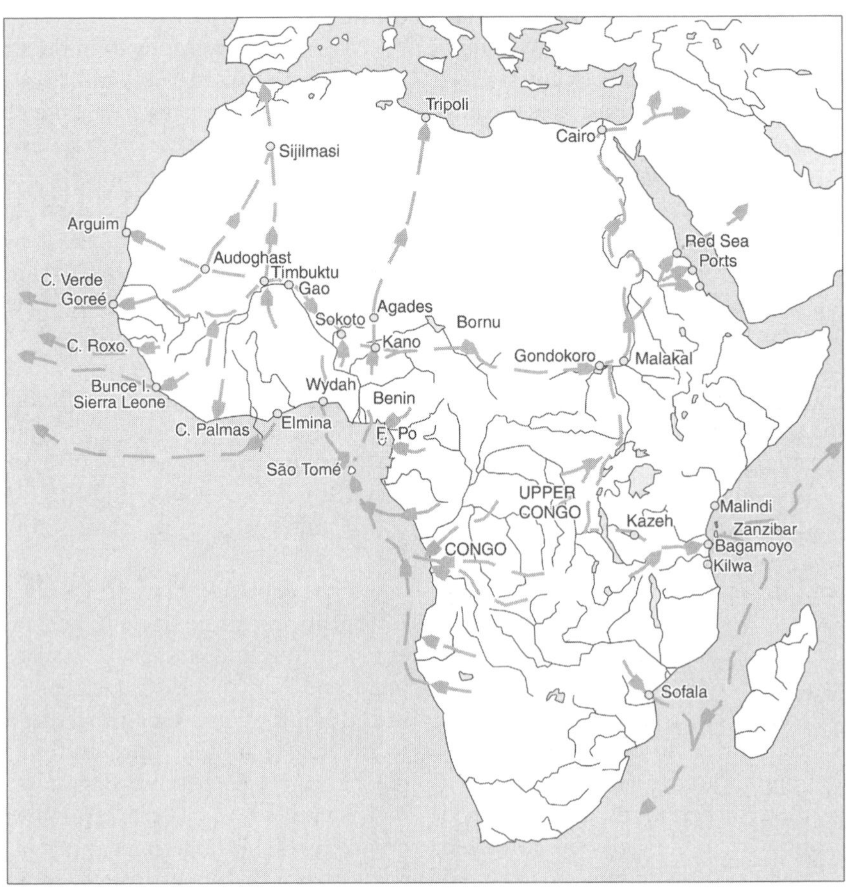

FIGURE 13.5. Routes and places important to an understanding of the African slave trade.

basin, which was the main zone of slave raiding. One route was from Arab ports on the Red Sea. Along the Red Sea coast, one can still see the remains of abandoned towns that were once flourishing slave ports. The main route to the interior was overland to Gondokoro and Malakal, then west and south to the upper Congo. The caravans that used the route were supported along the way by a long series of settlements.

One locus of the early and middle period of the slave trade was the island of Kilwa. The route from Kilwa skirted the southern highlands of what is now Tanzania to Cazembe's near Lake Mweru, in northeastern Zambia, on the border with the former Zaire (now the Democratic Republic of Congo). There is still a large Swahili-speaking community there.

Zanzibar was another locus of the trade. The Portuguese were displaced from the east coast of Africa by the Arabs of Muscat and Oman about 1650; they were pushed as far south as Mozambique, but managed to hold on south of the Ruvuma River. In 1832, trade and opportunities became interesting enough to Seyyid Said Barghash, the sultan of Oman, that he shifted his capital to Zanzibar.

The main east African route to the interior was from Zanzibar to Bagamoyo to Kazeh (headquarters of a powerful leader of the Wanyamwezi named Mirambo) to Ujiji, on Lake Tanganyika, and then across the lake into the upper Congo. In Gisenyi—a border town in northwestern Rwanda at the north end of Lake Kivu, where one can walk across the border into Goma in the former Zaire—one still finds houses built in the 19th century by people who were engaged in the slave trade. Many people in Gisenyi speak Kiswahili, the language of traders. This inner zone of east Africa from Gisenyi south to Cazembe's and stretching west of Lake Tanganyika into the drainage of the Lualaba and Lomami Rivers was the sphere of influence of Hamed bin Muhammad, more popularly known as Tippu Tip. Tippu Tip, an ivory and slave trader, was an urbane, learned man who was linked through marriage with powerful African families in the vicinity of present-day Tabora (Ingham, 1962: 66). He wrote up his exploits in a lively autobiography sometime before his death in 1895 (Tip, 1902–1903/1966).

An extended quote from Oliver and Mathew (1963: 274–275) gives some idea of the scope of Tippu Tip's operation. Note that many of the porters mentioned in the quote would have been captives, destined to be sold into slavery at the end of the journey.

> Size depended much, of course, on the length of time that the expedition had been absent from the coast. When that of Tippu Tip headed back towards Zanzibar after no less than twelve years of exploitation and trading, it numbered some 2,000 porters carrying a similar number of tusks and guarded by 1,000 askaris—and one may be sure that its size and prestige attracted hundreds of further followers. Such mammoth processions, returning after years of absence, spoke not only of the enterprise and fortune of their leaders, but also of the extensive credit facilities which were available to back them at the coast. Tippu tells how at the outset of this, his third and longest venture to the interior, Sultan Majid of Zanzibar himself was ready to intervene to ensure that he obtained the 50,000 dollars' worth of trade goods which he required; and although this was certainly beyond the ordinary scale, it gives some idea of the amount of Indian capital which might be locked up in the interior at any moment.

In summary, trade based on the capture and enslavement of people was sterile and self-defeating, but ever-escalating. A state had to be forever strong and dominant over its neighbors, or it would be conquered and its people enslaved. The parlous power relations between states further fed the trade of European and New World slavers, who supplied guns and gunpowder.

The Middle Passage

The "middle passage" was the dangerous journey by sea from Africa to the New

World. It was characterized by thoughtless brutalization, a great deal of crowding, and resultant disease and death. One well-known and characteristic example of crowding is provided by the *Brookes*, a British ship (Clarkson, 1836, Vol. 2: 238). The space allocation for a man was 6 feet × 1 foot, 4 inches × 1½ to 2 feet, and that for a woman was 5 feet × 1 foot, 4 inches × 1½ to 2 feet. In short, people were packed in like sardines. The *Brookes* was designed to accommodate 450 slaves, but on one voyage it carried 609. Liverpool merchants complained that their cargoes were being mishandled and that there was too much loss (indeed, there was a parliamentary debate on the issue in 1788). Slaves were allowed to exercise on deck in good weather, but not in bad weather. The journey could take as little as 5 weeks, but could last as long as 6 months. The sick were thrown overboard. Disease, particularly smallpox, was rampant and was spread especially quickly because of the physical proximity. If water ran short, some of the slaves were thrown overboard. Slaves were an economic commodity, a cargo. Mutinies and suicides were common. Most slaves went to the West Indies (Jamaica, Cuba, and Hispaniola [Haiti and the Dominican Republic]) and to Brazil. The United States and Mexico got smaller numbers.

The Impact on the Enslaved Persons

The majority of people captured as slaves were young. They were taken at night from their villages. Those who reached ships had endured a difficult, disorienting journey—in some cases, many hundreds of miles—in chains or wooden yokes. When families were captured, they were split up. People were further divided on ship, to keep those who spoke the same language from being together and thus being able to communicate and plan trouble. They were even further divided in the New World to maximize profit. Two quotations from a contemporary observer may convey some sense of the terror and despair the enslaved persons experienced.

> I have been to-day on board a slave-ship in the river, with 250 slaves. The men were chained in pairs; the women were kept apart. The young slaves were chearful, but the old ones were much cast down. At meals they were obliged to shout, and clap their hands, for exercise, before they begin to eat. I could then see shame and indignation in the faces of those more advanced in years. One woman, who spoke a little English, begged me to carry her home. She said she was from the opposite shore of the river to Freetown, that her husband had sold her for debt, and that she had left a child behind her: at the mention of the child, she wept. (Wadstrom, 1794/1968, Vol. 2: 83)

> An American slave-captain has been telling us that he lost a very fine slave, a few days ago, by the *sulks*—The man (said he) was a Mahometan, uncommonly well made, and seemed to be a person of consequence. When he first came on board, he was much cast down; but, finding that I allowed him to walk at large, he grew more easy. When my slaves became numerous, I put him in irons, like the rest, on which he lost his spirits irrecoverably. He complained of a pain at his heart, and would not eat. *The usual means* [that is, flogging with a cat-o'-nine-tails] was tried, but in vain; for he rejected food altogether, except when I stood by and made him eat. I offered him the best things in the ship, and left nothing untried; for I had set my heart on saving him. I am sure, he would have brought me 300 dollars in the W. Indies; but nothing would do. He said, from the first, he was determined to die, and so he did, after lingering 9 days. (Wadstrom, 1794/1968, Vol. 2: 84; emphasis in original)

Suppression

By the end of the 18th century, two factors came together to severely curtail first the slave trade, and then slavery. Abolitionist campaigns provided the moral argument against slavery while the expanding industrial revolution meant that slavery was becoming obsolete as industrial capitalists needed markets more than they needed unfree labor overseas. The suppression of the slave trade was carried out largely by the British and U.S. navies. In 1807, Britain outlawed the slave trade, and the United States outlawed the slave trade for U.S. carriers. In 1819, the United States outlawed the slave trade altogether, and the U.S. navy began to capture privateers. In 1833, after long parliamentary debates, Britain outlawed the institution of slavery, the Danes having done so earlier. Other European nations of the period quickly followed suit. Slavery as an institution in the United States was outlawed in 1863 with Lincoln's Emancipation Proclamation. Brazil finally outlawed slavery in 1895.

To suppress the trade, the British and U.S. navies patrolled near the west African coast and near the slavers' usual destinations. They often based their operations on islands that had formerly been used by slavers, such as Gorée in the harbor off Dakar, Senegal, and Bunce Island, off Freetown, Sierra Leone. If a ship was apprehended off the African coast, people were set ashore at the nearest point. No effort was made to return them to their homes; yet there are a few extraordinary stories of people who landed on the west coast, near Cape Verde, who traveled overland until they found their original villages in what is now Nigeria.

In Liberia, there is a place called Congo Town, where 1,000 people from the Congo were put ashore all at one time by the U.S. navy in 1860. Indeed, in the space of 2 months in mid-1860, over 4,000 "recaptured" Africans were released on the Liberian coast. The Liberian government, only 13 years old at the time, complained to the United States about these sudden intrusions on its sovereignty, although the United States did not recognize Liberia as a sovereign nation for another 2 years.

If a ship was apprehended in the Caribbean, the slaves were brought to processing centers in the Florida Keys. Eventually these people were repatriated to Africa—often to Sierra Leone or Liberia—though they usually did not return to their original homes.

The remaining slavers, after slavery had been outlawed, were called "renegades"; in trying to suppress them, the U.S. and British navies inadvertently made the trade even more vicious. Slave ships maintained even lower standards, and there were still more sickness and privation. If the ship was apprehended, the privateer drowned the cargo with weighted irons, destroying the evidence (see sidebar: "The Slave Trade—Horrid Barbarity"). The scene of the last trade was the Atlantic coast from Cabo Roxo to Sherbro Island, where there are thousands of inlets, estuaries, and islands in which to hide. The slavers would sneak out at night, and try to be well out to sea and out of reach by patrols by daybreak.

Some Consequences of the Slave Trade

Some scholars have argued that the slave trade left a "depopulated middle belt"

The Slave Trade—Horrid Barbarity

In February 1832, the *African Repository and Colonial Journal* carried the following news item under the headline "The Slave Trade—Horrid Barbarity":

The Fair Rosamond and the Black Joke, tenders to the Dryad frigate, have captured three slave vessels, which had originally 1800 slaves on board, but of which they succeeded in taking only 306 to Sierra Leone. It appears the Fair Rosamond had captured a lugger, with 106 Africans, and shortly afterwards saw the Black Joke in chase of two other luggers; she joined in the pursuit, but the vessels succeeded in getting into the Bonny River, and landed 600 slaves before the tenders could take possession of them. They found on board only 200, but ascertained that the rascals in command of the slavers had thrown overboard 180 slaves, manacled together, four of whom only were picked up. (*African Repository and Colonial Journal*, 1832: 388) across west Africa and in parts of the former Zaire and present-day Angola and Tanzania (Austen, 1987: 96; Oliver and Fage, 1962: 121; Church, 1957: 167; Gleave and White, 1969). Clearly, population densities are generally higher along the coast in west Africa, and there are large zones of high population densities in the Sahelian zone (the most notable examples being the closely settled zone around Kano, with its fine loessal soils, and the well-peopled area of Dagomba- and Mossi-speaking people in Burkina Faso). There was a long history of slave raiding by strong states from the north (Dagomba–Mossi, Kontagora, and the Fulani/Hausa states centered on Kano and Katsina), as well as from the south. The Aja people of Dahomey (present-day Benin) were so badly affected by the slave trade that their population declined after 1670 for the next 140 years, and recovered only in the early decades of the 20th century (Figure 13.6) (Manning, 1982: 343). It is unlikely that scholarship, in assessing the causes of the lightly peopled "middle belt," will ever be able to disentangle the complicated story of strong states and varied resource endowment (inferior in the zone now lightly peopled) from the history of slave raiding.

For Portuguese slavers working along the Gulf of Guinea in the 16th and 17th centuries, several strategically located islands—Fernando Po, São Tomé, and Príncipe—served as food supply and slave storage areas. Indeed, the initial settlement and development of São Tomé for sugar production were carried out by essentially enslaved people: Jews, driven from Spain by the 1492 Edict of Expulsion, plus exiles and convicts. The food plantations begun on these islands were intended to support the trade—that is, to grow provisions to feed the crew and the slaves on their journey. In order to do this, they had to have labor to grow the crops, which meant, of course, that the early destination of some of those enslaved was one or another of these islands. Many of the important New World crops introduced into Africa (e.g., maize, beans, cassava, sweet potatoes, peanuts, pineapples, tomatoes, avocado, papaya, red peppers, cacao, and tobacco) probably came through São Tomé.

One consequence of the slave trade was

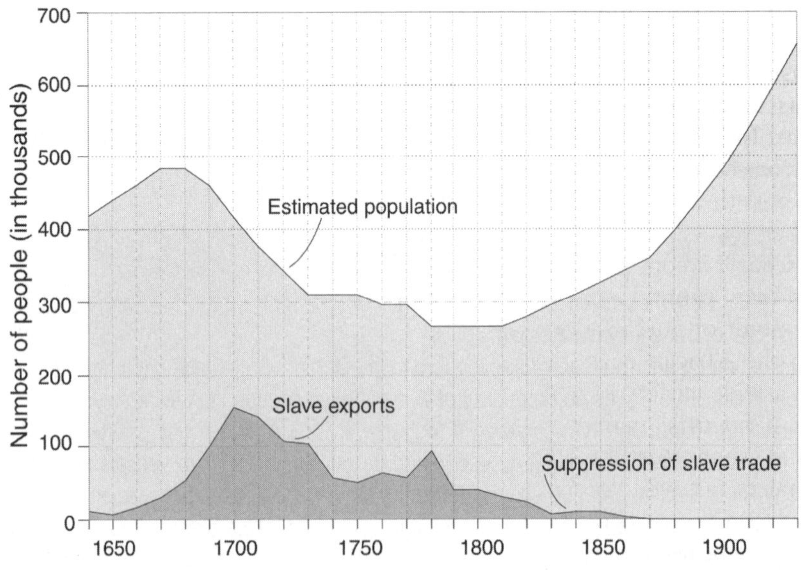

FIGURE 13.6. Slave exports and estimated population, Aja people, Dahomey, 1640–1930. *Source:* Data are from Manning (1982).

that it generated vast wealth for the European and New World interests who participated in it, both from the sale of people into human bondage, and from the income gained from the labor of slaves and their progeny. How much wealth was so generated is impossible to calculate, but it laid the basis for large maritime and mercantile companies in Europe (particularly England) and in the eastern ports of the United States; it provided the basis for the plantation economies of the southern United States and the Caribbean; and it played a role in Europe's industrialization.

The slave trade led to the creation of immense fortunes for individual families and companies in Europe, particularly in England, France, Portugal, and Spain. The trade itself was lucrative, but the wealth created in the plantations of the West Indies and South America, which were owned mainly by European families and companies, was also important. Thomas (1994: 28–29) has estimated that transfers of wealth to Europe from the 16th to the 19th centuries amounted to 884 million pounds sterling—an amount equivalent to over $100 billion in 1990s U.S. dollars. Gold and silver shipments from Spanish and Portuguese America accounted for 35% of the transfer, but the slave trade counted for 14%, and profits from the labor of those enslaved added another 28%. The balance was made up in money extracted from the East Indies by the Dutch, and British profits from India and China, relating to land taxes and the enforced sale of opium (discussed below).

The predatory commerce of the slave trade was doubly profitable to merchants—at both the point of purchase and the point of sale. On the African coast, they bought slaves with a wide variety of goods, including chains, handcuffs, manacles, firearms, powder, and shot (the day-to-day tools of enslavement), as well as manufactured goods and *pacotille*—assortments of cheap, brightly colored beads, bracelets, and gewgaws. Williams (1944: 65) provides a list taken from 1878:

> cotton and linen goods, silk handkerchiefs, coarse blue and red woolen cloths, scarlet cloth in grain, coarse and fine hats, worsted caps, guns, powder, shot, sabers, lead bars, iron bars, pewter basons [basins], copper kettles and pans, iron pots, hardware of various kinds, earthen and glass ware, hair and gilt leather trunks, beads of various kinds, silver and gold rings and ornaments, paper, coarse and fine checks [fabrics with a checkerboard pattern], linen ruffled shirts and caps, British and foreign spirits and tobacco.

European plantation agriculture in the Caribbean and southern United States set the stage for the industrial revolution by providing experience in organizing large-scale industrial production, by building markets for products, and by generating vast profits. Economic historians have argued about the degree to which the wealth associated with the "triangular trade" actually financed Europe's industrial revolution (Blaut, 1993; Robinson, 1987). Only part of the wealth fueled industrialization; much of it was devoted to increasing the estates of great landowners and the business reach of wealthy merchant companies. Nonetheless, some of the wealth from the slave trade itself, from the profits of plantations in the West Indies, and from income generated by manufacturing in response to the demand for products in Africa was used for investment in industrial development. James Watt and Matthew Boulton both received such financing for their respective enterprises—the steam engine, and cannon and piston manufacture. Anthony Bacon, who earlier had participated in the slave trade, set up an iron works in Wales and made a fortune from government contracts for artillery (Williams, 1944: 104).

Other institutions associated with the industrialization of Europe had their beginnings during the slave trade, or emerged out of the fortunes the trade created. In banking, Barclays Bank D.C.O. (the D.C.O. long stood for "Dominions, Colonies, and Overseas") was started by a Quaker family that engaged in the slave trade. Thomas Leyland, the Liverpool slave trader, created what later became the North and South Wales Bank, Ltd. In insurance, Lloyds of London, originally a coffee house listed in the *London Gazette* as the place to which runaway slaves should be returned, began its life by insuring slave consignments and slave ships (Williams, 1944: 104). There are no doubt other connections to be made between the slave trade and industrial developments, such as distilleries throughout Scotland, the tobacco industry in Glasgow, sugar refining in Bristol and Glasgow, cotton textiles in Manchester, iron and steel manufacturing in Birmingham, and shipbuilding and the shipping industry in Liverpool. It makes one wonder which of the name brands we see in today's bright advertisements could be traced back to an earlier fortune founded on the slave trade.

Perhaps the most profound and long-lasting effect of the slave trade was to disperse people of African descent throughout the Americas (and, more recently, in European cities). Their history of survival in the postslavery period, in the face of racist oppression, discrimination, and denial of fundamental human and economic rights, is one marked by fortitude and deep spiritual strength. They are part of the population that makes up the first world. They belong—and this fact and their rights pose an as-yet-unmet challenge to societies of first world nations. If the challenges of racism in the first world could be met, perhaps the larger challenges of creating social and economic justice among people in the third world could be met as well.

EXPANDING EUROPEAN POLITICAL AND ECONOMIC CONTROL IN ASIA

The course of empire in Asia in the 18th and 19th centuries was largely in the hands of the British, Dutch, and French, with only fragments of territory (Macao, Timor, Goa, and Damao) under Portuguese control (Palmer, 1957: 133, 169). The French empire consisted of French Indo-China (present-day Laos, Cambodia, and Vietnam), and a sprinkling of pocket colonies on the coast of India (Mahe, Karikal, Pondichery, Yanaon). The Dutch controlled a vast island archipelago (its Dutch East Indies), which has since become Indonesia.

The British gained control of the Malay States, the northern coast of the island of Borneo, and Hong Kong, but India was to become the "jewel in the crown" of Queen Victoria's empire. At the beginning of the 18th century, India was dotted with British, Portuguese, French, Dutch, and Danish trading outposts. The Mughal empire was declining and fragmenting. The British East India Company, with support from merchants who benefited from trade with the British, both fought off European competition and, by military conquest and playing one local leader off against another, gradually gained political and economic control of the vast subcontinent of South Asia by the middle of the 19th century. The British employed both direct and indirect rule in India, with the most strategic territories (eventually about 60% of the subcontinent) governed by the British, and the balance divided among over 600 "princely states" that were administered by local rulers under British tutelage. The East India Company governed British India until, following an Indian revolt that began 1857 and was brutally suppressed in 1858, the British Parliament made India a Crown Colony. In India, the British profited not only from international trade, but from collection of taxes on land and a tax on all salt sold.

Although never ruled by European powers, China, Japan, and Korea did not escape their imperial designs (Fairbank, Reischauer, and Craig, 1973). China, militarily weaker than the British, found itself unable to control its own commodity trade. The British East India Company established a monopoly over opium production and trade in India. Not wanting to debilitate the populations under their control, they became the world's biggest international drug pushers by exporting opium to China. Not surprisingly, the Chinese prohibited opium imports. In 1839, the Chinese destroyed a supply of opium that belonged to British merchants in Canton (present-day Guangzhou). This led to the so-called "opium wars," which forced China to allow opium into the country, and which created a string of "treaty ports" along the coast from the Gulf of Tonkin to Manchuria, as well as in China's interior.

The opium wars also established the principle of "extraterritoriality" (essentially, immunity for diplomats). Although formally independent states, China, Japan, and Korea signed treaties that gave European residents in "treaty ports" special privileges (Figure 13.7). They were not subject to local law, and they were given concessions on trade, tariffs, and customs duties. One can still find neighborhoods in Chinese cities, such as Shanghai and Tianjin (Tientsin), where Dutch, English, and French architectural styles indicate the former locations of affluent expatriate enclaves. One park in Shanghai is known for its infamous sign, long since removed: "No dogs or Chinese allowed."

Economic control was not limited to coastal ports. Foreign governments forced China to place in external hands various means of raising tax revenues, which went to pay foreign creditors. One traditional way to raise funds (used even before 119 B.C.) was a government monopoly on salt, whose

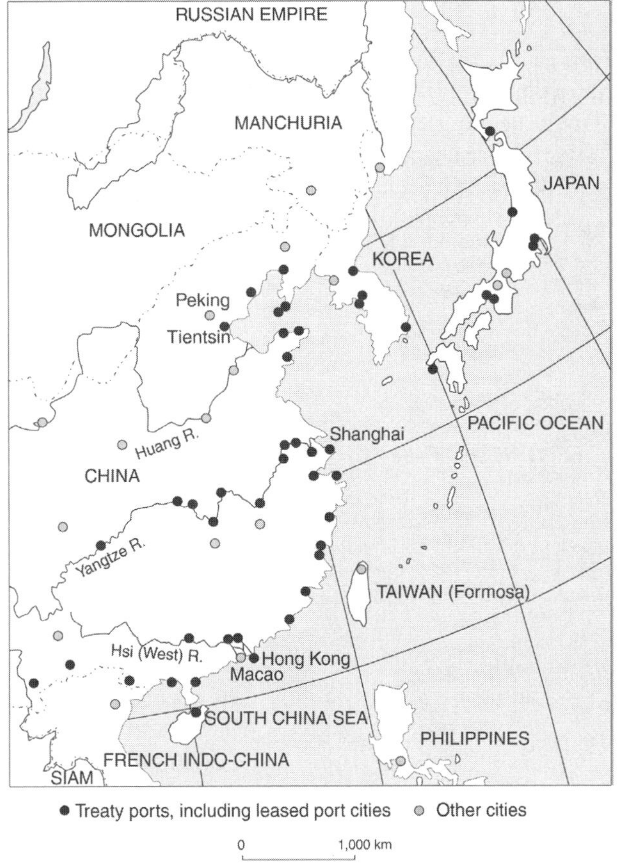

FIGURE 13.7. East Asian treaty ports as of 1898.

sale was taxed. Fairbank et al. (1973: 588) describe this as "a fiscal device for milking official taxes and private squeeze from a monopolized staple for which there was an inelastic demand." In 1911–1912, a six-power consortium (Great Britain, France, Germany, the United States, Japan, and Russia) insisted that China's salt taxes be collected by a modernized Salt Revenue Administration under the supervision of a British chief inspector. Foreign control did not stop with the Salt Revenue Administration, either: Foreigners held top posts in the Chinese Maritime Customs and Post Office administrations. Foreign steamships and gun boats plied Chinese inland rivers all the way to Hunan and Szechwan.

Japan became the exceptional case. After U.S. Admiral Perry's gunboat diplomacy opened Japan to trade in 1854, Japan embarked on a rapid process of internal reform and a program of planned modernization and industrialization. By the end of the 19th century, Japan began expanding its own empire to Taiwan, Korea, and Manchuria—a path that would later lead it into war with the other imperial powers in the region.

EUROPEAN EXPLORATIONS IN AFRICA

The 15th and 16th centuries are sometimes referred to as the "great age of European discovery." We have not treated it separately here, but have made it part of the story of colonial expansion—the usual direct consequence of a landfall by Europeans on a shore new to them. The European exploration of the interior of Africa, however, is worth a brief comment—in part because it set the stage for the "scramble for Africa" that was to ensue, and in part because the period of greatest activity by explorers coincides approximately with the period during which the slave trade was being suppressed. Not so coincidentally, this was also a time when the elites of commerce and government in Europe rethought and replanned future relationships with Africans, now that the slave trade was denied them.

Figure 13.8 is a graph showing the years during which European explorers began their expeditions in Africa. It indicates that there were two epochs. The first of these featured coastal explorations, which occurred mainly during the 16th century. Explora-

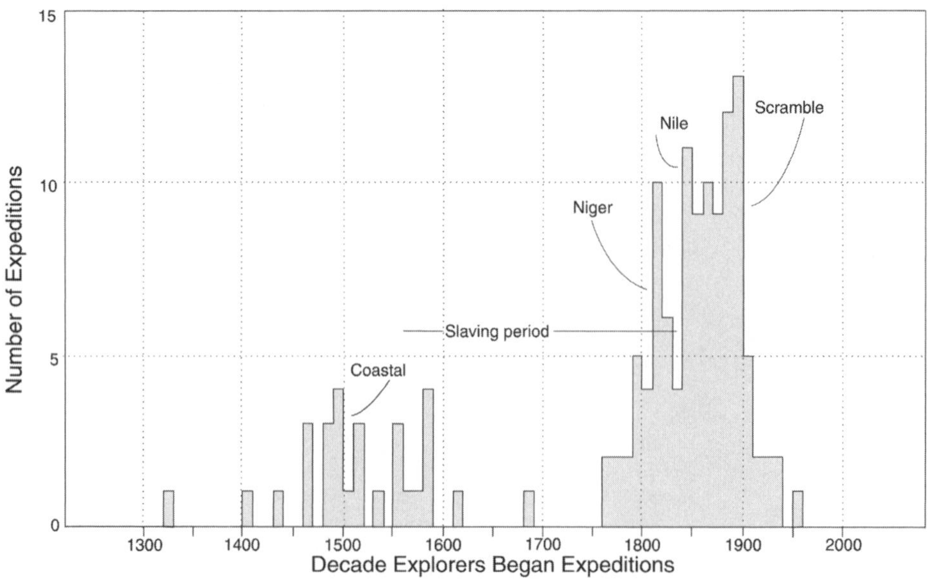

FIGURE 13.8. European explorers in Africa, 1300s through 1900s.

tion was conspicuously absent during the 17th and 18th centuries, the peak period of the slave trade. Toward the end of the 18th century, exploration was recommenced; this time it was directed toward inland zones.

Exploration was organized, for reasons that are not entirely self-evident, around questions of the courses and drainage basins of major river systems. The most famous puzzles concerned the Niger and the Nile. Which way did the Niger flow? What formed the true headwaters of the Nile? The problem of the Niger was attacked first; its exploration covered a period mainly between 1796, when Mungo Park reached the Niger at Segu, and 1830, when Richard and John Lander proved for Europeans that the Niger entered the Gulf of Guinea through the Oil Rivers (the Niger delta)—something that the local inhabitants already knew to be the case. (Such was European ignorance of the interior of west Africa that for a period of 100 years, as a consequence of Park's journey, a nonexistent east-to-west-trending mountain range called the Mountains of Kong came to be placed on nearly all maps [Bassett and Porter, 1991]. This range in many renditions was up to 2,455 miles [3,950 kilometers] long and was of considerable height, described in one gazetteer entry as having a "stupendous height" of 14,000 feet [4,267 meters].) The second great puzzle concerned the source of the Nile, and, for a time, the whereabouts of David Livingstone. Figure 13.8 shows an increased pace in explorations in the latter half of the 19th century, with no fewer than 59 European-led expeditions setting forth.

Expeditions to find the sources of rivers—gripping geographical puzzles that inflamed the European imagination—appear in hindsight to have been transparent covers for imperial ambition. The first Europeans to be in a place in Africa could claim priority over Europeans who arrived later. Hence the furor in Britain (see below) over France's sending a small military contingent of French officers and Senegalese troops (8 French officers and 120 Senegalese soldiers survived the trip) to Fashoda, on the banks of the Nile.

In the 18th and 19th centuries, the recently formed geographical societies, the new commercial and colonial societies, and the groups of private investors in France, Britain, and Belgium that financed the African expeditions were all interested in more than the answer to geographical puzzles. They saw possibilities for profit in commerce, trade, and control of mineral resources. The next section continues the story of exploration as part of the second phase of the global expansion of European colonialism.

COLONIALISM: THE SECOND PHASE IN AFRICA AND THE PACIFIC

In the wake of European explorers of Africa (e.g., Caillé, Clapperton, Burton, Baker, Speke, Barth, Livingstone, Stanley) came agents of chartered companies: the Royal Niger Company, the German Colonization Society, the United Africa Company (Unilever), the Imperial British East Africa Company (IBEA), and so forth. With the renewed interest in Africa, an international conference was convened in Berlin in 1884–1885 to establish the rules for dividing Africa among the European powers. The itch for colonial expansion was everywhere in Europe in 1885. A famous speech by Jules Ferry, delivered in the French Chamber of Deputies on July 28 of that year, advanced the standard arguments for colonial expansion—to establish trade, to accomplish a humanitarian mission ("It must be openly said that the superior races have rights over the inferior races"; Ferry, quoted in Brunschwig, 1966: 78), to increase a nation's political prestige—but did so in a way that generated wild enthusiasm. As is so often the case, the final argument was that other countries were already doing it.

> In Europe as it now exists, in this competitive continent where we can see so many rivals increasing in stature around us—some by

perfecting their armed forces or navies, and others through the enormous development produced by their ever-increasing population—in a Europe, or rather in a world, which is so constructed[,] a policy of containment or abstention is nothing other than the broad road leading to decadence! . . . To stand on one side from all European combinations and to regard any expansion toward Africa and the Far East as a snare and a rash adventure—this is a policy which, if pursued by a great nation, would, I assure you, result in abdication in less time than you could think. It would mean that we should cease to be a first-rate power and become a third- or fourth-rate power instead. Neither I, nor I imagine anyone here, can envisage such a destiny for our country. France must put itself in a position where it can do what others are doing. A policy of colonial expansion is being engaged in by all the European powers. We must do likewise. (Ferry, quoted in Brunschwig, 1966: 80)

The real scramble for Africa occurred because Britain's Prime Minister of that era, Lord Salisbury, decided in 1889 that the occupation of Egypt would have to be permanent. Other European powers at the time had the technology to dam the Nile and deprive Egypt of water. Britain decided that it had to beat others in gaining control of the headwaters of the Nile (Robinson and Gallagher with Denny, 1963).

On January 20, 1893, Victor Prompt, a French hydrologist, delivered a paper titled "Soudan Nilotique" that caused a sensation (Collins, 1969: 16). He asserted that whoever controlled Fashoda—a minor settlement on the left bank of the White Nile, some 600 kilometers upriver of Khartoum—could dam the Nile and thereby control Egypt. President Carnot subsequently permitted a French column to be formed to take Fashoda.

The British made agreements with King Leopold II of Belgium that allowed them to gain access to the Nile and block the French, while giving Britain a 25-kilometer-wide Cape-to-Cairo corridor. This was the Anglo-Congolese Agreement of 1894. Germany was angered by this action, and Leopold abrogated the treaty. Lord Salisbury had earlier bought off German interest in the headwaters of the Nile by trading Heligoland (a tiny but celebrated island in the North Sea that gets smaller by the year because it is so easily eroded) for an east–west boundary across the middle of Lake Victoria. The Kenya–Tanzania boundary from Lake Victoria to the Indian Ocean was contrived with a strategic jog in it so as to include Mount Kilimanjaro within the German sphere; flat, snow-topped Kibo (the most distinctive of Mount Kilimanjaro's three peaks) was presented as a kind of "birthday cake" to Bismarck.

In June 1896 (events moved more slowly in those days), Captain J. B. Marchand left for Africa to lead a French column to Fashoda—an expedition up the Oubangi and down the Bahr-el-Ghazal, a Nile tributary. After some hesitation, Lord Salisbury ordered General Horatio Herbert Kitchener and his Anglo-Egyptian army into the southern Sudan to deprive the French of rights "over any part of the territory situated upon the eastern slope of the watershed between the Nile and the Ubanghi" (Salisbury, quoted in Uzoigwe, 1974: 284). In April 1898, Kitchener defeated the Mahdists (Sudanese followers of the Mahdi) at the Atbara River and then took Omdurman, where his army machine-gunned down 11,000 Dervish soldiers. On September 19, 1898, he marched upon and confronted Marchand's expedition—a small military contingent of 8 Frenchmen and 120 Senegalese troops, which had reached Fashoda 2 months earlier, completing a journey that had taken 2 years. The French blinked first. The history of European colonial expansion is full of episodes like Fashoda—military adventures and diplomatic bargaining and boundary making in the chancelleries of Europe, with little or no thought given to the people living in the areas over which control was taken.

Figures 13.9, 13.10, and 13.11 show the rapid encroachment by European colonial powers on Africa. In 1880, Europe's colonies could be characterized as a set of discontinuous toeholds along the coast. By 1895, 10 years after the Berlin Conference, most of Africa (excepting only the Sahara,

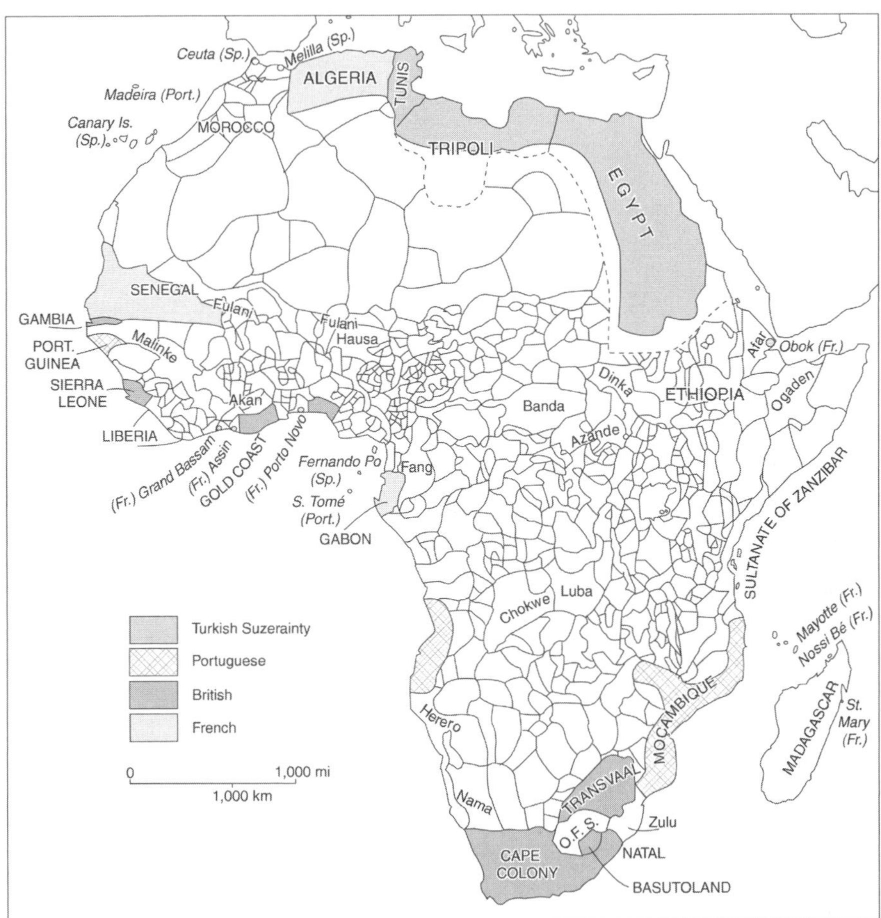

FIGURE 13.9. Status of European colonial expansion in Africa, 1880. *Sources:* Data are from Fage (1958, 1978) and Murdock (1959).

Sudan, and Morocco, and the independent states of Liberia and Ethiopia) had some external claimant. By 1914, the beginning of World War I, the process had been completed. Figures 13.9–13.11 have been drawn in such a way as to suggest that colonies were not being extended over ungoverned people and territories (as is so often suggested by the blank white paper of maps in historical atlases of Africa), but were encroaching upon and either subjugating (Akan), annihilating (Herero), or coopting (Hausa/Fulani) African political entities, however these may have been defined.

The scramble for Africa in the last two decades of the 19th century had a counterpart in the vast arena of the Pacific (Palmer, 1957: 133). The main rivalry was among the Americans, British, and French; from about 1875 to 1899, each took over island realms. The United States wrested the Philippines from Spain by force in 1899, and also gained control of the islands of Hawaii, Midway, Guam, Wake, and Samoa (in part). The British took the Gilberts, Ellice, part of the Solomons, Fiji, Tonga, and many other minor islands, although Australia and New Zealand subsequently assumed control in a number of instances.

The French gained control of many

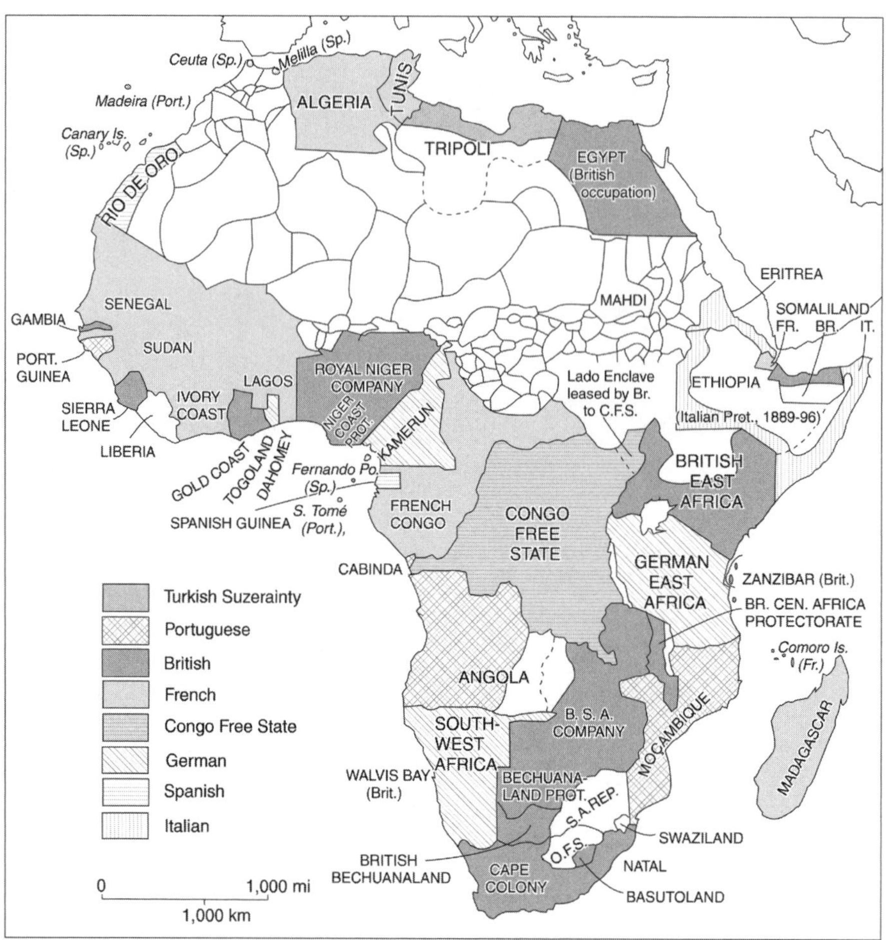

FIGURE 13.10. Status of European colonial expansion in Africa, 1895. *Sources:* Data are from Fage (1958, 1978) and Murdock (1959).

island groups in the Indian Ocean and in the Pacific. The Pacific islands of Mururoa and Sangutansa in the Tuamotu Archipelago, upwind of Tahiti, retain importance today as major sites for French tests of nuclear explosions. The facility became of even greater importance to the French when they lost Reggane, their Algerian/Saharan test site, during the Algerian war of independence. Among French territories at the end of the 19th century were New Caledonia, the Society and Liberty Islands, Tahiti, the Marquesas, Clipperton, and part of the New Hebrides.

The Germans came late to the competition for islands in the Pacific. In the 1880s, they claimed some Pacific island groups—Bismarck Island, Neu Mecklenberg, Neu Pommern (New Britain), the Marianas, Pelew, the Carolines, the Marshall Islands, and part of Samoa—and a part of New Guinea's northern coast.

In summary, throughout the tropics and subtropics, wherever there were lands and peoples not yet subject to European or U.S. hegemony, the ship of some northern nation soon arrived to change things. No place seemed too remote or insignificant to be fought over by the major colonial powers. Part of the competition had to do with doctrines of maritime power (control of sea lanes and strategic points); part of it was prideful competition goaded by chauvinistic nationalism; and part stemmed from speculation that valuable resources would be found in the newly claimed lands. Of these reasons for colonial expansion, perhaps the most fascinating concerns the historic importance of "command and control" points—islands and promontories dotted along the sea route from England, in particular. The British always made a habit of controlling pass routes as strategic constrictions to movement. Even two centuries later, how these place names still resonate in the ear: Gibraltar, Malta, Cyprus, Port Said, Suez, Aden, Singapore, and Hong Kong.

One might see colonialism in Africa as Europe's 19th-century reply to the abolition of the institution of slavery. Colonization is to a society as slavery is to an individual. If a nation is interested in economy of operation, stability of government, and a minimum of red tape and of meddling in local politics, there is no more effective mechanism than a colony—just as it is "better" for an employer to own employees (no unions, no fair employment practices, no competitive firms trying to hire away one's skilled labor). To the Victorian mind, the colony

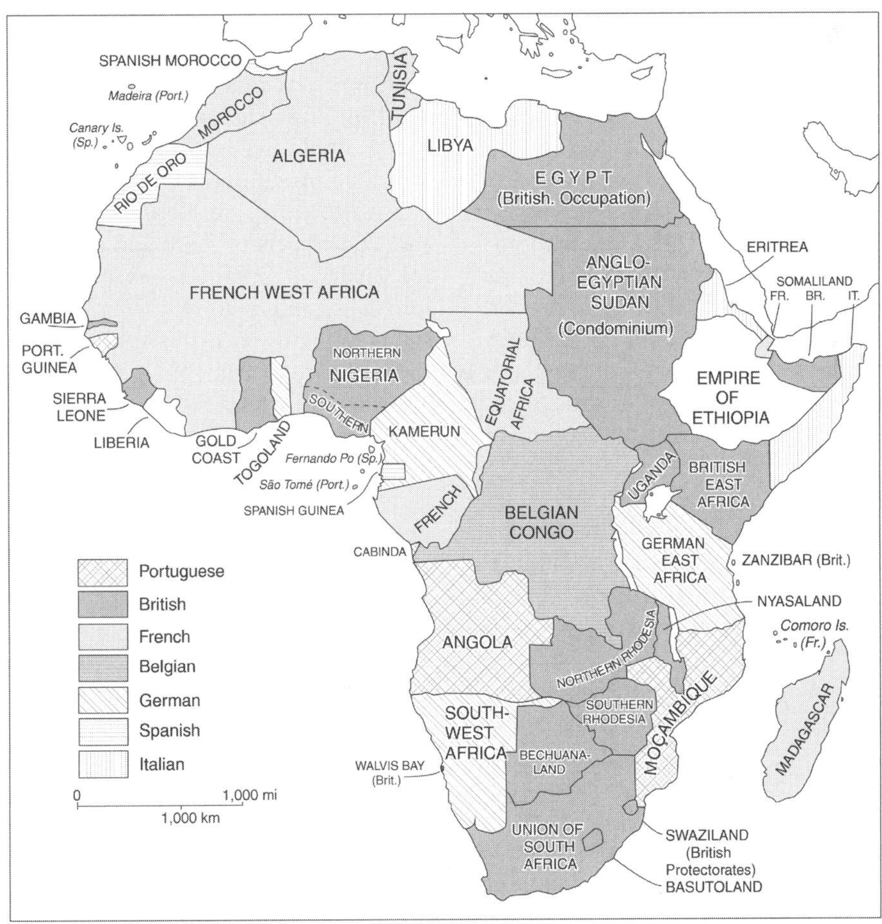

FIGURE 13.11. Status of European colonial expansion in Africa, 1914. *Sources:* Data are from Fage (1958, 1978).

seemed an appropriate, perfectly reasonable, and defensible institution: it could be used to stop "intertribal" warfare and the slave trade, to allow for the spread of literacy and the Christian faith, and to result in the economic development of the country and the uplifting of the people. The rapidly growing geographical and colonization societies of the day were seen as important instrumentalities in this overall task. Through their efforts, "the bare barren waste of the maps of the centre of that great continent [Africa] had blossomed into fertility, with waterways of thousands of miles and vast populations waiting for the birth of civilization and the olive branch of peace" (Freeman, 1961: 59).

Grand Strategies in Africa

Territorially, the French were most successful in Africa (Oliver and Crowder, 1981: 160–162). They established interior links between all coastal points of original penetration. Algeria was linked with the *sahel/ soudan*, the grasslands, across the Sahara. Senegal, Guinea, Côte d'Ivoire, Dahomey, Gabon—all became part of a larger uninterrupted land empire. The only parts of the French scheme that failed were establishing a land bridge to the River Nile, connecting the Nile with the equatorial and occidental empires, and perhaps ultimately connecting with French Somaliland (present-day Djibouti).

Britain's west African empire was fragmented, and apparently no real attempt was ever made to join the fragments together (Oliver and Crowder, 1981: 163–164; Uziogwe, 1985: 19 ff.). Britain took Nigeria, a large territory that always has been Africa's most populous country (its population was estimated at 139.8 million in 2004; World Bank, 2006a). Nigeria owes its size largely to the efforts of Lord Lugard, a handful of British officers, and African troops (mainly from the Gold Coast—present-day Ghana), who in 1903 finally brought the Muslim states of Sokoto, Kano, and Katsina into the British sphere. Lord Lugard, borrowing possibly from Marshal Lyautey's administrative policy in Morocco or from British experience in India and Fiji, opted for "indirect rule" in northern Nigeria, leaving the Sultan of Sokoto and the emirs of lesser states in charge of local affairs.

The grand British dream—to have Africa show pink (the usual color for the British Empire) on the map from Cairo to Cape Town—was that of Cecil Rhodes. This would require the British to extend their control across the length of Africa from north to south, and they very nearly succeeded. More generally, it is interesting how the British in the 19th century grabbed up the world's remaining grasslands. They nearly had the Argentine; they got Australia, east and central Africa, and the Sudan. Their concern was to have new outlets for white settlement, new sources of agricultural produce, and potential markets. There was substantial, well-financed research as to whether whites could live in the tropics (see Chapter 14). One little-appreciated feature of industrialization and development in Europe is that other parts of the world provided a vent for surplus population—an outlet that is no longer available to industrializing nations today. The migrant streams out of Europe to the Americas throughout the 19th century and in the first several decades of the 20th century were very large.

The British successes in claiming African territories were the occasions of failures for other European schemers (Oliver and Crowder, 1981: 164–167). For example, a rapprochement between Germans of South-West Africa (present-day Namibia) and the disgruntled Dutch-descended Boer farmers of the Orange Free State and the Transvaal got a quick response—the creation of British Bechuanaland, interposed between the two peoples who were considering an attempt to merge. The British had already cut off the Boer republics from the sea coast. Rhodes's mineral rights treaties with the Matabele people put the Union Jack in the Rhodesias, putting a stop to Portugal's dream of joining Angola with Portuguese East Africa (present-day Mozambique). It also put an end to German plans to link German East Africa with German South-West Africa, of which the Caprivi Strip, which reaches the banks of the Zambezi River above Victoria Falls, was an exploratory finger.

The British were unable to stop the Germans from acquiring a sphere in east Africa, the Cameroons, and Togoland; however, when the scramble was all over, the British had the people and the minerals, while the French had the space. The colonial boundaries agreed upon in the chancelleries of Europe were drawn without consultation with the people who became colonial subjects, and to them the borders made little sense. The map of colonial Africa features lots of arbitrarily chosen straight lines, meridians and parallels, and river courses. Cultural groups were at times purposely divided; for example, the Kru live in coastal settlements in southeastern Liberia and southwestern Côte d'Ivoire, the division being the Cavally River. Many Kru-speaking people worked on ships, and the French wanted an in-colony labor source. Similarly, Yoruba-speaking people found themselves divided between Nigeria and Dahomey (present-day Benin). The examples could be expanded endlessly.

World War I put the Germans out of the colonization business, with the colonial prizes being split and made into League of Nations mandates. Togoland became half French and half British. France and Britain also shared German Kamerun (or Cameroons). Britain and Belgium divided German East Africa, with Tanganyika going to Britain and Ruanda–Urundi to the Congo sphere. South-West Africa was mistakenly thought to have more problems than possibilities and was given entirely to the Union of South Africa, as a Class C mandate. South African control continued, despite many efforts by the International Court of Justice in the Hague and the world community to end South African administration. Finally, in 1990, Namibia held a plebiscite and became independent—the last colonial territory from the era of the scramble for Africa to do so.

One should not forget the Italians' imperial ambitions. They had long had designs on Tripoli and Cyrenaica on the Mediterranean coast; however, their dream of glory was to sweep over the east African horn by a pincer movement linking their Eritrean coast with their Somali coast by way of Ethiopia. For many years, their attempts failed utterly. They suffered a humiliating defeat at the hands of the Ethiopians at Adowa in 1896. The supreme moment for Italy finally came in 1936, when Italian troops took Addis Ababa from a young and dashing Haile Selassie, who fled to Europe and pled his country's case before the League of Nations. Although the League voted for sanctions against Italy, they were not enforced. Success for the Italians was short-lived, however, and the British chased them out of eastern Africa in the early years of World War II.

The Character of Colonial Rule in Africa

The character of colonial rule varied according to the colonizers and to the people and places colonized. The British entered the colonial field with a collective blank mind, a *tabula rasa* (Kaniki, 1985: 382). They had no preconceived model of a colony to be applied willy-nilly to all. In the words of their beloved Gilbert and Sullivan, they made "the punishment fit the crime." Each situation suggested its own solution. So, just like their improvisational recipes (1 dessert spoon of dripping, 1 egg cup of sugar, 3 breakfast cups of flour, 2 gills of water), their system of colonies was unstandardized and haphazard. There were crown colonies, protectorates, colonies and protectorates, condominiums (territories jointly ruled by two or more states), trusteeship territories, self-governing territories within the Empire (later the Commonwealth), high commission territories, and so forth. The three high commission territories of southern Africa are an interesting case in point. They were created originally at the insistence of three well-organized African peoples (the Swazi, Tswana, and Sotho), at the time the Union of South Africa was being established in the aftermath of the Anglo-Boer War, in the period 1902–1910. Basutoland (present-day Lesotho), Bechuanaland (Botswana), and Swaziland were expressly *not* included as part of the Union. As Moshoeshoe I, King of the Sotho, expressed it in a thank-you letter to Queen Victoria, his people wanted to "rest and live in the large folds of the blanket of England."

These three high commission territories were the responsibility of the Empire (later Commonwealth) Relations Office, but were administered like any colony—that is, in the manner prescribed by the Colonial Office. They were administered by the high commissioner, whose main job was to be British ambassador to the Union of South Africa, making him responsible to the Foreign Office. His office was in Cape Town, the legislative capital; he did his business in Pretoria, the administrative capital, 1,450 kilometers to the northeast. All three enclaves were landlocked, and Basutoland and Swaziland were almost entirely within the Union. The capital of Bechuanaland at the time, Mafeking, was not even in the country, but lay 8 kilometers inside the Union of South Africa. The railroad crossing Bechuanaland was owned by Southern Rhodesia but operated by the Union of South Africa.

To say the least, the British showed a certain degree of flexibility in meeting each situation. The main point was that they did not disturb indigenous institutions of governance or social organization when they found such institutions strongly entrenched and felt that they could use them in the maintenance of law and order. As noted earlier, Lord Lugard did not attempt to destroy the emirates of northern Nigeria; rather, he ruled through them. Indirect rule was a feature of British "native policy."

The British also made another far-reaching decision: that west Africa, the "white man's grave," was not suitable for European settlement. Laws were enacted prohibiting ownership of land by Europeans. The highlands of east and central Africa were not so designated, and after much discussion, European settlement was allowed and even encouraged in the colonies (but not in the protectorates). The British, in comparison with the French, emphasized education and the beginnings of internal government, as well as economic development. However, they dragged their feet on infrastructure, such as roads, railroads, electricity, and social services.

The French had a different idea (Coquery-Vidrovitch, 1985). Inspired, perhaps, by the ideals of the French revolution (*liberté, egalité, fraternité*), and deeply sure of the superiority of French culture, they attempted to create black Frenchmen and Frenchwomen. Cultural assimilation—complete cultural replacement in *France d'Outre Mer* (overseas France)—was their eventual goal. Local social structure, the richness of local myth, and indigenous political organization were of no concern to the French administrators. The basic approach to each of these was to let the anthropologists record it, but then to let it die and let the French way replace it. The French encouraged education, technical training, a modicum of self-government in the post-World War II years, and the beginnings of a vigorous labor union movement. But French settlement was encouraged too. Colonists came, bag and baggage, to the urban centers of French Africa. They came to stay—not like the British, to whom "up to town" was always London, and "home" was Britain. In Dakar, St. Louis, Abidjan, Bouaké, Conakry, and dozens of smaller interior towns, these French people were the *petit blancs*: the shopkeepers, stenographers, barbers, and auto mechanics. They were joined by many migrants from another French sphere of influence (Lebanon and Syria).

Ties were strong with the metropolitan country. Tariff barriers supported and protected marginal or infant plantations (e.g., plantings of bananas, or of the small oranges in Guinea whose oils are used in the manufacture of *eau de Cologne*). France always built its pyramid of power relations from Paris down into the territories. The pyramid was constructed of vertical pieces, not horizontal layers. Senegal and Guinea, the Côte d'Ivoire and Niger—these areas had little to do with one another, and this lack of integration and prior interrelations had a striking consequence. When de Gaulle granted independence to west and equatorial French African colonies in 1960, the lack of integration was suddenly apparent to all. The pyramid had nothing to hold it together, and Francophone Africa was balkanized almost overnight. Guinea went it alone. (General de Gaulle was so incensed by Guinea's vote of *non* that he ordered the country stripped bare of its colonial furnishings as the French occupants left. The very telephones were wrenched from their moorings and carted away.) The Mali Federation split into its component parts: Senegal and Soudan (Mali). The Côte d'Ivoire proclaimed a hollow-sounding *entente* between itself and Upper Volta (now Burkina Faso), Niger, and Dahomey.

The French viewed Algeria as an integral part of metropolitan France, just as the upper peninsula of Michigan is part of Michigan, or Alaska is part of the United States (Kassab, 1985: 420 ff.). After the Algerian revolution, at a time when de Gaulle sued for peace and agreed to Algerian independence, the French engaged in a bizarre propaganda exercise: They asserted that the "Saharan Departments," with their oil and nuclear test facilities, were not really part of Algeria at all. They published booklets about Algeria, with new maps (Figure 13.12), new figures for Algeria's population and land area, and so on, as if it had always been that way (Ambassade de France, 1961: 5). No one was taken in by this clumsy ruse, and the effort was soon abandoned.

The Belgians started with the advantage of inexperience and therefore a kind of naive "unprejudice" in colonial management, but they labored under a tremendous psychological burden—guilt (Slade, 1961; Ryckmans,

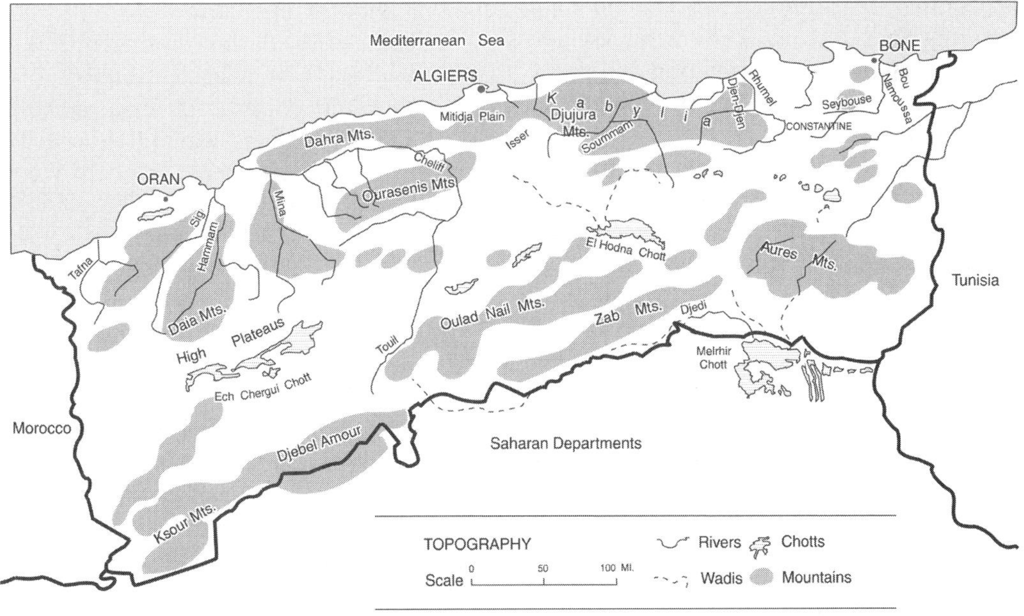

FIGURE 13.12. "Algeria" according to the public relations arm of the French government, 1961. *Source:* Adapted from Ambassade de France (1961).

1964; Coquery-Vidrovitch, 1985). Shamed for the merciless way the indigenous population had been exploited and murdered in the days of the Congo Free State (the personal state of Leopold II, King of the Belgians), they vowed to raise the indigenous people's standards of well-being to a high level before allowing them to undertake management of their own affairs. Education was widespread, but was held to secondary and technical levels. Medical orderlies were many; Congo-born doctors were almost nonexistent. The first Congolese student to enroll at the University of Louvain in law did so in 1958. Belgium, under pressure from the United States and other countries, agreed to grant independence to the Congo in 1960. The collapse that came soon after, in a vast, poorly interconnected country the size of the United States west of the Rocky Mountains, was not surprising.

Portuguese colonial policy in Guinea, Angola, and Mozambique from the 16th century on was informed by a peculiar mystique about civilization, assimilation, and colonial rule (Duffy, 1964). Like the French, the Portuguese colonists wanted the local people to acquire their culture. There was no color bar, only a cultural one. The Portuguese policy was one of complete isolation and paternalism. Their ideal was for the indigenous population to become *assimilado*—that is, assimilated to Portuguese culture. To demonstrate successful assimilation, a person had to pass a literacy test and an economic means test. As Catholics, the Portuguese discouraged missionary work by Protestant denominations, and those that existed had their activities carefully scrutinized. Economic development was slow in Portugal's colonies, as indeed it was for most rural folk in Portugal itself. Progress in the colonies, spread out over half a millennium, clearly moved at a snail's pace. In 1960, when the 500th anniversary of the death of Prince Henry the Navigator was being celebrated, some observers wryly commented that Portugal was "launching its Second Five Hundred Year Plan."

Legacy

The legacy of the colonial experience continues to permeate many aspects of economic and social life in third world countries. The legacy can be conveniently divided into five topics: boundaries and nations; infrastructure; economic dependencies; political and economic institutions; and a psychological residuum.

Boundaries and Nations

The colonizing powers delineated colonial borders, which in due course became international boundaries, at the time of decolonization. This process was especially problematic in Africa—where, at the time of the delineation of colonial boundaries, European powers had no firm basis on which to draw them, because resource and population distributions were largely unknown. Nonetheless, some of the more glaring absurdities in boundary configurations could have been avoided. Among numerous possibilities of territorial oddities and dysfunctional boundary making, we cite two: Cameroon and The Gambia (Figures 13.13 and 13.14).

Because the Berlin Conference had stressed access to navigable waterways as one important consideration in creating colonies, the Germans wanted to assert a claim on navigable water east of their colony of Kamerun (Figure 13.13). They finally got their opportunity by precipitating the Agadir crisis of 1911, which helped seal the colonial fate of Morocco. By accommodating France on Morocco, Germany got two land corridors, one to the Oubangi River and the other to the Congo River. Of course, World War I put an end to German colonies in Africa altogether; Kamerun was divided into British and French zones, and large sections on the east and south were reassigned to divisions of French Equatorial Africa.

The Gambia is a string bean of a country, stretching about 6 miles (10 kilometers) either side of the Gambia River, some 205 miles (330 kilometers) from the Atlantic

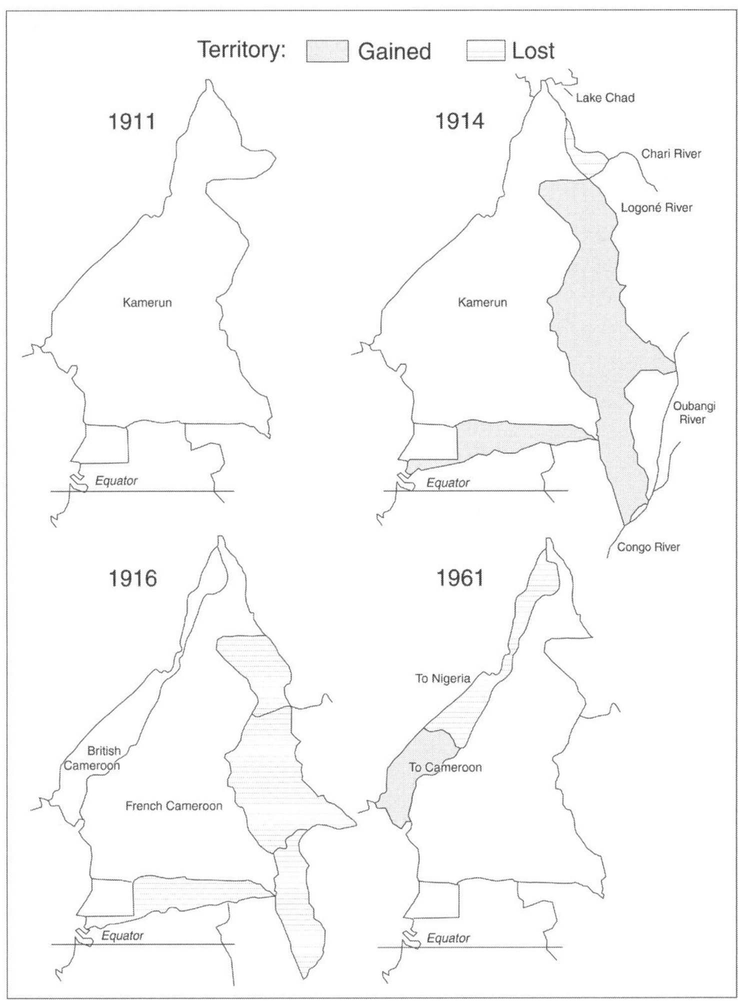

FIGURE 13.13. The changing boundaries of Cameroon. *Sources:* Data are from Njeuma (1989), Rudin (1968), and Central Intelligence Agency (1961).

coast, near Bathurst (now Banjul) eastward to Yabu Tenda (Figure 13.14). Its existence as a country can perhaps be traced to a long, irascible rivalry between Britain and France on the Senegambian coast—a feud that started in the 1670s and became "a constant succession of wars and treaties" over control of the river. The British had a fort at James Island, about 20 miles from the river's mouth, and the French had Albreda, a station 2 miles downstream. The Gambia's eastern boundary, set by the British as a 10-kilometer arc around Yabu Tenda, marks the head of navigation. With just over 900,000 people and a tiny land area, The Gambia has little potential for becoming a strong nation state.

With British control of the river, the French had to find other ways to reach the interior of Senegal and Soudan (Mali). They did so by building a railway from the excellent port at Dakar to Tambakounda (thus duplicating the avenue provided by the Gambia River) and on to Bamako, on the Niger. A more serious issue is the isolation of the Bas Casamance, a region of Senegal south

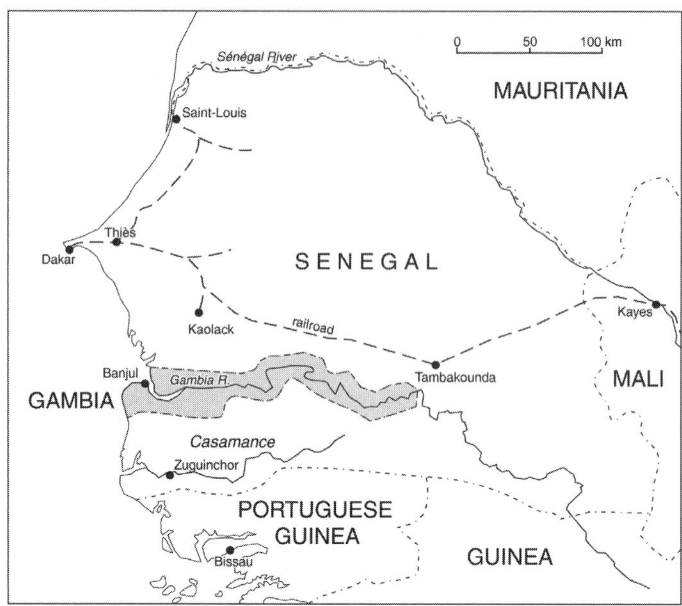

FIGURE 13.14. The Gambia. *Source:* Data are from l'Institut Géographique National (1954).

of The Gambia. Access to this region from Dakar involves crossing two international borders, or else a very long journey out of the way.

Infrastructure

In Chapter 14, we consider the incomplete, fragmented, incompatible system of rail transport created by colonial powers in most of the third world. Exceptions could be made for India, Argentina, and South Africa, where true networks were created. Elsewhere, particularly where territory was carved up into different European colonies (German, French, British, Portuguese, etc.), infrastructure was constructed principally for export of primary goods. It was rare for rail gauges to be the same as railroads crossed borders—and, in any case, railroads rarely crossed borders between colonies of rival imperial powers.

We could go on at length about the lack of development of other infrastructural work—roads, bridges, water supply, electricity, communications. One example must suffice. Sending telegrams and telexes or making telephone calls in Africa was, until recently, an adventure. The separation of British, French, Belgian, and other colonial systems from each other is illustrated by one of our favorite examples—making a telephone call from Kabale in southwestern Uganda to nearby Bukavu in the eastern portion of the former Zaire, two major regional towns only 195 kilometers apart. Until recently, the "trunk call" or long-distance call had to be routed as follows: Kabale → Kampala → London → Brussels → Kinshasa → Bukavu, with possible additional intermediate transfers through Nairobi and Kisangani. Things are finally changing in telecommunications in Africa because of microwave relay technology and satellites, so the routing of calls from place to place is losing the absurdities of an earlier era.

Economic Dependencies

Colonies were not allowed to develop their own manufacturing, but were required to specialize in producing a narrow range of primary commodities for export to the industrialized colonial powers. Colonizing powers shifted crops all over the world, so that people in each colony become dependent on a few cash crops to earn money, whereas the colonial countries diversified sources of supply of those commodities in order to ensure access to reliable, low-cost imports.

The economic or trade dependencies of former colonies may continue for decades to be closely tied to the former colonial occupiers. This may be a result of concessional trade agreements (a typical arrangement between France and its former African colonies), or it may be plain historical inertia or habit. The proportions of trade directed to former colonial metropoles is very high in many cases, showing how difficult it is for a country that produces few tradable commodities (be they minerals or crops) to break out of historic trading relationships (see also Chapter 16).

In 1960, most African countries were in the lower- and middle-income group (according to World Bank definitions), and they generally had between 15% and 20% of their trade with other third world countries. Over two-thirds of their trade was with industrial economies (Hance, 1967: 21). At a regional level, there may be even less basis for trade. For example, less than 10% of west Africa's trade was with other west African countries, even in the 1980s; the bulk of it was directed toward first world economies (Aryeetey-Attoh, 1997: 253).

Single-factor domination, or dependency on a single mineral, fuel, or crop for foreign exchange earnings, reaches extremes for certain countries (Table 13.1).

Political and Economic Institutions

Colonial powers established new institutions of labor and property, and restructured relations between classes, genders, and races to facilitate extraction of wealth. For example, a racial hierarchy was established, with Europeans at the top; Asians in the middle;

TABLE 13.1. Export Concentration in Certain Third World Countries

Country	HH index[a]	Principal export	Year of data
Angola	0.962	Crude oil	2004
Nigeria	0.962	Petroleum	2004
Iraq	0.961	Crude oil	2004
Equatorial Guinea	0.920	Petroleum	2004
Venezuela	0.870	Petroleum	2005
Sierra Leone	0.858	Diamonds	2004
Sudan	0.851	Oil and petroleum	2005
Libya	0.848	Crude oil	2004
Yemen	0.840	Crude oil	2005
Comoros	0.807	Vanilla	2004
Bahrain	0.795	Petroleum	2005
Iran	0.793	Petroleum	2005
Saudi Arabia	0.747	Petroleum	2003
Congo	0.743	Petroleum	2004
Falkland Islands	0.737	Wool	2004
Gabon	0.739	Crude oil	2005
Burkina Faso	0.699	Cotton	2005
New Caledonia	0.670	Ferronickels	2005

Source: Data are from United Nations Conference on Trade and Development (UNCTAD) (2008b).

[a]The Herfindahl–Hirschman (HH) index is a measure of the degree of concentration of exports, ranging in its standardized form from zero (no concentration at all) to 1 (a single product is exported). The

$$\text{HH index} = \frac{(\sum_{i=1}^{N} x_i^2 - N^{-1})}{(1 - N^{-1})}$$

where x_i is product i's fraction of total export earnings, and N is the number of products exported.

and sub-Saharan Africans, Native Americans, and other "indigenous peoples" at the bottom. Such a hierarchy was enshrined in South African apartheid laws until 1994. These and other less visible patterns of social differentiation created among the colonized people continue to exist worldwide and continue to be exploited by vested interests.

Colonial legislation and administration concerning money taxation, property titles in land, and the commercialization of agriculture linked to the international economy radically altered the nature of rural social relations in ways that are difficult to reverse (Bernstein, Johnson, and Thomas, 1992: 202). Such changes include the replacement of common property systems with private or state property, transfers of rights to resources, and land use changes (see Chapter 7). New local-level landlord classes emerged or were created, and these did not disappear with the end of colonial rule. For example, the skewed distribution of land ownership in Latin America that was produced under colonial rule continues to be a source of inequity, conflict, and uneven development.

The colonial system also created a highly centralized authoritarian state, but not always a competent or accountable state. The British established the elite Indian Civil Service, which became the postindependence "steel frame" of India. But the development of such capacities was exceptional. Among the most intractable problems of African nations in the postindependence period have been the weakness and ineffectiveness of the nation states. Nations gained their independence ill prepared to take the reins of government. The first president of Indonesia, Sukarno, was a trained geological engineer. Patrice Lumumba, the first prime minister of the Congo (later Zaire and now the Democratic Republic of Congo), had been a postal clerk, and President Kasavubu of the Congo had only partly completed training for the Roman Catholic priesthood.

According to the Swedish political scientist Goran Hydén (1983), there was no *moral foundation* for a public sector in the newly freed colonies. The public sector in the United States and Europe evolved slowly as economic development took place, and an ethos—a moral foundation for honest civil service—evolved with it. Both were "homegrown." In the colonies, a public sector based on European models of civil service was transferred intact to the educated elites, which assumed power. Lacking a similar tradition of public service, however, the elites in many cases behaved in corrupt ways. Most colonies at independence had virtually no industrial and commercial sectors (or such sectors as existed were controlled by expatriate interests), and for the educated elite, government was the easiest (sometimes about the only) avenue for advancement. According to Samatar and Samatar (1987), the new elites of independent nations became "rent seekers," intent on coopting funds from colonial development corporations, aid donors, UN agencies, and international banking and loan sources; in such a nation, the state became suspended over and disarticulated from the general population of the country. The state ignored the developmental problems of rural agricultural people in particular, and neither took from nor gave back to them. It did not help improve their productive capacities.

This has led to a pernicious secondary development: the belief in western donor nations and foundations and in international lending institutions (e.g., the World Bank) that third world states are so corrupt that ways have to be found to circumvent them in order to bring development to poor people. The emphasis placed by the Ford Foundation and the Rockefeller Foundation in the 1980s on small local entities—self-help groups, church groups, women's groups, village development committees, refugee groups, and nongovernmental organizations (NGOs)—reflected a view of the state as a barrier to development. The idea that the state can be circumvented is naive and misguided, and ways need to be found to empower the state to adopt policies and actions that benefit the poor, both in rural areas and in cities.

Psychological Residuum

The metropolitan governments that had colonial empires were of several minds about them. Administering them required governmental funds. They wanted the colonies to pay their way, but frequently colonies were a financial drain on their home governments. Plantations and mine operators within colonies may have been making a profit, but that did not necessarily mean that the governments themselves were. In the rivalry to be first and to claim colonial prizes, European powers, having obtained colonies, frequently set them aside and did little to develop them. This became particularly the case during the Great Depression of the 1930s and during World Wars I and II, when colonial administrators essentially were told to get on with their jobs without help from the mother countries. The colonies were expected to be self-sufficient. We mention this feature of colonial neglect and nondevelopment as background for considering what psychological effects several generations of colonial experience may have had.

We feel somewhat out of our depth here, but elements that may have entered the collective psyche of third world people are (1) a view that if something is to be done, the government should, and perhaps only the government *can*, do it; (2) a style of administration that may differ little from the top-down authoritarian style of a colonial district officer (D.O.); (3) a feeling that, given the technological superiority of the industrialized countries, any indigenous way of doing things must be inferior; and (4) views that divide groups within former colonies (urban vs. rural, the younger generation vs. the older). Philip Mbithi (1977: 30) catches this attitudinal gap nicely in describing agricultural extension in east Africa:

> The change agent in East Africa is a member of the educated elite, who became alienated from his illiterate parents when he went to school at the impressionable age of between six and eight, [and] spent at least 15 years "learning" western value systems, and life styles. He shares little with his rural folk and has no empathy with their thought processes. He may be arrogant or paternalistic but he does not recognize them as independent managers of their holdings. . . .
>
> The rural farmer has, for the past 70 years . . . been told repeatedly that he is backward, heathen, ignorant, illiterate and headed straight to "hell." . . . This orientation, [exalting] the supremacy of western technology, western value systems and western religions, saps self [assertiveness] and self identity from the humble rural farmer, and even makes him apologise for daring to see things differently. This approach generates a school-boy mentality among rural adults who are very willing to suspend their world view, abandon it and embrace that of the expert, who may have just recently scraped through an agricultural exam based on a narrowly designed curriculum.

CONCLUSIONS

It has been a little over 500 years since Europeans got the jump on everyone else. Since 1492, Europe has dominated world history and political economy, building on the initial advantage of having been the first among Old World peoples to exploit resources and people in the New World, the Americas (Blaut, 1993). Blaut titled his 1993 book *The Colonizer's Model of the World* with exquisite care, since it summarizes succinctly a European mindset in which Europe was the source, the origin, the center (core), its superior civilization diffusing outward to the periphery where dwelled the rest of the world's peoples, with their diverse but ineluctably inferior societies or civilizations (see Blaut, 1993: 8–17). In this chapter, we have surveyed some aspects of that half millennium—the first colonial phase, dominated by Portugal and Spain; the three centuries of the African slave trade (1570–1870s); and the second colonial phase, in which north European powers vied with Spain and Portugal and against one another, with the British and the French emerging in the 19th and early 20th centuries as colonial masters of much of the tropics and subtropics. We have reviewed the strategies the major colonial powers pursued to gain command and control of territory, resources, labor, and markets. Out of the competition emerged third world polities with absurd boundaries, fragmentary deformed infrastructures, high levels of dependency on single crops, and single metropoles. The 1960s saw the emergence of newly independent states that were not nations and nations that were not states. The new countries were ill prepared in institutions and trained cadres to develop resources productively for their people. In the next chapter, we explore the numerous and clever ways European colonizers controlled space and subject peoples (their movement, their labor, even their identity) in pursuit of the goals of empire.

14 Colonialism as Spatial and Labor Control System

> [So] they took away the Caribbean in April, Ambassador Ewing's nautical engineers carried it off in numbered pieces to plant it far from the hurricanes in the blood-red dawns of Arizona, they took it away with everything it had inside general sir, with the reflections of our cities, our timid drowned people . . . it's better to be left without the sea than to allow a landing of marines . . . they brought the Bible and syphilis, they made people believe that life was easy, mother, that everything is gotten with money. . . . I granted them the right to make use of our territorial waters in the way they considered best for the interests of humanity and peace among peoples.
>
> —Gabriel Garcia Marquéz (1976: 245–246)

THE TASK

European powers took over and held territories as colonies, first and foremost, to meet the needs of the colonizers. The nature of those needs and the methods of control and the response of the colonized peoples varied spatially and changed over time. As we have described in Chapter 13, European powers accumulated wealth for the first three centuries of the colonial era principally through the plunder of the Americas; the Atlantic slave–plantation production and trading complex; expansion and monopolization of the trade in luxury goods from and within Asia; and, later, collecting land taxes in India. As European economies were reshaped by the influx of wealth and the gathering steam of the industrial revolution, their needs changed. Particularly by the time of the scramble for Africa, the European powers were faced with the task of integrating the colonies ever more deeply into the colonizers' economies by bringing ever more aspects of life into a colonial regulated market system. Through this managed expansion of markets, and through the construction of new social and legal institutions, colonies were positioned in particular ways as suppliers of materials for the burgeoning industries in Europe, and increasingly as markets for the textiles, iron/steel products, and other manufactures the metropolitan countries produced. This task was more or less difficult, depending on the degree to which (1) the colonized people preferred to organize their livelihoods according to their own wishes, rather than to be brought into western economic relations involving wages, the use of currency, commodity pricing, and exchange rather than use values; and (2) the colonized people already had livelihood systems that satisfied their needs.

We are not arguing that colonized people had not previously engaged in trade or used currencies, or were unacquainted with the idea of "exchange value." People had always traded with others to some extent, but in many instances, nearly all needs were met within the context of households and small communities even if they were incorporated into larger nations or empires. If we view such "self-provisioning" societies as closed circles, the task of the colonialists was to break open those circles and force those living within them to use their time, their labor, and their subsequent purchasing power to respond to the demands of European colonial powers. In this chapter, we review the changing ways in which colonizing armies, trading companies, colonial administrators, and settler groups broke into the circles—all the while trying to do so cheaply, so as not to strain the budgets of the metropolitan countries. In short, this chapter explores "how they did it."

THE BEGINNINGS: INDIGENOUS EXPERIENCE OF COLONIZATION IN LATIN AMERICA

European colonization of Latin America was distinctive for several reasons. Latin America was the first region where Europeans conquered and came to control substantial territory (soon after 1492). This colonization had something of a feudal character, with loyal nobles and leaders receiving substantial land grants. It was the *destination*, not the source region, of the African slave trade; slaves figured prominently in the plantation labor system that developed in Brazil, the Caribbean, and Central America. Culturally, it was largely Iberian and Catholic (most areas and people were colonized by Spain and Portugal, and the church played an important role in social control). Finally, its political independence from Europe in the first decades of the 19th century, in the wake of the French revolution, resulted in a different colonialism—locally controlled, but still in a dependent relation with industrializing Europe and North America.

The indigenous people of Latin America tasted the bitter fruits of colonial rule virtually from the moment Columbus and his men set foot on land in the Caribbean in 1492. Conquest of the Aztec Empire in Mexico began by 1519, and the Incan realm in Peru was assaulted in 1531. South and Central America in 1492 was a vast, sparsely peopled land, with small pockets here and there of dense settlement. The arrival of the Spanish, Portuguese, and other Europeans not only brought external control, but triggered terrific population declines. Diseases to which the local people had no resistance, especially smallpox and measles, carried off entire populations. One estimate of pre-Columbian population of the western hemisphere put the figure at 57.3 million, over half of it in Mexico and the Andes (Stearns, Adas, and Schwartz, 1992: 398). On some Caribbean islands, everyone died; on the mainland, losses of 50–80% occurred (Stearns et al., 1992: 528). The population in Mexico was estimated as being 25.2 million in 1518 and 1.075 million in 1609—a catastrophic plunge to 4.5% of the original figure (Figure 14.1) (Cook and Borah, 1971: viii).

The conquest and colonial control of Latin America concentrated land ownership into large holdings, which in turn made possible two predominant kinds of agricultural systems: the *hacienda* and the plantation. *Haciendas* were large-scale quasi-feudal land holdings owned by Europeans on which indigenous laborers' families lived and produced subsistence crops for themselves, as well as supplying labor for the owners' commercial production. They tended to be located inland, producing livestock and agricultural commodities for the local market. Some scholars regarded *haciendas* as inefficient and as operated primarily to enhance the prestige of their owners. However, this was not necessarily so. Ward Barrett's (1970) study of the sugar *hacienda* owned for nearly four centuries (1535 to

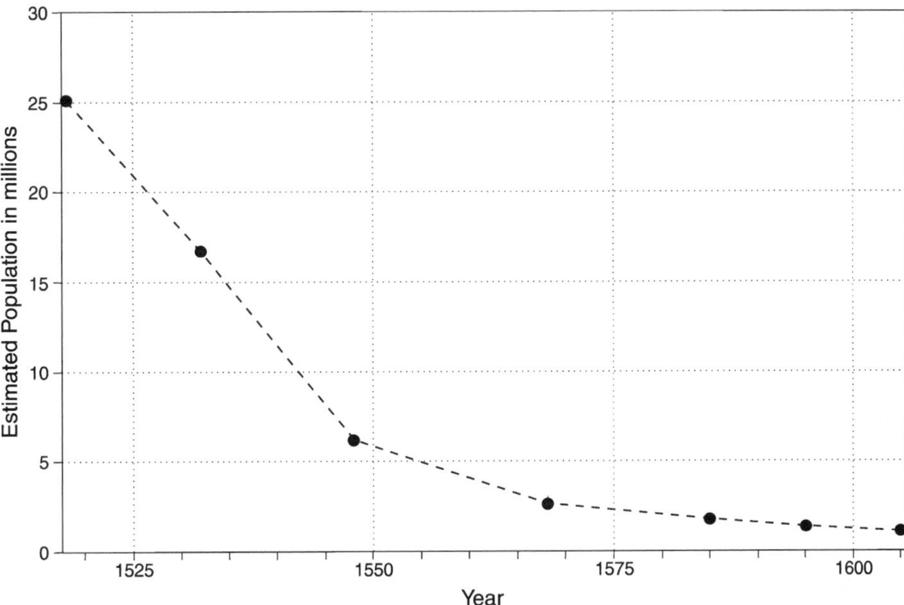

FIGURE 14.1. Population decline in 16th-century Mexico. *Source:* Data are from Cook and Borah (1971).

about 1910) by the Hernán Cortés family near Cuernavaca, Mexico, shows in exquisite detail how every aspect of production, even in the earliest years, was recorded and analyzed to make the operation profitable. For every laborer (skilled and unskilled), the plantation owners knew the work record, ethnic origin (Spanish, African-descended slave, mulatto, or Indian), approximate age, number of sick days, and food and clothing rations provided. Furthermore, they knew the cost and productivity of every step of production: in the cane fields, preparing seed beds, weeding, irrigating, and cutting; in the mill itself, in the press room, the furnace and boiling house, and the purgery (where brown sugar was made white, with molasses as a by-product); and in the carpentry shop, the pottery, the blacksmith shop, and the stable. Other workers were engaged as firewood cutters, as guards, or as muleteers and ox drivers who saw to plowing and transporting various supplies and the finished sugar and molasses (Barrett, 1970: 50 ff.).

Plantations, by contrast, were established primarily on the Caribbean islands and coastal Brazil to produce and process monocultural export crops using slave labor. These plantations constituted the agroindustrial part of the "triangular trade"—the immense, and immensely profitable, production and trading complex that, according to Blaut (1976, 1993), first perfected the systems of capital, industrial technologies, and management that led directly to the industrial revolution in Europe. Echoing the work of James (1938) and Williams (1944), Blaut (1993: 204) regards the West Indian slave-based plantation economy in the 17th and 18th centuries "as a highly advanced form of industrial system, implicitly the most advanced form in existence at that time." He has carried the argument further:

> Within the overall economic space which the Europeans controlled in the seventeenth and eighteenth centuries, they found it possible to advance the capitalist industrial production system—large-scale, organized, semi-mecha-

> nized—to its highest level, for that era, *mainly* in the plantation system, using slave labor, until the evolution of industrial production as an overall system had evolved sufficiently so that profits could be made even when the labor force was paid a living wage, a wage permitting subsistence and reproduction of the working class, and the system could then be centrated, imported into Europe itself. (Blaut, 1993: 204; emphasis in original)

Thus, in areas of established European settlement from the beginning of the 16th century on, Spanish and Portuguese control over land and the labor of the indigenous people was systematic, firm, and extensive. Many other areas were not occupied until much later, and European expansion was resisted by the various Native American peoples. The history of Latin America is replete with peasant revolts, slave uprisings, and (in recent times) strikes by miners and plantation workers. Vast amounts of land were taken over by settlers and made into large private estates (*latifundios*), while most people, particularly the indigenous population, lived as peasants, sharecroppers, or landless laborers. A divided society of haves and have-nots began early in Latin America. It is the precursor for the gulf between rich and poor that persists today in most Latin American countries. For example, in Brazil, the income of the top 20% of the population is 32.2 times that of the bottom 20%. Concentration in ownership of wealth (property and assets, from which income is generated) is even more extreme. It is thought that when countries exhibit income disparities much greater than 8:1, the seeds are sown for eventual revolt by the people at the lower end of the economic spectrum. One finds high levels of income disparity in other Latin American countries—for example, Panama, 25.1:1; Colombia, 22.9:1; Honduras, 21.8:1; and Chile, 18.8:1 (United Nations Development Programme [UNDP], 2004; see Chapter 2 for further discussion).

Even when independence came to Latin America (1791–1824), 300 years after Columbus's landfall, little changed in the long-established relationship between the indigenous population and Spanish and Portuguese settlers and colonial administrators. Independence was an event that benefited the local elite, who were freed from the colonial control of Spain or Portugal, and thenceforth able to run their own affairs. It was also a boon to Great Britain, which was trading and investing heavily in Latin America, and could now work with the local power structure. The pattern of dominance over land and local people continued undisturbed by the coming of independence, often well into the 20th century. There was great variation from country to country, and even within countries, in the living conditions and experiences of local peoples. In some places—for example, in the remote, dry, cold steppes of Patagonia; in southern Colombia; or in the Brazilian rain forest—they were left pretty much to themselves. In other places, such as central Mexico, they were subject to great control. Latin American nations had a quasi-colonial or at least dependent relationship with the main European colonial players in the late 19th and 20th centuries (as well as with the United States and Canada), because they traded mainly with these countries—supplying agricultural products and minerals, and importing manufactured goods. Latin American states, ruled by a tiny landed aristocracy, were prone to frequent coups as rival factions battled for control, and unstable governments were a result. Latin American politics has featured authoritarian rule, utter disregard for human and civil rights, and a chilling role for its military forces. Penny Lernoux (1984) has described it thus:

> Accustomed to a society in which the armed forces are controlled by civilian institutions, Americans do not always understand that the military in Latin America is often the only political party. It controls the government, the pursestrings, and the right of veto over the judicial system—not to protect national security but to enrich its members and ensure their domination of the civilian population. Those who object to this repressive and corrupt system, including some conservative

> businessmen, are tarred as "communist," an all-purpose epithet having nothing to do with Marxism. Thus US military aid perpetuates an anti-democratic political system in which the indigenous military serves as an occupying army, and the people are treated as the enemy.

The relations of the United States with Latin America and the Caribbean can also be interpreted in colonial/imperial terms—starting in 1823 with the Monroe Doctrine (which warned Europe not to meddle in the politics of newly independent Latin American states), but especially during the 20th century, an era ushered in by the Spanish–American War in 1898. The United States at one time or another has occupied and administered Panama, Cuba, Nicaragua, parts of Mexico (1914, 1916), Haiti (twice), the Dominican Republic, and Grenada. It has destabilized governments or aided coups in Brazil, Guatemala, Cuba, Chile, and Nicaragua (Lernoux, 1982). Furthermore, U.S. multinational firms in agriculture and mining essentially had their operational wishes met through cooptation of governing elites, giving rise to the term "banana republic." During much of the 20th century, the United Fruit Company (subsequently United Brands, and now Chiquita Brands International, Inc.), Gulf and Western, and similar U.S. companies dealt with dictators and totalitarian governments throughout Central America and the Caribbean: Trujillo in the Dominican Republic, Somoza in Nicaragua, Carías in Honduras, Martínez in El Salvador, Ubico in Guatemala, and so on.

DEATH AND TAXES IN INDIA

The south Asian encounter with Europe was quite different. In 1498, when Portuguese explorer Vasco da Gama became the first European to reach India by sea, the subcontinent was divided into a number of regional kingdoms whose social organization and technological and military prowess were equal or superior to those of the Europeans. The Portuguese established their first settlement in Goa in 1510, as part of their strategy to control the sea trade, both within Asia and between Asia and Europe. At that time, India produced goods prized in Europe (such as spices and fine textiles), but Europe produced little of interest to India. Portuguese traders used gold looted from the Americas to buy Indian goods, which they sold for huge profits in Europe. A century after the Portuguese, the Dutch, French, Danish, and British all began establishing trading ports, forming alliances with local power brokers, and seeking to expand their spheres of influence and trade.

The Europeans, however, were not the most significant actors in South Asia up to the 18th century. In 1526, Babar invaded India from the northwest and established the Mughal Empire. The Mughals expanded their rule over the next 180 years and eventually incorporated most of the subcontinent into their empire. The Mughals financed their empire through a system of taxation on land and on internal trade. The rate of land taxes tended to increase and decrease with the ruler's revenue needs (higher taxes during wartime, for example) and with good harvests and poor harvests. As the Mughal Empire began to decay after the death of Emperor Aurangzeb in 1707, regional powers, including the Europeans, sought to expand their influence. The British and their Indian allies defeated the French and their allies in an important battle in Bengal in 1757, making the British the dominant European power in India. As the British East India Company consolidated and expanded its position from the early 18th century onward, it gained the right to collect the land revenue in the areas it administered, and these taxes became the company's most important source of revenue. Thus began the "plunder of Bengal."

Whereas indigenous rulers often reduced taxes in years of poor harvests or failed crops, the East India Company was determined to maintain revenue flows, regardless of their effects on the populace. Thus Warren Hastings, the first Governor-General of

India, and his colleagues wrote the following in 1772 with reference to the plunder of Bengal (Hastings, Barker, Aldersey, Lane, Barwell, Harris, and Goodwin, 1772):

> The effects of the dreadful famine which visited these provinces in the year 1770, and raged during the whole course of that year, have been regularly made known to you by our former advices, and to the public by laboured descriptions, in which every circumstance of fact, and every act of language have been accumulated to raise compassion, and to excite indignation against your servants, whose unhappy lot it was to be the witnesses and spectators of the sufferings of their fellow creatures. But its influence on the revenues has been yet unnoticed, and even unfelt but by those from whom it is collected; for notwithstanding the loss of at least one third of the inhabitants of the province, and the consequent decrease of the cultivation, net collections of the year 1771 exceeded even those of 1768. . . . It was naturally to be expected that the diminution of the revenue should have kept an equal pace with the other consequences of so great a calamity; that it did not, was owing to its being violently kept up to its former standard.

This quote highlights the fact that the East India Company's governance of British India was accountable, first and foremost, for meeting the revenue demands of the company's shareholders back in England—with little or no accountability for the millions who were subjected to violence, starvation, and death in order to keep those revenues flowing into the shareholders' pockets, regardless of famine in India. Furthermore, whereas local rulers spent money locally, the East India Company repatriated its revenues to Britain, leaving little capital to be invested in India.

In succeeding years, the East India Company made the land revenue system more rigid and systematic, and increased tax rates. Furthermore, British policies supporting domestic industry helped to strangle Indian industry so that, by 1840, the British East India Company stated before a Parliamentary Select Committee that "this Company has in various ways, encouraged and assisted by our great manufacturing ingenuity and skill, succeeded in converting India from a manufacturing country into a country exporting raw produce" (quoted in Chaudhuri, 1971: 27). As Indian cotton flowed to British textile mills, Indians increasingly had to buy cloth manufactured in Britain.

COLONIAL RULE IN THE 19TH AND 20TH CENTURIES

Colonial Administration

The first task of colonial rule involved effective control of territory and people. Typically, the colonial power established a nested set of administrative units: provinces, districts, divisions, and wards. Unless a system of indirect rule was used—as in the so-called "princely states" in India, wherein the British ruled through the regency of local rulers, or in northern Nigeria, where rule was through the Muslim Fulani Emirs—a district was governed almost single-handedly by the district officer, or D.O., and the police contingent assigned to his district. This police constabulary was headed by another European and a small police force made up of indigenous people.

At one time, in about 1925, one could have identified about 1,000 European men who collectively had administrative control of nearly all of Africa. One could have done this by adding the district officers of the 31 districts of Kenya to the administrators of the 43 *cercles* of Haute Volta, the 88 *concelho* (or *circumscrição*) of Angola, the 126 *territoires* of the Belgian Congo, and so forth. The total comes to about 1,000—an amazingly small number for the basic control of a territory nearly four times the size of the United States.

Aiding the D.O. would be a small supplementary European staff: the agricultural officer, veterinary officer, forestry officer, health officer, and so forth. The small contingent would create its own society. In east Africa, the first structure established in any colonial administrative settlement was usually The Club, where colonial officers and their families could relax, drink their "sundowners" after work, and reinforce their various prejudices about the *watu* (people) or *wananchi* (common folk). From the 1920s on, the construction of landing strips (part of security considerations) also had high priority. An early infrastructural item to be built by and for the community of administrators was a golf course. Given sufficient size, such things as tennis courts, a church, and a squash court might be added.

The notion of social distance was fundamental to colonial control, as was the ever-present possibility of the use of force and violence. Colonial officers wore uniforms, and instantly recognizable uniforms were devised for all others who formed part of the administrative structure, whether they were *askaris* (soldiers), policemen, waiters, or train conductors. There were places the indigenous people were forbidden to enter. Audience with a colonial officer was arranged by petition. The D.O. had extraordinary administrative, legislative, and judicial power in all but the most serious of matters.

In practice, however, force alone was not sufficient to ensure that all policies were adhered to; European officers had to find other, less direct ways to accomplish their goals. Officers frequently did so by coopting and "empowering" local leaders. This practice had mixed results and was particularly problematic for the local leaders, caught between the people and the government. Maguire (1969: 7–8) described it well:

> Although . . . [indirect rule] sought in theory to foster traditional native authorities as a basis for the evolution of local administration, in practice the changes wrought did as much to transform as to consolidate tradition. Even indigenous chiefs, who had depended upon electors, elders, leaders of young men's societies and the people themselves for their initial selection and subsequent exercise of authority, found themselves increasingly estranged from this traditional context as they became simultaneously tied to and empowered by an alien colonial superstructure. The power of the chief increased in relation to these other traditional groups. At the same time, the chief lost the position of preeminence which the new employer, the British government, now enjoyed. In the eyes of both chief and people, the local incarnation of alien rule, the District Commissioner, assumed an aura of authority and the prerogatives of power.

The Colonial Organization of Space

Provinces and districts provided a framework for administering people, their movement, and resources. Commonly, district boundaries were drawn to surround a given cultural linguistic group, separating it from other groups. In colonial parlance, this separated "tribes" from one another. Colonial administrators liked to know where people were and who they were. This made it easier to control them, to count them, to tax them, and to call upon their labor. Nomadic pastoralists, whose very livelihood involved their having "no fixed address," were the bane of colonial officers who wanted things tidy.

Indeed, it has been argued that the notion of "tribe" itself is a European invention, socially constructed by the colonizers themselves. The sense of one's ethnicity is something real in Africa (the first question asked upon meeting someone on the road may be "Where are you going?", but the second is "Where do you come from?"). Before colonial intervention, ethnic identity was a generalized idea—diffuse, open-ended, relaxed, and mutually beneficial. Boundaries between African cultural groups in the period before British rule were flexible; there were arenas of ongoing contestation, but these were often ill defined or undefined (Ambler, 1988). Ranger (1983), Hobsbawm and Ranger (1983), Southall (1970), and others discuss the "invention of tradition"—that is, ethnic identification itself as a British invention used to identify, shape, and stabilize social structures in order to facilitate management.

Considerable interchange, intermarriage, and trade took place between groups. The territorial domain of a group was more open, with mixed shared margins (Kopytoff, 1987). The British colonial administrators wanted to fix ethnic groups in space so that they could be counted, taxed, and policed; so that their movement could be monitored or prevented; and so that their labor could be mobilized and controlled. It was during the colonial period that ethnicity became engraved on the map of Africa.

The notion of "tribe" has a fractal-like quality about it. Many readers will have encountered Benoit Mandelbrot's (1977) work on fractal geometry—that is, a form that is self-resembling, regardless of the scale at which it is examined. Stated another way, as you shift to larger scales and look at things in greater detail, there is the same complexity as you have observed at smaller scales. (Examples in nature are the pattern of stars, Brownian motion, turbulent flows, the cratered landscape of the moon, drowned coastlines, and dendritic forms—tree branchings or the stream paths of drainage basins.) Tribal or ethnic identity gets defined in different ways by different people, according to context. Figure 14.2 shows the distribution of tribes in west central Kenya according to three different sources (Murdock, 1959; *Atlas of Kenya*, 1959; Goldthorpe and Wilson, 1960). It covers an area of 1° of latitude × 1° of longitude, or about 12,300 square kilometers (4,750 square miles).

As the figure indicates, the tribal distributions mapped by Murdock and by the *Atlas of Kenya* are strikingly different. There is somewhat more similarity between the *Atlas of Kenya*'s and Goldthorpe and Wilson's mappings, but important differences still exist. Moreover, if you were to visit the area designated in all these maps, the people would be likely to use other names altogether in identifying their affiliations—subtribes or subsets. If you were using Goldthorpe and Wilson's map of tribes as a guide, no sooner would your feet be firmly planted on it than the paper would "dissolve" and you would drop through onto the map of subtribes below. You would note, first, that there are some discrepancies in placement of boundaries even between Goldthorpe and Wilson's two maps. Moreover, if you were to compare the names on this new "subtribal" level with the list provided in the *Atlas of Kenya*, you would find only partial agreement. The *Atlas of Kenya* lists (but does not locate on the map) 14 subgroups. The map by Goldthorpe and Wilson also shows 14 Luyia subgroups. In only 9 of the 14 cases, however, are the names the same, and you might wonder whether those who are called Samia, Gwe, Marachi, Kakaklua (or Lewi Lunala) and Tachioni (or Tatsoni) in the *Atlas of Kenya* list are among those named the Nyore, Isukha, Holo, Fafoyo, and Bugusu by Goldthorpe and Wilson. No doubt there are identifications at still more local scales of reference.

All this discussion of the looseness surrounding ethnic identity is not to assert an image of "happy Africa." Strife, conflict, and enslavement of some Africans by other Africans existed before colonial rule; however, the level of violence and carnage was minuscule in comparison to the genocidal butchery that has occurred in some African countries (notably Burundi, Rwanda, and Sudan) since independence, or elsewhere, such as in Cambodia and East Timor.

One of us once plotted on the map of Liberia the "wars" that occurred in different periods as Americo-Liberians established control over the hinterland. Although there were some very serious battles with much attendant slaughter, especially in what became northern Liberia, the "wars" were frequently characterized as "difficulties," "troubles," "disturbances," "skirmishes," "minor incidents," "conflicts," "hostilities," "small troubles," or "insubordination" (e.g., *African Repository*, 1863, 1879). The Third Grebo War of 1893 is typical of many of the skirmishes and battles of precolonial times. Regarding this war, Sir Harry Johnston (1906, Vol. 1: 286) stated: "These 'wars' were mostly skirmishes with small loss of life and many 'alarums and excursions' on both

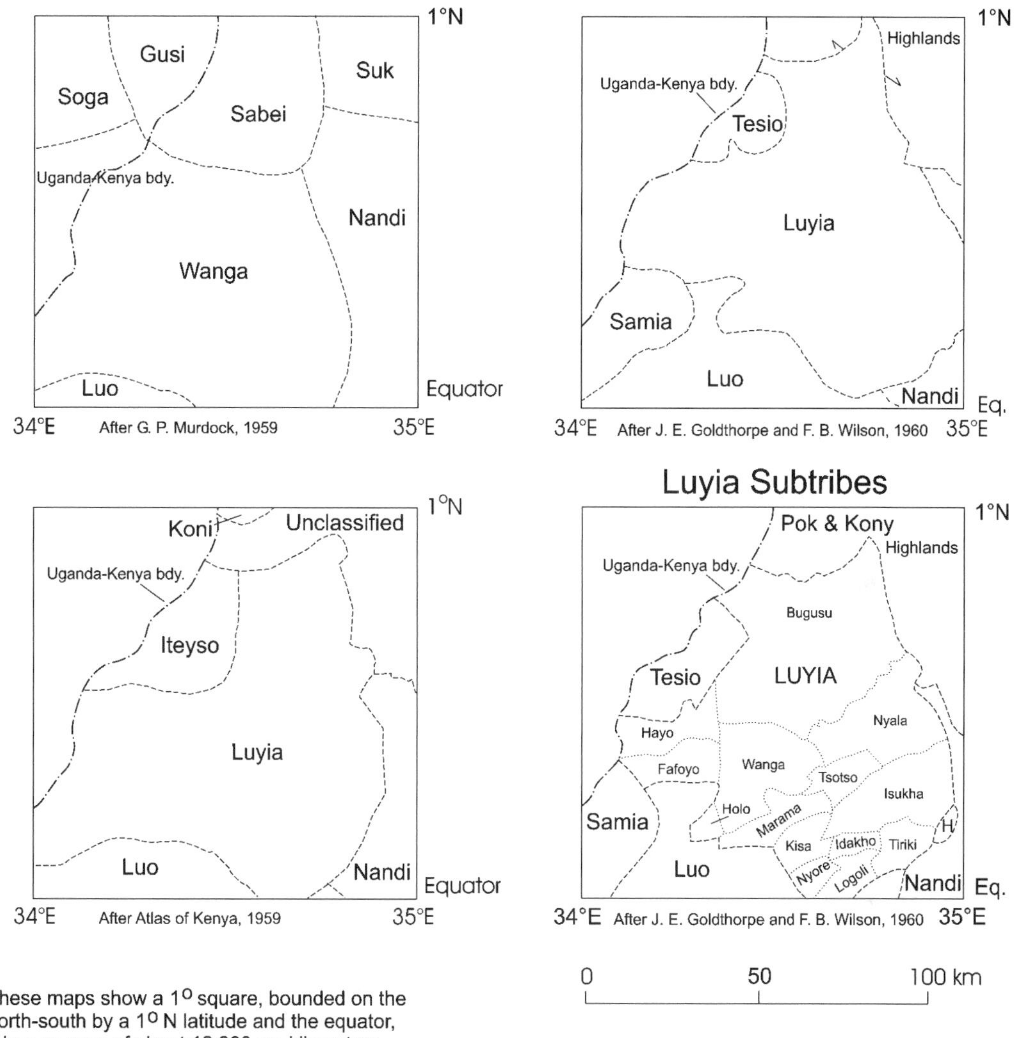

FIGURE 14.2. "Tribes" of west central Kenya, as defined in three different sources, and "subtribes" as defined in one of these. *Source:* (Top left) Adapted from Murdock (1959). Copyright 1959 by McGraw-Hill, Inc. Adapted by permission. (Middle left) Adapted from *Atlas of Kenya* (1959). (Upper and lower right) Adapted from Goldthorpe and Wilson (1960).

sides. . . . In 1896 fresh troubles arose with the Grebos, in which one or more Liberians were killed." During the colonial period as well, once *Pax Britannica* (or *Eintracht Germanica*, depending on the colonizer) was established, there was little direct killing and the countryside was peaceful.

In relation to the carnage witnessed in Rwanda in 1994 and since, one needs to consider ways in which colonial policies affected the social formation of the country. Colonial administrations often relied on one ethnic group to help in the administration of a colony. In part this was a matter of convenience, and in part it was a policy of "divide and rule." In the instance of Uganda, many Baganda served as agents of the British during the first two decades of the 20th century. Egyptians filled posts in the civil service and the army in the Anglo-Egyptian Sudan (a condominium). Similar situations existed with the Fulani in northern Nigeria, the Sikhs in India, and so forth.

When the Germans established colonial rule over the Banyarwanda, in what is now Rwanda and Burundi, they found a quasi-feudal society wherein two groups lived in a patron–client relationship: the cattle-rich Hima (or Tutsi) as patrons, and the Hutu as clients. This arrangement had existed for several hundred years (d'Hertefelt, 1965; de Heusch, 1964). As so often happened in colonial Africa, the German administrators (and the Belgians who succeeded them after World War I, when Ruanda and Urundi became League of Nations mandates under Belgian control) elected, for the most part, to rule indirectly through Tutsi royal leadership (d'Hertefelt, 1965: 434–435). There was thus an approximate 60-year period during which Hutu experienced Tutsi agency in controlling their lives. Few Rwandans at independence (1962) would have been able to remember what relations were like in precolonial days. Several generations of Hutu had grown up knowing only minority rule (whether Belgian or Tutsi) over the Hutu majority. The class and economic differentiations that emerged during and after the colonial era were there to exacerbate relations in the political struggle that ensued. The Hima/Tutsi patron group had control over much of the land and most of the livestock. The Hutu cultivated their patrons' land and managed their stock; as clients, they shared in the crops and products of the herd. With general high levels of poverty in Rwanda, a class struggle complicated by ethnic association has ensued over power and control of resources (Olson, 1995).

An intersecting set of controls on the residence and activities of colonized people was land classification. In British African territories, to use the terminology of the time, there was fundamentally a threefold division of land allocation: "native reserves," "scheduled areas," and "crown lands." The native reserves consisted of lands set aside for use by the indigenous population; the scheduled areas, such as the Kenya highlands, were lands alienated to European settlers; and crown lands were controlled by the colonial government itself, their ultimate use to be determined later "at the pleasure of the crown." The U.S. equivalent of "crown lands" is "federal lands."

There were many other special land use designations, which ensured government control of forests, protection of watersheds, control of stream flow and erosion, protection of grazing lands, and development of special uses. Land designated for such purposes included game reserves, conservation areas, controlled areas, and restricted areas for hunting. On the land classification map of colonial Kenya, one finds these additional designations: "crown forest," "native forest," "native leasehold areas," "native land units," "native settlement areas," "temporary native reserves," and "royal national parks and reserves."

In addition, strategic, concessionary, or military concerns sometimes led to special land designations. One of the most striking is the Diamantgebied 1 and 2 in what was once German South-West Africa, a strip of land over 100 kilometers wide and over 600 kilometers long (Figure 14.3). Under South African control, the entire coastal area comprising the Namib Desert was set aside in two "no-go" zones, largely because of the alluvial and surficial diamonds to be found in the area. Elsewhere, running from west to east across the entire country was the "police zone." This essentially empty buffer zone (designated as game parks) separated Ovamboland and two other reserves on the north from the rest of South-West Africa. European law prevailed to the south, and indigenous law to the north.

The result of colonial efforts to fix people in place—to tell them, "This is who

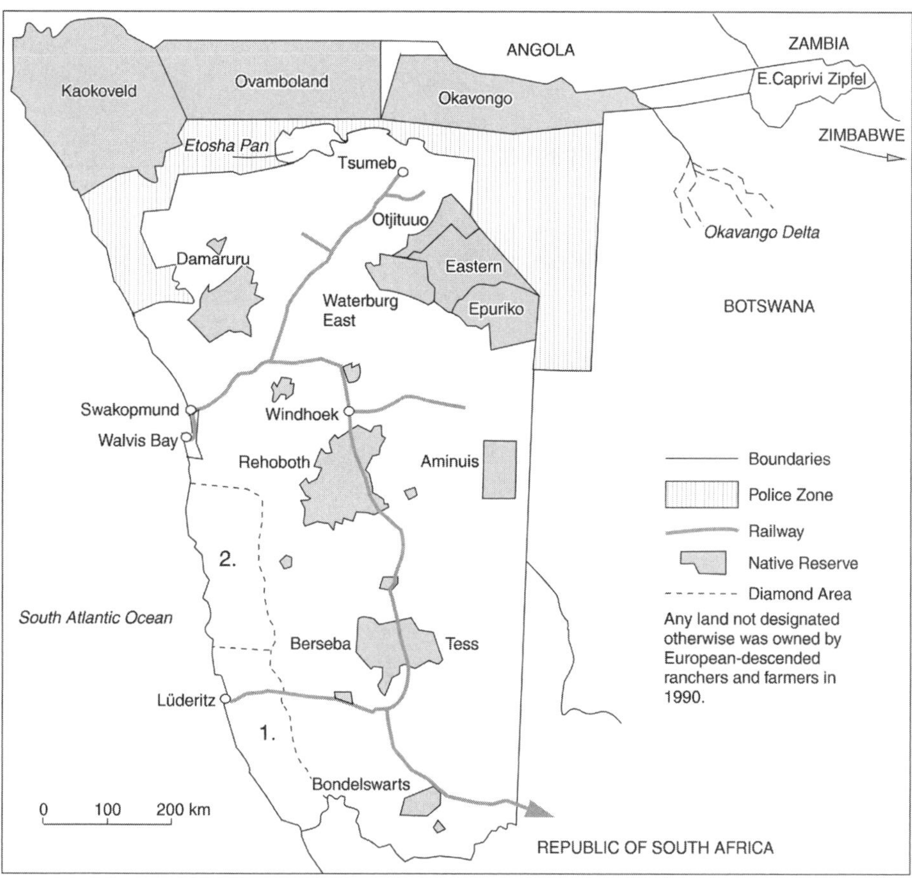

FIGURE 14.3. Land classifications in South-West Africa (preindependence period, before 1990). *Source:* Adapted from United Nations (1958b).

you are, and this is where you live"—was to disrupt livelihoods that depended on a more fluid and flexible relation to land and resources. Moreover, it frequently diminished absolutely, even devastatingly, the amount of land available to those colonized. A good example of this is provided by the map of Ukambani—that is, the land of the Kikamba-speaking peoples of Kenya (Figure 14.4). Before the arrival of the British, the people of Ukambani had access to large portions of the Kapiti and Athi Plains to their west, all of the Mua Hills, the eastern marches of Kitui, all of the Yatta Plateau, and areas to the south in the vicinity of the Chyulu Hills. Others (e.g., Maasai and Orwa pastoralists) used these areas too, of course, but there was much land, and grazing was plentiful for all. This is not the place to recount the history of all the alienations shown in Figure 14.4. The net effect of the removal of land and displacement and resettlement of people was to reduce the land available to the Akamba people by 68%, some of it (Mua Hills) high-potential agricultural land. Their homeland became restricted to two core areas: one in the western hill masses around Mbooni, and the other the smaller highland around Kitui Town. As land area was reduced, the numbers of Akamba increased (from about 200,000 in 1921, to over 800,000 in 1962, to 1,487,000 in 1979, and to 2,193,611 in 1999). In the 1930s, 1940s, and 1950s, there was much

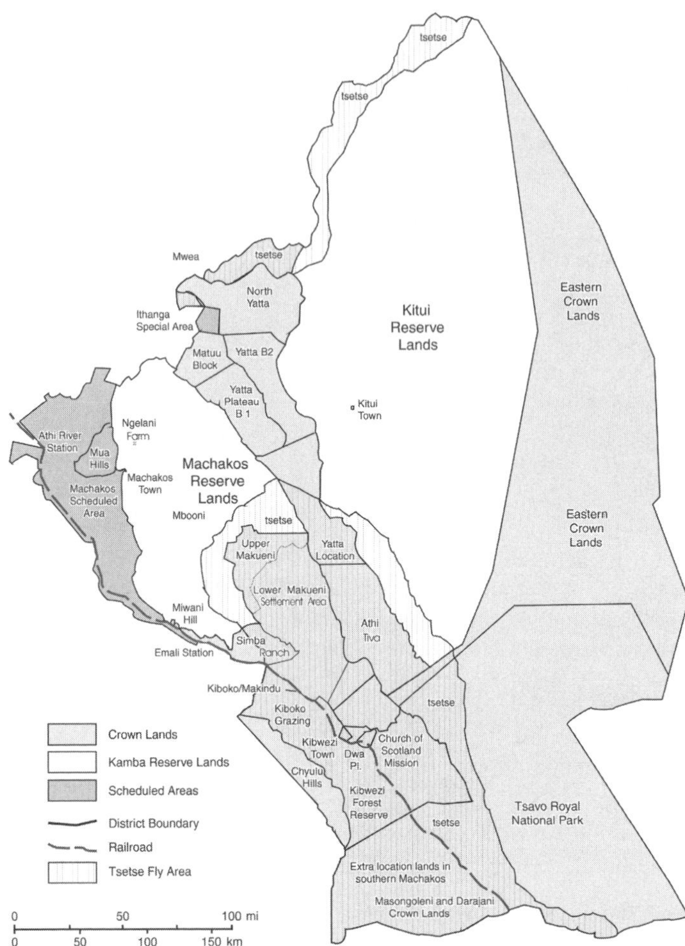

FIGURE 14.4. Land classifications in Machakos and Kitui Districts, Kenya. *Source:* Adapted from *Atlas of Kenya* (1959).

land fragmentation as successive generations of sons divided their fathers' land, and this was accompanied by spectacular land degradation and soil erosion. The colonial government then instituted compulsory terrace construction (see Chapter 10). These work programs were resisted, and protests over terracing were a feature of the struggle for independence. Once Kenyans were independent, a new attitude toward land ownership and stewardship began to emerge. In Ukambani, much land was brought into terracing voluntarily. Rostom and Mortimore (1991: 11) showed that terraced cropland increased in five divisions of Machakos District from 52% in 1948 to 96.3% in 1978. The story of land pressure consequent upon population growth in Ukambani is well known to students of land tenure and population pressure (Munro, 1975; Tiffen, Mortimore, and Gichuki, 1994).

The Colonial Organization of Transport

A quotation from a Nigerian geographer, Akin Mabogunje (1968: 143), sets the stage for competing rationales on how the transport systems of colonies might have been developed:

> At the time of their advent, the British could be said to have two choices before them. One was to improve the system of internal exchange in the hope that the increasing returns from this would lead to greater trading activities with Europe; the other was to concentrate on what they could profitably exploit and export from the country in the hope that this would have some incidental beneficial effect on internal exchange.
>
> To have taken first the choice would have meant that the British colonial venture was not to serve the interest of the British people but that of the Nigerians primarily. It would also imply that any development and innovations brought by them would be undertaken or accepted within the traditional order of importance among the cities. For example, if the railway were to be introduced, it would be first to link existing important centres, and only after would it serve less important centres. The exception would be the few smaller centres fortunate enough to lie on the direct link between two important centres.
>
> However, the British did not come to Nigeria to uphold or enhance the traditional system. In their concern to exploit the resources of the country in a way most remunerative to their imperial interest, they acted . . . in such a way as would appear to a "Nigerian" at the time as entirely arbitrary.

There were commonly two associated interests in the actual development of transport, which in its most costly and developmental form involved the construction of railways: the iron/steel industry of the home country, and the elaboration of means of circulation to serve colonial objectives. The iron/steel and heavy manufacturing industries of Britain in particular were interested in overseas outlets for their production, and the British Empire was the destination of many British exports of iron/steel, machinery, locomotives, and railway carriages—rising in the case of locomotives, for example, from 16% in 1870 to 59% in 1913 (Wolff, 1974: 15). After the Indian mutiny of 1857, the British government, through subsidies, promoted railway development throughout India. In the face of increasing protectionism in Germany and the United States toward the end of the 19th century, the British turned toward the "new Empire" (mainly its comparatively new colonies in Africa).

In a now classic article in the *Geographical Review* in 1963, Taaffe et al. (1963: 506) proposed a colonial model of transport evolution based on penetration from the coast for any of several purposes: "(1) the desire to connect an administrative center on the seacoast with an interior area of political and military control; (2) the desire to reach areas of mineral exploitation; (3) the desire to reach areas of potential agricultural export production." In essence, the goals were to control population and to extract resources. The points of supply were connected with the point of export, usually a port city that came to dominate the urban hierarchy—often termed a "primate city." Instead of enhancing interaction and communications among the people of the colony, transport policy in fact led to distorted, underdeveloped transport networks, badly interconnected and impervious to local needs.

A good example of transport development that ignores local needs is the Liberian American–Swedish Minerals Company rail line, opened in 1963. It connects the coastal port of Buchanan with the iron deposit at Mount Nimba, a long, knife-shaped ridge of very high-grade hematite (67%) that protrudes across the border from Guinea into north central Liberia. The rail line, some 270 kilometers long, carries alternating ore trains—one bound for the coast, the other for the interior. There is one siding, midway, where the trains can meet and pass each other. There are no other stops along the way through several zones of dense settlement, and no facilities for passengers. If the train went through outer space, it would be no less connected with the local population.

Figure 14.5 shows the rail network of west Africa. It is notably fragmentary, incomplete, and not interconnected. Something not shown on the map is that rail gauges in most instances change from one colonial power to the next, so that even if the systems were connected, freight cars would have to be placed on new sets of wheels and under-

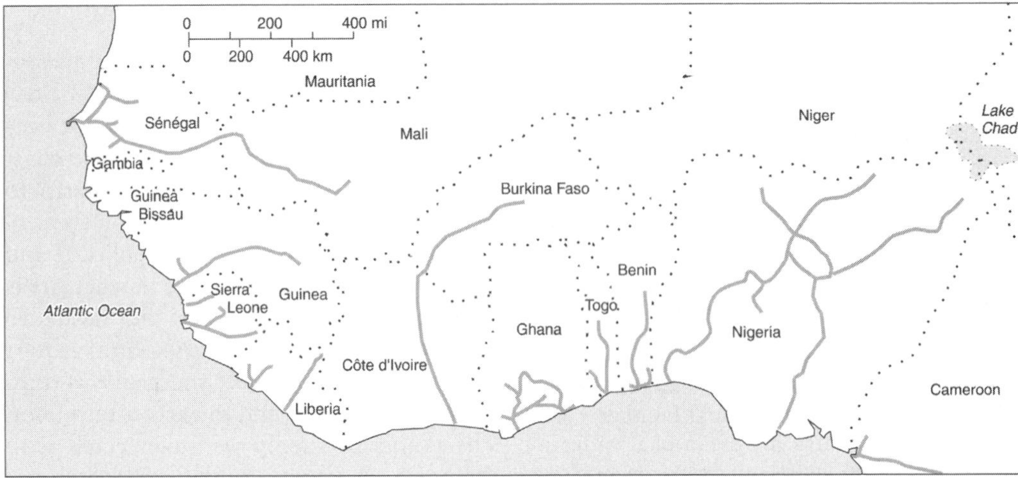

FIGURE 14.5. Railways in west Africa. *Source:* Data are from Church (1980) and Chi-Bonnardel (1973).

carriages (Siddall, 1969). Third world areas where true networks can be said to have been created are eastern Argentina, India, eastern China, and South Africa—all areas of high population density, great resource endowment, and early efforts to mobilize resources and connect the various parts of these countries. In most other instances, the networks in Asia, Latin America, and Africa reflect colonial objectives as outlined above, and are thus fragmented and incomplete.

The Form of Economic Exploitation

In the first round of colonization, and in the higher-latitude colonies of North America and Australia, Europeans decimated and displaced indigenous populations to "open up" territory and create European settler societies using settler labor. Later, in the colonial era, an important question was whether or not new colonies were suitable for permanent European settlement. The American Geographical Society, both in its journal, *Geographical Review*, and in its special publications, devoted considerable attention to human physiology and adaptation to different physical environments (hot, cool, wet, dry)—that is, climates of low latitudes and both low and high altitudes. A partial list of titles of research monographs published in the period 1920–1950 well illustrates the society's interest in acclimatization: Jefferson, *Recent Colonization in Chile* (1921), Jefferson, *The Peopling of the Argentine Pampa* (1926), Bowman, *The Pioneer Fringe* (1931), Joerg, *Pioneer Settlement* (1932), Price, *White Settlers in the Tropics* (1939), Pelzer, *Pioneer Settlement in the Asiatic Tropics* (1945), and Monge, *Acclimatization in the Andes* (1948).

There was also considerable concern about the relations of settlers with indigenous people. The idea is very old. The original meaning of the word "plantation" is "new settlement." Sir Francis Bacon wrote in 1625, "I like a plantation in a pure soil; that is, where people are not displanted, to the end to plant in others; for else it is rather an extirpation than a plantation" (Bacon, 1625/1899: 202). Of course, Bacon's "pure soil" did not exist, and extirpation was the rule in the Americas, Australia, and New Zealand. Over 300 years later, Europeans were still facing the contradictions of colonial settlement. Pierre Gourou (1946/1953) saw 20th-century European settlement in the tropics as facing an unsolvable dilemma.

If the European settlers did no manual labor, but served as overseers, the indigenous population would be exploited; however, if the Europeans intermarried with the local people, they were "bound to become half-castes," the implication being that they would lose their European culture and consciousness (Gourou, 1946/1953: 114). One route led to exploitation, the other to "decline."

In India, exploitation had taken a different form than Gourou considered, with British administrators collecting land revenue rather than overseeing labor. However, in much of Africa, and in plantation zones elsewhere, Europeans developed economies in which they were overseers. In these places, a crucial question became how to determine what proportion of able-bodied male labor (women were generally not considered) could be taken from the local subsistence economy without harming its productivity. If productivity was reduced, a problem of food supply for the local population would arise.

In the Belgian Congo, the Institut National pour l'Étude Agronomique du Congo Belge (INEAC) gave much thought to labor supplies and the potential disruption of local economies, because there were organizations with great needs for labor (Unilever and Union Minière), as well as expatriate farmers in Kivu and Haut Katanga provinces. According to estimates by INEAC, one could siphon off 15% of the male population for labor elsewhere without serious damage to the local economy. The International Cooperation Administration, the name in the mid-1950s of what subsequently became the U.S. Agency for International Development (USAID), used a figure of 30% of healthy adult males.

Colonial Organization of Labor

If a society is almost entirely self-provisioning (i.e., not dependent on trade or commerce for the things needed for daily life), a colonial occupier wishing to have local people provide labor has a problem—namely, that the local people may be satisfied with things as they are and unwilling to work. The solution of colonial administrators, frequently urged on by expatriate settlers, was to break apart the society's closed circle of self-sufficiency (referred to at the beginning of this chapter), making it necessary for those colonized to work. This was done by a diverse arsenal of techniques: taxes of all kinds (poll tax, hut tax); requirements that taxes be paid in currency, not in kind (currency was obtainable only through work for settlers); *corvée* or forced labor; forced conscription into military service or carrier corps (porters); outlawing of existing occupations in the society (e.g., that of warrior); land expropriation; and restrictions on movement of people and their stock. The strategy is summarized with chilling clarity in a speech by the governor of the East African Protectorate (Kenya), quoted in *The East African Standard* in 1913 (and in Wolff, 1974: 99): "We consider that taxation . . . is compelling the native to leave his reserve for the purpose of seeking work. Only in this way can the cost of living be increased for the native, and . . . it is on this that the supply of labour and the price of labour [depend]."

Southern Rhodesia (now Zimbabwe) provides a classic cautionary tale on "how to do it"—that is, how to create an indigenous labor force. The following summary is derived from a detailed paper on "labor proletarianization" by Giovanni Arrighi (1970). By "proletarianization," Arrighi refers to the creation of a proletarian class—a population dependent entirely on wage labor for its livelihood.

British colonial occupation in 1880 threw upper-caste Ndebele men out of work, since it deprived them of their role in fighting and expropriating land and cattle. They became structurally unemployed rather than join the peasant sector of the economy. Colonial control also released lower-caste Ndebele who had formerly served the upper-caste Ndebele.

Land was expropriated, but people were not moved from their ancestral lands.

The people were needed where they were. Land without people was of no value to the Europeans at the time. "It would be very shortsighted policy to remove these natives to reserves, as their services may be of great value to future European occupants," noted the Native Affairs Committee of Enquiry in 1911 (quoted by Arrighi, 1970: 208).

Taxation was introduced. At first, "payment in kind was accepted, but it was soon discouraged in order to induce Africans to earn their tax by wage labour" (Arrighi, 1970: 208). In the early days of settlement, forced labor was used. Later this practice was abandoned as a result of the African rebellions of 1896–1897, though the native commissioners still resorted to it in an informal way even into the 1920s. Land expropriation, which made large numbers of Africans landless, was a major measure responsible for the creation of Rhodesia's wage-earning population.

In 1903, a Department of Agriculture was set up to assist European agriculture, and it expanded its technical work rapidly: distributing improved seeds and plants, boring water holes, and conducting agricultural experiments. European farmers received financial assistance at subsidized rates. In 1905, the major burden of taxation was shifted from the Europeans to the Africans. In 1909, the British South Africa Company imposed a rent on unalienated land; thus all Africans living on these lands had to pay a rent. In addition, European landowners exacted various fees for grazing, dipping, and other "privileges" from Africans living on their farms.

It became customary for European landowners to market the produce of their tenants—a practice that prevented these Africans from underselling the Europeans. European-grown maize met with great success; production rose and prices fell. The effect of depressed prices made it less economical for Africans to grow maize—especially since they had high transport costs, because they were not close to railheads. Only 30% of Africans were within 25 miles of rail, but 75% of Europeans were that close. The net effect of a slump in prices in 1921 was to increase African participation in the labor market. In addition, extraterritorial labor was used from Mozambique, Northern Rhodesia (now Zambia), and Nyasaland (now Malawi); in 1922, such labor constituted 68% of the workforce. This helped to keep wages low.

Discretionary cash in due course became a necessity for Africans, given decades of participation in the market economy. Africans now wanted hoes, picks, cutlery, blankets, and clothing—even such luxuries as coffee, sugar, golden syrup, and corned beef. However, the insecurity of labor on European farms led African men to keep an interest in land and kinship groups on the reserves. They resisted change there, holding on to fragments of land. The terms of the Land Apportionment Act of 1931 barred Africans from purchasing land outside designated areas at a time when they might have done so. From 1931 to 1945, 100,000 Africans moved into reserves.

By the 1930s, the European farmers were in positions of political influence; they reversed previous governmental policy on nondiscrimination in commodity prices, replacing it with a two-price system for maize and cattle, which protected European settlers. There was a high rate of growth in the African population: The proportion of Africans living on the reserves rose from 54% in 1901 to 64% in 1922, and the trend continued. Because poorer land was brought into production, average crop yields fell. The "effort price" (the cost to participate) placed African farmers in a less favorable position to compete with Europeans.

Although considerable productive investment was made by African farmers in the form of carts, maize mills, and plows (440 plows in 1905 vs. 133,000 in 1945), one effect was to expand greatly the land a farmer cultivated. By 1926, overcrowding on the reserves was being noted. In 1943, the Department of Native Agriculture estimated that 62 out of 98 reserves were overpopulated, and that of those remaining, 19 were in or dangerously close to tsetse fly zones and not suitable for cattle keeping. From about 1943 onward, market forces, aided by governmental preferential and protectionist policies designed to serve the European settlers, became better established and widened the gap between European and African producers still further.

The results of the processes described above are vividly shown in three maps and a diagram (Figures 14.6–14.8 and Color Plate 14.1). Figure 14.6 shows the land alienations for Southern Rhodesia in 1961 (Roder, 1964). Note particularly the two roughly rectangular native areas (points A and B) near the center of the map, and the densely peopled zone to the east (point C), with its small squarish outlier (point D). In Figure 14.6, potentialities or recommended uses of land are indicated thus: I, specialized and diversified (fruit, tea, intensive livestock); II, intensive crop production (tobacco, maize); III, semiintensive crop production (livestock and crops); IV, semi-extensive ranching (some drought-resistant fodder crops); and V, extensive ranching only (XX refers to excessively broken topography that has no farming use). A dot map (Figure 14.7) shows population distribution for the same area in 1956 (Prescott, 1962: 561). The boundaries of the native reserves are easily discerned on the population map. Such high densities

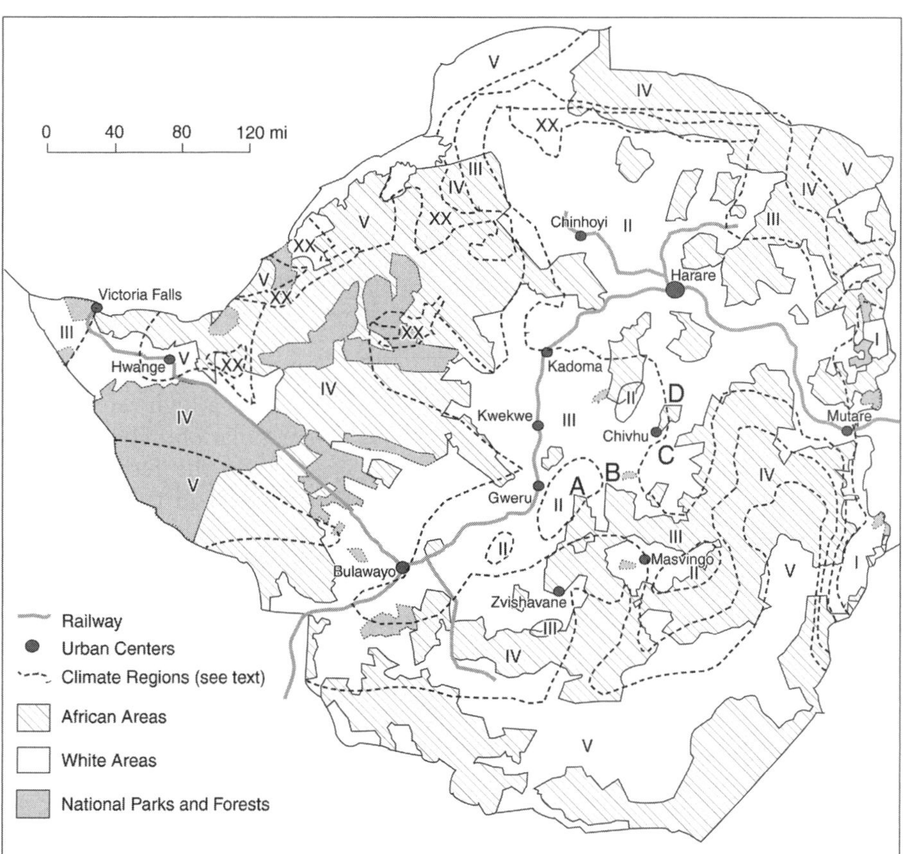

FIGURE 14.6. Land apportionment and climatic regions in Southern Rhodesia, 1961. Present-day city names are used in the map. *Source:* Adapted from Roder (1964). Copyright 1964 by Association of American Geographers. Adapted by permission of Blackwell Publishers, Ltd.

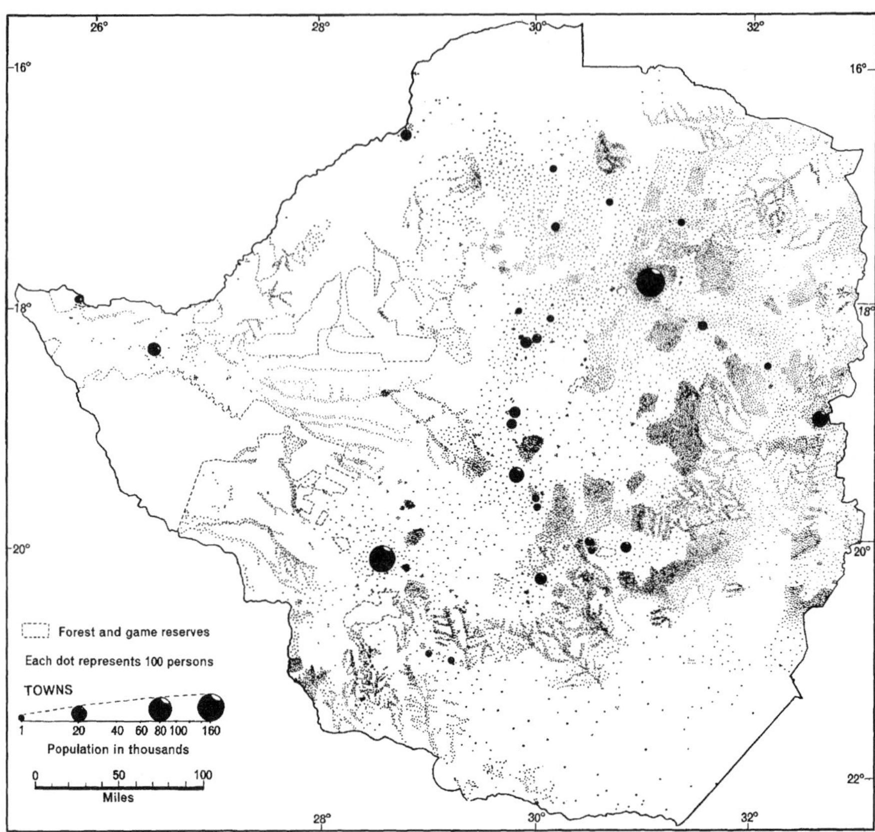

FIGURE 14.7. Population distribution in Southern Rhodesia, 1956. *Source:* Prescott (1962). Copyright 1962 by the American Geographical Society. Reprinted by permission.

were not sustainable in these areas, as noted above.

The most telling illustration of land deterioration is visible from space. Color Plate 14.1 (facing page 45) was taken by Landsat in November 1972 (Short, Lowman, Freden, and Finch, 1976: 390). In the scene, red indicates biomass. The pale white blotches coincident with native reserve areas are striking. These are areas where most of the ground cover has been removed through overgrazing and overcultivation. We can even note a change in land allocation between the time of the maps and the Landsat photograph. The squarish outlier on the right (point D), mentioned earlier, has apparently had a triangular piece of land added on its northern border, and that area has since been denuded of its vegetative cover. The growth of population and the buildup of pressure on land were constant concerns to the colonial administration. Over the years, from time to time, the government of Southern Rhodesia released portions of crown lands for use by the African population (Prescott, 1961). With each such reclassification and release of land, the balance between population and land changed (Figure 14.8). Over time, however, the continued growth of population diminished the amount of land available to the indigenous population. Readers with access to Google Earth may wish to study more recent imagery of the area. If one types "Harare" in the search line, and then scans a bit southwest of the city, one can see what changes have occurred since 1972.

Concerns over people's pressure on land and land degradation were what led William Allan, deputy director of agriculture for Northern Rhodesia in the 1930s, to originate and develop (1) his techniques for measuring "carrying capacity" in terms of indigenous systems of agriculture; (2) his notion of "critical population density" or CPD (the population density beyond which the land would begin an irreversible spiral of degradation—see Chapters 6 and 10); and (3) the idea of the "normal surplus"—the observation that since farmers planted in terms of growing enough even in years of poor rains (and thus low yields), there was frequently extra food available that people were willing to sell (Allan, 1965). These techniques, however, assumed that the indigenous systems of livelihood were stable and unchanging, and did not envisage the possibility that they might change or intensify.

KENYA: WHITE MAN'S COUNTRY

Since the Southern Rhodesian case has not revealed a number of the techniques at the disposal of colonial officers and settlers, we present some further observations on the development of the White Highlands of Kenya, along with some choice quotes to drive home the point that the key task was the mobilization of labor. In this instance, we are borrowing extensively from an excellent study by Wolff (1974).

Rationale

Britain went into Kenya and made it a part of what was then the "new Empire," in response to needs in the metropolitan economy. The British wanted to develop markets to which they could export textiles, clothing, metals, and machinery, which accounted for 70% of Britain's employment in manufacturing. They wished to have within the British Empire a source of raw cotton to reduce dependence on the United States, as well as a source of coffee to reduce dependence on Brazil (and the United States, which speculated in coffee, even though it did not produce it). Also, there was increasing protectionism in Germany and the United States, which was jeopardizing Britain's market for manufactured exports. Intense railway development took place in the 1850s. A major iron/steel industry was oriented toward railway supply, and had grown up beside a hitherto predominant textile industry. Investment was first in western Europe and the United States. After

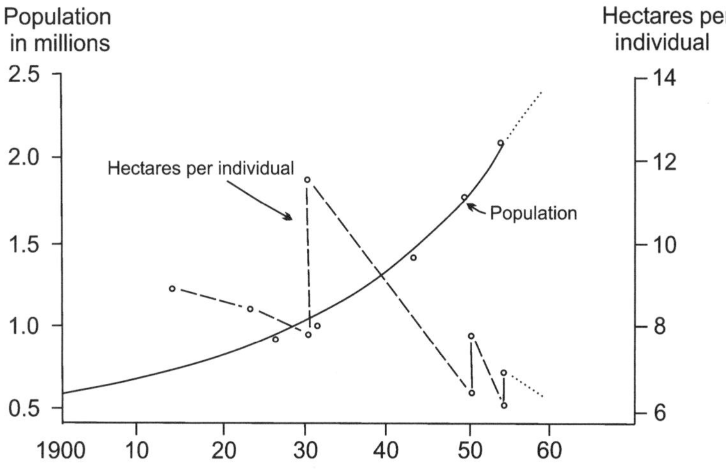

FIGURE 14.8. Release of crown lands to African farmers, Southern Rhodesia. *Source:* Adapted from Prescott (1961). Copyright 1961 by the Royal Geographical Society. Adapted by permission.

the Indian mutiny of 1857 and the U.S. Civil War, investment was directed to India, and then to eastern and southern Europe, Latin America, and the colonies. The latter half of the 19th century saw a reorientation of British capital flows to the "new Empire."

A second reason for gaining control of Kenya was to suppress the Arab slave trade, partly in response to the complaints of European traders. The British campaign against the Arab slave power continued well into the 1890s. In 1891, Gerald Portal carried out a *coup d'état* against the Sultan of Zanzibar and replaced his Arab administration with British personnel. William Mackinnon got Foreign Office support and a royal charter for the Imperial British East Africa Company (IBEA), and prevailed on the British to aid in suppression of the slave trade by military means and in construction of a railway to Uganda. The reasons for suppression were neither humanitarian nor religious; nor was suppression a cover for economic and political objectives. Suppression of the slave trade was simply *necessary* if British trade was to be supreme. Though the suppression was gradual, it led to the disruption of economic structures that had existed for decades, and it left agriculture and trade in a dismal state at the end of the 19th century.

The conventional literature on the creation of the White Highlands also cites other calamities of the 1890–1901 period—the smallpox epidemics of 1892 and 1898; the droughts of 1894, 1895, and 1899; locusts in 1894, 1895, and 1899; rinderpest epidemics in 1890, 1892, and 1894; and an influenza epidemic in 1899–1901—to explain how Europeans could have taken over territory of such apparent fertility and claim it to have been uninhabited. There was abundant evidence of village and field abandonment everywhere. Furthermore, it is in the nature of grazing lands that they are used seasonally and are not occupied permanently.

Once Britain took over from the IBEA, it faced a series of complex, interrelated tasks to make the colony serve the home country: attracting settlers; controlling and allocating the land; choosing suitable crops; protecting settlers at the expense of the local population; developing transport; and mobilizing labor. We consider each of these in turn.

Attracting Settlers

What sort of settlers should develop the East African Protectorate? The IBEA officials had been thinking that this would be done by Indians. But by 1900, a few dozen European settlers had arrived. In 1901, Sir Charles Eliot approved immigration of Indian settlers. In 1902, the Society to Promote European Immigration got Eliot to end the policy, though some searches in the Indian Punjab were made as late as 1906. Instead, Eliot sent a mission to South Africa; by 1905, he had 700 Afrikaner settlers, as well as over 250 British and others. This brought in capital and settler influences on future policy.

From 1904 to 1912, South African immigrants outnumbered British immigrants. Many other people responded as well, including Finns and Zionists (who toured the Uasin Gishu and Trans-Nzoia in the western highlands, searching for a possible site for a Jewish state).

John Ainsworth, an influential settler, said in 1906: "White people can live here and *will* live here, not . . . as colonists performing manual labor, as in Canada and New Zealand, but as planters, etc., overseeing natives doing the work of development" (quoted in Wolff, 1974: 54). Thus the settler model of yeoman farmer was rejected; instead, the model of estate and plantation overseer was adopted.

Controlling the Land

Which land to select was the next question. The Foreign Office pleaded for "jurisdiction over waste and uncultivated land in places where the native Ruler is incompetent whether from ignorance or otherwise, to exercise that jurisdiction" (quoted in Wolff, 1974: 62). The result was the Crown Ordinance of 1902, which placed land decisions in the hands of the British colonial administrators. The land commissioner could dispense land "on such terms and conditions as he may think fit" (quoted in Wolff, 1974: 62). Some African groups resisted the European encroachment. Several costly military expeditions were required. In 1897–1898, these accounted for 30% of expenditures in the East African Protectorate by Britain. There were punitive raids against the Nandi in 1895, 1900, 1902, 1903, and 1905. The 1905 raid required 12 companies of King's African Rifles and 1,000 Maasai "levies" (individuals conscripted involuntarily for military service). The British sold captured livestock to settlers and recovered the full costs of the punitive expeditions. (A decade later, 64,000 acres [25,900 hectares] of the best Nandi land were expropriated to become part of the Soldier Settler Scheme. The Nandi were paid at a rate of 6 shillings for each house that had to be vacated. The land was treated as unimproved and not subject to compensation.)

In 1904, Eliot wrote his Colonial Office supervisor in London: "Your lordship has opened this Protectorate to white immigration and colonization, and I think it is well that in confidential correspondence at least, we should face the undoubted issue, *viz.*, that white mates black in a very few moves. . . . There can be no doubt that the Masai and many other tribes must go under. It is a prospect which I view with equanimity and a clear conscience" (quoted in Wolff, 1974: 66).

The settlers demanded elimination of the requirement that a settler make physical improvements on the land (a provision similar to that in the U.S. Homestead Act, which gave the settlers five years to make improvements). The Crown Land Ordinance of 1915 marked a turning point. Leases were increased from 99 years to 999 years. Eliot listed areas for European settlement: Lumbwa, Nandi, the southern Rift Valley, Laikipia, Kenya Province, Kikuyu territory, and Ukambani as far east as Makindu.

Wealthy Englishmen used their influence to acquire large acreages. By 1912, five owners held 20% of all land alienated to Europeans. Fifty percent of the Rift Valley Province was held by two syndicates and four individuals: Lord Delamere and his two brothers; Major E. S. Grogan; the East Africa Estates Ltd.; and the East Africa Syndicate. Land that had sold for 6 pence in 1908 was resold in 1914 for 1 pound sterling, a 40-fold increase. Lord Delamere ultimately accumulated over one million acres (404,700 hectares) of the seven million acres (2,835,000 hectares) comprising the "scheduled areas."

Under the Soldier Settler Scheme of 1919, 2.5 million acres were parceled out as essentially free farms. Ultimately, 545 families (out of an original 1,245 farm plots) were taken up. Other land went to older settlers. There was speculation in land every step of the way. A 640-acre farm could be had for 80 pounds sterling, payable over 16 years. A 5,000-acre pastoral farm cost 10 pounds sterling per year.

In 1921 a rule was passed that all land, regardless of native tenure, remained crown land. Africans were tenants-at-will of the British crown. The British moved the Maasai out of the Rift Valley (northern part) onto the Laikipia; then they broke a treaty with the Maasai and moved them out of the Laikipia to the south of the Uganda Railway, and the vacated land was given to European settlers. The 1922 Land Tenure Commission said: "Every scrap of land to which the agricultural development of the country could be extended should be earmarked and made available for future alienation" (quoted in Wolff, 1974: 56).

Choosing Suitable Crops

John Ainsworth, in an influential article in 1906 (cited in Wolff, 1974: 72), warned that Kenya's settlers were too diversified and needed to produce a lot of a few things. They needed to do this to become attractive to buyers who would see Kenya as a substantial source—but what should they grow? At the time, cotton, coffee, and sisal seemed promising.

The 1901–1903 cotton crisis jeopardized the Lancashire supply of raw cotton because of speculation in the United States. This caused a loss of 2 million pounds sterling. The early 1900s were also the years when the boll weevil was wreaking havoc through the cotton plantations of the Old South in the United States. The Lancashire entrepreneurs got a royal charter and founded the British Cotton Growing Association to foster cotton growing in the empire. They were successful in some parts of the British Empire, but in Kenya cotton failed, largely because of an inadequate supply of labor and unacceptably low yields.

Sisal was popular in Kenya; the British thus followed Germany's lead in German East Africa, to counter the Mexico–New Orleans–New York "pernicious" monopoly on *henequen* (the name used for sisal in Mexico). The Germans had smuggled the plant out of Mexico and developed it in large sisal estates along the lines of rail in Tanga and Morogoro, in German East Africa. Wheat and maize were developed with governmental subsidies; maize was brought in to serve a local market.

In Ceylon, the coffee leaf disease essentially wiped out the industry, reducing output from 100 million pounds in 1874 to 18,000 pounds in 1913 (45,455 metric tons to 8 metric tons). With Britain so dependent on coffee imports (Table 14.1), the possibility of coffee production in Kenya seemed attractive. By 1922, Kenya had 700 coffee estates employing 35,000 Africans.

Protecting Settlers at the Expense of the Local Population

The Department of Agriculture gave every service and technical help it could to the settlers. The entire operation was designed to help European farming. A significant portion of the tax contribution of Africans was channeled into improving European settler agriculture. The administration provided military security. The Colonists Association requested lower railway rates, both for imports needed for agriculture and for crops exported. They also got their imports exempted from *ad valorem* duties. Agriculture in the African reserves was totally neglected until after the Mau Mau rebellion (1952–1955). Policies changed with the adoption of the Swynnerton plan, which directed governmental funds to farming in the reserve areas. The plan was summarized by Swynnerton (1955: 10), in words rich in irony: "Former government policy will be reversed and able, energetic or rich Africans will be able to acquire more land and bad or poor farmers less, creating a landed and a landless class. This is a normal step in the evolution of a country."

Developing Transport

The economic rationale for the railway to be built from Mombasa to Lake Victoria at Kisumu was trade between Uganda and Britain. When it came into operation, the railroad reduced freight costs from 7 shillings, 6 pence/ton mile to 2.5 pence/ton mile. This was a factor of 36:1. Trains also provided a considerable time saving over head-loaded porters.

There was a close relationship between the placement of the Uganda Railway and branch lines in Kenya and the creation of the scheduled areas, the seven-million-acre White Highlands (Figure 14.9). The scheduled areas, indeed, began as the railway track crossed the 5,000-foot (1,524-meter) con-

TABLE 14.1. British Coffee Imports: Value in Pounds Sterling

Date	British East Indies	United States	Latin America
1884	1,817,000	77,000	548,000
1904	611,000	486,000	1,217,000

Source: Data are from Wolff (1974: 75).

tour line at Kiu, southeast of Nairobi. Most of the highland urban places that emerged during the colonial period lay within the scheduled areas, and most of these were served by rail. By 1969 there were 13 urban places (population about 898,000) served by railway in the former scheduled areas, and only two (Nyeri and Kericho, with 21,000 people) not so served. On the other hand, six of the eight urban places in African lands were *not* served by rail—the exceptions being Kisumu, the terminus of the Uganda Railway on Lake Victoria, and Fort Hall (now Muranga, the two towns having a total of 37,000 people).

Mobilizing Labor

Europeans decided that to ensure an adequate supply of labor, coercion would be necessary. The experience of building the railway had reinforced this view. The African population was seen as a base on which to build. Settlers recommended that protectorate Africans not be allowed to work in the mines in South Africa. Among the British settlers' other policy goals regarding labor were (1) keeping Asians out, because settlers feared their competition; and (2) keeping labor migrants from Nyasaland (now Malawi) out, because the wages there were too high and the workers there were used to earning higher wages.

The settlers were endlessly creative in proposing taxes and other measures to the colonial administration to get African farmers to provide their labor. Lord Delamere suggested that the taxation be 1 rupee per palm tree, and also proposed taxing *Amerikani* (cotton cloth) and blankets. Other settlers suggested taxing blankets, wire, and beads. Testifying before the Labour Commission in 1912–1913, they urged that Africans get remission of taxes for a certain amount of labor on European farms.

Different kinds of taxation were tried, beginning with the 1902 hut tax. In 1903, a poll tax replaced the hut tax (there had been too much crowding in houses), and all adults became liable to taxation. In 1904, *ad valorem* duties were increased, but all agricultural implements, livestock for breeding purposes, and commercial seeds and seedlings were exempted. These, of course,

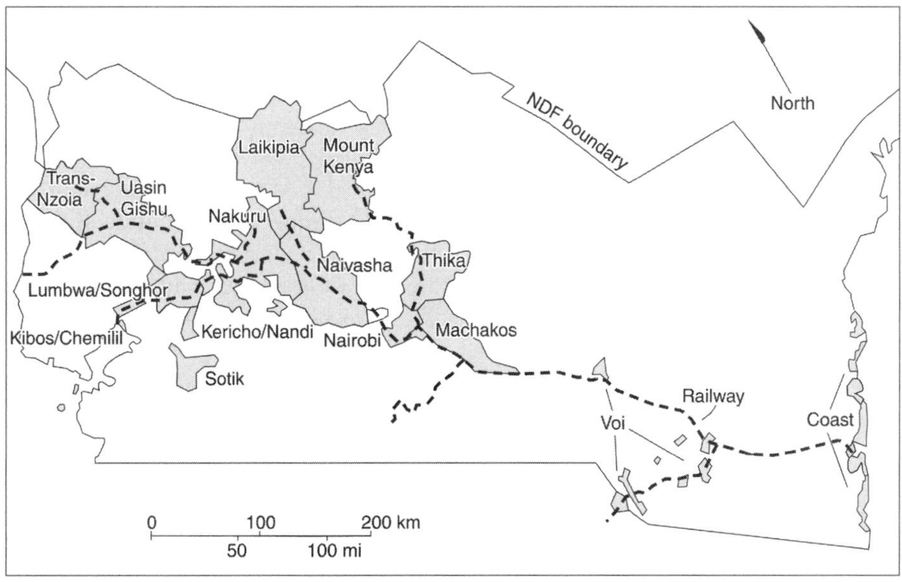

FIGURE 14.9. The scheduled areas of Kenya (including alienated lands outside the highlands) and their relationship to railway lines. *Source:* Adapted from *Atlas of Kenya* (1959).

were imported almost exclusively by Europeans. Over the years, tax rates increased. In 1910, the rate was 3 rupees; in 1915, it was 5 rupees; in 1920, it was 10 rupees or 2 months' labor. The British changed the currency system in 1920, replacing the rupee; this affected the coastal Indian and Arab traders, who henceforth were dependent on a British currency unrelated to India. Between 1912 and 1927, non-Africans were taxed at a rate of 30 shillings (15 rupees) for all males 18 or older. European direct taxes amounted to 7,500 pounds sterling; African direct taxes amounted to 558,044 pounds sterling. Africans paid as much of the custom duties as Europeans.

By the mid-1920s, the direct tax bill on Africans was 30% of total earnings, and the indirect (*ad valorem*) taxes from imports were 20% of the value of the goods. Overall, Africans paid 80% of the taxes collected in Kenya, and 85% of the amount collected as custom duties. Taxation served to inhibit capital accumulation among Africans, as well as to increase the labor supply.

Another line of pressure besides taxation involved governmental efforts to recruit labor, although the government went back and forth on the issue of whether it should be involved in such activities. In 1907 the government set up a Department of Native Affairs "specifically instituted to deal with the labour supply" (Wolff, 1974: 101). Settlers wanted recruitment of laborers to be a routine government task. The government tried to minimize its role, and this created a big conflict.

In 1909 the governor thought that squatting might be a solution. Land could be used in exchange for some days of work on call (180 days). It also meant that the farmer could call on women and children at times; this made for continuity in the labor supply. The number of squatters increased. By early 1930, there were 110,000 squatters.

A pass system was proposed, based on 100 years of experience in South Africa: "Under [the pass] system you get a disciplined native; you know where every native is, what his wages are and his employment" (Ainsworth, quoted in Wolff, 1974: 105). It was not instituted right away. The labor shortage continued. In 1915, the Native Registration Ordinance was passed; this was a pass system modeled on that of South Africa. Fear among Africans of being conscripted into the Carrier Corps (a large corps of head-loaded porters that supported the King's African Rifles) eased labor recruitment for the settlers, since if one worked for a settler, one could not be conscripted.

The pass had a place for citations. The employer could say, "He is a troublemaker." There was a severe fine for losing one's pass. The pass was helpful in tracking down laborers who deserted. All of this increased European control. When labor for the Uasin Gishu railway extension dwindled, the colonial secretary reluctantly approved forced labor.

One reason why the British colonial government tried all the labor mobilization techniques described above, leading ultimately to such severe measures as pass laws and forced labor, was that most African groups in Kenya already had a livelihood that met their needs. If their economies were largely self-contained and self-sustaining "circles," the government, at the urging of settlers, had to find a way to break apart those circles. They were not willing to do this by creating economic incentives for African farmers.

During World War I, the Carrier Corps was developed in the absence of roads and vehicles. Some 150,000 Africans served in the Carrier Corps (*kariakoo*). There were also 14,000 Africans in the armed forces. This was labor mobilization on a large scale. Recruitment was carried out with military expeditions, especially among the Akamba and Giriama. Of the 164,000 who served, 46,618 died in combat and from corps-related disease. Norman Leys (1925: 287) commented: "It is sad to read, in the earlier reports, of how great a boon we bestowed by stopping intertribal war. Since then, our own War has destroyed more life than a generation of intertribal wars."

The laborers on plantations, farms, and estates suffered physical effects. One survey showed that 80 per 1,000 was the mortality rate among African workers, not counting the unknown number who died the year they left employment. There was almost no medical service. Population estimates of Kenya give 4 million in 1902, falling to 2.5 million by 1921, and turning upward in 1923–1924.

Summary, and a Postscript on Brutality

In summary, the Kenya colonial government forced upon the indigenous population the following: comprehensive and high taxes; an all-inclusive pass system; official government pressure on Africans to work for the European settlers; forced labor; official support for squatting (which gave European farmers a resident labor force, including women and children, that could be called upon during periods of peak labor need); and absolute neglect of reserve agriculture. These and other features of the system assured an abundant, cheap wage labor supply. Furthermore, Africans had no way to improve their economic lot by themselves. They were prohibited from growing the main export cash crops: tea, coffee, sisal, pyrethrum, and dairy products. Africans were paid a lower price for surplus maize (a two-tiered price system favoring Europeans was used), and they found their livestock quarantined or subject to forced culling and sale at reduced rates. Not only did Africans have to get marketing licenses from the British, but they generally could not obtain leases to open shops in town. Moreover, Africans had no access to credit and were unable to accumulate capital. Wolff (1974: 136–138) stated: "[The British] created a modern labor force by withdrawing from the African population the possibility of earning sufficient income in any other way than by providing wage labor for Europeans." The British also encouraged European immigration in order to staff management-level positions. They invested large proportions of tax revenues paid by Africans directly in European agriculture.

Given the choice of having Europeans settle in Kenya, all other things followed. The settler class resembled a landed aristocracy more than it did an entrepreneurial group. After two decades, the colony required no further capital grants from London. Even so, with cheap land and labor, settlers barely survived, and many settlers quit and left (Wolff, 1974: 145). They failed in part because of poor economic times (the decade of world depression following the crash of the stock market in 1929), and partly through conspicuous display and lack of reinvestment, characteristic of many settlers who behaved like landed gentry.

In this discussion of Kenya, we have explored how colonial administrators carried out their dual responsibility of keeping administrative costs low while making colonies productive propositions for different interests, especially the home government and nearby settlers. They did this by establishing social distance between themselves and those colonized; by displaying military power; by organizing territory and permissible movement and activity within colonial territory (which involved manipulation of the ethnic identification of those colonized); by developing transport and communications for export and administrative purposes; and by resorting to a host of techniques designed to promote the interests of settlers and to force the indigenous population to provide labor.

Up to this point, however, the resort to physical violence and punishment has not been described. Perhaps it was more common in Portuguese and Belgian colonies, but it occurred in all French, British, and German colonies as well. It seems to have been most severe when the colonial officers were trying to get members of the indigenous population to do something they truly did not want to do or saw no sense in doing. A book on the social history of cotton in colonial Africa is full of instances of forced labor, imprisonment, fines, and disciplinary floggings in efforts to grow cotton in tropical Africa (Isaacman and Roberts, 1995). The cotton project in a sense was doomed from the start, given the prospects for growing better-quality, higher-yielding cotton at higher latitudes, such as Egypt, Spain, California, or Kazakhstan (see Chapter 11). We can suggest the brutality of the colonial labor process by quoting Osumaka Likaka, a contributor to the aforementioned book on cotton (Isaacman and Roberts, 1995: 209, wording in original draft retained):

> The *chicote*, a hippopotamus-hide whip, was widely used to discipline cotton cultivators both in prison and in the fields and was an integral part of a culture of terror. . . . For "poorly maintained fields" cotton cultivators received as many as twelve lashes. Generally, men were whipped in the fields in the sight of their wives and children. They were whipped naked by the policemen. Whipping was associated with insults and very often degrading practices such as the imitation of sexual intercourse. Some resisters were beaten undressed purposely at lumbar muscles until they ejaculated, experiencing the epitome of humiliation and shame.

The brutality of colonialism was not unique to Africa, but is integral to the colonial enterprise. The expropriation of land and wealth, and the means used to mobilize local labor to work on estates, farms, and plantations, had many similarities. Empires and their colonies—whether Roman, Dutch, Japanese, Incan, Spanish, or British—have had much in common in the ways they have worked and the impoverishing, demoralizing effects they have had on the lives of subject peoples.

15 The End of Colonialism and the Promise of Free Trade

Facing anticolonial resistance and independence movements throughout Africa and Asia, combined with U.S. pressures for a new world order and the emergent Cold War, the second wave of colonialism came to a precipitous end after World War II (see Chapter 13, Figure 13.1). Between 1950 and 1961, the number of colonies declined from 134 to 58; by the time Namibia became independent in 1990, only a handful of small, mostly island territories were left under colonial rule. In the chapters that follow, we use 1960 as a benchmark date against which to assess how global difference and inequality have changed since third world countries gained political independence. For practical purposes, 1960 was the end of European colonialism in Africa and elsewhere, as new, nominally sovereign nation states came into being.

In this era of developmentalist thinking, it was envisioned—both by third world political leaders and by first and second world policymakers—that political independence would bring prosperity. By the mid-1970s, it was clear that this promise was not being fulfilled. From the perspective of the periphery, political dependence had simply been replaced by economic dependence: The newly independent third world nations faced a post-1945 world order that remained stacked against them (Chapter 4). Adherents of neoliberal globalization have seen the solution in a move from state-led national regulation to deregulated global markets (Chapter 5). This is conventionally justified by appeal to the free trade doctrine: that unrestricted commodity exchange between places is the best way to advance their mutual prosperity. A few third world countries, particularly in east and southeast Asia, have come to benefit from significant participation in global markets. Yet many others experience persistent or increased poverty, and inequalities have increased within many countries of the first, former second, and third worlds (Chapter 2).

In this chapter, we examine how the colonial era came to an end, and what development possibilities were held out to the newly independent nation states. We show that Europeans did not give up their colonies easily, but only under pressure from determined independence movements within the third world, and from a newly powerful United States keen to break up colonial trading cliques. Once political independence was accepted, however, it was argued that free trade should reduce third world poverty. The doctrine of free trade argues that nation states can (and indeed should) differ in their economic contributions to the global economy, by specializing in the production of different commodities. The "right" international division of labor should make possible a differentiated but equitable system of codependent trading nations, all of which can share the benefits of specialization and trade. The second half of this chapter examines this doctrine in detail, to give readers a better understanding of this highly influential argument about how third world countries can supposedly "catch up" with the first world through free trade. Chapter 16 then assesses how free trade has worked in practice; subsequent chapters examine other ways in which third world nations are linked with the global economy, and the implications of these for prospects for a good life in the third world. Globalization is the talk of the global village, making it vital to understand the impacts of these linkages on those situated within the third world. At the same time, we look at attempts to contest negative impacts—both through calling principles of neoliberal globalization into question, and through pursuing alternative principles.

THE END OF COLONIAL TRADING BLOCS

Prior to World War II, global trading patterns were fragmented into quasi-independent colonial trading blocs, linking colonies closely and unequally with their colonizers. The principal linkages between these blocs took the form of trade among the colonial powers. These restrictive blocs existed despite much political rhetoric about the advantages of free trade. The United States had few colonies, and as a former colony itself had argued against colonialism. It had pursued protectionist trade policies since the days of Alexander Hamilton, nurturing U.S. capitalists as they developed globally competitive enterprises. Now, however, its policymakers envisioned an American century, if colonial trading blocs could be broken up so that U.S. firms could take advantage of a much more freewheeling world trading regime.

Political Independence

World War II provided conditions that made such a breakup possible. First, victory over the Axis powers of Germany, Italy, and Japan included the breaking up of those powers' own colonial blocs. Germany and Italy had few colonies, but Japan had come to exert colonial control over much of east and southeast Asia during the war. Second, the other European colonial powers became so heavily in debt to the United States during the war that the United States was able to secure a promise to break up their colonial blocs. In return for U.S. loans needed to pursue the war, and for U.S. aid in postwar reconstruction, Britain, France, Belgium, and Holland opened their blocs to trade with, and competition from, the United States and other first world nations.

Third, independence movements within the third world became increasingly effective. European colonial nations, focused on economic and political problems both internally and between the newly forming first and second worlds, no longer had the heart or the economic resources to fight for control over recalcitrant colonies; they were increasingly willing to abandon the mercantilist economic philosophies that saw colonialism as the key to economic prosperity. This did not mean that colonies were given up lightly. In their fight against a guerrilla war of independence in Indonesia, for example, Dutch soldiers joined forces with British and even Japanese forces to try to regain Dutch colonial mastery. (The Japanese had fought hard to bring Indonesia under Japanese rule during the war.) Bitter struggles of very different kinds occurred in India, Malaysia, Kenya, and many other places.

Women were disproportionately influential in making anticolonial struggles truly grassroots people's movements—mobilizing communities, organizing activities, and breaking old norms and expectations in the hope and promise that independence would translate into emancipation from all forms of colonization (Johnson-Odim and Strobel, 1999: xxxvii–xlii). Anticolonial movements achieved startlingly sudden success after literally centuries of struggle—a product of their own determination and ingenuity as much as of reduced interest by colonial powers—and brought into existence the collection of nation states that came to call themselves the third world. Yet emancipation of women, especially of women from marginalized classes and communities, did not generally follow. During nationalist struggles, women found themselves often marginalized in traditional support roles. Their attempts to use the struggle as an opportunity to challenge patriarchal norms was often suppressed by male leadership as a diversion from the "real" issues; this phenomenon became more noticeable after independence. Overlapping dichotomies between public and private, masculine and feminine, and modern and traditional in the making of new national identities and "invented traditions" worked too often to undermine the status of women as equal participants in postcolonial societies (Chatterjee, 1989; Enloe, 1989; Geiger, 1997). If the past had been a period when women were marginalized through Orientalist "colonial feminism" (Chapter 3), independence often became simply a continuation of similar forms of exclusions and inclusions from neocolonial structures and networks of power, albeit in less "black and white" ways.

A New World Order?

The post-1945 world order differed from the prewar one in a number of ways. First, the success of communist revolutions and takeovers in eastern Europe, China, North Korea, and Cuba introduced a new geopolitical dynamic—one that Agnew and Corbridge (1995) call the "Cold War geopolitical order." The alliance to defeat the Axis powers thus dissolved into a new conflict between capitalist and communist societies—one that newly emerging third world nations learned to turn to their advantage. A number of new third world regimes had a socialist political orientation, but also strong historical links to capitalist European states. They were willing to take help from either the first or the second world in seeking a third way that was neither European capitalism or Soviet communism. This triggered a scramble for influence over third world nations on the part of the first and second worlds, which was in some respects not unlike the scramble for Africa—except that third world elites now had some say about what kind of intervention was acceptable.

Second, outside the states that formed the second world (and their third world partners), a global economy was organized under the aegis of the United States, with multinational institutions and agreements designed to ease the worldwide flows of money and commodities. Even before the outcome of World War II was decided—in 1942, when the British seemed open to change—U.S. economists began meeting with their British counterparts (led by John Maynard Keynes) to plan this new world order. Keynesian policies had been at the heart of the New Deal, which picked the United States up out of the Great Depression (Chapter 4). After considerable debate about whether global connections in this postwar world should be shaped by market forces, or should follow a Keynesian state-oriented philosophy of giving power to global authorities such as a global central bank, the former strategy prevailed—albeit with the understanding that nation states had the right to control their borders.

The new structure was unveiled at the Bretton Woods conference in 1944. Complementing the anticipated dissolution of colonial trade blocs (even though the end of colonialism was not really contemplated at this time) were several other measures and proposals. It was agreed by the participating nations, under U.S. pressure, that international trade should be based on the free trade principle of comparative advantage developed by David Ricardo (Chapter 3), and that fixed exchange rates between all internationally traded national currencies were necessary to achieve this goal. It was agreed that the U.S. dollar would become the principal currency for international transactions, supplanting the British pound sterling, and that it should be anchored to a gold standard. The implications of this decision are examined in Chapter 21.

Two supranational, "multilateral" international financial institutions were founded to facilitate the international mobility of investment capital. The International Monetary Fund (IMF) was designed to facilitate the balanced expansion of world trade by promoting exchange rate stability through policy advice, as well as by providing short-term loans to countries in need of funds to address balance-of-payments problems. This was based on the assumption that global development requires the full convertibility of currencies in addition to free trade. The International Bank for Reconstruction and Development (IBRD), now a member institution of World Bank, was established to provide long-term, low-interest loans for reconstruction and development. The role of these agencies in the postwar global system is discussed in Chapter 22.

There were also discussions about creating parallel supranational agencies to coordinate both the trade of commodities (an international trading organization) and the international mobility of labor (an international labor organization). An international trade organization was proposed, which would regulate trade along Keynesian lines—according nation states the power to negotiate trade, and envisioning an approach to trade that prioritized full employment and labor standards (Drache, 2002). This failed to be enacted because of U.S. congressional opposition, but did result in the more voluntary and clumsy General Agreements on Tariffs and Trade (GATT; Chapter 16). There was (then, as now) little enthusiasm for any agency facilitating international migration, but the UN International Labour Organization (ILO), originally created by the League of Nations, continues to monitor international employment trends and developments in collective bargaining.

The Postcolonial World

Figure 15.1 shows the global division of labor between industry and the primary sector in 1960. This map displays the culmination of colonialism. Industrial employment was concentrated in the first and second worlds, whereas most former or current colonies of the third world (except Chile and Argentina) were dominated by employment in primary commodity production (minerals, fossil fuels, agricultural crops, fish, and timber). This reflected the colonial organization of the global economy (see Chapter 13). Note that this map only records the work of those who were paid a formal wage; it thus represents a biased picture that excludes most women's work, as well as that of a large number of people engaged in peasant agriculture and other traditional (but by western standards informal) employment. It is an accurate picture, however, of how policymakers in 1960 thought about employment and development. Generally, the independent third world nations saw industrialization, first world style, as the path to development. The question was how to achieve this: How could political independence be parlayed into economic wealth?

Two types of state strategies were under discussion. State-steered policies directly promoting industrialization—either emulating the state ownership of industry in the Soviet Union and certain social democratic European countries, or providing state protection of privately owned domestic industry from international competition—represented one path. Alternatively, it was argued that in a world of free and open com-

FIGURE 15.1. Global division of labor, 1960. *Source*: Data are from International Labour Organization (ILO, 1977).

petition, growth could be achieved through specialization and trade. The theory of free trade provided the rationale for this latter strategy. In this view, the existing specialization in primary commodity production in colonial countries reflected a comparative advantage; it was something they could do more efficiently than industrial production. Thus, instead of being a sign of backwardness or colonial exploitation, high employment in agriculture, fishing, or mining was seen as a rational basis for specialization and trade, and a more efficient and effective path to economic prosperity than state intervention to force the pace of industrialization. This implied that the spatial differentiation of production depicted in Figure 15.1 should continue as a foundation for economic growth, rather than being forced out of existence through state intervention. The capital accumulated through the export of primary commodities, it was argued, could then be parlayed into industrial production and services for domestic markets.

Outside the communist bloc, free trade was presented as the economic anchor for the new world order, and the principle of comparative advantage was seen as the determinant of international divisions of labor. U.S. policymakers in particular promoted free trade as bringing prosperity not only to the United States, but to all countries. Europeans were at first skeptical, but once the World Bank and the U.S. Marshall Plan had helped reconstruct Europe's industrial base (see Chapter 23), they were also ready to engage in global competition through trade, as were the Japanese. This resulted in a policy consensus in 1960 that provided many third world nations with a justification for what was the easier path anyway—supporting continued production and export of the primary commodities in which they already were specializing. There were important exceptions. For instance, Tanzania and India adopted more radical economic theories rationalizing state-organized industrialization as a substitute for specializing in and exporting primary commodities, and Brazil turned to import substitution policies after becoming frustrated with free trade approaches (see Chapter 17). South Korea, Taiwan, Singapore, and Hong Kong creatively combined state-driven export promotion and import substitution policies to underwrite industrialization, emulating European and U.S. policies dating back to the nineteenth century. After the formation of the World Trade Organization (WTO) in 1995, however, these strategies came to be condemned for interfering with the free markets that are supposed to guarantee prosperity via neoliberal globalization. The free trade doctrine is more popular than ever—and thus deserving of a critical examination.

THE FREE TRADE MODEL

The Basic Principle

If countries were self-sufficient, or in economists' jargon "autarkic," each would produce only the things demanded by its inhabitants. Supply would reflect local demand, making international trade unnecessary. Countries would then be more or less independent of one another; any geographical differences observed in production would be limited to international differences in what people need or desire (geographical differences in demand patterns). The free trade doctrine states that this is inefficient. In this view, each country should specialize in what it can do most effectively, producing a surplus that can be exported in return for imports of the other commodities needed by its populace.[1] The result would be an interdependent and much more differentiated international economic system: Each country would be more dependent on others, and more specialized in particular activities, than under autarky. The free trade doctrine concludes that even though specialization and trade undermine countries' self-sufficiency, they result in a more efficient system as long as countries make the right choices of what to specialize in. The right choice for each country is to specialize in activities for which it has a comparative advantage. If each country does this, the heightened efficiency of production allows more goods and services to be produced under specialization and trade than under autarky. These are the international gains from trade, and they can, in principle, be shared among all countries. Since each country stands to gain, faster economic growth is possible everywhere, meaning that trade is also a more rapid path to economic prosperity than is autarky. Finally, it should not matter at all what a country decides to specialize in, whether it is some set of industrial or primary products. All that matters is that it exploits that country's comparative advantage.

Thus countries in the periphery of the global economy should not regard their distinctive features—their physical environment or their labor and capital resources—as barriers to development. Instead, difference is a characteristic from which all can benefit in an interdependent economy; each country has something that it can do well and can contribute to the world. Consequently, societies should not isolate themselves from the rest of the world economy in order to pull themselves up by their own bootstraps. Differences between places are desirable, and should be exploited to the hilt through specialization and trade, in order to achieve development. It is important to recall that spatial divisions of labor are observable at all spatial scales; similarly, trade patterns link nations, but also regions, cities, and even neighborhoods. Yet it is at the international scale that most attention has been paid to the question of trade and development. Furthermore, only nation states are accorded the sovereignty to control trade, so most debates about trade policies address the international scale. This is also the focus of our discussion here—although there are also fascinating questions about the regional specializations, internal trade patterns, and geographical differences in development possibilities *within* nations (see Chapter 18).

The Logic of International Trade Theory

The free trade doctrine emerged in Britain at the height of colonialism—at a time when it had already used its geopolitical influence to facilitate its emergence as "the workshop of the world." One example should suffice. In the 16th and 17th centuries, India produced the best cotton textiles in the world. These were exported to Europe, where they were highly valued. Britain wished to develop its own infant textile industry, however, and used its colonial power to protect domestic producers by halting exports of Indian textiles to Britain. Instead, Britain arranged to dump Indian exports cheaply in continental Europe, undercutting domestic production (and thereby its competitors) there. Once the British industry was established, Britain imposed tariffs on Indian textile exports that drove up the price of all Indian textile exports to Europe. All Indian cotton textile exports to Europe were shipped via Britain, where they faced tariffs that were 5–25 times higher than those for British cotton textile exports (Frank, 1978a). Indian cotton textile producers could not compete with British exports in Europe or India, because British policies had eroded their comparative advantage. Cotton textile production in India declined dramatically and disappeared as an export commodity (Raffer, 1987: 134–137). Real textile prices fell to just 20% of their 1780 value by 1820 (Clingingsmith and Williamson, 2005), forcing Indian producers to shift to specializing in and trading raw cotton (until low-cost slave-produced U.S. cotton undercut Indian cotton exports, by the mid-19th century).

The free trade doctrine emerged simultaneously as a political doctrine and as an economic principle (Sheppard, 2005). Politically, the doctrine was popularized by the Anti-Corn Law League (ACLL), a group of Manchester cotton barons seeking to lower the cost of wheat (i.e., wage costs). They persuaded the British Tories to repeal tariffs on wheat imports in 1846, inaugurating the practice of free trade by the hegemonic global power until 1914. (Treasury bureaucrats calculated that Britain was well placed to benefit from free trade because it would be able to outcompete any European manufacturer.) David Ricardo (1817/1951) had offered an economic justification for the doctrine that, though studiously ignored by the ACLL because of its class analysis, became the foundation for international trade theory.

The question at the heart of the theory is whether geographical differences between places contribute to, or form the basis for overcoming, inequalities in the ability of their inhabitants to realize their development goals (see sidebar: "Sports—When Differences Are Okay"). As discussed above, the free trade doctrine states that any two countries can mutually benefit if each specializes in those activities for which it has a comparative advantage, producing a surplus, which is then freely traded with other countries that have employed the same principle to specialize in the production of other commodities.

The logic of (neoclassical) modern international trade theory extends this claim as follows:

1. Each country, because of its own unique characteristics, has a comparative advantage in some activity (i.e., there is some activity that can be more efficiently performed there than can any other activity), because of its particular endowment of land, resources, labor, and capital.
2. Rational capitalist entrepreneurs in a free market system will automatically choose to exploit this comparative advantage just by responding to market signals, making unnecessary any state intervention

Sports—When Differences Are Okay

Wherever you go in the world, you will find a section of the local newspaper devoted to organized sports. The results of soccer matches, cricket or baseball games, track and field competitions, bowling league playoffs, and so forth are reported there. Reports feature outstanding athletes and accounts of exciting games. That so much press space and local television and radio time are devoted to the outcomes of sporting competitions, whether the locale is Lusaka, Bangkok, Budapest, or Los Angeles, is remarkable. What lies behind this phenomenon?

The briefest answer is that sports are fun, interesting, and important to people. A more complex answer is that sports provide a venue wherein differences between people and groups of people are "okay"; they are socially sanctioned, permissible. Think about the structure of an athletic (or other game-like) competition. At the start, both sides are equal; the "rules of the game" apply equally to both sides; and at the end, there are winning and losing sides (unless, of course, there is a tie). In some cases, such as U.S. professional sports, great effort is devoted to leveling the playing field between seasons, by allowing the losers to draft the best new players.

People exhibit complex, contradictory attitudes toward treating life as a competition and seeking to make life fair. We know that people are not equal in respect to their individual capacities to cope with life's demands. Yet our foundation documents—constitutions and the like—assert such things as "All men are created equal." We set about finding ways to ensure that certain basic rights are preserved for all. On a political level, modern democratic ideals support basic equality in a variety of spheres: equality before the law, equal opportunity, civil and human rights, and so forth. In kin-based societies, similar concern for and attention to equality permeate social behavior. Judicial proceedings are often more concerned with restitution for the aggrieved party than they are with punishment of the guilty individual. The rights of individuals and obligations of individuals toward others are balanced and preserved in complex ways.

Thus, when someone argues—say, with respect to world trade policy or accusations of "dumping" of manufactured goods—that there should be a "level playing field," the person is appealing for equality in a competition. Although the imagery may have deeper roots than are at first apparent, this chapter illustrates how complex the matter is. We human beings love a contest, to be sure, but those of us who are well off have ambivalent feelings about equality when our economic well-being is at stake.

to ensure specialization in the appropriate activity.

3. If each country specializes in the activity for which it has a comparative advantage, and trades its surplus internationally, the world economy will produce more output than if each place remains self-sufficient.

4. Specialization and trade therefore constitute a more efficient organization for the global economy than autarkic national economies do.

5. When international prices are such as to make trade advantageous for countries, this increased output will be distributed as increased income from trade (compared to autarky) to all participating countries. How these gains from trade are distributed, however, is governed by international exchange rates for commodities (i.e., their relative prices in the international market).

The concept of "comparative advantage" is essential to the broad applicability of the free trade principle, and deserves explanation. A country has a comparative advantage for cloth production if, *relative to the costs of producing other commodities in that place*, it can produce cloth more cheaply than any other country can. It is thus not necessary to compare the absolute cost of cloth production between countries, but just to examine the cost of cloth production relative to that of other commodities in a place.

Ricardo thought that gold flows between countries would take care of any absolute price differences (he was much more interested in gold than in commodity flows). Suppose, to use Ricardo's classic example, that in England it costs 100 pounds sterling (£100) to produce cloth and £200 to produce wine, whereas in Portugal it costs £75 to produce cloth and £50 to produce wine. In absolute terms, England is more expensive for both commodities. By comparison to Portugal, however, England can produce cloth more cheaply than wine; the cost of cloth production is half that of wine production in England, whereas in Portugal the cost of cloth production is one and a half times higher that of wine production. It follows, of course, that if England has a comparative advantage in cloth, then Portugal must have a comparative advantage in wine (two-thirds the cost of cloth production in Portugal, compared to two times the cost of cloth production in England).

To apply this principle of comparative advantage to trade theory, England should specialize in cloth production and Portugal in wine production. It can then be deduced that cloth is traded from England to Portugal, that wine is traded from Portugal to England, and that the total output of the two countries is greater than would be the case if they each produced just enough of each commodity to meet domestic needs. This is true despite the fact that England is a more expensive producer of both commodities; a country can take advantage of this strategy for development even if in absolute terms it produces all goods more expensively than other countries do.

From this model of trade and development, using examples such as Ricardo's in which one nation produces a primary commodity and the other an industrial commodity, the following is argued: *If less developed countries exploit their comparative advantage in primary commodity production, in an institutional structure that guarantees free international trade, they will be able to reduce the gap between themselves and more developed industrialized countries.* As in all theories, however, certain simplifying assumptions are necessary to draw the definitive conclusions of free trade theory. It is generally assumed that:

- The extra transportation costs required to trade the goods internationally do not outweigh the benefits that result from specialization.
- Each country makes full use of its economic resources (i.e., there is no unemployment of labor or underutilization of capital).
- No firms make excess profits.
- All actors are fully informed and make rational, self-interested choices.
- Trade is in equilibrium: There is no trade surplus or deficit in any country.
- Sovereign countries can decide what policy to pursue.
- Neither country is so big that it could meet all the needs of both countries in both commodities. If Portugal, for example, proved to be capable of producing enormous amounts of both cloth and wine, then it could undersell England and eliminate British industry in both sectors.
- Foreign direct investment (FDI; see Chapters 20 and 21) can be ignored.
- The changes necessary for a country to become specialized can be made easily, without undermining the gains that are supposed to occur.

Of course, the actual state of affairs in third world nations diverges greatly from these assumptions. Third world countries typically have underutilized economic resources (especially an underemployed labor force); experience large and unpredictable labor and capital flows across their borders; and face significant social and political costs as a consequence of changing their specialization patterns (such as large landholders unwilling to abandon cash crops, or state export agencies committed to certain economic sectors) (see sidebar: "The Contested Intrusions of Trade"). Some have

The Contested Intrusions of Trade

The commercialization of agriculture in third world countries in the postcolonial era has often been a consequence of trade considerations, even when the crops grown are not for export. Too often, it has had unforeseen disruptive or self-destructive consequences. Irrigated wetlands along the Gambia River (which virtually defines the West African country of The Gambia; see Chapter 13, Figure 13.14) were promoted by external agencies and the national state in order to increase rice production. Excessive concentration on cash crop production of peanuts for export under colonial rule had brought Gambia to the point where huge amounts of food had to be imported. Irrigated rice production was supposed to substitute for these imports and place the Gambian economy on a more self-sufficient footing. Prior to this initiative, women had customary rights to use the wetlands for part-time rice growing, as their contribution to peasant household production. Yet commercial rice production was placed under male control, even though production schedules required continued and intensified rice growing by women, who thus simultaneously assumed a new burden and lost customary rights. In effect, this placed the commercial contributions of and income generated by women, in addition to their subsistence activities, under male control; it dramatically increased male power within households, without compensation for women. Women crafted various ways of contesting this reinforced gendered inequality, resorting in the final analysis to refusing to work or contracting their services for hire outside their families. As a consequence, the relationships among women's knowledge systems, agronomic expertise, and rice farming were ruptured; households were no longer able to pursue proper agricultural practices; and production fell off. The intrusions of commercial agriculture for the purposes of import substitution disrupted previous gendered power systems to the disadvantage of women, undermining rice production and reducing the sustainability of local agricultural practices. Yet those same women demonstrated that such intrusions can be successfully contested locally, shaping not only local social relations but national economies. In this case, their resistance to a patriarchal regime of rice production helped catalyze Gambia's shift from domestic rice to fruit and vegetable exports to Europe.

Source: Carney (1993).

small domestic markets that can be easily flooded by cheaper imports. There has been a great but inconclusive debate about whether the theory, and thus the free trade doctrine, is valid when one or more of these assumptions is relaxed. Increasingly, as assumptions are relaxed, economic theorists are discovering situations where one country loses once trade begins (particularly when trade is dominated by manufactures), and are proposing "strategic" trade policies—state interventions to rectify problems created by the trade of manufactures (Sen, 2005). Nonetheless, the free trade doctrine is more broadly accepted now than ever, as a core principle of neoliberal globalization. Using the doctrine of free trade as its justification, the WTO is now empowered to impose on nations and localities particular sets of trade-related rules and regulations devised in rounds of international negotiations going back to the first GATT, signed in 1947. The particulars of these rules, however, have more to do with power politics than with the doctrine of free trade.

Free Trade in Practice

The difficulty of applying principles of free trade to real situations can be exemplified by what actually happened in the case of England and Portugal (Raffer, 1987: 140–141). Portugal, a small country whose political importance as a sea power in the 18th century was declining rapidly in relation to England's, did indeed specialize in wine to be traded for (among other things) British cloth—to such an extreme that even food had to be imported. By the time the British had developed a trade treaty with France in

1786 for French wines at prices that undercut those of Portuguese producers, Portugal had been transformed from being more prosperous than England in the 17th century to being significantly poorer.

By the same token, after Britain instituted the free trade doctrine in 1846, many continental countries followed suit within a few years; Richard Cobden, leader of the ACLL, became a European celebrity. Yet by the 1860s most of these countries had abandoned free trade, because they realized that it was undermining domestic industrialization. The United States and most white settler colonies stuck with protectionism. As a result, Germany and the United States were beginning to outcompete British industry by the end of the 19th century, and Britain abandoned free trade after 1918. Today, third world countries are told to stick with specializing in their comparative advantage, even though first world countries prospered when they abandoned this policy. In a book title, Chang (2002) calls this *Kicking away the Ladder* that first world countries used to clamber to prosperity.

Obviously, the free trade doctrine's claim that it does not matter what countries specialize in contradicts experience. It is thus important to explore the idea of comparative advantage.

HOW IS COMPARATIVE ADVANTAGE DETERMINED?

Ghana specializes heavily in the production and export of cocoa (one-third of all exports in 2004) (UNCTAD, 2004a). This fact suggests that Ghana has a comparative advantage in this crop, and that continued production of cocoa (instead of, say, bananas) is Ghana's best choice for economic growth. This supposition is confirmed by calculating the Balassa index (measured as Ghana's share of world cocoa exports, divided by its share of total world exports) of "revealed comparative advantage" (Balassa, 1965). Comparative advantage is generally seen as quite permanent, based on fixed local characteristics. Thus it may be remarked that Ghana's location and climate favor cocoa over temperate crops (see Chapter 10). Although this is true, it does not explain why cocoa, of all possible tropical crops, is grown in Ghana; nor does it explain why most other tropical countries do not grow cocoa. A more common argument would be that Ghana's endemic shortage of capital and its surplus of underemployed labor (by first world standards) implies a comparative advantage in labor-intensive activities, such as cocoa production. It is important to note, however, that the general association in modern trade theory of factor availability with specialization—whereby countries specialize in production methods that rely heavily on locally abundant production factors—has been criticized on both theoretical and empirical grounds. As early as the 1950s, the U.S. economist Wassily Leontieff (1953) noted this paradox for trade theory: The United States and a number of other countries that would be expected to specialize in capital-intensive exports, in fact export more labor-intensive products. No trade theorist has been able to satisfactorily explain this paradox.

Again, the question of which labor-intensive activities Ghana should specialize in remains unanswered. The possibilities are enormous, ranging from peasant production of cocoa to industrial assembly of semiconductors in foreign-owned factories. How do we know that cocoa production really is Ghana's comparative advantage? Is Ghana a better place to grow cocoa than, say, to sew dresses?

Modern trade theory does not explain which labor-intensive activity should be engaged in, because it is presumed that capitalist entrepreneurs have made the right choice. If private entrepreneurs are allowed to choose those production activities that are most profitable locally, it is argued, they will choose those that reflect their country's comparative advantage. Thus the national state can leave it up to market forces to select the most appropriate activity. In this view, if private Ghanaian firms export cocoa, this must be because there is a comparative advantage in it. More generally, it is presumed that what places do generally matches their comparative advantage, unless the state has interfered—a rather circular argument.

Cocoa growing in Ghana certainly was not organized by the Ghanaian state (it dates back to colonial times), but it does not follow that rational local capitalists made this choice. There are plenty of cases, particularly in the third world, where the choices were not made by local actors at all. We associate west Africa with the production of cocoa, the Andean countries and Brazil with coffee, Central America with bananas, and Malaysia with rubber; we may thus be tempted to infer that these are indigenous products for which these places have a natural comparative advantage. Yet cocoa was originally found in Peru, coffee in Ethiopia, bananas in Indonesia, and rubber in the Amazon. Their current locations as cash crops are far from their biogeographical origins, because colonial powers in cooperation with European entrepreneurs reorganized their part of the global economy during the period of European colonialism. The emergence of the south Asian tea industry, for example, was a result of the success in 1851 by the British East India Company in breaking China's monopoly over the international market for tea, in the aftermath of China's defeat in the opium wars (for more examples, see Thomas, 1994). In short, the particular primary products now specialized in by third world nations, and presumed to represent their comparative advantage, were often brought there from elsewhere as part of a global colonial strategy to create and maintain reliable, inexpensive flows of primary commodities through geographical diversification of supply, with no concern for whether they would benefit the local populace.

We can go further than this. There are many examples of colonies with a comparative advantage in industrial products that was subsequently undermined in part through colonial policy. The case of Indian cotton textiles has been described above: Indian producers were forced to abandon industrial production and resort to growing raw cotton, as a result of British colonial policy. Similarly, when Europeans brought their manufactures to Africa, they found that Africans were already producing these products; indeed, Africans exported textiles and even iron to Europe, until colonial policies undermined African manufacturing and local elites acquired a taste for European styles (Raffer, 1987; Thornton, 1998). More extreme examples include the virtual elimination of indigenous peoples in North America and Australasia—actions that created favorable local conditions for European agricultural practices (notably private ownership and enclosure of agricultural land) and enabled the colonists to realize a comparative advantage for these places as suppliers of agricultural products to the world market. Beginning in the 1960s, U.S. food programs in Africa brought in food so cheaply that local farmers could not compete, and resorted instead to producing cash crops like cocoa for foreign markets. Local consumers acquired a taste for the European-style wheat-based products made available to them, such as bread, undermining local markets for tropical starches like manioc and sorghum—and thus increasing those countries' dependence on food imports (see Chapter 11). More recently, cotton farmers in Africa and elsewhere have protested at WTO meetings because national subsidies to U.S. cotton farmers are driving them out of business.

As trade theorists turned their attention to interindustry trade, they came to recognize that comparative advantages are not based on permanent local endowments. They now discuss how comparative advantage is continually being altered—both through state intervention and through the actions of local and nonlocal capitalists. The geographical concentration of a particular industry in a place alters its comparative advantage, as the industry coevolves with local conditions and local knowledge that reinforce its profitability. Some went on to conclude that there is a place for strategic trade policy (as in Japan and South Korea) to ensure that comparative advantages are created in those industries best placed to create the increasing returns that drive capital accumulation, innovation, and well-paid jobs (Krugman and Smith, 1994; Porter, 1990; Scott, 2006). Nevertheless, third world countries specializing in primary commodities are increasingly told to rely on free trade, neoliberal globalization, and market forces, instead of state intervention. These countries are advised to specialize in agriculture rather than industry, even though their farmers cannot compete with subsidized first world agriculture.

The location and size of markets for indigenous capitalists are also subject to interventions by political and economic actors that shape the geography of comparative advantage. No traveler to third world countries can fail to notice how consumption norms there have progressively converged on those of the residents of western industrialized nations; the landscape is replete with advertisements for Coca-Cola, Japanese autos, Hollywood films, and western designer (or imitation designer) clothing and accessories. If you are ever thirsty in a village in central Africa, eastern Ecuador, or west Sumatra, and are suspicious of the local beverages ("Don't drink the water"), a bottle of Coke or Fanta is almost always to be had—at prices far below those in the United States. Demand for these products is a result of both aggressive marketing campaigns and a more subtle diffusion of western cultural norms throughout the third world, undermining the profitability and comparative advantage of local producers.

National policies are also influential, notably those shaping overall income levels or income inequality, and those managing both national and regional supply and demand. Consider, for example, countries choosing to specialize in low-wage manufacturing to reduce unemployment (another seemingly rational third world response to the realities of current patterns of comparative advantage). Many third world nations have either deliberately or unintentionally kept wages low to attract investment (Lipietz, 1987; Marini, 1973). Yet this reduces domestic purchasing power and demand, forcing local producers to look either abroad or to national elites for their consumers. It is harder to compete in remote markets, and local elites are likely to demand prestige products for conspicuous consumption from abroad. In the first world, by contrast, Fordist economic management strategies subsidized massive increases in standards of living between 1945 and 1970, through closely articulated wage contracts, mass production strategies, government subsidies, and productivity increases (Lipietz, 1987). Such strategies have made these countries attractive locations for the production of manufactured goods. Thus different wage policies in the first and third worlds reinforce the advantages of first world locations as places to specialize in manufacturing.

With such examples in mind, it is important to remember that the international divisions of labor and patterns of specialization we observe cannot be assumed to represent the *best* spatial divisions of labor. Comparative advantage is continually being restructured by a variety of local and nonlocal actors, and it is heroic indeed to assume that the results of this approximate some theoretical economic equilibrium model, let alone that they are beneficial for all. Thus, even though national economic planners face increasing pressure to leave decisions about specialization to the market, an equally strong case can be made for the state to intervene and alter comparative advantage—particularly if there is reason to believe that not all comparative advantages are created equal.

DOES IT MATTER WHAT A COUNTRY SPECIALIZES IN?

From the perspective of the free trade doctrine, a well-informed nation state would not engage in trade unless it can be shown to be more beneficial than autarky. In this view, countries can expect to gain absolutely from trade. Inequalities in global development, however, depend not just on comparisons in the same place over time, but on comparisons between places. Trade theory offers an easy answer to this also, arguing that it does not matter what comparative advantage a country has, because trade levels the playing field. But does experience confirm that countries stand to gain equally from trade?

In trade theory, the distribution of the gains made from trade between the participating countries is supposed to be determined by international exchange rates between imports and exports, not by comparative advantage itself: Free trade does not guarantee fair trade. Intuitively, specialization increases the size of the economic pie available to participants, but when one country's share of the pie is greater, the other gets less. When two commodities are traded for each other, the closer the international exchange rate is to the exchange rate that would prevail domestically (between producers of the two goods within a country), then the smaller are the gains from trade that this country can expect from engaging in trade (see sidebar: "Exchange Rates and Gains from Trade").

If the global division of labor associated with specialization and trade is to reduce inequalities, trade has to result in greater relative benefits (or improved terms of trade) for third world countries than for first world countries. This would give third world countries the opportunity to invest their greater gains in economic growth that might close the gap separating them from the first world. If, however, third world countries accumulate smaller benefits than first world countries, then national policymakers face a dilemma. Engaging in trade may be better than not engaging in trade, but the wealthier partner benefits even more. Thus the poorer country faces the prospect that trade actually widens the wealth differential between the trading partners. The dilemma is difficult: Does the poorer country choose increased prosperity, widening the development gap, or autarky, with lower economic growth? Third world countries have evaluated this tradeoff differently. China, India, and other countries (e.g., Brazil)—particularly (but not exclusively) those with a large enough internal set of human and physical resources to make going it alone seem feasible—at times have followed policies that seem closer to autarky than to specialization and trade.

As we have discussed in Chapter 4, Raúl Prebisch (1959) examined the terms of trade governing the exchange of primary commodities exported from Latin America for manufactured imports in the 1950s. He found a steady decline in the terms of trade. The quantity of primary exports that had to be sold by Latin American countries to buy the same amount of industrial imports was steadily increasing. In other words, his research suggested that some kinds of commodities were (and are) more beneficial to specialize in than other kinds, and that the third world was getting the short end of the stick by inheriting a specialization in primary commodities. If correct, this suggests that some kinds of comparative advantage are more beneficial than others, implying that it matters a great deal how comparative advantages have been determined historically. It also suggests that there may be good reasons why a country should attempt to transform, and not just accept, its comparative advantage.

CONCLUSIONS

We have seen that an international economic differentiation had emerged by the end of colonialism—between third world countries producing mostly primary commodities, and first and second world countries where most manufacturing was clustered. This was a direct result of colonial policies, but it was suggested that the inequalities created could be overcome once political independence had been achieved. According to the free trade

Exchange Rates and Gains from Trade

The figure below contains two graphs illustrating the gains from trade for the example of England and Portugal, presented earlier in the chapter. The lower left-hand graph shows possible combinations of cloth and wine that Portugal could produce domestically for £30,000. Given that the cost of production of a bale of cloth is £75, and that for a barrel of wine is £50 in Portugal (see box on right-hand side of the figure), £30,000 could pay for the production of either 400 bales of cloth, or 600 barrels of wine, or some linear combination of the two. The line PP′ in the figure traces out all possible combinations. The upper right-hand graph (best read by turning the book upside down) shows possible combinations of cloth and wine that England could produce domestically for £30,000. Costs of production in England are higher: £100 for a bale of cloth and £200 for a barrel of wine (reflecting England's famous summer weather). The £30,000 would pay for 300 bales of cloth from English manufacturers, or 150 barrels of wine, or some linear combination of the two. The line EE′ traces out all possible combinations.

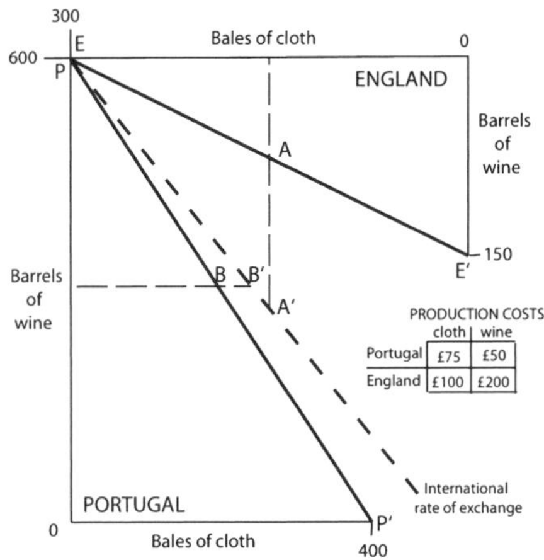

Calculating the gains from trade: An example.

The slopes of lines PP′ and EE′ represent the internal exchange rates for the two commodities—the rates at which Portuguese wine would be traded for Portuguese cloth, or English wine for English cloth, if no international trade were possible. In Portugal, one bale of cloth costs the same as one and a half barrels of wine, and the gradient of PP′ is 3/2. In England, one bale of cloth costs the same as half a barrel of wine, and the gradient of EE′ is 1/2. The flatter slope for England shows graphically that it has a comparative advantage in cloth; the steeper slope for Portugal shows its comparative advantage in wine. Any exchange rate of cloth for wine on the international market that lies between these two domestic ratios (i.e., between 3/2 and 1/2) represents a situation where both countries can gain, but the degree to which each gains from trade will depend on where within this range the actual international exchange rate lies. Consider the slope of the hypothetical international exchange rate in the figure, which in this case lies much closer to the exchange rate for Portugal (slope of PP′) than for England (slope of EE′). In this case, England will gain much more from trade than Portugal.

The length of the line segment AA′ shows the extra wine the English can buy in the international market at the international price, if they produce cloth and trade it with Portugal for wine instead of growing wine domestically. The length of the line segment BB′ shows the extra cloth the Portuguese can buy in the international market at this price, if they produce wine and trade it with England for cloth instead of producing cloth domestically. No matter how one compares these two line segments, England stands to gain more from this arrangement (i.e., experiences greater gains from trade) than Portugal. Portugal is better off than before, but its willingness to trade with England means that England benefits much more from trade than Portugal. If one of the purposes of trade is for Portugal to catch up economically with England, then trade does not help. For the English, however, it is a great idea under these conditions (if they can stay sober enough to appreciate it!).

doctrine, this kind of differentiation need not be disadvantageous for the third world. In this view, free trade is more beneficial for all countries than autarky, and a comparative advantage in primary commodities is as good as a comparative advantage in manufacturing. Proponents of free trade (many of whom were to be found in the first world) thus argued that the distinctive specialization of third world countries was in fact a good thing, and should be exploited through specialization and trade—both for the good of that country and for the good of the international economy.

In a sense, history and geography were supposed to be irrelevant. It did not matter how comparative advantage had been arrived at, or which commodities it favored in any particular country, because free trade would give everyone the chance of a fresh start. Yet if the gains from trade are inequitably distributed, and if some types of specialization are more beneficial than others, then these historical patterns of specialization matter a great deal: They shape starting positions on the uneven playing field of the global economy.

Reality differs greatly from the idealized world of international trade theory. International trade is not a free market where supply matches demand. Trade is typically unbalanced, with nations running surpluses or deficits; both monetary and nonmonetary barriers to free trade have been pervasive features of the world economy throughout history (see Chapter 16); transportation costs greatly complicate our ability to assess comparative advantage accurately; and a large proportion of trade is not even carried out through the marketplace. Considerable trading of commodities between governments is not subject to market pricing (e.g., purchases tied to intergovernmental aid agreements, or military expenditures; see Chapter 22), and even trade by private firms is often not governed by the market. At least 30% of all world trade is made up of international shipments of commodities between the subsidiaries of one or another transnational corporation, where prices are set by administrative rules rather than by the market (see Chapter 21). Finally, geopolitics is as important in shaping trade as market forces. International trade is governed by unequal political and legal negotiations, in the GATT and now the WTO, and trading blocs such as the North American Free Trade Agreement (NAFTA) or the European Union (EU) have become increasingly important. Yet the free trade doctrine is more popular than ever.

Spatial divisions of labor and comparative advantage have been manipulated by powerful nonlocal forces throughout history, and continue to be so manipulated today. As the examples offered earlier in this chapter suggest, many peripheral countries have had little say over their current comparative advantage. Activities ranging from Britain's deindustrialization of India, to contemporary trade barriers against the import of cheaper manufactured goods from the third world into the United States and the EU, suggest that those propounding the benefits of free trade see some commodities as far better to specialize in than others. Indeed, since 1846 the loudest proponents of free trade have been particularly active in manipulating comparative advantage and trade to their own advantage. If there are disproportionate benefits from trade, depending on the type of commodities a country specializes in, we must ask which countries benefit from the way in which spatial divisions of labor and international trade were organized in 1960 and have evolved since. We examine this from a third world perspective in Chapter 16.

NOTE

1. We use the word "commodities" to refer to all goods produced for the purpose of selling them to make a profit, and not the narrower popular definition that restricts the term to primary products (fossil fuels, minerals, agricultural products).

16 Trading Primary Commodities

In Chapter 15, we have seen that the free trade doctrine promised development through specialization and trade for countries specializing in primary commodities, as well as for those specializing in manufacturing. This must have seemed a risky strategy in one sense for former colonies: It was suggesting that they stake their economic prosperity on networks of mutual dependence, through trade, with former colonial exploiters. At the same time, however, the doctrine promised equal participation with all other sovereign nations—a sign that they really had achieved political independence. It also suggested that trade would take place on a level playing field, meaning that the ability of any country to correctly identify its comparative advantage would give it every opportunity to build on political independence and create economic independence. In this chapter, we examine what actually happened after 1960 as third world nations took part in global trading networks. We examine the experience of third world nation states exporting primary commodities to the first world in return for manufactured imports, and we ask whether such trading relations really constituted them as equal participants. We then examine reasons why too many third world countries find themselves unable to convert primary commodity trade into economic prosperity, and why trade may increase rather than decrease a country's economic dependence—thereby reinforcing the asymmetries in the global division of labor that were constructed during European colonialism. Chapter 17 examines industrialization as an alternative to continued specialization in primary commodity production.

WHO GAINS FROM PRIMARY COMMODITY SPECIALIZATION?[1]

The following generalizations can be made about the trade flows that accompanied the global division of labor in 1960 (see Figure 15.1 and Figure 16.1). First, world trade was dominated by two trading cliques: among first world and among second world nations. Together, these accounted for 58.7% of all exports. In this Cold War era, however, there was very little trade between the first and second worlds. Second, third world trade was predominantly with first world nations

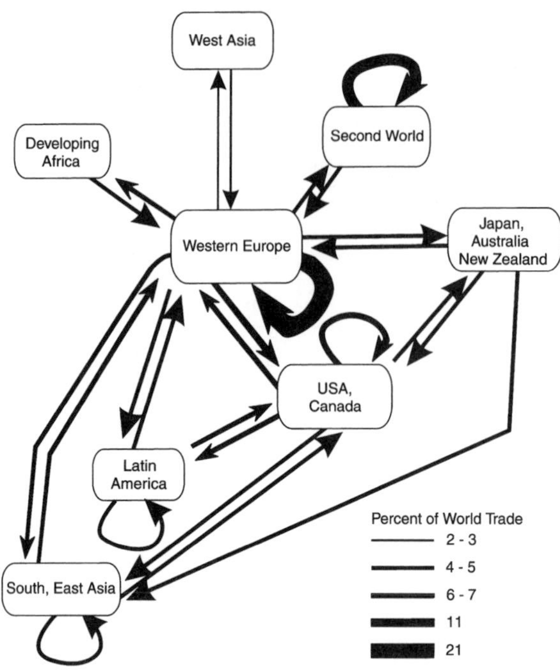

FIGURE 16.1. World trade flows, 1960. *Source:* Data are from United Nations Conference on Trade and Development (UNCTAD, 1965a).

(two-thirds of all exports, four-fifths of all imports). Unlike the strong flows among first and second world countries, only 5% of world trade was among third world nations; this illustrates well how trade patterns still reflected historical colonial relations. Third, the details of third world–first world trade patterns showed strong connections to old colonial spheres of influence, despite the new political independence of the third world. Africa and west Asia traded predominantly with western Europe, whose colonial governance they were now releasing themselves from. Latin America's dominant trading partner was North America, reflecting the political sphere of influence developed by the United States under the Monroe Doctrine. South and east Asia (excluding China, which was part of second world trading patterns) traded with Europe, North America, and Japan, reflecting a complex history of European and American colonialism and foreign policy, combined with the Japanese attempt in the 1930s and 1940s to establish a neocolonial "coprosperity sphere." The only notable trade between the second world and the third world was the second world's trade with the communist regime in Cuba.

Exports of primary commodities remain far more important to third world exporters than they are to first and second world importers. Unlike the first world, newly independent African and Asian nations were heavily dependent in 1968 on exporting primary products (food, fossil fuels, agricultural raw materials, and minerals), as was Latin America. This had not changed much by 2001 for Africa and west Asia (Figure 16.2, top), whereas industrialization in Latin America, but particularly in east and southeast Asia, was accompanied by a dramatic reduction in dependence on exporting primary products. In terms of imports (Figure 16.2, bottom), first world countries reduced their dependence on primary commodity imports from 30–70% in

1968 to 20–30% by 2001. Japan had the largest share of primary product imports—oil from the Middle East, and lumber and minerals from southeast Asia. On the other hand, industrialization in China has increased the demand for primary products to 21% of all imports in 2004. By 2001, 20–50% of export income for Latin America, west Asia, and Africa still depended on selling primary products to the first world. Yet these exports amounted to just 3% of the first world import bill (for reasons discussed in Chapter 18) (World Trade Organization [WTO], 2003).

Recall that according to free trade's proponents, it should not matter which products a country exports, as long as it has a comparative advantage in something. Yet, as discussed in Chapter 15, the gains from trade may be unequally distributed between the partners in a way that can enhance rather than reduce economic inequalities. Since the export of primary commodities for manufactures is still so important for the third world, it is worth examining in detail how the gains from trade have been shared between third world primary commodity exporters and first world exporters of manufactured goods.

It is important to point out that this is a highly contentious issue. The free trade doctrine is so widely accepted that its adherents have trouble accepting evidence that may contradict it, whereas critics are eager

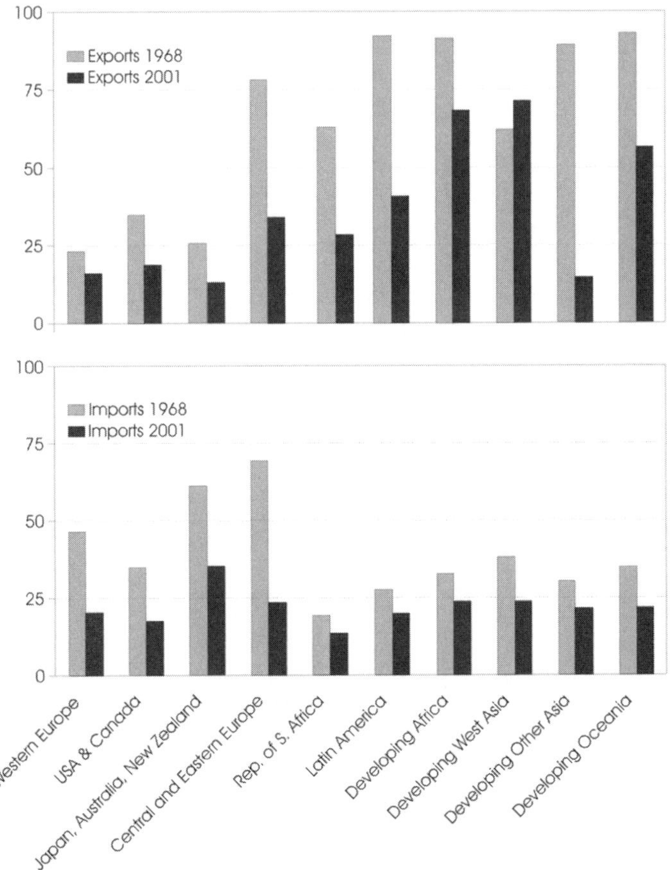

FIGURE 16.2. Export (top) and import (bottom) shares of primary products in world trade, 1968 and 2001. *Sources:* Data are from UNCTAD (2003a: Table 3.2).

to find any evidence that might undermine it. Depending on the measure used and the time periods compared, trade statistics have been used both to "prove" and to "disprove" the validity of the free trade principle. A direct way of determining how well a country does from trade is to examine its "terms of trade"—that is, the relative value of its exports compared to its imports. If this increases over time, this is evidence that the country is benefiting from trade, but a decrease suggests that trade is not in the long-term interest of that country. We compare several measures of the terms of trade over the entire period since the end of colonialism, in order to provide as complete a picture as possible.

One way to examine the history of the terms of trade is to examine the "price ratio" of a representative export compared to that of a representative import, taking care to compare products that have not changed their characteristics over time. Take the case of the international prices for bananas and steel (Figure 16.3). Between 1950 and 1993, the price of hot rolled steel plates from the United States increased at a far more rapid rate than the price of Central American bananas (see the lighter lines in the figure, with prices indicated by the left-hand axis). Banana prices almost tripled in 40 years, but steel prices increased sixfold. As a consequence, less and less steel could be purchased by Central American countries with the income made on a case of bananas (thick line on figure, with ratio indicated by right-hand axis). After 1993, the price gap closed, and the "purchasing power" of bananas (the amount of steel that could be imported with the income made from exporting a case of bananas) rose, but was still less than two-thirds of what it was in 1950. Other ways to approach the historical geographies of trade are to examine how the strategic values of specific commodities in the colonial period continued to guide the relations between ex-colonial powers and their former colonies, and the manner in which masculinity and femininity have been actively deployed in shaping the international political economy (Enloe, 1989).

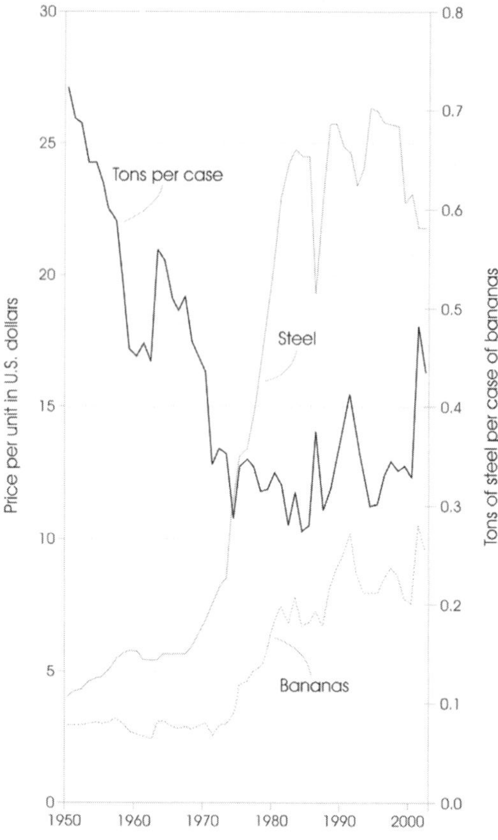

FIGURE 16.3. Trading bananas for steel, 1950–2002. *Sources:* Data are from UNCTAD (2003a), U.S. Bureau of Labor Statistics (2007) and Rangajaran (1978).

Although these changes are dramatic, they only compare two commodities, and thus raise the question of how representative this is of the general situation. A more complete measure is the "net barter terms of trade" (NBTT). This is a measure of the price of all exports relative to the price of imports, calculated by dividing the weighted average price of all third world primary product exports by the weighted average price of all third world manufactured imports. The weights used are the relative quantity of each commodity in the import and export baskets of third world nations. Spraos (1983) provides calculations going back to 1950, which we have updated to 2004 (Figure 16.4). These show that the NBTT dropped dramatically between 1951 and 2003, from 143 to just 45. This means that the price of primary commodity exports, relative to imported manufactures, fell to less than a third of its 1950 value. Note that when oil prices are included, the success of OPEC in reversing this trend for oil-exporting countries in the early 1970s and again in the early 1980s can clearly be seen; that by 1986, this advantage had disappeared; and that recent oil price increases have pushed it upward again.

The NBTT is also imperfect, however, because it does not take into account how the terms of trade can be affected by changes in the volume of exports or in production methods.[2] If a third world country can increase the quantity of its exports, then its ability to pay for imports, or its purchasing power, can increase even when the NBTT is declining. Figure 16.5 shows trends in purchasing power, also known as the "income terms of trade"—a measure of the quantity of imports that can be purchased with

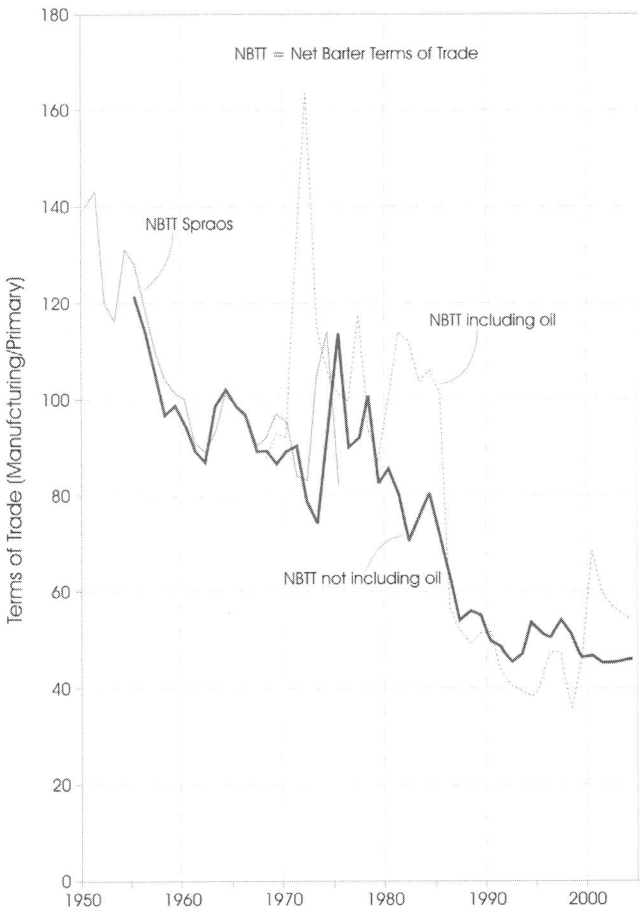

FIGURE 16.4. Terms of trade: Manufactured imports for third world primary commodity exports, 1950–2004. *Sources:* Data are from UNCTAD (1985a–2003a), United Nations (1985–2003), Spraos (1983), and Griffith-Jones and Harvey (1985).

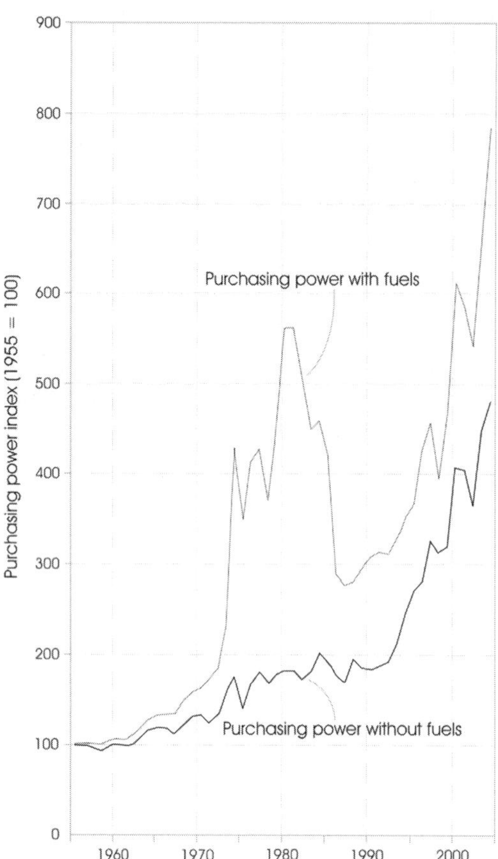

FIGURE 16.5. Purchasing power of third world primary commodity exports, 1955–2004. *Source:* Data are from United Nations (1960b–2003b).

the money made from primary commodity exports. When fuels are included, then purchasing power increased almost eightfold between 1955 and 2004, because the output of fuels from third world nations increased dramatically. If fuels are not included, representing the case of most (non-OPEC) third world primary commodity exporters, there was a fivefold increase. In this case, increased purchasing power means that third world countries are becoming increasingly committed to specializing in and exporting commodities with stagnant or falling NBTT, in order to purchase first world manufactures.

The value of manufactured goods actually imported by third world nations almost quadrupled between 1990 and 2004 alone (341% increase), growing even faster than purchasing power (which grew by 250%). Thus even these commitments to increased specialization and exports have not brought in the money needed by third world countries (particularly those with no oil resources and relatively little industrialization) to pay for manufactured imports. In Africa and the Middle East, continued heavy reliance on exporting primary commodities has limited manufacturing production and imports. In selected newly industrializing countries (NICs) in east and southeast Asia and Latin America, manufacturing imports and exports have exploded. Some of these countries are becoming "the first world within the third world": They are developing unequal trading relations with other third world primary commodity exporters that parallel those linking the first and third world described here—and are facing labor, environmental, and social costs internally.

ACCOUNTING FOR CHANGING TERMS OF TRADE

The long-term decline in the value of primary commodities exported by third world nations relative to the value of imported manufactured commodities, and the third world nations' persistent inability to pay for imports with the money made from exports, require detailed study because they challenge the validity of the claim that free trade tends to reduce inequalities between countries. A number of factors come into play other than simple political manipulation of markets. In part these relate to the nature of the commodities that many third world countries rely on for exports, and in part they stem from the situation that these countries occupy within the world economy, or their (geo)positionality. These two sets of factors are themselves related; as we have seen, the types of commodities exported by third world nations are in part the results of their colonial heritage—as are the manifold social and environmental changes that accompany specialization in such exports, including plantations, sex work, movements of domestic workers, and exotic monocultures (Enloe, 1989; Merchant, 1989). (For some ways in which the nature of agricultural exports has begun to change, see sidebar: "Contract Farming.")

Primary versus Manufactured Commodities

"Engel's law," named for 19th-century Prussian statistician Ernst Engel, postulates that as people become more wealthy, their demand for food products increases more slowly than their demand for manufactured goods (Kindelberger, 1968); there are limits on how much food they can consume, but not on how many shoes they can own. As a consequence, the increased consumption that comes with wealth is oriented more to manufactured commodities and services than to food, meaning that the demand for and price of the former will increase relative to the latter. This is consistent with the price trends suggested in Figures 16.3 and 16.4. Furthermore, many analysts have observed that the elasticity of demand is less for primary commodities than for manufactured commodities, meaning that demand does not change very much when prices are altered. Thus, if third world nations were to lower the price of their primary commodities, the increase in demand would not be dramatic and might not even compensate for the lost income from lower prices.

Production technologies have also improved more rapidly historically for manufactured commodities than for primary commodities. It is easier to introduce production line innovations and machines that reduce the cost of production, or to increase the technical sophistication of the product, on the factory floor than it is in fields and mines. In the absence of other changes, this should mean that the prices of manufactured products (for the identical products) *fall* relative to that of primary products, thus improving the terms of trade for third world nations. This has not happened, partly because manufactured commodities have become more sophisticated: A tractor is much more expensive now than it used to be, but is also a more complex machine. Yet even when productivity changes are taken into account in calculating the terms of trade, evidence still suggests that the prices of manufactures *rise* relative to those of agricultural commodities. This is not the case for minerals, but, as Spraos (1983: 112) points out, minerals generally become more expensive to produce over time because of the exhaustion of cheaper sources of nonrenewable resources; this should mean that their prices, and the corresponding terms of trade, *increase* relative to those of manufactured commodities. Thus, for both agricultural commodities and minerals, the effect of new production technologies on the terms of trade for third world primary commodity exporters should be more positive than we actually observe.

Improved transportation technologies always increase the potential gains from trade, but will affect commodities differently, depending on how important these costs are. Primary commodities are bulky, and transportation costs often represent a higher proportion of the cost of production, whereas manufactured commodities tend to have lower transportation costs relative to the value of the product. Because of the greater importance of transportation costs in the value of primary commodities, cheaper transportation will lower the delivered price of primary commodities more rapidly than that of manufactured commodities. This could account for part of the declining terms of trade, and need not represent a disadvantage for third world nations, because it is an income loss for transportation firms rather than manufacturers. We do not know, however, what proportion of the decline in terms of trade is attributable to falling transport costs.

The social regulation of wage costs varies significantly among nations. First, real

Contract Farming

Increasingly, the large absentee-owned or state-owned plantations and estates growing cash crops, which had dominated colonial and postcolonial agriculture in the third world, are being supplemented or replaced by a greater variety of farming operations producing a greater variety of export crops. Smallholders and peasant farmers, now recognized as frequently more efficient than large landowners, are exporting their crops as well as selling them in local markets. The crops they grow include not only coffee and bananas, but fresh cut flowers flown from Columbia to North America, or market vegetables flown from west Africa to France and the European Union (EU). In one way, food exporting is increasingly becoming the province of small entrepreneurs, and more families are being drawn into export markets.

This growth has occurred hand in hand with a rapid growth in "contract farming"—whereby the purchaser provides the farmer a guaranteed market for crops, and often some inputs and services; in exchange, the purchaser rather than the farmer specifies the quantity and quality of crops, and even the farming methods (Echánove and Steffen, 2005). Contracts may be with local middlemen (and some middlewomen). These middlemen utilize power and family networks within their countries, as well as contacts made with foreign buyers, to develop markets; they then seek out local farmers to supply the crops, specifying when and in what condition crops should be delivered. Theirs is often a risky business, but one that has the potential to create considerable wealth. Local state agencies or, increasingly, first world agribusinesses also contract with small local farmers.

Agribusiness benefits from contracting, because it allows contractual control over the production process without the need to own land or hire and supervise an agricultural labor force. Such a system transfers production risk from the contractor to the farmer, while giving agribusiness flexible yet stable control over sourcing and quality. "Contract crops are especially linked to demanding grade and quality standards—freshness, fragrance, appearance, color, weight, moisture content, shape, odor, absence of blemish, and so on—which allow the commodity to be classified, screened, and priced in the contract" (Watts, 1992: 79). When agribusiness companies face a market downturn, they may tighten quality evaluations and reject a higher proportion of the crop than they otherwise would. Farmers tend to engage in contract farming because they have few alternatives. Neoliberal economic policies have led to a situation in which contract production may be the only feasible means of obtaining access to credit, new technologies, and extension support, as well as providing a reasonably secure market for farmers' output.

Contract farming situations are so varied that it is difficult to generalize about their effects. The balance of risk and reward is usually tilted in favor of the purchaser rather than the farmer, and contract farming often means that growers lose autonomy as they come under the control of agribusiness companies. Thus banana growers under contract on the Caribbean island of St. Vincent must grow their bananas within a 10 minute walk of a motorable road, and the fruit must be picked and transported in an extremely careful and labor-intensive manner if the crops are to reach the coast without blemishes (Grossman, 1998). Blemishes turn into bruises, which people in the first world find objectionable on their bananas. However, small farmers have more bargaining power when they own their land and water supplies and have alternative sources of income (Porter and Phillips-Howard, 1997). Some farmers may resist by using agricultural inputs for their own crops, or by selling their output in markets when prices are above the contract price. Where contract farming competes for land and labor time with domestic food production, it often results in reduced food production. When contract production is male-dominated and food production is female-dominated, the results are often gender conflict and increased gender inequalities. There may also be increased concentration of land ownership and increased social differentiation. Finally, contract farming typically relies on agrochemicals that present both human and environmental risks, and on monocultural cropping that threatens biodiversity.

wages (the amount individuals can purchase with their money wages) are generally significantly higher in countries that mostly export manufactured commodities. Second, nations of the first world have more active and influential trade unions, and more broadly developed welfare state institutions, which together helped drive up real wages between 1945 and the early 1970s (see Chapter 17). Third, levels of unemployment and underemployment are lower in first and second world nations than in the third world. As production increases in first and second world countries, therefore, labor shortages lead to increased real wages, whereas the persistence of surplus labor tends to keep wages low in third world nations. One way in which first world entrepreneurs have dealt with the costs of increasing wages and taxes is to pass these on as price increases to their customers. This could help explain increases in the price of exports from first world nations relative to those from third world nations—no matter what commodities they are exporting. Given the current composition of world trade, this should result in improved terms of trade for first world manufactured exports relative to third world primary exports.

The "flexibility of production" is the ability of producers to respond rapidly to changing market conditions—producing more when prices are high, and less when they are low. Primary commodities are characterized by less production flexibility than manufactured commodities. The time necessary to bring into production tropical tree crops, which represent many of the cash crop exports from the third world, means that production must begin several years before the product can be brought to market. For minerals and fuels, production also must be planned years in advance: New mineral fields must be explored, and the big up-front costs of mining can only be amortized by continuing production for many years (Chapter 18). One consequence of this inflexibility is the existence of "boom–bust" cycles for many primary commodities. When production cannot be readily adjusted to market conditions, there is a tendency for periods of considerable undersupply and inflated prices to be followed by periods of oversupply and depressed prices. In the 1930s, for example, Brazil had so much excess coffee that it used the beans as fuel for trains. Boom–bust cycles make it difficult for third world primary commodity exporters to get the most out of their product. When prices are high, there are too few producers able to take advantage of them; when production levels are high, prices may be so depressed that little or no profits can be made.

The Positionality of Third World Nations

The five factors discussed above highlight differences between manufactured and primary commodities, which can account for deteriorating terms of trade simply in the types of products exported. These differences are important, because they suggest that the benefits from trade can depend greatly on which type of commodity a country happens to have its comparative advantage in. Yet the differences are not sufficient to explain asymmetries in the gains from trade. The relative geographic positionality of third world countries through history, both during and after colonialism, also matters. Even third world countries that have been able to specialize in and export manufactured goods experience at best stagnant terms of trade by comparison to first world manufactured exports. Furthermore, their demand for manufactured imports far outstrips the income made from exported manufactures: Between 1982 and 1996, terms of trade decreased by 7%, but purchasing power increased fivefold (Figure 16.6); this indicates that the quantity of manufactures needing to be produced for export, instead of for domestic markets, would have to expand more than fivefold in order to pay for these imports (Maizels, 2000; Sarkar and Singer, 1991). Specialization in low-wage export-oriented assembly of manufactured goods (Chapter 17) places third world export man-

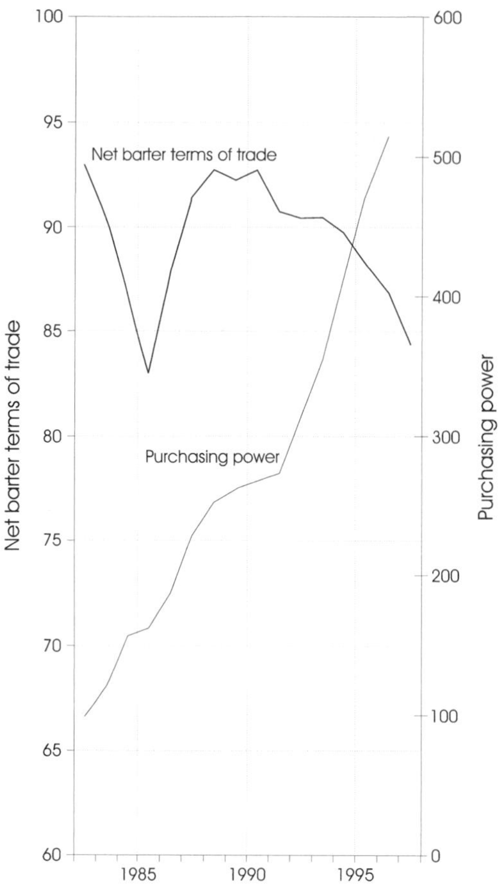

FIGURE 16.6. Terms of trade: Third world manufacturing exports versus first world manufacturing imports, 1982–1998. *Source*: Data are from Maizels (2000).

ufacturing in heavy competition with other third world countries, rather than with first world exports (Razmi and Blecker, 2005). (Of course, many third world manufacturing exporters are owned by first world corporations, which ultimately reap the profits either way; see Chapters 19 and 20).

To an even greater extent than in other arenas of exchange, international trade is characterized by political negotiations that greatly influence the conditions under which trade occurs. One generally accepted power of sovereign states is the power to control the flow of commodities across their borders—a power that seems in direct opposition to the doctrine of free trade, and is denigrated by free trade proponents as protectionism. International trade flows are subject to political decisions and negotiations at two levels. First, there exist bilateral arrangements between pairs of countries; individual nations may grant other nations the status of "most favored nation" (MFN). (They may also, on occasion, withdraw it: The United States withdrew MFN status for China between 1951 and 1980, withdrew it again temporarily after the 1989 Tian'anmen Square massacre, and has recently discussed doing this again.) Nation states may also prohibit trade with another nation, as the United States has done with Cuba since the latter's communist revolution. And influential nation states can also push the United Nations to impose a trade embargo, as the United States did on Iraq before leading the invasion of Iraq in 2003.

Second, there exist a number of supranational groups and agreements that, while affirming the right of nations to control trade, attempt to reduce discriminatory practices and reduce barriers to trade. As we have seen in Chapter 15, the United States was unwilling to hand over its power to regulate trade to a world trading organization in 1945, so instead the General Agreement on Tariffs and Trade (GATT) was founded. GATT, now absorbed into the WTO, is a supranational forum in which attempts are made to reach voluntary agreements about international prices, tariff reduction, and principles governing trade. The United Nations Conference on Trade and Development (UNCTAD), set up at the initiative of the Group of 77 in 1962, holds quadrennial conferences that focus on the trade and development problems of the third world. A number of formal agreements have also attempted to formulate contracts governing trade in certain areas between groups of countries. These include international commodity agreements, designed to reduce short-term uncertainty in commodity trade by, for example, setting up buffer stocks; the OPEC cartel, designed to control prices and production levels of petroleum; the Multi-Fibre Arrangement, initiated in 1973 by the United States, recognizing the right of first world nations to limit textile imports from third world countries when necessary to protect the importers' domestic textile industry from "disruptive" competition; and UN-sponsored trade embargoes, which have periodically been employed in an attempt to discipline "rogue" states, ranging from apartheid South Africa to Cuba, Iraq, and Serbia.

The most recent addition to these supranational arrangements and institutions is the WTO, created in 1995 during the "Uruguay round" of GATT negotiations. The WTO was set up, with a secretariat located in Geneva, as a new permanent organization to deal with trade issues at the global level. As such, it has several functions. It is a forum for governments to negotiate and sign agreements on the rules of international trade, as the GATT was. It also administers the latest version of GATT, in which signatory nations agreed to various measures to reduce barriers to trade: reducing tariffs by a third, eliminating quantitative nontariff barriers (NTBs), and reducing a variety of other NTBs (see next section). The most novel aspect of the WTO is that it is a place for national governments to settle trade disputes. A national government or governments can bring a complaint to the WTO if it believes another government is infringing its rights under the agreement. Negotiation is the first phase of the dispute process, but if the dispute is not resolved by negotiations, both sides bring in their lawyers and experts to present a case before a WTO panel of trade experts, who make a ruling on the case. If the ruling finds that a country is not living up to its obligations according to WTO trading rules, that country is required to change its laws or policies to bring them into line with the WTO ruling. If a government does not do so, it may be subject to retaliatory trade sanctions by the country or countries that brought the complaint.

The influence to date of political negotiation over trade practices shows how prices (and thus gains from trade) are influenced by political force at the negotiating table, and not just by the economic factors of demand, supply, and production and distribution technologies (for an analysis of these influences in the 1930s, see Hirschman, 1945). Countries whose situation in the world economy makes them more dependent on trade will be in a weaker bargaining situation in such negotiations. Those countries for which trade is less necessary can more easily walk away from the bargaining table if conditions are not to their liking, and will thus have the stronger hand. There are clear asymmetries between third and first world negotiators in this respect (see sidebar: "Power Hierarchies in the WTO").

First, exports to first world countries are far more important for third world countries seeking revenues to pay for imports, than exports to third world countries are for first world countries (Figure 16.7; note the liminal position of the European former second world). Since many third world nations rely heavily on first world imports to obtain necessary manufactured goods, luxuries, and even food—in order to foster economic growth, a prosperous lifestyle for their elites, and nutrition for the general populace—they cannot afford to disengage from first world–third world trade when terms of trade deteriorate.

Second, third world nations are more heavily specialized, trading only a limited number of commodities, whereas first world nations offer a broad spectrum of commodities on the international market. The three largest export commodities account for less than a third of total exports for countries in the core of the world economy, but make up between one-third and four-fifths of the exports of peripheral nations (Figure 16.8). Thus third world countries more closely follow the Ricardian free trade principle of relying on specialization in and export of a narrow range of commodities to foster economic growth than do first world nations. Figure 16.8 also estimates bargaining power by country type; bargaining power increases

Power Hierarchies in the WTO

The first round of trade negotiations under the auspices of the WTO, the "Doha round" initiated in 2001, is described as a "development agenda" for the third world. Yet the first world "Quad" negotiators set the terms in the form of the "Singapore issues," proposing that four new fields of economic policy be brought under the purview of the WTO (investment, competition, government procurement, and trade facilitation). These proposals would empower the WTO to regulate state practices for disciplining foreign investment, to judge whether government spending favored domestic firms, and to ensure that states would provide contracts only to globally competitive firms. Two groups sought to contest this: third world negotiators, and the anti-WTO social movements that had emerged after the 1999 Seattle protests.

Negotiations were reconvened in 2003 in Cancún (Mexico)—a city chosen, like Doha (Qatar), because its geography made it difficult for protestors to disrupt the meeting. Most third world countries indicated that they did not want to negotiate the Singapore issues during the run-up to the Cancún Ministerial; nevertheless, the Draft Cancun Ministerial Text included all four of the Singapore issues. The usual process for developing the Draft Text, in which the WTO Secretariat creates the draft text after meeting with member states, was not followed. Instead, the Chairman of the General Council prepared it "on his own responsibility." This ignored the "clearly stated views of Ministers of a large number of developing countries, and violate[d] the Doha principle that negotiations [on the new issues] can begin only if there is an explicit consensus" (Third World Network, 2003: 1).

Selected delegates from the anti-WTO social movements were allowed to join the negotiations (a post-Seattle concession), but those delegates did not have access to the key area where negotiations were taking place, which is known as the "Green Room." This is where the WTO's Director General organizes secret trade negotiations, carrying over a decades-old practice from the days of the GATT. Protestors were contained behind a steel fence, backed by a massive police presence, erected some 5 miles from the conference center.

Activists outside the fence developed strategies to communicate with their delegates inside the conference center. They scaled a construction crane across from the conference center, and hung a large banner ("*Que se vayan todos*"—"Get rid of all of them"), calling on the delegates to pack up and go home. Undoubtedly the most powerful signal that reached the convention center occurred after seven thousand activists marched from downtown Cancún toward the conference center, and were confronted at "kilometer zero" by steel walls and police lines. Unable to proceed further, a Korean farmer at the head of the delegation, Lee Kyung Hae, climbed the steel fence between the two massed forces, from where he led chants and then plunged a knife into his heart in protest. Lee's death cast a pallor over remaining discussions.

Inside the Center the G20+ bloc of third world countries, led by Brazil, India, China, and South Africa, pressed for increased market access for third world exports, the elimination of first world agricultural subsidies, and abandonment of the Singapore issues. When the Quad insisted on accepting the Singapore issues, the G20+ and their allies forcefully rejected the Draft Text. On the third evening the WTO secretariat called a Green Room meeting with delegates of a dozen countries, where the Quad continued to insist that the G20+ accept at least two of the Singapore issues. Talks collapsed the following afternoon when it became clear that neither side would capitulate.

After Cancún, the United States and the EU worked to undermine the G20+. The U.S. Trade Representative used the incentive of potential bilateral free trade agreements and the threat of reduced aid and access to U.S. markets to win over smaller states, dislodging countries such as Columbia and Costa Rica from the G20+. The United States and the EU courted India and Brazil, by offering that those countries join the United States, the EU, and Australia in a new negotiating group within the WTO, known as the Five Interested Parties. The IMF made support for the Doha round a de facto condition for a country receiving financial assistance, which meant that states that might have joined with the G20+ declined to do so. As of this writing, the Doha negotiations are stalled. Few predict a successful resolution.

Source: Wainwright (2006).

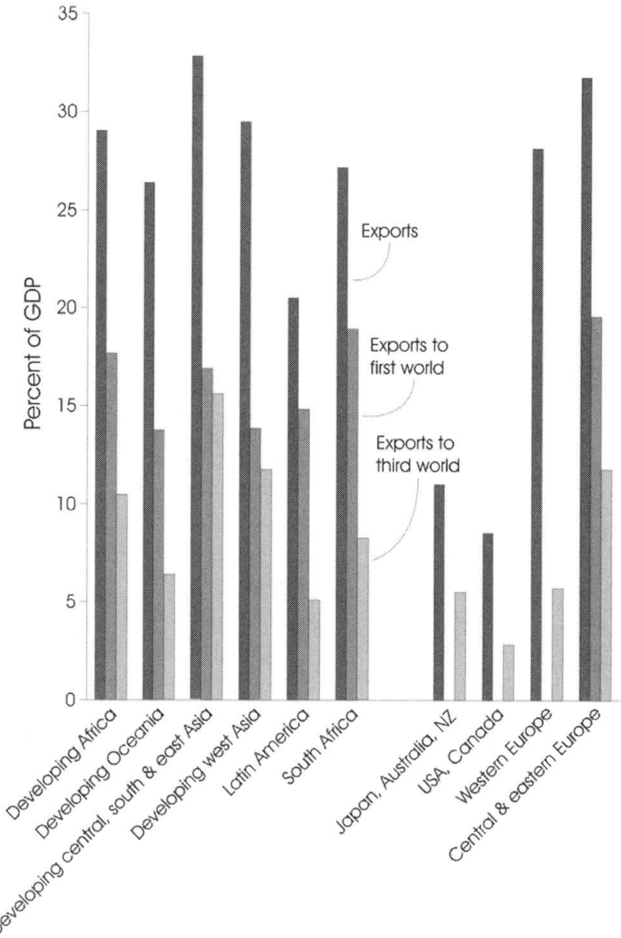

FIGURE 16.7. The importance of first world–third world trade by region, 2002. *Source:* Data are from UNCTAD (2003a).

with world market share and decreases with specialization (export share). Only two third world groupings approach first world bargaining power: the so-called NICs, and the low-income semiperiphery (itself dominated by rapidly industrializing China and India). Even oil exporters have low bargaining power.

Figure 16.9 shows the share of the three largest export commodities in total exports. Nations that specialize more heavily in a few commodities have less bargaining power in trade negotiations, because it is harder for them to shift their specialization to other commodities when prices are unfavorable. This is all the more difficult for primary commodity exporters, because the long lead time between investing in new production and the time when production begins makes them less flexible.

This sectoral specialization is reinforced by geographical specialization, which can further reduce the flexibility of third world nations. Third world nations tend to be more dependent on just a few nations as consumers for their exports, whereas first world nations spread their exports among more nations. In addition, the particular

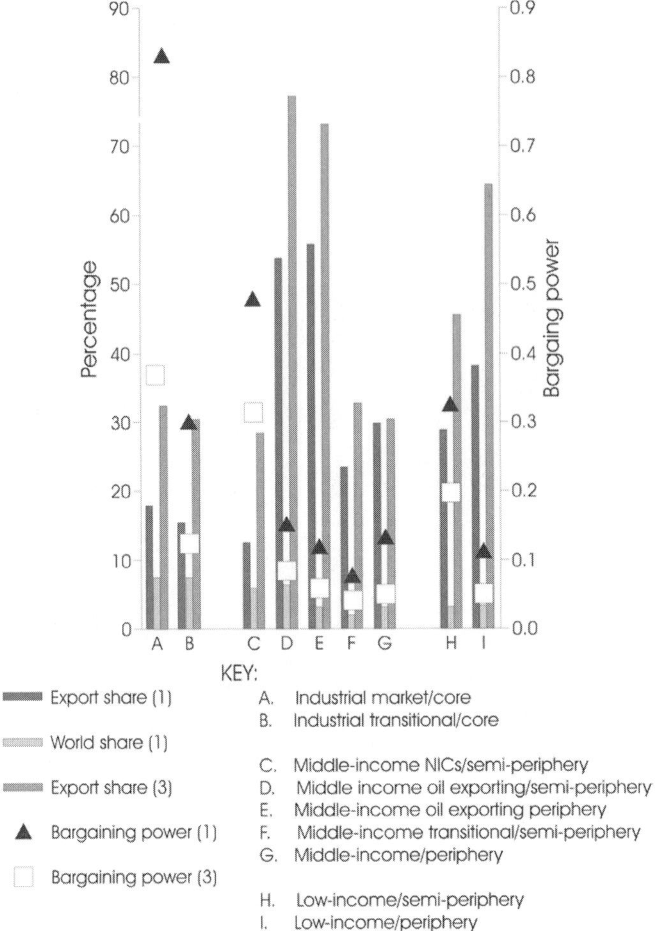

FIGURE 16.8. Export concentration, world market share, bargaining power, 2000–2001. *Source:* Data are from UNCTAD (2003a: Table 4.2D).

countries on which third world countries focus have changed little. As of 2002, after some 40 years of independence, Africa is still focused on western Europe for trade, as is west Asia (Figure 16.10). Latin America focuses on North America. South and east Asia retain strong connections with Japan, North America, and Europe, again reflecting historical spheres of political influence, such as Japan's "coprosperity sphere" of the 1930s and 1940s. Thus there is more to trade than can be explained by economics. Although to some degree these geopolitical clusters also reflect the fact that trade is easier over shorter distances, there are differences between third and first world nations within these clusters.

Third, trade flows from third world nations are bifurcating. Whereas exports from (parts of) south and east Asia have more than tripled since 1960, from 6% to 21% of world trade, Africa and Latin America have become relatively more isolated (compare Figures 16.1 and 16.10). Countries whose exports are quantitatively large, commanding a larger share of the international market, will have more bargaining power in trade negotiations. Like oligopolistic firms in a market, such countries can influence prices by changing the quantity exported.

First world nations dominate export totals, but also tend to have a larger share of the global market. In 2002, the three largest commodities of the United States made up only 16% of national exports, but constituted an average of 25% of world market share for these commodities. In Mexico, the three largest commodities made up 25% of all exports, with an average market share of just 4%.

As a rule of thumb, the bargaining power of countries engaged in international trade should be higher for countries with large world market shares, and for countries with more diversified mixtures of exports. This rule can be translated into a crude "bargaining power index" for a country by dividing the world market share of the country's principal exports by the share that those commodities represent of total exports. Let us take the example of the United States and Mexico: For the single largest commodity, this bargaining power index is 2.8 (17%/6%) for the United States (exporting aircraft), but just 0.5 (5%/10%) for Mexico (exporting crude oil). For the three largest exports, it is still 2.8 for the United States but only 0.2 for Mexico. More generally, countries in the periphery of the world economy have bargaining power indices that are just a small fraction of first world countries' bargaining power (Figure 16.11). Note, however that some third world semiperipheral countries exporting manufactured products—the NICs (see Chapter 17), China, and India (dominating the "low-income/semiperiphery" category)—have higher bargaining power indices, and indeed have benefited greatly from trade since 1980. The low-income periphery has very low bargaining power, however (see also Figure 16.8).

Fourth, competition among third world nations producing the same product can be severe. The importance of trade revenues to these nations and the inflexibility of production methods for primary commodities, combined with the high level of specialization, make it difficult to change the composition of exports; thus countries continue

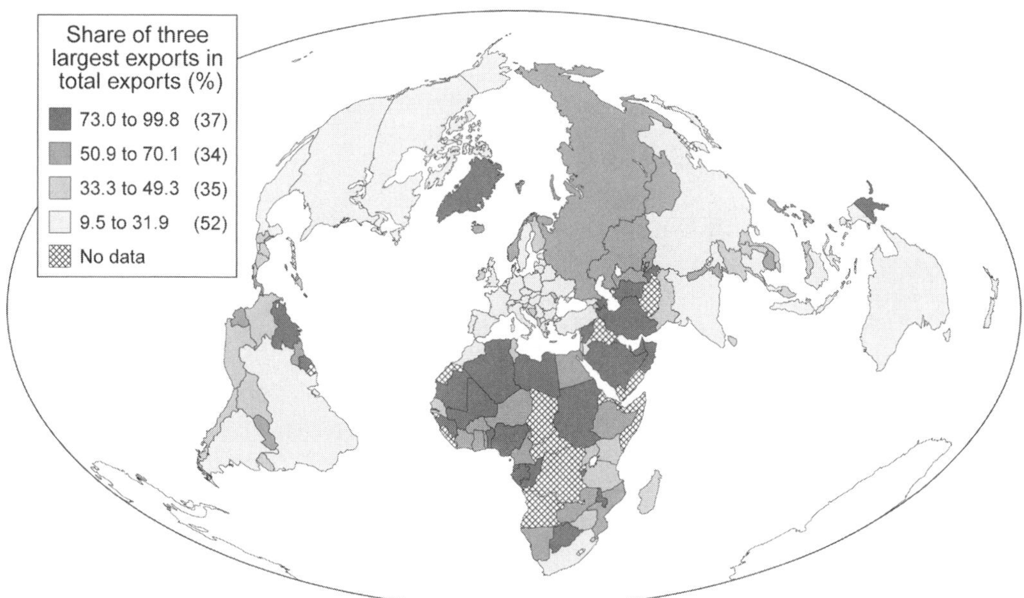

FIGURE 16.9. Export concentration, based on three largest commodities, 2002. *Source:* Data are from UNCTAD (2003a).

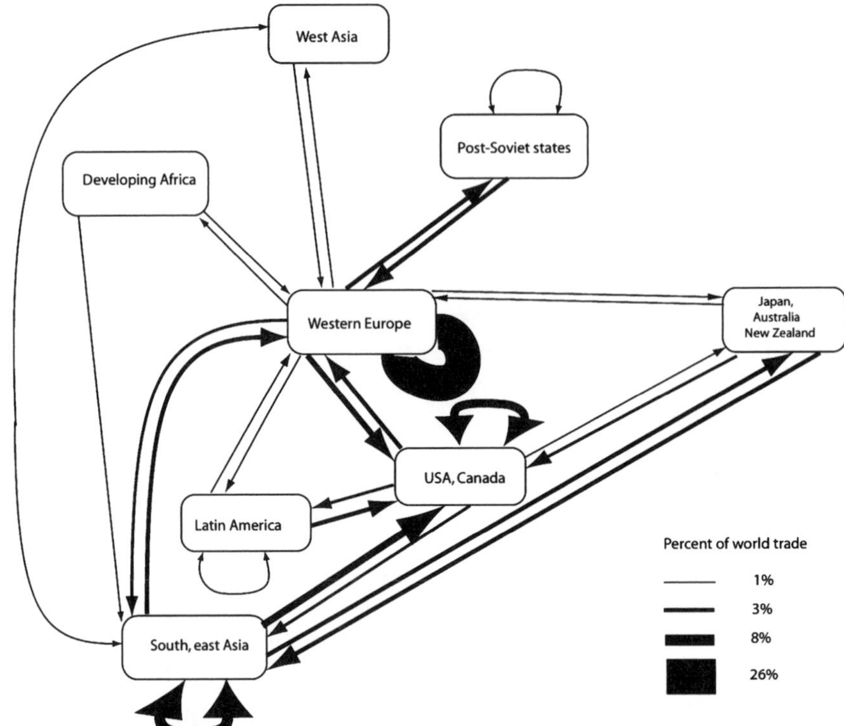

FIGURE 16.10. World trade flows, 2002. *Source:* Data are from UNCTAD (2003a).

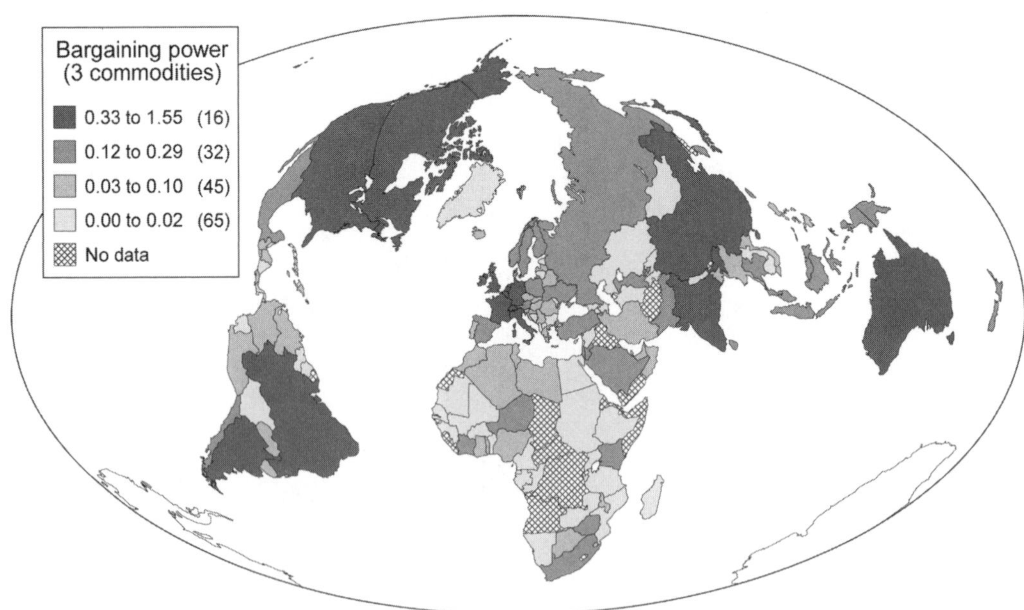

FIGURE 16.11. Trade bargaining power index, 2002. *Source:* Data are from UNCTAD (2003a).

to compete with one another in the same product, rather than seeking out alternatives. This problem is compounded by the fact that primary commodities are much more similar to one another, regardless of where they come from, than manufactured commodities are. A German tractor is seen as quite different from a U.S. tractor, but Ghanaian cocoa is very much like Indonesian cocoa (except, perhaps, to first world chocolate aficionados). As a consequence, whereas a general increase in the world price may slightly reduce demand for cocoa, if an individual country increases its price, then demand by external buyers for that country's cocoa will fall rapidly; cocoa-trading and chocolate companies will shift their purchases to other countries. Raffer (1987: 124) quotes estimates for Ghana in 1972 that a 1% increase in the price of its cocoa exports would lead to a 2–3% decline in demand, even though a 1% increase in the world price for cocoa would only lead to a 0.4% decline in demand.

The possibility of substituting one source of cocoa for another, and the need for third world nations to market their export surplus, can create cutthroat competition that drives prices down. As a consequence, whereas price decreases lead to only small increases in demand (Engel's law), price increases by individual countries lead to markedly reduced demand. In the case of Ghana, if the estimates above were used, the increased revenue per ton from a price increase would be more than offset by the decline in income from reduced sales, meaning that less income will be made from trade after the price increase than before. Although producers' cartels would be one way to avoid such problems, even under the most favorable conditions cartels bring only short-term benefits (see the discussion of OPEC in Chapter 18). First world nations find substitutes for, or ways of recycling, primary commodities whose price has increased. They also construct reserves of "strategic" minerals and even agricultural commodities, which can be drawn on when international prices are perceived to be too high. The long-term benefits from general increases in the price of primary commodities have been at best temporary and at worst counterproductive.

To summarize, third world policymakers face considerable problems in trying to increase their income from exporting primary commodities. Price decreases have relatively little effect on demand (Engel's law); attempts to force prices up by limiting output or simply increasing prices founder on the heavy competition among third world nations and the ability of first world customers to find other suppliers or to substitute products. In the absence of alternatives, the most effective way for a country to increase export incomes is to increase the quantity produced for export (which is how purchasing power has been increased in the face of declining or stagnating terms of trade; see Figure 16.5). Increases in specialization and export volume are no panaceas, however. At the national scale, they can make third world countries increasingly dependent on exporting a few primary commodities to a few first world nations, reducing their bargaining power and the prospects of long-term improvements in their terms of trade. Increased output combined with dependence keeps prices low, with highly differentiated local consequences. For example, the price paid by first world consumers for rugs from India has fallen dramatically. In the homes where these rugs are being woven, the children who were getting at least two full meals a day in the early 1990s now often go to sleep with half-empty stomachs. As rug weaving gets consolidated in the local areas and monopolies emerge, many men lose their jobs or are unable to make adequate livings. In the same families, children become child laborers, and their mothers get targeted by nongovernmental organizations (NGOs) for empowerment. A traditional way for countries to seek to improve the returns for their exporters is to impose trade barriers, but this has become increasingly controversial.

TRADE BARRIERS

One of the principal reasons for multinational negotiations concerning international trade, in GATT, UNCTAD, and other forums, has been to reduce the tendency for national governments to use their legal power to impose restrictions on imports or exports. Free trade proponents see such "trade barriers" as preventing realization of the free trade doctrine's promises. The first such restrictions are hurdles applied at the border: tariffs and NTBs. Tariffs are essentially taxes imposed on imports or exports at the national border. Export tariffs, which increase the effective price of exports, represent a way of directly raising tax revenues from exporters. Yet export tariffs reduce the international competitiveness of exports, and thus are rarely used—and only on commodities in considerable demand. Import tariffs, which essentially increase the cost of imports, are employed not only as a source of revenue for the state but as a part of national economic policy. By increasing the cost of imports, a country can make imported goods more expensive than those of domestic producers, and thus can inhibit foreign competition. Despite the rhetoric of free trade as the sine qua non for promoting global economic growth, and political negotiations directed at eliminating tariffs, import tariffs have consistently been selectively used to protect production in those sectors where cheaper foreign imports are perceived to threaten jobs and profits. At Doha, Qatar, in 2001, WTO ministers agreed to reduce and eliminate tariffs and NTBs, to enhance "market access" of foreign imports to domestic markets. They also sought to extend the scope of the agreements from primary commodities and manufactures to services.

A second set of restrictions shapes the geography of trade relations. An importing country may award MFN status to other countries, meaning that imports from these countries face tariff barriers that are no higher than those faced by the MFN. "Preferential trading arrangements" (PTAs) are agreements among certain countries to levy uniform tariffs and NTBs against one another that are even lower than MFN tariffs, and in some cases are zero ("free trade areas"). MFN status dates back to the 19th century, when Britain instituted free trade, but was built into GATT after 1945 and remains central to WTO negotiations. PTAs are much more recent: The first was formed in Europe in 1957 (the European Economic Community [EEC], now expanded to the European Union [EU]). Some, like the EU, are first world clubs, but others (like the North American Free Trade Agreement [NAFTA] of 1994) seek to connect the first and third worlds, and others again (e.g., the Mercado Común del Sur or Southern Common Market [MERCOSUR] in South America, founded in 1991; or the West African Economic and Monetary Union [WAEMU], founded in 1994) have only third world members. Since 1990, the number of PTAs has exploded to embrace most of the world in overlapping regional and geopolitical networks. Geographic rules of origin, often of intimidating complexity, are developed to determine which products count as originating within a country, and thus as eligible for MFN and PTA preferences, and which do not (Traub-Werner, 2007). Free trade proponents are deeply divided on whether such arrangements represent steps toward, or deviations from, free trade.

Tariff rates, expressed as a percentage of the price of the import at the point of importation, typically escalate. Traded commodities are typically linked into a commodity chain, ranging from the raw materials (e.g., raw cotton) to semifinished commodities (e.g., textiles) and finally to finished products (e.g., the T-shirt on your back). Tariff escalation means that the further along a commodity is in this chain, the higher the tariffs are (Figure 16.12). Escalation is typically the result of domestic manufacturers' lobbying for protection against cheap imports. For third world countries seeking to break into first world markets, escalation makes it that much harder to move from primary to man-

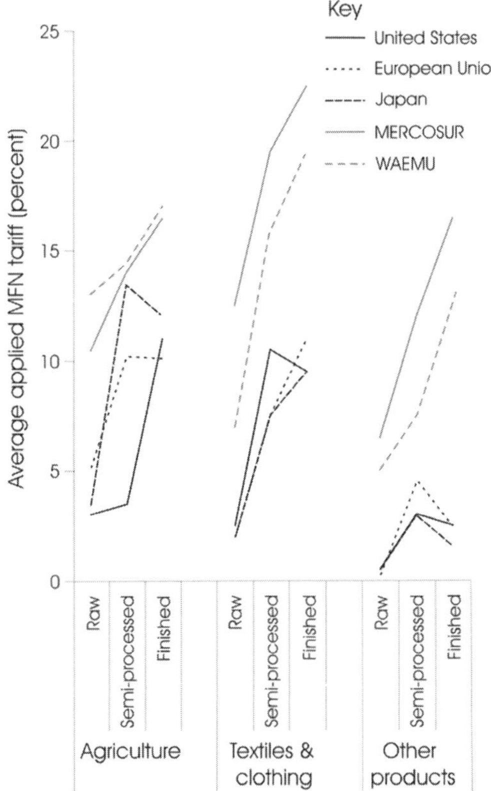

FIGURE 16.12. Tariff escalation for third world exports by importing country/region. MFN, most favored nation; MERCOSUR, Mercado Común del Sur (Southern Common Market); WAEMU, West African Economic and Monetary Union. *Source*: Data are from IMF and World Bank (2001).

ufactured imports. When such barriers are placed around a first world PTA, such as the EU, they create a Fortress Europe, which is hard to penetrate—unless you happen to be still closely connected to your European former colonizer. When Britain joined the EEC, it was required to eliminate preferential trading relations with current and former countries of the Commonwealth, causing considerable disruption. In 1993, Spain and France, which still own overseas territories that produce bananas (the Canary Islands, Guadeloupe, and Martinique), pushed through a regulation requiring that banana imports to the EU come from EU territories and former colonies in Africa, the Caribbean, and the Pacific. Tariffs in third world countries are often even higher, undermining south–south trade (see below).

In 1968, a generalized system of preferences (GSP) was agreed to, under third world pressure, which recognized the escalating nature of tariffs. Under the GSP, first world and second world nations provided preferential access to certain imports from selected third world nations, amounting in many cases to tariff reduction. The first country to implement this was the Soviet Union in 1965. In 2002, core industrialized nations granted GSP preferences, as did Russia, Belarus, Bulgaria, Estonia, and Turkey (UNCTAD, 2002b). GSP agreements tend to focus on manufactured imports, and are applied with the restriction that imports should not exceed certain quotas. This allows for controlled growth of imports beyond previously existing trade flows, but it is designed to protect domestic industry from undue "disruption" as a result of cheap imports. In 2001, 63% of imports to the "Quad" countries (the United States, Canada, Japan, and the EU) from the third world qualified for GSP, but only 42% received such preferential treatment (down from 51% in 1994) (UNCTAD, 2003b). GSPs are used like tariffs; coverage is more generous for imports that do not compete with well-organized domestic industries. For imports into the United States, for example, 67–100% of primary commodities receive GSP, whereas coverage for most manufactures is between 38% and 71% (except chemicals and precision machinery, for which coverage approaches 100%).

The WTO has sought to engineer a move from NTBs to tariffs (because the latter are seen as more "transparent"), but with little effect. NTBs take many forms, many of which are almost impossible to regulate (Table 16.1). Numerical quotas are particularly common, but there seems no limit to the human imagination when it comes to regulating trade. Observers are virtually unanimous that NTBs have been a greater

TABLE 16.1. Types of Nontariff Barriers (NTBs)

Type	Measures protecting domestic industry	Measures governing standards of production and consumption	Economic policies with indirect trade consequences
Quantitative restrictions	Import quotas; "voluntary" export constraints; embargoes; tariff quotas; discriminatory sourcing; labeling and packaging requirements	Banning of products (e.g., illegal drugs, environmentally unfriendly products)	State procurement policies requiring use of domestic contractors
Regulatory measures	Technical barriers: regulations; standards; certification and labeling requirements	Sanitary and phytosanitary measures: Product residues; specified treatment, testing, certification	State subsidies; trade facilitation offices; and state-owned production and transport
	Charges on imports and exports: surcharges; port taxes; storage taxes; prior deposits; licenses; etc.	Intellectual property issues	"Buy domestic" initiatives; domestic content restrictions
	Trade remedies: anti-dumping measures, countervailing duties	Labor or industrial standards: disallowing products produced using child labor or under exploitative working conditions, etc.	"Strategic" trade restrictions
	Customs regulations: formalities; rules of origin; inspection; licensing	Safeguard measures	Environmental and labor regulations; industrial policy

Source: Based on Morton and Tulloch (1977) and Organization for Economic Cooperation and Development (OECD, 2005).

barrier to trade than tariffs have been since the mid-1970s, and research consistently shows that they also escalate (cf. Colman & Nixson, 1986). Thirty percent of internationally traded commodities were subject to quantitative restrictions in the 1980s. There is a tendency to discriminate against third world imports. Of the 135 major NTBs known to GATT in 1987, 64 were directed against developing nations, particularly major exporters—with 23 directed against South Korea alone, the most successful third world competitor in the area of manufacturing (Euromonitor, 1989: Table 2.3). Bora, Kuwahara, and Laird (2002), examining just three kinds of NTBs from Table 16.1 (quotas, charges, and trade remedies), estimated that the Quad countries imposed NTBs in 2000 on some 42% of agricultural imports from the third world, and 17% of manufactures, but just 7% of minerals and fuels.

Reflect, for a moment, on the wide range of categories included in Table 16.1. These include not only obviously arbitrary restrictions, but also almost any attempt by the state to shape production and trade. Even regulations to promote environmental or workers' welfare can be, and are, appealed to the WTO as examples of "protectionism." This was why first world farmers and workers joined the 1999 anti-WTO protests in Seattle. For neoliberals, all NTBs should be eliminated, because all state "interference" in the market is presumed to be socially undesirable as the market can solve all problems. In their view, it makes sense for WTO procedures to extend "behind the border" to shape local policies and revisit local ethics (e.g., that whales should, or should not, be hunted for food—see sidebar: "The WTO behind the Border"). Does this make sense?

NTBs applied to third world imports are more frequently applied against manufactured imports that are seen as threatening domestic industry—clothing, processed food, electrical equipment, and textiles (Morton and Tulloch, 1977: 178). (For some creative applications of NTBs, see sidebar: "The WTO, Intellectual Property, and Patenting Plants.") Yet they can also hurt third world primary commodity producers and exports. Ongoing domestic agricultural subsidies in North America, Japan, and the EU ($231 billion in U.S. dollars, averaging 31% of production costs, in the Organization for Economic Cooperation and Development [OECD] in 2001; Lankes, 2002) have become a lightning rod in WTO negotiations. For example, they have driven west African cotton farmers into bankruptcy, because these farmers are unable to compete with their better-paid first world counterparts.

The use of regulatory controls tends to disadvantage third world nations, which are less well equipped to learn about such regulations in a timely manner, to adapt exports rapidly to satisfy such restrictions, or to negotiate effectively with the importing nations in cases of disagreement about the application of regulations. The EU, for example, has spent much energy designing product guidelines and quality measures that all its members adhere to; as a result, domestic regulatory agencies automatically exempt all intra-EU trade from inspection. Smaller exporters are more disadvantaged than the larger exporters. Quotas tend to take current trading patterns as their starting point, meaning that larger exporters get bigger quotas. But economically influential countries also simply have more bargaining power. For example, the Multi-Fibre Arrangement, restricting Chinese textile exports and creating space for textile exports from Central America, the Caribbean, and Africa, was terminated in January 2005—creating enormous potential for lower-wage Chinese firms. In addition, smaller exporters find regulatory measures even more difficult to

The WTO behind the Border

- *Case 1*: In 1996, Massachusetts enacted a law barring companies that do business with the brutal military regime in Myanmar from bidding for large public contracts in Massachusetts. The EU argued that under WTO rules, the Massachusetts restriction is unfair "to the trade and investment community," and that it breaches current WTO rules on government procurement. Massachusetts questioned whether doing business with a brutal military regime is fair. Similar economic sanctions had been used in the antiapartheid movement in the United States in the 1980s and have been credited for hastening the transition to democracy in South Africa.

  The existence of this WTO challenge affected other efforts to use economic sanctions to uphold human rights. Hoping to avoid trouble in the WTO, in 1998 the Clinton administration actively lobbied the Maryland state legislature to stop the adoption of a selective purchasing law against Nigeria. The proposal subsequently lost by one vote.

- *Case 2*: India's law excluded plants and animals from patenting, in order to maintain local control over these life forms. This helps maintain low prices for some pharmaceuticals and legitimates local healing practices. The WTO stipulated, however, that "developing" countries must move toward allowing foreign companies the right to patent local plant varieties. The United States complained to the WTO that India had violated its obligations by not moving fast enough toward compliance. The WTO agreed, forcing India to grant market monopolies to corporations on the basis of patents given by other countries.

Source: Adapted from Mander and Barker (1999). Copyright 1999 by the International Forum on Globalization. Adapted by permission.

The WTO, Intellectual Property, and Patenting Plants

The "Uruguay round" of GATT negotiations not only created the WTO; for the first time, it broadened the scope of multilateral trading agreements to include rules regulating Trade-Related Aspects of Intellectual Property Rights (TRIPS). Western corporations, concerned that they were losing sales and royalties to companies in third world countries with weak patent systems, lobbied for and largely drafted the provisions of TRIPS. This agreement requires all signatory nations to implement a specified minimum standard of law protecting intellectual property rights (IPRs), as well as effective enforcement mechanisms. For example, patent protection must be available for inventions for at least 20 years. Countries that do not follow WTO rules can be brought before WTO dispute resolution panels and are subject to trade sanctions if they do not come into compliance.

The economic rationale for IPRs is that producers of new knowledge should be rewarded, and that this should be done by giving these producers a short-term monopoly over the use of their innovations. The notion of IPRs is a cultural product of Anglo-Saxon thinking and is not universally shared around the world. This is important to note because knowledge, in contrast to physical things, is not consumed when it is shared; rather, it is increased and enriched as the various users interact, rework it, and spread it farther. This collaborative and expansive aspect of knowledge and innovation, which complicates the very notion of intellectual property, is not recognized in the TRIPS agreement. If TRIPS covered only things such as pirating software, movies, and designer clothes, this absence would not be of much concern. But TRIPS also significantly extends the scope of IPRs to living organisms. Nations must provide patents for microorganisms, and plant varieties must be protectable by patents or by a special system that protects breeders' rights. Thus, by privatizing knowledge and restricting the free sharing of plant varieties, "the WTO legal regime will privatize biotech discoveries, mak[ing] them available only if large profits are made—and can threaten biodiversity by promoting (and paying for, valuing) monoculture" (Mushita and Thompson, 2002: 74).

In 1992, the U.S. Patent and Trademark Office granted a U.S. company (W. R. Grace) a patent on all forms of transgenetic cotton, and the European Patent Office granted the same company a patent on genetically transformed soybeans. Such all-embracing patents effectively allow individual corporations ownership over all genetic engineering of these plants. This is equivalent to granting one company the exclusive right to all innovations in, say, minivans. It effectively prevents farmers from pursuing traditional practices of adapting plants for their environment, or even from keeping seeds from entire plant species, without compensating the corporation that owns the patent. However, companies must access biodiversity to produce their new plant varieties. This biodiversity has been developed and nourished by third world farmers operating under the shared and collaborative approach to knowledge. It is their collective and freely shared work that is taken without compensation, turned into corporate intellectual property, and sold back to them at monopoly prices. Often termed "biopiracy," this is merely the most recent step in a scramble, extending back to colonial times, by first world governments and entrepreneurs to gain control over the commercial development of plants and animals found in third world nations and traditionally utilized by their inhabitants (Juma, 1989).

Grassroots struggles against such biopiracy are gaining force. For example, Anupreeta Das (2006) reports:

> India's centuries-old traditional knowledge, preserved and orally passed down through generations of households, is now going digital. Over the coming months, India will unveil a first-of-its-kind encyclopedia of 30 million pages, containing thousands of herbal remedies and eventually everything from indigenous construction techniques to yoga exercises. The project represents a 21st-century approach to safeguarding intellectual property of the ancient variety. The Traditional Knowledge Digital Library . . . aims to prevent foreign entrepreneurs from claiming Indian lore as novel, and thus patenting it.

deal with. Taken together, NTBs show the same tendencies as tariff barriers to increase the difficulties faced by third world exporters seeking first world markets (particularly those attempting to specialize in and export manufactured goods), and, within the third world, to favor those countries that already export manufactures. Barriers to trade with the first world represent an incentive to increased trade among third world countries, however, and this might help reduce the degree to which current trade patterns are oriented toward the first world (absent "beggar thy neighbor" strategies within the third world).

CHALLENGING THE TRADE REGIME

The difficulties faced by third world nations in trading with the first and second worlds, as discussed above, have led to many suggestions about how to rethink third world trade, in ways that go beyond the interventions described above. These alternatives seek to promote alternative economic practices to the production and exchange of commodities for profit, but also to shift the geography of trade away from being seen as an exchange among nation states.

One is that that trade among third world nations (south–south trade; Nyrere, 1983) should be expanded. Within south and east Asia, such expansion has occurred: Between 1960 and 2002, south–south trade within this region expanded from 1.8% to 8.3% of world trade. Indeed, this has become the most intense regional trading network in the world, other than the EU. Yet the global share of other south–south trade has grown more slowly (from 3.5% in 1960 to 4% in 1993, but to only 5.2% in 2002), and the share of south–south trade outside south and east Asia—that is, among west Asian, African, and Latin American countries—has actually fallen (from 2.5% in 1960 to 2.1% in 2002). At the same time, south–south trade has more than doubled as a proportion of all exports from third world countries, from 17% to 39%.

Certainly, third world countries have been reluctant to reduce south–south trade barriers, or to take into account the deleterious effects of trade on other third world nations. Tariffs are higher on average (Figure 16.12), and OPEC-led oil price increases in the 1970s (Chapter 18) were far more deleterious for third world than for first world nations (although OPEC has set up development funds setting aside a percentage of oil income to be used for development aid in the third world).

Beyond the lack of cooperation, however, a fundamental difficulty in promoting south–south trade is that third world nations, particularly those that are geographical neighbors, tend to occupy a similar positionality in the global economy. Many attempts have been made to create PTAs linking third world nations, to overcome the endemic problem of small, low-wage domestic markets. These have included the East African Community, the Central American Common Market, the Economic Community of West African States, and the Association of Southeast Asian Nations (ASEAN). Only ASEAN has met with substantial success, in large part because its members have shifted from primary to manufactured products. In other south–south PTAs, as for much south–south trade outside south and east Asia, countries tend to trade very similar products and are unable to provide among themselves the manufactured inputs that they need. Another way of putting this is to say that although primary commodities may be a comparative advantage for trade with the first world, this is not adequate for the creation of a coherent third world trading bloc.

The transition to manufactured exports in south and east Asia, and selected NICs elsewhere, has proven somewhat advantageous for these countries, but this may not generalize to south–south trade in general. South–south trade of primary commodities for manufactures risks reproducing the inequities that we have discussed for first world–third world trade. When some third world nations (the NICs) become the source of manufactured commodities for other third world nations, then there is the danger that the gains from trade will again be distributed among trading partners in such a way as to benefit NICs, relative to third world nations that continue to concentrate on exporting primary products. A tripartite world trade hierarchy may be emerging: industrialized core countries with skilled manufacturing labor forces on top, semiperipheral industrializing but often low-wage-oriented countries in the middle, and peripheral and primary commodity exporting countries at the bottom. We show in Chapter 17 that countries in the middle level of this hierarchy are following strategies earlier pioneered by the United States, Japan, and Germany of state-led development rather than free trade.

In short, south–south trade may well not be the panacea for resolving difficulties that stem from confronting the free trade doctrine with the reality of geographical inequality shaped by long-term geopolitical processes. An interesting new south–south arrangement that also seeks to challenge free trade is the Bolivaran Alternative for the Americas (ALBA), connecting Venezuela, Cuba, and Bolivia. ALBA seeks to promote not only south–south exchange, but exchange based on national needs rather than profits. Other alternatives include fair trade, barter, and local exchange trading systems (LETS).

Fair trade initiatives seek to ensure that third world producers get fairer compensation for the commodities they produce and export than that provided through the declining terms of international trade. Fair trade constructs networks linking small producers in diverse localities across the third world with retailers and consumers in the first world who are willing to pay more in the name of free trade. Fair trade networks typically purchase directly from producers; seek to foster long-term trading relations; encourage cooperatives and environmentally responsible producers; and offer agreed-upon minimum prices, together with technical assistance and market information (Barratt-Brown, 1993; Nicholls and Opal, 2005). The third world producers in these networks typically grow agricultural products (coffee, tea, cocoa, bananas, cotton). Fair trade has boomed into its own industry, tapping into first world consumer activism; is supported by a variety of NGOs; and has shifted from specialty and alternative retailers to become an option (alongside organic agriculture) in many supermarket chains. Fair trade sales increased almost five-fold between 1998 and 2005, to $1.6 million U.S. dollars worldwide (Raynolds and Long, 2005). At the same time, debates have emerged about the conditions under which commodities can be classified and labeled as fair trade products, and about the effectiveness of such monitoring and labeling systems. In the process, fair trade is increasingly presented as simply a market niche of international commodity trade, another choice for consumers preferring its products—what some might call "feel-good consumerism."

Barter is the direct reciprocal exchange of goods and services, as when a doctor takes food in return for medical advice. Barter trade does not involve money, and thus often remains unreported in accounting schemes measuring capitalist exchange, such as the gross domestic product (GDP). Typically, barter is constructed as something that occurs largely in the third world—a "traditional" means of exchange gradually being superseded by the "true" commodity exchange for money that typifies a "developed" capitalist society. Yet barter is common in the first world also (think of swap meets, household labor, eBay, craigslist, or barn raising). Barter is also constructed as local exchange, and thus as inefficient in a globalized world. Yet big firms also engage in barter—calling it "reciprocal trade"—which accounts for some 15% of international trade ($843 billion in U.S. dollars; *www.irta.com/ReciprocalTradeStatistics.aspx*).

LETS seek both to substitute exchange within local communities for long-distance trade, and to provide alternatives to regular commodity exchange for money through the development and use of local currencies (e.g., locally printed paper notes exchangeable for an hour of labor) for exchange. LETS are envisaged as making communities more sustainable by reducing their dependence on trade with the outside world. Local currencies also foster alternatives to the production and exchange of commodities for profit, because such credits can only be used for local exchange, and no interest can be earned. They enable even the poorest to accumulate credits and participate in exchange, because anyone can offer labor, skill, and knowledge in return for credits in the local currency. LETS have flourished since Ithaca, New York introduced its system in 1989, spreading rapidly throughout local communities in the first world; however, very few exist in the third world, and these are found mostly in Latin America. Yet the LETS principle of gaining local credit in return for contributing to the community has deep historical roots and remains central to informal economic activities in the third world (Chapter 19; see also Chapter 24 sidebar, "Buddhist Economics").

CONCLUSIONS

It is clear that first world nations benefit from third world countries specializing in the export of primary commodities, as can be seen in the changing terms of trade. Agricultural commodities and even minerals show low price elasticity, and improvements in manufacturing productivity and transportation technologies have primarily benefited the first world and its workers. There is little basis for regional cooperation among third world nations: They produce very similar commodities; their trade constitutes just a small part of world trade; they are often dependent on just a few exports to a few countries; and their concerns are frequently marginalized in bilateral and multilateral trade agreements. There have been major attempts to bring the world closer to the ideals of free trade theory, with agreements to eliminate or reduce tariffs and NTBs; these have been reinforced by the WTO, which has the power to enforce such agreements. Yet the barriers that remain continue to burden third world countries disproportionately, and the evidence suggests that if free trade were possible, third world nations would continue to suffer from inequities. Their specialization in primary commodities and low-wage assembly work, combined with their relative situation within the global economy, means that they occupy a disadvantaged position on the uneven playing field of international trade.

South–south trade may not hold out great possibilities for improving this situation. The similar situation of many third world nations in the global economy, and the likelihood that more industrial third world nations may benefit disproportionately from south–south trade, together may reproduce within the third world (among both countries and regions) the kinds of differences and inequalities between the first and third worlds that we have discussed in the bulk of this chapter (Nyrere, 1983). Yet the alternative is not to abandon trade and exchange; many alternative trading practices and geographies are being explored in and beyond the third world.

NOTES

1. We are grateful to Jun Zhang, Todd Federenko, and John Benson for their help in collecting the data on which the following sections are based.

2. John Spraos (1983) developed another measure, the "employment-corrected double factorial terms of trade," to take account of changes in both productivity and employment. For agricultural products, this decreased steadily between 1960 and 1978; for minerals (excluding fuels), it showed no overall upward or downward trend. We have not been able to update these figures.

17 Peripheral Industrialization

Paths and Strategies

Chapter 16 has shown the difficulties faced by third world countries that attempt to exploit comparative advantages in primary commodities in order to speed up economic growth and reduce disparities in wealth between themselves and first world nations. However, we have also seen that comparative advantages are not fixed, but can be fundamentally reconstructed through actions taken both within and outside those nations. This offers a way out of the trap of specializing in primary commodities that does not entail international economic isolation. Many third world nations have experienced at best a limited shift of employment into industrial activities, meaning that most third world residents have experienced little change in their role in the global spatial division of labor since 1960. Substantial industrialization has occurred in a few countries, however. Refusing to accept historically constructed comparative advantages, as laid down by ruling market prices, these "newly industrializing countries" (NICs) have taken concerted action to create competitive advantages in certain industrial commodities.

This alternative requires action to restructure the relative profitability of different economic sectors to favor those with greater possibilities of enhancing economic growth—typically seeking to engineer a shift from primary commodities to manufacturing (and services). Third world governments intuitively grasped this before the fungibility of comparative advantage gained the attention of the "new" trade theorists. Industrialization policies, initiated by the state and national elites, have been persistent and important aspects of state economic development and growth strategies in the third world. Taking the historical experience of first or second world nations as a model, third world governments have tried various ways of altering domestic conditions of comparative advantage. There is no country where a convincing argument can be made that the state's role was minimal.

The term "industrialization" can be misleading, however, since it can refer to such activities as the processing of raw materials, the increased use of capital equipment in agriculture, construction activities, services, and utilities. Although all of these are important economic activities, discussion of industrialization in the third world really refers to the ability of third world nations to manufacture industrial goods domestically, for sale at home or abroad (steel, machinery, transportation equipment, textiles, refrigerators, paper clips, etc.). This particular subset of activities, which we associate with the "industrial revolution," is often referred to as "manufacturing" (also an ambiguous term). Whenever possible, in this chapter we examine manufacturing rather than industrialization, although at times we resort to "industrialization" in the broader sense for the simple reason that more specific information is missing.

It is important to note the gendered nature of the terms "industrialization" and "manufacturing." On the one hand, these have come to be dominated by male labor forces—notwithstanding the importance of a female workforce in certain sectors, places, and times (e.g., the clothing industry; "Rosie the Riveter" in the United States during World War II; export-processing zones [EPZs] today). Although women's presence in these sites is critical, the politics of masculinity and femininity also shapes more general discourses about and attitudes toward industry and manufacturing. The overlapping binaries of global–local and masculine–feminine also carry across into a dichotomous construction of industrialized–nonindustrialized (manufacturing–nonmanufacturing). In these overlapping binaries, the nonindustrialized (or less industrialized) sector, city, region, or country becomes constructed as dependent—as the victim and the one to be uplifted (empowered, emancipated) by that which is more industrialized, independent, and powerful (Nagar, Lawson, McDowell, and Hanson, 2002; Roberts, 2004). This construction acquires particular dominance once industrialization is represented as the handmaiden of development, and once industrial transnational corporations (TNCs) are seen as the vehicle for globalizing manufacturing (Chapter 20).

We first examine the growth of manufacturing in the world economy, to put third world experiences in perspective. We then examine the historical experiences of the first and second world countries as they industrialized, and the various approaches tried by third world nations. We are particularly interested in asking whether there is some magic formula for industrialization—a foolproof recipe for success—and whether we can expect all third world nations to emulate such often-cited success stories as South Korea (or the United States).

CHANGES IN THE POSTWAR GLOBAL GEOGRAPHY OF MANUFACTURING

Since 1960, there has been a steady but certainly not spectacular increase in the global share of manufacturing taking place in the third world, as measured by the United Nations and the World Bank. The economic importance of manufacturing to a country is usually measured by the "value added" during the manufacturing process (manufacturing value added, or MVA), defined as the difference between the cost of nonlabor inputs and the cost of the final product. This difference comprises wages, profits, rents, interest payments, and net taxes, together representing the actual increase in market value during the process of manufacturing process.

Between 1960 and 1975, the largest absolute increase in the share of manufacturing value occurred in the second world countries of state socialism, which were pursuing evidently successful economic policies to stimulate the production of capital goods (Figure 17.1). The third world was the fastest-growing region in percentage terms (44% increase), but these percentages were calculated on a very small base. Since 1975, the percentage of world MVA in the first world has slightly increased (shifting from Europe to Japan). The world's share of manufacturing in the (former) Soviet second world imploded after 1990, falling from 18% to just 6%. This decline was matched by significant increases in third world manufacturing, entirely concentrated in south and

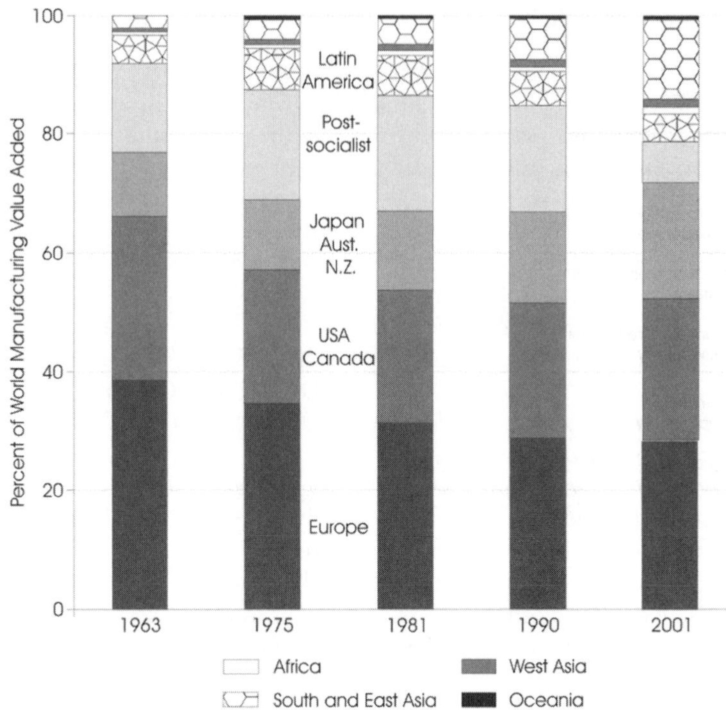

FIGURE 17.1. World shares of manufacturing production, 1963–2001. *Sources:* Data for 1963 are from United Nations Industrial Development Organization (UNIDO, 1985); data for 1975–1990 are from UNIDO (1992); data for 2001 are from World Bank (2008).

east Asia; Latin American NICs have lost world share, and there remains little manufacturing elsewhere.

Yet even by the early 1990s, the opportunity to obtain work in the manufacturing sector was still very limited for a third world resident. As Figure 17.2 shows, most third world nations were still distinguished from the first and second worlds by their low proportion of workers in industry (broadly defined). Furthermore, with population growth, 10-fold discrepancies in MVA per capita persist between most third world nations and the first world (Figure 17.3).

Distribution of Manufacturing within the Third World

The very uneven geographical distribution of manufacturing is even more stark at the country scale (Figure 17.3). MVA per capita ranges from over $4,800 in Singapore (ninth highest in the world) to just $3.80 in the Democratic Republic of the Congo. A very few third world nations have captured the lion's share of peripheral manufacturing, with 60% in just 10 countries and one-third in China and South Korea alone. Table 17.1 shows how membership in this elite group has changed significantly, shifting from Latin America toward east Asia. Half of the six Latin American nations in the top 10 in 1963 had disappeared by 1992, whereas the number of south and east Asian nations had tripled, from two to six. The only other nation in the top 10 since 1992 is Turkey, and there are no African members at all.[1] Note that total MVA depends on the size of an economy, biasing this list toward larger third world countries. On a per capita basis,

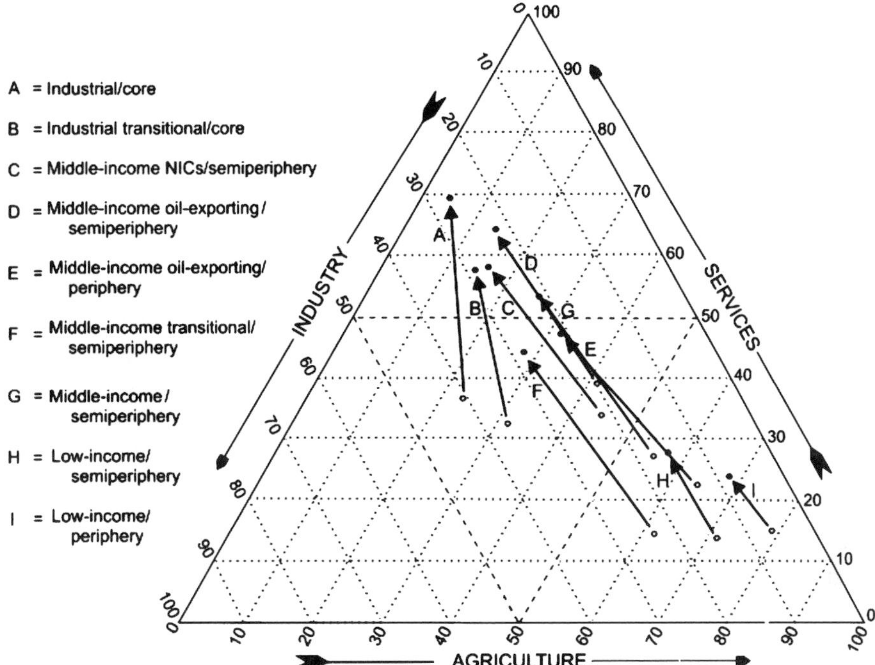

FIGURE 17.2. Regional trends in the division of labor, 1960–2001. *Sources:* Data for 1960 are from the International Labour Organization (ILO, 1977); the most recent data (for years between 1997 and 2001) are from the ILO (2003).

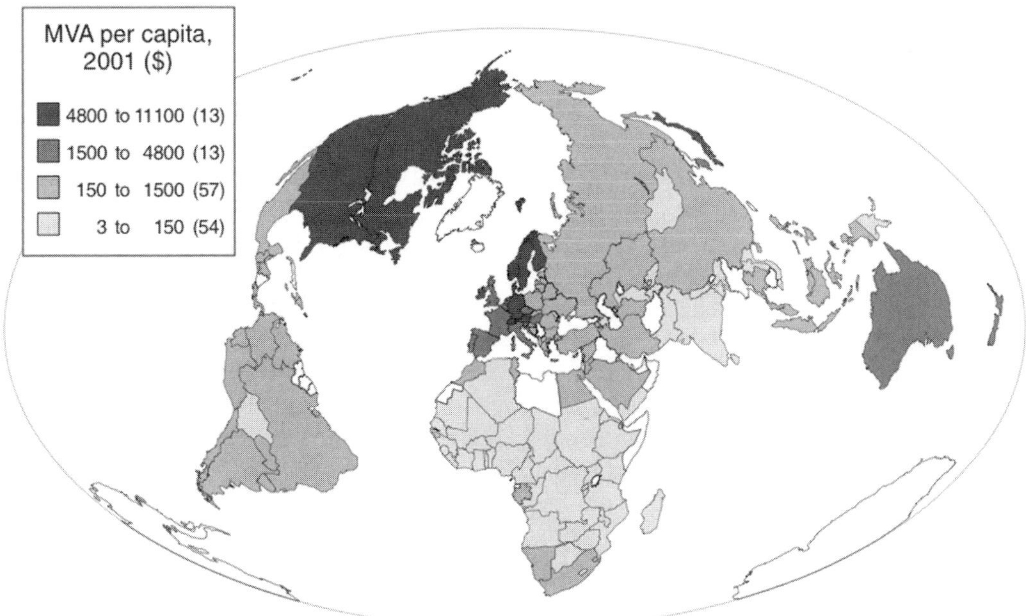

FIGURE 17.3. The global distribution of MVA per capita, 2001. *Source:* Data are from World Bank (2003).

the leading third world countries in 1992 included Singapore and Hong Kong, alongside South Korea, Mexico, and Argentina.

The term "NICs" was coined to describe those third world nations showing significant success in developing a globally competitive manufacturing sector. There is no universal agreement as to which nations are NICs. Almost every definition includes South Korea, Hong Kong, Taiwan, and Singapore, Brazil and Mexico, and now China and India. This group includes small nations with a proportionately large manufacturing sector (Singapore); those whose large size makes their contribution to global manufacturing significant, despite the small proportion of their economy in manufacturing (India); those that have always had to rely on manufacturing because of a limited resource base (the city states of Hong Kong and Singapore); and those that have made a spectacular transition from specialization in agriculture to specialization in manufacturing (South Korea and Taiwan). It is thus a heterogeneous club, and one whose membership fluctuates with the changing industrial fortunes of its more marginal members. Yet NICs are the obvious examples to focus on as we attempt to understand the dynamics of industrialization in the third world.

Manufacturing and Services

One difficulty in discussing manufacturing is how to distinguish it from service activities (Sayer and Walker, 1992; Walker, 1985). Services are conventionally separated from manufacturing, because a service is often not a tangible good. Most services cannot be taken away and consumed at the customer's leisure, but constitute human activities whose benefits must be consumed at the point and time of production. Yet the distinction is problematic: Services frequently are also commodities produced under specific working conditions and sold for a profit, and in many cases they include a tangible product (such as a haircut, a legal contract, or a bowl of soup). Increasingly, services can also be provided at a distance. Among the fastest-growing nonagricultural activities in India are "call centers"; these employ some 200,000 young Indian women and men who either answer the phone when you call a customer service hot line, or place a sales call to you. They are trained to speak English in your dialect, may work under assumed names that do not sound foreign, and are armed with up-to-date information about where you live in case you decide to chat with them. It is often hard to tell that such calls connect you with the far side of the world (where lower wages more than compensate for long-distance phone rates). Furthermore, as we have discussed in Chapter 16, international trade in services is increasingly discussed alongside manufacturing. In short, the distinction between services and manufacturing is at best fuzzy.

"Informal" Manufacturing

The global statistics cited above are based on a particular definition of manufacturing—one that follows the conventional representation of industrialization in the first world: factories employing manufacturing workers and producing goods to be sold in regular markets, for which industrial statistics are readily collected. Any visitor to Brazil, India, Indonesia, or Mali would be struck, however, by the numerous manufacturing activities that go on in tiny shops or in public spaces—activities that surely are inadequately represented in such statistics. Walking down the commercial streets of Jakarta, one sees furniture makers, textile weavers, moped and bicycle repairers, wood carvers, and metalworkers making a variety of manufactured goods. In many senses, these activities are more evident in the landscape than are the larger factories hidden in industrial estates.

Some of this work no doubt is counted in national statistics, but it is hard to estimate exactly how much. Much is defined as belonging to the "informal sector," even though it is still producing a manufactured commodity, because the product is bartered or purchased outside usual market channels and thus not subject to state supervision, record collection, and taxation. "Informal" manufacturing (and retail) activities not only are represented as a marginal economic category—as imperfect by comparison to formal manufacturing—but also are gendered, raced, and classed as the domain of those who need help to be brought into the international development project. They are often characterized as occupying a liminal positionality between rural peasant livelihoods and an urban industrial and service workforce—a space occupied by circuits connecting urban and rural livelihood strategies, whose elimination would indicate the completion of capitalist development.

In the 1980s, much attention was paid to the activities of the large and growing informal manufacturing and service sectors in third world nations. Such "black market" activities are also present to an increasing degree in the first world (the informal sector in Italy is said to be worth 20% of the gross domestic product [GDP]; think also of drug dealers in the United States). They were prevalent under state socialism and remain an important part of everyday life in post-socialist societies. Yet their presence in the third world has received particular notice. In one view, they have been regarded as parasitic on the formal economy: They are seen as siphoning off nontaxable revenues, as undermining proper manufacturing activities, and as symptomatic of a dualism that reflects an incomplete modernization of third world societies (see Chapter 4). More recently, a more positive developmentalist interpretation has emerged, emphasizing the positive contributions of the informal sector to capitalist industrialization. In this view, informal activities exemplify the entrepreneurial talent and potential of individuals who create opportunities out of seemingly impossible economic circumstances in third world slums (Maloney, 2004). Informal activities are regarded also as a source of cheap goods and services, which help lower living costs and production costs in the formal sector. Note, however, that in most of these discussions, unpaid (mostly female) household work—which clearly also belongs to the informal sector—has received little

TABLE 17.1. The 10 Largest Third World Manufacturing Nations (% Third World MVA), 1963–2001

Country	1963	1975	1981	1992	2001
China				18.0	22.2
South Korea	—	2.9	4.9	12.0	10.3
Brazil	19.6	22.7	22.7	14.5	8.0
India	13.5	9.1	8.6	5.6	4.1
Mexico	10.7	12.4	13.9	10.4	4.1
Thailand	—	—	—	4.8	3.1
Indonesia	—	—	2.8	4.0	3.1
Argentina	9.0	8.4	4.9	8.0	2.3
Turkey	3.4	4.2	3.7	3.2	1.9
Malaysia	—	—	—	—	1.8
Iran	—	2.1	—	2.4	—
Philippines	2.8	2.5	2.6	—	—
Hong Kong	—	—	2.3	—	—
Venezuela	3.8	3.1	2.5	—	—
Peru	2.8	2.3	—	—	—
Chile	2.4	—	—	—	—
Egypt	2.1	—	—	—	—
Top 10	70.1	70.0	68.6	83.9	59.1

Note. Table includes all third world countries ranked in the top 10 at least once. Order in table is according to the size of MVA in 1992. No data are available for China before 1992, or for Taiwan, whose manufacturing sector is approximately as large as that of South Korea. — means not in top 10 for that year.

Sources: Data for 1963–1981 are from UNIDO (1985); data for 1992 are from World Bank (1994: Table 3); data for 2002 are from World Bank (2008).

attention in either the third or the first world, even though it absorbs up to half of society's labor time.

There is ambivalence about the informal sector, which reflects contrasting perspectives on development. Those endorsing development and neoliberal globalization evaluate the informal sector in terms of whether it helps or hinders capitalist economic growth. In this view, the informal sector is a residue of precapitalist practices that will eventually be replaced by "real" capitalist firms—notwithstanding its potential to catalyze the transition to a formal capitalist economy. Note, however, that such a perspective relies on a false dualism, which constructs the informal sector as a distinctive feature of the third world that is absent in the first world. Those critical of such perspectives from the core see the informal sector as a repository of capitalist and noncapitalist production practices, existing to a greater or lesser extent in all parts of the world. On the one hand, this suggests that the informal sector fills various niches in the capitalist economy by flexibly providing low-cost goods and services, albeit often involving what might be considered exploitative and/or illegal practices. Second, some see the informal sector as a starting place in the search for alternative approaches to manufacturing. In this view, although unpleasant practices occur within the informal sector, it reproduces preexisting socially embedded noncapitalist practices (e.g., nonmarket and cooperative production; forms of Islamic and Buddhist economic practice), and it therefore provides a space within which new alternatives can be tried out in the search for alternatives to first-world-style capitalism (Gibson-Graham, 1996, 2006).

Notwithstanding the importance of the informal sector, especially for average families in third world nations, state industrialization policies have focused on the formal, industrial sector. We examine the evolution of such policies, in order both to analyze the successes and failures of peripheral industrialization, and to provide a case study of state involvement in economic development.

PATHS TO FIRST AND SECOND WORLD INDUSTRIALIZATION

In the 1950s, when industrialization policies began to be implemented in many of the NICs, third world nations shared a similarly marginal positionality in the world economy. The first world nations were focusing on postwar reconstruction; in particular, the United States was attempting to reconstruct economic links between Allied and Axis powers in Europe and east Asia in the face of the impending Cold War. Similarly, the Soviet Union was engaged in constructing the second world trade bloc that became known as the Council for Mutual Economic Assistance, or COMECON (an agreement coordinating production and trade among the communist countries of eastern Europe, focused on the Soviet Union). Little attention was devoted to third world development (indeed, in many cases independence movements were being opposed by industrial powers; see Chapter 15), and even less money was directed toward it. In 1946 $1 billion was allocated to European borrowers, whereas lending through the U.S. Export–Import Bank to Latin America declined from an average of $70 million a year during the war to $30 million (Ballance and Sinclair, 1983: 21). Could industrial policy offer a way to transform this marginal positionality?

The industrialization experiences of the industrial nations represented the only examples for third world nations to draw on, and they are worth some attention because they are often misrepresented. The success of the industrial revolution in Europe in the 19th century, and the heavy emphasis on rebuilding the industrial base in Europe and Japan in the postwar years, both suggested successful industrialization paths for third world nations to emulate. The two most obvious parallels to the situation faced by the third world were the cases of the United

States and Germany in the 19th century. Like the third world today, they were once much less industrialized than Britain, which represented the core of the global economy at that time. They were able to overcome this advantage, however, overtaking Britain between 1870 and 1913 in terms of industrial production, and becoming larger exporters of manufacturing by 1957 (Figure 17.4). Japan provides a similar, more recent success story.

We have seen one example of how Britain manipulated prices and trade to advance its industrial production—its manipulation of comparative advantage in order to undermine competition from Indian cotton textiles (see Chapter 15). State intervention in the domestic sphere was also central to the

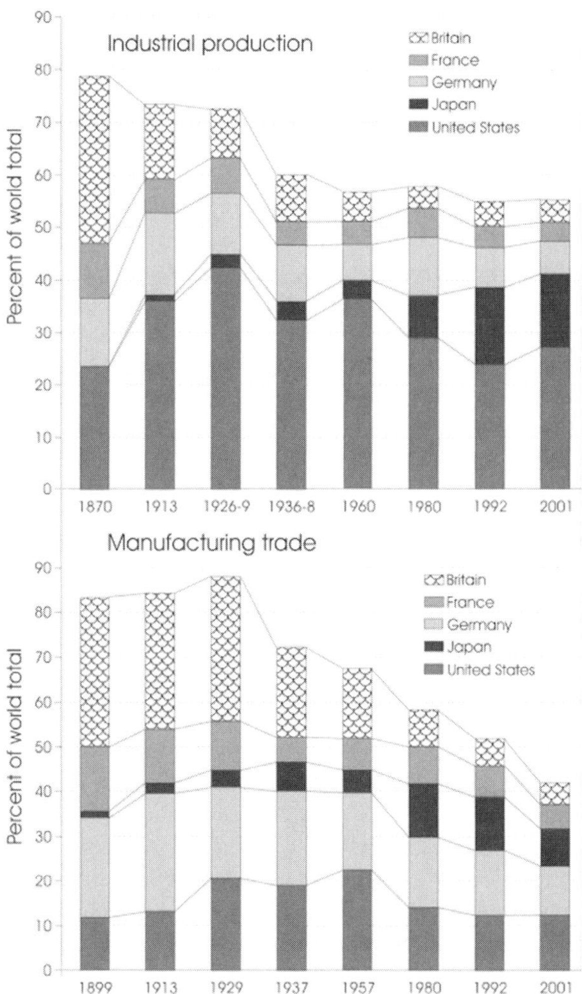

FIGURE 17.4. World leadership in industrial production and manufacturing trade, 1870–2001. *Sources:* In A, data for 1870–1938 are from Dicken (1992), who used data from Hilgert (1945); data for 1960–1992 are from World Bank (1994), and for 2001 from World Bank (2003: Table 4.2). In B, data for 1899–1980 are from Dosi, Pavitt, and Soete (1990: Table 3.6); data for 1992 are from UNCTAD (1994a: Tables 4.1, A.13), and for 2001 from UNCTAD (2003a: Tables 3.2.1A and 4.1A). *Note.* Data for 1930–1935 in A and for 1930–1936 in B are not included because of the distorting effect of the Great Depression.

ability of Germany and the United States to overtake Britain as industrial nations. Such policies created trade barriers to protect and nurse domestic industry until it became internationally competitive, after which time the gospel of free trade was adopted (Chang, 2002). Japan also consistently limited access to its markets by foreign importers in key industries, and ironically has been roundly criticized for doing this by Americans and Europeans in recent years. NICs have also deployed this approach, now known as "import substitution industrialization" (ISI; see below and Chapter 20), and they too have been criticized widely by established first world industrial powers for doing so.

State-led coordination of industrialization also includes actions to ensure the existence of markets for the commodities produced in the manufacturing sector. Although it is often claimed that the market takes care of coordinating demand and supply, and needs no help from the state, in fact most industrialization paths have relied heavily on state policies for coordinating and regulating supply and demand—policies that structure the incentives to which firms respond. In part, such policies address the degree to which markets are to be sought at home or abroad; as we describe later, this has been a key difference in postwar third world industrialization policies. In part, they address which kinds of domestic markets to emphasize: consumer demand, or the demand for "capital goods" (goods that are purchased primarily by other firms). It is instructive to compare the strategies followed in the first and second worlds after 1945. Both groups of nations emphasized industrialization to serve domestic markets, but first world nations placed more emphasis on consumer goods, whereas second world nations focused on capital goods.

First World Fordism and Thereafter

As discussed in Chapter 4, the first world prior to the mid-1970s was characterized as a "virtuous cycle" of wealth creation and economic growth developed under Keynesian policies of economic management of national demand and supply. To recall, "Fordism," as such policies have been termed, encouraged national economic growth through the mass production of consumer goods, complemented by increasing purchasing power (Lipietz, 1987). The latter was necessary to ensure that there was enough demand to purchase the consumer goods manufacturers produced. In the United States, for example, the federal government provided subsidies for the construction of housing and the spread of suburbanization, triggering demand for the construction industry, automobiles, and household appliances (Walker, 1981). In Europe, the increasing scope of the welfare state ensured that even the least well off could consume at comfortable levels, at least by world standards. In both places, increased availability of consumer credit also stimulated consumption. State spending in the defense industry, fueled by the Cold War and its warmer outbreaks in Korea and Vietnam, also created demand for industries in the military–industrial sector (Markusen, Hall, Campbell, and Dietrick, 1991). The 1950s and 1960s were indeed a period of great technical progress in mass production, enabling first world (usually male) blue-collar workers to be paid higher wages and preventing deficit spending from becoming too extreme.

The increasingly low cost of primary products imported from the third world, relative to the price of manufactures, kept production costs low and made room for wage increases. After 1973, however, real wages and consumer purchasing power stagnated and then declined, while unemployment increased. State policies shifted as well, from supporting consumption and the welfare state to adopting "supply-side" policies that included deregulating markets and privatizing many state-run services (Chapter 5). The economic advantages of mass production were undermined by flexible production and new communication technologies, making smaller factories more competitive with larger ones. There is general agreement that an important shift from Fordism to what is now called "neoliberalism" occurred in the first world after 1973, but third world countries experienced this differently (Amin, 1994; Boyer and Durand, 1997; Leitner, Peck, and Sheppard, 2007a; Leitner, Sziarto, Sheppard, and Maringanti, 2007b).

State Socialism and Heavy Industrialization

In the state socialist (nominally communist) governments of the second world, particularly in the more industrialized states of eastern Europe and the Soviet Union, a very different course of postwar demand management was embarked on. Much of the heavy industry had been destroyed during World War II, creating a shortage that the arms buildup of the Cold War exacerbated. Primary emphasis was thus placed on encouraging the production of capital goods. This focus on capital goods in turn left little capacity for producing consumer goods. In addition, the relative self-sufficiency of COMECON meant that few consumer goods were imported. Overall, then, growth depended more on producers' than on consumers' purchasing power, and consumer demand was neglected. Thus the rapid growth of manufacturing in the postwar period (Figure 17.1) was not matched by increased consumer wealth; this situation created a rising gap in individual prosperity between the first and second worlds. In the same vein, little attention was paid to the social and environmental consequences of heavy industrialization, and wasted urban and industrial landscapes began to appear, reminiscent of the worst of the 19th-century industrial revolution in western Europe and North America.

Productivity increases were also slower, and there was less reliance on cheap third world imports—a result of the attempt to make COMECON as self-sufficient as possible. Finally, there were considerable inefficiencies in the storage and distribution of products, particularly agricultural products. The stark differences in consumer goods and quality of material life between eastern and western Europe, resulting from these policies, were principal reasons for the populist rejection of state socialism at the end of the 1980s. After 1989, under advice and pressure from the first world and the Bretton Woods institutions, these societies began a transition to capitalism (Smith and Pickles, 1998).

FACTORS FACED BY THIRD WORLD NATIONS CONSIDERING INDUSTRIALIZATION

In the 1950s and 1960s, industrialization in the third world was seen as a national initiative, the pursuit of which could promote domestic goals. Not only did the example of the more prosperous nations suggest industrialization as the path to development; it also seemed rational in the light of internal conditions in third world nations, as well as their historical situation in the global economy. Domestically, there was a highly unequal distribution of wealth between small elite groups and an overwhelming number of very poor people. Industrialization promised a bigger economic pie, and it seemed possible that at least a small slice of this increased wealth could be given to the poor without compromising the economic interests of the elites. Industrialization now, with the promise of redistribution later, could foster political support from rich and poor alike, making it a much more palatable policy than redistribution now—particularly as there was very little to redistribute (Ballance and Sinclair, 1983). Externally, national governments were very aware of the difficulty of achieving economic prosperity through specialization in primary commodities; they were also concerned that economic influence from industrialized nations could undermine political independence from colonialism, which was now becoming possible. Furthermore, the fact that first world financial resources were focused on reindustrializing Europe and Japan at this time suggested to third world nations that they could not rely on help from outside, but had to undertake their own industrialization initiatives.

Industrialization therefore held out the promise of increased wealth and prosperity, economic independence, and a way out of the trap of specialization and trade in primary commodities. The challenge was how to alter internal economic conditions in a way that would favor investment in industry over investment in agriculture or investment abroad. Although the U.S., German, and Japanese experiences suggested models for third world policies, the situation faced by would-be NICs was more challenging than those these three nations had faced.

First, the trading position in the world economy was, and is, different. Whereas Germany and the United States could take advantage of cheap primary commodities imported from the colonized third world (and, in the case of the United States, cheap immigrant labor power and abundant land resources), third world nations as a group have no such trade relations to exploit, since they *are* the third world. Second, the global power of more industrialized competitors was significantly less in the 19th century. At the height of Britain's economic power in 1870, the rising industrial powers had to compete against the established industrial economies of Britain and France, which were producing about 40% of global manufacturing and whose manufactured exports accounted for some 47% of world trade in manufactures. In 1960, by contrast, the established industrial nations against which the third world had to compete were producing more than 90% of manufacturing output and were responsible for 88% of world manufacturing exports (Dicken, 1992; World Bank, 1994b; Dosi, Pavitt, and Soete, 1990).

Closely related to this were important differences in internal economic conditions. Whereas incomes in the United States, in Germany, and later in Japan were high by global standards, incomes were and remain generally very low in the third world. This is important, because low incomes make it difficult to develop domestic markets for industrial products. Enormous differences in technological know-how also existed (and still exist). In an analysis of South Korea, Amsden (1989, 1990) has argued that the technical advances made in industrialized nations, and the continued investment there in research and development, have made it all but impossible for third world nations to compete with the first world through invention or innovation of new production methods and products. Such strategies were much more feasible for Germany and the United States in the 19th century. Finally, there is a greater prevalence of foreign branch plants in third world nations, primarily from the first world. In the 19th century, the large multinational concerns were trading corporations, primarily concerned with opening up North America and Asia and with shipping products from there to Europe. The development of industrial production in Germany or the United States was in the hands of domestic entrepreneurs. By contrast, industrialization in most third world nations has been undertaken by foreign as well as (and in many cases instead of) domestic firms.

These internal conditions are, of course, closely bound up with one another and with the relative position of third world nations in the global economy. For example, the technological hegemony of the already industrialized nations is closely related to their economic power. It reinforces low-wage policies in the third world, since this is the only way they can compensate for their technological disadvantages. Such technological disadvantages also induce third world countries to attract foreign investors in order to benefit from their technological know-how. Low wages in turn mean that indigenous firms have little incentive to develop new technologies, which historically have been a response to the pressure of increasing labor costs. More generally, investors in low-wage locations tend to utilize older technologies of mass production that require intense unskilled labor, rather than bringing with them state-of-the-art production methods. The tendency to exploit cheap labor locations for mass production during certain stages in an industry's life cycle has been documented by several authors (see sidebar: "The Profit/Product Cycle and Low-Wage Locations").

In selecting an industrialization strategy under these conditions, newly independent third world nations had to decide how to stimulate industrial production while securing adequate markets for the commodities produced. With respect to stimulating production, three possibilities were suggested by the experiences of previously industrialized nations and by theories of economic development: (1) encouraging domestic elites to invest their wealth in industry by stimulating the development of an indigenous entrepreneurial class; (2) encouraging foreign investment in domestic industry; or (3) having the state assume ownership of industrial production. The first approach characterized the most successful cases of industrialization in Europe and North America, but proved difficult to achieve. Wealth creation within third world nations specializing in primary commodities was highly polarized, and it was hard to discourage elites from investing abroad the part of their wealth that was not used for conspicuous consumption.

First world corporations were expanding abroad, making the second option attractive to some, since this represented a potential quick source of investment funds. Foreign firms have only been willing to invest in certain third world nations, however, and there remain important questions about whether the presence of foreign firms helps or hinders third world industrialization and wealth creation (see Chapter 21). Foreign ownership also raises questions about the desirability of excessive dependence on the rest of the world—questions similar to the ones we have examined with respect to trade policy (see Chapters 15 and 16). Desires for autonomy, together with suspicions about the motives of foreign firms, mean that third world states tend to see foreign investment as a temporary solution.

State ownership of industry has consistently met with severe disapproval if not political and economic sanctions from the first world. As a result, this policy has been pursued only when political ideologies or economic inequalities are strong enough to override these objections, and in countries willing and able to withstand such external pressure. Some countries—notably China, India, Cuba, North Korea, Vietnam, Nicaragua, Zimbabwe, and Tanzania—actively pursued such policies under the influence of socialist development philosophies. A much larger group of countries saw nationalization (the transfer of ownership of selected firms from private entrepreneurs to the state) as a quick way of reducing foreign ownership in the 1960s, when few benefits seemed to accrue from foreign-owned firms. With the dissolution of the second world, it became very hard to find external partners supportive of state ownership. The first and second options have thus been turned to more often. States have turned to the second option of foreign investment when the first one of indigenous capitalism fails, as has often been the case.

With respect to decisions about securing viable markets for manufactures, the choice is between domestic and foreign markets. The domestic market often is quite limited by the low incomes of the majority of the population, particularly in countries that are small and/or have highly unequal distributions of wealth. In addition, foreign imports have long dominated domestic markets, and domestic consumers have come to value foreign goods, making it hard for domestic firms to compete. Production for foreign markets has meant attempting to export to first world markets, with their considerable purchasing power. But third world firms have faced even greater difficulties in competing with first world producers in their home territories, compounded by the high tariffs and nontariff barriers (NTBs) that first world nations have erected

The Profit/Product Cycle and Low-Wage Locations

It has been suggested that most industries go through a typical life cycle during which the locations utilized by the industry change, as laid out in the adjacent table. This has been variously labeled a "product cycle" (Vernon, 1966) or "profit cycle" (Markusen, 1985), depending on whether the theorist sees the cycle as being driven by technological changes or by profit considerations. Once an industry develops mass production to serve established markets (in cases where cost savings from unskilled, labor-intensive mass production are significant), especially for industries with geographically widespread markets, relocation of the process of mass production in low-wage locations becomes attractive. Fröbel et al. (1980) describe this in a book titled *The New International Division of Labour.*

The Life Cycle of an Industry

Stage in life cycle	Profitability	Technology	Location
1. Initial invention	Marginal/uncertain	Craft-intensive	Places or laboratories with favorable conditions for creative and inventive activities
2. Innovation; establishment of market niche	High "windfall" profits	Intensive use of skilled labor; small- batch production	Accessible to skilled labor, suppliers, and/or initial markets, as well as to venture capital
3. Established market share and product recognition	Normal profits	Mass production facilities; use of unskilled labor and assembly line production	Relocation of factories for carrying out unskilled, labor-intensive production to low-wage locations
4a. Decline (replacement by different products, better technologies)	Subnormal or negative profits	Rationalization of production costs; factory closings, more intensive work processes, deskilling of jobs	Closure of less profitable locations and relocation to places of cheaper labor and less rigid labor or environmental regulation; demand for state support to keep factories open or prevent relocation
4b. Regeneration (innovation of new products as previous ones decline in sales)	As for stages 1, 2	As for stages 1, 2	Near research and development laboratories; as for stage 2

Stage 4 suggests that investments in low-wage locations are vulnerable to competition from even cheaper locations, to which firms facing subnormal profits can relocate. Over the last 15 years, in low-wage assembly industries ranging from electronics to clothing, many firms that left the first world in the 1980s to take advantage of lower wages in Central and South America, and in NICs in east and southeast Asia, have relocated again to places like China. Even China is now losing firms to places like Vietnam, where wages are lower still. In short, stage 3 industries (i.e., the ones that third world countries can most easily compete for) are not a secure source of long-term employment.

This "race to the bottom" means that states governing low-wage locations strategize to keep labor costs low, and to offer other subsidies to the private sector in order to attract and retain stage 3 industries. However, the race to the bottom is complicated by other considerations. It is important to remember that low-wage locations are not all in third world nations. Production may be just as efficient in lower-wage regions within the first world, and now particularly in eastern Europe, if more productive technologies can be applied there and if semiskilled workers who may be more socialized into factory work can be employed. Countries such as the Czech Republic are currently more attractive than many third world nations. Although labor costs are somewhat higher than in the third world, the Czech Republic offers a highly productive labor force with a strong industrial tradition, located close to major European markets in a country that has joined the European Union.

against manufactures threatening their domestic industries (Chapter 16). The relative merits of these strategies has dominated discussions about third world industrialization policies since the 1950s, with two broad groups of policies emerging. ISI (mentioned earlier) aims to encourage manufacture for domestic markets, discouraging competing imports; export-oriented industrialization (EOI) concentrates on industrial production for foreign markets.

INDUSTRIALIZATION STRATEGIES IN THE PERIPHERY

Import Substitution

ISI involves state intervention to encourage domestic production for domestic markets, with the goal of catalyzing domestic industry as a competitive substitute for imported commodities. The state provides assistance and incentives for manufacturers seeking to serve domestic markets, while limiting competition from more efficient foreign firms. The expected outcome is a reduced level of imports of manufactured commodities, and thus an improved balance of trade. Thus even if the nation continues to export primary commodities, the reduced import bill brought about by this substitution should compensate for the relatively meager gains from trade associated with such exports, and should thus improve the trade balance. ISI as an official industrialization policy was first implemented in Latin America in response to disrupted trade during the two world wars and the Depression, and was seen as a way out of the imbalanced trade relations identified by Prebisch and the Economic Commission for Latin America (ECLA) (see Chapter 4). It spread widely throughout the third world during the 1950s, however, becoming the initial policy pursued in the Asian NICs that we now associate with EOI.

ISI policy used the following types of instruments to increase the profitability of, or improve the comparative advantage of, domestic producers serving domestic markets. Import tariffs were imposed on the products selected for ISI, making competing imports more expensive and effectively raising a protective wall behind which domestic industry could be competitive in domestic markets, even if it was unable to compete globally. By contrast, import tariffs on those inputs required by industries supported under ISI were eliminated. The rate of exchange of the domestic currency was raised, increasing its value relative to other currencies. This also made imports not subject to tariffs cheaper and exports more expensive, which both disadvantaged exporters of primary goods (thus implicitly favoring investment in industry) and made the imported inputs for ISI cheaper. Rather than waiting for the market to react to these restructured incentives, the state also gave direct support to producers or potential producers of commodities selected for ISI who were prepared to expand domestic protection.

In Brazil, which is often cited as the paradigmatic case for ISI, the state reduced tariffs on imports needed by the businesses engaged in ISI; set up a development bank to ease financing of domestic industry; increased the exchange rate; and followed a mixed policy of state ownership in some sectors and encouragement of foreign firms to undertake ISI production in others. The sectors targeted by this policy in Brazil (as in most countries adopting ISI in the 1950s) were consumer industries, especially those that reflected current patterns of domestic demand. By the late 1970s, Brazil was able to supply the bulk of domestic demand for steel, textiles, transportation equipment, and pharmaceuticals (Evans, 1979).

India, which prior to independence had already developed a significant industrial sector devoted to consumer goods, was an important exception to this focus on consumer industries. Since World War I, consumer goods production had been growing in India as a result of colonial ISI policies sanctioned by the British. After independence, India turned to emphasize the production of capital goods—notably energy, iron/steel, and cement—during the first two 5-year plans in the 1950s (Kemp, 1983). Production in the capital goods sector had stagnated by the 1970s, however, and most industrial growth under ISI was occurring in the consumer goods sector.

The size and nature of economic growth under ISI depend on the size and composition of the domestic market, and on the effect of output levels on the profitability of production. ISI is more viable in larger, wealthier, and less unequal countries, because a larger domestic market makes it easier for domestic production facilities to attain enough sales to be able to engage in mass production. The size of the Brazilian market even induced U.S. and European firms to set up branch plants in Brazil after ISI began, in order to avoid the tariff barriers. Smaller, poorer, and more unequal countries were more difficult for domestic producers to serve efficiently and less attractive for foreign firms, because total demand was seen as being too small to support efficient mass production.

The mix of consumer goods produced was tailored to current patterns of domestic demand. In countries with a highly unequal income distribution, the principal markets were to be found in elite populations. Consequently, ISI has predominantly involved the production of western-style consumer goods for middle-income populations (much as Fordism in the first world has): TVs, automobiles, refrigerators, and so forth. Such commodities are also attractive because their relatively complex technology offers the possibility of improving the technical prowess of domestic producers. Since these elite populations also benefited most from industrial expansion, this created a "virtuous cycle" whereby increased output led to increased purchasing power within a restricted social group, further increasing demand for these products. This cycle enhanced social inequality between the elite and the remainder of the population.

With respect to production methods, the availability of unskilled but very cheap labor in most third world nations favored the use of labor-intensive technologies, involving assembly line production where work could be divided into a series of simple tasks to be repetitively performed by individual workers. This meant that in the case of more complex products (e.g., automobiles), third world factories at least initially tended to concentrate on product assembly rather than on technological development, considerably limiting the development of technological know-how and learning. Over time, however, in selected industries and places, workers and managers have acquired the expertise to engage in more sophisticated production methods. Such industries and places also became sites where labor organized, creating a relative well-paid male labor force and an incipient middle class. In Mexico, for example, ISI clustered in the center of the country, around Mexico City. A politically active male labor force developed around these industries, and state spending on welfare, health, housing, and education expanded. This encouraged nuclear families in which the men worked and the women stayed at home (as in the United States at this time; Cravey, 1998).

Although ISI was widely hailed in the 1950s as the way for peripheral countries to shift from dependence on primary exports to industrial development, it is currently out of favor for both practical and ideological reasons. Practically, ISI has had little effect on one of its principal goals: reducing imports. Indeed, in many cases it has had the opposite effect. Reduced imports of commodities selected for ISI were accompanied by increased imports of the inputs necessary to manufacture these commodities. With the help of reduced tariffs on such imports, capital goods such as machinery, equipment for assembly lines, and semifinished products as inputs to be assembled on those lines took up an increasing share of imports. The more sophisticated consumer goods targeted for ISI in fact tend to rely more on imported inputs than basic consumer goods do. Thus ISI, as implemented, paradoxically led to an increased reliance on manufactured imports rather than a reduced reliance. This was a greater challenge for the third world than for the United States, Germany, and Japan, because of the ease with which such inputs could be exported from the first world—reducing the need and incentive to produce them domestically.

Second, there was little diversification of the sectors supported by ISI beyond those producing sophisticated consumer goods. The problem of increased imports of capital goods could theoretically be overcome by extending ISI policies to cover industries producing those intermediate and basic capital goods that were being imported in increasing quantities, but this transition proved difficult. Markets for such goods are too small in many third world countries to make local production for domestic consumption efficient. Even in third world nations with large markets, notably Brazil and India, success in some basic industries (e.g., the iron/steel industry) has not laid the foundation for a substantial diversification of ISI. One reason for this is the difficulty of successfully acquiring, developing, or applying the kind of complex technological know-how necessary for implementing, for example, a state-of-the-art machine tool industry. Whereas Germany and the United States made a successful transition to ISI in capital goods through a series of innovations and focused research and development in chemicals, energy, electrical equipment, and transport equipment, as well as through improved production methods—all of which eventually enabled them to take international market share from the British—it has proven much more difficult for third world nations to succeed.

State policies prioritizing the current structure of consumer demand in selecting industries to support, or "market-based" ISI (Colman and Nixson, 1986: 281), also inhibited the diversification of ISI. The production of sophisticated consumer goods for the middle class and elite, though seemingly a sensible response to market signals, produced commodities that the vast majority of the population could not afford; moreover, the production methods used did not necessarily catalyze mass industrial employment. ISI policies prioritizing basic goods manufacturing sectors would have resulted in much more intensive employment of unskilled labor. Such basic consumer industries did exist and were growing in third world nations, but they did not receive the favored treatment that the state allotted to ISI sectors. Those who did gain employment in ISI increased their incomes and were able to participate to some degree in increased prosperity and the consumption of sophisticated consumer goods, but the bulk of the population was still left out. Thus, in responding to market signals, ISI tended to reproduce the economic inequality that those signals reflected.

Third, ISI did not reduce social and regional inequalities. Employment in ISI factories meant exceptionally good working conditions by Latin American standards, with reasonable pay in unionized industries. Yet, because ISI did not diversify industrialization adequately into other commodities, a relatively small but highly influential group of workers and their families benefited from working in these factories—a group that came to be known as a "labor aristocracy."

The other principal beneficiaries of ISI were the factory owners, workers in state agencies involved in this industrial policy, and those better-off consumers benefiting from state-subsidized production of consumer goods they could afford. In the 1950s and 1960s, during the period when ISI became the focus of industrial policy, income inequalities increased in Brazil and Mexico (1950–1963) and in Argentina (1953–1961). The poorest income groups, often rural peasants, faced a declining income share, while middle-income urban groups at times increased their share of income (Bennoldt-Thomsen, Evers, Müller-Plantenberg, Müller-Plantenberg, and Schoeller, 1979: 223; Colman and Nixson, 1986: 78).

The industries supported by ISI were concentrated disproportionately in the large cities that had developed under colonial and other external influences. Thus they were situated at locations that already had a large potential labor market; a disproportionate share of middle-class and elite consumers; and ready access both locally to the centers of national political power, and globally to the world market for the import of essential inputs. This exacerbated regional and urban–rural economic inequalities and rural–urban migration, increasing the attractiveness of these cities for commodity production and heightening the dualism between "traditional" rural and "modern" urban regions in third world societies (see Chapter 19).

These three problems reinforced one another. Limited domestic demand made diversification difficult, which increased rather than decreased import bills, which in turn reinforced social and spatial inequality. Thus ISI in the third world, despite its success in the first world, did not lead to the broad general increase in incomes that was necessary to reinforce the viability of domestically oriented industries. In short, the promise that ISI would provide a greater pie from which all could benefit was not fulfilled. Those who see market mechanisms as the key to third world development (Chapter 5), and are ideologically opposed to state-led development and trade barriers, capitalized on these failures to urge wholesale abandonment of ISI. Forgetting or ignoring how ISI-like policies were crucial to the successful industrialization of many first world countries, they have argued with considerable force and influence that third world countries should accept and exploit their comparative advantages in resource-intensive and labor-intensive production, rather than attempting to alter them through this kind of state intervention. The failure of ISI to live up to its expectations, combined with the rising influence of neoliberal ideas, has placed much pressure on Latin American and other proponents of ISI to shift to an export-oriented approach. In particular, the success of Hong Kong, Singapore, South Korea, and Taiwan has typically been pointed to as exemplifying how EOI could succeed for third world industrialization where ISI had failed.

Export Orientation

One feature that distinguishes industrial policy in these four Asian countries from that pursued in the Latin American NICs is the occurrence of an early shift to developing a capital goods sector that emphasized sales in foreign markets—a form of EOI—instead of trying for ISI in these areas. We focus here on South Korea and Taiwan, because they exemplify the challenge faced by most third world nations seeking to achieve a transition from producing primary commodities to manufacturing products. Both South Korea and Taiwan specialized in exporting agricultural commodities in the early 1950s, whereas the city states Hong Kong and Singapore never had a significant specialization in primary commodities. Both South Korea and Taiwan initially employed ISI, but Taiwan turned to EOI in 1957, followed by South Korea in 1960. By 1981, South Korea's share of third world manufactured output was 5%, and its share of third world manufactured exports was 16%; for Taiwan, the figures were 3% and 18%, respectively.

These remarkable success stories have been widely hailed as examples of how economic growth can be achieved through accepting the principle of growth through specialization based on comparative advantage, and exporting the products of this specialization—in other words, as examples of how rigorous application of free market principles will bring about economic prosperity. When the World Bank and the International Monetary Fund (IMF) require second and third world countries to undergo structural adjustment as a precondition for receiving loans (see Chapter 23), their argument is often based on the argument that EOI, responding to rather than seeking to shape market forces, is the way to go. A detailed examination of South Korea or Taiwan calls such claims into question, however.

EOI attempts to achieve industrial growth through successful competition in international markets, rather than reliance on domestic demand. Although it is undoubtedly true that successful penetration of global markets has been essential to economic growth in South Korea and Taiwan, it does not follow that this has been a result of accepting and exploiting current comparative advantages. In both countries, the state played an active role in reconstructing domestic conditions in order to provide incentives for export-oriented producers, thus creating new comparative advantages (Webber and Rigby, 1996). This was achieved by the state's working closely with and directing private sector firms, in a coordinated industrial policy very different from the more *laissez-faire* economic role of the state that is currently the rage among proponents of neoliberal globalization (Chapter 5). It certainly has not meant this in Taiwan and South Korea, whose policies have deviated substantially from those propounded under structural adjustment. The United States is widely regarded as having one of the least regulated economies but at the same time one of the least export-oriented economies. South Korea and Taiwan are examples of the opposite extreme—state-run economic development combined with extreme EOI.

In South Korea, large industrial conglomerates (*chaebols*) that are closely connected to the state have come into existence, and state control over financial institutions has made the interests of financial capital subordinate to those of industrial capital. In addition, the state has intervened to keep labor costs low through political actions controlling and suppressing unionization and other social movements, and stabilizing food prices (Amsden, 1989). The shift toward EOI was partly associated with reductions in state support for ISI between 1960 and 1967: Tariff barrier legislation was changed to designate such barriers as the exception rather than the rule (although 68% of all imports were still subject to tariffs in 1984), and currency exchange was substantially deregulated. At the same time, however, state intervention has been crucial to the shift to EOI. Substantial tax subsidies exist for the export-oriented iron/steel, chemical, and electronics industries; tariffs are lower on inputs for EOI industries; state-subsidized capital lending favors EOI industries; and the Foreign Exchange Demand and Supply Plan strictly controls how currency earned through exports may be used (Webber and Rigby, 1996).

In Taiwan, state-owned enterprises accounted for more than 10% of its gross national product (GNP) from 1951 to 1980 (Wade, 1990). These enterprises are particularly concentrated in heavy industry, including some of the most successful export subsectors (shipbuilding, rolled steel, petrochemicals, machinery, and automobile parts). The state has directed firms into the export sector by providing export incentives, which averaged 11% of industrial revenues in the 1960s and 1970s. When firms in the export sectors need to import supplies that cannot be obtained from Taiwanese firms, they need pay no duties on such imports. For imports that compete with products made by domestic firms, however, a cascading structure of import tariffs remains in place (like those depicted in Chapter 16, Figure 16.12). Nominal tariff rates averaged 31% in 1981 (UNCTAD, 1990a).

Thus, instead of relying on existing comparative advantages calculated from the relative prices of different products, in South Korea and Taiwan the state has manipulated those prices in order to create new comparative advantages in industries for which these countries previously had no advantage at all. Successful exports have been the key to industrial growth, but on terms dictated by the national states rather than the international market. This kind of EOI would perhaps be better named "export-promoting industrialization," yet it would be inaccurate to label even South Korea or Taiwan as export-promoting in their strategy. They have in fact simultaneously pursued import substitution and export promotion, shifting the emphasis between these and between the sectors in which they are applied, depending on judgments made about what seems to be effective for national economic growth in a particular sector and point in time.

A form of EOI that more closely matches the free trade prescription does exist in a number of other third world nations. This involves the construction of factories employing large numbers of unskilled workers to produce labor-intensive products (e.g., textiles), or to carry out labor-intensive production tasks (e.g., the assembly of computers), with the purpose of exporting the product abroad. In this case the firm involved—usually, but by no means always, foreign-owned—locates labor-intensive production in a place where underemployment and underdevelopment have kept wages very low, thereby exploiting a de facto comparative advantage of low labor costs. Unlike the South Korean or Taiwanese strategies, which seek to support and coordinate new indigenous industries and competitive advantages through export promotion, this state-led strategy exploits (and reinforces) current locational advantages by creating places for export processing (EPZs; see sidebar: "Export-Processing Zones"). These zones attract foreign investment to process commodities for export abroad, in a clearly demarcated space within which governance regimes hold down wages, block workplace health and safety provisions, and avoid any environmental regulation. The goal is to keep costs low enough (and profits high enough) to compensate for the extra transportation and organizational costs associated with TNCs using such locations. The brutal working conditions under which EPZs producer cheap goods for first world consumers have been contested by such groups as United Students Against Sweatshops (Chapter 24).

In Mexico, a shift from ISI to EOI after 1976 has had profound geographical and social effects (Cravey, 1998). Geographically, mass production for the domestic market around Mexico City declined, as low-wage assembly production flourished in the *maquiladoras* along the Mexican side of the U.S.–Mexico border, for export to the U.S. market. Low-wage jobs in the *maquiladoras*, targeting unskilled women, were substituted for better-paid unionized male jobs in the interior of the country. Socially, the state has cut back substantially on social spending of all kinds, and the fringe benefits negotiated by unions in the older region have not been made available to *maquiladora* workers. There has also been a regendering of family relations, from "housewifization" (Cravey, 1998: 45) in the older industrial region to female proletarianization in the *maquiladoras*. In the former regime, women had to struggle against social forces keeping them at home and out of the labor market. Under the current regime, young women receive the jobs—but also the resentment of men who are underemployed, excluded from this labor force. These women face a double-edged sword. On the one hand, they have the opportunity of paid employment, as well as the often contradictory forms of empowerment and emancipation associated with moving from rural peasant households to industrial urban work. On the other hand, opportunities for advancement are very limited, and the working environment

Export-Processing Zones

Export-processing zones (EPZs) are geographical districts established by state agencies, particularly but not exclusively in third world countries, which are reserved for the location of industries producing products for export. The products are not sold in domestic markets, providing a rationalization for the state to provide four types of benefits for industries locating in EPZs (Thrift, 1989): (1) eased import regulations for inputs used to produce commodities for export; (2) no duty on exports, no foreign exchange control, and a general freedom to repatriate profits; (3) provision of infrastructure and factory buildings, often at subsidized rates; and (4) tax holidays and other subsidies for firms. Ireland opened the first EPZ, next to Shannon Airport, in 1956. Eight third world countries in Asia and Latin America followed suit between 1962 and 1970, but the real growth began in the 1970s. In 1975 there were 31 EPZs in 18 countries, expanding to more than 110 in at least 68 mostly developing countries in 1990, employing over 500,000. By 2003, there were over 5,000 EPZs; 90% of these are in the third world, employing some 42 million workers. The geographical distribution is highly uneven. Whereas Latin America has the most EPZs (3,300 in Central America), employing 2.5 million, Asia accounts for three-quarters of all EPZ employment (30 million in China alone) in some 750 EPZs. Africa has just 1% of the global total (Boyenge, 2003).

The figure below shows the locations of EPZs based on 1990 information. This map shows all countries with at least one EPZ, and for countries with several EPZs it shows the locations of the largest concentrations. EPZs are concentrated along the coast of China, in the NICs of southeast Asia, in Mexico just south of the U.S. border, and in the Dominican Republic (the main Caribbean location). There are also a number in India, in Central America and northern South America, and at scattered locations in northern Africa. They are not all at coastal locations; some are near airports. The map shows, however, that two types of locations are valued: proximity to first world nations, and places in the third world that act as gateways to the world economy. The latter in particular are reminiscent of, and in many cases replicate, the locations once favored by colonial powers as trading *entrepôts*.

Export-processing zones, 1990. *Sources*: Data are from Thrift (1989), Wilson (1989), and World Bank (1992).

EPZs compete on the basis of a low-wage, compliant workforce, making them particularly suited for the kind of mass production identified in stage 3 of the industry life cycle (see "The Profit/Product Cycle . . ." sidebar). Two types of industries that fall into this category—textile manufacturing and the assembly of electronic and electrical goods—have been predominant. Workers recruited to EPZs must be willing to carry out repetitive, unskilled tasks for long hours and low wages. In 1980, wages in U.S. dollars ranged between 17¢ (in the Philippines) and $1 an hour (in Mexico), and the working week is often 45–55 hours. There has been heavy recruitment of young female workers, who are perceived to have been socialized to be both docile and dexterous assembly workers. Women, particularly between the ages of 17 and 23, make up about three-quarters of the EPZ workforce worldwide (World Bank, 1992). Workers complain repeatedly about long hours without overtime; dangerous working conditions; and supervisors who force them to work at high speed, whether or not they are healthy.

The close collaboration of the national state and foreign firms within EPZs makes it extremely difficult to organize workers so as to improve working conditions. In many cases, organizing has been harshly suppressed.

> After a year-long clandestine campaign intended to build strength while avoiding firings and harassment, workers organizing unions at the Choishin and Cimatextiles factories, owned by a Korean-based company . . . , went public on July 9, 2001. While the union campaign initially caught the company off-guard, within 48 hours, workers report, a campaign of violent intimidation began, including a death threat against one union leader, surveillance of union workers, and the stoning of a union meeting place. [This] culminated on July 18 and 19 with two days of violence in the factories when mobs, reportedly orchestrated by supervisors who said they would close the plants if the union wasn't ousted, attacked union supporters, threatening to lynch them while throwing rocks, bottles, and food. During the attack, union supporters were urged to resign or face further violence. (U.S. Labor Education in the Americas Project [US/LEAP], 2001).

The contribution of EPZs to national economic growth depends on a number of factors: their long-term viability in competition with other EPZs and with more efficient capital-intensive technologies applied in higher-wage locations; their ability to generate foreign exchange; their demand for goods and services from domestic industries located outside the EPZs (or their "local multiplier effect"—see Chapter 21); the income generated from employment in the EPZs; and the skill and knowledge learned by EPZ workers that could eventually be transferred to other domestic industries. The net benefits of EPZs are subject to considerable debate. Estimates suggest that foreign exchange revenues, though at times considerable in nominal terms, are much reduced because many companies in EPZs ship in their own inputs (often from their own factories in other parts of the world), assemble them, and ship the product out again. The proportion of inputs purchased from domestic firms outside the EPZs was just 3% in Malaysia and 2% in Mexico, but 30–40% in the Asian NICs in the late 1970s. In addition, profits may be repatriated. Employment in EPZs, while significant in some countries, in many cases has had little effect on joblessness or wealth creation (Thrift, 1989). The spread of EPZs has also increased competition among countries seeking investors in such zones, increasing the subsidies that must be offered to potential investors, and thus lowering net benefits for the host countries.

is brutal and repressive. Furthermore, some face great personal danger, including rape and murder, in a context where *maquila* women are frequently perceived as out of place when they leave the home (Wright, 2004). Mexican women contest such working conditions and exclusions from public space, however, drawing on a tradition of labor and social activism, as well as parallel struggles in other EPZs. These are just part of the emergent contestations of low-wage EOI employment (see sidebar: "Just Garments").

CONCLUSIONS

There has been a worldwide shift away from ISI and toward EOI as the favored strategy for promoting third world industrialization in recent years. Detailed examination of state industrialization policies in the third world does not, however, suggest that this represents some natural sequence. Successful nations have mixed the two strategies flexibly, adapting to changing conditions, without necessarily relying on market forces in either case. It is reasonable to generalize that all third world states with some success at industrialization have profited from a "developmentalist state"—a national state that has intervened actively in coordinating and restructuring the incentives for domestic industry, as well as in creating domestic social conditions that are favorable for private firms (notably controlling unionization and strikes, and keeping food costs and wages low) (Evans, 1995). There are many developmentalist third world states that have spectacularly failed to achieve industrialization, however; this raises the difficult question of why some have succeeded whereas others have not.

There is much controversy about why such nations as South Korea and Taiwan have been successful. It is possible to point to conditions in these countries that favored industrialization. These include extensive inflows of U.S. foreign aid beginning in the 1950s (because of their geopolitical situation as Asian "bastions" against communism at the start of the Cold War); successful early land reform programs, which eliminated land-owning elites as a political and economic force (encouraged by the United States in order to undermine support for peasant resistance movements); a strong sense of national independence in the face of real or perceived external economic and political threats (Japan, North Korea, and China in the case of South Korea; China in the case of Taiwan and, until 1997, Hong Kong); strategic location within global trading and investment networks (Hong Kong and Singapore); and authoritarian national states that retained legitimacy through a strong sense of national unity and a willingness to sacrifice for long-term growth, as well as through domestic and foreign military and diplomatic support.

Another factor pointed to is the use of highly focused national industrial policies, in which the state used its partial autonomy to subsidize industry, in a manner that was both flexible and well-informed enough to ensure that more efficient enterprises were rewarded and less efficient ones penalized. Amsden (1990) has also argued that in South Korea, considerable success was achieved by compensating for the technological advantages of first world nations with a system of workplace organization that made considerable cost savings on the factory floor possible through work teams and the development of robotics. She describes this as technological improvement through learning how to apply

Just Garments

The Just Garments textile factory, in Soyapango, El Salvador, was the only EPZ plant in the country with workplace democracy (i.e., a unionized workforce participated in running the company). It was founded in a factory that had been closed by its former Taiwanese owners in response to local attempts to organize the workforce. An international campaign coordinated by activists from the United States and Taiwan, supplementing local action, persuaded Tainan Enterprises to sign an agreement under which it provided the capital, machinery, and technical support to establish a unionized facility, with a two-person board of directors (one each from Tainan and the El Salvadoran textile workers' union, Sindicato de Trabajadores de la Industria Textil). Two major U.S. retailers also participated: Gap Inc. (under pressure during the campaign) and Lands' End placed orders and pledged technical support to the nascent enterprise after it reopened in April 2003. Just Garments sought to survive through the production and marketing of "sweat-free" clothing in the United States. It engaged in a fund-raising campaign to keep production afloat in the face of political opposition from within El Salvador, snubbing by most major first world retailers, and the higher cost of their product by comparison to nonunionized operations. Just Garments closed its doors on May 15, 2007.

existing technologies better, rather than through developing new technologies.

The crucial question, however, is whether such success stories can be generalized into an ideal, "best-practice" industrialization policy for the rest of the third world. Attempts to find a single approach to industrialization in the third world—whether this be ISI or EOI, free competition or state-run industries—share a single vision about national economic policy. In this view, the appropriate internal conditions and a matching policy will suffice to bring about industrialization. Depending on the philosophy of the analyst or consultant, nations are asked to open their markets through deregulation and privatization; to develop a social partnership among industry, workers, and the state; to coordinate industrialization through the state; or to nationalize private industry. Following a developmentalist world view, it is common to point to already industrialized countries as the model for any of these (e.g., the United States, Germany, Japan, or Britain, respectively). When nations with limited manufacturing are urged to copy some other country, however, it is important to recall that that the complex factors shaping industrialization and economic growth tend to be misleadingly attributed to some simple formula, such as "free market" policies. In fact, earlier-industrializing nations practiced technology pirating and imperialism, and virtually all of them once protected their infant industries.

Such advice is notable more for its failures than its successes. Failures are generally attributed to the inability of state institutions to follow the proposed policies closely enough, or to various internal conditions that are seen both as very difficult to change and as barriers to industrialization (the lack of a "culture of entrepreneurship," corruption, or the physical geography of a nation). However, the appropriate path to industrialization depends on the situation of a country within the global economy as well as on internal conditions, implying that universal solutions may make little sense. We have argued in this chapter that third world countries today face a very different and much more difficult situation than that which Germany, the United States, and Japan successfully overcame. Within the third world, the situation again varies from country to country, meaning that appropriate policies may vary. For example, South Korean and Taiwanese firms are now fanning out to operate assembly plants in parts of the third world where wages are lower than in their home countries, creating new, asymmetrical mutual dependencies within the third world. What distinguishes South Korea and Taiwan from many African nations has as much to do with the way in which the state creatively responded to the conditions facing each country, evolving unique combinations of policies that happened to be successful, as it has with the internal characteristics of sub-Saharan African states. There also remains the difficult and unresolved question of whether it is even possible for all states in a global competitive system to achieve industrial development and prosperity, or whether the prosperity of some countries is dependent on the poverty of others, as Wallerstein (1979) has suggested (see Chapter 4).

NOTE

1. The Republic of South Africa ranked 11th in 2001.

18 The Earth's Crust as Resource

Industrialization, particularly combined with long-distance trade, engendered distinctive claims by humans on the earth's biophysical environment. First, industrialization demands large quantities of cheap energy, available to order. The industrial revolution quickly exceeded the local availability of energy in the forms generally used to date: biomass (fuelwood, charcoal, animal power) and water power. It was rapidly determined that fossil fuels—coal, and later oil and natural gas—provided energy in forms that were easy to access, transportable to where they were needed, and capable of producing a lot of energy quickly. The new transportation technologies that emerged as part of the industrial revolution dramatically lowered trade costs, entailing a parallel shift from animals (humans, horses, and oxen) and wind to coal and oil. Second, metals were central to the industrial revolution. Metals had been used for thousands of years to make tools (not to mention the use of gold and silver in jewelry and coinage), but the mass production associated with industrial factories vastly increased demand for metals—particularly for the machinery invented to speed industrial production. (Of course, industrialization would not have been possible without making cheap labor available—for example, by displacing rural households from their land—but that is not the focus of this chapter.)

Fossil fuels and metals are available in the earth's crust, so human exploration and exploitation of the biophysical environment shifted from renewable resources located at, near, or above the earth's surface toward nonrenewable resources mined from underneath. The atmospheric, hydrologic, and carbon cycles, as well as soils and vegetation, are in principle renewable. These cycles replenish the availability of energy, water, organic substances, and other soil nutrients within the time span of human society, and vegetative matter daily, with different societal implications that stem from geographical location within these cycles and from human use. Although these cycles have often been disrupted by human action, their potential as renewable resources still exists. By contrast, the geological cycles of the earth's crust are so slow that over the span of human history, the availability of such resources can be regarded for all intents and purposes as fixed. Whereas biomass, water, and solar power are the results of the earth's ongoing heat exchange with the sun, fossil fuels store previously accumulated energy from the sun, in the form of carbon from ancient plants and animals, within the earth. Use of the latter means drawing down the bank of energy accumulated over the millennia, rather than living within our means (contemporaneous energy flows from the sun). The themes of geographical differences in resource availability, and of the interrelationship between commodity production and the "natural resource" base, are common to discussions of renewable and nonrenewable resources—but nonrenewability poses distinct challenges.

CHARACTERISTICS OF RESOURCES IN THE EARTH'S CRUST

It is common to label as "natural resources" chemicals of the earth's crust that humans find to be useful for one purpose or another. In common parlance, "natural" is often interpreted as meaning that these resources are useful by their very nature, but this is misleading. It is not the chemical or physical properties of a mineral that make it useful, but human perceptions, knowledge, and power. Iron only became a resource at that time when, and in those places where, people discovered how it could increase their ability to manipulate the biophysical environment for social purposes, making tools and machinery. Uranium is only a resource for societies with the political power to produce nuclear energy (as defined by the Nuclear Nonproliferation Treaty) and with the will to assume the risks of nuclear power stations. Water is only a resource for those individuals who, and social groups that, occupy the geographical locations near it and have the social and political power to utilize it (think of riparian water rights, or conflicts over Native American fishing rights). Thus what makes a mineral a resource is not some universal property of that mineral, but is contextual; it depends on whether society establishes a use value for it. As Carl Sauer (1925: 36–37) put it, a natural resource is a cultural achievement. When we use the adjective "natural," we mean simply that the location and molecular structure of chemicals in the earth's crust depend on biophysical processes that to a large degree have been independent of human action.

With the exception of oil and natural gas, most of these resources are obtained by mining the earth's crust for minerals, from which the necessary chemical elements are extracted. Only oil, natural gas, coal, mercury, and gold are found close to a pure state in nature with any regularity. Thus iron is obtained from iron ores, which are in fact composed of iron oxides and other chemicals. The availability of all minerals currently sought as resources by humankind is limited by three features.

First, they tend to be rare. The most common minerals are iron (representing approximately 6% of the earth's crust) and aluminum (8.5%). Of the others, only magnesium (2.8%), cobalt (2.5%), and potassium (1.7%) represent more than 1% of the earth's crust. Table 18.1 provides a list of minerals and fossil fuels in heavy demand, together with their availability and their most popular uses. (Most gases are not listed despite high demand [e.g., oxygen], because their availability is so great that there is no foreseeable shortage.) The table is subdivided into (mostly fossil) fuels, iron, ferrous metals, and nonferrous metals (plus silicon). Less common metals that are typically found with another, more common, metal are listed after that metal and slightly indented.

Second, the degree of purity of these minerals, within the ores of the earth's crust where they are found, varies greatly. It is typically assumed that the relationship between the quantity of a mineral in the earth's crust and the degree of purity of ores containing it can be described by a bell-shaped curve. In Figure 18.1, the vertical axis represents the quantity of the mineral found in the earth's crust at any given concentration, and the horizontal axis represents different levels of

TABLE 18.1. Global Mineral Resources: Uses, Availability, and Demand

Mineral (1)	Use (2)	Reserves (3)	Resources (4)	World output (5)	U.S. demand (6)	Growth rate of world demand (7)	Units (8)
Coal	Energy	100,912	20,000,000	5,159	1,094	2.5%	Mil. short tons
Oil	Energy	1,150	3,000	252	8.6	2%	BBarrels
Natural gas	Energy	6,400	9,000	112	27.5	2.5%	Tr. cu. ft.
Uranium	Nuclear energy	2,500	3,557	68	16	5%	Th. MT
Iron	Many	160,000	370,000	1,520	62	3%	M. MT
Nickel	Alloys	62,000	140,000	1,500	221	3.8%	Th. MT
Manganese	Alloys	430,000	5,200,000	9,790	790	−0.5%	Th. MT
Chromium	Alloys	600,000	12,000,000	18,000	270	1%	Th. MT
Vanadium	Alloys	13,000	38,000	43.5	4.2	2%	Th. MT
Cobalt	Magnets/alloys	7,000	13,000	52.4	11	1%	Th. MT
Molybdenum	Alloys	8,600	19,000	163	34.2	−1%	Th. MT
Rhenium	Alloys/catalysts	2,400	10,000	43.2	35.8	5%	MT
Tungsten	Cutting agent	2,000	6,200	76.5	11.6	−0.4%	Th. MT
Tantalum	Microelectronics	43,000	150,000	1910	646	2%	MT
Copper	Electronics, pipes	470,000	940,000	14,900	2,270	3.3%	Th. MT
Tellurium	Semiconductors	26,000	47,000	113	75		MT
Zinc	Galvanizing, dies	230,000	460,000	10,100	1,370	3.2%	Th. MT
Cadmium	Electroplating	600	1,800	18	0.43	2.3%	Th. MT
Germanium	Fiber optics	3,000	Immense	90	27	3%	MT
Indium	Nuclear reactors	2,800	6,000	455	115	7%	MT
Aluminum	Many	250,000,000	320,000,000	165,000	10,500	1.9%	Th. MT
Titanium	Paints/aircraft	110	5,000	88	27	4%	Th. MT
Tin	Plating	6,100	11,000	280	65.8	1.8%	Th. MT
Lead	Batteries/pipes	67,000	140,000	2,380	1,540	1%	Th. MT
Antimony	Flame retardant	1,800	3,900	117	34	0.5%	Th. MT
Bismuth	Alloys	330	680	5.2	2.4	5%	MT
Silver	Photography	270,000	570,000	20,300	7,720	2.9%	MT
Gold	Many	42,000	90,000	2,450	195	7%	Th. MT
Platinum	Electronics/alloys	71,000	80,000	218	98	4.9%	MT
Mercury	Scientific equip.	120,000	240,000	1,600	245	0%	MT
Zirconium	Heat resistance	38,000	72,000	870	40	2.4%	MT
Barite	Drilling	200,000	740,000	7,620	2,800	−4%	Th. MT
Niobium	Alloys/cutting	4,400	5,200	33	7.2	2%	Th. MT
Selenium	Photocopying	82,000	170,000	1,350	600	5%	MT
Sulfur	Chemicals		5,000,000	64,000	12,400	1.8%	Th. MT
Phosphate	Fertilizer	18,000,000	50,000,000	148,000	40,000	2.3%	Th. MT
Potash	Fertilizer	8,300,000	17,000,000	31,000	6,100	1.8%	Th. MT
Silicon	Alloys, electronics	Immense	Immense	5,100	577	6%	Th. MT

Note. Abbreviations: MT, metric tons; Th., thousand; Mil., million; BBarrels, billions of barrels; Tr. cu. ft., trillion cubic feet; n.a., not available.

Sources: Data are from Energy Information Administration (2006), Gordon, Bertram, and Graedel (2006), and U.S. Geological Survey (USGS, 2006).

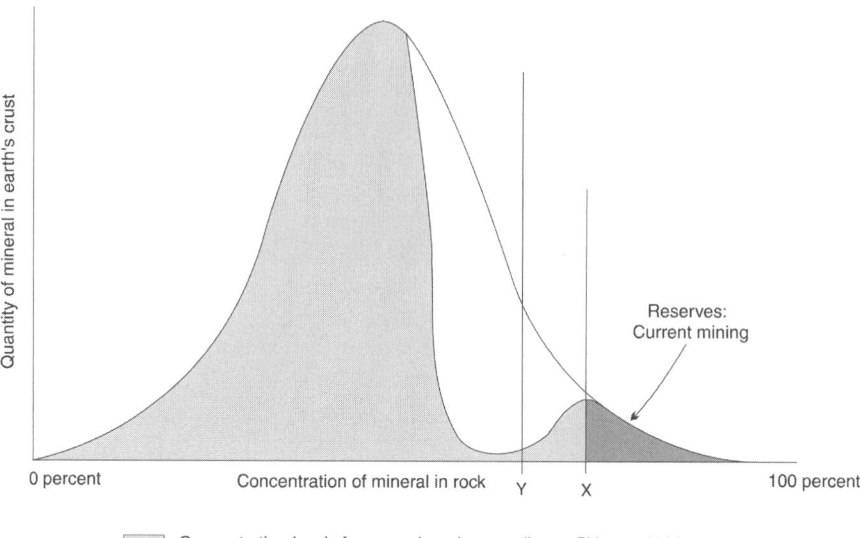

FIGURE 18.1. Mineral availability at varying ore concentration levels. *Source:* Adapted from Skinner (1980).

concentration of the mineral as a percentage of other elements making up the rock from which it can be extracted. To take the example of iron, the right-hand extreme of this graph refers to iron ores such as hematite (for which up to 90% of the rock is iron), while the left-hand extreme includes those orange sandstones whose color is evidence that they contain iron, but at very low levels of concentration. The total area under the curve is the total quantity of that mineral in the earth's crust.

The difficulty of exploiting any mineral rises as the purity of its ores decreases, and there is a point below which extracting minerals from an ore is infeasible or uneconomic. We represent this on Figure 18.1 by darkly shading levels of concentration (above *X*%) that are high enough to make the ore usable for exploiting the natural resource it contains, given the current state of knowledge about minerals extraction and the economics of mineral extraction. The total quantity in this darkly shaded area is known as the global "reserve" of this mineral. As can be seen, this leaves large quantities of the mineral that cannot be used, because it occurs in ores whose purity is too low. Although improved mining techniques or higher prices can push this boundary to the left (from *X*% down to *Y*%), there remains a level of concentration below which the energy required to extract a resource is so high that more resources would be consumed in extracting it than could ever be gained from its exploitation. For example, it is impossible for us to imagine that humankind will ever be able to use sandstone as an iron ore. This problem is further complicated by debates about whether the bell curve in Figure 18.1 accurately represents the distribution of rare minerals by levels of purity (see sidebar: "Are Scarce Minerals Even Scarcer?").

Third, the geographical distribution of resources is highly irregular. Geologists have provided much knowledge about the geological forms in which minerals occur, and the conditions under which extraordinary, exploitable concentrations of them exist. There is no space in this book to detail these geological processes, but it is worth noting the following. The fossil fuels—coal, oil, and natural gas—are found in sedimentary rock formations, since they are formed when organic matter has been overlain by other sedimentary matter and compressed over a period of many millions of years. Certain types of iron ore are found in sedimentary rock formations similar to those containing coal; yet many of the metallic minerals (with the additional exception of aluminum) are found in exploitable form in igneous and metamorphic rocks, or in rock formations that have been heavily penetrated by igneous intrusions, such as mountain chains. These minerals are often found in the same regions, and sometimes in the same rock veins. Seawater also contains many useful minerals in small concentrations, some of which precipitate out naturally. Manganese, for example, occurs as nodules on the ocean floor (beyond the ownership of national governments), and much money has been spent by first world governments to develop ways of economically recovering these nodules. Indeed, questions of profitability have come to lie at the center of understanding the geography of minerals production in particular, and resources in general. One of the most effective ways of accumulating profits remains the ability to convert aspects of the biophysical environment into commodities—a process that typically involves what David Harvey (2003) dubs "accumulation by dispossession."

EXPLORING FOR MINERAL RESOURCES

Before a mineral can be exploited, it must be located; thus the first stage in extracting natural resources is exploration. There are plenty of maps purporting to show the mineral concentrations of the world, but all of them suffer from the same problems: inaccuracy and bias. Although geologists understand quite well the general processes by which mineral concentrations form, exploitable concentrations are rare and highly localized geographically, and geological knowledge is not precise enough to pinpoint the location of such concentrations with sufficient accuracy. Even for those minerals that we regard as our most important natural resources, large areas of the globe have not yet even been prospected in the detail necessary to identify whether the conditions might be right for the occurrence of exploitable concentrations. In those cases where prospecting has revealed rock formations that seem to have the potential for exploitable mineral concentrations, only great effort makes it possible to determine whether exploitable concentrations exist, and (if so) exactly where they are. For instance, in the early 1970s it was estimated to cost $10 million "to give just a 50 percent chance of finding just one economic deposit of a major nonferrous metal" in an area already known to be promising geologically (Rees, 1990: 70). The average cost of exploring for uranium during the 1970s was $2,055 per ton of resources found (Crowson, 1990).

There is also a distinct geographical bias to mineral exploration, and thus to our knowledge about global mineral resources—a bias that has resulted in far less information about and exploration in third world nations than about and in other parts of

Are Scarce Minerals Even Scarcer?

The geologist Brian Skinner (1980) suggests that the distribution of minerals by concentration is very different for rare minerals, taking a form closer to that of the lighter gray-shaded area in Figure 18.1 (see Skinner's Figure 4). "Rarely do the scarce minerals . . . form separate minerals. Instead they are present as randomly distributed atoms trapped . . . in minerals of the . . . abundant elements" (Skinner, 1980: 162). He feels that we are now exploiting such minerals at levels of concentration above X% on this graph. As we improve our technologies to shift this boundary down toward Y%, however, we will experience little increase in available reserves, except for such common minerals as iron and aluminum. If Skinner is right, we will have a lot more difficulty increasing our global supply of most of the minerals we use today as resources than others suggest.

the world. First, the detailed mapping of bedrock geology that traditionally has been used to identify useful sources of minerals has been carried out more intensively and over a much longer time period in Europe (including the Russian Federation), North America, Australia, and South Africa than elsewhere. Countries with the demand for minerals and the money to invest in exploiting them have concentrated their efforts within their own national territories, turning to other nations only when domestic supplies run short. Second, costs of exploration are generally higher in third world locations, in part because initial geological mapping has been less extensive, and in part because the costs of sending and equipping a minerals exploration expedition are higher. Third, the potential benefits are less, both because third world mineral locations tend to be farther from the major consumers of these resources in the industrial nations of the first world (see below) and because of political risks (the locations of many potential minerals are within the territories of nations that nationalized a number of mineral resources exploited by foreign companies in the late 1960s and 1970s). In 2005, 32% of all global expenditures on non-fuel-related mineral exploration were invested in Canada and Australia alone—greater than Latin America and Pacific/southeast Asia combined. Sixty percent of global expenditures was spent on looking for gold (47%) and diamonds (Metals Economics Group, 2005).

Although precise figures are not available, certainly less than 10% of global mineral exploration is carried out by third world organizations, and most of this is by state-owned corporations within their own national territories. Indeed, so little money is available for this purpose from third world nations that the United Nations and the World Bank have developed special loan programs for mineral exploration. In general, about one-quarter of all exploration occurs in third world nations; this is mostly financed by companies from the first world whose overall commitment to exploration in the third world has been quite small (with the notable exception of oil). European companies were investing just 20% of their exploration expenditures in the third world in the late 1970s, and North American companies were spending less than 10% (Rees, 1990: 63). With these biases in the process of exploration, it is impossible to tell to what degree the concentrations of fossil fuels and mineral fields in the first world, which appear on most maps of global mineral resources, are indicators of an actual geographical advantage or simply of our ignorance about third world geological resources. Consider, however, the case of petroleum (Figure 18.2), where attempts have been made to map this bias (Odell and Rosing, 1983).

EXPLOITING MINERAL RESOURCES

Even if we could draw an accurate map of global geological resources, it would only indicate locations of potential supply, not those where minerals are produced. "Exploration costs pale into insignificance besides the expenditure required to bring a new find into production" (Rees, 1990: 70). Although resources are produced by biophysical processes, their exploitation is a commercial activity driven by dictates of production costs and markets. Increasingly, mining in both the private and public sectors is driven by considerations of profitability. Profitability depends not only on the difficulty of getting the resource out of the ground, but also on accessibility to markets (i.e., the geography of consumption), on the current price obtainable for that mineral, on estimates of the likelihood that the political climate will allow continued exploitation in future years, and on variations in local production costs from place to place.

As with any economic activity, the revenue obtained from sales of a geological resource can be divided up among four components: the costs of capital equipment

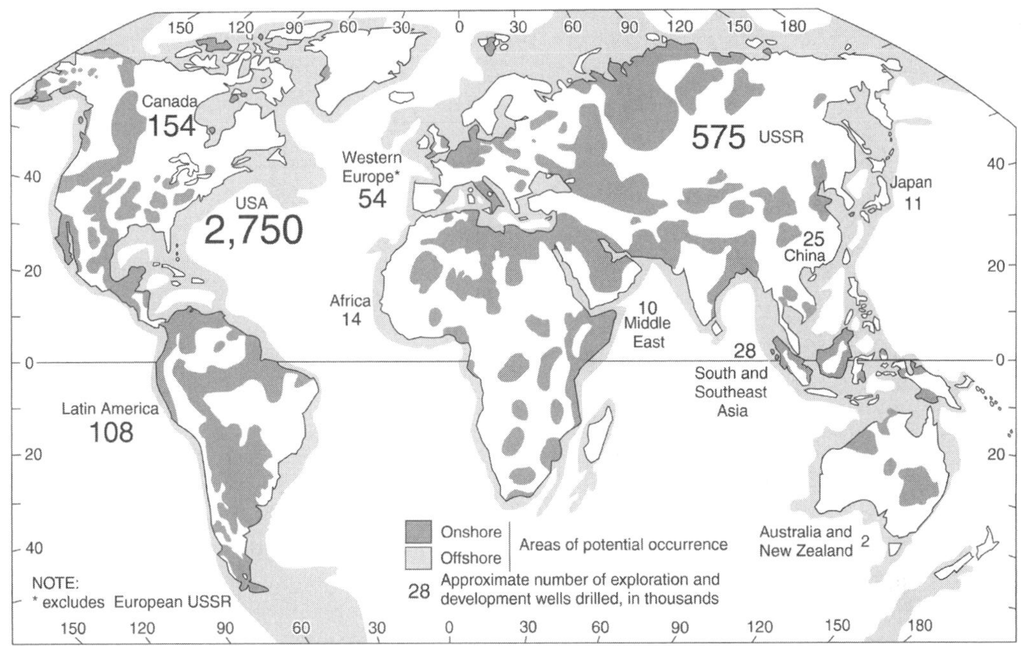

FIGURE 18.2. Potential petroliferous areas and levels of oil exploration. *Sources:* Adapted from Odell and Rosing (1983: 27), Odell (1988: 91). Copyright 1983 by Kogan Page, London.

and nonlabor inputs, or capital goods; labor costs; rents and payments to government; and profits. Large capital costs pay for mining equipment, and for the living quarters and services necessary to support the mine workers in what are often remote areas. These costs are payable before any mining begins, and are increased by the fact that it takes years before any profits can be realized to recoup this investment (and to pay back with interest the loans taken out to finance it). Third world governments often cannot afford these costs; multinational organizations have not lent much money for such risky ventures in the third world; and private enterprise calculates that the lack of infrastructure, remoteness, and perceived political risk of third world locations make them relatively expensive for this kind of long-term investment.

An indication of the nature of these differences in the case of copper mining is given in Table 18.2. The costs of mining and milling, which are labor-intensive activities, are higher for an ore of comparable purity in first world than in third world locations (compare the third and fourth columns for Australia vs. Zambia, or for South Africa vs. the Philippines). This reflects the much higher wages earned by (mostly unionized) first world miners, together with their better working hours, health care benefits, and retirement benefits. Yet despite these differences, the cost of production that would allow a copper-mining company to break even on its investment are often lower for an ore of comparable quality in the first world (now compare the third and fifth columns for the same countries). Break-even costs will depend on the costs of marketing the ore (especially its distance from consumers, who are mostly in the first world); the costs of up-front capital investments; and government subsidies and royalties. Taken together, all these costs put third world locations at a disadvantage. The location of mines, then, depends less on maps of geological fields than on the geography of pro-

TABLE 18.2. Comparative Production Costs for Copper, 1978

Country	Share of western world production (%)	Average ore grade[a]	Mining and milling cost[a]	Break-even cash cost[b]
Australia	3.6	204	253	59
Canada	10.6	74	112	78
South Africa	3.4	55	142	7
United States	22.3	65	73	132
Chile	17.0	118	83	78
Papua New Guinea	3.3	65	53	66
Peru	6.0	119	87	100
Philippines	4.3	51	39	103
Zaire	7.0	493	173	89
Zambia	10.6	244	166	132

Source: Data are from Crowson (1981: 50). Adapted from Rees (1990). Copyright 1990 by Methuen and Co. Adapted by permission of Routledge, Ltd.

[a]Figures represent an index, relative to an average of 100 for all first and third world production.

[b]Mining, milling, administration, taxes, and marketing. Index number: 100 equals first world average.

duction and marketing costs. A comparison of Figure 18.3 (showing global patterns of oil consumption and production) with Figure 18.2 is instructive in this regard. Compare the areas of petroliferous geological formations with both levels of exploration and levels of production in South America and Africa, relative to the United States and Europe. Traditionally, third world countries have played a minor role in the production of most of the world's important mineral resources. In 1987, the first world produced

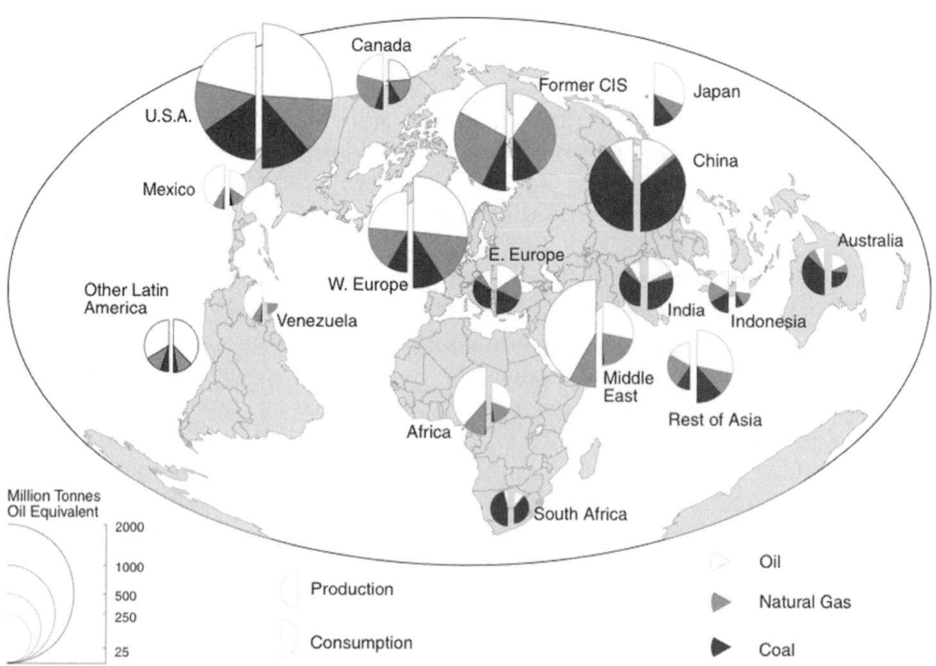

FIGURE 18.3. World geography of oil, natural gas, and coal production and consumption, 2002. CIS, Commonwealth of Independent States (the former USSR). *Source*: Data are from Energy Information Administration (2006).

96% of global magnesium, 73% of zinc, 71% of lead, 67% of bauxite (for aluminum) and nickel, 58% of iron ore, 54% of crude oil, and 53% of copper (Rees, 1990). Over the last two decades, however, third world shares have increased (Figure 18.4).

CONSUMING MINERAL RESOURCES

Global patterns of mineral consumption, even more than production patterns, are shaped by social, economic, and political factors. Consumption depends on what a particular society regards as useful natural resources, and on how necessary those resources are to the lifestyle and production system of that society. Take the example of nuclear power. Norway does not use it, in part because of the cheap availability of hydroelectric power. Austrian consumers have voted not to consume it for reasons of principle. Many third world governments would have no scruples about nuclear power, but political and economic factors limit their access to it. The Nuclear Nonproliferation Treaty requires each country wishing to use nuclear power to be certified by the current nations with nuclear capability that the planned use of nuclear power is peaceful—a process that must include consideration of the country's perceived political stability—before production (and consumption) can begin. A small group of countries has ignored this restriction. Some pay significant costs in the form of political and economic censure (Iran, North Korea), whereas others

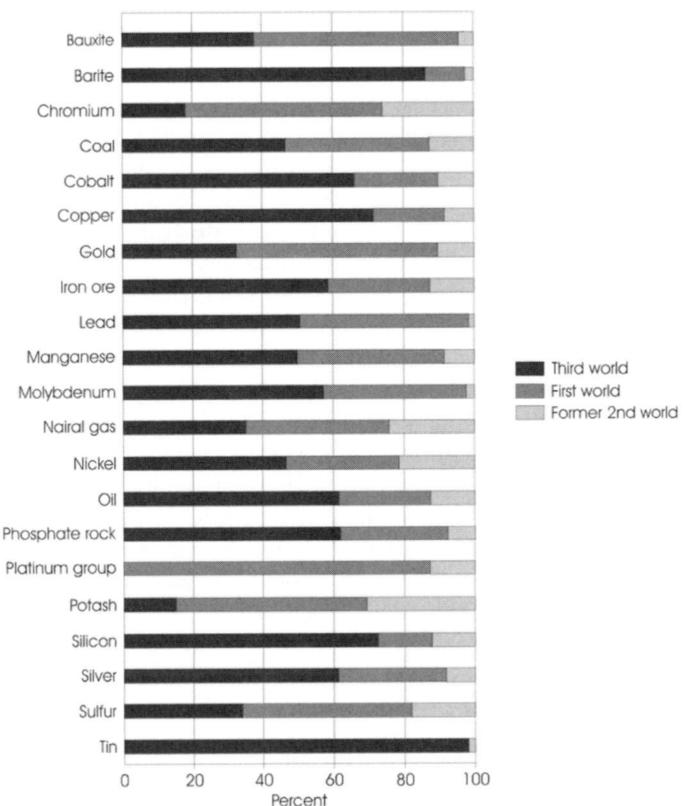

FIGURE 18.4. Regional shares of world production, 2002. *Sources*: Data are from Energy Information Administration (2003), U.S. Geological Survey (USGS, 2006).

that have aligned themselves closely with the United States (Israel, Pakistan, India) receive no censure at all. Such political barriers are compounded by the immense costs of nuclear power and the lack of domestic purchasing power for energy in general.

Figure 18.3 shows consumption patterns for oil, gas, and coal. Rates of consumption in the first world greatly exceed those in the third world. In 2005, the United States, including industry, consumed 40 times as much fossil fuel per person than Africa—an increase from the 29:1 ratio in 1993 (Porter and Sheppard, 1998). By contrast, the gap is narrowing in east Asia, where fossil fuel consumption is exploding alongside rapid industrialization and urbanization in China and southeast Asia. Per capita U.S. consumption still exceeds that in China by more than 10:1, but China's sheer size means that growing demand in east Asia is beginning to affect global minerals trading patterns and prices.

TRADING MINERAL RESOURCES

The trade of mineral resources, like that of any commodity, involves comparing demand and supply at each place. Trade occurs between those places with a net surplus of a resource and those with a net deficit, which is why an understanding of the geography of production and consumption patterns is important to making sense of the flow of resources between countries. Two broad generalizations may be made about global trade in minerals. First, overall trade volumes for minerals, as for other primary commodities, has been dominated by first world exports. Second, third world nations generally have been net exporters of minerals, until recently exporting largely to the first world. At first sight, these two generalizations seem contradictory, but they reflect prevalent disparities in consumption and production between the first and third worlds. First world countries have long dominated global production for reasons discussed above. In 1990, third world production accounted for more than half of global production for just three resources: tin, oil, and cobalt (Rees, 1990). First world exports, generally to other first world markets, have thus been larger.

At the same time, global consumption has been even more skewed toward first world nations than has global production: First world countries consume even more than they produce, whereas third world countries as a group produce more than they consume, and are thus net exporters. As an example, consider Figure 18.5, based on the production and consumption of oil (Figure 18.3). This map shows that trade does not simply match areas with excess production with the nearest areas of excess consumption; instead, economic relations are influenced by history, geography, and politics. In the absence of such factors, we would expect much larger flows from Russia toward western Europe and the United States. Yet during the Cold War, North America and (to a lesser degree) western Europe were reluctant to be dependent on socialist countries for oil. In return, the nations of the former second world developed a broad self-sufficiency in most minerals, to avoid any dependence on first world nations during the Cold War. These countries' contributions to world minerals trade thus remained small until the dissolution of the Council for Mutual Economic Assistance (COMECON) in the 1990s.

This long-standing pattern of global minerals trade is beginning to change. First, former members of the second world are trading more with other regions than they used to. Second, consumption is beginning to explode in those third world countries, particularly in east Asia, that have been experiencing rapid industrialization. For the first time, global demand and prices are being shaped by these developments, particularly in China. The prices of oil and other minerals have increased rapidly in the first few years of the 21st century, driven largely by this new geography of consumption. China has signed a 30-year contract to import cop-

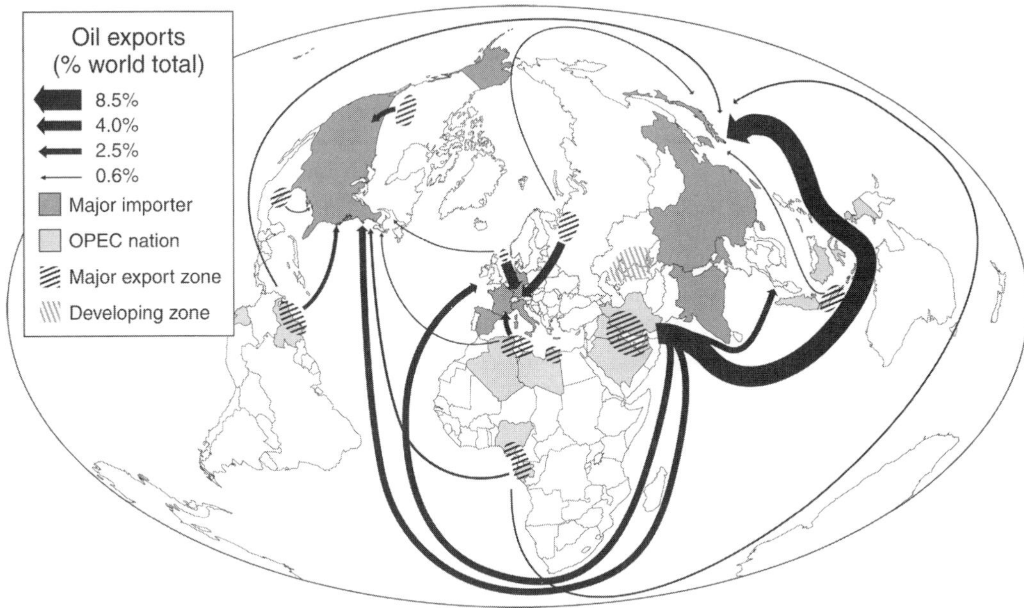

FIGURE 18.5. World oil trade, 2002. *Source*: Data are from Energy Information Administration (2006).

per from Chile, and its representatives have been traveling throughout Africa, offering financial aid in return for similar minerals-trade contracts. It is also importing huge amounts of coal from Australia. Third, the proportion of world minerals production, and thus of exports, stemming from the third world has been increasing. (Compare Figure 18.4 with Figure 11.5 in Porter and Sheppard, 1998: 219.) Trading patterns are thus increasingly influenced by developments in the third world. These developments are beneficial for third world minerals exporters, at least for the time being (thereby encouraging these countries to continue specializing in primary commodities; see Chapter 16). They are also creating new geopolitical conflicts between first world and third world countries over access to underexploited mineral resources, such as oil around the Caspian Sea (see sidebar: "Oil, OPEC, and Development"). Finally, they are increasing the speed at which mineral resources are likely to run out.

THE FUTURE OF MINERAL RESOURCES

We all worry about mineral resources running out, but no one can tell exactly how long they will last. Estimates of the quantities in the earth's crust, their availability for human exploitation, and the rate at which they will be consumed vary widely, since these estimates are based on assumptions made in different ways by different forecasting agencies for different purposes. Two things are sure, however. Current western lifestyles, to which many people worldwide currently aspire, are based on heavy consumption of some very rare minerals in the earth's crust. Making these lifestyles available to all people in the world would mean that we will run out of resources very quickly indeed because of this reliance on rare materials. Thus the lifestyles of the first world are not environmentally sustainable, except by maintaining current geographical and social inequalities in wealth.

Oil, OPEC, and Development

Consider for a moment how global production and consumption of oil have evolved over time. This will give some insight into the way in which social, economic, political, and cultural forces intersect with biophysical processes to produce the oil fields and oil-trading patterns of the world. Before 1859, no maps of oil fields were drawn, for the simple reason that oil was not yet regarded as a natural resource. Its utility as a source of energy was not well known, and other sources seemed quite sufficient. If such maps had been drawn in 1901, the only source of supply depicted would have been the United States, and the only export would have been to Europe (in small quantities). Yet demand for oil rapidly exceeded this source of supply, beginning a trend that persists to this day: the search for new sources of supply for Europe and later North America. By 1935, the map would have begun to show sources of supply in Iran, Venezuela, Iraq, Kuwait, the Soviet Union, and Saudi Arabia, with the principal point of excess demand still being Europe. At that time, known oil fields in the first world were becoming exhausted; this led to prospecting by first world nations in new locations. In the 1910s and 1920s, the discovery of huge fields in the Middle East—an area dominated by European colonial powers at that time—prompted a radical shift in production patterns. British Petroleum moved into Iran as early as 1913. In the 1930s, a British–French–American consortium set up operations in Iraq; British Petroleum and American Gulf moved into Kuwait; and the Arabian-American Oil Company (ARAMCO) began operating in Saudi Arabia. These were newly created countries, carved out of the Ottoman Empire after 1918 under French and British supervision, from a region with no previous history of sovereign nation states. It was populated by distinct and often rival groups, but borders between them had been fuzzy and flexible—unlike the fixed borders that are placed around nation states. European powers ignored this fluidity, defining borders and selecting initial rulers. Three wide-ranging, fluid Muslim empires were thus broken up into 23 nations with client rulers, as European notions of political order were imposed on the Middle East.

For example, the British created Kuwait as a miniature sheikdom on the edge of Iraq in the 1930s—over the strong objections of the many Kuwaitis and Iraqis who supported unification—in order to deny Iraq access to the sea. In the subsequent histories of these nations, immense wealth accrued to the small number of Kuwaitis, compared to continued relative poverty in a populous Iraq, where oil revenues per capita were far smaller.

The dominance of the Middle East as a point of oil production steadily increased, but local concerns about limited revenues as a result of U.S.–European control over oil production triggered the formation in 1960 of a political economic bloc: the Organization of the Petroleum Exporting Countries (OPEC). In 1973, in response to the Yom Kippur War between Israel and surrounding Arab states, OPEC moved to use its nation states' sovereignty to place oil production within a cartel that ensured greater local ownership of oil companies and greatly increased oil royalties. The unique success of this third world production cartel, increasing oil prices and oil incomes 10-fold in 7 years, can be traced to a number of factors. First, world exports had come to be dominated by third world producers. Second, these producers shared many characteristics that eased collaboration: language; Muslim religion (extending to non-Middle East oil exporters, Nigeria and Indonesia, although oil is in southern Nigeria, whereas the Muslims are in the north); colonial relations with Europe; and the presence of European and American oil companies that had become extremely rich on the basis of their oil fields. Third, the first world had become heavily dependent on cheap oil as its prime source of energy for industry and transportation. Oil companies were promulgating an extremely optimistic picture of oil availability and oil prices at this time—much more optimistic than the oil industry's own estimates of oil resources could possibly justify (Odell and Rosing, 1983).

OPEC's actions triggered a historically unprecedented rise in world prices (see adjacent figure). This resulted in an "oil crisis" in 1973 and again in 1979, during which Europeans and Americans spent hours lining up at gas stations and the price of oil exploded (for OPEC, these certainly were not crises!). Even under these uniquely favorable conditions, however, these windfalls, huge as they were, lasted only a decade. By 1986, oil prices were again as low in real terms (i.e., adjusted for inflation) as they had been before the 1973 oil crisis. The cartel had been undermined by both external responses and internal differences. In the first world, oil consumption gradually declined, as a result of increased fuel efficiency and conversion to other energy sources: natural gas, coal, and nuclear power. Oil companies and national governments also spent billions searching for and drilling new oil fields outside OPEC—on Alaska's north slope, in Europe's North Sea, and in nations such as Mexico. The United States and other countries also created strategic energy reserves that would buttress them against future such threats to their energy independence. Internally, OPEC's unity fell apart as the interests of small nations (which had accumulated more than enough oil money to create immense wealth, and were willing to produce more oil at lower prices) clashed with those of populous OPEC members (which still had widespread poverty and wanted to keep prices high). The windfall profits to OPEC from the oil crisis did not improve the lives of the majority of the residents of OPEC nations. Large chunks supported opulent lifestyles for a few, and much flowed into the coffers of western banks, which then lent it back to the third world with interest (see Chapter 22).

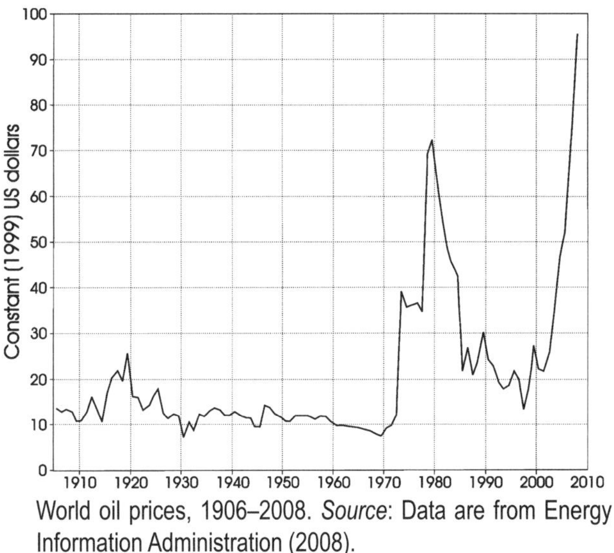

World oil prices, 1906–2008. *Source*: Data are from Energy Information Administration (2008).

Such economic and political differences were compounded by war. Since 1983, a three-stage Persian Gulf war has undermined OPEC's coherence and the Middle East's dominance of global oil production.

1. In 1980, Iraq invaded Iran, seeking to control oil fields along the Iran–Iraq border. The United States supported these attacks against the country that had thrown out its American-backed Shah and taken Americans hostage. Saddam Hussein met with President Reagan's envoy Donald Rumsfeld in 1983, and thereafter gained access to cluster bombs and chemical and biological weapons technology. The war ended in 1988, at a cost of over a million lives and no change in the border.
2. In 1990, Iraq invaded Kuwait, after a long-running border dispute that affected each nation's ability to drill and exploit the immense oil field running under the Iraqi–Kuwait border, as well as Kuwaiti attempts to get Iraq to repay debts accumulated during the war with Iran. A week before this invasion, the U.S. ambassador allegedly told Hussein that the United States "had no opinion on . . . your border dispute with Kuwait." The United States assembled a multilateral military force, under UN support and U.S. control, that in 1991 invaded Kuwait and Iraq from Saudi Arabia (itself having been promised U.S. support against both external and domestic threats to the Saudi regime). External observers have estimated that during the ensuing 10 years—as Iraq coped with international sanctions, external support for Kurdish and Shiite independence movements, and daily military air incursions—up to 100,000 civilians died (mostly women and children).

3. Trumped-up charges, promulgated by Rumsfeld (then U.S. Secretary of Defense), about the presence in Iraq of weapons of mass destruction triggered a U.S.-led invasion of Iraq in 2003, with no Arab or UN support. At this writing, this occupation continues—with 60,000 civilian deaths to date, but without significant resumption of Iraqi oil exports.

The concurrence of oil fields and Muslim-majority countries extends beyond OPEC. After the dissolution of the second world, its oil fields have also become available to world markets. Particularly rich oil fields in the former Soviet countries surrounding the Caspian Sea have become a new focus for geopolitical struggle. These fields are no longer under Russian political control but are exploited by Russian, and now western, firms. They are close to the rapidly growing oil markets of east and south Asia, but also in an area where U.S. military influence has increased markedly after the 2002 invasion of Afghanistan (another country invented by the British along with the Russians).

Estimating Reserves and Resources

Consider again Table 18.1, which includes the U.S. Bureau of Mines estimates of the availability of scarce resources. Two sets of figures are given: one estimating reserves, or the quantities of each mineral currently known to exist in concentrations that can be exploited via available technology (column 3); the other estimating resources, or current "guesstimates," as to how much of this mineral will ever be found, in concentrations that will ever be exploitable (column 4). The latter estimates are, of course, larger than the former (which represent the more conservative estimates).

Even estimates of reserves vary from one expert to another. There is very little agreement on estimates of ultimately recoverable resources. These estimates depend on two sets of assumptions, which are subject to extreme uncertainty, and consequently are argued about and manipulated for various purposes. One has to do with what percentage of a mineral is likely to be found at different concentrations. As discussed earlier, the common assumption is a bell-shaped curve, but this also may be too optimistic (Figure 18.1). The second set of assumptions is an estimate of the effort a society will eventually expend in order to extract the mineral. This is based on guesses about how efficient extraction technologies will become, and on how high the price of the mineral will eventually rise (since extraction must be profitable). The more optimistic this assumption, the larger the darkly shaded area in Figure 18.1.

Differences in either of these assumptions can drastically affect estimates of resources. For example, in 1977 the U.S. Geological Survey (USGS) estimated the resources of iron as 130 billion tons, whereas another survey arrived at the figure of 1,500 billion tons—more than 10 times as large. Although both surveys agreed on the first assumption and on the total amount of iron in the earth's crust, the latter was more optimistic about mining technology: It assumed that mining to depths of 2.5 kilometers below the earth's surface would eventually be profitable, as opposed to the figure of 1 kilometer used by the USGS. Although USGS estimates of resources are the figures most often quoted, there are reasons to believe that even these figures, with their more conservative view of mining technology, may be excessive. They assume that all these recoverable resources will be found; that all resources can be reached, even those under ice caps and cities; that all deposits of adequate quality are large enough in size to be economically exploitable and do not consist of a series of widely scattered but very small high-quality deposits, which are hard to find and uneconomical to mine; and that the distribution of ore quantities by quality is represented by Figure 18.1.

These uncertainties mean that every

estimate of resources is based on a series of assumptions whose nature will depend on the organization making the forecast. The economic geographers Odell and Rosing (1983) showed, for example, that oil industry estimates of global oil resources of 1,600 billion barrels of oil in 1978 excluded alternative oil sources such as oil shales, and also underestimated oil resources in third world locations, which they perceived as politically risky. Table 18.3 shows their comparison of oil industry estimates with those of the U.S. and Soviet governments in the 1970s. Publishing low estimates, of course, increases perceptions of scarcity and helps maintain higher prices—a strategy that other analysts argue is persistently followed by the mineral industry (Barnet, 1980; Tanzer, 1980).

How Long Will They Last?

Minerals in the earth's crust are nonrenewable resources; we cannot rely on geological or biological processes to replace any of them within the time span of human society. The length of time before the resources of a mineral run out is generally calculated from estimates of the quantity available and likely to be discovered in the foreseeable future, and from the average rate of growth of output. If we assume that world demand will not increase, we can calculate a *static* index of lifetimes, by simply dividing the amount available by the annual output (given in column 5 of Table 18.1). Table 18.4 contains such estimates for 37 of the minerals and fossil fuels of Table 18.1, in columns 2 (for reserves) and 5 (for U.S. estimates of resources). From column 7 in Table 18.1, however, we see that demand is not constant, but increasing on an annual basis by anywhere from 1% to 6% per year. A 6% annual increase means that demand will double every 11 years, and that static estimates are clearly overoptimistic.

A *dynamic* calculation of lifetimes takes into account annual increases in demand, by assuming that current growth rates of demand will continue forever. This leads to shorter lifetimes (columns 3 and 6 of Table 18.4). For example, oil will last for 50–100 years if demand does not increase, but for just 25–45 years if world demand increases at current rates of 2.3% annually. These dynamic estimates are clearly "business as usual" projections. We do not know how rapidly demand will increase in the future, because trends change. In first world countries, demand for oil increased by 3% annually between 1974 and 1979, decreased by 6% a year until 1983, and increased again thereafter. Such uncertainty is unfortunate, because small differences in estimated rates of increase in demand mean very large differences in the lifetimes of resources. Table 18.5 takes different official estimates of oil resources and calculates lifetimes based on different plausible estimates of rates of growth in world demand. Estimates vary from 25 to 96 years, depending on which of these assumptions or speculations the reader accepts as most plausible—clearly a big difference!

The estimates discussed thus far are based on current consumption behavior, which of course includes the great global inequities in consumption. Accordingly, assuming that future rates of growth in demand will be like today's rates also assumes that these inequities will remain.

TABLE 18.3. Alternative Estimates of Oil Resources in the Third World (Billions of Barrels, 1978)

Region	Oil industry	Grossling (USGS)	Ministry of Geology (USSR)
Latin America	150–230	490–1,225	686
Africa	120–170	470–1,200	730
South/southeast Asia	55–80	130–325	409

Source: Adapted from Odell and Rosing (1983: 32). Copyright 1983 by Kogan Page, London.

TABLE 18.4. Estimates of the Lifetimes of Minerals (Years)

	Reserves			Resources			
Mineral (1)	Static lifetime (2)	Dynamic lifetime (3)	Redistributive lifetime (4)	Static lifetime (5)	Dynamic lifetime (6)	Redistributive lifetime (7)	Goeller and Zucker: % left in 2100 A.D. (8)
Coal	20	16	4	3877	185	836	—
Oil	5	4	6	12	11	16	—
Natural gas	57	36	11	80	44	15	—
Uranium	37	22	7	52	27	10	—
Iron	105	48	118	243	71	273	14%
Nickel	41	25	13	93	40	29	0%
Manganese	44	66	25	531	Long	301	0%
Chromium	33	36	102	667	203	2032	88%
Vanadium	299	97	141	874	147	414	77%
Cobalt	134	85	29	248	124	54	0%
Molybdenum	53	74	11	117	Long	25	0%
Rhenium	56	27	3	231	53	13	0%
Tungsten	26	29	8	81	102	24	0%
Tantalum	23	19	3	79	48	11	0%
Copper	32	22	9	63	34	19	0%
Tellurium	230	n.a.	16	416	n.a.	29	22%
Zinc	23	17	8	46	29	15	0%
Cadmium	33	24	64	100	52	191	0%
Germanium	33	23	5	Long	Long	Long	0%
Indium	6	5	1	13	10	2	0%
Aluminum	1,515	81	1,088	1,939	122	1,393	0%
Titanium	1	1	0	57	30	8	0%
Tin	22	18	4	39	29	8	0%
Lead	28	25	2	59	46	4	0%
Antimony	15	14	2	33	29	5	0%
Bismuth	63	29	6	131	41	13	0%
Silver	13	10	2	28	20	3	0%
Gold	17	12	10	37	19	21	0%
Platinum	326	60	33	367	61	37	42%
Mercury	75	75	22	150	150	45	0%
Zirconium	44	30	43	83	46	82	0%
Barite	26	Long	3	97	Long	12	0%
Niobium	133	65	28	158	71	33	0%
Selenium	61	29	6	126	42	13	0%
Sulfur	22	20	5	78	48	18	0%
Phosphate	122	58	21	338	95	57	—
Potash	268	98	62	548	134	127	—
Silicon	Very long	Very long	Very long	Very long	Very long	Very long	—

Note. —, no estimates published; n.a., not available.

Sources: Data in column 8 are from Goeller and Zucker (1984). Other data represent our own calculations from Table 18.1

Thus the static and dynamic estimates of lifetimes do not consider any equalization of mineral resource use among peoples and countries (unless North Americans and Europeans were to reduce their consumption, which for U.S. residents would mean using just one-fifth of what they use today). The remaining estimates in Table 18.4 consider the implications of qualitative increases in resource consumption in the third world. "Redistributive" estimates (columns 4 and 7) calculate the length of time a mineral or fossil fuel will last if per capita rates of consumption throughout the globe were immediately increased to match current U.S. levels, and thereafter remain constant. Some lifetime estimates are so short that half a dozen of our minerals should already be gone, based on calculations made for the first edition of this book! A more plausible scenario is represented in column 8. This describes the percentage of current resources that will remain in 2100 A.D. if per capita demand in the first world countries does not increase after 2000 A.D., whereas per capita demand in the third world increases gradually to reach a level of one-half of current per capita demand in the developed world in the year 2100 A.D. In this case also, it has been estimated that only five minerals will still be available in the earth's crust by 2100: iron, chromium, vanadium, tellurium, and platinum (Goeller and Zucker, 1984).

Projections such as those of Table 18.4 are of course very crude, and there is no reason why any of them should be accurate. Yet they clearly show that, with a few exceptions, the time until the mineral reserves are exhausted is limited. This time can be further reduced by profit-maximizing strategies of mineral exploitation. Thus, taking the example of a North Sea oil field, Odell and Rosing (1976) showed that if a company employs a profit-maximizing geographical pattern of drilling, this does not maximize the total quantity of oil that can be extracted. Furthermore, the residual oil cannot be subsequently extracted once the profit-maximizing strategy has been completed.

Mineral lifetimes can be lengthened by reducing per capita consumption, by recycling the minerals found in industrial and household wastes, by increasing the durability of goods made with those minerals, and by finding less scarce substitutes. From a global point of view, some argue that substitution combined with efficient recycling can make lifetimes effectively infinite (the cornucopian thesis; see Chapter 6). Although there are minerals with no known substitutes (iron, aluminum, magnesium, phosphorus, manganese, and fluorine), these are all fairly abundant and themselves represent substitutes for scarcer metals (copper, zinc, lead, nickel, and cobalt).

Special attention should be paid to sources of fuel, however. Fossil fuel is known as a "flow resource," because it is used up when it is consumed; this rules out recycling as a method for increasing lifetimes. Furthermore, increased rather than decreased energy supplies will be necessary to exploit productively the less concentrated ores that form a large part of the estimated resources. Yet it is clear from Table 18.4 that oil, natural gas, and uranium are in particularly short supply. In terms of nonrenewable

TABLE 18.5. Estimating the Lifetime of Oil Resources (Years)

	Assumed growth rate of world demand			
Estimated resources (bil. barrels)	1.5%	2.5%	4.5%	7.5%
1,500	50	43	32	25
4,500	96	76	53	39

Sources: Data on assumed growth rates are from Odell and Rosing (1983); lifetime estimate data represent our calculations using the dynamic method.

natural resources, then, major alterations in use patterns will become necessary. The only long-term options are increased conservation, decreased material consumption levels in the developed world, and renewable sources of energy.

Conservation contributed significantly to decreased per capita demand for gasoline after the OPEC oil crisis of the 1970s, particularly in the United States, where there was a 30% reduction between 1970 and 1986. More efficient automobiles, and the substitution of the more common coal for oil as a source of industrial and commercial energy, were the principal mechanisms through which this occurred. Yet habits developed in times of cheap energy and unprecedented wealth are hard to break. The very structure of North American cities makes energy hard to conserve. They were constructed as part of an era of personal transportation and individual-dwelling heating systems, which are more wasteful than the mass transit and district heating found in, say, northern Europe. U.S. and European consumers returned to their gas-guzzling ways as real oil prices fell after 1982, buying sport utility vehicles and building exurban communities. Oil, automobile, real estate, and other durable goods corporations actively encouraged such profit-making behavior (for them), and neoliberalizing states tended to turn a blind eye to these "market logics," despite such actions as signing the 1997 Kyoto Protocol on climate change—even when politicians were not actively in the pockets of such powerful patrons. (At this writing, the United States has signed, but has not ratified, the Kyoto Protocol.)

Although overconsumption of mineral resources in first world countries is clearly contributing to an unsustainable use of our global environment, unfortunately it does not follow that the adoption of strategies to prolong these resources' lifetimes is necessarily beneficial to third world nations. If the use of mineral resources shifts from mining them to recycling them, then third world countries that have come to rely on selling their natural resources to finance development will have to pursue other paths to economic growth. This will bring difficult adjustments, because these countries have come to rely heavily on such exports, despite questions about the wisdom of such a strategy of specialization and trade (see Chapter 16). When materials are recycled, it is in the places of greatest consumption that the best opportunities will exist for making money from mineral resources, and these include few places in the third world. Similarly, a shift from geographically localized to more widespread minerals (such as using silicon from sand for fiber optic wiring, instead of copper wires) will mean that a greater number of places will be able to produce the resources in demand.

Second, recycling in first world countries can have at least undesirable short-term side effects on selected third world locations. Although the great strides made in Germany in plastics recycling reduced solid waste there, the supply of recycled plastics outstripped domestic demand. As a consequence, these plastics have been marketed to third world nations, such as Indonesia. One consequence of this has been that informal sector workers there, who used to make their living from the unhealthy practice of sifting through garbage for plastic bags, were displaced from even this marginal activity as a result of the importation of cheaper recycled plastics from Germany. More broadly, lacking more positive options, a number of third world localities have agreed to import and process or store waste from first world countries producing waste at a faster pace than can be absorbed by local dumping and incineration facilities—including medical and nuclear waste.

Third, concern about environmental degradation in first world countries has led to considerable pressure on third world nations to conform to high environmental standards through such activities as reducing factory pollution, introducing environmentally friendly production practices, and stopping the indiscriminate destruction of tropical rainforests. Although these are important and perhaps vital changes, and are widely supported in the third world, its policymakers have argued that this once again tilts the playing field against third world nations. Whereas Europe and North America could industrialize in the 19th century without taking the effort to protect the environment, third world nations are being pressured to take a more difficult and costly path to industrialization, while already competing with more sophisticated industries elsewhere (see Chapter 17). It has been suggested that third world nations need extra resources to enable them to meet these potentially conflicting goals of industrialization and development, but little help has been forthcoming. Lacking such assistance, third world countries have been able to negotiate exceptions to the obligations of the Kyoto Protocol that recognize this difficulty—underwriting rapid, pollution-creating industrialization in places like China.

RENEWABLE ENERGY FROM THE BIOSPHERE

For most of recorded history, people have used renewable sources of energy, such as sunshine, wood, dried dung, agricultural wastes, and falling water. The sun, of course, is our most important energy source. When we heat our houses or cook dinner, we are simply "topping up," adding to the heat provided by the interaction of the sun and the earth's atmosphere. Without their help, we would have to heat the house, or our lentil stew, from absolute zero (–273.15°C)! Rural third world people still probably obtain more than 90% of their energy from renewable sources, although this has become increasingly difficult. The industrialized economies, by contrast, fueled their development largely with nonrenewable energy (especially coal and oil); natural gas and subsequently nuclear power have been more recent contributors to energy output (McDonald, 1981). Industrialization and urbanization in the third world have also been closely associated with the availability of nonrenewable energy—at least for those who can afford it. Table 18.6 shows the changing mix of energy sources through time.

Inevitably, the production of nonrenewable resources follows a "boom and bust" cycle. The summit of this cycle has recently been dubbed "Hubbert's peak," after U.S. geophysicist Marion King Hubbert. As one source peaks, energy is devoted to the next alternative, each marked by a time lag between the rate of proved discovery and the rate of production. The case of the United States (Figure 18.6), where for oil the time lag was about 10.5 years and Hubbert's peak was reached in the mid-1950s (McDonald, 1981), shows a sort of fugal chase through nonrenewable energy resources:

discovery > production > substitution
    discovery > production > substitution
        discovery > production > substitution

TABLE 18.6. Changing Mix of World Energy Sources

	Percentage contribution to total energy used					
Energy source	1875	1900	1925	1950	1975	1995
Wood, vegetation	60	39	26	21	13	10
Coal	38	58	61	44	27	17
Oil	2	2	10	25	40	40
Natural gas	<1	1	2	8	15	23
Other sources (mainly hydroelectric and nuclear)	<1	<1	1	2	5	10

Sources: Adapted from Haggett (1975: 200). Copyright 1975 by Peter Haggett. Adapted by permission of Addison-Wesley Educational Publishers, Inc. Data for 1995 are from World Resources Institute (1996b).

Figure 18.6 shows how this has played out worldwide, shifting from a 60% reliance on biomass in the late 19th century to a 40% reliance on oil a century later. Current debates about how soon oil will run out, and when it will reach $100 or even $200 a barrel, are dominated by disputes about when Hubbert's peak was, or will be, reached for the world as a whole. In 1995, oil and natural gas amounted to 63% of the global energy market; just 13% consisted of renewable fuels, largely accounted for by third world consumption—dried dung (for cooking and heating), wood and vegetable refuse (with firewood and charcoal constituting the bulk of this category), and plant materials fed to animals. The world's 400 million draft animals, serving two billion people worldwide, will continue to make major contributions to agricultural tasks—plowing fields, turning pumps and threshers, and transporting goods to market (Lazlo, 1981: 242). Of course, renewable sources of energy have become increasingly popular in the first world as possible substitutes for fossil fuels. Hydroelectric power, wind and wave turbines, biomass substitutes for gasoline and diesel, photovoltaic cells to concentrate solar energy, and geothermal sources are all the rage—each pushed by particular grassroots initiatives, energy providers, and state agencies. Estimates in the United States suggest that each of these alternative energy sources is of comparable efficiency, in terms of energy output relative to energy input (Figure 18.7). Yet the abilities of first world countries to obtain oil cheaply from the third world, combined with vested economic and political interests in fossil and nuclear fuels, have tilted the playing field away from renewable alternatives.

The third world participates differentially in the consumption of nonrenewable resources. Oil-producing countries of the third world export most of their product, generally to the first world, and some have gained substantial windfall profits as a result of this (see the "Oil, OPEC, and Development" sidebar, above). Nevertheless, the costs to local environments and residents have been significant, triggering resistance (see Chapter 24 sidebar, "Nigerian Women Shock Shell"). Oil-importing countries may pay a heavy price for their

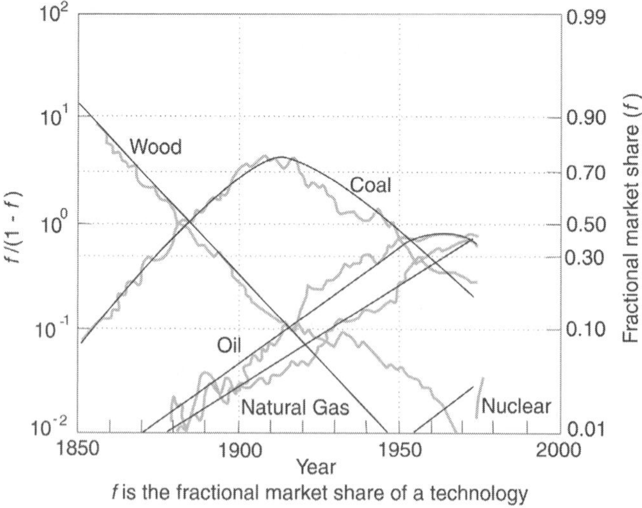

FIGURE 18.6. History of primary energy substitution in the United States, 1850–1975. *Source:* Adapted from McDonald (1981). Copyright 1981 by the International Institute for Applied Systems Analysis. Adapted by permission.

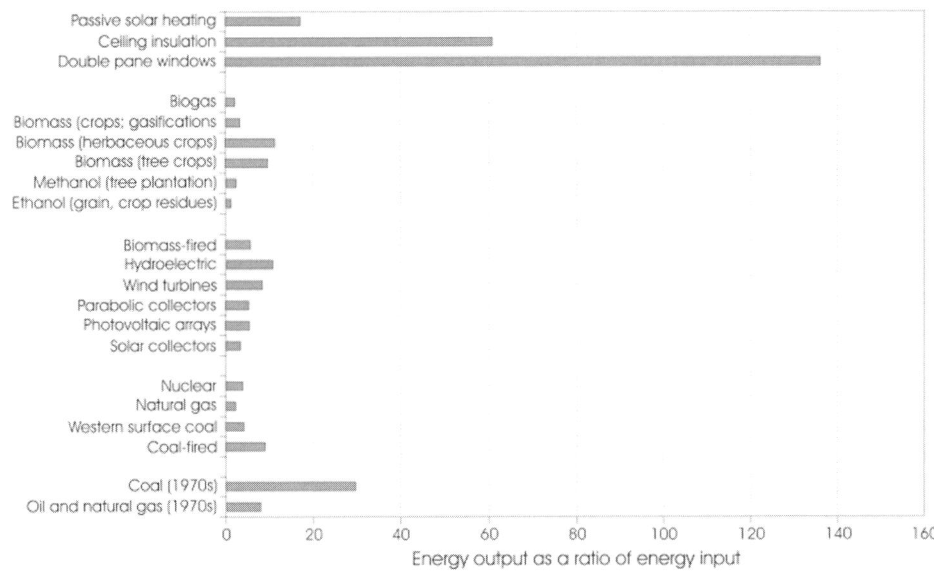

FIGURE 18.7. Efficiency of alternative energy sources, United States. *Source*: Land Institute (2004).

oil and other imported fuels (which must be bought with hard currency), although they need these fuels for industry, transportation, and urbanization. At the same time, the third world continues to actively utilize and retain substantial expertise in the use of noncommercial renewable energy sources, unlike the virtual abandonment of such alternatives, until very recently, in the first world (Figure 18.7). Table 18.7 gives continental (and, by extension, first world–third world) comparisons in the per capita consumption of commercial and noncommercial energy. Although wood and charcoal are certainly sold and therefore "commercial," in this instance "commercial" means oil, natural gas, coal, and nuclear energy, and "noncommercial" means wood, charcoal, dried dung, and agricultural waste products (rice hulls, maize cobs, etc.). The percentages tell the story. The industrialized world derives about 1% of its energy from noncommercial sources, whereas African dependence on noncommercial fuels is 64%. Asia and Latin America rely on noncommercial fuels for about a quarter of their energy consumption. The ratios of commercial (essentially nonrenewable) energy use between first world and

TABLE 18.7. Per Capita Energy Consumption (in Kilograms of Oil or Equivalents)

	Africa	Asia	Latin America	Industrialized countries	World
Commercial	155	401	853	4,419	1,502
Noncommercial	276	119	291	58	132
Total	431	520	1,144	4,477	1,634
Noncommercial (as % of total)	64.0	29.7	25.4	1.3	8.1

Source: O'Keefe and Kristoferson (1984: 186). Copyright 1984 by the Royal Swedish Academy of Sciences. Reprinted by permission.

third world economies are 28.5:1 (Africa), 11.0:1 (Asia), and 5.2:1 (Latin America).

As noted above, there are huge social and geographical differences within third world countries. Urban elites live a lifestyle based, as in the first world, on consuming huge amounts of nonrenewable energy with an unsustainable ecological footprint (Chapter 6). The vast majority of the rural population, and some of the urban poor, extract their energy mainly from the biosphere (not the nonrenewable lithosphere), with a much smaller ecological footprint. Forests and woodlands can provide fuel and construction material on a sustained basis if managed properly. Hosier and Boberg (1992: 18) found that many areas of Tanzania could provide a steady supply of firewood and charcoal, as long as the young shoots of trees that had been cut down were protected from goats and cattle, and natural coppicing was managed. This management consists of pruning away all but one or two of the sprouts, so that a tree rather than a bush regrows from the stump. Where forest areas have been degraded (as in Shinyanga and Kondoa), it is the combined result of overgrazing/overbrowsing, fire, cultivation, and wood cutting, not of wood cutting alone.

Various factors have combined to make it increasingly difficult for third world residents to draw energy sustainably from their immediate environment. Although it is popular to blame the residents themselves for local ecological devastation, the causes typically lie further afield. First, governments replace local mixed ecosystems with fenced-off monoculture forestry plantations or create wildlife preserves, excluding locals from a variety of ecological resources that once underwrote their well-being, including energy (Chapter 7). The original forest vegetation is an expression of the fact that particular communities of plants, animals, and humans evolved together in that particular environment in the first place. Similarly, creation of wildlife preserves from which humans are excluded (unless they are in Land Rovers) also challenges ecosystems that had coevolved with local cultural practices for centuries. Gade and Perkins-Belgram (1986) question the reliance on fast-growing exotic species (eucalyptus, wattle, pine) grown in plantations and afforestation schemes. They argue that such an approach is maladaptive in the long term.

Second, novel practices of profit making diffuse in, undermining the viability of local ecosystems. We have all read about the devastation in forested areas in Brazil and Central America: Such areas are logged, and cattle ranching replaces tropical forests for a few years, but the ranches are abandoned when soils become toxic and the grass cover becomes too impoverished even to support livestock (Fearnside, 1986; Hecht and Cockburn, 1989; Nations and Komer, 1983). Losses in Asia and the Pacific are no less pronounced (Messerschmidt, 1987; Ranjitsinh, 1979; Smil, 1983). There is a lesson here: *Adaptation* by local people is generally more successful than *adoption* administered from above or outside. Third, the displacement of local populations from their land, without the availability of alternative livelihood chances, increases impoverishment and people's need for noncommercial energy sources: They simply cannot afford to buy cooking oil, so they must search for fuelwood and dung.

As stocks of firewood are used up, people must walk farther to collect fuel. In Kenya, some households devote as much as 15 hours per week to fuelwood collection (O'Keefe and Kristoferson, 1984: 170). This certainly damages the ecosystem, but not because people are behaving wastefully or irrationally. Indeed, their impact on the biophysical environment is much smaller than our own. Furthermore, gathering fuel has often been gendered as a feminine practice, and the time devoted to it undermines the opportunities for women and girls to gain an education and a job. Although this gendered practice is shaped heavily by class (e.g., girls of better-off families in a village might go to school instead of on fuel-gathering treks), it nevertheless contributes to reproducing existing gendered economic and political hierarchies in the household and the village.

Local alternatives do exist, and there is plenty of local know-how to draw on. Reforestation that utilizes indigenous tree species could meet the varied local needs for fuel, small timber, and fodder, while also rehabilitating the environment, preserving biological diversity, stopping soil erosion, and regulating runoff and stream flow. However, this can become more difficult in contexts where commodification pressures make short-run incomes more important than long-term sustainability. For instance, in many rural communities in North India, poor families have turned to growing eucalyptus for quick income through sale of timber, even though they are acutely aware that eucalyptus reduces yields of fruits such as mango and jamun. It is now generally recognized by "development experts" and "communities" alike that fuel requirements, and the health risks associated with cooking over open fires in small enclosed spaces, could be reduced with more efficient stoves and heaters. Where such projects have succeeded, they have usually involved adaptation of an existing technological practice, not adoption of a technology introduced from elsewhere. The lesson is clear: On the one hand, local ecological and technological know-how should not be overlooked. Various technological institutes have been working on these problems, drawing on local expertise throughout the third world, but as yet are without the resources to implement their ideas in ways that best meet the diverse needs of families currently forced to overexploit local resources. On the other hand, there is a need for nonlocal strategies to address the broader-scale processes, such as those described above, that undermine local possibilities.

What energy will replace oil and natural gas in the 21st century? Arguments for nuclear energy have become more muted, given the technical, political, ecological, and economic problems of long-term storage of radioactive spent fuels and the cost of decommissioning reactors, but nuclear energy still enjoys powerful support in the first and third worlds. Thus far most of the newer "soft" technologies (biogas, solar energy, wind, ocean waves, geothermal energy, ethanol, etc.) have made only limited contributions to meeting the energy needs of third world people. Biogas is becoming important in China and India. Although solar heating of water has had some success, solar cookers may not function on cloudy days, and need frequent adjustment to ensure that the cookers track the sun properly; moreover, women generally cook at the end of the day (about the time the sun sets). Persistent, strong winds are largely absent in the tropics, so wind energy is seldom a useful option there.

There is promise for photovoltaics, the energy technology that provides energy for satellites. The attributes of photovoltaics are summarized by Hayes (1977: 26): "They have no moving parts, consume no fuel, produce no pollution, operate at ambient temperatures, last a long time, require little maintenance, and normally consist of silicon, the second most abundant element in the earth's crust." Another good feature of solar energy is that it is essentially ubiquitous. No economies of scale are gained by concentrating solar energy generation in large power plants; indeed, energy generation is best placed close to where the energy is to be used. This property has made it difficult for large energy firms to control solar energy production. This in turn is one reason why growth has been slow, despite the steadily declining costs of solar power generation, which are now comparable to those of fossil fuels and much lower than those of nuclear energy. Although ultimately solar energy may be the best hope for abundant, inexpensive, nonpolluting energy for everyone, wood, dung, and plant materials are destined to be the major energy sources for most rural third world people for the foreseeable future (Eckholm, 1979). The challenge is for them to meet their needs without destroying their surroundings.

CONCLUSIONS

We have seen that the availability of minerals is not simply a question of geology. Human processes and societal practices condition what makes a chemical element a resource or mineral that we seek to exploit. These same practices influence the locations where such resources are sought, and thus their effective availability. Finally, even though biophysical processes largely independent of human action determine the scarcity and geographical distribution of these resources, the socioeconomic systems within which humans seek to use them condition their extraction, availability, and future scarcity. In this sense, "natural" resources do not determine human practices; rather, there is a complex interdependence between human and biophysical systems that we still do not fully understand. Geographical differences are a part of this complexity—differences between different regions of the world in the power to define, extract, and use resources, as well as in knowledge, beliefs, and everyday practices of resource use. The high degree of interdependence of these practices—how the use of resources in industrial societies conditions their availability for those living in other places and future times, and how even waste recycling by European households can affect the livelihoods of Indonesian families—illustrates how closely all our diverse current and future lives are intertwined.

19 Urbanization, Migration, and Spatial Polarization

Since societies first developed permanent urban settlements—up to 5,000 years ago in present-day Iraq, Egypt, China, Pakistan, Nigeria, and Mexico—cities and migration have been closely interrelated. The creation of this distinctive settlement pattern entailed the spatial concentration of people—initially elites and their dependents—who were previously dispersed across space. Cities were centers of religious, military, political, and economic power, engendering a polarization between urbanizing elites and their associates, and the rural hinterlands on whose surplus they relied for their own prosperity. The contemporary geography of these processes has become a great deal more complicated than such city–hinterland dynamics. Nevertheless, urbanization, societal change, migration, and spatial polarization remain closely interlinked. In this chapter, we explore these relationships and their implications for the third world. We pay particular attention to two aspects: how these relationships have coevolved with industrialization and associated nonrenewable resource extraction (Chapters 17 and 18), and how they have been shaped by the distinctive geopolitical situation of the third world since colonialism. We also examine how these processes play out within third world cities, which are rapidly becoming places that not only are emblematic of the distinctive socioeconomic challenges of third world societies, but also are global centers of accumulation, consumption, and high-tech living—in other words, of first world lifestyles within the third world.

As we will see, the particular characteristics and challenges of third world urbanization and spatial polarization are bound up with global-scale processes. Towns and cities were essential to the organization and administration of large colonies by a handful of Europeans. Colonialism often turned the spatial orientation and settlement patterns of third world societies inside out, as they became externally dependent rather than internally oriented. Industrialization and urbanization are closely related, because cities provide access to the necessary labor forces and infrastructure. Industrialization and urbanization have long been associated with spatial difference and inequality in the first world. Urban–rural differences are marked by divisions of labor between agricultural and nonagricultural activities, but also are associated with inequalities in wealth, population change, norms and values, and influence over national affairs. As postcolonial third world states pursued development, the inside-out settlement geography inherited from colonialism often catalyzed particularly strong spatial polarization, itself engendering migration. Third world cities became the homes and sources of power for political and economic elites, often receiving preferential treatment (Lipton, 1977; Walton, 1977). In South Korea, for example, industrialization has brought with it tremendous problems of congestion in the cities of Seoul and Pusan, as well as enhanced inequalities in prosperity and opportunity between these cities and much of rural South Korea. Challenging international inequalities in economic development through urbanization and industrialization has thus often reinforced spatial inequalities within nations. Even countries with relatively little industrialization suffer from great inequalities in accessibility to nonagricultural jobs in different parts of the country, as these activities concentrate in cities. Seeking to enhance their livelihood chances, people are moving in ever-increasing numbers from the rural third world to the "mega-cities" of the third world—but also to first world cities.

The cities of a national urban system differ dramatically from one another in terms of their size, composition, and rates of growth. Such differences are a central theme of many discussions of third world urbanization, which identify "urban polarization" (whereby a country's mega-cities seem to contain the bulk of all economic and population growth) as a pressing urban problem. Such intranational differentiation in turn reflects differences in the ways in which these cities are plugged into the global urban system: Mega-cities are often more closely connected with similar cities in other countries than with the national urban system. Most of the major cities of the third world grew under colonialism as *entrepôts* through which resources were extracted for Europe, and remain today the principal funnels through which third world nations and the global economy interact. Dramatic livelihood gradients also exist within cities. Jakarta, the capital of Indonesia, has the highest average per capita income of any region in the country—but also the highest disparities in income and wealth, and the highest rates of malnutrition. These disparities are more evident in third world cities than in most first world cities, because different social classes are not as segregated into separate parts of the city, but live and work side by side. Neoliberal globalization has underwritten such inequalities, and the third world mega-cities that are becoming global centers of prosperity and opportunity are also national centers of destitution and despair.

THE GROWTH OF CITIES AND THE CIRCULATION OF POPULATION

A Historical Geography of Urbanization

Since cities are often viewed as symbols of modernity, and as the vehicles through which industrial capitalism was mobilized in the first world and has been transmitted to the third world, it is important to recall that the first city-based societies long predated capitalism and developed in places that we now associate with the third world. The earliest cities developed between 3800 and 2800 B.C. in the sophisticated civilizations of the Tigris and Euphrates valleys (of contemporary Iraq), the Hwang Ho valley (China), the Indus valley (Pakistan), and the Nile valley (Egypt). These "independent inventions" of the efficacy of urban life were joined in the 14th century A.D. by city-based Aztec and possibly Mayan civilizations of Central America. When Cortéz reached the Aztec capital of Tenochtitlan in 1519 A.D., he was shocked at its size, which at 150,000–200,000 inhabitants was comparable to the largest city in Europe at that time—Paris (Sanders, 1976). Indigenous city-based civilizations also existed in Africa, notably the Yoruba civilization of what is now Nigeria and Benin (Mabogunje, 1962), whose largest city attained a population estimated as 50,000–60,000 by 1500 A.D.—also larger than all but a handful of European cities.

The efficacy of cities as centers for the accumulation of wealth and population can be traced back to their earliest days. Scholars studying the first cities point out that they were centers of religious and military power, and that this power permitted them to accumulate wealth on the basis of agricultural labor (Sjoberg, 1960; Wheatley, 1971). Agricultural populations in these areas had long attained the capacity to produce an agricultural surplus beyond their subsistence needs, as a result of both the natural fertility of their environments and agricultural innovations (notably domestication of seeds and animals, as well as irrigation). The capacity to produce a surplus need not translate into the actual accumulation of surplus, however. As we have seen, subsistence-based societies may utilize this capacity as a reserve to be drawn on when necessary, rather than as a fund to invest in growth. The religious and military elites who settled in early cities are thought to have been the forces behind a successful organization of agricultural populations to work harder, thereby converting their capacity to produce surplus into greater agricultural output. This was achieved through a distinctive form of urban–rural trade: religious and military "protection" from the cities, in return for a share of the rural surplus (in the form of tithes and offerings of food brought to the cities). Making an offer that rural populations could not refuse, these elites were able to increase agricultural output—providing the means to support increasing numbers of nonagricultural activities and urban dwellers, and to accumulate urban wealth. Several extensive precapitalist empires of Asia and the Middle East seem to have had their origins in such schemes.

By the 14th century, urbanization had diffused into Europe, but no region of the Old World had a particular concentration of urban societies. Cities developed not only as centers for local control and accumulation, but increasingly as nodes in a chain of long-distance trading networks scattered across what we now call the third world, connecting Europe with China by way of central Asia, and with south and east Asia by way of the Middle East (Abu-Lughod, 1989). Cities were becoming the centers of mercantile capitalism—islands of relatively well-developed market systems and commodity production within their own regions, and nodes in the intercontinental circulation of commodities (Blaut, 1993). In short, cities were beginning to take on the role they still play today: connecting local communities, cultures, and economies with constantly evolving national and international systems.

In Europe, the coincidence of colonialism and capitalism triggered historically unprecedented rates of urbanization. The industrial revolution in Europe was preceded by an agricultural revolution—a cluster of innovative agricultural and land enclosure practices that vastly increased the productivity of agriculture. Much of the rural population became superfluous to agricultural production and was displaced, or attracted, to cities. By no means all industrial activities were urban. Yet cities attracted industrial activities in need of a cheap workforce, as well as rural–urban migrants who were seeking work because they could no longer live off the land.

The spatial restructuring associated with industrial capitalism brought varying fortunes for different cities and regions within Europe. Some prosperous cities that had been ideally located to profit from agricultural production were unable to attract the new activities of industrial commodity production and trade, and stagnated. Other places, previously little more than hamlets, proved to be well located for the new industries and grew explosively. Still others—particularly national capitals and trade nodes—weathered the transition from an agricultural to an industrial economy without breaking stride, continuing to grow. As cities became increasingly connected into national systems of commodity production and trade, a hierarchical size structure of cities developed, in which a city's size and influence reflected its economic and political importance within that system. National systems in turn became part of an international urban system. Those cities that became intermediaries in the international movement of commodities, people, and money took on a special status: they were often dubbed "world" or "global" cities (Beaverstock, Smith, and Taylor, 2000; Friedmann, 1986; Knox and Taylor, 1995; Sassen, 2002).

The size and importance of a city have long been associated with its involvement, and that of the region within which it is associated, in larger-scale circulation processes and the geopolitical spaces created to smooth circulation. This involvement enables a city to attract population and to accumulate wealth in quantities far beyond those that can be generated from its immediate hinterland. The fortunes of European cities were already dictated by their articulation with Asian-based systems of trade and conquest in 1000 A.D. (Tilly, 1994: 7). As the fortunes of different European countries and principalities in long-distance trading networks rose and fell, other European cities such as Bruges, Venice, Antwerp, and Amsterdam entered and then left the list of Europe's 10 largest cities (Bairoch, 1988; Braudel, 1986). The top of this list was dominated by longer-term trends that initially favored Paris, reflecting its regional importance within the highly centralized French nation state.

At the global scale, the successes of the Ottoman, Chinese, Japanese, and Mogul Empires prior to European capitalism and colonialism were reflected in the size of their largest cities. Paris and London were the only European cities that were large by world standards in 1700, and European travelers were in awe of the prosperity of Peking (now Beijing), Constantinople (now Istanbul), and Delhi. Yet Paris and London became two of the world's three largest cities by 1900, as France and Britain pushed aside other European colonial powers. London, at the center of the first world economy of global scope, had distanced itself from Paris as the world's largest city. European cities were then joined and overtaken by New York and other U.S. cities as the United States succeeded Britain as the globally hegemonic power. Until 1945, then, the size and population growth dynamics of the world's cities reflected their geopolitical influence (Chase-Dunn, 1985).

This association of the population size of cities with their economic dynamism and political influence broke down, however, during the explosion of third world cities after the end of colonialism. By 1990, only three of the world's largest urban agglomerations were located in the first world (and just two in 2003), signaling a shift in the center of gravity of urbanization toward the third world (Table 19.1; Figure 19.1). The rate of growth of cities in the third world is unprecedented in recorded history. In 1950, 340 million people, or approximately 36% of all urban dwellers, lived in third world cities; by 1990 this had quintupled to 1.5 billion people, or 62% of all urban dwellers. In short, the world's urban population has shifted from first world dominance (back) to third world dominance, but this has not been paralleled by a shift of the economic and political core of the global economy to the third world. Indeed, the lack of employment chances for the many rural–urban migrants whose movements have swelled the size of third world cities has led many to describe third world societies as "overurbanized." First world societies have also experienced a congregation of poor, underprivileged migrants (often members of ethnic minorities) in the central areas of their largest cities, where they find limited opportunities to improve their lives. But the scope of poverty is less, and metropolitan areas as a whole are economically more dynamic and influential, in the first world.

TABLE 19.1. The World's Largest Cities, 1700–2003 (Populations in Millions)

1700	1800	1900	1925	1960	1990	2003
Istanbul (0.7)	Beijing (1.1)	London (6.4)	New York (7.7)	New York (14.2)	Tokyo (25.0)	Tokyo (35.0)
Yedo (Tokyo) (0.7)	London (0.9)	New York (4.2)	London (7.7)	Tokyo (11.0)	São Paulo (18.1)	Mexico City (18.7)
Beijing (0.65)	Guangzhou (0.8)	Paris (3.3)	Tokyo (5.3)	London (9.0)	New York (16.1)	New York (18.3)
London (0.6)	Yedo (0.7)	Berlin (2.7)	Paris (4.8)	Shanghai (8.8)	Mexico City (15.1)	São Paulo (17.9)
Paris (0.5)	Istanbul (0.6)	Chicago (1.7)	Berlin (4.0)	Paris (7.2)	Shanghai (13.4)	Mumbai (17.4)
Ahmadabad (0.4)	Paris (0.5)	Vienna (1.7)	Chicago (3.6)	Buenos Aires (6.8)	Bombay (12.2)	Delhi (14.1)
Osaka (0.4)	Naples (0.4)	Tokyo (1.5)	Ruhr district (3.4)	Los Angeles (6.5)	Los Angeles (11.5)	Calcutta (13.8)
Isfahan (0.4)	Hangchow (0.4)	St. Petersburg (1.4)	Buenos Aires (2.4)	Ruhr district (6.4)	Buenos Aires (11.4)	Buenos Aires (13.0)
Kyoto (0.4)	Osaka (0.4)	Manchester (1.4)	Osaka (2.2)	Beijing (6.3)	Seoul (11.0)	Shanghai (12.8)
Hangchow (0.3)	Kyoto (0.4)	Philadelphia (1.4)	Philadelphia (2.1)	Osaka and Moscow (tie) (6.2)	Rio de Janeiro and Beijing (tie) (10.9)	Jakarta (12.3)

Sources: Data for 1700–1925 are from Chandler (1987); data for 1960 and 1990 are from United Nations (1993d); data for 2003 are from United Nations (2003d).

Urbanization and Migration

As industrial capitalism gained momentum during the 18th century, the level of urbanization changed little in Europe, with city dwellers averaging 12% of the total population (lower in Russia). During the 19th century, however, the share of the population living in cities tripled, and the total urban population increased from 19 to 108 million (Bairoch, 1988). Much of this increase was fueled by rural–urban migration. Perhaps two-thirds of the increase in urban populations was accounted for by rural–urban migrants and their subsequent offspring (the remainder being attributable to natural increase). The majority of these moves were over short distances, but the increasingly global scope of European capitalism triggered migration to other continents. An increasing proportion of European rural out-migrants sought their fortunes in (or were deported to) the New World and European colonies. Some 50 million people left Europe between 1840 and 1930—as many emigrants as there were rural–urban migrants within Europe. It has been estimated that in the absence of this out-migration, the population of Europe might be 1.2 billion today, almost twice the current population (Davis, 1974). For example, Ireland would have 12 million people rather than the 3 million now living there, if so many people had not been driven out by the potato blight famine (1845–1850) brought on by Ireland's English landlords' specializing so much in wheat production for international markets that potatoes became the staple food crop of their tenant farmers. The other intercontinental migration flows during the 18th and 19th centuries were also shaped by processes of colonialism: the slave trade (45 million between 1620 and 1850; Chapter 13) and the movement of indentured labor from east and south Asia to European colonies in Africa, the Caribbean, and Southeast Asia (12–37 million between 1850 and 1940) (Castles and Miller, 2003).

Many European intercontinental migrants settled in rural areas, but they also had dramatic impacts on the growth of cities in North America, Australia, and South

America. Between 1850 and 1910, the urban population in North America increased by a factor of 12 (nearly four times faster than European urban growth), and the level of urbanization tripled to reach the European level of 40%. Between 1850 and 1930 (when international migration was dominated by outflows from Europe), rates of urbanization in North America, Australia, and South America closely tracked rates of immigration of European immigrants (Berry, 1993). Indeed, there was a close relationship between cycles of migration, urbanization, and capital investment in Britain and those observed in the United States, Canada, and Australia. Between 1870 and 1910, higher periods of emigration from Britain were accompanied by significant outflows of capital and a slowing down of urbanization there, and by a boom in urban construction and population growth in North America (Thomas, 1972). In short, the close connection between international migration on the one hand and capital flows and economic conditions in Europe on the other meant that rapid rates of growth and urbanization in Europe coincided with slower rates in Europe's white settler colonies, and vice versa.

During the Great Depression of the 1930s, international migration dropped dramatically—from 13 million annually in 1920 to just 2 million by 1930 and 5 million in 1940. By 1950 international migration had climbed again to levels reached in the 1910s, but the geography of migration flows at the end of the colonial era, and its consequent impact on the geography of urbanization, began to change. Prior to the 1960s, immigration regulations in the three principal destination nations (the United States, Canada, and Australia) were explicitly racist in their intent, favoring British and other European immigrants. As a result, intercontinental migration remained dominated by migration to Europe's (now former) settler colonies, along with some migration from Central America and east Asia to North America (Figure 19.2a). Such official restrictions and quotas were scaled back, reflect-

FIGURE 19.1. Urban agglomerations with more than a million inhabitants, 2003. *Source:* Data are from United Nations (2003d).

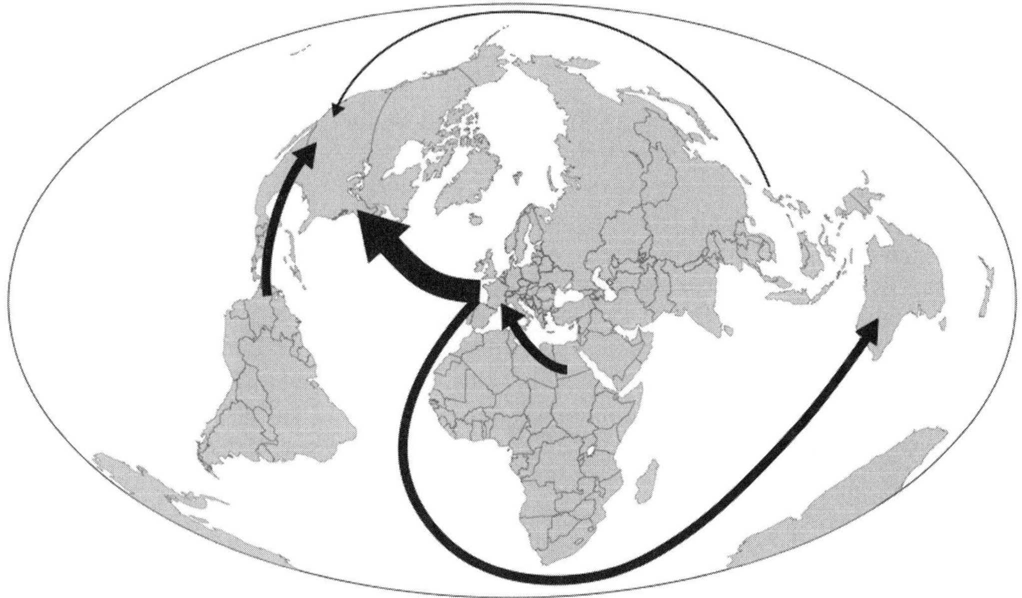

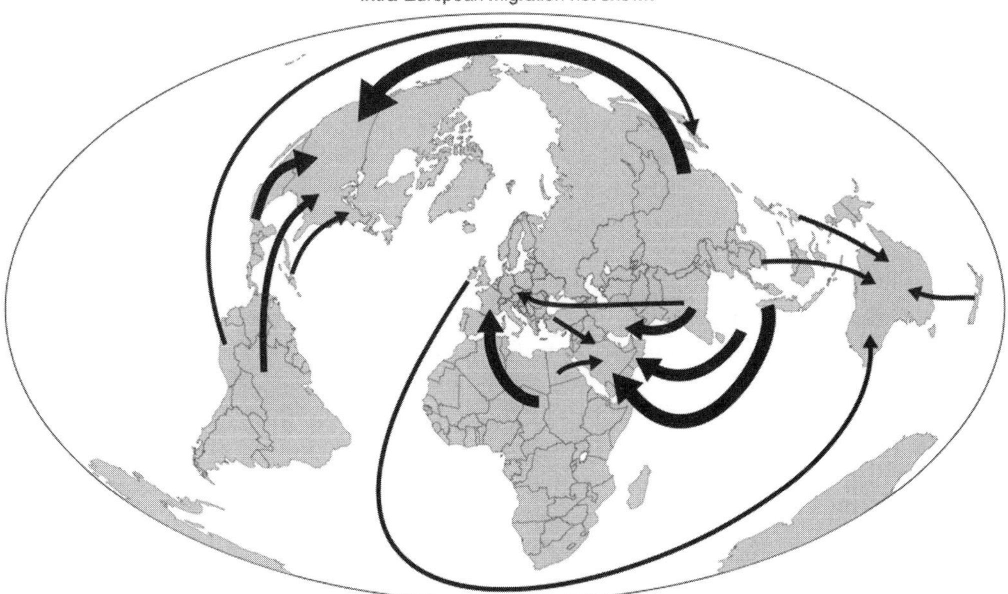

FIGURE 19.2. Intercontinental migration flows: (a) 1960–1964; (b) 1970–2000. Data for a are from Mazur (1994); data for b are from Castles and Miller (2003).

ing an absence of sufficient potential European immigrants to meet domestic needs (Castles and Miller, 2003). Thus intercontinental migration has come to be dominated by migration from the third to the first world, and from south and southeast Asia to selected (by now prosperous) oil-rich states in the Middle East (Figure 19.2b). In the United States, patterns of immigration that were 75% European in the 1950s had become 75% Latin American and Asian by the 1980s (most were admitted as relatives of previous immigrants). These shifts were a result of the long-term effects of U.S. interventions in Vietnam and Central America, and of changes in quota systems that had previously favored European immigrants. Australia's immigrants changed from 55% British to 18% British and 45% Asian in the same period. Former colonizing nations, such as Britain, France, and the Netherlands, for the first time experienced significant immigration of culturally and ethnically distinct populations from outside Europe. A combination of colonial citizenship policies (which gave certain rights to residents of former colonies), moral obligations, and deteriorating economic and political conditions have resulted in periods of intense immigration of north and west Africans (into France); east Africans, Caribbean islanders, and south Asians (into Britain); and southeast Asians and Melanesians (into The Netherlands). This shift toward increasingly global flows has been accompanied by accelerating numbers of migrants; a feminization of international migration (an increasing share of female migrants); and the institutionalization of international migration as states seek to attract temporary labor (to Europe, North America, and the Middle East), to send underemployed workers overseas (from places like the Philippines), and to retain connections with successful emigrants (such as nonresident Indians) (Leitner, 2000). In response to increasing disparities in livelihood chances accompanying globalization, the number of south–north migrants more than doubled between 1980 and 1990 (from 48 to 110 million). The number of international migrants (defined as those living abroad for at least a year) increased by 13% during the 1990s (to 174 million, 6% of the world's population). About half of these are women (United Nations, 2006a).

The institutionalization of migration has become particularly important. Prior to 1945, European out-migrants were often encouraged to pursue their desire to seek a better life elsewhere: Except for restrictions associated with the forced out-migration of convicts, they were welcomed in and actively recruited to move to the colonies. Thus surplus rural European populations, unable to find employment in industrializing cities, could move (or be sent) abroad. After 1945, countries that attempted to restrict out-migration (notably in the second world) were castigated for interfering with individuals' liberty to seek better lives, and thereby with their human rights. Third world countries have been encouraging their surplus populations to seek employment abroad, at least temporarily, through a variety of labor export policies aimed at reducing unemployment at home and enhancing remittances home from workers abroad. (In 2002, estimated remittances substantially exceeded official development aid [ODA], as discussed in Chapter 23.) Yet potential first world, and oil-rich OPEC, receiving states have developed increasingly elaborate institutional barriers in the form of immigration policies.

Permanent migration has become increasingly difficult as migration outflows shifted from Europe to the third world. Instead, and in close collaboration with the labor needs of domestic capitalists, various guest and temporary worker policies have been developed under which in-migrants are directed to certain industrial sectors in the first world, and are expected to return home after a fixed period of stay. Northern European countries initiated "guest worker" programs in the 1960s to make up for domestic labor shortages (much as the United States did with its 1940s Bracero Program for

Mexican farm workers), recruiting southern Europeans and subsequently north Africans and Turks to work in jobs ranging from factory assembly lines to street cleaning. The two other principal flows of guest workers have been from southern African nations and homelands into apartheid South Africa, and from south and southeast Asian and populous north African and Middle Eastern nations into Middle Eastern OPEC states after 1973. By and large, these flows have drawn selectively on relatively skilled and active men and women, willing to take on lower-status work than they are qualified for at home in return for better pay. (Their political and social rights are curtailed, relative to those of permanent immigrants and citizens.) Over time, particularly in Europe, many of these temporary migrants have become effectively permanent and have been joined by their families, as a consequence of ongoing demand for guest workers and of international and domestic opposition to attempts to send guest workers home. Such issues are still actively under discussion in both Europe and the former white settler colonies of North America, Australia, and New Zealand.

Other migrants arrive as asylum seekers and refugees, granted exceptional status on human rights grounds. The number of international refugees rose from 2 million in 1975 to 15 million in 1995, declining over the subsequent decade to 10 million. Internally displaced persons—refugees who do not migrate abroad—amount to another 6 million. Policies for regulating, controlling, and deporting such individuals have moved to the center of political debate in the first world, particularly in Europe, where a postwar legacy of fair treatment has been undermined by construction of a supranational regulatory regime controlling the entry of asylum seekers and refugees into the European Union (Leitner, 1997). Yet the burdens of managing refugees and asylum seekers are in fact far greater in the third world. The disruptions of war and political conflict, famine, and economic crisis have created many localized streams of refugees and asylum seekers across international borders. Just 4% of the world's refugees have come to North America, and another 24% to Europe; 61% remain in Africa and Asia (United Nations, 2006a), along with as many internally displaced persons. Africa has shouldered almost twice the responsibility with only a 30th of the wealth of the first world—a burden that the United Nations and charitable organizations seek to alleviate. Refugees face considerable barriers to entering the first world: They are required to prove their refugee status by using criteria developed in the receiving countries, and often find themselves placed in camps or segregated housing, with limited access to economic opportunity.

In short, people seeking to migrate abroad in search of better livelihood chances, displaying the same "pioneer spirit" attributed to European migrants to North America, face increased institutional barriers. One response has been undocumented migration—migration that is not legally sanctioned. (It's worth recalling that Native Americans regarded white settlers in North America as illegal immigrants, fencing in Native land without permission, but had neither the political autonomy nor the military wherewithal to prevent such movements.) Undocumented migrants have to overcome huge, often life-threatening risks en route; are subject to exploitation by human traffickers both during the trip and once they arrive; and can be sent home at a moment's notice. Even more so than legal immigrants, they often have to take jobs of lower status than they had at home and are qualified for. Nevertheless, their desire for better lives means that they disregard such risks and obstacles. There is increased trafficking in undocumented migrants, even as first world countries devote increasing resources to prevention and to their interdiction, detection, and expulsion. Traffickers offer to smuggle undocumented migrants across the border, at considerable cost. Migrants face three risks: They may not be brought into the country they contracted for; they may die en route, since forms of transportation can be brutal; and they may find themselves trapped in indentured or forced labor (United Nations, 2006b). This last has become increasingly common, particularly for women. Arriving migrants are under the control of traffickers, who may refuse to return their identity documents and force them to work under slave-like conditions to pay off debts accrued en route.

The feminization of migration reflects a variety of processes. As noted above, one-half of all permanent and "guest" migrants are now female. These are a mixture of women joining their (male) partners or relatives who have previously migrated, and women striking out on their own to improve their livelihoods. They often face greater differences in livelihood chances than their male compatriots, as a result of patriarchal relations in the households, villages, and countries where they reside that marginalize their life chances at home (see sidebar: "Migration in Bangladesh"). Female migrants fill demands for domestic servants, nurses, waitresses, and sweatshop and sex workers—less desirable occupations than those filled by male migrants. Refugee populations are also 50% female (25% girls under 18; half of all refugees are children). Women forced to flee their homes are often caught in a reinforced vicious cycle of abuse, "exposed to sexual exploitation throughout the refugee experience. Sexual and gender-based violence ranges from harassment, domestic violence and rape to . . . the withholding of food or other essential[s] unless paid for with sex" (United Nations, 2006a: 66). It is estimated that 77% of those held by human traffickers in indentured and slave-like working conditions are women, almost 90% of whom are trapped in the sex trade (United Nations, 2006b). The worse the conditions faced by international migrants, the more likely it is that these migrants are female.

Many migrants live modestly, so they can send whatever money they save home to help their families. These remittances have become a major source of money for the migrants' countries of origin (Russell, 1992). International remittances of all kinds sent by migrants back to the third world increased from $32 billion in 1990 to $167

Migration in Bangladesh

Pryer (1992: 148–149) tells the story of Momena, who was born in the village of Kahimari in southwestern Bangladesh. She was married to a nearby landowner at 16 and lived with his extended family for 6 years, in a wealthy household that treated her harshly. She was allowed to eat only once a day and was frequently beaten. She finally fled with her three children home to her father, who arranged a divorce. She was then married again to a farmer with just 1 acre of land, with whom she had a fourth child. She was poor but happy. However, her second husband died, and his brothers took title to his land without her knowledge. During the first harvest, they gave her only enough grain to feed her family for 1 month. She left and lived with her brother's family for 3 months in the southern market town of Kulna. She then had to move out, taking a dwelling in a slum settlement and finding a job as a domestic servant.

Working all day, Momena sent the three meals that she received as in-kind wages back home to her young children. Her employer and brother helped whenever they could with food and charity. At 14, her son went to work as a rickshaw driver. Momena lost her job as domestic servant when her employer replaced her with an orphaned girl from their home village. She invested the small sum of capital they provided her in the black-market smuggling and trading of Indian saris, which increased her income until her money was seized on the Indian border 6 months later. She then resorted to trading on credit, which, combined with a Bangladeshi ban on the sale of Indian saris, drastically reduced her income. By October 1986, her household was in extreme poverty and high debt, and the nutritional survival of the household was in jeopardy as well. The only person escaping undernourishment was her son.

billion by 2005 (all figures here are in U.S. dollars). This is approximately the same as all foreign direct investment (FDI) flows to the third world (Chapters 20 and 21), and twice the total of all ODA. Remittances to India and China exceeded $21 billion each, and in Togo, Lesotho (a prime source of workers for South Africa dating back to apartheid), and Jordan (the major place of settlement of displaced Palestinians), they exceeded 20% of the gross domestic product (GDP) (World Bank, 2006b).

The highly complex nature of contemporary international migration patterns makes it difficult to describe their broad effects on first world or third world urbanization. Many of these migrants move from rural to urban areas, and have considerable impacts on individual cities and nations in particular time periods, but generalizations are difficult. International estimates show that the diversification of international migration streams, and the increased importance of Europe as a destination for migration, are factors enhancing urbanization in many parts of the first world (Berry, 1993). This replaces the earlier dynamic whereby international migration created contrasting urbanization histories between Europe and other parts of the first world. As international migration is generally adding to urban populations in the first world, however, domestic migration no longer has much effect on levels of urbanization. Less than 25% of the first world population lives in rural areas, so domestic rural–urban migration can no longer be regarded as a major driving force of urbanization. Domestic migration is mostly urban–urban migration. This can contribute to significant shifts of urban population from one city to another, but by definition cannot affect the size of the total urban population. Indeed, some analysts argue that first world urban systems have undergone an "urbanization transition," much as the first world previously experienced a demographic transition (see Chapter 6). In this interpretation, migration was of increasing importance as a contributor to urbanization, relative to natural increase, as cities attracted rural–urban migration. As rural–urban migration has diminished, however, the contributions of migration relative to those of natural increase have become small (Ledent, 1982).

Within the third world, domestic rural–urban migration persists as the driving force behind urban population growth. Between 1950 and 2005, the urban population in the third world increased almost eightfold (from 285 million to 2.2 billion people), while the percentage of third world residents living in cities more than doubled (from 17% to 41%; Figure 19.3). In both relative and absolute terms, this represents the most rapid growth of urban populations over a 40-year period that humankind has ever experienced, and growth rates have been even greater for the largest cities. This rapid increase is almost entirely attributable to in-migration, in a manner that does not seem consistent with even the early stages of an urbanization transition. For example, India has shown no signs of entering such a transition, and Egypt's experience seems to be the converse of the first world model (Figure 19.4). The persistence of rapid rural–urban migration, reflecting widespread displacement of rural populations and desires to leave miserable and oppressive livelihood conditions, unabated by the apparent lack of opportunity for new migrants in the cities, does not fit the European experience and has become a vexing and widely discussed problem for researchers and policymakers.

By 2005, 76% of Latin Americans lived in cities—a proportion comparable to first world percentages (Figure 19.5). At these high levels, urbanization has slowed in Latin America, but the concentration of populations in the largest cities is continuing as people move from smaller to larger cities. The level of urbanization is just half this in Asia and Africa (37%). Urban populations in Africa are increasing by 5% a year. When the relationship between per capita GNP and levels of urbanization is examined (Figure 19.6), African countries tend to have lower per capita gross national product (GNP) by

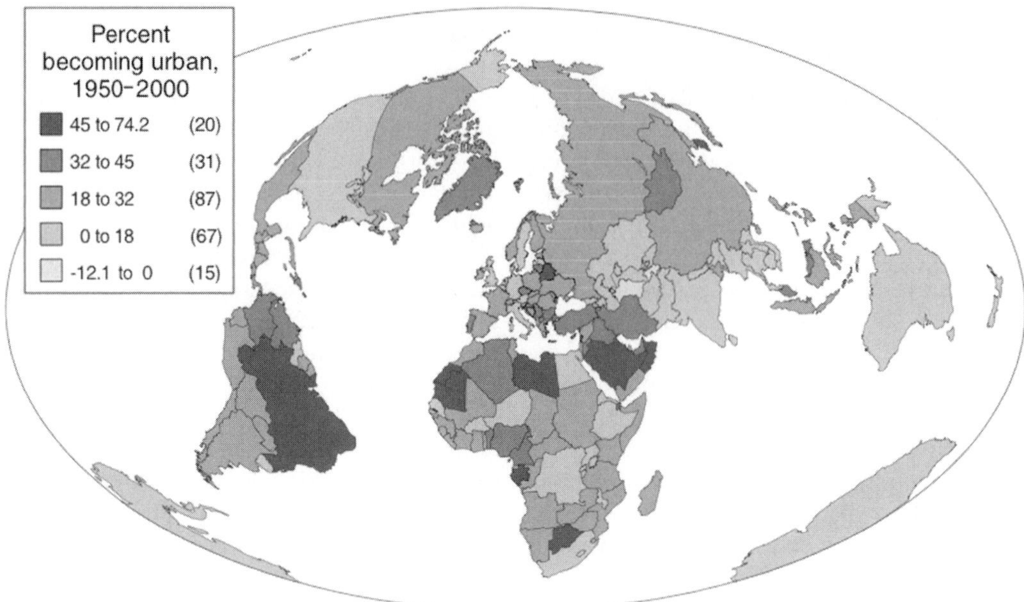

FIGURE 19.3. Change in urbanization, 1950–2000. *Source:* Data are from United Nations (2003d).

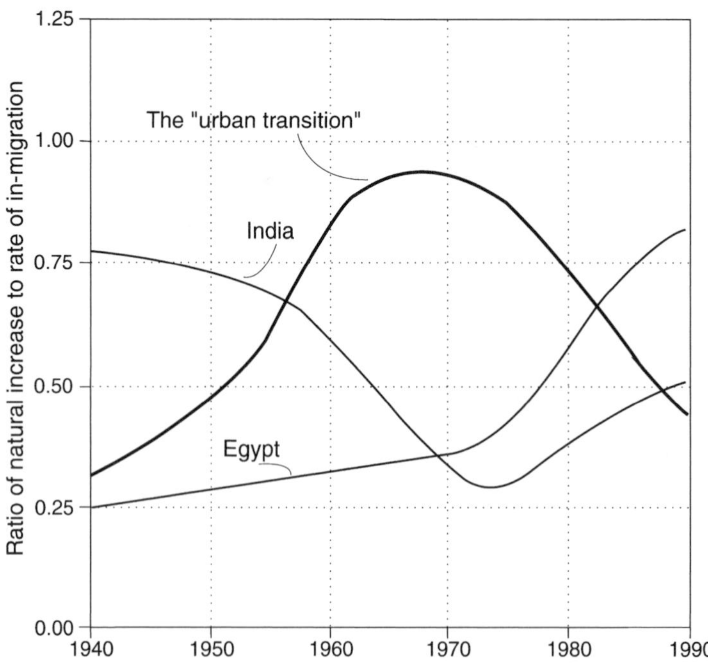

FIGURE 19.4. The "urban transition" in Egypt and India? *Source:* Adapted from Ledent (1982). Copyright 1982 by Regional Research Institute. Adapted by permission.

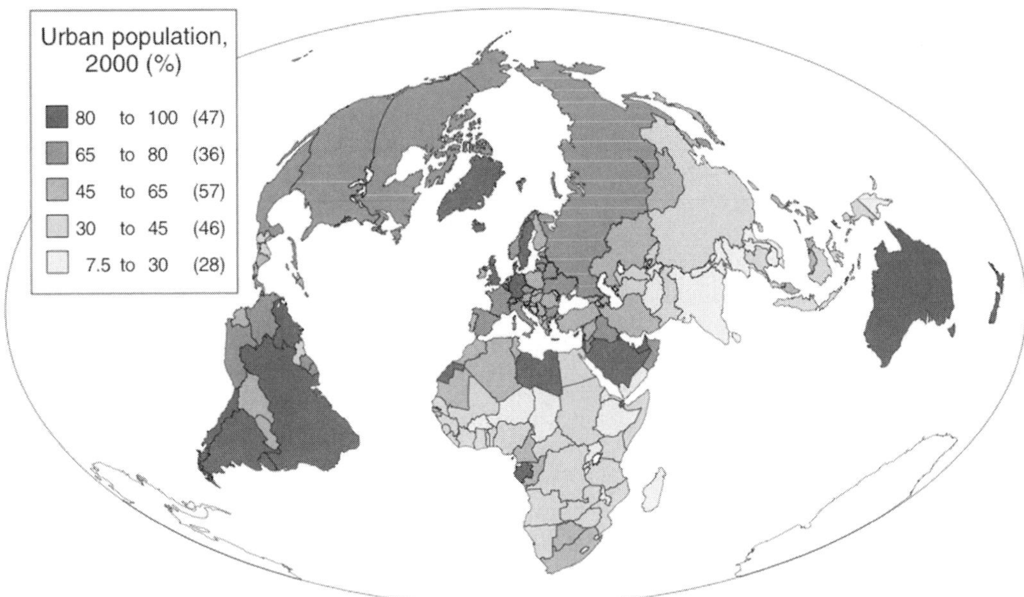

FIGURE 19.5. Levels of urbanization, 2000. *Source:* Data are from United Nations (2003d: 123).

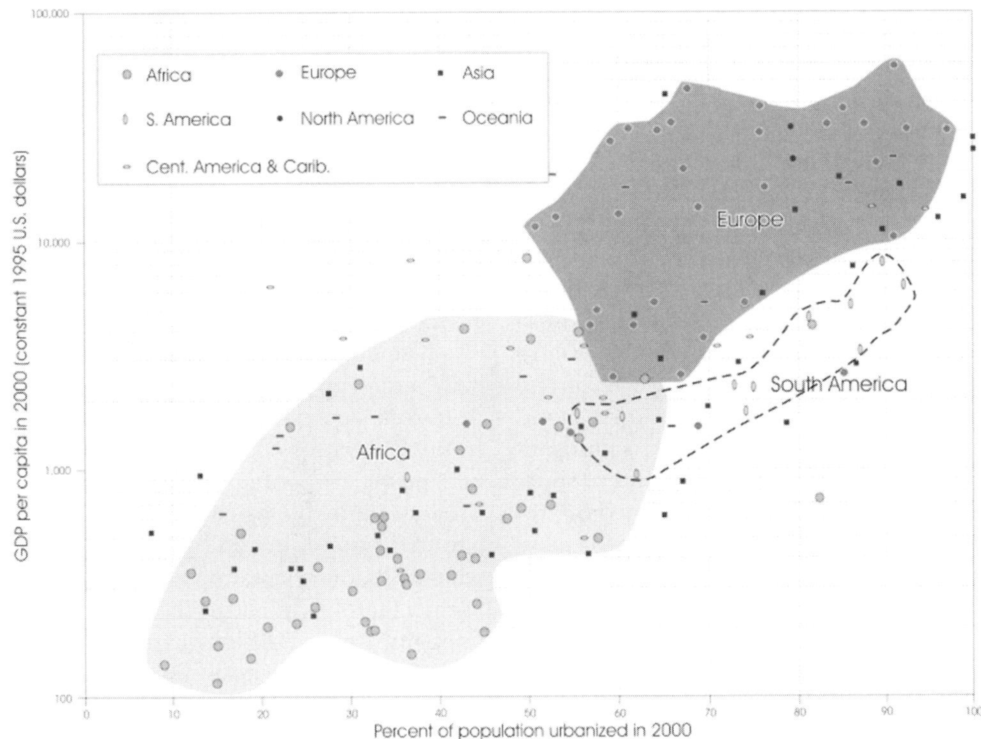

FIGURE 19.6. Urbanization and per capita GNP, 2000. *Sources:* Data are from World Bank (2008) and United Nations (2003d).

comparison to urbanization levels, whereas the reverse is the case in Europe.

THIRD WORLD CITIES AND POLARIZED SPATIAL DEVELOPMENT

An examination of the relationship between migration and urban growth suggests some important differences between urbanization as experienced in the first world and the forms of urbanization currently underway in the third world—differences that go beyond the demographic changes described above. First, patterns of international migration indicate that third world cities are connected to the global economy in different ways than are first world cities (Berry, 1976; Vining, 1982). Second, cities in the first world seem to have been capable of providing opportunities for urban immigrants to obtain employment. Even though its cities have become major centers of poverty and of polarized livelihood opportunities for urban residents along lines of class and race, nonetheless there has been some balance between population growth and overall economic dynamism in these cities. In the third world, however, urban population growth in the large cities has continued, regardless of the economic situation. Third, this disparity not only is a characteristic of the urban system as a whole, but is particularly problematic for the largest cities, which seem to attract a disproportionate share of urban population growth. By contrast, first world urban systems have experienced significant phases of counterurbanization, and of shifts of growth momentum away from the largest cities, since the 1970s. The first of these three differences has been an important underlying reason for the other two, making it important to examine the economic interdependencies linking cities to one another and to the global system in the third world. In this section, we examine how these links affect the roles played by third world cities in their own national economies, and what the implications are for interurban differentiation in the national urban system.

European Origins: Colonial Cities and Uneven Development

Perhaps the salient characteristic of most third world cities is that their location and character in most cases have been conditioned by European colonial influence, notwithstanding the extensive precolonial history of urbanization in selected regions throughout the third world. In regions where there was little indigenous urbanization, colonial contact dramatically altered the spatial organization of the administered or conquered territory. Even in regions with preexisting urban systems, many precolonial settlements were abandoned or declined in importance, because their locations were no longer suitable for the new, externally oriented, colonial space economy. In Peru, for example, the highland cities of the Incas were abandoned, as Spanish colonists built new cities on the coast and the spatial organization of the economy was turned inside out. Interdependencies between the settlements located within Peru (as well as with other parts of the Andes settled by the Incas) declined in importance relative to connections with Europe, meaning that central and internally oriented settlements lost momentum relative to coastal and externally oriented ones.

The colonial space economy was typically organized to gain access to internal resources efficiently and to extract them from the territory for the use of the colonial power; this organization reflected the situation and role of colonies in this international system. In addition to using rivers, whose natural orientation made them useful for penetration inland, the colonial power built railroads and highways into the interior, to locations whose mineral resources, labor forces, or soil and climate conditions made them suitable for colonial purposes. The result was a dendritic transportation network, which effectively transformed more internally oriented and organic trading systems into a managed, externally oriented extraction system (see Chapter 14).

Colonial cities were built at the principal junctions and the mouths of these networks, to serve as political and economic *entrepôts* between a colony and the broader international system of which it was a part—in other words, to administer the territory and facilitate extraction of its resources. Typical locations chosen by colonial powers for cities included coastal points of transshipment, where commodities could be transferred to oceangoing vessels; strategic locations, where the national and international transportation system was in need of defense; and inland locations, in the cooler highlands of tropical colonies, which were suitable for European settlement and agriculture.

Such transformations occurred even in cases where external control over domestic society was incomplete. In the Dutch East Indies (Indonesia), for example, local control was left in the hands of indigenous elites as long as they were capable of meeting the purposes of the colonizing power. A particularly telling case is China, which never was colonized. Its long history of internal orientation and self-sufficiency was turned inside out as China became increasingly dependent on external trade. China's defeat in the opium wars, securing British control over the crucial opium exports to China, represented a defining moment in this process of trade dependence. As a result, China acceded to a series of European-run "treaty ports" along the Chinese coast, including dendritic transportation routes running inland from each port (see Chapters 13 and 14, and Figure 13.7). The momentum of economic growth shifted from the interior to coastal areas, and remains there today. The principal region benefiting from the recent rapid industrialization in China is Guangzhou province, on the southern coast close to Hong Kong—one of the last treaty ports, returned to Chinese control on July 1, 1997. China's experience shows clearly that external orientation and economic dependence can occur even when a country retains political independence.

The colonial cities were in many senses more closely connected with the international colonial system than with their own local hinterlands—a pattern that has persisted in many cases to the present day. Cultural life and norms were dominated by foreign influence; politics were determined by outside agendas and considerations; and the formal economy was dominated by transactions involving colonial imports/exports and products serving the wishes of colonial officials and their employees, in ways that left out many of the lower-class residents of these towns (see Chapter 14). Thus, whereas from an external perspective colonial cities represented modern outposts in a backward society (exemplified in Arthur Lewis's "dual economy"; see Chapter 4), from a local perspective these cities were enclave economies. Hoselitz (1955) defined such cities as "parasitic," meaning that they grew at the expense of their own hinterlands, as opposed to "generative" cities, whose dynamism would have contributed to the welfare of their hinterlands. He argued that an excessively strong external orientation was often associated with parasitism. In the terminology of dependency and world system theory, parasitic colonial cities were engaged in extracting surplus from their hinterland—part of which was siphoned off by these cities, but the bulk of which was transferred to the core ("metropolitan") countries and their trading cities.

In the early 1960s, when so much of Africa was declaring independence, western analysts recognized this parasitic role but argued that political independence would bring with it a process of modernization, whereby these cities would shift to become generative of local development (Taaffe et al., 1963). The previous experience of the United States was regarded as an example that others would follow (Figure 19.7). It was hypothesized that independence would result in a more internally oriented and better-connected space economy, enhancing

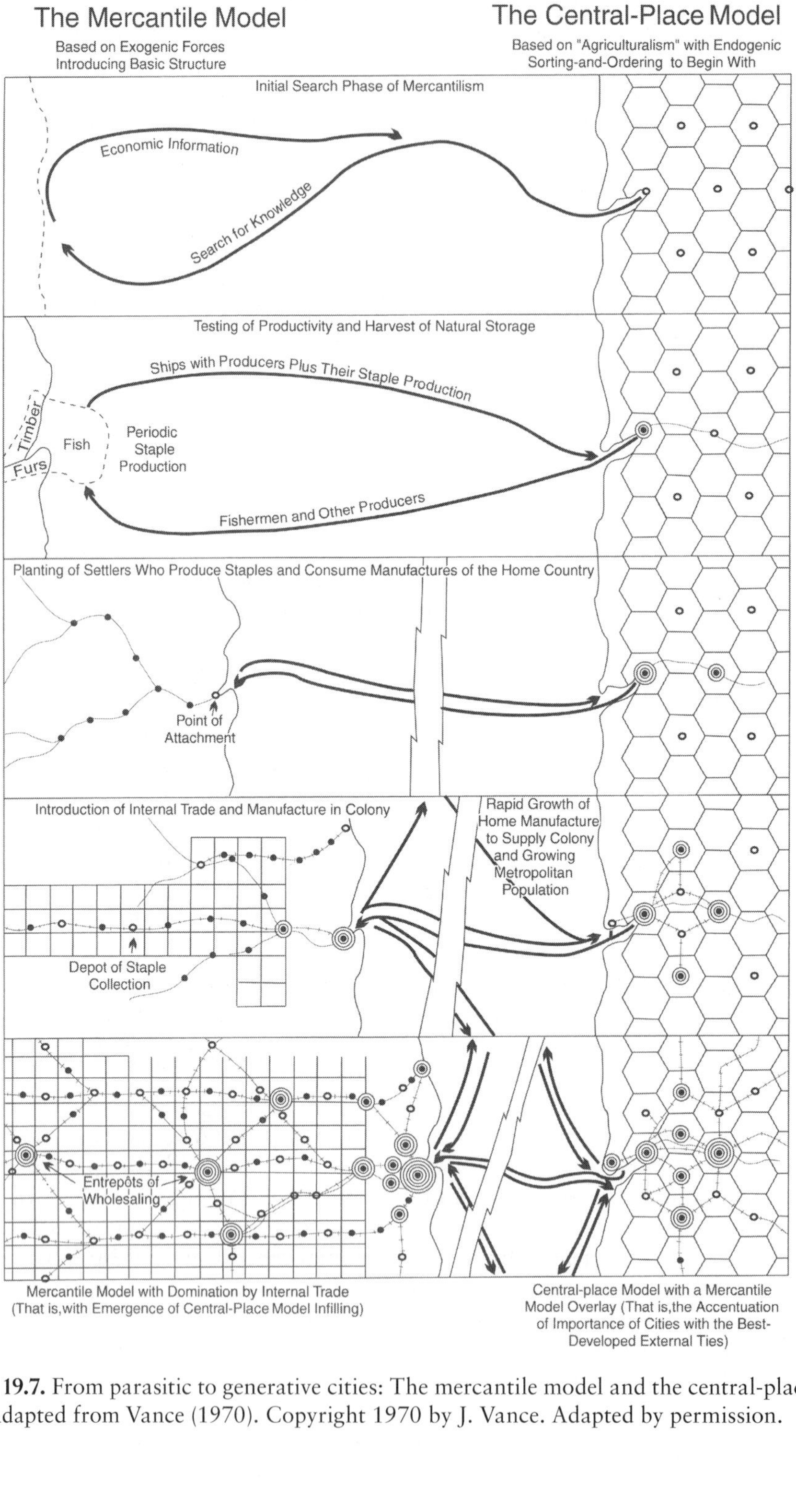

FIGURE 19.7. From parasitic to generative cities: The mercantile model and the central-place model. *Source:* Adapted from Vance (1970). Copyright 1970 by J. Vance. Adapted by permission.

interaction between indigenous cities and facilitating more balanced spatial development patterns. At independence, however, the existence of a few externally oriented, parasitic colonial cities meant that most newly independent third world nations inherited an urban system characterized by a high degree of "primacy"—a large size gap between the largest city and other regional centers, implying a disproportionate concentration of urban population in one or two major cities, by comparison to the experience of first world nations (Berry, 1961; Sheppard, 1982).

Urbanization after Independence

In much of the third world, political independence did not result in a more internally oriented and geographically balanced spatial system. Even today, many third world countries remain dependent on external trade, often relying on products similar to those exported under colonialism to generate income for economic growth (Chapter 16). Industrialization also has remained externally oriented, particularly given the failure of import substitution industrialization (ISI; see Chapter 17). Low wages, together with the difficulty of preventing capital from leaking abroad (Chapter 22), have meant that third world economic growth continues to rely on other first world countries for markets, essential inputs, and technologies. The physical infrastructure of these countries is symptomatic of this persistent external orientation (see Figure 14.5).

By the same token, the largest third world cities have retained a strong external orientation, functioning as cities whose activities are influenced at least as much by international trade and finance as by developments within their own national territories. Although independence brought a new political status to national capital cities, even this has not reduced concerns about whether the largest cities continue to be parasitic. In addressing these concerns, it is necessary to pay attention to political, cultural, and economic processes that may be acting to reinforce or reduce differences between metropolises and the smaller cities making up the remainder of the national urban system, as well as to consider how the geography of a country and the development of communication among its cities and regions may be affecting this process.

The metropolises are, first of all, concentrations of national political and economic power. In most cases, the national political capital is also the largest city, but there are of course exceptions to this rule. Thus Tanzania and Brazil chose new inland locations for their national capitals, taking this function away from the principal coastal cities that previously had served this purpose. This was a conscious attempt to reverse the external orientation of the space economy by moving important functions inland. The strategy has had little success, however, since Dodoma and Brasilia remain little more than figurehead capitals (much like Washington, D.C., in the 19th century)—places where members of political elites spend as little time as possible, and where few other activities have agglomerated. In both India and China, European influence did not completely undermine sophisticated internally oriented urban systems, but superimposed an external orientation onto them. Consequently, their capital cities are not the largest cities, nor are they on the coast. Beijing, the center of Chinese imperial rule in the 19th century, was the largest city until it was overtaken by the coastal city of Shanghai, a British treaty port. New Delhi, capital of India, was founded by the British in 1921 on the fringe of Delhi, the inland capital of Muslim India. Delhi was the largest city in 1700, but by 1800 it had been superseded by the new colonial coastal cities of Mumbai and Kolkatta (formerly Bombay and Calcutta). Both countries today are characterized by a very low degree of urban primacy compared to other third world nations (and indeed most first world nations).

Cities and their residents have consistently been favored by national elites in third world countries, because they represent concentrations of political and economic power (Lipton, 1977). States have acted to keep food prices low, disadvantaging farmers in the hinterland, to secure the political support of low-income urban populations. This has effectively meant that the interregional terms of trade between cities trading manufactures and services, and rural areas from which agricultural products are obtained in exchange, have been stacked in favor of the cities. State spending on public services has also typically favored urban populations, as have many foreign aid initiatives, and urban populations benefit from better utilities and health conditions. State policies seeking to reduce urban–rural differences were pursued in the transitional countries, where state socialist regimes devoted considerable effort to equalizing conditions in rural and urban areas (Table 19.2), and in third world countries with socialist or social democratic state policies, such as Cuba, Tanzania, and Costa Rica. If urban populations have been favored because cities are foci of power, this is particularly the case for the politically most important and prestigious cities. Because national capitals have important symbolic value and high visibility, national governments, often in close collaboration with the mayors and councils of the capital cities, are particularly keen to invest there in order to create symbols of their own success. Regional centers are left to the responsibility of local governments, which often have very limited resources at their disposal, although secondary cities with powerful local elites may do better than those without (Smith, 1985).

The historical location of colonial cities at strategic locations in the externally oriented transportation system, and the subsequent conversion of these into the principal cities of the newly independent state, have combined political advantage with economic advantage at these locations. These cities provide two types of advantages for urban economic activities. As large cities—with large and diverse labor forces; large local markets; urban services and utilities; and universities and other educational and research facilities—they provide agglomeration advantages that other locations do not have. These advantages of site are reinforced by advantages of situation. Strategic location on the transportation system often means that these cities are also ideally located from the point of view of accessibility, both to other parts of the country and to the world economy. In countries with a strong state role in the economy, and in times when the state exerts this influence to regulate foreign or domestic investors, capital cities provide the additional political advantage of access to the corridors of political power.

The degree to which these factors of site, situation, and politics give capital cities and other large cities critical advantages

TABLE 19.2. Household Health Conditions in Urban and Rural Areas, 1995

	Safe drinking water (%)		Access to sanitation (%)	
Country types	Urban	Rural	Urban	Rural
Industrial market/core	98.2	94.3	97.5	93.6
Industrial transitional/core	97.8	97.0	94.2	91.7
Middle-income NICs/semiperiphery	90.8	56.8	94.6	51.4
Middle-income oil-exporting/ semiperiphery	93.6	72.2	95.9	54.4
Middle-income transitional/semiperiphery	100.0	98.4	100.0	99.4
Low-income/semiperiphery	97.3	95.4	91.4	74.0
Middle-income oil-exporting/periphery	81.5	55.0	66.8	44.2
Middle-income/periphery	85.7	56.0	79.0	56.8
Low-income/periphery	64.7	47.9	65.2	28.6

Source: Data are from World Resources Institute (1996a).

over competing locations depends on the historical geographical context, but in many cases they have enabled the largest cities to prosper in the face of wide-ranging economic and political changes. Consider, for example, ISI, which favors domestic markets, and export-oriented industrialization (EOI), which favors exporting to foreign markets (see Chapter 17). In principle, ISI should favor cities that are central within the national market, whereas EOI should favor those accessible to foreign markets. A dramatic example of this has been the development of the *maquiladora* region and its cities along the northern Mexican border, far from Mexico City, as a result of the export processing that has developed there for the U.S. market. This reversed the sociospatial system of work and gender relations that had emerged earlier under ISI, in which Mexico City was the center of industrialization, on the basis of a male unionized workforce and nuclear families (unlike the female low-wage workforce of the *maquiladoras*, with many single women and female-headed households) (Cravey, 1998). Yet there are many cases where no such shift has occurred. Rio de Janeiro and São Paulo (Brazil), Seoul and Pusan (South Korea), and Bangkok (Thailand) have continued to attract industrial and service activities and population, regardless of whether ISI or EOI dominates industrial policy. This is in part because political and site factors may be more important than accessibility, but also because the externally oriented spatial organization of many third world societies makes the major cities not only accessible to external markets, but also close to domestic markets.

Indeed, the external orientation of the space economy, combined with the high costs of building and maintaining new transportation infrastructure where population densities are low and topography is difficult, has often inhibited the filling in of the communications network envisaged in modernization theory (as visualized in Figure 19.7). There is a cycle of cumulative causation. An externally oriented communications system makes it difficult for other cities to develop as separate poles away from the major cities occupying strategic locations. The failure of such alternatives in turn reinforces external orientation. Thus, instead of the development of cities at a variety of locations, each with distinct advantages for particular activities, one or a very few locations become advantageous for all kinds of activities. The result can be a backwash of development, or a draining of surplus, from other parts of the country into the largest cities.

Urban economists argue that sooner or later the exploding size of very large cities will create disadvantages of its own—agglomeration disadvantages that will override such backwash effects and create opportunities for new growth poles to emerge in peripheral locations. Indeed, these very large cities suffer from enormous congestion, overcrowding, and pollution (see the next section). Yet these evident problems seem to have little effect in stemming the flow of people and activities to the largest cities. Indeed, much evidence suggests that improved transportation and communications technologies are increasing the pull of the largest cities and reinforcing the spatial polarization of development. Migration studies show that migration to the largest cities is often not directly from rural areas, but follows a stepping-stone pattern. Rural residents migrate first to the local town, then to the regional city, and only later to the largest cities. Now, however, improved information flows and public transportation frequently encourage people to move directly from distant rural areas to the metropolises.

The persistence of rural–urban migration, even though there are very few opportunities for migrants to attain a "good life" in the urban destination, is symptomatic of the way in which the roots of urbanization seem to differ in the third world from the conventional economic explanations that apply to first world cities. There are clearly aggregate income differences between rural and urban areas, but many studies have shown that the job chances available to new in-migrants are not sufficient to make the move economically worthwhile for these individuals. Other mechanisms must be taken into account. First, migration is actually a highly heterogeneous process. Whereas young single men may be going to the city to try their chances at making money, younger women may see the city as a place of social and cultural opportunity, and older women may move to help look after the children of their relatives (Chant, 1992). Second, "push factors"—factors inducing migrants to leave their rural residences—may be more important in the decision to leave than are the possible attractions of the metropolis. For example, women who face patriarchal domestic situations in which they are denied access to resources, are forced into familial traditions that they wish to avoid, or are denied the opportunity to challenge cultural norms may regard a move as desirable, no matter how difficult economic conditions are in the destination (see the sidebar "Migration in Bangladesh," above).

Third, migration is not an isolated action, but is typically part of a chronological sequence of previous moves by household members and friends to the same destination—a phenomenon referred to as "chain migration." Migration has a history. Previous migrants return with (realistic or misleading) information about urban opportunities, or with (actual or promised) opportunities for employment for new migrants. In their desire to demonstrate their own success in the city, they often paint an overly positive picture of livelihood chances to those left behind. Although there may be niches that individuals with privileged contacts can take advantage of, in many cases new migrants follow the paths of their predecessors on the basis of unrealizable promises of help from previous migrants, or false beliefs about urban opportunities.

Fourth, migration is often not an individual act of permanent relocation, but part of a collective household strategy. Although this is true of migration everywhere, it is particularly true in the third world, where ties of kinship remain stronger and where the opportunities available to individuals are fewer. Migrations may make little sense as individual actions, but a great deal of sense as part of a household strategy. Rural–urban migration both relieves the rural household of the need to support some of its members directly, and also provides the household with ways of diversifying possible sources of income and employment (much like the Pokot agricultural practices described in Chapter 12). As in the case of guest workers, migrants leave with the hope and obligation of remitting any earnings to household members remaining in rural areas. (Of course, what counts as a household varies across space and time, and households are generally heterogeneous—made up of people whose age, gender, and familial position situate them differently. As a result, there may be as much conflict as collective action, with people migrating to get away from familial conflict rather than to help their relatives.) Migration may also be regarded as a temporary strategy—a phenomenon known as "circular migration" (Standing, 1985). Migrants move to the city for a season, planning to return when their labor is needed in the rural area or if they fail to find a reasonable source of employment and income.

Household-based migration both artificially swells the apparent number of urban residents (by including in this number many who are only temporarily in the city) and reinforces strong ties between urban and rural areas at the household level. These ties make it easier for potential migrants to undertake the risk of migrating, and make them more willing to accept poorly paid and irregular employment in the city, at least in the short term. Migrants may have the resources of the larger household to fall back on if the migration is unsuccessful. Extension of the geographic scope of rural household activities to include activities within the urban realm also ties the fortunes of rural communities more closely to those of urban neighborhoods.

Cities in the third world are not only places through which political, economic, and demographic changes in the global system are linked to those of localities; they also play important roles as cultural *entrepôts*. Cultural influences from the first world—in the form of dress fashions, pop music, social norms, movies, food, and TV—show up first and foremost in the largest cities, where direct connections to the first world are strongest. It may be, however, that these cultural norms have the strongest influence in secondary cities, where they are not matched by political and economic dynamism (Armstrong and McGee, 1985). Western cultural values and consumption norms have diffused to the far reaches of the third world, through the hierarchy of secondary cities and villages into rural areas, as a result of the circulation of people between cities and their hinterlands. Coca-Cola, baseball caps, and/or TVs have become symbols of third world rural conceptions of a good life that remains unattainable without adequate waged employment. The diffusion of first world consumption norms down the urban hierarchy, while employment opportunities in the production process remain concentrated in the metropolises, places secondary cities in a contradictory location between seemingly limitless rural expectations and very limited urban possibilities. Secondary cities accelerate rural–urban migration, as migrants seek nearby paid employment to realize their first world images of the good life. At the same time, the inability of secondary cities to fulfill migrants' goals means that they often move on to swell the populations of the largest third world cities, reinforcing spatial polarization.

DIFFERENCE WITHIN THIRD WORLD CITIES

The differentiation and polarization that can be observed in the development of cities as a whole in the third world—which we can attribute to the historical geography of urbanization, migration, and economic growth, and to the role of third world cities as *entrepôts* between global and local processes—have their counterparts at the intraurban scale. As in the fractal patterns of chaos theory, in which each closer examination of a structure reveals the same patterns of difference as observed at larger scales, the differentiation within third world cities is as marked as that between cities and their hinterlands, or between first and third world nations. This is true not only of third world cities, of course. Such differentiation can be observed, and is increasing, even in the most prosperous "global cities" at the core of the first world (Sassen, 1991). Nor is it the case that these differences are identical in large and small cities throughout the third world. Lacking space to address the important geographical complexities, however, we restrict ourselves here to conveying an impression of urban morphology and life in very large third world cities by drawing directly on the experience of one of us (ES) in Jakarta, Indonesia.[1]

Spatial Structures

European colonialists introduced a distinctive spatial structure to third world cities, even in those cases where indigenous cities were adopted as colonial cities (see Chapter 14). European city planning brought with it networks of wide streets in residential and commercial areas, built for the large-scale mechanical forms of transportation that were so essential to colonial production and administration. It also created new foci for the cities—railroad stations, governors' offices, and barracks. City plans spatially segregated colonists, merchants (often ethnically distinct from the majority population), and indigenous people into different parts of the city, as well as zoning different commercial and residential activities into different areas. These reflected state-of-the-art ideas about urban form in Europe, adapted to the proposed functions of colonial cities, but they differed greatly from indigenous urban morphologies. Except for ceremonial centers for rulers and religious observance, indigenous cities had been much more organic in form—with little separation of activities and classes into different zones of the city, and with networks of winding, narrow, unmarked streets through which only local residents could navigate easily.

After independence, European ideas about urban spatial structure were adopted by the new political elites and adapted to the images they wished to propagate. In Jakarta, for example, the Indonesian government built a new city center on the inland fringe of the older Dutch harbor of Batavia (Figure 19.8). The heart of this area is a government complex focused on Independence Square with its *Monas* obelisk, surrounded by the president's palace and other national buildings. Reminiscent of Washington, D.C., the new city center was designed not only as a symbol of modernity and independence—the building of a modern emancipated society onto Indonesian tradition—but also as a symbol of national unity. It was supposed to embody Indonesia's new five principles (*pancacila*) guaranteeing "unity within diversity," and thus to unite a wide-ranging group of 13,000 islands with more than 300 languages and ethnic groups (although many such groups have also viewed it as an embodiment of Javanese "imperialism").

Radiating out from this center, both connecting it to the port and providing a framework for urban expansion to the south, is a set of broad western-style urban arterial roads. Urban planners also designated zones for commercial, industrial, and residential

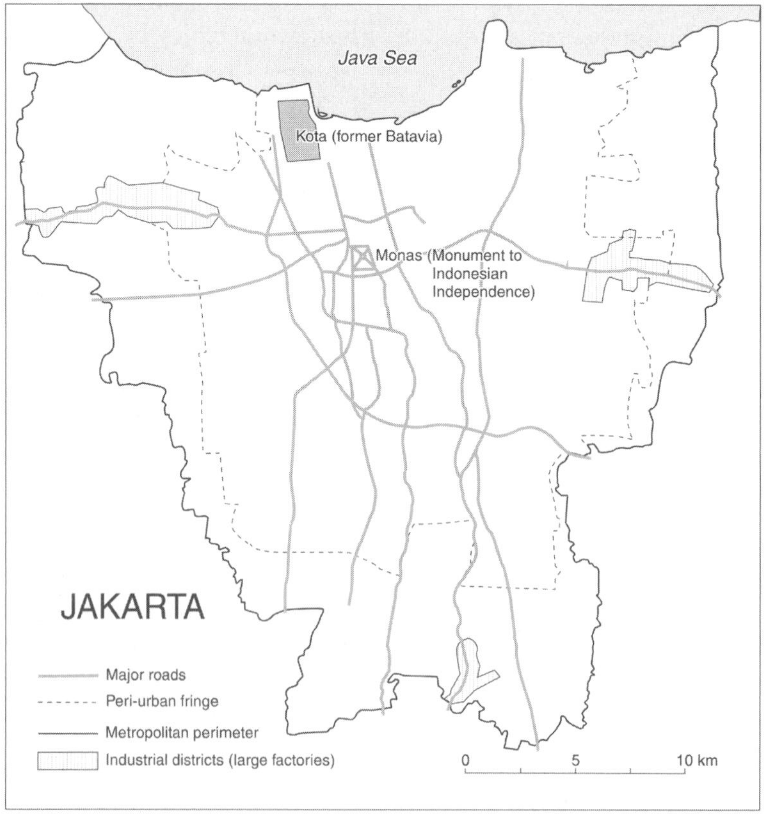

FIGURE 19.8. Jakarta, Indonesia. *Source:* Adapted from Browder, Bohland, and Scarpacci (1995). Copyright 1995 by the American Planning Association. Adapted by permission.

activities, again emulating western planning. Although the details differ, a similar approach was taken throughout the third world—from Lima to Manila, from Cairo to Cape Town. These frameworks for a modern independent city have been overtaken, however, by two principal events: the speedy growth of third world metropolises, and the social contradictions of development. Rapid growth can outpace any plan, creating congestion, crowding, and pollution. In the case of Jakarta, the metropolitan area grew by 2 million people during the 1970s, and by another 2.7 million people during the 1980s, doubling in size to 9.2 million inhabitants. This amounted to an average of 650 new people each day for 20 years (almost half of them being in-migrants)—a rate of growth that would outpace the best-financed first world urban plans.

Beyond these problems of rapid growth, the role of third world metropolises as the principal points of contact between first world development and the third world periphery has meant that poverty and wealth, kinship and capitalism, and indigenous and market economies have all come together within third world cities. This can be seen not only in the physical structures making up the built environment of these metropolises, but in their spatial arrangement. Housing ranges from whitewashed, bright, air-conditioned houses for the national political, economic, and military elite, through row housing in planned developments for the small middle class, to large quantities of slum and squatter housing. About 80% of the people of Jakarta live in *kampungs* ("villages") scattered around the city. *Kampungs*, like similar developments throughout the third world, started as informal settlements—places where new immigrants built their own shacks, in a city unable or unwilling to provide housing for them. In many cases, such settlers began as squatters, occupying land owned by the state or by absentee owners, or land on which planners would never build housing estates. In Jakarta, these can be found along railroad tracks, in flood plains, or literally built out over the canals and ponds of the city (see Plates 19.1 and 19.2). In hillier towns such as Lima, Peru, or Managua, Nicaragua, they will be found on hillsides deemed too steep or dangerous to settle. As a consequence of having to occupy locations unsuitable for other more formal activities, squatter settlers actually expose themselves to a disproportionate risk from environmental hazards (floods, mudslides, and earthquakes).

The spatial organization of these settlements reflects their organic evolution and the settlement structures of the rural areas from which so many squatter settlers came: narrow, unmarked streets winding around what to first world eyes seems like a chaotic clustering of housing. These paths, too narrow for most four-wheeled vehicles, offer a stark contrast in their appearance and traffic usage to main thoroughfares, which are often congested to the point of a virtual standstill with all manner of transportation.

Despite their informal beginning, and occasional attempts by the state to eliminate them, squatter settlements in many cases have been transformed from their beginnings as cardboard and corrugated iron shacks. Individual dwellers resisted attempts to clear them out, illegally tapped into electricity lines, and obtained paid work that allowed them to improve their houses (see Plate 19.3). Grassroots movements have formed in the settlements, and these have been highly successful in both providing services for the community and organizing community governance—in some cases, along lines that maximize the participation of all community members in decision making. Over time, some settlements have gained a status of de facto permanence, and the government and foreign aid donors have become willing to invest heavily in improving the physical environment of these settlements.

In Jakarta, a 20-year *kampung* improvement program in the more established *kampungs* has raised streets above flood level and paved them, and has provided drainage ditches, toilets, and showers. *Kampung*

PLATE 19.1. Squatter housing along railroad tracks is a gateway for new urban immigrants to Jakarta. Informal traders lay out their wares on the tracks, stepping aside as the trains pull through.

PLATE 19.2. The many canals of northern Jakarta, sinks for refuse of every description, are unowned space that squatter housing can colonize. Rattan, poled through the waterways, is being unloaded for furniture manufacture.

PLATE 19.3. *Kampung* housing is more permanent and roomy than squatter housing, and its owners at least have an informal right (if no legal right) to the land. Housing construction materials range from wood to cement and tiles; a small but permanent store provides for immediate needs and basic employment possibilities. Washing occurs in the space behind the store, but there is no running water.

housing now ranges from minimal dwellings stacked on top of one another to comfortable middle-class housing with gardens; floods are less frequent, and health and education have improved. Such settlements remain legally marginal and poorly provided for, however. Most residents have no legal title to the land on which they have built their dwellings, meaning that in principle they could be evicted overnight. For most residents, toilets and showers are communal, sometimes in appallingly unhealthy conditions, and water comes from pumps. In northern Jakarta (the original colonial Dutch port, now dominated by *kampungs*), groundwater supplies have been drawn down so far that saltwater from the ocean has flooded the aquifers in the northern third of the city. *Kampung* residents here have to buy water in 5-gallon cans, paying up to 30 times more than the wealthy pay for piped water in southern parts of the city (see Plate 19.4).

As some *kampungs* become regularized, however, the continual flow of in-migrants requires new searches for places to live. Cardboard boxes are covered with plastic sheets and placed along and even between train tracks, built out farther over the canals, or built on land held by speculators or urban planners for future developments. Provision of public housing by the government, in order to replace squatter settlements with more regular housing, is a rarely used option in the third world. Hong Kong and Singapore have very large public housing programs, accommodating more than half their population. In Jakarta, by contrast, publicly financed housing is limited in quantity and only available to loyal government employees.

Despite an organization of intraurban space that provides for a general separation of low- from high-income housing, there is in fact considerable intermixing of income groups. Although intraurban inequalities are greater than in first world cities of comparable size, low- and high-income families in fact are less segregated from one another. Not only is there a range of income groups in the *kampung* settlements, reflecting the differing fortunes of their inhabitants over the years; clusters of low-income housing can also be found within the high-income estates, on small plots of land taken over by squatters, and on land as yet unoccupied by housing for the wealthy. As a consequence of this intermixing, and of the huge income differences within the city (which are greater in Jakarta than in any other region of Indonesia), the architecture of the wealthy housing is highly defensive, with high wrought iron fences in the front and concrete walls up to 4 meters high capped by broken glass in the back.

The social differences and disparities evident in housing structures can also be found in manufacturing, services, and office activities. The most visible component of manufacturing on the urban landscape is in the form of factories on industrial estates, owned by domestic entrepreneurs and foreign firms, and engaged in both ISI and EOI (often labor-intensive) (see Figure 19.8). Yet at the same time, along the main thoroughfares and scattered through the residential districts, many small manufacturers operate out of small rented spaces, their own dwellings, and unclaimed open spaces, engaged in the micromanufacture of such commodities as textiles, clothing, furniture, and ornaments. Retailing runs the spectrum from brand-new air-conditioned shopping centers with high-fashion stores, visited by the elite in their Mercedes (see Plate 19.5); through market buildings constructed by the state in an attempt to get retailers off the street; to salespeople in living rooms, in front gardens, on street corners, or walking the streets (see

PLATE 19.4. The fresh water under most of the *kampungs* in northern Jakarta has been replaced by seawater as a result of overuse and lack of sewage systems. Water sellers negotiate the narrow streets, bringing fresh water to households at a price many times that paid in southern Jakarta by middle-class households for running water.

PLATE 19.5. Ratu Plaza is a stainless steel shopping center, offering the latest in European fashion to social elites whose drivers wait outside by the Mercedes. Access is carefully controlled.

Plate 19.6). Office activities similarly range from 30-story office towers sharing the main thoroughfares with five-star hotels, and serving larger domestic firms, foreign corporations, and the government, to doctors', notaries', and accountants' tiny offices in any available space on and off the streets.

The differences between buildings that seem to have come straight from the portfolios of New York architects, and work and living spaces very much like those found in small villages, reflect the polarized nature of third world metropolitan economies, particularly the importance of the informal sector (see below). These contrasts are heightened, however, by the spatial intermingling of the different land uses, including rural activities no longer found in first world cities. The shadows of brand-new office buildings fall across *kampungs* clustered at their bases; herds of goats can be found walking through housing estates; street sellers set up business immediately outside retail complexes; and a cassava field can be found squeezed between a Japanese hotel and a clogged urban artery (see Plate 19.7). This complex intermingling of nonagricultural activities with one another, and with agricultural activities, creates urban forms so different from those familiar to the residents of first world cities that Terry McGee (1991) has speculated whether first world conceptions of urbanization are even appropriate for understanding Asian cities. These patterns certainly pose continual headaches for third world officials seeking to "modernize" their cities so that they look more like those of the first world.

PLATE 19.6. An informal trader selling cut fruit and vegetables has managed to upgrade from pans carried on a yoke around her shoulders to a cart on wheels. In the tent behind, another informal trader is selling *soto ayam* (chicken noodle soup) to customers.

PLATE 19.7. Modern hotels and office buildings, many built during a worldwide surplus of real estate capital in the early 1980s, line the main arterial road. Between these glass and concrete towers are open fields planted in cassava, papaya, and bananas; *kampung* settlements; and mosques of all sizes for Jakarta's mostly Muslim population.

Modernity and the Informal Sector

At first sight, urban life in a third world metropolis seems to violate many conceptions of modern life. To a first world visitor, there seems to be disorder or even chaos everywhere—not only the difficulty that a traveler always faces when confronted with a new culture, but the mixing of apparently very different lifestyles. In the trip in from the airport, the beat-up and overpriced taxi (overpriced compared to what "locals" pay) weaves its way among Range Rovers, trucks, bicycles, pedicabs, and families on foot—a traffic chaos that seems as if there should be an accident at every corner. The 30-meter trip from the curb to the hotel receptionist requires the traveler to negotiate handcarts selling food, a woman and child begging, someone offering to change money, and two officials in $500 suits arguing about interest rates. Stepping out of the hotel for an evening stroll, turning a corner deposits the visitor in an ill-lit winding street where getting lost can take only minutes, and where he or she is regarded as if being from another planet.

In fact, these contrasts and juxtapositions are just another dimension of modernity. In the 19th century, European novelists described the chaos of urban street life as characteristic of modernism in Paris and London (Harvey, 1989). This seemed to disappear in many first world metropolises during the postwar boom, as city streets came to be dominated by cars rather than pedestrians. It can now be found in third world metropolises, yet takes a particular form that reflects these cities' positionality—simultaneously occupying the core of their national space economy, and located within the periphery of the global system. The role of the informal sector in third world metropolises is central to the forms that modernity is taking here. Definitions of the "informal sector" vary, but generally it is regarded as referring to economic activities that are unlicensed, unregistered, or illegal, as well as activities in which goods are bartered for one another rather than exchanged for money. Informal sector activities include selling vegetables on the street corner, acting as a courier, engaging in prostitution, running drugs, selling plastic containers door to door, bartering for medical care, guarding parked cars, or using one's own car as a temporary taxi. The informal sector includes many of the only options open to new in-migrants and longer-term residents alike, struggling to gain a foothold in a metropolitan economy that has few conventional jobs to offer. Many people holding conventional jobs also utilize the informal sector, however, as a supplementary source of income. Lower-level public sector workers (including school and university teachers) are often paid salaries too low to support their families, and turn to the informal sector for help.

Such activities are not a peculiarity of third world cities. They have also increased in importance in first world cities during the last 20 years, as the ability of the mainstream economy to provide jobs and shelter for first world urban residents has markedly declined. Often referred to as the "black market," or simply as "criminal activities," the informal sector has been endemic to second world cities (both before and after the "quiet revolutions" of 1989 that brought down the Berlin Wall and eastern Europe's communist governments) and is increasingly common in first world cities. Nevertheless, informal sector activities are particularly prevalent in third world cities; they reflect the close links between rural households and rural–urban migrants, the traditionally very different nature of economic activities under kinship and capitalism, and the lack of mainstream opportunities for both urban and rural inhabitants.

From the perspective of third world elites and many development theorists, informal activities were long regarded as undesirable. They were seen as being in some sense part of a traditional rather than a modern economy; they did not fit well with, and even undercut, mainstream economic activities; they were socially undesirable or hazardous; and, above all, they generated no taxes. Indeed, in most cases it was not even possible to quantify their contribution to the urban economy, because they remained unrecorded in conventional statistics.

As a consequence, there have been numerous attempts to eliminate aspects of the informal sector, and consequently to modernize cities. In Jakarta, for example, a number of multistory concrete markets were built, providing retail space that licensed retailers were supposed to rent, as part of an attempt to modernize the urban retail sector by getting traders off the streets. Yet the rents paid in these buildings are beyond the means of small traders, and they force up the prices of retailers who can afford them. Furthermore, the ability of street traders to bring their goods into the *kampungs*, or to elite estates where servants can purchase them, gives them a locational advantage over traders in the markets. Finally, street trading is a valuable source of income for many urban residents with no access to conventional jobs. For these reasons, street trading retains an economic niche, playing an essential social role that makes it hard to eliminate in the name of modern retailing. Indeed, Jakarta authorities now turn a blind eye to street traders who cluster around the entrances to the state-built markets, selling fruits from the family farm, plastic bags scavenged from garbage dumps, or T-shirts bought on consignment.

It is not only informal activities that are frowned on in the name of modernization. For example, *becaks* (pedicabs; see Plate 19.8) have repeatedly been criticized as an antiquated and inefficient form of transportation in Jakarta, because they clog up the streets and slow down cars and trucks. In 1984, authorities banned *becaks* from main thoroughfares, confiscating about 40,000 of them in 3 years and dumping them in the ocean. Once again, however, the importance of *becaks* to the city has made them impossible to eliminate (see sidebar: "The *Becak* Driver: Informality and Inequality"). They

PLATE 19.8. Carrying up to three people and their shopping, the *becak* (pedicab) is small enough to negotiate *kampung* streets. *Becak* driving is a brutal way to earn a living, but also one of the best opportunities for new male in-migrants. Drivers quickly develop massive calves, but can rarely get the nutrition necessary to maintain their health.

The *Becak* Driver: Informality and Inequality

Sarah works as a maid for expatriate foreigners in Jakarta. She and her husband have a small dwelling in a *kampung*, and have managed to save enough money to purchase a *becak* (pedicab; see Plate 19.8 in text). Through an informal contract, they charge Suparno, a new young immigrant living in a shanty settlement by the canal, a daily fee to drive the *becak* for them. By working hard, Suparno can make just enough from his passengers to get by, after paying this fee. For Suparno, this is better than most informal sector opportunities in the short term. He has enormous calf muscles, but because of the sheer physical effort involved in driving the *becak* with up to three riders plus parcels, combined with his poor nutrition and the pollution from trucks and buses using poor-quality gasoline, his health will deteriorate before too long.

The arrangement between Sarah and Suparno benefits both, but in a way that maintains the inequality between them. Suparno has at least found quasi-reliable employment in the informal sector, unlike many of his friends, but he is only making enough to prevent himself from starving. The members of Sarah's family are carefully accumulating the money from Suparno's fee, so that they can replace the *becak* with a *bajaj* (a three-wheeled minicab, imported from India, with a small lawn-mower-type motor). *Bajajs* are not much faster than *becaks*, but they can carry more and generate more income. The economic situation of Sarah and her family remains very vulnerable. Their plan to accumulate money and move up to a better source of income will come to nothing if she loses her job, her husband loses his, or someone becomes sick. Yet their chances of improving their situation are much better than Suparno's, and are increased because his prospects are so limited that he is willing to pay to work for them.

are a source of income for young male in-migrants seeking their first jobs; they provide a source of capital to the lower-middle-class families owning them; and they are among the very few types of vehicles small enough to serve the *kampungs*—in the course of which they also have to use the urban thoroughfares. Indeed, enterprising individuals fish them out of the ocean again, repaint them, and sell them back to be redeployed on the streets of Jakarta.

More recent analyses of the informal sector suggest that it plays an essential role in the functioning of cities like Jakarta. Free market analysts have praised the informal sector as the epitome of free market entrepreneurialism, seeing the proprietors of such "microenterprises" as small capitalists who are willing to take risks, and imaginative in identifying niches to be filled with new products and services. In this view, informal activities should be supported because they represent a form of nascent capitalism capable of lifting third world economies from the doldrums of underdevelopment and excessive state control. From a political economy perspective, it is argued that the informal sector helps keep prices and wages low. Prices are subsidized by the unpaid family and informal sector labor used to produce and distribute them, and when prices are low, money wages also can be lower. In this view, the informal sector contributes to underdevelopment in many third world nations by reinforcing the cycle of low-wage employment and underemployment, but it will be tolerated in practice precisely because it is essential to a low-wage economy.

The form taken by informal sector activities will vary over time and among cities, depending on opportunities available in the formal urban economy; on the rate and needs of urban in-migrants; on the role of the city in the national and global systems; and on the success of the state in providing public services that substitute for, or repress, informal activities. In South Korea, for example, successful industrialization and relatively low income inequalities have reduced the need of its urban residents to rely on the informal sector for their livelihood. In Thailand, prostitution has become a very significant informal sector activity, as a result of international marketing of sex tourism to first world males who cannot find or cannot afford such activities at home. Facing rural poverty, families are induced to send their young girls (and some boys) to Bangkok as part of a household subsistence strategy, with a deadly consequence: Northern Thailand has among the fastest-growing HIV/AIDS infection rates in the world (Chapter 8).

In Rio and Bogota, informal housing settlements have become centers of the drug trade (like inner city neighborhoods in U.S. cities), because of the lack of other opportunities, the surplus of young men with little access to regular employment, and the impossibility of police control and surveillance in these areas. In Singapore and Hong Kong, where land is at a premium, a longstanding commitment by the state to build high-rise public housing has kept informal housing to a minimum. Yet, notwithstanding these variations, the informal sector is an essential part of the urban economy in third world cities. In this sense, informal activities are not the remnants of a traditional indigenous activity that will disappear with capitalist development, but an essential part of modernity in cities that are highly differentiated socially and often have a parasitic rather than symbiotic relationship with their own third world hinterlands.

Neoliberal Globalization and Third World Urban Glitter

The market logics and openings of national territories that have accompanied globalization are beginning to transform selected third world cities in dramatic ways. We offer just a few examples here, to illustrate some of these changes. In Malaysia, Kuala Lumpur has developed into a shiny glass and concrete downtown, dominated by modern and postmodern office buildings, including the Petronas twin towers—until recently, the highest building in the world. (Petronas is the Malaysian state oil company.) Between Kuala Lumpur and the new international airport, the state has invested in two new towns. Cyberjaya, opened in 1999, vies to become a major third world information technology and communication (ITC) center. Next to it, Putrajaya, still in development, is the new home for most of Malaysia's national state office buildings and office workers—almost a new capital city (although to date the parliament has stayed in Kuala Lumpur), built around artificial lakes, with architecture that eclectically combines postmodern and Islamic features. Bangalore, attracting to India ITC investments from around the world, has an ambitious new plan that will quintuple the size of the metropolitan area, including an ITC metropolis 50% larger in area than Paris. Taipei, capital of Taiwan, now has the world's highest building (101 Taipei, at 500 meters, 50 meters taller than the Empire State Building), surrounded by half a dozen enclosed shopping complexes filled with the hottest European, American, and Japanese designer stores. Even Paris could not offer as rich a selection to well-heeled consumers. New condominiums are as expensive in Taipei as in Manhattan. Across the river from the old colonial Bundt in Shanghai, the epicenter of Chinese urbanization since China reopened itself to the world economy, an ambitious new district of commercial and residential buildings is emerging literally from the cleared earth. It includes 30 square kilometers of special economic zones (cf. Chapter 17), and a variety of space-age architectural styles in its commercial districts. The western edge of Pudong, the Lujiazui Finance and Trade Zone, planned as China's global financial hub, now has some 20 million square feet of grade A office space—about 80% of the total office space in midtown and downtown Manhattan together. Its Shanghai World Financial Center will become one of the tallest buildings in the world: 100 floors and almost 500 meters.

Then there is Dubai. This tiny emirate on the Persian Gulf is investing its oil wealth into a long-term development plan—vying to become the place where Europeans and Americans buy vacation condominiums. Through a combination of a marina now largely completed, and islands being built into the Persian Gulf (three of which are shaped like palm trees, plus a cluster forming a map of the world), Dubai intends to have as much floor space as all of Manhattan. There are plans for the next entry in the tallest building stakes: Burj Dubai, at 705 meters! As of 2006, approximately one-sixth of the world's high-rise construction cranes had been brought to Dubai to realize these plans. The desert emirate offers broad beaches, warm and calm waters, cheap plastic and dental surgery, water parks, golf courses, horse tracks, high-end retailing, state of the art soccer and cricket facilities (the International Cricket Council recently moved here from London), ice skating, and a ski slope. It also seeks to reconstruct its historical role, before the advent of European colonialism, as a major *entrepôt* between Europe and Asia. The Dragon Mart in Dubai is the largest Chinese wholesale market outside east Asia, with 1,200 Chinese employees. Dubai is also the hub for one of the world's fastest-growing airlines, Emirates, and the 18th largest cargo airport in tonnage in the world (comparable with New York and London).

Yet this glitter of modernity cannot come into existence without running up against those parts of the city and rural hinterland where very different livelihoods are practiced (Benjamin, 2000). Massive differences in lifestyle, wealth, and the power to pursue a better life persist. The new buildings come into existence by formalizing first-world style property relations. Unambiguous land titles are created and recorded in geographical information systems, which allow land to be claimed for redevelopment. New transportation corridors are built through slums. Land is zoned to displace microenterprises and street traders from newly designated residential districts. The streets themselves are transformed from open-air markets into high-speed movement corridors. In the process, the liminal and marginal city spaces where very poor and new in-migrants can find housing and eke out their livelihoods become harder and harder to create. At the same time, privatization policies mean that residents must pay higher prices for basic utilities, or even for their children to attend state-run schools, and are cut off from services if they are unable to pay. Through exploiting loopholes in urban policies, self-help organizing, activist initiatives and protests against such policies and actions, poor residents craft spaces to pursue alternative survival strategies (Bond and McInnes, 2007; Oldfield and Stokke, 2007). But this is becoming harder to do, even as more people are attracted to the lights and excitement of the big cities.

CONCLUSIONS

Common processes drive urbanization throughout the world. Cities are defined by a spatial division of labor, and by the trade of nonagricultural goods for primary commodities, between cities and their rural hinterlands. Broader-scale processes affecting industrialization and trade are also vital to the economic health of cities. Cities, as clusters of people in built-up areas, are equally the result of patterns of demographic change: more localized rural–urban migration, as well as interurban and international population movements. Finally, cities are places where political power and influence accumulate, and where new cultural and social norms are often constructed. Despite such commonalities, however, urbanization processes are evolving in distinct ways in different parts of the world, with particular social and spatial consequences.

Urbanization in the third world is occurring in magnitudes and at speeds unprecedented in human history, posing huge challenges to societies attempting to manage change. This general challenge is compounded by the extreme degree to which urbanization is congregating in one, or a very few, cities within each third world country. These places of rapid demographic and economic growth all too frequently stand in stark contrast to the bulk of that country's territory, which is experiencing stagnation and underdevelopment. Cities act as *entrepôts* between international processes (of increasing influence) and local livelihoods. The extreme external orientation of many third world economic and political systems means that the large cities are more closely linked with other cities across the world than with their own national territories. This makes such cities parasitic on, rather than generative of, growth in their national hinterlands. External orientation, excessive rates of urbanization, spatially polarized patterns of change, and increasing urban–rural disparities have thus gone hand in hand in many third world countries.

The situation is different in many first world nations. The largest cities of these nations include world "mega-cities" instrumental to the functioning of the international urban system, and many of their cities are heavily linked to the international political economy through trade, capital flows, and population movements. Yet despite these international connections, their national economies are more self-sufficient, and growth in the largest cities need not occur at the expense of underdevelopment in their hinterlands. In third world countries, transportation and communications improvements often accelerate spatial polarization by increasing the concentration of population and economic activities in the largest cities; in first world countries, the opposite can frequently be observed. Even though places like New York, London, and Paris remain the largest national cities, spatial restructuring has shifted the momentum of growth among other cities and regions on a number of occasions. Thus, in the United States, the 1970s were years when the older industrial cities of the northeastern "rust belt" lost much of their growth momentum to cities in the southern and western "sun belt." There have even been well-documented examples of "exurbanization"—the movement of people and some economic activities out beyond the metropolitan fringe into rural areas. The result of such changes has not been an equalization of welfare and opportunity among the cities and regions of first world nations, but the disparities and persistent spatial development differences are much less evident than in the third world.

Steady immigration in the face of limited opportunities within the formal economy has resulted in extremes of poverty and wealth within third world cities that are rarely found elsewhere. Parallel extremes exist in the range of economic enterprises in those cities. The larger first world cities are experiencing similar increases in social and economic polarization, in part as a consequence of an inability to provide employment for all, and in part as a consequence of the disappearance of state-supported social services for the least well off. This polarization is compounded by the fact that many of those worst affected are people of color and women. It has been observed that this polarization is most extreme within the "global cities" of the first world (Sassen, 1991). These cities are the destinations for many of the international population movements reaching the first world, and have also become containers for indigenous communities of color. Many end up in a flourishing sweatshop industry in low-rent spaces within the inner cities of the first world (not to mention sex work), in a period of time when there is reduced state regulation of working conditions, creating a burgeoning secondary labor market of poorly paid workers with few opportunities for advancement. There are also burgeoning informal sectors in these cities. Noting the street corner windshield cleaners, day labor markets, illegal taxis, congestion, street people, drug businesses, and back-street sweatshops, observers of New York, Los Angeles, and London increasingly compare them to Mexico City and Jakarta.

Notwithstanding their similarities, third world cities retain distinctive characteristics reflecting their relative position within the world economy. Despite the desperate conditions under which too many people must struggle in first world cities, the extremes of urban impoverishment are much greater in the third world. The spatial organization of these cities also makes the extremes more evident, since poverty and wealth are frequently found cheek by jowl; in first world cities, by contrast, urban land markets and state policies have combined to separate the wealthy and the poor into different parts of the city. The everyday confrontation of wealth with poverty reinforces the frustration of each group with the other. The wealthy, impatient with what they see as the inability of the poor to improve themselves, assent to draconian methods to force modernization and distance poverty from at least their everyday experience. Squatter settlements are razed, street traders harassed, and the homeless transported out of the city. The poor—experiencing the close linkage between their poverty and others' wealth, and aware of the indifference of states, international firms, and financial organizations to their plight—contest these moves in a variety of ways. These range from passive resistance to petty crime to street demonstrations. Demonstrations are increasingly resorted to in cases where states have found fewer resources for, and shown less interest in, improving the lives of the urban masses. Yet third world cities can also be places of positive social experiments (see sidebar: "Curitiba and Puerto Alegre"). Thus the polarization that is associated with third world cities' acting as *entrepôts* for global processes of development and underdevelopment, operating at a variety of scales, has made these cities increasingly important sites of public unrest. Rural areas were the sources of many of the most visible revolutionary and anticolonial movements within the third world in the 20th century, but cities may increasingly become the loci for such actions in this millennium—as evidenced in the cities of Palestine and Iraq, and recent unrest in suburban immigrant settlements in France.

NOTE

1. Descriptions of Jakarta are based on joint field research by Helga Leitner and ES, undertaken primarily in 1986–1987. Several of the photographs also were taken by Helga Leitner.

Curitiba and Porto Alegre

Curitiba, a Brazilian city of 1.5 million residents, has come to be seen as a worldwide model for environmentally sustainable urbanism. Land use planning has created a built environment in which residents are connected to workplaces and other destinations by light rail rapid transit. Two-thirds of its (largely middle-class) population uses this rather than automobiles and engage in voluntary recycling. About 22,000 poorer families earn food in return for recycling; and there have been rapid improvements in health and child mortality.

Porto Alegre, a city of 1.3 million inhabitants in southern Brazil, has gained a worldwide reputation for its participatory city budgeting process (as well as for hosting the World Social Forum). Each year, 16 district assemblies rank local spending priorities through public debate. These 16 "Great Assemblies" are held in each district, where city officials report on the previous year and present their investment plan. Each district produces one set of rankings for 12 major in-district "themes," and another for cross-cutting efforts that affect the entire city. These are complemented by thematic and citywide assemblies. Finally, a municipal budget council, with 42 representatives (one from each district and thematic assembly), sets overall spending priorities. The process involves some 40,000 city residents, disproportionately the poor, and takes 9 months. Through citizen initiative, participatory budgeting has broadened its scope to cover more of the city's budget, and responsibility for the leadership and design of meetings has shifted from executive branch officials toward citizens and their elected delegates. Porto Alegre has provided water and sewers for 98% of its population; spends 40% of its budget on health and education; and has increased public housing fivefold (Baiocchi, 2002; de Sousa Santos, 1998).

Sources: The description of Curitiba is based on Rabinovitch (1992). The description of Porto Alegre draws heavily on Goldsmith (n.d.).

20 Transnational Production

During the 20th century, particularly after Bretton Woods, a new agent entered the everyday lives of third and first world residents—one capable of exerting control over production in other countries even when those countries are politically independent. This agent, the "transnational corporation" (TNC), has become a major player in shaping economic processes within the third world, including the location of industrial activities and the growth of large cities. A TNC owns facilities (e.g., factories, mines, sales offices) in more than one country for the production and distribution of its products (Jenkins, 1987). When a TNC opens a facility in another country, this entails not only a flow of money capital from one country to another in order to underwrite production abroad, but also the exertion of direct organizational control from one country over production in the other. In this sense, production in a TNC is truly transnational in scope, transcending limits to the geography of production imposed by national political boundaries.

The investment activity engaged in by TNCs is referred to as "foreign direct investment" (FDI)—the investment of money abroad, in facilities over which the investor has a degree of direct control. We talk of the country where a TNC has its headquarters as being the "home country" for such investment, whereas the country to which FDI is directed is the "host country." It is important to note that any focus on transnational production and FDI, as in this and the following chapter, is a gendered, masculine account of what counts as important—one that prioritizes the formal economy and the top-down impact of large-scale economic agents of globalization (Freeman, 2001; Nagar et al., 2002; Roberts, 2004). Yet its structuring influence on the livelihood possibilities of men and women around the world demands that we pay attention to it.

The growth of transnational production raises a series of questions for national governments seeking economic growth. On the one hand, it may be a quick and effective source of investment. For example, eastern European countries actively sought to attract FDI in order to give their economies a quick boost after the revolutions of 1989. On the other hand, foreign capital poses a threat to national identity and autonomy. Excessive foreign ownership is seen as a sign of weakness and dependence ("Buy American!"), and the international mobility of transnational investment makes it more difficult for nation states to regulate the behavior of privately owned firms. Foreign firms may stimulate local business, but they also have the resources to drive local entrepreneurs out of business. This poses problems for third world governments attempting to use FDI to jump-start domestic industry (see Chapter 17). Despite such reservations, TNCs have become major players in the global economy. In this chapter, we examine the growth and geographical patterns of transnational production, and try to account for why it has grown and spread. In Chapter 21, we discuss factors shaping the impact of foreign-owned production on third world economies.

THE GROWTH OF TRANSNATIONAL PRODUCTION

Up to the third quarter of the 19th century, the surplus of capital accumulating in certain countries, particularly in Britain, was typically lent to (usually expatriate) independent entrepreneurs and their corporations in other countries, to expand commodity production there. Lenin (1916/1970) referred to this direct export of money as "imperialism" (see Chapter 4), although by the time he wrote about it this form of imperialism was declining in significance relative to FDI. Prior to 1914, another form of international enterprise had been influential in European colonial empires—the multinational trading companies, such as the East India Company (Britain and Holland each had one) or the Hudson's Bay Company. Trading companies made their profits by supplying exotic and primary products to Europe, rather than engaging in production abroad, and were allotted considerable political and military power by their home countries to pursue these goals in the colonies and on the high seas. Like TNCs, they exploited their considerable size and diminished corporate risk, as well as their state charters, to engage in projects that otherwise would not have been attractive to private firms (see Chapter 3). Their fortunes waned as European powers took direct control over the colonies, from which they had organized the extraction of primary products, and with the increasing profitability of FDI.

Dunning (1988) provides a concise history of the growth of transnational production. In 1914 (as Britain's 80-year free trade policy was winding up), British TNCs dominated the world economy (Figure 20.1); they invested heavily in the production of primary commodities (55%) and railroad construction (20%), largely within the British Empire. The United States was a secondary player, investing mostly (72%) in primary commodity production in Canada and Latin America. In all, about three-fifths of foreign-owned production was in places that are now part of the third world, mostly in colonial possessions (see Chapter 14). FDI declined in importance for European TNCs between the two world wars (1914–1938), whereas U.S. firms increased their foreign presence. FDI was still dominated by investment in primary products in what we now call the third world, which by now was the home for almost two-thirds of foreign-owned production.

FDI more than doubled during the postwar Fordist boom in the first world (1945–1960), growing faster than world trade. This expansion was dominated by U.S. TNCs, reflecting the shift of global economic supremacy from Britain to the United States. About two-thirds of all new investment and new foreign branch plants in this period were U.S. owned. By 1960, the relative importance of foreign investment for U.S. and British TNCs had reversed the imbalance that had existed in Britain's favor in 1914 (Figure 20.1); this peak of U.S. influence lasted until 1973.

Despite this growth of FDI, the attractiveness of the third world as a host for for-

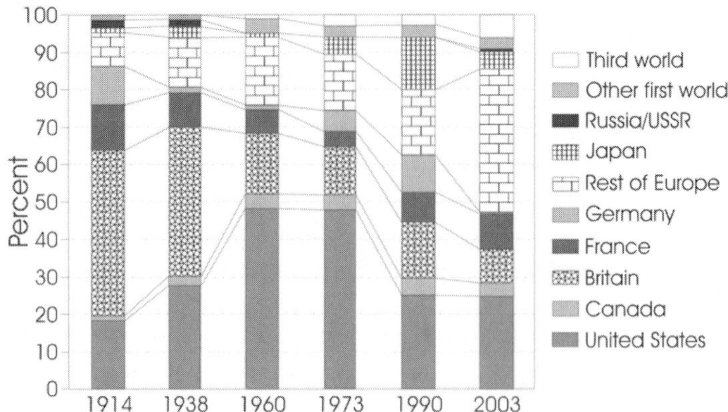

FIGURE 20.1. Foreign direct investment (FDI) by host country, 1914–2003. *Sources:* Data for 1914–1973 are from Dunning (1988: Table 3.1); data for 1983 are from United Nations (1992c); data for 1994 are from United Nations (1995); and data for 2003 are from United Nations (2004).

eign investors declined rapidly during this period. Ninety-five percent of new FDI was in the first world, so the third world share of all foreign-owned production dropped dramatically, from two-thirds in 1945 to one-third in 1960. British investments abandoned newly independent colonies, focusing instead on Canada, Australia, and South Africa. U.S. and European TNCs concentrated on European expansion, locating foreign production within Europe to avoid import tariffs. There was also a sectoral change, as FDI shifted away from primary products and into manufacturing (Table 20.1). Only Japanese TNCs did not follow this trend, continuing to invest in primary commodity production in third world locations, two-thirds of which were in Asia. There was also a decreased interest in investing in new "greenfield" plants at new locations, as mergers and acquisitions became increasingly common ways of acquiring foreign production.

From the late 1960s to the early 1980s, the relative importance of FDI in the global economy declined, under development agendas led by nation states. The FDI flowing to third world countries had declined to just 3% by 1980, triggered in part by a wave of nationalization of foreign-owned primary commodity production by third world states in the 1960s and early 1970s. International bank lending had flourished as FDI stagnated, but in the early 1980s a third world debt crisis triggered the most rapid expansion of FDI yet experienced, as bank lending collapsed (Chapter 23). Within 5 years (1985–1990), FDI quadrupled, doubling again by 1996. During this expansion, the U.S. share of FDI declined substantially (from 40% in 1983 to 20% by 1996), to be replaced by German, Japanese, and other European TNCs. Much of the new FDI continued to flow to the first world, especially to the United States and Europe, but the share going to the third world was increasing (to a third of the global total by 1996–1997)—particularly to the newly industrializing countries (NICs) of southeast Asia. By 1997, FDI constituted more than half of all capital flows to the third world.

The 1997 Asian financial crisis was followed by a renewed boom of FDI worldwide, increasing by 350% between 1997 and 2001 to $1.2 trillion in U.S. dollars, declining to just $600 billion in 2003 in the wake of the "dot.com bust" in the first world, and increasing again to $900 billion by 2005. This unprecedented volatility closely followed the changing fortunes of financial markets. The

TABLE 20.1. The 10 Largest TNCs, 1962–2003

Company (home country)	Activity	Sales (U.S. $, millions)	Host country	GDP[a] (U.S. $, millions)
1962				
General Motors (U.S.)	Automobiles	14,660	Argentina	14,430
Standard Oil (Ind.) (U.S.)	Oil	9,480	Venezuela	8,290
Ford Motor Co. (U.S.)	Automobiles	8,090	Turkey	7,660
Shell (Neth.)	Oil	6,020	Philippines	6,010
General Electric (U.S.)	Electrics	4,790	Peru	4,900
Unilever (Neth./U.K.)	Food	4,140	Nigeria	4,190
Mobil/Socony (U.S.)	Oil	3,930	Thailand	4,050
U.S. Steel (U.S.)	Steel	3,470	Indonesia	3,630
Texaco (U.S.)	Oil	3,270	Algeria	3,170
Gulf (U.S.)	Oil	3,100	S. Korea	3,000
1972				
General Motors (U.S.)	Automobiles	30,435	Argentina	32,000
Exxon (U.S.)	Oil	20,309	Switzerland	22,000
Ford (U.S.)	Automobiles	20,194	Denmark	16,500
Shell (Neth.)	Oil	14,060	Venezuela	15,000
General Electric (U.S.)	Electrics	10,239	Indonesia	11,000
Chrysler (U.S.)	Automobiles	9,759	S. Korea	10,000
IBM (U.S.)	Electronics	9,532	Peru	9,000
Mobil Oil (U.S.)	Oil	9,166	Chile	9,000
Unilever (Neth.)	Chems, food	8,864	Thailand	8,500
Texaco (U.S.)	Oil	8,692	Philippines	8,000
1983				
Exxon (U.S.)	Oil	88,561	Mexico	145,130
Shell (Neth.)	Oil	80,550	Indonesia	78,320
General Motors (U.S.)	Automobiles	74,582	S. Korea	76,640
Mobil (U.S.)	Oil	54,607	Nigeria	64,570
British Petroleum (U.K.)	Oil	49,195	Turkey	47,840
Ford (U.S.)	Automobiles	44,455	Peru	47,640
IBM (U.S.)	Electronics	40,180	Thailand	40,430
Texaco (U.S.)	Oil	40,068		
Du Pont (U.S.)	Chemicals	35,378	Philippines	34,640
Standard Oil (Ind.) (U.S.)	Oil	27,635	Hong Kong	27,500
1993				
General Motors (U.S.)	Automobiles	133,622	Indonesia	126,364
Ford (U.S.)	Automobiles	108,521	Iran	110,258
Exxon (U.S.)	Oil	97,825	Turkey	99,696
Shell (Neth.)	Oil	95,134	Ukraine	94,831
Toyota (Japan)	Automobiles	85,283	Hong Kong	77,828
Hitachi (Japan)	Electronics	68,581	Israel	69,762
IBM (U.S.)	Electronics	62,716	Greece	67,270
Matsushita (Japan)	Electronics	61,385	Venezuela	61,137
General Electric (U.S.)	Electrical	60,823		
Daimler-Benz (Ger.)	Automobiles	59,102	Malaysia	57,568
2003				
Wal-Mart Stores (U.S.)	Retail	246,525	Turkey	237,972
General Motors (U.S.)	Automobiles	186,763	Saudi Arabia	188,479
ExxonMobil (U.S.)	Oil	182,466	Saudi Arabia	188,479
Royal Dutch/Shell (U.K./Neth.)	Oil	179,431	Greece	173,045
BP (U.K.)	Oil	178,721		
Ford Motor (U.S.)	Automobiles	163,871	Finland	161,549
DaimlerChrysler (Ger.)	Automobiles	141,421	Thailand	143,163
Toyota Motor (Japan)	Automobiles	131,754	Iran	136,833
General Electric (U.S.)	Electronics	131,698	Argentina	129,735
Mitsubishi (Japan)	Trading	109,386	Israel	103,689

Sources: Data for firms for 1962 are from Dunning and Pearce (1985); data for firms for 1973, 1983, and 1993 are from *Fortune* magazine (1973a, 1973b, 1984, 1994, 2003). Data for countries are from World Resources Institute (1996a) and World Bank (2008).

[a]GDP figures for the 1962 listings are actually those for 1965. Otherwise, GDP data are for the years indicated.

U.S. share of outward FDI flows has continued to fall, to 16%. FDI stayed away from the third world in the wake of the 1997 crisis but has since returned, with new inward FDI flows to the third world representing 36% of the global total. Much of the growth has been in the primary sector, where mineral and fossil fuel prices and profits are booming again. Third world countries have put much effort into developing new regulations to ease and attract FDI, except in Latin America, where progressive regimes have installed restrictions (including nationalization of gas production in Bolivia). The last decade has also seen a boom in FDI *from* the third world (i.e., in the growth of third world TNCs headquartered in the third world; see below).

Increasingly, FDI flows are not resulting in the construction of new factories or job creation. Overseas mergers and acquisitions have recently come to dominate FDI outflows. These represent cases where new foreign ownership comes into existence, and a flow of FDI is recorded in the statistics, but it is simply a change in ownership. Too often, the result is not new jobs but unemployment, as the new owner "rationalizes" its new assets and closes factories. Mutual funds and hedge funds are also increasingly putting their money into FDI-type investments. This includes "round-tripping," where money is sent abroad only to return to the same country in a form recorded as direct investment. It also includes "trans-shipping," whereby FDI money is recorded as flowing to select locations (such as offshore financial centers [OFCs]; see Chapter 22) where it is placed in "special-purpose entities" and holding companies that then ship the money elsewhere. Again, it is questionable whether such flows create new factories and jobs. Indeed, even traditional TNCs have become more concerned with short-term profit taking than with long-term investment strategies, responding to their shareholders' desires for immediate returns on their investments (United Nations, 2006c).

The United Nations (2006c) estimated that some 77,000 TNCs (almost double the number in 1993) employed 62 million workers (more than double the number in 1993) in 770,000 foreign affiliates worldwide (triple the number in 1993), with a total accumulated value of FDI stocks of over $10 trillion in U.S. dollars (quadrupling since 1993). Total sales of these foreign affiliates had reached $22.2 trillion (quadrupling since 1993). Some 10% of the value of world output is produced by TNCs, and two-thirds of all world exports are in their hands (Dicken, 2003). Approximately one-third of this is within-firm trade—commodity shipments between branches of the same TNC, which are not governed by the market forces envisaged by the free trade doctrine (Chapter 15).

The largest 100 TNCs own 10% of worldwide FDI, employ almost 15 million workers (7.4 million in overseas operations), and generate over $6 trillion (U.S. dollars) in sales (half from overseas operations). Table 20.1 traces the 10 largest individual TNCs from 1962 to 2003, showing how their sales compare to the gross domestic products (GDPs) of selected countries. Several trends can be seen here. First, the sales of these largest TNCs have consistently matched the GDPs of all but the biggest third world nations (see the right-hand columns of this table). Between 1962 and 1983, only four third world nations had GDPs greater than the sales of the largest TNC, largely because of their huge population size (China, India, Brazil, and Mexico). By 1993, these had been joined by South Korea and Argentina. Second, the mix of these largest TNCs has changed, as automobile and petroleum-extracting firms are gradually infiltrated by TNCs engaged in electrical and electronics production. Most recently, the retailer Walmart (formerly Wal-Mart), with its worldwide chain of "big box" stores, has leapfrogged to the top of the table in terms of sales (but not assets). Third, Japanese and German firms are beginning to make inroads into an elite group of TNCs traditionally dominated by U.S., British, and Dutch firms.

THE GEOGRAPHY OF TRANSNATIONAL PRODUCTION

Overall, since World War II FDI has grown rapidly, has shifted from primary production to manufacturing and services, and now has shifted back to the primary sector; has relocated from third world to first world host countries, and to some degree back again; and is beginning to come also from the third world. There has been a corresponding shift in the largest home countries, where TNCs are headquartered: from Britain to the United States (1945–1973), and subsequently to the European Union (EU) (Figure 20.1).

FDI Flows and Stocks

The geography of FDI ownership networks (Figure 20.2) is even more dominated by north–north flows than is the case for international trade (Figure 16.10), and has become increasingly so since 1980. Most of the flows are within Europe and between Europe and North America. Interregional FDI has become important in south and east Asia, dominated by FDI from Taiwan, South Korea, and Hong Kong (which still has a quasi-independent status) into low-wage Chinese export-processing zones (EPZs); and Chinese FDI flowing to Hong Kong and South Korea. In global terms, Africa and west Asia (notwithstanding recent significant increases) are "off the map." In 1980 they received significant FDI, but by 2003 the entire FDI in Africa (mostly to South Africa, Egypt, and Nigeria) was less than 1% of the global total. Latin America and the post-Soviet world receive a very small share of global FDI.

Almost half a century after independence, FDI from the first to the third world

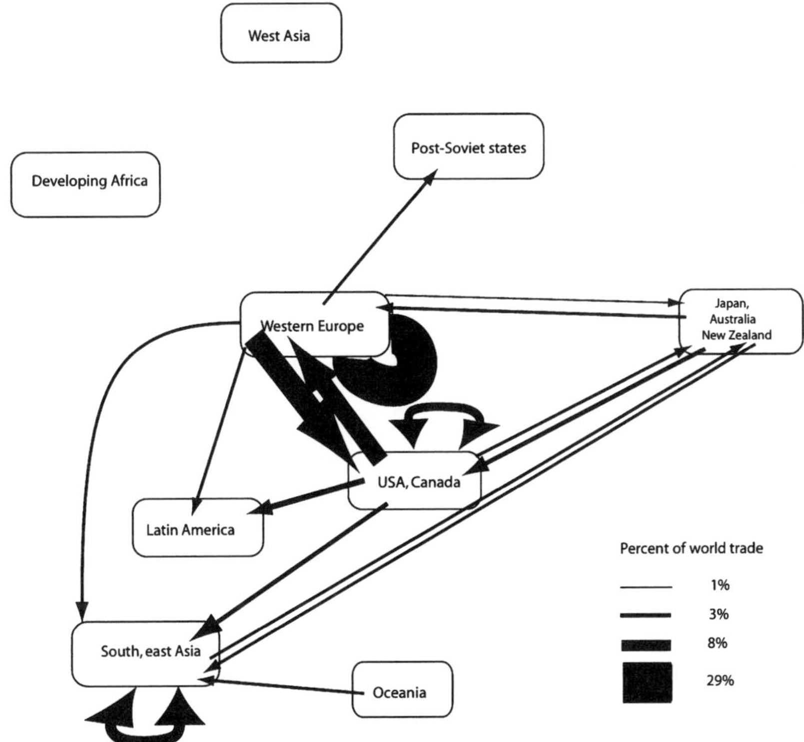

FIGURE 20.2. World FDI flows, 2003. *Source:* Data are from United Nations Conference on Trade and Development (UNCTAD, 2008a).

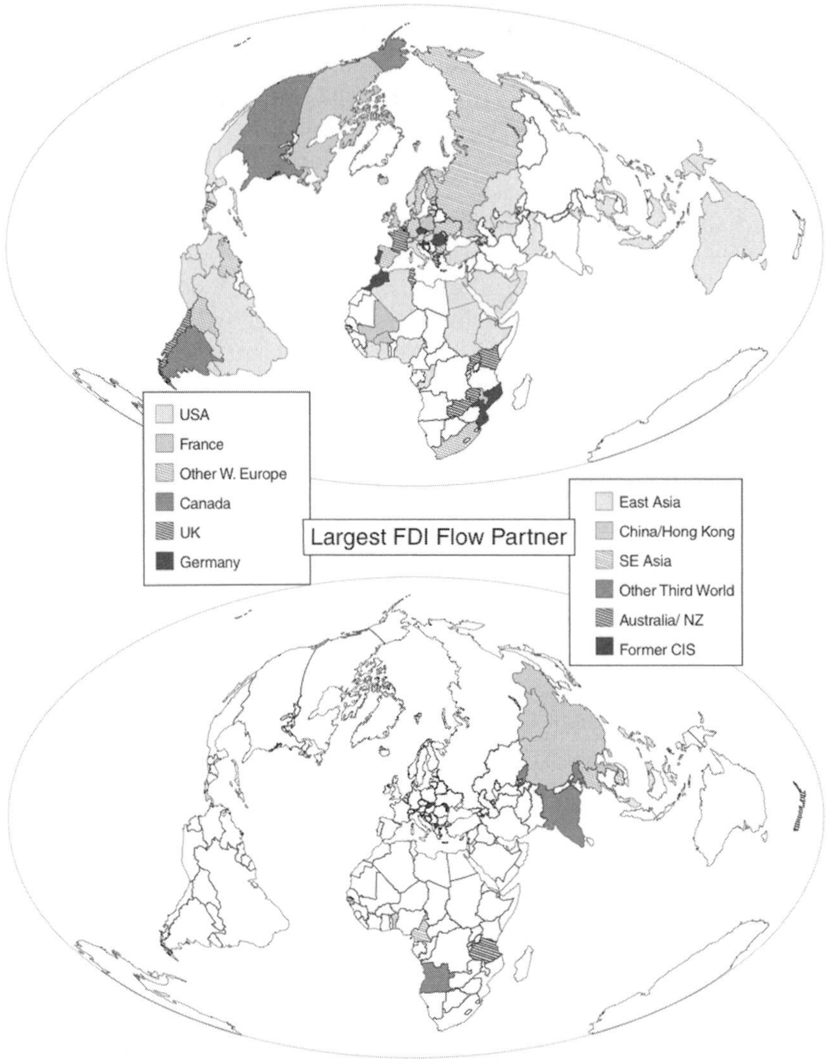

FIGURE 20.3. Dominant host countries for FDI flows, 2002. CIS, Commonwealth of Independent States. *Source:* Data are from UNCTAD (2008a).

is still shaped by geopolitics and colonial histories. Figure 20.3 shows, for each host country, which home country was the source of the largest FDI flows in 2002. The top map shows countries dominated by North American and European partners; the bottom shows those dominated by other home countries. U.S. TNCs still rule south of the Rio Grande, except in Cuba, Nicaragua, Venezuela, Bolivia, and the southern cone, as well as in west Asia. Britain is present in east Africa, and France in west Africa. Southeast Asian countries dominate southern and eastern Asia (India's dominant partner is Mauritius, but almost certainly because FDI is trans-shipped through there from elsewhere), and a few southern African countries.

FDI flow data fluctuate a lot from year to year. A more reliable indicator of the long-term power geographies of FDI is to look at "accumulated stocks"—the total

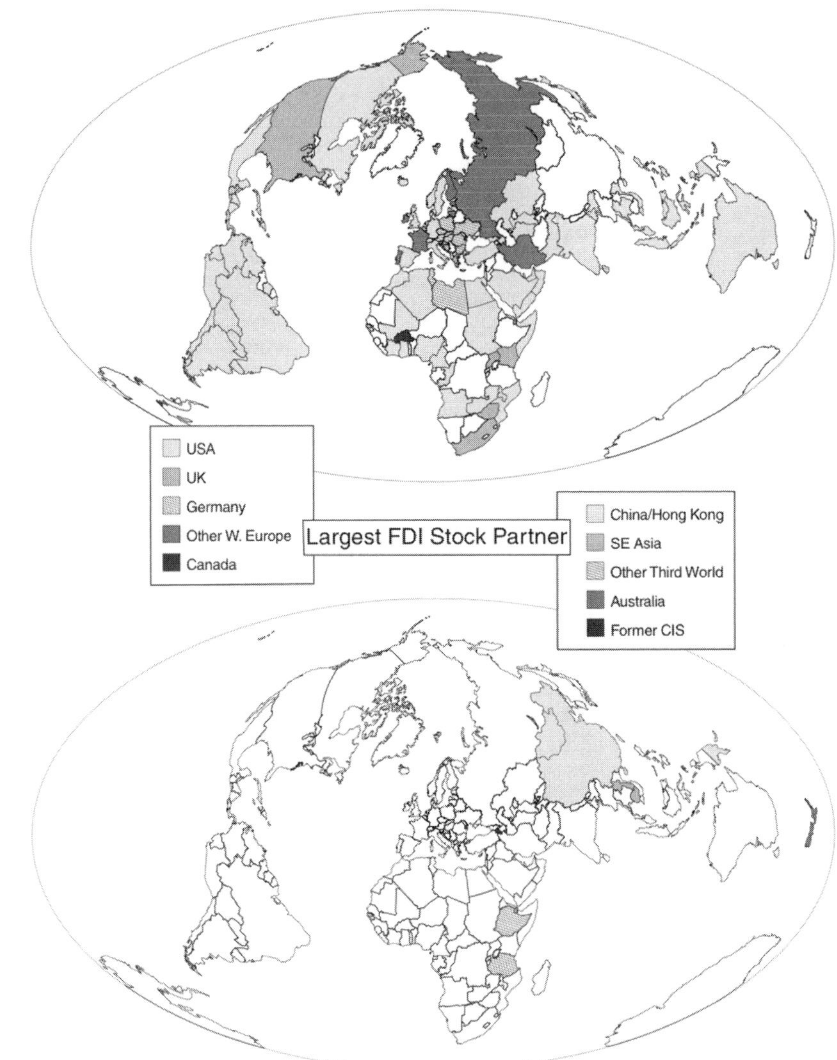

FIGURE 20.4. Dominant host countries for FDI stocks, 2002. *Source:* Data are from UNCTAD (2008a).

current value of all past investments from a country (Figure 20.4). Here U.S. dominance in Latin America (again excepting Cuba) is unambiguous, as is its presence in sub-Saharan Africa, the Middle East, and south and southeast Asia. This reflects U.S. dominance in FDI outflows between 1945 and 1975, and its interests in oil-producing regions and geostrategic Asian partners. U.S. FDI has stayed away from countries labeled by the United States as pariah states: Libya, Iraq, North Korea, Syria, and Iran. Britain only dominates a few former colonies in east and south Africa, and Germany only in Tunisia and Libya. Patterns in southeast Asia are much like those for FDI flows, since FDI here has been dominated by recent investments. Note that neither Japan nor France dominates anywhere.

In 1990, U.S.-owned FDI in the third world favored Latin America (62%) and south and east Asia (28%), whereas Japan's

FDI favored Asia. Western Europe had a fairly equal distribution across the different third world regions. The United Kingdom had almost half (48%) of its investments in south and east Asia; France had 64% of its third world affiliates in Africa, where its most extensive colonial territories were; and Germany had 56% of its third world affiliates in Latin America, the predominant third world destination for German emigrants. Australia and New Zealand concentrated almost exclusively on south and east Asia (Porter and Sheppard, 1998).

The geographical patterns described above do not tell us much about the distribution of FDI across the third world. FDI is concentrated overwhelmingly in just a few third world nations deemed to be attractive locations: Brazil, Mexico, Argentina, China, Hong Kong, Malaysia, Turkey, South Korea, and Taiwan (note the complete absence of Africa; the little FDI reaching this continent clusters in South Africa, Egypt, Nigeria, Morocco, and Sudan). These are all NICs.

Turning to examine the importance of FDI for third world economies, we find that its presence has almost tripled since 1990. The value of accumulated inward FDI stocks as a percentage of GDP increased from 9.8% to 24%, higher than for the first world (21%) (United Nations, 2006c). Within the first world, European countries have the largest presence of FDI (mostly intra-European flows), whereas in the large U.S. economy it is 13%, and in Japan just 2%. In the Caribbean, inward FDI exceeds GDP (mostly because of OFCs on selected islands; Chapter 22); and in southeast Asia it is 43% of GDP. It is lowest in west Asia (12%) and south Asia (6%). Yet it varies dramatically from country to country within the same region. In Liberia and Hong Kong, it is several times larger than GDP, but in Libya, Somalia, Cuba, Iran, Iraq, Kuwait, Afghanistan, Bhutan, and Nepal, it is almost zero. In order to make sense of these patterns, it is necessary to investigate the diverse geographical investment strategies followed by TNCs.

Third World TNCs

As noted above, although the first world is still the home for the vast majority of TNCs, the number and influence of third-world-based TNCs (largely headquartered in Asia) are increasing. About 12% of all FDI now comes from the third world, particularly from Hong Kong, Taiwan, Singapore, China, South Africa, Malaysia, Mexico, and South Korea. Fifteen of the world's top 200 TNCs are headquartered in the third world, largely in Asia. Table 20.2 lists the largest of these and shows how these have changed since 1990, which may be compared with Table 20.1. Since 1990, Chinese TNCs have made a dramatic appearance on this stage. The two largest third world TNCs are oil corporations, which are becoming involved in prospecting for oil overseas with the assent of various other third world governments. Indeed, six of the top eight third world TNCs are petroleum corporations—and all are state-owned rather than private corporations. This confirms the shift in FDI toward primary products, driven by rapid industrialization in Asia.

A key question is whether third world TNCs are more willing to invest in other third world countries (creating south–south FDI flows alongside south–south trade), and, if so, what the consequences of this will be for the third world. Like first world TNCs, third world TNCs invest heavily in the United States, the United Kingdom, and The Netherlands (Europe's largest FDI hosts), but also in Hong Kong, China, Singapore, Japan, and Malaysia. Significant FDI also flows through Caribbean OFCs (United Nations, 2006c). There is thus evidence of some south–south FDI, but largely to countries where first world FDI also goes. Three trends can be discerned in this recent growth of south–south FDI. First, TNCs from NICs like Taiwan and South Korea have specialized in operating global chains of low-wage overseas assembly operations, particularly in textiles and electronics, which are plugged into global commodity chains (see below).

TABLE 20.2. The Largest Third World Nonfinancial TNCs, 1993 and 2003

Fortune ranking (2003)	Company	Home country	Activity	Sales (U.S. $, millions)
1993				
	Samsung	South Korea	Electronics	51,531
	Daewoo	South Korea	Electronics	30,893
	Petroleo Brasiliero	Brazil	Petroleum	15,263
	Hyundai	South Korea	Automobiles	10,544
	Chinese Petroleum	Taiwan	Petroleum	10,075
	Jardine Matheson	Hong Kong	Diversified	8,424
	LG Electronics	South Korea	Electronics	7,565
	Yukong	South Korea	Petroleum	6,901
	Souza Cruz	Brazil	Tobacco	3,721
	Hutchison Whampoa	Hong Kong	Diversified	3,202
	Tatung	Taiwan	Electronics	3,121
2003				
69	China National Petroleum	China	Petroleum	44,864
70	Sinopec	China	Petroleum	44,503
94	Hyundai Motor	Korea	Automobiles	38,459
95	Pemex	Mexico	Petroleum	37,974
115	Samsung	South Korea	Trading	32,960
189	Petrobrás	Brazil	Petroleum	22,612
191	Indian Oil	India	Petroleum	22,506
204	Petronas	Malaysia	Petroleum	21,430
205	LG International	South Korea	Trading	21,394
230	China Mobile Communications	China	Telecom	19,783
248	Sinochem	China	Trading	18,763
261	LG Electronics	South Korea	Electronics	17,836
275	SK Global	South Korea	Trading	17,152
279	Korea Electric Power	South Korea	Energy	17,075

Sources: Data are from United Nations (1995c; Box I.1) and *Fortune* (2003).

These firms are shifting assembly work from low-wage to even lower-wage locations: from NICs, to Central America, to China, and now to places like Vietnam and Laos. The second trend is the boom of third world FDI investments in the primary sector, notably petroleum. China in particular is seeking permission to drill for oil in Africa, Latin America, and west Asia, in order to secure oil supplies for domestic industrialization and urbanization. In return, it is offering foreign aid and expertise in infrastructure development, without the conditions imposed by institutions like the World Bank (Chapter 23). The third trend is the transshipment of FDI through offshore banking nodes.

With just a few countries dominating FDI from the third world, whose TNCs pursue strategies similar to those of the first world, it is not clear that this will catalyze broad-based wealth creation in the third world. On the one hand, the ongoing polarization of income inequalities within the third world will be reinforced as the owners and executives of third world TNCs prosper, whereas their workers often remain miserably paid. The owners congregate in the elite spaces of third and first world metropolises, whereas their workers are scattered through the EPZs. On the other hand, host countries for third world FDI stand to prosper from the recirculation back home of profits made overseas, whereas their third world hosts experience low-wage employment, health/safety issues, and the extraction of minerals and fuels for use elsewhere in the third world. For example, Taipei has prospered despite the relocation of low-wage assembly employment to China, because of its new role as a node for producer services and research and development for Taiwanese TNCs. Indeed, the prosperity accompanying the growth of domestic corporations in places like South Korea and Taiwan is making even parts of the first world into cheap FDI hosts (see sidebar: "The Secret in Alabama"). Yet Taiwanese branch plants in China, southeast Asia, and Central America have gained a reputation for at times life-threatening working conditions, as well as brutal antiunion activism.

If south–south FDI operates to the advantage of the home countries, then the growth of third world TNCs may reinforce already existing inequities between NICs and other third world countries—inequities that compound those separating the first and third worlds. In order to determine how likely this is, it is necessary to learn whether third world TNCs behave differently from first world TNCs. Do they perhaps make a more positive contribution to economic growth in third world host countries? Some such differences have been identified, such as smaller facilities, more extensive use of joint venture arrangements with local owners, a greater tendency to locate outside the largest metropolitan areas, and greater reliance on local inputs. To date, however, there is little evidence; it is also not clear whether such differences are attributable to the third world origin of branch plants, or to the smaller size of third world TNCs and the particular niches they have been able to exploit in the global economy. Since all TNCs share the same capitalist goals of profitability and growth, the latter explanation is certainly plausible. The possibility must thus seriously be entertained that these asymmetries, paralleling those of trade and industrialization, may reinforce inequalities between host nations and home nations within the third world.

CONCEPTUALIZING TRANSNATIONAL PRODUCTION

Explaining Transnational Production

Any attempt to explain FDI must be capable of answering three questions (Dunning, 1988). First, we must explain how foreign subsidiaries in a country can compete successfully with domestically owned firms. FDI will only expand in a country if foreign subsidiaries can outcompete indigenous entrepreneurs. Usually the comparison is made between foreign subsidiaries of TNCs and local firms with at most a few domestic facilities. In this comparison, the subsidiaries of TNCs have several inherent advantages because of their access to the resources of large organizations—ones that are geographically, and often sectorally, much more diverse in their activities than local firms are. TNCs own certain resources that local firms would have to purchase or otherwise obtain: a large bank of capital, innovations, knowledge, and expertise on which subsidiaries can draw, all of which make it easier to finance, equip, and manage a new enterprise. Size also gives TNCs' subsidiaries certain

The Secret in Alabama

On May 25, 2005, *The Korea Herald*, an English-language Seoul newspaper, called attention in an editorial to a newly opened Hyundai assembly plant in Alabama, asking what the secret was that enabled Hyundai to produce technologically cutting-edge automobiles in the United States. "The secret is simple; it is a lower cost, just as in the tens of thousands of Korean manufacturing facilities going to China and Southeast Asia." Enumerating the $14 hourly nonunionized wages in Alabama, 1,744-acre site and $250 million in tax breaks provided by Alabama, minimal healthcare costs, and no pension plan for nonunionized workers, the editorial argued that land, labor, healthcare, and pension costs are higher in South Korea—"a sad reminder of the detrimental effect on the economy by the treacherously high property prices here and our powerful unions" (*The Korea Herald*, 2005).

advantages of scale. Larger organizations can purchase inputs more cheaply; can give their subsidiaries advantages in the market through the use of internationally popular brand names (which enhance sales) and the use of monopoly power to influence prices; and can reduce uncertainty by arranging long-term contracts between different subsidiaries of a TNC, instead of having to deal with independent firms.

The international geographical scope of a TNC provides further advantages. It has better access to worldwide information on markets, new technologies, and products; it can drive local firms out of business by temporarily reducing a subsidiary's prices below the local cost of production, because profits made in other countries can be used to subsidize the local subsidiary; and it is less dependent on local political or social conditions, because it can more easily relocate its activities to other nations.

Second, we must explain why corporations prefer to have their own subsidiaries abroad. Even if a foreign corporation can outcompete local firms, it may not be in the best interest of the corporation to become involved as a local producer. A TNC may decide that it is better to produce at home and simply export the product to other nations, or to purchase its foreign inputs from a foreign firm instead of setting up a production facility abroad. One motivation is to increase global influence, in the expectation that this will also increase profits and growth (Hymer, 1976). Foreign subsidiaries may enable a corporation to expand its share of global markets, and thus to increase its economic power to set prices, undercut smaller competitors, and influence consumer tastes. A more geographically diverse corporation is less subject to unexpected events in particular nations. Unwanted developments in one place that could increase the cost of production there, such as regulations to reduce pollution or union actions to increase wages, can be combated by relocating (or threatening to relocate) production to places that do not have these "problems."

Capitalism flourishes by expanding into new areas of social life and new places. Large corporations that dominate domestic markets can grow by either expanding into new domestic arenas, or expanding abroad. Geographical expansion promises access to new markets for a firm that may be running out of new customers in its current markets, or helps maintain a presence in current foreign markets. Finally, extended ownership reduces uncertainty and transaction costs associated with market-based economic transactions. Instead of relying on others to deliver an input when it is needed, of appropriate quality, and at the right price, production within the corporation promises greater control over transactions and reduces their risk and cost (although some argue that this is less of an advantage in an era of flexible production and supply-side economic policies; see, e.g., Scott, 1988). The state where a TNC is headquartered will also encourage outward FDI, expecting expansion abroad to result in more profits flowing back home. As noted in Chapter 14, colonialism made it possible for European firms to be contracted to build infrastructure and supply necessary inputs in European colonies (much like U.S. firms with no-bid contracts in Iraq at this writing). After 1945, U.S.-led programs to rebuild postwar western Europe and Japan not only stimulated U.S. exports (Chapter 15), but made it easier for U.S. firms to rebuild and expand their overseas investments in these countries.

Third, if TNCs can compete successfully with indigenous firms and it is in their interest to do so, we must ask how locations for foreign subsidiaries are selected. FDI is highly concentrated in a relatively few nations, and in particular cities and regions within those nations; it is important to understand why some places are able to attract foreign subsidiaries, whereas most are not. Each TNC seeks certain attributes of a place that make it attractive for investment. Depending on the nature of the TNC, these may be the presence of certain natural resources; access to a large enough market to make local production worthwhile; the availability of cheap labor or other inputs; political and social stability; or simply the adequacy of infrastructure. Locations within a country satisfying one or more of these conditions include resource sites, EPZs (see Chapter 17), and large cities. Actions by the state also influence the location of FDI.

The Geographical Strategies of TNCs

The strategies pursued by TNCs can be divided into two broad groups—cloning and geographical specialization. "Cloning" simply means duplicating abroad exactly the same activities that are invested in at home. Cloning may entail duplicating the identical production activities abroad, as when U.S. oil corporations relocated oil drilling operations from Oklahoma to the Middle East, or when General Motors built automobile assembly plants in Brazil, behind its tariff barriers, during the era of import substitution industrialization (ISI). Increasingly, cloning also includes the duplication of retailing and service facilities, as in the spread of Walmart-style "big box" retailing worldwide, or the opening of Price Waterhouse accounting offices in global cities in Europe, Asia, and Latin America (Beaverstock et al., 2000).

One reason for this is to take advantage of lower production costs in foreign locations, while still selling the product in the same markets as before. This was the strategy of western oil corporations when they expanded to the Middle East in the 1930s. The abundance of, and ease of access to, the resource more than compensated for the fact that the product still had to be shipped back to markets in the home country, because the cost savings at the foreign location exceeded the extra transport costs of shipping it back to current markets. Factories may be relocated to EPZs today for the same reason: Lower costs and local subsidies trump other considerations. A second reason is to compete in foreign markets. This may be driven by conditions in the host country, such as the saturation of domestic markets: New markets abroad can function as a spatial fix for domestic limitations. But there are pull factors also: Foreign countries with prosperous or large domestic markets are attractive in their own right. Sales in foreign markets can be catalyzed by establishing a sales office abroad to facilitate exports, but in many cases this is insufficient. When a nation imposes tariffs or nontariff barriers (NTBs) limiting imports, or when domestic political conditions make foreign-produced commodities unpopular, then production within the territory of the foreign market may be the only way of gaining or maintaining sales abroad. Market-seeking geographical expansion also occurs for other reasons, such as the need to be close to consumers when custom-designed products are produced, or the need to speed the delivery of products (Schoenberger, 1988). Choice of which particular host nation to enter is also driven by such intangibles as TNCs' perceptions of the difficulties and risks faced there, which in turn depend on perceived linguistic, cultural, and political differences, and on preexisting economic and geopolitical connections.

When Latin American nations engaged in ISI in the 1950s and 1960s, U.S. firms could only compete by opening facilities in these nations, since tariffs made imports too expensive. They were also encouraged to do so because indigenous firms did not have the know-how or experience to supply the domestic market. More recently, Asian automobile producers have built assembly operations in North America and the EU so that they are not disadvantaged by being typecast as foreign producers taking jobs away from domestic workers. Much of the expansion of U.S. FDI into Europe during the 1980s can be attributed to a similar strategy (Dunning, 1988). Britain has traded on this by advertising itself as having lower wages and more compliant unions than other European nations, although it is now losing ground to the lower-wage skilled labor markets of the new EU member states of the former second world.

"Geographical specialization" refers to a TNC's geographical division of its operations in order to undertake different tasks in different places. Global, national, regional, and divisional headquarters' activities will typically be located in major cities, with access to the specialized producer services, global communications networks, skilled labor forces, political connections, and lifestyle opportunities that ease management, control, and long-term planning, and that attract corporate executives. Research and development (R&D)-intensive activities will be located in clusters of related activities, where technical labor forces can be assembled, and where local competition and "buzz" (Bathelt, Malmberg, and Maskell, 2004) accelerate the circulation of knowledge (think of Silicon Valley; see Saxenian, 1994). Production facilities can be split up and located in places around the world where production costs can be minimized, taking into account the geographies of political and economic risk. Finally, sales offices are located close to the most lucrative markets. The result is a spatial division of labor within corporations.

Over the last two decades, the challenges of coordinating and operating such corporate networks (Dicken, Kelly, Olds, and Yeung, 2001) have diminished. Low real energy costs and technological advances (air freight, containerized shipping) have reduced transportation costs. Global cyberspace can be utilized to coordinate global operations on an almost instantaneous basis through corporate "intranets" (exclusionary proprietary computer networks). National differences in the regulations governing local corporate operations have diminished, as states throughout the third world have adopted market-friendly "good governance" principles and protection of firms' property rights, bending over backward to attract FDI. For example, the agreement on Trade-Related Aspects of International Property Rights (TRIPS), signed at the end of the "Uruguay round" of the General Agreement on Tariffs and Trade (GATT) in 1994 and subsequently incorporated into the World Trade Organization (WTO), requires signatory nations to recognize commonly defined copyright rules governing such things as the rights of performers; appellations of origin; industrial and integrated circuit layout designs; patents and trademarks; and monopolies for developers of new varieties and genetic modifications of plants and animals. It also specifies enforcement procedures and remedies. By reducing intracorporate geographical barriers and smoothing the regulatory landscape, such changes have made it easier for corporations to undertake "just-in-time" production, whereby bits and pieces are shipped from one plant to another to arrive just at the moment they are needed, saving on wastage and on storage and inventory costs (replacing "just-in-case" approaches, in which large quantities of everything a TNC might possibly need are stored, often for months; see Sayer and Walker, 1992).

TNCs typically follow some combination of horizontal diversification and vertical integration. "Horizontal diversification" refers to investing in a variety of economic sectors, in order to avoid overreliance on the global fortunes of any one area of the economy. Some TNCs have become holding companies that are so diversified that they seem to be invested in everything from mining to fast food. "Vertical integration" refers to extending control along the commodity chain governing the production of a particular commodity. A "commodity chain" describes the sequence of production activities that begin with nature and end with sale to the consumer (Gereffi, 1996). For petroleum, this extends from exploring for oil through drilling, to refining oil and producing petrochemicals, to manufacturing Tupperware and operating gas stations (think of Exxon Mobil). Another extends from cotton fields to textile mills, sewing operations, and finally clothing stores. Some commodity chains are demand-driven, beginning at the retail end, as when Walmart places orders that trigger activities all the way back to cotton farming. Others are producer-driven, as in the case of oil. The distinction depends largely on where along the commodity chain the greatest economic power is located. All TNCs are involved in one or more commodity chains. Sometimes the entire commodity chain may be within the hands of a single TNC; in other cases, different TNCs specialize in different aspects. As noted above, for example, South Korean and Taiwanese textiles TNCs have specialized in the stage of assembling clothing, locating these operations wherever they can minimize labor costs. This enables firms like Walmart to sell cheap clothing without gaining a worse reputation for exploiting third world women; they can wash their hands by claiming that others, from the third world, are responsible for such reprehensible acts.

Along a commodity chain, corporate strategies of geographical specialization draw on two approaches. In some cases, the plants of a TNC are connected into a "global production line": The product is literally moved from one location to the next at different stages in the production process. Thus clothing may be designed in New York, where the firm can draw on the expertise of fashion designers and their knowledge of the latest fashion trends. The design may then be taken to northeastern Italy, where the cloth can be woven or printed in one of its many small firms that are world-famous for their textile crafts. The cloth may then be shipped to China, where the plentiful supply of labor at very low wages reduces the cost of the labor-intensive process of cutting and sewing the fabric into clothing. The final product is then returned to New York City for sale in Bloomingdale's. This is a common strategy for products whose value is high by comparison to their weight (such as computers). In other cases, the arrangement may look more like a "global assembly line": The product is assembled in one place, using parts produced in many different countries and localities. This is common for bulkier objects like automobiles and aircraft.

No matter which strategy is pursued, the result is that plants in different locations specialize in different aspects of the production process; this creates an international division of labor within the corporation, building on preexisting global divisions of labor. Geographical specialization has multiple advantages for TNCs. First, it can minimize global production costs by moving labor-intensive activities to places where labor costs and fringe benefits are low (and workers' rights are not supported or even recognized), and by moving environmentally costly activities to remote locations and places where there is little environmental regulation. Second, it can dramatically reduce state regulation. The global reach of a TNC makes it less dependent on any particular national territory and its government. Even the U.S. government has found it increasingly difficult to persuade U.S. companies to conform to U.S. norms and laws when operating abroad, or to persuade them to align with U.S. foreign policy (such as economic boycotts). As countries compete increasingly intensively for FDI, the result can become a "race to the bottom," whereby minimal labor costs and labor/environmental regulations in third world locations, desperate for FDI, result in pressure to lower wages, disempower unions, and loosen environmental regulations in the first world. Third, the use of many plants in a variety of locations enhances a TNC's ability to continue business as usual in the face of developments in particular places that might threaten production, through "global sourcing." When the workers in one branch plant go on strike, or when a state agency attempts to close a facility for violating environmental regulations, a TNC can draw on alternative sources at its facilities elsewhere. Finally, global reach enables a TNC to access information and political influence worldwide, enabling it to manipulate internal accounting rules to take advantage of differences in exchange rates or to avoid high tax regimes (known as "transfer pricing"; see Chapter 21).

Foreign Ownership and Local Economic Development

Much has been written about whether TNCs help or hinder local economic development, particularly in the third world. We examine the different kinds of impacts that any new investment can have on a locality, with particular reference to FDI, in Chapter 21. It is worth noting, however, that the very different positions on this issue parallel the differences between core and peripheral perspectives on development, globalization, and the third world (Chapters 4 and 5). The World Social Forum, for example, focuses on the negative consequences of TNCs in the third world (see Chapter 24 sidebar, "Another World Is Possible").

Those conceptualizing the impact of foreign-owned firms on local development can be broadly divided into two groups. First are those who believe that TNCs exemplify the development of monopolistic practices that undermine competition. In this view, monopolistic corporations distort economic forces of development in the following ways: by creating rather than eliminating barriers to free competition; by abusing their power in order to create demand for and overprice their products; by undermining the ability of local firms to develop; by forming parasitic cartels; and by reaping excessive monopoly profits, which are extracted from the host nations in a form of unequal exchange (Baran and Sweezy, 1966; Barnet and Müller, 1974; Eichner, 1976). Because TNCs gain from this, whereas the places where their branch plants are located experience distorted development, FDI is argued to enhance underdevelopment in host countries while accelerating development in home countries—thereby increasing disparities between home and host nations. Since third world countries are far more likely to be host nations than home nations, this reinforces the dependence of ordinary people in the third world on foreign, first world capital. All such analysts agree that such "monopoly capitalism," a consequence of the local dominance of a few large foreign corporations, is worse than competitive capitalism. Some turn to state regulation to control monopolistic tendencies; others argue that the only solution is to subject foreign subsidiaries to state or workers' control. This view was popular in the third world during the era when state-led development was popular (Chapter 4).

In contradistinction to this view stand those scholars who believe that FDI is fundamentally a positive force. These include both neoclassical and new institutional economists and certain Marxists, unified in the belief that what is good for a corporation is good for the place where it locates (Dunning, 1988; Warren, 1980). From a neoclassical and neoliberal standpoint, corporations engage in FDI to overcome impediments to the operation of market forces imposed by national borders, state regulation, and geographical distance. Such barriers are viewed as inhibiting economic development. Consequently, the ability of TNCs to move capital around the globe, avoiding and breaking down the effectiveness of these barriers for investments within the corporation, is seen as making TNCs more efficient than the actual world economy and therefore as making them a positive force for economic prosperity. Marxists holding this positive view see capitalism as an essential precondition for further progress, and TNCs as "pioneers of capitalism" that are useful for stimulating the development of indigenous capitalism. The general conclusion is that TNCs foster competitive capitalism, promoting development in the places where they are active, and thus should be encouraged. In the third world, this view came to replace the former perspective among national elites and within the United Nations after 1980, as neoliberal perspectives on globalization emerged (Chapter 5). Yet ordinary people in the third world, and many also in the first world, remain skeptical that FDI is beneficial.

There is also disagreement about the ability of localities to take advantage of inward FDI to enhance the prospects of their residents. The outcome for a particular place will depend on the local impact of two key processes: the advantages that accrue to enterprises when they agglomerate; and the increased ability of a TNC to disinvest from locations rapidly if another, better place can be found in the global economy. The advantages of agglomeration mean that places with a history of industrialization in general, especially when they are closely identified with a particular industry, accrue a series of characteristics that promote further economic growth there (very much like the idea of polarized development; see Chapter 4). This advantage historically has characterized those regions of the world that have already enjoyed a prosperous history as cores of industrial production, but more recently new nodes seem to be emerging—cities like Seoul, Taipei, or Shanghai, or places where development is now being driven by information technology and communication (ITC), such as Bangalore and Hyderabad. In this view, in an increasingly flattened world, any place able to identify its competitive advantage (i.e., the activities that it is best able to undertake) can attract to itself a beneficial mix of growing, closely related, and technologically dynamic industries (Porter, 1990; Scott, 2006; Storper, 1997). This very growth, however, is contingent on the continued prosperity of the industries agglomerated there, which is not guaranteed. Evolving local conditions—such as higher wages paid to an increasingly unionized workforce, outdated buildings and infrastructure, a polluted environment, or simply changing locational needs—may become increasingly onerous. The second process, the mobility of capital and the flexibility of transnational production systems, then comes into play. Mobility makes it easier for industries to relocate to places that do not have these burdens, and for new industries to develop at completely new locations.

This means that the successes of individual corporations and the economic prosperity of core industrial regions that benefit from these successes are not eternal, even though they can certainly persist for extensive periods of time. They will be challenged repeatedly by competition from new firms, new growth industries, and new production locations. As investment flows become more mobile, both core and peripheral regions come under greater competitive pressure, with the possible result that economic and spatial restructuring of FDI patterns become more frequent and unpredictable. Such challenges have not resulted in a diffusion of industrial development evenly throughout the world economy, however, even though we have observed periodic shifts in the economic and geographical cores of industrial growth. Cores and peripheries do not melt away, but reappear in new places.

Notwithstanding the implied possibility that transnational production could facilitate real industrial development in a host country under the right conditions, much of the third world has experienced limited and often unsuccessful industrialization. Many policymakers have come to see FDI as the most attractive "quick fix" to catalyze economic development, but the putative benefits of FDI continue to elude most third world residents. For example, as noted above, Bangalore and Hyderabad have exploded as global nodes for ITC activities, challenging Silicon Valley. Indian- and foreign-owned firms are now engaged in everything from operating help-line numbers for first world consumers, to developing software and even providing medical consulting for first world hospitals. Yet the majority of the residents of these cities remain deeply impoverished, often becoming the victims of local policies that seek to remake these places as technologically cutting-edge global cities. Indeed, their desperation can be exploited in order to enhance the profits of local ITC operations and the competitive advantage of these cities; impoverished residents can constitute a labor force willing to undertake the undesirable underside of even supposedly clean industries, such as reprocessing toxic e-waste. Monetary costs are lowered for the key investors in the locality, at the human cost of poor people's bodies exposed to unhealthy working and living conditions. In order to gauge the likely success of such strategies, as third world governments (along with those of the former second world) aggressively comb the world for foreign investors, it is important to know more about who is likely to benefit from FDI, in which kinds of ways, and in which contexts. Understanding this will allow decisions to be made about whether and in what form FDI should be encouraged—important questions that elude any definitive answer (see Chapter 21).

21 Foreign Branch Plants and Economic Growth

The chairman of General Motors once unforgettably remarked, "What is good for General Motors is good for America." This captures the idea that the growth of large corporations is good for the countries where they operate—or is at least good for the countries where they are headquartered. In this chapter, we examine the applicability of this proposition to countries of the third world.

THE FOREIGN DIRECT INVESTMENT MULTIPLIER

The level of foreign direct investment (FDI) by a "home country" (where transnational corporations [TNCs] are headquartered) in a "host country" (where branch plants are located) can be measured by either the stock or the flow of FDI. The "stock" is the present economic value of all previous forms of FDI (plant, equipment, and stocks of unused inputs and unsold outputs), and represents the accumulated presence of TNCs in the host country. The "flow" of FDI is the annual net change in FDI stock, and can be positive or negative. New FDI coming from the host nation, and profits from last year's FDI that are reinvested in the host nation, represent positive FDI flow, adding to FDI stock (Figure 21.1). Negative FDI flow, reducing the stock of FDI, is defined as occurring when TNCs repatriate profits to the home country, or when they disinvest from their subsidiaries by transferring ownership entirely or in part to private residents or the government of the host country. These are recorded as a flow of FDI from the home to the host country.

Officials of both host and home countries hope that FDI will create further economic growth through multiplier effects in their countries. Encouraging the inflow of FDI can stimulate rapid growth by drawing on external resources, but this is only effective as a development tool if this inflow leads to further beneficial impacts. Such indirect effects are termed "multiplier effects" because they multiply the impact of the initial investment. Multipliers—whether in the form of shorter-term impacts on employment and other local firms, or of longer-term broader development impacts—certainly exist, but the extent to which they affect

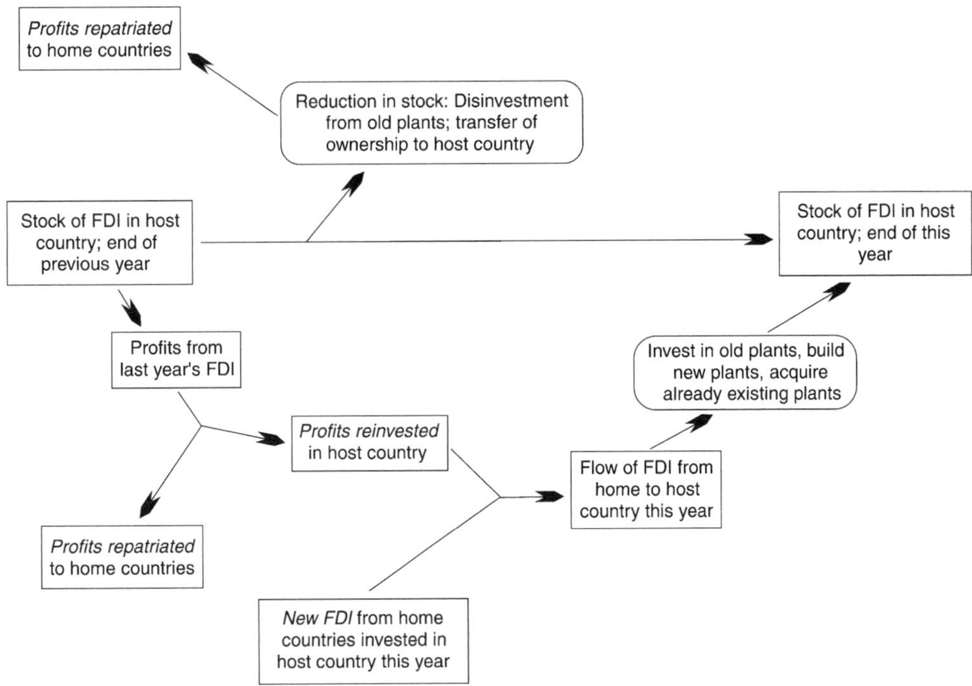

FIGURE 21.1. The annual round of FDI.

local development depends on their geographical and social distribution.

Supporters of TNC investment as an "engine" of development argue that sufficient multiplier effects accumulate locally, among a broad enough group of people, to boost local economic prosperity in a way that more than compensates for the cost and effort of attracting FDI. Critics of TNCs argue that these potentially beneficial effects "leak out" of the locality to benefit other places abroad, or, to the degree that they do accumulate locally, they do so in a way that does not compensate for the cost and effort of attracting FDI. When a third world nation makes an effort to attract FDI, such as a General Motors plant, it does so in the belief that such leakages can be contained and that net local multiplier effects are of sufficient quantity and quality to make the effort worthwhile. If expectations are not fulfilled, then what is good for General Motors may be "good for America" if that is where the benefits leak back to, but it will not benefit a host country such as Mexico that has encouraged General Motors to locate there. As in the case of deteriorating terms of trade for third world nations, a disproportionate flow of the benefits of FDI back to the home country can enhance international inequalities instead of reducing them, even though selected social groups and regions within Mexico may benefit.

The principal home nations for FDI have actively promoted the foreign activities of their firms through such institutions as the Overseas Private Investment Corporation in the United States and the Export–Import Bank in Japan, presumably in the belief that home countries benefit from multiplier effects leaking back from the host countries. As TNCs have become more genuinely transnational or even global in their strategies, however, great concern has developed that multiplier effects' leakages from host countries do not automatically return to home countries. With investments in many places around the globe, the multiplier effects leaking out of one host country may be redirected to another host country. Thus even the home nations are increasingly asking whether they benefit from FDI. U.S. consumers wonder whether they really are "buying American" by buying a Saturn, or whether such a purchase in fact provides more opportunities for workers abroad than purchasing a Toyota made in Tennessee does (see Chapter 17 sidebar, "Export-Processing Zones," and Wright, 2006).

The United Nations, once critical of the impact of FDI on the third world (United Nations Centre on Transnational Corporations [UNCTC], 1983), has argued more recently that "transnational corporations play a critical role in the allocation of resources world-wide, in improving the competitiveness of both host and home countries in the new world economy and in stimulating processes of economic integration" (United Nations, 1992b: 5). We evaluate this claim by looking at the types of multiplier effects that can stem from an initial FDI in a third world nation, and where these end up. It is always possible to pick individual empirical examples of FDI that represent either dramatic success stories for the host society or complete disasters, but it is much harder to generalize about the relative importance and impact of local multiplier impacts versus leakages. Examining the different possibilities, however, makes it possible to draw up a checklist that can be used to evaluate any particular case.

MONETARY FLOWS

The most obvious impact of FDI is the flow of money itself. Indeed, one scheme often used by economists to judge the impact of FDI is to measure its "balance-of-payments" effect: Do FDI inflows exceed FDI outflows? There is much more to monetary flows than FDI itself, but we begin there.

Gains and Losses for Countries/Regions

First, let us consider the initial capital flows (Figure 21.1). The balance of inflows less outflows is the net flow of investment capital resulting from a nation's role as a host for FDI. A similar calculation can be made for home countries: New FDI outflows, and profits from FDI stocks abroad that remain in the host country, can be subtracted from the repatriated earnings flowing into the home country from FDI stocks abroad. Table 21.1 shows the balance of capital flows at the end of the 1970s, before the FDI boom. The totals at the bottom of the table show that despite the power to repatriate profits, host countries gained investment capital from FDI overall, whereas home countries showed a loss. There were important regional differences, however. Latin America was the only third world region that gained from hosting FDI, whereas Japan and Australia were the only first world countries to lose as hosts. Individually, Canada and West Germany experienced net outflows as hosts, largely because repatriation from very large stocks of FDI outweighed new FDI inflows. The exceptional gains from hosting FDI in Brazil, Argentina, and Mexico were made because less than half of the profits were being repatriated from these countries (UNCTC, 1983: Annex Table II.13). The high losses in Indonesia and west Asia came at a time when western oil corporations were appropriating windfall profits from the second phase of the oil crisis.

If we add together the net gains from being a host and a home country (the overall balance in the right-hand column of Table 21.1), the United States gained FDI, whereas Europe lost. Overall, there was a net flow of FDI capital from the third to the first world in this period. Most of the net flow of FDI reflected a redistribution of wealth among the first world nations, from Europe and Canada to the United States.

Second, we must go beyond FDI flows to analyze what happens to the money

TABLE 21.1. Balance of Capital Flows from FDI, 1978–1980 (Annual Averages, U.S. Dollars, Millions)

	As host country			As home country			
Country/region	FDI inflow	Repatriated profits	Balance	Repatriated earnings	FDI outflow	Balance	Overall balance
United States	10,205	–2,398	7,807	17,766	–19,547	–1,781	6,026
Canada	1,138	–1,976	–838	747	–2,617	–1,870	–2,708
Britain	3,756	–1,761	1,995	2,571	–5,756	–3,185	–1,190
West Germany	1,257	–2,275	–1,018	434	–4,262	–3,828	–4,846
France	2,902	–184	2,718	294	–2,359	–2,065	653
Rest of Europe	4,914	–2,525	2,389	2,225	–4,053	–1,828	561
Japan	173	–509	–336	1,015	–2,552	–1,537	–1,873
Austral./N.Z./ S. Africa	1,644	–1,920	–276	443	–417	26	–250
Latin America	4,902	–2,828	2,074	145	–229	–84	1,990
Brazil	2,118	–617	1,501	—	—	—	—
Mexico	1,376	–349	1,027	—	—	—	—
Argentina	366	–224	142	—	—	—	—
Dev. Africa	1,594	–1,861	–267	36	–51	–15	–282
West Asia	–1,074	–4,173	–5,247	63	–250	–187	–5,434
Southeast Asia, Oceania	2,468	–3,994	–1,526	88	–160	–72	–1,598
Malaysia	688	–84	604	—	—	—	—
Indonesia	229	–2,526	–2,297	—	—	—	—
South Korea	44	–56	–12	—	—	—	—
Total	33,879	–26,404	7,475	25,827	–42,253	–16,426	–8,951

Source: United Nations Centre on Transnational Corporations (UNCTC), 1983: Table II.2).

recorded as flowing into a country. New FDI recorded as entering a country may not actually flow from the home to the host country. For example, less than one-third of the capital invested by U.S. firms in third world host countries between 1966 and 1972 was raised in the United States (Jenkins, 1987: 96). Moreover, capital that is recorded as flowing into a country may not stay there, particularly in the third world. FDI inflows are typically spent on wages, machinery, buildings, and other fixed equipment used in production. Building contractors may well be local, but most third world nations do not produce their own machinery. If the money is used to purchase imported production equipment, the capital flows out again—perhaps back to the very country from which it came (see Chapter 23). New FDI entering a country also may not represent new sources of investment funds for development. If the money is spent on taking over an already existing enterprise, then any net gain to the country is far less than the size of the FDI flow. Three emerging trends have accelerated this process since the 1980s. First, mergers and acquisitions became very popular forms of direct investment in other companies, by TNCs and other firms. Second, widespread privatization of government-owned companies (particularly in telecommunications, finance, and oil production) in the third world, the former second world, and the European Union (EU) have often led to a transfer of ownership to TNCs. Third, debt-for-equity swaps, whereby unpaid debts to foreign banks have been addressed by conceding partial ownership to the creditor, became popular solutions to third world debt crises (see Chapter 23).

Gains and Losses for Corporations

In the discussion above, we have looked at the monetary gains and losses for the territories affected by FDI; it remains to examine evidence about the gains and losses for the corporations involved in FDI. Corporations would not engage in FDI if they did not believe it to be profitable, and the evident success of large TNCs (see Chapter 20, Table 20.1) suggests that they are usually right. Evidence on rates of profit is difficult to obtain, as corporations guard this information jealously. The evidence that does exist, however, suggests that there are substantial profits from FDI, particularly in developing countries (Table 21.2). This table is distorted to some degree by the exceptionally high profits associated with U.S. petroleum investments in Organization of the Petroleum Exporting Countries (OPEC) member states, but with one exception, rates of profit are significantly higher in developing countries. The exception is manufacturing, which only began to give higher rates of return for U.S. firms in the third world in the late 1970s.

Corporations can make mistakes, and there have been spectacular cases where TNCs have incurred massive losses, particularly when national governments moved to nationalize their factories. Many TNCs see investment in the third world as more risky than in the first world, partly because of real difficulties such as inadequate infrastructure and the costs of locating far from markets, but also because of estimates and perceptions of political risk. Perceptions of risk reflect not only previous bad experiences with nationalization and political conflict, but biases and lack of information about nations with different cultural and political characteristics. Accurate or not, these perceptions induce TNCs to withhold from investing in certain places unless they can be reasonably sure that profits will more than compensate for the risk, or until the governments of those nations are prepared to subsidize the investment to ensure what the corporation judges to be an adequate rate of return.

FDI is very often preceded by negotiation with local officials in order to set the terms of the investment and the subsidies from the host country, and there is plenty of opportunity in these negotiations for a TNC's representatives to make a better deal. Third world officials typically have limited experience with such negotiations, and only the firm has adequate information about its profits and needs. Thus it is reasonable to expect that many negotiations favor the corporation above and beyond its own estimates of the return needed to compensate for perceived risk. To put it otherwise, the higher profits in developing countries recorded in Table 21.2 may be attributable as much to the ability of TNCs to negotiate profitable terms as to the efficiency of their third world branch plants.

Transfer Pricing

Although statistics such as those summarized above can be analyzed, their accuracy is very questionable because of the ability of corporations to engage in the practice of "transfer pricing." We have seen in Chapter 20 that many of the transactions engaged in

TABLE 21.2. Rate of Return on U.S. FDI (%)

	1974		1981	
Economic sector	First world	Third world	First world	Third world
All sectors	13.4	53.6	11.5	22.5
Petroleum	11.0	133.3	19.8	49.0
Manufacturing	14.0	13.9	8.2	12.5
Other	14.2	20.9	10.6	18.0
Worldwide average	23.0		14.4	

Source: UNCTC (1983: Annex Table II.5).

by branch plants, and a considerable share of international trade in general, are with other branch plants of the same corporation. These transactions are governed by the price that branch plants pay one another for the goods and services exchanged. Such transfer, or administrative, prices can be set in principle by the corporation in any way it wishes, and need not conform closely to prices in the open market. It is very difficult to obtain information on transfer prices, but attempts to estimate them in the third world have shown considerable divergence from free market prices. Vaitsos (1974) calculated that, on average, the price paid by TNC branch plants in Colombia for inputs imported from other branches of the same corporation was 250% of the open market price for pharmaceuticals inputs, and 125–150% of the market price for other inputs. Prices for some individual inputs were as much as 3,000 times higher than the market price.

The idea that corporations charge themselves prices that exceed open-market prices may seem irrational, because the same input could be obtained more cheaply from outside the firm. Yet what is best for the corporation as a whole may be very different from what is best for an individual plant in that corporation, or for the place where that plant is located. Transfer pricing can occur in a number of circumstances (Jenkins, 1987).

Inflated transfer prices can be a means of transferring profits made from one branch plant to another, without declaring them as profits, by making the former pay a high price to the latter. Internal accounting systems record this as a cost at the former plant, making its declared profitability less than its actual profitability. If there are reasons for disguising how high profits are in a country, such a transaction with a branch plant located abroad enables profits to leak out of the country unrecorded. This will be advantageous if the branch plant is located in a country where there are high taxes on corporate profits or limits on profit remittances, or where excessive profits would be resented (see sidebar: "Closing Ford (Netherlands)").

Certain aspects of agreements made by

Closing Ford (Netherlands)

The U.K. newspaper *The Manchester Guardian* (Boyle, 1981) reported on April 29, 1981, that on April 25, workers at the Ford assembly plant in Amsterdam were told that the plant would be closed on September 30. The managing director, insisting that the decision had been taken without influence from global headquarters in Detroit, blamed a shift from profits in 1976 of $5 million (U.S. dollars) to a loss in 1980 and 1981 of $20 million. The Dutch Multinational Companies Research Foundation, examining information from the works council and company documents, discovered the following:

- Tax advantages made it attractive for Ford of Europe to maximize declarations of profits in Britain and minimize these in The Netherlands.
- Dividends paid to Detroit headquarters, on its Ford (Netherlands) shares, increased from 39% to 75% in the late 1970s.
- Parts shipped to Amsterdam from Ford (Britain) were charged a 23% handling charge when they passed through Ford (Belgium).
- Parts supplied from Ford (Germany) jumped in price by 20% in 1 year (four times the inflation rate).
- All profits from Ford (Netherlands) were repatriated to Ford (Detroit), while finance for investment had to be borrowed from Ford (Detroit) at interest rates up to 50% greater than those available from Dutch banks.
- Ford (Netherlands) was used for short-term runs of popular cars, requiring frequent costly retooling, which was not taken into account in estimating the efficiency of the plant.

corporations with host countries are tied to the costs of production, and manipulating production costs through transfer prices is a way for a branch plant to take maximum advantage of such agreements. Suppose a host country has agreed to provide a potential foreign investor with subsidies that will lower local production costs to make them competitive with production costs elsewhere. Inflated transfer prices can be used by the firm to make local costs of production seem higher than they really are, and thus to induce the host country to offer higher subsidies than those that might really be necessary. Governments generally do not have the power or information necessary for independent judgments of a corporation's internal pricing practices; this makes it difficult to guard against such actions.

Finally, international transfer prices may incorporate an exchange rate between the currency used for payment and that of the supplier, set internally by the corporation, which differs from official rates. This enables money to be moved between currencies, in order to take advantage of currency rate fluctuations or to avoid restrictions on the import or export of currencies.

Transfer pricing is a very common practice, with the potential to undermine attempts by a country to regulate the operations of foreign firms within its territory. What is debated is the degree to which such prices deviate from "reasonable" (generally defined as open-market) prices, and the reasons for these deviations. Proponents of FDI argue that transfer prices do not differ much from market prices, and that when they do differ, it is because state regulation has distorted market prices from their proper value—and the firm is simply correcting these distortions. Critics of FDI argue that the results of the Vaitsos (1974) study are typical. They further contend that the practice of transfer pricing enhances the mobility of capital and makes it even more difficult for countries to design policies to ensure that the benefits of FDI accrue not only to the corporations undertaking the investment, but also to the residents of the places in which the investment occurs.

This debate is all but impossible to resolve. Usually it is not even possible to collect the necessary information on transfer prices; market prices are also hard to measure, and there is disagreement about whether market prices are the appropriate norm. We can conclude, however, that transfer pricing makes it very difficult to determine the profitability of firms' subsidiaries and the accumulation and flow of profits with any degree of accuracy. Given the prevalence of such practices, it can be hypocritical to castigate governments for engaging in international "dumping" practices (i.e., artificially lowering the prices of exports), when transfer pricing by corporations is neither criticized nor regulated.

IMPACT ON LOCAL FIRMS

FDI multipliers affect indigenous firms and capitalists in the host country in two ways. First, the presence of branch plants may stimulate demand for, and investment in, local firms that buy from or sell to the branch plant. Second, FDI will affect local firms that compete directly with the branch plant because they produce the same commodity. We are concerned with the difference that foreign ownership makes. We would like to know whether externally owned branch plants have more or fewer links to related local activities than do locally owned firms, and whether the presence of foreign-owned plants has a different impact on local competitors than that of locally owned plants.

To address the first issue, we must examine the intensity of a branch plant's linkages with local firms, particularly those that could provide it with inputs and services. If a branch plant obtains most of these inputs locally, then this implies that the branch plant stimulates local firms. If, on the other hand, large quantities of these inputs and services are imported, then the multiplier effects are leaking out of the country, limiting the local benefits of FDI. There are several celebrated cases of branch plants operating as "enclaves" within the host territory, meaning that the plants have only minimal interaction with the locality in which they are situated. These "cathedrals in the desert" are usually either engaged in resource exploitation or located in export-processing zones (EPZs).

A foreign TNC may invest in constructing a mine, but all of the equipment and technical know-how may be imported (even the prefabricated housing for workers), and the product itself may be exported for processing somewhere else (later to be reimported in finished form and at higher prices). Externally owned copper mines in Chile only spent 17% of their capital locally in the 1920s, including wages and taxes, although by the 1950s this had risen to 70%. Aluminum branch plants in the Caribbean nations spent just 25–40% locally in the 1960s (Jenkins, 1987: 104–108). In EPZs (see Chapter 17), branch plants may amount to little more than platforms for assembling imported parts and exporting the products, with only such basic services as cleaning, security, and gasoline purchased locally. Only 0.3% of the parts used by export-oriented branch plants in Mexico in the 1970s were purchased locally (United Nations, 1991c: 49); in 1987, Japanese electronics branch plants in Asia were purchasing just 36% locally (Jenkins, 1987: 108).

The association of enclave economies with foreign ownership is far from predictable. FDI in sectors that serve domestic markets rather than export their products often has much stronger local linkages than the image of enclaves would suggest. It is also possible, in certain sectors and locations, that local capitalists may also function as enclaves because of the locational characteristics of that industry in that place.

A large number of studies have compared the propensity of branch plants to purchase locally to that of locally owned firms, in both peripheral regions of the first world and the third world. Many of these show that externally owned firms have fewer local linkages (and thus larger leakage effects) than locally owned ones—one of the few cases of clear differences between the behavior of externally and locally owned firms (Jenkins, 1987). Branch plants are part of a corporation that is capable of providing a broad range of inputs and expertise to which local firms may not have access. In addition, branch plants are part of the international strategy of the parent corporation, and the best interest of the corporation may diverge substantially from that of a branch plant. A local capitalist may also use foreign firms rather than local ones, but it is easier for a branch plant to do so; indeed, branch plants are often compelled to purchase inputs from other subsidiaries of the same corporation even when the same input is available locally. When it is economically advantageous for a plant to purchase certain inputs locally, we would expect a local capitalist to do so, but a branch plant may have other priorities.

Even where significant linkages are established locally, not all residents of the locality benefit from these. If the linkages encourage local firms to employ workers at minimal wages and under miserable working conditions, or if they represent payoffs to local state officials in order to remain in business (a situation certainly not restricted to officials in third world countries—consider the celebrated examples of Lockheed's payoffs to Japanese officials in the 1970s, and Italian payoffs to Italian officials discovered in the 1990s), then the benefits accrue to local elites and may well contribute more to income inequality than to general prosperity. If linkages encourage related firms to overexploit the environment (e.g., if timber mills clear-cut rainforests) or to produce hazardous commodities, then they are not beneficial in the long term even when the immediate benefits seem positive. It is important, therefore, to examine who gains from these linkages, not just where they occur.

Consider now the impact of FDI on

those local firms in direct competition with the branch plants. In the pro-FDI view, branch plants are members of efficient and technologically superior TNCs, which pose new and tougher standards of competition for local capitalists and will drive inefficient local firms out of business. FDI breaks down barriers to market competition, and anything that breaks down these barriers must be beneficial, because more competition means more efficiency. In the anti-FDI view, this tougher competition tips the balance against local capitalists, because they do not have the resources to compete with TNCs. Consequently, even efficient local producers will go bankrupt, as branch plants use the oligopolistic power of their parent corporations to eliminate local competition. Empirical studies show that higher levels of FDI are generally associated with lower use of domestic savings for investment, which could be a result of externally owned plants driving domestic ones out of business (United Nations, 1992c: 115). A locality will then become dependent on foreign firms with little interest in the welfare of its residents.

TNCs' branch plants tend to be larger than domestically owned firms, to employ a more capital-intensive technology, and to show higher productivity; all these factors reinforce the idea that they can outcompete local firms. Very often, however, such comparisons are plagued by the fact that apples are being compared with oranges. TNCs tend to invest in more capital-intensive and oligopolistic sectors with good growth prospects, and a strict comparison ought to be with domestic firms operating in the same niche of the economy. When such precise comparisons have been possible, few systematic differences between domestic and externally owned plants have emerged (Jenkins, 1987); however, whether this is because TNCs have no advantages or because local firms have had to adapt to the practices of TNCs is not clear.

Historical studies of the entry and growth of TNCs can distinguish between these possibilities, and indeed in some countries, such as Kenya, the elimination of domestic producers by TNCs has been found to occur (Langdon, 1981). Even here, however, the impact of this on the locality is not easily described. It can be interpreted variously as: (1) an increasing dependence on "disinterested" and foreign capital, which has used its power to eliminate indigenous industry; (2) a change that is of incidental importance to local development, because local capitalists would have behaved similarly to foreign owners (Jenkins, 1987); or (3) a healthy process of competition, eliminating inefficient local firms and releasing capital that can be invested more productively elsewhere (United Nations, 1992c: 124).

TECHNOLOGICAL TRANSFER

Technological change (i.e., the development of new production methods and new products) is recognized as one of the fundamental means of enhancing long-term economic growth, and TNCs dominate private spending on research and development (R&D) of new technologies and products. It is important, therefore, to investigate whether FDI accelerates technological change in host countries. Technological development in a place can occur in several ways: through investing in R&D, through transferring technologies to host countries, and through adapting imported technologies to local needs. We examine the impact of TNCs in each of these areas.

There is little evidence that TNCs carry out much R&D in third world host countries. TNCs invest two to three times more of their effort in R&D than other firms do, but between 67% and 90% of R&D investment by U.S. and European TNCs stays at home, and almost all of the rest is invested in other first world countries. The very few studies examining the relative propensity of externally and locally owned firms to engage in R&D in the third world suggest that externally owned branch plants, though increasingly engaged in R&D, spend a lower proportion of their revenue on R&D than do the host economies in which they are located (United Nations, 1992c: 146). Branch plants are also likely to devote more effort to adapting imported technology to local conditions, and less to R&D, than locally owned firms.

TNCs contribute to the international transfer of technologies in three ways. First, whenever a branch plant is built abroad, technology is imported into the host nation in the form of capital equipment, shop floor production methods, and management systems through which the equipment and methods are employed. Compared to local firms in the third world, TNCs invest much more in "research-intensive" sectors, such as chemicals, machinery, and electrical equipment. This may mean that TNCs are bringing better technologies into host nations than those used by indigenous firms, but statistics can be misleading. Investment in research-intensive computing machinery, for example, will not bring in much new technology if the only activity carried out in the host nation is the assembly of semiconductors by unskilled workers.

Technology transfer also occurs when a local firm enters into a contract with a foreign firm. Such arrangements range from subcontracting, in which the local firm gains limited technological knowledge during the process of adapting the product to the needs of the foreign corporation; to licensing agreements, whereby the local firm is licensed to produce the foreign corporation's products; to cooperative strategic agreements for the development of new technologies and products. Strategic agreements have become a particularly important global strategy by which TNCs share in and accelerate the development of technological know-how, but fewer than 3% of strategic agreements in the 1980s involved firms outside the first world. The United Nations (1992c: 155–156) suggested that strategic agreements were actually slowing technology transfer from the first to the third world.

The difficulties and costs of technology transfer have made it common for third world firms to pursue a third strategy: to ignore copyright laws and illegally copy products and processes developed and patented in other countries. This has become particularly common in electronics; massive production of bootleg copies of music recordings and computer software occurred in southeast Asia in the 1980s. Many high-fashion items such as clothing, perfumes, and watches have also been reproduced and sold well below the price of the genuine articles, though still at a considerable profit. Copyright laws are designed to prevent this. They suspend market principles in order to encourage R&D in new technologies, by giving an innovator exclusive right to a product for a number of years as compensation for the cost and effort invested in its development. Until recently, a number of third world nations refused to sign international copyright treaties, implicitly encouraging technological imitation of foreign products, and making it impossible for TNCs to retain exclusive worldwide control over certain technologies.

This type of copying only works for certain types of commodities, and only competes with the foreign investors within third world countries—although it should not be forgotten that this type of illicit copying also goes on in first world countries. Considerable international pressure was brought to bear on third world nations in the late 1980s, however, to sign treaties protecting intellectual property rights (IPRs). Third world countries face a dilemma. Such treaties make technological transfer slower and more expensive, and place it further under the control of foreign companies, but refusal to sign such agreements brings about retaliation from TNCs and their home countries. This retaliation now has a basis in international law, in the 1994 Trade-Related Aspects of Intellectual Property Rights (TRIPS) agreement (see Chapter 20).

Technology transfer can also occur in the reverse direction, when TNCs import new products and processes from the third to the first world. This is relatively rare, but it is vital in certain areas. The best-known case is that of pharmaceuticals. First world TNCs, drawing on the knowledge of indigenous people about the medicinal properties of plants, have identified organisms in tropical rainforests that can form the basis for new drugs. TNCs can patent any new products developed from these organisms, giving them exclusive rights, without having to compensate a host nation for the essential contribution of its biodiversity and local knowledge. By contrast, local people have neither the resources or the expertise to seek patents, even if they wished to do so. This form of technology transfer has expanded with the development of genetic engineering: Firms can use very small quantities of genes taken from third world ecosystems to create new genes, which they then again can patent as their own products. Even though this amounts to the same kind of unsanctioned appropriation of others' knowledge that the enforcement of IPRs is supposed to prevent, there are no legal mechanisms in the World Trade Organization (WTO) or elsewhere to prevent this form of reversed technology transfer (Chapter 16).

A third form of technology transfer occurs when imported technologies are altered and adapted locally. This ranges from altering machinery so that smaller quantities can be produced for local markets, to all kinds of shop floor practices that adapt a product or a production method more closely to local conditions. It is extraordinarily difficult to measure the degree to which this occurs, let alone the influence of TNCs in this process, but there is evidence that externally owned plants in the third world are more likely to be involved in adapting old technologies than in developing new ones. Such adaptations seem minor, but can have considerable long-term developmental impacts. Amsden (1990) argues that they were key to the ability of South Korean firms to close the technological gap with first world countries, fueling successful industrialization. It is important to note, however, that this progress has occurred in Korean-owned industrial complexes, so it is a result of indigenous industrial policy rather than of FDI.

When technologies are transferred to a country, it does not follow that they are appropriate for that locality. There has been much debate about whether the production methods employed by TNCs, which are often more capital-intensive than the methods of domestic firms, are appropriate in localities where there is a surplus of labor. There has also been much debate about whether the products themselves are appropriate for the countries in which they are sold. No general conclusions can be drawn on these questions; they have to be examined on a case-by-case basis.

The prices that host countries pay for technologies are also important. As prices increase, the benefits that those technologies bring relative to the cost of obtaining them will fall. Prices are determined as part and parcel of the negotiations governing FDI. Negotiating terms will depend on the relative power of the negotiators, and there is reason to expect that TNCs have more bargaining power. Additional restrictions are often part of such agreements. It may be stipulated that equipment, service contracts, and other inputs must be purchased from the foreign firm providing the technology, effectively increasing its price. Restrictions may also be placed on the export of anything manufactured with the purchased technology, so that local firms cannot compete abroad with the corporation offering the technology. In the 1970s, between 14% and 83% of all such contracts in Latin America included the former restrictions, and between 21% and 99% included the latter restrictions (Jenkins, 1987: 81).

In sum, the very incomplete evidence does not strongly support the argument that TNCs equalize the availability of technology between home and host countries, at least for third world host countries.

LABOR

FDI can affect the labor force in three ways: the numbers of people employed; job types and opportunities for advancement; and the ability to obtain better working conditions. TNCs employed some seven million workers in the third world in 1992. In very few countries did this amount to more than 5% of the economically active population, meaning that the direct impact of TNCs on employment numbers was small, although it would also be necessary to count those jobs created in locally owned firms as a result of FDI. The number of such jobs depends on the intensity of linkages between branch plants and indigenous firms, discussed above. Externally owned plants generally employ a significant number of foreigners, usually in well-paid positions. Such expatriates, often relocated to these countries by the parent corporation to help manage the firm, are growing fewer but still make up 0.5% of employment in U.S. affiliates abroad and 3% in Japanese firms (United Nations, 1992c: 178). Externally owned firms employ fewer workers per dollar invested than indigenous firms do. It can be concluded, then, that branch plants generally have a lower propensity to employ local people than locally owned firms do. External ownership usually does not reduce employment, but this evidence suggests that the same quantity of domestic capital is likely to have a greater employment impact.

One positive impact that TNCs have had on employment numbers in third world nations is a stronger tendency to hire women. About 29% of employees in externally owned firms in the third world were female in the mid-1980s; most of these were in manufacturing. Indeed, most of the two million workers hired in TNC affiliates located in EPZs are women (United Nations, 1992c: 184). This suggests that TNCs have helped extend employment opportunities to a group that was previously marginalized in the formal job market. It is important, however, to bear in mind the limited opportunities for advancement and the working conditions associated with these jobs.

With respect to the types of jobs created, and employees' opportunities for career advancement and skill development, the impact of FDI depends greatly on the local context. Unskilled, low-wage, and routine employment represents one extreme. These jobs typically involve labor-intensive assembly of clothing, textiles, or electronic equipment, often located in EPZs, as well as routine "back-office" data-processing activities in the service industry (i.e., entering data into global computer information bases, such as airline ticketing systems). The low wages paid in the third world represent considerable cost savings for foreign firms. American Airlines has estimated that it has saved $3.5 million a year by relocating back-office activities to China and Barbados (United Nations, 1992c: 186). The low wages contribute little spending power in the host economy per worker, and prospects for improved skills and social advancement are limited. Jobs are created, but they do not promise a bright future for the workers hired; nor do they contribute much to the host country.

The gendered nature of such "dead-end" jobs is also important. They are occupied overwhelmingly by women; this is justified on the basis of gender stereotypes representing women as more dexterous, more docile, and more willing to work long hours in repetitive, low-wage jobs. Little is learned in such jobs that can lead to career advancement or social mobility, so the appearance of increased female participation in the economy often masks a reality in which women continue to face limited opportunities. When the creation of such jobs in low-wage areas is part of a global corporate strategy of exporting unskilled work while retaining skilled jobs within the core regions of the global economy, the most significant benefits to workers from FDI—that is, the skills and the higher wages and salaries—are retained within the home countries of FDI and in the possession of investors and top management (see sidebar: "Women Working in Export Processing"; see also Chapters 5 and 17).

At the other extreme are skilled employees who are well paid, are regularly offered training to improve their skills and adapt to new conditions, and have opportunities to advance within the corporation or take their marketable skills elsewhere. The involvement of TNCs in the import substitution sector in Latin America created in some cases a unionized, well-paid, and largely male workforce—similar to that found in equivalent industries in the first world. Such workers have prospered relative to those in other sectors, and have contributed more wealth to the host economy, but the developmental impact is still being debated. Some argue that these workers represent a new middle class bridging rich and poor, of the sort that has characterized first world 20th-century society. Others suggest that they are members of a "labor aristocracy" who owe their prosperity and allegiance to foreign capital and to the state regimes that encouraged FDI, and whose success has distanced them from the concerns of the bulk of the population. Still others believe that these workers have the potential to put pressure on national governments to create better working conditions and social programs for the population as a whole.

It is very difficult to sort out to what degree the kinds of jobs created are different from those that would be found in locally owned firms. Skilled workers and managers receive more intensive training, and TNCs may spend more on education and training than indigenous firms (United Nations, 1992c: 175–176). Yet if trained personnel tend to stay within these corporations (as has been observed, for example, in Turkey),

Women Working in Export Processing

A July 1993 article in the *Asian Women Workers Newsletter*, cited the next year in an anonymous journal article (*Connexions*, 1994), describes conditions among women working in export processing in China. In the Japanese-owned San Mei electronics plant in Zhuhai, one of the Special Economic Zones in southern China, women on the assembly line earn $49 a month. This is relatively high pay compared to wages in other locations, which average $38 monthly for 7 days' work a week, and from which women must pay $19 monthly for food plus $5 for dormitory lodging. The All-China Trade Union admits that violations of workers' rights are common. Dangerous or toxic conditions are frequent; the pace of work is kept very high; workers are harshly and on occasion violently treated; and many foreign companies forbid unionization. Bonuses are paid for extra output, but even a single day's absence will eliminate all bonuses. In April 1993, 600 women at a Canon factory went on strike for 3 days because their wages ($62.50 a month) were far below those paid in state enterprises (approaching $100). Two thousand San Mei workers also struck in May, arguing that a 16% wage increase was barely matching spiraling inflation in Zhuhai. The Canon workers' demands were met, although they complained that the state forced them back to work and pressured 12 workers to "resign." The San Mei workers were not successful.

Conditions among women working in EPZs in Mexico are similar. A U.S. anthropologist who did participatory fieldwork in the *maquiladora* region of Mexico describes her experiences thus (Fernandez-Kelly, 1984: 238):

> The weekday evening shift began at 3:45 and ended at 11:30 P.M. A bell rang at 7:30 to signal . . . a half hour dinner break. We worked, in total, forty-eight hours a week for the minimum wage, an hourly rate of about U.S. $0.60. . . . My new job was to sew a narrow bias around the cuff openings of men's shirts. My quota of 162 pairs of sleeves every hour meant one every 2.7 seconds. After six weeks as a direct production operator, I still fell short of this goal by almost 50 percent.

then the benefits to the host region will be less, because these skills are not made available to local firms. Large corporations' employees are less likely to leave, so the benefits of a greater investment in training by TNCs are counteracted by a lower probability that the skills thus derived will diffuse more broadly within the host country. When host country residents work within a TNC, they tend to absorb part of the culture of that corporation, which in practice means the culture of business that the corporation has developed within its home country. This may range from shop floor work habits (e.g., punctuality, meeting goals, and competition with others) to philosophies about methods of management, worker–employee relations, entrepreneurial attitudes, and the importance of markets and private ownership of production. From a diffusionist and pro-TNC viewpoint, the spread of western business attitudes to the third world is seen as good for development. From a more critical perspective, however, it is seen as a form of cultural diffusion that may push countries onto an inappropriate development path. This poses a dilemma for third world governments.

The third way in which TNCs influence the labor force of host countries is their influence on compensation and working conditions, as well as on social benefits provided by the state. Labor unions have traditionally played an important role in these areas in first world nations, and analogous organizations exist in most countries. We examine how the presence of FDI affects such processes. Once again, the potential effects operate in two directions. On the one hand, the large size and organizational structure of externally owned branch plants offer good conditions for union organizing. Some of the largest and most militant labor unions in third world nations have developed in such plants, particularly in mines and in market-oriented import-substituting industries. Thus the presence of FDI may facilitate unionization. This is not the intent of TNCs, but a side effect of the labor process used.

Large TNCs have developed considerable expertise in working with labor organizations. In some cases they are more willing than indigenous entrepreneurs to countenance unions as a result of positive experiences in first world countries, but in other cases they use their power to prevent unionization. The latter has occurred particularly in corporations that for ideological reasons have never allowed unionization, or whose emphasis is on low-wage assembly activities. In these latter cases, particular groups of workers are chosen precisely because they are believed to be less likely to organize or protest working conditions.

Perhaps the most important aspect of FDI that undermines unionization is its transnational scope. Labor unions, and legislation adopted by states to improve working conditions and provide social programs, operate largely at a national scale. The international mobility and flexibility associated with FDI mean that TNCs can "vote with their feet" by moving production out of countries where union activity and labor organization, evaluated in the context of the other locational advantages that this host country possesses, seem excessive. The international mobility of TNCs always has the potential to undermine the national power of workers' movements. Whether this potential will be realized will depend on the perceived necessity of FDI to the host country. This is a problem faced by all government regulation of FDI, and governments have become increasingly willing to adapt to the requirements of foreign investors in recent years. Compliant governments, on occasion with explicit support from the U.S. government, have used political and military power to control or roll back labor rights and suppress unionization, or to create EPZs where such rights are suspended (see Chapter 17). As Melissa Wright (2006) has shown in the Mexican *maquiladoras*, and as documented in videos such as *The Global Assembly Line*

(Da Art Video, 1986) and *China Blue* (Bullfrog Films, 2005), workers (particularly women) are victimized in and beyond the factories where they work, for challenging the presumption that they should be grateful to have factory work at all.

FDI AND THE STATE

The one institution with the political power to alter the arrangements and conditions governing FDI, and to harness multiplier effects for national development, is the nation state. The state can regulate the operation of foreign and domestic firms within its territory. At the same time, however, the growth of transnational production is undermining the ability of a state to exercise this power, and states are increasingly likely to use this power to encourage rather than to regulate FDI.

Most third world countries have state agencies whose approval must be obtained before any FDI is permitted. Approval has traditionally been difficult to obtain, and it has been used to control the sectors and locations where FDI is possible, as well as the degree of foreign ownership allowed. The state may refuse permission to invest in sectors that it regards as economically or politically strategic, and/or in sectors where it regards the national interest to be threatened by foreign ownership. The state has also frequently required that a significant proportion of the ownership of the foreign subsidiary be in local hands; that is, it has encouraged joint ventures between local and external owners, rather than outright external ownership. The most important debating point here is whether majority control can be in foreign hands.

States can also control the operation of already existing branch plants. The most extreme of these is "nationalization" (i.e., expropriating the ownership of a facility from its foreign owners, and placing it in the hands of the state). Although nationalization of foreign firms has been very rare in the first world, it was a real risk faced by TNCs during the 1970s in the third world, particularly in natural resource industries. The wave of nationalization peaked in 1975, with 85 nationalizations worldwide, but by the end of the 1970s it had fallen off to approximately 16 a year (UNCTC, 1983: 11). Since 1985, nationalization has practically stopped (United Nations, 1992c: 287). It is important to note that nationalization need not be as extreme as the word implies. First, it usually involves considerable compensation to the foreign owner. When a TNC perceives compensation to be inadequate, then it has recourse to courts of international law, or may seek to work with other TNCs or home countries to boycott the offending host. Second, a TNC may itself seek nationalization. In 1969 the Anaconda copper mine in Chile, fearing the imminent election of a socialist government, asked for nationalization with compensation instead of a joint venture arrangement offered by the Christian Democratic government, so that it could remove its capital from Chile and reinvest it in Australia and the United States (Jenkins, 1987: 183).

Nationalization is often the last resort, used when other approaches seem inadequate, to assert national identity or facilitate a transition to socialism. A range of other measures is available to regulate the operation of externally owned plants and to reduce the leakage of multiplier effects out of the country. These include increasing local ownership, seeking to direct more of the profits into local hands, and restricting performance. Performance restrictions include laws requiring a minimum degree of local content in the products of externally owned enterprises, regulations stipulating technological transfer, or regulations reducing imports or increasing exports.

Measures discriminating against FDI in domestic facilities face two common problems. First, it is assumed that local owners will behave differently from branch plants (i.e., that a greater proportion of the multiplier effects of domestic investments will be retained to promote local economic welfare). As suggested above, the evidence in favor of this assumption is at best patchy. Second, domestic regulation is considerably hampered by a fundamental difference in the geographic scale at which states and TNCs exert territorial control. National governments have no control over operations outside their territory, and this places severe upper limits on the degree to which they can regulate TNCs. It is very difficult for the state even to obtain accurate information on the profitability of FDI; profits hidden through transfer pricing allow a TNC to present its plants as less profitable than they really are, and to claim that state regulations will force the branch plant out of business. More importantly, the inconvenience of excessive regulation can be avoided by simply disinvesting from the offending host and relocating production elsewhere. The threat of disinvestment is an important bargaining chip making it harder to regulate FDI.

As investment capital becomes more mobile, and as national governments become more reliant on FDI to stimulate employment and growth, TNCs gain more leverage over state policy. In fact, the tables have turned in the negotiations between national governments and TNCs. From the waves of nationalization in the early 1970s, national state policies have progressively shifted in the 1980s and particularly since 1990 from regulating FDI to encouraging it. In 1991, 20 third world countries, 10 countries from the former second world, and Japan and Sweden all took legal measures to reduce the regulation of current FDI or to encourage new FDI. Even India, which for 40 years had strictly controlled FDI in an attempt to promote domestic entrepreneurs, reversed its policy to allow automatic approval for FDI in 34 high-priority industries, as long as the FDI covers the cost of the capital equipment imported for use in the branch plant (United Nations, 1992c: 82–83). Only two countries have increased their regulation of FDI. Significantly, they are two major home countries for FDI: the United States and Switzerland.

There has also been a wave of bilateral agreements between home and host countries promoting FDI, increasing from 92 in the 1970s to 162 in the 1980s, with a further 54 in 1990 and 1991 alone (United Nations, 1992c: 77). Many of these are agreements made by south and east Asian countries, and the transitional economies of eastern Europe and the former Soviet Union, with all parts of the first world; by African countries with Europe; and by Latin American countries with the United States. The EU has introduced regulations allowing the free movement of investment capital among its member countries and associated members of the European Economic Area, thus promoting FDI among first world countries. Finally, there has been a rapid worldwide increase in the willingness of states to privatize the ownership of state-run economic activities. In the third world, TNCs are often the only institutions with the resources to purchase large state-run operations. Privatization is thus often the mirror image of nationalization, increasing FDI. Privatizations quintupled (to 130) between 1985 and 1990 (United Nations, 1992c).

A parallel shift in attitudes toward TNCs and FDI has occurred in supranational agencies. The Organization for Economic Cooperation and Development (OECD) Declaration on International Investment and Multinational Enterprises evolved from a 1976 agreement that concentrated on developing a code of conduct stipulating ethical behavior for TNCs (Workshop on the OECD Investment Declaration and Bylaws, 1977), to a broader set of binding policy instruments obligating OECD member countries to minimize regulation of FDI from other OECD countries. (In 1991, this was strengthened to include mandatory periodic evaluations of policies on a country-by-country basis.) In 1983, the UNCTC designed a Code of Conduct for Transnational Corporations, specifying the kinds of conduct that signatory nations would regard as permissible and proper (UNCTC, 1983: 110), and based on the belief that TNCs were outcompeting indigenous firms and distorting local development. By 1992, renamed the United Nations Transnational Corporations and Management Division, the UN agency was recommending elimination of all restrictions on FDI and trade, unless it could be clearly established that the national interest is threatened. This is based on a belief that free competition in general, and FDI in particular, are generally beneficial for economic growth (United Nations, 1992c).

This implies that policymakers' earlier concerns that TNCs use their power to pursue unfair practices (e.g., transfer pricing or tying technology sales to agreements to purchase other inputs from the same corporation) have been replaced by discourses representing trade and investment policies or local content requirements as inappropriate government interference that interferes with the benefits of FDI. Whether or not the practices of TNCs have changed, it is clear that attitudes toward them have been transformed. As a result, national policies now emphasize different measures designed to entice FDI, including "tax holidays" (exemption from all tax obligations for a period of time), exemptions from trade barriers, provision of infrastructure, and investment grants. These are typically offered in package deals to prospective foreign investors. There are also general measures reducing state regulation of all private investors in a country, deregulating financial and goods markets, and privatizing state-owned enterprises. Countries compete with one another to introduce such policies, fearing that FDI will go where the "investment climate" is most favorable.

Cases certainly exist where FDI has been redirected from one nation to another by the use of such measures, but it is debatable whether their effectiveness makes the effort worthwhile and whether they bring FDI to more third world countries than before. As more and more nations enter this competition, there develops a bidding war for FDI, which tends to increase the size and expense of packages that must be offered by any country to encourage FDI. As the packages become more favorable to TNCs, any net benefits for host nations, to the extent that these do not coincide with the interests of the TNC, diminish. Eventually a point will be reached where it will be wiser to encourage locally owned firms, but it is unclear when this may happen. Furthermore, such policies do not make it any easier for the most disadvantaged countries to attract FDI. Such countries may offer the most pervasive and generous arrangements, but at great risk to their financial health and often to little effect. Thus the playing field governing the international competition for FDI is not leveled.

What prospects do such policies hold for third world nations, in a situation where the elimination of state socialism has drawn significant amounts of FDI to eastern Europe and away from the third world? Some pro-FDI, promarket analysts criticize such measures because they interfere with free competition, but many see any move to reduce regulation of market forces and investment behavior as the best path to economic growth and prosperity for all, regardless of the historical and geographical context within which such policies are pursued. Anti-FDI and antimarket analysts see them as essentially undermining economic development, by redirecting national wealth into the hands of large, private foreign firms. Yet even many critics support FDI on pragmatic grounds. The shortage of domestic capital and consumers, the paucity of foreign aid, and the unpleasant experiences of borrowing money on the private market (see Chapter 23) together make FDI the only game in town. Many third world nations now argue that FDI enables an accumulation of capital, savings, and technological know-how, and that this accumulation can be used to stimulate domestic entrepreneurs whose success will eventually marginalize the importance of foreign investors.

CASE STUDY: TOURISM AND DEVELOPMENT[1]

Third world mass tourism is largely dominated by foreign-owned "branch plants"—large hotels and resorts typically owned by U.S., European, and Japanese (but also now Singaporean and Hong Kong) global hotel chains. Can such tourism be an engine for development for third world countries, an alternative source of hard currency for investment (McMichael, 1996: 82)? One enduring factor in favor of tourism for third world locations is their "comparative advantage" in having locales with climate, seas, sand beaches, wilderness, and/or Pleistocene fauna that cannot be matched in much of the developed world.

Tourism is reputedly the largest business in the world. According to Mieczkowski (1990), it constituted 12% of the world's economy in 1988 and, when domestic and international receipts were combined, exceeded $2 trillion in value. In 2003, transport, travel, and other commercial services in world exports constituted 30% of total trade and were valued at nearly $1.8 trillion (World Tourism Organization, 2006); this figure does not include domestic receipts. In 2000, the number of international tourist arrivals was 696.8 million; after September 11, 2001, it declined slightly, by 0.6% (Infoplease, 2006).

Tourism inverts the usual logic of location theory in economic geography. Generally, in the production of an economic good, raw materials are exploited at one or more locations, transported to a place to be processed, moved to their markets, and distributed to the consumers, who are willing to travel a particular distance for the good or service. We will go to the front doorstep each morning for the newspaper, to the corner grocery for a loaf of bread, downtown for new clothes, and perhaps to a large city for special camera equipment or arthroscopic knee surgery. With tourism—take, for example, wild game viewing—the product is "finished" in its original state and marketed by shipping the consumers to the source of raw materials. That is, the consumers are moved to and through the product. The novel dimensionality of tourism makes aggressive marketing essential. Thus much of the industry makes extraordinary efforts in advertising its wares, filling the potential visitor's mind with seductive images of the "four S's": sun, sand, sea, and sex.

Many organizations play some role in making international tourism possible. The three major groups of players are tour operators, airline operators, and hotel operators. There is considerable interaction and "vertical integration" among these three sectors of the industry. For example, there is a great deal of linkage among travel agents, consolidators (who purchase blocks of airline tickets), tour operators, airlines, hotels, and local agents. Frequently special discounts are arranged on travel and hotel accommodations, and these tend to favor the major carriers and the larger hotel chains. In 1993, about 75% of all "revenue passenger kilometers" flown by international scheduled airlines (both domestic and international flights) were flown by first world carriers. The 25 top airlines carried 75.3% of passengers. The hotels used by tourists are found mainly in the first world (see Table 21.3). Africa, south Asia, and the Middle East accounted for 5.7% of hotel rooms worldwide in 1992. These three regions attracted only about 6% of international tourists in 1992, but since this percentage represented nearly 29 million travelers, it likewise represented an important source of revenue—over $13.3 billion (World Tourism Organization, 1994: 190, 198). Multinational hotel chains provide a large share of the rooms and services used by international tourists. Of the world's 11 million hotel rooms, the 20 largest hotel chains accounted for over

TABLE 21.3. Hotel Rooms Worldwide, 1992

Region	Number of rooms (thousands)	Percent of all hotel rooms
Africa	361	3.2
Americas	4,427	39.1
East Asia/Pacific	1,344	11.9
Europe	4,906	43.3
Middle East	164	1.4
South Asia	120	1.0
Total	11,323	100.0

Source: Data are from World Tourism Organization (1994: 206).

4.5 million, or 41% (Lundberg and Lundberg, 1993: 108).

In order to build a tourist industry, governments in third world countries commonly decide that they must attract the providers of the necessary elements: transport, accommodation, and touristic activities. To do so, host country governments may resort to concessions to increase the incentive of hotel chains, airlines, and travel companies to invest or participate. Incentive packages may include any number of economic attractions: free land, exemption from import duties, liberal depreciation allowances, tax holidays, long-term loans and loan guarantees, interest rate subsidies, and equipment grants. The government, while proffering incentive packages to potential hotel developers, usually assumes a set of infrastructural responsibilities all its own. These are the ancillary requirements of tourists: roads, hotel site preparation, electricity, water, sewers and sewage treatment, airport extensions and upgrading, telecommunications, harbor facilities, medical facilities, and so forth, all of which may take imported equipment and personnel to build.

It is notoriously difficult to calculate the costs and benefits of tourism. In one study of Kenya, the researchers tried to estimate the "leakage" of tourist expenditures on beach and safari package holidays—that is, money spent that did not stay in Kenya (Sinclair and Stabler, 1991). Foreign interests gained most of the benefit from 1990 tourist stays in Kenya in the two main forms these took: game viewing and beach holidays on the Indian Ocean. Britton (1982, cited in Sinclair and Stabler, 1991: 200), claimed a "75 to 78% leakage from developing countries where airline and hotel [are both] owned by non-nationals, and between 55 and 60% for [a foreign-owned] airline, but [a] locally owned hotel." Some third world countries are profoundly dependent on the tourist industry. Tourism is sometimes the leading earner of hard currency for a country—for example, Barbados (60.1%) and Jamaica (33.5%) (Harrison, 1992: 12). A further complication is the seasonality of tourism. There are seasons with almost no traffic—times when hotel occupancy rates are low, restaurants and nightclubs are nearly empty, and staff members are let go. Hotels must calculate break-even points, taking into account high-season and low-season business. If the occupancy rate and charge per room do not multiply to give a particular threshold figure, a hotel is operating at a loss. An average occupancy rate of about 60% may be required to meet both fixed and variable costs (Gee, Makens, and Choy, 1989: 309).

One of the economic benefits claimed for the tourist industry is the direct creation of jobs for local people and the "multiplier effect" of tourism, which generates jobs in supporting industries, both formal and informal. The jobs available in the tourist industry itself—as waiters/waitresses, bartenders, kitchen staff, cleaners, sweepers, musicians, porters, drivers, and security guards—may be low-level and in most cases comparatively unskilled, but such jobs often pay better than alternatives, such as farming in the rural countryside (Gartner, 1996). A low-skilled employee (e.g., a bellhop) may make 10 times as much a day (including tips) as a construction worker (Gartner, personal communication). The tourist industry also gives opportunity for people in the informal sector to get into the act—hustlers, touts, unlicensed guides, beach and street hawkers, vehicle "attendants," pavement sellers, prostitutes, drug dealers, and moneychangers. The multiplier effect extends as well to jobs created in supplying secondary goods and services needed on a recurring basis by the tourist industry: fresh vegetables and fruit, meat, fish, flowers, beverages, furnishings, laundry, and dry cleaning (indeed, almost any service that society provides).

The most controversial aspect of the presence of international tourists has to do with culture contact, cultural misunderstandings, and cultural change (Nash, 1996; Rossel, 1988). Although the ideal form for tourist experience would involve a social encounter between equals, with mutual respect between tourists and host country people, in third world tourism this is commonly not the case. To the "four S's" mentioned earlier, the tourist may add another: servility. According to Turner and Ash (1975: 207), the domain of the tourist, the "pleasure periphery," is the place where money buys unquestioning servility. The bulk of the tourist trade in most third world countries is run by TNCs or expatriate residents. For the most part, the contact local people have with international tourists is as employees in low-level positions in hotels and other tourist-related firms. Once a tourist enclave has been built, the circulation of traffic is frequently controlled and restricted, to keep out the "undesirable poor." Increasing social differentiation commonly accompanies the growth of tourism. Another consequence for the people of the tourist destinations may be increased commodification—the inevitable spread of market relations. Indigenous art, dance, carving, painting, weaving, basketry, and other handicrafts, which may have been functional and even sacred within traditional societies, may become changed or even cheapened when pressed to serve as mere entertainments and curios for tourists.

To return to our original question: Could tourism be a way to promote development? Could it be a vehicle for bettering the social and economic well-being of people in third world locations? Given the global structure of tourism and the power of first world major players (tour operators, airline operators, and hotel operators), it will be a difficult task. The task will be to ensure that the management of tourist enterprises comes more fully and firmly under local control; that employment at all levels of skill and responsibility goes to local people; and that the benefits of playing host to tourists from elsewhere stay as much as possible within a country. There are signs, nonetheless, that third world individuals engaged in tourism and governmental tourism boards understand the problems and are finding ways to change tourism to the benefit of the local economy and society, but it will be a long and daunting effort (Wall, 1993).

CONCLUSIONS

We have seen that it is extremely hard to make any universal statements about the benefits and costs of FDI. Too much depends on the type of industry, the geographical and social distribution of multiplier effects, the information available to national governments, and the actual negotiations between potential investors and host countries. Despite this, governments are adopting more liberal policies toward FDI. It may be believed that FDI is good for the population. Yet domestic elites benefiting from foreign investment can also utilize their contacts to the global market and their domestic influence to pressure the state into encouraging FDI. Such actions often comply with external pressures from foreign investors, their home countries, and multinational agencies seeking to eliminate barriers to FDI.

Gauging the gains to be made from attracting more FDI is reminiscent of the dilemma faced by third world nations seeking to promote free trade (see Chapter 17). Some new FDI is better for the host country than no investment. If the gains accrue disproportionately to home countries, however, or to selected host countries that are already advantaged within the third world, then FDI can widen the economic inequalities within and between third world nations, and between these and the rest of the world. Yet FDI is not the only option, despite current rhetoric to the contrary. This belief does not adequately take into account states' powers to control investment within their territories, and the willingness of some third world states to exercise this power. South Korea, Taiwan, and Brazil have achieved considerable economic growth while limiting FDI to a small and selective role within the national economy (Webber and Rigby, 1996). As with industrialization, successful policies will stem from innovative state initiatives addressing the broad interests of the population, rather than from copying others.

NOTE

1. The reader is referred to the first edition of *A World of Difference*, which devoted an entire chapter (Chapter 24) to tourism and development.

22 Money and Global Finance Markets

with Bongman Seo

In this chapter and the next, we examine how third world countries gain access to money. Any individual or country seeking to pursue a capitalist path to economic prosperity must be able to accumulate capital. One important source is the profits earned from international trade (Chapters 15 and 16); another is foreign direct investment (FDI) (Chapters 20 and 21); and a third is migrants' remittances (Chapter 19). But money flows in and out of countries in a variety of other ways, and these are also important to trace. These include international lending by banks; the international purchase of stocks and bonds; speculation against national currencies; the redistribution of funds by international financial institutions; foreign aid; and various forms of unrecorded "gray" and "black" money flows (including "capital flight"—money that elites send abroad, unrecorded flows of legitimately earned money, and laundered money from illegal activities). In this chapter, we focus on money that flows by means of global financial markets. In Chapter 23, we turn our attention to the question of third world debt.

It is important to recall that a focus on money has the effect of marginalizing other ways of valuing societal activities and trajectories of change. It adopts the same narrow lens as a focus on global national income (GNI) (see Chapter 2)—excluding from consideration all those human activities that are not paid for, and assuming that the societal and ecological value of everything is proportional to its price. In particular, the activities that dominate the livelihoods of women across the world (in the household), and of other marginalized groups who support themselves outside the formal market, are left completely out of the picture. We do not endorse such a position. Yet it is increasingly the case that people and places are judged by their ability to accumulate wealth and capital—judgments that affect their livelihood possibilities. For example, the debts run up by third world countries in the 1980s resulted in the imposition by their creditors of structural adjustment programs that closely circumscribed the forms that development and livelihoods could take, often with negative effects on the disadvantaged

Bongman Seo, PhD, is Assistant Professor of economic geography, Graduate School of Economics, Hitotsubashi University, Tokyo, Japan.

people in these societies (Chapter 23). Thus, notwithstanding the narrow nature of any focus on money, it is important to understand how it circulates, where it piles up, and who determines these flows.

These days, it seems that money can be moved anywhere in the world with a click of a computer mouse. We might conclude, therefore, that money must be ubiquitous. Yet we know from the news that this is not the case. We read of the International Monetary Fund (IMF) telling Russia how to manage its finances, and of third world countries complaining that they cannot raise funds from the international banking community, even as the United States runs up chronic current account deficits with no apparent difficulty. How can we make sense of this? We begin by sketching a nation's budget, as a vehicle for understanding how these various flows of money intersect in a place, before turning our attention to money flows themselves and how they have been shaped by the international monetary system. The second section describes this process, beginning with Bretton Woods, when the U.S. dollar replaced the British pound as the default currency for international transactions. Every country is empowered to print its own national currency, but a few are accepted for international payments, conferring special advantages on the countries that issue these currencies, along with certain obligations. We discuss how the Bretton Woods system failed, how there has been a gradual move away from the dollar, and how nation states and the money they print are less and less central to global finance with the emergence of offshore financial centers (OFCs) and petrodollars.

The third section describes shifts in the geography of global finance accompanying the internationalization of finance markets. Some believe that the fluidity of global finance has made geography irrelevant, but this is not the case. First, even globalized financial institutions do not treat all places indifferently. Second, different banking systems persist in different places, notwithstanding substantial pressure for all banking systems to converge on the U.S./U.K. market-based norm. A different (bank-based) system has long existed in some other countries (notably Japan, parts of continental Europe, and southeast Asia). Islamic banking systems are also emerging in some places, catalyzed by petrodollars. Third, financial transactions remain heavily concentrated in a handful of first world cities (London, New York, and Tokyo). Finally, we examine changing global patterns of private bank lending to the third world, using the example of global syndicated loans (paralleling previous examinations of capital flows tied to trade and FDI in Chapters 16 and 20, respectively).

THE BALANCE OF PAYMENTS, AND CROSS-BORDER MONEY FLOWS

Like your own household, every territory needs money to guard against a rainy day, invest in improvements, and pay for a little fun. Every nation state has the power to control the money crossing its border, even though almost all nation states are increasingly unwilling to regulate money flows in this way. Yet countries can, and do, monitor these flows of money, by calculating the "balance of payments." This balance is the result of two kinds of flows. Money crosses the national border as payments for goods and services, defined as the "current account." But there are also longer-term obligations—the international transfer of debts and credits, known as the "financial account." (The IMF sets the rules for these calculations.)

The current account measures a nation state's net earnings from participating in the global economy in any given year (much like the income your household makes from the wages and salaries received in return for its labor, and interest earned on savings and investments, minus all expenditures). For a nation state, the principal components are the trade balance (export revenues minus payments for imports); the FDI balance (net inward FDI flows and repatriated profits);

the balance of earnings on portfolio lending (dividends and interest from loans abroad minus debt payments on loans from abroad); and net "current transfers" (remittances from emigrants).[1] As for your household, if income exceeds expenditures, then wealth is accumulating. In the third world, however, with a few prominent exceptions, countries have a persistent current account deficit (as do the United States and the United Kingdom in the first world): On average, the savings of residents, together with the profits of domestically located economic activities, are less than outlays. Thus many third world countries seek to reduce their current account deficit through some combination of a positive trade balance, more inward FDI (and fewer repatriated profits), or more remittances from its emigrants (as India attempts through courting its nonresident Indians). As we have learned, the viability of such options often depends on circumstances beyond a country's control.

A second way of addressing a current account deficit is to borrow money or obtain aid from abroad, thereby incurring indebtedness to and dependence on foreign creditors. The financial account records such longer-term transactions. It counts up all "capital transfers" (the international transfer of financial assets, including debt forgiveness) and the value of any "nonproduced, nonfinancial" assets acquired abroad (including land, resources, and patents). To all these, we add foreign aid and other financial transfers involving foreign governments and supranational organizations (like the IMF).

There is a convention, dating back to 18th-century England (Poovey, 1998), that financial accounts must balance out any surplus or deficit in current accounts. In balance-of-payments statistics, therefore, any current account deficit is exactly balanced by a financial account surplus. In practice, however, this is not the case. Worldwide "errors and omissions" in such accounts are substantial (amounting to $150 billion in U.S. dollars in 2005),[2] and large components of these are gray and black money. These include capital flight (money sent abroad by domestic elites—and firms—seeking to avoid taxes, deposited in Swiss and other OFC bank accounts, which do not report this information to international regulators), as well as illegal economic transactions (smuggling, the global drug trade, and some laundered money). Brown (2006) estimates these as totaling $250 billion in 2005–2006, which is about the size of Turkey's economy.

Balance-of-payments statistics are by no means sufficient to track the geography of money. Not only do they miss some vital gray and black money flows, but they also do not record the final destinations of money flows. Substantial sums recorded as flowing across a national border may simply be passing through. Money may just be making a "round trip"—flowing from country A to country B in one form, and then returning to country A in another form. Or country B may simply act as a "turntable": Money flows in from A to B, only to be immediately reinvested in country C (Brown, 2006). Yet balance-of-payments statistics do highlight who is short of money, where those shortfalls are recorded, and where debts are accumulating.

Note, however, that your ability to accumulate debt also depends crucially on whether anyone will lend you money. Rich households often find it easy to live beyond their means because bankers are willing to loan them money, whereas poor people have difficulty even obtaining a small loan. The same applies at the national scale. It is possible for the United States to run up massive current account deficits with little hindrance, because others (notably China) are willing to buy U.S. Treasury bonds to finance this deficit. By contrast, Niger is forced to live close to its means, slowing economic growth and limiting public services, because no one is willing to lend it money.

Current account surpluses are rare in all world regions (Figure 22.1a). Since 1970, the first world, the Organization of the Petroleum Exporting Countries (OPEC) member nations in north Africa and the

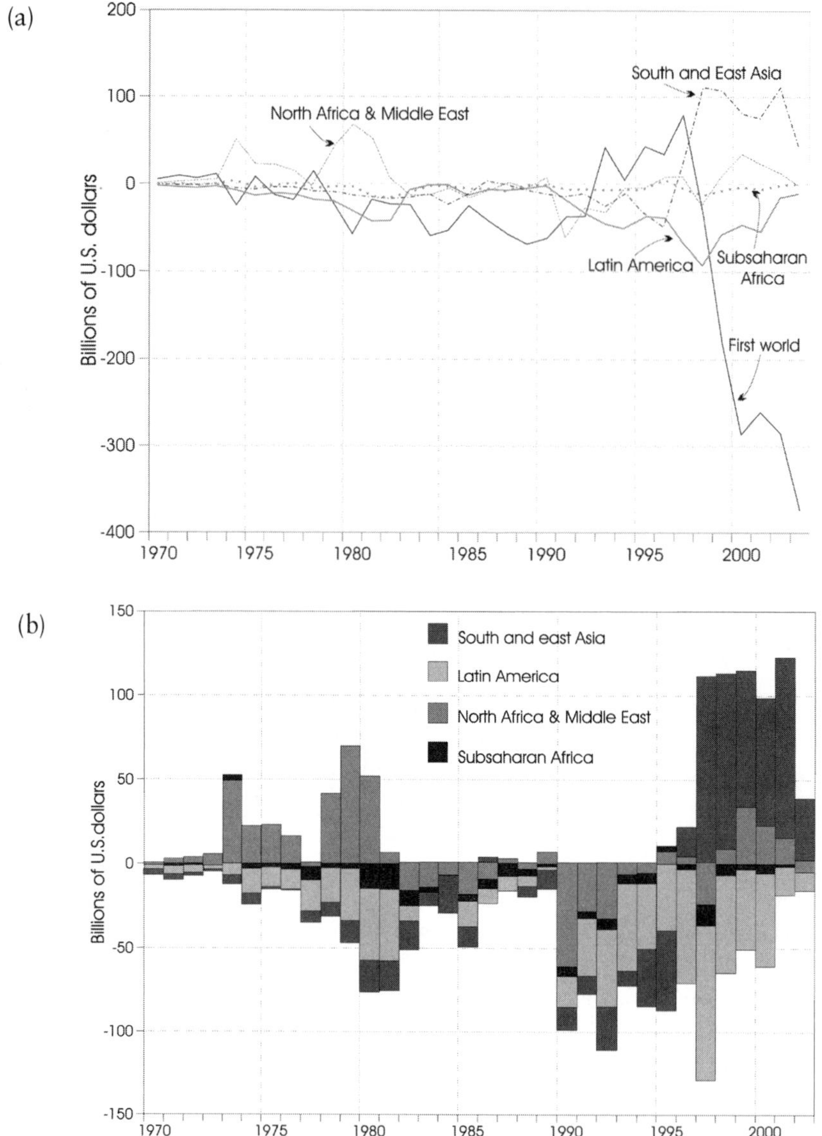

FIGURE 22.1. Current account balances 1970–2003: (a) World regions; (b) Third world regions. *Source:* Data are from World Bank (2008).

Middle East, and south and east Asia have each run surpluses for short periods of time. The first world managed this prior to the OPEC "oil crisis" and during the "new economy" information technology and communications (ITC) boom of the 1990s. Oil exporters did so during the 1970s "oil crisis" and when oil prices boomed after 2000. South and east Asia have recently developed a substantial surplus (helping underwrite current first world debts, along with OPEC members). Figure 22.1b focuses on the third world. It shows how non-oil-producing third world countries ran up current account deficits during the 1970s oil crisis, borrowing money to pay for oil imports (see, e.g., the short video *A Matter of Interest*; Leeds Animation Workshop,

1990). These deficits fell after 1982, primarily because the 1980s debt crisis made it impossible for these countries to borrow new money (Chapter 23). Current account deficits redeveloped in the 1990s, reflecting trade deficits. Selected Asian economies (notably China) subsequently were able to generate current account surpluses through exports, but Latin America has remained in debt. Sub-Saharan Africa barely appears.

Countries, unlike households, can increase the availability of money—either by simply printing more money, or by offering government bonds for sale. The current U.S. experience shows that influential countries issuing international currencies can finance ongoing debts through selling bonds, but this is not an option for most third world countries. Printing money also does not help, particularly in a world of globalized financial and currency markets. If the Indian state increases money supply by printing more rupees, the exchange rate of the rupee relative to other currencies, and thus the purchasing power of the national currency in international markets, will fall unless India can show a corresponding increase in economic productivity. Indeed, currency markets have become a means by which anonymous investors, overwhelmingly situated within the first world, can penalize countries that they judge to be failing to perform up to their expectations. This happened in Mexico in 1994–1995, with significant inequitable impacts. During the 1997 Asian crisis, the value of currencies collapsed throughout southeast Asia and South America as money was withdrawn from countries in these regions.

Ideally, nation states can balance out current account deficits or surpluses through financial accounts. As shown above, most countries suffer from chronic current account deficits, but show different abilities to cope with them through financial transactions. Third world countries are relatively constrained both in borrowing to pay for deficits and in lending with their surpluses, compared to first world countries. In order to understand this, we need to trace the development of the post-World War II global financial system.

A BRIEF HISTORY OF GLOBAL MONETARY SYSTEMS

Bretton Woods and the Marshall Plan

Thus far, we have examined the ways in which money flows across borders to balance out deficits and surpluses of individual countries. Such cross-border financial settlements require, however, an institutional framework within which cross-border money flows are transacted. First of all, we need a system of monetary exchange so that country A can exchange its own currency for country B's currency, in order to buy country B's goods denominated in its currency. Second, we need to prepare a systemwide safety net, to support the system in case of financial crises and defaults. These institutional arrangements are critical for underwriting global financial and monetary systems. The former refers to "a whole system of creating, buying and selling credit money with the help of international banks and global capital markets," whereas the latter governs "the relationship between national currencies" largely through foreign exchange rates (Strange, 1994: 49).

The foundation for the postwar monetary system was laid at the Bretton Woods conference in 1944 (Chapter 15). In 1941, Harry D. White of the U.S. Treasury Department started working on a proposal for a postwar international monetary order. British economist John Maynard Keynes subsequently offered an alternative proposal, for an international currency (Mikesell, 1994). Both proposals sought to restore stability in international payments and exchange after the disruptions of the Great Depression and World War II, while preserving national economic autonomy (Ingham, 1994). The negotiation procedures reflected global hegemony. Only the U.S. and U.K. proposals were considered in pre-Bretton Woods negotiations and the 1944 Bretton Woods conference, while U.S. and U.K. delegates collaborated to dismiss others' opinions. Indeed, the Bretton Woods conference was just "a drafting meeting, with the substance having been largely settled *beforehand* by the U.S. and U.K. delegations and supported by the Canadians" (Mikesell, 1994: 34; emphasis added).

Recall that the Bretton Woods system consisted largely of three elements: a fixed currency exchange regime, the IMF, and the International Bank for Reconstruction and Development (IBRD). Under this arrangement, all national currencies were to have a fixed exchange rate with the U.S. dollar, whose value was in turn fixed as $35 per ounce of gold. This gold–dollar convertibility seemed sensible, as the United States had massive gold reserves at the time (71% of global monetary gold in 1949; Brett, 1983: 173), as well as a substantial international trade surplus with Japan and Europe ($19.5 billion between 1945 and 1947; Brett, 1985).

However, in order to maintain the fixed gold–dollar convertibility, the United States needed to balance the amount of dollar liquidity in circulation with its gold reserves in Fort Knox (the site of the U.S. Bullion Depository). In other words, soundness of the U.S. economy was critical in maintaining the stability of the international financial system because the United States (replacing the United Kingdom) became the holder of the key global currency, and thus the only country that could control the supply of international liquidity. Domestic politics played an important role in the birth of the fixed exchange rate system. The U.S. Treasury Department took over monetary control from the Federal Reserve and, along with other domestic interests, preferred a fixed to a floating exchange rate. These interests had been preoccupied with domestic stabilization since the 1930s, and were "wary of the possible costs of internationalism" implied in a floating exchange rate system (Ingham, 1994: 43).

The IMF was designed to stabilize exchange relationships between currencies by providing a regulatory framework for convertibility and supplementary liquidity for countries in need (Cohen, 2002). To execute these roles, the IMF needed to maintain an international reserve of funds. At Bretton Woods, each member country agreed to contribute assigned credits toward the reserve, according to a formula with variable weights given to each country's gold holdings, national income, foreign trade, and population (Mikesell, 1994). The initial international reserve of the IMF was $9.1 billion, although Keynes argued that this was too small to accommodate the financial needs for postwar rebuilding in Europe (Ingham, 1994; Mikesell, 1994). As Keynes predicted, a "dollar shortage" arose. Except for the United States, into the 1950s other countries had far too few dollars to pay for their imports and were not in a position to earn dollars through a trade surplus, because the war had destroyed so many production facilities in Europe and Japan.

Despite the many negotiations behind the Bretton Woods conference, the system was not in operation during the immediate postwar years (Ingham, 1994). There was the dollar shortage, compounded by the failure of the U.S. financial system to recirculate its trade surplus in the form of international liquidity; its gold reserves were hoarded in Fort Knox instead (Ingham, 1994). In order to provide extra global liquidity, the United States, as the only capable creditor, launched various aid programs through the IBRD; in addition, the Marshall Plan (1947–1951) provided European allies with $12.5 billion worth of goods and services. These aid programs were designed to facilitate the recovery of European allies regarded as tempted by developments in the second world, and had the additional benefit of increasing demand for U.S. exports by providing these countries with funds to buy them. These funds were targeted at Europe and Japan, but not the third world. Latin America had prospered economically during the war from greatly increased exports to the United States, but lost these advantages as attention shifted to shielding western Europe from socialist ideas and the Soviet Union.

The End of Bretton Woods and the Rise of Empire

The Bretton Woods system overcame its dollar shortage problem, as convertibility among European currencies was restored in 1958, but new circumstances threatened its stability. The new threat was a dollar surfeit outside the United States, driven by a deteriorating U.S. trade balance and by growing U.S. military and aid expenditures (Cohen, 2002). The United States simply printed money to cover its debt—a fiscal policy that lacked prudence and increased the supply of dollars relative to U.S. reserves. By 1961, the dollars held outside the United States actually exceeded the total of all gold and dollar reserves within the United States (a "dollar overhang").

The United States had greatly benefited from its aid programs to allies, giving them the means to buy U.S. goods and services, but this had unintended long-term consequences. The dollar injections from the United States stimulated rapid productivity increases in first world allies' economies, which began to challenge U.S. dominance of global production and finance. The U.S. trade surplus dwindled throughout the 1960s, and finally, in 1971, the United States recorded its first trade deficit since 1945. This shift in the U.S. current account balance meant that the United States started to provide the international monetary system with liquidity in the form of net payments for its imports, rather than a recirculation of its surplus. This change put strains on the fixed exchange rate (gold–dollar convertibility), because it became increasingly difficult for the U.S. economy to provide extra liquidity matching the rates of economic growth outside the United States.

The other important phenomenon was the rise of the United States as a geopolitical superpower. This increased the global dollar surfeit through military spending and aid during the 1960s. The Vietnam War (1964–1975) dramatically increased overseas military expenditures. Coupled with current account deficits, military and aid expenditures inflated the amount of dollars circulating beyond the reach of the U.S. government. An overseas Eurodollar market developed in the late 1950s. After its 1956 invasion of Hungary, the Soviet Union became concerned that its U.S. deposits could be confiscated, and transferred these dollar accounts to a former Soviet-owned bank in Paris, La Banque Commerciale pour l'Europe du Nord. The name "Eurodollar" is believed to come from its telex answer-back code: "Euro-bank" (Clarke, 2004: 77). Eurodollars expanded (Table 22.1) as more dollar accounts were opened in Europe, where bank regulations were less stringent. Even U.S. banks began to borrow Eurodollars. All these circumstances increased the quantity of dollars beyond U.S. control, undermining the ability of the U.S. government to manage its monetary policies.

By 1971, the dollars outside the United States were 4.5 times greater than U.S. domestic gold and currency reserves. Countries outside the United States sensed the danger associated with such large dollar holdings, and began to convert their dollars into gold, seeing gold as more valuable than its fixed exchange rate with the dollar. When the French government converted large amounts of its dollar reserves into gold, this precipitated a crisis. The United States responded by unilaterally abrogating the Bretton Woods agreement. U.S. President Richard Nixon devalued the dollar substantially in relation to other currencies, and eliminated the fixed exchange rate between dollars and gold. This removed any attempt to provide an external basis for the value of money, introducing new uncertainties and sources of speculation into international finance markets.

However, it is important to note, again, that the end of the dollar–gold con-

TABLE 22.1. The Emergence of Eurodollars

Year	Net size of Eurodollar market[a]	U.S. overseas military and aid expenditures[b]	U.S. banks' Eurodollar borrowings[c]
1964	9,000		
1965	11,500		
1966	14,500	6,300	2,685
1967	17,500	7,300	3,655
1968	25,000	7,000	6,016
1969	37,500	6,900	12,118
1970	46,000	7,200	10,949
1971	54,000	7,300	3,300

Note: The first year for which data are available is 1964. Data are in millions of U.S. dollars.
Source: Adapted from Dickens (2005: Tables 8.1 and 8.2). Copyright 2005 by Edward Elgar Publishing Ltd. Adapted by permission. Dickens used data from the following sources:
[a]Bank for International Settlements, Annual Report, various years.
[b] and [c] U.S. White House, International Economic Report, March 1973; Federal Reserve Bulletin, various issues.

vertibility was partly driven by domestic economic conditions. Just as the Bretton Woods system had been closely calibrated with domestic U.S. interests at its inception, its termination was pushed by the U.S. Treasury Secretary as "desirable in terms of the country's 'national interests' " (Gowa, 1983: 157). Facing a deteriorating trade balance, rising military costs, and domestic recession, the U.S. government believed that dollar–gold convertibility left little latitude for the United States' domestic and international policy. U.S. policymakers argued that pegged exchange rates between the U.S. dollar and other major currencies worsened the U.S. trade balance by allowing cheaper foreign goods, especially from Germany and Japan, to penetrate U.S. markets, whereas expensive U.S. goods were uncompetitive in foreign markets (Gowa, 1983). The U.S. economy was largely domestic, so concerns about domestic stability outweighed those of global finance.

Ruggie (1982) has characterized the Bretton Woods system as "embedded liberalism," because it "provided for the liberalization of world trade while ensuring, through capital controls and fixed exchange rates, that governments did not have to sacrifice systems of social protection and macroeconomic policy geared to the achievement of domestic objectives, such as full employment and growth" (Held et al., 1999: 201). Under this system, capital flows were mainly official (from government to government), and the intensity and extensity of capital flows were relatively limited (Hanson, Honohan, and Majnoni, 2003). The end of the Bretton Woods system signaled the rise of new types of financial flows handled by internationally active private financial firms. Nevertheless, Bretton Woods remains influential through its two still-dominant international financial institutions: the IMF and the World Bank (Chapter 23).

The Flexible Exchange Rate System and Global Imbalances since the 1970s

The end of fixed currency regimes triggered a new mobility, flexibility, and unpredictability in international financing. Three aspects of this shift are important: governments' ability to control currency fluctuation; the increasingly international nature of international currencies; and the deregulation and integration of finance markets. Flexible exchange rates have increased fluctuations of currency values and encouraged investment into or out of a particular currency, depending on differences in interest rates and guesses as to whether that currency will be revalued or devalued. Flexible exchange rates also make the long-run value of debts much more unpredictable. When an international currency is revalued, debts taken out in that currency become greater in real terms and more difficult for the debtor to pay. When it is devalued, the debt becomes less in real value, and the creditor loses money.

The transition to flexible exchange rates was not smooth. An early attempt to keep the fixed exchange rate system between currencies without gold–dollar convertibility, the 1971 Smithsonian Agreement, failed when the U.S. dollar and other major currencies were destabilized by speculative attacks against them in 1972 and 1973 (Obsfeld and Taylor, 2005). The transition was completed when major currencies were floated against the U.S. dollar in March 1973. The U.S. dollar retained its prominence, however, as the principal currency for international transactions. As noted above, the holder of the prime international currency can manipulate global markets in its favor more easily than other countries can, and this is what the United States set out to do.

The United States took advantage of the new regime, devaluing the U.S. dollar against currencies of its main trading partners throughout the 1970s. The devalued dollar was expected to improve the competitive position of the United States in international trade, making its exports cheaper and its imports more expensive, but the U.S. trade balance continued to deteriorate. Inflation also rose rapidly, because of costlier U.S. imports, increased oil prices, and increasing real wages under Fordism (Chapter 4). Dollar devaluation was contested by "surplus" countries (others running a current account surplus), however, as it reduced the value of their dollar-denominated assets and reserves, and worsened their trade balance. Thus surplus countries—particularly Germany and Japan—began to intervene in U.S. monetary policy, putting considerable pressure on the United States to act more responsibly and eliminate its trade deficit, in order to shore up the value of the dollars they held. In fact, they reinvested part of their trade surpluses in the U.S. financial markets, mainly in Treasury bonds, to increase demand for dollars. This would prevent the dollar from depreciating too far, thereby maintaining the value of their assets and reserves.

In 1978, with the United States facing both inflation and recession, President Jimmy Carter moved to increase the value of the dollar against other currencies—a revaluation that continued until 1983. In order to do this, the U.S. Federal Reserve Bank increased its dollar reserves and reduced the supply of dollars, while increasing the supply of foreign money by issuing government bonds (IOUs) in yen and deutschmarks to raise these funds. This further undermined the status of the dollar as an international currency, however, by legitimizing the use of other national currencies for international payments (Parboni, 1988: 47). But the surplus economies also did not want their currencies to appreciate much against the dollar, because their export-led economic strategy favored cheaper currencies to maintain price competitiveness of their goods in the United States (Eichengreen, 2007). These monetary policies, maintaining the status of the dollar as an international currency, have kept the United States at the center of global finance, but the United States has failed to reverse what has become a historical shortage of investment in research and development (R&D) for the civilian economy, as well as in public and private infrastructure, education, and training. The declining strength of the U.S. economy relative to other first world economies has meant that even extensive dollar devaluations have not produced the export surplus necessary to bolster the international strength of the dollar (Eichengreen, 2007).

Such imbalances have persisted. The U.S. economy has recorded trade deficits since 1971, except for 1973 and 1975. The size of these deficits has exploded since 2000, doubling from \$377 billion in 2000 to \$764 billion in 2006. The U.S. current account deficit is presently financed by the current account surpluses of the oil-producing countries and emerging economies of Asia, including China and Japan (IMF, 2007a).

As in 1971, persistent deficits pose credibility problems for the dollar as an international currency. The advent of the euro in 1999, as a supranational European currency, has posed threat to the dollar as the key currency for both international transactions and currency reserves. The euro has consistently expanded its role as reserve currency, raising its share from some 18% in 1999 to over 25% in 2006 (IMF, 2007a), and has appreciated against the dollar since its inception. In addition, occasional threats to the dollar as an international currency emanate from the third world. In 2000, President Hugo Chavez of Venezuela began an initiative under which Venezuela's oil was traded in Latin America on a barter basis instead of for U.S. dollars, and Iraq under Saddam Hussein required that its oil exports be paid for in euros. Iran, Malaysia, and Indonesia have also considered switching to euros (Nunan, 2004). The likelihood of an abrupt exodus from the dollar to other currencies for international transactions still seems small, but some diversification into nondollar assets is inevitable, given the weakening U.S. economy. Policy coordination among major economies—seeking to sustain an adequate supply of dollars without undermining their value or intervening to manipulate exchange rates among the euro, the Japanese yen, the Swiss franc, the Chinese renminbi, and the U.S. dollar—had thus been deemed necessary to ameliorate global imbalances (IMF, 2007b). Other third world nations are not major players in this policy coordination, but their economic prospects are particularly vulnerable to changes in the value of the dollar, because they have few currency reserves to pay for imports and carry a heavy international debt burden.

Limits to National Regulation: Eurocurrency Markets and OFCs

The Eurodollar market that emerged after 1945 has diversified into a Eurocurrency market, in which a bank's deposits are denominated in currencies other than that bank's domestic currency. British Midland Bank is considered to have initiated the Eurodollar market, offering a 1.875% rate of interest for 30-day deposits at a time when U.S. Federal Regulation Q kept the ceiling for the same deposit in U.S. banks below 1% (Schenk, 1998). In other words, dollar deposits in London yielded more interest income than did those in the United States, and dollar holders started to move their accounts to London across the Atlantic. Regulatory asymmetry between the United States and the United Kingdom thus played an important role in creation of the Eurocurrency market.

The Eurocurrency market became a major center for currency exchange after the 1960s, embracing such other major currencies as the deutschmark and yen. A considerable increase in currency in circulation—including petrodollars, dollars flowing out of the United States as a result of its growing deficit, and private corporate funds being invested in financial markets rather than expanded production—led to a 23-fold expansion of the Eurocurrency market in just 13 years, from $44 billion in 1969 to $1,020 billion in 1982; it further expanded to more than $3,000 billion in the early 1990s (Brett, 1983: 209–212; Brett, 1985: 230; Martin, 1994: 258).

The Eurocurrency market has had three important implications for international currency flows. First, its acceptance of deposits in other currencies has reduced reliance on the U.S. dollar for international transactions. Second, it became an important focus in the 1970s for making large long-term loans from first world to third world nations, facilitating the 1980s third world debt crisis (Chapter 23). Third, the large deposits of national currencies held in the Eurocurrency market have reduced the ability of states to control currency exchange rates. Currencies are bought and sold on the Eurocurrency market and other offshore markets in such quantities that it has become very difficult for national governments to respond. By 1998, the average amount of currency traded *daily* by private currency brokers exceeded

$1 trillion—more than the total assets held by all national central banks.

The Eurocurrency market is described as an "offshore" market, because the currency held in its accounts lies beyond the reach of its national regulatory authority. Yet offshore currency transactions must occur somewhere that can accommodate their anarchistic nature. This necessity is met by a few small territories and nations serving as OFCs, which provide "tax havens" for offshore transactions. For such countries, with few human or natural resources, hosting offshore transactions has been an attractive development strategy. In practice, OFCs amount to little more than clusters of small offices or post office boxes in these nations. These are typically registered as subsidiaries of various first world banks, which accept deposits in a variety of key currencies; these can be loaned to residents from other countries without worries about such restrictions as loan asset ratios (requiring banks to hold a certain proportion of all loaned funds as bank assets). Almost all OFC transactions are electronic. The integration of these small island economies into global monetary circuits has made them vulnerable to whims of the global economy, as they catalyze further spatio-temporal fixes to global capitalism (Harvey, 1982; Roberts, 1994). The Cayman Islands boasted 546 banks from around the world in 1992, but only six banks in its capital, George Town, could cash a check (Roberts, 1994). The number of OFCs has grown from 25 in the 1970s to 72 by 2005, each typically linked to a global financial center (Christensen, 2007). Main OFCs include the Cayman Islands, the Bahamas, and the Netherlands Antilles in the Caribbean, as well as Hong Kong, Singapore, Bahrain, and Panama—but even London was designated an OFC in 2007!

Policymakers and activists in developed economies, notably the Tax Justice Network (see *www.taxjustice.net/cms/front_content.php?idcat=2*), have become concerned recently about tax leakages from transnational corporations (TNCs), which use administrative pricing to attribute part of their profits to subsidiaries in OFCs where there are minimal corporate taxes. It is estimated that the U.S. Treasury alone loses $100 billion a year, over a third of America's annual budget deficit, from such tax evasion (*The Economist*, 2007). Gray and black money also flows through anonymous accounts registered in these otherwise proper vacation destinations.

The 1970s Oil Crisis and the Emergence of Petrodollars

In the midst of trying to adjust to the new, post-Bretton Woods monetary system, the global economy was hit hard when OPEC quadrupled oil prices in 1973 (see Chapter 18 sidebar, "Oil, OPEC, and Development"). This simultaneously catalyzed an economic recession in many countries, even as it dramatically increased global financial liquidity. The current account surplus of oil-exporting nations increased from $3 billion in 1973 to an average of $41.4 billion a year between 1974 and 1981. The two booms in current account surpluses (Figure 22.1) closely followed those in oil prices. The OPEC countries could not spend this much money domestically, so much of it (42% of the OPEC current account surplus between 1975 and 1978) was deposited in the banks of first world nations (Hallwood and Sinclair, 1981: 88). These surplus "petrodollars" became available for lending to third world and first world nations that were running balance-of-payments deficits because of the newly expensive oil imports. Thus first world banks effectively recycled the petrodollars, as loans, back to the places from which they had originated as oil payments, although certainly not in amounts that matched each country's needs.

This recycling of petrodollars was not accompanied by growth in the borrowing economies, especially in Latin America. Borrowed money was spent to purchase expensive imports and buy out politicians, and was rerouted to secret accounts in foreign countries. First world countries raised interest rates to fight against inflation, increasing the burden of interest payments on borrowing countries at a time when their exporters suffered from depressed demand in the first world (Yergin and Stanislaw, 2002). The outcome was one of the worst such crises in history—the 1980s third world debt crisis (Chapter 23).

THE GEOGRAPHIES OF INTERNATIONALIZED FINANCIAL MARKETS

In a book provocatively subtitled *The End of Geography*, Richard O'Brien (1992: 1–2) suggests that "location will continue to matter while physical barriers exist. . . . Yet, as markets and rules become integrated, the relevance of geography and the need to base decisions on geography will alter and often diminish. Money . . . will largely succeed in escaping the confines of the existing geography." He imagines a world in which the combination of technological progress with national financial deregulation (i.e., market-based financial systems) is expected to reduce the impact of geographical difference and distance on information availability. This is argued to result in an efficient market, in which the price of financial commodities reflects the decisions of rational actors based on available information, and no excess profits are possible (Shleifer, 2000). According to this logic, as long as good data are available, it does not matter much where financial transactions take place. Reality remains more complex, however. Global finance is dominated by first world banks, financial institutions/markets, and banking systems, albeit with considerable geographical unevenness and with third world innovations and contestations.

Competitive Deregulation and the Internationalization of Banking

Deregulation has transformed the finance industry since the 1980s. Major countries have implemented a competitive deregulation of national financial markets, seeking to retain financial transactions within their boundaries. In October 1986, the London stock exchange underwent a "big bang," eliminating much government restriction on stock and bond trading in an attempt to sustain London's future as a global financial center; Tokyo followed suit in 1997. Technological developments, especially information technologies, have expanded the geographical scope of, and reduced temporal barriers to, financial transactions. Stock exchanges are always open somewhere (Figure 22.2). The combined outcome is a much flatter space of global finance, in which financial flows are freer and financial firms face fewer barriers to setting up shop in distant regional markets.

These changes have adversely affected banks' profitability. Previously, banks internationalized their operations in response to the internationalization of their corporate customers, to provide them with services in overseas markets and retain them as customers. This changed dramatically in the 1980s: As nonbank financial firms and capital markets began to steal banks' traditional customers, powerful foreign competitors penetrated domestic financial markets, and banks were forced to internationalize. By 2004, the 25 largest banks in the world "held over 10.2 trillion U.S. dollars in assets, employed 916,000 staff and generated 36% of their total banking income" in foreign countries (Slager, 2006: 1).

Despite this interweaving of national financial markets into a globally integrated market, there remain distinct geographies to banks' behavior. First, even the largest and most globalized banks, from different countries of origin, show unequal degrees of globalization (Slager, 2006). Continental European banks have recorded the strongest increase since the 1980s, whereas U.S. and U.K. banks have experienced a slight decrease, and Japanese banks showed a significant decrease in the second half of the 1990s (Slager, 2006). Second, there is a "home market" effect: Even the largest

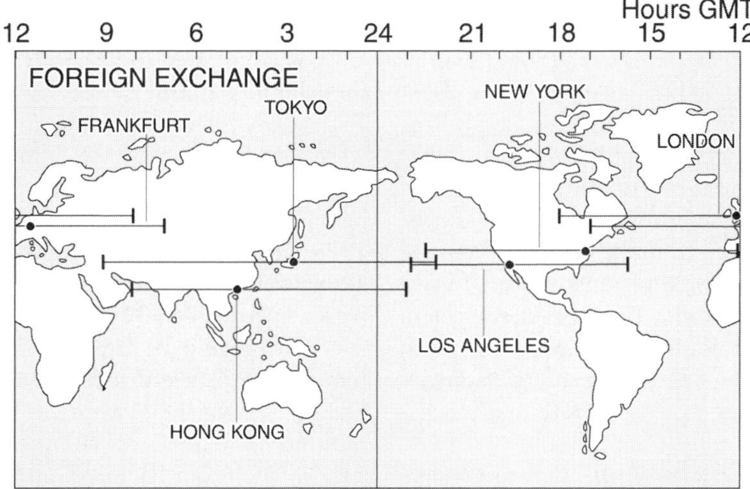

FIGURE 22.2. The 24-hour global finance markets. *Source*: Adapted from Thrift (1989). Copyright 1989 by Blackwell Publishers, Ltd. Adapted by permission.

banks show a home bias, holding a much higher portion of domestic assets than would be predicted by economic models of optimal geographical diversification (Buch, Driscoll, and Østergaard, 2004, quoted in Slager, 2006). European banks decreased their share of home assets in the 1990s, whereas U.S. and Japanese banks increased their home market share (Slager, 2006). It is interesting to note that the European banks' globalization accelerated as their own regional market experienced a strong growth in the second half of the 1990s.

Third, the experience of Japanese banks in the 1990s suggests that globalization is not irreversible; domestic conditions also matter. Banks adjust their spatial reach according to their domestic and international environment. In the 1980s, Japanese banks almost monopolized the top 10 of the world's largest banks, and were expected to replace American and European banks. Yet an economic recession stemming from the collapse of the Japanese stock and real estate markets in the early 1990s resulted in Japanese banks partly retreating from international markets in the second half of the 1990s, as they made strategic adjustments to address nonperforming domestic loans.

The Geography of Financial Systems

Market-Oriented and Bank-Oriented Systems

We have noted above that the Bretton Woods institutions, the United States, and the United Kingdom placed considerable pressure on all countries to adopt a common, market-oriented financial system. In a market-oriented system, used in the United States and United Kingdom, it is argued that market signals (such as stock prices, interest rates, and foreign exchange rates) will lead to an optimal capital allocation. The principal alternative is a bank-oriented system. In a bank-oriented system—characteristic of Japan and southeast Asia, but also of European countries like Germany—banks use relational ties with firms and other market participants to monitor firms' behavior and market situations, and to optimize the allocation of financial resources.

As financial firms, including banks, expand operations into foreign markets, they must adjust to different regulatory systems and financial customs. Thus any convergence to a common regulatory system is advantageous for global banks, as it significantly reduces their transaction costs. The market-oriented system is consistent with neoliberal principles. Its international acceptance was facilitated by the 1990s recession in Japan, together with the 1997 Asian financial crisis and emergent neoliberal globalization, which created skepticism about the effectiveness of their bank-oriented system. Proponents of market orientation argued that relational ties and corruption in this system weakened the monitoring role of banks, which then failed to make prudent financial decisions. Many Asian countries were forced to move away from a bank-oriented system under structural adjustment programs, and in 1997 the Japanese "big bang" spurred conversion there also to a more market-oriented system.

However, it is doubtful that any single financial system can best serve the full variety of economic structures, cultures, and development trajectories that persist around the world. It is argued, for example, that whereas a market-based system may better serve customers in capital-rich countries, a bank-oriented one is better for countries facing the capital shortages that are common in the third world (Rajan and Zingales, 1998).

Islamic Financial Practices

Even as bank-based systems have come under pressure to reform to a market-based system, the circulation of petrodollars has catalyzed the growth of what is known as "Islamic finance." Islamic finance differs from other forms of financial transaction because it promotes profit-and-loss sharing between lenders and borrowers, as well as economic and social development aligned with interpretations of Islamic norms. For example, the lender shares part of the borrower's earnings and losses instead of charging interest (which is illegal under Islamic law). In the early 1970s, as petrodollars began to proliferate, space was created for the emergence of an Islamic financial system consistent with Muslim religious values and supportive of Islamic political and economic self-determination (Pollard and Samers, 2007; Warde, 2000). An intergovernmental Islamic Development Bank, formed at the 1974 Organization of the Islamic Conference, is considered to be the "cornerstone of the Islamic banking system" (Warde, 2000: 75). Many private Islamic financial firms were also established across the Middle East during the 1970s (the Dubai Islamic Bank being the first private Islamic bank), and in 1979 Pakistan became the first country to adopt a full Islamicization of its banking sector (Warde, 2000).

The incipient Islamic financial system began to face difficulties in the 1980s. Steadily falling real oil prices in the 1980s reduced oil earnings, enhancing the bargaining power of Islamic bankers who were lending to OPEC governments with cash flow problems. At the same time, however, new financial needs (e.g., remittances by the increasing numbers of migrant workers, and black currency trading) catalyzed the development of new types of Islamic financial firms outside the existing banking system (Warde, 2000). Increased competition, and limited investment opportunities for Islamic banks, cut into profits and encouraged short-term speculative activities by Islamic financial firms. Consequently skepticism rose about whether *Shari'a* (Islamic law) was being strictly followed in Islamic finance, leading to some transformations in Islamic finance, such as the development of a series of regulatory institutions located in the Gulf States (Pollard and Samers, 2007).

Islamic banking is now common in the OPEC countries of the Middle East, and in other Islamic countries such as Pakistan, Malaysia, and Brunei; the first Islamic bank serving Muslim populations in the first world was founded in Britain in 2004. Islamic banking is gaining significant attention from global finance. Malaysia drew attention from other Islamic countries in the 1990s, when Prime Minister Mahathir Mohammed successfully "harnessed Islam to his goal of economic growth through the embrace of high technology and modern finance" (Warde, 2000: 85). Mohammed combined practical and nationalistic approaches, devising new financial products for Islamic capital markets, and developing Labuan as an OFC for Islamic finance. Malaysian success, despite resistance from conservative Gulf nations, has opened up new possibilities for Islamic finance, which is now becoming integrated into global financial circuits. Western banks, such as Citibank, are opening Islamic banking subsidiaries in Islamic countries; conversely, Islamic institutions are developing financial products for non-Muslim customers and establishing foreign branch banking networks. There is already a family of Dow Jones Islamic Market Indexes, with a total capitalization of $19 trillion in 2007, growing at over 10% annually (see *www.djindexes.com*).

Places of Finance

Although money circulates globally, the detailed knowledge necessary to make wise decisions about borrowing and lending is often tacit and localized. Face-to-face contact remains essential to making the judgments and establishing the trust necessary for financial transactions (Leyshon and Thrift, 1997; Thrift, 1994). Every financial product has particular information requirements and an explicit geographical scope of operations (Clark, 1997). Knowledge of general national economic trends may suffice for investing in foreign currency markets, and this implies that a few financial centers can offer worldwide coverage; however, investment banking transactions such as mergers and acquisitions require intensive knowledge about specific firms. This is not readily accessible from a distance. Rather, it requires the existence of geographically dispersed financial centers that focus on specific regions and industries.

Financial centers host a network of diverse financial products with different informational contents and corresponding spatial scopes (Coakley, 1992). A network of financial centers ranging from global financial centers to local ones has developed to handle different mixes of financial products with different market sizes (Figure 22.3). Financial centers have also developed different specializations, reflecting the historical trajectories and regulatory environments of specific places. For example, in 1997 European banks accounted for over 55% of international lending, whereas 8 of the 10 largest corporate finance institutions were U.S. banks. As is well known, Switzerland is the dominant center for private banking (personal asset management), due to its respect for customer secrecy, whereas London dominates institutional investment management (Walter, 1998).

Financial centers are not just physical offices where trading occurs, but repositories of financial knowledge production, where tacit knowledge, locally specific customs, and business relations among financial firms and their clients are crucial to success or failure (Thrift, 1994). Once this is recognized, it makes sense that there is a persistent and uneven geographical network of financial centers, notwithstanding globalized and homogenized financial markets. This network is still dominated by London, New York, and Tokyo, with the influence of regional and local centers shifting in response to the multiscalar dynamics of global capitalism.

The Changing Financial Space of Flows: The Case of Global Syndicated Lending

The 1980s saw an unprecedented integration of national financial markets, with emerging networks of financial centers intermediated by cross-border penetration of financial firms organizing their activities at the global scale. This set the tone for an explosion of global financial markets, with substantial growth in the size of financial flows and assets, particularly after the mid-1990s. According to McKinsey Global Institute (2007), the total worldwide value of financial stock grew from $12 trillion in 1980 to $53 trillion in 1993 and over $140 trillion in 2005. A major reason for this increase is the growth

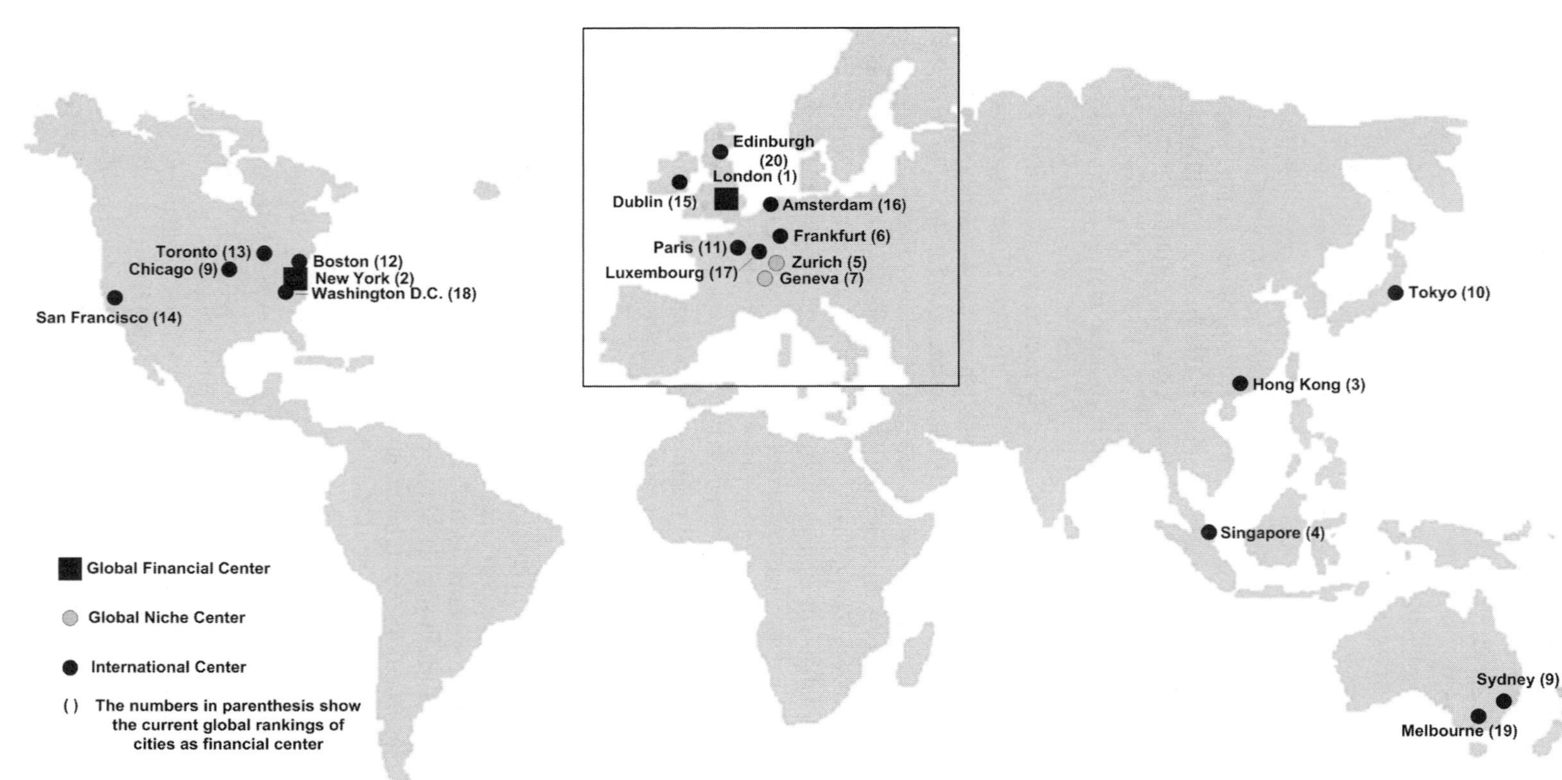

FIGURE 22.3. The 20 largest global financial centers, 2008. *Source*: Data are from Yeandle, Mainelli, and Harris (2007).

of private capital flows since the early 1990s (World Bank, 2008). These private capital flows have also introduced unprecedented volatility into the market, triggering a new type of financial crisis in the 1990s (Chapter 23). This volatility has been particularly marked for flows to the third world, where explosive growth in flows (mostly to a handful of countries denoted as "emerging" markets) reversed after the 1997 Asian financial crisis, only to rebound after 2000.

In order to gain some sense of the position of third world countries in this rapidly evolving space of private financial flows, within networks of finance firms and finance centers, we consider the example of global syndicated loans. These are loans provided to a borrower in a particular country by a loan "syndicate"—a group of banks that agree to provide the loan collectively under a common contract. Global syndicated loans, used here because of the availability of geographically referenced data (Loan Pricing Company, 2001), are reasonable proxies for international bank loans in general.

Notwithstanding discourses about the speed and mobility of global finance and the end of geography, these financial flows show distinct and persistent geographical patterns, summarized in Figure 22.4. First, world regional finance markets are becoming increasingly interconnected (often by flows of less than 1% of global loans, which are not depicted in Figure 22.4). As in the cases of trade and FDI (Chapters 16 and 21), these flows are dominated by connections among North America, western Europe, and industrialized Asia (Japan, South Korea, Taiwan, Hong Kong, and Singapore). Modest connections have also been emerging among the peripheral regions. By the late 1990s, only eastern Europe and the Caribbean were not directly connected with the vast majority of the other peripheral regions (Seo, 2005). At face value, expanded circuits mean that syndicates and borrowers both enjoy diversified business opportunities. Yet the asymmetrical nature of these circuits means that while expanded circuits favor loan syndicates, providing them with a greater choice of borrower nodes, they also make peripheral nodes vulnerable to decisions made in the three core markets.

Second, the strength of interregional flows has varied over time—further evidence of volatility. Between 1986–1992 and 1993–1997, interregional flows strengthened in relative terms between western Europe and many peripheral regions (southeast Asia, Oceania, the Middle East and north Africa, south Asia, and Central America), whereas North America strengthened its linkages to South America and southeast Asia, and industrial Asia reinforced its connection with the other two major markets. The 1997 Asian financial crisis restructured these dynamics. Between 1993–1997 and 1998–2000, southeast Asia's connections with the three core regions shrank substantially again, although South America maintained its linkages. This was compounded by a rush of mergers and acquisitions in Europe in the late 1990s, which drew in money from North America as well as within the Eurozone. As a result, an emerging tripartite structure of the mid-1990s gave way to a reinforced bipolar circuit connecting North America with Europe, as circuits from and into industrialized Asia shrank after 1997 (Figures 22.4b and 22.4c).

Third, global financial markets and cross-border flows have distinct geographies that shape the vulnerability and dependence of third world countries on first world lenders. Although third world countries have diversified their lender base, peripheral regions have remained heavily dependent on banks from first world regions (Seo, 2004). Endogenous local lenders in the third world countries are currently somewhat inchoate, accounting for less than 10% of total loans. In Latin America, banks from North America and western Europe have been almost equally dominant lenders. Western European lenders further strengthened their presence in eastern Europe and sub-Saharan Africa in the late 1990s, as they caught up with U.S. lenders in these markets. In south-

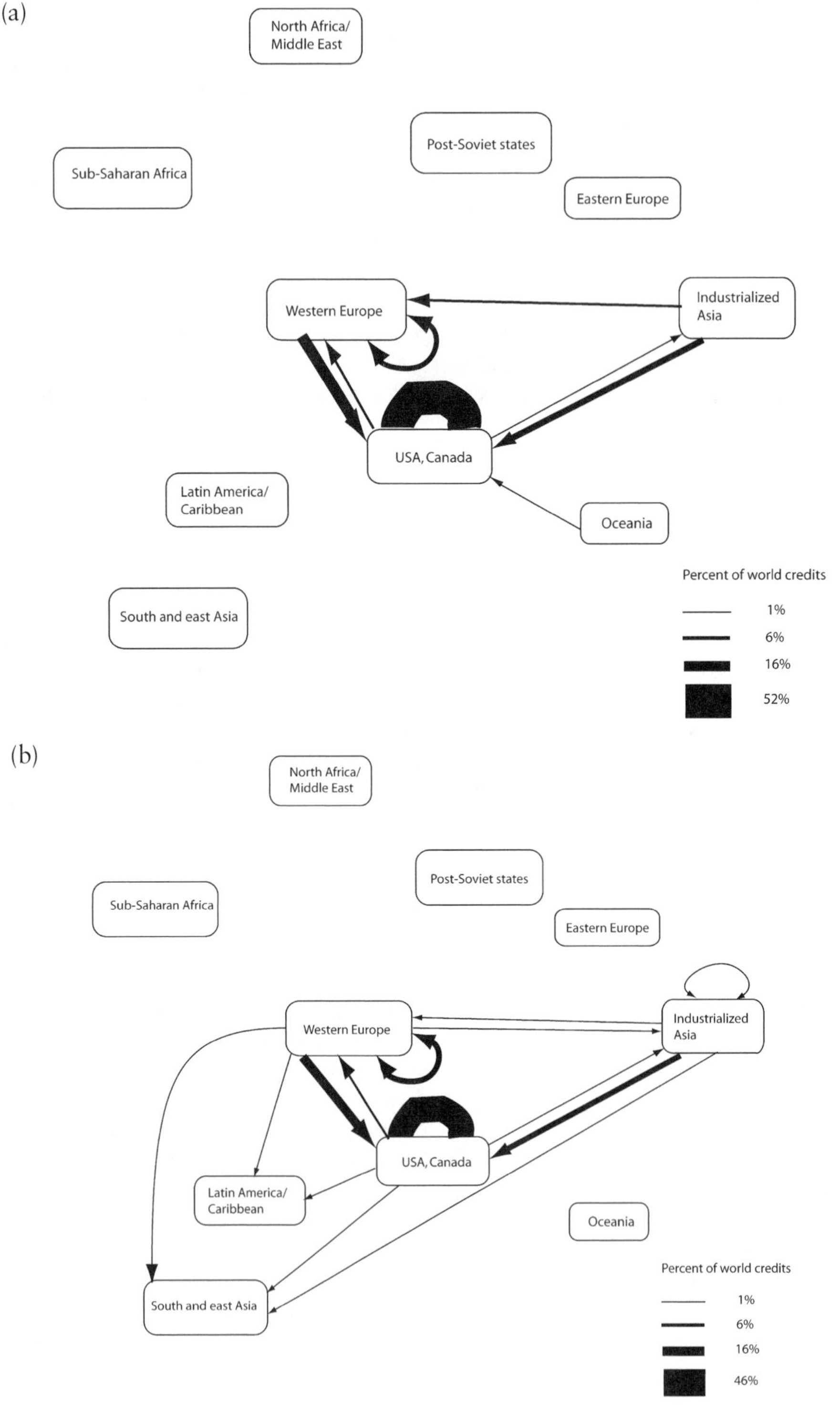

FIGURE 22.4. Global flows of syndicated credits, 1986–2000: (a) 1986–1992; (b) 1993–1997; (c) 1998–2000. *Source:* Data are from Seo (2005).

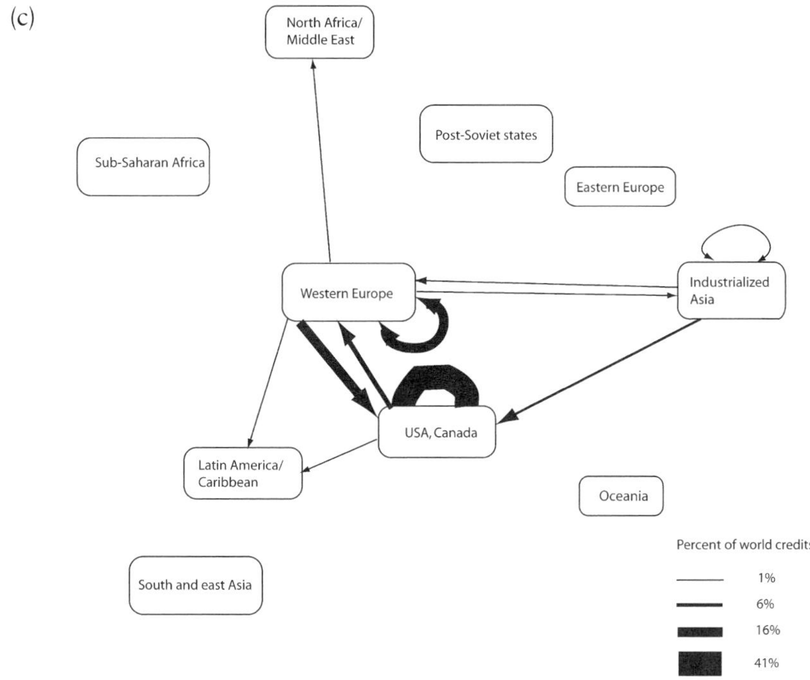

FIGURE 22.4. *(cont.)*

east Asia, the dominance of Japanese lenders until the early 1990s has been challenged, initially by U.S. lenders and subsequently by western European ones.

CONCLUSIONS

We have begun this chapter by examining how countries manage money flows across their borders through balance of payments in both the current account and the financial account. By closely examining these accounts, we can learn about the linkages between flows of commodities and services, and those of different types of money. In order to mediate cross-border money flows, international financial and monetary institutions are needed. During the years immediately after World War II, the United States and its allies established a global financial and monetary order through the Bretton Woods system, supported by the IMF and World Bank. The operation of the Bretton Woods system in the 1950s and 1960s depended on the U.S. economy and its dollar reserves; the United States and its dollar emerged as the principal hegemon and key currency, respectively. The Bretton Woods system ended in the early 1970s, however, when the faltering U.S. economy could no longer support it. Despite this, and repeated crises in the world economy, Wall Street–U.S. Treasury–IMF neoliberals still believe in the invisible hand of financial markets dominated by the first world. Alternatives to the U.S. market-based model, the bank-based approach favored in Asia or Islamic finance receive short shrift. Although many trends in global finance have imposed the idea of convergence on bank-based systems onto third world countries, it is time to consider the coexistence of different financial systems for diverse economies.

The financial globalization facilitated by competitive deregulation and the development of information and communication technologies has eliminated many spatial constraints on financial transactions, thereby challenging nation states' ability to govern money flows. Yet global financial centers maintain their dominance over other challengers, even as financial centers with special characters have emerged as OFCs. Financial institutions have shown similar strategic sensitivity in creating business opportunities over space. Recent global finance has witnessed new geographies of money rather than the end of geography. Certain places remain marginalized in these ongoing transformations, however. In particular, third world lenders and borrowers have limited access to global financial markets, further complicating their challenges.

NOTES

1. The IMF now also includes foreign aid loans, grants, and gifts in the current account. We exclude them from this category, to keep the focus on money earned from internationalized networks of commodity production.

2. From here on in this chapter, and throughout Chapter 23, monetary values are given in U.S. dollars unless otherwise indicated.

23 Borrowing Money

Aid, Debt, and Dependence

with Bongman Seo

When ambitions exceed available funds (profits, savings, and the other financial inflows discussed in Chapter 22), countries, like individuals, must borrow money to finance new economic plans. Like poor households, third world nations have traditionally been short of money and find it difficult to qualify for credit. Deteriorating terms of trade in the export of primary products, combined with the need to import manufactured goods, create imbalances in the current account (see Chapters 17 and 22). These difficulties are reinforced by the low wages paid to working people in most third world nations. Low wages reduce domestic markets for indigenous producers (increasing the need for imports) in some interpretations, reducing the gains that a nation can make from trade; and they also minimize the domestic savings available for governments or firms to borrow. It is thus necessary for third world countries to borrow money to finance economic growth. Governments and firms can issue bonds and other IOUs. By selling these in international markets, they receive money now that will be paid back later, with interest (although many in the third world find this difficult, because global rating organizations do not give them a high bond and credit risk rating). Other ways of gaining access to funds include foreign aid and grants and loans from international financial institutions (the Bretton Woods institutions, but also various development banks).

Those in the third world seeking to borrow money—whether a large national government dealing with international financial organizations or a poor female entrepreneur seeking $25 from a local moneylender to purchase some chickens—face a number of hurdles. Many find it all but impossible to borrow money at all. Those able to borrow money face other problems: The moneylenders tell them what they are supposed to do with it, and there are long-term risks associated with whether the debts accrued can be paid off. On two occasions between the end of Bretton Woods in the 1970s and 2008, the many local and individual crises faced by borrowers have concatenated into global-scale financial crises: the 1980s third world debt crisis across the newly industrializing countries (NICs) of Latin America; and the 1997 Asian financial crisis across Southeast and East Asia. In both cases, the IMF imposted structual adjustment policies. Lenders were criticized for triggering the crises by their imprudent loans and the speed with which they withdrew money when a problem occurred. However, the means by which these crises were resolved tended to help global financial institutions weather the storm, while triggering widespread impoverishment and loss of wealth mostly to the poor across the third world. Third world elites are the first to gain access to and benefit from the money lent, often find ways to channel parts of it into their personal bank accounts, and engage in capital flight (shipping their wealth abroad to Switzerland and other offshore financial centers [OFCs]) at the first sign of crisis. The endemic nature of these crises for the third world has triggered criticisms of finance markets over the last 15 years, as well as alternative proposals ranging from debt relief to microfinance.

LENDERS AND LOANS

As shown in Table 23.1, countries seeking funds have several different sources to tap, distinguished by the type of lender and the terms under which the money is lent. (We include foreign direct investment [FDI] flows here, since these constitute a major source of long-term funds and are increasingly sought after by third world nations, even though they are tied to institutions engaged in investment rather than lending.) Most lending is public—either "bilateral" (from one government to another) or multilateral (from international financial institutions such as the World Bank, the International Monetary Fund [IMF], the United Nations, or any of the regional development banks, including the Inter-American Development Bank, the African Development Bank, and the Asian Development Bank). These are the only institutions that may engage in "concessional" lending (loans at below-market rates of interest, or interest-free loans and grants). The major private lenders are banks (lending money or purchasing government bonds) and nonfinancial firms (often as FDI; see Chapters 20 and 21). Bilateral lending is often criticized, because it serves the interests of the lender more than those of the borrower. Multilateral agencies are supposed to avoid biases, but, as we will see, national governments with higher quotas (e.g., the United States) can exert considerable influence over how and where these funds are spent.

Money is lent for various purposes under different terms. Thus, when national governments make short-term loans at market rates as export credits, they are simply advancing money for a year or less in order to enable another country to purchase the lender's exports. Such loans are clearly tied closely to bilateral trade and arms purchase agreements. Longer-term bilateral grants and loans at below-market rates are forms of foreign aid (official development aid [ODA]), but other long-term loans may be made at market rates for a variety of reasons.

When we examine the historical geography of all lending to third world regions (Figure 23.1), two clear peaks can be discerned since 1970: petrodollars recirculated to the third world during the late 1970s and early 1980s, and monies lent to southeast Asia in the late 1990s when the first world was experiencing massive, speculative economic growth associated with the "new" information economy. Each of these was followed by a sharp decline, marking the two third world financial (debt) crises. During the first boom, the principal beneficiaries were the industrializing and oil-exporting countries of Latin America (Mexico, Venezuela, Brazil, Argentina, and Chile) and the Middle East. These regions then suffered the brunt of the 1980s debt crisis. Lending to east (including southeast) Asia grew steadily during the first boom, continued during the 1980s crisis, and dominated the second boom during the mid-1990s—only to be reversed during the 1997 Asian finance crisis (Chapter 22). Since the late 1990s, lending has diversified toward the big potential markets of China and India. China has in fact become a major creditor since 2000, as a principal purchaser of U.S. Treasury bonds. Africa and Oceania were not major losers in either crisis, but this is simply because no one was willing to lend them much money even during the boom

TABLE 23.1. Types of International Lending

Type of lender	Terms of loan: Below market rates (concessional)	At market rates (nonconcessional): Short-term	At market rates (nonconcessional): Long-term
Governments (bilateral)	Bilateral ODA	Export credits	Other official flows
Supranational institutions (multilateral)	IBRD/IDA loans	IMF balance-of-payments credits	Other World Bank loans
Private banks		Short-term loans	Long-term loans, government bonds
Private firms		Capital advances	FDI
Individual investors		Stock purchases	Bond purchases

Note. ODA, official development aid; IBRD, International Bank for Reconstruction and Development; IDA, International Development Association; IMF, International Monetary Fund; FDI, foreign direct investment.

years, when lending was profligate. It is not surprising that analysts discuss Africa's "lost development decades."

Figure 23.2 shows the changing importance of different types of lending. From 1970 to the 1980s debt crisis, FDI dominated, followed by foreign aid and export credits. During the crisis, private funds (FDI and private bank lending) were withdrawn, leaving foreign aid and public lending to take up the slack. This pattern was repeated during the second boom and the 1997 crisis, with a third cycle apparently underway since 2004. (The white areas at the top of the graph, during 1986–1988 and 2002–2004, mark moments when third world countries were repaying debts after a crisis. In 1986–1988, they had to repay previously accrued export

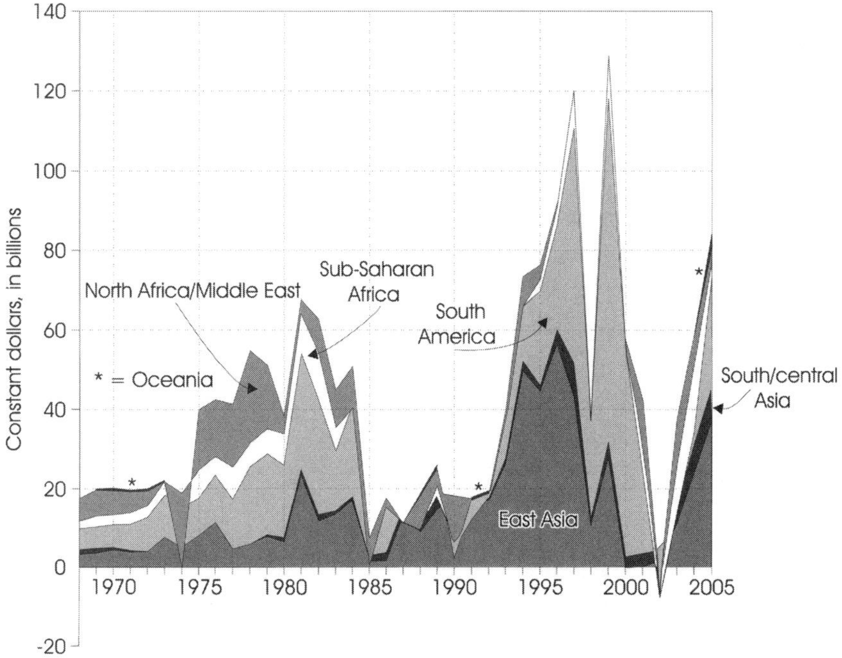

FIGURE 23.1. Third world lending by region, 1968–2005. *Source:* Data are from Organization for Economic Cooperation and Development (OECD, 2007).

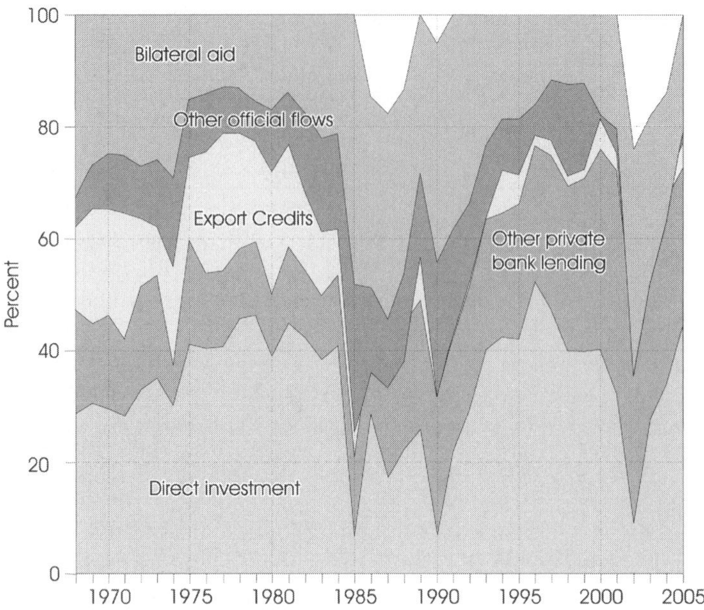

FIGURE 23.2. Third world lending by type, 1968–2005. *Source:* OECD (2007).

credits; in 2002–2004, they were repaying other official flows.) Note that whereas the second crisis was felt most dramatically in 1998–2000 in Asian and some other countries, it was not until the end of the "new economy" financial bubble (in 2001) that private funds were withdrawn from the third world as a whole.

To summarize, private lending dominates in good times and disappears in bad times, leaving public lenders to pick up the pieces (Christensen, 2007). Booms and busts coincide with booms and busts in the global money and credit available for lending. The first crisis coincided with the end of the OPEC oil boom, dramatically reducing the petrodollars in circulation; the second crisis coincided with the end of the first world 1990s information technology boom.

The burden imposed by financial flows on the third world depends not only on the size of lending relative to the capacity to repay loans, but also on the degree to which lending creates debt. Grants and FDI do not create debt, and in 1970 such non-debt-creating borrowing was large enough to cover the majority of current account deficits in the third world. Debt-creating lending was larger than non-debt-creating lending, but not a great deal larger, and almost 70% of this was from public sources. Beginning in 1974, current account deficits grew very rapidly, becoming much larger than the non-debt-creating borrowing and forcing countries into debt to finance this deficit. In 1980, debt-creating borrowing had increased to almost three times the non-debt-creating flows, and more than half of this was privately financed. By 1988, private financing had largely disappeared, to be replaced by non-debt-creating borrowing and increasingly by FDI. Yet debt-creating private lending returned to selected third world countries in the 1990s, as private bank lending increased its share to almost 40% by 2000, also displaying high volatility (Figure 23.1).

In the remainder of this chapter, we examine the three major sources of third world financing (other than FDI): bilateral foreign aid and its ties to foreign policy; bank lending and associated financial crises; and World Bank/IMF lending and development programs, which have come to define the geography of lending today to countries of the third (and former second) world.

BILATERAL FOREIGN AID

As noted above, "bilateral foreign aid" refers to financial transfers from a lending to a borrowing government for purposes related to "development." This can occur in a number of ways. The classic example is providing finance to support a specific project, such as dam construction, highway improvement, hospital construction, or the purchase of agricultural equipment. A second form is the provision of material goods, particularly food aid. A third is provision of human labor, ranging from sending volunteers overseas to work with the local populace (as in the U.S. Peace Corps program), to providing consultants for the public or private sector, to training third world residents either at home or abroad. Expenditures on research for development purposes are a fourth form, including funding research at tropical agriculture research stations in the third world (see Figure 10.10) or at first world universities tackling specific third world problems (such as tropical diseases). Finally, when third world debt is forgiven or rescheduled, any savings to the third world nation are also counted as foreign aid; this made up about one-fifth of all foreign aid disbursed by first world nations in 1990–1991 (Organization for Economic Cooperation and Development [OECD], 1992).

Thus significant components of foreign aid are not spent directly on development in third world nations; indeed, an increasing proportion of the money never leaves the country of origin except in an accounting sense. The OECD (1992: 27) has noted "an increase in spending on development in donor countries, largely consisting of subsidies to NGOs [nongovernmental organizations], research of interest to developing countries, costs associated with the administration of aid programs, and the financing of facilities for nationals of developing countries receiving education or training in a reporting donor country." Military aid, direct support for the military of the borrowing nation, also does not enhance development; however, we have no comparable information on the real size of this, because the member countries of the OECD (which compiles the other statistics) have agreed to exclude military expenditures from their compilations (OECD, 1992: 86).

It is very difficult to evaluate the degree to which foreign aid helps third world residents. Three elements are central to such an evaluation, each of which is tricky to analyze: the motives under which the money is provided (altruism or self-interest?); the long-term distribution of the benefits of aid between donor and recipient countries (the question of tied aid); and the vision of development for which it is provided (the appropriateness of foreign aid).

Motives for Foreign Aid

Since foreign aid involves providing concessional financial support for third world nations, this is often regarded as an act of selfless generosity. Even if this were true, the amounts involved do not suggest great generosity. At the 1970 UN General Assembly, donor governments promised to spend 0.7% of their global national income (GNI) on foreign aid. On average, first world nations have provided 0.33% of their gross national product (GNP) as foreign aid during the last 20 years. Some nations have progressively increased their contribution, with The Netherlands and the Scandinavian countries providing close to 1% of their GNP, but others have fallen back—notably Great Britain, the United States, and Australia. The United States is the least generous first world nation with the exception of Greece, providing just 0.16% of its GNI, although the absolute size of its aid still exceeds that of any other nation. U.S. foreign aid amounts to $22 billion annually—$73 per U.S. resident, or the cost to the United States of 7 weeks of the

Iraq War (according to Pentagon budget requests). Those third world nations wealthy enough to provide foreign aid have been more generous. Average contributions by OPEC nations were negligible in 1970, rose to 8% of GNP at the height of the oil crisis, and have since declined. Currently, Kuwait, Saudi Arabia, and China are the largest third world ODA donors.

Foreign aid is not allocated to nations simply on the basis of need. Major global powers have used aid as a part of foreign policy, helping nations whose political support they find to be strategically important. Thus the United States has a track record of focusing foreign aid on countries that contain U.S. military bases, and/or that are of geopolitical or strategic importance to U.S. foreign policy (Figure 23.3). The bulk of U.S. foreign aid has been directed to countries with a small proportion of the third world population whose political regimes and geopolitical position are aligned with those of the United States, even though too often they have autocratic governments and/or armed forces actively engaged in maintaining internal order. In 1986, the Reagan administration objected to attempts by the U.S. Congress to reduce foreign aid, because the amount proposed would have been too small to meet foreign policy goals. By 1994, there was general agreement among U.S. policymakers that U.S. foreign aid had been primarily a tool of foreign policy, and that the terms of its continuation should be evaluated on this basis. After 2001, the George W. Bush administration argued for increased foreign aid appropriations, on the grounds that these would help the "war on terror."

First world nations also are more likely to provide aid to those third world nations with which they have had historical connections (such as former colonies), with which they have significant economic linkages (often because of such historical connections), or where they perceive that the aid is being used in a way that they define as "productive." Figure 23.4 shows which first world nations are relied on by the third world for foreign aid, illustrating these geopolitical, historical, and economic connections. The United States aid goes to its

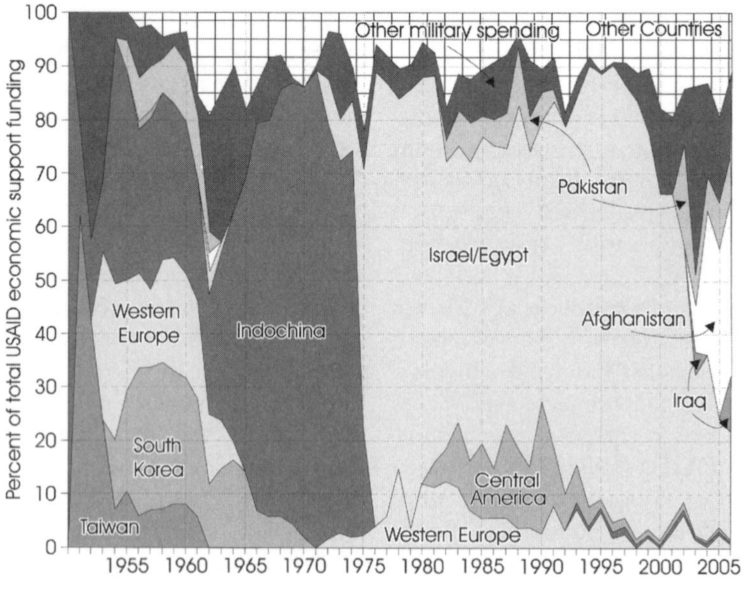

FIGURE 23.3. The political nature of U.S. aid, 1951–2005. USAID, U.S. Agency for International Development. *Source:* Adapted from Ruttan (1996). Copyright 1996 by Vernon W. Ruttan. Adapted by permission.

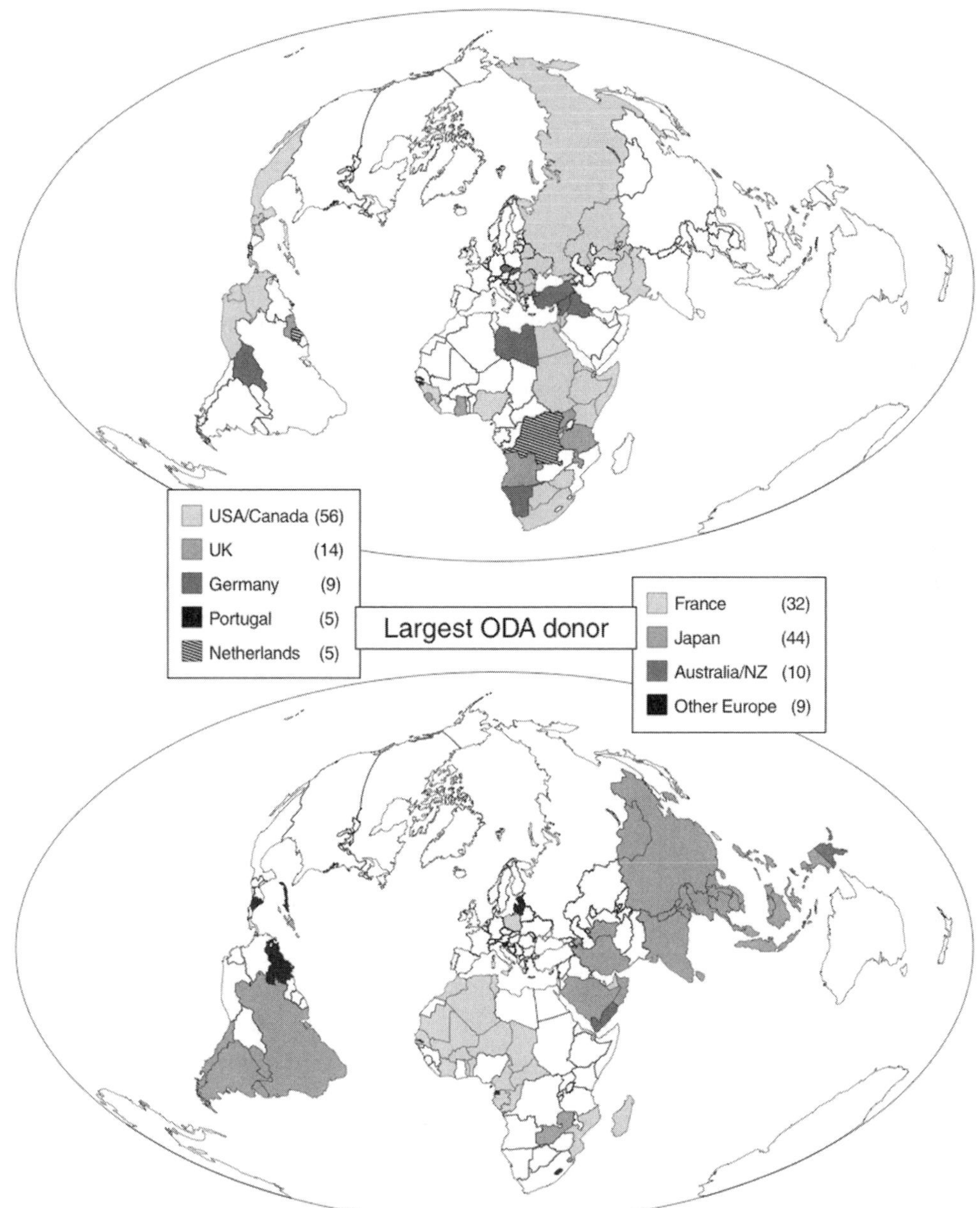

FIGURE 23.4. Dominant sources of foreign aid, 2001–2002. *Source:* Data are from OECD (2004).

geopolitical backyard, Latin America, as well as to strategic geopolitical locations in the Middle East, northeast Africa, around Afghanistan, and in the former Soviet sphere. Japan's presence is strongest in east, southeast, and south Asia; the Middle East (a principal source of oil); and the southern cone of South America (where it has strong trade relations). Francophone Africa relies on France, and Germany dominates aid to Turkey and Namibia (a former colony). The remaining areas of sub-Saharan Africa and South America receive most of their aid from other European nations.

The Strings Attached to Foreign Aid

Foreign aid entering a country need not stay there. Foreign aid agreements often stipulate that part of the aid money be spent on purchasing products from the donor country. This is termed "tied aid," and means that in practice a certain proportion of the aid money leaks back to the nation of origin. Aid has not always been tied in this way. The practice of tied aid originated in the competition among first world nations for third world export markets. The United States invented tied aid in the early 1960s, at a time when the U.S. trade surplus was shifting to a deficit, and when there was concern that certain countries such as Turkey were using U.S. aid money to purchase inputs from European competitors. In 1960, 41% of U.S. foreign aid (excluding food aid and export credits, which are tied by definition) was spent on U.S. products; by 1965, this had risen to 95% (Payer, 1974: 29). Japan and the European nations followed suit in self-defense.

Food aid—food sent to third world nations—is a special form of tied aid. It is aid in material form, purchased by the donor government from its farmers and food corporations. It can reduce hunger in the short term (as long as it reaches those in need), but has the longer-run effect of undermining domestic agriculture in the recipient nation. Farmers in the recipient nation cannot compete with free imported food, and reduce their production of domestic food crops. This is compounded by shifts in dietary preferences. The cheap food made available may induce residents to shift, for example, from indigenous grains to imported wheat, which cannot be grown cost-effectively in tropical climates. Alternatively, first world food products may be preferred because they are associated with prosperous lifestyles. All this leads sooner or later to increased food and seed imports, and thus to reduced self-sufficiency (Colman and Nixson, 1986: 187–188, 261–262).

Tied aid can take many forms. British aid to build a dam in Kenya, for example, may require the purchase of Land Rovers for use on the project. U.S. agricultural aid to El Salvador may specify use of International Harvester tractors, Cargill seed corn, and the hiring of U.S. agronomists. Japanese aid for developing an iron mine in Indonesia may require the use of Japanese building materials and geologists. From the receiving country's point of view, tied aid has two kinds of disadvantages. First, it reduces the amount of foreign aid that can be spent domestically, meaning that the country must rely more on the secondary longer-term impact of foreign aid on development, and less on the immediate impact of the money lent. The size of this disadvantage thus depends on the details of the project being financed. Of course, in some cases tied purchases may represent essential inputs that are simply not available domestically and would have to be imported anyway. Second, the existence of ties reduces the ability of the third world nation to choose the best price and most appropriate equipment when money is spent on imported materials. Prices will tend to be higher, because the supplier knows that there is little competition. Furthermore, the equipment available under the tied aid agreement may not be particularly appropriate.

It has been conservatively estimated that 10–20% of the value of foreign aid was lost as a result of tied aid in selected countries in the 1960s (Colman and Nixson, 1986: 188–189; United Nations Conference on Trade and Development [UNCTAD], 1967b), and the amount is almost certainly greater today. This would amount to $8–16 billion of the foreign aid provided in 2005 being handed back to donor countries. The degree to which aid is tied varies significantly by donor country. In 1998, 16% of Japan's foreign aid was tied, compared to 49% for the United States, 52% for Germany, and 65% for Britain. Yet Japan's low figure is also not as altruistic as it seems. Because Japanese goods are the most competitive on international markets, countries with untied aid are more likely to purchase Japanese products anyway. This illustrates how tied aid is still used by first world nations to compete with one another in trading with the third world.

The Appropriateness of Foreign Aid

The impact of the foreign aid that does remain in a country depends greatly on its form and purpose. Donor nations and multilateral organizations attempt to identify the type of foreign aid that is best for third world nations, but the stories of failure are legion: tractors that removed the topsoil or could not be repaired; dams that ruined the water table; foreign aid that ended up in the pockets of corrupt politicians; food aid that was stolen and resold by warlords or merchants; and charity payments that were largely spent on administrative costs and the salaries of local representatives. Thus the story of foreign aid is one of both fundamental successes and spectacular disasters. The key to success or failure is the appropriateness of the foreign aid expenditure, both to a recipient nation's internal conditions and to its evolving situation in the world economy.

Appropriateness takes several forms. First, there is the appropriateness of the technology used in a development project. Machinery and equipment marketed by first world firms may be appropriate for the countries where it was developed, but not at all appropriate when taken to the third world: Local resources may be different (e.g., gas stoves may be useless if natural gas is hard to come by); the environmental impact of the technology may be different (e.g., topsoil may be ruined by plowing too deeply, or forests by clear-cutting); the scale of the technology may be much too large ("small is beautiful"); or local labor skills may not match the knowledge necessary to operate the technology.

Although skills can be learned, it does not follow that acquiring the skills to operate a new technology is the most appropriate use of local residents' skills and knowledge. We have seen that third world residents have a sophisticated knowledge of local conditions, evolving practices, rules, and skills to make the most of these. Local knowledge is not necessarily superior; changing local conditions, an increased integration into national and global processes, and a lack of opportunity to judge the long-term consequences of short-term decisions can all make local knowledge fallible or out of date. Local residents are adept at identifying when imported technologies are inappropriate, and may respond by ignoring them or simply by persisting with tried and true approaches. Although donors may dismiss this as ignorance, in many cases their decision turns out to be in fact the best one. An unwillingness to adopt imported technologies may often be the result of realizing its limitations in the local context, or its inability to supplant current practices adequately, rather than any lack of understanding of how to use it (Blaut, 1987).

Imported knowledge may provide access to materials, practices, and approaches that can be combined effectively with local knowledge to significantly improve local residents' well-being, but it is necessary to integrate an understanding of local conditions and practices with that of the imported ones. Several small-scale projects have succeeded in using first world knowledge to develop novel and appropriate local technologies by combining the expertise of locals and nonlocals, rather than by imposing the latter's expertise on the former. Developing technology in this way is a time-consuming and delicate process, however, and does not easily lead to the large-scale profitability that corporations expect from the new products and processes they develop in a first world context. Furthermore, the local representatives and political contacts used to diffuse imported technologies within third world nations frequently have more interest in the money to be made than in the appropriateness of technologies.

A second way in which the appropriateness of foreign aid must be assessed is in terms of the types of projects supported. Although the countries seeking foreign aid would like to have the money made available for any purpose that they judge appropriate, those offering the aid have insisted on determining how it will be used. The vast majority of bilateral and multilateral aid is provided under the condition that it be spent on a particular project approved by the donor (Colman and Nixson, 1986: 186). Usually this has meant that aid is provided for specific projects: building the Aswan Dam in Egypt; implementing the transmigration resettlement program in Indonesia; improving shanty towns in Colombia; or underwriting the Green Revolution in India. Many of these projects have involved the construction of large pieces of physical infrastructure, providing large and prestigious technological achievements to enhance the reputation of recipient politicians. Too often, however, they have not brought the scope of development promised, and have had unintended and undesirable social and environmental side effects (see the discussion of dams in Chapter 7). Thus there has been a gradual shift toward smaller-scale and less visible projects, such as improvement of shanty towns.

When countries seeking aid propose a number of possible projects, a donor country will typically carry out a cost–benefit analysis of these alternatives, picking those that are judged to have the greatest estimated net benefits. From the donor's viewpoint, this is an attempt to ensure that the money is used in ways the donor sees as productive. Yet there is considerable controversy about the adequacy of cost–benefit analysis as a way of judging potential benefits from a project. A cost–benefit analysis attempts to convert all costs and benefits associated with a project into money, and then subtracts the costs from the benefits to obtain a "bottom line" estimate of its net benefits. In order to do this, it is necessary to identify all the potential costs and benefits; to place a monetary value on phenomena that are not usually measured in monetary terms (what is the monetary value of a life saved, of secondary education, of birth control, of an acre of rainforest?); and to calculate the "discount rate" (e.g., what is a $1,000 benefit in the year 2015 worth in today's money?). Given the wide range of social and environmental changes associated with development, and given that these must be examined over a long time period, estimates of the discount rate and of the value of nonmonetary phenomena can have a crucial impact on whether the cost–benefit analysis has a positive or a negative outcome.

Such estimates are necessarily subjective; they are based on the perceptions of the (often first world) cost–benefit analysts and on economic assumptions stressing free competition. This also assumes that development is best measured in monetary terms. For example, the value of a man who is prevented from contracting AIDS may be measured in terms of the savings in hospital costs, plus the value of the wages he may make for the extra years he can work. Valuing his life in terms of wages presumes that his value to society depends on his wages, and not on his many other potential contributions.

Such analyses are often readily accepted by political and economic elites in third world nations, despite the technical criticisms that have been made (Mishan, 1967). They argue that any foreign aid is better than no aid, so there is little choice but to accept the conditions under which donor countries are willing to offer it. Many members of political and economic elites have studied in first world universities, where they have learned to accept the assumptions behind such analyses. Furthermore, there are significant personal financial benefits for individuals in third world nations who act as local representatives and facilitators for such projects, and members of political and economic elites are in the best position to receive such benefits. (This is not simply a third world problem. Consider the many stories of political corruption in the United States.)

Recognizing the problems of using cost–benefit analysis to pick foreign aid projects does not mean, however, that such analyses are irrelevant, or that any project supported by a third world government should be picked. What may be good from the perspective of the government (avoiding social unrest, ensuring the support of influential elites or foreign states) may have little to do with development. It does, however, point to the necessity for critical analysis of how such decisions are made, from a perspective that seriously attends to the development perceptions and needs of those with little access to state decision makers. From the perspective of potential recipients, first world views of what is appropriate too often take precedence over third world views. This attitude on the part of first world donors is bound up with the postcolonial mentality that the wealthy countries know what is best for everyone else.

This brings up a third, deeper level at which the appropriateness of foreign aid must be judged: development ideology. In the early 1990s, there was a shift away from needs- and project-based lending toward lending tied to neoliberal reforms in third world countries, as coordination of foreign aid among first world nations increased under the auspices of the OECD, and with the emergence in first world nations of neoliberal development discourses. In its 1992 report, the OECD argued that foreign aid should be oriented toward facilitating the operation of free markets at an international scale, arguing that free competition is the best guarantor of development in the third world:

> The long term interests of the OECD countries are inextricably bound up with the effective functioning of the global economy. . . . These basic conditions cannot be achieved without substantial political, economic, and social development in the developing countries. . . . The new orientation of many developing countries towards democracy and market-based economic strategies creates a historic opportunity to achieve a more secure and prosperous world. . . . Developing countries committed to market-based reforms, democratization, and good government should be given priority in the allocation of development assistance. . . . Encouragingly, the dialogue indicates that the developing countries themselves—especially in Latin America and Africa—are taking the lead in supporting change. . . . Donors should therefore limit investments in public enterprises and focus institutional support on areas that help foster competition and the private sector and that improve a government's ability to provide basic social services. . . . The concerns and culture of aid agencies are thus drawing closer to those of policy makers in other areas. (OECD, 1992: 8, 9, 19, 31, 32, 49)

In short, it was argued that ODA should now be coordinated more closely with other global policies aimed at enhancing market-oriented development (Chapter 5); that this would benefit both donor and recipient nations; that aid should complement, rather than substitute for, market forces; and that such shifts would coordinate the practice of foreign aid more closely with structural adjustment policies (see below). Although donors consider the internal conditions of third world nations and their situation in the global economy as important factors in examining the kinds of economic changes to which a market-oriented approach may lead, they do not question the overall desirability of this approach. A further shift occurred between 2001 and 2008, as the Bush administration led a global push to tie foreign aid to antiterrorist initiatives.

Of course, donor countries will shape the conditions under which their money is released for foreign aid. The appropriateness of the aid will depend on whether the technologies, projects, and development philosophies of the donor nations do indeed foster the welfare of residents of recipient nations. When donor countries define the appropriateness of their terms according to their notion of development, then this amounts to propagating a diffusionist approach to development (Chapter 4). A better guarantee for appropriate foreign aid would be a genuine exchange of ideas and perspectives between donor organizations and the citizens of recipient nations whose welfare is the target of the aid. Such an exchange would not presume the superiority of first world models of development, but would critically examine their appropriateness.

BANK LENDING, DEBT, AND CRISES

The provision of credit essentially entails borrowing money from where there is a surplus and lending it where there is a shortage. This involves moving money from one sector or region to another, but also from one point in time to another. As we have seen in Figure 23.2, private lending to the third world twice grew rapidly when cash was abundant worldwide, but in each case a crisis followed the boom. The 1973–1982 petrodollar boom engendered a third world debt crisis of global proportions, vastly magnifying the long-term challenge of raising funds to finance economic growth. The 1990s saw an explosive growth of private liquidity in the system, which is believed to be partly responsible for a series of financial crises in Mexico, Thailand, Indonesia, South Korea, and (most recently) Argentina.

Financial crises are no longer exceptional, but rather a latent systemic issue in this era of globalized economic transactions. They are not confined to a small number of countries with scandalous political economic affairs; more than 130 countries experienced either financial crises or serious banking problems between 1980 and 1995. Here we discuss two representative cases of financial crises in the 1980s and 1990s: the 1980s debt crisis and the 1997 Asian financial crisis.

Petrodollars and the 1980s Debt Crisis

From 1978 to 1982, third world current account deficits exploded. Banks were flush with petrodollars to be recirculated; increasing commodity prices and rapidly growing NICs during the late 1970s made banks optimistic about the third world; and non-OPEC third world countries needed cash to pay the high prices charged for oil imports.

The surplus of capital combined with a shortage of conventional opportunities meant that investors did not always carefully examine the risk of lending to third world nations, or the difficulty of realizing projects for which the money was lent. Financial institutions generally lend more money than they have, but in 1980 they were lending between 14 and 30 times as much money as they possessed, two-thirds of which was being lent to the third world (Watson, Methieson, Kincaid, and Kalter, 1986: 28, 94). A few third world nations were able to borrow easily, almost at will. According to a former director of the Bank of Brazil, Brazil had an "automatic" line of credit to obtain $1.5 billion a month in new loans up to the middle of 1982 (Brett, 1985: 294). From the perspective of third world countries, rates of inflation (because of the oil crisis) exceeded the rates of interest on the loans that were negotiated, meaning that the effective rate of interest (the rate of interest minus the rate of inflation) was negative (Colman and Nixson, 1986: 194). This created the impression that the loan would be easy to pay back.

The geographical distribution of long-term loan commitments within the third world was highly uneven. In 1979–1981, about 60% of all long-term bank loan commitments for the third world went to just five countries (Argentina, Brazil, Mexico, South Korea, and Venezuela) (Watson et al., 1986). Other third world nations, unable to convince international banks of their creditworthiness, had little success in obtaining long-term financing. The entire continent of Africa obtained just $4.8 billion in long-term loan commitments in 1979—less than half the money committed to Mexico alone.

Although both lenders and borrowers were optimistic about the prospects of repayment in the late 1970s, circumstances changed, to the considerable disadvantage of third world borrowers. First, the United States implemented policies to protect the declining value of the dollar in the late

1970s, resulting in an increased value of the dollar and in greatly increased interest rates (see Chapter 22). When the value of the dollar increased, so did the effective size of the debts, almost all of which were in dollars. In Mexico in 1982, for example, the exchange rate of pesos per dollar almost doubled, meaning that its external debts also almost doubled as a fraction of Mexico's gross domestic product (GDP). Almost all long-term loans had been negotiated on terms that included adjustable interest rates, meaning that the interest due in any year was indexed to general interest rates in that year. Catalyzed by U.S. Federal Reserve Bank policy, world interest rates rose in the early 1980s, meaning that the amount of interest to be paid on outstanding long-term loans also increased. Effective rates of interest (the real costs of paying back loans) increased even more rapidly than nominal interest rates, from negative values as low as –9% in 1979 to a positive rate of 22% in 1982 (Corbridge, 1993: 39).

These finance market developments were coupled with developments in international trade that reduced the amount of export income countries were making (income needed to pay off debts). The prices of primary commodities, led by oil prices, fell significantly in the early 1980s, reducing the income to be made from primary commodity exports. First world nations also significantly decreased their demand for third world manufactures—in part because of a general reduction in demand during economic crises, and in part because of policies increasing tariff barriers in order to protect first world industrial jobs from cheaper third world imports. In short, the debt burden increased, while export incomes needed to pay these debts were stagnating. Between 1973 and 1983, the outstanding debt owed by third world nations increased fivefold, to $810 billion (Cuddington and Smith, 1985: 3).

Another kind of private financial flow became extremely important during this period: "capital flight." This refers to economic, political, or military elites' moving their personal wealth (however gained) abroad to Swiss banks or other OFCs, where it escapes taxes and state supervision. This makes it unavailable for domestic investment or for reducing the national debt. Rojas-Súarez (1991) estimates that capital flight from 13 (mostly Latin American) countries rose from $47 billion a year in 1978 to $100 billion in 1982, when the first debt crisis started, and to $184 billion in 1988, by which time it amounted to more than three-quarters of the external debt of those countries.

There were scattered renegotiations of payment schedules for nations that had fallen behind in the late 1970s, but things came to a head in August 1982 when Mexico, one of the major debtors, announced that it could no longer pay its debts and asked for a 3-month moratorium on repayments (later extended). Mexico would have needed to spend nearly half of its export income just to pay its debt obligations (i.e., the sum of principal and interest on loans coming due) for that year. The situation was even worse elsewhere. Argentina's debt service amounted to 83% of its export income, and in Brazil the figure was 103% (Edwards, 1988: Table 12)! The average for the 19 largest debtor countries was 31%, much greater than the 15% average for all third world countries (Figure 23.5).

Most of these countries were running a trade deficit, making it all but impossible to pay their debts. Brazil sought a moratorium on repayment in November, followed by Venezuela in February 1983, and then Chile, Peru, Ecuador, Uruguay, and 20 other countries by the end of 1983 (Figure 23.6). This was not only a crisis for the debtor countries; at least as importantly, it was a crisis for many major private financial institutions, and thereby for the entire global financial system. Forty-nine percent of all third world debt was owed to private institutions by 1982 (McFadden, Eckhaus, Feder, Hajivassilou, and O'Connell, 1985: 185), and some of the signature international

FIGURE 23.5. Debt service as a percentage of export income, 1983. *Source:* Data are from World Resources Institute (1988).

FIGURE 23.6. Diffusion of private debt rescheduling, 1979–1984. *Source:* Data are from Corbridge (1993: 52).

banks were heavily overinvested in the third world. The debts owed by Mexico to the nine largest U.S. banks in 1981 amounted to 50% of the total capital possessed by those banks, with a further 45% owed by Brazil and 20% by Argentina. Thus loans to these three countries alone exceeded these banks' assets by 15%, and by the end of 1984 the overhang had grown to 32% (Corbridge, 1993). Smaller first world banks were similarly exposed (Guttentag and Herring, 1985: 130–131).

Even conservative analysts feared that the international financial system could not survive defaults by major third world debtors, and a series of acrimonious negotiations ensued to delay repayments or refinance the loans. These involved the banks and the countries seeking moratoria, but also the IMF and first world governments, which were being asked to support bridging loans to debtor countries in order to defuse the crisis. It was hard for third world governments simply to refuse to pay back their loans. They still required external funds for development, and defaults would have made it impossible to borrow again in the future—not to mention potential first world retaliation in other international arenas, such as trade embargoes or seizure of foreign exchange reserves (as against Iraq and other "rogue" nations in the 1990s). Banks certainly were willing to restructure loan agreements, since partial payment was better than none, but third world nations had to pay a price for this.

Beyond its effect on livelihoods in the third world, the 1980s debt crisis catalyzed a dramatic change in the role of and influence over third world governments. It provided an opportunity for the World Bank and the IMF, recent converts from state-led development to neoliberal principles, to initiate "structural adjustment" programs. The IMF played a major role in brokering the Mexico debt renegotiation and most of the subsequent ones. Although these institutions did not lend a lot of money, their stamp of approval was necessary for third world countries to attract other lenders. Under structural adjustment (see below), they compelled third world states to move away from state-led to market-friendly development strategies. Only South Korea—with its high degree of state steering of the economy, including a large deficit in public spending and heavy involvement in the financing of industrial enterprises—was able to avoid such a restructuring (Park, 1985). (Measures were also taken to prevent a recurrence of the heavy exposure of international banks to risky loans to third world countries, including stronger regulation of lender behavior and a greater international integration of financial markets.)

Banks responded by imposing their own moratorium on lending to third world nations. Private lending dropped by 90% between 1982 and 1987 (Corbridge, 1993), even though the needs of third world nations had increased. The burden placed on governments and on multinational institutions by this withdrawal of the private sector led to two U.S. proposals in the mid-1980s, directed at the debt problems of the large debtor nations. The Baker Plan in 1985 called on private banks to join with the IMF in providing increased lending to nations agreeing to adopt structural adjustment, but the banks refused to cooperate, further reducing their lending. The Brady Plan of 1989 tried to place this lack of interest in a positive light by praising banks for their willingness to reduce debts. The Brady Plan called on the IMF and the World Bank, with help from Japan, to commit substantial funds to defray the costs that large debtors would have to pay to reduce their debts to private banks. Banks could choose from a number of options, including writing off a third of the value of the debt; allowing the debtor to buy back the debt at a cash discount; and "debt–equity" or "debt–nature" swaps, in which banks would be granted ownership of economic activities or land in the debtor country in lieu of outstanding debts. This last option proved the most popular. Banks benefited from such arrangements, gaining both property and substantial fees in return for agreeing to reduce debts that were practically unpayable. After the 1980s crisis, banks shifted their strategies to emphasizing loans and offering banking services to the world's approximately eight million high-net-worth individuals, wherever they are located, known in the trade as "hen-wees" (Christensen, 2007).

The 1997 Asian Financial Crisis

The early 1990s saw the emergence of a new global financial environment where private capital flows increased dramatically, replacing previously dominant official flows (Ito and Krueger, 2001). From 1994 on, there was a huge increase in global liquidity (McKinsey Global Institute, 2007); this flowed towards parts of the third world (rapidly growing economies in southeast Asia, India, and Latin America), and the former second world of eastern Europe (Mukherjea, 1999). Initially everything seemed fine, as money surpluses in the first world were reinvested in, and facilitated the growth of, these countries. In return, bankers in developed economies earned higher returns than domestic ones. But money does not always make the world go around. It sometimes panics the world, creating what becomes labeled as a "crisis."

Since the late 1980s, surplus liquidity in the first world started to find opportunities in southeast Asian countries. Thailand was one of the early beneficiaries of cheap credit flows into the region, recording over 8% real GDP growth on average during the first half of the 1990s. Exports expanded by nearly 20% annually during this period, and the stock and property markets boomed. However, boom turned to bust when trade deficits started to mount in 1995, and when the stock and property markets started to collapse in late 1996. Many loans, especially those related to stock and property markets, became nonperforming (meaning that the borrowers could not pay the interest, much less the principal). As a result, many financial firms experienced losses from nonperforming loans and even failed. In March 1997, it was announced that the largest financial company in Thailand, Finance One, troubled by the property loan crises, would be rescued by the 12th largest, Thai Danu Bank. The failure of Finance One precipitated the collapse of the stock market, and the Stock Exchange of Thailand had to suspend transactions of banks, nonbank financial institutions, and securities companies' stocks.

Another panic situation developed in the currency market. Before 1997, the Thai baht was pegged to the U.S. dollar at around 25 baht per dollar. When the economic slowdown in Thailand became apparent in 1996, financial firms (including hedge funds) undertook a series of speculative attacks on the baht. Defending against these threats to its value, the Bank of Thailand used almost two-thirds of the entire foreign reserves to buy baht in the market. They also raised the interest rate to 19.5% by the end of June 1997. These government interventions stabilized the baht exchange rate until July 1997, when the Thai government announced a shift to a floating exchange rate system and let the baht float against other currencies. The baht exchange rate fell to 40 baht per dollar by October, at which point Thailand was in the middle of a full-fledged financial crisis that started to affect neighboring countries, the hardest hit being Indonesia and South Korea.

Another form of economic turmoil was already unfolding in South Korea. Although macroeconomic indicators showed no signs of trouble, the South Korean economy had warning signs including high debt-to-equity ratios and low profitability in its *chaebols* (Korean business conglomerates) in the first half of the 1990s, alongside rapid accumulation of short-term liabilities to foreigners and deteriorating bank balance sheets (Mishkin, 2006). Warning signs became a reality in 1997 when six *chaebols* underwent bankruptcy, including Kia and Hanbo (ranked 8th and 14th, respectively). The bankruptcies of *chaebols* and other companies shook the financial sector, as foreign lenders decided not to extend the maturity dates of their loans to South Korean banks, and foreign investors started to withdraw their money from the stock market (Mishkin, 2006). The South Korean government attempted to intervene to restore the stability of the financial system, but turned out to be short-handed, as few currency reserves were left. Thus when the tide of crisis reached South Korea in October, its government was nearly helpless, able only to raise interest rates in its defense of the financial system against the stock market crash and speculative attacks on the Korean won. However, high interest rates triggered further bankruptcies of small and medium-size firms that had little financial buffer against external shocks. In just 2 months, the Korea Composite Stock Price Index was halved in value to 500, and the won lost 47% of its value. The South Korean economy plunged into negative 5.4% growth in the second half of 1997, and the government had no choice but to embrace IMF structural reforms in return for what was then the largest bailout package in history ($58 billion).

The damage had been done. The effect of the economic crisis extended far beyond crashing stock indexes and depreciated currencies. Unemployment in South Korea skyrocketed from less than 3% in 1997 to 7% in 1998. In particular, unskilled manual workers lost almost 13% of their jobs, and manufacturing workers suffered a 4.1% wage cut. As a result, income inequality widened between the rich and the poor (Moon, 1999). Economic hardships in turn took tolls on social life, as suicides and divorces rose by nearly 50%, and drug addiction and the crime rate increased dramatically (Mishkin, 2006). In other words, the Asian financial crisis was as much a social crisis as an economic one.

Capital flight again played a role during and after the 1997 crisis. Beja (2006) shows that capital flight from southeast Asia grew with neoliberal globalization, showing a small peak after the first debt crisis, but a much larger peak after the Asian crisis (see also Epstein, 2005). As of 2002, the stock of capital flight from Indonesia, Malaysia, the Philippines, and Thailand had reached $1 trillion, three times the size of these countries' external debt. More generally, Henry (2007) estimates that capital flight from the third world averaged $160 billion annually (in 2000 dollars) between 1977 and 2003, amounting to an accumulated wealth significantly exceeding the external debt of these countries since 1998. In short, if these elites had invested their money at home, their countries would not be in debt.

Explaining the 1990s Crises

Mainstream economists argue that the 1997 Asian crisis and other 1990s financial crises (including the European currency crisis of 1992–1993 and the Mexican peso crisis of 1994) differed from the 1982 debt crisis. They attribute the earlier (so-called "balance-of-payments") crisis to deteriorating trade deficits and capital flight, but argue that the 1990s crises were compounded by unstable exchange rates due to rapid short-term speculative international capital movements (Ito and Krueger, 2001). Drastic currency depreciation and the resulting financial fragility created panic.

But there are three views of what exactly caused the 1990s crises. "Fundamentalists" argue that weakening economic fundamentals, especially deteriorating trade deficits and lack of financial governance, are to blame (Ito and Krueger, 2001). In this view, the Asian countries practiced "crony capitalism" (Corsetti, Pesenti, and Roubini, 1999). At the corporate level, cozy relations between government and business created a moral hazard, as financial firms made investments to firms without properly evaluating the riskiness of projects "under the impression that the return on investment was somewhat 'insured' against adverse shocks" (Corsetti et al., 1999: 307). For example, in 1996 20 out of the 30 largest *chaebols* in South Korea recorded profit rates that were lower than their cost of capital, and seven were considered bankrupt. On the financial side, the dominance in Asia of relationship banking meant that investment decisions were based on the nature of bank–customer relationships rather than on market signals. Thus loans were continually extended to companies despite deteriorating profitability. Capital market liberalization and cheap capital inflows compounded overlending and the accumulation of nonperforming loans. International banks aggravated this problem by excessively lending to domestic financial firms of crisis-affected countries without proper risk assessment. In 1996, "the ratio of short term external liabilities to foreign reserve—a widely used indicator of financial fragility—was above 100 percent in Korea, Indonesia and Thailand" (Corsetti et al., 1999: 308). This analysis called into question the Asian development model, and was used to legitimize the following aspects of IMF-induced structural reform, even in South Korea (Republic of Korea, 1997):

- Tightened monetary and fiscal policy: a regime of high interest rates.
- Reform of the financial sector: strengthened supervision; timely exits by troubled firms; conformity to the Basel standard; and accelerated entry by foreign financial institutions.
- Trade liberalization.
- Capital account liberalization.
- Transparent corporate governance and corporate structure; reform of *chaebols*.

These measures were intended to transplant the Anglo-American model of capitalism to Asia, and to integrate the region into the "best practices" of neoliberalism. However, even some IMF insiders disagreed with this approach, notably its own chief economist, Joseph Stiglitz:

> The last set of financial crises had occurred in Latin America in the 1980s. . . . There, the IMF had correctly imposed fiscal austerity. . . . So, in 1997 the IMF imposed the same demands on Thailand. . . . As the crisis spread to other East Asian nations—and even as evidence of the policy's failure mounted—the IMF barely blinked, delivering the same medicine to each ailing nation that showed up on its doorstep. . . . I thought this was a mistake. . . . The problem was not imprudent government, as in Latin America; the problem was an imprudent private sector—all those bankers and borrowers, for instance, who'd gambled on the real estate bubble. . . . High interest rates might devastate highly indebted East Asian firms, causing more bankruptcies and defaults. Reduced government expenditures would only shrink the economy further. (Stiglitz, 2000: 56)

"Institutionalists" have argued that financial crises were not confined to so-called crony capitalist countries in Asia, so more general explanations are necessary. Webber (2001) suggests that the crisis in Asia was attributable to the emerging nature of finance. First, financial flows were no longer counterbalancing commodity flows but were self-perpetuating, changing the value of money and assets in their destination countries. They were also continually exposed to manipulations and speculations; consequently, financial flows became increasingly independent from the dynamics of the real economy. Chang, Park, and Yoo (1998) argue, by contrast, that the crisis was due to the dismantling of the Asian development model. They argue that financial liberalization and weakened governance made the economy vulnerable to external shocks. Highly critical of IMF-induced one-size-fits-all neoliberal reform, they stress the need for state action to ameliorate often erratic global financial flows.

The "capitalist crisis school" analyzes why crises continue to occur despite many policy prescriptions aimed at minimizing crises through coordinated efforts by governments and international organizations. Drawing on empirical evidence of overaccumulation since the 1970s, Harvey (2003) contends that that these crises are normal products of the workings of capitalism. He argues that surpluses in the capitalist system are absorbed through a "spatio-temporal fix." By this, he means a combination of "temporal displacement through investment in long-term capital projects or social expenditures . . . [and] spatial displacements through opening up new markets, new production capacities, and new resource, social, and labour possibilities elsewhere" (Harvey, 2003: 109). Overaccumulation in the primary circuit of capital (the realm of immediate production and consumption) can be absorbed by the secondary circuit (fixed capital—e.g., plant and equipment, and housing) or the tertiary circuit (social infrastructure—e.g., health care and education), but overaccumulation in the latter two circuits can trigger "more general crises"(Harvey, 2003: 112). He argues that the Asian financial crisis was a localized devaluation that was part of "a cascading and proliferating series of spatio-temporal fixes" throughout regions outside the triad of the United States, Japan, and Europe. This enabled the capitalist system to avoid major setbacks at the expense of instability in regional economies, as capital is continually redirected between places. Such "switching crises" (Harvey, 2003: 121) were facilitated by free-flowing finance capital. As international competition escalates, "either the weakest succumb and fall into serious crises of localized devaluation or geopolitical struggles arise between regions" (2003: 124).

Responding to Financial Crises

Policy responses to financial crises since the 1980s have been largely shaped by the neoliberal discourses of major international financial institutions, including the Bank of International Settlements (BIS) and the IMF. The BIS had been set up in the 1930s to cope with financial instability, but was almost abolished by the Bretton Woods negotiators. It reemerged as a meeting place for central bankers when the Bretton Woods system collapsed in the early 1970s. The BIS shares its promarket ideology with the Bretton Woods institutions but goes further in insisting on the role of a regulatory environment for proper workings of markets (Patomäki, 2001). For instance, the BIS responded to the 1980s debt crisis by implementing the capital adequacy ratio (the so-called "BIS ratio") to monitor the risk exposure of the internationally active banks that partially caused the crisis. These new regulatory tools were easily circumvented by new types of financial firms and products, however, and financial crises recurred throughout the 1990s. Recurring financial crises have not changed anything within the governing organizations. In the aftermath of the Asian financial crisis, Tony Blair and Gordon Brown (then U.K. Prime Minister and Chancellor of the Exchequer, respectively) argued that the revision of the existing BIS-centered regime and enhanced coordination between the IMF and World Bank would be sufficient to create a new and safer global financial regime (Patomäki, 2001). However, yet another crisis occurred in Argentina, which had followed the stipulated procedures for developing a sound financial system (Mishkin, 2006).

Other problems in the present neoliberal governance regime are the ways in which ideas and interests are mediated and reproduced within the Bretton Woods organizations. Tickell (2000: 96; emphasis in original) argues that the promarket regulatory regime entails the danger of bias by representing mainly the view of the Wall Street–U.S. Treasury–IMF complex:

> This is geopolitically important even when the proposals represent a sensible technocratic response because they are not only a response to American—and sometimes European—particularities, but the only place in which serious debate can be made is *within* already powerful states. Just as with other aspects of the emergent international rule regime, there remains a very real danger that international rules normalize American and Euro-American interests, as well as practices.

L'Association pour la Taxation des Transactions pour l'Aide aux Citoyens (ATTAC) represents one of the most active NGOs contesting this neoliberal global finance regime. Originating with an editorial in the French newspaper *Le Monde Diplomatique* at the peak of the Asian financial crisis in December 1997, its main objective has been to introduce a "Tobin tax" to curb speculative financial flows. Bernard Cassen (2004: 156) defines ATTAC as an "action oriented movement for popular education." It has spread throughout the European Union (EU), Canada, African and Latin American countries, and Japan. The Tobin tax is named after American economist and Nobel laureate James Tobin, who proposed a tax on financial transactions, warning that "excessive international—or better, inter-currency—mobility of private financial capital" poses a danger to macroeconomic stability and national economic autonomy (Tobin, 1978: 153). He suggested that the excessive mobility of capital would transmit economic disturbances through massive foreign exchange transactions, forcing national governments to sacrifice other economic policy objectives (Patomäki, 2001). He recommended that a small tax on all currency transactions would slow down capital mobility. Spahn (1996) has proposed amending the Tobin tax scheme by introducing a two-tier tax system, in which a minimal tax rate will be applied to most regular transactions, with surcharges charged in time of speculative attacks.

Critics argue that the finance industry would find ways to evade such restrictions by developing new financial products or shifting the location of transactions to tax havens, with the implication that a Tobin tax may create liquidity problems without deterring speculative transactions with substantially higher profit margins than tax rates. The possibility of tax evasion should not mean giving up on the idea of taxing financial transactions, however (Patomäki, 2001). The Tobin tax is not a panacea for current financial anomalies, but is one easy way of creating space for alternative financial regimes that would require new ideas and contest existing norms and customs.

In 2001, at the end of the second crisis (Figure 23.2), the overall distribution of third world debt levels still matched that at the height of the 1980s debt crisis (compare Figure 23.7 with Figure 23.5). The only difference was that this indebtedness had become geographically more widespread, across Africa and the former second world. Sixty-three countries labored under either large debts or large debt burdens (Figure 23.8). Nearly $3.7 trillion in debt was generating $550 billion in annual debt service payments to lenders. In 2006, the world's 60 poorest countries paid $41 billion annually to service their debts—approximately the value of the foreign aid they received (Christensen, 2007). This was despite attempts since 1997 to reduce indebtedness (see the next section).

Not all influential financial measures have emerged from first world policymakers and the international financial institutions, however. First, Bangladesh's Grameen Bank has gained notice for its practice of lending money to poor, often female, potential entrepreneurs. The poor have often proven to be good credit risks who use these loans wisely (see sidebar: "Lending to the Poor"). This approach, now known as "microfinance," has spread around the third world and also to the first world. Second, Venezuela and five other Latin American countries opened an alternative international finance institution, Banco del Sur, in December 2007, with $7 billion in initial assets. Third, a number of third world countries have begun "sovereign-wealth funds"—state-run investment funds used to invest in domestic development and companies abroad. *The Economist* (2007) estimates that such funds (85% of which are of Third World origin) could approach $12 trillion by 2015.

MULTILATERAL LENDING: THE IMF, THE WORLD BANK, AND STRUCTURAL ADJUSTMENT

There are many multinational institutions for funneling money to different parts of the

FIGURE 23.7. Debt service as a percentage of export income, 2001. *Source:* Data are from World Bank (2003: Table 4.17).

FIGURE 23.8. Large debtors and large debt burdens, 2001. *Source:* Data are from World Bank (2003: Table 4.16).

Lending to the Poor

Nurjahan was married at 12, but was abandoned by her husband a year later, 3 months pregnant. She returned to the family that had raised her, working as a cook while raising her son. She was landless, and had never earned more than $37.50 a year until she was offered a loan by the Grameen Bank. Five years after that loan, her annual income was $250; she owned two goats, a pregnant cow, 10 hens, and two-thirds of an acre of land (which she had purchased for $1,000); and she employed two farmhands to assist with the rice harvest.

The Grameen Bank was founded in 1983 by Muhammad Yunus (for which he received the 2006 Nobel Peace Prize), a professor of economics in the city of Chittagong, Bangladesh, after he met Sophia Katoon, a 22-year-old furniture maker working 7 days a week. Sophia looked twice her age and lived in abject poverty, because she had to sell her output to a money lender in return for borrowing money to pay for her inputs. With a loan from Professor Yunus of a few dollars, within a few months Sophia had increased her income seven times and repaid the loan. Calculating that she was paying money lenders more than 3,000% interest a year, Professor Yunus founded the Grameen Bank to provide "microcredit" loans to the poorest of the poor. Average loans of a little more than $100 were made without requiring collateral or security from the borrower. The borrower also determined which business activity to use the loan for, and the bank helped make this successful. Rates of interest were only as high as needed to keep the bank solvent. Borrowers purchased one, and only one, share in the bank apiece; together, they owned 98% of its shares, and received dividends on any profits made.

In October 1983, the Grameen Bank Project was transformed into an independent bank by government legislation. It is owned by the rural poor. Its borrowers own 90% of its shares, with the remaining 10% owned by the government. Today, the Grameen Bank operates in 95% of the villages of Bangladesh, loaning over $722 million annually to 7.2 million borrowers (see *www.grameen-info.org*). Ninety-seven percent of these are women, in part because they are poor, and in part because they have proven to be exceptionally reliable and successful in using the loans to develop microenterprises. Ninety-eight percent of all loans have been repaid on time, and 54% of borrowers have raised their incomes above the poverty line.

The bank's startling success, confounding the principles of banking, has launched imitators and a current fascination with "microcredit" worldwide. On the one hand, it has empowered poor people, particularly women, to succeed as entrepreneurs. On the other hand, it fosters market-based approaches to poverty production, resonating with recent emphases on poverty reduction in the World Bank (Weber, 2002).

world, but the Bretton Woods institutions remain most influential (see Chapter 15). The World Bank provides long-term development assistance and investment funds (i.e., loans with a maturity of more than 5 years) to nations in need, supplemented by loans made available through bilateral arrangements between countries. Aside from the actions of UN agencies, two of the three World Bank affiliates—the International Bank for Reconstruction and Development (IBRD) and the International Development Association (IDA)—provide the majority of all multilateral development finance. The IMF, charged with making short-term financial loans to countries with balance-of-payments problems, makes smaller loans, but has become central to multilateral lending schemes throughout the third and the former second worlds.

The World Bank and the IMF are similar institutions with complementary tasks—so similar in their history, structure, and policies that they are virtually twin institutions. They opened for business in 1947, with 44 mostly first world member nations. Since then, the number of members has grown to 185 as of 2007—with third world nations joining during the 1960s and 1970s, and nations from the former second world in the late 1980s and early 1990s. The two institutions are housed across the street from each other in Washington, D.C. The president of the World Bank is from the United States, appointed by the U.S. President, whereas the executive director of the IMF is European (with a U.S.-appointed deputy director). This provides some balance of power among two-thirds of the triad of first world regions. Their political decision-making systems and systems of financing are also broadly equivalent. Each institution is financed in the first instance by money lent to it by the national governments of member countries. When its members vote on actions to be taken by the institution, the vote of each nation is weighted by the size of its contribution. Since first world nations have lent the bulk of these assets, the World Bank and the IMF are very much first world institutions, despite their international charters (Peet, 2003).

The International Monetary Fund

The IMF was founded to promote international monetary collaboration, based on the Bretton Woods assumption that global development is best achieved through the free trade of commodities and the full convertibility of currencies. Prior to World War II, first world nations had manipulated their exchange rates in order to steer trade and achieve a trade balance, offering different rates to different trading partners. It was agreed at Bretton Woods, under U.S. pressure, that free trade should be based on the free market principle of comparative advantage rather than on government action, and that universal, fixed exchange rates for all nations were necessary to achieve this goal. The IMF was intended to oversee making national currencies convertible in this sense, and to deal with any problems that might ensue. It monitors a code of conduct agreed to by member countries, requiring members to inform or consult with the IMF whenever they introduce policies that influence the balance of payments or otherwise affect monetary conditions in other member countries. In the event that member countries run out of international currencies to pay for imports, the IMF is also given a certain amount of money from which it can make short-term loans (on a less-than-3-year basis) to deal with such cash flow crises.

Each of the IMF's 185 member countries provides a contribution, called its "quota," to the capital base of the IMF. The size of this contribution is fixed by a country's GDP, its international monetary reserves, and payments and receipts on its national account. Three-quarters of the contribution must be in international currencies, and the remainder in its own domestic currency. A member's quota is thus closely related to the size of its economy, which both determines the influence of a member over IMF lending policies and sets limits on the amount of money it can borrow. All lending policies must be approved by a 20-member executive board—including one member from each of the five countries with the largest quota, one from each of the two largest borrowers from the previous year, and 13 others elected at large by the members. The number of votes a country has in this at-large election is proportional to the size of its quota. When the executive board votes on lending policies, its members also have unequal votes, in proportion to their own quotas (Payer, 1974: 218). Most decisions require an 85% majority (Girling, 1985: 96), which gives both the United States (with 17% of the votes) and the EU countries a de facto veto over lending decisions. The U.S. executive director is bound by law to vote according to the instructions of the U.S. Secretary of the Treasury (Strange, 1973: 284).

The amount that countries can borrow also depends on their quotas. In 2007, the IMF had approximately $327 billion in quotas, representing the approximate limit of its funding capacity. A country can borrow automatically up to 25% of its contribution (the "reserve tranche"), but if it wishes to borrow more it needs permission from the IMF, and must also conform to IMF conditions as part of this agreement (Torp, 1993).

Loans exceeding a member's quota by more than 25% require ongoing consultation with IMF experts, as well as agreement by that country to IMF "surveillance," or monitoring of how well the country conforms to IMF lending conditions.

Throughout the history of the IMF, an important condition has been attached to loans: They are only to be made if the country concerned adopts policies to deal with its financial problems that the IMF considers appropriate for stabilizing the balance of payments (Brett, 1985: 69). The nature of such IMF conditionality has varied over time, shifting in the 1980s from a Keynesian to a neoliberal philosophy (i.e., from state-led to market-oriented development).

Such conditions can only be imposed on member countries that are seeking to borrow from the IMF, but the imposition of such conditions is selective. Whereas third world countries, more recently former state socialist nations of the second world, and even the United Kingdom have had to accept such conditions to receive IMF money, the IMF has lent considerable amounts of money to the United States, financing 10% of the U.S. deficit between 1960 and 1967 without imposing stabilization conditions (Payer, 1974: 219). The IMF has shown no signs recently of imposing conditions on the United States, despite the unprecedented size and global impact of its current deficit. Even when conditions are imposed on loans to first world nations, they are frequently much less stringent than those required of the third world: "Information placed before the Executive Board [of the IMF] showed that the number of performance criteria in stand-by agreements for members in Latin America and Asia had on average been much greater than for members in Europe" (Dell, 1981: 12).

The World Bank

The World Bank was created in response to pressure for an institution capable of providing longer-term development assistance and investment funds to nations in need, beyond those made available through bilateral arrangements between countries. It has two main components. The IBRD was the original World Bank institution, and is charged with making development loans at slightly concessional rates. Its members subscribe with a specified share of the total assets of the IBRD. This share is proportional to the size of the member's economy and determines the proportion of votes held by a member. The United States, for example, contributes 17% of the total assets and has 17% of the votes over World Bank policies. Adding Canada, the EU, and Japan to the United States makes up a majority of all contributions and votes. While member contributions form a financial foundation for the IBRD, most of its funds are raised on world financial markets. The World Bank's excellent credit rating (it has never defaulted on a loan, has always made a profit, and is backed by the world's governments) allows it to borrow at rock-bottom rates on the private market, and to lend to countries at slightly lower interest rates than private institutions charge.

The limited size and geographical scope of IBRD loans led to the formation in 1962, under third world pressure, of the IDA. The IDA was set up to provide concessional financing to third world nations, with the finance coming largely from grants by World Bank member countries; its lending policies are governed by almost the same weighted voting system as that of the IBRD. IDA loans are highly concessional. There is no interest (but a 0.757% annual finance charge), and the first repayments on the loans are not due for 10 years. The money lent by the IDA steadily increased to reach 50% of all new World Bank lending in the early 1990s. Throughout, the lending strategy of the IBRD and the IDA has been to identify and finance specific development projects in third world countries—ones that, according to the World Bank's analysis, have a well-defined lifetime and a positive cost–benefit ratio.

The World Bank has often conformed to the wishes of the United States. A U.S. Treasury study in 1982 found that in the previous 10 years, the United States had been able to use its lending policies to ensure that World Bank lending was consistent with U.S. foreign policy on 85% of those decisions for which the United States had a specific objective it was pursuing (Girling, 1985). Initially, the IBRD's policies were conservative. It had to borrow much of its money in private financial markets, meaning that, like private banks, this money had to be lent at nonconcessional rates (although to a wider spectrum of countries and at the low end of commercial interest rates). The IBRD was very careful to lend only for projects that seemed beneficial according to standard financial principles, meaning that it favored secure, low-risk investments. In this early period, the majority of its loans were to first world nations damaged by World War II (many of which had signed the Bretton Woods agreement).

The development policies pursued by the World Bank diversified significantly during the 1970s. First, its research department began stressing the importance of the redistribution of wealth, and of supporting poorer families and enterprises in the informal sector, through a policy of "basic needs." In this view, development could be accelerated by providing for the basic needs of the least well off, rather than through liberalizing foreign trade and investment. This change of philosophy had only a limited effect on lending policies, however, and during the 1980s World Bank policies shifted back to promoting exports and liberalizing investment. Second, the World Bank's traditional lending strategy of financing specific projects became increasingly problematic, because too few projects were meeting its own criteria for success. Thus it began to diversify its activities, allowing up to 25% of its lending to be used for the more general purpose of long-term balance of payments financing in order to promote "structural adjustment" in third world economies (Brett, 1985: 293). This shift blurred the distinctions between World Bank and IMF activities, and marked the onset of a phase of unprecedented close cooperation between the two institutions in the 1980s as a joint structural adjustment policy developed.

Structural Adjustment

Structural adjustment was introduced by the World Bank as part of a loan to Jamaica in 1979 providing temporary balance-of-payments relief for escalating oil prices, and became more widespread beginning in 1982. It represented a convergence between the World Bank's lending policies and those of the IMF, and facilitated cooperation between the two institutions. The debt crisis had catapulted the IMF into a position of considerable influence, and IMF conditionality became a standard prerequisite for obtaining World Bank structural adjustment loans during the 1980s. Although World Bank structural adjustment loans and IMF structural adjustment facilities remained formally separate programs, operated by independent institutions, their timing and conditions converged to the point where they could be combined as *de facto* structural adjustment packages.

Structural adjustment conditions included three components: (1) deflationary policies to correct budgetary imbalances (including tight control over state spending, limits to the money supply, increased interest rates on credit, and wage reductions); (2) expenditure-switching policies promoting export-oriented growth (including currency devaluation, export promotion, tax reforms, and deregulation of imports); and (3) institutional reforms designed to liberalize trade and promote market efficiency (including deregulation of prices, exchange rates, and interest rates; elimination of barriers to international trade, investment, and currency flows; and privatization of state-run activities) (Mengisteab and Logan, 1995; Stein, 1992; Torp, 1993). While these conditions were extremely ambitious and wide-ranging, the intended longer-term effect was to increase the influence of market forces relative to the state, to harmonize such policies across countries, and to open up the countries to unrestricted spatial competition with the rest of the world. Third world nations had little choice but to accept these conditions, in order to qualify for loans from first world financial institutions. Because they were often trained in the first world, and because they were benefiting themselves from market-oriented reforms, third world elites endorsed this shift to neoliberal principles. This was despite evidence that state intervention had been crucial to stimulating industrialization and development, both in the first world and in successful NICs (Chang, 2002; Wade, 1996: 408–421).

Structural adjustment policies diffused rapidly throughout the third world, and also the second world, during the 1980s. Seventeen agreements were signed between 1979 and 1981, and another 65 between 1982 and 1985, with 33 third world nations plus Yugoslavia and Romania (Watson et al., 1986: 103). By the end of the 1980s, more than 1.4 billion people had been directly affected. Geographically, from an initial orientation toward east Africa in 1982, structural adjustment spread to west Africa and particularly to Latin America by 1986, and to Asia by 1989 (Figure 23.9). By April 1993, structural adjustment had diffused throughout the third world (and eastern Europe), only passing over the Middle Eastern OPEC countries and the southeast Asian NICs (Figure 23.10).

Proponents generally suggested that the short-term costs of structural adjustment would eventually pay off as longer-term benefits from market-led development. Yet workers and the least well off bore the brunt of structural adjustment (see sidebar: "Structural Adjustment versus Sustainability"). Increasing social and economic inequality generated considerable domestic political opposition to, and public protest against, structural adjustment from populist and grassroots groups throughout the third world. Even the World Bank began to take note of some of the inequities and the political resistance, and there was some discussion of structural adjustment with a human face. The downsides of structural adjustment were highlighted during the 1997 crisis, as the IMF in particular came under fire for its inflexibility (as discussed above), and during the 1999 protests at the World Trade Organization (WTO) meeting in Seattle, which catalyzed worldwide activist opposition to neoliberal globalization. As a result, the Bretton Woods institutions dropped the language of structural adjustment altogether.

From Structural Adjustment to Poverty Reduction

In 1999, the World Bank closed the books on the term "structural adjustment" (just as it was coming under intense worldwide criticism), announcing a new Poverty Reduction Strategy Program (PRSP). Much of the rhetoric surrounding this initiative stressed that it would be participatory instead of imposed from above, and would listen to the voices of the poor. Indeed, during the 1990s the World Bank worked with NGOs to undertake poverty assessments and "participatory rapid/rural appraisals" throughout the third world, using intensive interviews to record and publicize the "voices of the poor" (Narayan, Patel, Schafft, Rademacher, and Koch-Schulte, 2000). The PRSP stressed three priorities: opportunity, empowerment, and (increasingly) security. Yet, notwithstanding this discursive framework of a new approach influenced by the poor and sensitive to their needs, the PRSP has reproduced many of the features of structural adjustment. In order to participate, countries have to produce a Poverty Reduction Strategy Paper for approval, much as they had to produce a report detailing their structural adjustment policies. They can then qualify for the IMF's short-term Poverty Reduction and Growth Facility (PRGF) and the World Bank's Poverty Reduction Support Credits.

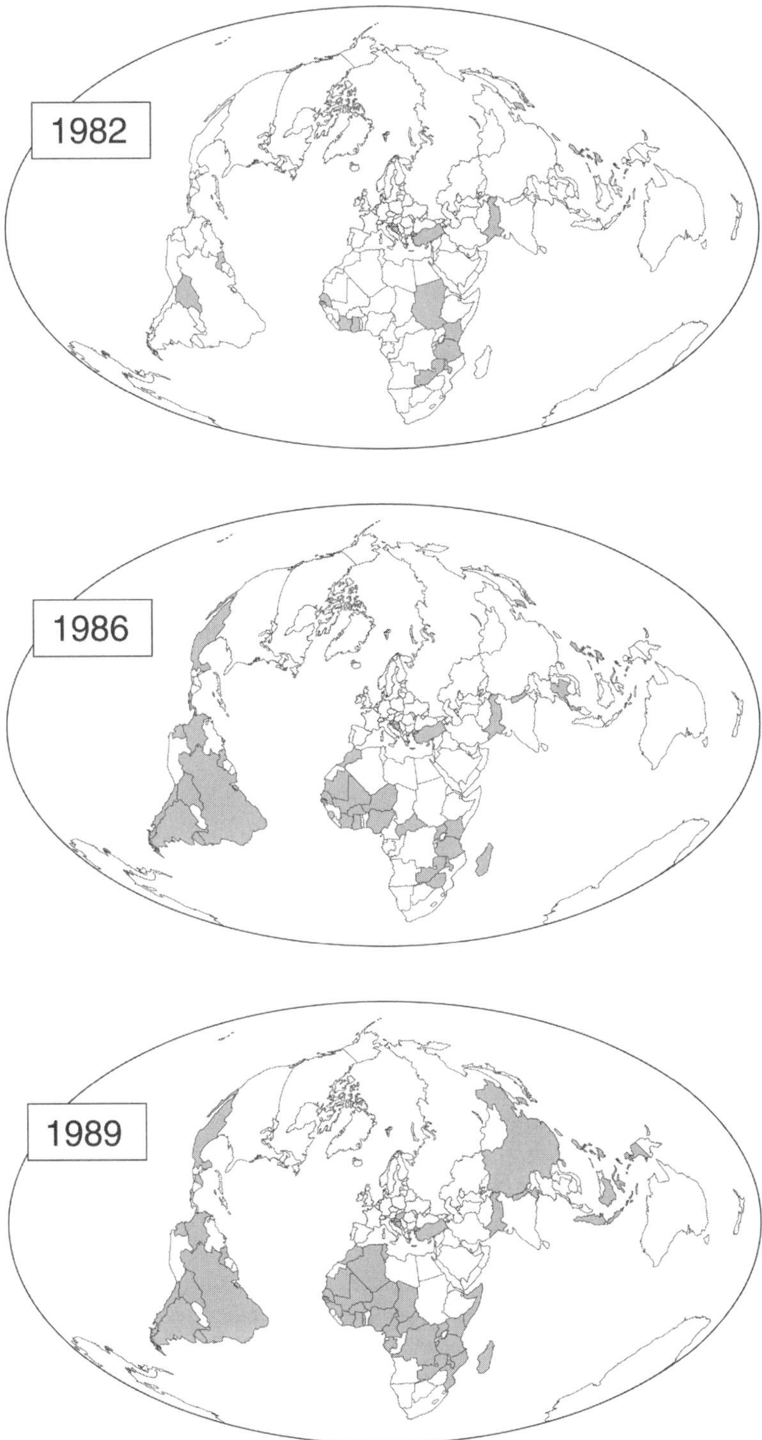

FIGURE 23.9. Geographical spread of IMF/World Bank structural adjustment programs: 1982 (top), 1986 (middle), and 1989 (bottom). *Sources:* Data are from Webb and de Melo (1992) and World Bank (1996).

FIGURE 23.10. Cumulative geographical diffusion of IMF/World Bank structural adjustment programs, 1979–1993. *Sources:* Data are from Webb and de Melo (1992) and World Bank (1996).

The PRSP was designed to replace structural adjustment as a country's comprehensive development strategy. The qualifying conditions for these loans, as laid out in the strategy report, were initially almost identical to those used under structural adjustment, and have not changed a great deal since. Indeed, the IMF (2000) stated that the PRGF was planned to retain "many of the key features of the [Enhanced Structural Adjustment Facility]." "Remarkably quickly, . . . agencies from the UN through all the significant bilaterals and most large NGOs welcomed and engaged the process" (Craig and Porter, 2006: 82). The complicity of NGOs with first world developmentalist agendas, even as they claim to be empowering local residents in the third world, has engendered increased resistance (see Chapter 24 sidebar, "A Journey of *Sangtins*").

In certain ways, the PRSP goes beyond the more purely neoliberal policies of structural adjustment. A central role for the state in development policies has again been acknowledged; much more stress is laid on tailoring the program to local conditions; and there is a strong intention to prioritize immediate improvement for the least well

Structural Adjustment versus Sustainability

After structural adjustment, which promoted export-oriented agriculture, Jamaican farmers saw interest rates on agricultural credit climb to 23%. Other consequences—notably increased unemployment, lower wages, and reduced health and education services—meant that female-headed households were particularly hard hit by structural adjustment. Women already faced higher unemployment, lower wages, and greater responsibility for maintaining their families. Loss of government subsidies made the price of kerosene unaffordable, forcing women to cut wood for fuel. Forested hillsides, particularly those surrounding urban areas, are being denuded by this additional and very time-consuming task. The resulting environmental degradation is due to development policies, not population growth (Development Alternatives with Women for a New Era, 1993).

off over other development issues. Nevertheless, there persist fundamental beliefs in the market as (in principle) the most effective means for achieving these goals, and in the necessity for first world experts to monitor the third world if development is to happen (to ensure good governance and, when necessary, to penalize deviations) (Craig and Porter, 2006).

The Heavily Indebted Poor Countries Initiative

Responding to increasing global outcry against the dependence created by third world indebtedness (and to bankers' concerns that they would not get their money back), in 1996 the World Bank and the IMF introduced a second program in parallel to the PRSP: the Heavily Indebted Poor Countries (HIPC) Initiative. This was presented as the first comprehensive multilateral third world debt relief program. Forty-one countries were chosen (on economic but also geopolitical grounds), accounting for just 39% of poor countries' debt (Christensen, 2007). The IMF proposed to pay for this by liquidating its gold reserves, but backed down after objections from the World Gold Council. The HIPC Initiative was instead pursued on a pay-as-you-go basis, which limited the number of recipients. Potential grantees had to demonstrate conformance to the usual neoliberal reforms (privatization, tax reform, and a balanced budget) before receiving any debt relief. After 3 years of such reforms, if approved, a "decision point" became possible—the moment when a relief package could be assembled. After another 3 years of good behavior, a "completion point" could be reached when serious debt reduction became possible (defined as reducing debt service to a sustainable level). Grantees also had to participate in poverty reduction initiatives.

Not surprisingly, given all these conditions, just six countries had reached completion by 2000, and no relief had been disbursed. (Eventually $3.7 billion was released, in most cases as small annual amounts spread out over decades.) After massive "drop the debt" rallies at the Group of Eight (G8) meeting in Birmingham, England, in 1999, a second (supposedly faster and more generous) program was initiated: HIPC2. Yet only 18 of the original HIPC2 countries had reached completion by 2006. The countries granted relief accounted for only 18% of the outstanding third world debt, amounting to some $43 billion (three-quarters of which had not been paid out by 2006), with little relation between the relief granted and development needs. Debt burdens declined, but this was also occurring prior to these countries' entry into HIPCs.

The turn of the millennium brought large-scale calls for a "debt jubilee." Under pressure from prominent artists like Bono, together with British Prime Minister Tony Blair, the 2005 G8 meeting in Gleneagles, Scotland, pledged to "make poverty history" in the form of the Multilateral Debt Relief Initiative. Some 42 low-income countries with $38.2 billion in debt may be eligible, but eligibility again depends on neoliberal conditionality. Prospective payouts are projected to be only $950 million annually over 30 years, to be shared by the 42 countries that already owe more than this in annual debt service. The net present value of these payments (taking into account inflation over the 30 years) is just $10–15 billion (Christensen, 2007).

CONCLUSIONS

Third world nations continue to be unable to generate significant domestic finance for investment, because they are caught in a vicious cycle of low wages, export income volatility from primary commodities, and limited industrialization. There was a brief flurry of finance from private financial institutions during the 1980s, but the timing and consequences of this were such as to create a global debt crisis, driving private finance away from most third world nations again. By the end of the 1980s, the mix of international lending once again looked as it had at the end of the 1970s, with lending bolstered primarily by foreign aid and by public sector bilateral and multilateral loans; however, important differences had emerged.

There was a general shift in the balance of thinking about development, toward a general acceptance of the principle that freely operating markets are the best guarantors of economic growth. The IMF and the World Bank were enormously successful in propagating the worldwide acceptance by nations of structural adjustment policies based on this thinking (see Figures 23.9 and 23.10), and similar ideas now even govern the distribution of foreign aid. Bilateral official or private donors also insist on agreements being reached with the IMF and the World Bank before they are willing to support balance-of-payments or development financing (Torp, 1993: 1). Conformity with market principles has thus become a precondition for third world countries to borrow the money they so desperately need to finance growth, and these nations have had little choice but to accept such policies. Indeed, this situation is not unique to third world nations, as all nations are increasingly forced to tune their policies to the judgment of financial markets.

A new financial crisis swept the third world in the summer of 1997, dramatically undercutting the economic viability of the very countries that avoided the debt crisis of the 1980s. South Korea, Hong Kong, and several would-be southeast Asian NICs (Indonesia, Thailand, and Malaysia) had been plunged into debt, forcing them to seek new loans coordinated by the IMF to avoid economic meltdown. A few comments are in order. First, the crisis was not precipitated by failures to pay back loans, but by international financial markets' speculating on the value of these nations' currencies and the lack of governmental resources to counter speculation. Second, global model success stories of third world industrialization seemed to turn into economic basket cases overnight. Third, the causes of the financial speculation lay in beliefs that the failure of these nations to adopt first-world-style market economies free of untoward government intervention had made them vulnerable, and the prescribed solution was thus structural adjustment.

Now neoliberal discourses are encircling policymakers around the world. The failures of Asian NICs in 1997 have pushed policymakers to rethink those few success stories where state intervention has created a generative path of industrialization and growth in third world nations. The perspective that state socialist planning provides an alternative development path has also been widely discredited by the collapse of state socialism in the second world in favor of capitalism. Moreover, many skeptics have pointed to the ongoing history of authoritarianism in many third world states. Whether because of a professed belief that encouraging freer markets is the best policy for third world nations (many third world elites are trained in the first world, some spending time in the Bretton Woods institutions), or because economic and political elites have calculated that they stand to gain more by encouraging such policies, third world governments have become increasingly willing to cooperate in pursuing the successors to structural adjustment, and to conform to the standard principles governing lending in both the public and private sectors—often in the face of widespread domestic opposition. This has posed an unprecedented challenge to alternative visions of development (see Chapter 24).

Appendix: The 2008–2009 Global Finance Crisis

In October 2008, a new global finance crisis came to a head, with the potential to profoundly reshape global geographies of development. It differs from the third world debt crisis of the 1980s and the Asian financial crisis of 1997 in two respects: It began in the heart of global finance (the nexus of Wall Street–London), rather than on the periphery. It is also of far greater magnitude than those two, and thus is more comparable to the 1929 Wall Street crash that triggered the Great Depression in the United States. It has demonstrated that financial crises cannot be blamed on third world governance failures or crony practices in Asian bank-based finance systems, and has reinforced skepticism about the viability of neoliberal policies also in the first world. Yet the crisis is linked to recurrent instabilities of global finance and periodic crises characterizing globalizing capitalism since 1945.

Particularly since the 1980s, financial globalization has been characterized by increasingly flexible exchange rates; deregulation of finance markets; the growing influence of finance on other first world economic sectors; the rapid growth of a shadow banking sector immune from regulation (including hedge funds and private equity groups sponsored and operated by banks), particularly in London's aggressively deregulated finance center; and securitization (the conversion of concrete assets into tradable financial securities). London had become the financial center also for U.S. shadow banking by 2007. Taken together, these changes created an explosion of speculative capital looking for outlets worldwide, an indicator that the commonsense idea that changes in the so-called real economy drive outcomes in a supposed financial superstructure had become archaic.

Investment capital, that fled emerging economies during the 1997 crisis (see Chapter 20, pp. 502, 504), recovering its losses with the help of the Wall Street–Treasury–IMF complex, combined with the boom of financial fictitious capital in the global north, to pour into the ITC sector. This created a speculative boom centered on Silicon Valley that burst in 2001 (creating an economic crisis in the San Francisco Bay region). As stocks crashed in 2001 and stagnated thereafter, and as profits in nonfinancial sectors steadily fell, the U.S. government adopted a consumption-led growth policy in which newly expanded housing ownership and housing equities, along with credit card loans, became central elements in sustaining the U.S. economy. In doing so, the ITC bubble was successfully replaced with a housing bubble spreading to a variety of rapidly globalizing cities around the world. In addition, globally circulating fictitious capital catalyzed new bubbles in commodities and food (the explosion of fuel, mineral, and food prices in 2007, that drove some 100 million people into poverty and 44 million into malnutrition, was due as much to speculative investment as to any global imbalance in demand/supply). This was underwritten by the U.S. Federal Reserve bank's pursuit of a low-interest policy during the early 2000s; a cheap money policy that, *inter alia*, channeled some U.S. $11,000 million of debt into the housing and finance sectors. In short, exhibiting close collaboration between Wall Street operators and Washington regulators, Federal Reserve Chairman Alan Greenspan underwrote the emergence of a series of asset price bubbles: blowing bubbles, bursting them, and managing the fallout. This culminated with the unmanageable real estate boom.

Once again, U.S. fiscal policymaking in the 2000s was complicated by the need to manage global finance in an increasingly unbalanced and unequal global economy: Global gulfs between production and consumption, and the need to retain the status of the U.S. dollar as an international currency. First, U.S. consumers were the focus of global production. The export-oriented industrialization policies propagated across the third world since the 1980s depended on the capacity of U.S. consumers to buy ever-increasing quantities of imports. The culture of consumption intensified (also in other wealthy regions ranging from the United Kingdom to Singapore), and U.S. consumers were enjoined (by President George W. Bush after the 9/11 attacks) that consumption is patriotic. Yet real incomes were stagnant or declining for the majority in the United States, which compounds the problems of underconsumption that always plague capitalism. In this case, rapid economic growth in third world low-wage manufacturing required increased purchasing power in the first world, where most global purchasing power became concentrated. With stagnating real incomes in North America and Europe, and Japan in the midst of its own economic crisis, a New Wall Street System with new actors, new practices, and new dynamics, emerged to address the gap.

Wealthy households could draw on their rapidly increasing financial gains (dividends and gains through asset bubbles) to purchase SUVs, "McMansions," and tropical vacations. Middle and lower income households relied on credit cards and second mortgages to boost their consumption, and finally on subprime loans to buy new houses that they could fill with commodities. However, this "upside-down world" of fictitious capital could not last forever. Worries over inflation moved the Federal Reserve to raise interest rates from 1 to 5.25 percent in 2004–2006, as the U.S. housing boom waned in the summer of 2005 and the U.S. economy slowed down in 2006. U.S. households, unable to pay their rapidly increasing mortgages or faced with negative equity—houses whose value had shrunk below that of the mortgage—moved out, often leaving both the house and contents behind. By 2007, U.S. household debt amounted to $1,200 billion, equal to the U.S. GDP for that year. Total U.S. indebtedness was $3,500 billion, the remainder equally shared by corporations and the Federal government, subsidizing nonhousehold consumption of capital and military goods—increases in the latter due to new wars in Iraq and Afghanistan.

Second, there was the challenge of supporting the dollar as the United States fell into ever-deeper trade and fiscal deficits. The dollar's value and viability as the international currency could only be maintained as long as foreign governments and investors (particularly from Japan and China) remained willing to continue purchasing dollars and federal bonds. Low interest rates on the dollar catalyzed a "carry trade," with currency speculators profiting from buying dollars and converting them into other currencies and assets with higher interest rates, building on existing zero-interest Japanese yen carry trading. In addition the U.S. dollar rapidly fell in value relative to other currencies during 2002–2004, particularly against the Euro, improving the competitiveness of U.S. exporters and TNCs, and reducing its debt burden.

During the real estate bubble, the U.S. housing market experienced one of the steepest price hikes in history, enhancing the wealth of property owners. Culminating a gradual upward trend since the 1960s, homeownership grew from 64 percent in 1994 to 69 percent in 2005. During 2000-2007 the outstanding amount of mortgage-backed securities (MBS) almost doubled. But subprime mortgages grew 800 percent, amounting to one quarter of all total outstanding MBS by 2006–2007. Most homeowners drew on their newfound wealth to finance expanded consumption. Subprime loans offered rich and poor households the opportunity to buy houses that they could not otherwise afford, on the grounds that the rising value of their house would enable them to pay off mortgages whose very low initial payments would later grow rapidly as interest rates adjusted upward in two to three years.

This worked during the first half of the 2000s, as rising house values enabled borrowers to refinance their mortgages, often at a lower rate, and lenders could refinance without jeopardizing their risk exposure. The house of cards came tumbling down, however, when the real estate boom waned. Subprime mortgage-backed securities were highly dependent on cash flow from prepayments on subprime mortgages, making them heavily dependent on continuing house price increases. New subprime mortgages had been financed by securitizing existing mortgages; by 2005–2006 about 80 percent of current subprime mortgage originations were being securitized in order to finance new loans. Their securitization functioned as follows: Risky subprime loans with "junk" credit ratings (BBB or lower) were sliced and diced with innumerable other securitized assets, and sold to investors as collateralized debt obligations (CDOs). In these packages, risky subprime mortgage-backed securities were packaged with AAA-rated securities. These packages were in turn subdivided into "tranches" of differing risk and return. The low default rate of subprime mortgages, combined with the ingenuity of Wall Street's financial alchemists, created AAA-rated CDOs that claimed to provide the impossible: low risk and high return. Banks used a shadow banking system (i.e., structured investment vehicles, SIVs) and conduits to purchase the supposedly least risky tranches. Regulators allowed the banks to load up on these without burdening their balance sheet. Hedge funds sponsored by banks bought "equity" tranches, so risky that credit rating agencies would not even rate them. These tranches were then repackaged into other securities with even more opaque content and value.

In the glut of fictitious capital, these various securities were sold to eager buyers with money to burn, by recently hired financial "wizards" with little training, and by scam artists like Bernard Madoff and Sir Allen Stanford. They were rated highly by the credit rating agencies Moody's, Standard and Poor's, and Fitch, whose fees are paid by those issuing the securities. Sellers were not required to inform buyers of the content of CDOs and SIVs, and buyers did not care. Instead they took out insurance against any future loss of value, particularly credit-default swaps (CDSs). By November 2008, estimates of CDS-style insurance amounted to as much as US $65,000 billion, significantly exceeding global GDP. When the real estate market crashed, buyers lost trust in these (now "toxic") securities, prices collapsed across the board, and insurance contracts could not be paid. In two short months, three of New York's (and the world's) five investment banks disappeared, with the survivors converting themselves to commercial banks (to take advantage of Federal bailout money). Iceland went bankrupt, and the U.S. government bailed out AIG (the principal seller of credit-default insurance—"too big to fail"). Banks around the world, at the center of what had become a massive devalorization of financial assets and loss of trust, closed, were bailed out, and/or partially nationalized. By October 2008, governments had put $5,000 billion into bailing out globalized finance. Within 6 months, perceptions had shifted from seeing capitalism as triumphant to peering into the abyss of its possible demise (on the October 3–10 cover of *The Economist*). Global governance norms are in question, and the effects of the crisis are concatenating across the world—particularly affecting, again, the vulnerable global south.

During the early stages of the crisis in 2007, promarket analysts were quick to characterize the crisis as having been caused by corruption and greed: blaming the poor, again, for taking out "liars' loans" in the United States and the United Kingdom; and blaming Wall Street's "culture of greed." Market imperfections thus catalyzed a necessary correction to the markets, from which they should emerge stronger. Yet by late 2008 the consensus located blame in the heart of the financial system, the complexity of which had been thought to be controllable through mathematically engineered programs, and the governance of which was seen as following best practices: deregulation and privatization. As a result, norms of global governance and geographies are in flux as policymakers scramble for quick fixes to the crisis. The future of neoliberalism and market-led globalization is in question. At the national scale, governments have turned to reregulation, Keynesian-style state spending to enhance domestic demand, bailing out some of the entities in trouble (largely institutions of global finance, which caused the problem in the first place), and reprioritizing national economies relative to the global economy. The crisis has also sparked a broader geographic coalition of states that seek to shape global governance: The G8 has become the G20; NICs are lecturing the United States and the United Kingdom on the importance of a developmental state; China is being invited to become a major player in the IMF; and there are geopolitical struggles over hegemony in the emerging global financial architecture—especially regarding the standing of U.S. influence in the IMF and the World Bank and whether the U.S. dollar will continue as the key currency. In addition, labor unions have become reinvigorated, and activists working for alternative approaches to globalization, such as those in the World Social Forum, are energized as never before.

Struggles over the shape of global governance, and the viability of capitalism, are taking place at the same time that the ability to earn one's livelihood across the global north and global south is declining. As of March 2009, unemployment is rising dramatically, deindustrialization is rampant, international trade and investment are slumping, migrant workers are being sent home and remittances are disappearing, and urban real estate values and urban growth are collapsing. General Motors, the second largest TNC in 2003, is essentially bankrupt. More than 20 million low-wage assembly workers have been laid off in China's coastal export processing zones, returning to the countryside where there are few means to support them. African countries were unable to attract private capital in 2008, turning financial surpluses into deficits and making the countries unable to afford the kinds of Keynesian stimulus packages taking place in the first world and in NICs. NICs themselves have up to $3,000 billion of debt that will fall due in 2009. The primary commodity price booms of 2007 have gone bust, undermining exports and employment in export production in the non-NIC resource-rich third world. Dubai, the poster child for how third world cities can become global and how countries can make the most of the windfall of valuable nonrenewable resources (see Chapter 19, pp. 496–497), is in desperate straits. As Dubai's population declines rapidly, and foreign experts and condo owners have left and South Asian construction workers are without work, Dubai's less spectacular and debt-ridden neighbor, Abu Dhabi, is being asked to bail out Dubai.

While Wall Street investors and the like have taken the most spectacular falls, there is no doubt that the crisis is having the worst impact on the impoverished of the global south. There, life chances have changed little over the last thirty, or fifty years: Households, particularly women and children, live in degraded rural environments or urban slums and seek to make ends meet in squatter settlements, informally employed, indebted to money lenders, subject to the whims of global markets and climate fluctuations, and are below the radar of politicians (except when their votes are needed). The World Bank estimates that an additional 65 million people are (re)entering the ranks of the very poor as a result of this crisis, compounded by an additional 200,000–400,000 childhood deaths annually.

In short, the world finds itself in a liminal moment; of peril and opportunity. There is, perhaps, no better time to let our geographical imagination loose, to look toward different worlds.

24 Toward Different Worlds

Idlers do not make history: they suffer it!

—PETER KROPOTKIN (1887/1993: 119)

In a world where the very idea of "public" is being threatened, for educators to feign neutrality is irresponsible. . . . The way to develop critical global literacy is only through direct engagement with diverse ideas. . . . Teaching is biased when it ignores multiple perspectives and does not allow interrogation of its own assumptions and propositions. Partisan teaching on the other hand, invites diversity of opinion but does not lose sight of the aim of the curriculum: to alert students to global injustice, to seek explanations, and to encourage activism.

—BILL BIGELO AND BOB PETERSON (2002: 5)

More than 60 years since some of the bloodiest battles of World War II (Iwo Jima, the Battle of the Bulge, etc.), to say nothing of the Holocaust or of Hiroshima and Nagasaki—and more than 90 years after even greater carnage was wrought on the battlefields of France (e.g., Verdun—61,000 casualties in a single day)—the first world cannot look back on either the 20th century or the beginning of the 21st with any sense of satisfaction that it was the instrument that diffused peace, justice, and economic prosperity throughout the world (Eliot, 1948; Steiner, 1971). Although interstate war on a global scale has been avoided for some 60 years, violence has not. Violence takes a variety of interrelated forms. Global economic, environmental, and cultural changes challenge and undermine the sustainability of local livelihoods, practices, and beliefs, especially (but not only) in the global south. Ecosystems and nonhuman livelihoods are transformed and destroyed in the name of human progress. Women are subjected to domestic and reproductive violence and, with others, to forced migration and human trafficking. Military, police, paramilitary organizations, and guerrilla forces are deployed in struggles for control over territories, resources, and people, in what are now somewhat euphemistically called "the new wars" (cf. Duffield, 2002). Anticorporate activists attack businesses, fields, and laboratories. In the name of religion, some take reprisal against others seen as threatening their values and beliefs.

Other, less violent worlds often seem impossible—but then the most surprising things happen. After 1945, people throughout Asia, Africa, and the Caribbean took matters into their own hands to overturn what seemed to be the immutable violence of colonialism, building on independence movements in South America a century earlier. In the late 1980s, similar "velvet revolutions" swept the second world. On February 15, 2003, and then again on March 15 (the beginning of the U.S.-led invasion of Iraq that has resulted directly or indirectly in the deaths of at least 90,000 [estimates run to over a million] Iraqi civilians), millions took to the streets to demonstrate against this rush to war. Never before had such crowds of people gathered, against wishes of parties and states, to stop a war before it had begun (Retort, 2005: 3). The Cable News Network (CNN) reported protests in 2,000 cities in 98 countries. Protests took place throughout Europe, North America, and Australia. In the Middle East, they occurred in Turkey, Egypt, Syria, Lebanon, Jordan, Palestine, Morocco, and Yemen—most notably in Cairo and Rabat, where demonstrations were illegal. Across Asia, there were protests in Japan, South Korea, Thailand, Indonesia, Bangladesh, Nepal, India, and Pakistan. In Africa, protests took place in Sudan and South Africa; in Latin America, they occurred in Mexico, Honduras, Colombia, Brazil, Argentina, Ecuador, and Chile. Protestors included not only the residents of such metropolises as San Francisco, Madrid, Jakarta, Lahore, Johannesburg, and Mexico City, but also peasants and laborers from "indigenous" and rural communities who undertook journeys for several hours to join protests—whether in the mountainous areas of Honduras, or the so-called "backwater" district towns of Azamgarh and Ballia in north India (Faust and Nagar, 2003).

On each of these occasions, powerful forces suddenly found their global agendas challenged by everyday people. Each of these events was marked by a flourishing of many different dreams of alternative worlds to those promoted through more dominant agendas. Certainly, the worldwide opposition to the U.S. invasion of Iraq was shared by people with very different visions of alternatives to warfare. In protest after protest, people repeated that this was not a people's war and that military warfare cannot be separated from economic warfare. Third world protestors made connections between U.S. foreign policy and domestic policies in their own countries, tried to develop a historical understanding of the United States' role in militarily enforcing a so-called "geopolitical stability," and argued that the war in Iraq could not be seen in isolation from the fifth Afghan War and the occupation of Palestine (Faust and Nagar, 2003).

On each occasion, the dreams motivating grassroots uprisings turned out to be hard to realize. We cannot often make the future of our own choosing. For most protestors, neither independence from colonialism nor the end of state socialism in Europe resulted in the utopian visions motivating most of the protestors whose actions catalyzed change. By the same token, it is hard not to feel disheartened at the bloodshed and horror that have followed the U.S. occupation of Iraq. Yet the hope generated by such protests, and the political critiques that have emerged therein, have not faded. Dreams of different worlds endure.

Since the end of the Cold War, two contrary processes have been at work: the globalizing, totalizing integration of finance and economic production in the care of *multinational* corporations, and the localizing fragmentation of *multicultural* identities and conflict in an eruption of ethnic, racial, political, and class conflicts. The effect, which concatenates through the world at every scale, is the intensification of divisions between a handful of wealthy, empowered elites and an impoverished and sociopolitically disempowered majority. The decades since the European colonies achieved formal independence have brought increased globalization of economic and social life in the third world, with large and increasing disparities in wealth and income, continued privation and poverty for billions of people, and serious (in some cases, irreversible) environmental degradation (Johnston, Taylor, and Watts, 2002). These decades have also been a time when the United States has come to acquire unprecedented (some would say imperial) power (Hardt and Negri, 2000; Harvey, 2003; Smith, 2005). This is not the world of difference that is good for humanity, or for the environments in which human communities are sustained.

What countervailing forces could be brought to bear on such divisive tendencies in the global system to sustain the hopes of the millions who oppose military, socioeconomic, and ecological violence? At first, the possibilities seem daunting. You have probably encountered the phrase "Everything is socially constructed." Implicit, and indeed visible, in the word "con*struct*ed" is "structure." We have devoted most of this book to exploring the various structures in and through which human beings give multiple forms and meanings to their practices. These include social/cultural structures, biophysical resource structures, and economic/political structures. In the cultural sphere, social worlds are remarkably varied and enduring. In a world with between 3,000 and 4,000 speech communities or languages, and even more numerous cultures, there are great differences in how people identify themselves, the interests they champion, and the categories they create for themselves and others.

Yet it is important to remember that such diversity exists only when there is a viable environment for communities to live in and have sustainable livelihoods. As Nettle and Romaine (2000: 5) point out in the case of the world's languages, "Where communities cannot thrive, their languages are in danger. When languages lose their speakers, they die." Indeed, the extinction of over 300 Australian aboriginal and Native American languages is not a thing of the past. As the voices of those who speak these languages continue to vanish, some estimate that about half the known languages in the world have disappeared over the past 500 years (Nettle and Romaine, 2000: 2). Crystal (2000) suggests that we may be losing one language every 2 weeks. The losses are greatest among indigenous and rural peoples, often as a direct or indirect result of development policies. Consider the Ugong (Nettle and Romaine, 2000: 10):

> In the late 1970s the Electricity Generating Authority of Thailand built two hydroelectric dams on the two branches of the River Kwai. These dams flooded the locations of two Ugong villages and the inhabitants were relocated elsewhere. With the unity of the villages destroyed and their speakers scattered . . . Ugong has literally been swamped and the speakers immersed in Thai villages.

Like the sociocultural world, the biophysical world of the tropics and subtropics is complex and easily injured. Those who live there possess a hard-earned knowledge of their environments and evolved management practices that have worked without doing irreparable harm to the environment. Their knowledges represent outcomes of what Richard Norgaard (1994: 27–28, 35 ff., 81–103) calls "coevolutionary processes"—processes in which all of nature (including humans) participate over periods of time, and in which the consequences of actions and events are unforeseeable. Unfortunately, rapid increases in capitalist production and privatization of basic resources have created new and intensified demands on the biosphere to yield products to support higher consumption, involving exports to people elsewhere; these demands have placed the soils, vegetation, and water of the tropics and subtropics under tremendous stress. Indeed, the commonly expressed fear that "the next world war will be a war over water" does not seem particularly remote when one considers major battles over water that have been (and are being) fought in places such as Cochabamba in Bolivia and the Narmada Valley of India.[1] At the same time, it is hard to sustain any romantic ideas about the efficacy, superiority, or innocence of "indigenous knowledges"—or, for that matter, of "western science," which so often serves established power structures. With Peet and Watts (1996: 262), we agree that "the term 'the social construction of nature' overestimates the transformative powers of human practice and . . . underestimates the significance of nonmanipulable nature." As these authors assert, "Reason must be reasoned rather than rejected, science should be changed and used differently, not abandoned" (Peet and Watts, 1996: 261).

When we turn to economic and political structures, we hear much talk of how globalization is removing possibilities for action from the hands of individuals—and even nation states. We are conditioned to think of power in terms of the nation state, but states have been persuaded to see their role in the neoliberal era as expanding economic growth by facilitating the desires of corporate elites, both through changing domestic policy and through participating in international agreements, which expand corporate trading rights, investment rights, and property rights.

> In 1990 more than half of America's exports and imports, by value, were simply transfers of such goods and services *within* global corporations. . . . Under these conditions, globalization is everything but universalist in its consequences. It assigns communities, regions, and nation-states new niches or specialized roles (including marginalization) in the global economy. (McMichael, 1996: 112, 117; emphasis in original)

A central feature of the current round of economic globalization has been a change in the division of labor from *social* (within economic sectors of a given country) to *technical* (within industries operating in several countries). There has been a transfer of manufacturing to third world countries, particularly to China and to export-processing zones (EPZs), where taxes, duties, and labor costs are low. In the first world, these shifts have resulted in corporate downsizing, mergers, and acquisitions; worker wage cuts and layoffs; disappearance of health and retirement benefits; unemployment and labor instability; and deskilling of the workforce.

The world's financial markets have become global in scope, and are open for business on a 24/7 basis. Philip McMichael (1996: 116) quotes a former chairman of Citicorp, who describes currency traders "facing 200,000 trading room monitors across the world" as conducting "a kind of global plebiscite on the monetary and fiscal policies of governments issuing money." Finance markets and multinational agencies seem to sit in judgment over the policies of nation states, threatening financial crisis if policies are not pursued that are consistent with their market-based thinking. The world's multinational corporations seemingly get more powerful, while individuals become less so. States, rather than weakened bystanders in this process, have been actively changing the rules of the game in ways that support corporate power. Politics increasingly acts as the servant of capital, and does its bidding: to protect or guarantee investments, ensure domestic tranquility, and see that contracts are honored. In short, nations have become agents of transnational corporations (TNCs) and global finance, drawing them further from responsibilities to their citizens.

There is a wonderfully prescient and witty scene in the 1976 film *Network*, in which Paddy Chayefsky, who wrote the screenplay, has a business tycoon, Arthur Jensen, explain to the hapless TV personality Howard Beale how the global economy works (see sidebar: "Arthur Jensen Explains the Global System to Mr. Beale"). The global system Arthur Jensen describes is a fantasy; the real global system is not like it, nor is it as benign. However, we believe that within the dialectical relationship between "agency" and "structure," there is much scope for agents (both individually and in groups) to act effectively and to make a difference. We use this final chapter to explore this aspect of our world of difference and its future. Our hope is to illuminate ways in which women, men, transgendered people, and children, both individually and as cooperating collectives, can create spaces in the hegemonic power of 21st-century capitalism to envision and build alternative economic systems—alternative ways of producing, consuming, relating to other people, and using the environment sustainably.

Neither the modernization/development project, nor the neoliberal globalization project currently underway, is sustainable in the long term. Given the quantity of resources needed, using present technologies, to pro-

Arthur Jensen Explains the Global System to Mr. Beale

In Paddy Chayefsky's screenplay for *Network*, the business tycoon Arthur Jensen describes his view of the global economy to Howard Beale, the "mad as hell" TV news broadcaster:

Jensen: You have meddled with the primal forces of nature, Mr. Beale, and I won't have it, is that clear?! You think you merely stopped a business deal—that is not the case! The Arabs have taken millions of dollars out of this country, and now they must put it back. It is ebb and flow, tidal gravity, it is ecological balance! You are an old man who thinks in terms of nations and peoples. There are no nations! There are no peoples! There are no Russians! There are no Arabs! There are no Third Worlds! There is no West! There is only one holistic system of systems, one vast and immane, interwoven, interacting, multivariate, multi-national, dominion of dollars! Petro-dollars, electro-dollars, multi-dollars, Reichmarks, rubles, rin, pounds and shekels! It is the international system of currency that determines the quality of life on this planet! That is the natural order of things today! That is the atomic, sub-atomic, and galactic structure of things today! And you have meddled with the primal forces of nature, and you will atone! Am I getting through to you, Mr. Beale? You get up on your little twenty-one-inch screen, Mr. Beale, and howl about America and democracy. There is no America. There is no democracy. There is only IBM and ITT and AT and T and Dupont, Dow, Union Carbide, and Exxon. Those *are* the nations of the world today. What do you think the Russians talk about in their councils of state? Karl Marx? They get out their linear programming charts, statistical decision theories, minimax solutions and compute the price–cost probabilities of their transactions and investments just like we do. We no longer live in a world of nations and ideologies, Mr. Beale. The world is a college of corporations, inexorably determined by the immutable by-laws of business. The world is a business, Mr. Beale! It has been since man crawled out of the slime, and our children will live, Mr. Beale, to see that perfect world without war and famine, oppression and brutality—one vast and ecumenical holding company, for whom all men will work to serve a common profit, in which all men will hold a share of stock, all necessities provided, all anxieties tranquilized, all boredom amused. And I have chosen you to preach this evangel, Mr. Beale.

Howard (humble whisper): Why me?

Jensen: Because you're on television, dummy.

Source: Chayefsky (1976/1995: 205–206). Copyright 1976 by Metro-Goldwyn-Mayer Inc. and United Artists. Reprinted by permission of Applause Books.

vide a "middle-class lifestyle" to millions in the first world and increasingly in the third world, it is clear that a comparable level of resource use and lifestyle cannot be extrapolated to all of the world's people (even if we assume that improvements in technology will occur). If we accept that humankind should live in balance with nature's renewable stock of resources, and if we admit that the world's demographic future holds a population approaching 10 billion by the year 2050, it is obvious that our ideas about ourselves and what we consider to be a "good life" need to change. Ultimately, only a just world can be a safe world. To live harmoniously with nature and humankind—to negotiate a tricky "sustainability transition"—will necessitate reshaping human consciousness and mentality (Kates, 1995).

CONTESTING NEOLIBERAL GLOBALIZATION AND DEVELOPMENTALISM

> The US government is willing to put the interests of a wealthy sector of society ahead of human life. To say that this is a war for oil is not entirely true. . . . When you have a president with such an atrocious domestic policy, with the

> schools falling apart, with Medicare falling apart, the war is a way to deflect criticism. If anyone sets himself up against "evil incarnate," which in this case is Saddam Hussein, they are bound to look good by comparison. This has been US state policy since the Cold War, making the public scared of enemies overseas in order to entrench and support the political leaders at home. It really works off the fear of people. . . . we have a duty to show the rest of the world that there are Americans who oppose what is going on and are fighting it. . . . It's unethical to be silent and capitulate in front of power, when your society is supportive of some of the worst killing that is going on. It's criminal to be silent.
>
> —JAMIE, quoted in KAY (2003)

Jamie was one of the several thousand high school students who stunned the United States with their sophisticated political analyses during the student walkout that immediately followed the 2003 U.S. invasion of Iraq. Jamie criticized the political power that serves the interests of the wealthy while snatching the meager resources and privileges of the poor, and observed that processes at the "domestic" level or national scale are inseparable from those taking the form of an imperial invasion of an oil-rich third world country. But Jamie also equated silence with complicity. Indeed, the actions embraced by U.S. high school students in March 2003 sent a clear message to the world that despite benefiting from corporate globalization in many ways, they were capable of critically reflecting on and standing up against violence and injustice, and that the opportunity and responsibility to use this power lies with all of us. In our closing remarks, we provide glimpses into a few of the many ways in which people throughout the world are claiming this creative power to collectively conceptualize and enact alternative practices, and to ensure that different worlds can flourish even in the face of the neoliberal "military–industrial–entertainment complex" (Retort, 2005: 37). Before we look at examples of alternative practices, however, it may be useful to reflect on the idea of "contestation" and how it can provide a useful framework for appreciating these interventions and visions.

What might it mean to confront or contest neoliberal globalization and developmentalism? Does every act of speaking out count as resistance to the system? Or does it make sense to analytically distinguish among different kinds of actions that seek to critique, challenge and/or transform the dominant systems? Although such distinctions are somewhat arbitrary, for the purpose of analytical clarity we can specify three ways in which collectives have frequently contested neoliberal development and globalization agendas (cf. Katz, 2004). To begin with, there is *resistance*, such as that seen in the ongoing anti-WTO protests as well as those of 1999 in Seattle, 2003 in Cancún, and 2005 in Hong Kong, and in the demonstrations in Genoa during the Group of Eight (G8) meetings and the post-Genoa debate of 2001. Such resistance seeks to launch a direct attack on neoliberalism by objecting both to its "imaginaries and practices"[2] and to its harmful effects, particularly on disadvantaged groups and locations (Leitner et al., 2007b). Such oppositional activism is a worthy goal, but there are two problems with looking for contestation solely or primarily in this form. First, it suffers from some of the same artificial binaries that characterize the neoliberal globalization discourses:

> Typically framed in terms of the impact of "the global" on "the local," these discourses conjure up inexorable market and technological forces that take shape in the core of the global economy and radiate out from there. A number of other binaries map on to the global/local dichotomy. In addition to active/passive and dynamic/static, these include economics/culture, general/specific, abstract/concrete, and very importantly, dichotomous understandings of time and space, in which time is accorded active primacy, while space appears as a passive container. This conflation of the "the global" with dynamic, technological–economic forces restlessly roving the globe defines its inexorable—and inexorably masculine—character. By the same token,

"the local" appears as a passive, implicitly feminine recipient of global forces whose only option is to appear as alluring as possible. (Hart, 2002: 12–13)

Second, as Gibson-Graham (1996, 2006) and Katz (2004) argue, not all contestation seeks directly to undermine dominant forces, but seeks instead to practice alternatives that survive through their *resilience* in the face of the globalization project. Instead of attacking globalization, such alternatives seek to *rework* from below the ideological meanings, cultural practices, and values embedded in relations of domination, described in a word as "hegemony." Such instances of resilience and reworking of hegemony involve both imaginaries and practices, and they are far more pervasive on the ground than both neoliberalism's proponents and also many of its critics tend to acknowledge (Leitner et al., 2007b).

Sadly, scholarly and activist literatures as well as progressive media continue to present both globalization and efforts to contest it as top-down processes. Thus we hear of alternative global imaginaries of various hues and shades, ranging from anarchism and revolutionary Islam to socialism, Buddhism (see sidebar: "Buddhist Economics"), class struggle, and the multitude (Hardt and Negri, 2000, 2004; Harvey, 2000). We read about global initiatives such as fourth world movements; the World Social Forum (see sidebar: "Another World is Possible"); the Association pour la Taxation des Transactions pour l'Aide aux Citoygens (ATTAC; see Chapter 23); and a range of conferences on gender, violence, and HIV/AIDS, as well as on sustainable futures and environments. We also learn of transnational alliances of labor activists and consumer activists (e.g., United Students Against Sweatshops). But we rarely hear of initiatives and struggles led by local collectives across the globe to acquire different forms and degrees of alternative practices. Sometimes these take the form of local small-scale technologies for rain harvesting, or people's science movements that seek to recast scientific knowledge from the perspective of the marginalized communities. Sometimes they involve inventing new forms of communal or worker-owned production and local exchange or barter systems, at times by negotiating international donor funding on their own terms. Still others seek alternative paths to knowledge production that address local questions of marginalization and deprivation—by examining those issues in relation to regional, national, and global processes; and by producing knowledge for consumption, evaluation, and action by local communities in languages that seem far removed from the domain of the English-speaking global elites (see sidebar: "A Journey of *Sangtins*"). And somewhere in the middle of this spectrum stretching from the very global to the very local lie initiatives at the national and regional scale, such as the ones we have witnessed in Venezuela (see sidebar: "The Untelevised Venezuelan Revolution"), Cuba, and Chiapas, Mexico (home of the Zapatistas); in the National Alliance of People's Movements in India; and in the fair trade movement. Each of these seeks to create alternative political economies, social institutions, and exchange systems.

The overwhelming tendency to regard both "globalization" and "antiglobalization" as top-down processes can be countered by starting with the often neglected places and people frequently invoked as mere victims of neoliberal policies, and as "too local" and insignificant to have any impact on the mighty forces of the states, corporations, and imperial nations. The sidebar "Nigerian Women Shock Shell" can give us some clues. Behind the resistance that the world witnessed on the waterfronts of Warri in August 2002, there were probably years of resilience and reworking in which the Ijaw, Ilaje, and Itsekiri women learned to (1) cope with the ecological and socioeconomic horrors of oil drilling; (2) develop understandings and critiques of the socioeconomic processes that forced their communities to pay the costs for a form of "national" development that primarily benefited the multinational oil

Buddhist Economics

Buddhism is, foremost, an ethical and philosophical system whose purpose is to reduce human suffering and misery—a practical, applied goal. It argues that existence is sorrow; that sorrow is created by desire; that sorrow ceases when desire ceases; and that one can achieve this state by following the "noble eightfold path" (right belief, right resolve, right speech, right conduct, right occupation, right effort, right contemplation, and right meditation). Its logic leads ineluctably to a philosophy of nonviolence and vegetarianism. One could argue that many of our desires are directed toward *wants* (rollerblades, an iPod) rather than *needs* (food, shelter, respect). The German economist Ernst Schumacher (1973), in *Small Is Beautiful*, expanded one of the eight noble paths—right occupation or livelihood—into a chapter on "Buddhist economics." It becomes a way of simplifying life and reducing the quantity of resources needed to support it.

Here are representative quotes presenting a contrary view (contrary, that is, to neoclassical economics) on resource use, labor, mechanization, and transport (one has to ignore the sexist features of Schumacher's account):

> It is not wealth that stands in the way of liberation but the attachment to wealth; not the enjoyment of pleasurable things but the craving for them. . . . Since consumption is merely a means to human well-being, the aim should be to obtain the maximum of well-being with the minimum of consumption. (57)
>
> The Buddhist point of view takes the function of work to be at least threefold: to give a man a chance to utilise and develop his faculties; to enable him to overcome his ego-centeredness by joining with other people in a common task; and to bring forth the goods and services needed for a becoming existence. (54–55)
>
> [There are] two types of mechanization which must be clearly distinguished: one that enhances a man's skill and power and one that turns the work of man over to a mechanical slave, leaving man in a position of having to serve the slave. . . . The carpet loom is a tool, a contrivance for holding warp threads at a stretch for the pile to be woven round them by the craftsmen's fingers; but the power loom is a machine, and its significance as a destroyer of culture lies in the fact that it does the essentially human part of the work. (55)
>
> [The modern economist's] fundamental criterion for success is simply the total quantity of goods produced during a given period of time. . . . From a Buddhist point of view, this is standing the truth on its head by considering goods as more important than people and consumption as more important than creative activity. (56)
>
> From the point of view of Buddhist economics, therefore, production from local resources for local needs is the most rational way of economic life, while dependence on imports from afar and the consequent need to produce for export to unknown and distant peoples is highly uneconomic and justifiable only in exceptional cases and on a small scale. . . . The Buddhist economist would hold that to satisfy human wants from faraway sources rather than from sources nearby signifies a failure rather than a success. (59)

companies and the Nigerian state and economic elites; and (3) make decisions about what kinds of alliances they were going to build against the colonial and neocolonial "divide and rule" policies to confront the situation, how they were going to make their case, which negotiations and concessions they would be willing to make, and when and how they would put their own lives and personal security on the line. Our point here is not that we should always look for similar forms of contestation. Rather, we believe that considering the imaginaries and practices of diverse local and nonlocal actors can provide new insights into the ways that contestation works in multiple and contextually

Another World Is Possible

The committee of Brazilian organizations that conceived of and organized the first World Social Forum (Porto Alegre, January 25–30, 2001), after evaluating the results of that Forum and the expectations it raised, drew up a Charter of Principles to guide the continued pursuit of that initiative. Approved and adopted in São Paulo on April 9, 2001, by the organizations that made up the World Social Forum Organizing Committee, the charter was approved with modifications by the World Social Forum International Council on June 10, 2001. Here are several extracts from the charter:

1. The World Social Forum is an open meeting place for reflective thinking, democratic debate of ideas, formulation of proposals, free exchange of experiences and interlinking for effective action, by groups and movements of civil society that are opposed to neoliberalism and to domination of the world by capital and any form of imperialism, and are committed to building a planetary society directed towards fruitful relationships among Humankind and between it and the Earth. . . .
3. The World Social Forum is a world process. All the meetings that are held as part of this process have an international dimension.
4. The alternatives proposed at the World Social Forum stand in opposition to a process of globalization commanded by the large multinational corporations and by the governments and international institutions at the service of those corporations' interests, with the complicity of national governments. They are designed to ensure that globalization in solidarity will prevail as a new stage in world history. This will respect universal human rights, and those of all citizens—men and women—of all nations and the environment[,] and will rest on democratic international systems and institutions at the service of social justice, equality and the sovereignty of peoples.
5. The World Social Forum brings together and interlinks only organizations and movements of civil society from all the countries in the world, but it does not intend to be a body representing world civil society. . . .
8. The World Social Forum is a plural, diversified, non-confessional, non-governmental and non-party context that, in a decentralized fashion, interrelates organizations and movements engaged in concrete action at levels from the local to the international to build another world. . . .
10. The World Social Forum is opposed to all totalitarian and reductionist views of economy, development and history and to the use of violence as a means of social control by the State. . . .
11. As a forum for debate, the World Social Forum is a movement of ideas that prompts reflection, and the transparent circulation of the results of that reflection, on the mechanisms and instruments of domination by capital, on means and actions to resist and overcome that domination, and on the alternatives proposed to solve the problems of exclusion and social inequality that the process of capitalist globalization with its racist, sexist and environmentally destructive dimensions is creating internationally and within countries. . . .
13. As a context for interrelations, the World Social Forum seeks to strengthen and create new national and international links among organizations and movements of society, that—in both public and private life—will increase the capacity for non-violent social resistance to the process of dehumanization the world is undergoing and to the violence used by the State, and reinforce the humanizing measures being taken by the action of these movements and organizations.
14. The World Social Forum is a process that encourages its participant organizations and movements to situate their actions, from the local level to the national level and seeking active participation in international contexts, as issues of planetary citizenship, and to introduce onto the global agenda the change-inducing practices that they are experimenting in building a new world in solidarity.

Source: World Social Forum (2002).

A Journey of *Sangtins*

In Awadhi (see *Note* below), *sangtin* is a term of solidarity, of reciprocity, of enduring friendship among women; it is used by a woman to refer to a close female companion who sees her through the trials and tribulations of life. Founded in 1998 by a group of local women in the Sitapur district of the Indian state of Uttar Pradesh, the organization Sangtin was renamed in 2006 as Sangtin Kisaan Mazdoor Sangathan (Sangtin Peasants and Workers Organization) or SKMS. SKMS works for the socioeconomic, political, and intellectual empowerment of rural peasants and workers, and organizes both women and men in 60 villages of Sitapur (Sangtin, 2005; Sangtin Writers, 2006; Sangtin Writers and Nagar, 2006).

The writing and publication of the book *Sangtin Yatra* (2004) were critical to the intellectual growth and political vision of SKMS. *Sangtin Yatra* was fired by a desire to imagine how the organization could become a true *sangtin* for the most marginalized women of Sitapur. Through the collective writing of this book by nine *sangtins* from different socioeconomic and institutional locations, SKMS came to articulate its deep commitment to enhancing the ability of the least powerful individuals and groups to challenge and change—in their favor—existing power relationships that place them in subordinate economic, social, and political positions. At the same time, *Sangtin Yatra* has also inspired a vision that aims to empower the local communities intellectually by questioning the very idea of who is on the margins. SKMS believes that those who are pushed to the society's margins are not actually "marginal" people living outside mainstream society; they are, in fact, the core of society. Rather than thinking of marginalized communities as people who need to be connected with the mainstream, SKMS works toward eliminating the structures that create the margins in the first place. Below we present a segment from the last pages of *Sangtin Yatra*, translated into English as *Playing with Fire* (Sangtin Writers and Nagar, 2006):

> The resources made available to the rural poor can be likened to a cumin seed in the mouth of a camel: they are too small to have an impact. Even the minimal amounts of goods and amenities allocated to people living and dying under these conditions diminish little by little as they make their way through different levels of the system. Similarly, the interrelationships between the processes and politics of globalization, development, and NGOization push us to work actively toward undoing these knotlike puzzles in our own minds. After all, a person breathing in the remotest village is entitled to decide for herself how, why, and for whom the whole globe has become a village and for whom the whole world is still constituted by a village, settlement or district. What kinds of inequalities and social violence does the existence of these two worlds indicate?
>
> Let us also focus for a moment on the ugly face of violence that has shaken up the soul of our country. If the culmination of a debate over Babri Mosque and Ram Janmbhoomi acquires the face of a nationwide communal riot after the destruction of a four-hundred-year old mosque-shaped structure, and some ten years later, a violent incident in a train compartment transforms itself into a communal slaughter in Gujarat, then developing an awareness and understanding of such tragedy also becomes a critical part of our work and social responsibility. It is only when we place this matter on our agenda that our people will be able to grasp how events such as the Mandir–Masjid debate and the massacre of Muslims in Gujarat shape the communal politics of our own districts and villages. To accomplish this, we will have to develop a historical understanding of communalism. Let us consider the creation of India in 1947 for a moment. At that time, Pakistan was created separately from India, and subsequently Bangladesh was carved out by splitting Pakistan. Without understanding the background and multidimensional histories of these events, how can we begin to grasp the complexities of Indo–Pak partition and the contemporary communal politics? It is high time that the ordinary women and men of our villages be given the opportunities to develop a clear and in-depth understanding of these issues. We believe that we must play an important role in shaping such understandings in our own communities.
>
> . . . We also believe that if our main aim behind advancing all of these understandings and reflections is to do concrete and meaningful work in the lives of the poorest rural women, then we must also deepen our acquaintance with writings and reflections related to women and feminisms, and the various debates

and conversations on caste, class, race, and religion that have emerged from time to time in various women's movements. Only then will we be in a position to continue our work on the ground without giving up the courage and confidence to intervene continuously in the politics of knowledge production.

And in the End . . .

When in the lukewarm sun of December 2002, the nibs of nine pens started pouring out on paper and transforming themselves into this chronicle, our eyes were wet and our hearts were filled with a pain and restlessness. We had never imagined that a journey that started with remembering and understanding the tears, scoldings and beatings of our Ammas, Babus and Dadis would one day lead us to distinguish between livelihoods and social movements. But today we know very well that it is only when we juxtaposed the stories of our personal lives and saw them with new lenses that we were able to arrive at a point where it is becoming possible for us to honestly re-evaluate the inequalities pervasive in our work-field.

In other words, if we could not have built a collective understanding about how Garima's pangs of hunger as a child were different from Radha's, perhaps we would have also failed to see the manner in which the full reins of our organization, which profess to work with Dalit and oppressed women, end up gathering in the hands of the Sawarns. And if we had not grappled with the deep-seated double standards associated with untouchability and *purdah* in our own hearts, where would we have found the insights and determination to question the double standards in the thoughts and actions of celebrated figures in the worlds of NGOs and academia?

The strong bond that moved us from ink to tears has today brought us all the way from tears to dreams. If there are new hopes along with new shapes and colors in these dreams, we are also aware of the new complications, dangers and risks that reside there. And we are also aware that at the very least, this collective journey of creation has united us in a closed fist.

We hope that this fist would continue to become stronger, and that we will gain the support and strength of many many fists like ours. Only then will we be able to create a world where small groups like ours would have the heart to dream big dreams with ordinary people for their happiness—on our own terms, by the force of our own thoughts, and in our own languages.

Note. Awadhi, or the language of Awadh, is predominantly spoken in the rural areas of central and eastern Uttar Pradesh, including the districts of Bahraich, Barabanki, Faizabad, Gonda, Hardoi, Lakheempur, Lucknow, Raibareli, Sitapur, Sultanpur, and Unnao.

Source: Sangtin Writers and Nagar (2006: 129–131).

specific ways. It can help to make sense of the mutually constitutive relationships between the global and the local, to reconceptualize and recast these relationships, and thereby to envision and make different worlds.

WORKING TOGETHER TOWARD DIFFERENT WORLDS

> Around the world, activists are piggy backing on the ready-made infrastructures supplied by the global corporations. This can mean cross-border unionization, but also cross-sector organizing—among workers, environmentalists, consumers, even prisoners, who may all have different relationships to one multinational [corporation]. . . . Thanks to Monsanto, farmers in India are working with environmentalists and consumers around the world to develop direct-action strategies that cut off genetically modified foods in the field and in the supermarkets. Thanks to Shell Oil and Chevron, human rights activists in Nigeria, democrats in Europe, [and] environmentalists in North

America have united in a fight against the unsustainability of the oil industry. Thanks to the catering giant Sodexho-Marriott's decision to invest in Corrections Corporation of America, university students are able to protest against the exploding US for-profit prison industry simply by boycotting the food in their campus cafeteria. Other targets include pharmaceutical companies who are trying to inhibit the production and distribution of low-cost AID[S] drugs, and fast-food chains. Recently, students and farm workers in Florida have joined forces . . . to boycott Taco Bell on university campuses. . . . Students facing corporate takeover of their campuses by the Nike swoosh have linked up with workers making its branded campus apparel, as well as with parents concerned at the commercialization of youth, and church groups campaigning against child labor—all united by their

The Untelevised Venezuelan Revolution

The Revolution Will Not Be Televised, a movie by the independent Irish film makers Kim Bartley and Donnacha O'Briain, records what was one of history's shortest-lived *coups d'état.* Hugo Chavez, elected president of Venezuela in 1998, emerges as a people's hero beloved by his nation's working class, and as a tough-as-nails, quixotic opponent to the power structure that would see him deposed. Bartley and O'Briain were inside the presidential palace on April 11, 2002, when he was forcibly removed from office. They were also present 48 hours later when, remarkably, he returned to power amid the cheers of his aides. The film is a document about political muscle and an extraordinary portrait of the man *The Wall Street Journal* credits with making Venezuela "Washington's biggest Latin American headache after the old standby, Cuba."

Neoliberalism came to Caracas with a vengeance in 1989. Confronted by recession, the government of that time responded with a typical austerity package: Spending on health and education was cut, and price rises were imposed on basic commodities and foodstuffs. The measures provoked popular outrage. When the price of gasoline was doubled, and private bus owners increased their fares in turn, the outrage erupted into widespread rioting. Over 300 people died. These cataclysmic events were to have a profound, formative influence on Hugo Chavez, then a young army officer.

Chavez's election in 1998 not only marked a turning point in Venezuela; it sent ripples of change throughout Latin America, where the same economic model had been in the ascendancy during the late 1980s and 1990s. Prior to Chavez, Latin American governments had either acquiesced in or enthusiastically endorsed the "voodoo economics" of neoliberalism. While governments elsewhere in the region enacted legislation to transform public goods (water, energy) into private commodities, the Chavez administration introduced a new constitution to ensure that vital assets were kept out of private hands. (Venezuela's wealthy would have expected to benefit handsomely from the privatization of assets, such as the state oil company Petróleos de Venezuela, S.A., as had been the experience of elites throughout Latin America.) The new constitution also restored rights—severance pay, for example—that previous administrations had abolished. In addition, health care and education were made free of charge, for the first time in Venezuela's history. The Chavez administration effectively threw the neoliberal project in Latin America into reverse.

In recent years, popular protests in Mexico, Peru, and Bolivia have also succeeded in overturning proposed privatizations. However, the neoliberal project in Latin America still has one crucial item on the agenda—the Free Trade Agreement of the Americas (FTAA). Realization of the FTAA has been a key policy goal of the George W. Bush administration. (At this writing, it remains to be seen what President Barack Obama's position on the FTAA will be.) The Chavez administration has stated its opposition to the FTAA; nonetheless, it may no longer be the region's lone voice. Indeed, the subsequent electoral successes of Luis Ignacio da Silva ("Lula") in Brazil, Lucio Gutierrez in Ecuador, and Evo Morales in Bolivia have sent a clear signal to the world that for millions in Latin America, neoliberalism is an idea whose time has long gone.

Sources: Jones (2007), and Power, Bartley, O'Briain, and Zoido (2002).

Nigerian Women Shock Shell

> Shell and ChevronTexaco gas flare and oil spills has polluted our river and atmosphere. For the first time women from Itsekiri, Ijaw, and Ilaje decided to put an end to these predicaments. . . . We Itsekiri, Ijaw, and Ilaje are one[;] no division, no divide and rule.
>
> —BIMPE EBELEYE, an Ilaje woman (quoted in VOLHEIM, 2004b: 282)

> Our roofs are destroyed by their chemical. No good drinking water in our rivers . . . even the fishes we catch in our rivers . . . smell of crude oil . . . They intimidate us with soldiers, police, navy and tell us that cases of spill are caused by us. . . . Thirty years till now, what do we have to show by Chevron, apart from this big yard and all sorts of machines making noise?
>
> —FELICIA ITSERO, an Ijaw mother and grandmother (quoted in VOLHEIM, 2004b: 283)

Nigeria is the world's sixth largest oil exporter, accounting for approximately a 12th of the oil imported by the United States The United States is looking into doubling its Nigerian oil imports in an effort to be less reliant on the Middle East. Sales of crude oil account for more than 85% of the Nigerian government's revenue. Operating in partnership with the Nigerian National Petroleum Company are five TNCs: the British/Dutch Shell, the Italian Azienda Generale Italiana Petroli, the French Elf-Aquitaine, and the U.S. giants ChevronTexaco and ExxonMobil. The claim of these oil companies that their activities are conducted under the highest environmental standards was loudly protested by Ken Saro-Wiwa, a passionate spokesperson for the Movement of the Survival of the Ogoni People. Saro-Wiwa was hanged in 1995 for speaking out. But his execution gave birth to even louder protests.

At the crack of dawn on August 8, 2002, the calm waterfronts of Warri in Nigeria came alive with boats of various shapes and sizes—each full to capacity with women singing, in various dialects, sorrowful dirges lamenting the pitiful conditions of the Niger Delta. Later that day, 3,000 women from the Ijaw, Itsekiri, and Ilaje communities seized the Ogunnu operational headquarters of ChevronTexaco and Shell, barricaded the gates, and forced work to stop. An Ilaje leader vowed, "All will not be well for the oil companies in our areas until they start treating us as human beings that deserve a good life." In the violent confrontations that followed with armed soldiers and police, scores of women were seriously injured, one was beaten unconscious, one was shot to death, and others were tear-gassed.

But this violence only added fuel to the fire. Between August 14 and 23, 100 Ilaje women took over a smaller Ewan oil platform. These protests were the latest expressions of all-women demonstrations that had begun on July 8 with a 10-day siege of ChevronTexaco's offices in Escravos near Warri. The Itsekiri women, after taking over an offshore oil terminal, used a time-tested cultural shaming tactic: They threatened to remove their clothes. Public nudity, a local taboo, would have embarrassed the 1,000 oil workers on the terminals who held these older women in high esteem. On July 16, Ijaw women took over four oil flow stations, 50 miles southeast of Escravos. These combined actions cost ChevronTexaco $3 million in lost revenue.

Sources: Adapted from Volheim (2004a, 2004b).

> different relationship to a common global enemy.
>
> —KLEIN (2004: 222–223)

We do not intend to end this book by thanking a handful of TNCs. We quote Naomi Klein because her examples suggest that each campaign or alliance evolves through its own particular logic, requirements, networks, and relationships. They also show how supposedly local issues can have broader impacts through spatial strategies—strategies that take advantage of possibilities created by neoliberal globalization, and that connect different initiatives (without collapsing them into a unitary movement). Throughout the pages of *A World of Difference*, we have argued against structures, rules, and relationships that tend to eliminate difference by homogenizing diverse ways of living and being for humans and for nature. Universal norms and standards, when defined and imposed from above—whether in the name of civilization, modernization, development, free trade, or emancipation—are almost always likely to create relationships where those in elite and privileged locations come to prevail by directly or indirectly dominating, silencing, or unilaterally speaking for the non-elite and the unprivileged.

The same is also true in the realm of contestation. Any attempt to create a blueprint, a methodology, or a formula about how to contest neoliberalism across scales or communities risks slipping into a project that produces a new universalism. This is a real danger for those of us who inhabit the relatively privileged spaces of the first world as teachers, students, professionals, consumers, or activists. Yet the strategies, analyses, and visions of contestation can be transformed into a systematic and sustainable commitment only when a movement evolves organically from its own needs and with its own tools, as the journeys of many collectives suggest (see, e.g., Notes from Nowhere [2003] and the sidebar "A Journey of *Sangtins*," above). This does not, in any way, limit the scope for alliances across places, geographical scales, and socioeconomic, cultural, or institutional differences. Rather, it suggests that a commitment to "preserve" the differences that many of us have come to value in this world—differences of language, clothing, cuisine, music, arts, nature, and so on—is not merely about struggling to make spaces for humans and various plant and animal species; social categories and identities; and cultures and economies to live and thrive on equal, nonviolent, and nondominating terms. It is also about creating spaces where multiple visions of a good life can be articulated, nourished, and enacted, to create many worlds of difference.

Certain individuals from the third world have put in an appearance in the course of this book. We have met Wambua Muathe and some of his relatives in the first chapter. In Chapter 9 and subsequent chapters, Kitemu wa Nguli and his family have described aspects of the environment they use. They have told of how they plant their crops, deal with tricky rains, and classify and evaluate their soils. Kitemu has spoken of his family's difficulties with agricultural vermin. Mbeke and Mbula, wives of Kitemu, have the unremitting tasks of obtaining water and firewood. In other chapters, we have traced the kinship links between Njeri Wang'ati and Rebeka Njau; surveyed the medicines available from Dr. Mtemi Alahu Maswumale in northeastern Tanzania; met Momena, a migrant, and Nurjahan, a Grameen Bank loan recipient, both in Bangladesh; and Sarah and Suparno, the latter a *becak* driver, in Jakarta. Some 10 named Pokot people have been introduced in Chapter 12.

It would be naive to think that we can ever fully "know" their thoughts about the materials covered in this book. However, their presence in this book serves to remind us—the authors and the readers—that whatever we produce and learn as "knowledge" about encountering and contesting development has to be subjected to their critical scrutiny and evaluation as well. These are the people who live third world lives, and together we have to find the ways to strive for a just and equitable world.

If this book has raised your burden of awareness—of both the complexities and unequal consequences of these forces for (and across) the third world, and the possibilities of working together toward better worlds—then this is a beginning. Reflect on your own positionality within these processes; familiarize yourself with other parts of the world; and then ask yourself what you can do, with whom, and how (see sidebar: "One Way to Begin . . .").

NOTES

1. In April 2000, Bolivia grabbed the world's attention when the city of Cochabamba erupted in a public uprising over water prices. In 1999, following World Bank advice, Bolivia had granted a 40-year lease to a subsidiary of the Bechtel Corporation, giving it control over the water on which more than half a million people survive. Immediately the company doubled and tripled water rates for some of South America's poorest families. For more details and reports of this struggle, see Democracy Center (n.d.).

2. "Imaginaries and practices" include (but are not restricted to) values, beliefs, institutional and popular rhetoric, everyday rules, regulations, and activities that together impart meanings and give legitimacy and support to a given social structure in a specific time and place.

One Way to Begin . . .

There are many ways in which one can begin to work with one's burden of awareness, both as an individual and as a member of different communities or collectives. There are, of course, personal choices that each of us makes—for example, whether to buy a sport utility vehicle or a hybrid car; whether to carpool; or whether to live without a car. Similarly, in a country like the United States, where on average food travels over 1,000 miles before being consumed, we make choices about how we should eat. These are choices with consequences: The outcry against conditions under which sweatshop labor toils in factories producing for U.S.-based multinational corporations led thousands of students in the 1990s to boycott clothing made in such sweatshops. Many of these protestors opted to primarily use secondhand clothing.

As members of various local communities, we continually make choices about how we connect or build reciprocities with our neighbors, peers, and coworkers. As members of society, we have the power to take a range of actions and stances on such issues and policies as those involving treatment and representations of undocumented immigrants, poverty, and refugees (and on the attitudes of our families, friends, peers, and teachers toward them), or the many forms of violence we find around us (ranging from regional and international warfare in the name of national security, development, and global peace, to domestic violence, classism, racism, and homophobia). These actions include direct action, voting, and creating discussions and dialogues that question common-sense views on controversial issues: issues of power and difference, us and them, development and backwardness, terror and patriotism . . .

Why don't you begin a new dialogue, embarking on your own journey to creatively embrace your own burden of awareness?

References

Abu-Lughod, J. (1989). *Before European hegemony: The world system A.D. 1250–1350.* New York: Oxford University Press.

Adams, W. (1990). *Green development: Environment and sustainability in the third world.* New York: Routledge.

Adams, W. (1992). *Wasting the rain: Rivers, people and planning in Africa.* Minneapolis: University of Minnesota Press.

African Academy of Sciences. (1989). *Environmental crisis in Africa: Scientific response.* Nairobi: Academy Science.

African Repository. (1863). Message of the President of Liberia. . . . *39*(3), 76–85.

African Repository. (1879). Insubordination of the Greboes. *55*(4), 123.

African Repository and Colonial Journal. (1832). The slave trade—Horrid barbarity. *7*(12), 388.

Aglietta, M. (1979). *A theory of capitalist regulation.* London: New Left Books.

Agnew, J., and Corbridge, S. (1995). *Mastering space: Hegemony, territory and international political economy.* London: Routledge.

Ahlburg, D. A. (1998). Julian Simon and the population growth debate. *Population and Development Review*, *24*(2), 317–327.

Ahmed, L. (1992). *Women and gender in Islam: Historical roots of a modern debate.* New Haven, CT: Yale University Press.

Alexander, L. T., and Cady, J. G. (1962). *Genesis and hardening of laterite in soils* (Technical Bulletin No. 1282). Washington, DC: Soil Conservation Service.

Allan, A. Y. (1969). *Maize diamonds.* Kitale, Kenya: National Agricultural Research Station.

Allan, W. (1965). *The African husbandman.* New York: Barnes and Noble.

Alvares, C. (1992). *Decolonising history.* Goa: The Other India Bookstore.

Alvarez, S. E. (1998). Latin American feminisms go global. In Alvares, S. E., Dagnino, E., and Escobar, A. (Eds.), *Cultures of politics, Politics of cultures: Re-visioning Latin American social movements* (pp. 293–324). Boulder, CO: Westview Press.

Ambassade de France. (1961, May). *Basic data on Algeria.* New York: Service de Presse et d'Information.

Ambio. (1986). *Ambio index, 1972–1986.* Stockholm: Royal Swedish Academy of Sciences.

Ambler, C. H. (1988). *Kenyan communities in the age of imperialism: The central region in the late nineteenth century.* New Haven, CT: Yale University Press.

Amin, A. (Ed.). (1994). *Post-Fordism: A reader.* Oxford: Blackwell.

Amin, S. (1974). *Accumulation on a world scale.* New York: Monthly Review Press.

Amin, S. (1988). *Eurocentrism.* New York: Monthly Review Press.

Amin, S., Arrighi, G., Frank, A. G., and Wallerstein, I. (1982). *Dynamics of the global crisis.* New York: Monthly Review Press.

Amsden, A. H. (1989). *Asia's next giant: South Korea and late industrialization.* Oxford: Oxford University Press.

Amsden, A. H. (1990). Third world industrialization: "Global Fordism" or a new model? *New Left Review*, *182*, 5–31.

Anderson, R. E. (1952). *Liberia: America's African friend*. Chapel Hill: University of North Carolina Press.

Andiema, R., Dietz, T., and Kotomei, A. (2003). *Participatory evaluation of development interventions for poverty alleviation among (former) pastoralists in West Pokot, Kenya*. Amsterdam: Pokot Development Research Group, AGIDS/CERES.

Appadurai, A. (1996). *Modernity at large*. Minneapolis: University of Minnesota Press.

Approach. (1964, September). Desert survival. *26*.

Armstrong, A. H. (2004). Globalization from below: AIDWA, foreign funding, and rendering anti-violence campaigns. *Journal of Developing Societies*, *20*, 39–55.

Armstrong, W., and McGee, T. R. (1985). *Theatres of accumulation: Studies in Asian and Latin American urbanization*. London: Methuen.

Arrighi, G. (1970). Labour supplies in historical perspective: A study of the proletarianization of the African peasantry in Rhodesia. *Journal of Development Studies*, *6*, 197–234.

Aryeetey-Attoh, S. (1997). *Geography of sub-Saharan Africa*. Upper Saddle River, NJ: Prentice Hall.

Ash, T. G. (2005). *Free world*. London: Penguin.

Atlas of Kenya. (1959). Nairobi: Survey of Kenya.

Austen, R. (1987). *Africa in economic history*. Portsmouth, NH: Heinemann.

Bacon, F. (1625). Of plantations. In *Bacon's essays and wisdom of the ancients*. Boston: Little, Brown (1899).

Bagú, P. (1949). *Economiá de la sociedad colonial*. Buenos Aires: El Ateneo.

Baiocchi, G. (2002). Synergizing civil society: State–civil society and democratic decentralization in Porto Alegre, Brazil. *Political Power and Social Theory*, *15*, 3–86.

Bairoch, P. (1988). *Cities and economic development: From the dawn of history to the present*. Chicago: University of Chicago Press.

Balakrishnan, R. (2007, February 4). Cancer drug patent woes mount for Novartis. *DNA: Daily News and Analysis*, *www.dnaindia.com/report.asp?NewsID=1077991*

Balassa, B. (1965). Trade liberalization and "revealed comparative advantage." *Manchester School of Economic and Social Studies*, *33*, 92–123.

Ballance, R. H., and Sinclair, S. W. (1983). *Collapse and survival*. London: Allen & Unwin.

Bandarage, A. (1997). *Women, population and global crisis: A political–economic analysis*. London: Zed Books.

Baneria, L. (1989). Gender and the global economy. In MacEwan, A., and Tabb, W. (Eds.), *Instability and change in the world economy* (pp. 241–258). New York: Monthly Review Press.

Banuri, T. (1990). Development and the politics of knowledge: A critical interpretation of the social role of modernization theories in the development of the third world. In Marglin, A., and Marglin, S. (Eds.), *Dominating knowledge: Development, culture, and resistance* (pp. 29–72). New York: Oxford University Press.

Baran, P., and Sweezy, P. (1966). *Monopoly capital: An essay on the American economic and social order*. New York: Monthly Review Press.

Barndt, D. (2002). *Tangled routes: Women, work and globalization on the tomato trail*. Lanham, MD: Rowman & Littlefield.

Barnet, R. J. (1980). *The lean years: Politics in the age of scarcity*. New York: Simon and Schuster.

Barnet, R. J., and Müller, R. (1974). *Global reach: The power of the multinational corporation*. New York: Simon and Schuster.

Barnett, T., and Blaikie, P. (1992). *AIDS in Africa: Its present and future impact*. New York: Guilford Press.

Barratt-Brown, M. (1974). *The economics of imperialism*. Harmondsworth, UK: Penguin Books.

Barratt-Brown, M. (1993). *Fair trade: Reform and realities in the international trading system*. London: Zed Books.

Barrett, W. (1970). *The sugar hacienda of the Marqueses del Valle*. Minneapolis: University of Minnesota Press.

Bartholomew, J. (1950). *The advanced atlas of modern geography*. London: Meiklejohn.

Bassett, T. J., and Porter, P. W. (1991). "From the best authorities": The Mountains of Kong in the cartography of west Africa. *Journal of African History*, *32*, 367–413.

Basu, A. M. (1997). The politicization of fertility to achieve non-demographic objectives. *Population Studies*, *51*(1), 5–18.

Bates, M. (1952). *Where winter never comes: A study of man and nature in the tropics*. New York: Scribner.

Bathelt, H., Malmberg, A., and Maskell, P. (2004). Clusters and knowledge: Local buzz, global pipelines and the process of knowledge creation. *Progress in Human Geography*, *28*, 31–56.

Beaverstock, J., Smith, R., and Taylor, P. J. (2000). World-city network: A new metageography? *Annals of the Association of American Geographers*, *90*, 123–134.

Beja, E. L., Jr. (2006). Was capital fleeing southeast Asia? *Asia Pacific Business Review*, *12*, 261–283.

Benenson, A. S. (Ed.). (1990). *Control of communicable diseases in man* (15th ed.). Washington, DC: Public Health Association.

Benjamin, S. (2000). Governance, economic settings and poverty in Bangalore. *Environment and Urbanization*, *12*, 35–56.

Bennett, P. R. (1974). Remarks on a little-known Africanism. *Ba Shiru*, *6*(1), 69–71.

Bennoldt-Thomsen, V., Evers, T., Müller-Plantenberg, C., Müller-Plantenberg, U., and Schoeller, L. (Eds.). (1979). *Lateinamerika: Analysen und Berichte*, *3*. Berlin: Olle and Walter.

Berlin, I. (1979). *Against the current: Essays in the history of ideas*. London: Chatto and Windus.

Bernard, E. J. (2007, November 27). UNAIDS reduces estimate of global HIV prevalence to 33 million. *AIDSmap News*. (Accessed 12/21/08 from *www.aidsmap.com/en/news/6E2EF486-C363-438C-9804-881C05E7053C.asp*)

Berner, R. A., and Lasaga, A. C. (1989). Modeling the geochemical carbon cycle. *Scientific American*, *260*(3), 74–81.

Bernstein, H., Johnson, H., and Thomas, A. (1992). Labour regimes and social change under colonialism. In Allen, T., and Thomas, A. (Eds.), *Poverty and development in the 1990s* (pp. 185–202). Oxford: Oxford University Press.

Berry, B. J. L. (1961). City-size distributions and economic development. *Economic Development and Cultural Change*, *9*, 573–587.

Berry, B. J. L. (Ed.). (1976). *Urbanization and counterurbanization*. Beverly Hills, CA: Sage.

Berry, B. J. L. (1993). Transnational urbanward migration, 1830–1980. *Annals of the Association of American Geographers*, *83*, 389–405.

Bhabha, H. (1994). *The location of culture*. London: Routledge.

Biever, C. (2005, June 11). Melting permafrost pulls plug on Arctic lakes. *New Scientist* (2503).

Bigelow, B., and Peterson, B. (Eds.). (2002). *Rethinking globalization: Teaching for justice in an unjust world*. Milwaukee, WI: Rethinking Schools.

Blaikie, P. (1985). *The political economy of soil erosion in developing countries*. London: Longman.

Blaikie, P. (1995). Changing environments or changing views? *Geography*, *80*, 203–214.

Blaut, J. (1963). The ecology of tropical farming systems. *Revista Geografica*, *28*, 47–67.

Blaut, J. (1976). Where was capitalism born? *Antipode*, *8*(2), 1–11.

Blaut, J. (1987). Diffusionism: A uniformitarian critique. *Annals of the Association of American Geographers*, *77*, 30–47.

Blaut, J. (1992). Fourteen ninety-two. *Political Geography*, *11*, 355–385.

Blaut, J. (1993). *The colonizer's model of the world: Geographical diffusionism and Eurocentric history*. New York: Guilford Press.

Board on Science and Technology for International Development. (1996). *Lost crops of Africa: Grains*. Washington, DC: National Academy Press.

Bolin, B. (1970). The carbon cycle. *Scientific American*, *223*(3), 124–132.

Bollig, M. (1990). Ethnic conflicts in northwest Kenya: Pokot–Turkana raiding 1969–1984. *Zeitschrift für Ethnologie*, *115*, 73–90.

Bollig, M. (1993). Intra- and interethnic conflict in northwest Kenya: A multicausal analysis of conflict behaviour. *Anthropos*, *88*, 176–184.

Bollig, M. (1998). Moral economy and self-interest: Kinship, friendship, and exchange among the Pokot (N.W. Kenya). In Schweizer, T., and White, D. R. (Eds.), *Kinship, networks, and exchange* (pp. 137–157). Cambridge, UK: Cambridge University Press.

Bollig, M. (2000). Staging social structures: Ritual and social organization in an egalitarian society—the pastoral Pokot of northern Kenya. *Ethnos*, *65*, 341–365.

Bollig, M., and Schulte, A. (1999). Environmental change and pastoral perceptions: Degradation and indigenous knowledge in two African pastoral communities. *Human Ecology, 27*, 493–514.

Bond, P., and McInnes, P. (2007). Decommodifying electricity in postapartheid Johannesburg. In Leitner, H., Peck, J., and Sheppard, E. (Eds.), *Contesting neoliberalism: Urban frontiers* (pp. 179–204). New York: Guilford Press.

Booth, D. (1985). Marxism and development sociology: Interpreting the "impasse." *World Development, 13*, 761–787.

Bora, B., Kuwahara, A., and Laird, S. (2002). *Quantification of non-tariff measures* (UNCTAD Policy Issues in International Trade and Commodities No. 18). New York: United Nations.

Borchert, J. R. (1953). Regional differences in the world atmospheric circulation. *Annals of the Association of American Geographers, 43*, 14–26.

Boserup, E. (1965). *The conditions of agricultural growth.* Chicago: Aldine.

Boserup, E. (1970). *Women's role in economic development.* New York: St. Martin's Press.

Bot, A., Nachtergaele, F., and Young, A. (2000). *Land resource potential and constraints at regional and country levels.* Rome: Land and Water Division, Food and Agriculture Organization of the United Nations.

Bouvier, L. F., and Grant, L. (1994). *How many Americans?: Population, immigration and the environment.* San Francisco: Sierra Club Books.

Bowman, I. (1931). *The pioneer fringe* (Special Publication No. 13). New York: American Geographical Society.

Box, E. O., and Meentemeyer, V. (1991). Geographic modeling and modern ecology. In Esser, G., and Overdieck, D. (Eds.), *Modern ecology* (pp. 773–804). Amsterdam: Elsevier.

Boyenge, J.-P. (2003). *ILO database on export processing zones.* Geneva: International Labour Organization.

Boyer, R., and Durand, J.-P. (1997). *After Fordism.* London: Macmillan.

Boyle, B. (1981, April 29). Ford's policy strangles Dutch plant. *The Guardian* [Manchester, UK], 9.

Brandt, W. (1980). *North–south: A program for survival.* London: Pan Books.

Brandt, W. (1983). *North–south: Cooperation for world recovery.* London: Pan Books.

Braudel, F. (1986). *The perspective of the world.* New York: Harper and Row.

Brecher, J., Costello, T., and Smith, B. (2000). *Globalization from below: The power of solidarity.* Cambridge, MA: South End Press.

Breemer, J. P. van den, Drijver, C. A., and Venema, L. B. (1995). *Local resource management in Africa.* New York: Wiley.

Brenner, R. (1977). The origins of capitalist development: A critique of neo-Smithian Marxism. *New Left Review, 104*, 23–93.

Brett, E. A. (1983). *International money and capitalist crisis.* London: Heinemann.

Brett, E. A. (1985). *The world economy since the war: The politics of uneven development.* London: Macmillan.

Brewer, A. (1980). *Marxist theories of imperialism.* London: Routledge and Kegan Paul.

Britton, S. (1982). The political economy of tourism in the third world. *Annals of Tourism Research, 9*, 331–358.

Broek, J. O. M, and Webb, J. W. (1978). *A geography of mankind.* New York: McGraw-Hill.

Bromley, D. W. (1991). *Environment and economy: Property rights and public policy.* Oxford: Blackwell.

Browder, J. O., Bohland, J. R., and Scarpacci, J. L. (1995). Patterns of development on the metropolitan fringe: Urban fringe expansion in Bangkok, Jakarta, and Santiago. *Journal of the American Planning Association, 61*, 310–327.

Brown, B. (2006). *What drives global capital flows?: Myth, speculation and currency diplomacy.* Basingstoke, UK: Palgrave/Macmillan.

Brown, L. R. (1995). *Who will feed China?: Wake-up call for a small planet.* New York: Norton.

Brown, L. R., and Wolf, E. C. (1985). *Reversing Africa's decline* (Worldwatch Paper No. 65). Washington, DC: Worldwatch Institute.

Brown, L. R., et al. (1984–2007). *State of the world.* New York: Norton.

Brown, Lynn R. (2004). Economic growth rates in Africa: The potential impact of HIV/AIDS. In Kalipeni, E., Craddock, S., Oppong, J. R., and Ghosh, J. (Eds.), *HIV and AIDS in Africa: Beyond epidemiology* (pp. 291–303). Oxford: Blackwell.

Brunschwig, H. (1966). *French colonialism, 1871–1924.* New York: Praeger.

Buckman, H. O., and Brady, N. C. (1962). *The nature and properties of soils.* New York: Macmillan.

Bull, D. (1982). *A growing problem: Pesticides and the third world poor.* Oxford: Oxfam.

Bullfrog Films. (1995). *Who's counting?: Marilyn Waring on sex, lies and global economics* [Film, T. Nash, Director]. Montreal: National Film Board of Canada (Producer).

Bullfrog Films. (2005). *China blue.* Micha X. Peled [Film Director]. Oley, PA: Bullfrog Films.

Cairncross, F. (1997). *The death of distance: How the communications revolution will change our lives.* London: Orion Business Books.

Callahan, D. (1971). Introduction. In Callahan, D. (Ed.), *The American population debate* (pp. xi–xv). Garden City, NY: Doubleday.

Campbell, C. (2004). Migrancy, masculine identities, and AIDS: The psychosocial context of HIV transmission on the South African gold mines. In Kalipeni, E., Craddock, S., Oppong, J. R., & Ghosh, J. (Eds.), *HIV and AIDS in Africa: Beyond epidemiology* (pp. 144–154). Oxford: Blackwell.

Cardoso, F. H. (1977). *The originality of the copy: ECLA and the idea of development.* Cambridge, UK: University of Cambridge, Centre of Latin American Studies.

Cardoso, F., and Faletto, R. (1979). *Dependency and development.* Berkeley: University of California Press.

Carney, J. (1993). Converting the wetlands, engendering the environment: The intersection of gender with agrarian change in The Gambia. *Economic Geography*, *69*, 329–348.

Carruthers, I. D. (1969). *Issues in selection and design of rural water projects* (Discussion Paper No. 68). Nairobi: Institute for Development Studies, University of Nairobi.

Carter Center. (2005). Committed to international health through Guinea worm disease eradication: The Carter Center Guinea Worm Disease Eradication Program. *www.cartercenter.org/health/guinea_worm/index.html*

Cassen, B. (2004). Inventing ATTAC. In Mertes, T. (Ed.), *A movement of movements: Is another world really possible?* (pp. 152–174). London: Verso.

Castles, S., and Miller, M. J. (2003). *The age of migration* (3rd ed.). New York: Guilford Press.

Centers for Disease Control and Prevention. (2005). *The impact of malaria, a leading cause of death worldwide. www.cdc.gov/malaria/impact/index.htm*

Centers for Disease Control and Prevention. (2006). *Human immunodeficiency virus type 2. www.cdc.gov/hiv/resources/factsheets/hiv2.htm*

Centers for Medicare and Medicaid Services. (2008). *Historical national health expenditures data.* Department of Health and Human Services, Washington, DC. Accessed 12/9/2009 from *www.cms.hhs.gov/NationalHealthExpendData/02_NationalHealthAccountsHistorical.asp*

Central Bureau of Statistics. (1999). *1999 census of population and housing, Government of Kenya, Vol. 1. www.cbs.go.ke/pdf/authority/pdf*

Central Intelligence Agency (CIA). (1961). *Cameroon.* Washington, DC: CIA.

Ceres. (1976, May–June). New Sahel threats. -.

Chamberlain, H. S. (1899). *Die Grundlagen des Neunzehnten Jahrhunderts.* Munich: F. Bruckmann (1904).

Chandler, T. (1987). *Four thousand years of urban growth: An historical census.* Lampeter, UK: Edwin Mellon Press.

Chang, H.-J. (2002). *Kicking away the ladder: Development strategy in historical perspective.* London: Anthem Press.

Chang, H.-J., Park, H.-J., and Yoo, C. G. (1998). Interpreting the Korean crisis: Financial liberalisation, industrial policy and corporate governance. *Cambridge Journal of Economics*, *22*, 735–746.

Chang, J.-H. (1968). The agricultural potential of the humid tropics. *Geographical Review*, *58*, 333–361.

Chang, J.-H. (1970). Potential photosynthesis and crop productivity. *Annals of the Association of American Geographers*, *60*, 92–101.

Chant, S. (Ed.). (1992). *Gender and migration in developing countries.* London: Belhaven.

Chase-Dunn, C. (1985). The system of world cities, A.D. 800–1975. In Timberlake, M. (Ed.), *Urbanization in the world-economy* (pp. 269–292). New York: Academic Press.

Chatterjee, P. (1989). Colonialism, nationalism and colonized women. *American Ethnologist*, *16*, 622–633.

Chaudhuri, K. N. (Ed.). (1971). *The economic development of India under the East India*

Company 1814–58. Cambridge, UK: Cambridge University Press.

chavezthefilm.com. (2002a). The revolution will not be televised: Neoliberalism public pain, private gain. *www.chavezthefilm.com/html/backgrd/neolib.htm*

chavezthefilm.com. (2002b). The revolution will not be televised: Synopsis. *www.chavezthefilm.com/html/film/synopsis.htm*

Chayanov, A. V. (1966). *The theory of peasant economy*. Homewood, IL: American Economic Association.

Chayefsky, P. (1976). *Network*. In P. Chayefsky, *The collected works of Paddy Chayefsky: The screenplays* (Vol. 2, pp. 115–226). New York: Applause Books (1995).

Chenery, E. M. (1960). *An introduction to the soils of the Uganda protectorate*. Kampala: Kawanda Research Station.

Chi-Bonnardel, R. van. (1973). *The atlas of Africa*. New York: Free Press.

Chilcote, R. (1984). *Theories of development and underdevelopment*. Boulder, CO: Westview Press.

Christensen, J. (2007). Dirty money: Inside the secret world of offshore banking. In Hiatt, S. (Ed.), *A game as old as empire: The secret world of economic hit men and the web of global corruption* (pp. 41–67). San Francisco: Berrett-Koehler.

Church, R. J. H. (1957). *West Africa*. London: Longmans, Green.

Church, R. J. H. (1980). *West Africa* (8th ed.). London: Longman.

Clark, G. L. (1997). Pension funds and urban investment: Four models of financial intermediation. *Environment and Planning A, 29*, 1297–1316.

Clarke, W. M. (2004). *How the city of London works*. London: Sweet and Maxwell.

Clarkson, T. (1836). *History of the rise, progress, and accomplishment of the abolition of the African slave-trade by the British Parliament* (2 vols.). New York: J. S. Taylor.

Clingingsmith, D., and Williamson, J. G. (2005). *Mughal decline, climate change, and Britain's industrial ascent: An integrated perspective on India's 18th and 19th century deindustrialization* (NBER Working Paper No. 11730). Cambridge, MA: National Bureau of Economic Research.

Coakley, J. (1992). London as an international financial centre. In Budd, L., and Whimster, S. (Eds.), *Global finance and urban living: A study of metropolitan change* (pp. 52–72). London: Routledge.

Coale, A. J. (1974). The history of the human population. In Scientific American (Ed.), *The human population* (pp. 14–25). San Francisco: Freeman.

Co-Chairs' Statement, Asian–African Subregional Organizations Conference, Bandung, Indonesia. (2003, July 29–30). *www.aseansec.org/15478.htm*

Cohen, B. (2002). Bretton Woods system. In Jones, R. J. B. (Ed.), *Routledge encyclopedia of international political economy* (pp. 95–102). London: Routledge.

Colchester, M. (1994). Sustaining the forests: The community-based approach in south and south-east Asia. *Development and Change, 25*, 69–100.

Coleman, D. C. (1996). *Fundamentals of soil ecology*. San Diego, CA: Academic Press.

Collins, J. L. (1987). Labor scarcity and ecological change. In Little, P. D., Horowitz, M. M., with Nyerges, A. E. (Eds.), *Lands at risk in the third world: Local level perspectives* (pp. 19–37). Boulder, CO: Westview Press.

Collins, R. O. (Ed.). (1969). *The partition of Africa*. New York: Wiley.

Colman, D., and Nixson, F. (1986). *Economics of change in less developed countries*. New York: Barnes and Noble.

Commoner, B. (1975, August–September). How poverty breeds overpopulation (and not the other way around). *Ramparts, 13*(10), 21–25, 58–59.

Conant, F. P. (1965). *Korok:* A variable unit of physical and social space among the Pokot of East Africa. *American Anthropologist, 67*, 419–434.

Conant, F. P. (1966). *Oren Pokot: The "way" of the Pokot*. Unpublished manuscript.

Conant, F. P. (1973). *Sexual bias and ecological realities in east Africa*. Paper presented at the annual meeting of the American Anthropological Association, New Orleans, LA.

Conant, F. P. (1981). Thorns paired, sharply recurved: Cultural controls and range quality in east Africa. In Spooner, B. (Ed.), *Anthropology and desertification* (pp. 111–122). London: Academic Press.

Conant, F. P. (1982a). Refugee settlements and vegetation change: A multistage Landsat data analysis of a semi-arid region in Kenya. In

Cook, J. J. (Ed.), *International symposium on remote sensing of the environment* (pp. 449–461). Ann Arbor: Environmental Research Institute of Michigan.

Conant, F. P. (1982b). Strength, reproductive capacity, and the division of labor in east Africa. In Edgerton, R., and Kennedy, J. G. (Eds.), *Culture and ecology: Eclectic perspectives* (Special Publication No. 15, pp. 26–55). American Anthropological Association.

Conklin, H. (1957). *Hanunoo agriculture*. Rome: Food and Agriculture Organization.

Connexions (1994, *44*, 9). No ground to stand on . . .

Cook, S. F., and Borah, W. (1971). *Essays in population history: Vol. 1. Mexico and the Caribbean*. Berkeley: University of California Press.

Coquery-Vidrovitch, C. (1985). The colonial economy of the former French, Belgian and Portuguese zones, 1914–35. In Boahen, A. A. (Ed.), *General history of Africa: VII. Africa under colonial domination 1880–1935* (pp. 351–381). Paris: UNESCO.

Corbridge, S. (1993). *Debt and development*. Oxford: Blackwell.

Corbridge, S. (1998). "Beneath the pavement only soil": The poverty of post-development. *Journal of Development Studies*, *34*(6), 138–148.

Corsetti, G., Pesenti, P., and Roubini, N. (1999). What caused the Asian currency and financial crisis? *Japan and the World Economy*, *11*, 305–373.

Cournot, A. (1838). *Recherches sur les principes mathématiques de la théorie des richesses*. Paris: Hachette.

Cowen, M. P., and Shenton, R. W. (1996). *Doctrines of development*. London: Routledge.

Craddock, S. (2004). Introduction: Beyond epidemiology: Locating AIDS in Africa. In Kalipeni, E., Craddock, S., Oppong, J. R., and Ghosh, J. (Eds.), *HIV and AIDS in Africa: Beyond epidemiology* (pp. 1–10). Oxford: Blackwell.

Craig, D., and Porter, D. (2006). *Development beyond neoliberalism? Governance, poverty reduction and political economy*. New York: Routledge.

Cravey, A. (1998). *Women and work in Mexico's maquiladoras*. Lanham, MD: Rowman & Littlefield.

Crehan, K. (1983). Women and development in north western Zambia: From producer to housewife. *Review of African Political Economy*, *27–28*, 51–66.

Crow, B., and Sultana, F. (2002). Gender, class and access to water: Three cases in a poor and crowded delta. *Society and Natural Resources*, *15*, 709–724.

Crowson, P. C. F. (1981, March). Reversing the declining investment in metals exploration. *Metals and Minerals*, 49–53.

Crowson, P. C. F. (1990). A perspective on worldwide exploration for minerals. In Tilton, J. E., Eggert, R. G., and Landsberg, H. H. (Eds.), *World mineral exploration: Trends and economic issues* (pp. 21–103). Washington, DC: Resources for the Future.

Crystal, D. (2000). *Language death*. Cambridge, UK: Cambridge University Press.

Cuddington, J. T., and Smith, G. W. (1985). International borrowing and lending: What have we learned from theory and experience? In Smith, G. W., and Cuddington, J. (Eds.), *International debt and the developing countries* (pp. 3–17). Washington, DC: World Bank.

Curtin, D. W. (2005). *Environmental ethics for a postcolonial world*. Lanham, MD: Rowman & Littlefield.

Curtin, P. D. (1969). *The Atlantic slave trade: A census*. Madison: University of Wisconsin Press.

Daily Nation [Kenya]. (2004, October 17). Police break up land pressure group rally.

Daily Nation [Kenya]. (2004, December 18). Italy gives a Sh1b loan for irrigation.

Daily Nation [Kenya]. (2005, February 28). Civic leaders demand end to tree-felling.

Dalby, D., and Church, J. R. H. (1973). *Drought in Africa*. London: Centre for African Studies, School of Oriental and African Studies, University of London.

Das, A. (2006, February 9). India: Breathe in, and hands off our yoga. *The Christian Science Monitor*. *www.csmonitor.com/2006/0209/p07s02-wosc.htm*

Datoo, B. A. (1978). Toward a reformulation of Boserup's theory of agricultural change. *Economic Geography*, *54*, 135–144.

Davis, K. (1974). The migrations of human populations. In the Scientific American editors (Eds.), *The human population* (pp. 53–68). San Francisco: Freeman.

de Barros, J. (1552). *Decadas da Asia* (Decade I, Book 2, Chapter 2). Lisboa.

de Heusch, L. (1964). Nationalisme et lutte des classes au Rwanda. In Fröhlich, W. (Ed.), *Afrika im Wandel seiner Gesellschaftsformen* (pp. 96–108). Leiden, The Netherlands: E. J. Brill.

Dell, S. (1981). *On being grandmothery: The evolution of IMF conditionality.* Princeton, NJ: Princeton University Press.

Democracy Center. (n.d.). Bechtel vs. Bolivia: The Bolivian water revolt. *www.democracyctr.org/bolivia/investigations/water*

Department of Veterinary Services. (1953). *Cattle census West Suk District, 1952–53* (Ref. No. Stock/1/59, typescript). Kapenguria, Kenya: Department of Veterinary Services.

de Pina, R. (ca. 1500). *Chronica del Rey Dom Joao II.* Lisboa.

Derrida, J. (1976). *Of grammatology.* Baltimore, MD: Johns Hopkins University Press.

de Sousa Santos, B. (1998). Participatory budgeting in Porto Alegre: Toward a redistributive democracy. *Politics and Society, 26,* 461–510.

De Souza, A. R. (1986). To have and to have not: Colonialism and core–periphery relations. *Focus, 36*(3), 14–19.

Development Alternatives with Women for a New Era. (1993). A View from the South. *Connexions, 41,* 8–9, 39.

Dhanraj, D. (Producer/director). (1993). *Something like a war* [Film]. London: Channel 4; New York: Women Make Movies.

d'Hertefelt, M. (1965). The Rwanda of Rwanda. In Gibbs, J. L., Jr. (Ed.), *Peoples of Africa* (pp. 403–440). New York: Holt, Rinehart and Winston.

Diamond, J. (1997). *Guns, germs and steel.* New York: Norton.

Dicken, P. (1992). *Global shift* (2nd ed.): *The internationalization of economic activity.* New York: Guilford Press.

Dicken, P. (2003). *Global shift* (4th ed.): *Reshaping the global economic map in the 21st century.* New York: Guilford Press.

Dicken, P., Kelly, P. F., Olds, K., and Yeung, H. W.-C. (2001). Chains and networks, territories and scales: Towards a relational framework for analysing the global economy. *Global Networks, 1,* 89–112.

Dickens, E. (2005). The Eurodollar market and the new era of global financialization. In Epstein, G. A. (Ed.), *Financialization and the world economy* (pp. 210–219). Northampton, MA: Edward Elgar.

Dietz, T. (1987). *Pastoralists in dire straits* (Report No. 49). Amsterdam: Nederlandse Geografische Studies.

Dietz, T. (1996). *Entitlements to natural resources: Contours of political environmental geography.* Amsterdam: International Books.

Dietz, T., and de Leeuw, W. (1999). The Arid and Semi-Arid Lands Programme in Kenya. In Sterkenburg, J., and van der Wiel, A. (Eds.), *Integrated area development: Experiences with Netherlands aid in Africa* (pp. 37–57). The Hague: Ministerie van Buitenlandse Zaken.

Dietz, T., van Haastrecht, A., and Schomaker, M. (1983a, July). *Locational development profile, Lelan Location, West Pokot District, Kenya* (Regional Development Research, West Pokot). Amsterdam: University of Amsterdam and Kerio Valley Development Authority.

Dietz, T., van Haastrecht, A., and Schomaker, M. (1983b, August). *Locational development profile, Sekerr Location, West Pokot District, Kenya* (Regional Development Research, West Pokot). Amsterdam: University of Amsterdam and Kerio Valley Development Authority.

Dietz, T., van Haastrecht, A., and Schomaker, M. (1983c, May). *Locational development profile, Sook Location, West Pokot District, Kenya* (Regional Development Research, West Pokot). Amsterdam: University of Amsterdam and Kerio Valley Development Authority.

Dietz, T., and van Woersem, B. (1996). *The Arid and Semi-Arid Lands Programme in Kenya, with a focus on West Pokot, Elgeyo Marakwet and Kajiado Districts.* Unpublished report.

Dirlik, A. (1997). *The postcolonial aura: Third world criticism in the age of global capitalism.* Boulder, CO: Westview Press.

Disney, H. J. de S., & Haylock, J. W. (1956). The distribution and breeding behavior of the Sudan dioch (*Quelea q. aethiopica*) in Tanganyika. *East African Agricultural Journal, 20,* 141–147.

Dos Santos, T. (1970). The structure of dependence. *American Economic Review, 60,* 231–236.

Dosi, G., Pavitt, K., and Soete, L. (1990). *The economics of technical change and international trade.* London: Wheatsheaf.

Drache, P. (2002). When labour and investment standards almost mattered: A putative history lesson in trade politics that ought not to be forgotten. In McBride, S., Dobuzinskis, L., Griffin Cohen, M., and Busumtwi-Sam, J. (Eds.), *Global instability: Uncertainty and new vision in political economy* (pp. 9–28). Amsterdam: Kluwer.

Drèze, J., and Sen, A. (Eds.). (1990–1991). *The political economy of hunger* (3 vols.). New York: Oxford University Press.

Duffield, M. (2002). *Global governance and the new wars: The merging of development and security.* London: Zed Books.

Duffy, J. (1964). Portugal in Africa. In Quigg, P. (Ed.), *Africa* (pp. 84–98). New York: Praeger.

du Guerny, J. (2002). *The elderly, HIV/AIDS and sustainable rural development: Dimensions. www.fao.org/sd/2002/PE0101a_en.htm*

Dunford, M. (1990). Theories of regulation. *Environment and Planning D: Society and Space, 8*, 297–322.

Dunning, J. H. (1988). *Explaining international production.* London: Unwin Hyman.

Dunning, J. H., and Pearce, R. D. (1985). *The world's largest industrial enterprises, 1962–1983.* New York: St. Martin's Press.

Durkheim, E. (1893). *De la division de travail social.* Paris: F. Alcan.

The East African Standard. (2005, February 5). Why the Pokot won't stop firing from all flanks.

The East African Standard. (2005, March 5). Kenya: Land of ironies.

Echánove, F., and Steffen, C. (2005). Agribusiness and farmers in Mexico: The importance of contractual relations. *Geographical Journal, 171*, 166–176.

Eckholm, E. (1979). *Planting for the future: Forestry for human needs.* Washington, DC: Worldwatch Institute.

Eckholm, E., and Brown, L. R. (1977). *Spreading deserts: The hand of man* (Worldwatch Paper No. 13). Washington, DC: Worldwatch Institute.

Economic Commission for Latin America (ECLA). (1951). *Theoretical and practical problems of economic growth.* Santiago, Chile: ECLA, United Nations.

The Economist. (2007, May 24). Sovereign wealth funds: The world's most expensive club. *www.economist.com/finance/displaystory.cfm?story_id=9230598*

Edgerton, R. B. (1971). *The individual in cultural adaptation.* Berkeley: University of California Press.

Edgerton, R. B., and Conant, F. P. (1964). *Kilapat*: The "shaming party" among the Pokot of East Africa. *Southwestern Journal of Anthropology, 20*, 404–418.

Educational TV and Film Center. (1986). *The global assembly line.* Lorraine Gray [Film Director]. Washington, DC: Educational TV and Film Center.

Edwards, C. (1988). The debt crisis and development: A comparison of major theories. *Geoforum, 19*, 3–28.

Ehret, C. (1969). Cushites and the highland and plains Nilotes. In Ogot, B. A., and Kierman, J. A. (Eds.), *Zamani: A survey of East African history* (pp. 158–176). New York: Humanities Press.

Ehrlich, P. R. (1968). *The population bomb.* New York: Ballantine Books.

Ehrlich, P. R., and Ehrlich, A. H. (1970). *Population, resources, environment: Issues in human ecology.* San Francisco: Freeman.

Eichengreen, B. (2007). *Global imbalances and the lessons of Bretton Woods.* Cambridge, MA: MIT Press.

Eichner, A. S. (1976). *The megacorp and oligopoly.* Cambridge, UK: Cambridge University Press.

Eisenstadt, S. (1965). *Modernization, protest and change.* Englewood Cliffs, NJ: Prentice-Hall.

Ekins, P. (1993). Making development sustainable. In Sachs, W. (Ed.), *Global ecology: A new arena of political conflict* (pp. 91–103). London: Zed Books.

El Saadawi, N. (1994, June). *Thinking and acting: The challenge of global feminism.* Keynote Lecture, National Women's Studies Association Annual Conference, Ames, IA.

Eliot, T. S. (1948). *Notes toward the definition of culture.* London: Faber and Faber.

Elson, D., and Pearson, R. (1981). Nimble fingers make cheap workers: An analysis of women's employment in third world export manufacturing. *Feminist Review, 7*, 87–107.

Emmanuel, A. G. (1972). *Unequal exchange.* New York: Monthly Review Press.

Energy Information Administration. (2003). *International energy annual 2003.* Washington, DC: U.S. Government Printing Office.

Energy Information Administration. (2006). *International energy outlook 2005.* Washington, DC: U.S. Government Printing Office.

Energy Information Administration. (2008).

Official energy statistics from the U.S. government. *www.eia.doe.gov/international*

Enloe, C. (1989). *Bananas, beaches and bases: Making feminist sense of international politics.* Berkeley: University of California Press.

Epstein, G. A. (Ed.). (2005). *Capital flight and capital controls in developing countries.* Northampton, MA: Edward Elgar.

Escobar, A. (1988). Power and visibility: Development and the intervention and management of the third world. *Cultural Anthropology, 3,* 428–443.

Escobar, A. (1992). Reflections on "development": Grassroots approaches and alternative politics in the third world. *Futures, 24,* 411–436.

Escobar, A. (1995). *Encountering development.* Princeton, NJ: Princeton University Press.

Esteva, G. (1992). Development. In Sachs, W. (Ed.), *The development dictionary* (pp. 6–25). London: Zed Books.

Euromonitor. (1989). *Third world economic handbook.* Bury St. Edmunds, UK: St. Edmundsbury Press.

Evans, P. (1979). *Dependent development: The alliance of multinational, state, and local capital in Brazil.* Princeton, NJ: Princeton University Press.

Evans, P. (1995). *Embedded autonomy: State and industrial transformation.* Princeton, NJ: Princeton University Press.

Fage, J. D. (1958). *An atlas of African history.* London: Arnold.

Fage, J. D. (1978). *An atlas of African history* (2nd ed.). New York: Africana.

Fairbank, J. K., Reischauer, E. O., and Craig, A. M. (1973). *East Asia: Tradition and transformation.* Boston: Houghton Mifflin.

Faust, D. R., and Nagar, R. (2003). *The global movement against the war on Iraq* (Pamphlet). People's Geography Project.

Fearnside, P. M. (1986). Spatial concentration of deforestation in the Brazilian Amazon. *Ambio, 15,* 74–81.

Fernandez-Kelly, M. P. (1984). *Maquiladoras*: The view from the inside. In Sacks, K. B., and Remy, D. (Eds.), *My troubles are going to have trouble with me* (pp. 203–215). New Brunswick, NJ: Rutgers University Press.

Focus on the Global South and GRAIN. (2004). *World Food Day: Iraqi farmers aren't celebrating. www.grain.org/nfg/?id=253*

FOIL [Forum of Indian Leftists]. (1996). *Those that be in bondage: Child labor and IMF strategy in India* (FOIL Pamphlet No. 1). *www.proxsa.org/economy/labor/chldlbr.html*

Food and Agriculture Organization (FAO). (2000). *Agricultural knowledge and information system for rural development (AKIS/RD): Strategic vision and guiding principles.* Rome: FAO.

Food and Agriculture Organization (FAO). (2006). *FAOSTAT. faostat.fao.org*

Ford, J. (1971). *The role of trypanosomiases in African ecology.* Oxford: Clarendon Press.

Fortune. (1973a, May). *Fortune*'s directory of the 100 largest industrial corporations. 220–249.

Fortune. (1973b, September). *Fortune*'s directory Part II. 202–209.

Fortune. (1984, August 20). The *Fortune* international 500. 175–220.

Fortune. (1994, July 25). The global 500. *130,* 2, 138–196.

Fortune. (2003, May 12). The Fortune 1000. *147,* 9.

Foucault, M. (1980). *Power/knowledge: Selected interviews and other writings, 1972–1977.* London: Harvester Press.

Foucault, M. (1991). Governmentality. In Burchell, G., Gordon, C., and Miller, P. (Eds.), *The Foucault effect: Studies in governmentality* (pp. 87–104). London: Harvester Wheatsheaf.

Frake, C. O. (1962). Cultural ecology and ethnography. *American Anthropologist, 62,* 53–59.

Frank, A. G. (1967). *Capitalism and underdevelopment in Latin America.* New York: Monthly Review Press.

Frank, A. G. (1978a). *Dependent accumulation and underdevelopment.* London: Macmillan.

Frank, A. G. (1978b). *World accumulation 1492–1789.* New York: Monthly Review Press.

Freeman, C. (2001). Is local:global as feminine:masculine? Rethinking the gender of globalization. *Signs, 26,* 1007–1036.

Freeman, T. W. (1961). *A hundred years of geography.* Chicago: Aldine.

Friedman, T. L. (2005). *The world is flat: A brief history of the twenty-first century.* New York: Farrar, Straus and Giroux.

Friedmann, J. (1966). *Regional development policy: A case study of Venezuela.* Cambridge, MA: MIT Press.

Friedmann, J. (1986). The world city hypothesis. *Development and Change, 17,* 69–84.

Fröbel, F., Heinrichs, J., and Kreye, O. (1980). *The new international division of labour.* Cambridge, UK: Cambridge University Press.

Fukuyama, F. (1989). The end of history? *The National Interest, 16,* 3–16.

Furtado, C. (1966). *Subdesarrollo y estanciamento en America Latina.* Buenos Aires: C.E.A.L.

Gadamer, H.-G. (1993). *Truth and method* (2nd rev. ed.). New York: Continuum.

Gade, D. W., and Perkins-Belgram, A. N. (1986). Woodfuels, reforestation, and ecodevelopment in highland Madagascar. *GeoJournal, 12,* 365–374.

Gadgil, M., and Guha, R. (1995). *Ecology and equity: The use and abuse of nature in contemporary India.* New York: Routledge.

Galtung, J. (1971). A structural theory of imperialism. *Journal of Peace Research, 2,* 81–116.

Gardner, C. (2005). Mercury rising. *www.oceanconcervancy.org/site/PageServer?pagename=bpm_feature_3*

Garrow, D. (1986). *Bearing the cross.* New York: Morrow.

Gartner, W. C. (1996). *Tourism development: Principles, processes and policies.* New York: Van Nostrand Reinhold.

Gee, C. Y., Makens, J. C., and Choy, D. J. L. (1989). *The travel industry.* New York: Van Nostrand Reinhold.

Geertz, C. (1963). *Agricultural involution: The processes of ecological change in Indonesia.* Berkeley: University of California Press.

Geiger, S. (1997). *Tanu women: Gender and culture in the making of Tanganyikan nationalism 1955–1965.* Portsmouth, NH: Heinemann.

Gelens, H. F., Kinyanjui, H. C. K., and van de Weg, R. F. (Eds.). (1976). *Soils of the Kapenguria area* (Reconnaissance Soil Survey Report No. R2, Kenya Soil Survey). Nairobi: Ministry of Agriculture, Republic of Kenya.

Gereffi, G. (1996). Global commodity chains: New forms of coordination and control among nations and firms in international industries. *Competition and Change: The Journal of Global Business and Political Economy, 1,* 427–439.

Gersmehl, P., Kammrath, W., and Gross, H. (1980). *Physical geography.* Philadelphia: Saunders College and Holt, Rinehart and Winston.

Gesler, W. (1991). *The cultural geography of health care.* Pittsburgh: University of Pittsburgh Press.

Gibbon, E. (1776–1787). *The decline and fall of the Roman Empire.* New York: Knopf (1993).

Gibson-Graham, J. K. (1996). *The end of capitalism (as we know it).* Oxford: Blackwell.

Gibson-Graham, J. K. (2006). *A postcapitalist politics.* Minneapolis: University of Minnesota Press.

Giddens, A. (1991). *Modernity and self-identity.* Stanford, CA: Stanford University Press.

Gidwani, V. (2002). The unbearable modernity of "development"? An essay on canal irrigation and development planning in western India. *Progress in Planning, 58*(1), 1–80.

Girling, R. H. (1985). *Multinational institutions and the third world.* New York: Praeger.

Gischler, C. E. (1979). *Water resources in the Arab Middle East and north Africa.* Cambridge, UK: Middle East and North African Studies Press.

Glassman, J. (2001). From Seattle (and Ubon) to Bangkok: The scales of resistance to corporate globalization. *Environment and Planning D: Society and Space, 19,* 513–533.

Glassman, J., and Samatar, A. (1997). Development geography and the third-world state. *Progress in Human Geography, 21,* 164–198.

Gleave, M. B., and White, H. P. (1969). The west African middle belt: Environmental fact or geographer's fiction? *Geographical Review, 59*(1), 123–139.

Gobineau, J. A., Comte de. (1853–1855). *Essai sur l'inegalité des races humaines.* Paris: Firmin-Didot.

Goeller, H., and Zucker, A. (1984). Infinite resources: The ultimate strategy. *Science, 223,* 456–462.

Goldman, A. (1991). Tradition and change in postharvest pest management in Kenya. *Agriculture and Human Values, 8*(1–2), 99–113.

Goldman, A. (1995). Threats to sustainability in African agriculture: Searching for appropriate paradigms. *Human Ecology, 21*(3), 291–334.

Goldschmidt, W. R. (1969). *Kambuya's cattle: The legacy of an African herdsman.* Berkeley: University of California Press.

Goldschmidt, W. R. (1976). *The culture and behavior of the Sebei.* Berkeley: University of California Press.

Goldschmidt, W. R. (2006). *The bridge to humanity: How affect hunger trumps the selfish gene.* New York: Oxford University Press.

Goldsmith, W. W. (n.d.). Participatory budgeting in Brazil. *www.plannersnetwork.org/publications/brazil_goldsmith.pdf*

Goldthorpe, J. E., and Wilson, F. B. (1960). *Tribal maps of east Africa and Zanzibar* (East African Studies No. 13). Kampala: East African Institute of Social Research.

Good, C. M. (1987). *Ethnomedical systems in Africa: Patterns of traditional medicine in rural and urban Kenya.* New York: Guilford Press.

Goode's world atlas (19th ed., Espinshade, E. B., Jr., Ed.). (1995). Chicago: Rand McNally.

Gordon, R. B., Bertram, M., and Graedel, T. E. (2006). Metal stocks and sustainability. *Proceedings of the National Academy of Sciences USA, 103,* 1209–1214.

Gore, A. (1992). *Earth in the balance: Ecology and the human spirit.* New York: Penguin Books.

Gould, P. (1993). *The slow plague: A geography of the AIDS pandemic.* Oxford: Blackwell.

Gould, S. J. (1981). *The mismeasure of man.* New York: Norton.

Gourou, P. (1946). *The tropical world: Its social and economic conditions and its future status.* New York: Wiley (1953).

Gowa, J. (1983). *Closing the gold window: Domestic politics and the end of Bretton Woods.* Ithaca, NY: Cornell University Press.

Graham, S., and Marvin, S. (2001). *Splintering urbanism: Networked infrastructures, technological mobilities and the urban condition.* London: Routledge.

Graves, B. (1998). Political discourse—theories of colonialism and postcolonialism: "Can the subaltern speak?" *www.postcolonialweb.org/poldiscourse/spivak/spivak2.html*

Greenland, D. J., and Lal, R. (1977). *Soil conservation and management in the humid tropics.* Chichester, UK: Wiley.

Gregory, D. (2004). *The colonial present.* Oxford: Blackwell.

Grieser, M., Gittelsohn, J., Shankar, A. V., Koppenhaver, T., Legrand, T. K., Marindo, R., Mahvu, W. M., and Hill, K. (2001). Reproductive decision making and the HIV/AIDS epidemic in Zimbabwe. *Journal of Southern African Studies, 27*(2), 225–243.

Griffith-Jones, S., and Harvey, C. (1985). *World prices and development.* Aldershot, UK: Gower.

Grootaert, C. (1998). Social capital: The missing link? In World Bank (Ed.), *Social capital initiative working paper.* Washington, DC: World Bank.

Grossman, L. (1998). *The political ecology of bananas: Contract farming, peasants, and agrarian change in the eastern Caribbean.* Chapel Hill: University of North Carolina Press.

Guha, R. (2000). *The unquiet woods: Ecological change and peasant resistance in the Himalaya.* Berkeley: University of California Press.

Gupta, A. (1998). *Postcolonial developments: Agriculture in the making of modern India.* Durham, NC: Duke University Press.

Guttentag, J. M., and Herring, R. (1985). Commercial bank lending to developing countries: From overlending to underlending to structural reform. In Smith, G. W., and Cuddington, J. T. (Eds.), *International debt and the developing countries* (pp. 129–151). Washington, DC: World Bank.

Haggett, P. (1975). *Geography: A modern synthesis.* New York: Harper.

Hallwood, P., and Sinclair, S. (1981). *Oil, debt and development: OPEC in the third world.* London: Allen & Unwin.

Hance, W. A. (1967). *African economic development.* New York: Praeger.

Hanson, J. A., Honohan, P., and Majnoni, G. (2003). Globalization and national financial systems: Issues of integration and size. In Hanson, J. A., Honohan, P., and Majnoni, U. (Eds.), *Globalization and national financial systems* (pp. 1–34). New York: World Bank and Oxford University Press.

Harcourt, G. C. (1972). *Some Cambridge controversies in the theory of capital.* Cambridge, UK: Cambridge University Press.

Hardin, G. (1969). *Population, evolution, and birth control: A collage of controversial ideas, assembled by Garrett Hardin.* San Francisco: Freeman.

Hardin, G. (1974). Living on a lifeboat. *BioScience, 24*(10), 561–568.

Hardt, M., and Negri, A. (2000). *Empire.* Cambridge, MA: Harvard University Press.

Hardt, M., and Negri, A. (2004). *Multitude: War and democracy in the age of empire.* London: Penguin Books.

Harrison, D. (1992). *Tourism and the less developed countries.* New York: Wiley.

Hart, G. (2002). *Disabling globalization: Places of power in post-apartheid South Africa.* Berkeley: University of California Press.

Hartmann, B. (1995). *Reproductive rights and wrongs: The global politics of population control* (rev. ed.). Boston: South End Press.

Hartmann, B. (1999). Population, environment and security: A new trinity. In Silliman, J., & King, Y. (Eds.), *Dangerous intersections: Feminist perspectives on population, environment and development* (pp. 1–23). Cambridge, MA: Southend Press.

Harvey, D. (1974). Population, resources, and the ideology of science. *Economic Geography, 50*, 256–277.

Harvey, D. (1982). *The limits to capital*. Oxford: Blackwell.

Harvey, D. (1989). *The condition of postmodernity*. Oxford: Blackwell.

Harvey, D. (2000). *Spaces of hope*. Berkeley: University of California Press.

Harvey, D. (2003). *The new imperialism*. Oxford: Oxford University Press.

Harvey, D. (2005). *A brief history of neoliberalism*. Oxford: Oxford University Press.

Hastings, W., Barker, R., Aldersey, W., Lane, T., Barwell, R., Harris, J., and Goodwin, H. (1772, November 3). Letter published in *Sixth report from the Committee of Secrecy appointed to enquire into the state of the East India Company, the 26th of April 1773*, 300.

Hawley, S. (2003). Turning a blind eye: Corruption and the UK Export Credits Guarantee Department. *www.thecornerhouse.org.uk/pdf/document/correcg.pdf*

Hayes, D. (1977). *Energy for development: Third world options*. Washington, DC: Worldwatch Institute.

Hecht, S., and Cockburn, A. (1989). *The fate of the forest*. London: Penguin Books.

Hecksher, E. (1919). The effects of foreign trade on the distribution of income [in Swedish]. *Ekonomisk Tidskrift, 21*, 497–512.

Heijnen, J. D., and Conyers, D. (1971). Impact studies of rural water supply. In Tschannerl, G. (Ed.), *Water supply* (Research Paper No. 20, pp. 53–65). Dar es Salaam: Bureau of Resource Assessment and Land Use Planning, University of Dar es Salaam.

Heilbroner, R. L. (1963). *The great ascent: The struggle for economic development in our time*. New York: Harper and Row.

Held, D., McGrew, A., Goldblatt, D., and Perraton, J. (1999). *Global transformations: Politics, economics and culture*. Stanford, CA: Stanford University Press.

Henfrey, C. (1981). Dependency, modes of production, and the class analysis of Latin America. *Latin American Perspectives, 8*, 17–54.

Henry, J. S. (2007). The mirage of debt relief. In Hiatt, S. (Ed.), *A game as old as empire: The secret world of economic hit men and the web of global corruption* (pp. 219–262). San Francisco: Berrett-Koehler.

Hermanson, M. H., and Brosowski, J. R. (2005). History of Inuit community exposure to lead, cadmium and mercury in sewage lake sediments. *Environmental Health Perspectives, 113*, 1308. *64.233.161.104/search?q=cache:h2nV6nW14tUJ:ehp.niehs.gov/docs/2005/7985*

Herskovits, M. J. (1926). The cattle complex in East Africa. *American Anthropologist, 23*, 230–272, 362–380, 494–528, and 633–664.

Hewitt, T., and Smyth, I. (1992). Is the world overpopulated? In Allen, T., and Thomas, A. (Eds.), *Poverty and development in the 1990s* (pp. 78–96). Oxford: Oxford University Press.

Hilgert, F. (1945). *Industrialization and foreign trade*. Geneva: League of Nations.

Hirschman, A. O. (1945). *National power and the structure of foreign trade*. Berkeley: University of California Press.

Hirschman, A. O. (1958). *The strategy of economic development*. New Haven, CT: Yale University Press.

Hirschman, A. O. (1961). Ideologies of economic development in Latin America. In Hirschman, A. O. (Ed.), *Latin American issues: Essays and comments* (pp. 3–42). New York: Twentieth Century Fund.

Hirst, P., and Thompson, G. (1996). *Globalization in question: The international economy and possibilities of governance*. Cambridge, UK: Polity Press.

Hitler, A. (1925). *Mein Kampf*. Boston: Houghton Mifflin (1943).

Hobsbawm, E., and Ranger, T. (Eds.). (1983). *The invention of tradition*. Cambridge, UK: Cambridge University Press.

Hollis, M., and Nell, E. (1975). *Rational economic man*. Cambridge, UK: Cambridge University Press.

Holloway, M. (1994). Trends in women's health: A global view. *Scientific American, 271*(2), 76–83.

Homer-Dixon, T. F. (1999). *Environment, scar-*

city, and violence. Princeton, NJ: Princeton University Press.

Hoselitz, B. (1955). Generative and parasitic cities. *Economic Development and Cultural Change, 3*, 278–294.

Hosier, R., and Boberg, J. (1992). *Charcoal production and environmental degradation: Environmental history, selective harvesting, and post-harvest management.* Stockholm: Stockholm Environment Institute.

Howe, G. (1981). Dependency theory, imperialism, and the production of surplus value on a world scale. *Latin American Perspectives, 8*, 82–102.

Howe, R. W. (1965). Losses caused by insects and mites in stored foods and feeding stuffs. *Nutrition Abstract Reviews, 35*, 285–303.

Hunter, J. M., Rey, L., Chu, K. Y., Adekolu-John, E. O., and Mott, K. E. (1993). *Parasitic diseases in water resources development: The need for intersectoral negotiation.* Geneva: World Health Organization.

Huston, P. (1979). *Third world women speak out.* New York: Praeger.

Hydén, G. (1983). *No shortcuts to progress: African development management in perspective.* Berkeley: University of California Press.

Hymer, S. (1976). *The international operation of foreign firms: A study of direct investment.* Cambridge, MA: MIT Press.

Ianni, O. (1971). *Imperialismo y cultura de la violencia en América Latina.* Mexico City: Siglo XXI Editores.

Infoplease. (2006). Travel statistics. *www.infoplease.com/ipa/A0855290.html*

Ingham, G. (1994). States and markets in the production of world money: Sterling and the dollar. In Corbridge, S., Martin, R., and Thrift, N. (Eds.), *Money, power and space* (pp. 29–48). Oxford: Blackwell.

Ingham, K. (1962). *A history of east Africa.* London: Longmans, Green.

Inikori, J. E. (1992). Africa in world history: The export slave trade from Africa and the emergence of the Atlantic economic order. In Ogot, B. A. (Ed.), *General history of Africa: V. Africa from the sixteenth to the eighteenth century* (pp. 74–112). Paris: UNESCO.

l'Institut Géographique National. (1954). *Carte administrative de l'Afrique Occidentale Française* (Carte No. 73). Paris: Direction de la Documentation.

Intergovernmental Panel on Climate Change (IPCC). (2007a). *Climate change 2007. www.ipcc.ch*

Intergovernmental Panel on Climate Change (IPCC). (2007b, April). *Climate change 2007: Impacts, adaptation and vulnerability.* (Working Group II contribution to the IPCC Fourth Assessment Report). Brussels: IPCC.

Intermediate Technology Development Group (ITDG). (2003, April). US $0.4 billion lost through rustling and conflicts. *ITDG East Africa Peace Bulletin* (Issue 1). *www.itdg.org/html/itdg_eastafrica/peace1_news.htm*

International Institute for Tropical Agriculture (IITA). (1986). *IITA annual report and research highlights 1985.* Ibadan, Nigeria: IITA.

International Labour Organization (ILO). (1977). *Labour force estimates and projections, 1975–2000.* Geneva: ILO.

International Labour Organization (ILO). (2003). *Key indicators of the labour market.* Geneva: ILO.

International Monetary Fund (IMF). (2000, February 9). Overview: Transforming the Enhanced Structural Adjustment Facility (ESAF) and the Debt Initiative for the Heavily Indebted Poor Countries (HIPCs). *www.imf.org/external/np/esafhipc/1999*

International Monetary Fund (IMF). (2007a). The COFER (Currency Composition of Official Foreign Exchange Reserves) database. *www.imf.org/external/np/sta/cofer/eng/index.htm*

International Monetary Fund (IMF). (2007b). *The multilateral consultation on global imbalances* [IMF Issues Brief, March]. Washington, DC: IMF *www.imf.org/external/np/exr/ib/2007/041807.pdf*

International Monetary Fund (IMF) and World Bank. (2001). *Market access for developing countries' exports.* Washington, DC: IMF and World Bank.

Inter Press Service, Women and Law in Southern Africa Research Trust, Southern Africa AIDS Information Dissemination Service (IPS/WLSA/SAfAIDS). (2001). *Gender, rights and HIV/AIDS: Setting an agenda for meeting the challenges in Africa.* Harare, Zimbabwe: IPS 2001 Annual Support Group Meeting.

Isaacman, A., and Roberts, R. (Eds.). (1995). *Cotton, colonialism and social history in sub-Saharan Africa.* London: Heinemann.

Ismail, Q. (1999). Discipline and colony: *The*

English Patient and the crow's nest of postcoloniality. *Postcolonial Studies*, 2, 403–463.

Itard, J. (1801). *The wild boy of Aveyron*. New York: Appleton-Century-Crofts (1962).

Ito, T., and Krueger, A. (2001). Introduction. In Ito, Y., and Krueger, A. (Eds.), *Regional and global capital flows* (pp. 1–10). Chicago: University of Chicago Press.

Jackson, I. J. (1969). Tropical rainfall variations over a small area. *Journal of Hydrology*, *8*, 99–110.

Jackson, I. J. (1977). *Climate, water and agriculture in the tropics*. London: Longman.

James, C. L. R. (1938). *The black Jacobins: Toussaint L'Ouverture and the San Domingo revolution*. London: Secker and Warburg.

Jarrett, T. (1957). *Tsetse fly survey: West Suk, 1957*. Kabete, Kenya: Veterinary Department.

Jayne, T. S., Villarreal, M., Pingali, P., and Hemich, G. (2004). *Interaction between the agricultural sector and the HIV/AIDS pandemic: Implications for agricultural policy* (ESA Working Paper No.04-06). *www.sarpn.org.za/documents/d0000788/index.php*

Jefferson, M. (1921). *Recent colonization in Chile* (Research Series No. 6). New York: American Geographical Society.

Jefferson, M. (1926). *The peopling of the Argentine pampa* (Research Series No. 16). New York: American Geographical Society.

Jenkins, R. (1987). *Transnational corporations and uneven development: The internationalization of capital and the third world*. London: Methuen.

Jessop, B. (1999). Reflections on globalisation and its logics. In Olds, K., Dicken, P., Kelly, P., Kong, L., and Yeung, H. W.-C. (Eds.), *Globalisation and the Asia-Pacific: Contested territories* (pp. 19–38). London: Routledge.

Jevons, W. (1871). *The theory of political economy*. London: Macmillan.

Joerg, W. L. G. (Ed.). (1932). *Pioneer settlement* (Research Series No. 14). New York: American Geographical Society.

Johnson, A. J. (1877). *Johnson's new illustrated family atlas of the world*. New York: A. J. Johnson.

Johnson, S. (1995). *The politics of population: The International Conference on Population and Development, Cairo 1994*. London: Earthscan.

Johnson-Odim, C. (1991). Common themes, different contexts: Third world women and feminism. In Mohanty, C., Russo, A., and Torres, L. (Eds.), *Third world women and the politics of feminism* (pp. 314–327). Bloomington: University of Indiana Press.

Johnson-Odim, C., and Strobel, M. (1999). Series editors' introduction: Conceptualizing the history of women in Africa, Asia, Latin America and the Caribbean, and the Middle East and north Africa. In Johnson-Odim, C., and Strobel, M. (Eds.), *Restoring women to history* (pp. xvii–li). Bloomington: Indiana University Press.

Johnston, H. (1906). *Liberia* (2 vols.). London: Hutchinson.

Johnston, R. J., Taylor, P., and Watts, M. J. (Eds.). (2002). *Geographies of global change: Remapping the world* (2nd ed.). Oxford: Blackwell.

Joint United Nations Programme on HIV/AIDS (UNAIDS). (2005). *www.unaids.org/en/geographical+area/by+region.asp*

Jones, B. (2007). *Hugo!: The Hugo Chavez story from mud hut to perpetual revolution*. Hanover, NH: Steerforth Press.

Joy, C. R. (Ed.). (1947). *Albert Schweitzer: An anthology*. New York: Harper.

Juma, C. (1989). *The gene hunters: Biotechnology and the scramble for seeds*. London: Zed Books.

Kabeer, N. (1994). *Reversed realities: Gender hierarchies in development thought*. London: Verso.

Kabeer, N., and Subrahmanian, R. (Eds.). (1999). *Institutions, relations and outcomes: A framework and case-studies for gender-aware planning*. New Delhi: Kali for Women.

Kafka, F. (1948). *Tagbücher, 1910–1923*. New York: Schocken Books.

Kahn, H., and Wiener, N. J. (1967). *The year 2000: A framework for speculation in the next thirty-three years*. New York: Macmillan.

Kaler, A. (1998). A threat to the nation and a threat to the men: The banning of Depo-Provera in Zimbabwe, 1981. *Journal of Southern African Studies*, *24*(2), 347–376.

Kaler, A. (2000). "Who has told you this thing?": Toward a feminist interpretation of contraceptive diffusion in Rhodesia, 1970–1980. *Signs*, *25*(3), 677–708.

Kalof, L., and Satterfield, T. (Eds.). (2005). *The Earthscan reader in environmental values*. London: Earthscan.

Kamat, S. (2002). *Development hegemony: NGOs and the state in India*. New Delhi: Oxford University Press.

Kaniki, M. H. Y. (1985). The colonial economy: The former British zones. In Boahen, A. A. (Ed.), *General history of Africa: VII. Africa under colonial domination 1880–1935* (pp. 382–419). Paris: UNESCO.

Kaplan, R. (1994, February). The coming anarchy: How scarcity, crime, overpopulation, and disease are rapidly destroying the social fabric of our planet. *Atlantic Monthly*, 44–76.

Kassab, A. (1985). The colonial economy of north Africa. In Boahen, A. A. (Ed.), *General history of Africa: VII. Africa under colonial domination 1880–1935* (pp. 420–440). Paris: UNESCO.

Kates, R. W. (1995). Labnotes from the Jeremiah experiment: Hope for a sustainable transition. *Annals of the Association of American Geographers*, *85*(4), 623–640.

Katz, C. (2004). *Growing up global*. Minneapolis: University of Minnesota Press.

Kaufmann, D., Kray, A., and Mastruzzi, M. (2005). *Governance matters: IV. Governance indicators for 1996–2004* (World Bank Policy Research Working Paper Series). Washington, DC: World Bank.

Kay, J. (2003, March 22). Ann Arbor, Michigan high school students speak out against war. *www.wsws.org*

Kelley, A. C., and Schmidt, R. M. (1996). Toward a cure for the myopia and tunnel vision of the population debate: A dose of historical perspective. In Ahlburg, D., Kelley, A. C., and Mason, K. O. (Eds.), *The impact of population growth on well-being in developing countries* (pp. 11–35). Berlin: Springer-Verlag.

Kemp, T. (1983). *Industrialization in the non-Western world*. London: Longman.

Kenya Land Commission. (1934). *Evidence and memoranda* (3 vols.). London: His Majesty's Stationery Office.

Kevles, D. J. (1985). *In the name of eugenics: Genetics and the uses of human heredity*. New York: Knopf.

Kindelberger, C. P. (1968). *International economics*. Homewood, IL: Richard D. Irwin.

Kipling, R. (1917). *Collected verse of Rudyard Kipling*. Garden City, NY: Doubleday.

Kitching, G. (2001). *Seeking social justice through globalization: Escaping a nationalist perspective*. University Park: Pennsylvania State University Press.

Klein, N. (2004). Reclaiming the commons. In Mertes, T. (Ed.), *A movement of movements: Is another world really possible?* (pp. 219–229). London: Verso.

Knight, C. G., and Newman, J. L. (Eds.). (1976). *Contemporary Africa: Geography and change*. Englewood Cliffs, NJ: Prentice-Hall.

Knox, P., and Taylor, P. J. (Eds.). (1995). *World cities in a world-system*. Cambridge, UK: Cambridge University Press.

Kopytoff, I. (1987). *The African frontier: The reproduction of traditional African societies*. Bloomington: Indiana University Press.

The Korea Herald. (2005, May 25). Editorial: The secret in Alabama. *http://beuni.com/be_new/?document_sr1500064301&mid=u_e_sisa_01*

Kropotkin, P. (1887). Anarchism: Its philosophy and ideal. In Woodcock, G. (Ed.), *Peter Kropotkin: Fugitive writings* (p. 93). Cheektowaga, NY: Black Rose Books (1993).

Krugman, P., and Smith, A. (Eds.). (1994). *Empirical studies of strategic trade policies*. Chicago, IL: University of Chicago Press.

Laboratory of Climatology (C. W. Thornthwaite Associates). (1962–1965). *Average climatic water balance data of the continents* (Vol. 15). Centerton, NJ: The Lab.

Laclau, E. (1971). Feudalism and capitalism in Latin America. *New Left Review*, *67*, 19–39.

Lal, D. (1985, June). The misconceptions of "development economics." *Finance and Development*, 10–13.

Lal, R. (1987). Managing the soils of sub-Saharan Africa. *Science*, *236*, 1069–1076.

Land Institute. (2004). *Efficiency of alternative energy sources*. Salina, KS: Land Institute.

Lang, H., and Bollig, M. (n.d.). Demography of human populations in arid areas. *www.uni-koeln.de/sfb389/study_groups/group4/group4.htm*

Lang, S. (2002). The NGO-ization of feminism: Institutionalization and institution building within the German women's movements. In Smith, B. (Ed.), *Global feminisms since 1945* (pp. 290–304). New York: Routledge.

Langdon, S. (1981). *Multinational corporations in the political economy of Kenya*. London: Macmillan.

Lankes, H. P. (2002, September). Market access for developing countries. *Finance and Devel-*

opment: A Quarterly Magazine of the IMF, 39, 8–13.

Latouche, S. (1993). *In the wake of the affluent society: An exploration of post-development*. London: Zed Books.

Latour, B. (1993). *We have never been modern*. New York: Harvester Wheatsheaf.

Lazlo, E. (1981). Animal power: A major source of rural energy. *Ambio, 10*, 242–243.

Lazreg, M. (1988). Feminism and difference: The perils of writing as a woman on women in Algeria. *Feminist Studies, 14*, 81–107.

Learmonth, A. T. A. (1988). *Disease ecology: An introduction*. Oxford: Blackwell.

Ledent, J. (1982). The factors of urban population growth: Net inmigration versus natural increase. *International Regional Science Review, 7*, 99–126.

Lee, R. B. (1984). *The Dobe !Kung*. New York: Holt, Rinehart and Winston.

Leeds Animation Workshop (Producer). (1990). *A matter of interest* [Video]. Leeds, UK: Leeds Animation Workshop.

Leitner, H. (1997). Reconfiguring the spatiality of power: The construction of a supranational migration framework for the European Union. *Political Geography, 16*, 123–143.

Leitner, H. (2000). The political economy of international migration. In Sheppard, E., and Barnes, T. (Eds.), *A companion to economic geography* (pp. 450–467). Oxford: Blackwell.

Leitner, H., Peck, J., and Sheppard, E. (2007a). Squaring up to neoliberalism. In Leitner, H., Peck, J., and Sheppard, E. (Eds.), *Contesting neoliberalism: Urban frontiers* (pp. 311–328). New York: Guilford Press.

Leitner, H., Sziarto, K. M., Sheppard, E., and Maringanti, A. (2007b). Contesting urban futures: Decentering neoliberalism. In Leitner, H., Peck, J., and Sheppard, E. (Eds.), *Contesting neoliberalism: Urban frontiers* (pp. 1–25). New York: Guilford Press.

Lenin, V. I. (1916). *Imperialism: Highest stage of capitalism*. Peking: Foreign Languages Press (1970).

Lenin, V. I. (1917). *The state and revolution*. London: Lawrence and Wishart (1933).

Leontieff, W. (1953). Domestic production and foreign trade: The American capital position re-examined. *Proceedings of the American Philosophical Society, 97*, 332–349.

Lerner, D. (1957). *The passing of traditional society*. Glencoe, IL: Free Press.

Lernoux, P. (1982). *Cry of the people*. New York: Penguin Books.

Lernoux, P. (1984). *Fear and hope: Toward political democracy in Central America*. New York: Field Foundation.

Levins, R. (1990). The struggle for ecological agriculture in Cuba. *Capitalism, Nature, Socialism, 5*, 121–141.

Lewis, W. A. (1954). Economic development with unlimited supplies of labour. *Manchester School of Economic and Social Studies, 22*, 139–191.

Leys, N. (1925). *Kenya*. London: Hogarth Press.

Leyshon, A., and Thrift, N. (1997). *Money/space: Geographies of monetary transformation*. London: Routledge.

Lim, L. (1983). Capitalism, imperialism and patriarchy: The dilemma of third-world women workers in multinational factories. In Visvanathan, N., Duggan, L., Nisonoff, L., and Wiegersma, N. (Eds.), *The women, gender and development reader* (pp. 216–229). London: Zed Books (1997).

Lindblom, G. (1920). The Akamba. *Archives d'Etudes Orientales, 17*, 1–607 [Uppsala].

Lipietz, A. (1987). *Mirages and miracles*. London: Verso.

Lipton, M. (1977). *Why poor people stay poor: Urban bias in world development*. Cambridge, MA: Harvard University Press.

Little, P. D., and Horowitz, M. M, with Nyerges, A. E. (Eds.). (1987). *Lands at risk in the third world: Local level perspectives*. Boulder, CO: Westview Press.

Littlefield, A., Lieberman, L., and Reynolds, L. T. (1982). Redefining race: The potential demise of a concept in physical anthropology. *Current Anthropology, 23*(6), 641–656.

Loan Pricing Company. (2001). *Dealscan database*. New York: Loan Pricing Company.

Low-Beer, D. (2005). [Review of E. Kalipeni et al. (Eds.). (2004). *HIV and AIDS in Africa: Beyond epidemiology*]. *Annals of the Association of American Geographers, 95*, 478–481.

Lundberg, D. E., and Lundberg, C. B. (1993). *International travel and tourism*. New York: Wiley.

Luxemburg, R. (1915). *The accumulation of capital: An anti-critique*. London: Routledge and Keegan Paul (1951).

Mabogunje, A. L. (1962). *Yoruba towns*. Ibadan: Ibadan University Press.

Mabogunje, A. L. (1968). *Urbanization in Nigeria*. London: University of London Press.

MacLeish, A. (1978). *Riders on the earth*. Boston: Houghton Mifflin.

Madeley, R., Jelley, D., Epstein, P., and O'Keefe, P. (1984). The promise and problems of global health. *Ambio, 13*(3), 182–188.

Maguire, G. A. (1969). *Toward "Uhuru" in Tanzania: The politics of participation*. Cambridge, UK: Cambridge University Press.

Maizels, A. (2000). *The manufactures terms of trade of developing countries with the United States, 1981–97* (Working Paper No. 36). London: Queen Elizabeth House.

Maloney, W. (2004). Informality revisited. *World Development, 32*(7), 1159–1178.

Malthus, T. R. (1798). *An essay on the principle of population*. New York: Cambridge University Press (1992).

Mandelbrot, B. B. (1977). *The fractal geometry of nature*. New York: Freeman.

Mander, J., and Barker, D. (1999). The World Trade Organization: Processes and rulings. *www.ifg.org/analysis/wto/inv_govt.htm*

Mandeville, B. (1714). *The fable of the bees: or, private vices, publick benefits*. Harmondsworth, UK: Penguin Books (1970).

Manning, P. (1982). *Slavery, colonialism and economic growth, 1940–1960*. Cambridge, UK: Cambridge University Press.

Marini, R. (1973). *La dialéctica de la dependencia*. Mexico City: Ediciones Era.

Markusen, A. (1985). *Profit cycles, oligopoly and regional development*. Cambridge, MA: MIT Press.

Markusen, A., Hall, P., Campbell, S., and Dietrick, S. (1991). *The rise of the gun belt: The military remapping of industrial America*. New York: Oxford University Press.

Marquéz, G. G. (1976). *Autumn of the patriarch*. New York: Harper and Row.

Martens, J. (2005, October). *A compendium of inequality* (FES Briefing Paper). *www.fes.de/globalization*

Martí, J. (1891). *Obras completas: XIX. Estados Unidos y América Latina*. Havana: Patronato del Libro Popular (1961).

Martin, G. J. (1973). *Ellsworth Huntington: His life and thought*. Hamden, CT: Archon Books.

Martin, P. M. (1981). The Portuguese in Africa, c. 1450–1650. In Oliver, R., and Crowder, M. (Eds.), *The Cambridge encyclopedia of Africa* (pp. 141–145). Cambridge, UK: Cambridge University Press.

Martin, R. (1994). Stateless monies, global financial integration and national economic autonomy: The end of geography? In Corbridge, S., Martin, R., and Thrift, N. (Eds.), *Money, power and space* (pp. 253–278). Oxford: Blackwell.

Marx, K. (1867). *Das Kapital: Kritik der politischen Ökonomie*. Hamburg: Meissner.

Marx, K. (1877). Letter to Otechestvanige Zapiski. In Marx, K., and Engels, F. (Eds.), *Collected works* (pp. 196–201). New York: International Publishers (1989).

Mascarenhas, A. C. (1967). *Some aspects of food shortages in Tanganyika, 1923–45*. Kampala: East African Institute of Social Research.

Mascarenhas, A. (1971). Agricultural vermin in Tanzania. In Ominde, S. H. (Ed.), *Studies in east African geography and development* (pp. 259–267). London: Heinemann.

Masefield, G. B. (1950). *A short history of agriculture in the British colonies*. Oxford: Clarendon Press.

Masha, I. (2004). An economic assessment of Botswana's national strategic framework for HIV/AIDS. In Haacker, M. (Ed.), *The macroeconomics of AIDS* (pp. 287–310). New York: International Monetary Fund.

Massey, D. (1999). Imagining globalization: Power-geometries of time–space. In Brah, A., Hickman, M. & Mac an Ghaill, M. (Eds.), *Global futures: Migration, environment and globalization* (pp. 27–44). New York: St. Martin's Press.

Massey, D. (2005). *For space*. Thousand Oaks, CA: Sage.

Mazur, L. A. (Ed.). (1994). *A reader on population, consumption and the environment*. Washington, DC: Island Press.

Mbithi, P. M. (1977). Human factors in agricultural management in east Africa. *Food Policy, 2*, 27–33.

McClelland, D. (1961). *The achieving society*. Princeton, NJ: Van Nostrand.

McCully, P. (1996). *Silenced rivers: The ecology and politics of large dams*. London: Zed Books.

McDonald, A. (1981). *Energy in a finite world*. Laxenburg, Austria: International Institute for Applied Systems Analysis.

McEwan, C. (2002). Postcolonialism? In Desai, V., and Potter, R. B. (Eds.), *The companion to development studies* (pp. 127–131). London: Arnold.

McFadden, D., Eckhaus, R., Feder, G., Hajivassilou, V., and O'Connell, S. (1985). Is there life after debt?: An econometric analysis of the creditworthiness of developing countries. In Smith, G. W., and Cuddington, J. T. (Eds.), *International debt and the developing countries* (pp. 179–209). Washington, DC: World Bank.

McGee, T. R. (1991). Presidential address: Eurocentrism in geography—The case of Asian urbanization. *Canadian Geographer, 35*, 332–344.

McKinsey Global Institute. (2007). Perspective: Mapping the global capital markets. *www.mckinsey.com/mgi*

McMichael, P. (1996). *Development and social change: A global perspective.* Thousand Oaks, CA: Pine Forge Press.

Meade, J. (1961). *A neoclassical theory of economic growth.* London: Allen & Unwin.

Meade, M. S., Florin, M. W., and Gesler, J. W. (Eds.). (1988). *Medical geography.* New York: Guilford Press.

Meentemeyer, V. (1984). The geography of organic decomposition rates. *Annals of the Association of American Geographers, 74*(4), 551–560.

Mehta, U. S. (1999). *Liberalism and empire.* Chicago: University of Chicago Press.

Mekuria, S. (Ed.). (1995, Winter–Spring). Female genital mutilation in Africa: Some African views. *ACAS Bulletin, 44–45. www.prairienet.org/acas/bulletin/mekuria.html*

Menger, C. (1871). *Grundsätze der Volkswirtschaftslehre.* Vienna: Braumüller.

Mengisteab, K., and Logan, I. (1995). *Beyond economic liberalization: Structural adjustment and the alternatives.* London: Zed Books.

Merchant, C. (1989). *Ecological revolutions: Nature, gender and science in New England.* Chapel Hill: University of North Carolina Press.

Merchant, C. (1992). *Radical ecology: The search for a livable world.* New York: Routledge.

Messerschmidt, D. A. (1987). Conservation and society in Nepal: Traditional forest management and innovative development. In Little, P. D., Horowitz, M., and Nyerges, A. E. B. (Eds.), *Lands at risk in the third world: Local-level perspectives* (pp. 373–397). Boulder, CO: Westview Press.

Metals Economics Group. (2005). *World exploration trends, 2005.* Halifax, NS: Metals Economics Group.

Metts, R. L. (2001). The fatal flaw in the disability adjusted life year. *Disability and Society, 16*, 449–452.

Mexican Solidarity Network. (2006). *Zapatismo. www.mexicosolidarity.org/node/146*

Mieczkowski, Z. (1990). *World trends in tourism and recreation.* New York: Lang.

Mies, M. (1980). Capitalist development and subsistence production: Rural women in India. *Bulletin of Concerned Asian Scholars, 12.*

Mies, M., and Shiva, V. S. (1993). *Ecofeminism.* London: Zed Books.

Mikesell, R. F. (1994). *The Bretton Woods debates: A memoir.* Princeton, NJ: Princeton University Press.

Mill, J. S. (1862). *On liberty; Representative government; The subjection of women: Three essays.* London: Oxford University Press (1966).

Milne, G. (1935). Some suggested units of classification and mapping, particularly for east African soils. *Soil Research, 4*, 183–198.

Mishan, E. J. (1967). *The costs of economic growth.* London: Staples Press.

Mishkin, F. S. (2006). *The next great globalization: How disadvantaged nations can harness their financial systems to get rich.* Princeton, NJ: Princeton University Press.

Mitchell, T. (2002). *Rule of experts: Egypt, technopolitics and modernity.* Berkeley: University of California Press.

Mohanty, C. (1984). Under Western eyes: Feminist scholarship and colonial discourses. *Boundary, 2*, 333–358.

Mohanty, C. (2003). *Feminism without borders: Decolonizing theory, practicing solidarity.* Durham, NC: Duke University Press.

Monge, C. (1948). *Acclimatization in the Andes.* Baltimore: Johns Hopkins University Press (for distribution by the American Geographical Society).

Montagu, A. (1964). *Man's most dangerous myth: The fallacy of race.* Cleveland, OH: World.

Monteith, J. L. (1965). Light distribution and photosynthesis in field crops. *Annals of Botany (N.S.), 29*(113), 17–37.

Monteith, J. L. (1966). The photosynthesis and transpiration of crops. *Experimental Agriculture, 2*, 1–14.

Monteith, J. L. (1972). Solar radiation and productivity in tropical ecosystems. *Journal of Applied Ecology, 9*, 747–755.

Moon, H. (1999). *Impacts of the economic crisis on income distribution and policy implications.* Seoul: Korea Development Institute.

Moran, E. F. (1987). Socioeconomic considerations in acid tropical soils research. In Sanchez, P., Pushparajah, E., and Stoner, E. (Eds.), *Management of acid tropical soils for sustainable agriculture* (pp. 227–244). Bangkok: International Board for Soil Research and Management.

Morris, M. D. (1979). *Measuring the condition of the world's poor: The physical quality of life index.* New York: Pergamon Press.

Morton, K., and Tulloch, P. (1977). *Trade and developing countries.* New York: Wiley.

Mukherjea, S. (1999). The syndicated loan market in emerging markets. In Mukherjea, S. (Ed.), *Syndicated lending: A handbook for borrowers in emerging markets* (pp. 3–12). London: Euromoney.

Munro, J. F. (1975). *Colonial rule and the Kamba: Social change in the Kenya highlands, 1889–1939.* Oxford: Clarendon Press.

Murdock, G. P. (1959). *Africa: Its peoples and their culture history.* New York: McGraw-Hill.

Musambyai, K. (2003). Banditry and conflict in the Kapotur triangle: An alternative menu for resolution. *Regional Development Dialogue, 2*, 135–154.

Mushita, A. T., and Thompson, C. B. (2002). Patenting biodiversity? Rejecting WTO/TRIPS in Southern Africa. *Global Environmental Politics, 2*, 65–82.

Myers, S. L., Revkin, A. C. Romero, S., and Krauss, C. (2005, October 20). Old ways of life are fading as the Arctic thaws. *The New York Times. www.nytimes.com/2005/20/20/science/earth/20arctic.ready.html?hp=&adxnnl=1&*

Myrdal, G. (1957). *Rich lands and poor.* New York: Harper.

Naess, A. (1990). Sustainable development and deep ecology. In Engel, J. R., and Engel, J. G. (Eds.), *Ethics of environment and development: Global challenge, international response* (pp. 87–96). Tucson: University of Arizona Press.

Nagar, R., Lawson, V., McDowell, L., and Hanson, S. (2002). Locating globalization: Feminist (re)readings of the subjects and spaces of globalization. *Economic Geography, 78*(3), 257–284.

Naoroji, D. (1871). *Poverty and un-British rule in India.* New Delhi: Publications Division, Ministry of Information and Broadcasting, Government of India (1962).

Narayan, D., Patel, R., Schafft, K., Rademacher, A., and Koch-Schulte, S. (2000). *Can anyone hear us?* Washington, DC: Oxford University Press and World Bank.

Narayan, U. (1997). *Dislocating cultures: Identities, traditions and third world feminism.* New York: Routledge.

Nash, D. (1996). *Anthropology of tourism.* Oxford: Pergamon Press.

Nash, J., and Safa, H. I. (1980). Introduction. In Nash, J., and Safa, H. I. (Eds.), *Sex and class in Latin America: Women's perspectives on politics, economics and the family in the third world* (pp. x–xiii). New York: J. F. Bergin.

National Geographic Society. (Ed.). (1993). Global warming debate [Special issue]. *Research and Exploration, 9*(2), 142–249.

National Research Council. (1982). *Ecological aspects of development in the humid tropics.* Washington, DC: National Academy Press.

National Research Council. (1986). *Pesticide resistance: Strategies and tactics for management.* Washington, DC: National Academy Press.

Nations, J. D., and Komer, D. I. (1983). Central America's tropical rainforests: Positive steps for survival. *Ambio, 12*, 232–238.

Nettle, D., and Romaine, S. (2000). *Vanishing voices: The extinction of the world's languages.* Oxford: Oxford University Press.

Newman, J. L., and Matzke, G. E. (1984). *Population patterns, dynamics, and prospects.* Englewood Cliffs, NJ: Prentice-Hall.

Ngugi, D. N., Karau, P. K., and Nguyo, W. (1978). *East African agriculture.* London: Macmillan.

Nicholls, A., and Opal, C. (2005). *Fair trade: Market-driven ethical consumption.* London: Sage.

Nisonoff, L. (1997). Introduction to Part 3. In Visvanathan, N., Duggan, L., Nisonoff, L., and Wiegersma, N. (Eds.), *The women, gender and development reader* (pp. 177–190). London: Zed Books.

Njeuma, M. Z. (1989). *Introduction to the his-*

tory of Cameroon. New York: St. Martin's Press.

Nobile, A. (1999). . . . Thought to be erotic . . . [Exhibit commentary]. Vancouver: Museum of Anthropology, University of British Columbia.

Norgaard, R. B. (1994). *Development betrayed: The end of progress and a coevolutionary revisioning of the future*. New York: Routledge.

Norman, C. (1978). *Soft technologies, hard choices* (Worldwatch Paper No. 21). Washington, DC: Worldwatch Institute.

Notes from Nowhere. (Ed.). (2003). *We are everywhere: The irresistible rise of global anticapitalism*. London: Verso.

Nunan, C. (2004). Petrodollar or petroeuro? A new source of global conflict. In Douthwaite, R., and Jopling, J. (Eds.), *Growth: The Celtic cancer* (pp. 125–129). Dublin: Foundation for the Economics of Sustainability.

Nyrere, J. K. (1983). South–south option. In Gauhar, A. (Ed.), *South–south strategy* (pp. 9–16). London: Third World Foundation.

O'Brien, R. (1992). *Global financial integration: The end of geography*. London: Royal Institute of International Affairs.

O'Connor, J. (1998). *Natural causes: Essays in ecological Marxism*. New York: Guilford Press.

Obare, O. (2008, February 24). Cattle rustlers using mobile phones. *The East African Standard*. *www.eastandard.net/news/?id=1143982334&cid=159*

Obare, O., and Maero, T. (2005, April 30). Herdsmen flee into Uganda to avoid arrest. *The East African Standard*.

Obsfeld, M., and Taylor, A. M. (2005). *Global capital markets: Integration, crisis, and growth*. New York: Cambridge University Press.

Odell, P. (1988). Draining the world of energy. In Johnston, R. J., and Taylor, P. J. (Eds.), *A world in crisis?* (pp. 79–100) Oxford: Blackwell.

Odell, P., and Rosing, K. E. (1976). *The optimal development of the North Sea's oil fields*. London: Kogan Page.

Odell, P. R., and Rosing, K. E. (1983). *The future of oil*. New York: Nichols.

Office of the Special Adviser on Gender Issues and Advancement of Women. (2005). *Gender mainstreaming*. *www.un.org/womenwatch/osagi/gendermainstreaming.htm*

Office of Technology Assessment (OTA). (1988). *Enhancing agriculture in Africa: A role for U.S. development assistance*. Washington, DC: U.S. Government Printing Office.

Ohlin, B. (1933). *Interregional and international trade*. Cambridge, MA: Harvard University Press.

Ohmae, K. (1995). *The end of the nation state: The rise of regional economies*. New York: Free Press.

O'Keefe, P., and Kristoferson, L. (1984). The uncertain energy path: Energy and third world development. *Ambio*, *8*, 168–170.

Oldfield, S., and Stokke, K. (2007). Political polemics and local practices of organizing and neoliberal politics in South Africa. In Leitner, H., Peck, J., and Sheppard, E. (Eds.), *Contesting neoliberalism: Urban frontiers* (pp. 139–156). New York: Guilford Press.

Oliver, R., and Crowder, M. (1981). *The Cambridge encyclopedia of Africa*. Cambridge, UK: Cambridge University Press.

Oliver, R., and Fage, J. D. (1962). *A short history of Africa* (2nd ed.). Baltimore: Penguin Books.

Oliver, R., and Mathew, G. (1963). *History of east Africa*. Oxford: Clarendon Press.

Olson, J. M. (1995). Behind the recent tragedy in Rwanda. *GeoJournal*, *35*(2), 217–222.

Ong, A. (1987). *Spirits of resistance and capitalist discipline: Factory women in Malaysia*. Albany: State University of New York Press.

Organization for Economic Cooperation and Development (OECD). (1992). *Development cooperation: 1992 report*. Paris: OECD.

Organization for Economic Cooperation and Development (OECD). (2004). Recipient aid charts. *www.oecd.org/dac/stats/recipientcharts*

Organization for Economic Cooperation and Development (OECD). (2005). *Looking beyond tariffs: The role of non-tariff barriers in world trade*. Paris: OECD.

Organization for Economic Cooperation and Development (OECD). (2007). OECD development database on aid from DAC members online. *www.oecd.org/dataoecd/50/17/5037721.htm*

Over, M. (2004). Impact of the HIV/AIDS epidemic on the health sectors of developing countries. In Haacker, M. (Ed.), *The macroeconomics of AIDS* (pp. 311–344). New York: International Monetary Fund.

Owen, D. F. (1973). *Man in tropical Africa.* New York: Oxford University Press.

Paalova, J., and Lowe, I. (2005). *Environmental values in a globalising world: Nature, justice and governance.* London: Routledge.

Palma, G. (1981). Dependency and development: A critical overview. In Seers, D. (Ed.), *Dependency theory: A critical reassessment* (pp. 20–78). London: Frances Pinter.

Palmer, R. R. (1957). *Atlas of world history.* Chicago: Rand McNally.

Parboni, R. (1988). U.S. economic strategies against Western Europe: From Nixon to Reagan. *Geoforum, 19,* 45–54.

Park, Y.-C. (1985). Korea's experience with external debt management. In Smith, G. W., and Cuddington, J. T. (Eds.), *International debt and the developing countries* (pp. 289–328). Washington, DC: World Bank.

Parmar, P. (Director), and Walker, A. (Executive Producer). (1993). *Warrior marks* [Film]. New York: Women Make Movies.

Parsons, T. (1948). *The structure of social action.* New York: McGraw-Hill.

Parsons, T. (1961). Some considerations on the theory of social change. *Rural Sociology, 26,* 219–239.

Parsons, T. (1966). *Societies: Evolutionary and comparative perspectives.* Englewood Cliffs, NJ: Prentice-Hall.

Pasinetti, L. L. (1981). *Structural change and economic growth.* Cambridge, UK: Cambridge University Press.

Patomäki, H. (2001). *Democratising globalisation: The leverage of the Tobin tax.* London: Zed Books.

Paul, D. B. (1986). The history of the eugenics movement and of its multiple effects on public policy. *Scientific American, 254,* 27–31.

Paulson, T. (2001, March 22). Bill Gates' war on disease, poverty is an uphill battle. *Seattle Post-Intelligencer* (accessed 12/12/2008: *http://seattlepi.nwsource.com/africa/overview22.shtml*)

Payer, C. (1974). *The debt trap: The International Monetary Fund and the third world.* New York: Monthly Review Press.

Paz, O. (1972). *The other Mexico: Critique of the pyramid.* New York: Grove Press.

Peet, R. (1985). *Global capitalism: Theories of social development.* London: Routledge.

Peet, R. (2003). *Unholy trinity: The IMF, World Bank and WTO.* London: Zed Books.

Peet, R., and Watts, M. (Eds.). (1996). *Liberation ecologies: Environment, development, social movements.* London: Routledge.

Peluso, N., and Watts, M. (2001). Violent environments. In Peluso, N., and Watts, M. (Eds.), *Violent environments* (pp. 3–38). Ithaca, NY: Cornell University Press.

Pelzer, K. J. (1945). *Pioneer settlement in the Asiatic tropics* (Special Publication No. 29). New York: American Geographical Society.

Perelman, M. (2000). *The invention of capitalism: Classical political economy and the secret history of primitive accumulation.* Durham, NC: Duke University Press.

Peristiany, J. G. (1951). The age-set system of the pastoral Pokot. *Africa, 21,* 188–206.

Peristiany, J. G. (1954). Pokot sanctions and structure. *Africa, 24,* 17–25.

Petras, J. (1981). Dependency and world system theory: A critique and new directions. *Latin American Perspectives, 8,* 148–155.

Pkalya, R., Adan, M., and Masinde, I. (2003). *Conflict in Northern Kenya. www.itdg.org/html/itdg_eastafrica/conflict_in_northern_kenya.htm*

Plucknett, D. L., and Smith, N. J. H. (1986). Sustaining agricultural yields. *BioScience, 36,* 40–45.

Polanyi, K. (1964). Sortings and "ounce trade" in the west African slave trade. *Journal of African History, 5*(3), 381–393.

Polanyi, K. (1971). *Primitive, archaic and modern economics: Essays of Karl Polanyi* (G. Dalton, Ed.). Boston: Beacon Press.

Pollard, J., and Samers, M. (2007). Islamic banking and finance: Postcolonial political economy and the decentering of economic geography. *Transactions of the Institute of British Geographers, 32,* 313–330.

Poovey, M. (1998). *A history of the modern fact: Problems of knowledge in the sciences of wealth and society.* Chicago: University of Chicago Press.

Population Reference Bureau. (1986). *1986 world population data sheet.* Washington DC: Population Reference Bureau.

Population Reference Bureau. (2002). *2002 world population data sheet.* Washington DC: Population Reference Bureau.

Population Reference Bureau. (2003). *2003 world population data sheet.* Washington DC: Population Reference Bureau.

Porter, G., and Phillips-Howard, K. (1997). Comparing contracts: An evaluation of contract farming schemes in Africa. *World Development, 25*, 227–238.

Porter, M. (1990). *The competitive advantage of nations*. New York: Free Press.

Porter, P. W. (n.d.). *Adaptation in ecological context: Studies of four east African societies*. Unpublished manuscript.

Porter, P. W. (1958). *Benin to Bahia: A chronicle of Portuguese empire in the south Atlantic in the fifteenth and sixteenth century, with comments on a chart of Jorge Reinel*. Minneapolis: James Ford Bell Book Trust.

Porter, P. W. (1976a). Climate and agriculture in East Africa. In Knight, C. G., and Newman, J. L. (Eds.), *Contemporary Africa: Geography and change* (pp. 112–139). Englewood Cliffs, NJ: Prentice-Hall.

Porter, P. W. (1976b, February 23). *Agricultural development and agricultural vermin in Tanzania*. Paper presented at the annual meeting of the American Association for the Advancement of Science, Boston.

Porter, P. W. (1979). *Food and development in the semi-arid zone of East Africa* (Foreign and Comparative Studies/African Studies No. 32). Syracuse, NY: Maxwell School of Citizenship and Public Affairs, Syracuse University.

Porter, P. W. (1987). Wholes and fragments: Reflections on the economy of affection, capitalism, and the human cost of development. *Geografiska Annaler, 69B*(1), 1–14.

Porter, P. W. (2006). *Challenging nature: Local knowledge, agroscience, and food security in Tanga Region, Tanzania*. Chicago: University of Chicago Press.

Porter, P. W., and Porter, P. G. (1993). *Eight months in Tanzania*. Unpublished journal (kept during field work, 1992–1993, in Tanga Region, Tanzania).

Porter, P. W., and Sheppard, E. S. (1998). *A world of difference: Society, nature, development*. New York: Guilford Press.

Postel, S. (1988). Controlling toxic chemicals. In Brown, L. R., et al. (Eds.), *State of the world 1988* (pp. 118–136). New York: Norton.

Postel, S. L., Daily, G. C., and Ehrlich, P. R. (1996). Human appropriation of renewable fresh water. *Science, 271*, 785–788.

Power, D., Bartley, K., O'Briain, D., and Zoido, A. (2002). *The revolution will not be televised* [Film]. [Wolverhampton, U.K.]: Venezuela Solidarity Campaign.

Prebisch, R. (1959). Commercial policy in the underdeveloped countries. *American Economic Review, 49*, 251–273.

Prescott, J. R. V. (1961). Overpopulation and overstocking in the native areas of Matabeleland. *Geographical Journal, 127*, 212–225.

Prescott, J. R. V. (1962). Population distribution in Southern Rhodesia. *Geographical Review, 52*(4), 559–582.

Price, A. G. (1939). *White settlers in the tropics* (Special Publication No. 23). New York: American Geographical Society.

Price Jones, D. (1974). Selectivity in pesticides: Significance and enhancement. In Price Jones, D., and Solomon, M. E. (Eds.), *Biology in pests and disease control* (pp. 178–195). Oxford: Blackwell.

Pryer, J. (1992). Purdah, patriarchy and population movement: Perspectives from Bangladesh. In Chant, S. (Ed.), *Gender and migration in developing countries* (pp. 139–153). London: Belhaven.

Quesnay, F. (1753–1758). *Tableau économique*. Versailles: Privately printed.

Rabinovitch, J. (1992). Curitiba: Towards sustainable urban development. *Environment and Urbanization, 4*(2), 62–73.

Radwan, L. (ca. 1995) Average daily river flows and diurnal fluctuations: Issues from data in the tropics. *www.geogr.unipd.it/g_acqua/2.3-RADWAN.html*

Raffer, K. (1987). *Unequal exchange and the evolution of the world system*. London: Macmillan.

Rahnema, M. (1992). Poverty. In Sachs, W. (Ed.), *The development dictionary: A guide to knowledge as power* (pp. 158–176). London: Zed Books.

Rahnema, M., and Bawtree, V. (Eds.). (1997). *The post-development Reader*. London: Zed Books.

Rajan, R. G., and Zingales, L. (1998). Which capitalism? Lessons from the east Asian crisis. *Journal of Applied Corporate Finance, 11*, 40–48.

Ramani, K. (2001, December 11). The guns of Kerio Valley and the looming danger. *The East African Standard*.

Rangan, H. (2000). *Of myths and movements: Rewriting Chipko into Himalayan history*. New York: Verso.

Rangarajan, L. (1978). *Commodity conflict*. London: Croom Helm.

Ranger, T. (1983). The invention of tradition in colonial Africa. In Hobsbawm, E., and Ranger, T. (Eds.), *The invention of tradition* (pp. 211–262). Cambridge, UK: Cambridge University Press.

Ranjitsinh, M. K. (1979). Forest destruction in Asia and the South Pacific. *Ambio*, *8*, 192–201.

Rassool, N. (1999). *Literacy for sustainable development in the age of information*. Clevedon, UK: Multilingual Matters.

Raynolds, L. J., and Long, M. A. (2007). Fair/alternative trade: Historical and empirical dimensions. In Raynolds, L. J., Murray, D., and Wilkinson, J. (eds.), *Fair trade: The challenges of transforming globalization* (pp. 15–32). London: Routledge.

Razmi, A., and Blecker, R. (2005). *The limits to export-led growth: An empirical study* (Department of Economics Working Paper No. 2005-02). Amherst: University of Massachusetts, Amherst.

Rees, J. A. (1990). *Natural resources: Allocation, economics and policy*. London: Routledge.

Republic of Korea. (1997, December 5). *IMF stand-by arrangement: Summary of the economic program*. Seoul. (available from: *www.imf.org/external/np/oth/korea.htm*)

Retort. (2005). *Afflicted powers: Capital and spectacle in a new age of war*. London: Verso.

Revkin, A. C. (2005a, May 29). Ocean warmth tied to African drought. *The New York Times*, D3.

Revkin, A. C. (2005b, October 4). A new measure of well-being from a happy little kingdom. *The New York Times*, D1, D6.

Reynolds, J. E. (1982). *Community underdevelopment, ethnicity, and stratification in a rural destination: Mnagei, Kenya*. Unpublished doctoral dissertation, University of Washington.

Ricardo, D. (1817). *On the principles of political economy and taxation*. Cambridge, UK: Cambridge University Press (1951).

Richards, P. (1985). *Indigenous agricultural revolutions: Ecology and food production in west Africa*. London: Hutchinson.

Riddell, J. (1970). *The spatial dynamics of modernization in Sierra Leone: Structure, diffusion and response*. Evanston, IL: Northwestern University Press.

Rist, G. (1997). *The history of development: From western origins to global faith*. Cape Town: University of Cape Town Press.

Roberts, D. (1997). *Killing the black body: Race, reproduction and the meaning of liberty*. New York: Pantheon Books.

Roberts, S. (1994). Fictitious capital, fictitious spaces: The geography of offshore finance flows. In Corbridge, S., Martin, R., and Thrift, N. (Eds.), *Money, power and space* (pp. 91–115). Oxford: Blackwell.

Roberts, S. (2004). Gendered globalization. In Kofman, E., Peake, L., and Staehili, L. (Eds.), *Mapping women, making politics: Feminist perspectives on political geography* (pp. 127–140). New York: Routledge.

Robinson, C. (1987). Capitalism, slavery, and bourgeois historiography. *History Workshop*, *23*, 122–141.

Robinson, R., and Gallagher, J., with Denny, A. (1963). *Africa and the Victorians: The official mind of imperialism*. London: Macmillan.

Roder, W. (1964). The division of land resources in Southern Rhodesia. *Annals of the Association of American Geographers*, *54*, 41–58.

Rogers, B. (1980). *The domestication of women: Discrimination in developing societies*. London: Kogan Page.

Rojas-Súarez, L. (1991). Risk and capital flight in developing countries. In International Monetary Fund (IMF) (Ed.), *Determinants and consequences of international capital flows* (pp. 83–93). Washington DC: IMF.

Rose, N. (1999). *Powers of freedom: Reframing political thought*. Cambridge, UK: Cambridge University Press.

Ross, L. (1994). Sterilization and "de-facto" sterilization. *Womensstruggle*, *1*(4), 20.

Rossel, P. (Ed.). (1988). *Tourism: Manufacturing the exotic*. Copenhagen: International Working Group for Indigenous Affairs.

Rosset, P., and Benjamin, M. (Eds.). (1994a). *The greening of the revolution: Cuba's experiment with organic agriculture*. Melbourne: Ocean Press.

Rosset, P., and Benjamin, M. (1994b). Cuba's nationwide conversion to organic agriculture. *Capitalism, Nature, Socialism*, *5*(3), 79–97.

Rostom, R. S., and Mortimore, M. (1991). *Land use profile, environmental change and dryland management in Machakos District, Kenya, 1930–1990* (Working Paper No. 58). London: Overseas Development Institute.

Rostow, W. W. (1960). *The stages of economic*

growth: A non-communist manifesto. Cambridge, UK: Cambridge University Press.

Rowley, J. (1993). *Grasshoppers and locusts: The plague of the Sahel.* London: Panos Institute.

Roy, A. (2004, August 16). *Tide? Or Ivory Snow? Public power in the age of empire.* Speech given in San Francisco. *www.democracynow.org/static/Arundhati_Trans.shtml*

Ruddiman, W. F. (2003). The anthropogenic greenhouse era began thousands of years ago. *Climatic Change, 61,* 261–293.

Rudin, H. R. (1968). *Germans in the Cameroons, 1884–1914.* Hamden, CT: Archon Books.

Ruggie, J. (1982). International regimes, transactions, and change: Embedded liberalism and the postwar economic order. *International Organization, 36,* 379–415.

Russell, S. S. (1992). Migrant remittances and development. *International Migration, 30,* 267–286.

Ruttan, V. W. (1986). Toward a global agricultural research system: A personal view. *Research Policy, 15,* 307–327.

Ruttan, V. W. (1994). Constraints on the design of sustainable systems of agricultural production. *Ecological Economics, 10,* 209–219.

Ruttan, V. W. (1996). *United States development assistance policy.* Baltimore: Johns Hopkins University Press.

Ryckmans, P. (1964). Belgian "colonialism." In Quigg, P. W. (Ed.), *Africa* (pp. 69–83). New York: Praeger.

Sachs, J. D. (2004, June 19). *Stages of economic development.* Speech given at the Chinese Academy of Arts and Sciences, Beijing.

Sachs, J. D. (2005). *The end of poverty: Economic possibilities for our time.* London: Penguin Books.

Sachs, J. D., Mellinger, A. D., and Gallup, J. L. (2001, March). The geography of poverty and wealth. *Scientific American,* 71–75.

Sachs, W. (1990). On the archaeology of the development idea. *Lokayan Bulletin, 8,* 7–37.

Sachs, W. (Ed.). (1992). *The development dictionary: A guide to knowledge as power.* London: Zed Books.

Said, E. W. (1978). *Orientalism.* New York: Vintage.

Sainath, P. (2006, April 1). Where shining India meets great depression. *The Hindu, www.hindu.com/2006/04/01/stories/2006040100731000.htm*

Samatar, A. I. (1999). *An African miracle: State and class leadership and colonial legacy in Botswana development.* Portsmouth, NH: Heinemann.

Samatar, A., and Samatar, A. I. (1987). The material roots of the suspended African state: Arguments from Somalia. *Journal of Modern African Studies, 25*(4), 669–690.

Samuelson, P. A. (1953–1954). Prices of goods and factors in general equilibrium. *Review of Economic Studies, 21,* 1–20.

Sanchez, P., and Cochrane, T. T. (1980). Soil constraints in relation to major farming systems in tropical America. In *Priorities for alleviating soil related constraints to food production in the tropics* (pp. 107–139). Los Baños, Philippines: International Rice Research Institute.

Sanders, W. T. (1976). The population of the central Mexican symbiotic region, the Basin of Mexico, and the Teotihuacán Valley in the sixteenth century. In Denevan, W. M. (Ed.), *The native population of the Americas in 1492* (pp. 85–150). Madison: University of Wisconsin Press.

Sangtin. (2005, March 18). *Sangtin, Sitapur: Missions, objectives and challenges.* Unpublished manuscript.

Sangtin Writers. (2006). *Still playing with fire: Intersectionality, activism, and NGOized feminism.* Paper presented at the Transnational Feminist Praxis Workshop, Minneapolis.

Sangtin Writers, and Nagar, R. (2006). *Playing with fire: Feminist thought and activism through seven lives in India.* Minneapolis: University of Minnesota Press; New Delhi: Zubaan.

Sarkar, P., and Singer, H. W. (1991) Manufactured exports of developing countries and their terms of trade since 1965. *World Development, 19,* 333–340.

Sassen, S. (1991). *The global city: New York, London, Tokyo.* Princeton, NJ: Princeton University Press.

Sassen, S. (Ed.). (2002). *Global networks, linked cities.* London: Routledge.

Sauer, C. O. (1925). *The morphology of landscape.* Berkeley: University of California Press.

Saunders, K. (2002a). Introduction. In Saunders, K. (Ed.), *Feminist post-development thought: Rethinking modernity, post-colonialism and representation* (pp. 1–38). London: Zed Books.

Saunders, K. (Ed.). (2002b). *Feminist post-development thought: Rethinking modernity, post-colonialism and representation*. London: Zed Books.

Saxenian, A. (1994). *Regional advantage: Culture and competition in Silicon Valley and Route 128*. Cambridge, MA: Harvard University Press.

Sayer, A., and Walker, R. (1992). *The new social economy: Reworking the division of labor*. Oxford: Blackwell.

Schenk, C. R. (1998). The origins of the Eurodollar market in London: 1955–1963. *Explorations in Economic History, 35*, 221–238.

Schneider, H. K. (1956). The interpretation of Pokot visual art. *Man*, No. 108.

Schneider, H. K. (1957). The subsistence role of cattle among the Pokot in east Africa. *American Anthropologist, 59*, 278–300.

Schneider, H. K. (1959). Pokot resistance to change. In Bascom, W., and Herskovits, M. J. (Eds.), *Continuity and change in African cultures* (pp. 114–167). Chicago: University of Chicago Press.

Schneider, H. K. (1964). Economics in east African aboriginal societies. In Herskovits, M. J., and Harwitz, M. (Eds.), *Economic transition in Africa* (pp. 53–75). Evanston, IL: Northwestern University Press.

Schoenberger, E. (1988). From Fordism to flexible accumulation: Technology, competitive strategies and international location. *Environment and Planning D: Society and Space*, 6, 245–262.

Schumacher, E. F. (1973). *Small is beautiful: Economics as if people mattered*. New York: Harper and Row.

Scott, A. J. (1988). *New industrial spaces*. London: Pion.

Scott, A. J. (2006). *Global city-regions*. Oxford: Oxford University Press.

Scott, J. C. (1985). *Weapons of the weak: Everyday forms of peasant resistance*. New Haven, CT: Yale University Press.

Scott, J. C. (1994). *State simplifications: Nature, space and people* (Working Paper No. 3, Series 10). Minneapolis: MacArthur Program on Peace and International Cooperation in Developing Societies, University of Minnesota.

Scott, R. M. (1962). The soils of East Africa. In Russell, E. W. (Ed.), *The natural resources of east Africa* (pp. 67–76). Nairobi: East African Literature Bureau.

Scott, R. M. (1969). The soils of East Africa. In Morgan, W. T. W. (Ed.), *East Africa: Its peoples and resources* (pp. 95–105). London: Oxford University Press.

Seager, J. (2003). *The Penguin atlas of women in the world* (3rd ed.). New York: Penguin Books.

Seager, J. (2009). *The Penguin atlas of women in the world* (4th ed.). New York: Penguin Books.

Seillière, E. (1903). *Le compte de Gobineau et l'aryanisme historique. La philosophie de l'imperialisme*. Paris: Plon-Nourrit et Cie.

Semple, E. C. (1911). *Influences of geographic environment*. New York: Henry Holt.

Sen, A. (1981). *Poverty and famines: An essay on entitlement and deprivation*. New York: Oxford University Press.

Sen, A. (1987). *Hunger and entitlements: Research for action*. Helsinki: World Institute for Development Economics Research, United Nations University.

Sen, S. (2005). International trade theory and policy: What is left of the free trade paradigm? *Development and Change, 36*, 1011–1029.

Seo, B. (2004). *Relational networks and geographies of global banking*. Unpublished doctoral dissertation, University of Minnesota.

Seo, B. (2005). Geopolitical economy of global syndicated credit markets. In Le Heron, R., and Harrington, J. W. (Eds.), *New economic spaces: New economic geographies* (pp. 55–72). London: Ashgate.

Sharman, A. (1970). Nutrition and social planning. *Journal of Development Studies*, 6, 76–91.

Sheppard, E. (1982). City size distributions and spatial economic change. *International Regional Science Review*, 7, 127–152.

Sheppard, E. (2002). The spaces and times of globalization: Place, scale, networks, and positionality. *Economic Geography, 78*, 307–330.

Sheppard, E. (2005). Free trade: The very idea! From Manchester boosterism to global management. *Transactions of the Institute of British Geographers, 30*, 151–172.

Shiva, V. (1991). *Ecology and the politics of survival*. New Delhi: Sage Publications and United Nations University Press.

Shiva, V. (1993). Reductionist science as epistemological violence. In Nandy, A. (Ed.), *Science, hegemony and violence* (pp. 232–255). Delhi: Oxford University Press.

Shleifer, A. (2000). *Inefficient markets: An introduction to behavioral finance.* Oxford: Oxford University Press.

Shohat, E. (1998). Introduction. In Shohat, E. (Ed.), *Talking visions: Multicultural feminism in a transnational age* (pp. 1–63). New York: New Museum of Contemporary Art; Cambridge, MA: MIT Press.

Short, N. M., Lowman, P. D., Jr., Freden, S. C., and Finch, W. A., Jr. (1976). *Mission to earth: Landsat views of the world.* Washington, DC: National Aeronautics and Space Administration.

Sidaway, J. D. (2002). Post-development. In Desai, V., and Potter, R. B. (Eds.), *The companion to development studies* (pp. 16–20). London: Arnold.

Siddall, W. R. (1969). Railroad gauges and spatial interaction. *Geographical Review, 59*, 29–57.

Siderius, W., and Njeru, E. B. (1976). *Soils of Trans-Nzoia District* (Kenya Soil Survey Report No. 28). Nairobi: Ministry of Agriculture, Republic of Kenya.

Silva, J. A. (Ed.). (1985). *Soil-based agrotechnology transfer.* Honolulu: Benchmark Soils Project, University of Hawaii.

Simon, J. (1981). *The ultimate resource.* Princeton, NJ: Princeton University Press.

Simon, J. (1996). *The ultimate resource 2.* Princeton, NJ: Princeton University Press.

Simon, K. H. (1929). *Slavery.* London: Hodder and Stoughton.

Sinclair, M. T., and Stabler, M. J. (Eds.). (1991). *The tourism industry: An international analysis.* Wallingford, UK: C. A. B. International.

Sjoberg, G. (1960). *The preindustrial city.* Glencoe, IL: Free Press.

Skinner, B. J. (1980). A second Iron Age ahead? In Skinner, B. J. (Ed.), *Earth's energy and mineral resources* (pp. 158–169). Los Altos, CA: W. Kaufmann.

Slade, R. (1961). *The Belgian Congo.* London: Oxford University Press.

Slager, A. (2006). *The internationalization of banks: Patterns, strategies and performance.* Basingstoke, UK: Palgrave/Macmillan.

Slater, D. (2004). *Geopolitics and the postcolonial: Rethinking north-south relations.* Oxford: Blackwell.

Smil, V. (1983). Deforestation in China. *Ambio, 12*, 226–231.

Smith, A. (1776). *An inquiry into the nature and causes of the wealth of nations.* London: A. Strahan and T. Cadell.

Smith, A., and Pickles, J. (Eds.). (1998). *Theorizing transition: The political economy of post-communist transformations.* London: Routledge.

Smith, C. (1985). Class relations and urbanization in Guatemala: Toward an alternative theory of urban primacy. In Timberlake, M. (Ed.), *Urbanization in the world-economy* (pp. 121–167). New York: Academic Press.

Smith, N. (2005). *The end game of capitalism.* London: Routledge.

Smith, R. C. (1854). *Smith's first book in geography.* New York: Burgess.

Sneddon, C. S. (2000). "Sustainability" in ecological economics, ecology and livelihoods: A review. *Progress in Human Geography, 24*(4), 521–549.

Snyder, L. L. (1939). *Race: A history of modern ethnic theories.* London: Longman, Greens.

Soja, E., and Tobin, R. (1977). The geography of modernization: Paths, patterns and processes of spatial change in developing countries. In Abu-Lughod, J. (Ed.), *Third world urbanization* (pp. 155–164). Chicago: Maaroufa Press.

Solcomhouse. (2005). Permafrost. *www.solcomhouse.com/Permafrost.htm*

Solomon, M. E. (1949). The natural control of animal populations. *Journal of Animal Ecology, 18*(1), 1–35.

Solow, R. M. (1956). A contribution to the theory of economic growth. *Quarterly Journal of Economics, 70*, 65–94.

Southall, A. W. (1970). The illusion of tribe. *Journal of Asian and African Studies, 5*, 28–50.

Spahn, P. B. (1996). The Tobin tax and exchange rate stability. *Finance and Development, 33*(2), 24–27.

Spivak, G. (1988a). Can the subaltern speak. In Nelson, C., and Grossberg, L. (Eds.), *Marxism and the interpretation of culture* (pp. 271–313). Urbana: University of Illinois Press.

Spivak, G. C. (1988b). *In other worlds: Essays in cultural politics.* London: Routledge.

Spivak, G. C. (2000). Discussion: An afterword on the new subaltern. In Chatterjee, L., and Jeganathan, P. (Eds.), *Subaltern studies XI:*

Community, gender and violence (pp. 305–334). Delhi: Permanent Black.

Spraos, J. (1983). *Inequalising trade?* Oxford: Clarendon Press.

Spring, G. M. (1932). *The vitalism of Count Gobineau.* New York: Institute of French Studies.

Stack, C. (1974). *All our kin: Strategies for survival in a black community.* New York: Harper and Row.

Stack, C. (1996). *Call to home.* New York: Basic Books.

Standard and Poor's current statistics. (1996, January). New York: Standard and Poor's.

Standing, G. (Ed.). (1985). *Labour circulation and the labour process.* London: Croom Helm.

Stanecki, K. A. (2000, July). *The AIDS pandemic in the 21st century: The demographic impact in developing countries.* Paper presented at the XIIIth International AIDS Conference, Durban, South Africa.

Stanecki, K. A. (2004). *The AIDS pandemic in the 21st century.* Washington, DC: U.S. Bureau of the Census.

Stavrianos, L. S. (1988). *The world since 1500: A global history* (5th ed.). Englewood Cliffs, NJ: Prentice-Hall.

Stearns, P. N., Adas, M., and Schwartz, S. B. (1992). *World civilizations: Vol. 1. Beginnings to 1750.* New York: HarperCollins.

Stein, H. (1992). Deindustrialization, adjustment, the World Bank and the IMF in Africa. *World Development, 20,* 83–95.

Steiner, G. (1971). *In Bluebeard's castle: Some notes towards the redefinition of culture.* New Haven, CT: Yale University Press.

Stevens, S. (1987). Chernobyl fallout: A hard rain for the Sami. *Cultural Survival, 11*(2), 1–9.

Stewart, J. I. (1988). *Response farming in rainfed agriculture.* Davis, CA: WHARF Foundation Press.

Stewart, J. I., and Hash, C. T. (1982). Impact of weather analysis on agricultural production and planning decisions for the semiarid areas of Kenya. *Journal of Applied Meteorology, 21*(4), 477–494.

Stiglitz, J. (2000, April 17). The insider: What I learned at the world economic crisis. *The New Republic,* 56.

Stiglitz, J. (2002). *Globalization and its discontents.* London: Allen Lane.

Stone, R. (1995). If the mercury soars, so may health hazards. *Science, 267,* 957–958.

Storper, M. (1997). *The regional world: Territorial development in a global economy.* New York: Guilford Press.

Strand, P., Selnaes, T. D., Boe, E. Harbitz, O., and Andersson-Sorlie, A. (1992). Chernobyl fallout: Internal doses to Norwegian population and the effect of dietary advice. *Health Physics, 63,* 385–392.

Strange, S. (1973). IMF: Monetary managers. In Cox, R., and Jacobson, H. (Eds.), *The anatomy of influence: Decision-making in international organizations.* New Haven, CT: Yale University Press.

Strange, S. (1994). From Bretton Woods to the casino economy. In Corbridge, S., Martin, R., and Thrift, N. (Eds.), *Money, power and space* (pp. 49–62). Oxford: Blackwell.

Sundborg, A., and Rapp, A. (1986). Erosion and sedimentation by water: Problems and prospects. *Ambio, 15*(4), 215–225.

Sunkel, O. (1973). Transnational capital and national disintegration in Latin America. *Social and Economic Studies, 22,* 132–176.

Swarr, A. L., and Nagar, R. (2004). Dismantling assumptions: Interrogating "lesbian" struggles for identity and survival in India and South Africa. *Signs, 29*(2), 491–516.

Swyngedouw, E. (1997). Neither global nor local: "Glocalization" and the politics of scale. In Cox, K. (Ed.), *Spaces of globalization: Reasserting the power of the local* (pp. 137–166). New York: Guilford Press.

Swynnerton, R. J. M. (1955). *A plan to intensify the development of African agriculture.* Nairobi, Kenya: Government Printer.

Taaffe, E. J., Morrill, R. L., and Gould, P. R. (1963). Transport expansion in underdeveloped countries: A comparative analysis. *Geographical Review, 53,* 503–529.

Tallantire, A. C. (1975). A preliminary study of the food plants of the West Nile and Madi Districts of Uganda. *East African Agricultural and Forestry Journal, 40,* 233–255.

Tanzer, M. (1980). *The race for resources: Continuing struggles over minerals and fuels.* New York: Monthly Review Press.

Taylor, J. G. (1979). *From modernization to modes of production.* London: Macmillan.

Taylor, P. J., Watts, M. J., and Johnston, R. J. (2002). Geography/globalization. In Johnston, R. J., Taylor, P. J., and Watts, M. (Eds.),

Geographies of global change: Remapping the world (pp. 1–18) Oxford: Blackwell.

Tax, M., with Agosin, M., Aidoo, A. A., Menon, R., Rosca, N., and Sala, M. (1999). Power of the world: Culture, censorship, and voice. In Silliman, J., and King, Y. (Eds.), *Dangerous intersections: Feminist perspectives on population, environment, and development* (pp. 108–132). Cambridge, MA: South End Press.

Thatcher, M. (1987/2008). Interview for Woman's Own ("no such thing as society"). Margaret Thatcher Foundation, *www.margaretthatcher.org/speeches/displaydocument.asp?docid=106689*

Third World Network. (2003). *Comment by Third World Network on Cancun text of 13 September.* Press release, Cancun.

Thomas, A. (1994). *Third world atlas* (2nd ed.). Washington, DC: Taylor and Francis.

Thomas, B. (1972). *Migration and urban development: A reappraisal of British and American long cycles.* London: Methuen.

Thomas, D. B. (1978). *Some observations on soil conservation in Machakos District, Kenya, with special reference to terracing* (Soil and Water Conservation in Kenya, Occasional Paper No. 27). Nairobi: Institute for Development Studies, University of Nairobi.

Thompson, J., Porras, I. T., Tumwine, J. K., Mujwahuzi, M. R., Katui-Katua, M., Johnstone, N., and Wood, L. (2004). *Drawers of water II: Assessing long-term change in domestic water use in west Africa* (International Institute for Environment and Development, Sustainable Agriculture and Rural Livelihoods [SARL] Project Summary). *www.iied.org/pubs/pdfs/9049IIED.pdf*

Thornthwaite, C. W. (1948). An approach toward a rational classification of climate. *Geographical Review, 38,* 55–94.

Thornton, J. (1998). *Africa and Africans in the making of the modern world.* Cambridge, UK: Cambridge University Press.

Thrift, N. (1989). The geography of international economic disorder. In Johnston, R. J., and Taylor, P. J. (Eds.), *A world in crisis?* (pp. 12–67). Oxford: Blackwell.

Thrift, N. (1994). On the social and cultural determinants of international financial centers. In Corbridge, S., Martin, R., and Thrift, N. (Eds.), *Money, power and space* (pp. 327–355). Oxford: Blackwell.

Tickell, A. (2000). Dangerous derivatives: Controlling and creating risks in international money. *Geoforum, 31,* 87–99.

Tiffen, M., Mortimore, M., and Gichuki, F. (1994). *More people, less erosion: Environmental recovery in Kenya.* New York: Wiley.

Tilly, C. (1994). Entanglements of European cities and states. In Tilly, C., and Blockmans, W. P. (Eds.), *Cities and the rise of states in Europe, A.D. 1000 to 1800* (pp. 1–27). Boulder, CO: Westview Press.

Tinker, I. (1976). The adverse impact of development on women. In Tinker, I., and Bramsen, B. M. (Eds.), *Women and world development* (pp. 22–34). Washington, DC: Overseas Development Council.

Tip, T. (1902–1903). *Hame maisha ya Hamed bin Muhammed el Murkebi, yaani Tippu Tip, kwa maneno yake mwenyewe* [Translated into English by W. H. Whitley]. Nairobi: East African Literature Bureau (1966).

Tobin, J. (1978). A proposal for monetary reform. *Eastern Economic Journal, 4,* 153–159.

Tönnies, F. (1887). *Community and society.* East Lansing: Michigan State University Press (1957).

Torp, F. (1993). *Stabilization and structural adjustment.* London: Routledge.

Traub-Werner, M. (2007). Free trade: A governmentality approach. *Environment and Planning A, 39*(6), 1441–1456.

Trinh, T. M.-H. (1989). *Woman, native, other: Writing postcoloniality and feminism.* Bloomington: Indiana University Press.

Truman, Harry S. (1949, January 20). *Presidential inaugural address. www.americanrhetoric.com/speeches/harrystrumaninauguraladdress.html*

Tschannerl, G. (1971). *Water supply as part of rural development* (Paper No. 91). Kampala: Makerere University, Universities Social Sciences Council.

Tuan, Y. F. (1996). *Cosmos and hearth: A cosmopolite's viewpoint.* Minneapolis: University of Minnesota Press.

Turner, B. L., II. (Ed.). (1990). *The earth as transformed by human action: Global and regional changes in the biosphere over the past 300 years.* Cambridge, UK: Cambridge University Press.

Turner, B. L., II, and Ali, A. M. S. (1996). Induced intensification: Agricultural change in Bangladesh with implications for Malthus and Boserup. *Proceedings of the National Academy of Sciences USA, 93*, 14984–14991.

Turner, L., and Ash, J. (Eds.). (1975). *The golden hordes: International tourism and the pleasure periphery.* London: Constable.

United Nations. (1948a–2004a). *Demographic yearbook.* New York: United Nations, Population Division.

United Nations. (1958b). *South-West Africa* (Map No. 1099). New York: United Nations.

United Nations. (1960b–2003b). *International trade statistics yearbook.* New York: United Nations.

United Nations. (1980c). *Equality, development and peace: Report of the World Conference of the United Nations Decade for Women, Copenhagen, Denmark, July 14–30* (U.N. Doc. A/CONF.94/35). New York: United Nations.

United Nations. (1991c–2006c). *World investment report.* New York: United Nations.

United Nations. (1993d). *World urbanization prospects: The 1992 revision.* New York: United Nations.

United Nations. (2003d). *World urbanization prospects: 2003 revision.* New York: United Nations.

United Nations. (2006a). *The state of the world's refugees: Human displacement in the new millenium.* Oxford: Oxford University Press.

United Nations. (2006b). *Trafficking in persons: Global patterns.* New York: United Nations, Office on Drugs and Crime

United Nations Centre on Transnational Corporations (UNCTC). (1983). *Transnational corporations in world development: Third survey.* New York: United Nations.

United Nations Conference on Trade and Development (UNCTAD). (1965a–2004a). *Handbook of international trade and development statistics* [after 1999, *UNCTAD handbook of statistics*]. New York: United Nations.

United Nations Conference on Trade and Development (UNCTAD). (1967b). *UNCTAD secretariat: Progress report* (No. TD/Supp. 8). New York: United Nations.

United Nations Conference on Trade and Development (UNCTAD). (2002b). *About GSP. www.unctad.org/Templates/Page.asp?intItemID=2309&lang=1*

United Nations Conference on Trade and Development (UNCTAD). (2003b). *Trade preferences for LDCs: An early assessment of benefits and possible improvements.* New York: United Nations Conference on Trade and Development.

United Nations Conference on Trade and Development (UNCTAD). (2008a). Foreign direct investment statistics. *www.unctad.org/fdistatistics*

United Nations Development Programme (UNDP). (1996–2005). *Human development report.* New York: United Nations Development Programme.

United Nations Educational, Scientific, and Cultural Organization (UNESCO). (1971). *Scientific framework for world water balance* (Technical Papers in Hydrology No. 7). Paris: UNESCO.

United Nations Industrial Development Organization (UNIDO). (1985). *World industry in the 1980s.* Vienna: United Nations.

United Nations Industrial Development Organization (UNIDO). (1992). *Handbook of industrial statistics, 1992.* Vienna: United Nations.

Urdang, S. (1983). The last transition: Women and development in Mozambique. *Review of African Political Economy, 27–28*, 8–32.

U.S. Bureau of Labor Statistics. (2007). *Producer prices and price indices. www.bls.gov/data/home.htm*

U.S. Census Bureau. (2009). *International data base. www.census.gov/ipc/www/idb/worldpopinfo.html*

U.S. Department of Commerce. (1976). *Business statistics 1975.* Washington, DC: U.S. Government Printing Office.

U.S. Department of Commerce. (1992). *Business statistics 1963–1991.* Washington, DC: U.S. Government Printing Office.

U.S. Geological Survey (USGS). (2000). *Mercury in the environment* (FactSheet No. 146-00). *www.usgs/themes/factsheet/146-00*

U.S. Geological Survey (USGS). (2006). *World mineral summaries, 2006.* Washington, DC: U.S. Government Printing Office.

U.S. Labor Education in the Americas Project (US/LEAP). (2001). *Maquila* workers attacked for organizing a union. *www.usleap.org/Maquilas/Choi/ChoiNL8-31-01.html*

Uzoigwe, G. N. (1974). *Britain and the conquest of Africa: The age of Salisbury.* Ann Arbor: University of Michigan Press.

Uzoigwe, G. N. (1985). European partition and conquest of Africa: An overview. In Boahen,

A. A. (Ed.), *General history of Africa: VII. Africa under colonial domination 1880–1935* (pp. 19–44). Paris: UNESCO.

Vaitsos, C. (1974). *Inter-country income distribution and transnational enterprises.* Oxford: Clarendon Press.

Vance, J. (1970). *The merchant's world.* Englewood Cliffs, NJ: Prentice-Hall.

Vatn, A. (2001). Environmental resources, property regimes, and efficiency. *Environment and Planning C: Government and Policy, 19,* 665–680.

Vernon, R. (1966). International investment and international trade in the product cycle. *Quarterly Journal of Economics, 80,* 90–207.

Vining, D. R., Jr. (1982). Migration between the core and the periphery. *Scientific American, 247*(6), 44–53.

Volheim, E. (2004a). Flare up!: Niger Delta women take on oil companies. In Yuen, E., Burton-Rose, D., and Katsiaficas, G. (Eds.), *Confronting capitalism: Dispatches from a global movement* (pp. 278–281). Brooklyn, NY: Soft Skull Press.

Volheim, E. (2004b). Testimonies and declarations: Women speak out. In Yuen, E., Burton-Rose, D., and Katsiaficas, G. (Eds.), *Confronting Capitalism: Dispatches from a global movement* (pp. 282–285). Brooklyn, NY: Soft Skull Press.

Wackernagel, M., and Rees, W. (1996). *Our ecological footprint: Reducing human impact on the earth.* Gabriola Island, British Columbia: New Society.

Wade, R. (1990). *Governing the market.* Princeton, NJ: Princeton University Press.

Wade, R. (1996). Japan, the World Bank, and the art of paradigm maintenance: "The east Asian miracle" in political perspective. *New Left Review, 217,* 3–37.

Wadstrom, C. B. (1794). *An essay on colonization, particularly applied to the western coast of Africa, with some free thoughts on cultivation and commerce.* New York: A. M. Kelley (1968).

Wagongo, V. O. (2003). Traditional range condition and trend assessment: Lessons from Pokot and Il Chamus pastoralists of Kenya. *Anthropologist, 5,* 79–87.

Wainwright, J. (2007). Spaces of resistance in Seattle and Cancun. In Leitner, H., Peck, J., and Sheppard, E. (Eds.), *Contesting neoliberalism: Urban frontiers* (pp. 179–203). New York: Guilford Press.

Walker, R. (1981). A theory of suburbanization. In Dear, M., and Scott, A. J. (Eds.), *Urbanization and urban planning in market societies* (pp. 383–430). London: Methuen.

Walker, R. (1985). Is there a service economy? The changing capitalist division of labor. *Science and Society, 49,* 42–83.

Wall, G. (1993). International collaboration in the search for sustainable tourism in Bali. *Journal of Sustainable Tourism, 1,* 38–47.

Wallerstein, I. (1979). *The capitalist world economy.* Cambridge, UK: Cambridge University Press.

Wallerstein, I. (1984). *The politics of the world-economy.* Cambridge, UK: Cambridge University Press.

Walras, L. (1874). *Élements d'économie politique pure.* Lausanne, Switzerland: Corbaz.

Walter, I. (1998). *Globalization of markets and financial center competition* (New York University Salomon Center, Working Paper Series No. S-98-31). New York: New York University.

Walton, J. (1977). *Elites and economic development: Comparative studies on the political economy of Latin American cities.* Austin: Institute of Latin American Studies, University of Texas.

Warde, I. (2000). *Islamic finance in the global economy.* Edinburgh: Edinburgh University Press.

Waring, M. (1988). *If women counted: A new feminist economics.* New York: Harper & Row.

Warner, D. (1969). *Rural water supply and development: A comparison of nine villages in Tanzania.* Dar es Salaam: Economic Research Bureau, University of Dar es Salaam.

Warren, B. (1980). *Imperialism: Pioneer of capitalism.* London: New Left Books.

Watson, M., Methieson, D., Kincaid, R., and Kalter, E. (1986). *International capital markets: Development and prospects* (Occasional Paper No. 43). Washington, DC: International Monetary Fund.

Watts, M. (1992). Living under contract: Work, production politics, and the manufacture of discontent in a peasant society. In Pred, A., and Watts, M. (Eds.), *Reworking modernity: Capitalisms and symbolic discontent* (pp.

65–105). New Brunswick, NJ: Rutgers University Press.

Watts, M. (2001). Petro-violence: Community, extraction, and political ecology of a mythic commodity. In Peluso, N., and Watts, M. (Eds.), *Violent environments* (pp. 189–212). Ithaca, NY: Cornell University Press.

Watts, M., and Bassett, T. J. (1985). Crisis and change in African agriculture: A comparative study of the Ivory Coast and Nigeria. *African Studies Review, 28*(4), 3–27.

Webb, S., and de Melo, M. (1992). *Adjustment lending and mobilization of private and public resources for growth* (Country Economics Department, Policy and Research Series No. 22). Washington, DC: World Bank.

Webber, M. (2001). Finance and the real economy: Theoretical implications of the financial crisis in Asia. *Geoforum, 32*, 1–13.

Webber, M., and Rigby, D. (1996). *The Golden Age illusion: Rethinking postwar capitalism.* New York: Guilford Press.

Weber, H. (2002). The imposition of a global development architecture: The example of microcredit. *Review of International Studies, 28*, 537–555.

Weil, C., and Kvale, K. M. (1985). Current research on geographical aspects of schistosomiasis. *Geographical Review, 75*(2), 186–216.

Weil, C., and Scarpaci, J. (Eds.). (1992). *Health and health care in Latin America during the last decade: Insights for the 1990s* (Minnesota Latin American Series No. 3). Minneapolis: University of Minnesota.

Wheatley, P. (1971). *The pivot of the four quarters.* Edinburgh: Edinburgh University Press.

White, G. F., Bradley, D. S., and White, A. U. (1972). *Drawers of Water: Domestic water use in East Africa.* Chicago: University of Chicago Press.

Widstrand, C. G. (1973). Pastoral peoples and rural development: A case study. *Annales Academiae Regiae Scientiarum Upsaliensis, 17*, 35–54.

Wignaraja, P., Hussain, A., Sethi, H., and Wignaraja, G. (1991). *Participatory development: Learning from south Asia.* Tokyo: United Nations University Press.

Wilbanks, T. J. (1994). Sustainable development in geographic perspective. *Annals of the Association of American Geographers, 84*(4), 541–556.

Williams, C. C., and Millington, A. C. (2004). The diverse and contested meanings of sustainable development. *Geographical Journal, 170*, 99–104.

Williams, E. E. (1944). *Capitalism and slavery.* Chapel Hill: University of North Carolina Press.

Willmott, C. J., and Feddema, J. J. (1992). A more rational climatic moisture index. *Professional Geographer, 44*(1), 84–88.

Wilson, P. A. (1989). *The global assembly industry* (Working Paper No. 89-05). Austin: Institute of Latin American Studies, University of Texas.

Wisner, B. (1989). *Power and need in Africa.* Trenton, NJ: Africa World Press.

Wolf, E. C. (1988). Avoiding a mass extinction of species. In Brown, L. R., et al. (Eds.), *State of the world 1988* (pp. 101–117). New York: Norton.

Wolff, R. D. (1974). *The economics of colonialism: Britain and Kenya, 1870–1930.* New Haven, CT: Yale University Press.

Wood, G. (1997). States without citizens: the problem of the franchise state. In Hulme, D., and Edwards, M. (Eds.), *NGOs, states and donors: Too close for comfort?* (pp. 79–92). New York: St. Martin's Press, in association with Save the Children.

Workshop on the OECD Investment Declaration and Bylaws, Washington, DC. (1977). *The OECD guidelines for multinational enterprises.* Washington, DC: Institute for International and Foreign Trade Law, Georgetown University Law Center.

World Bank. (1992). *Export processing zones.* Washington, DC: Country Economics Department, World Bank.

World Bank. (1993). *World development report 1993: Investing in health.* New York: Oxford University Press.

World Bank. (1994). *World development report 1994.* New York: Oxford University Press.

World Bank. (1996). *World development report 1996: From plan to market.* New York: Oxford University Press.

World Bank. (2003). *World development indicators, 2003.* Washington, DC: World Bank.

World Bank. (2004a). *HIV/AIDS: Data. web. worldbank.org/WBSITE/EXTERNAL/TOPICS/EXHEALTHNUTRITION . . .*

World Bank. (2004b). *HIV/AIDS in east Asia and Pacific.* Washington, DC: World Bank.

World Bank. (2004c). *HIV/AIDS in south Asia.* Washington, DC: World Bank.

World Bank. (2004d). *AIDS regional update: Latin America and the Caribbean.* Washington, DC: World Bank.

World Bank. (2004e). *AIDS regional update: Middle East and north Africa.* Washington, DC: World Bank.

World Bank. (2004f). *AIDS regional update: Europe and central Asia.* Washington, DC: World Bank.

World Bank. (2004g). Distribution of income or consumption. *www.worldbank.org/data/lodi2001/pdfs/tab_28.pdf*

World Bank. (2005a). *Global development finance.* Washington, DC: World Bank.

World Bank. (2005b). *World development indicators, 2005.* Washington, DC: World Bank.

World Bank. (2006a). *Nigeria: Country brief. web.worldbank.org/WBSITE/EXTERNAL/COUNTRIES/AFRICASEXT/NIGERIAEXTN/0,,menuPK:368906~page:141132~piPK:141107~theSite:38896,00.html*

World Bank. (2006b). *Global economic prospects 2006: Economic implications of remittances and migration.* Washington, DC: World Bank.

World Bank. (2008). *World development indicators and global development finance online database. www.worldbank.org/data/onlinedatabases/onlinedatabases.html*

World Climate Report. (2004). Ups and downs. *www.worldclimatereport.com/index.php/2004/03/22/ups-and-downs*

World Commission on Dams (WCD). (2000). *Dams and development: A new framework for decision-making.* London: Earthscan. (Also available at *www.dams.org*)

World Commission on Environment and Development (Brundtland Commission). (1987). *Our common future.* Oxford: Oxford University Press.

World Health Organization (WHO). (1999a). *Dioxins and their effects on human health. www.who.int/mediacentre/factsheets/fs225/en/index.html*

World Health Organization (WHO). (1999b). *World celebrates African health success story.* Press release, WHO/AFRO. *www.afro.who.int/press/1999/pr19991110.html*

World Resources Institute. (1988). *World resources 1988–89.* New York: Basic Books.

World Resources Institute (in collaboration with the United Nations Environment Programme and the United Nations Development Programme). (1994). *World resources 1994–95: People and the environment.* New York: Oxford University Press.

World Resources Institute. (1996a). *World resources 1996–97* [Database diskette], Washington, DC.

World Resources Institute. (1996b). *World resources 1996–97: A guide to the global environment.* New York: Oxford University Press.

World Social Forum. (2002). World Social Forum Charter of Principles. *www.forumsocialmundial.org.br/main.php?id_menu=4&cd_language=2*

World Tourism Organization. (1994). *Compendium of tourism statistics.* Madrid: World Tourism Organization.

World Tourism Organization. (2006). *Tourism and the world economy.* Madrid: World Tourism Organization. *http://unwto.org/facts/eng/economy.htm*

World Trade Organization (WTO). (2003). *International trade statistics 2002.* Washington, DC: WTO.

Wright, M. W. (2001). Feminine villains, masculine heroes, and the reproduction of Ciudad Juárez. *Social Text, 69*(19), 93–114.

Wright, M. W. (2004). From protests to politics: Sex work, women's worth and Ciudad Juárez modernity. *Annals of the Association of American Geographers, 94,* 369–386.

Wright, M. W. (2006). *Disposable women and other myths of global capitalism.* London: Routledge.

Yale Center for Environmental Law and Policy. (2005a). *2005 environmental sustainability index: Benchmarking national environmental stewardship.* New Haven, CT: Yale Center for Environmental Law and Policy; New York: Center for International Earth Science Information Network, Columbia University.

Yale Center for Environmental Law and Policy. (2005b, January 26). *2005 environmental sustainability index.* Press release. *www.yale.edu/esi*

Yapa, L. (1993a). What are improved seeds?: An epistemology of the Green Revolution. *Economic Geography, 69*(3), 254–273.

Yapa, L. (1993b). *What causes poverty?* Paper presented at the Association of American Geographers annual meeting, San Francisco.

Yapa, L. (1996a). What causes poverty? A postmodern view. *Annals of the Association of American Geographers*, *86*(4), 707–728.

Yapa, L. (1996b). Improved seeds and constructed scarcity. In Peet, R., and Watts, M. (Eds.), *Liberation ecologies: Environment, development, social movements* (pp. 69–85). London: Routledge.

Yeandle, M., Mainelli, M., and Harris, I. (2007). *The Global Financial Center Index 2*. *www.zyen.com/Activities/On-line%20surveys/GFCI.htm*

Yergin, D., and Stanislaw, J. (2002). *The commanding heights: The battle for the world economy*. New York: Touchstone Books.

Young, R., and Fosbrooke, H. (1960). *Smoke in the hills*. Evanston, IL: Northwestern University Press.

Zea, L. (1963). *The Latin American mind*. Norman: University of Oklahoma Press.

Zimmerer, K. S., and Bassett, T. J. (Eds.). (2003). *Political ecology: An integrative approach to geography and environment–development studies*. New York: Guilford Press.

Index

Page numbers followed by letters indicate *f* for figures, *n* for notes, *t* for tables

About the Authors

Eric Sheppard is Regents Professor of Geography and Associate Director of the Interdisciplinary Center for the Study of Global Change, University of Minnesota. Among his awards are Distinguished Scholarship Honors, Association of American Geographers; Fellow, Center for Advanced Study in the Behavioral Sciences; Fesler–Lampert Professor in Humanities, University of Minnesota; and Scholar of the College of Liberal Arts, University of Minnesota. He is coauthor or coeditor of *The Capitalist Space Economy, A Companion to Economic Geography, Scale and Geographic Inquiry, Reading Economic Geography, Politics and Practice in Economic Geography,* and *Contesting Neoliberalism,* and has published over 100 articles in such journals as the *Annals of the Association of American Geographers; Transactions of the Institute of British Geographers; Environment and Planning A; Environment and Planning D: Society and Space; Journal of Regional Science;* and *Antipode.*

Philip W. Porter is Professor Emeritus, University of Minnesota, where he taught geography from 1957 to 2000. He specialized in African geography, with particular emphasis on livelihood systems and the biophysical environments in which they are pursued, as well as the political economies in which they are embedded. His first research was in Liberia and he subsequently did research in Kenya, Tanzania, and Uganda. His awards include Scholar of the College of Liberal Arts, Lifetime Achievement Award of the Association of American Geographers (AAG), and the Robert McC. Netting Award, Cultural and Political Specialty Group of the AAG. He has published over 70 articles, plus numerous book reviews and editorials, in such journals as *Annals of the Association of American Geographers, American Anthropologist, Antipode, Focus, Geografiska Annaler, Journal of African History, Journal of Geography,* and *Professional Geographer.*

David R. Faust is the Librarian for South Asia at the Ames Library of South Asia, University of Minnesota. He has written in *Antipode; Ethics, Place & Environment;* and *Economic and Political Weekly* on development politics, nongovernmental organizations, and the disjunctures related to English-medium education in India.

Richa Nagar is Professor of Gender, Women, and Sexuality Studies at the University of Minnesota. She is coauthor of *Playing with Fire: Feminist Thought and Activism through Seven Lives in India* and coeditor of *Critical Transnational Feminist Praxis.* Her articles on space and communal politics among South Asians in postcolonial Tanzania and the politics of empowerment in India have appeared in *Signs; Feminist Studies; Gender, Place, and Culture; Environment and Planning D: Society and Space; Economic Geography; Antipode; Ecumene; Women's Studies International Forum; Economic and Political Weekly;* and *Comparative Studies of South Asia, Africa, and the Middle East.*